UNLEASHING GOD'S TRUTH, ONE VERSE AT A TIME.®

THE MACARTHUR
BIBLE
COMMENTARY

John MacArthur

THOMAS NELSON
Since 1798

NASHVILLE DALLAS MEXICO CITY RIO DE JANEIRO

THE MACARTHUR BIBLE COMMENTARY

Copyright © 2005 by John MacArthur

All rights reserved. No portion of this book may be reproduced, stored in a retrieval system, or transmitted in any form by any means-electronic, mechanical, photocopy, recording, scanning, or other-except for brief quotations in critical reviews or articles, without the prior written permission of the publisher.

Published in Nashville, Tennessee by Thomas Nelson.

Published in association with the literary agency of Wolgemuth & Associates, Inc.

Thomas Nelson, Inc., titles may be purchased in bulk for educational, business, fundraising, or sales promotional use. For information, please email SpecialMarkets@ThomasNelson.com

John MacArthur
"Unleashing God's Truth, One Verse at a Time®"
"Unleashing God's Truth, One Verse at a Time" is a trademark of Grace to You.
All rights reserved.

Unless otherwise indicated, Scripture quotations are from the
NEW KING JAMES VERSION © 1982 by Thomas Nelson. All rights reserved

Interior design and typesetting by Kristy L. Edwards, Smyrna, Tennessee

ISBN-10: 0-7852-5066-2
ISBN-13: 9-780-7852-5066-1

Printed in the United States of America
22 23 24 25 TRM 43 42 41

CONTENTS

PREFACE

And Ezra opened the book in the sight of all the people . . . they read distinctly from the book, in the Law of God; and they gave the sense, and helped them to understand the reading—Nehemiah 8:5, 8 (NKJV)

Although this momentous renewal of interest in Scripture occurred over 2,400 years ago (c. 445 B.C.), this has been the primary need of every subsequent generation, i.e., to read and understand—for the purpose of obedience—the Bible and to thereby know the blessing of God (Rev. 1:3). Therefore, I have undertaken, with the encouragement of Wayne Kinde at Thomas Nelson and the editorial partnership of Dr. Richard Mayhue, executive vice president of The Master's College and Seminary, to create a one-volume commentary which will meet this spiritual need in the twenty-first century.

The core around which this one-volume commentary has been arranged is the original notes of *The MacArthur Study Bible* published in 1997. Since then, (1) those notes have been thoroughly reviewed for accuracy and clarity, with appropriate revisions and corrections. (2) The outline for each book (located with the Introduction) has been integrated into the commentary. (3) A Further Study section has been added at the end of the commentary for each book which contains a bibliography of several other commentaries which can be consulted to expand on one's studies. (4) Most significantly, over 300 new maps, charts, diagrams, and word studies have been added to the over 350 found in the original *MacArthur Study Bible* for a total of almost 700 study/teaching aids, in addition to the commentary material.

This one-volume commentary on the whole Bible is in itself a minilibrary which will be especially advantageous to those with financial and/or space limitations. To greatly expand the value of this commentary, one's studies can be vastly enhanced with the additional use of *The MacArthur Topical Bible*.

Everyone from new believers to pastors can benefit from this study tool. Its purpose and design are to make the precious truths of Scripture understandable and consequently obeyed by the people of God. May God's promise to Joshua over 3,400 years ago be just as real today because you have used this volume to know, understand, and obey the Word of God.

This Book of the Law shall not depart from your mouth, but you shall meditate in it day and night, that you may observe to do according to all that is written in it. For then you will make your way prosperous, and then you will have good success —Joshua 1:8 (NKJV)

THE NATURE AND PURPOSE OF THE
BIBLE

The Bible is a collection of 66 documents inspired by God. These documents are gathered into two testaments, the Old (39) and the New (27). Prophets, priests, kings, and leaders from the nation of Israel wrote the OT books in Hebrew (with two passages in Aramaic). The apostles and their associates wrote the NT books in Greek. The two testaments go from creation to consummation, eternity past to eternity future.

The OT record starts with the creation of the universe and closes about four hundred years before the first coming of Jesus Christ.

The flow of history through the OT moves along the following lines:

Creation of the universe

Fall of man

Judgment flood over the earth

Abraham, Isaac, Jacob (Israel)—fathers of the chosen nation

The history of Israel

Exile in Egypt—430 years

Exodus and wilderness wanderings—40 years

Conquest of Canaan—7 years

Era of Judges—350 years

United Kingdom—Saul, David, Solomon—110 years

Divided Kingdom—Judah/Israel—350 years

Exile in Babylon—70 years

Return and rebuilding the land—140 years

The details of this history are explained in the 39 books divided into 5 categories:

The Law—5 (Genesis—Deuteronomy)
History—12 (Joshua—Esther)
Wisdom—5 (Job—Song of Solomon)
Major Prophets—5 (Isaiah—Daniel)
Minor Prophets—12 (Hosea—Malachi)

After the completion of the OT, there were four hundred years of silence, during which God did not speak or inspire any Scripture. That silence was broken by the arrival of John the Baptist announcing that the promised Lord Savior had come. The NT records the rest of the story from the birth of Christ to the culmination of all history and the final eternal state.

While the thirty-nine OT books major on the history of Israel and the promise of the coming Savior, the twenty-seven NT books major on the person of Christ and the establishment of the church. The four Gospels give the record of His birth, life, death, resurrection, and ascension. Each of the four writers views the greatest and most important event of history, the coming of the God-man, Jesus Christ, from a different perspective. Matthew looks at Him through the perspective of His kingdom; Mark through the perspective of His servanthood; Luke through the perspective of His humanness; and John through the perspective of His deity.

The Book of Acts chronicles the impact of the life, death, and Resurrection of Jesus Christ, the Lord and Savior—from His Ascension, the consequent coming of the

Holy Spirit, and the birth of the church, through the early years of gospel preaching by the apostles and their associates. Acts records the establishment of the church in Judea, Samaria, and into the Roman Empire.

The twenty-one epistles were written to churches and individuals to explain the significance of the person and work of Jesus Christ, with its implications for life and witness until He returns.

The NT closes with Revelation, which starts by picturing the current church age, and culminates with Christ's return to establish His earthly kingdom, bringing judgment on the ungodly and glory and blessing for believers. Following the millennial reign of the Lord Savior will be the last judgment, leading to the eternal state. All believers of all history enter the ultimate eternal glory prepared for them, and all the ungodly are consigned to hell to be punished forever.

To understand the Bible, it is essential to grasp the sweep of that history from creation to consummation. It is also crucial to keep in focus the unifying theme of Scripture. The one constant theme unfolding throughout the whole Bible is this: God for His own glory has chosen to create and gather to Himself a group of people to be the subjects of His eternal kingdom, to praise, honor, and serve Him forever and through whom He will display His wisdom, power, mercy, grace, and glory. To gather His chosen ones, God must redeem them from sin. The Bible reveals God's plan for this redemption from its inception in eternity past to its completion in eternity future. Covenants, promises, and epochs are all secondary to the one continuous plan of redemption.

There is one God. The Bible has one Creator. It is one book. It has one plan of grace, recorded from initiation, through execution, to consummation. From predestination to glorification, the Bible is the story of God redeeming His chosen people for the praise of His glory.

As God's redemptive purposes and plan unfold in Scripture, five recurring motifs are constantly emphasized:

- the character of God
- the judgment for sin and disobedience
- the blessing for faith and obedience
- the Lord Savior and sacrifice for sin
- the coming kingdom and glory

Everything revealed on the pages of both the OT and NT is associated with those five categories. Scripture is always teaching or illustrating: (1) the character and attributes of God; (2) the tragedy of sin and disobedience to God's holy standard; (3) the blessedness of faith and obedience to God's standard; (4) the need for a Savior by whose righteousness and substitution sinners can be forgiven, declared just, and transformed to obey God's standard; and (5) the coming glorious end of redemptive history in the Lord Savior's earthly kingdom and the subsequent eternal reign and glory of God and Christ.

It is essential as one studies Scripture to grasp these recurring categories like great hooks on which to hang the passages. While reading through the Bible, one should be able to relate each portion of Scripture to these dominant topics, recognizing that what is introduced in the OT is also made more clear in the NT.

Looking at these five categories separately gives an overview of the Bible.

1. The Revelation of the Character of God

Above all else, Scripture is God's self-revelation. He reveals Himself as the sovereign God of the universe who has chosen to make man and to make Himself known to man. In that self-revelation is established His standard of absolute holiness. From Adam and Eve through Cain and Abel and to everyone before and after the Law of Moses, the standard of righteousness was established and is sustained to the last page of the NT. Violation of it produces judgment, temporal and eternal.

In the OT, it is recorded that God revealed Himself by the following means:

- creation—primarily through man—who was made in His image
- angels
- signs, wonders, and miracles
- visions
- spoken words by prophets and others
- written Scripture (OT)

In the NT, it is recorded that God revealed Himself again by essentially the same means, but more clearly and fully:

- Incarnation—the God-man, Jesus Christ, who was the very image of God
- angels
- signs, wonders, and miracles
- visions
- spoken words by apostles and prophets
- written Scripture (NT)

2. The Revelation of Divine Judgment for Sin and Disobedience

Scripture repeatedly deals with the matter of man's sin, which leads to divine judgment. Account after account in Scripture demonstrates the deadly effects in time and eternity of violating God's standard. There are 1,189 chapters in the Bible. Only four of them don't involve a fallen world: the first two and the last two—before the Fall and after the creation of the new heaven and new earth. The rest is the chronicle of the tragedy of sin.

In the OT, God showed the disaster of sin—starting with Adam and Eve, to Cain and Abel, the patriarchs, Moses and Israel, the kings, priests, some prophets, and Gentile nations. Throughout the OT appears the relentless record of continual devastation produced by sin and disobedience to God's law.

In the NT, the tragedy of sin becomes more clear. The preaching and teaching of Jesus and the apostles begin and end with a call to repentance. King Herod, the Jewish leaders, and the nation of Israel—along with Pilate, Rome, and the rest of the world—all reject the Lord Savior, spurn the truth of God, and thus condemn themselves. The chronicle of sin continues unabated to the end of the age and the return of Christ in judgment. In the NT, disobedience is even more flagrant than OT disobedience because it involves the rejection of the Lord Savior, Jesus Christ in the brighter light of NT truth.

3. The Revelation of Divine Blessing for Faith and Obedience

Scripture repeatedly promises wonderful rewards in time and eternity that come to people who trust God and seek to obey Him. In the OT, God showed the blessedness of repentance from sin, faith in Himself, and obedience to His Word—from Abel, through the patriarchs, to the remnant in Israel—and even Gentiles who believed (such as the people of Nineveh).

God's standard for man, His will, and His moral law were always made known. To those who faced their inability to keep God's standard—recognized their sin, confessed their impotence to please God by their own effort and works, and asked Him for forgiveness and grace—there came merciful redemption and blessing for time and eternity.

In the NT, God again showed the full blessedness of redemption from sin for repentant people. There were those who responded to the preaching of repentance by John the Baptist. Others repented at the preaching of Jesus. Still others from Israel obeyed the gospel through the apostles' preaching. And finally, there were Gentiles all over the Roman Empire who believed the gospel. To all those and to all who will believe through all of history, there is blessing promised in this world and the world to come.

4. The Revelation of the Lord Savior and Sacrifice for Sin

This is the heart of both the OT, which Jesus said spoke of Him in type and prophecy, and the NT, which gives the biblical record of His coming. The promise of blessing is dependent on grace and mercy given to the sinner. Grace means that sin is not held against the sinner. Such forgiveness is dependent on a payment of sin's penalty to satisfy holy justice. That requires a substitute—one to die in the sinner's place. God's chosen substitute—the only one who qualified—was Jesus.

Salvation is always by the same gracious means, whether during OT or NT times. When any sinner comes to God, repentant and convinced he has no power to save himself from the deserved judgment of divine wrath, and pleads for mercy, God's promise of forgiveness is granted. God then declares him righteous because the sacrifice and obedience of Christ is put to his account.

In the OT, God justified sinners that same way, in anticipation of Christ's atoning work. There is, therefore, a continuity of grace and salvation through all of redemptive history. Various covenants, promises, and epochs do not alter that fundamental continuity, nor does the discontinuity between the OT witness nation, Israel, and the NT witness people, the church. A fundamental continuity is centered in the Cross, which was no interruption in the plan of God, but is the very thing to which everything else points.

Throughout the OT, the Savior and sacrifice are promised. In Genesis, He is the seed of the woman who will destroy Satan. In Zechariah, He is the pierced one to whom Israel turns and by whom God opens the fountain of forgiveness to all who mourn over their sin. He is the very One symbolized in the sacrificial system of the Mosaic Law. He is the suffering substitute spoken of by the prophets. Throughout the OT, He is the Messiah who would die for the transgressions of His people; from beginning to end in the OT, the theme of the Lord Savior as a sacrifice for sin is presented. It is solely because of His perfect sacrifice for sin that God graciously forgives repentant believers.

In the NT, the Lord Savior came and actually provided the promised sacrifice for sin on the Cross. Having fulfilled all righteousness by His perfect life, He fulfilled justice by His death. Thus, God Himself atoned for sin, at a cost too great for the human mind to fathom. Now, He graciously supplies on their behalf all the merit necessary for His people to be the objects of His favor. That is what Scripture means when it speaks of salvation by grace.

5. The Revelation of the Kingdom and Glory of the Lord Savior

This crucial component of Scripture brings the whole story to its God-ordained consummation. Redemptive history is controlled by God, so as to culminate in His eternal glory. Redemptive history will end with the same precision and exactness with which it began. The truths of eschatology are neither vague nor unclear—nor are they unimportant. As in any book, how the story ends is the most crucial and compelling part—so with the Bible. Scripture notes several very specific features of the end planned by God.

In the OT, there is repeated mention of an earthly kingdom ruled by the Messiah, Lord Savior, who will come to reign. Associated with that kingdom will be the salvation of Israel, the salvation of Gentiles, the renewal of the earth from the effects of the curse, and the bodily resurrection of God's people who have died. Finally, the OT predicts that there will be the "uncreation" or dissolution of the universe, and the creation of a new heaven and new earth—which will be the eternal state of the godly—and a final hell for the ungodly.

In the NT, these features are clarified and expanded. The King was rejected and executed, but He promised to come back in glory, bringing judgment, resurrection, and His kingdom for all who believe. Innumerable Gentiles from every nation will be included among the redeemed. Israel will be saved and grafted back into the root of blessing from which she has been temporarily excised.

Israel's promised kingdom will be enjoyed, with the Lord Savior reigning on the throne, in the renewed earth, exercising power over the whole world, having taken back His rightful authority, and receiving due honor and worship. Following that kingdom will come the dissolution of the renewed, but still sin-stained creation, and the subsequent creation of a new heaven and new earth—which will be the eternal state, separate forever from the ungodly in hell.

Those are the five topics that fill up the Bible. To understand them at the start is to know the answer to the question that continually arises—Why does the Bible tell us this? Everything fits into this glorious pattern. As you read, hang the truth on these five hooks and the Bible will unfold, not as sixty-six separate documents, or even two separate testaments—but one book, by one divine Author, who wrote it all with one overarching theme.

My prayer is that the magnificent and overwhelming theme of the redemption of sinners for the glory of God will carry every reader with captivating interest from beginning to end of the story. Christian—this is your story. It is from God for you—about you. It tells what He planned for you, why He made you, what you were, what you have become in Christ, and what He has prepared for you in eternal glory.

The Holy Scriptures

KEY TEACHINGS OF THE
BIBLE

We teach that the Bible is God's written revelation to man, and thus the sixty-six books of the Bible given to us by the Holy Spirit constitute the plenary (inspired equally in all parts) Word of God (1 Cor. 2:7–14; 2 Pet. 1:20, 21).

We teach that the Word of God is an objective, propositional revelation (1 Cor. 2:13; 1 Thess. 2:13), verbally inspired in every word (2 Tim. 3:16), absolutely inerrant in the original documents, infallible, and God-breathed. We teach the literal, grammatical-historical interpretation of Scripture, which affirms the belief that the opening chapters of Genesis present creation in six literal days (Gen. 1:31; Ex. 31:17).

We teach that the Bible constitutes the only infallible rule of faith and practice (Matt. 5:18; 24:35; John 10:35; 16:12, 13; 17:17; 1 Cor. 2:13; 2 Tim. 3:15–17; Heb. 4:12; 2 Pet. 1:20, 21).

We teach that God spoke in His written Word by a process of dual authorship. The Holy Spirit so superintended the human authors that, through their individual personalities and different styles of writing, they composed and recorded God's Word to man (2 Pet. 1:20, 21) without error in the whole or in the part (Matt. 5:18; 2 Tim. 3:16).

We teach that, whereas there may be several applications of any given passage of Scripture, there is but one true interpretation. The meaning of Scripture is to be found as one diligently applies the literal, grammatical-historical method of interpretation under the enlightenment of the Holy Spirit (John 7:17; 16:12–15; 1 Cor. 2:7–15; 1 John 2:20). It is the responsibility of believers to ascertain carefully the true intent and meaning of Scripture, recognizing that proper application is binding on all generations. Yet the truth of Scripture stands in judgment of people; never do people stand in judgment of it.

God

We teach that there is but one living and true God (Deut. 6:4; Is. 45:5–7; 1 Cor. 8:4), an infinite, all-knowing Spirit (John 4:24), perfect in all His attributes, one in essence, eternally existing in three persons—Father, Son, and Holy Spirit (Matt. 28:19; 2 Cor. 13:14)—each equally deserving worship and obedience.

God the Father

We teach that God the Father, the first person of the Trinity, orders and disposes all things according to His own purpose and grace (Ps. 145:8, 9; 1 Cor. 8:6). He is the Creator of all things (Gen. 1:1–31; Eph. 3:9). As the only absolute and omnipotent ruler in the universe, He is sovereign in creation, providence, and redemption (Ps. 103:19; Rom. 11:36). His fatherhood involves both His designation within the Trinity and His relationship with mankind. As Creator, He is Father to all men (Eph. 4:6), but He is Spiritual Father only to believers (Rom. 8:14; 2 Cor. 6:18). He has decreed for His own glory all things that come to pass (Eph. 1:11). He continually upholds, directs, and governs all creatures and events (1 Chr. 29:11).

In His sovereignty, He is neither author nor approver of sin (Hab. 1:13), nor does He abridge the accountability of moral, intelligent creatures (1 Pet. 1:17). He has graciously chosen from eternity past those whom He would have as His own (Eph. 1:4–6); He saves from sin all those who come to Him through Jesus Christ; He adopts as His own all those who come to Him; and He becomes, upon adoption, Father to His own (John 1:12; Rom. 8:15; Gal. 4:5; Heb. 12:5–9).

God the Son
We teach that Jesus Christ, the second person of the Trinity, possesses all the divine excellencies, and in these He is coequal, consubstantial, and coeternal with the Father (John 10:30; 14:9).

We teach that God the Father created "the heavens and the earth and all that is in them" according to His own will, through His Son, Jesus Christ, by whom all things continue in existence and in operations (John 1:3; Col. 1:15–17; Heb. 1:2).

We teach that in the Incarnation (God becoming man) Christ surrendered only the prerogatives of deity but nothing of the divine essence, either in degree or kind. In His Incarnation, the eternally existing second person of the Trinity accepted all the essential characteristics of humanity and so became the God-man (Phil. 2:5–8; Col. 2:9).

We teach that Jesus Christ represents humanity and deity in indivisible oneness (Mic. 5:2; John 5:23; 14:9, 10; Col. 2:9).

We teach that our Lord Jesus Christ was virgin-born (Is. 7:14; Matt. 1:23, 25; Luke 1:26–35); that He was God incarnate (John 1:1, 14); and that the purpose of the Incarnation was to reveal God, redeem men, and rule over God's kingdom (Ps. 2:7–9; Is. 9:6; John 1:29; Phil. 2:9–11; Heb. 7:25, 26; 1 Pet. 1:18,

19).

We teach that, in the Incarnation, the second person of the Trinity laid aside His right to the full prerogatives of coexistence with God, assumed the place of a Son, and took on an existence appropriate to a servant while never divesting Himself of His divine attributes (Phil. 2:5–8).

We teach that our Lord Jesus Christ accomplished our redemption through the shedding of His blood and sacrificial death on the Cross and that His death was voluntary, vicarious, substitutionary, propitiatory, and redemptive (John 10:15; Rom. 3:24, 25; 5:8; 1 Pet. 2:24).

We teach that on the basis of the efficacy of the death of our Lord Jesus Christ, the believing sinner is freed from the punishment, the penalty, the power, and one day the very presence of sin; and that he is declared righteous, given eternal life, and adopted into the family of God (Rom. 3:25; 5:8, 9; 2 Cor. 5:14, 15; 1 Pet. 2:24; 3:18).

We teach that our justification is made sure by His literal, physical Resurrection from the dead and that He is now ascended to the right hand of the Father, where He now mediates as our Advocate and High Priest (Matt. 28:6; Luke 24:38, 39; Acts 2:30, 31; Rom. 4:25; 8:34; Heb. 7:25; 9:24; 1 John 2:1).

We teach that in the Resurrection of Jesus Christ from the grave, God confirmed the deity of His Son and gave proof that God has accepted the atoning work of Christ on the Cross. Jesus' bodily resurrection is also the guarantee of a future resurrection life for all believers (John 5:26–29; 14:19; Rom. 4:25; 6:5–10; 1 Cor. 15:20, 23).

We teach that Jesus Christ will return to receive the church, which is His body, unto Himself at the Rapture and, returning with His church in glory, will establish His millennial kingdom on earth (Acts 1:9–11; 1 Thess. 4:13–18; Rev. 20).

We teach that the Lord Jesus Christ is the one through whom God will judge all mankind (John 5:22, 23):

   a. Believers (1 Cor. 3:10–15; 2 Cor. 5:10);

   b. Living inhabitants of the earth at His glorious return (Matt. 25:31–46); and

   c. Unbelieving dead at the Great White Throne (Rev. 20:11–15).

As the mediator between God and man (1 Tim. 2:5), the head of His body the church (Eph. 1:22; 5:23; Col. 1:18), and the coming universal King who will reign on the throne of David (Is. 9:6, 7; Ezek. 37:24–28; Luke 1:31–33), He is the final judge of all who fail to place their trust in Him as Lord and Savior (Matt. 25:14–46; Acts 17:30, 31).

God the Holy Spirit

We teach that the Holy Spirit is a divine person, eternal, underived, possessing all the attributes of personality and deity, including intellect (1 Cor. 2:10–13), emotions (Eph. 4:30), will (1 Cor. 12:11), eternality (Heb. 9:14), omnipresence (Ps. 139:7–10), omniscience (Is. 40:13, 14), omnipotence (Rom. 15:13), and truthfulness (John 16:13). In all the divine attributes He is coequal and consubstantial with the Father and the Son (Matt. 28:19; Acts 5:3, 4; 28:25, 26; 1 Cor. 12:4–6; 2 Cor. 13:14; and Jer. 31:31–34 with Heb. 10:15–17).

We teach that it is the work of the Holy Spirit to execute the divine will with relation to all mankind. We recognize His sovereign activity in the creation (Gen. 1:2), the Incarnation (Matt. 1:18), the written revelation (2 Pet. 1:20, 21), and the work of salvation (John 3:5–7).

We teach that a unique work of the Holy Spirit in this age began at Pentecost when He came from the Father as promised by Christ (John 14:16, 17; 15:26) to initiate and com-plete the building of the body of Christ. His activity includes convicting the world of sin, of righteousness, and of judgment; glorifying the Lord Jesus Christ and transforming believers into the image of Christ (John 16:7–9; Acts 1:5; 2:4; Rom. 8:29; 2 Cor. 3:18; Eph. 2:22).

We teach that the Holy Spirit is the supernatural and sovereign agent in regeneration, baptizing all believers into the body of Christ (1 Cor. 12:13). The Holy Spirit also indwells, sanctifies, instructs, empowers them for service, and seals them unto the day of redemption (Rom. 8:9–11; 2 Cor. 3:6; Eph. 1:13).

We teach that the Holy Spirit is the divine teacher who guided the apostles and prophets into all truth as they committed to writing God's revelation, the Bible (2 Pet. 1:19–21). Every believer possesses the indwelling presence of the Holy Spirit from the moment of salvation, and it is the duty of all those born of the Spirit to be filled with (controlled by) the Spirit (Rom. 8:9–11; Eph. 5:18; 1 John 2:20, 27).

We teach that the Holy Spirit administers spiritual gifts to the church. The Holy Spirit glorifies neither Himself nor His gifts by ostentatious displays, but He does glorify Christ by implementing His work of redeeming the lost and building up believers in the most holy faith (John 16:13, 14; Acts 1:8; 1 Cor. 12:4–11; 2 Cor. 3:18).

We teach, in this respect, that God the Holy Spirit is sovereign in the bestowing of all His gifts for the perfecting of the saints today and that speaking in tongues and the working of sign miracles in the beginning days of the church were for the purpose of pointing to and authenticating the apostles as revealers of divine truth, and were never intended to be characteristic of the lives of believers (1 Cor. 12:4–11; 13:8–10; 2 Cor. 12:12; Eph. 4:7–12; Heb. 2:1–4).

Man

We teach that man was directly and immediately created by God in His image and likeness. Man was created free of sin with a rational nature, intelligence, volition, self-determination, and moral responsibility to God (Gen. 2:7, 15–25; James 3:9).

We teach that God's intention in the creation of man was that man should glorify God, enjoy God's fellowship, live his life in the will of God, and by this accomplish God's purpose for man in the world (Is. 43:7; Col. 1:16; Rev. 4:11).

We teach that in Adam's sin of disobedience to the revealed will and Word of God, man lost his innocence; incurred the penalty of spiritual and physical death; became subject to the wrath of God; and became inherently corrupt and utterly incapable of choosing or doing what is acceptable to God apart from divine grace. With no recuperative powers to enable him to recover himself, man is hopelessly lost. Man's salvation is thereby wholly of God's grace through the redemptive work of our Lord Jesus Christ (Gen. 2:16, 17; 3:1–19; John 3:36; Rom. 3:23; 6:23; 1 Cor. 2:14; Eph. 2:1–3; 1 Tim. 2:13, 14; 1 John 1:8).

We teach that because all men were in Adam, a nature corrupted by Adam's sin has been transmitted to all men of all ages, Jesus Christ being the only exception. All men are thus sinners by nature, by choice, and by divine affirmation (Ps. 14:1–3; Jer. 17:9; Rom. 3:9–18, 23; 5:10–12).

Salvation

We teach that salvation is wholly of God by grace on the basis of the redemption of Jesus Christ, the merit of His shed blood, and not on the basis of human merit or works (John 1:12; Eph. 1:4–7; 2:8–10; 1 Pet. 1:18, 19).

Election

We teach that election is the act of God by which, before the foundation of the world, He chose in Christ those whom He graciously regenerates, saves, and sanctifies (Rom. 8:28–30; Eph. 1:4–11; 2 Thess. 2:13; 2 Tim. 2:10; 1 Pet. 1:1, 2).

We teach that sovereign election does not contradict or negate the responsibility of man to repent and trust Christ as Savior and Lord (Ezek. 18:23, 32; 33:11; John 3:18, 19, 36; 5:40; 2 Thess. 2:10–12; Rev. 22:17). Nevertheless, since sovereign grace includes the means of receiving the gift of salvation as well as the gift itself, sovereign election will result in what God determines. All whom the Father calls to Himself will come in faith and all who come in faith the Father will receive (John 6:37–40, 44; Acts 13:48; James 4:8).

We teach that the unmerited favor that God grants to totally depraved sinners is not related to any initiative of their own part nor to God's anticipation of what they might do by their own will, but is solely of His sovereign grace and mercy (Eph. 1:4–7; Titus 3:4–7; 1 Pet. 1:2).

We teach that election should not be looked upon as based merely on abstract sovereignty. God is truly sovereign but He exercises this sovereignty in harmony with His other attributes, especially His omniscience, justice, holiness, wisdom, grace, and love (Rom. 9:11–16). This sovereignty will always exalt the will of God in a manner totally consistent with His character as revealed in the life of our Lord Jesus Christ (Matt. 11:25–28; 2 Tim. 1:9).

Regeneration

We teach that regeneration is a supernatural work of the Holy Spirit by which the divine nature and divine life are given (John 3:3–8; Titus 3:5). It is instantaneous and is accomplished solely by the power of the Holy Spirit through the instrumentality of the Word of God (John 5:24), when the repentant sinner, as enabled by the Holy Spirit, responds in faith to the divine provision of salvation. Genuine regeneration is manifested by fruits worthy of repentance as demonstrated in righteous attitudes and conduct. Good works will be its proper evidence and fruit (1 Cor. 6:19, 20; Eph. 5:17–21; Phil. 2:12b; Col. 3:12–17; 2 Pet. 1:4–11). This obedience causes the believer to be increasingly conformed to the image of our Lord Jesus Christ (2 Cor. 3:18). Such a conformity is climaxed in the believer's glorification at Christ's coming (Rom. 8:16, 17; 2 Pet. 1:4; 1 John 3:2, 3).

Justification

We teach that justification before God is an act of God (Rom. 8:30, 33) by which He declares righteous those who, through faith in Christ, repent of their sins (Luke 13:3; Acts 2:38; 3:19; 11:18; Rom. 2:4; 2 Cor. 7:10; Is. 55:6, 7) and confess Him as sovereign Lord (Rom. 10:9, 10; 1 Cor. 12:3; 2 Cor. 4:5; Phil. 2:11). This righteousness is apart from any virtue or work of man (Rom. 3:20; 4:6) and involves the placing of our sins on Christ (Col. 2:14; 1 Pet. 2:24) and the imputation of Christ's righteousness to us (1 Cor. 1:2, 30; 6:11; 2 Cor. 5:21). By this means, God is enabled to "be just, and the justifier of the one who has faith in Jesus" (Rom. 3:26).

Sanctification

We teach that every believer is sanctified (set apart) unto God by justification and is therefore declared to be holy and is therefore identified as a saint. This sanctification is positional and instantaneous and should not be confused with progressive sanctification. This sanctification has to do with the believer's standing, not his present walk or condition (Acts 20:32; 1 Cor. 1:2, 30; 6:11; 2

Thess. 2:13; Heb. 2:11; 3:1; 10:10, 14; 13:12; 1 Pet. 1:2).

We teach that there is also, by the work of the Holy Spirit, a progressive sanctification by which the state of the believer is brought closer to the likeness of Christ through obedience to the Word of God and the empowering of the Holy Spirit. The believer is able to live a life of increasing holiness in conformity to the will of God, becoming more and more like our Lord Jesus Christ (John 17:17, 19; Rom. 6:1–22; 2 Cor. 3:18; 1 Thess. 4:3, 4; 5:23).

In this respect, we teach that every saved person is involved in a daily conflict—the new creation in Christ doing battle against the flesh—but adequate provision is made for victory through the power of the indwelling Holy Spirit. The struggle nevertheless stays with the believer all through this earthly life and is never completely ended. All claims to the eradication of sin in this life are unscriptural. Eradication of sin is not possible, but the Holy Spirit does provide for victory over sin (Gal. 5:16–25; Phil. 3:12; Col. 3:9, 10; 1 Pet. 1:14–16; 1 John 3:5–9).

Security

We teach that all the redeemed, once saved, are kept by God's power and are thus secure in Christ forever (John 5:24; 6:37–40; 10:27–30; Rom. 5:9, 10; 8:1, 31–39; 1 Cor. 1:4–9; Eph. 4:30; Heb. 7:25; 13:5; 1 Pet. 1:4, 5; Jude 24).

We teach that it is the privilege of believers to rejoice in the assurance of their salvation through the testimony of God's Word which, however, clearly forbids the use of Christian liberty as an excuse for sinful living and carnality (Rom. 6:15–22; 13:13, 14; Gal. 5:13, 16, 17, 25, 26; Titus 2:11–14).

Separation

We teach that separation from sin is clearly

called for throughout the Old and New Testaments, and that the Scriptures clearly indicate that in the last days apostasy and worldliness will increase (2 Cor. 6:14–7:1; 2 Tim. 3:1–5).

We teach that out of deep gratitude for the undeserved grace of God granted to us and because our glorious God is so worthy of our total consecration, all the saved should live in such a manner as to demonstrate our adoring love to God and so as not to bring reproach upon our Lord and Savior. We also teach that separation from any association with religious apostasy, and worldly and sinful practices is commanded of us by God (Rom. 12:1, 2; 1 Cor. 5:9–13; 2 Cor. 6:14–7:1; 1 John 2:15–17; 2 John 9–11).

We teach that believers should be separated unto our Lord Jesus Christ (2 Thess. 1:11, 12; Heb. 12:1, 2) and affirm that the Christian life is a life of obedient righteousness demonstrated by a beatitude attitude (Matt. 5:2–12) and a continual pursuit of holiness (Rom. 12:1, 2; 2 Cor. 7:1; Heb. 12:14; Titus 2:11–14; 1 John 3:1–10).

The Church

We teach that all who place their faith in Jesus Christ are immediately placed by the Holy Spirit into one united spiritual body, the church (1 Cor. 12:12, 13), the bride of Christ (2 Cor. 11:2; Eph. 5:23–32; Rev. 19:7, 8), of which Christ is the head (Eph. 1:22; 4:15; Col. 1:18).

We teach that the formation of the church, the body of Christ, began on the day of Pentecost (Acts 2:1–21, 38–47) and will be completed at the coming of Christ for His own at the Rapture (1 Cor. 15:51, 52; 1 Thess. 4:13–18).

We teach that the church is thus a unique spiritual organism designed by Christ, made up of all born-again believers in this present age (Eph. 2:11–3:6). The church is distinct from Israel (1 Cor. 10:32), a mystery not revealed until this age (Eph. 3:1–6; 5:32).

We teach that the establishment and continuity of local churches is clearly taught and defined in the New Testament Scriptures (Acts 14:23, 27; 20:17, 28; Gal. 1:2; Phil. 1:1; 1 Thess. 1:1; 2 Thess. 1:1) and that the members of the one spiritual body are directed to associate themselves together in local assemblies (1 Cor. 11:18–20; Heb. 10:25).

We teach that the one supreme authority for the church is Christ (Eph. 1:22; Col. 1:18) and that church leadership, gifts, order, discipline, and worship are all appointed through His sovereignty as found in the Scriptures. The biblically designated officers serving under Christ and over the assembly are elders (males, who are also called bishops, pastors, and pastor-teachers; Acts 20:28; Eph. 4:11) and deacons, both of whom must meet biblical qualification (1 Tim. 3:1–13; Titus 1:5–9; 1 Pet. 5:1–5).

We teach that these leaders lead or rule as servants of Christ (1 Tim. 5:17–22) and have His authority in directing the church. The congregation is to submit to their leadership (Heb. 13:7, 17).

We teach the importance of discipleship (Matt. 28:19, 20; 2 Tim. 2:2), mutual accountability of all believers to each other (Matt. 18:15–17), as well as the need for discipline for sinning members of the congregation in accord with the standards of Scripture (Matt. 18:15–22; Acts 5:1–11; 1 Cor. 5:1–13; 2 Thess. 3:6–15; 1 Tim. 1:19, 20; Titus 1:10–16).

We teach the autonomy of the local church, free from any external authority or control, with the right of self-government and freedom from the interference of any hierarchy of individuals or organizations (Titus 1:5). We teach that it is scriptural for true churches to cooperate with each other for the presentation and propagation of the faith. Local churches, however, through their pastors and their interpretation and application of Scripture, should be the sole judges of the measure and method of their cooperation (Acts 15:19–31; 20:28; 1 Cor. 5:4–7, 13; 1 Pet. 5:1–4).

We teach that the purpose of the church is to glorify God (Eph. 3:21) by building itself up in the faith (Eph. 4:13–16), by instruction of the Word (2 Tim. 2:2, 15; 3:16, 17), by fellowship (Acts 2:47; 1 John 1:3), by keeping the ordinances (Luke 22:19; Acts 2:38–42) and by advancing and communicating the gospel to the entire world (Matt. 28:19; Acts 1:8).

We teach the calling of all saints to the work of service (1 Cor. 15:58; Eph. 4:12; Rev. 22:12).

We teach the need of the church to cooperate with God as He accomplishes His purpose in the world. To that end, He gives the church spiritual gifts. First, He gives men chosen for the purpose of equipping the saints for the work of the ministry (Eph. 4:7–12) and He also gives unique and special spiritual abilities to each member of the body of Christ (Rom. 12:5–8; 1 Cor. 12:4–31; 1 Pet. 4:10, 11).

We teach that there were two kinds of gifts given to the early church: miraculous gifts of divine revelation and healing, given temporarily in the apostolic era for the purpose of confirming the authenticity of the apostles' message (Heb. 2:3, 4; 2 Cor. 12:12); and ministering gifts, given to equip believers for edifying one another. With the New Testament revelation now complete, Scripture becomes the sole test of the authenticity of a person's message, and confirming gifts of a miraculous nature are no longer necessary to validate a person or his message (1 Cor. 13:8–12). Miraculous gifts can even be counterfeited by Satan so as to deceive

even believers (Matt. 24:24). The only gifts in operation today are those non-revelatory, equipping gifts given for edification (Rom. 12:6–8).

We teach that no one possesses the gift of healing today, but that God does hear and answer the prayer of faith and will answer in accordance with His own perfect will for the sick, suffering, and afflicted (Luke 18:1–8; John 5:7–9; 2 Cor. 12:6–10; James 5:13–16; 1 John 5:14, 15).

We teach that two ordinances have been committed to the local church: baptism and the Lord's Supper (Acts 2:38–42). Christian baptism by immersion (Acts 8:36–39) is the solemn and beautiful testimony of a believer showing forth his faith in the crucified, buried, and risen Savior, and his union with Him in death to sin and resurrection to a new life (Rom. 6: 1–11). It is also a sign of fellowship and identification with the visible body of Christ (Acts 2:41, 42).

We teach that the Lord's Supper is the commemoration and proclamation of His death until He comes, and should be always preceded by solemn self-examination (1 Cor. 11:23–32). We also teach that whereas the elements of Communion are only symbolically representative of the flesh and blood of Christ, the Lord's Supper is nevertheless an actual Communion with the risen Christ who is present in a unique way, fellowshiping with His people (1 Cor. 10:16).

Angels

Holy Angels

We teach that angels are created beings and are, therefore, not to be worshiped. Although they are a higher order of creation than man, they are created to serve God and to worship Him (Luke 2:9–14; Heb. 1:6, 7, 14; 2:6, 7; Rev. 5:11–14).

Fallen Angels

We teach that Satan is a created angel and the author of sin. He incurred the judgment of God by rebelling against his Creator (Is. 14:12–17; Ezek. 28:11–19), by taking numerous angels with him in his fall (Matt. 25:41; Rev. 12:1–14), and by introducing sin into the human race by his temptation of Eve (Gen. 3:1–15).

We teach that Satan is the open and declared enemy of God and man (Is. 14:13, 14; Matt. 4:1–11; Rev. 12:9, 10), the prince of this world who has been defeated through the death and Resurrection of Jesus Christ (Rom. 16:20), and that he shall be eternally punished in the lake of fire (Is. 14:12–17; Ezek. 28:11–19; Matt. 25:41; Rev. 20:10).

Last Things (Eschatology)

Death

We teach that physical death involves no loss of our immaterial consciousness (Rev. 6:9–11), that there is a separation of soul and body (James 2:26), that the soul of the redeemed passes immediately into the presence of Christ (Luke 23:43; 2 Cor. 5:8; Phil. 1:23), and that, for the redeemed, such separation will continue until the Rapture (1 Thess. 4:13–17) which initiates the first resurrection (Rev. 20:4–6), when our soul and body will be reunited to be glorified forever with our Lord (1 Cor. 15:35–44, 50–54; Phil. 3:21). Until that time, the souls of the redeemed in Christ remain in joyful fellowship with our Lord Jesus Christ (2 Cor. 5:8).

We teach the bodily resurrection of all people, the saved to eternal life (John 6:39; Rom. 8:10, 11, 19–23; 2 Cor. 4:14), and the unsaved to judgment and everlasting punishment (Dan. 12:2; John 5:29; Rev. 20:13–15).

We teach that the souls of the unsaved at death are kept under punishment until the final resurrection (Luke 16:19–26; Rev. 20:13–15), when the soul and the resurrection body will be united (John 5:28, 29). They shall then appear at the Great White Throne judgment (Rev. 20:11–15) and shall be cast into hell, the lake of fire (Matt. 25:41–46), cut off from the life of God forever (Dan. 12:2; Matt. 25:41–46; 2 Thess. 1:7–9).

The Rapture of the Church

We teach the personal, bodily return of our Lord Jesus Christ before the seven-year Tribulation (1 Thess. 4:16; Titus 2:13) to translate His church from this earth (John 14:1–3; 1 Cor. 15:51–53; 1 Thess. 4:15–5:11) and, between this event and His glorious return with His saints, to reward believers according to their works (1 Cor. 3:11–15; 2 Cor. 5:10).

The Tribulation Period

We teach that immediately following the removal of the church from the earth (John 14:1–3; 1 Thess. 4:13–18) the righteous judgments of God will be poured out upon an unbelieving world (Jer. 30:7; Dan. 9:27; 12:1; 2 Thess. 2:7–12; Rev. 16), and that these judgments will be climaxed by the return of Christ in glory to the earth (Matt. 24:27–31; 25:31–46; 2 Thess. 2:7–12). At that time, the Old Testament and Tribulation saints will be raised and the living will be judged (Dan. 12:2, 3; Rev. 20:4–6). This period includes the seventieth week of Daniel's prophecy (Dan. 9:24–27; Matt. 24:15–31; 25:31–46).

The Second Coming and the Millennial Reign

We teach that after the Tribulation period, Christ will come to earth to occupy the throne of David (Matt. 25:31; Luke 1:32, 33; Acts 1:10, 11; 2:29, 30) and establish His messianic kingdom for a thousand years on the earth (Rev. 20:1–7). During this time, the resurrected saints will reign with Him over Israel and all the nations of the earth (Ezek. 37:21–28; Dan. 7:17–22; Rev. 19:11–16). This reign will be preceded by the overthrow of the Antichrist and the false prophet, and by the removal of Satan from the world (Dan. 7:17–27; Rev. 20:1–6).

We teach that the kingdom itself will be the fulfillment of God's promise to Israel (Is. 65:17–25; Ezek. 37:21–28; Zech. 8:1–17) to restore them to the land which they forfeited through their disobedience (Deut. 28:15–68). The result of their disobedience was that Israel was temporarily set aside (Matt. 21:43; Rom. 11:1–26), but will again be awakened through repentance to enter into the land of blessing (Jer. 31:31–34; Ezek. 36:22–32; Rom. 11:25–29).

We teach that this time of our Lord's reign will be characterized by harmony, justice, peace, righteousness, and long life (Is. 11; 65:17–25; Ezek. 36:33–38), and will be brought to an end with the release of Satan (Rev. 20:7).

The Judgment of the Lost

We teach that following the release of Satan after the thousand-year reign of Christ (Rev. 20:7), Satan will deceive the nations of the earth and gather them to battle against the saints and the beloved city, at which time Satan and his army will be devoured by fire from heaven (Rev. 20:9). Following this, Satan will be thrown into the lake of fire and brimstone (Matt. 25:41; Rev. 20:10); whereupon Christ, who is the judge of all people (John 5:22), will resurrect and judge the great and small at the Great White Throne judgment.

We teach that this resurrection of the unsaved dead to judgment will be a physical resurrection; whereupon receiving their judgment (John 5:28, 29), they will be committed to an eternal, conscious punishment in the lake of fire (Matt. 25:41; Rev. 20:11–15).

Eternity

We teach that after the closing of the Millennium, the temporary release of Satan, and the judgment of unbelievers (2 Thess. 1:9; Rev. 20:7–15), the saved will enter the eternal state of glory with God, after which the elements of this earth are to be dissolved (2 Pet. 3:10) and replaced with a new earth wherein only righteousness dwells (Eph. 5:5; Rev. 20:15, 21, 22). Following this, the heavenly city will come down out of heaven (Rev. 21:2) and will be the dwelling place of the saints, where they will enjoy forever fellowship with God and one another (John 17:3; Rev. 21; 22). Our Lord Jesus Christ, having fulfilled His redemptive mission, will then deliver up the kingdom to God the Father (1 Cor. 15:23–28) that in all spheres the triune God may reign forever and ever (1 Cor. 15:28).

DEALING WITH
GOD'S WORD

Here are tips on how to get the most out of the study of this "divine handbook." These pointers will help answer the most crucial question of all, "How can a young man cleanse his way?" The psalmist responds, "By taking heed according to Your Word" (Ps. 119:9).

Why Is God's Word So Important?

Because it contains God's mind and will for your life (2 Tim. 3:16, 17). It is the only source of absolute, divine authority for you as a servant of Jesus Christ.

It is infallible in its totality. "The law of the Lord is perfect, converting the soul; the testimony of the Lord is sure, making wise the simple" (Ps. 19:7).

It is inerrant in its parts. "Every word of God is pure; He is a shield to those who put their trust in Him. Do not add to His words, lest He rebuke you, and you be found a liar" (Prov. 30:5, 6).

It is complete. "For I testify to everyone who hears the words of the prophecy of this book: If anyone adds to these things, God will add to him the plagues that are written in this book; and if anyone takes away from the words of the book of this prophecy, God shall take away his part from the Book of Life, from the holy city, and from the things which are written in this book" (Rev. 22:18, 19).

It is authoritative and final. "Forever, O Lord, Your word is settled in heaven" (Ps. 119:89).

It is totally sufficient for your needs. "That

the man of God may be complete, thoroughly equipped for every good work" (2 Tim. 3:16, 17).

It will accomplish what it promises. "So shall My word be that goes forth from My mouth; it shall not return to Me void, but it shall accomplish what I please, and it shall prosper in the thing for which I sent it" (Is. 55:11).

It provides the assurance of your salvation. "He who is of God hears God's words" (John 8:47; cf. 20:31).

How Will I Benefit from Studying God's Word?

Even with today's wealth of books and computer helps, the Bible remains the only source of divine revelation and power that can sustain Christians in their "daily walk with God." Note these significant promises in the Scripture.

The Bible is the source of truth. "Sanctify them by Your truth; Your word is truth" (John 17:17).

The Bible is the source of God's blessing when obeyed. "But He said, 'More than that, blessed are those who hear the word of God and keep it'" (Luke 11:28).

The Bible is the source of victory. "The sword of the Spirit, which is the word of God" (Eph. 6:17).

The Bible is the source of growth. "As newborn babes, desire the pure milk of the word, that you may grow thereby" (1 Pet. 2:2).

The Bible is the source of power. "For I am

not ashamed of the gospel of Christ, for it is the power of God to salvation for everyone who believes, for the Jew first and also for the Greek" (Rom. 1:16).

The Bible is the source of guidance. "Your word is a lamp to my feet and a light to my path" (Ps. 119:105).

What Should Be My Response to God's Word?

Because the Bible is so important and because it provides unparalleled eternal benefits, then these should be your responses:

Believe it (John 6:68, 69).
Honor it (Job 23:12).
Love it (Ps. 119:97).
Obey it (1 John 2:5).
Guard it (1 Tim. 6:20).
Fight for it (Jude 3).
Preach it (2 Tim. 4:2).
Study it (Ezra 7:10).

Who Can Study the Bible?

Not everyone can be a Bible student. Check yourself on these necessary qualifications for studying the Word with blessing:

Are you saved by faith in Jesus Christ (1 Cor. 2:14–16)?
Are you hungering for God's Word (1 Pet. 2:2)?
Are you searching God's Word with diligence (Acts 17:11)?
Are you seeking holiness (1 Pet. 1:14–16)?
Are you Spirit-filled (Eph. 5:18)?

The most important question is the first. If you have never invited Jesus Christ to be your personal Savior and the Lord of your life, then your mind is blinded by Satan to God's truth (2 Cor. 4:4).

If Christ is your need, stop reading right now and, in your own words with prayer, turn away from sin and turn toward God: "For by grace you have been saved through faith, and that not of yourselves; it is the gift of God, not of works, lest anyone should boast" (Eph. 2:8, 9).

What Are the Basics of Bible Study?

Personal Bible study, in precept, is simple. I want to share with you five steps to Bible study which will give you a pattern to follow.

Step 1—Reading. Read a passage of Scripture repeatedly until you understand its theme, i.e., the main truth of the passage. Isaiah said, "Whom will he teach knowledge? And whom will he make to understand the message? Those just weaned from milk? Those just drawn from the breasts? For precept must be upon precept, precept upon precept, line upon line, here a little, there a little" (Is. 28:9, 10).

Develop a plan on how you will approach reading through the Bible. Unlike most books, you will probably not read it straight through from cover to cover. There are many good Bible reading plans available, but here is one that I have found helpful.

Read through the Old Testament at least once a year. As you read, note in the margins any truths you particularly want to remember, and write down separately anything you do not immediately understand. Often as you read, you will find that many questions are answered by the text itself. The questions to which you cannot find answers become the starting points for more in-depth study using commentaries or other reference tools.

Follow a different plan for reading the New Testament. Read one book at a time repetitiously for a month or more. This will help you to retain what is in the New Testament and not always have to depend on a concordance to find things.

If you want to try this, begin with a short book, such as 1 John, and read it through in one sitting every day for thirty days. At the end of that time, you will know what is in the book. Write on index cards the major theme of each chapter. By referring to the cards as you do your daily reading, you will begin to remember the content of each chapter. In fact, you will develop a visual perception of the book in your mind.

Divide longer books into short sections and read each section daily for thirty days. For example, the Gospel of John contains twenty-one chapters. Divide it into three sections of seven chapters. At the end of ninety days, you will finish John. For variety, alternate short and long books, and in less than three years you will have finished the entire New Testament—and you will really know it!

Step 2—Interpreting. In Acts 8:30, Philip asked the Ethiopian eunuch, "Do you understand what you are reading?" Or put another way, "What does the Bible mean by what it says?" It is not enough to read the text and jump directly to the application; we must first determine what it means; otherwise the application may be incorrect.

As you read Scripture, always keep in mind one simple question: "What does this mean?" To answer that question requires the use of the most basic principle of interpretation, called the analogy of faith, which tells the reader to "interpret the Bible with the Bible." Letting the Holy Spirit be your teacher (1 John 2:27), search the Scripture He has authored, using cross-references, comparative passages, concordances, indexes, and other helps. For those passages that yet remain unclear, consult your pastor or godly people who have written in that particular area.

Errors to Avoid. As you interpret Scripture, several common errors should be avoided.

1. *Do not draw any conclusions at the price of proper interpretation.* That is, do not make the Bible say what you want it to say, but rather let it say what God intended when He wrote it.

2. *Avoid superficial interpretation.* You have heard people say, "To me, this passage means," or "I feel it is saying." The first step in interpreting the Bible is to recognize the four gaps we have to bridge: language, culture, geography, and history (see below).

3. *Do not spiritualize the passage.* Interpret and understand the passage in its normal, literal, historical, grammatical sense, just like you would understand any other piece of literature you were reading today.

Gaps to Bridge. The books of the Bible were written many centuries ago. For us to understand today what God was communicating then, there are several gaps that need to be bridged: the language gap, the cultural gap, the geographical gap, and the historical gap. Proper interpretation, therefore, takes time and disciplined effort.

1. *Language.* The Bible was originally written in Greek, Hebrew, and Aramaic. Often, understanding the meaning of a word or phrase in the original language can be the key to correctly interpreting a passage of Scripture.

2. *Culture.* The culture gap can be tricky. Some people try to use cultural differences to explain away the more difficult biblical commands. Realize that Scripture must first be viewed in the context of the culture in which it was written. Without an understanding of first-century Jewish culture, it is difficult to understand the Gospels. Acts and the Epistles must be read in light of the Greek and Roman cultures.

3. *Geography.* A third gap that needs to be closed is the geography gap. Biblical geography makes the Bible come alive. A good Bible atlas is an invaluable reference tool that can help you comprehend the geography of the Holy Land.

4. *History.* We must also bridge the his-

tory gap. Unlike the scriptures of most other world religions, the Bible contains the records of actual historical persons and events. An understanding of Bible history will help us place the people and events in it in their proper historical perspective. A good Bible dictionary or Bible encyclopedia is useful here, as are basic historical studies.

Principles to Understand. Four principles should guide us as we interpret the Bible: literal, historical, grammatical, and synthesis.

1. *The Literal Principle.* Scripture should be understood in its literal, normal, and natural sense. While the Bible does contain figures of speech and symbols, they were intended to convey literal truth. In general, however, the Bible speaks in literal terms, and we must allow it to speak for itself.

2. *The Historical Principle.* This means that we interpret a passage in its historical context. We must ask what the text meant to the people to whom it was first written. In this way, we can develop a proper contextual understanding of the original intent of Scripture.

3. *The Grammatical Principle.* This requires that we understand the basic grammatical structure of each sentence in the original language. To whom do the pronouns refer? What is the tense of the main verb? You will find that when you ask some simple questions like those, the meaning of the text immediately becomes clearer.

4. *The Synthesis Principle.* This is what the Reformers called the *analogia scriptura.* It means that the Bible does not contradict itself. If we arrive at an interpretation of a passage that contradicts a truth taught elsewhere in the Scriptures, our interpretation cannot be correct. Scripture must be compared with Scripture to discover its full meaning.

Step 3—*Evaluating.* You have been reading and asking the question, "What does the Bible say?" Then you have interpreted, asking the question, "What does the Bible mean?" Now, it is time to consult others to insure that you have the proper interpretation. Remember, the Bible will never contradict itself.

Read Bible introductions, commentaries, and background books which will enrich your thinking through that illumination which God has given to other men and to you through their books. In your evaluation, be a true seeker. Be one who accepts the truth of God's Word even though it may cause you to change what you always have believed, or cause you to alter your life pattern.

Step 4—*Applying.* The next question is: "How does God's truth penetrate and change my own life?" Studying Scripture without allowing it to penetrate to the depths of your soul would be like preparing a banquet without eating it. The bottom-line question to ask is, "How do the divine truths and principles contained in any passage apply to me in terms of my attitude and actions?"

Jesus made this promise to those who would carry their personal Bible study through to this point: "If you know these things, blessed are you if you do them" (John 13:17).

Having read and interpreted the Bible, you should have a basic understanding of what the Bible says, and what it means by what it says. But studying the Bible does not stop there. The ultimate goal should be to let it speak to you and enable you to grow spiritually. That requires personal application.

Bible study is not complete until we ask ourselves, "What does this mean for my life and how can I practically apply it?" We must take the knowledge we have gained from our reading and interpretation and draw out the practical principles that apply to our personal lives.

If there is a command to be obeyed, we obey it. If there is a promise to be embraced, we claim it. If there is a warning to be followed, we heed it. This is the ultimate step: we submit to Scripture and let it transform our lives. If you skip this step, you will never enjoy your Bible study and the Bible will never change your life.

Step 5—Correlating. This last stage connects the doctrine you have learned in a particular passage or book with divine truths and principles taught elsewhere in the Bible to form the big picture. Always keep in mind that the Bible is one book in sixty-six parts, and it contains a number of truths and principles, taught over and over again in a variety of ways and circumstances. By correlating and cross-referencing, you will begin to build a sound doctrinal foundation by which to live.

What Now?

The psalmist said, "Blessed is the man who walks not in the counsel of the ungodly, nor stands in the path of sinners, nor sits in the seat of the scornful; But his delight is in the law of the Lord, and in His law he meditates day and night" (Ps. 1:1, 2).

It is not enough just to study the Bible. We must meditate upon it. In a very real sense we are giving our brain a bath; we are washing it in the purifying solution of God's Word.

BIBLE BOOK
ABBREVIATIONS

The Old Testament

Genesis . . . . .Gen.	2 Chronicles . . . . .2 Chr.	Daniel . . . . .Dan.
Exodus . . . . .Ex.	Ezra . . . . .Ezra	Hosea . . . . .Hos.
Leviticus . . . . .Lev.	Nehemiah . . . . .Neh.	Joel . . . . .Joel
Numbers . . . . .Num.	Esther . . . . .Esth.	Amos . . . . .Amos
Deuteronomy . . . . . . .Deut.	Job . . . . .Job	Obadiah . . . . .Obad.
Joshua . . . . .Josh.	Psalms . . . . .Ps.	Jonah . . . . .Jon.
Judges . . . . .Judg.	Proverbs . . . . .Prov.	Micah . . . . .Mic.
Ruth . . . . .Ruth	Ecclesiastes . . . . .Eccl.	Nahum . . . . .Nah.
1 Samuel . . . . .1 Sam.	Song of Solomon . . . .Song	Habakkuk . . . . .Hab.
2 Samuel . . . . .2 Sam.	Isaiah . . . . .Is.	Zephaniah . . . . .Zeph.
1 Kings . . . . .1 Kin.	Jeremiah . . . . .Jer.	Haggai . . . . .Hag.
2 Kings . . . . .2 Kin.	Lamentations . . . . . . .Lam.	Zechariah . . . . .Zech.
1 Chronicles . . . . .1 Chr.	Ezekiel . . . . .Ezek.	Malachi . . . . .Mal.

The New Testament

Matthew . . . . .Matt.	Ephesians . . . . .Eph.	Hebrews . . . . .Heb.
Mark . . . . .Mark	Philippians . . . . .Phil.	James . . . . .James
Luke . . . . .Luke	Colossians . . . . .Col.	1 Peter . . . . .1 Pet.
John . . . . .John	1 Thessalonians . . . . .1 Thess.	2 Peter . . . . .2 Pet.
Acts . . . . .Acts	2 Thessalonians . . . . .2 Thess.	1 John . . . . .1 John
Romans . . . . .Rom.	1 Timothy . . . . .1 Tim.	2 John . . . . .2 John
1 Corinthians . . . . . . .1 Cor.	2 Timothy . . . . .2 Tim.	3 John . . . . .3 John
2 Corinthians . . . . . . .2 Cor.	Titus . . . . .Titus	Jude . . . . .Jude
Galatians . . . . .Gal.	Philemon . . . . .Philem.	Revelation . . . . .Rev.

Key to Parenthetical References

( )	exact text
(cf.)	corroborative text
(see)	amplifying/clarifying text
(contra.)	contrasting text

LIST OF
CHARTS, MAPS, AND ARTICLES

LIST OF
WORD STUDIES

The Progress of Revelation

OLD TESTAMENT

	Book	Approximate Writing Date	Author
1.	Job	Unknown	Anonymous
2.	Genesis	1445–1405 B.C.	Moses
3.	Exodus	1445–1405 B.C.	Moses
4.	Leviticus	1445–1405 B.C.	Moses
5.	Numbers	1445–1405 B.C.	Moses
6.	Deuteronomy	1445–1405 B.C.	Moses
7.	Psalms	1410–450 B.C.	Multiple Authors
8.	Joshua	1405–1385 B.C.	Joshua
9.	Judges	ca. 1043 B.C.	Samuel
10.	Ruth	ca. 1030–1010 B.C.	Samuel (?)
11.	Song of Solomon	971–965 B.C.	Solomon
12.	Proverbs	971–686 B.C.	Solomon primarily
13.	Ecclesiastes	940–931 B.C.	Solomon
14.	1 Samuel	931–722 B.C.	Anonymous
15.	2 Samuel	931–722 B.C.	Anonymous
16.	Obadiah	850–840 B.C.	Obadiah
17.	Joel	835–796 B.C.	Joel
18.	Jonah	ca. 760 B.C.	Jonah
19.	Amos	ca. 755 B.C.	Amos
20.	Hosea	755–710 B.C.	Hosea
21.	Micah	735–710 B.C.	Micah
22.	Isaiah	700–681 B.C.	Isaiah
23.	Nahum	ca. 650 B.C.	Nahum
24.	Zephaniah	635–625 B.C.	Zephaniah
25.	Habakkuk	615–605 B.C.	Habakkuk
26.	Ezekiel	590–570 B.C.	Ezekiel
27.	Lamentations	586 B.C.	Jeremiah
28.	Jeremiah	586–570 B.C.	Jeremiah
29.	1 Kings	561–538 B.C.	Anonymous
30.	2 Kings	561–538 B.C.	Anonymous
31.	Daniel	536–530 B.C.	Daniel
32.	Haggai	ca. 520 B.C.	Haggai
33.	Zechariah	480–470 B.C.	Zechariah
34.	Ezra	457–444 B.C.	Ezra
35.	1 Chronicles	450–430 B.C.	Ezra (?)
36.	2 Chronicles	450–430 B.C.	Ezra (?)
37.	Esther	450–331 B.C.	Anonymous
38.	Malachi	433–424 B.C.	Malachi
39.	Nehemiah	424–400 B.C.	Ezra

INTRODUCTION TO THE
PENTATEUCH

The first five books of the Bible (Genesis, Exodus, Leviticus, Numbers, Deuteronomy) form a complete literary unit called the Pentateuch, meaning "five scrolls." The five independent books of the Pentateuch were written as an unbroken unity in content and historical sequence, with each succeeding book beginning where the former left off.

The first words of Genesis, "In the beginning God created" (Gen. 1:1) imply the reality of God's eternal or "before time" existence and announce the spectacular transition to time and space. While the exact date of creation cannot be determined, it certainly would be estimated to be thousands of years ago, not millions. Starting with Abraham (c. 2165–1990 B.C.) in Genesis 11, this book of beginnings spans over 300 years to the death of Joseph in Egypt (c. 1804 B.C.). There is then another gap of almost 300 years until the birth of Moses in Egypt (c. 1525 B.C.; Ex. 2).

Exodus begins with the words, "Now these are the names" (Ex. 1:1), listing those of the family of Jacob who went down to Egypt to be with Joseph toward the end of Genesis (Gen. 46ff.). The second book of the Pentateuch, which records the escape of the Israelites from Egypt, concludes when the cloud which led the people through the wilderness descends upon the newly constructed tabernacle.

The first Hebrew words of Leviticus may be translated, "Now the LORD called to Moses" (Lev. 1:1). From the cloud of God's presence in the tabernacle of meeting (Lev. 1:1), God summons Moses in order to prescribe to him the ceremonial law which told Israel how they must approach their holy Lord. Leviticus concludes with, "These are the commandments which the Lord commanded Moses for the children of Israel on Mount Sinai" (Lev. 27:34).

Numbers, much like Leviticus, begins with God commissioning Moses at the tabernacle of meeting, this time to take a census in preparation for war against Israel's enemies. The book's title in the Hebrew Bible accurately represents the content—"Wilderness." Due to lack of trust in God, Israel did not want to engage its enemies militarily in order to claim the Promised Land. After forty additional years in the wilderness for their rebellion, Israel arrived on the plains of Moab.

Despite the fact that "It is eleven days' journey from Horeb by way of Mount Seir to Kadesh Barnea" (Deut. 1:2), the journey took Israel forty years because of their rebellion against God. Moses preached the book of Deuteronomy as a sermon on the plains of Moab in preparation for God's people to enter the land of covenant promise (Gen. 12:1–3). The title *Deuteronomy* is from the Greek phrase *deuteros nomos,* meaning "second law." The book focuses on the restatement and, to some extent, the reapplication of the law to Israel's new circumstances.

Moses was the human author of the Pentateuch (Ex. 17:14; 24:4; Num. 33:1, 2;

Deut. 31:9; Josh. 1:8; 2 Kin. 21:8); thus, another title for the collection is "The Books of Moses." Through Moses, God revealed Himself, His former works, Israel's family history, and its role in His plan of redemption for mankind. The Pentateuch is foundational to all the rest of Scripture.

Quoted or alluded to thousands of times in the OT and in the NT, the Pentateuch was Israel's first inspired body of Scripture. For many years, this alone was Israel's Bible. Another common title for this section of Scripture is *Torah* or Law, nomenclature which looks at the didactic nature of these books. The Israelites were to meditate upon it (Josh. 1:8), teach it to their children (Deut. 6:4–8), and read it publicly (Neh. 8:1ff.). Just before his death and Israel's move into the Promised Land, Moses set forth the process by which public reading would make its way into human hearts and change their relationship with God, and ultimately their conduct: "Gather the people together, men and women and little ones, and the stranger who is within your gates, that they may hear and that they may learn to fear the LORD your God and carefully observe all the words of this law" (Deut. 31:12).

The relationships between the commands is important. The people must: (1) gather to hear the law in order to learn what is required of them and what it has to say about God; (2) learn about the Lord in order to fear Him based on a correct understanding of who He is; and (3) fear God in order to be correctly motivated to obedience and good works. Good works performed for any other reason will be improperly motivated. The priests taught the law to the families (Mal. 2:4–7) and the parents instructed the children within the home (Deut. 6:4ff.). Instruction in the law, in short, would provide the right foundation for the OT believer's relationship with God.

Because the Israelites' knowledge of the world in which they lived came through the Egyptians, as well as their ancestors the Mesopotamians, there was much confusion about the creation of the world, how it got to its present state, and how Israel had come into existence. Genesis 1–11 helped Israel understand the origin and nature of creation, human labor, sin, marriage, murder, death, bigamy, judgment, the multiplicity of languages, cultures, etc. These chapters established the worldview which explained the remainder of Israel's first Bible, the Pentateuch.

The later portion of Genesis explained to Israel who they were, including the purpose God had for them as a people. In Genesis 12:1–3, God had appeared to Abraham and made a threefold promise to give them a land, descendants, and blessing. Years later, in a ceremony typical of Abraham's culture, God recast the threefold promise into a covenant (Gen. 15:7ff.). The remainder of Genesis treats the fulfillment of all three promises, but focuses especially on the seed or descendants. The barrenness of each of the patriarch's chosen wives taught Israel the importance of trust and patience in waiting for children from God.

The rest of the Pentateuch looks at the way in which the promises of Genesis 12:1–3 expand in the Abrahamic covenant and achieve their initial stages of fulfillment. Exodus and Leviticus focus more on the blessing of relationship with God. In Exodus, Israel meets the God of their fathers and is led forth by Him from Egypt to the Promised Land. Leviticus underscores the meticulous care with which the people and priests were to approach God in worship and every dimension of their lives. Holiness and cleanness come together in simple and practical ways. Numbers and Deuteronomy focus on the journey to and preparation for the land. The Pentateuch treats many issues related to Israel's relationship with their God. But the underlying theme of the Pentateuch is the initial, unfolding fulfillments of God's promises made to Abraham.

THE FIRST BOOK OF MOSES CALLED
GENESIS

Title

The English title, Genesis, comes from the Greek translation (Septuagint, LXX), meaning "origins"; whereas, the Hebrew title is derived from the Bible's very first word, translated "in the beginning." Genesis serves to introduce the Pentateuch (the first five books of the OT) and the entire Bible. The influence of Genesis in Scripture is demonstrated by being quoted over thirty-five times in the NT, with hundreds of allusions appearing in both testaments. The story line of salvation begins in Genesis 3 and is not completed until Revelation 21 and 22 where the eternal kingdom of redeemed believers is gloriously pictured.

Author and Date

While (1) the author does not identify himself in Genesis and (2) Genesis ends almost three centuries before Moses was born, both the OT (Ex. 17:14; Num. 33:2; Josh. 8:31; 1 Kin. 2:3; 2 Kin. 14:6; Ezra 6:18; Neh. 13:1; Dan. 9:11, 13; Mal. 4:4) and the NT (Matt. 8:4; Mark 12:26; Luke 16:29; 24:27, 44; John 5:46; 7:22; Acts 15:1; Rom. 10:19; 1 Cor. 9:9; 2 Cor. 3:15) ascribe this composition to Moses, who is the fitting author in light of his educational background (cf. Acts 7:22). No compelling reasons have been forthcoming to legitimately challenge Mosaic authorship. Genesis was written after the Exodus (c. 1445 B.C.), but before Moses' death (c. 1405 B.C.). For a brief biographical sketch of Moses, read Exodus 1–6.

Background and Setting

The initial setting for Genesis is eternity past. God, by willful act and divine Word, then spoke all creation into existence, furnished it, and finally breathed life into a lump of dirt which He fashioned in His image to become Adam. God made mankind the crowning point of His creation, i.e., His companions who would enjoy fellowship with Him and bring glory to His name.

The historical background for the early events in Genesis is clearly Mesopotamian. While it is difficult to pinpoint precisely the historical moment for which this book was written, Israel first heard Genesis sometime prior to crossing the Jordan River and entering the Promised Land (c. 1405 B.C.).

Genesis has three distinct, sequential geographical settings: (1) Mesopotamia (chs. 1–11); (2) the Promised Land (chs. 12–36); and (3) Egypt (chs. 37–50). The time frames of these three segments are: (1) Creation to c. 2090 B.C.; (2) 2090–1897 B.C.; and (3) 1897–1804 B.C. Overall, Genesis covers more time than the remaining books of the Bible combined.

Historical and Theological Themes

In this book of beginnings, God revealed Himself and a worldview to Israel which contrasted, at times sharply, with the worldview of Israel's neighbors. The author made no attempt to defend the existence of God or to present a systematic discussion of His person and works. Rather, Israel's God distinguished Himself clearly from the alleged gods of her neighbors. Theological foundations are revealed which include God the Father, God the Son, God the Holy Spirit, man, sin, redemption, covenant, promise, Satan and angels, kingdom, revelation, Israel, judgment, and blessing.

Genesis 1–11 (primeval history) reveals the origins of the universe, i.e., the beginnings of time and space and many of the firsts in human experience, such as marriage, family, the Fall, sin, redemption, judgment, and nations. Genesis 12–50 (patriarchal history) explained to Israel how they came into existence as a family whose ancestry could be traced to Eber (hence the "Hebrews"; Gen. 10:24, 25) and even more remotely to Shem, the son of Noah (hence the "Semites"; Gen. 10:21). God's people came to understand not only their ancestry and family history, but also the origins of their institutions, customs, languages, and different cultures, especially basic human experiences such as sin and death.

Because they were preparing to enter Canaan and dispossess the Canaanite inhabitants of their homes and properties, God revealed their enemies' backgrounds. In addition, they needed to understand the actual basis of the war they were about to declare, in light of the immorality of killing, consistent with the other four books that Moses was writing (Exodus, Leviticus, Numbers, and Deuteronomy). Ultimately, the Jewish nation would understand a selected portion of preceding world history and the inaugural background of Israel as a basis by which they would live in their new beginnings under Joshua's leadership in the land that had previously been promised to their original patriarchal forefather, Abraham.

Genesis 12:1–3 established a primary focus on God's promises to Abraham. This narrowed their view from the entire world of peoples in Genesis 1–11 to one small nation, Israel, through whom God would progressively accomplish His redemptive plan. This underscored Israel's mission to be "a light to the Gentiles" (Is. 42:6). God promised land, descendants (seed), and blessing. This three-fold promise became, in turn, the basis of the covenant with Abraham (Gen. 15:1–20). The rest of Scripture bears out the fulfillment of these promises.

On a larger scale, Genesis 1–11 sets forth a singular message about the character and works of God. In the sequence of accounts which make up these chapters, a pattern emerges which reveals God's abundant grace as He responded to the willful disobedience of mankind. Without exception, in each account God increased the manifestation of His grace. But also without exception, man responded in greater sinful rebellion. In biblical words, the more sin abounded, the more did God's grace abound (cf. Rom. 5:20).

One final theme of both theological and historical significance sets Genesis apart from other books of Scripture, in that the first book of Scripture corresponds closely with the final book. In the Book of Revelation, the paradise which was lost in Genesis will be regained. The apostle John clearly presented the events recorded in his book as future resolutions to the problems which began as a result of the curse in Genesis 3. His focus is on the effects of the Fall in the undoing of creation and the manner in which God rids His creation of the curse effect. In John's own words, "And there shall be no more curse" (Rev. 22:3).

Not surprisingly, in the final chapter of God's Word, believers will find themselves back in the Garden of Eden, the eternal paradise of God, eating from the Tree of Life (Rev. 22:1–14). At that time, they will partake, while wearing robes washed in the blood of the Lamb (Rev. 22:14).

Interpretive Challenges

Grasping the individual messages of Genesis which make up the larger plan and purpose of the book presents no small challenge since both the individual accounts and the book's overall message offer important lessons for faith and works. Genesis presents creation by divine fiat, *ex nihilo*, i.e., "out of nothing." Three traumatic events of epic proportions—the Fall, the universal flood, and the dispersion of nations—are presented as historical backdrop in order to understand world history. From Abraham on, the pattern is to focus on God's redemption and blessing.

The customs of Genesis often differ considerably from those of modern times. They must be explained against their ancient Near Eastern background. Each custom must be treated according to the immediate context of the passage before any attempt is made to explain it based on customs recorded in extrabiblical sources or even elsewhere in Scripture.

Genesis by content is comprised of two basic sections: (1) Primitive history (Gen. 1–11) and (2) Patriarchal history (Gen. 12–50). Primitive history records four major events: (1) creation (Gen. 1; 2); (2) the Fall (Gen. 3–5); (3) the flood (Gen. 6–9); and (4) the dispersion (Gen. 10; 11). Patriarchal history spotlights four great men: (1) Abraham (Gen. 12:1–25:8); (2) Isaac (Gen. 21:1–35:29); (3) Jacob (Gen. 25:21–50:14); and (4) Joseph (Gen. 30:22–50:26).

The literary structure of Genesis is built on the frequently recurring phrase "the history/genealogy of" and is the basis for the following outline.

Outline

I. THE CREATION OF HEAVEN AND EARTH (1:1–2:3)

1:1 This description of God creating heaven and earth is understood to be: (1) recent, i.e., thousands not millions of years ago; (2) *ex nihilo*, i.e., out of nothing; and (3) special, i.e., in six, consecutive, twenty-four-hour periods called "days" and further distinguished as such by this phrase, "the evening and the morning." Scripture does not support a creation date that makes the earth any more than about ten thousand years old. *In the beginning.* While God exists eternally (Ps. 90:2), this marked the beginning of the universe in time and space. In explaining Israel's identity and divine purpose for being to her on the plains of Moab, God wanted His people to know about the origin of the world in which they found themselves. *God.* Elohim, which means "supreme one," is a general term for deity and a specific name for the true God, though it is used also at times, in a relative sense, for pagan gods (31:30), angels (Ps. 8:5), men (Ps. 82:6), and judges (Ex. 21:6). Moses made no attempt to defend the existence of God, which is assumed; nor did he explain what He was like in person or how He works, which is treated elsewhere (cf. Is. 43:10, 13). All are to be believed by faith. (cf. Heb. 11:3, 6). *created.* This word is used here of God's creative activity alone, although it occasionally is used elsewhere of matter which already existed (Is. 65:18). Context demands, in no uncertain terms, that this was a creation without preexisting material (as does other Scripture: cf. Is. 40:28; 45:8, 12, 18; 48:13; Jer. 10:16; Acts 17:24). A simple decree from God brought the created thing into being. Matter emerged from that which was immaterial. Out of nothing, in an instant, the universe—with all its space and matter—was made by God's decree. The universe—at least its energy and

mass—began to exist in some form. *the heavens and the earth.* All of God's creation is incorporated into this summary statement which includes all six, consecutive days of creation.

1:2 *without form, and void.* This means "not finished in its shape and, as yet, uninhabited by creatures" (cf. Is. 45:18, 19; Jer. 4:23). The Hebrew expression signifies a wasteland, a desolate place. The earth was an empty place of utter desolation, existing in a formless, barren state, shrouded in darkness and water or mist of some sort. It suggests that the very shape of the earth was unfinished and empty. The raw material was all there, but it had not yet been given form. God would quickly (in six days) decorate His initial creation (v. 2–2:3). *deep.* Sometimes referred to as primordial waters, this is the term used to describe the earth's water-covered surface before the dry land emerged (vv. 9, 10). The earth's surface was a vast ocean—a global, primordial sea that covered the entire planet. Water, so vital to the nourishment of the life that was to come, was already earth's most prominent feature. Jonah used this word to describe the watery abyss in which he found himself submerged (Jon. 2:5). *Spirit of God.* The earth's creative agent enveloped, surrounded, and guarded its surface. Not only did God the Holy Spirit participate in creation, but so did God the Son (cf. John 1:1–3; Col. 1:16; Heb. 1:2).

1:3–5 This is day one of God's creation.
1:3 *God said.* God effortlessly spoke light into existence (cf. Pss. 33:6; 148:5), which dispelled the darkness of verse 2. *light.* That which most clearly reveals and most closely approximates God's glory (cf. Dan. 2:22; 1 Tim. 6:16; James 1:17; 1 John 1:5). Like Him, light illuminates and makes all else known. Without light, all creation would remain cold and dark. What form this light

took is not clear. But light itself, the reality of light, was created on day one and instantly separated day from night. The greater and lesser lights (the sun and moon) were created later (vv. 14–19) on the fourth day. Here, God was the provider of light (2 Cor. 4:6) and will in eternity future be the source of light (cf. Rev. 21:23).

1:4 *good.* This light was good for the purposes it was intended to serve (cf. v. 31).

1:4–5 *divided . . . called.* After the initial creation, God continued to complete His universe. Once God separated certain things, He then named them. Separating and naming were acts of dominion and served as a pattern for man, who would also name a portion of God's creation over which God gave him dominion (2:19, 20). The creation of light also inaugurated the measurement of earth's time by periods of day and night. Regular intervals of light began to be interspersed with intervals of darkness.

1:5 *first day.* God established the pattern of creation in seven days which constituted a complete week. *Day* can refer to: (1) the light portion of a twenty-four-hour period (1:5, 14); (2) an extended period of time (2:4); or (3) the twenty-four-hour period which basically refers to a full rotation of the earth on

its axis, called evening and morning. On the other hand, this cannot mean an age, but only a day, reckoned by the Jews from sunset to sunset (vv. 8, 13, 19, 23, 31). *Day* with numerical adjectives in Hebrew always refers to a twenty-four-hour period. Comparing the order of the week in Exodus 20:8–11 with the creation week confirms this understanding of the time element. Such a cycle of light and dark means that the earth was rotating on its axis, so that there was a source of light on one side of the earth, though the sun was not yet created (v. 16).

1:6–8 This is day two of God's creation.

1:6 *firmament.* The Hebrew word speaks of something spread out. God commanded the water to separate, and He placed an expanse, or a "firmament," between the water that remained on the earth and the water that now rose above the expanse. The imagery is that of a vast expanse, a protective layer that overlays the earth and divides the waters below from the waters above. The expanse in-between includes the earth's breathable atmosphere.

1:7 *under the firmament.* This refers to subterranean reservoirs (cf. 7:11). ***above the firmament.*** This could possibly have been a

The Pentateuch

Book	Key Idea	The Nation	The People	God's Character	God's Role	God's Command
Genesis	Beginnings	Chosen	Prepared	Powerful Sovereign	Creator	"Let there be!"
Exodus	Redemption	Delivered	Redeemed	Merciful	Deliverer	"Let my people go!"
Leviticus	Worship	Set Apart	Taught	Holy	Sanctifier	"Be holy!"
Numbers	Wandering	Directed	Tested	Just	Sustainer	"Go in!"
Deuteronomy	Renewed Covenant	Made Ready	Retaught	Loving Lord	Rewarder	"Obey!"

Nelson's Complete Book of Bible Maps & Charts (Nashville: Thomas Nelson Publishers, 1996) 3. © 1993 by Thomas Nelson, Inc.

canopy of water vapor which acted to make the earth like a hothouse, provided uniform temperature, inhibited mass air movements, caused mist to fall, and filtered out ultraviolet rays, and thereby extending life.

1:9–13 This is day three of God's creation.

1:9–10 dry land. This was caused by a tremendous, cataclysmic upheaval of the earth's surface, and the rising and sinking of the land, which caused the waters to plunge into the low places, forming the seas, the continents and islands, the rivers and lakes (cf. Job 38:4–11; Ps. 104:6–9).

1:11 whose seed is in itself. This is the basis of the principle of reproduction that marks all life (cf. vv. 22, 24, 28). God made the vegetation not only capable of reproduction, but also ready for it. He created fully mature vegetation with seed already in it, ready to be dispersed.

1:11–12 according to its kind. God set in motion a providential process whereby the vegetable kingdom could reproduce through seeds which would maintain each one's unique characteristics. The same phrase is used to describe the perpetuating reproduction of animals within their created species (vv. 21, 24, 25), and indicates that evolution, which proposes reproduction across species lines, is a false explanation of origins.

1:14–19 This is day four of God's creation.

1:14 lights. Cf. verse16. For three days, there had been light (v. 4) in the day as though there were a sun, and lesser light at night as though there were the moon and stars. God could have left it that way, but He did not. He created the "lights, sun, moon, and stars," not for light, but to serve as markers for signs, seasons, days, and years. From now on there would be light-bearing bodies that would perpetually shine on the earth at the proper intervals and seasons. What had

been a disembodied blanket of diffused supernatural light was superseded by a universe full of light-bearing bodies. The alternation between day and night continued, but now heavenly bodies provided the varying degrees of light. The entire panoply of heaven was complete and fully functioning on the day God made it. **signs.** The Hebrew word means "beacons" or "signals." It suggests that the heavenly bodies were set in place to serve as markers to indicate times and seasons. These certainly included: (1) weather (Matt. 16:2, 3); (2) testimony to God (Pss. 8; 19; Rom. 1:14–20; (3) divine judgment (Joel 2:30, 31; Matt. 24:29); and (4) navigation (Matt. 2:1, 2). **seasons.** It is the earth's movement in relation to the sun and moon that determines the seasons and the calendar.

1:15–19 two great lights . . . to divide the light from the darkness. It was God (not some other deity) who created the lights. Israel had originally come from Mesopotamia, where the celestial bodies were worshiped, and more recently from Egypt, where the sun was worshiped as a primary deity. God was revealing to them that the very stars, moons, and planets which Israel's neighbors had falsely worshiped were the products of His creation. Later, they became worshipers of the "host of heaven" *(see note on 2 Kin. 17:16),* which led to their being taken captive out of the Promised Land. Tragically, the world's population would choose to worship the creation rather than the Creator (Rom. 1:25).

1:20–23 This is day five of God's creation.

1:20 living creatures. These creatures, including the extraordinarily large ones, included all sorts of fish and mammals, even dinosaurs *(see notes on Job 40:15–41:1).*

1:22 blessed. This is the first occurrence of the word *bless* in Scripture. God's admonition to "be fruitful and multiply" was the substance of the blessing.

1:24–31 This is day six of God's creation.

1:24–25 cattle ... beast. This probably represents all kinds of large, four-legged animals. The Hebrew word translated "cattle" speaks of livestock and animals that can be domesticated. Sheep, goats, and oxen would no doubt be included. All are known primarily for their uses to humanity.

1:24 beast of the earth. Different from and larger than the clan of cattle, this would include dinosaurs like Behemoth (Job 40:15ff.).

1:26 Us ... Our. This is the first clear indication of the triunity of God (cf. 3:22; 11:7). The very name of God, Elohim (1:1), is a plural form of El. The plural pronouns introduce a plurality of relationships in the Godhead. They suggest both communion and consultation among the members of the Trinity. They also signify perfect agreement and clear purpose. **man.** The crowning point of creation, a living human, was made in God's image to rule creation. **Our image ... likeness.** This speaks of the creation of Adam in terms that are uniquely personal. It establishes a personal relationship between God and man that does not exist with any other aspect of creation. It is the very thing that makes humanity different from every other created animal. It explains why the Bible places so much stress on God's hands-on creation of Adam. He fashioned this creature in a special way—to bear the stamp of His own likeness. It suggests that God was, in essence, the pattern for the personhood of man. The image of God is personhood, and personhood can function only in the context of relationships. Man's capacity for intimate, personal relationships needed fulfillment. Most important, man was designed to have a personal relationship with God. It is impossible to divorce this truth from the fact that man is an ethical creature. All true relationships have ethical ramifications. It is at this point that God's communicable attributes come into play. Man is a living being capable of embodying God's communicable attributes (cf. 9:6; Rom. 8:29; Col. 3:10; James 3:9). In his rational life, he was like God in that he could reason and had intellect, will, and emotion. In the moral sense, he was like God because he was good and sinless. However, it did not bestow deity upon man.

1:26–28 have dominion ... subdue. This defined man's unique relation to creation, i.e., man was God's representative in ruling over the creation. The command to rule separated him from the rest of living creation and defined his relationship as above the rest of creation (cf. Ps. 8:6–8).

1:27 male and female. Cf. Matthew 19:4; Mark 10:6. While these two persons equally shared God's image and together exercised dominion over creation, they were by divine design physically diverse in order to accomplish God's mandate to multiply, i.e., neither one could reproduce offspring without the other.

1:28 blessed. This second blessing (cf. v. 22) involved reproduction and dominion. Be fruitful and multiply; fill the earth and subdue it. God, having just created the universe, created His representative (dominion) and representation (cf. v. 26, image and likeness). Man would fill the earth and oversee its operation. Subdue does not suggest a wild and unruly condition for the creation because God Himself pronounced it "good." Rather, it speaks of a productive ordering of the earth and its inhabitants to yield its riches and accomplish God's purposes.

1:29-30 for food ... for food. Prior to the curse (3:14–19), both mankind and beasts were vegetarians.

1:31 very good. What had been pronounced good individually (vv. 4, 10, 12, 18, 21, 25) was now called "very good" collectively. There were no flaws or omissions.

The work was complete in every sense. God was pleased with it. A whole universe now existed where nothing had existed only a week earlier. It was a vast cosmos full of countless wonders, each of which displayed the glory and wisdom of a good and perfect Creator. The words anticipated God's conclusion that it was "not good" for a man to be alone (2:18), which occurred on the sixth day.

2:1-3 This is day seven of God's creation.
These words affirm that God had completed His work. Four times it is said that He finished His work, and three times it is said that this included all His work. Present processes in the universe reflect God sustaining that completed creation, not more creation (cf. Heb. 1:3).

2:2 ended . . . rested. God certainly did not rest due to weariness; rather, establishing the pattern for man's work cycle, He only modeled man's need for rest. The entire work of creation was complete. With the dawn of the seventh day, God ceased from creating. When God works there is no dissipation of His energy. He cannot be fatigued, and He doesn't need rejuvenation. The Hebrew word translated "rested" simply means that He abstained from creative work. He had completed all of creation, so there was nothing more for Him to create. Later, the Sabbath ordinance of Moses found its basis in the creation week (cf. Ex. 20:8–11). The Sabbath was God's sacred, ordained day in the weekly cycle. Jesus said, "The Sabbath was made for man" (Mark 2:27) and verse 3 stated that God "sanctified" or set apart the Sabbath day because He rested in it. Later, it was set aside for a day of worship in the Mosaic Law (see note on Ex. 20:8). No ordinance mandating Sabbath rest and worship is expressly instituted here. There were no restrictions governing what Adam could and could not do on the seventh day of the week. All of that came later, with the giving of the law to Israel. The specific ceremonial requirements outlined in the Mosaic Sabbath laws would have been superfluous in Eden. Everything about Adam's life before he sinned was precisely what the Sabbath laws pictured. In a sense, Israel's Sabbath observances were designed to show in microcosm what life in Eden was designed to be. And this aspect of Moses' Law was merely a ceremonial reminder of what God's original design for human life involved. Adam would have lived in a perpetual Sabbath rest, if he had not fallen into sin. Hebrews 4:4 distinguishes between physical rest and the redemptive rest to which it pointed. Colossians 2:16 makes it clear that the Mosaic "Sabbath" has no symbolic or ritual place in the New Covenant. The church began worshiping on the first day of the week to commemorate the Resurrection of Christ (see note on Acts 20:7).

II. The Generations of the Heavens and the Earth (2:4–4:26)

A. Adam and Eve in Eden (2:4–25)

2:4–25 the history of. This section fills in the details of man's creation on day six which were not included in 1:1–2:3. How did Moses obtain this account, so different from the absurd fictions of the pagans? Not from any human source, for man was not in existence to witness it. Not from the light of reason, for though intellect can know the eternal power of the Godhead (Rom. 1:18–20) and that God made all things, it cannot know how. None but the Creator Himself could give this data and, therefore, it is through faith that one understands that the worlds were formed by the Word of God (Heb. 11:3).

2:4–5 *before any plant.* Verse 4 gives a summary of days one and two, before the vegetation of day three.

2:6 *mist went up.* This should be translated "flow." It indicates that water came up from beneath the ground as springs and spread over the whole earth in an uninterrupted cycle of water. After the Fall, rain became the primary means of watering the earth and allowed for floods and droughts that did not exist originally. Rains also allowed God to judge through floods and droughts.

2:7 *formed.* Many of the words used in this account of the creation of man picture a master craftsman at work shaping a work of art to which he gives life (1 Cor. 15:45). This adds detail to the statement of fact in 1:27 (cf. Ps. 139:14, 15; 1 Tim. 2:13). Made from dirt, a man's value is not in the physical components that form his body, but in the quality.

2:8 *garden . . . Eden.* The Babylonians called the lush green land from which water flowed *edenu;* today, the term *oasis* describes such a place. This was a magnificent garden paradise, unlike any the world has seen since, where God fellowshiped with those He created in His image. It was also a garden with minerals, including every precious stone. The exact location of Eden is unknown; if "eastward" was used in relationship to where Moses was when he wrote, then it could have been in the area of Babylon, the Mesopotamian valley.

2:9 *tree of life.* There was nothing harmful in the tree itself or in the fruit of the tree. This was a real tree, with special properties to sustain eternal life. Placed in the center of the garden, it must have been observed by Adam, and its fruit perhaps eaten by him, thus sustaining his life (v. 16). Such a tree, symbolic of eternal life, will be in the new heavens and new earth (*see note on Rev. 22:2*). *tree . . . knowledge.* Cf. verse 16;

3:1–6, 11, 22. It was perhaps given that title because it was a test of obedience by which our first parents were tried, whether they would be good or bad—obey God or disobey His command. If Adam didn't disobey, he would never know evil; but when he disobeyed, he experienced evil because evil is disobedience.

2:10 *out of.* That is to say "the source," which likely refers to some great spring gushing up inside the garden from a subterranean reservoir. There was no rain at that time.

2:11 *Pishon . . . Havilah.* The locations are uncertain. This represents pre-flood geography, now dramatically altered.

2:12 *Bdellium.* This is a gum resin and refers more to appearance than color, i.e., it had the appearance of a pale resin.

2:13 *Gihon . . . Cush.* The river location is uncertain. Cush could be modern-day Ethiopia.

2:14 *Hiddekel . . . Assyria.* The post-flood Tigris River runs northwest to southeast east of the city of Babylon through the Mesopotamian Valley. *Euphrates.* A river that runs parallel (northwest to southeast) to the Tigris and empties into the Persian Gulf after joining the Tigris.

2:15 *tend and keep it.* Work was an important and dignified part of representing the image of God and serving Him, even before the Fall. Cf. Revelation 22:3. Adam was made the gardener in Eden. This was an easy and pleasant assignment because it was a source of great joy. It was the only work he was given to do—if such an occupation can even be called "work" in a sweatless, weedless, curse-free environment. His only responsibility was to make sure that the trees and plants had appropriate care. He was a guardian and steward of its wonders and resources.

2:17 *surely die.* To die has the basic idea of separation. It can mean spiritual separation, physical separation, and/or eternal separation. At the moment of their sin, Adam and Eve died spiritually but, because God was merciful, they did not die physically until later (5:5). There is no reason given for this prohibition, other than it was a test *(see note on v. 9)*. There was nothing magical about that tree, but eating from it after it had been forbidden by God would indeed give man the knowledge of evil—since evil can be defined as disobeying God. Man already had the knowledge of good.

2:18 *not good.* When God saw His creation as very good (1:31), He viewed it as being, to that point, the perfect outcome to His creative plan. However, in observing man's state as not good, He was commenting on his incompleteness before the end of the sixth day because the woman, Adam's counterpart, had not yet been created. The words of this verse emphasize man's need for a

companion, a helper, and an equal. He was incomplete without someone to complement him in fulfilling the task of filling, multiplying, and taking dominion over the earth. This points to Adam's inadequacy, not Eve's insufficiency (cf. 1 Cor. 11:9). Woman was made by God to meet man's deficiency (cf. 1 Tim. 2:14).

2:19 This was not a new creation of animals. They were created before man on the fifth and sixth days (1:20–25). Here, the Lord God was calling attention to the fact that He created them "out of the ground" as He did man; but man, who was a living soul in the image of God, was to name them, thus signifying his rule over them.

2:20 *gave names to.* Naming is an act of discerning something about the creature so as to appropriately identify it; also it is an act of leadership or authority over that which was named. This was Adam's first task. He

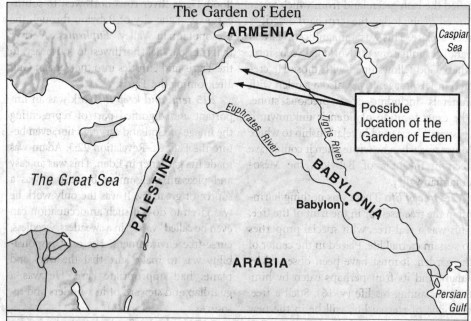

The Garden of Eden may have been located near the Tigris River, which the Bible calls Hiddekel (2:14).

The MacArthur Bible Handbook, by John MacArthur (Nashville: Thomas Nelson Publishers, 2003) 7. © 2003 by Thomas Nelson, Inc.

had to look at the characteristics of each creature and give it a fitting name. It is the Creator's privilege to name what He creates. Man was made in God's image, so it was appropriate that God would delegate to man something of His own sovereign prerogative. There is no kinship with any animal since none was a fitting companion for Adam.

2:21 *one of his ribs.* Ribs is better translated "sides," including surrounding flesh ("flesh of my flesh," v. 23). Divine surgery by the Creator presented no problems. This would also imply the first act of healing in Scripture. The woman was also created in God's image, but instead of being made out of material in the earth, she was created with material from the man. Eve's genetic structure was derived from and therefore perfectly harmonious with Adam's.

2:23 *bone of my bones.* Adam's poem focuses on naming the delight of his heart in this newly found companion. The man *(ish)* names her "woman" *(isha)* because she had her source in him (the root of the word *woman* is *soft*). She truly was made of bone from his bones and flesh from his flesh. (cf. 1 Cor. 11:8). The English words *man/woman* sustain the same relationship as the Hebrew words, hinting at that original creation.

2:24 *leave . . . be joined to.* The marital relationship was established as the first human institution. The responsibility to honor one's parents (Ex. 20:12) does not cease with leaving and the union of husband with wife (Matt. 19:5; Mark 10:7, 8; 1 Cor. 6:16; Eph. 5:31), but does represent the inauguration of a new and primary responsibility. *Joined* carries the sense of a permanent or indissoluble union, so that divorce was not considered (cf. v. 16). "One flesh" speaks of a complete unity of parts making a whole, e.g., one cluster, many grapes (Num. 13:23) or one God in three persons (Deut. 6:4); thus, this mari-

tal union was complete and whole with two people. This also implies their sexual completeness. One husband and one wife constitute the married pair to reproduce. The "one flesh" is primarily seen in the child born of that union, the one perfect result of the union of two. Cf. Matthew 19:5, 6; Mark 10:8; 1 Cor. 6:16; Ephesians 5:31. Permanent male/female monogamy was and continues to be God's only design and law for marriage. God has ordained and acknowledges sexual conduct only in the marriage relationship between a man and woman. All other sexual behavior is excluded.

2:25 *both naked . . . not ashamed.* With no knowledge of evil before the Fall, even nakedness was shameless and innocent. Shame is produced by the consciousness of the evil in something. They had no shame because they had no knowledge of evil. There was a beauty in the shameless wonder of that original marriage. They found their complete gratification in the joy of their one union and their service to God. With no inward principle of evil to work on, the solicitation to sin had to come from without, and it would.

B. The Fall and Its Outcomes (3:1–24)

3:1 *the serpent.* The word means "snake." The apostle John identified this creature as Satan (cf. Rev. 12:9; 20:2) as did Paul (2 Cor. 11:3). The serpent, a manifestation of Satan, appears for the first time before the Fall of man. The rebellion of Satan, therefore, had occurred sometime after 1:31 (when everything in creation was good), but before verse 1. Cf. Ezekiel 28:11–15 for a possible description of Satan's dazzling beauty and Isaiah 14:13, 14 for Satan's motivation to challenge God's authority (cf. 1 John 3:8). Satan, being a fallen archangel and, thus, a supernatural spirit, had possessed the body of a snake in its pre-Fall form (cf. v. 14 for post-Fall form).

more cunning. Deceitful; cf. Matthew 10:16.
to the woman. She was the object of his attack, being the weaker one and needing the
protection of her husband. He found her
alone and unfortified by Adam's experience
and counsel. Cf. 2 Timothy 3:6. Though sinless, she was temptable and seducible. ***Has
God . . . said?*** In effect Satan said, "Is it true
that He has restricted you from the delights
of this place? This is not like one who is truly
good and kind. There must be some mistake." He insinuated doubt as to her understanding of God's will, appearing as an angel
of light (2 Cor. 11:14) to lead her to the supposed true interpretation. She received him
without fear or surprise, but as some credible
messenger from heaven with the true understanding, because of his cunning.

3:2–3 In her answer, Eve extolled the
great liberty that they had; with only one exception, they could eat all the fruit.

3:3 *nor shall you touch it.* This appears to
be an addition to the original prohibition as
recorded (cf. Gen. 2:17). Adam may have so
instructed her for her protection. It could
also mean that Eve, apparently beginning to
feel God's restriction was too harsh, added to
the harshness of it.

3:4–5 *not . . . die.* Satan, emboldened by
Eve's openness to him, spoke this direct lie.
This lie actually led her and Adam to spiritual death (separation from God). So Satan
is called a liar and murderer from the beginning (John 8:44). His lies always promise
great benefits (cf. v. 5). Eve experienced this
result—she and Adam did know good and
evil; but by personal corruption, they did
not know as God knows in perfect holiness.

3:6 *good . . . pleasant . . . desirable.* Eve's
deception took three forms. That the tree
was *good* for food appealed to her physical
appetite—an illicit appetite provoked by a
selfish discontent and a distrust of God. That
its was *pleasant* to the eyes excited her emo-

tional appetite—as covetousness grew in her
heart, the forbidden fruit looked better and
better. And that the fruit was *desirable* to
make one wise provoked her intellectual appetite—she desired knowledge and was
tempted by the false promise that it would
make her like God. She decided that Satan
was telling the truth and she had misunderstood God, but she didn't know what she
was doing. It was not overt rebellion against
God, but seduction and deception to make
her believe her act was the right thing to do
(cf. v. 13). The NT confirms that Eve was deceived (2 Cor. 11:3; 1 Tim. 2:14; Rev. 12:9).
he ate. A direct transgression without deception *(see note on 1 Tim. 2:13, 14).*

3:7 *opened . . . knew . . . sewed.* The innocence noted in 2:25 had been replaced by
guilt and shame (vv. 8–10) and, from then
on, they had to rely on their conscience to
distinguish between good and their newly
acquired capacity to see and know evil. The
serpent had promised them enlightenment—what they received was a hideously
twisted caricature. It opened their eyes to the
meaning of guilt, but it made them want to
hide their eyes in shame. Sin instantly destroyed their innocence. Even the holy gift of
their physical relationship was polluted with
a sense of shame. Gone was the purity of it.
Now present were wicked and impure
thoughts they had never known before.
Sewing fig leaves together as a covering was a
noble effort to cover their sin and mask their
shame. Ever since, clothing has been a universal expression of human modesty.

3:8 God appeared, as before, in tones of
goodness and kindness, walking in some
visible form (perhaps Shekinah light as He
later appeared in Ex. 33:18–23; 34:5–8, 29;
40:34–38). He came not in fury, but in the
same condescending way He had walked
with Adam and Eve before.

3:9 *"Where are you?"* The question was

God's way of bringing man to explain why he was hiding, rather than expressing ignorance about man's location. Shame, remorse, confusion, guilt, and fear all led to their clandestine behavior. There was no place to hide. See Psalm 139:1–12.

3:10 *Your voice.* The sound in verse 8 probably was God calling for Adam and Eve. Adam responded with the language of fear and sorrow, but not confession.

3:11 Adam's sin was evidenced by his new knowledge of the evil of nakedness, but God still waited for Adam to confess to what God knew they had done. The basic reluctance of sinful people to admit their iniquity is here established. Repentance is still the issue. When sinners refuse to repent, they suffer judgment; when they do repent, they receive forgiveness.

3:12 *The woman whom You gave.* Adam pitifully attempted to put the responsibility on God for giving him Eve. That only magnified the tragedy in that Adam had knowingly transgressed God's prohibition, but still would not be open and confess his sin, taking full responsibility for his action, which was not made under deception (1 Tim. 2:14).

3:13 *The serpent deceived me.* The woman's desperate effort to pass the blame to the serpent, which was partially true (1 Tim. 2:14), did not absolve her of the responsibility for her distrust and disobedience toward God.

3:14 *to the serpent.* The cattle and all the rest of creation were cursed (see Rom. 8:20–23; cf. Jer. 12:4) as a result of Adam's and Eve's eating, but the serpent was uniquely cursed by being made to slither on its belly. It probably had legs before this curse. Now, snakes represent all that is odious, disgusting, and low. They are branded with infamy and avoided with fear. Cf. Isaiah 65:25; Micah 7:17.

3:15 After cursing the physical serpent, God turned to the spiritual serpent, the lying seducer, Satan, and cursed him. *bruise your head . . . bruise His heel.* This "first gospel" is prophetic of the struggle and its outcome between "your seed" (Satan and unbelievers, who are called the devil's children in John 8:44) and her seed (Christ, a descendant of Eve, and those in Him), which began in the garden. In the midst of the curse passage, a message of hope shone forth—the woman's offspring called "He" is Christ, who will one

The Fall

The Fall refers to that moment in time when human beings first disobeyed God. Genesis 3 tells the painful episode. What Eve set in motion, Adam confirmed and completed by joining her. They sinned together. The willful decision of Adam and Eve created a state of rebellion between the creation and her Creator.

The expression "the Fall" comes from the Bible itself. The apostle Paul uses the word in summarizing the human condition in Romans 3:23, "For all have sinned and fall short of the glory of God." It carries with it the sense of defeat and destruction. Great cities fell. So did people. But another fall preceded all these—the fall of the angel Lucifer, who became known as Satan (Is. 14:12–15).

The Bible makes it clear that the Fall brought sin into every subsequent person's life: "Therefore, just as through one man sin entered the world, and death through sin, and thus death spread to all men, because all sinned" (Rom. 5:12). One's capacity for sin is inborn. A person is a sinner before he has the opportunity to sin. All have inherited the effects of Adam's fall.

day defeat the serpent. Satan could only "bruise" Christ's heel (cause Him to suffer), while Christ will bruise Satan's head (destroy him with a fatal blow). Paul, in a passage strongly reminiscent of chapter 3, encouraged the believers in Rome, "And the God of peace will crush Satan under your feet shortly" (Rom. 16:20). Believers should recognize that they participate in the crushing of Satan because, along with the Savior and because of His finished work on the cross, they also are of the woman's seed. For more on the destruction of Satan, see Hebrews 2:14, 15; Revelation 20:10.

3:16 *conception . . . pain.* This is a constant reminder that a woman gave birth to sin in the human race and genetically passes it on to all her children. She can be delivered from this curse by raising godly children, as indicated in 1 Timothy 2:15 *(see notes there).* **Your desire . . . he shall rule.** Just as the woman and her seed will engage in a war with the serpent, i.e., Satan and his seed (v. 15), because of sin and the curse, the man and the woman will face struggles in their own relationship. Sin has turned the harmonious system of God-ordained roles into distasteful struggles of self-will. Lifelong companions, husbands and wives, will need God's help in getting along as a result. The woman's desire will be to lord it over her husband, but the husband will rule by divine design (Eph. 5:22–25). This interpretation of the curse is based upon the identical Hebrew words and grammar being used in 4:7 *(see note there)* to show the conflict man will have with sin as it seeks to rule him.

3:17 *Because you have heeded.* The reason given for the curse on the ground and human death is that man turned his back on the voice of God, to follow his wife in eating that from which God had ordered him to abstain. The woman sinned because she acted independently of her husband, disdaining

his leadership, counsel, and protection. The man sinned because he abandoned his leadership and followed the wishes of his wife. In both cases, God's intended roles were reversed.

3:17–18 *Cursed is the ground for your sake.* God cursed the object of man's labor and made it reluctantly, yet richly, yield his food through hard work. Weeds and thorns would henceforth infest the ground. Pain, weariness, and sweat would make life difficult. Adam was thus condemned to a life of labor, tilling the cursed earth.

3:19 *return to the ground.* I.e., to die (cf. 2:7). Man, by sin, became mortal. Although he did not physically die the moment he ate (by God's mercy), he was changed immediately and became subject to all the sufferings and miseries of life, to death, and to the pains of hell forever. Adam lived 930 years (5:5).

3:21 *tunics of skin.* It is appropriate that those bearing the guilt of sin should cover themselves. God Himself demonstrated this when He killed animals to use their skins as a covering for the fallen couple. This was a graphic object lesson showing that *only* God can provide a suitable covering for sin, and that the shedding of blood is a necessary part of the process (Heb. 9:22). The first physical deaths should have been the man and his wife, but it was an animal—a shadow of the reality that God would someday kill a substitute to redeem sinners.

3:22 *like one of Us. See note on 1:26.* This was spoken out of compassion for the man and woman, who only in limited ways were like the Trinity, knowing good and evil—not by holy omniscience, but by personal experience (cf. Is. 6:3; Hab. 1:13; Rev. 4:8).

3:22–23 *and live forever. See note on 2:9.* God told man that he would surely die if he ate of the forbidden tree. But God's concern may also have been that man not live forever in his pitifully cursed condition. Taken in the broader context of Scripture, driving the man and his wife out of the garden was an act of merciful grace to prevent them from being sustained forever by the tree of life.

3:24 cherubim. Later in Israel's history, two cherubim or angelic figures guarded the ark of the covenant and the Holy of Holies in the tabernacle (Ex. 25:18–22), where God communed with His people. *flaming sword.* An unexplainable phenomenon, perhaps associated directly with the cherubim or the flaming, fiery Shekinah presence of God Himself.

C. Murder of a Brother (4:1–24)

4:1 Adam knew Eve his wife. The act of sexual intercourse was considered the only means by which God Himself gave children. He was acknowledged as the sovereign giver of all life.

4:2 she bore again. Some think the boys may have been twins, since no time element intervenes between verses 1 and 2. *keeper of sheep . . . tiller of the ground.* Both occupations were respectable; in fact, most people subsisted through a combination of both. God's focus was not on their vocation, but on the nature of their respective offerings.

4:3 fruit of the ground. This speaks of produce in general.

4:4 firstborn . . . fat. The best animals.

4:4–5 Abel's offering was acceptable (cf. Heb. 11:4), not just because it was an animal, nor just because it was the very best of what he had, nor even that it was the culmination of a zealous heart for God, but because it was in every way obediently given according to what God must have revealed (though not recorded in Genesis). Cain, disdaining the divine instruction, just brought what he wanted to bring: some of his crop.

4:5–6 very angry. Rather than being repentant for his sinful disobedience, Cain was violently hostile toward God, whom he could not kill, and jealous of his brother, whom he could kill (cf. 1 John 3:12; Jude 11).

4:7 do well . . . be accepted? God reminded Cain that if he had obeyed God and offered the animal sacrifices God had required, his sacrifices would have been acceptable. It wasn't personal preference on God's part, or disdain for Cain's vocation, or the quality of his produce that caused God to reject his sacrifice. *sin lies at the door.* God told Cain that if he chose not to obey His commands, ever-present sin, crouched and waiting to pounce like a lion, would fulfill its desire to overpower him (cf. 3:16).

4:8 The first murder in Scripture (cf. Matt. 23:35; Luke 11:51; Heb. 12:24). Cain rejected the wisdom spoken to him by God Himself, rejected doing good, refused to repent, and crouching sin thus pounced and turned him into a killer. Cf. 1 John 3:10–12.

4:9 Am I my brother's keeper? Cain's sarcasm was a play on words, based on the fact that Abel was the "keeper" of sheep. Lying was the third sin (unacceptable worship and anger being the first two) resulting from Cain's attitude of indifference toward God's commands. Sin was ruling over him (v. 7).

4:10 voice . . . blood. A figure of speech to indicate that Abel's death was well known to God.

4:11 cursed from the earth. A second curse came from God, affecting just the productivity of the soil Cain would till. To a farmer like Cain, this curse was severe, and meant that Cain would all his life be a wanderer, "a fugitive and a vagabond" (vv. 12, 14).

4:14 anyone . . . kill me. This shows that the population of the earth was, by then, greatly increased. As a wanderer and scavenger in an agrarian world, Cain would be easy prey for those who wanted his life.

4:15 mark. While not described here, it involved some sort of identifiable sign that he was under divine protection which was mercifully given to Cain by God. At the same time, the mark that saved him was the lifelong sign of his shame.

4:16 Nod. An unknown location.

4:17 Cain knew his wife. Cain's wife obviously was one of Adam's later daughters (5:4). By Moses' time, this kind of close marriage was forbidden (Lev. 18:7–17), because of genetic decay. **Enoch.** His name means "initiation," and was symbolic of the new city where Cain would try to mitigate his curse.

4:19 two wives. No reason is given on Lamech's part for the first recorded instance of bigamy. He led the Cainites in open rebellion against God (cf. 2:24) by his violation of marriage law.

4:20 Jabal. He invented tents and inaugurated the nomadic life of herdsmen so common in the Middle East and elsewhere.

4:21 Jubal. He invented both stringed and wind instruments.

4:22 Tubal-Cain. He invented metallurgy.

4:23–24 Lamech killed someone in self-defense. He told his wives that they need not fear any harm coming to them for the killing because, if anyone tried to retaliate, he would retaliate and kill them. He thought that if God promised sevenfold vengeance on anyone killing Cain, He would give seventy-seven-fold vengeance on anyone attacking Lamech.

D. Hope in the Descendants of Seth (4:25, 26)

4:25 Seth. With Cain removed as the older brother and heir of the family blessing, and with Abel dead, God graciously gave Adam and Eve a godly son through whom the seed of redemption (3:15) would be passed all the way to Jesus Christ (Luke 3:38).

4:26 men began to call on the name of the LORD. As men realized their inherent sinfulness with no human means to appease God's righteous indignation and wrath over their multiplied iniquities, they turned to God for mercy and grace in hopes of a restored personal relationship.

III. THE GENERATIONS OF ADAM (5:1–6:8)

5:1–6:8 the genealogy of Adam. Ten specific families are mentioned. Most likely, in accord with other biblical genealogies, this listing is representative rather than complete (cf. Ruth 4:18–22).

A. Genealogy—Adam to Noah (5:1–32)

5:1–32 Adam . . . Noah. The genealogy links Adam to the Noahic family which not only survived the Flood, but also became first in God's post-Flood world. Two recurring phrases carry redemption history forward: "and he had sons and daughters," "and he died." These lines, which get repeated for each successive descendant of Adam, echo two contrasting realities; God had said "you shall surely die" (2:17), but He had also commanded them to "be fruitful and multiply" (1:28).

5:1 the likeness of God. See notes on 1:26.

5:2 called them Mankind. In naming man, God declared His own dominion over all creation (Matt. 19:4; Mark 10:6).

5:3 in His own likeness, after His image. The human image and likeness in which God created mankind was procreatively passed to the second generation and to all subsequent generations.

5:5 nine hundred and thirty years. These are literal years marking unusual length of life. The pre-Flood environment, provided by the earth being under a canopy of water, filtered out the ultraviolet rays of the sun and produced a much more moderate and healthful condition. *See notes on 1:7; 2:6.* **and he died.** God told Adam that, if he ate of the tree, he would surely die (2:17). It included spiritual death, immediately and then physical death, later.

5:24 walked with God . . . was not, for God took him. The life of Enoch provides the only break in the chapter from the incessant comment, "and he died." Cf. 4:17, 18; 1 Chronicles 1:3; Luke 3:37; Hebrews 11:5; Jude 14. Only one other man is said to have enjoyed this intimacy of relationship in walking with God—Noah (6:9). Enoch experienced being taken to heaven alive by God, as did Elijah later (2 Kin. 2:1–12).

5:25–27 Methuselah. This man lived the longest life on record. He died in the year of the Flood judgment (cf. 7:6).

5:29 This one will comfort us. Comfort would come through the godly life of Noah, who is an "heir of the righteousness" which is according to faith (Heb. 11:7).

B. Rampant Sin Prior to the Flood (6:1–8)

6:1–4 The account that follows records an act of degradation that reveals the end-point of God's patience.

6:1 Such long lifespans as indicated in the record of chapter 5 caused a massive increase in earth's population.

6:2 the sons of God saw the daughters of men. The sons of God, identified elsewhere almost exclusively as angels (Job 1:6; 2:1; 38:7), saw and took wives of the human race. This produced an unnatural union which violated the God-ordained order of human marriage and procreation (Gen. 2:24). Some have argued that the sons of God were the sons of Seth who cohabited with the daughters of Cain; others suggest they were perhaps human kings wanting to build harems. But the passage puts strong emphasis on the angelic versus human contrast. The NT places this account in sequence with other Genesis events and identifies it as involving fallen angels who indwelt men *(see notes on 2 Pet. 2:4, 5; Jude 6).* Matthew 22:30 does not necessarily negate the possibility that angels are capable of procreation, but just that they do not marry. However, to procreate physically, demons had to possess human, male bodies.

6:3 My Spirit. Cf. Genesis 1:2. The Holy Spirit played a most active role in the OT. The Spirit had been striving to call people to repentance and righteousness, especially as Scripture notes, through the preaching of Enoch and Noah (1 Pet. 3:20; 2 Pet. 2:5; Jude 14). **one hundred and twenty.** The span of time until the Flood (cf. 1 Pet. 3:20), in which man was given opportunity to respond to the warning that God's Spirit would not always be patient.

6:4 giants. The word *nephilim* is from a root meaning "to fall," indicating that they were strong men who "fell" on others in the sense of overpowering them (the only other use of this term is in Num. 13:33). They were already in the earth when the "mighty men" and "men of renown" were born. The fallen ones are not the offspring from the union in verses 1 and 2.

6:5 his heart was only evil continually. This is one of the strongest and clearest statements about man's sinful nature. Sin begins in the thought-life *(see notes on James 1:13–15).* The people of Noah's day were exceedingly wicked, from the inside out. Cf. Jeremiah 17:9, 10; Matthew 12:34, 35; 15:18, 19; Mark 7:21; Luke 6:45.

6:6 sorry . . . grieved. Sin sorrowed God who is holy and without blemish (Eph. 4:30). Cf. Exodus 32:14; 1 Samuel 15:11; Jeremiah 26:3.

6:7 God promised total destruction when His patience ran out (cf. Eccl. 8:11).

How Old Were the Patriarchs?

ADAM 930 years (Gen. 5:5)

SETH 912 years (Gen. 5:8)

ENOSH 905 years (Gen. 5:11)

ENOCH 365 years (Gen. 5:23)

METHUSELAH 969 years (Gen. 5:27)

LAMECH 777 years (Gen. 5:31)

NOAH 950 years (Gen. 9:29)

~~~The Flood~~~

SHEM 600 years (Gen. 11:10,11)

EBER 464 years (Gen. 11:16,17)

TERAH 205 years (Gen. 11:32)

ABRAHAM 175 years (Gen. 25:7)

ISAAC 180 years (Gen. 35:28)

JACOB 147 years (Gen. 47:28)

JOSEPH 110 years (Gen. 50:26)

The patriarchs who lived before the Flood had an average lifespan of about 900 years (Gen. 5). The ages of post-Flood patriarchs dropped rapidly and gradually leveled off (Gen. 11). Some suggest that this is due to major environmental changes brought about by the Flood.

The MacArthur Bible Handbook, by John MacArthur (Nashville: Thomas Nelson Publishers, 2003) 9. © 2003 by Thomas Nelson, Inc.

6:8 But Noah found grace. Lest one believe that Noah was spared because of his good works alone (cf. Heb. 11:7), God makes it clear that Noah was a man who believed in God as Creator, Sovereign, and the only Savior from sin. He found grace for himself, because he humbled himself and sought it (cf. 4:26). *See notes on Isaiah 55:6, 7;* he was obedient, as well (v. 22; 7:5; James 4:6–10).

IV. The Generations of Noah (6:9–9:29)

A. Preparation for the Flood (6:9–7:9)

6:9 a just man . . . perfect . . . walked. Cf. Ezekiel 14:14, 20; 2 Peter 2:5. The word order is one of increasing spiritual quality before God: just is to live by God's righteous standards; *perfect* sets him apart by a comparison with those of his day; and that he *walked with God* puts him in a class with Enoch (5:24).

6:11 corrupt . . . filled with violence. Cf. verses 3, 5. The seed of Satan, the fallen rejectors of God, deceitful and destructive, had dominated the world.

6:13 I will destroy them with the earth.

Destroy did not mean annihilation, but rather referred to the Flood judgment, both of the earth and its inhabitants.

6:14 *ark.* This was a hollow chest, a box designed to float on water (Ex. 2:3). ***gopherwood.*** Probably cedar or cypress trees are in view, abundant in the mountains of Armenia.

6:15, 16 While the ark was not designed for beauty or speed, these dimensions provided extraordinary stability in the tumultuous floodwaters. A cubit was about eighteen inches long, making the ark 450 feet long, 75 feet wide, and 45 feet high. A gigantic box of that size would be very stable in the water, impossible to capsize. The volume of space in the ark was 1.4 million cubic feet, equal to the capacity of 522 standard railroad box cars, which could carry 125,000 sheep. It had three stories, each fifteen feet high; each deck was equipped with various rooms (lit. "nests"). "Pitch" was a resin substance to seal the seams and cracks in the wood. The "window" may have actually been a low wall around the flat roof to catch water for all on the ark.

6:17 *floodwaters.* Other notable Scriptures on the worldwide Flood brought by God include: Job 12:15; 22:16; Psalm 29:10; Isaiah 54:9; Matthew 24:37–39; Luke 17:26, 27; Hebrews 11:7; 1 Peter 3:20; 2 Peter 2:5; 3:5, 6.

6:18 *But I will establish My covenant with you.* In contrast with the rest of the created order which God was to destroy, Noah and his family were not only to be preserved, but they were to enjoy the provision and protection of a covenant relationship with God. This is the first mention of covenant in Scripture. This pledged covenant is actually made and explained in 9:9–17 *(see notes there).*

6:19, 20 There are fewer than 18,000 species living on earth today. This number may have been doubled to allow for now-extinct creatures. With two of each, a total of 72,000 creatures is reasonable as indicated in the note on verses 15 and 16; the cubic space could hold 125,000 sheep and, since the average size of land animals is less than a sheep, perhaps less than 60 percent of the space was used. The very large animals were surely represented by young. There was ample room also for the one million species of insects, as well as food for a year for everyone (v. 21).

7:1 *righteous.* Cf. 6:9; Job 1:1.

7:2, 3 *seven . . . seven.* The extra six pairs of clean animals and birds would be used for sacrifice (8:20) and food (9:3).

7:3 *to keep the species alive.* God could use them to replenish the earth.

7:4 God allowed one more week for sinners to repent. ***rain . . . forty days and forty nights.*** A worldwide rain for this length of time is impossible in post-Flood, atmospheric conditions, but not then. The canopy that covered the whole earth *(see note on 1:7),* a thermal water blanket encircling the earth, was to be condensed and dumped all over the globe (v. 10).

B. The Flood and Deliverance (7:10–8:19)

7:11 *month . . . day.* The calendar system of Noah's day is unknown, although it appears that one month equaled thirty days. If calculated by the Jewish calendar of Moses' day, it would be about May. This period of God's grace was ended (cf. v. 4; 6:3, 8). ***all the fountains of the great deep were broken up.*** The subterranean waters sprang up from inside the earth to form the seas and rivers (1:10; 2:10–14), which were not produced by rainfall (since there was none), but by deep fountains in the earth. Such a catastrophe would also easily explain why so many of the earth's mountain ranges give evidence of having once been under the sea. ***the windows of heaven.*** The celestial waters in the canopy encircling the globe were dumped on the earth and joined with the terrestrial

The Flood Chronology

1. In the 600th year of Noah (second month, tenth day), Noah entered the ark (Gen. 7:4,10,11).

2. In the 600th year of Noah (second month, seventeenth day), the flood began (Gen. 7:11).

3. The waters flooded the earth for 150 days (5 months of 30 days each), including the 40 days and 40 nights of rain (Gen. 7:12,17,24; 8:1).

4. In the 600th year of Noah (seventh month, seventeenth day), the waters began to recede (7:24; 8:1).

5. The waters receded to the point that (600th year, seventh month, seventeenth day) the ark rested on Ararat (Gen. 8:3,4).

6. The waters continued to abate so that (600th year, tenth month, first day) the tops of the mountains were visibile (Gen. 8:5).

7. Forty days later (600th year, eleventh month, tenth day) Noah sent out a raven and a dove (Gen. 8:6). Over the next 14 days, Noah sent out two more doves (Gen. 8:10,12). In all, this took 61 days or two months and one day.

8. By Noah's 601st year on the first month, the first day, the water had dried up (Gen. 8:12,13).

9. Noah waited one month and twenty-six days before he disembarked in the second month, the 27th day of his 601st year. From beginning to end, the Flood lasted one year and ten days from Gen. 7:11 to Gen. 8:14.

The MacArthur Study Bible, by John MacArthur (Nashville: Word Publishing, 1997) 26. © 1993 by Thomas Nelson, Inc.

and the subterranean waters (cf. 1:7). This ended the water canopy surrounding the earth and unleashed the water in the earth; together, these phenomena began the new system of hydrology that has since characterized the earth (see Job 26:8; Eccl. 1:7; Is. 55:10; Amos 9:6). The sequence in this verse, indicating that the earth's crust breaks up first, then the heavens drop their water, is interesting because the volcanic explosions that would have occurred when the earth fractured would have sent magma and dust into the atmosphere, along with gigantic sprays of water, gas, and air—all penetrating the canopy and triggering its downpour.

7:16 *the Lord shut him in.* No small event is spared in the telling of this episode, although the details are sparse.

7:19 *all the high hills.* This describes the extent of the flood as global. Lest there be any doubt, Moses adds "under the whole heaven" (cf. 2 Pet. 3:5–7). There are over 270 flood stories told in cultures all over the earth, which owe their origin to this one global event.

7:20 The highest mountains were at least twenty-two and one-half feet under water, so that the ark floated freely above the peaks. This would include the highest peak in that area, Mount Ararat (8:4), which is c. 17,000 feet high. That depth further proves it was not a local flood, but a global flood.

7:24 *one hundred and fifty days.* These days included the forty-day-and-night period of rain (7:12, 17). The flood rose to its peak at that point (cf. 8:3). It then took over two and one-half months before the water receded to reveal other mountain peaks (8:4, 5), over four and one-half months before the dove could find dry land (8:8–12), and almost eight months before the occupants could leave the ark (8:14).

8:1 *Then God remembered Noah.* God's covenant with Noah brought provision and protection in the midst of severe judgment. The remnant was preserved and God initiated steps toward reestablishing the created order on earth. *the waters subsided.* God used the wind to dry the ground; evaporation returned water to the atmosphere.

8:4 *the mountains of Ararat.* These were in the region of the Caucasus, also known as ancient Urartu, where the elevation exceeded 17,000 feet.

8:7–12 *a raven . . . a dove.* Ravens survive on a broad range of food types. If any food was available outside the ark, the raven could survive. In contrast, a dove is much more selective in its food choices. The dove's choice of food would indicate that new life had begun to grow; thus Noah and his family could also survive outside the ark.

8:14–16 Noah and his family had been in the ark for 378 days (cf. 7:4, 10, 11).

8:17–19 *be fruitful and multiply.* In the process of replenishing the created order that He had judged with destruction, God repeated the words of the blessing which He had put upon non-human creatures (1:22). Noah faced a new world where longevity of life began to decline immediately; the earth was subject to storms and severe weather, blazing heat, freezing cold, seismic action, and natural disasters.

C. God's Noahic Covenant (8:20–9:17)

8:20 *built an altar.* This was done as an act of worship in response to God's covenant faithfulness in sparing him and his family.

8:21 *smelled a soothing aroma.* God accepted Noah's sacrifice. ***curse . . . destroy.*** Regardless of how sinful mankind would become in the future, God promised not to engage in global catastrophe by flood again (cf. 9:11). *See notes on 2 Peter 3:3–10* for how God will destroy the earth in the future.

8:22 *While the earth remains.* With many alterations from the global flood, God reestablished the cycle of seasons after the catastrophic interruption.

9:1 *blessed Noah . . . Be fruitful and mul-* ***tiply, and fill the earth.*** God blessed Noah and recommissioned him to fill the earth (cf. 1:28).

9:2, 3 *the fear of you.* Man's relationship to the animals appears to have changed, in that man is free to eat animals for sustenance (v. 3).

9:4 *blood.* Raw blood was not to be consumed as food. It symbolically represented life. To shed blood symbolically represented death (cf. Lev. 17:11). The blood of animals, representing their life, was not to be eaten. It was, in fact, that blood which God designed to be a covering for sin (Lev. 17:11).

9:5 *beast . . . man.* Capital punishment was invoked upon every animal (Ex. 21:28) or man who took human life unlawfully. Cf. John 19:11; Acts 25:11; Romans 13:4 for clear NT support for this punishment.

9:6 *For in the image of God.* The reason man could kill animals, but neither animals nor man could kill man, is because man alone was created in God's image.

9:9–17 This is the first covenant God made with man, afterwards called the Noahic covenant. *See note on verse 16.*

9:9, 10 *with you . . . with your descendants, . . . with every living creature.* The covenant with Noah included living creatures as was first promised in 6:18.

9:11 *by the waters.* The specific promise of this covenant, never to destroy the world again by water, was qualified by the means of water, for God has since promised to destroy the earth with fire one day (2 Pet. 3:10, 11; Rev. 20:9; 21:1).

9:12 *the sign of the covenant.* The rainbow is the perpetual, symbolic reminder of this covenant promise, just as circumcision of all males would be for the Abrahamic covenant (17:10, 11).

9:15 *I will remember.* Not simple recognition, but God's commitment to keep the promise.

Major Mountains of the Bible

Mt. Ararat (in modern Turkey), where Noah's ark came to rest (Gen. 8:4).

Mt. Carmel, where Elijah was victorious over the prophets of Baal (1 Kin. 18:9–42).

Mt. Ebal (opposite Mt. Gerizim), where Moses commanded that an altar be built after the Hebrews entered the Promised Land (Deut. 27:4).

Mt Gerizim where Jesus talked with the Samaritan woman at the well (John 4:20).

Mt. Gilboa, where King Saul and his sons were killed in a battle with the Philistines (1 Chr. 10:1,8).

Mt. Hermon, a mountain range that marked the northern limit of the conquest of Canaan (Josh 11:3,17).

Mt. Lebanon, the source of cedar wood for Solomon's temple in Jerusalem (1 Kin. 5:14,18).

Mt. Moriah, where Abraham brought Isaac for sacrifice (Gen. 22:2) and the location of Solomon's temple (2 Chr. 3:1).

Mt. Olivet, or Mt. of Olives, where Jesus gave the discourse on His Second Coming (Matt. 24:3).

Mt. Pisgah, or Nebo, where Moses viewed the Promised Land (Deut. 34:1).

Mt. Seir, south of the Dead Sea, the location to which Esau moved after Isaac's death (Gen. 36:8).

Mt. Sinai, or Horeb (near Egypt), where the law was given to Moses (Ex. 19:2–25).

Mt. Tabor, 6 miles east of Nazareth, served as a boundary between Issachar and Zebulun; also Barak launched his attack on Sisera from Tabor (Judg. 4:6–15).

Mt. Zion, originally limited to the SW sector (2 Sam. 5:7), was later used of all Jerusalem (Lam. 1:4).

9:16 *the everlasting covenant.* This covenant with Noah is the first of five divinely originated covenants in Scripture explicitly described as "everlasting." The other four include: (1) Abrahamic (Gen. 17:7); (2) priestly (Num. 25:10–13); (3) Davidic (2 Sam. 23:5); and (4) new (Jer. 32:40). The term *everlasting* can mean either (1) to the end of time and/or (2) through eternity future. It never looks back to eternity past. Of the six explicitly mentioned covenants of this kind in Scripture, only the Mosaic or old covenant was nullified.

D. The History of Noah's Descendants (9:18–29)

9:18 *Ham was the father of Canaan.* Canaan's offspring, the idolatrous enemies of Israel whose land Abraham's descendants would later take (15:13–16), becomes a primary focus in chapter 10. This notation is important since Moses was writing the Pentateuch just before the Israelites took Canaan (see Introduction: Author and Date,

Background and Setting).

9:19 *from these the whole earth.* All people who have ever lived since the Flood came from these three sons of Noah (cf. 10:32). The "one blood" of Acts 17:26 is that of Adam through Noah. All physical characteristics of the whole race were present in the genetics of Noah, his sons, and their wives.

9:21 *was drunk.* Fermentation, which leads to drunkenness, may have been caused by changed ecological conditions as a result of the flood. Noah may have taken off his clothes because of the heat, or been involuntarily exposed due to his drunkenness.

9:22 *saw the nakedness.* There is no reasonable support for the notion that some perverse activity, in addition to seeing nakedness, occurred. But clearly, the implication is that Ham looked with some sinful thought, if only for a while until he left to inform his brothers. Perhaps he was glad to see his father's dignity and authority reduced to such weakness. Maybe he thought his brothers might share his feelings so he eagerly told them. If so, they did not share his attitude (v. 23).

9:24 *younger son.* This is used in the sense of "youngest son."

9:25–27 *Cursed be Canaan.* The shift from Ham to his son Canaan established the historic legitimacy of Israel's later conquest of the Canaanites. These were the people with whom Israel had to do battle shortly after they first heard Moses' reading of this passage. Here, God gave Israel the theological basis for the conquest of Canaan. The descendants of Ham had received a sentence of judgment for the sins of their progenitor. In 10:15–20, the descendants of Canaan are seen to be the earlier inhabitants of the land later promised to Abraham.

9:26 *may Canaan be his servant.* Conquered peoples were called servants, even if they were not household or private slaves. Shem, the ancestor of Israel, and the other "Semites" were to be the masters of Ham's descendants, the Canaanites. The latter would give their land to the former.

9:27 *dwell in the tents.* This means that spiritual blessings would come to the Japhethites through the God of Shem (v. 26) and the line of Shem from which Messiah would come.

V. THE GENERATIONS OF SHEM, HAM, AND JAPHETH (10:1–11:9)

A. The Nations (10:1–32)

10:1–32 See the map "The Nations of Genesis 10" for the locations of Noah's descendants.

10:5 *were separated . . . according to his language.* This act describes the situation after the Tower of Babel account in chapter 11.

10:6–20 *The sons of Ham.* Many of these were Israel's enemies.

10:8–10 *Nimrod.* This powerful leader was evidently the force behind the building of Babel (see 11:1–4).

10:10 *Babel.* This city was the beginning of what later would prove to be Babylon, the eventual destroyer of God's people and His city Jerusalem (c. 605–539 B.C.).

10:11 *to Assyria and built Nineveh.* This was Israel's primary enemy from the East. Nimrod was Israel's prototypical ancient enemy warrior, whose name in Hebrew means "rebel" (cf. Mic. 5:6).

10:15–19 *Canaan.* A notable shift occurs in this section away from place names to the inhabitants themselves (note the "ite" ending). These are not only the cursed people of Canaan's curse for the scene at Noah's drunkenness, but also they are those who possessed the Promised Land which Israel as a nation needed to conquer. But the Noahic curse alone did not determine their guilt, for God said to Abram that the iniquity of the Amorites must first be complete before his descendants could occupy the Promised Land (15:16).

10:21–31 The sons of Shem, i.e., Semitic people.

10:21 *Japheth the elder.* This is better translated "the elder brother of Japheth" which would make Shem the oldest of Noah's three sons.

10:25 *the earth was divided.* This looks ahead to the dispersion of nations at Babel (11:1–9).

B. Dispersion of the Nations (11:1–9)

11:1 *one language and one speech.* God, who made man as the one creature with whom He could speak (1:28), was to take the gift of language and use it to divide the race, because the apostate worship at Babel indicated that man had turned against God in pride (vv. 8, 9).

11:2 *as they journeyed from the east.* God had restated His commission for man to "be fruitful and multiply and fill the earth" (9:7). It was in the course of spreading out that the events of this account occurred.

11:3, 4 *let us make bricks . . . build our-selves a city, and a tower . . . make a name for ourselves.* While dispersing, a portion of the post-Flood group, under the leading of the powerful Nimrod (10:8–10), decided to stop and establish a city as a monument to their pride and for their reputation. The tower, even though it was a part of the plan, was not the singular act of rebellion. Human pride was, and it led these people to defy God. They were refusing to move on, i.e., scattering to fill the earth as they had been instructed. In fact, this was Nimrod's and the people's effort to disobey the command of God in 9:1 and, thus, defeat the counsel of heaven. They had to make bricks, since there were few stones on the plain.

11:4 *whose top is in the heavens.* The tower would not actually reach to the abode

of God and the top would not represent the heavens. They wanted it to be a high tower as a monument to their abilities, one that would enhance their fame. In this endeavor, they disobeyed God and attempted to steal His glory.

11:6 *nothing . . . withheld.* They were so united that they would do all they desired to do.

11:7 *let Us.* See note on 1:26 (cf. 3:22).

11:8 *scattered them abroad.* God addressed their prideful rebellion at the first act. They had chosen to settle; He forced them to scatter. This account tells how it was that the families of the earth "were separated, everyone according to his language" (10:5) and "were divided on the earth after the flood" (10:32).

11:9 *its name is called Babel.* This is linked to a Hebrew word meaning "to con-

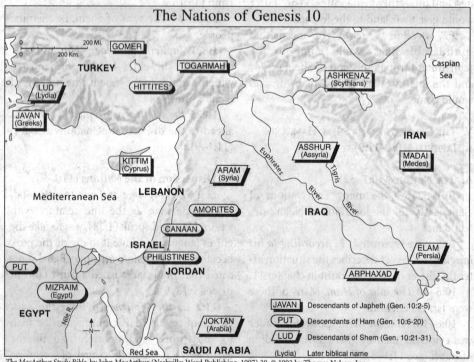

The Nations of Genesis 10

GOMER

TURKEY

TOGARMAH

Caspian Sea

ASHKENAZ (Scythians)

LUD (Lydia)

HITTITES

JAVAN (Greeks)

IRAN

ASSHUR (Assyria)

MADAI (Medes)

KITTIM (Cyprus)

ARAM (Syria)

Euphrates

Tigris River

Mediterranean Sea   LEBANON

AMORITES

IRAQ

CANAAN

ISRAEL

ELAM (Persia)

PHILISTINES

PUT

JORDAN

ARPHAXAD

MIZRAIM (Egypt)

EGYPT   Nile R.

—N—

JAVAN   Descendants of Japheth (Gen. 10:2-5)

PUT   Descendants of Ham (Gen. 10:6-20)

LUD   Descendants of Shem (Gen. 10:21-31)

JOKTAN (Arabia)

Red Sea   SAUDI ARABIA   (Lydia)   Later biblical name

The MacArthur Study Bible, by John MacArthur (Nashville: Word Publishing, 1997) 30. © 1993 by Thomas Nelson, Inc.

fuse." From this account, Israel first understood not only how so many nations, peoples, and languages came about, but also the rebellious origins of their archetypal enemy, Babylon (cf. 10:5, 20, 31). *scattered them.* Because they would not fill the earth as God had commanded them, God confused their language so that they had to separate and collect in regions where their own language was spoken.

VI. THE GENERATIONS OF SHEM: GENEALOGY OF SHEM TO TERAH (11:10–26)

11:10–26 *Shem . . . Abram.* This represents the genealogy of Shem (v. 10). Israel, upon hearing this section read, learned how the generation who survived the Flood related to their own father, Abram (v. 26), later known as Abraham (cf. 17:5). The shortening of lifespans was in effect.

11:14 *Eber.* This man was the progenitor of the Hebrews (i.e., Eber's descendants).

11:26 *seventy years.* This was the age that Terah began to father children. Abram was born later when Terah was 130 (c. 2165 B.C.). Cf. 11:32 with 12:4.

VII. THE GENERATIONS OF TERAH (11:27–25:11)

A. Genealogy (11:27–32)

11:27 *Abram.* The name means "exalted father." Cf. 17:5.

11:28 *Ur of the Chaldeans.* A prosperous, populous city in Mesopotamia.

11:31 *from Ur . . . to Haran.* Cf. Acts 7:2–4; Hebrews 11:8–10. Abram traveled northwest along the Euphrates River to Haran, a crossroads trading town in northern Mesopotamia or Syria, the best route from which to come down into Canaan and avoid crossing the great desert with all his people

and animals (see 12:4).

B. The Abrahamic Covenant: His Land and People (12:1–22:19)

1. Journey to the Promised Land (12:1–9)

12:1–3 *the Lord . . . to Abram.* This passage contains the promise whose fulfillment extends all through Scripture (either in fact or in expectation) and ultimately to Revelation 20. The Abrahamic covenant proper is introduced in verses 1–3, actually made in 15:18–21, reaffirmed in 17:1–21, then renewed also with Isaac (26:2–5) and Jacob (28:10–17). It is an everlasting covenant (17:7, 8; 1 Chr. 16:17; Ps. 105:7–12; Is. 24:5) which contains four elements: (1) seed (17:2–7; cf. Gal. 3:8, 16 where it refers to Christ); (2) land (15:18–21; 17:8); (3) a nation (v. 2; 17:4); plus (4) divine blessing and protection (v. 3). This covenant is unconditional in the sense of its ultimate fulfillment of a kingdom and salvation for Israel (*see notes on Rom. 11:1–27*), but conditional in terms of immediate fulfillment (cf. 17:4). Its national importance to Israel is magnified by its repeated references and point of appeal throughout the OT (cf. 2 Kin. 13:23; 1 Chr. 16:15–22; Neh. 9:7, 8). Its importance spiritually to all believers is expounded by Paul (*see notes on Gal. 3; 4*). Stephen quoted 12:1 in Acts 7:3.

12:1 *To a land.* Abram was still in Haran (11:31) when the call was repeated (Acts 7:2) to go to Canaan.

12:2 *name great.* Abram's magnificent reputation and legacy was fulfilled materially (13:2; 24:35), spiritually (21:22), and socially (23:6).

12:3 *I will curse him who curses you.* Those who *curse* Abram and his descendants are those who treat him lightly, despise him, or treat him with contempt. God's curse for such lack of respect and disdain was to involve the most harsh of divine judgments. The opposite was to be true for those who bless him and his people. *in you all the families of the earth shall be blessed.* Paul identified these words as "the gospel to Abraham beforehand" (Gal. 3:8).

12:4 *Haran.* *See note on 11:31.* They must have been there for some time because they accumulated a group of people (probably servants).

12:5 *they came to . . . Canaan.* C. 2090 B.C.

12:6 *Shechem.* A Canaanite town located in the valley between Mt. Ebal and Mt. Gerizim (cf. Deut. 27:4, 12) west of the Jordan River about fifteen miles and north of Jerusalem about thirty miles. Moreh was most likely a resident of the area for whom the tree was named. *Canaanites were then in the land.* Moses was writing approximately 700 years after Abram entered the land (c. 1405 B.C.). The Canaanites, of whom he wrote, were soon to be the opponents of Israel as they entered Canaan.

12:7 *I will give this land.* Cf. 13:15; 15:18; 17:7, 8; Galatians 3:16. God was dealing with Abram, not in a private promise, but with a view toward high and sacred interests far into the future, i.e., the land which his posterity was to inhabit as a peculiar people. The seeds of divine truth were to be sown there for the benefit of all mankind. It was chosen as the most appropriate land for the coming of divine revelation and salvation for the world. *altar to the LORD.* By this act, Abram made an open confession of his religion, established worship of the true God, and declared his faith in God's promise. This was the first true place of worship ever erected in the Promised Land. Isaac would later build an altar also to commemorate the Lord's appearance to him (26:24, 25), and Jacob also built one in Shechem

(33:18–20).

12:8 *Bethel . . . Ai.* Bethel, seven miles north of Jerusalem, was named later by Abraham (28:19). Ai was two miles east of Bethel, where Joshua later fought (Josh. 7; 8).

12:9 *toward the South.* Abram moved toward the Negev into a less desirable area for raising crops but better for his vocation as a herdsman, perhaps engaging also in merchant activity.

2. Redemption from Egypt (12:10–20)

12:10 *a famine in the land.* Famine was not an unusual phenomenon in Canaan; two other major food shortages also occurred during the patriarchal period (26:1; 41:56). The severity and timing of this one forced Abram, soon after his arrival and travel in the Promised Land (vv. 5–9), to emigrate to Egypt, where food was usually in abundant supply. Still holding to God's promise, he did not return to Ur, though matters were extremely difficult (cf. Heb. 11:15).

12:11 *woman . . . beautiful.* At sixty-five, Sarai was still young and exceptionally attractive, being only half the age she was to be when she died (127). The patriarchs lived long; Abram was 175 when he died.

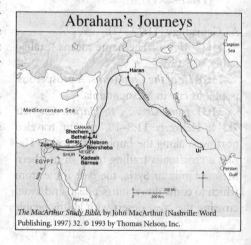

Abraham's Journeys

The MacArthur Study Bible, by John MacArthur (Nashville: Word Publishing, 1997) 32. © 1993 by Thomas Nelson, Inc.

12:12, 13 Abram's fear of Sarai's being taken to Pharaoh's harem and his being killed led him to disguise his true relationship to her (cf. 20:13). Abram sought on his own initiative to take care of his future, attempting to assist God in fulfilling His promises.

12:13 sister. This was a lying half-truth, since Sarai was Abram's half-sister (20:12).

12:15 taken to Pharaoh's house. Egyptian officials did take notice of Sarai and informed their monarch of her beauty. The result was not unexpected; she ended up in Pharaoh's harem.

12:17 the LORD plagued Pharaoh... with great plagues. The separation of Abram and Sarai was critical enough to evoke the Lord's personal and dramatic intervention. Abram engineered the ruse to protect himself (v. 13, "that I may live"), apparently without too much thought being given to Sarai; but

God's reaction focused on the protection of Sarai ("because of Sarai").

12:18, 19 What is this you have done to me?... take her and go. Somehow, and it remains unexplained, the plagues uncovered the deceit of Abram for Pharaoh. The monarch of Egypt humiliated Abram with his questions, showing more character than Abram gave him credit for and sending Abram out of his country.

12:20 sent him away. Abram's lie brought him and his extended family to an ignominious exit from Egypt—one which the servants must have talked about among themselves, with some loss to Abram's integrity and reputation in their eyes. See note on 13:9.

3. Division of the land (13:1–18)

13:1–4 Significantly, after the disastrous situation in Egypt, Abram journeyed back to

The Life of Abraham

Event	Old Testament	New Testament
The birth of Abram	Gen. 11:26	
God's call of Abram	Gen. 12:1–3	Heb. 11:8
The entry into Canaan	Gen. 12:4–9	
Abram in Egypt	Gen. 12:10–20	
Lot separates from Abram	Gen. 13:1–18	
Abram rescues Lot	Gen. 14:1–17	
Abram pays tithes to Melchizedek	Gen. 14:18–24	Heb. 7:1–10
God's covenant with Abraham	Gen. 15:1–21	Rom. 4:1–25
		Gal. 3:6–25
		Heb. 6:13–20
The birth of Ishmael	Gen. 16:1–16	
Abraham promised a son by Sarah	Gen. 17:1–27	Rom. 4:18–25
		Heb. 11:11, 12
Abraham intercedes for Sodom	Gen. 18:16–33	
Lot saved and Sodom destroyed	Gen. 19:1–38	
The birth of Isaac	Gen. 21:1–7	
Hagar and Ishmael sent away	Gen. 21:8–21	Gal. 4:21–31
Abraham challenged to offer Isaac as sacrifice	Gen. 22:1–19	Heb. 11:17–19
		James 2:20–24
The death of Sarah	Gen. 23:1–20	
The death of Abraham	Gen. 25:1–11	

where he had erected an altar and there he again worshiped (see 12:8).

13:5 flocks and herds. Wealth in the ancient world was measured, not by land owned, but by the size of one's herds and the possession of silver, gold, and jewels (cf. v. 2; Job 1:1–3).

13:6, 7 Not unexpectedly, conflict occurred because of crowded conditions and limited grazing space. Both uncle and nephew had accrued much on the slow trip from Ur via Haran and Egypt to the Bethel/Ai region.

13:7 Perizzites. A Canaanite tribe. Cf. 34:30; Deuteronomy 7:1; Judges 1:4; 3:5, 6; 1 Kings 9:20, 21; Ezra 9:1.

13:8 we are brethren. Abram's reaction in resolving the strife between the two households and their personnel portrayed a different Abram than seen in Egypt; one whose attitude was not self-centered. Waving his right to seniority, he gave the choice to his nephew, Lot.

13:9 Is not the whole land before you? Abram gladly called on Lot to select for himself (vv. 10, 11) what he desired for his household and flocks. After Lot's choice had been exercised, then Abram would accept what was left for him. Perhaps this did much to restore, in the eyes of the servants, Abram's integrity and reputation (see note on 12:20).

13:10 (before the Lord destroyed Sodom and Gomorrah). When Moses was writing (700 years after Abram came to Canaan) the devastation of that region had long before occurred by divinely initiated catastrophe (19:23–29), totally obliterating any evidence of its agricultural richness. **like the garden of the Lord . . . like . . . Egypt.** This twofold appraisal of the Jordan valley, with its meadows on either side of the river to which Lot was so strongly attracted, highlighted its lush and fertile nature. Moses, reading this to the Jews

about to enter Canaan and likening it to the Garden of Eden, referred hearer and reader to God's revelatory description of it (Gen. 2:8–15). Likening it to an obviously well-known and well-irrigated region of Egypt referred them to a place the Jews had likely known well in their sojourn in Egypt. **Zoar.** Cf. 4:2. A town located at the south end of the Dead Sea, whose name means "small place" (see 19:22).

13:11, 12 An excellent yet selfish choice, from a worldly point of view, but disastrous spiritually because it drew Lot into the wickedness of Sodom (v. 13).

13:13 the men of Sodom were exceedingly wicked. Lot's decisions put him in dangerous proximity to those cities whose names would become a byword for perversion and unbridled wickedness. Their evil is the theme of chapter 19.

13:14–17 With Lot gone, the Lord reaffirmed His covenant promise with Abram (Gen. 12:1–3). Strikingly and unmistakably, the Lord deeded the land (v. 14—look in all directions, and v. 17—walk in all directions) in perpetuity to Abram and his descendants, whom He declared would be definitely innumerable (v. 16—as the dust).

13:18 the terebinth trees of Mamre. A distinctively large grove of trees owned by Mamre the Amorite (14:13) located c. nineteen miles southwest of Jerusalem at Hebron whose elevation exceeds 3,000 feet. **built an altar.** Cf. 12:7, 8; 13:4. He was devoted to the worship of God.

4. Victory over the kings (14:1–24)

14:1–12 Raiding, conquering, and making other kings and city-states subservient vassals were all part of the world of the Fertile Crescent in Abraham's day. These locations mentioned range from Shinar in the east (the region of Babylon in Mesopotamia)

Travels of the Patriarchs

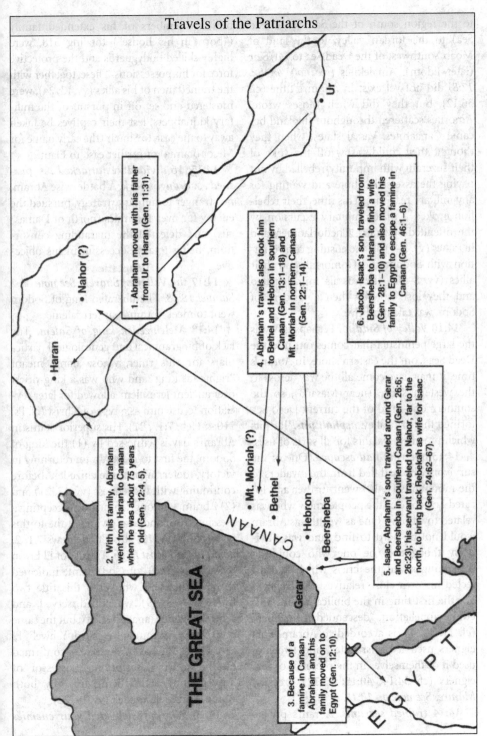

1. Abraham moved with his father from Ur to Haran (Gen. 11:31).

2. With his family, Abraham went from Haran to Canaan when he was about 75 years old (Gen. 12:4, 5).

3. Because of a famine in Canaan, Abraham and his family moved on to Egypt (Gen. 12:10).

4. Abraham's travels also took him to Bethel and Hebron in southern Canaan (Gen. 13:1–18) and Mt. Moriah in northern Canaan (Gen. 22:1–14).

5. Isaac, Abraham's son, traveled around Gerar and Beersheba in southern Canaan (Gen. 26:6; 26:23); his servant traveled to Nahor, far to the north, to bring back Rebekah as wife for Isaac (Gen. 24:62–67).

6. Jacob, Isaac's son, traveled from Beersheba to Haran to find a wife (Gen. 28:1–10) and also moved his family to Egypt to escape a famine in Canaan (Gen. 46:1–6).

Ur

Nahor (?)

Haran

Mt. Moriah (?)

Bethel

Hebron

Beersheba

Gerar

CANAAN

THE GREAT SEA

EGYPT

Nelson's Complete Book of Bible Maps & Charts (Nashville: Thomas Nelson Publishers, 1996) 19. © 1993 by Thomas Nelson, Inc.

to the region south of the Salt Sea (Dead Sea) to the Jordan valley, to the land of Moab, southwest of the Dead Sea to Mt. Seir (later Edom). Amalekites *(see note on Ex. 17:8)* did not yet exist in Abram's time (cf. 36:12), but they did when Moses wrote. Amorites scattered throughout the land became Canaanites. Vassal states, when they thought they could throw off the yoke of their suzerain with impunity, rebelled by not paying the assessed tribute and waiting for any military response. This time, their rebellion evoked a major military excursion by the offended suzerain, Chedorlaomer, and his allies (vv. 5–7); in the ensuing confrontation with Sodom and Gomorrah and their allies (vv. 8–10), the vassals miscalculated and they lost. Lot, by then a resident of Sodom, was taken captive.

14:10 *Valley of Siddim.* Perhaps this was the large peninsula that comes out into the Dead Sea from the eastern shore. In Abram's time, it may have come all the way across to the western shore (near Masada), so the southern one-third of the current Dead Sea formed this dry valley. ***asphalt pits.*** Tar pits which provided sealants for all sorts of uses.

14:13 *one who had escaped.* One of the survivors who had fled from the invaders to the mountains (v. 10) went further and located Lot's uncle (the people knew who was related to whom). One as wealthy as Abram would not be hard to find, and was obviously thought to be one who could do something about the crisis which had affected his own close relatives. ***the Hebrew.*** For the first time in the biblical record, this ethnic appellation, "descended from Eber" (cf. 11:15–17), is accorded to Abram. Foreigners used it of Israelites, and Israelites used it of themselves in the presence of foreigners (cf. 34:14; 40:15; 43:32). ***trees of Mamre.*** See note on 13:18.

14:14 *trained servants.* Abram's private militia, members of his extended family ("born in his house") totaling 318, were highly skilled bodyguards and the protective force for his possessions. These, together with the trained men of his allies (vv. 13, 24), were mustered and set off in pursuit of the military kidnappers, lest their captives be taken away to the east, to Shinar (the early name for Mesopotamia) or further east, to Elam.

14:15, 16 *divided . . . attacked . . . pursued . . . brought back.* A battle-wise Abram, no stranger to military strategy, pursued the enemy for over 150 miles (north of Damascus) and defeated the marauding consortium, being totally successful in his objective.

14:17 *the Valley of Shaveh.* *See note on 2 Samuel 18:18.* The liberated king of Sodom went to meet Abram near Jerusalem.

14:18 *Melchizedek king of Salem.* The lack of biographical and genealogical particulars for this ruler, whose name meant "righteous king" and who was a king-priest over ancient Jerusalem, allowed for later revelation to use him as a type of Christ (cf. Ps. 110:4; Heb. 7:17, 21). His superior status in Abram's day is witnessed by (1) the king of Sodom, the first to meet Abram returning in victory, deferring to Melchizedek before continuing with his request (vv. 17, 21) and (2) Abram, without demur, both accepting a blessing from and also giving a tithe to this priest-king (vv. 19, 20). Cf. Hebrews 7:1, 2. ***priest of God Most High.*** The use of El Elyon (Sovereign Lord) for God's name indicated that Melchizedek, who used this title two times (vv. 18, 19), worshiped, served, and represented no Canaanite deity, but the same one whom Abram also called Yahweh El Elyon (v. 22). That this was so is confirmed by the added description, "Possessor of heaven and earth," being used by both Abram and Melchizedek (vv. 19, 22).

14:20 *Who has delivered your enemies*

into your hand. Credit for victory over a superior military coalition correctly went to the Sovereign Lord (El Elyon) and not to Abram's prowess *(see note at vv. 15, 16).* To Melchizedek, and to Abram too, this amounted to true worship of the true God. *a tithe.* This is the first mention in Scripture of giving ten percent (cf. 28:22). This ten-percent offering was purely voluntary, and may only have been a tenth of the best, not a tenth of the total *(see note on Heb. 7:4).* This tenth is not like the required tenths given to Israel in the Mosaic Law *(see notes on Num. 18:21–24; Deut. 14:22; 26:12).*

14:21–24 If Abram acceded to the king of Sodom's request, he would have allowed that wicked king to attribute Abram's wealth to the king's generosity, thus distorting the clear testimony of the Lord's blessings on his life. To accept such payment would belie his trust in God. Such a personal commitment would not be foisted upon his allies, who could make their own decisions. As for his own servants, their meals taken from the spoils was sufficient compensation. Undoubtedly, the servants remembered their master's reaction and testimony; it overcame much of the negative aspects in the memory of the earlier exit from Egypt *(see notes on 12:20; 13:9).*

5. The covenant ratified (15:1–21)

15:1 *I am your shield.* God served Abram as his divine protector (cf. Pss. 7:10; 84:9).

15:2 *I go childless.* In response to God's encouragement and admonition (v. 1), Abram showed what nagged at him. How could God's promise of many descendants (13:16) and of being a great nation (12:2) come about when he had no children? *Eliezer of Damascus.* To Abram, God's promise had stalled; so adoption of a servant as the male heir—a well-known contemporary Mesopotamian custom—was the best

officially recognizable arrangement to make it come to pass, humanly speaking.

15:3–5 The question, "What will You give me?" (v. 2) became an accusation, "You have not given me!" (v. 3). The Lord's rejection of Abram's solution (v. 4) preceded God's reiterated promise of innumerable descendants (v. 5).

15:5 Cf. Romans 4:18.

15:6 *believed . . . accounted . . . for righteousness.* The apostle Paul quoted these words as an illustration of faith in contrast to works (Rom. 4:3, 9, 22; Gal. 3:6; James 2:23). Abram was justified by faith. *See notes on Romans 4; Galatians 3* for a fuller discussion of justification by faith.

15:7 *to give you this land to inherit it.* That a specifically identifiable land (see vv. 18–21) was intimately linked with Abram's having many descendants in God's purpose and in the Abrahamic covenant was clearly revealed and, in a formal ceremony (vv. 9–21), would be placed irrevocably beyond dispute.

15:8 *how shall I know that I will inherit it?* A question not of veiled accusation at the delayed fulfillment but of genuine request for information and assurance. In response, God affirmed His covenant with Abram in a remarkable ceremony (vv. 9–21).

15:9, 10 *cut them in two.* The sign of ancient covenants often involved the cutting in half of animals, so that the pledging parties could walk between them, affirming that the same should happen to them if they broke the covenant (see Jer. 34:18, 19).

15:12 *sleep.* God put him to sleep, because the covenant did not involve any promise on Abram's part; therefore, he would not walk through the pieces as a pledge (see v. 17).

15:13, 14 The words of God in the covenant ceremony assured Abram that his descendants would definitely be in the land, although a painful detour into Egypt would delay fulfillment until long after his demise. Cf. Acts. 7:6, 7.

15:13 *four hundred years.* This represents an approximated number which is precisely 430 years (cf. Ex. 12:40).

15:16 *the iniquity of the Amorites is not yet complete.* A delay in judgment occasioned the delay in covenant fulfillment. Judgment on Egypt (v. 14) would mark the departure of Abram's descendants for their land, and judgment on the Canaanites (broadly defined ethnically as Amorites) would mark their entrance to that land.

15:17 *smoking oven . . . burning torch.* Cf. Exodus 13:21. These items symbolized the presence of God, who solemnly promised by divine oath to fulfill His promises to Abram by alone passing through the animal pieces (vv. 9–11).

15:18–21 *river of Egypt to the . . . Euphrates.* Scripture records both general (Ex. 23:31; Num. 13:21; Deut. 11:24; 1 Kin. 8:65; 2 Kin. 14:25; Is. 27:12) and specific (Num. 34:1–12; Josh. 15:1, 2; Ezek. 47:15–20; 48:1, 28) descriptions of the Promised Land, centering on the ancient land of Canaan. Such precise geographic demarcation will not allow for any redefinitions which would emasculate God's promise of its specificity.

Dreams in Genesis	
Scripture	**Person**
Gen. 15	Abraham
Gen. 20	Abimelech of Gerar
Gen. 28	Jacob
Gen. 31:11–13	Jacob
Gen. 31:24	Laban
Gen. 37	Joseph
Gen. 40	Chief butler
Gen. 40	Chief baker
Gen. 41	Pharaoah
Gen. 46:2–4	Jacob

The river of Egypt was most probably what be-came known as the Wadi El Arish, the southern border of Judah. ***Kenites . . . Jebusites.*** The various peoples who inhabited the land are named. Such precise detailing of the nations in the land of Canaan attests again to the specificity of the Promised Land in God's promises.

6. Rejection of Hagar and Ishmael (16:1–16)

16:1 See Galatians 4:21–31, where Paul uses Hagar as an illustration.

16:3 *gave her to her husband.* After ten childless years (cf. 12:4), Sarai resorted to the custom of the day by which a barren wife could get a child through one of her own maidservants (v. 2, "I shall obtain children by her"). Abram, ignoring divine reaction and assurance in response to his earlier attempt to appoint an heir (cf. 15:2–5), sinfully yielded to Sarai's insistence, and Ishmael was born (v. 15).

16:5 *My wrong be upon you! . . . I became despised.* Sarai, not anticipating contemptuous disregard by Hagar (v. 4) as the result of her solution for barrenness, blamed Abram for her trouble and demanded judgment to rectify the broken mistress-servant relationship. Abram transferred his responsibility to Sarai, giving her freedom to react as she wished (v. 6, "your maid is in your hand"). Sarai treated Hagar so badly that she left.

16:7 *the Angel of the LORD.* This special individual spoke as though He were distinct from Yahweh, yet also spoke in the first person as though He were indeed to be identified as Yahweh Himself. Hagar, in seeing this angel, believed she had seen God (v. 13). Others had the same experience and came to the same conclusion (cf. 22:11–18; 31:11–13; Ex. 3:2–5; Num. 22:22–35; Judg. 6:11–23; 13:2–5; 1 Kin. 19:5–7). The Angel of the

Abraham—Justified by Faith

In Genesis 15:6, we are told that when Abraham "believed" in the Lord, it was "accounted" to him for "righteousness." The apostle Paul quoted these words as an illustration of faith over and against works (Rom. 4:3, 9, 22; Gal. 3:6). Abraham was regenerated by faith, and so are we!

This quotation is one of the clearest statements in all Scripture about justification. Abraham's faith is not a meritorious work. It is never the ground of justification—it is simply the channel through which it is received and it, too, is a gift. His faith was "accounted" or "imputed" to him, which is a term used in both financial and legal settings. It means to take something that belongs to someone and credit to another's account. It is a one-sided transaction. Abraham did nothing to accumulate it: God simply credited it to him. In this case, God took His own righteousness and credited it to Abraham as if it were actually his. This God did because Abraham believed in Him.

The "righteousness" imputed to Abraham is unique: (1) God is its source (Is. 45:8); (2) it fulfills both the penalty and precept of God's law. Christ's death as a substitute pays the penalty exacted on those who failed to keep God's law, and His perfect obedience to every requirement of God's law fulfills God's demand for comprehensive righteousness (2 Cor. 5:21; 1 Pet. 2:24; see Heb. 9:28); and (3) because God's righteousness is eternal (Ps. 119:142; Is. 51:8; Dan. 9:24), the one who receives it from Him enjoys it forever.

Lord, who does not appear after the birth of Christ, is often identified as the preincarnate Christ. *See note on Exodus 3:2.* **Shur.** This location was south of Palestine and east of Egypt, which meant that Hagar attempted to return home to Egypt.

16:8 *Hagar, Sarai's maid.* Both the salutation and the instruction (v. 9, "Return . . . submit") given by the angel and the response by Hagar treated the mistress-servant relationship as if it were still intact. Rebelling and absconding was not the solution (v. 9).

16:10 *I will multiply.* A servant she might have been, but mother of many she would also become, thus making Abram the father of two groups of innumerable descendants (see 13:16; 15:5).

16:11 *call his name Ishmael.* With her son's name meaning "God hears," Hagar the servant could never forget how God had heard her cry of affliction.

16:12 *a wild man . . . against every man.* The untameable desert onager (wild donkey) best described the fiercely aggressive and independent nature Ishmael would exhibit, along with his Arabic descendants.

16:13 *You-Are-the-God-Who-Sees.* Recognizing the angel as God and ascribing this new name to Him arose from Hagar's astonishment at having been the object of God's gracious attention. The theophany and revelation led her to call Him also "The One Who Lives and Sees Me" (v. 14).

16:15 *his son . . . Ishmael.* C. 2079 B.C.

16:16 *eighty-six years old.* Abram was seventy-five when he left Haran (12:4). There would be a thirteen-year interval until 17:1 picks up the narrative again.

7. The covenant confirmed (17:1–27)

17:2 *My covenant between Me and you.* This is another reaffirmation of God's unilateral covenant with Abram, which did not mean that there would be no responsibilities falling upon its recipients. *See notes on verses 7–9; 12:1–3; 15:13–21.*

17:4 *many nations.* The threefold reaffirmation of the divine promise of many descendants, perhaps including Isaac's and Ishmael's, brackets the change of name (vv. 4–6), giving it significant emphasis.

17:5 *your name shall be Abraham.* Cf. 11:27. The new name, meaning "father of many nations," reflected Abraham's new relationship to God as well as his new identity based on God's promise of seed. Cf. Romans 4:17.

17:6 *kings shall come from you.* This promise highlights the reality of more than one people group, or nation in its own right, coming from Abraham.

17:7 *I will establish My covenant.* This relationship was set up at God's initiative and also designated as an "everlasting covenant" (v. 7), thus applying to Abraham's posterity with equal force and bringing forth the declaration "I will be their God" (v. 8). This pledge became the dictum of the covenant relationship between Yahweh, i.e., Jehovah, and Israel.

17:8 *all the land of Canaan.* God's reaffirmation of His covenant promises to Abraham did not occur without mention of the land being deeded by divine right to him and his descendants as "an everlasting possession." Cf. Acts 7:5.

17:9 *you shall keep My covenant.* Despite repeated disobedience by the patriarchs and the nation, God's faithfulness to His cove-nant commitment never wavered (e.g., Deut. 4:25–31; 30:1–9; 1 Chr. 16:15–18; Jer. 30:11; 46:27, 28; Amos 9:8; Luke 1:67–75; Heb. 6:13–18). Divine attestations of Abraham's obedience (22:16–18; 26:3–5) were pronounced years after the formal establishment of His covenant (12:1–3; 15:12–18). Though the nation was apostate, there was always an obedient remnant of faithful Israelites (see Zeph. 3:12, 13).

17:11 *a sign of the covenant.* Circumcision (cutting away the male foreskin) was not entirely new in this period of history, but the special religious and theocratic significance then applied to it was entirely new, thus identifying the circumcised as belonging to the physical and ethnical lineage of

Old Testament Names for God

1. **Elohim,** meaning "God," a reference to God's power and might (Gen. 1:1; Ps. 19:1)
2. **Jehovah** (sometimes spelled Yahweh), a reference to God's divine salvation (Gen. 2:4)
3. **El-Elyon,** meaning "The most high God" (Gen. 14:17–20; Is. 14:13, 14)
4. **El-Roi,** meaning "The strong one who sees" (Gen. 16:12)
5. **El-Shaddai,** meaning "The God of the mountains" or "God almighty" (Gen. 17:1; Ps. 91:1)
6. **Jehovah-Jireh,** meaning "The Lord will provide" (Gen. 22:13, 14)
7. **Jehovah-Rapha,** meaning "The Lord our healer" (Ex. 16:26)
8. **Jehovah-Nissi,** meaning "The Lord our banner" (Ex. 17:15)
9. **Jehovah-Maccaddeshem,** meaning "The Lord thy sanctifier" (Ex. 31:13)
10. **Jehovah-Shalom,** meaning "The Lord is peace" (Judg. 6:24)
11. **Jehovah-Rohi,** meaning "The Lord my shepherd" (Ps. 23:1)
12. **Jehovah-Sabbaoth,** meaning "The Lord of Hosts" (Is. 6:1–3)
13. **El-Olam,** meaning "The everlasting God" (Is. 40:28–31)
14. **Jehovah-Tsidkenu,** meaning "The Lord our righteousness" (Jer. 23:6)
15. **Jehovah-Shammah,** meaning "The Lord who is present" (Ezek. 48:35)
16. **Adonai,** meaning "Lord," a reference to the lordship of God (Mal. 1:6)

Abraham (cf. Acts 7:8; Rom. 4:11). Without divine revelation, the rite would not have had this distinctive significance; thus, it remained a theocratic distinctive of Israel (cf. v. 13). There was also a health benefit; since disease could be kept in the folds of the foreskin, removing it prevented that. Historically, Jewish women have had the lowest rate of cervical cancer. But the symbolism had to do with the need to cut away sin and be cleansed. It was the male organ which most clearly demonstrated the depth of depravity because it carried the seed that produced depraved sinners. Thus, circumcision symbolized the need for a profoundly deep cleansing to reverse the effects of depravity.

17:12 *eight days old.* This same time frame was repeated in Leviticus 12:3.

17:14 *shall be cut off from his people.* Being cut off from the covenant community meant loss of temporal benefits stemming from being part of the special, chosen, and theocratic nation, even to the point of death by divine judgment.

17:15 *Sarai . . . Sarah.* Fittingly, since Sarai ("my princess") would be the ancestress of the promised nations and kings, God changed her name to Sarah, taking away the limiting personal pronoun *my,* and calling her "princess" (v. 16).

17:16 *mother of nations.* Cf. 17:5.

17:17 *fell on his face and laughed, and said in his heart.* A proper reaction of adoration over God's promises was marred by the incredulity of Abraham. He knew he was to be a father (12:2; 15:4), but this was the first mention that his barren, old wife was to be the mother.

17:18 *Oh, that Ishmael might live before You!* Abraham's plea for a living son to be the designated beneficiary of God's promises betrayed just how impossible it was for him and Sarah to have children (cf. Rom. 4:17).

17:19–21 Again, patiently but firmly rejecting Abraham's alternative solution, God emphatically settled the matter by bracketing His gracious bestowal of much posterity to Ishmael (see 25:12–18) with affirmations that, indeed, Sarah's son would be the heir of the "everlasting covenant." For the first time, God named the son.

17:19 *call his name Isaac.* The name of the promised son meant "he laughs," an appropriate reminder to Abraham of his initial, faithless reaction to God's promise.

17:23–27 *that very same day.* Without delay, Abraham fully carried out God's command on himself, on "every male," and on "all the men of his house" (vv. 23, 27).

8. Birth of Isaac foretold (18:1–15)

18:1 *the LORD appeared.* This is another instance of a theophany. Abraham, perhaps, did not recognize at first that one of his visitors, whom he humbly greeted, entertained (vv. 2–8), and properly sent away (v. 16), was Yahweh. *trees of Mamre. See note on 13:18.*

18:3 *My Lord.* Although perhaps first used as the customary respectful address of a host to a visitor, later in their interchange it was used knowingly by Abraham of his true and sovereign Lord, whom he addressed as "Master" (vv. 22, 30–32), and whom he must have recognized when the visitor spoke of Himself as "LORD" (v. 14).

18:9–13 Despite a promise clearly reminiscent of God's words to Abraham, Sarah reacted with similar incredulity as her husband had done (cf. 17:17). She was not thinking of divine miracle but of divine providence working only within the normal course of life, being convinced that, at their age, bearing children was not possible.

18:10, 14 Cf. Romans 9:9.

18:14, 15 A rhetorical question ("Is anything too hard?) and divine declaration ("At the appointed time"), coupled with obvious knowledge of her thoughts ("laughed within herself"), made Sarah fearfully perceive her total misperception of God's working.

9. Sodom and Gomorrah (18:16–19:38)

18:17, 18 *Shall I hide from Abraham what I am doing?* The Lord's reason for permitting Abraham to know of judgment in advance underscored his special role in the plan of God and the certain outcome of His covenant with Abraham—many offspring and great blessing.

18:18 Cf. Galatians 3:8.

18:19 *For I have known him, in order that he may command.* An expression of divine confidence, i.e., a tribute to faithfulness, obedience, and consistency.

18:20 *Because the outcry . . . is great.* The iniquity of the two cities, by then complete (cf. 15:16), had reached the point of no return before the Lord, who demonstrated before Abraham how justly He assessed the time for judgment (v. 21, "I will go down now and see").

18:23 *Would You also destroy the righteous with the wicked?* The intercession for the two wicked cities began with a question that portrayed Abraham's acute awareness of God's mercy toward the righteous and the distinction He made between the good and the bad (v. 25).

18:24 *fifty righteous.* Among the righteous was Lot (see 2 Pet. 2:7, 8).

18:25 *Shall not the Judge of all the earth do right?* Abraham's clear understanding of God's character being able only to do what is good and totally above reproach was affirmed with this rhetorical question.

18:27 *I who am but dust and ashes.* Abraham's negotiation, far from being crassly or selfishly manipulative, humbly and compassionately expressed his concern

for people (cf. 13:8, 9) and particularly interceded for the place where his nephew Lot and his family lived. He did not intend to anger the Lord by his repeated requests (vv. 28, 30, 32).

18:32 *for the sake of ten.* That the number of righteous people necessary to forestall judgment had been reduced from fifty to ten may have reflected Abraham's awareness both of the intense wickedness of the cities as well as Lot's ineffective witness there. Abraham probably had the whole of Lot's family in mind.

18:33 *the LORD went His way . . . Abraham returned to his place.* Nothing more could be done; the judgment was inevitable.

19:1 *two angels.* These were the angels who, with God, had visited Abraham (18:22). They had taken human form (v. 10; called "men"). ***Lot was sitting in the gate.*** Since city officials and other prominent citizens conducted the community's affairs at the gate, Lot participated there as a judge (v. 9).

19:2 *please turn in to your servant's house.* Lot's invitation to the two angels (vv. 1–3) to partake of his hospitality was most likely not just courtesy, but an effort to protect them from the known perversity of the Sodomites (cf. v. 8, "this is the reason").

19:3 *he insisted strongly.* Such was Lot's concern for these strangers that their stated preference to pass the night in the town square could not be permitted.

19:4 *the men of the city . . . all the people.* Both the size of the lustful mob of men boisterously milling around Lot's house and the widespread nature of Sodom's immoral perversion received emphasis both from the additional qualifiers used ("all the people from every quarter" and "both old and young") and the request made (v. 5, "know them *carnally*"). Even acknowledging legitimate exaggeration in this use of *all* would not detract from this emphasis—this was indeed a wicked city.

19:5 know them carnally. They sought homosexual relations with the visitors. God's attitude toward this vile behavior became clear when He destroyed the city (vv. 23–29). Cf. Leviticus 18:22, 29; 20:13; Romans 1:26; 1 Corinthians 6:9; 1 Timothy 1:10 where all homosexual behavior is prohibited and condemned by God.

19:6–8 Lot's response betrayed tension in his ethics; his offer to gratify their sexual lust contradicted his plea not to act "so wickedly." Such contradiction made clear also the vexation of spirit under which he lived in wicked Sodom (cf. 2 Pet. 2:6, 7).

19:8 do to them as you wish. The constraints of Eastern hospitality and the very purpose for which Lot had invited the visitors in (vv. 2, 3) compelled Lot to offer his daughters for a less deviant (see notes on Rom. 1:24–27) kind of wickedness, so as to protect his guests. This foolish effort shows that while Lot was right with God (2 Pet. 2:7, 8), he had contented himself with some sins and weak faith rather than leaving Sodom. But God was gracious to him because he was righteous, by faith, before God.

19:9 keeps acting as a judge. Their accusation suggests Lot had made moral pronouncements before, but his evaluation was no longer tolerable. **pressed hard.** Homosexual deviation carries an uncontrollable lust that defies restraint. Even when blinded, they tried to fulfill their lust (v. 11).

19:10, 11 Lot was now being protected by those whom he had earlier sought to protect.

19:13 the LORD has sent us to destroy it. With the wickedness of the city so graphically confirmed (vv. 4–11), divine judgment was the only outcome, but Lot's family could escape it (vv. 12, 13). Cf. Jude 7.

19:14 seemed to be joking. Lot's warning of imminent judgment fell within the category of jesting, so concluded his sons-in-law (or perhaps his daughters' fiancés).

19:16 the LORD being merciful to him. This reason, elsewhere described as God having remembered Abraham (v. 29), is why, in the face of Lot's seeming reluctance to leave ("lingered"), the angels personally and forcefully escorted him and his family beyond the city's precincts.

19:17–21 An urbanized lifestyle was apparently superior to a lonely one in the mountains and might be why Lot, playing upon the mercy already shown him, negotiated for an alternative escape destination—another city. The angel's reply (v. 21) indicated that this city was included in the original judgment plan, but would be spared for Lot's sake.

19:24 brimstone . . . from the Lord out of the heavens. When morning came (v. 23), judgment fell. Any natural explanation, about how the Lord used combustible sulfur deposits to destroy that locale, falters on this emphatic indication of miraculous judgment. Brimstone could refer to any inflammable substance; perhaps, a volcanic eruption and an earthquake with a violent electrical storm "overthrew" (v. 25) the area. That area is now believed to be under the south end of the Dead Sea. Burning gases, sulfur, and magma blown into the air all fell to bury the region.

19:26 his wife looked back. Lot's wife paid the price of disregarding the angelic warning to flee without a backward glance (v. 17). In so doing, she became not only encased in salt, but a poignant example of disobedience producing unwanted reaction at Judgment Day (cf. Luke 17:29–32), even as her home cities became bywords of God's judgment on sin (cf. Is. 1:9; Rom. 9:29; 2 Pet. 2:5, 6).

19:29 the cities of the plain. The best archeological evidence locates Sodom and

Gomorrah at the south of the Dead Sea region, i.e., in the area south of the Lisan Peninsula that juts out on the east *(see note on 14:10)*. **God remembered Abraham.** Cf. 18:23–33.

19:30 afraid to dwell in Zoar. Perhaps this was so because the people there felt he was responsible for all the devastation, or he feared more judgment on the region might hit the city (vv. 17–23).

19:31–36 The immoral philosophy of Sodom and Gomorrah had so corrupted the thinking of Lot's daughters that they contrived to be impregnated by their own father. They were virgins (v. 8), the married daughters were dead (v. 14), and there were no men left for husbands (v. 25). In fearing they would have no children, they concocted this gross iniquity.

19:37, 38 The two sons born of incest became the progenitors of Moab and Ammon, Israel's longstanding enemies.

10. Philistine encounter (20:1–18)

20:1 Gerar. A Philistine city on the border between the Promised Land and Egypt, about ten miles south of Gaza.

20:2 She is my sister. Twenty-five years after leaving Egypt in disgrace because of lying about his wife (12:10–20), Abraham reverted to the same ploy. **Abimelech.** This king who took Sarah into his harem was most likely the father or grandfather of the Abimelech encountered by Isaac. See note on 26:1.

20:3 God came . . . in a dream. Again, Abraham's Lord intervened to protect Sarah, who had joined in the lie of her husband (v. 5), deceiving a king who earnestly protested his innocence and integrity before God (vv. 4–6). Together with his aides, Abimelech demonstrated proper submission to the warning of God (v. 8).

20:6 withheld you from sinning. Notwithstanding God's restraint of Abimelech,

he was still required to restore Sarah to forestall judgment.

20:7 he is a prophet. Abraham, in spite of his lie, still served as God's intermediary and intercessor for Abimelech (cf. vv. 17, 18). This is the first time the Hebrew term for "prophet" is used in Scripture. Here, it identified Abraham as one recognized by God to speak to Him on behalf of Abimelech. Usually, it is used to describe not one who speaks to God on behalf of someone, but one who speaks to someone on behalf of God.

20:9 deeds . . . not to be done. The confrontation between prophet and king attested to the grievous nature of Abraham's actions. It proved humiliating for the prophet of God to be so rebuked by a heathen king.

20:11–13 Abraham offered three reasons for his lie: (1) his perception from the horrible vices in Sodom that all other cities had no fear of God, including Gerar; (2) his fear of death as a mitigating factor for what he had done; and (3) his wife actually being his half-sister as justification for lying and hiding their marital status. Abraham did not need fraud to protect himself. God was able to provide safety for him.

20:16 rebuked. This is better translated "justified."

11. Isaac's birth (21:1–34)

21:1 the LORD visited Sarah. To the aged couple (vv. 2, 5, 7), exactly as promised, a son was born and the twenty-five year suspense was finally over with the earlier laughter of derision now turning to rejoicing (v. 6). The barrenness of Sarah (11:26) had ended.

21:4 circumcised. *See note on 17:11.*

21:5 Isaac . . . born to him. C. 2065 B.C. God fulfilled His promise to Abraham (12:2; 15:4, 5; 17:7).

21:8 weaned. This usually occurred in the second or third year.

21:9 the son of Hagar . . . scoffing. The

celebration of Isaac's passage from infancy to childhood witnessed the laughter of ridicule (an intensive form of the Hebrew verb for laughing) and offended Sarah, causing her to demand the expulsion of Ishmael and his mother from the encampment (v. 10).

21:10 Cast out ... not be heir. Legal codes of Abraham's day, e.g., of Nuzi and of Hammurabi, forbade the putting out of a handmaiden's son if a rightful, natural heir was born. Sarah's request, thus, offended (1) social law, (2) Abraham's sensibilities, and (3) his love for Ishmael (v. 11). Abraham, however, was given divine approval and assurances to overcome his scruples before sending Hagar and Ishmael out into the wilderness (vv. 12–15). Cf. Galatians 4:22–31.

21:12 Cf. Romans 9:7; Hebrews 11:18.

21:13 Cf. verse 18; *see notes on 16:11, 12.* Ishmael was about seventeen years old, a customary time for sons to go out to set up their own lives.

21:14 Wilderness of Beersheba. A wide, extensive desert on the southern border of Israel.

21:17 God heard the voice of the lad. When desperation turned the lad's voice of scoffing into a cry of anguish at probable death from thirst (vv. 15, 16), God heard him whose name had been given years before when God had heard Hagar's cries (16:11). It reminded the mother of the promise made to Abraham about her son (17:20). *angel of God.* This is the same person as the Angel of the Lord. See note on Exodus 3:2.

21:18 *See note on verse 13.*

21:21 Wilderness of Paran. This was located in the northeast section of the Sinai peninsula, the area called Arabia.

21:22–34 A parity treaty formally struck between Abimelech and Abraham guaranteed the proper control and sharing of the region's limited water resources and also assured the king of the patriarch's fair and equitable treatment for years to come.

21:31 Beersheba. This site is about forty-five miles southwest of Jerusalem.

21:32 the land of the Philistines. Abraham had contact with early migrations of Aegean traders who settled along the southwest coastal regions of Canaan and who were the predecessors of the twelfth century B.C. influx of Philistines, the future oppressors of Israel.

21:33 tamarisk tree. This tree functioned as a reminder of the treaty between two, well-known contemporaries, and also as a marker of one of Abraham's worship sites. the Everlasting God. A divine name appropriately signifying to Abraham the unbreakable and everlasting nature of the covenant God had made with him, notwithstanding his being only a resident alien and a sojourner in the land (cf. 23:4).

12. Abraham's act of faith with Isaac (22:1–19)

22:1 God tested Abraham. This was not a temptation; rather, God examined Abraham's heart (cf. James 1:2–4, 12–18).

22:2 Take . . . your son . . . and offer him. These startling commands activated a special testing ordeal for Abraham, i.e., to sacrifice his "only son" (repeated three times by God, vv. 2, 12, 16). This would mean killing the son (over twenty years old) and with that, ending the promise of the Abrahamic covenant. Such action would seem irrational, yet Abraham obeyed (v. 3). *Moriah.* Traditionally associated with Jeru-salem, this is the site on which Solomon's temple would be built later (cf. 2 Chr. 3:1).

22:4 third day. With no appearance of reluctance or delay, Abraham rose early (v. 3) for the two-day trip from Beersheba to Moriah, one of the hills around Jerusalem.

22:5 the lad and I will go . . . we will

come back. The three-day journey (v. 4) afforded much time to reflect upon God's commands but, without wavering or questioning the morality of human sacrifice or the purposes of God, Abraham confidently assured his servants of his and Isaac's return and went ahead with arrangements for the sacrifice (v. 6). Hebrews 11:17–19 reveals that he was so confident in the permanence of God's promise, that he believed if Isaac were to be killed, God would raise him from the dead *(see notes),* or God would provide a substitute for Isaac (v. 8).

22:9, 10 Abraham's preparations to kill his only son clearly evidenced his trust in God. Cf. Hebrews 11:17–19.

22:11 *Angel of the Lord. See note on Exodus 3:2.*

22:12 *now I know.* Abraham passed the test (v. 1). He demonstrated faith that God responds to with justification. *See note on James 2:21.*

22:13 *instead of his son.* The idea of substitutionary atonement is introduced, which would find its fulfillment in the death of Christ (Is. 53:4–6; John 1:29; 2 Cor. 5:21).

22:15–18 In this formal reaffirmation of His Abrahamic covenant, the Lord mentioned the three elements of land, seed, and blessing, but with attention directed graphically to the conquest of the land promised (v. 17, "shall possess the gate of their enemies").

22:16, 17 Cf. 12:1–3; 15:13–18; 17:2, 7, 8, 9; Hebrews 6:13, 14.

22:17 *possess the gate of their enemies.* Cf. 24:60. This refers to conquering enemies, so as to control their city.

22:18 Cf. Acts 3:25.

C. Abraham's Promised Seed
(22:20–25:11)

1. Rebekah's background (22:20–24)
22:20–24 *it was told.* This is clear indica-

tion that, despite geographical separation, information about family genealogies flowed back and forth in the Fertile Crescent region. This update advised most notably of a daughter, Rebekah, born to Isaac's cousin, Bethuel (v. 23). It also reminds the readers that Abraham and Sarah had not lost all ties with their original home. Abraham's brother, Nahor, still lived back in Mesopotamia, though he had not seen him for about sixty years.

2. The death of Sarah (23:1–20)
23:1, 2 Although Sarah's age—the only woman's age at death recorded in Scripture—might suggest her importance in God's plan, it more importantly reminds of the birth of her only son when she was well beyond childbearing age (at ninety years of age, cf. 17:17) and of God's intervention to bring about the fulfillment of His word to her and Abraham. Sarah's death occurred c. 2028 B.C.

23:2 *Hebron. See note on 13:18.*

23:3 *the sons of Heth.* A settlement of Hittites whose original home was in Anatolia (modern-day Turkey), who had already been established in Canaan far from their homeland.

23:4 *Give me property.* Negotiations for the purchase ("give" signifies here "sell") of Hittite property was properly conducted in accordance with contemporary Hittite custom, with Abraham wanting to pay the fair market value for it (v. 9).

23:6 *a mighty prince among us.* Rank and reputation accorded Abraham a place of leadership and respect, leading his neighbors (the Hittites) to freely offer their best sepulchers to him. They went on and arranged for Abraham to purchase a cave that belonged to a wealthy neighbor called Ephron (vv. 7–9), unknown to Abraham.

23:10 *dwelt.* Lit. "was sitting," perhaps at

the city gate where business was usually transacted.

23:11 *I give you the field.* This suggests not that Ephron felt generous, but that he was constrained by Hittite feudal polity, which tied ownership of land with service to the ruler. Passing the land to Abraham would pass also feudal responsibilities to Abraham, making him liable for all taxes and duties. Ephron was apparently anxious to do this; thus, the offer to give the land.

23:14, 16 *shekels of silver, currency of the merchants.* Precious metals were not made into coins for exchange until centuries later. Merchants maintained the shekel as the standard weight of value for business transactions. A shekel weighed less than one-half ounce.

23:17, 18 With the words of the transaction, the careful description of the property, and the payment of the stated price all done before witnesses and at the proper place of business, ownership of the land officially passed to Abraham. It was still binding years later in the time of Jacob (49:29–32; 50:12, 13).

23:19 *after this.* Once the purchase had been made, Abraham buried Sarah. Moses notes the place is Hebron in Canaan, to which his initial readers were soon headed when they entered the land.

23:20 *So the field and the cave ... were deeded.* This is an important summary because finally, after years of nomadic wandering, Abraham owned a small piece of real estate in the midst of all the land divinely promised to him and his descendants. The cave also became, many years later, the family burial plot for Abraham, Isaac, Rebekah, Leah, and Jacob (cf. 25:9; 49:31; 50:13), with Rachel being the exception (35:19).

3. Isaac's marriage to Rebekah (24:1–67)
    24:2 *the oldest servant ... who ruled.*

Eliezer, at eighty-five years of age, had risen to steward, or "chief of staff," a position of substantial authority (indicated in v. 10). He would have received all Abraham's wealth if he had no son (see 15:1, 2); yet, when Isaac was born, the inheritance became Isaac's. So not only had he loyally served his master despite having been displaced by another heir (cf. 15:2–4), but he also faithfully served that heir (v. 67).

24:2–4 *put your hand under my thigh ... and ... swear.* See note on verse 9.** A solemn pledge mentioning the Lord's name and formalized by an accepted customary gesture indicated just how serious an undertaking this was in Abraham's eyes. At his age (v. 1), Abraham was concerned to perpetuate his people and God's promise through the next generation; so he covenanted with his servant to return to Mesopotamia and bring back a wife for Isaac.

24:3, 4 Matrimonial arrangements were made by parents, and chosen partners were to come from one's own tribe. It was apparently customary to marry one's first cousin. But Abraham's higher motive was to prevent Isaac from marrying a Canaanite pagan after Abraham's death, possibly leading the people away from the true God.

24:6, 7 *do not take my son back there.* Should the expected scenario not materialize (v. 5), then the dictates of the oath were lifted (v. 8), but the option of Isaac going was summarily rejected because it suggested a nullification of God's promise and calling for the Land of Promise (v. 7).

24:7 *He will send His angel before you.* A statement of Abraham's faith that the 450-mile expedition to Mesopotamia was clearly under divine oversight.

24:9 *his hand under the thigh.* An ancient Near Eastern custom by which an intimate touch affirmed an oath (cf. 47:29).

24:10 *city of Nahor.* This is, no doubt, the home of Abraham's brother, Nahor (22:20).

24:12–14 The steward's prayer manifests not only his trust in God to direct affairs, but also the selflessness with which he served Abraham. His patience after prayer (v. 21), his worship at answered prayer (v. 26), and his acknowledgment of divine guidance (v. 27) also portrayed his faith.

24:14 *camels a drink.* Hospitality required giving water to a thirsty stranger, but not to animals. A woman who would do that was unusually kind and served beyond the call of duty. Rebekah's servant-attitude was revealed (vv. 15–20) as was her beauty and purity (v. 16).

24:20 *all his camels.* A single camel can hold up to twenty-five gallons, and he had ten of them. Serving them was a great task as she filled them all (v. 22).

24:22 *shekel. See note on 23:14, 16.*

24:24 *I am the daughter of.* In formal introductions, an abbreviated genealogy provided for specific identification (cf. 22:23). She was Isaac's cousin.

24:29–31 *Laban.* From what is revealed about his character (ch. 29), there is reason to believe that his sight of all the presents and the camels generated the welcome.

24:33 *I will not eat until.* The first order of business was to identify his master and to explain his assignment, but not without emphasizing the blessings of God upon his master and upon his trip (vv. 34–48) and also not without immediately seeking to conclude his task and return home (vv. 49, 54–56). This is the portrait of a committed, faithful, and selfless servant.

24:49 *right . . . left.* An expression indicating the matter of which way to go next.

24:50, 51 The servant's conviction and focus was obvious and intense, precluding anything but immediate acknowledgment of God's leading and anything less than a full compliance with his request from Rebekah's father and brother (vv. 50, 51).

24:53 By this dowry, Rebekah was betrothed to Isaac.

24:54 Send me away to my master. Protocol and courtesy demanded a messenger be dismissed by the one to whom he had been sent.

24:57, 58 *Will you go with this man?* Commendably, Rebekah concurred with an immediate departure and showed her confident acceptance of what was providentially coming about in her life.

24:59 *her nurse.* See 35:8.

24:60 *they blessed Rebekah and said.* Little did they realize that their conventional prayer, wishing numerous offspring to Rebekah, conformed with God's promises of many descendants to Abraham through Sarah and Isaac. They also wished for her offspring to be victorious over their enemies ("possess their gates"), perhaps echoing God's promises of possession of the Canaanites' land (13:17; 15:7, 16; 17:8).

24:62 *Beer Lahai Roi.* See 16:14. Located on the northern Egyptian border, about twenty-five miles northwest of Kadesh Barnea. Isaac lived there after Abraham's

---

Key Word

Heavens: 1:1, 8, 9; 2:1; 8:2; 11:4; 14:22; 24:3; 28:12—The Hebrew word for heavens may refer to the physical heavens, the sky and the atmosphere of earth (2:1, 4, 19), or to the dwelling place of God (Ps. 14:2), the spiritual heaven. The expression is related to the term for "to be high, lofty." The physical heavens of creation testify to God's glorious position and also to His creative genius (Ps. 19:1, 6).

death (25:11).

24:63 to meditate. How God drew Isaac from home to where Hagar encountered the Angel of the Lord (cf. 16:14) remains unknown, but he was in the right place to meet the caravan returning with his fiancée. Perhaps he was prayerfully contemplating the circumstances of his life and the void left by his mother's death (v. 67), as well as thinking about and hoping the steward would not return from a failed mission.

24:65 she took a veil and covered herself. Convention demanded the designated bride veil her face in the presence of her betrothed until the wedding day.

24:67 his mother Sarah's tent. Isaac, thus, established his acceptance of Rebekah as his wife before he had seen her beauty. When he did see her, "he loved her."

4. Isaac—the only heir (25:1–6)

25:1–4 Abraham's sons through Keturah (a concubine, cf. v. 6; 1 Chr. 1:32) a wife of lower status than Sarah, became the progenitors of various Arab tribes to the east of Canaan.

25:5, 6 Conferring gifts upon these other sons, then sending them away, and also con-

---

Couples in Love

Solomon and his bride show all of the affection and romance that people universally associate with being in love (Song 2:16). Theirs is one of a number of stories about romantic love told in the Bible.

Isaac and Rebekah	(Gen. 24:1–67) A father seeks and finds a wife for his son, and the young couple love each other deeply.
Jacob and Rachel	(Gen. 29:1–30) Jacob labors 14 years for his father-in-law in order to gain Rachel as his wife.
Boaz and Ruth	(Ruth 3–4) Legal technicalities bring together a Moabite widow and a wealthy landowner of Bethlehem, and through them a king is descended.
Elkanah and Hannah	(1 Sam. 1–2) A woman is loved by her husband despite being childless, and God eventually blesses her with the birth of a son, who becomes a mighty judge over Israel.
David and Michal	(1 Sam. 18:20–30) Genuine love is manipulated by a jealous king, but instead of ridding himself of his nemesis, the ruler gains a son-in-law.
Solomon and the Shulamite	(Song of Solomon) The commitments and delights of two lovers are told in a beautiful romantic poem.
Hosea and Gomer	(Hos. 1:1–3:5) God calls the prophet Hosea to seek out his adulterous spouse and restore the relationship despite what she has done.
Christ and the Church	(Eph. 5:25–33) Having won His bride's salvation from sin, Christ loves and serves her as His own body, thereby setting an example for human husbands everywhere.

The MacArthur Bible Handbook, by John MacArthur (Nashville: Thomas Nelson Publishers, 2003) 179. © 2003 by Thomas Nelson, Inc.

ferring the estate upon Isaac ensured that Isaac would be considered as the rightful heir without competition or threat from his half-brothers. The steward, Eliezer, had informed Rebekah's relatives that all of Abraham's estate was Isaac's (cf. 24:36).

5. The death of Abraham (25:7–11)

25:8 gathered to his people. A euphemism for death, but also an expression of personal continuance beyond death, which denoted a reunion with previously departed friends (c. 1990 B.C.). Cf. Matthew 8:11; Luke 16:22, 23.

25:9, 10 his sons . . . buried him. Abraham's funeral brought together two sons who would perhaps otherwise have remained somewhat estranged from each other (cf. 35:29). He was buried in the place which he had purchased at Hebron (ch. 23).

VIII. The Generations of Ishmael (25:12–18)

25:12–18 the genealogy of Ishmael. With the death of Abraham and the focus shifting to Isaac, the record confirms God's promise of twelve princes to Ishmael (cf. 17:20, 21).

25:13–16 Arab tradition has it that these are their earliest ancestors.

25:16 by their towns and their settlements. In addition to serving as a testimony to God's promises (17:20), information such as this genealogy helped Israel to understand the origins of their neighbors in central and northern Arabia.

IX. The Generations of Isaac (25:19–35:29)

A. Competition Between Esau and Jacob (25:19–34)

25:20 Padan Aram. This refers to the "plain of Aram" in upper Mesopotamia near Haran to the north-northeast of Canaan.

25:21 she was barren. Confronted by twenty years of his wife's barrenness (vv. 19, 26), Isaac rose to the test and earnestly turned to God in prayer, obviously acknowledging God's involvement and timing in the seed-promise.

25:22 struggled together within her. The very uncomfortable condition of her pregnancy ("why am I like this?") prompted Rebekah, undoubtedly following the example of her husband, to turn earnestly to God in prayer. She learned directly from the Lord that the severe jostling in her womb prefigured the future antagonism between the two nations to arise from her twin sons (v. 23).

25:23 the older shall serve the younger. This was contrary to the custom in patriarchal times when the elder son enjoyed the privileges of precedence in the household and, at the father's death, received a double share of the inheritance and became the recognized head of the family (cf. Ex. 22:29; Num 8:14–17; Deut. 21:17). Grave offenses could annul such primogeniture rights (cf. Gen. 35:22; 49:3, 4; 1 Chr. 5:1) or the birthright could be sacrificed or legally transferred to another in the family, as here (vv. 29–34). In this case, God declared otherwise since His sovereign elective purposes did not necessarily have to follow custom (cf. Rom. 9:10–14, esp. v. 12).

25:24 days were fulfilled. Esau and Jacob were born c. 2005 B.C.

25:25 red. This would be the linguistic basis for calling Esau's country "Edom" (cf. v. 30).

25:27, 28 The difference between the two sons manifested itself in several areas: (1) as progenitors—Esau of Edom and Jacob of Israel; (2) in disposition—Esau a rugged, headstrong hunter preferring the outdoors and Jacob a plain, amiable man preferring the comforts of home; and (3) in parental favoritism—Esau by his father and Jacob by

The Life of Jacob

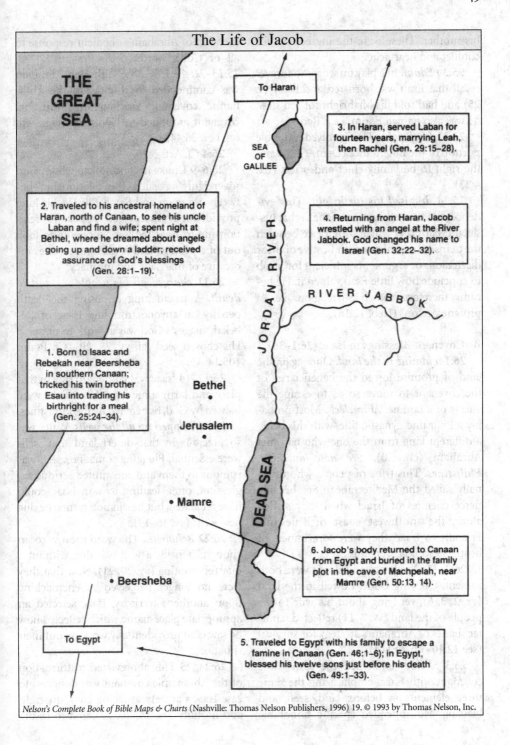

THE GREAT SEA

To Haran

SEA OF GALILEE

3. In Haran, served Laban for fourteen years, marrying Leah, then Rachel (Gen. 29:15–28).

2. Traveled to his ancestral homeland of Haran, north of Canaan, to see his uncle Laban and find a wife; spent night at Bethel, where he dreamed about angels going up and down a ladder; received assurance of God's blessings (Gen. 28:1–19).

4. Returning from Haran, Jacob wrestled with an angel at the River Jabbok. God changed his name to Israel (Gen. 32:22–32).

JORDAN RIVER

RIVER JABBOK

1. Born to Isaac and Rebekah near Beersheba in southern Canaan; tricked his twin brother Esau into trading his birthright for a meal (Gen. 25:24–34).

• Bethel

• Jerusalem

DEAD SEA

• Mamre

6. Jacob's body returned to Canaan from Egypt and buried in the family plot in the cave of Machpelah, near Mamre (Gen. 50:13, 14).

• Beersheba

To Egypt

5. Traveled to Egypt with his family to escape a famine in Canaan (Gen. 46:1–6); in Egypt, blessed his twelve sons just before his death (Gen. 49:1–33).

Nelson's Complete Book of Bible Maps & Charts (Nashville: Thomas Nelson Publishers, 1996) 19. © 1993 by Thomas Nelson, Inc.

his mother. These were the ingredients for conflict and heartache.

25:30 *Edom.* In a play on words to forever recall that Esau was born red and hairy (v. 25) and had sold his birthright for red stew, he was also named Edom, i.e., "Red."

25:31 *birthright.* This involved a double portion of the inheritance (Deut. 21:17) and the right to be family chief and priest (Ex. 4:22).

25:34 *despised his birthright.* This evidences the final evaluation of the verbal tussle and bartering which took place between the twins, all of which was indicative of prior discussions or arguments sufficient for Jacob to conclude how little Esau valued it. He became, therefore, known as irreligious, i.e., "a profane person" (Heb. 12:16).

B. Covenant Blessings to Isaac (26:1–35)

26:1 *a famine in the land.* Once again the land of promise forced the beneficiaries of the covenant to move so as to escape the effects of a famine. ***Abimelech.*** Most probably a Philistine dynastic title, with this being a different king from the one who had met Abraham (ch. 20). *See note on 20:2.* ***Philistines.*** This tribe of people who originally sailed the Mediterranean Sea became fierce enemies of Israel when they settled along the southwest coast of Palestine. Friendly to Isaac, they were forerunners of hostile descendant enemies.

26:2–11 Obedience and deceit were both present. Obeying God to dwell in the land (vv. 2, 3, 6), yet lying about his wife to the people of the land (vv. 7–11) reflected familiar shades of Abraham's strategy for survival (see 12:10–14; 20:1–4).

26:3–5 God confirmed the Abrahamic covenant with Isaac, emphasizing the same three elements as before: land, seed, and blessing. He appended specific honorable

mention of Abraham's obedient response to all of God's words. *See notes on 12:1–3; 15:13–21; 17:2, 7, 8, 9.* Although Abraham was commended for his deeds, the Abrahamic covenant was an unconditional covenant grounded in God's sovereign will (cf. Lev. 26:44, 45).

26:4 Cf. Acts 3:25.

26:6–9 Unlike his ancestor to whom God sovereignly revealed the relationship between Abraham and Sarah (20:3), this king providentially discovered Rebekah's relationship to Isaac by just happening to look out of a window and witnessing caresses indicative of marriage and intimacy.

26:11 *charged all his people . . . put to death.* A pagan king imposing the death penalty on anyone troubling Isaac or Rebekah suggests God was at work to preserve His chosen seed (cf. vv. 28, 29). Cf. Psalm 105:14, 15.

26:12–14 Isaac was content to stay in that place and farm some land. His efforts were blessed by God, but envied by the Philistines.

26:15 *stopped up all the wells.* Water was so precious in that desert land that wells were essential. Plugging someone's well was ruinous to them and constituted serious aggression, often leading to war. Isaac could have retaliated, but he did not; rather, he dug new wells (vv. 16–19).

26:22 *Rehoboth.* The word means "room enough." Finally, a well was dug without a quarrel erupting (vv. 20, 21). Now that they were no longer perceived as encroaching upon another's territory, Isaac selected an appropriate place-name which reflected how he saw God providentially working out their situation.

26:24, 25 This abbreviated reaffirmation of the Abrahamic covenant was designed to ease Isaac's anxiety at facing envy, quarrels, and hostility (vv. 14, 20, 27), and to assure

Isaac that he had reasoned right—fruitfulness in posterity would prevail. That it was a significant reminder to Isaac is seen in a response reminiscent of his father; he built an altar of worship to mark the spot of God's appearance to him (12:7).

26:26 Abimelech . . . and Phichol. Because ninety years had passed since Abraham was visited by men with the same names, they must have been titles rather than proper names (cf. 21:22). *See note on verse 1.*

26:28 an oath . . . a covenant. In a mirror image of a former occasion (21:22–32), Abimelech, in the company of a friend and the highest ranking officer in his army (v. 26), sought after a treaty with one they estimated to be superior and stronger than themselves and a possible threat (v. 29). Isaac, on the other hand, perceived them as hostile (v. 27). The outcome was most desirable for both—peace between them (v. 31).

26:30 Ratification of a covenant often involved a banquet.

26:33 Beersheba. Lit. "the well of the oath." The very place where his father Abraham had made an oath with another Abimelech and Phichol *(see note on v. 26)* and which Abraham had named Beersheba (21:32).

26:35 grief of mind. Esau's choice of wives from among neighboring Hittite women saddened his parents. His action had deliberately ignored the standard set by Abraham for Isaac (24:3). Cf. 27:46.

C. Jacob's Deception for the Blessing (27:1–40)

27:1 Isaac was old. Blind Isaac evidently thought he was near death (v. 2) and would not live much beyond his current 137 years, which was the age of Ishmael when he died (25:17). He certainly did not expect to live another forty-three years as he actually did

(35:28; cf. 30:24, 25; 31:41; 41:46, 47; 45:6; 47:9 to calculate Isaac's age at 137 and his twin sons' ages at 77 years old).

27:4 my soul may bless you. Ignoring the words of God to Rebekah (25:23), forgetting Esau's bartered birthright (25:33), and overlooking Esau's grievous marriages (26:35), Isaac was still intent on treating Esau as the eldest and granting him the blessing of birthright, and so arranged for his favorite meal before bestowing final fatherly blessing on his favorite son.

27:5 Now Rebekah was listening. Desperation to secure patriarchal blessing for Jacob bred deception and trickery, with Rebekah believing her culinary skills could make goat's meat taste and smell like choice venison (vv. 8–10) and make Jacob seem like Esau (vv. 15–17).

27:12 I shall seem to be a deceiver to him. To his credit, Jacob at first objected. The differences between him and Esau would surely not fool his father and might result in blessing being replaced with a curse as a fitting punishment for deception.

27:13 Let your curse be on me. With his mother accepting full responsibility for the scheme and bearing the curse should it occur, Jacob acquiesced and followed Rebekah's instructions.

27:15 choice clothes of her elder son. Esau, having been married for thirty-seven years (cf. v. 1; 26:35), would have had his own tents and his own wives to do for him; so how and why Rebekah came by some of his best clothes in her tent is unknown. Perhaps these garments were the official robes associated with the priestly functions of the head of the house, kept in her house until passed on to the oldest son. Perhaps Esau had, on occasion, worn them, thus their smell of the field (v. 27).

27:20 Because the LORD your God brought it to me. Isaac's perfectly legitimate question in verse 20 (hunting took time and Jacob had come so quickly with goats from the pen) afforded Jacob an escape route—confess and stop the deceit. Instead, Jacob, with consummate ease, knowing he needed Isaac's irrevocable confirmation even though he had bought the birthright, ascribed success in the hunt to God's providence. A lie had to sustain a lie, and a tangled web had begun to be woven (vv. 21–24). Although Jacob received Isaac's blessing that day, the deceit caused severe consequences: (1) he never saw his mother after that; (2) Esau wanted him dead; (3) Laban, his uncle, deceived him; (4) his family life was full of conflict; and (5) he was exiled for years from his family. By the promise of God, he would have received the birthright (25:23). He didn't need to scheme this deception with his mother.

27:27–29 Finally, with all lingering doubts removed, Isaac pronounced the blessing upon Jacob, although the opening words show he thought the one receiving it was Esau, the man of the field. His prayer-wish called for prosperity and superiority and ended with a repeat of God's words to Abraham (v. 29c; cf. 12:1–3). The words indicated that Isaac thought the covenantal line should have continued through his eldest son, Esau.

27:33 Isaac trembled exceedingly. Visibly shocked when the scandal was uncovered by the entrance of Esau, the father, remembering the Lord's words to Rebekah (25:23), refused to withdraw the blessing and emphatically affirmed its validity—"indeed he shall be blessed" and a little later "indeed I have made him your master" and also "you shall serve your brother" (vv. 37, 40). His sudden realization at having opposed God's will all those years likely made the shock even more severe.

27:34 Bless me—me also. Esau fully expected to receive the blessing, for he had identified himself to his father as the firstborn (v. 32). Anguished at losing this important paternal blessing and bitterly acting as the innocent victim (v. 36), Esau shifted the blame for the loss of birthright and blessing to Jacob and pleaded for some compensating word of blessing from his father (vv. 36, 38).

27:39, 40 The prayer-wish called for prosperity and inferiority, i.e., maintaining the validity of the words to Jacob and replacing "be master over your brethren" with "you shall serve your brother" (vv. 29, 40). This secondary blessing would not and could not undo the first one.

27:40 you shall break his yoke from your neck. In later history, the Edomites, who descended from the line of Esau, fought time and again with Israel and shook off Israelite control on several occasions (2 Kin. 8:20; 2 Chr. 21:8–10; 28:16, 17).

D. Blessing on Jacob in a Foreign Land (27:41–32:32)

1. Jacob sent to Laban (27:41–28:9)

27:41 The days of mourning for my father. Evidently, Esau also thought his father was on the verge of death (27:1) and so, out of respect for his aged father, he postponed murder. Isaac lived another forty-three years (see note on v. 1).

27:45 bereaved also of you both in one day? Rebekah understood that she stood to lose both her sons since, after the murder of Jacob, the avenger of blood, i.e., the next nearest relative, would track down and execute Esau.

27:46 daughters of Heth. These are local Hittite women. See notes on 23:3; 26:35.

28:1, 2 take yourself a wife from there. Anxious for the safety of her son, Rebekah easily convinced her husband that the time had come for him to seek a non-Canaanite wife back in their homeland and preferably from near kinsmen (vv. 2, 5), just as Rebekah had been sought for Isaac (see 24:1–4).

28:2 Padan Aram. See note on 25:20.

28:3, 4 This extra patriarchal blessing unveiled where Isaac was in his thinking. He had come to understand that the divine blessings would go through Jacob, to whom the Abrahamic covenant promises of posterity and land also applied—quite the reversal of prior wishes and understanding (cf. 27:27–29). The lack of land possession at that time, described by the phrase "in which you are a stranger," did not deter at all from the certainty of God's promise.

28:3 God Almighty. Significantly, El Shaddai was the name Isaac chose to use when blessing Jacob. It was the name of sovereign power with which God had identified Himself to Abraham in covenant reaffirmation (17:1), an encouraging factor to both him and his son.

28:5 Isaac sent Jacob away. C. 1928 B.C. This must have been a hard departure for the domestic Jacob.

28:9 So Esau went to Ishmael. Marrying back into the line of Abraham through the family of Ishmael seemed to have been a ploy to gain favor with his father (vv. 6, 8), and show an obedience similar to his brother's (v. 7). He hoped by such gratifying of his parents to atone for past delinquencies and, maybe, have his father change the will. He actually increased iniquity by adding to his pagan wives (26:34, 35) a wife from a family God had rejected.

2. Angel at Bethel (28:10–22)

28:10–15 For the first time, and significantly while Jacob was on his way out of the land of Canaan, God revealed Himself to Jacob and confirmed the Abrahamic cov-

enant with him in all of its three elements of land, seed, and blessing (vv. 13, 14). Later, God would remind Jacob of this event when He instructed him to return to the land (31:13) and Jacob would remind his household of it when he instructed them to cleanse their homes before they could return to Bethel (35:3).

28:10 Haran. See note on 11:31.

28:11 a certain place. Identified in verse 19 as Bethel, about fifty miles north of Beersheba, and about six miles north of Jerusalem. There, Jacob spent the night in an open field.

28:12 a ladder . . . angels of God were ascending and descending. This is a graphic portrayal of the heavenly Lord's personal involvement in the affairs of earth, especially as they related to divine covenant promises in Jacob's life (vv. 13–15). This dream was to encourage the lonely traveler. God's own appointed angelic messengers ensured the carrying out of His will and plans. More than likely, the angels traversed a stairway rather than a ladder.

28:15 will keep you . . . will bring you back. A most timely, comforting, and assuring promise which remained engraved on Jacob's heart during his sojourn in Haran (see 30:25). His forced departure from Canaan did not and would not abrogate any of God's promises to him.

28:18–21 a pillar. Marking a particular site as of special religious significance by means of a stone pillar was a known practice. A libation offering, a change of place-name, and a vow of allegiance to the Lord in exchange for promised protection and blessing completed Jacob's ceremonial consecration of Bethel, i.e., "House of God." See note on 31:13.

28:22 a tenth. Tithing, though not commanded by God, was obviously already known and voluntarily practiced, and served

to acknowledge God's providential benefi-
cence in the donor's life *(see note on 14:20)*. Jacob may have been bargaining with God, as if
to buy His favor rather than purely worshiping God with his gift; but it is best to translate
the *if* (v. 20) as "since" and see Jacob's vow and
offering as genuine worship based on confidence in God's promise (vv. 13–15).

3. Disagreements with Laban (29:1–30)

29:1–4 Conveniently meeting at his destination, shepherds who knew both Laban
and Rachel reflected the directing hand of
God upon his life, just as promised (28:15).

29:2, 3 *A large stone.* Perhaps due to the
fact that this well of precious, stored water
could evaporate rapidly in the sun, or
be filled with blowing dust, or used indiscriminately, it had been covered and its use
regulated (vv. 7, 8).

29:5 *Laban the son of Nahor?* Genealogical fluidity in the use of "son," meaning
male descendant, occurred in Jacob's inquiry
after Laban, because he was actually Nahor's
grandson (cf. 22:20–23).

29:6–8 It appears that Jacob was trying to
get these men to water their sheep immediately and leave, so he could be alone with
Rachel for the meeting.

29:9 *speaking with them.* The language of
Haran was Aramaic or Chaldee and evidently
was known by Abraham and his sons. There
is no comment on how these patriarchs
spoke with the Canaanites and Egyptians in
their travels, but it is reasonable to assume
they had become skilled linguists, knowing
more than Hebrew and Aramaic.

29:10–14 Customary greetings and personal introductions ended ninety-seven
years of absence since Rebekah had left *(see
notes on 25:21; 27:1)*, and Laban's nephew
was welcomed home.

29:14 *a month.* Tradition in that ancient
area allowed a stranger to be looked after for
three days. On the fourth day, he was to tell
his name and mission. After that, he could
remain if he worked in some agreed-upon
way (v. 15).

29:17 *eyes were delicate.* This probably
means that they were a pale color rather than
the dark and sparkling eyes most common.
Such paleness was viewed as a blemish.

29:18–30 Love and working to provide
his service as a dowry (vv. 18–20) combined
to make Jacob remain during the first seven
years in Laban's household, almost as an
adopted son rather than a mere employee.
But Jacob, the deceiver (27:1–29), was about
to be deceived (vv. 22–25). Local marriage
customs (v. 26), love for Rachel, and more
dowry desired by Laban (vv. 27–30) all conspired to give Jacob, not only seven more
years of labor under Laban, but two wives
who were to become caught up in jealous
childbearing competition (30:1–21).

29:23 The deception was possible because
of the custom of veiling the bride and the

Sons of Jacob		
Mother	**Son**	**Birth**
Leah	Reuben	Gen. 29:32
	Simeon	Gen. 29:33
	Levi	Gen. 29:34
	Judah	Gen. 29:35
	Issachar	Gen. 30:18
	Zebulun	Gen. 30:20
Bilhah	Dan	Gen. 30:6
	Naphtali	Gen. 30:8
Zilpah	Gad	Gen. 30:11
	Asher	Gen. 30:13
Rachel	Joseph	Gen. 30:24
	Benjamin	Gen. 35:18

dark of the night (v. 24).

29:23, 30 went in to. This is a euphemism for consummating marriage.

29:27, 30 It appears that Laban agreed to give Rachel to Jacob after the week of wedding celebration for Leah's marriage to him, and before the seven years of labor.

29:28 Rachel as wife also. Such consanguinity was not God's will (see note on Gen. 2:24), and the Mosaic code later forbade it (Lev. 18:18). Polygamy always brought grief, as in the life of Jacob.

4. Promised seed (29:31–30:24)

29:31 Leah was unloved . . . Rachel was barren. There was quite a contrast when the one dearly beloved (vv. 18, 20, 30) had no children, whereas the one rejected did. Jacob might have demoted Leah, but God took action on her behalf. Leah had also prayed about her husband's rejection (v. 33) and had been troubled by it, as seen in the names given to her first four sons (vv. 32–35).

30:1 or else I die! A childless woman in ancient Near Eastern culture was no better than a dead wife and became a severe embarrassment to her husband (see v. 23).

30:2 Am I in the place of God? Although spoken in a moment of frustration with Rachel's pleading for children and the envy with which it was expressed, Jacob's words do indicate an understanding that, ultimately, God opened and closed the womb.

30:3 on my knees. When the surrogate gave birth while actually sitting on the knees of the wife, it symbolized the wife providing a child for her husband.

30:1–21 The competition between the two sisters/wives is demonstrated in using their maids as surrogate mothers (vv. 3, 7, 9, 12), in declaring God had judged the case in favor of the plaintiff (v. 6), in bartering for time with the husband (vv. 14–16), in accusing one of stealing her husband's favor (v.

15), and in the name given to one son—"wrestled with my sister" (Naphtali, v. 8). The race for children was also accompanied by prayers to the Lord or by acknowledgment of His providence (vv. 6, 17, 20, 22; also 29:32, 33, 35). This bitter and intense rivalry, all the more fierce though they were sisters and even though they occupied different dwellings with their children as customary, shows that the evil lay in the system itself (bigamy), which as a violation of God's marriage ordinance (Gen. 2:24) could not yield happiness.

30:14 mandrakes. Jacob had eight sons by then from three women, and about six years had elapsed since his marriages. The oldest son, Reuben, was about five. Playing in the field during wheat harvest, he found this small, orange-colored fruit and "brought them to his mother Leah." These were superstitiously viewed in the ancient world as "love apples," an aphrodisiac or fertility-inducing narcotic.

30:15, 16 This odd and desperate bargain by Rachel was an attempt to become pregnant with the aid of the mandrakes, a folk remedy which failed to understand that God gives children (vv. 6, 17, 20, 22).

30:20 now my husband will dwell with me. This was the plaintive cry of one still unloved (cf. 29:31), as confirmed by Jacob's frequent absence from her home. She hoped that having six children for Jacob would win his permanent residence with her. **Zebulun.** The name means "dwelling," signifying her hope of Jacob's dwelling with her.

30:21 Dinah. Although not the only daughter to be born to Jacob (cf. 37:35; 46:7), her name is mentioned in anticipation of the tragedy at Shechem (ch. 34).

30:22 Then God remembered Rachel. All the desperate waiting (see 30:1) and pleading climaxed at the end of seven years with God's response. Then Rachel properly ascribed her delivery from barrenness to the Lord, whom she also trusted for another son (vv. 23, 24).

30:24 Joseph. C. 1914 B.C. His name means "he will add" or "may he add," indicating both Rachel's thanks and her faith that God would give her another son.

5. Departure from Aram (30:25–31:55)

30:25 Send me away . . . to my country. Fourteen years of absence had not dulled Jacob's acute awareness of belonging to the land God had given to him. Since Mesopotamia was not his home and his contract with Laban was up, he desired to return to "my own place" and "my country." Jacob's wish to return to Canaan was not hidden from Laban (v. 30).

30:27 by experience. Lit. "by divination." See note on Deuteronomy 18:9–12.

30:28 Name me your wages. On the two occasions that Laban asked this of Jacob, it was to urge him to stay. The first time (29:15), Laban had sought to reward a relative but, this time, it was because he had been rewarded since "the LORD has blessed me for your sake" (v. 27). Jacob readily confirmed Laban's evaluation in that "little" had indeed become "a great amount" (v. 30) since he had come on the scene. Laban's superficial generosity should not be mistaken for genuine goodness (see 31:7). He was attempting to deceive Jacob into staying because it was potentially profitable for him.

30:31–36 What shall I give you? Laban wanted Jacob to stay and asked what it would take for him to do so. Jacob wanted nothing except to be in a position for God to bless him. He was willing to stay, but not be further indebted to the scheming and selfish Laban. He offered Laban a plan that could bless him while costing Laban nothing. He would continue to care for Laban's animals, as he had been doing. His pay

would consist of animals not yet born—animals which would seem the less desirable to Laban because of their markings and color. None of the solid color animals would be taken by Jacob and, if any were born into Jacob's flocks, Laban could take them (they were considered as stolen). Only those animals born speckled, spotted, striped, or abnormally colored would belong to Jacob. Evidently, most of the animals were white (sheep), black (goats), and brown (cattle). Few were in the category of Jacob's request. Further, Jacob would not even use the living speckled or abnormally colored animals to breed more like them. He would separate them into a flock of their own kind, apart from the normally colored animals. Only the spotted and abnormally colored offspring born in the future to the normally colored would be his. Since it seemed to Laban that the birth of such abnormally marked animals was unlikely to occur in any significant volume from the normally colored, he agreed. He believed this to be a small and favorable concession on his part to maintain the skills of Jacob to further enlarge his herds and flocks. Jacob, by this, put himself entirely in God's hands. Only the Lord could determine what animals would be Jacob's. To make sure Jacob didn't cheat on his good deal, Laban separated the abnormally marked from the normal animals in Jacob's care (v. 34–36).

31:1, 2 Of materialistic bent and envious at Jacob's success, Laban's sons grumbled at what they saw as the depleting of their father's assets, thus hurting their own inheritance. If Jacob heard of this, so did Laban, and that knowledge rankled him to the point of surliness toward his son-in-law (cf. 31:20). Profiting from God's blessings through Jacob (30:27, 30) was one thing, but seeing only Jacob blessed was quite another matter and elicited no praise or gratitude to

God from Laban.

31:3 *Return to the land.* When Jacob sought to leave at the end of his contract (30:25), it was not right in God's timing. Now it was, so God directed Jacob's departure and, in confirmation, assured him of His presence. So after another six years, it was time to go (vv. 38–41).

31:4 *called . . . to the field.* In the privacy of the open field, Jacob's plans could be confidentially shared with his wives.

31:5 *your father's . . . my father.* This was a contrast, perhaps not intentional, but nevertheless noticeable, since their father signaled rejection toward him; whereas the God of his father had accepted him.

31:6–9 As Jacob explained it, his unstinting service to their father had been met by Laban with wage changes intended to cripple his son-in-law's enterprise, but God had intervened by blocking the intended hurt (v. 7) and overriding the wage changes with great prosperity (v. 9).

31:10–12 *See notes on 30:37–42.*

31:11 *the Angel of God.* Cf. 21:17. The same as the Angel of the Lord (16:11; 22:11, 15). *See note on Exodus 3:2.*

31:13 *I am the God of Bethel.* The Angel of God (v. 11) clearly identified Himself as the Lord, pointing back as He did so to the earlier critical encounter with God in Jacob's life (28:10–22).

31:14–16 The two wives concurred that, in the context of severely strained family relationships, their inheritance might be in question since the ties that bind no longer held them there. They also agreed that God's intervention had, in effect, refunded what their father had wrongfully withheld and spent.

31:19 *household idols.* Lit. *teraphim* (cf. 2 Kin. 23:24; Ezek. 21:21). These images or figurines of varying sizes, usually of nude goddesses with accentuated sexual features,

either signaled special protection for, inheritance rights for, or guaranteed fertility for the bearer. Or perhaps possession by Rachel would call for Jacob to be recognized as head of the household at Laban's death. *See notes on verses 30, 44.*

31:20 *stole away.* Because of fear at what Laban might do (v. 31), Jacob dispensed with the expected courtesy he had not forgotten before (30:25) and clandestinely slipped away at an appropriate time (v. 19). With all his entourage, this was not a simple exit. Laban's gruffness (vv. 1, 2) exuded enough hostility for Jacob to suspect forceful retaliation and to react by escaping what danger he could not know for sure.

31:21 *the river . . . mountains of Gilead.* These are the Euphrates River and the area south of Galilee to the east of the Jordan

---

Key Word

Inheritance: 31:14; 48:6—meaning "possession" or "property," is linked to the promises of God, particularly those involving the Promised Land (Gen. 13:14–17). When this word is used of the Promised Land, it does not merely refer to what a person wills to his children, although this is a common meaning. Rather God, Creator of the world, granted His people a specific parcel of ground. He fixed its boundaries and promised to deliver it to them. However, the concept of Israel's inheritance transcends a simple association with the land. David and Jeremiah both affirm that God Himself is the real inheritance of His people (Ps. 16:5; Jer. 10:16). God's people can find joy and fulfillment in their relationship with God. Nothing this world can offer as an inheritance compares with God Himself (1 Pet. 1:4).

River, respectively.

31:23 seven days' journey. That it took so long for Laban's band to catch up with a much larger group burdened with possessions and animals indicates a forced march was undertaken by Jacob's people, probably motivated by Jacob's fear.

31:24 Be careful . . . neither good nor bad. God again sovereignly protected, as He had done for Abraham and Isaac (12:17–20; 20:3–7; 26:8–11), to prevent harm coming to His man. In a proverbial expression (cf. Gen. 24:50; 2 Sam. 13:22), Laban is cautioned not to use anything in the full range of options open to him, "from the good to the bad," to alter the existing situation and bring Jacob back.

31:26 my daughters like captives. Laban evidently did not believe that his daughters could have possibly agreed with the departure and, thus, must have left under duress.

31:27–29 Laban's questions protested his right to have arranged a proper send-off for his family and functioned as a rebuke of Jacob's thoughtlessness toward him.

31:30 why . . . steal my gods? Longing to return to Canaan (cf. 30:25) might excuse his leaving without notice, but it could not excuse the theft of Laban's teraphim (v. 19). Laban's thorough search for these idols (vv. 33–35) also marked how important they were to him as a pagan worshiper. *See notes on verses 19, 44.*

31:31 afraid. A reasonable fear is experienced by Jacob, who had come to find a wife and stayed for at least twenty years (v. 38) under the selfish compulsions of Laban.

31:34, 35 One dishonest deed needed further dishonesty and trickery to cover it up.

31:35 the manner of women. Rachel claimed she was having her menstrual period.

31:37 judge between us both! Rachel's theft and dishonest cover-up had precipi-

tated a major conflict between her father and her husband which could only be resolved by judicial inquiry before witnesses.

31:38–42 Jacob registered his complaint that he had unfairly borne the losses normally carried by the owner and had endured much discomfort in fulfilling his responsibility. Jacob also delivered his conclusion that, except for the oversight of God, Laban may very well have fleeced him totally.

31:42 Fear of Isaac. Also see "the Fear of his father Isaac" (v. 53). This was another divine name, signifying Jacob's identification of the God who caused Isaac to reverence Him.

31:43 Laban pled his case, amounting to nothing more than the manifestation of his grasping character, by claiming everything was his.

31:44 let us make a covenant. Although Laban did regard all in Jacob's hands as his—after all Jacob had arrived twenty years before with nothing—nevertheless, the matter was clearly ruled in Jacob's favor, since Laban left with nothing. A treaty was struck in the customary fashion (vv. 45–51) in which they covenanted not to harm one another again (v. 52). With heaps of stones as testaments to the treaty named and in place (vv. 47–49), with the consecration meals having been eaten (vv. 46, 54), and with the appropriate oaths and statements made in the name of their God (vv. 50, 53), the agreement was properly sanctioned and concluded and, thus, they parted company. All contact between Abraham's kin in Canaan and Mesopotamia appears to have ended at this point.

31:47–49 Jegar Sahadutha . . . Galeed . . . Mizpah. The first two words mean in both Aramaic and Hebrew, "heap of witnesses." The third word means "watchtower."

31:53 God of Nahor. Laban's probable syncretistic paralleling of the God of Abraham with that of Nahor and Terah, his

Jacob Returns to Canaan

? Exact location questionable

Mediterranean Sea

Sea of Chinnereth

Jordan River

Shechem · Succoth · Mahanaim?

Jabbok R.

Penuel

Bethel · Ai

Ephrath

Hebron · Dead Sea

Beersheba

0 — 40 Mi.
0 — 40 Km.

—N—

The MacArthur Study Bible, by John MacArthur (Nashville: Word Publishing, 1997) 63. © 1993 by Thomas Nelson, Inc.

brother and father, respectively, elicited Jacob again using "the Fear of Isaac," a reference to the true God (v. 42), for he certainly could not give credence to any of Laban's syncretistic allusions.

6. Angels at Mahanaim and Penuel (32:1–32)

32:1 The angels of God. With one crisis behind him and before him the suspense of having to face Esau, Jacob was first met by an angelic host, who must have reminded him of Bethel, which served also as a timely reminder and encouragement of God's will being done on earth (28:11–15).

32:2 God's camp . . . Mahanaim. Meaning "double camp," i.e., one being God's and one being his own. It was located east of the Jordan River in Gilead near the River Jabbok. Cf. Song 6:13.

32:3 Seir . . . Edom. The territory of Esau south of the Dead Sea.

32:7 greatly afraid and distressed. Jacob had sought reconciliation with Esau (vv. 4, 5), but the report of the returning envoys (v. 6) only confirmed his deepest suspicions that Esau's old threat against him (27:41, 42) had not abated over the years, and his coming with force signaled only disaster (vv. 8, 11). Jacob prepared for the attack by dividing his company of people and animals.

32:9–12 Commendably, notwithstanding the plans to appease his brother (vv. 13–21), Jacob prayed for deliverance, rehearsing God's own commands and covenant promise (v. 12; see 28:13–15), acknowledging his own anxiety, and confessing his own unworthiness before the Lord. This was Jacob's first recorded prayer since his encounter with God at Bethel en route to Laban (28:20–22).

32:13–21 The logistics of Jacob's careful appeasement strategy (550 animals Esau would prize) may highlight his ability to plan, but it highlights even more, given the goal statement at the end (v. 20), his failure to pray and believe that God would change Esau's heart.

32:22–32 This unique, nightlong wrestling match at Peniel ends with the ninety-seven year old Jacob having a change of name (v. 28) and the place having a new name assigned to it (v. 30) in order to memorialize it for Jacob and later generations. The limp with which he emerged from the match (vv. 25, 31) also served to memorialize this event.

32:22 Jabbok. A stream, sixty to sixty-five miles long, east of the Jordan River which flows into that river midway between the Sea of Galilee and the Dead Sea (c. forty-five miles south of the Sea of Galilee).

32:24 a Man wrestled. The site name, Peniel, or "face of God," given by Jacob (v. 30) and the commentary given by Hosea (Hos. 12:4) identifies this Man with whom Jacob wrestled as the Angel of the Lord who is also identified as God, a preincarnate appearance of the Lord Jesus Christ. *See note on Exodus 3:2.*

32:28 no longer . . . Jacob, but Israel. Jacob's personal name changed from one meaning "heel-catcher" or "deceiver" to one meaning "God's fighter" or "he struggles with God" (cf. 35:10). **with God and with men.** An amazing evaluation of what Jacob had accomplished, i.e., emerging victorious from the struggle. In the record of his life, "struggle" did indeed dominate: (1) with his brother Esau (chs. 25–27); (2) with his father (ch. 27); (3) with his father-in-law (chs. 29–31); (4) with his wives (ch. 30); and (5) with God at Peniel (v. 28).

32:30 Peniel. *See note on verse 24.*

32:32 not eat the muscle that shrank. This might refer to the sciatic muscle/tendon. The observation that up to Moses' time ("to this day") the nation of Israel did not eat this part of a hindquarter intrigues because it bears no mention elsewhere in the OT, nor is it enshrined in the Mosaic Law. It does find mention in the Jewish Talmud as a sacred law.

E. Esau's Reunion and Reconciliation with Jacob (33:1–17)

33:1, 2 Esau was coming. Jacob hastily divided his family into three groups (cf. 31:7) and went ahead of them to meet his brother. The division and relative location of his family in relationship to the perceived danger gives tremendous insight into whom Jacob favored.

33:3, 4 Fearfully and deferentially, Jacob approached his brother as an inferior would a highly honored patron; while gladly and eagerly, Esau ran to greet his brother without restraint of emotion. "They wept" because, after twenty-one years of troubling separation, old memories were wiped away and

murderous threats belonged to the distant past; hearts had been changed, brothers reconciled. See verse 10.

33:5–11 Family introductions (vv. 5–7) and an explanation of the gift of 550 animals (vv. 8–10; cf. 32:13–21) properly acknowledged the gracious provision of the Lord upon Jacob's life (vv. 5, 11). The battle for generosity was won by Jacob when Esau, who initially refused to take anything from his brother, finally agreed to do so (v. 11).

33:10 your face . . . the face of God. Jacob acknowledged how God had so obviously changed Esau, as indicated by his facial expression which was not one of sullen hate but of brotherly love, divinely wrought and restored.

33:15 Let me find favor. Jacob did not want to have Esau's people loaned to him for fear something might happen to again fracture their relationship.

33:16, 17 to Seir . . . to Succoth. With Esau's planned escort courteously dismissed, they parted company. Jacob's expressed intention to meet again in Seir (*see note on 32:3*), for whatever reason, did not materialize. Instead, Jacob halted his journey first at Succoth, then at Shechem (v. 18). Succoth is east of the Jordan River, twenty miles east of Shechem, which is sixty-five miles north of Jerusalem, located between Mt. Ebal and Mt. Gerizim.

F. Events and Deaths from Shechem to Mamre (33:18–35:29)

33:18 came safely. C. 1908 B.C. A reference to the fulfillment of Jacob's vow made at Bethel when, upon departure from Canaan, he looked to God for a safe return. Upon arrival in Canaan, he would tithe his possessions (28:20–22). Presumably, Jacob fulfilled his pledge at Shechem or, later, at Bethel (35:1).

33:19 bought the parcel of land. This

purchase became only the second piece of real estate legally belonging to Abraham's line in the Promised Land (cf. 23:17, 18; 25:9, 10). However, the land was not Abraham's and his descendants simply because they bought it but, rather, because God owned it all (Lev. 25:23) and gave it to them for their exclusive domain (*see notes on 12:1–3*).

33:20 *erected an altar.* In the place where Abraham had first built an altar (12:6, 7), Jacob similarly marked the spot with a new name, incorporating a new name (32:28), "God, the God of Israel," declaring that he worshiped the "Mighty One." "Israel" perhaps foreshadowed its use for the nation with which it rapidly became associated, even when it consisted of not much more than Jacob's extended household (34:7).

34:1–31 The tawdry details of the abuse of Dinah and the revenge of Levi and Simeon are recounted in full, perhaps in order to highlight for the readers about to enter Canaan how easily Abraham's descendants might intermingle and marry with Canaanites, contrary to patriarchal desires (cf. 24:3; 27:46; 28:1) and God's will (Ex. 34:6; Deut. 7:3; Josh. 23:12, 13; Neh. 13:26, 27).

34:1 *to see the daughters.* Little did Dinah (see 30:20, 21) realize that her jaunt to the nearby city to view how other women lived would bring forth such horrific results.

34:2 *saw . . . took . . . violated.* Scripture classifies Shechem's action as forcible rape, no matter how sincerely he might have expressed his love for her afterwards (v. 3) and desire for marriage (vv. 11, 12). Other expressions in the account underscore the clearly unacceptable nature of this crime, e.g., "defiled" (vv. 5, 13), "grieved and very angry" (v. 7), "a disgraceful thing . . . which ought not to be done" (v. 7), and "treat our sister like a harlot" (v. 31).

34:5 *Jacob held his peace.* In the absence of further data, Jacob's reticence to respond should not be criticized. Wisdom dictated that he wait and counsel with his sons; but their reaction, grief, anger, and vengeance hijacked the talks between Jacob and Hamor (v. 6) and led, finally, to Jacob's stern rebuke (v. 30).

34:6–10 The prince of Shechem painted a picture of harmonious integration (v. 16, "become one people"). However, Shechemite self-interest and enrichment actually prevailed (v. 23).

34:7 *in Israel.* Already Jacob's household is being called by the name God had given him as father of the coming nation (32:28).

34:13–17 Feigning interest in the proposals put forward and misusing, if not abusing, the circumcision sign of the Abrahamic covenant (*see notes on 17:11–14*), Jacob's sons conned both father and son into convincing all the men to submit to circumcision because the outcome would be to their favor with marriages (v. 9) and social, economic integration (v. 10).

34:19 *He was more honorable.* This means that the men agreed to such an excruciating surgery (vv. 24, 25) because they had so much respect for him and because they anticipated mercenary benefit (v. 23).

34:20 *gate of their city.* The normal place for public gatherings.

34:25–29 A massacre of all males and the wholesale plunder of the city went way beyond the reasonable, wise, and justly deserved punishment of one man; this was a considerably more excessive vengeance than the Mosaic Law would later legislate (cf. Deut. 22:28, 29).

34:27 *The sons of Jacob.* Simeon and Levi set in motion the barbarity of that day and attention validly falls upon them in the narrative (vv. 25, 30; cf. 49:5–7), but their brothers joined in the looting, thereby approving murder and mayhem as justifiable retribution for the destroyed honor of their sister (v. 31).

34:30 *You have troubled me.* Vengeance exacted meant retaliation expected. Total loss of respect ("making me obnoxious") and of peaceful relations (v. 21) put both him and them in harm's way with survival being highly unlikely. This threat tested God's promise of safety, giving Jacob cause for great concern (28:15; 32:9, 12). *Perizzites. See note on 13:7.*

35:1 *Bethel.* This was the place where God confirmed the Abrahamic covenant to Jacob (28:13–15).

35:2–4 *Put away the foreign gods.* Moving to Bethel necessitated spiritual preparation beyond the level of an exercise in logistics. Possession of idolatrous symbols such as figurines, amulets, or cultic charms (v. 4, "earrings") were no longer tolerable, including Rachel's troubling teraphim (31:19). Idols buried out of sight, plus bathing and changing to clean clothes, all served to portray both cleansing from defilement by idolatry and consecration of the heart to the Lord. It had been eight or ten years since his return to Canaan and, appropriately, time enough to clean up all traces of idolatry.

35:4 *terebinth tree . . . Shechem.* Possibly this was the same tree as in Abraham's day (12:6).

35:5 *the terror of God.* A supernaturally induced fear of Israel rendered the surrounding city-states unwilling and powerless to intervene and made Jacob's fear of their retaliation rather inconsequential (34:30).

35:7 *built an altar there.* Through this act of worship, fulfillment of his vow (28:20–22), and renaming the site, Jacob reconfirmed his allegiance to God, who also affirmed His commitment to Jacob by reappearing to him, repeating the change of name (v. 10; cf. 32:28), and rehearsing the Abrahamic promises (vv. 11, 12). In response, Jacob also repeated the rite he had performed when he first met God at Bethel (v. 14) and reaffirmed its name (v. 15).

35:11 *kings shall come from your body.* God's words, here included for the first time since His promises at Abraham's circumcision (17:6, 16), served as a reminder of future royalty.

35:13 *went up.* The presence of God was there in some visible form.

35:14 A common way to make a covenant (*see note on 28:18–21*).

35:16 *Ephrath.* A more ancient name for Bethlehem (v. 19; 48:7; cf. 5:2).

35:18 *Ben-Oni . . . Benjamin.* The dying mother appropriately named her newly born son "Son of my sorrow," but the grieving father named him "Son of my right hand," thus assigning him a place of honor in the home. Rachel's prayer at the birth of her firstborn was answered (30:24).

35:20 The memorial to Rachel could still be seen in Moses' day, about one mile north of Bethlehem.

35:21 *tower of Eder.* This was likely a watchtower for shepherds, near Bethlehem.

35:22 *the sons of Jacob.* The birth of Benjamin in Canaan (v. 18) furnished reason to simply review the sons born outside of Canaan, with only one sad note preceding it, i.e., the sin of Reuben, which tainted the qualifier "Jacob's firstborn" in the listing (see 49:3, 4; Deut. 22:30; 1 Chr. 5:1, 2).

35:27 *Mamre . . . Hebron. See note on 13:18.*

35:29 *his sons Esau and Jacob.* C. 1885 B.C. Isaac's funeral brought his two sons back together, as Abraham's funeral had done for Isaac and Ishmael (25:9). Jacob, back in the land before his father's death, fulfilled yet another part of his Bethel vow (28:20, "come back to my father's house in peace").

X. The Generations of Esau (36:1–37:1)

Altars in the Old Testament

1. Built by Noah	Gen. 8:20
2. Built by Abra- ham in Shechem, in Hebron, and in Moriah	Gen. 12:7, 8; 13:18; 22:2, 9
3. Built by Isaac	Gen. 26:25
4. Built by Jacob at Shechem and at Bethel	Gen. 33:20; 35:1–7
5. Built by Moses	Ex. 17:15
6. Built by Balak	Num. 23:1, 4, 14
7. Built by Joshua	Josh. 8:30
8. Built by the tribes living east of the Jordan	Josh. 22:10
9. Built by Gideon	Judg. 6:24
10. Built by Manoah	Judg. 13:20
11. Built by Israel	Judg. 21:4
12. Built by Samuel	1 Sam. 7:15, 17
13. Built by Saul	1 Sam. 14:35
14. Built by David	2 Sam. 24:25
15. Built by Jer- oboam	1 Kin. 12:32, 33
16. Built by Ahab	1 Kin. 16:32
17. Built by Elijah	1 Kin. 18:31, 32

36:1–19 The taking up of "the history of Jacob" (37:2), the next patriarch, is preceded by a fairly detailed genealogy of Esau, to which is appended both the genealogy of Seir the Horite, whose descendants were the contemporary inhabitants of Edom and a listing of Edomite kings and chiefs. Jacob's and Esau's posterities, as history would go on to show, would not be in isolation from each other as originally intended (vv. 6–8). They were to become bitter enemies engaged with each other in war.

36:1 *Edom.* Cf. verse 8; *see note on 25:30; see Introduction to Obadiah.*

36:7 *too great for them to dwell together.* Crowded grazing and living conditions finally clinched the decision by Esau to move permanently to Edom, where he had already established a home (cf. 32:3; 33:14, 16). Since it was Abraham's descendants through Isaac and Jacob who would possess the land, it was fitting for God to work out the circumstances, providentially keeping Jacob's lineage in the land and moving Esau's lineage out. It is not revealed if Esau had understood and came to accept the promises of God to Jacob, although his descendants surely sought to deny Israel any right to their land or their life.

36:8 *Mount Seir.* This was divinely assigned as Esau's place (Deut. 2:5; Josh. 24:4).

36:10–14 Cf. 1 Chronicles 1:35–37.

36:15 *the chiefs.* This term, "ruler of a thousand," apart from one exception (Zech. 12:5, 6), is used exclusively for the tribal princes or clan leaders, the political/military leaders in Edom. It may suggest a loosely formed tribal confederacy.

36:20–28 Cf. 1 Chronicles 1:38–42.

36:31–39 *kings . . . before any king . . . of Israel.* Sandwiched in the genealogical details of Edom is a statement prophetically pointing to kingship in Israel (17:6, 16; 35:11; 49:10; Num. 24:7, 17, 18; Deut. 17:14–20). The kings' list does not introduce a dynasty, each ruler not being the son of his predecessor. *Kings* more likely suggests rule over a more settled people than tribal groups.

36:43 *father of the Edomites.* The closing title of the genealogy calls attention to the Lord's words to Rebekah at the birth of her sons, "two nations are in your womb" (25:23); here was the nation from the older son.

37:1 *father was a stranger.* This by-line into the story of Jacob's son, Joseph, informs the reader that Jacob's father, Isaac, hence his sons as well, though in the land, had not yet entered into possession of their inheritance. They were still alien residents. *land of Canaan.* Actually Jacob and his family were in Hebron (v. 14). *See note on 13:18.*

XI. THE GENERATIONS OF JACOB (37:2–50:26)

A. Joseph's Dreams (37:2–11)

37:2 *Joseph, being seventeen years old.* Eleven years had passed since he had entered the land of Canaan with his family (cf. 30:22–24), since Joseph was born six years before departing from Haran. *a bad report.* Whether Joseph brought this at his own initiative or reported back at the father's demand on four of his brothers (e.g., v. 14) is not elaborated upon, nor specifically cited as the cause of the brothers' intense dislike of Joseph (cf. vv. 4, 5, 8, 11, 18, 19).

37:3, 4 Overt favoritism of Joseph and tacit appointment of him as the primary son by the father (*see note on v. 3*) conspired to estrange him from his brothers. They hated and envied him (vv. 4, 5, 11) and could not interact with him without conflict and hostility. Joseph must have noticed the situation.

37:3 *tunic of many colors.* The Septuagint (LXX) favored this translation of the Hebrew phrase used by Moses, although some prefer "a long-sleeved robe" or "an ornamented tunic." It marked the owner as the one whom the father intended to be the future leader of the household, an honor normally given to the firstborn son.

37:5–10 The content of the dreams which Joseph recounted exacerbated fraternal hostility, with the second one also incurring paternal rebuke. The dream symbolism needed no special interpretation to catch its significant elevation of the favored son to ruling status over his brothers (vv. 8–10).

37:11 *kept the matter in mind.* Unlike the brothers, who immediately rejected any meaning to Joseph's words, yet, still allowed the dream to sorely irritate them into greater resentment of their brother (v. 19), the father, notwithstanding his public admonishment of Joseph, continued to ponder the meaning of the dreams.

B. Family Tragedy (37:12–38:30)

37:12–17 The assignment to Shechem brought Joseph providentially to Dothan, a site more convenient for contact with merchants using the main trade route on their way to Egypt.

37:12, 14 *Shechem . . . Hebron.* Shechem (*see note on 12:6*) was located c. fifty miles north of Hebron (*see note on 13:18*).

37:17 *Dothan.* Almost fifteen miles north of Shechem.

37:18–27 The brothers' plans for murder and cover-up, the fruit of hate and envy, were forestalled by two brothers: first by Reuben, who intended to effect a complete rescue (vv. 21, 22), and then by Judah who, prompted by a passing merchants' caravan, proposed a profitable alternative to fratricide (vv. 25–27).

37:25 *Ishmaelites.* A people-group also known as Midianites (cf. vv. 28, 36; 39:1). The descendants of Ishmael and of Abraham through Keturah and Midian (25:1, 2) were sufficiently intermarried or were such inveterate travelers and traders that they were viewed as synonymous groups. These were coming west from Gilead. *Gilead. See note on 31:21.*

37:27 This criminal behavior would later be prohibited by the Mosaic legislation (Ex. 21:16; Deut. 24:7)

37:28 *twenty shekels of silver.* This was the average price of a slave at that time in the second millennium B.C. Although most slaves were part of the booty of military conquest, private and commercial slave-trading

Joseph's Journey to Egypt

Mediterranean Sea

Sea of Chinnereth

Dothan
Shechem
GILEAD
Bethel
Gaza
Hebron
Dead Sea
NEGEV

To Egypt

CANAAN

—N—

0   100 Mi.
0   100 Km.

The MacArthur Study Bible, by John MacArthur (Nashville: Word Publishing, 1997) 70. © 1993 by Thomas Nelson, Inc.

was also common. Joseph was sold into slavery c. 1897 B.C.

37:29 Reuben . . . tore his clothes. Although he was absent at the time of the sale, he would be held responsible for the treachery, and so joined in the cover-up (vv. 30–35). His grief manifested how much he had actually wanted to rescue Joseph (see 42:22).

37:31–35 The deceiver of Isaac (27:18–29) was deceived by his own sons' lie. Sin's punishment is often long delayed.

37:35 grave. This is the first OT use of this term for the abode of the dead (in 35:20, it is used to refer to an earthly burial plot). It is a general Hebrew term meaning the place of the dead (*Sheol*—used sixty-five times in the OT), referring either to the body in its decaying form or to the soul in its conscious afterlife.

37:36 Potiphar. He was a prominent court official and high-ranking officer in Egypt, perhaps captain of the royal bodyguard (cf. 40:3, 4). His name, a most unusual grammatical form for that period, either meant "the one whom the god Ra has given" or "the one who is placed on earth by Ra," making it a descriptive epithet more than a personal name. *See note on 40:3, 4.*

38:1–30 The Judah Interlude, as it is sometimes known, is bracketed by references to the sale of Joseph to Potiphar (37:36; 39:1). Such a parenthesis in the Joseph story demands some reason why a chapter laced with wickedness, immorality, and subterfuge should of necessity be placed in this spot. The answer is that the events recorded are chronologically in the right place, being contemporary with the time of Joseph's slavery in Egypt (v. 1, "at that time"). The account is also genealogically in the right place, i.e., with Joseph gone (seemingly for good), with Reuben, Simeon, and Levi out of favor (for incest and for treachery), Judah would most likely accede to firstborn status. It provides a contrast because it also demonstrates the immoral character of Judah, as compared with the virtue of Joseph. Canaanite syncretistic religion and inclusivism threatened to absorb the fourth and later generations of Abraham's heirs, but Egyptian exile and racial exclusivism produced not loss of their ethnic identity, but the preservation of it.

38:1 Adullamite. Adullam was a town about one mile northwest of Hebron.

38:2–5 Judah's separation from his brethren was marked by more than the geographical; it involved integration. His Canaanite wife had three sons for his family line.

38:6–10 Two sons were executed by the Lord, one for unspecified wickedness and one for deliberate and rebellious rejection of the duty to marry a relative's widow, called a levirate marriage. This was a rather dubious distinction for the line of Judah to gain. For details on levirate marriage according to later Mosaic Law, *see note on Deuteronomy 25:5–10;* see Ruth: Interpretive Challenges.

38:11 Remain a widow . . . till my son. Taking her father-in-law at his word and residing at her father's household as a widow would do, Tamar vainly waited for Judah's third son to protect the inheritance rights of her deceased husband (v. 14) and finally resorted to subterfuge to obtain her rights (vv. 13–16). In so doing, she may have been influenced by Hittite inheritance practices which called the father-in-law into levirate marriage in the absence of sons to do so.

38:12 Timnah. The specific location in the hill country of Judah is unknown. Cf. Joshua 15:10, 57; Judges 14:1.

38:13 shear his sheep. Such an event was frequently associated in the ancient world with festivity and licentious behavior characteristic of pagan fertility-cult practices.

38:14, 15 Feeling that no one was going to give her a child, Tamar resorted to disguising herself as a prostitute, obviously knowing she could trap Judah, which says little for his moral stature in her eyes. Judah's Canaanite friend, Hirah (vv. 1, 20), called her a shrine-prostitute (v. 21), which made Judah's actions no less excusable just because cultic prostitution was an accepted part of Canaanite culture. He solicited the iniquity by making the proposal to her (v. 16), and she played the role of a prostitute, negotiating the price (v. 17).

38:18 signet and cord, and your staff. A prominent man in the ancient Near East endorsed contracts with the cylinder seal he wore on a cord around his neck. Her request for the walking stick suggests it also had sufficient identifying marks on it (cf. v. 25, "please determine whose these are"). The custom of using three pieces of identifica-

tion is attested to in Ugaritic (Canaanite) literature.

38:20–23 It was not good for one's reputation to keep asking for the whereabouts of a prostitute.

38:24 let her be burned! Double standards prevailed in that Judah, no less guilty than Tamar, commanded her execution for immorality. Later, Mosaic legislation would prescribe this form of the death penalty for a priest's daughter who prostituted herself or for those guilty of certain forms of incest (Lev. 20:14; 21:9).

38:26 more righteous than I. This was not an accolade for her moral character and faith, but a commendation by Judah for her attention to inheritance rights of her family line and his shameful neglect thereof. Her death sentence was rescinded.

38:29 Perez. This first of the twins, born of prostitution and incest to Tamar, nevertheless came into the messianic line, which went through Boaz and Ruth to King David (Ruth 4:18–22; Matt. 1:3). His name means "breach" or "pushing through."

C. Vice Regency over Egypt (39:1–41:57)

39:1 Potiphar. See note on 37:36. **Ishmaelites.** See note on 37:25.

39:2 The LORD was with Joseph. Any and all ideas that Joseph, twice a victim of injustice, had been abandoned by the Lord are summarily banished by the employment of phrases highlighting God's oversight of his circumstances, e.g., "with him" (vv. 3, 21), "made all he did prosper" (vv. 3, 23), "found/gave him favor" (vv. 4, 21), "blessed/ blessing" (v. 5), and "showed him mercy" (v. 21). Neither being unjustly sold into slavery and forcibly removed from the land (37:28), nor being unjustly accused of sexual harassment and imprisoned (vv. 13–18) were events signaling even a temporary loss of divine superintendence of Joseph's life and God's purpose for His people, Israel.

39:2–4 *successful . . . overseer of his house.* This involved authority as the steward of the whole estate (v. 5, "house and field" and v. 9, "no one greater"), one of the criteria for which was trust. No doubt, Joseph was conversant in the Egyptian language (*see note on 29:9*).

39:5 *blessing of the LORD.* Joseph was experiencing fulfillment of the Abrahamic covenant, even at that time before Israel was in the land (see 12:1–3).

39:6 *except for the bread which he ate.* Since Joseph proved trustworthy enough to need no oversight, his master concerned himself only with his own meals or his very own personal affairs. Joseph himself remarked that Potiphar had delegated to him so much that he no longer knew the full extent of his own business affairs (v. 8); in fact, he knew only what was set before him (v. 6).

39:9 *this great wickedness.* Joseph explained, when first tempted, that adultery would be a gross violation of his ethical convictions which demanded (1) the utmost respect for his master and (2) a life of holiness before his God. Far more was involved than compliance with the letter of an ancient Near Eastern law code, many of which did forbid adultery, but rather obedience to the moral standards belonging to one who walked with God, and that long before Mosaic law-code prescriptions applied (cf. Ps. 51:4).

39:10–18 Her incessant efforts to seduce Joseph failed in the face of his strong convictions not to yield nor be compromised. At flashpoint, Joseph fled! Based on false accusations, Joseph was deemed guilty and imprisoned. Cf. 2 Timothy 2:22 for a NT picture of Joseph's attitude.

39:12 *his garment.* See 37:31–35 for the other time one of Joseph's cloaks was used in a conspiracy against him.

39:17 *Hebrew servant.* This term was used by Potiphar's wife as a pejorative, intended to heap scorn upon someone considered definitely unworthy of any respect. Its use may also suggest some latent attitudes toward dwellers in Canaan, which could be aggravated to her advantage. Potiphar's wife also neatly shifted the blame onto her husband for having hired the Hebrew in the first place (vv. 16–18) and stated this also before the servants (v. 14).

39:19, 20 The death penalty for adultery may not have applied to a charge of attempted adultery, attempted seduction or rape (cf. vv. 14, 18), so Potiphar consigned Joseph to the prison reserved for royal servants, from where, in the providence of God, he would be summoned into Pharaoh's presence and begin the next stage of his life (cf. chs. 40; 41). *See note on 40:3, 4.*

39:21 *showed him mercy.* God did not permit this initial painful imprisonment to continue (cf. Ps. 105:18, 19).

39:22, 23 Once again Joseph, though in circumstances considerably less comfortable than Potiphar's home, rose to a position of trust and authority and proved to be trustworthy enough not to need any oversight.

40:1 *the king of Egypt.* He should be identified as Senusert II, c. 1894–1878 B.C.

40:2 *the chief butler and the chief baker.* Both these occupations and ranks in Pharaoh's court are attested in existing ancient Egyptian documents. The butler was the king's cupbearer, who gave him his drinks. The baker cooked his bread. Both had to be trustworthy and beyond the influence of the monarch's enemies.

40:3, 4 *captain of the guard.* See note on 37:36. If this was Potiphar, the captain of the guard, then Joseph's former master directed him to attend to the two royal servants remanded into his custody until sentence was past. This prison was also called "the house of the captain of the guard" (v. 3), "his lord's house" (v. 7), and "dungeon" (40:15; 41:14), unless Joseph had been moved to another penal facility.

40:5 *dream.* Oneiromancy, the science or practice of interpreting dreams, flourished in ancient Egypt because dreams were thought to determine the future. Both Egypt and Babylon (Dan. 2:2) developed a professional class of dream interpreters. Deut-eronomy 13:1–5 shows that such dream interpreters were part of ancient false religion and were to be avoided by God's people. By some 500 years later, a detailed manual of dream interpretation had been compiled. Unlike Joseph, neither butler nor baker understood the significance of their dreams (cf. 37:5–11).

40:8 *Do not interpretations belong to God?* Joseph was careful to give credit to his Lord (cf. 41:16). Daniel, the only other Hebrew whom God allowed to accurately interpret revelatory dreams, was just as careful to do so (Dan. 2:28). Significantly, God chose both men to play an important role for Israel while serving pagan monarchs and stepping forward at the critical moment to interpret their dreams and reveal their futures.

40:9–13 *the chief butler.* Consistent with his duty as the cupbearer to the king, he dreamed of a drink prepared for Pharaoh. It was a sign that he would be released and returned to his position (v. 13).

40:14, 15 *remember me.* This was a poignant appeal to the butler, whose future was secure, to speak a word for Joseph's freedom, because he knew butlers had the ear of kings. The butler quickly forgot Joseph (v. 23), until his memory was prompted just at the right moment two years later (41:1, 9).

40:15 *the land of the Hebrews.* Giving this designation to the land of Canaan indicates that Joseph understood the land promise of the Abrahamic covenant.

40:16 *the interpretation was good.* The chief baker, noting some similarity in the dreams, was encouraged to request interpretation of his dream. Joseph's words employ a subtle play on words: the butler's head would be "lifted up" (v. 13) but the baker's would be "lifted off" (v. 18).

40:20 *Pharaoh's birthday.* The Rosetta Stone (discovered in A.D. 1799, a trilingual artifact from Egyptian antiquity, c. 196 B.C., whose Greek inscription enabled linguists to understand the language of hieroglyphics) records a custom of releasing Pharaoh's prisoners; but, at this party held for his servants, Pharaoh rendered two very different kinds of judgment (vv. 21, 22).

41:1 *the river.* Probably the Nile River, which dominated Egyptian life.

41:8 *no one who could interpret.* The combined expertise of a full council of Pharaoh's advisers and dream experts, all of whom had been summoned into his presence, failed to provide an interpretation of the two disturbing dreams. Without knowing it, they had just set the stage for Joseph's entrance on the scene of Egyptian history. Compare a similar situation almost 1,200 years later in Babylon with Daniel (Dan. 2:1–45).

41:9 *Then the chief butler spoke.* With his memory suitably prompted, the butler apologized for his neglect ("I remember my faults"), and informed Pharaoh of the Hebrew prisoner and his accurate interpretation of dreams two years earlier (vv. 10–13).

41:14 *Then Pharaoh sent and called Joseph.* The urgent summons had Joseph in front of Pharaoh with minimum delay, in prized, clean-shaven Egyptian style for a proper appearance.

41:16 *It is not in me; God will give.* Deprecating any innate ability, Joseph advised at the very outset that the answer Pharaoh desired could only come from God.

41:25 God has shown. Joseph's interpretation kept the focus fixed on what God had determined for Egypt (vv. 28, 32).

41:33–36 After interpreting the dream, Joseph told Pharaoh how to survive the next fourteen years. Incongruously, Joseph, a slave and a prisoner, appended to the interpretation a long-term strategy for establishing reserves to meet the future need, and included advice on the quality of the man to head up the project. Famines had ravaged Egypt before, but this time divine warning permitted serious and sustained advance planning.

41:37–41 To Pharaoh and his royal retinue, no other candidate but Joseph qualified for the task of working out this good plan, because they recognized that he spoke God-given revelation and insight (v. 39). Joseph's focus on his Lord had quickly taken him from prison to the palace (v. 41).

41:38 Spirit of God. The Egyptians did not understand about the third person of the triune Godhead. They merely meant that God had assisted Joseph, thus "spirit" would be more appropriate than "Spirit."

41:41 set you over all the land of Egypt. The country-wide jurisdiction accorded to Joseph receives frequent mention in the narrative (vv. 43, 44, 46, 55; 42:6; 45:8).

41:42 signet ring . . . garments . . . gold chain. These are emblems of office. A reward of clothing and jewelry suitable to the new rank accompanied Pharaoh's appointment of Joseph as vizier, or prime minister, the second-in-command (v. 40; 45:8, 26). Joseph wore the royal seal on his finger, authorizing him to transact the affairs of state on behalf of Pharaoh himself.

41:43–45 Other awards appropriate to promotion were also bestowed on Joseph, namely official and recognizable transportation (v. 43), an Egyptian name (v. 45), and an Egyptian wife (v. 45). Further, the populace

was commanded to show deference for their vizier (v. 43, "bow the knee"). All these dreams had been revealed by God, in a rare display of manifesting truth through pagans, so that Joseph would be established in Egypt as a leader and, thus elevated, could be used for the preservation of God's people when the famine came to Canaan. Thus, God cared for His people and fulfilled His promises (*see note on 45:1–8*).

41:43 the second chariot. This signified to all that Joseph was second-in-command.

41:45 Zaphnath-Paaneah. This name probably means "The Nourisher of the Two Lands, the Living One." It could also mean "God speaks and He lives." However, certainty of that meaning still eludes scholars. Foreigners are known to have been assigned an Egyptian name.

41:46 thirty years old. C. 1884 B.C. Only thirteen years had elapsed since his involuntary departure from "the land of the Hebrews" (cf. 40:15). Joseph had been seventeen when the narrative commenced (37:2).

41:50 On. One of the four great Egyptian cities, also called Heliopolis, which was known as the chief city of the sun god, Ra. It was located c. nineteen miles north of ancient Memphis.

41:51, 52 Manasseh . . . Ephraim. The names meaning "forgetful" and "fruitful," assigned to his sons together with their explanations, depict the centrality of God in Joseph's worldview. Years of suffering, pagan presence, and separation from his own family had not harmed his faith.

41:54–57 The use of hyperbole with *all* (vv. 54, 56, 57) emphatically indicates the widespread ravaging impact of famine far beyond Egypt's borders. She had become indeed the "breadbasket" of the ancient world.

41:55, 56 Go to Joseph. After seven years, Joseph's authority remained intact, and Pharaoh still fully trusted his vizier. He dispensed the food supplies by sale to Egyptians and others (v. 47).

D. Reunion with Family (42:1–45:28)

42:1–3 Jacob's sons were traumatized in the famine, and Jacob was reluctant to let his family return to Egypt, not knowing what would happen to them (v. 4). But, with no other choice left, he dispatched them to buy grain in Egypt (v. 2).

42:4 Benjamin. See 35:16–19. He was the youngest of all, the second son of Rachel, Jacob's beloved, and the favorite of his father since he thought Joseph was dead.

42:6 bowed down. Without their appreciating it at the time, Joseph's dream became reality (37:5–8). Recognition of Joseph was unlikely because: (1) over fifteen years had elapsed and the teenager sold into slavery had become a mature adult; (2) he had become Egyptian in appearance and dress; (3) he treated them without a hint of familiarity (vv. 7, 8); and (4) they thought he was dead (v. 13).

42:9–22 The brothers' final evaluation after being imprisoned for three days, after protesting the charge of espionage, and after hearing the royal criterion for establishing their innocence (vv. 15, 20), revealed their guilty conscience and their understanding that vengeance for their wrongdoing to Joseph had probably arrived (vv. 21, 22). Calling themselves "honest men" (v. 10) was hardly an accurate assessment.

42:9 remembered the dreams. Joseph remembered his boyhood dreams about his brothers bowing down to him (37:9) as they were coming true.

42:15 By the life of Pharaoh. Speaking an oath in the name of the king would most likely have masked Joseph's identity from the brothers. Perhaps it also prevented them from grasping the significance of his declaration, "I fear God" (v. 18). **unless your**

Key Word

Spirit: 6:3; 7:22; 41:38—related to a verb meaning "to breathe" or "to blow." It can signify breath (Job 9:18; 19:17), wind (Gen. 8:1; Ex. 10:13), air (Eccl. 1:14; Is. 26:18), the breath of life (whether animal or human, see Gen. 6:17; 7:15), disposition or mood (Gen. 41:8; Ezek. 21:7), an evil or distressing spirit (1 Sam. 16:14–16), or the Spirit of God (Gen. 1:2; Ps. 51:11). The spirit of life is the gift of God to all creatures (Job 12:10; 33:4; Eccl. 12:7). The endowment of God's Holy Spirit is a special gift to believers, which brings spiritual life (Pss. 51:10, 11; 143:10), power (Judg. 6:34), wisdom and understanding (Is. 11:2), and divine revelation that leads to a better understanding of God's Word and His perfect ways (Is. 61:1, 2; Joel 2:28).

---

youngest brother comes. Joseph wanted to find out if they had done the same or a similar thing to Benjamin as to himself.

42:19, 20 If you are honest men. Joseph took their assessment of themselves at face value when exhorting them to respond to his proposals, but still asked for a hostage.

42:21 anguish of his soul. The brothers had steeled their hearts when selling Joseph to the Midianites (37:28, 29), but they could not forget the fervent pleading and terror-filled voice of the teenager dragged away as a slave from home. Reuben reminded them of his warning at that time and the consequence.

42:22 blood . . . required of us. This declaration referred to the death penalty (9:5).

42:24 took Simeon. He did not keep Reuben, the firstborn, hostage but Simeon, the oldest brother, who willingly participated in the crime against Joseph (37:21–31).

42:28 God has done. Their guilty conscience and fear of vengeance from God surfaced again in this response to the money with which they had purchased the grain being returned and found in the one sack which had been opened. Later, upon discovering that all their money had been returned, their fear increased even further (v. 35).

42:36 Jacob could not handle the prospect of losing another son, and he did not trust the brothers who had already divested him of two sons by what he may have thought were their intrigues. *All . . . against me.* The whole situation overwhelmed Jacob, who complained against his sons (cf. 43:6) and would not release Benjamin (v. 38).

42:37 The always salutary Reuben generously made his father an offer easy to refuse—killing his grandsons.

43:3 *solemnly warned us.* The seriousness of Joseph's words portended failure for another mission to buy food, unless the criterion he had set down was strictly met.

43:9 *I myself will be surety for him.* Reuben's offer to guarantee the safety of Benjamin had been rejected (42:37, 38), but Judah's was accepted (v. 11) because of the stress of the famine and the potential death of all (v. 8) if they waited much longer (v. 10).

43:11 *a little.* Likely, this was a significant present because they had little left. But there was no future at all past the little, if they did not get grain in Egypt.

43:14 Jacob's acquiescence to let Benjamin go (v. 13) ended with prayer for the brothers' and Benjamin's safety and with a cry of being a helpless victim of circumstances. Pessimism had apparently set into his heart and deepened after the loss of Joseph.

43:23 *Your God . . . has given.* This is an indication of Joseph's steward either having come to faith in God or having become very

familiar with how Joseph talked of his God and life. So concerned were the brothers to protest their ignorance of the means of the money being returned and to express their desire to settle this debt (vv. 20–22) that they missed the steward's clear reference to the God of Israel ("the God of your father") and his oversight of events in which he had played a part ("I had your money").

43:26 *bowed down.* Again, Joseph's boyhood dream (37:5–8) had become reality (cf. 42:6).

43:29 *God be gracious.* Joseph easily used the name of God in his conversation, but the brothers did not hear the name of their own covenant God being spoken by one who looked just like an Egyptian (cf. 42:18).

43:30 *to weep.* Joseph was moved to tears on several occasions (42:24; 45:2, 14, 15; 46:29).

43:32 *not eat food with the Hebrews.* Exclusivism kept the Egyptians sensitive to the social stigma attached to sharing a meal table with foreigners (cf. 46:34). Discrimination prevailed at another level, too: Joseph ate alone, his rank putting him ahead of others and giving him his own table and setting.

43:33 *the firstborn . . . the youngest.* To be seated at the table in birth order in the house of an Egyptian official was startling—how did he know this of them? Enough clues had been given in Joseph's previous questions about the family and his use of God's name for them to wonder about him and his personal knowledge of them. Obviously, they simply did not believe Joseph was alive (44:20) and certainly not as a personage of such immense influence and authority. They had probably laughed through the years at the memory of Joseph's dreams of superiority.

43:34 *Benjamin's serving.* Favoritism shown to Rachel's son silently tested their attitudes; any longstanding envy, dislike, or animosity could not be easily masked. However, none surfaced.

44:2 *my cup, the silver cup.* Joseph's own special cup, also described as one connected with divination (vv. 5, 15) or hydromancy (interpreting the water movements), was a sacred vessel symbolizing the authority of his office of Egyptian vizier. Mention of its superstitious nature and purpose need not demand Joseph be an actual practitioner of pagan religious rites. *See note on verse 15.*

44:5 *divination.* *See note on Deuteronomy 18:9–12.*

44:7–9 The brothers, facing a charge of theft, protested their innocence by pointing first to their integrity in returning the money from the last trip, and then by declaring death on the perpetrator and slavery for themselves.

44:12 *began with the oldest.* Again, there was a display of inside knowledge of the family, which ought to have signaled something to the brothers. *See note on 43:33.*

44:13 *tore their clothes.* This is a well known ancient Near Eastern custom of visibly portraying the pain of heart being experienced. They were very upset that Benjamin might become a slave in Egypt (v. 10); Benjamin appears to have been speechless. They had passed a second test of devotion to Benjamin (the first in v. 34).

44:14 *fell before him.* Again, the dream had become reality (cf. 37:5–8; 42:6); but now prostrate before him, they had come to plead for mercy, both for their youngest brother Benjamin and for their father Jacob (vv. 18–34).

44:15 *practice divination.* *See notes on verses 2, 5.* Joseph, still disguising himself as an Egyptian official before his brothers, permitted them to think it so.

44:16 *Then Judah said.* Judah stepped forward as the family spokesman since it was he who came with his brothers to Joseph's house and he who pled with him (cf. vv. 14, 18); Reuben, the firstborn, had been eclipsed. ***God has found out the iniquity.*** Judah, showing how his heart had changed, acknowledged the providence of God in uncovering their guilt (note the "we" in the questions), and did not indulge in any blame-shifting, even on to Benjamin.

44:18–34 An eloquent and contrite plea for mercy, replete with reference to the aged father's delight in and doting upon the youngest son (vv. 20, 30) and the fatal shock should he be lost (vv. 22, 29, 31, 34). Judah's evident compassion for Jacob and readiness to substitute himself for Benjamin in slavery finally overwhelmed Joseph. These were not the same brothers of yesteryear (45:1).

45:1–8 Stunned by the revelation of who it really was with whom they dealt, the brothers then heard expressed a masterpiece of recognition of and submission to the sovereignty of God, i.e., His providential rule over the affairs of life, both good and bad. *See note on 41:43–45.*

45:6 *these two years.* Joseph would have been thirty-nine years old and away from his brothers for twenty-two years (37:2).

45:7 *to preserve a posterity.* These are words reflecting, on Joseph's part, an understanding of the Abrahamic covenant and its promise of a nation (cf. chs. 12; 15; 17).

45:8 *father to Pharaoh.* A title which belonged to viziers and which designated one who, unrelated to Pharaoh, nevertheless performed a valuable function and held high position, which in Joseph's case was "lord of all Egypt" (v. 9). A new and younger Pharaoh now reigned, Senusert III, c. 1878–1841 B.C.

45:10 *land of Goshen.* This area, located in the northeast section of the Egyptian delta region, was appropriate for grazing the herds of Jacob (cf. 47:27; 50:8). Over 400 years later, at the time of the Exodus, the Jews still lived in Goshen (cf. Ex. 8:22; 9:26).

45:14, 15 Reconciliation was accomplished with much emotion, which clearly showed that Joseph held no grudges and had forgiven his brothers, evidencing the marks of a spiritually mature man. *See note on 50:15–18.* It had been twenty-two years since the brothers sold Joseph into slavery.

45:16 *So it pleased Pharaoh.* The final seal of approval for Joseph's relatives to immigrate to Egypt came unsought from Pharaoh (vv. 17–20).

45:24 *troubled along the way.* This was a needed admonition because they would have so much sin to think about as they readied their confession to their father.

45:26 *Jacob's heart stood still.* Like his sons (v. 3), Jacob was stunned by the totally unexpected good news. Even though the record is silent on the matter, this was the appropriate occasion for the sons to confess their crime to their father.

E. Transition to the Exodus (46:1–50:26)

1. Journey to Egypt (46:1–27)

46:1 *offered sacrifices.* The route to Egypt for Jacob went via Beersheba, a notable site about twenty-five miles southwest of Hebron and a favorite place of worship for both Abraham and Isaac (21:33; 26:25).

46:2–4 *God spoke . . . in the visions.* Jacob's anxiety about his departure to Egypt was allayed by the Lord's approval and confirmation of his descendants returning as a nation. God had previously appeared/spoken to Jacob in 28:10–17; 32:24–30; 35:1, 9–13.

46:4 *hand on your eyes.* A promise of dying peacefully in the presence of his beloved son (cf. 49:33).

46:6 *went to Egypt.* C. 1875 B.C. They remained 430 years (Ex. 12:40) until the Exodus in 1445 B.C.

46:8–27 The genealogical register, separately listing and totaling the sons per wife and handmaid, is enveloped by notification that it records the sons/persons of Jacob who went to Egypt (vv. 8, 27). Ancient Near Eastern genealogies could include historical notes as is true here, namely the death of Er and Onan (v. 11), and that Laban gave the handmaids to his daughters (vv. 18, 25).

46:8 *the children of Israel.* This was the first time that author Moses referred to the family as a whole in this way, although "in Israel" had been used by the sons of Jacob before (cf. 34:7).

46:26 *sixty-six persons.* The total of verses 8–25 is seventy, from which Er, Onan, Manasseh, and Ephraim need to be deleted.

46:27 *seventy.* Jacob, Joseph, Manasseh, and Ephraim should be added to the sixty-six. The seventy-five of Acts 7:14 included an additional five people, born in the land, which were added in the LXX reading of 46:8–27 (cf. Ex. 1:5; Deut. 10:22). These five included two sons of Manasseh, two sons of Ephraim, and one grandson of the latter. *See note on Exodus 1:5.*

2. Occupation in Goshen (46:28–47:31)

46:28 *sent Judah before him.* Once again Judah was the leader going ahead as Jacob's representative, not Reuben. *See note on 44:16.* **Goshen.** *See note on 45:10.*

46:31–34 Joseph's instructions about his preparatory interview with Pharaoh were designed to secure his relatives a place somewhat separate from the mainstream of Egyptian society. The social stigma regarding the Hebrews (43:32), who were shepherds also (v. 34), played a crucial role in protecting Israel from intermingling and losing their identity in Egypt. *See note on 43:32.*

47:1–6 *in the land of Goshen.* By informing Pharaoh of where he had located his family (cf. 45:10; 46:28) and, then, by having the family's five representatives courteously request permission to reside in Goshen (vv. 2, 4), Joseph, wise to court procedures, paved the way for Pharaoh's confirmation and approval (v. 6).

47:7, 10 *Jacob blessed Pharaoh.* The aged patriarch's salutations pronounced, undoubtedly in the name of God, a benediction on Pharaoh Senusert III (*see note on 45:8*) for his generosity and his provision of a safe place for Jacob's family. Though Senusert III had ascended to the throne before the famine ended, he honored his father's commitments.

47:9 *my pilgrimage . . . few and evil.* Since neither Jacob nor his fathers had actually possessed the land of Canaan, describing life as a pilgrimage was a fitting evaluation to give. In addition, his years seemed few in contrast to those of the two who had visited Egypt long before him—Abraham and Isaac (175 and 180 years, respectively). Still overshadowed with pessimism, the days were "evil," in the sense of toil and trouble, of many sorrows, distresses, and crises. *See note on 48:15.*

47:11 *land of Rameses.* An alternative designation for Goshen (cf. 46:34; 47:1, 6), with this name perhaps used later to more accurately describe the region for Moses' contemporary readers. *See note on Exodus 1:11* regarding the name Rameses ("Raamses" being the alternate spelling in Exodus). This region is also called Zoan elsewhere (cf. Ps. 78:12, 43).

47:12 *according to the number in their families.* A rationing system was evidently in operation.

47:13–24 When the famine finally exhausted the Egyptians' supply of money, Joseph accepted animals in exchange for grain (v. 17). After the animals ran out, the people were desperate enough to exchange their land (vv. 19, 20). Eventually, Pharaoh owned all the land, except what was the priests' (v. 22), though the people were allowed to work the land and pay one-fifth of its yield to Pharaoh (v. 24). Whatever may have been the land-tenure system at that time, some private land ownership did at first exist, but finally, as in a feudal system, all worked their land for Pharaoh. Landed nobility did lose out and declined during major social reforms undertaken under Senusert III. This is the first record in Scripture of a national income tax, and the amount was twenty percent. Later, after the Exodus, God would prescribe tithes for Israel as national income taxes to support the theocracy (see Mal. 3:10).

47:15 *when the money failed.* The severity of the famine finally bankrupted all in Egypt and Canaan. With no monetary instruments available as a medium of exchange, a barter system was established (vv. 16–18).

47:16–18 Land soon replaced animals as the medium of exchange.

47:25, 26 The extra measures imposed by Joseph to control the impact of the famine, i.e., moving parts of the population into cities (v. 21) and demanding a one-fifth tax on crop yields (v. 24), did not affect his approval ratings (v. 25). Whatever the gain to Pharaoh, the people obviously understood that Joseph had not enriched himself at their expense.

47:27, 28 *grew and multiplied.* For seventeen years, Jacob was witness to the increase; he had a glimpse of God's promise to Abraham, Isaac, and himself in the process of being fulfilled.

47:29 *your hand under my thigh.* Cf. Abraham and Eliezer in Genesis 24:9. *do not bury me in Egypt.* With the customary sign of an oath in that day, Joseph sincerely promised to bury Jacob, at his request, in the family burial cave in Canaan (cf. 49:29–32).

47:31 Cf. Hebrews 11:21.

3. Blessings on the Twelve Tribes (48:1–49:28)

48:3–6 After summarizing God's affirmation of the Abrahamic covenant to himself, Jacob/Israel, in gratitude for Joseph's great generosity and preservation of God's people, formally proclaimed adoption of Joseph's sons on a par with Joseph's brothers in their inheritance, thus granting to Rachel's two sons (Joseph and Benjamin) three tribal territories in the land (cf. v. 16). This may explain why the new name, Israel, was used throughout the rest of the chapter.

48:4 Cf. Acts 7:5.

48:8 *Who are these?* Blind Jacob asked for identification of Joseph's sons before he would pronounce their blessings. Perhaps, at this point, he recollected the time of blessing before his own father and the trick played on blind Isaac (27:1–29).

48:14 *guiding his hands knowingly.* Intentionally crossing his hands, Jacob altered what Joseph expected to happen and placed his right hand on the youngest, not on the firstborn. When Joseph attempted to correct Jacob's mistake (vv. 17, 18), he learned that Jacob knew exactly what he was doing (vv. 19, 20). The patriarchal blessing took on prophetic significance with such action and words, since Ephraim would be the most influential of the two to the extent that Ephraim would become a substitute name for Israel (*see note on v. 19*).

48:15 *blessed Joseph.* With hands on the sons' heads, Jacob uttered the prayer-wish for Joseph, which indicated by his wording that these two would be taking his son's place under Abraham and Isaac. *See note on verses 3–6.*

48:15, 16 Pessimism no longer overshadowed Jacob's testimony; he recognized that every day had been under God's hand or that

of His angel (*see note on 16:13*). This was a different evaluation of his life than previously given (47:9).

48:16 *redeemed me.* This is the first mention of God as redeemer, deliverer, or Savior.

48:19 *younger brother shall be greater.* Ephraim did indeed become the dominant tribe of the ten northern tribes, eventually being used as the national designate for the ten tribes in the prophets (Is. 7:2, 5, 9, 17; Hos. 9:3–16).

48:21 *bring you back.* Dying Jacob gave voice to his undying trust in God's taking his descendants back to Canaan.

48:22 *one portion . . . with my sword.* Jacob's history does not record any conquest of Amorite land. He did purchase property from the children of Hamor (Gen. 33:19) but that was not by conquest. At some time, this military event had actually occurred, but for some unknown reason, it finds no other mention in God's revelation.

49:1–28 With Judah and Joseph receiving the most attention (vv. 8–12, 22–26), the fa-

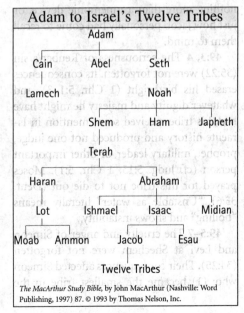

Adam to Israel's Twelve Tribes

Adam
Cain — Abel — Seth
Lamech — Noah
Shem — Ham — Japheth
Terah
Haran — Abraham
Lot — Ishmael — Isaac — Midian
Moab — Ammon — Jacob — Esau
Twelve Tribes

The MacArthur Study Bible, by John MacArthur (Nashville: Word Publishing, 1997) 87. © 1993 by Thomas Nelson, Inc.

ther's blessing portrayed the future history of each son, seemingly based upon their characters up to that time. The cryptic nature of the poetry demands rigorous analysis for correlating tribal history with Jacob's last word and testament. See Moses' blessing on the tribes in Deuteronomy 33, c. 1405 B.C.

49:1 in the last days. The key expression leading into the poetic content of Jacob's prediction for each son often signifies the last days in prophetic literature (Is. 2:2; Ezek. 38:16) or points more generally to "the latter days" (Deut. 4:30; 31:29), i.e., in the sense of "in subsequent days."

49:2–27 The names of the sons are not given in birth order (cf. 29:32–30:24; 35:18), nor in the pattern of wife, then handmaid (cf. 46:8–25). The order is as per the mother: (1) the six sons of Leah; (2) one son of Bilhah; (3) two sons of Zilpah; (4) one son of Bilhah; and (5) the two sons of Rachel. Other than the reversal of Leah's fifth and sixth sons, the others remain in chronological order in relation to their mothers. No other pattern is discernible. It may have been nothing more than a mnemonic device, or just how Jacob personally had come to recall them to mind.

49:3, 4 The seriousness of Reuben's sin (35:22) were not forgotten. Its consequences erased his birthright (1 Chr. 5:1–3), and whatever dignity and majesty he might have had, his tribe received scant mention in Israelite history and produced not one judge, prophet, military leader, or other important person (cf. Judg. 5:15; 1 Chr. 5:1). Moses prayed for this tribe not to die out (Deut. 33:6). "Unstable as water" literally means "boiling" and shows instability.

49:5–7 The cruelty and anger of Simeon and Levi at Shechem were not forgotten (34:25). Their consequences affected Simeon who: (1) became the smallest tribe in the second census of Moses (Num. 26:14); (2) was omitted from the blessing of Moses (Deut. 33:8); and (3) later shared territory with Judah (Josh. 19:1–9). Levi was "scattered" (v. 7) throughout Israel; they became, by God's grace and through their loyalty to God (Ex. 32:26), the priestly tribe and residents of the cities of refuge. Neither possessed their own designated region in the land, although Levi's priestly position was certainly a privileged one (cf. Deut. 33:8–11; Josh. 21:1–3). "Hamstrung" means to cut the leg tendons as a means of destroying the animal's usefulness.

49:8–12 As strong as a young lion and entrenched as an old lion, to Judah's line belonged national prominence and kingship, including David, Solomon, and their dynasty (640 years after this), as well as "the one to whom the scepter belongs, " i.e., Shiloh, the cryptogram for the Messiah, the one also called the "Lion of the Tribe of Judah" (Rev. 5:5). On the march through the wilderness, Judah went first (Num. 10:14) and had the largest population in Moses' census (cf. Num. 1:27; 26:22). This language (vv. 11, 12) de-

---

Key Word

Seed: 1:11, 29; 13:15, 16; 15:18; 17:19; 28:14; 48:19—the Hebrew word for seed can literally mean a plant's seed (1:11, 12) or can figuratively mean one's descendants (13:15). In Genesis, it refers specifically to the coming Messiah, in God's promise that the woman's seed would crush the serpent (3:15; Num. 24:7; Is. 6:13; Gal. 3:16). As such, the term takes on great importance in the Bible: Through Abraham's *seed*, both collectively in Israel and singularly in Christ, God would reach out to save His people (15:3).

scribes prosperity so great that people will tie a donkey to a choice vine, letting it eat because there is such abundance; wine will be as plentiful as water and everyone will be healthy. This is likely a millennial prophecy.

49:13 Although Zebulun's territory did not border the Mediterranean Sea or the Sea of Galilee, the tribe was situated to benefit from the important trade route, the Via Maris, traversed by sea traders moving through her territory.

49:14, 15 Issachar, an industrious, robust, hardy, and stalwart tribe, lived up to the name of their founder whose name meant "man of wages" (cf. 1 Chr. 7:1–5; 12:32).

49:16–18 Dan, whose name meant "judge," fathered an aggressive tribe that would also judge in the nation but would not be known for moral stature or religious faithfulness (cf. Judg. 13:2; 18:1ff.; 1 Kin. 12:28–30; 2 Kin. 10:29). Dan would later abandon its land allotment (Josh 19:40–48) and migrate to the extreme north of Israel (Judg. 18:1–31). Jacob's closing cry expressed hope for Dan in the day when salvation would indeed come to Israel. Dan, however, is omitted in the list of tribes in Revelation 7:4–8.

49:19 Settling in Transjordan exposed Gad's people to invasions, making them valiant fighters worthy of victory and commendation (cf. 1 Chr. 5:18–22; 12:8–15).

49:20 Asher benefited much from occupying the agriculturally rich coastal region north of Carmel, and provided gourmet delights for the palace. Cf. Joshua 19:24–31.

49:21 Deer-like speed and agility marked Naphtali's military prowess (cf. Judg. 4:6; 5:18). The song of Deborah and Barak, who hailed from Naphtali (Judg. 4:6), is representative of his eloquent words (Judg. 5).

49:22–26 Addressed to Joseph, but applicable to his two sons (cf. 48:15–20), these words thrust forth a contrasting experience of growth and prosperity alongside hostility and conflict. Verses 23 and 24 may be a biography of Joseph. No other tribe had such direct reference to the Lord God (vv. 24, 25) in their blessing as addressed to Joseph. The four names for God well reflect Joseph's emphasis on the sovereignty of his God, no matter the misfortune and grief which attended his way (cf. v. 23). Samuel was from Ephraim, Gideon from Manasseh.

49:27 The warlike nature of the small tribe of Benjamin became well known, as exhibited in their archers and slingers (Judg. 20:16; 1 Chr. 8:40; 12:2; 2 Chr. 14:8; 17:17) and in the brazen defense of their wickedness in Gibeah (Judg. 19; 20). Both Sauls in the Bible were from this tribe: the first king in Israel (1 Sam. 9:1, 2) and the apostle Paul (Phil. 3:5).

4. The death and burial of Jacob in Canaan (49:29–50:14)

49:29–32 Jacob's dying instructions were fully carried out (cf. 50:12–14). See 23:6–20.

Key Word

Jews: from a root meaning "to praise" or "to give thanks." Jacob used this term during his blessing of his son Judah in Genesis 49:8: "Judah, your brothers will praise you." A Jew may be a person from the tribe of Judah (Num. 10:14), or an Israelite living in the geographical region known as Judah (see Jer. 7:30). During the post-exilic period, "Jew" referred to the Israelites as a people group. The use of the term *Jew* is also found in the New Testament. Jesus is called "the King of the Jews" (Matt. 27:29). Later, Paul clarified that the true Jew is a person marked by "circumcision of the heart" (Rom. 2:28, 29).

Joseph—A Type of Christ

Joseph	Parallels	Jesus
37:2	A shepherd of his father's sheep.	John 10:11, 27–29
37:3	His father loved him dearly.	Matt. 3:17
37:4	Hated by his brothers.	John 7:4,5
37:13, 14	Sent by father to brothers.	Hebrews 2:11
37:20	Ohters plotted to harm them.	John 11:53
37:23	Robes taken from them.	John 19:23, 24
37:26	Taken to Egypt.	Matt. 2:14, 15
37:28	Sold for the price of a slave.	Matt. 26:15
39:7	Tempted.	Matt. 4:1
39:16–18	Falsely accused.	Matt. 26:59, 60
39:20	Bound in chains.	Matt. 27:2
40:2, 3	Placed with two other prisoners, one who was saved and the other lost.	Luke 23:32
41:41	Exalted after suffering.	Phil. 2:9–11
41:46	Both 30 years old at the beginning of public recognition.	Luke 3:23
42:24; 45:2,14,15; 46:29.	Both wept.	John 10:35
45:1–15	Forgave those who wronged them.	Luke 23:34
45:7	Saved their nation.	Matt. 1:21
50:20	What men did to hurt them, God turned to good.	1 Cor. 2:7, 8

The MacArthur Study Bible, by John MacArthur (Nashville: Word Publishing, 1997) 89. © 1993 by Thomas Nelson, Inc.

49:31 *there I buried Leah.* Honor was finally accorded to Leah in death and in Jacob's request to be buried alongside his wife, as were his fathers. Burial alongside Rachel, the beloved wife, was not requested.

49:33 *Jacob . . . breathed his last. C. 1858 B.C. gathered to his people.* *See note on 25:8.*

50:2, 3 *physicians to embalm.* Joseph summoned medical men, who were fully capable of embalming, rather than the religious embalmers in order to avoid the magic and mysticism associated with their practices. Usually in Egypt, mummifying was a forty-day process, which included gutting the body, drying it, and wrapping it.

50:3–6 Once normal embalming and mourning had been properly observed according to Egyptian custom, Joseph was free to seek permission to conduct a funeral in Canaan.

50:7–11 Out of respect for Joseph, a substantial escort accompanied him and all his relatives into the land of Canaan. This extraordinary event gave assurance to later generations because the bodies of the three patriarchs were in Canaan and Joseph's bones awaited transport there when, as per Joseph's last words, God's promises to the three began to be fulfilled.

5. The death of Joseph in Egypt (50:15–26)

50:15–18 The brothers' guilty consciences reasserted themselves and caused them to underestimate the genuineness of Joseph's forgiveness and affection for them. Jacob's concern to plead on his sons' behalf equally underestimated Joseph's words and actions toward his brethren.

50:19 *am I in the place of God?* This concise question tweaked their memory of Joseph's explanation of how God had put him where he was (cf. 45:3–8), in the place God intended him to be at that time.

50:20 *but God meant it for good.* Joseph's wise, theological answer has gone down in history as the classic statement of God's sovereignty over the affairs of men. *See note on 45:1–8.*

Other Types of Christ in the Old Testament

Certain persons and practices recorded in the Old Testament serve as hints, clues, and pre-illustrations of what Jesus Christ would accomplish by His life, death, and resurrection. In most cases, the similarities or parallels are pointed out in the New Testament. The following people are some of those mentioned as representing, in a narrow way, what Christ accomplished perfectly:

1. Adam	Romans 5:14; 1 Corinthians 15:45
2. Abel	Genesis 4:8, 10; Hebrews 12:24
3. Aaron	Exodus 28:1; Hebrews 5:4, 5; 9:7, 24
4. David	2 Samuel 8:15; Philippians 2:9
5. Jonah	Jonah 1:17; Matthew 12:40
6. Melchizedek	Genesis 14:18–20; Hebrews 7:1–17
7. Moses	Numbers 12:7; Hebrews 3:2
8. Noah	Genesis 5:29; 2 Corinthians 1:5
9. Samson	Judges 16:30; Colossians 2:14–15
10. Solomon	2 Samuel 7:12, 13; 1 Peter 2:5

The following events and practices also prefigure Christ:

1. Ark	Genesis 7:16; 1 Peter 3:20, 21
2. Atonement sacrifices	Leviticus 16:15, 16; Hebrews 9:12, 24
3. Bronze serpent	Numbers 21:9; John 3:14, 15
4. Mercy seat	Exodus 25:17–22; Romans 3:25; Hebrews 4:16
5. Passover lamb	Exodus 12:3–6, 46; John 19:36; 1 Corinthians 5:7
6. Red heifer	Leviticus 3:1; Ephesians 2:14, 16
7. Rock of Horeb	Exodus 17:6; 1 Corinthians 10:4
8. Scapegoat	Leviticus 16:20–22
9. Tabernacle	Exodus 40:2; Hebrews 9:11; Colossians 2:9
10. Veil of the tabernacle	Exodus 40:21; Hebrews 10:20

50:24 God will surely visit you. Joseph died just as he had lived, firmly trusting in God to carry out His promises (cf. Heb. 11:22). Almost four centuries later, Moses took Joseph's remains out of Egypt (Ex. 13:19) and Joshua buried them at Shechem (Josh. 24:32). **to Abraham, to Isaac, and to Jacob.** The death of Jacob had finally allowed for the three patriarchs to be mentioned together.

50:26 one hundred and ten years old. C. 1804 B.C. Joseph's span of life was consid-

Further Study

Davis, John J. *Paradise to Prison: Studies in Genesis.* Grand Rapids: Baker, 1975.

MacArthur, John. *The Battle for the Beginning.* Nashville: Word, 2001.

Morris, Henry M. *The Genesis Record.* Grand Rapids: Baker, 1976.

ered, at that time in Egypt, an ideal lifespan. Amenemhet III (c. 1841–1792 B.C.) was the reigning Pharaoh. Exodus picked up the his-

THE SECOND BOOK OF MOSES CALLED
EXODUS

Title

The Greek Septuagint (LXX) and the Latin Vulgate versions of the OT assigned the title Exodus to this second book of Moses because the departure of Israel from Egypt is the dominant historical fact in the book (19:1). In the Hebrew Bible, the opening words, "And (or now) these are the names," served as the title of the book. The opening "and" or "now" in the Hebrew title suggests that this book was to be accepted as the obvious sequel to Genesis, the first book of Moses. Hebrews 11:22 commends the faith of Joseph who, while on his deathbed (c. 1804 b.c.), spoke of the "departure" or the "exiting" of the sons of Israel, looking ahead over 350 years to the Exodus (c. 1445 b.c.).

Author and Date

Mosaic authorship of Exodus is unhesitatingly affirmed in Scripture. Moses followed God's instructions and "wrote all the words of the Lord" (24:4), which included at the least the record of the battle with Amalek (17:14), the Ten Commandments (34:4, 27–29), and the Book of the Covenant (20:22–23:33). Similar assertions of Mosaic writing occur elsewhere in the Pentateuch: Moses is identified as the one who recorded the "starting points of their journeys" (Num. 33:2) and who "wrote this law" (Deut. 31:9).

The OT corroborates Mosaic authorship of the portions mentioned above (see Josh. 1:7, 8; 8:31, 32; 1 Kin. 2:3; 2 Kin. 14:6; Neh. 13:1; Dan. 9:11–13; Mal. 4:4). The NT concurs by citing Exodus 3:6 as part of "the book of Moses" (Mark. 12:26), (1) by assigning Exodus 13:2 to "the law of Moses," which is also referred to as "the law of the Lord" (Luke 2:22, 23), (2) by ascribing Exodus 20:12 and 21:17 to Moses (Mark 7:10), (3) by attributing the law to Moses (John 7:19; Rom. 10:5), and (4) by Jesus' specifically declaring that Moses had written of Him (John 5:46, 47).

At some time during his forty-year tenure as Israel's leader, beginning at eighty years of age and ending at 120 (7:7; Deut. 34:7), Moses wrote down this second of his five books. More specifically, it would have been after the Exodus and obviously before his death on Mount Nebo in the plains of Moab. The date of the Exodus (c. 1445 B.C.) dictates the date of the writing in the fifteenth century B.C.

Scripture dates Solomon's fourth year of reign, i.e., when he began to build the temple (c. 966/65 B.C.), as being 480 years after the Exodus (1 Kin. 6:1), thus establishing the early date of 1445 B.C. for the Exodus. Jephthah noted that, by his day, Israel had possessed Heshbon for 300 years (Judg. 11:26). By calculating backward and forward from Jephthah, and taking into account different periods of foreign oppression, judgeships and kingships, the wilderness wanderings, and the initial entry and conquest of Canaan under Joshua, this amounts to 480 years and, thus, the early date is confirmed.

Scripture also dates the entry of Jacob

and his extended family into Egypt (c. 1875 B.C.) as being 430 years before the Exodus (12:40), thus placing Joseph in what archeologists have designated as the Twelfth Dynasty, the Middle Kingdom period of Egyptian history, and placing Moses and Israel's final years of residence and slavery in what archeologists have designated as the Eighteenth Dynasty, or New Kingdom period. Further, Joseph's rule as vizier over all of Egypt (Gen. 45:8) precludes his having served under the Hyksos (c. 1730–1570 B.C.), the foreign invaders who ruled during a period of confusion in Egypt and who never controlled all of the country. They were a mixed Semitic race who introduced the horse and chariot as well as the composite bow. These implements of war made possible their expulsion from Egypt.

Background and Setting
Eighteenth Dynasty Egypt, the setting for Israel's dramatic departure, was not a politically or economically weak and obscure period of Egyptian history. Thutmose III, for example, the pharaoh of the oppression, has been called the "Napoleon of Ancient Egypt," the sovereign who expanded the boundaries of Egyptian influence far beyond their natural borders. This was the dynasty which over a century before, under the leadership of Amose I, had expelled the Hyksos kings from the country and redirected the country's economic, military, and diplomatic growth. At the time of the Exodus, Egypt was strong, not weak.

Moses, born in 1525 B.C. (80 years old in 1445 B.C.), became "learned in all the wisdom of the Egyptians" (Acts 7:22) while growing up in the courts of Pharaohs Thutmose I and II and Queen Hatshepsut for his first 40 years (Acts 7:23). He was in self-imposed, Midianite exile during the reign of Thutmose III for another 40 years (Acts

7:30), and returned at God's direction to be Israel's leader early in the reign of Amenhotep II, the pharaoh of the Exodus. God used both the educational system of Egypt and his exile in Midian to prepare Moses to represent his people before a powerful pharaoh and to guide his people through the wilderness of the Sinai peninsula during his final 40 years (Acts 7:36).

Moses died on Mount Nebo when he was 120 years old (Deut. 34:1–6), as God's judgment was on him for his anger and disrespect (Num. 20:1–3). While he looked on from afar, Moses never entered the Promised Land. Centuries later, he appeared to the disciples on the Mount of Transfiguration (Matt. 17:3).

Historical and Theological Themes
In God's timing, the Exodus marked the end of a period of oppression for Abraham's descendants (Gen. 15:13), and constituted the beginning of the fulfillment of the covenant promise to Abraham that his descendants would not only reside in the Promised Land, but would also multiply and become a great nation (Gen. 12:1–3, 7). The purpose of the book may be expressed like this: To trace the rapid growth of Jacob's descendants from Egypt to the establishment of the theocratic nation in their Promised Land.

At appropriate times, on Mt. Sinai and in the plains of Moab, God also gave the Israelites that body of legislation, the law, which they needed for living properly in Israel as the theocratic people of God. By this, they were distinct from all other nations (Deut. 4:7, 8; Rom. 9:4, 5).

By God's self-revelation, the Israelites were instructed in the sovereignty and majesty, the goodness and holiness, and the grace and mercy of their Lord, the one and only God of heaven and earth (see especially chs. 3; 6; 33; 34). The account of the Exodus and the events that followed are also the subject of other major biblical revelation (cf. Pss. 105:25–45; 106:6–27; Acts 7:17–44; 1 Cor. 10:1–13; Heb. 9:1–6; 11:23–29).

Interpretive Challenges

The absence of any Egyptian record of the devastation of Egypt by the ten plagues and the major defeat of Pharaoh's elite army at the Red Sea should not give rise to speculation on whether the account is historically authentic. Egyptian historiography did not permit records of their pharaohs' embarrassments and ignominious defeats to be published. In recording the conquest under Joshua, Scripture specifically notes only three cities which Israel destroyed and burned (Josh. 6:24; 8:28; 11:11–13). The conquest, after all, was primarily one of takeover and inhabitation of property virtually intact, not a war designed to destroy. The date of Israel's march into Canaan will not be confirmed or questioned, therefore, by examining extensive burn levels at many other city-sites of a later period.

Despite the absence of any extrabiblical, ancient Near Eastern records of the Hebrew bondage, the plagues, the Exodus, and the conquest, archeological evidence corroborates the early date. All the pharaohs, for example, of the fifteenth century left evidence of interest in building enterprises in Lower Egypt. These projects were obviously accessible to Moses in the delta region near Goshen.

The typological significance of the tabernacle has occasioned much reflection. Ingenuity in linking every item of furniture and every piece of building material to Christ may appear most intriguing; however, if NT statements and allusions do not support such linkage and typology, then hermeneutical caution must rule. The tabernacle's structure and ornamentation for efficiency and beauty are one thing, but finding hidden meaning and symbolism is unfounded. How the sacrificial and worship system of the tabernacle and its parts meaningfully typify the redeeming work of the coming Messiah must be left to those NT passages which treat the subject.

Outline

I. Israel in Egypt (1:1–12:36)
  A. The Population Explosion (1:1–7)
  B. The Oppression Under the Pharaohs (1:8–22)
  C. The Maturation of Israel's Deliverer—Moses (2:1–4:31)
  D. The Confrontation with Pharaoh (5:1–11:10)
  E. The Preparation for Departure (12:1–36)
II. Israel Enroute to Sinai (12:37–18:27)
  A. Exiting Egypt and Panicking (12:37–14:14)
  B. Crossing the Red Sea and Rejoicing (14:15–15:21)
  C. Traveling to Sinai and Grumbling (15:22–17:16)
  D. Meeting with Jethro and Learning (18:1–27)
III. Israel Encamped at Sinai (19:1–40:38)
  A. The Law of God Prescribed (19:1–24:18)
  B. The Tabernacle of God Described (25:1–31:18)
  C. The Worship of God Defiled (32:1–35)
  D. The Presence of God Confirmed (33:1–34:35)
  E. The Tabernacle of God Constructed (35:1–40:38)

I. ISRAEL IN EGYPT (1:1–12:36)

1:1–12:36 This section recounts Israel's final years in Egypt before the Exodus.

A. The Population Explosion (1:1–7)

1:1–5 Genesis also reported the names and the number of Jacob's descendants who came to Egypt (Gen. 35:23; 46:8–27).

1:5 seventy persons. Cf. Genesis 46:8–27. Acts 7:14 reports seventy-five with the addition of five relatives of Joseph included in the LXX, but not the Hebrew text.

1:6–8 This summary of a lengthy period of time moves the record from the death of Joseph (c. 1804 B.C.), the last recorded event in Genesis, to the radical change in Israel's history, i.e., from favor before Egypt's pharaoh to disfavor and enslavement (c. 1525–1445 B.C.).

1:7 The growth of the nation (cf. 12:37) was phenomenal. It grew from seventy men to 603,000 males, twenty years of age and older, thus allowing for a total population of about two million (Num. 1:46) departing from Egypt. The seed of Abraham was no longer an extended family, but a nation. The promise that his descendants would be fruitful and multiply (Gen. 35:11, 12) had, indeed, been fulfilled in Egypt.

B. The Oppression Under the Pharaohs (1:8–22)

1:8 there arose a new king. This king is either to be identified as one of the Hyksos kings (see Introduction) during a period of political disintegration, or as Pharaoh Amose I, founder of what archeologists have designated as the Eighteenth Dynasty of the New Kingdom period in Egyptian history. It is probably best to take this new king, who knew not Joseph, as a Hyksos ruler. Furthermore, the term arose signifies "rose against," which accords well with a foreign seizure of

the Egyptian throne. The Hyksos (c. 1730–1570 B.C.) came from outside Egypt (cf. Acts 7:18).

1:9–12 This represents another summary of a fairly lengthy period of time, as indicated by the population continuing to grow in spite of increasing hardship imposed on Israel.

1:9 the people. An Egyptian pharaoh designated Israel as a nation, marking the first time the term people or nation is used of them.

1:10, 11 join our enemies . . . set task-masters over them. Israel was assessed both as a threat to national security and as an economic asset—slavery would, therefore, control the danger and maximize their usefulness.

1:11 supply cities, Pithom and Raamses. These are places where both provisions and military hardware were stored. Archeological identification has not been finally definitive, with some three to five options being put forward for them. Pithom is usually taken as a center of solar worship in northern Egypt, and Raamses as Qantir in the eastern delta region. In addition, the city might very well have been renamed under the reign of the later, powerful pharaoh, and that name was better known to Israel later on (cf. the case of Laish, or Leshem, renamed Dan in Gen. 14:14; Josh. 19:47; Judg. 18:29).

1:13 the Egyptians. The native inhabitants continued to enslave Israel. Between verses 12 and 13, a major change in Egyptian history took place—the Hyksos were driven out (c. 1570 B.C.).

1:14 hard bondage—in mortar, in brick. Archeologists have uncovered reliefs and paintings confirming the Egyptian practice of imposing forced labor on prisoners and slaves. These paintings also show foremen and guards watching construction work while scribes registered data on tablets.

1:15–17 *the midwives feared God.* These brave, older women reverenced their God and, thus, obeyed Him and not man. They obviously understood that children were a gift from God and that murder was wrong. The two midwives mentioned by name were probably the leading representatives of their profession, since it is unlikely that such a burgeoning population had only two midwives to deal with all the births.

1:15, 16 The failure of rigorous bondage to suppress population growth necessitated that different measures be taken; hence, the royal order to the Hebrew midwives to murder male infants at birth.

1:16 *birthstools.* Lit. "two stones" on which the women sat to deliver.

1:19, 20 Rather than trying to argue for a justifiable lie on the part of midwives seeking to protect God's people, it is better to take it as a statement of what was actually true: God was directly involved in this affair of birth and national growth. This is the key to understanding why no decree of Pharaoh would work out as he intended it, and why Hebrew women were so healthy and gave birth with ease.

1:22 The failure of the extermination program demanded of the midwives finally caused Pharaoh to demand that all his subjects get involved in murdering newborn boys.

C. The Maturation of Israel's Deliverer— Moses (2:1–4:31)

2:1, 2 Since Moses was born soon after the general decree of 1:22 was given (c. 1525 B.C.), the issuer of the decree was Thutmose I.

2:3, 4 The careful actions of Moses' mother to construct the ark of bulrushes, to set Moses afloat close to the royal bathing place, and to have his sister watch to see what would happen, indicate a hope that something would work out right for the child.

2:5 *the daughter of Pharaoh.* She has been identified, possibly, as Hatshepsut or another princess; in either case, she was a princess whom God providentially used to override Pharaoh's death decree and protect the life of His chosen leader for the Israelites.

2:10 *became her son.* The position of "son" undoubtedly granted Moses special privileges belonging to nobility, but none of these persuaded Moses to relinquish his native origin. Rather, as the NT advises, his spiritual maturity was such that when he came of age, "he refused to be called the son of Pharaoh's daughter" (Heb. 11:24). The formal education in the court of that time meant that Moses would have learned reading, writing, arithmetic, and perhaps one or more of the languages of Canaan. He would also have participated in various outdoor sports, e.g., archery and horseback riding, two favorites of the Eighteenth Dynasty court.

2:11 *when Moses was grown.* The narrative skips over all details of Moses' life as the adopted son of an Egyptian princess prior to the event which led to his flight into Midian.

2:11, 12, 16–21 Two injustices aroused Moses' indignation with different conse-

Pharaohs of Moses' Time		
1. Thutmose I (Ex. 1:22)	1526–1512 B.C.	At Moses' birth (c. 1525 B.C.)
2. Thutmose II (Acts 7:22)	1512–1504 B.C.	During Moses' adolescence
3. Thutmose III (Ex. 2:15)	1504–1450 B.C.	During Moses' Midian exile
4. Amenhotep II (Ex. 5:1ff.)	1450–1425 B.C.	At the Exodus (c. 1445 B.C.)

quences: one resulted in his leaving home, having killed an Egyptian who beat an Israelite; the other resulted in his finding a new home as an Egyptian who helped the Midianite daughters of Reuel, and in his finding a wife. Undoubtedly, Reuel and his family soon discovered Moses was not really an Egyptian.

2:14 Cf. Acts 7:27, 28, 35.

2:15 *Midian.* The Midianites, descendants of Abraham and Keturah (Gen. 25:1–4), settled in the Arabian Peninsula along the eastern shore of the Gulf of Aqabah.

2:18 *Reuel.* He was also known as Jethro (3:1), who may very well have been a worshiper of the true God (cf. 18:12–23), notwithstanding his being also the priest of Midian.

2:21–23 The narrative skips over the unimportant details of this forty-year period and moves the record ahead quickly to the finding of a new home and family and to the moment when Moses returned to his people.

2:23–25 The hardship imposed upon Israel finally brought forth a collective cry for relief. The response of God is presented in four words: *heard, remembered, looked upon,* and *acknowledged.* This signaled that a response was forthcoming.

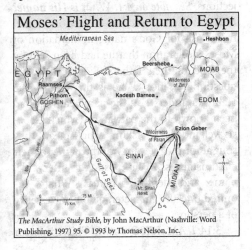

Moses' Flight and Return to Egypt

The MacArthur Study Bible, by John MacArthur (Nashville: Word Publishing, 1997) 95. © 1993 by Thomas Nelson, Inc.

2:24 *remembered His covenant.* The unilateral covenant God made with Abraham (Gen. 12:1–3; 15:1–21; 17:1–22) and confirmed with Isaac (Gen. 26:2–5) and with Jacob (Gen. 28:10–15; 35:9–15) specifically promised a geographically recognizable territory to the descendants of Abraham through Isaac and Jacob. Because of them, too, the world would be blessed.

3:1 *Moses was tending the flock.* Moses worked as a shepherd while living with his father-in-law, a life and occupation quite different from the privilege and prestige associated with his life in Pharaoh's court. *Horeb.* An alternative name for Mt. Sinai (cf. 19:11; Deut. 4:10). Traditionally, this mountain has been identified with Jebel Musa, "the mountain of Moses." *Horeb* is the Hebrew for the non-Semitic place-name, Sinai, located in the southern part of the Sinai Peninsula. *the mountain of God.* This is known as such because of what took place there, later in Israel's history. This name for the mountain suggests that the Book of Exodus was written by Moses after the events at Sinai. Others suggest that it was already known as a sacred mountain prior to the call of Moses, but it seems best to relate the name to what God did for Israel there.

3:2–4 Moses' attention was drawn to a most unusual sight, that of a burning bush which was not being consumed by the fire within. A supernatural event is the only viable explanation. Natural explanations of certain types of flowers with gaseous pods or oil glands fail, in that, after forty years of work in the desert, Moses would surely have ignored something normal. This was so different that it aroused his curiosity and demanded further examination. God was in the bush speaking, clearly a miraculous event.

3:2 *The Angel of the* LORD. Lit. "messenger of Yahweh" who, in context, turns out to be the Lord Himself talking to Moses (cf. Acts 7:30).

3:5–10 Cf. Acts 7:33, 34.

3:5 *Do not draw near this place. Take your sandals off.* This is a sign of reverence in a holy place, one set apart from the norm because God was present there. These commands prevented Moses from rashly intruding, unprepared, into God's presence.

3:6 *I am the God of your father.* God's opening words, although important for Moses to hear, point the reader back to 2:24—showing that the God of Israel has remembered His people and has begun to take action (cf. Matt. 22:32; Mark 12:26; Luke 20:37; Acts 3:13; 7:32). ***Moses hid his face.*** A fitting reaction of reverent fear in the presence of the divine was modeled by Moses.

3:7, 8 *I have surely seen . . . have heard.* The emphasis is on God's having been well aware of the desperate situation of Israel. The result: He promised to deliver them from Egyptian oppression. Here, and in the next two verses, the repetitive manner in describing what God saw and would do served to underscore all the more His personal involvement in the history of His people whom He had sent into Egypt.

3:8 *to a good and large land, to a land . . . to the place.* Three descriptions of the land to which Israel was going to be taken emphatically underscored the land-promise of the Abrahamic covenant. ***flowing with milk and honey.*** A formal and graphic way of describing a fertile land of bounteous provision. ***of the Canaanites and the Hittites.*** A specific identification of the territory to which Israel was going; her Promised Land was currently inhabited by other peoples.

3:10 *I will send you.* The divine summons made Moses both leader and deliverer of Israel and ambassador of God before Pharaoh.

3:11 *Who am I . . . ?* The first response is an objection from Moses to the divine summons, an expression of inadequacy for such a serious mission. It sounded reasonable, for after forty years of absence from Egypt, what could he, a mere shepherd in Midian, do upon return?

3:12 *I will certainly be with you.* The divine promise, one given also to the patriarchs, Abraham, Isaac, and Jacob, should have been sufficient to quell all the chosen agent's fears and sense of inadequacy for the task. ***you shall serve God on this mountain.*** A second divine promise signified the future success of the mission, suggesting that Israel would not be delivered simply out of bondage and oppression, but rescued to worship (cf. Acts 7:7).

3:13 *Then Moses said.* Was Moses at this point crossing the line from reasonable inquiry to unreasonable doubt? God's patient replies instructing Moses on what He would do and what the results would be, including Israel's being viewed with favor by the Egyptians (3:21), ought to caution the reader from hastily classifying Moses' attitude as altogether wrong from the very beginning of the interaction between him and the Lord. A response of divine anger comes only in 4:14 at the very end of Moses' questions and objections. *See note on 4:1.* ***What is His name?*** Moses raised a second objection. Israel might ask for God's name in validation of Moses' declaration that he had been sent by the God of their fathers. Significantly, the question was not "Who is this God?" The Hebrews understood the name Yahweh had been known to the patriarchs (which Genesis well indicates). Asking "what" meant they sought for the relevancy of the name to their circumstances. "Who?" sought after title, name, and identity; whereas "What?" inquired into the character, quality, or essence of a person.

3:14 *I AM WHO I AM.* This name for

Moses' Five Excuses
1. "I am a nobody" (Ex. 3:11)
God's response (Ex. 3:12)
2. "I am not a theologian" (Ex. 3:13)
God's response (Ex. 3:14, 15)
3. "I am unconvincing" (Ex. 4:1)
God's response (Ex. 4:2–9)
4. "I am not a preacher" (Ex. 4:10)
God's response (Ex. 4:11, 12)
5. "I am really not interested" (Ex. 4:13)
God's response (Ex. 4:14–17)

God points to His self-existence and eternality; it denotes "I am the One who is/will be," which is decidedly the best and most contextually suitable option from a number of theories about its meaning and etymological source. The significance in relation to "God of your fathers" is immediately discernible: He is the same God throughout the ages. The Hebrew consonants *Yhwh* (usually written *Yahweh*), when combined with the vowels from the divine name *Adonai* (Master or Lord), gave rise to the name "Jehovah" in English. Since the name *Yhwh* was considered so sacred that it should not be pronounced, the Massoretes inserted the vowels from *Adonai* to remind themselves to pronounce it differently when reading instead of saying *Yahweh*. Technically, this combination of consonants is known as the "tetragrammaton."

3:15–22 Having provided Moses with His name in response to his second inquiry, God then furnished him with two speeches, one for Israel's elders (vv. 16, 17) and one for Pharaoh (v. 18b). Also included was notification of the elders' positive response to Moses' report (v. 18a), of Pharaoh's refusal to grant them their request (v. 19), of God's miraculous, judgmental reaction (v. 20), and of Israel's plundering of the Egyptians, who found themselves responding favorably to the departing nation's request for silver, gold, and clothing (vv. 21, 22). The last of these harkens back to God's promise to Abraham that his descendants would come out of the land of their affliction with great possessions (Gen. 15:14).

3:15 Cf. Matthew 22:23; Mark 12:26; Acts 3:13.

3:16 *elders.* Lit. "bearded ones," which indicated the age and wisdom needed to lead.

3:17 *land of. See notes on 3:8.*

3:18 *three days' journey.* The request for a three-day journey to worship, in the light of (1) direct promises of deliverance from Egypt, (2) worship at Horeb, and (3) entrance into Canaan, was not a ruse to get out and then not return, but an initial, moderate request to highlight the intransigence of Pharaoh. He just would not let these slaves leave under any conditions (v. 19)!

3:22 *See note on 12:36.*

4:1 *Then Moses answered and said.* In a third objection, Moses gave an unworthy response, after the lengthy explanation by God to Moses in 3:14–22. At this point, the hypothetical situation proposed became more objection than reasonable inquiry.

4:2–9 In response to the hypothetical situation of Israel's rejecting God as having appeared to him, Moses was given three signs to accredit him as the chosen spokesman and leader. Note the purpose stated: "That they may believe that the LORD God . . . appeared to you" (v. 5). Two of these signs personally involved Moses right then and there—the rod to snake and back, the hand leprous and healed. No matter what the situation Moses could envision himself facing, God had sufficient resources to authenticate His man, and Moses was not to think otherwise.

4:10 *I am not eloquent.* With his fourth argument, Moses focused on his speech disability, describing himself literally as not being "a man of words," as being "heavy in mouth and heavy in tongue," i.e., unable to articulate his thoughts in fluent, flowing speech. An ancient document, *The Tale of the Eloquent Peasant,* suggests that eloquence was important in Egyptian culture, something which Moses would have well known from his time in the court. *neither before nor since You have spoken.* This is a pointed and inappropriate, if not impolite, criticism that somehow in all the discussion, God had overlooked Moses' speech disability. Unless this disability changed, Moses believed that he could not undertake the assigned task (cf. 6:12).

4:11, 12 *Who has made man's mouth?* Three rhetorical questions from God shut the door on any complaints or criticisms about being clumsy of speech. The follow-up command, "Therefore, go!" including its promise of divine help in speech, forbade all such objections.

4:13–16 Moses' fifth and final statement, notwithstanding the opening supplication, "O my Lord," was a polite way of bluntly saying, "Choose someone else, not me!" The anger of God toward this overt expression of reluctance was appropriate, yet the Lord still provided another way for His plan to move forward unhindered. Providentially (v. 27), Aaron would meet his brother Moses, and positively respond to being the spokesman.

4:15 *and I will teach you.* The plural pronoun *you* means that God had promised to assist both of them in their newly appointed duties.

4:16 *you shall be to him as God.* Aaron would speak to the people for Moses, even as Moses would speak to Aaron for the Lord.

4:17 *this rod . . . with which you shall do the signs.* Moses, despite God's anger at his unwillingness, retained superiority in that he had the instrument by which miracles would

be done so that it was identified as "the rod of God" (v. 20).

4:18 *Please let me go.* Courtesy toward the father-in-law for which he worked was not overlooked because of the divine call to service as national leader. Exactly how much was explained of the encounter at the burning bush remains unknown, but the purpose for the return, "and see whether they are still alive," suggests that specific details of the call for Moses to be leader/deliverer were left unsaid, in contrast to the full explanation given to Aaron (v. 28).

4:20 *sons.* Gershom (2:22) and Eliezer (18:4).

4:21 *I will harden his heart.* The Lord's personal and direct involvement in the affairs of men so that His purposes might be done is revealed as God informed Moses what would take place. Pharaoh was also warned that his own refusal would bring judgment on him (v. 23). Previously, Moses had been told that God was certain of Pharaoh's refusal (3:19). This interplay between God's hardening and Pharaoh's hardening his heart must be kept in balance. Ten times (4:21; 7:3; 9:12; 10:1, 20, 27; 11:10; 14:4, 8, 17) the historical record notes specifically that God hardened the king's heart, and ten times (7:13, 14, 22; 8:15, 19, 32; 9:7, 34, 35; 13:15) the record indicates the king hardened his own heart. The apostle Paul used this hardening as an example of God's inscrutable will and absolute power to intervene as He chooses, yet obviously never without loss of personal responsibility for actions taken (Rom. 9:16– 18). The theological conundrum posed by such interplay of God's acting and Pharaoh's acting can only be resolved by accepting the record as it stands and by taking refuge in the omniscience and omnipotence of the God who planned and brought about His deliverance of Israel from Egypt, and in so doing also judged Pharaoh's sinfulness. *See note at 9:12.*

4:22 *My son, My firstborn.* To the ancient Egyptians, the firstborn son was special and sacred, and the Pharaoh considered himself the only son of the gods. Now, he heard of a whole nation designated as God's firstborn son, meaning "declared and treated as first in rank, preeminent, with the rights, privileges, and responsibilities of being actually the firstborn." The Lord pointedly referred to the nation collectively in the singular in order to show that He was a father in what He would do, i.e., bring a nation into existence, then nurture and lead him (cf. Deut. 14:1, 2). Divine sonship, as in the pagan world's perverted concept of a sexual union between the gods and women, was never so much as hinted at in the way God used the term to express His relationship with Israel, who were His people, a treasured possession, a kingdom of priests, and a holy nation (cf. 6:7; 19:4–6).

4:24–26 The presence of Zipporah's name indicates that the personal pronouns refer to Moses. She, judging by her action of suddenly and swiftly circumcising her son, understood that the danger to her husband's life was intimately connected to the family's not bearing the sign of the covenant given to Abraham for all his descendants (Gen. 17:10–14). Her evaluation, "You are a husband of blood to me," suggests her own revulsion with this rite of circumcision, which Moses should have performed. The result, however, was God's foregoing the threat and letting Moses go (v. 26a). The reaction of God, at this point, dramatically underscored the seriousness of the sign He had prescribed. *See note on Jeremiah 4:4.*

4:29, 30 The "leadership team" functioned as instructed: Aaron told all, and Moses performed all the signs given to him (vv. 2–9).

4:31 *So the people believed . . . then they bowed . . . and worshiped.* Just as God predicted, they responded in belief at the signs and in worship at the explanation of God's awareness of their misery.

D. The Confrontation with Pharaoh (5:1–11:10)

5:1 *Let My people go.* With this command from Israel's Lord, the confrontation between Pharaoh and Moses, between Pharaoh and God, began. It was a command Pharaoh would hear often in the days leading up to the Exodus.

5:2 *Who is the* LORD? In all likelihood, Pharaoh knew of Israel's God, but his interrogative retort insolently and arrogantly rejected Him as having any power to make demands of Egypt's superior ruler.

5:3–5 As a follow-up to Pharaoh's rejection, the spokesmen rephrase more specifically their request, together with a warning of possible divine judgment upon Israel for their failure to obey their God. Pharaoh saw this simply as a ruse to reduce the hours put in by his slave work force.

5:6–9 Showing his authority to give orders to Israel, Pharaoh immediately increased their workload and the severity of their bondage. By adding, "let them not regard false words," he showed his negative evaluation of God's words.

5:10 *taskmasters . . . and their officers.* When combined with "officers of the children of Israel" (v. 15), a three-level command structure is seen to have been in place—Egyptian section leaders, labor gang bosses, and Israelite foremen.

5:11 *straw.* Ancient documents from Egypt show that straw was used as a necessary component of bricks; it helped bind the clay together.

5:15–19 The formal labor complaint at the highest level was rejected with an emphatic evaluation of laziness on the part of Israel and a demand that production not slack.

5:20–21 The leadership team evidently knew of the lodging of the formal labor complaint and waited outside the royal hall in order to meet Israel's representatives. The meeting was definitely not a cordial one, with accusations raised both about the propriety of and the authority of the words and actions of Aaron and Moses toward Pharaoh.

5:22, 23 Moses returned to the LORD. Whether Moses and his brother remonstrated with the foremen about their strong and wrong evaluation remains a moot point. Rather, the focus is upon Moses, who remonstrated with the Lord in prayer. Evidently, Moses did not anticipate what effect Pharaoh's refusal and reaction would have upon his own people. Confrontation with Pharaoh, so far, had provoked both angry resentment of Israel by the Egyptians and of Moses by Israel. This was not the expected scenario!

6:1 Now you shall see. The Lord announced, in response to Moses' prayer, that finally the stage had been set for dealing with Pharaoh, who, in consequence, would only be able to urge Israel to leave.

6:2–5 God spoke to Moses and reminded him of His promises to the patriarchs. Once again, the focal point of the covenant was the land of Canaan deeded to their descendants by divine decree. The fact that this covenant was remembered meant obvious removal from Egypt.

6:2, 3 I am the LORD. The same self-existent, eternal God, Yahweh, had been there in the past with the patriarchs; no change had occurred in Him, either in His covenant or promises.

6:3 God Almighty . . . LORD . . . not known. Since the name Yahweh was spoken before the flood (Gen. 4:26) and later by the patriarchs (Gen. 9:26; 12:8; 22:14; 24:12), the special significance of Yahweh, unknown to them, but to be known by their descendants, must arise from what God would reveal of Himself in keeping the covenant and in redeeming Israel. *See notes on 3:13, 14.*

6:4 My covenant. The Abrahamic covenant (cf. Gen. 15:1–21; 17:1–8).

6:6–8 God instructed Moses to remind Israel of what they had previously been told: of God's remembering the covenant with Abraham, of His seeing their misery, of His delivering them from it, of His granting to them the land of Canaan, and, thus, taking them there. The repetitive "I will" (seven times) marked God's personal, direct involvement in Israel's affairs. Bracketed, as they were, by the declaration, "I am Yahweh," denoted certainty of fulfillment.

6:9 because of anguish of spirit. The bondage was so great that it blocked out even the stirring words Moses had just delivered to them (vv. 6–8).

6:12 uncircumcised lips? See notes on *4:10.*

6:14–27 The genealogical information formally identified Moses and Aaron as descendants of Levi, third son of Jacob by Leah. It also listed Aaron's son, Eleazar, and grandson, Phinehas, both of whom would become Israel's high priests. Mention of Levi in company with Reuben and Simeon recalled, perhaps, the unsavory background belonging to these three tribal fathers (Gen. 49:3–7) and emphasized that the choice of Moses and Aaron was not due to an exemplary lineage. This is intended to be a representative genealogy, not a complete one.

6:28–7:5 A summary of the mission to Egypt resumes the narrative after the genealogical aside on Moses and Aaron.

7:1 as God to Pharaoh. Moses, as the spokesman and ambassador for God, would speak with authority and power. ***your***

prophet. Aaron, as the divinely appointed spokesman for Moses, would forthrightly deliver the message given to him. Cf. Acts 14:11–13, where Barnabas and Paul were perceived in a similar situation.

7:4 *My armies and My people.* The first term in this double designation of Israel occurred originally in 6:26. The nation was described as organized like an army with its different divisions (its tribes) and also as God's military instrument upon the Canaanites. The second term with its possessive pronoun revealed the incongruity of Pharaoh's acting as though these people belonged to him.

7:5 *know that I am the* LORD. This purpose of the Exodus finds repeated mention in God's messages to Pharaoh and in God's descriptions of what He was doing (cf. 7:16; 8:10, 22; 9:14, 16, 29; 14:4, 18). Some of the Egyptians did come to understand the meaning of the name Yahweh, for they responded appropriately to the warning of the seventh plague (9:20), and others accompanied Israel into the wilderness (12:38). In the final analysis, Egypt would not be able to deny the direct involvement of the God of Israel in their rescue from bondage and the destruction of Egypt's army.

7:9 *Show a miracle.* Pharaoh's desire for accreditation would not go unanswered. That which God had done for Moses with the rod (4:2–9), and Moses had copied for Israel (4:30, 31), also became the sign of authority before Pharaoh (cf. 7:10).

7:11 *magicians.* Magic and sorcery played a major role in the pantheistic religion of Egypt. Its ancient documents record the activities of the magicians, one of the most prominent being the charming of serpents. These men were also styled "wise men" and "sorcerers," i.e., the learned men of the day and the religious as well (the word for sorcery being derived from a word

meaning "to offer prayers"). Two of these men were named Jannes and Jambres (cf. 2 Tim. 3:8). Any perceived supernatural power came from Satan (cf. 2 Cor. 11:13–15). *enchantments.* By means of their "secret arts" or "witchcraft," the wise men, sorcerers, and magicians demonstrated their abilities to perform a similar feat. Whether by optical illusion, sleight of hand, or learned physical manipulation of a snake, all sufficiently skillful enough to totally fool Pharaoh and his servants, or by evil power, the evaluation given in the inspired record is simply "they also did in like manner." However, the turning of rods into snakes, and later turning water into blood (7:22) and calling forth frogs (8:7), were not the same as trying to create lice from inanimate dust (8:18–19). At that point, the magicians had no option but to confess their failure.

7:12 *Aaron's rod swallowed up their rods.* The loss of the magicians' rods in this fashion gave evidence of the superiority of God's power when Aaron's rod gulped theirs down.

7:14–10:29 The obvious miraculous nature of the ten plagues cannot be explained by identifying them with natural occurrences to which Moses then applied a theological interpretation. The specific prediction of, as well as the intensity of, each plague moved it beyond being normal, natural phenomena. The notification of the specific discriminatory nature of some of the plagues, distinguishing between Hebrew and Egyptian (cf. 8:23; 9:4, 6; 10:23), or Goshen and the rest of the land (cf. 8:22; 9:26), as they did, also marks the supernatural nature of these events.

7:15 *in the morning.* Apparently, Pharaoh habitually went to the river for washing or, more likely, for the performance of some religious rite. Three times Moses would meet him at this early morning rendezvous to warn of plagues, i.e., the first, fourth, and seventh (8:20; 9:13). *by the river's bank.* The first confrontation of the plague cycle took place on the banks of the Nile River, the sacred waterway of the land, whose annual ebb and flow contributed strategically and vitally to the agricultural richness of Egypt. Hymns of thanksgiving were often sung for the blessings brought by the Nile, the country's greatest, single economic resource.

7:17 *blood.* The Hebrew word does not denote red coloring such as might be seen when red clay is washed downstream, but denotes actual substance, i.e., blood.

7:19, 20 *the waters . . . all the waters.* The use of different words, "waters, streams, rivers, ponds, and pools," indicates graphically the extent of the plague. Even buckets of wood and stone filled with water and kept inside the homes could not escape the curse of their contents being turned into blood.

7:22 *the magicians . . . did so with their enchantments.* How ludicrous and revealing that the magicians resorted to copycat methodology instead of reversing the plague. What they did, bringing just more blood, did serve, however, to bolster Pharaoh's stubbornness.

7:24 *dug all around the river.* The only recourse was to tap into the natural water table, the subterranean water supply. Evidently, this was the water which was available to the magicians to use (v. 22).

7:25 *seven days.* An interval of time occurred before another warning was delivered, indicating that the plagues did not occur rapidly in uninterrupted succession.

8:1 *Go to Pharaoh.* The warning for the second plague was delivered to Pharaoh, presumably at his palace. Warnings for the fifth (9:1) and eighth (10:1) plagues also occurred at the palace.

8:2 *smite.* The verb God used also meant "to plague." Various terms (lit. from the Hebrew), namely *plagues* (9:14), *strike* (12:13), and *pestilence* (9:3, 15), were employed to impress them with the severity of what was happening in Egypt. *frogs.* That Egyptians favored frogs was seen in the wearing of amulets in the shape of a frog and in the prohibition against intentionally killing frogs, who were considered sacred animals. The croaking of frogs from the river and pools

The Ten Plagues on Egypt

The Plague	Egyptian Deity	The Effect
1. Blood (7:20)	Hapi	Pharaoh hardened
2. Frogs (8:6)	Heqt	Pharaoh begs relief, promises freedom (8:8), but is hardened (8:15)
3. Lice	Hathor, Nut	Pharaoh hardened (8:19)
4. Flies (8:24)	Shu, Isis	Pharaoh bargains (8:28), but is hardened (8:32)
5. Livestock diseased (9:6)	Apis	Pharaoh hardened (9:7)
6. Boils (9:10)	Shekhmet	Pharaoh hardened (9:12)
7. Hail (9:23)	Geb	Pharaoh begs relief (9:27), promises freedom (9:28), but is hardened (9:35)
8. Locusts (10:13)	Serapis	Pharaoh bargains (10:11), begs relief (10:17), but is hardened (10:20)
9. Darkness (10:22)	Ra	Pharaoh bargains (10:24), but is hardened (10:27)
10. Death of firstborn (10:29)		Pharaoh and Egyptians beg Israel to leave Egypt (12:31–33)

of water signaled to farmers that the gods who controlled the Nile's flooding and receding had once again made the land fertile. The god Hapi was venerated on this occasion because he had caused alluvial deposits to come downstream. Further, the frog was the representation, the image, of the goddess Heqt, the wife of the god Khum, and the symbol of resurrection and fertility. The presence of frogs in such abundance, all over everywhere outside and inside the houses (vv. 3, 13), however, brought only frustration, dismay, and much discomfort, rather than the normal signal that the fields were ready for cultivating and harvesting.

8:7 the magicians did so. Once again, instead of reversing the plague, the magicians in demonstrating the power of their secret arts only appeared to increase the frog population to the added discomfort of the people. Their power was not sufficient enough to do more than play "copycat." That the magicians could duplicate but not eradicate the problem was, however, sufficient to solidify royal stubbornness.

8:8 Entreat the LORD. Using the Lord's name and begging for relief through His intervention was more a point in negotiation and not a personal or official recognition of Israel's Lord.

8:9 remain in the river only. A specific detail like this in Moses' question indicates that the Nile and the waters had returned to normal and, again, continued to support life.

8:10 Tomorrow. Having been granted the privilege to set the time when the Lord would answer Moses' prayer for relief, Pharaoh requested a cessation only on the next day. Presumably, he hoped something else would happen before then so that he would not have to acknowledge the Lord's power in halting the plague, nor be obligated to Moses and his God. But God answered the prayer of Moses, and Pharaoh remained obstinate (v. 15).

8:16 Without prior warning, the third plague descended on the country. The same absence of warning occurred for the sixth (9:8, 9) and the ninth (10:21) plagues. A threefold pattern surfaces: prior warning at the river, then at the palace, and then no warning given. **lice.** The Hebrew term is preferably taken to designate tiny, stinging gnats barely visible to the naked eye. Those priests, who fastidiously kept themselves religiously pure by frequent washing and by shaving off body hair, were afflicted and rendered impure in their duties.

8:17 All the dust of the land ... throughout all the land. The record emphasizes by its repetition of "all" and "land" the extent and severity of this pestilence.

8:19 This is the finger of God. The failure of the magicians to duplicate this plague elicited from them this amazing evaluation, not only among themselves, but publicly before Pharaoh, who nevertheless remained recalcitrant, unwilling to acknowledge the power of God (cf. Luke 11:20).

8:21 swarms. The LXX translates "swarms" as "dog-fly," a bloodsucking insect. The ichneumon fly, which deposited its eggs on other living things so the larvae could feast upon it, was considered the manifestation of the god Uatchit. "The land was corrupted because of the swarms" (v. 24) is hardly an evaluation propitious for any insect god! Whatever the specific type of fly might have been, the effect of the plague was intense and distressful.

8:22 set apart the land of Goshen. For the first time in connection with the plagues, God specifically noted the discrimination to be made—Israel would be untouched. The term *sign* (v. 23) describes the distinction which was being drawn and which was also specifically noted for the fifth, seventh, ninth, and tenth plagues. Coupled with the repeated emphasis on "My people" in God's pronouncements, the specific distinguishing between Israel in Goshen and Egypt itself highlighted both God's personal and powerful oversight of His people.

8:23 Tomorrow. The plague warning on this occasion stated exactly when it would strike, giving Pharaoh and his people opportunity to repent or yield. *Tomorrow* was also the due time for the fifth, seventh, and eighth plagues (9:5, 18; 10:4), and "about midnight" was the stated time for the ninth plague to begin (11:4). *See note on 11:4.*

8:26 sacrificing the abomination of the Egyptians. An attempt at appeasement by compromise on the part of Pharaoh—"Go, sacrifice . . . in the land"—was countered by Moses' pointing out that Israel's sacrifices would not be totally acceptable to the Egyptians, who might even react violently—"will they not stone us?" This evaluation Pharaoh immediately understood. Either their strong dislike of shepherds and sheep (Gen. 46:34) or Israel's sacrificial animals being sacred ones in their religion brought about Egyptian aversion to Israel's sacrifices.

8:27–29 We will go . . . I will let you go. The first declaration showed the decision to travel no less than three days beyond Egyptian borders was a non-negotiable item. The second declaration showed Pharaoh trying to keep that decision to travel and sacrifice strictly under his authority and not as a response to the Lord's request for His people.

8:28 Intercede for me. This was an abbreviated request, applying not only to himself but also for the removal of the plague as previously asked in connection with the second plague (8:8).

8:29 let Pharaoh not deal deceitfully. Moses' closing exhortation underscored the deceptive nature of the king's words.

8:31 Not one remained. This declaration

of the total divine removal of the flies—a demonstration of God's answering Moses' entreaty—did not persuade Pharaoh at all. Once again, removed from the humiliating effects of a plague, his stubborn resistance resurfaced (v. 32).

9:3 in the field. Apparently stabled livestock did not succumb to the pestilence. Although incredibly severe, some animals were still alive afterwards for Egypt to continue without total loss to an economy which depended on domesticated animals. A few months later, when the seventh plague struck, there were still some cattle, which, if left in the field, would have died (9:19). **horses . . . camels.** Horses, which were common in the period, had been brought into military service by the Hyksos. See Introduction: Author and Date. Camels were a domesticated animal by this time in the fifteenth century B.C. **a very severe pestilence.** In listing the different kinds of livestock, the severe nature of the plague was underscored as one which would for the first time target personal property. Egyptian literature and paintings substantiate how valuable livestock was to them. Whatever the exact nature of this pestilence—anthrax, murrain, or other livestock disease—it was clearly contagious and fatal. Religious implications were obvious: Egypt prized the bull as a sacred animal with special attention and worship being given to the Apis bull, the sacred animal of the god Ptah. Heliopolis venerated the bull, Mnevis. Further, the goddess Hathor, represented by a cow, or a cow-woman image, was worshiped in several cities.

9:4 nothing shall die. The additional declaration on the safety of Israel's livestock graphically underscored the miraculous nature of what God was about to do and the distinction being made between Israel and Egypt. It emphasized Israel's protection and to whom she really belonged.

9:5 *appointed a set time.* The prophetic and miraculous nature of this plague is highlighted by stating "tomorrow" and, by noting "on the next day," it happened as predicted (v. 6).

9:6 *of the livestock . . . of Israel, not one died.* The distinction being made received added emphasis with this double declaration that Israelites suffered absolutely no loss in livestock.

9:7 *Then Pharaoh sent.* This time the king had to check on the veracity of the protection afforded Israel. Whatever his own rationalizations or theories about it might have been, they only confirmed him in his resistance and disobedience, despite finding out that it was true, "indeed, not even one . . . was dead."

9:9 *boils that break out in sores on man and beast.* For the first time, human health was targeted.

9:10 *ashes from the furnace.* Aaron and Moses took two handfuls of ash, not just from any furnace, but from a lime kiln or brick-making furnace. That which participated so largely in their oppressive labor became the source of a health hazard for the oppressors!

9:11 *magicians could not stand.* A side comment indicates that these men (who in Egyptian eyes were men of power) had been so sorely afflicted that they could not stand, either physically or vocationally, before God's spokesmen. Although they are not mentioned after the third plague, they apparently had continued to serve before Pharaoh and were undoubtedly there when plagues four and five were announced. Their powerlessness had not been sufficient as yet for Pharaoh to dispense with their services—an outward symbol, perhaps, of Pharaoh's unwillingness to acknowledge the total sovereignty of the God of Israel.

9:12 *the* LORD *hardened.* For the first time, apart from the words to Moses before the plagues began (cf. Ex. 4:21; 7:3), the statement is made that God hardened Pharaoh's heart. In the other instances, the record observes that Pharaoh hardened his own heart. Each instance records "as the Lord commanded," so what happened did so from two closely related perspectives: (1) God was carrying out His purpose through Pharaoh, and (2) Pharaoh was personally responsible for his actions as the command of verse 13 implies. *See note on 4:21.*

9:14 *My plagues.* God's use of the possessive pronoun specified what should have become abundantly clear to Pharaoh by then, namely, that these were God's own workings. *to your very heart.* This was apparently a colloquial expression denoting someone's being made to feel the full force of an act, to feel it strike home!

9:14–19 After sounding again the customary demand to release God's people for worship (v. 13), and after delivering a warning of how His plagues would really have an impact (v. 14), God provided more information and issued certain preliminary instructions:

1. A threefold purpose pertained to the plagues, namely, the Egyptians would recognize that Yahweh was incomparable, that His power would be demonstrated through them, and that His name, character, attributes, and power, would be known everywhere. Egypt could not keep other nations from knowing about her humiliation by the plagues of Israel's Lord.

2. A declaration that whatever royal authority Pharaoh had, it had been because of God's sovereign and providential control of world affairs, which included putting Pharaoh on his throne. This was a telling reminder that He was what He declared Himself to be, the one and only true and immanent Lord.

3. A reminder of the worst scenario for

Egypt if Yahweh had chosen, in lieu of the preceding plagues, to strike the people first—they would have perished. In other words, God had been gracious and longsuffering in the progression of the plagues.

4. A declaration that the weather about to be unleashed by the incomparable God was unlike anything previously recorded in Egypt's entire history, or "since its founding" or "since it became a nation."

5. An instruction as to how the Egyptians could avoid severe storm damage and loss of property. Grace again was afforded them.

9:16 See Romans 9:17 where Paul indicates God's sovereignty over Pharaoh.

9:20, 21 *who feared . . . who did not regard.* Some heard the instruction and obeyed; others, like their national leader, did not "regard the word of the LORD"—a graphic expression of refusal to heed divine instruction.

9:23, 24 *fire darted . . . fire mingled.* The violent, electrical thunderstorm brought with it unusual lightning, or "fireballs," which zigzagged (lit. "fire taking hold of itself") to and fro on the ground with the hail.

9:26 *Only in the land of Goshen.* The discriminatory nature of this plague was unannounced beforehand, but the national distinction previously declared and observed again prevailed. Although unstated, those who were in the strife-torn regions and who obeyed instructions obviously found their livestock safe and sound.

9:27 *I have sinned this time.* Any improvement in Pharaoh's theological understanding, notwithstanding the following confession of a righteous Lord and of a wicked people, was rendered suspect by the face-saving caveat "this time." Lacking repentance, it brushed aside all previous reaction and disobedience as having no significance.

9:28 *it is enough.* Moses' reply (v. 30)

indicated that such an evaluation was not one of repentance or one of fearing the Lord and acknowledging His power.

9:31, 32 *flax and the barley were struck . . . the wheat and the spelt were not struck.* A very brief bulletin on which crops were damaged and which were not placed this plague in February. All four crops mentioned were important economic resources. Wheat would be harvested only a month later than flax and barley together with the aftercrop "spelt" or "rye." God's timing of the disaster to two crops left room for Pharaoh to repent before the other crops might be destroyed.

9:34 *sinned yet more.* Pharaoh's culpability increased because when he saw God answer Moses' prayer—an entreaty he had requested (v. 28)—still all his admissions and promises were promptly swept aside. *he and his servants.* For the first time mention is made of the stubborn resistance of Pharaoh's entourage, all of whom had hardened their hearts. The striking contrast emerges in God's directions to Moses for the next plague: He had hardened their hearts for a purpose (10:1).

10:2 *that you may tell . . . that you may know.* The release from Egypt, accompanied by these great acts of God, was designed to become an important and indelible part in recounting the history of Israel to succeeding generations. It would tell just who their God was and what He had done. *the mighty things . . . done.* Lit. "to deal harshly with" or "to make sport of," and describing an action by which shame and disgrace is brought on its object.

10:3 *How long will you refuse?* The question asked of Pharaoh struck a contrast with the opening words of God to Moses (v. 1), "I have hardened his heart." What God did cannot erase personal responsibility from Pharaoh to hear, repent, and submit. Under the cumulative weight of seven plagues, the time had come to deliver a challenge to reconsider and obey. This is God's grace operating parallel with His own sovereign purposes.

10:4–6 The extent and intensity of the locust plague was such that it would be unique in Egyptian history—nothing like any locust problem during the previous two generations, nor like any locust swarm in the future (v. 14). Locust invasions were feared in Egypt, to the point that the farmers often prayed to the locust god to ensure the safety of their crops. The humiliation of their god was total, as was the damage: "There remained nothing green" (v. 15).

10:7 *How long shall this man?* The first "How long?" question in this encounter dealt with the desired response from Pharaoh (v. 3), whereas this second "How long?" question pointed out their impatience at Pharaoh's intransigence. Their advice—to give in—was the best choice. *Egypt is destroyed?* The advisers negatively evaluated the state of the country after seven plagues, and suggested that Pharaoh was refusing to acknowledge how desperate the situation really was, even before the agriculture was completely destroyed. Stubborn resistance did not necessarily rob them of all reason, and the better part of wisdom, this time, demanded acquiescence to Moses' request.

10:8 *Who are the ones that are going?* For the first time Pharaoh tried to negotiate a deal before the threatened plague struck. Adroitly, he suggested in his question that only representatives of Israel, perhaps only the men (v. 11), need go out to worship.

10:10 *The* LORD *had better be with you.* Sarcastic threats demonstrated the unyielding and unreasonable obstinacy of Pharaoh. Egyptian women did accompany their men in religious celebration but, in Israel's case, if the men went out then the women and chil-

dren were in effect hostages bidding them return.

10:11 *driven out.* For the first time, God's two spokesmen were angrily dismissed from the throne room.

10:12 *all that the hail has left.* This reminder of the previous plague, in which God had graciously restrained the extent of agricultural damage, appeared also in the warning of the plague given to Pharaoh and his advisers (v. 5) and in the description of the damage done by the locusts (v. 15).

10:13 *an east wind.* God used natural means, most probably the spring hot wind, or "sirocco," to bring the locusts into the country from the Arabian peninsula.

10:16 *in haste.* A recognition on the part of Pharaoh that his country now faced a crisis brought forth a hurried confession to Aaron and Moses, which again was merely an expedient course of action.

10:17 *forgive my sin.* Again, this was an attempt by Pharaoh to sound earnest in his response, and again he appealed for Mo-ses to pray for removal of the plague. He referred to it this time as "this death," or "deadly plague," phrases which highlighted the severity of Egypt's condition.

10:19 *west wind.* In answer to prayer, wind direction reversed as the Lord caused the locusts to be blown eastward out of the country. The completeness of their removal received emphasis. That none remained in the country was apparently something unusual, perhaps somewhat distinct from previously known locust invasions. The absence of locusts was a challenging reminder of the power of the Lord, who had brought it all to pass.

10:21, 22 *darkness . . . felt . . . thick darkness.* Such a description of the ninth plague, which occurred without warning, pointed to the most unusual nature of the three-day darkness that now prevented the people from leaving their homes. That Israel had light in their dwellings and went about their normal activity emphasizes the supernatural nature of this plague. It takes attention away from trying to explain the darkness solely in terms of the Khamsin, the swirling sandstorms of the day. The LXX did, however, string together three Greek words, two for darkness and one for storm, to portray the nuance of the Hebrew. In so doing, it may unwittingly have given some credence to a severe sandstorm. Theologically, such thick darkness directly challenged the faithfulness of the sun god, Ra, to provide warmth and sunshine from day to day, and also prevented any daily worship rituals from taking place.

10:24 "Go . . . Let your little ones also go with you." Pharaoh's deceitful and manipulative negotiating skills rose to the occasion: Let the people go but keep back their livestock as the hostage forcing their return. He had not yet understood that partial obedience to the Lord's directions was unacceptable.

10:25 See 3:18 for remarks on the request to leave for worship, suggesting something less than permanent departure.

10:28 "Get away from me! ... you shall die!" Pharaoh's obstinacy and resistance reached a new height when he summarily dismissed Moses and Aaron and this time added a death threat.

10:29 never see your face again. Moses concurred, but from another perspective than that of Pharaoh. All negotiations and requests ceased immediately. Moses would be summoned to see Pharaoh again after the tenth plague (12:31), but that would be to hear him finally concede defeat.

11:1–3 And the LORD said. This should be read as "the LORD had said." In a parenthetical paragraph, the narrative recorded that which God had already said to Moses during the three days of darkness, priming him for

Pharaoh's summons, and priming Israel to receive Egyptian jewelry and other goods. An aside explained Egyptian generosity as occasioned by divine intervention (cf. 12:35, 36). This also included a healthy respect by Egypt's leaders and people for Israel's leader.

11:4–8 Then Moses said. Moses' response to Pharaoh's threat continued with his giving warning of the final plague and leaving with great indignation. The death threat delivered by Pharaoh evoked one from God. The "get out!" from Pharaoh to Israel's and God's spokesmen would be met by the "get out" from the Egyptians to Israel.

11:4 About midnight. The day was not specified, as in previous plagues by "tomorrow." It took place either the same day of the final confrontation with Pharaoh or a few days later. If the instructions for the Passover (12:1–20) were not given during the days of darkness, then four days minimum would be required to set the stage for that special feast day, i.e., from the tenth to the fourteenth day (12:3, 6). *See note on 8:23.* **I will go out.** God was, of course, involved in all previous plagues through whatever means He chose to use, but this time, to warrant personal attention, God stated that He Himself (emphatic personal pronoun used) would march throughout the land. Note the repeated "I will" statements in the Passover instructions (12:12, 13).

11:5 the firstborn. The firstborn held a particularly important position in the family and society, not only inheriting a double portion of the father's estate, but also representing special qualities of life and strength (cf. Gen. 49:3). In Egypt, the firstborn would ascend to the throne and continue the dynasty. Whatever significance might have been attached religiously, politically, dynastically, and socially, it was all stripped away by the extent and intensity of the plague— namely the execution of all the firstborn of all classes of the population, including their animals.

11:6 So drastic was this plague that its uniqueness in Egypt's history, already past and yet to come, was noted in the warning.

11:7 In contrast to the turmoil and grief experienced in Egyptian territory, all remained tranquil in Israelite territory—so much so that not even a dog barked. That the Lord had made and was making a sharp distinction between the two peoples was a fact to which none could be blind.

E. The Preparation for Departure (12:1–36)

12:1 *the* LORD *spoke.* Most probably, the instructions on the Passover (vv. 1–20) were also given during the three days of darkness in order to fully prepare Israel for the grand finale, their Exodus from Egypt. *in the land.* Later, while Israel was in the wilderness, Moses wrote (23:14–17; Deut. 16:1–8) and indicated that the detailed instructions for this very special feast day in Israel's religious calendar were not like those of the other special days, all which were given after the nation had already left Egypt. This one, the Passover, was inextricably linked to what took place in the Exodus, and that connection was never to be forgotten. It became indelibly entrenched in Israel's tradition and has always marked the day of redemption from Egypt.

12:2 *This month.* The month of Abib (March/April), by divine decree, became the beginning of the religious calendar, marking the start of Israel's life as a nation. Later in Israel's history, after the Babylonian captivity, Abib would become Nisan (cf. Neh. 2:1; Esth. 3:7).

12:3–14 The detailed instructions for the Passover included what animal to select, when to kill it, what to do with its blood, how to cook it, what to do with leftovers, how to dress for the meal, the reason why it was being celebrated "in haste," and what the shed blood signified.

12:5 *Your lamb shall be without blemish.* A kid goat was an alternative choice. Any flaw would render it unfit to represent a pure, wholesome sacrifice given to Yahweh.

12:6 *at twilight.* Lit. "between the two evenings." Since the new day was reckoned from sunset, the sacrificing of the lamb or kid was done before sunset while it was still day fourteen of the first month. *Twilight* has been taken to signify either that time between sunset and the onset of darkness, or from the decline of the sun until sunset. Later Moses would prescribe the time for the sacrifice as "at twilight, at the going down of the sun" (Deut. 16:6). According to Josephus, it was customary in his day to slaughter the lamb at about 3:00 P.M. This was the time of day that Christ, the Christian's Passover lamb (1 Cor. 5:7), died (Luke 23:44–46).

12:9 *Do not eat it raw.* A prohibition, with health implications, also distinguished them from pagan peoples who often ate raw flesh in their sacred festivals.

12:12 *against all the gods.* The tenth plague was a judgment against all Egyptian deities. The loss of the firstborn of men and beasts had far-reaching theological implications, namely, the impotence of the pagan deities, many of whom were represented by animals, to protect their devotees from such nationwide tragedies. The great cry of grief (11:6; 12:30) may also have bemoaned the incapability of the nation's gods.

12:14 *a memorial.* The details of how this Passover Day was to be memorialized in future years were laid down (vv. 14–20), and then repeated in the instructions to the elders (vv. 21–27). Prescribing the eating of unleavened bread for seven days, demanding a thorough house-cleaning from leaven

(v. 15), issuing a stern warning of banishment for eating leaven (v. 15), and bracketing the seven days with special holy days (v. 16) served to proclaim the importance of the nation's remembering this event.

12:16 prepared by you. See note on verse 46.

12:19 a stranger. Provision was made right at the beginning for non-Israelites to be included in the nation's religious festivals. Failure to comply with the regulations on leaven would result in banishment for the alien as well.

12:22 bunch of hyssop. Certain identification is impossible, but this could be the jar-joram plant. **lintel ... the two doorposts.** The top and two sides of the doorway.

12:23 the destroyer. This is most likely the Angel of the Lord (cf. 2 Sam. 24:16; Is. 37:36). See note on 3:2.

12:25 The promise of entering the land again received emphasis. Israel was not to think of the Exodus as merely a departure from Egypt, but rather as a departure from one land in order to enter another land, which would be their own, in strict accordance with the specifics of the Abrahamic covenant for his descendants through Isaac and Jacob (cf. Gen. 17:7, 8).

12:26, 27 In the annual commemoration of the Passover, parents were obligated to teach their children its meaning. It became customary for the youngest child of a Jewish family to elicit the father's formal explanation of what happened in connection with the original observance of the meal in Egypt.

12:31 Rise, go out ... serve the LORD. Finally, Pharaoh's response to the repeated "Let My people go!" became "Leave my people!" with no attempt at further negotiation, but total acquiescence. His subjects, fearing more deaths, concurred and hastened Israel's departure (v. 33), driving them out with no time wasted (v. 39).

12:32 bless me also. Undoubtedly, this final request from Pharaoh, whose heart was certainly not repentant (14:8), temporarily conceded defeat and acknowledged Moses and his God as the victors and as those who had the power and resources to bless him.

12:36 they plundered the Egyptians. Cf. 3:20, 21; Genesis 15:14. This was not done with deceit, but rather a straightforward request (cf. 11:2, 3).

II. Israel Enroute to Sinai (12:37–18:27)

12:37–18:27 This section recounts the march of the Israelites from Egypt to Mt. Sinai.

A. Exiting Egypt and Panicking (12:37–14:14)

12:37 Rameses to Succoth. One of the cities Israel built (1:11) headed up the itinerary for the journey through the wilderness to Canaan. Succoth is first mentioned in Genesis 33:17 as an encampment designated by the word *Succoth*, which means "booth." Although there is later a town by that name east of the Jordan River (cf. Judg. 8:5–16), this is rather a place near Egypt (cf. 13:20; Num. 33:5, 6). **six hundred thousand men on foot.** A conservative estimate based on the number of men, probably the fighting men twenty years of age and above, would give a population of two million. Israel's population had exploded from the seventy who entered with Jacob in 1875 B.C. to the two million who left with Moses in 1445 B.C. See note on 1:7.

12:38 A mixed multitude. Other Semitic peoples, other races, and perhaps some native Egyptians accompanied the departing nation. They preferred to be identified with the victorious nation and Jehovah God. Later, some of these became the troublemakers with whom Moses had to deal (Num. 11:4).

12:40, 41 *four hundred and thirty years.* Abraham had originally been told that his descendants would be aliens mistreated in a foreign land for 400 years, using a figure rounded to hundreds (see Gen. 15:13).

12:43–51 Additional regulations given for the holding of the Passover contained prohibitions on any uncircumcised foreigner, stranger, or hired servant being a valid participant. To partake of this meal, non-Israelites had to be "as a native of the land" (v. 48). *See note on Jeremiah 4:4.*

12:46 *break . . . bones.* Christ, the Christian's Passover lamb (1 Cor. 5:7), had no bones broken (John 19:36).

12:50 *so they did.* On two occasions (see also v. 28) Moses emphasized the complete obedience of the nation in response to the Lord's commands to them: a contrast to the disobedience they would demonstrate in the near future.

12:51 *on that very same day.* What would be for the nation in their new land a special Sabbath day, was for them at that time the day on which their journey began.

13:2–10 Further explanation tied their departure to the divine promise of entrance and residence in a new land where commemoration of the Exodus would occur through annual observance of this seven-day feast. Again the pedagogical opportunity afforded was not to be overlooked (vv. 8, 16).

13:2 *Consecrate to Me all the firstborn.* Since the firstborn of Israel, of both man and animal, were untouched by the tenth plague, it was fitting that they be set aside as special to God. Note the closing emphasis: "it is Mine." Further instruction followed on the law relating to the firstborn males once they were in their assigned territory (vv. 11–16). This divine demand was closely linked to the day of departure (12:51, "on that very same day") and the Feast of Unleavened Bread (v. 3, "this day" and v. 4, "on this day . . . in the month of Abib"). See Luke 2:7, where Christ was referred to as Mary's firstborn.

13:8 *for me when I.* A personalized application of God's working belonged to the first generation who experienced the Exodus. Later generations could only say "for us, when we" in the sense of "our nation," but without loss to the significance of how God

Chronology of the Exodus

Date	Event	Reference
Fifteenth day, first month, first year	Exodus	Exodus 12
Fifteenth day, second month, first year	Arrival in Winderness of Sin	Exodus 16:1
Third month, first year	Arrival in Wilderness of Sinai	Exodus 19:1
First day, first month, second year	Erection of Tabernacle	Exodus 40:1, 17
	Dedication of Altar	Numbers 7:1
	Consecration of Levites	Numbers 8:1–26
Fourteenth day, first month, second year	Passover	Numbers 9:5
First day, second month, second year	Census	Numbers 1:1, 18
Fourteenth day, second month, second year	Supplemental Passover	Numbers 9:11
Twentieth day, second month, second year	Departure from Sinai	Numbers 10:11
First month, fortieth year	In Winderness of Zin	Numbers 20:1, 22–29; 33:38
First day, fifth month, fortieth year	Death of Aaron	Numbers 20:22–29; 33:38
First day, eleventh month, fortieth year	Moses' Address	Deuteronomy 1:3

The MacArthur Study Bible, by John MacArthur (Nashville: Word Publishing, 1997) 111. © 1993 by Thomas Nelson, Inc.

Key Word

Passover: 12:11, 21, 27, 43, 48; 34:25—lit. "to pass" or "to leap over." The Passover celebration commemorated the day God spared the firstborn children of the Israelites from the death plague brought on Egypt. The Lord "passed over" those who sprinkled the blood from the Passover lamb on their doorposts (Ex. 12). Passover, as specified in the Law of Moses, reminds the Israelites of God's great mercy on them (see Lev. 23:5–8; Num. 28:16–25; Deut. 16:1–8). In the New Testament, Jesus also celebrated the Passover feast with His disciples (Matt. 26:2, 18). Christ became the ultimate Passover Lamb when He sacrificed Himself for sins (John 1:29; 1 Cor. 5:7; 1 Pet. 1:19).

---

had brought about such an important day in the nation's history. There was an intended personalized application of the law of the firstborn as well (v. 15, "I sacrifice . . . my sons I redeem").

13:9 Later generations would translate this figurative and proverbial expression (cf. Prov. 3:3; 6:21) into the physical reality of phylacteries—the leather prayer boxes which were strapped on the left arm and on the forehead. Four strips of parchment inscribed with certain words (13:1–16; Deut. 6:4–9; 11:13–21) were placed inside these boxes. The imagery of the proverbial mode of speech signified that their conduct was to be that of someone who could verbally recall what God's Law demanded of them. Yahweh, who had rescued them, had also provided the standards of life for them.

13:12, 15 See Luke 2:23.

13:17 by way of the land of the Philistines. Travelers going east and northeast out of Egypt had two good options: "the way of the sea," or "the way of Shur." The first route, the most direct and shortest, was dotted with Egyptian fortresses which monitored arrivals and departures to and from Egypt. A little further north, Philistine territory also presented a military threat. The lack of battle readiness on Israel's part deleted the first option, and God chose the second option (v. 18; 15:22). In any case, God had told Moses to lead the people to Horeb or Sinai, the mountain of God (3:1), and not to take them immediately into Canaan (3:12).

13:18 the Red Sea. An alternative designation, quite in accord with the Hebrew term, would be "Sea of Reeds," or perhaps "Sea of papyrus marshes." The difficulty of precisely locating other names associated with the crossing of the Red Sea (see 14:2) has occasioned much debate on the location of the crossing. Four views have generally emerged: It was located (1) in the northeastern region of the delta—but this would have been in effect "the way of the sea" and would not have been three days' journey from Marah (15:22, 23); (2) in the northern end of the Gulf of Suez—but this rules out entry into the wilderness of Shur (15:22); (3) in the vicinity of Lake Timsah or the southern extension of present day Lake Menzaleh—but probably more than three days from Marah; and (4) in the Bitter Lakes region, satisfying, in terms of geography and time, all objections to the other options.

13:19 the bones of Joseph. In fulfillment of their solemnly sworn duty and responsibility (Gen. 50:24–26), the Israelites took Joseph's coffin with them. Some 360 years earlier he had foreseen the day when God would bring about the Exodus, and his instructions about his bones being carried to the Promised Land indicated just how certain he was of Israel's departure for Canaan (cf. Gen. 50:24–26; Heb. 11:22). After the years of wilderness wanderings, Joseph's remains reached their final resting place in Shechem (Josh. 24:32).

13:20 *Etham at the edge of the wilderness.* The Hebrew name of this place may be a transliteration of the Egyptian *Khetem,* meaning "fortress." A line of fortresses (*see note on v. 17*) stretched from the Mediterranean Sea to the Gulf of Suez. Even if the site remains unknown so that pinpointing it is not possible, it was surely a place bordering on the desert area to the east of Egypt.

13:21 *a pillar of cloud . . . a pillar of fire.* This was the means by which God led the people. It was a single column, being cloud by day and fire by night (cf. 14:24), and was associated with the Angel of God (14:19; 23:20–23) or the Angel of God's presence (Is. 63:8, 9). *See note on 3:2.* It was the pillar from which the Lord also spoke to Moses (33:9–11).

14:3, 4 *Pharaoh will say . . . I will harden.* Pharaoh was kept abreast of Israelite progress and, when he heard of the change of direction, he assumed they were lost in unfamiliar territory and were trapped, closed in by desert, sea, and marsh. God intervened again and the stage was set for the final confrontation and the most spectacular display of divine power.

14:5 *Why have we done this?* Hardened hearts lost all sensitivity to the recent tragedy and focused instead on the loss of the economic benefit Israel's enslavement had provided. Those who had urged the Israelites to leave quickly now had the urge to force them to return.

14:7 *six hundred choice chariots.* Chariots, introduced by the Hyksos (see Introduction: Author and Date), featured prominently in the army of Egypt, and these

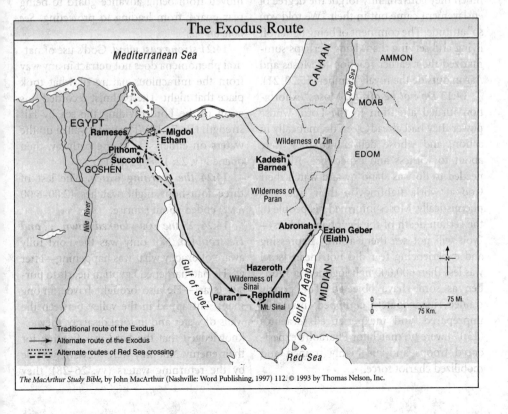

The Exodus Route

Mediterranean Sea

CANAAN

AMMON

Dead Sea

MOAB

EGYPT

Rameses
Migdol
Etham
Pithom
Succoth
GOSHEN

Nile River

Wilderness of Zin

Kadesh Barnea

EDOM

Wilderness of Paran

Abronah
Ezion Geber (Elath)

Hazeroth
Wilderness of Sinai
Paran
Rephidim
Mt. Sinai

Gulf of Suez

Gulf of Aqaba

MIDIAN

—N—

0   75 Mi.
0   75 Km.

→ Traditional route of the Exodus
⇢ Alternate route of the Exodus
▨▨▨ Alternate routes of Red Sea crossing

Red Sea

The MacArthur Study Bible, by John MacArthur (Nashville: Word Publishing, 1997) 112. © 1993 by Thomas Nelson, Inc.

"choice" ones belonged to an elite, specialized unit.

14:8 *Israel went out with boldness.* The confidence shown by Israel in their departure is in sharp contrast to the fear they exhibited when they became aware of the pursuing force (v. 10).

14:10 *cried out to the* LORD. The initial reaction of the people on seeing the Egyptians' approach was to turn to the Lord in anxious prayer. But prayer soon turned to complaints with Moses as the target of their dismay.

14:11 *no graves in Egypt.* In light of Egypt's excessive preoccupation with death and various funerary and mortuary rituals, the bitter irony of Israel's questions marked how easily they had forgotten both bondage and rescue.

14:12 *serve the Egyptians?* Just how much they conveniently forgot the degree of enslavement came out in their "We told you so" attitude. The comment of being better off living and serving than dying perhaps summarized their earlier reaction to Moses and Aaron outside the royal chambers (5:20, 21).

14:13 *Do not be afraid.* Moses' exhortation turned attention to the Lord, whose power they had already seen dramatically in action, and whose deliverance they were about to witness and experience. All they needed to do was stand by and watch their God at work, fighting on their side. Euphemistically, Moses informed his people of the certain death of the Egyptian soldiers— "you will not see them again!" Expressing and experiencing fear did not mean Israel was less than 600,000 fighting men in number, as some have objected. The poorly trained, inadequately equipped, militarily unprepared, and inexperienced Israelites (13:17) were no match for Pharaoh's experienced troops and his highly trained and mobilized chariot force.

14:14 *The* LORD *will fight.* This has been and will be true throughout the history of Israel (cf. 1 Sam. 17:47; 2 Chr. 14:10, 11; 20:15; Ps. 24:8; Zech. 14:3).

B. Crossing the Red Sea and Rejoicing (14:15–15:21)

14:15 *Why do you cry to Me? . . . go forward.* The Lord's promise of deliverance overruled all despair and sense of hopelessness.

14:16, 17 *lift up your rod.* For the grand, triumphant finale, the rod which had previously been used to bring in different plagues on the Egyptians now divided the water, opening up a valley through which Israel would walk and in which Egypt's army would drown.

14:19 *stood behind them.* The Angel of the Lord, and the pillar of cloud and fire, moved from being advance guard to being rear guard, from leading to protecting. *See note on 3:2.*

14:21 *strong east wind.* God's use of natural phenomena does not detract in any way from the miraculous nature of what took place that night. The psalmist recorded this event as the Lord dividing the sea by His strength (Ps. 74:13). The wind walled up the waters on either side of the pathway, then opened (v. 22; 15:8; Ps. 78:13).

14:24 *the morning watch.* The last of three four-hour night watches (2:00–6:00 A.M.) ended about sunrise.

14:24, 25 *the* LORD *looked down . . . and He troubled.* Not only was the Lord fully aware of exactly what was happening—after all, He had hardened Egyptian hearts to pursue Israel—He also brought havoc among them. Entrapped in the valley between the walls of water and in total disarray, they acknowledged that the Lord was fighting for their enemy. Not only were they swept aside by the returning waters (vv. 26–28), they were also hindered from driving their chariots forward by a sudden cloudburst (Ps. 77:17–19).

14:29–31 The stark difference between Israel and Egypt is again rehearsed: One nation is obstinate and defeated, their dead on the shores of the sea, having acknowledged the Lord victorious; the other nation is alive on the shores, having traversed the sea on dry ground, acknowledging the work of the Lord, reverencing and believing Him and His servant, Moses.

15:1–18 The structure of the song now sung by the nation contains four stanzas (vv. 1–5; 6–10; 11–13; and 14–17) and a one-line closing declaration (v. 18). Stanzas one and two end with "They sank," a refrain emphasizing the finality of the enemy army's defeat. Stanzas three and four end with reference to God's Holy Place (vv. 13, 17).

More is involved than in easily observing these break points of the song. The flow of thought and emphasis is also interesting. Stanza one briefly introduces God's powerful victory (vv. 1–5). Stanza two graphically repeats the victory and then inserts the arrogant and vengeful assertions of victory by the enemy to show how puny they were (vv. 6–10). Stanza three concisely summarizes the victory after asking an appropriate question (vv. 11–13). Further, since the victory was essential for Israel's rescue, the stanza also introduces them. Stanza four picks up and expands on Yahweh's leading His people to their divinely assigned home and the consequent fear by other nations as they hear of Israel's dramatic rescue from such a powerful enemy nation (vv. 14–17). The closing line sums it all up: The Lord reigns! A narrative interlude (vv. 19, 20) reminds one of the theme behind the song, and introduces the antiphonal response of Miriam and her band of women (v. 21).

15:1 *I will sing.* The Israelites began their song in the first person, effectively personalizing the community's song as individually relevant, each person heralding Yahweh's victory and declaring who and what He was to them (cf. the possessive pronouns in v. 2).

15:6 O Lord. The forthright declarations of the opening stanza (vv. 1–5) are most appropriately followed by this vocative form of address in the rest of the song (vv. 6, 11, 16, 17), since the focus of attention is on His working and intervention.

15:15 *Edom . . . Moab . . . Canaan.* Edom and Moab were on the eastern border of the Jordan; Canaan or Palestine was to the west.

15:16, 17 An expression of confidence in the promises that God had made to Abraham 700 years earlier (see Gen. 12; 15; 17).

15:18 *reign forever.* This speaks of the eternal, universal kingship of the Lord (cf. Ps. 145:13).

15:20 *the prophetess.* Miriam was the first woman to be given this honor. She claimed that the Lord had spoken through her (Num. 12:2). She apparently played an important role in these rescue events because the prophet Micah states that God delivered Israel by the hand of Moses, Aaron, and Miriam (Mic. 6:4). Other women to receive this rare honor were Deborah (Judg. 4:4); Huldah (2 Kin. 22:14); Isaiah's wife (Is. 8:3); Anna (Luke 2:36); and Philip's four daughters (Acts 21:9).

C. Traveling to Sinai and Grumbling (15:22–17:16)

15:24 *complained against Moses.* Israelite memory of victory displayed a remarkable brevity. The personalized declarations of their ode to the Lord sung three days earlier vanished into thin air. Their belief of Moses faded out of the picture (14:31). Their question about drinking water roughly brushed aside all recent affirmations of God's being worthy of praise because He had done wonders and was clearly taking them to their land.

15:25 *waters were made sweet.* Since there is no known tree which would naturally make unpalatable water drinkable, this must have been a miracle by which God demonstrated His willingness and ability to look after His people in a hostile environment. Marah is usually associated with modern day Ain Hawarah, where the waters still remain brackish and unpleasant. ***tested them.*** "To subject to difficulty in order to prove the quality of someone or something" is one way to explain the meaning of the Hebrew word used. Later, at Rephidim (17:1–7), at Sinai (20:20), and at Taberah (Num. 11:1–3; 13:26–33), God did just that to Israel. This is something which no one can do to God (Deut. 6:16). He needs no testing in character or deed, but man certainly does need proving.

15:26 *the* LORD *who heals.* Since this is what He is, Jehovah-Rapha, obedience to divine instruction and guidance will obviously bring healing, not the consequence of plagues like those visited upon Egypt. This specific promise is limited in context to Israel, most likely for the duration of the Exodus only.

15:27 *Elim.* The next stopping place, most probably in modern day Wadi Garandel, had an abundant water supply. God would and did lead them aright.

16:1 *Wilderness of Sin.* More details of the camp sites in the journey from Rameses to Succoth and beyond are found in Numbers 33:5–11. That itinerary also lists the next stop as having been Dophkah (Num. 33:12). Identifying it with modern Debbet er Ramleh locates it in the southwest of the Sinai peninsula on a direct line between Elim and Sinai. ***fifteenth day . . . second month.*** Thirty days after their departure from Rameses.

16:2 *the whole congregation . . . complained.* What characterized them as a whole was this attitude of negativism. Faced with the scarcity of resources in the wilderness, they hankered after the abundant resources they had experienced in Egypt. The country which had enslaved them looked good in comparison to the wilderness. Again, their complaining so soon after benefiting from the miracles done by the Lord on their behalf points only to their short-term memory and self-centeredness.

16:3 *died by the hand of the* LORD. Incredibly, Israel's complaint still acknowledged the intervention of the Lord in their affairs. Sarcastically, they voiced a preference for dying in Egypt. The hand of the Lord which they had glorified in song (15:6) only a month beforehand, they now pretended would have been better used to kill them in Egypt.

16:4 *I will rain bread.* God's gracious answer to their complaining was to promise an abundance of the bread they missed. God's directions on how to gather it would also test their obedience to Him (vv. 4, 5, 16, 26–28). *See note on 16:31.*

16:5 The same principle on a larger scale would feed the nation during and after the sabbatical year (cf. Lev. 25:18–22).

16:6 *you shall know.* Israel's short-term memory loss would be short-lived because that very day of complaint would witness not only God's provision for them, but also would powerfully remind them of who had brought them out of Egypt, namely, the Lord their God (cf. vv. 11, 12).

16:7 *the glory of the* LORD. In seeing the start of the provision of daily bread on the next day, Israel would also see the Lord's glory, an appropriate term to use because what He did showed His presence with them. *Glory* typically refers to God's manifested presence, which makes Him impressive and

The Cycle of Good and Bad in Scripture

A GREAT GOOD . . .	. . . FOLLOWED BY A GREAT EVIL
The world is created (Gen. 1–2).	Adam and Eve rebel and fall into sin, resulting in shame, fear, pain, toil and death (Gen. 3).
Noah is obedient in preparing for the flood and his survival in the ark (Gen. 6:13–22; 7:23).	Noah falls into a drunken stupor and nakedness which embarrasses his sons and leads to Canaan's curse (Gen. 9:20–25).
God delivers the people from the Egyptians by parting the Red Sea (Ex. 14:21–31).	The people complain about a lack of water (Ex. 15:22–25).
God gives the Ten Commandments to Moses (Ex. 20:1–17).	The people worship a golden calf (Ex. 32:1–6).
Aaron and his sons begin their spiritual leadership (Lev. 9:1–24).	Aaron's two oldest sons offer "profane fire" before the Lord and are killed as a result (Lev. 10:1–3).
David affirms God's covenant with him (2 Sam. 6).	David commits adultery with Bathsheba and arranges for the murder of her husband Uriah (2 Sam. 11:1–27).
Elijah triumphs over the prophets of Baal on Mount Carmel (1 Kin. 18:20–46).	Elijah flees in fear from the wrath of Jezebel and complains that God does not take care of him (1 Kin. 19:1–18).
Jonah successfully proclaims repentance to pagan Nineveh (Jon. 3).	Jonah expresses disappointment in Nineveh's repentance and complains about a lack of personal comfort (Jon. 4).
Peter affirms that Jesus is the Messiah of God (Matt. 16:16).	Peter is rebuked by Jesus for attempting to subvert God's purposes (Matt. 16:22–23).
Jesus enters Jerusalem to cheering crowds (Luke 19:28–40).	Jesus is crucified after angry mobs demand His death (Luke 23:13–49).
Barnabas makes a generous gift to the church of the proceeds from a land sale (Acts 4:36–37).	Ananias and Sapphira attempt to deceive Peter about a similar act of "charity" and are slain by God as a result (Acts 5:1–11).

Nelson's Complete Book of Bible Maps & Charts (Nashville: Thomas Nelson Publishers, 1996) 56. © 1993 by Thomas Nelson, Inc.

leads to worship. *your complaints.* Set in the context of instruction on how the Lord would act to provide for them, the fourfold repetition of this phrase (vv. 6–9) served to highlight God's gracious response in contrast to their ungracious grumbling against Him. For an effective poetic presentation of this contrast, see Psalm 78:17–25.

16:13 *quails.* The psalmist removed all doubt about whether these birds of the partridge family were not real birds but something else, for he called them "feathered fowl" and in the preceding line of the parallelism referred to the coming of the quails as God having "rained meat" on them (Ps. 78:27). Upon return to their former habitat, these migratory birds would often fall to the ground, exhausted from prolonged flight. In ancient Egyptian paintings, people were shown catching quails by throwing nets over the brush where they were nesting.

16:16, 32 *Omer.* Slightly more than two quarts.

16:18 See 2 Corinthians 8:15, where Paul applies this truth to Christian giving.

16:22–30 The provision of manna on six days only but none on the seventh was a weekly lesson on the nature of the Sabbath as a different day. It taught the people to keep the Sabbath properly, and acted as a challenge to obey God's commands.

16:31 *Manna.* The arrival of the quails in much quantity (v. 13) was totally overshadowed by the arrival of manna the next morning. Despite the different descriptions given for its form and taste (vv. 14, 31), the name chosen for it derived from the question they asked. "Manna" was an older form of their question, "What is it?" The psalmist referred to manna as the "bread of heaven" and "angels' food" which rained down after God had opened the windows of heaven (Ps. 78:23–25). Natural explanations for the manna, such as lichen growing on rocks or insect-excreted granules on tamarisk thickets, are totally inadequate to explain its presence in sufficient quantity on the ground under the dew every day except the Sabbath for the next forty years (v. 35) to satisfy every family's hunger. It was supernaturally produced and supernaturally sustained to last for the Sabbath.

16:32–36 *lay it up before the* Lord. Provision was made for memorializing the giving of the manna. When the tabernacle was finally constructed, the pot of manna was placed inside the ark. Succeeding generations would be reminded, when they came for worship, of the faithfulness of the Lord in caring for His people (cf. Heb. 9:4).

17:1 *Rephidim.* To be identified as modern day Wadi Refayid.

17:2 *the people contended.* This time the people, reacting to Moses' leading them to a waterless site, quarreled with him or laid a charge against him. So intense was their reaction that Moses thought he was about to be stoned (v. 4). Significantly, the nation had not come to Rephidim without divine guidance (v. 1), portrayed by the column of fire and cloud. The people, in the midst of their emotional response, simply could not see that right before their eyes was the evidence of God's leading.

17:4 *Moses cried out to the* Lord. The leader turned to God in prayer, whereas the people, instead of following his example, turned on their leader. Moses' petition was not an isolated incident. His life was characterized by prayer (cf. 15:25; 32:30–32; Num. 11:2, 11; 12:13; 14:13, 19) and by turning to God for solutions to problems and crises.

17:5, 6 *Go on before . . . I will stand before.* By these words in His instructions to Moses, the Lord reinforced both the position of Moses as leader and Himself as present to act. He answered the people's charge against Moses and their underlying challenge of His presence (v. 7). In fact, He intervened miraculously.

17:7 *Massah and Meribah.* Appropriate names, "Testing" and "Contending," were assigned to this place, a disappointing culmination to all they had experienced of God's miraculous care and guidance (cf. Ps. 95:7, 8; Heb. 3:7, 8).

17:8 *Amalek came and fought.* The Amalekites took their name from Amalek, the grandson of Esau, and dwelt as a nomadic people in the Negev. Israel first encountered their military at Rephidim in the wilderness (vv. 8–13; Deut. 25:17, 18). As a result, the Amalekites were doomed to annihilation by God (v. 14; Num. 24:20; Deut. 25:19), but it would not be immediate (v. 16). The Amalekites defeated disobedient Israel at Hormah (Num. 14:43–45). Saul failed to destroy them as God ordered (1 Sam. 15:2, 3, 9). David later fought and defeated the Amalekites (1 Sam. 30:1–20). In Hezekiah's day, the Amalekite remnant in the land was finally destroyed by Hezekiah (c. 716–687 B.C.). The final descendants of Agag (Esth. 3:1), the Amalekite king in Saul's day, were destroyed in Persia at the time of Esther and Mordecai (c. 473 B.C.; Esth. 2:5, 8–10).

17:9–13 Through the circumstances they experienced, Israel had learned how God provided food and water. They had to learn through warfare that God would also bring about defeat of hostile neighbors.

17:9 *Joshua.* The name of Moses' aide-de-camp, or personal minister (24:13; 33:11; Josh. 1:1), appears here for the first time in Exodus. His assignment to muster a task force was part of his being groomed for military leadership in Israel. Actually, at this stage his name was still Hoshea, which later changed to Joshua at Kadesh just before the reconnaissance mission in Canaan (Num. 13:16). At this stage, Israel could not be de-

scribed as a seasoned army and was not even militarily prepared and trained. *See Introduction to Joshua: Author and Date.* ***the rod of God.*** The staff which Moses held up in his hands was no magic wand. Rather, it had been previously used to initiate, via His chosen leader, the miracles which God did and about which He had informed Moses in advance. It became, therefore, the symbol of God's personal and powerful involvement, with Moses' outstretched arms perhaps signifying an appeal to God. The ebb and flow of battle in correlation with Moses' uplifted or drooping arms imparted more than psychological encouragement as the soldiers looked up to their leader on the hilltop, and more than Moses' interceding for them. It demonstrated and acknowledged their having to depend upon God for victory in battle and not upon their own strength and zeal. It also confirmed the position of Moses both in relation to God and the nation's well-being and safety. They had angrily chided him for their problems, but God confirmed his appointment as leader.

17:10 *Hur.* Caleb's son and the grandfather of Bezalel, the artisan (cf. 31:2–11; 1 Chr. 2:19, 20).

17:14 *Write this for a memorial . . . and recount it.* Moses would have learned writing and record-keeping in Pharaoh's school of government. Official Hebrew records, other than Scripture, were also to be kept, in this case especially for the purpose of remembering the victory in the very first battle in which they nationally engaged. God referred to "the book," so Moses had evidently already begun it. This was not, then, the initial entry into what perhaps became known as "The Book of the Wars of Yahweh" (Num. 21:14). Writing it was essential, so the facts could be verified and needed not to depend upon human memory or solely oral tradition. ***blot out the remembrance.*** The sentence of national extinction which the Amalekites proclaimed for Israel (cf. Ps. 83:4–7) passed by divine decree upon the Amalekites. The sentence was partially realized in Saul's and David's day (cf. 1 Sam. 15:1–9; 2 Sam. 1:1; 8:11, 12), after which it is scarcely mentioned again. However, due to Saul's disobedience in sparing Agag, the Amalekite king and some of his people (1 Sam. 15:7–9), he lost his throne (v. 23). Samuel killed Agag (v. 33), but some Amalekites remained to return a few years later to raid Israel's southern territory, even capturing David's family (1 Sam. 30:1–5). David killed all but four hundred (1 Sam. 30:16, 17) who escaped. It was a descendant of Agag, Haman, who tried to exterminate the Jews later in Esther's day (cf. Esth. 3:1, 6).

17:15 The-LORD-Is-My-Banner. By titling the altar with this designation for the Lord, Yahweh-Nissi, Moses declared the Lord Himself to be the standard of His people.

17:16 The LORD has sworn. The difficulty of the Hebrew text permits an alternative translation: "a hand is upon/toward/against the throne/banner of Yahweh," with the sense of supplication, or of taking an oath. Contextually, the significance is clear, whatever the translation adopted: The ongoing problem with Amalek was not merely one nation hostile toward another; it was a war between God and Amalek.

D. Meeting with Jethro and Learning (18:1–27)

18:1 Jethro . . . heard of all. The intelligence-gathering ability of ancient peoples should not be underestimated. Quickly and thoroughly, the news of significant events in other lands passed from one place to another, very often via the merchant caravans which traversed the Fertile Crescent, or through ambassadors and other official contacts between nations. In Jethro's case, whatever knowledge he had gleaned of Israel's progress had been supplemented with information from Zipporah and her sons after Moses sent them ahead to her home (v. 2).

18:7–12 Moses' testimony elicited responses of praise and sacrifice from Jethro, evidence of his belief. Further, he understood fully the incomparability of Yahweh (v. 11). The priest of Midian (v. 1) was surely no worshiper of Midian's gods. Since Midianites were generally regarded as idolaters (cf. Num. 25:17, 18; 31:2, 3, 16), Jethro must be viewed as remarkably different from his contemporaries, a difference highlighted by Aaron and the elders worshiping and fellowshiping together with him (v. 12).

18:12 to God. Since the name Yahweh is always used in connection with sacrifices prescribed for Israel in the Pentateuch, the switch to Elohim must have some significance here, particularly after Jethro had himself used the name of Yahweh in his response to Moses. Despite the strong declaration of his faith and understanding, Jethro was a believing Gentile, therefore, a proselyte and an alien. In this situation, the Lord was relating to the Israelite and Gentile world simultaneously, thus the use of Elohim rather than Yahweh, the unique covenant name for Israel.

18:13–27 Jethro's practical wisdom was of immense benefit to Moses and Israel, and has been lauded as an example of delegation and management organization by efficiency experts for centuries—and still is. Woven into Jethro's advice were statements about God and the virtues of godly men that cause one to respect this man as having his newfound faith well integrated into his thinking. Indeed, he fully recognized that Moses needed divine permission to enact his advice (v. 23). Moses apparently did not immediately implement Jethro's solution, but waited until the law had been given (cf. Deut. 1:9–15).

18:21 These same spiritual qualities were required of NT leaders (see Acts. 6:3; 1 Tim. 3:1–7; Titus 1:6–9).

III. Israel Encamped at Sinai (19:1–40:38)

19:1–40:38 This section outlines Israel's activities during their approximately eleven month stay at Sinai (cf. 19:1 with Num. 10:11).

A. The Law of God Prescribed (19:1–24:18)

19:3–8 The Israelites discerned the familiar pattern, in shortened form, of a suzerainty (superior-subordinate relationship) treaty in God's words: a preamble (v. 3), a historical prologue (v. 4), certain stipulations (v. 5a), and blessings (vv. 5b–6a). The acceptance in solemn assembly would normally be recorded in the final treaty document. Here, it follows upon presentation of the treaty to them (vv. 7, 8). *See note on 24:7.*

19:3 *from the mountain.* The sign which the Lord had given particularly to Moses when he was still in Midian (3:12), that God had indeed sent him, was now fulfilled; he was with the people before the mountain of God. *house of Jacob ... children of Israel.* In employing this dual designation for the nation, the Lord reminded them of their humble beginnings as descendants of Abraham through Isaac and Jacob, who had been with them in Egypt, and of their status now as a nation (children = people).

19:4 *bore you on eagles' wings.* With a most appropriate metaphor, God described the Exodus and the journey to Sinai. Eagles were known to have carried their young out of the nests on their wings and taught them to fly, catching them when necessary on their outspread wings. Moses, in his final song, used this metaphor of God's care for Israel and especially noted that there was only one Lord who did this (Deut. 32:11–12).

19:5, 6 Three titles for Israel, "a special treasure," "a kingdom of priests," and "a holy nation" were given by the Lord to the nation, contingent upon their being an obedient and covenant-keeping nation. These titles summarized the divine blessings which such a nation would experience: belonging especially to the Lord, representing Him in the earth, and being set apart to Him for His purposes. These ethnically and morally expanded what it meant to have brought them to Himself. "For all the earth is mine," in the midst of the titles, laid stress upon the uniqueness and sovereignty of the Lord and had to be understood as dismissing all other claims by the so-called gods of other nations. It was more than the power of one god over another in Israel's situation; it was the choice and power of the only Lord. See 1 Peter 2:9, where Peter uses these terms in the sense of God's spiritual kingdom of the redeemed.

19:8 *Then all the people answered together.* Presented with the details of God's bilateral, conditional covenant (note the "if you will obey ... then you shall be" in v. 5), the people, briefed by their elders, responded with positive enthusiasm. The Lord's response to them does not take it as a rash promise by the people (cf. Deut. 5:27–29).

19:9 *and believe you forever.* The Lord designed the upcoming encounter with Him so as to forestall any later accusation that Moses had himself compiled the law and had not met with the Lord on the mountain. It would also lead to great deference being accorded Moses by the people.

19:10 *consecrate them.* How serious this step was for the nation was emphasized for them by two days of special preparation. The inward preparation for meeting with God was mirrored in the outward actions of maintaining bodily cleanliness.

19:12, 13 The proper approach to a holy

God could not have been better emphasized than by imposing a death penalty upon those who violated the arbitrary boundaries which God had set around the mountain. Even animals could not encroach upon this sacred area (cf. Heb. 12:20).

19:15 *do not come near your wives.* This was so they would be ceremonially clean (see Lev. 15:16–18).

19:16 *thunderings and lightnings.* The dramatic visual presentation of God's presence on the mountain, accompanied by thick cloud and trumpet blast, more than impressed the onlookers with God's majesty and power. They trembled, but so did Moses (Heb. 12:21). The unusual was happening, not the usual phenomena from volcanic activity, as some writers have proposed.

19:24 *the priests.* With the law still to be given, no priesthood had been established in Israel. These priests must have been the first-born in each family who served as family priests because they had been dedicated to the Lord (cf. 13:2; 24:5). Their place would be taken over later by the Levites (Num. 3:45).

20:1 *all these words.* This general description of the commands to follow also received from Moses the title "Ten Commandments" (34:28; Deut. 4:13). By this emphasis on God Himself speaking these words (cf. Deut. 5:12, 15, 16, 22, 32, 33), all theories on Israel's borrowing legal patterns or concepts from the nations around them are unacceptable.

20:3–17 The Ten Commandments, also known as the Decalogue, which follow upon the opening historical prologue (v. 2), are formed as a precept or direct command given in the second person. This form was something rather uncommon in that day. Ancient Near Eastern law codes for the most part were casuistic, or case law, in form, i.e., an "if . . . then" construction written in the third person, wherein a supposed offense

was followed by a statement of the action to be taken or penalty to be exacted. The Ten Commandments may also be grouped into two broad categories: the vertical, man's relationship to God (vv. 2–11), and the horizontal, man's relationship to the community (vv. 12–17). Concisely listed prohibitions mark the second category, with only one exception—an imperative plus its explanation (v. 12). Explanation or reason appended to a prohibition marks the first category. By these Ten Commandments, true theology and true worship, the name of God and the Sabbath, family honor, life, marriage, and property, truth, and virtue are well protected. *See note on 24:7.*

20:3 *before Me.* Meaning "over against Me," this is a most appropriate expression in light of the next few verses. All false gods stand in opposition to the true God, and the worship of them is incompatible with the worship of Yahweh. When Israel departed from the worship of the only one and true God, she plunged into religious confusion (Judg. 17; 18).

20:4–6 The mode or fashion of worship appropriate to only one Lord forbids any attempt to represent or caricature Him by use of anything He has made. Total censure of artistic expression was not the issue; the absolute censure of idolatry and false worship was. Violations would seriously affect succeeding generations because the Lord demanded full and exclusive devotion, i.e., He is a jealous God (cf. 34:14; Deut. 4:24; 5:9). The worship of man-made representations was nothing less than hatred of the true God.

20:5, 6 *to the third and fourth generations . . . thousands.* Moses had made it clear that children were not punished for the sins of their parents (Deut. 24:16; see Ezek. 18:19–32), but children would feel the impact of breaches of God's law by their parents' generation as a natural consequence of

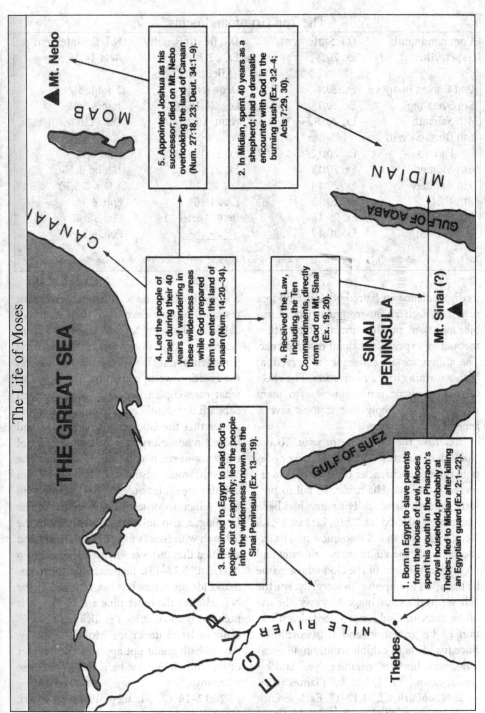

The Life of Moses

THE GREAT SEA

CANAAN

MOAB

▲ Mt. Nebo

5. Appointed Joshua as his successor; died on Mt. Nebo overlooking the land of Canaan (Num. 27:18, 23; Deut. 34:1–9).

2. In Midian, spent 40 years as a shepherd; had a dramatic encounter with God in the burning bush (Ex. 3:2–4; Acts 7:29, 30).

MIDIAN

GULF OF AQABA

4. Led the people of Israel during their 40 years of wandering in these wilderness areas while God prepared them to enter the land of Canaan (Num. 14:20–34).

4. Received the Law, including the Ten Commandments, directly from God on Mt. Sinai (Ex. 19; 20).

SINAI PENINSULA

Mt. Sinai (?) ▲

GULF OF SUEZ

3. Returned to Egypt to lead God's people out of captivity; led the people into the wilderness known as the Sinai Peninsula (Ex. 13–19).

1. Born in Egypt to slave parents from the house of Levi, Moses spent his youth in the Pharaoh's royal household, probably at Thebes; fled to Midian after killing an Egyptian guard (Ex. 2:1–22).

EGYPT

NILE RIVER

Thebes

Nelson's Complete Book of Bible Maps & Charts (Nashville: Thomas Nelson Publishers, 1996) 30. © 1993 by Thomas Nelson, Inc.

The Ten Commandments			
Commandment	O.T. Statement	O.T. Death Penalty	N.T. Restatement
1st Polytheism	Ex. 20:3	Ex. 22:20; Deut. 6:13-15	Acts 14:15
2nd Graven Images	Ex. 20:4	Deut. 27:15	1 John 5:21
3rd Swearing	Ex. 20:7	Lev. 24:15,16	James 5:12
4th Sabbath	Ex. 20:8	Num. 15:32-36	Col. 2:16 nullifies
5th Obedience to Parents	Ex. 20:12	Ex. 21:15-17	Eph. 6:1
6th Murder	Ex. 20:13	Ex. 21:12	1 John 3:15
7th Adultery	Ex. 20:14	Lev. 20:10	1 Cor. 6:9,10
8th Theft	Ex. 20:15	Ex. 21:16	Eph. 4:28
9th False Witness	Ex. 20:16	Deut. 18:16-21	Col. 3:9,10
10th Coveting	Ex. 20:17	_____	Eph. 5:3

The MacArthur Study Bible, by John MacArthur (Nashville: Word Publishing, 1997) 124. © 1993 by Thomas Nelson, Inc.

its disobedience, its hatred of God. Children reared in such an environment would imbibe and, then, practice similar idolatry, thus themselves expressing hateful disobedience. The difference in consequence served as both a warning and a motivation. The effect of a disobedient generation was to plant wickedness so deeply that it took several generations to reverse.

20:7 take the name . . . in vain. To use God's name in such a way as to bring disrepute upon His character or deeds was to irreverently misuse His name. To fail to perform an oath in which His name had been legitimately uttered (cf. 22:10, 11; Lev. 19:12; Deut. 6:13) was to call into question His existence, since the guilty party evidently had no further thought of the God whose name he had used to improve his integrity. For the believer in the church age, however, the use of the name of God is not a needed verification of his intention and trustworthiness since his life is to exhibit truth, on all occasions, with his "yes" meaning "yes" and his "no" meaning "no" (Matt. 5:37; James 5:12).

20:8 Sabbath. Cf. 31:12–17. Each seventh day belonged to the Lord and would not be a work day, but one set apart (i.e., holy) for rest and for time devoted to the worship of Yahweh. The term *Sabbath* is derived from "to rest or cease from work." The historical precedent for such a special observance was the creation week; a span of time equal to what man copied weekly in practice. Each Sabbath day should have reminded the worshiper that the God whom he praised had indeed made everything in both realms of existence in six, twenty-four hour days. The Sabbath would also stand, therefore, as a counter to evolutionary ideas prevalent in false religion. Moses, in the review of the Decalogue, also linked the observance of the Sabbath with Israel's Exodus from Egypt and specified that this was why Israel was to keep it (Deut. 5:12–15). Significantly, the command for the Sabbath is not repeated in the NT, whereas the other nine are. In fact, it is nullified (cf. Col. 2:16, 17). Belonging especially to Israel under the Mosaic economy, the Sabbath could not apply to the believer of the church age, for he is living in a new economy.

20:12–16 Cf. Matthew 19:18–19; Mark 10:19; Luke 18:20.

20:12 *Honor your father and your mother.* The key to societal stability is reverence and respect for parents and their authority. The appended promise primarily related the command to life in the Promised Land and reminded the Israelite of the program God had set up for him and his people. Within the borders of their territory, God expected them not to tolerate juvenile delinquency, which at heart is overt disrespect for parents and authority. Severe consequences, namely capital punishment, could apply (cf. Deut. 21:18–21). One of the reasons for the Babylonian exile was a failure to honor parents (Ezek. 22:7, 15). The apostle Paul individualized this national promise when he applied the truth to believers in his day (cf. Matt. 15:4; Mark 7:10; Eph. 6:1–3).

20:13–15 Cf. Romans 13:9.

20:13 *murder.* The irreversible nature of the divinely imposed sentence of death on every manslayer who killed another intentionally (cf. 21:12; Num. 35:17–21) stands without parallel in ancient Near Eastern literature and legal codes (cf. Gen. 9:5, 6). Further, the sacredness of human life stands out in the passages dealing with unintentional manslaughter. The accident of death still carried with it a penalty of banishment to the city of refuge until the death of the high priest for the one who killed, but not with intent. Careful appraisal of the word Moses used (one of seven different Hebrew words for killing, and one used only forty-seven times in the OT) suggests a broad translation of "to kill, slay" but denoting the taking of life under a legal system where he would have to answer to the stipulations of a legal code, no matter whether he killed unintentionally or intentionally. By this command, people would be reminded and exhorted to strive after carefulness in the affairs of life so that, on the person-to-person level, no one would die by their hand. *See note on 21:12–14* (cf. Matt. 5:21; James 2:11).

20:14 *adultery.* Applicable to both men and women, this command protected the sacredness of the marriage relationship. God had instituted marriage at the creation of man and woman (Gen. 2:24) and had blessed it as the means of filling the earth (Gen. 1:28). The penalty for infidelity in the marital relationship was death (Lev. 20:10). Adultery was also referred to as "a great sin" (Gen. 20:9) and a "great wickedness and sin against God" (cf. Gen. 39:9; Matt. 5:27; James 2:11).

20:15 *steal.* Any dishonest acquiring of another's goods or assets greatly disturbs the right to ownership of private property, which is an important principle for societal stability. Stealing seriously questions God's unquestionable ability to properly provide for His people.

20:16 *false witness.* Justice is not served by any untruthful testimony. Practically all societies have recognized this principle and adjure all witnesses in courts to tell the truth and nothing but the truth.

20:17 *covet.* The thoughts and desires of the heart do not escape attention. A strong longing to have what another has is wrong. This tenth command suggests that none of the previous nine commandments are only external acts with no relation to internal thoughts (cf. Matt. 15:19; Rom. 7:7; 13:9).

20:18 *trembled and stood afar off.* The people fearfully withdrew from the cluster of phenomena accompanying this theophany, this appearance of God on the mountain. They instinctively placed Moses in the position of mediator between them and God, because such was the gap between them and their holy God that they feared they were not fit to live in His presence (v. 19).

20:19 *let not God speak.* Fearing for their

lives, the nation asked Moses to be their mediator (cf. Heb. 12:18–21).

20:20 Instructed not to respond to the phenomena with fear, they were also told that proper fear, i.e., awe and reverence of God, deterred sin.

20:22–26 Sacrifices, offerings, and altars were not unknown to Israel and were already part of certain worship ceremonies. Neither the earthen nor stone altars would have even a hint of being shaped to represent something more specific, so the restrictions on the form and the method of building would ensure the appropriateness and propriety of their worship. Leviticus 1–7 outlines the Mosaic sacrifices.

21:1 *judgments.* These are a combination of casuistic (case law) and apodictic (direct command) precepts laid down, as a detailed enlargement of the Decalogue, the framework for judging and resolving civil disputes in Israel. Such a combination continued to confirm the uniqueness of Israel's law among the different ancient Near Eastern law-codes. Later in a special ceremony, God entitled these precepts "The Book of the Covenant" (24:7).

21:2–11 The law of the slave guaranteed freedom after a specified period of six years unless the slave himself elected permanent servitude, but this would be service in a context not of abuse, but of love (v. 5). Any permanent, involuntary servitude for a Hebrew slave to a Hebrew master was obviously undesirable for Israelite society and was unknown in Israel (cf. Lev. 25:39–55). Provision was also made to ensure the proper treatment of female slaves, who could not deliberately be left destitute by wrongful action on the part of their master.

21:12–14 The laws relating to personal injury (vv. 15–36) from man or animal were preceded by the most serious of injuries,

homicide. The death penalty was prescribed for intentional homicide only (see 20:13), whereas for unintentional homicide the penalty was banishment to an appointed place, which later God revealed were the cities of refuge (cf. Num. 35:6–24; Deut. 19:1–13). No degree of sanctuary applied to one guilty of premeditated murder. Death by accident at the hand of another is something unplanned by man, but which God let happen. The law did afford sanctuary, but away from home and vengeful relatives, often for life, because there the person guilty of involuntary manslaughter remained until the death of the high priest (Num. 35:25, 28).

21:15, 17 Disrespect for parents seen in physical and verbal abuse of them by their children was so serious that it was designated a capital offense. Commandment five was a serious matter! Other ancient law codes, e.g., the Code of Hammurabi, also respected parental authority and prescribed severe consequences, although not the death penalty.

21:17 Cf. Matthew 15:4; Mark 7:10.

21:20, 21, 26, 27 Punishment of slaves was considered the right of the owner (Prov. 10:13; 13:24), but did not allow for violence. Judges were to decide the appropriate punishment if the slave died (v. 20). If the slave lived a few days, it was evidence that the owner had no intent to kill, and the loss of the slave was punishment enough (v. 21). A beating without death ensuing was construed as a disciplinary matter, not a homicidal one. Any permanent personal injury brought freedom and loss of a master's investment. The master's power over the slave was thus limited, which made this law unprecedented in the ancient world.

21:22 Compensation was mandatory for accidentally causing a premature birth, even if no injury resulted to either mother or child. Judges were brought into the legal process so that damages awarded were fair and were not calculated out of vengeance.

21:23, 24 Cf. Leviticus 24:19, 20; Deuteronomy 19:21. The principle of retaliation, or *lex taliones,* applied if injury occurred to either mother or child. The punishment matched, but did not exceed, the damage done to the victim. The welfare of a pregnant woman was protected by this law so that unintentional maltreatment constituted culpable negligence. Significantly for the abortion debate, the fetus was considered a person; thus, someone was held accountable for the baby's death or injury.

21:24 Cf. Matthew 5:38.

21:30 Animal owners were held responsible for death or injuries caused by their animals. Since the owner was guilty of negligence and not of an intentional crime, he was able to make payment to escape the death penalty. Again, judges are brought into the process to ensure that no vengeful decisions are made.

21:32 *shekels.* A shekel weighs four-tenths an ounce; thirty shekels would weigh twelve ounhes. Christ was betrayed for the price of a slave (Zech. 11:12, 13; Matt. 26:14, 15).

22:3 *If the sun has risen on him.* The culpability of a householder's actions against an intruder depended on whether the break-in (lit. "digging through" the mud walls) was at night or in the daytime. At night, quick evaluation of an intruder's intentions was not as clear as it might be in daytime, nor would someone be awake and on hand to help.

22:11 *an oath of the* Lord. This is, presumably, an oath of innocence which would bind the two parties to a dispute over lost goods and preclude any further legal action being taken.

22:16 *If a man entices . . . pay the bride-price.* The male was held accountable for premarital intercourse and the victim was seen as having been exploited by him, for which he paid a price (cf. Deut. 22:22–29).

22:18 *sorceress.* A woman who practices occultism.

22:19 The degree of sexual perversion in Canaanite culture was such that bestiality was fairly commonplace (cf. Lev. 18:23, 24). Hittite laws, for example, even permitted cohabitation with certain animals.

22:20 *utterly destroyed.* Lit. "put to the ban" or "devoted to sacred use," which in this case meant death (cf. Josh. 7:2ff.).

22:22 *widow or fatherless child.* God reserved His special attention for widows and orphans who often had no one to care for them. He also reserved a special reaction, His wrath, for those who abused and exploited them. This wrath would work out in military invasions as the sword reduced the abusers' families to the same status of being without spouse or parents.

22:25 *interest.* One way in which the people showed their concern for the poor and needy was to take no business advantage of them. Charging interest was allowable (Lev. 25:35–37; Deut. 23:19, 20; 24:10–13), but not when it was exorbitant or worsened the plight of the borrower. The psalmist identified a righteous man as one who lends money without excessive interest (Ps. 15:5).

22:28 See Acts 23:5, where Paul apparently violated this law, not knowing to whom he spoke.

22:31 *holy men to Me.* All these laws and regulations caused Israel to be set apart in conduct, not just in name. The special calling as Yahweh's firstborn son (4:22) and as His treasured possession, a kingdom of priests and a holy nation (19:5, 6), mandated ethical uprightness. *eat meat torn.* Flesh of an animal killed by another and lying in the field became unclean by coming into contact with unclean carnivores and insects and with putrefaction by not having had the blood drained properly from it. A set-apart lifestyle impacted every area of life, including the location and source from where a person collected his meat.

23:1–9 This is a list of miscellaneous laws, which includes the protection of equitable and impartial justice for all. False testimony, undiscerningly following a majority, favoring one over another, and accepting bribes, all contribute to the perversion of true justice. The attitude of impartiality was to include the helping of another with his animals, regardless of whether he was friend or foe. If no help was given, his livelihood could very well be adversely affected, which was a situation that others in the community could not allow to happen.

23:10, 11 *seventh year.* A sabbatical year of rest after six years of farming benefited both the land and the poor. This pattern of letting a field lie fallow appears to have been unique with Israel.

23:13 Idolatry was to be avoided right down to the level of not causing the name of other deities to be remembered. This perhaps served also as a prohibition of intermarriage with other nations, for in the marriage contract recognition was given to the deities of the parties involved, which would have had the effect of putting God on a par with pagan gods.

23:14–19 Requiring all males to be present for three specified feasts at a central sanctuary would have had a socially and religiously uniting effect on the nation. The men must trust the Lord to protect their landholdings while on pilgrimage to the tabernacle (cf. 34:23, 24). All three feasts were joyful occasions, being a commemoration of the Exodus (the Feast of Unleavened Bread), an expression of gratitude to God for all the grain He had provided (the Feast of Harvest), and a thanksgiving for the final harvest (the Feast of

Ingathering). Alternative names appear in the biblical record for the second and third feasts: the Feast of Weeks (34:22) or Firstfruits (34:22; Acts 2:1), and the Feast of Tabernacles or Booths (Lev. 23:33–36). For additional discussions, see, Leviticus 23:1–24:9; Numbers 28; 29; Deuteronomy 16.

23:19 *not boil a young goat.* Canaanite ritual, according to excavations at Ras Shamra (ancient Ugarit), called for sacrificial kids to be boiled in milk, but the damaged Ugaritic text does not clearly specify mother's milk. If it were so, then it is understandable that Israel was being prevented from copying pagan idolatrous ritualism. Another option suggests that the dead kid was being boiled in the very substance which had sustained its life, hence the prohibition. Until more archeological information comes to light, the specific religious or cultural reason remains as supposition.

23:23 *My Angel.* This is usually taken to be a reference to the Angel of Yahweh, who is distinguished from the Lord who talks about Him as another person. *See note on 3:2.* Yet, He is identified with Him by reason of His forgiving sin and the Lord's name being in Him (v. 21). Neither Moses nor some other messenger or guide qualify for such descriptions. The key to victory in the upcoming takeover of the land would not be Israel's military skill, but the presence of this angel, who is the preincarnate Christ.

23:24 *sacred pillars.* Stone markers of pagan shrines were absolutely intolerable once the land had been taken from the tribes just mentioned in the previous verse.

23:25, 26 Proper worship brought with it due rewards, not only good harvests and a good water supply, but also physical health, including fertility and safe pregnancies.

23:28 *hornets.* This figurative expression of the panic-producing power of God parallels "My fear" (v. 27), which was the obvious effect of "My angel" having been the advance guard to the conquest (v. 23). In anticipation of the conquest of their land, Israel was being given another reminder that victory depended on God and not their own efforts alone. Fear and panic did play a strategic role in the victories in Transjordan and Canaan (Num. 22:3; Josh. 2:9, 11; 5:1; 9:24). An alternative non-figurative view is based upon the bee or wasp being a heraldic symbol of Egyptian pharaohs whose steady succession of military strikes into Canaan year after year God providentially used to weaken Canaan prior to the invasion by Israel.

23:29, 30 The occupation would be a gradual but effective process taking longer than a year to accomplish, but ensuring full control of a land in good condition and not left desolate by a sweeping and destructive warfare. The reference to the multiplication of wild beasts if the land was desolated underscores the fertility of the land and its ability to support life.

23:31 *I will set your bounds.* God gave both broad and more detailed geographic descriptions of the land. Even limited demarcation of borders was sufficient to lay out the extent of their possession. It would extend from the Gulf of Aqabah to the Mediterranean Sea and from the desert in the Negev to the river of the northern boundary.

23:32 *make no covenant.* International diplomacy, with its parity or suzerainty treaties, was not an option open to Israel in dealing with the tribes living within the designated borders of the Promised Land (Deut. 7:1, 2). All these treaties were accompanied by the names of the nations' gods, so it was fitting to deliver a charge not to make a treaty (covenant) with them, nor to serve their pagan gods. The situation with other nations outside the land being given to Israel was different (cf. Deut. 20:10–18).

24:4 *twelve pillars.* Unlike pagan stone markers (23:24), these were built to represent the twelve tribes and were placed alongside the altar Moses had erected in preparation for a covenant ratification ceremony. They did not mark the worship site of a pagan deity.

24:5 *young men.* This is most probably a reference to firstborn children who officiated until the law appointed the Levites in their place.

24:7 *the Book of the Covenant.* Civil, social, and religious laws were received by Moses on Mt. Sinai, orally presented (v. 3), then written down (v. 4), and read to the people. This Book contained not only this detailed enlargement of the Decalogue

Old Testament Appearances of the Angel of the Lord

1. He wrestled with Jacob.	Gen. 32:24–30
2. He redeemed Jacob from all evil.	Gen. 48:16
3. He spoke to Moses from the burning bush.	Ex. 3:2
4. He protected Israel at the Red Sea.	Ex. 14:19
5. He prepared Israel for the Promised Land.	Ex. 23:20–23; Is. 63:9; 1 Cor. 10:1–4
6. He reassured Joshua.	Josh. 5:13–15
7. He commissioned Gideon.	Judg. 6:11,12
8. He instructed Samson's parents.	Judg. 13:3–18
9. He ministered to Elijah.	1 Kin. 19:7
10. He saved Jerusalem.	Is. 37:36
11. He preserved three godly Hebrew men.	Dan. 3:25

(20:22–23:33), but also the Ten Commandments themselves (20:1–17) and the preliminary abbreviated presentation of the treaty (19:3–6). *See notes on 19:3–8; 20:3–17.*

24:8 sprinkled it on the people. By this act, Moses, in response to the positive acceptance and assertion of obedience by the people after hearing the Book of the Covenant read to them, officially sealed the treaty with blood, a not uncommon custom (cf. Gen. 15:9–13, 17). Half of the blood used had been sprinkled on the altar as part of the consecration ceremony. The representatives of Israel were thereby qualified to ascend the mountain and participate in the covenant meal with Yahweh (24:11; cf. Heb. 9:20).

24:9, 11 they saw God. The representatives accompanying Moses up the mountain, as per God's instructions, were privileged to have seen God without being consumed by His holiness. Precisely what they saw must remain a moot point and must stay within the description given, which focuses only on what was under His feet. This perhaps indicates that only a partial manifestation took place such as would occur before Moses (33:20), or when the elders, in the presence of divine majesty, beauty, and strength (cf. Ps. 96:6), did not dare raise their eyes above His footstool.

24:10 paved work of sapphire stone. The description sounds like a comparison with lapis lazuli, an opaque blue, precious stone much used in Mesopotamia and Egypt at that time.

24:12 tablets of stone. For the first time, mention is made of what form the revelation of the law would take: tablets of stone. They were also called the "tablets of the Testimony" (31:18) and the "tablets of the covenant" (Deut. 9:9).

24:14 Hur. *See note on 17:10.*

24:16–18 This was the first (ending in 32:6) of two (forty days and forty nights each) trips to Sinai (cf. 34:2–28). The awe-inspiring sight of God's glory cloud, the Shekinah, resting on the mountain and into which Moses disappeared for forty days and nights, impressed everyone with the singular importance of this event in Israel's history. During these days Moses received all the instructions on the tabernacle and its furnishings and accoutrements (chs. 25–31). The settling of the Shekinah upon the tabernacle at its completion impressed the Israelites with the singular importance of this structure in Israel's worship of and relationship to Yahweh (40:34–38).

25:1–40:38 The primary focus of attention in the closing chapters is upon the design and construction of the central place of worship for the nation. In preparation for occupation of their land, they had been given a system of law to regulate individual and national life, to prevent exploitation of the poor and the stranger, and to safeguard against polytheism and idolatry. That these safeguards were needed was confirmed by the idolatrous golden calf incident (32:1–35). The very detailed and divinely given blueprint of the tabernacle removes all speculation about whether it has any comparison with, or was somehow derived from, the little portable sanctuaries belonging to various tribal deities. The origin of the tabernacle was found in God and delivered to Moses by special revelation (cf. 25:9, 40; 26:30; Heb. 8:5).

B. The Tabernacle of God Described (25:1–31:18)

25:2 an offering . . . willingly. Voluntarily and freely the people were given opportunity to contribute to the nation's worship center from the list of fourteen components and materials needed to build the tabernacle. One wonders how much of their contribution came originally from Egyptian homes and had been thrust into the hands of the Israelites right before the Exodus (cf. 12:35, 36). The people responded with such joy and enthusiasm that they finally had to be restrained from bringing any more gifts (35:21–29; 36:3–7). A similar response occurred centuries later, when King David requested gifts to build the temple (1 Chr. 29:1–9).

25:4 blue, purple, and scarlet thread. These colors were produced by dying the thread: blue from a shellfish, purple from the secretion of a murex snail, and crimson from powdered eggs and bodies of certain worms, which attached themselves to holly plants. Deriving different colored dyes from different natural sources demonstrates a substantial degree of technical sophistication with textiles and fabrics. **fine linen.** Egypt had a reputation for excellence in producing finely twined linens.

25:5 ram skins dyed red. With all the wool removed and then dyed, it resembled moroccan leather. **acacia wood.** A hard, durable, close-grained, and aromatic desert wood avoided by wood-eating insects. It was considered good for cabinet-making, and could also be found in sufficient quantities in the Sinai peninsula.

25:6 spices. For the many years of Bible history, Arabia was highly respected for the variety of balsams she exported.

25:7 onyx stones. Sometimes thought to be chrysoprase quartz, a product known to the Egyptians and with which Israel was no doubt familiar. The LXX translated it as beryl.

25:8 I may dwell. The tabernacle, a noun derived from the verb "to dwell," was an appropriate designation for that which was to be the place of God's presence with His people. His presence would be between the cherubim and from there He would meet with Moses (v. 22).

25:9 tabernacle. The Pentateuch records five different names for the tabernacle: (1) "sanctuary," denoting a sacred place or set apart, i.e., holy place; (2) "tent," denoting a temporary or collapsible dwelling; (3) "tabernacle," from "to dwell," denoting the place of God's presence (as well as other titles); (4) "tabernacle of the congregation, or meeting"; and (5) "tabernacle of the testimony."

25:11 pure gold. The technology of the day was sufficient to refine gold.

25:16 the Testimony. This designation for the two tablets of stone containing the Ten Commandments which were placed inside the ark explains why it was also called "the ark of the testimony" (v. 22), and shows why it was appropriate to call the whole structure "the tabernacle" or "the tent of the testimony." "The ark of the covenant of the Lord of all the earth" (Josh. 3:11) and "the holy ark" (2 Chr. 35:3) were alternative designations.

25:17 mercy seat. The lid or cover of the ark was the "mercy seat" or the place at which atonement took place. Between the Shekinah glory cloud above the ark and the tablets of law inside the ark was the blood-sprinkled cover. Blood from the sacrifices stood between God and the broken law of God.

25:18 cherubim. Forged as one piece with the golden cover of the ark were two angelic beings rising up on each end and facing one another, their wings stretching up and over forming an arch. Cherubim, associated with the majestic glory and presence of God (cf. Ezek. 10:1–22), were appropriately woven into the tabernacle curtains and the veil for the Holy of Holies (26:1, 31), for this place was where God was present with His people. Scripture reveals them as the bearers of God's throne (1 Sam. 4:4; Is. 37:16) and the guardians of the Garden of Eden and the tree of life (Gen. 3:24).

25:30 showbread. Each week a new batch

of twelve loaves of bread was laid on a table on the north side of the Holy Place. The utensils for this table were also made of refined gold (v. 29). This "Bread of His Presence" was not set out in order to feed Israel's God, unlike food placed in pagan shrines and temples, but to acknowledge that the twelve tribes were sustained constantly under the watchful eye and care of their Lord. The bread was eaten in the Holy Place each Sabbath by the priests on duty (Lev. 24:5–9). The showbread is understood to typify the Lord Jesus Christ as the bread which came from heaven (John 6:32–35).

25:31 lampstand. Situated opposite the table of showbread on the south side of the Holy Place stood an ornate lampstand, or menorah, patterned after a flowering almond tree. It provided light for the priests serving in the Holy Place. Care was taken, according to God's instructions (27:20, 21; 30:7, 8; Lev. 24:1–4), to keep it well supplied with pure olive oil so that it would not be extinguished. The lampstand is seen as typifying the Lord Jesus Christ, who was the true light which came into the world (John 1:6–9; 8:12).

25:39 talent. Approximately seventy-five pounds.

25:40 Cf. Hebrews 8:5.

26:1 ten curtains. The beauty of these curtains could be seen only from the inside, the thick outer protective covering of goats' hair drapes, and ram and badger skins (v. 14) hiding them from the view of anyone except the priests who entered.

26:7 eleven curtains. The extra length of the outer drapes doubled as a covering for the front and back of the tabernacle structure (vv. 9–13).

26:15–29 The frame or trellis work, on which the curtains and outer coverings were draped also received precise instructions. The portability of the whole structure was obvious. Throughout the wilderness wanderings, it could be quickly dismantled and readied for transport, and just as rapidly put up again.

26:30 pattern. Again (cf. 25:40), the warning was sounded that the blueprint must be carefully followed. Nothing was to be left to human guesswork, no matter how skilled the craftsmen might have been.

26:31–34 A veil, similar in design to the inner curtains (see note on 26:1), divided the tabernacle into the Holy Place and the Most Holy, or literally the Holy of Holies.

26:36 screen. Another curtain or veil, without the embroidered cherubim motif, was made to cover the entrance way into the Holy Place.

27:1 altar. The largest piece of equipment, also known as the "altar of burnt offering" (Lev. 4:7, 10, 18), was situated in the courtyard of the tabernacle. It was covered, not in gold as the items inside the Holy Place, but in bronze. Like the other pieces of furniture and equipment, it was also built to be carried by poles (vv. 6, 7).

27:3 All the altar's utensils and accessories were also made of bronze, not gold.

27:9 the court of the tabernacle. The dimensions of the rectangular courtyard space, bordered by curtains and poles around the tabernacle were also precisely given (vv. 9–19; 150 feet by 75 feet). The outer hangings were high enough, five cubits or seven and one-half feet, to block all view of the interior of the courtyard (v. 18). Entry into the courtyard of God's dwelling place was not freely gained from all quarters.

27:16 gate of the court. The curtain forming the covering for the entrance way into the courtyard was colored differently from that which surrounded the oblong courtyard. Clearly, there was only one way to enter this very special place where God had chosen to place the evidence of His dwelling with His people.

The Plan of the Tabernacle

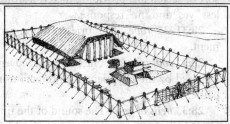

The tabernacle was to provide a place where God might dwell among His people. The term tabernacle sometimes refers to the tent, including the Holy Place and the Most Holy Place, which was covered with embroidered curtains. But in other places it refers to the entire complex, including the curtained court in which the tent stood.

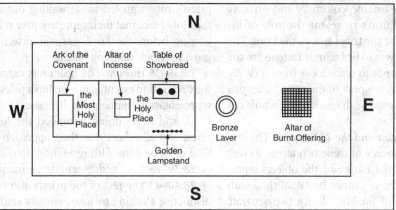

This illustrations shows relative positions of the tabernacle furniture used in Israelite worship. The tabernacle is enlarged for clarity.

The MacArthur Study Bible, by John MacArthur (Nashville: Word Publishing, 1997) 134. © 1993 by Thomas Nelson, Inc.

27:20, 21 *pure oil of pressed olives.* The clear oil from crushed unripened olives granted almost a smoke-free light. The people were to provide the fuel to maintain the light needed by the high priest and his priestly staff in the Holy Place.

28:1 *minister to Me as priest.* The threefold repetition of this phrase in the opening words about Aaron's priestly wardrobe would appear to stress the importance of his role in the religious life of the nation. Aaron's sons were part of the priesthood being set up. The Hebrew text groups the sons in two pairs, the first pair being Nadab and Abihu, both of whom died because of wanton disregard of God's instructions (Lev. 10:1, 2). Aaron and his descendants, as well as the

tribe of Levi, were selected by God to be Israel's priests—they did not appoint themselves to the position. The law clearly defined their duties for worship and the sacrifices in the tabernacle and for the individual worshiper and the nation's covenantal relationship to God.

28:2 *for glory and for beauty.* The garments were designed to exalt the office and function of the priesthood, vividly marking out Aaron as a special person playing a special mediatorial role—they were "holy" vestments. In the OT priestly system for the nation of Israel, such dress maintained the priest-laity distinction.

28:3 *gifted artisans.* This was the first reference in God's instructions to Moses that certain men would be especially empowered by Him to work skillfully on this construction project.

28:5–13 *ephod.* Whenever Aaron entered the sanctuary, he carried with him on his shoulders the badge and the engraved stones that were representative of the Twelve Tribes.

28:15–30 *the breastplate of judgment.* The twelve precious stones, each engraved with a tribe's name, colorfully and ornately displayed Aaron's representative role of intercession for the tribes before the Lord. The breastplate was to be securely fastened to the ephod so as not to come loose from it (v. 28; 39:21). Thus, to speak of the ephod after this was done would be to speak of the whole ensemble.

28:30 *Urim and the Thummim.* The etymological source of these two terms, as well as the material nature of the objects represented by them, cannot be established with any degree of finality. Clearly, two separate objects were inserted into the breastplate and became, thereby, an essential part of the high priest's official regalia. Aaron and his successors bore over their heart "the judgment of the children of Israel," i.e., "judgment" in the sense of giving a verdict or decision. The passages in which the terms appear (Lev. 8:8; Num. 27:21; Deut. 33:8; 1 Sam 28:6; Ezra 2:63; Neh. 7:65) and those which record inquiries of the Lord when a high priest with the ephod was present (Josh. 9:14; Judg. 1:1, 2; 20:18; 1 Sam. 10:22; 23:2, 4, 10–12; 1 Chr. 10:14) allow for the following conclusions: (1) that these two objects represented the right of the high priest to request guidance for the acknowledged leader who could not approach God directly, as Moses had done, but had to come via the God-ordained priestly structure, and (2) that the revelation then received gave specific direction for an immediate problem or crisis, and went beyond what could be associated with some

sort of sacred lots providing merely a wordless "yes" and "no" response.

28:31–35 *robe.* The priest's outer garment.

28:32 *coat of mail.* A flexible metal covering used by the Egyptians for protection in battle.

28:33 *bells of gold.* The sound of the tinkling bells sewn on the hem of the high priest's robe signaled those waiting outside the Holy Place that their representative ministering before the Lord was still alive and moving about, fulfilling his duties.

28:36–38 *turban.* The headdress carried the declaration essential to worship a priestly representation, namely the holiness of the Lord, and in so doing reminded the high priest and all others that their approach to God must be done with reverence.

28:39 *tunic . . . sash.* An undergarment.

28:40–43 The rest of the priests also had distinctive clothing to wear, visually setting them apart from the ordinary citizen. Failure to comply with the dress regulations when serving in the sanctuary brought death. Such a severe consequence emphasized the importance of their duties and should have motivated the priests not to consider their priestly role as a mundane, routine, and thankless task.

29:1–18 *hallow.* The ones chosen to begin the priesthood could not enter into office without Moses' conducting a solemn, seven-day investiture (vv. 4–35; Lev. 8:1–36), involving washing, dressing, anointing, sacrificing, daubing and sprinkling with blood, and eating.

29:19, 20 Daubing blood on the right ear, hand, and big toe symbolically sanctified the ear to hear the Word of God, the hand to do the work of God, and the foot to walk in the way of God.

29:27, 28 *wave offering . . . heave offering. See note on Leviticus 7:30–32.*

The Furniture of the Tabernacle

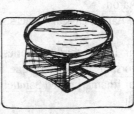

Ark of the Covenant
(Ex. 25:10–22)
The ark was most sacred of all
the furniture in the tabernacle.
Here the Hebrews kept a copy of
the Ten Commandments, which
summarized the whole covenant.

Bronze Laver
(Ex. 30:17–21)
It was to the laver of bronze
that the priests would come
for cleansing. They must be
pure to enter the presence
of God.

Altar of Burnt Offering
(Ex. 27:1–8)
Animal sacrifices were
offered on this altar, located in
the court in front of the
tabernacle. The blood of the
sacrifice was sprinkled on
the four horns of the altar.

Golden Lampstand
(Ex. 25:31–40)
The gold lampstand stood in
the holy place, opposite the table
of showbread. It held seven
lamps, flat bowls in which a wick
lay with one end in the oil of
the bowl and the lighted end
hanging out.

Table of Showbread
(Ex. 25:23–30)
The table of showbread was
a stand on which the
offerings were placed.
Always in God's presence on
the table were the 12 loaves
of bread representing the 12
tribes.

Altar of Incense
(Ex. 30:1–10)
The altar of incense inside
the tabernacle was much
smaller than the altar of burnt
offering outside. The incense
burned on the altar was a
perfume of a sweet-smelling
aroma.

Nelson's Complete Book of Bible Maps & Charts (Nashville: Thomas Nelson Publishers, 1996) 38. © 1993 by Thomas Nelson, Inc.

29:40 *ephah . . . hin.* Four to six gallons and six to eight pints, respectively.

29:42 *throughout your generations.* Perhaps this phrase intends a prophetic reminder or confirmation of a long history for Israel.

29:45 *I will dwell.* That He would be their God and they would be His people was one thing; but that He would also dwell or taber-nacle with them was a very important reality in the experience of the new nation. They were to understand not only the transcendence of their God, whose dwelling place was in the heaven of heavens, but also the immanence of their God, whose dwelling place was with them. Their redemption from Egypt was for this purpose (v. 46).

Priests in the Old Testament

Name	Identification	Scripture
Aaron	Older brother of Moses; first high priest of Israel	Ex. 28, 29
Nadab and Abihu	Evil sons of Aaron	Lev. 10:1, 2
Eleazar and Ithamar	Godly sons of Aaron; Eleazar—Israel's second high priest	Lev. 10:6; Num. 20:26
Phinehas	Son of Eleazar; Israel's third high priest whose zeal for pure worship stopped a plague	Num. 25:7-13
Eli	Descendant of Ithamar; raised Samuel at Shiloh	1 Sam. 1–4
Hophni and Phinehas	Evil sons of Eli	1 Sam. 2:12–36
Ahimelech	Led a priestly community at Nob; killed by Saul for befriending David	1 Sam. 21, 22
Abiathar	Son of Ahimelech who escaped the slayings at Nob	1 Sam. 22:20-23; 2 Sam. 20:25
Zadok	High priest during the reign of David and Solomon	2 Sam. 15; 1 Kin. 1
Jehoiada	High priest who saved Joash from Queen Athaliah's purge	2 Kin. 11; 12
Uriah	Priest who built pagan altar for evil King Ahaz	2 Kin. 16:10-16
Hilkiah	High priest during the reign of Josiah	2 Kin. 22; 23
Elishama and Jehoram	Teaching priests during the reign of Jehoshaphat	2 Chr. 17:7-9
Amariah	High priest of Bethel; confronted Amos the prophet	2 Chr. 19:11
Jahaziel	Levite who assured Jehoshaphat of deliverance from an enemy	2 Chr. 26:14-17
Azariah	High priest who stood against Uzziah when the ruler began to act as a prophet	2 Chr. 26:16-20
Ezra	Scribe, teacher, and priest during the rebuilding of Jerusalem after the Babylonian captivity	Ezra 7-10; Neh. 8
Eliashib	High priest during the time of Nehemiah	Neh. 3:1; 13:4, 5
Shelemiah	Priest during the time of Nehemiah; was in charge of administering storehouses	Neh. 13:13
Pashhur	False priest who persecuted the prophet Jeremiah	Jer. 20:1-6
Amaziah	Evil priest of Bethel; confronted Amos the prophet	Amos 7:10-17
Joshua	First high priest after the Babylonian captivity	Hag. 1:1, 12; Zech. 3

30:1–10 altar . . . incense. The design for this piece of furniture for the Holy Place was not given with the other two (25:23–40), but follows the instructions about the priesthood, perhaps, because it was the last piece to which the high priest came before he entered the Holy of Holies once a year. Right after Aaron's consecration ceremony had been noted, his duties of (1) ensuring proper incense was offered continually upon this altar and (2) annually cleansing the altar with blood from the atonement offering (v. 10) received attention.

30:6 before the veil. This places the altar outside of the "Holy of Holies" in the Holy Place. Hebrews 9:3, 4 speaks of the altar in the "Holy of Holies" in the sense of its proximity to the ark and in relation to its cleansing on the Day of Atonement. The priests could not go beyond it on any other day.

30:9 strange incense. See verse 38.

30:12 census. The reason for the numbering of all males of military age (v. 14) was not stated, but its seriousness surfaces in the dire warning given about a plague and the use of the term *ransom* in connection with it (cf. 1 Chr. 21).

30:13 shekel of the sanctuary. A shekel weighed about four-tenths of an ounce (cf. Lev. 5:15; 27:3, 25; Num. 3:47; 7:13ff.).

30:18–21 laver of bronze. The washing of hands and feet was mandatory before engaging in priestly duties. Again, the seriousness of being ceremonially purified is seen in the warning of death if this washing is neglected. Nothing casual was being done in the sanctuary or out in the courtyard.

30:22–33 Nothing was left to chance or to human ingenuity. The ingredients for making the anointing oil were carefully spelled out. Using anything different was totally unacceptable and brought with it the penalty of death (v. 33). This was to be a unique blend.

Key Word

Anointed: 29:29, 36; 30:26; 40:9, 15—a verb meaning "to wet or daub a person with olive oil." Kings, priests, and prophets were anointed at the beginning of their service (Num. 8:12; 16:32; 2 Sam. 2:4; 5:3; 1 Kin. 19:15–16). This ritual identified a person or object as set apart for God's special purposes. During the Exodus, many holy objects were anointed, including the tabernacle itself. Anointing oil was an exquisite and expensive blend of oil and spices (Num. 7:1). This special oil symbolized the consecration of the tabernacle and its furnishings to God.

Using it for any other purpose also erased its holy status as set apart for use in the tabernacle and made it no different from the ordinary and the mundane.

30:25, 35 art of the perfumer. The skill of the perfumer was obviously already well known in Israel, a trade which they undoubtedly observed in Egypt.

30:34–38 incense. God also listed the ingredients for the unique blend of incense prescribed for use at the altar of incense. Making anything different would have been to make "strange incense" (v. 9) and would also result in death (v. 38). Personal use rendered its holy status null and void. Nadab and Abihu were executed for violating this command (cf. Lev. 10:1, 2).

31:1–11 God identified two men by name as specially chosen and divinely endued with ability, or Spirit-filled, to make all He had revealed to Moses (cf. 28:3; 36:1). None of the craftsmen were left untouched by divinely bestowed understanding in the intricacy of their work. They were called "gifted artisans," suggesting previously developed skill. They were to make all that is prescribed in Exodus 25–30.

31:12–17 See note on 20:8.

31:18 two tablets of the Testimony. See note on 25:16. **written with the finger of God.** A figurative way (anthropomorphism) of attributing the law to God.

C. The Worship of God Defiled (32:1–35)

32:1 make us gods. Such was the influence of the polytheistic world in which they lived that the Israelites, in a time of panic or impatience, succumbed to a pagan worldview. What made it even more alarming was the rapidity with which pagan idolatry swept in despite recent, real-life demonstrations of God's greatness and goodness toward them. But they weren't just requesting gods, but gods to lead them forward—"that shall go before us." The pagan worldview had robbed them of seeing God as having led them out of Egypt and, instead, they scornfully attributed the Exodus to Moses (cf. Acts. 7:40).

32:4 a molded calf. The young bull, which Aaron caused to be fashioned, was a pagan religious symbol of virile power. A miniature form of the golden calf, although made of bronze and silver, was found at the site of the ancient Philistine city of Ashkelon. Since it dates to about 1550 B.C., it indicates that calf worship was known not only in Egypt, but also in Canaan prior to the time of Moses. In worshiping the calf, the Israelites violated the first three commandments (20:3–7).

32:5 feast to the LORD. Syncretism brought about the ludicrous combination of an idol, an altar, and a festal celebration held in a bizarre attempt to honor the true God.

32:6 rose up to play. The Hebrew word allows for the inclusion of drunken and immoral activities so common to idolatrous fertility cults in their revelry (see the description in vv. 7, 25). Syncretism had robbed the people of all ethical alertness and moral discernment (cf. 1 Cor. 10:7).

32:7 your people. In alerting Moses to the trouble in the camp, God designated Israel as Moses' people, a change of possessive pronoun Moses could not have missed. Beforehand, God had acknowledged them as "My people." In pleading with God for Israel and in responding to God's offer to make of him a great nation (v. 10), Moses maintained what he knew to be true, given the Exodus and the divine promises to the patriarchs (vv. 12, 13), and designated them correctly as "Your people" (v. 11).

32:10 make of you a great nation. God could have consumed all the people and started over again with Moses, just like he had done earlier with Abraham (Gen. 12).

Key Word

Consecrate: 28:3, 41; 29:9, 33, 35; 30:30; 32:29—this verb means "to make holy," "to declare distinct," or "to set apart." The word describes dedicating an object or person to God. By delivering the Israelites from slavery in Egypt, God made the nation of Israel distinct. Through His mighty acts of deliverance, God demonstrated that the Israelites were His people, and He was their God (6:7). By having the people wash themselves at Mount Sinai, the Lord made it clear that He was claiming a special relationship with them (19:10).

32:13 Israel. Another name for Jacob, which means "one who strives with God" (cf. Gen. 32:28).

32:14 the LORD relented from the harm. Moses' appeal for God to change His mind, to relent, succeeded because God had only threatened judgment, not decreed it. A divine intention is not an unchangeable divine decree. Decrees or sworn declarations (cf. Gen. 22:16–18; Ps. 110:4) or categorical statements of not changing or relenting (cf. Jer. 4:28; Ezek. 24:14; Zech. 8:14, 15) are unconditional and bind the speaker to the stated course of action regardless of the circumstances or reactions of the listeners. Intentions retain a conditional element and do not necessarily bind the speaker to a stated course of action (cf. Jer. 15:6; 18:8–10; 26:3, 13, 19; Joel 2:13; Jon. 3:9, 10; 4:2).

32:19 broke them. Moses pictured the nation breaking God's commandments by actually breaking the tablets on which they were written.

32:22–24 Aaron, held responsible by Moses for what had taken place in the camp (vv. 21, 25), endeavored to avoid responsibility for the people's actions by shifting the blame to their propensity to do evil, and also for the presence of the golden calf by representing it as having just popped out of the fire all by itself.

32:23 See Acts. 7:40.

32:26 *Whoever is on the* LORD*'s side.* Only the tribe of Levi responded to the call to take action in response to this situation which demanded judgment be inflicted. They had understood that neutrality could not exist in the open confrontation between good and evil. Family and national ties were superseded by submission to the Lord to do His will, which in this situation was to wield the sword of God's judgment to preserve His honor and glory.

32:28 They apparently killed those who persisted in idolatry and immorality (cf. Num. 25:6–9).

32:32 *blot me out of Your book.* Nothing more strongly marked the love of Moses for his people than his sincere willingness to offer up his own life rather than see them disinherited and destroyed. The book to which Moses referred, the psalmist entitled "the book of the living" (Ps. 69:28). Untimely or premature death would constitute being blotted out of the book. The apostle Paul displayed a similar, passionate devotion for his kinsmen (Rom. 9:1–3).

D. The Presence of God Confirmed (33:1–34:35)

33:2–6 Good news included bad news! Entry into the Promised Land was not forfeited, but God's presence on the way was withdrawn. What was a sworn covenant-promise to the patriarchs just could not be broken: what was assured—the divine presence on the way—could be set aside because of sin (cf. 23:20–23). The removal of their jewelry depicted outwardly of the people's sorrow of heart. It was a response analogous to donning sackcloth and ashes.

33:2 *See notes on 3:8.*

33:7 *the tabernacle of meeting.* In the time prior to the construction of the tabernacle, Moses' tent became the special meeting place for Moses to talk intimately, "face to face" (v. 11), with God. No doubt, the people watching from afar were reminded of the removal of God's immediate presence.

33:12–17 Again, Moses entered earnestly and confidently into the role of intercessor before God for the nation whom he again referred to as "Your people" (vv. 13, 16). Moses clearly understood that without God's presence they would not be a people set apart from other nations, so why travel any further? Moses' favored standing before the Lord comes out in the positive response to his intercession (v. 17).

33:18–23 Cautionary measures were needed for God to respond only in part to Moses' request to see more of Him than he was already experiencing (cf. Num. 12:8)—otherwise he would die. Notwithstanding God's being gracious and compassionate to whomever He chose, Moses could not see God's face and live. Whatever he saw of God's nature transformed into blazing light is referred to as "God's back" and was never subsequently described by Moses (cf. John 1:18; 1 John 4:12).

33:19 See Romans 9:15.

34:1 *Cut two tablets of stone.* Renewal of the covenant meant replacement of the broken, original tablets on which God had personally written the Ten Commandments (cf. 32:19).

34:2–28 Moses' second period of forty days and nights on Mt. Sinai (cf. chs. 25–32).

34:6, 7 Here is one of the testimonies to the character of God.

34:7 *See note on 20:5, 6.*

34:11 *See note on 3:8.*

34:12–17 *See note on 23:32.* This time the

admonition on international treaties included a warning of how idolatry could easily ensnare them, by seemingly innocent invitations to join the festivities like a good neighbor or by intermarriage, because these events would require recognition of the contracting parties' deities. Their future history demonstrated the urgency of such instruction and the disaster of disobeying it.

34:18 *See note on 12:14.*

34:19, 20 *See note on 13:2.*

34:21 *See note on 20:8.*

34:22, 23, 26 *See note on 23:14–19.*

34:29–35 The first time on the mount (24:12–32:14), unlike the second, had not left Moses with a face which was reflecting some radiance associated with being in the presence of the Lord for an extended period of time. On the first occasion, mere mention was made of Moses' being gone forty days and nights (24:18). On the second, mention was made of the forty day and night absence, but adding that Moses had been there with the Lord neither eating nor drinking (v. 28), which appears to draw attention to the different nature of the second visit. It, in comparison with the first, was not interrupted by the Lord's sending Moses away because of sin in the camp (32:7–10). A compliant people feared the evidence of God's presence. When not speaking to the Lord or authoritatively on His behalf to the people, Moses veiled his face. The apostle Paul advised that the veil prevented the people from seeing a fading glory and related it to the inadequacy of the old covenant and the blindness of the Jews in his day (*see notes on 2 Cor. 3:7–18*).

E. The Tabernacle of God Constructed (35:1–40:38)

35:1–40:38 In this section, the Israelites constructed the tabernacle as God so prescribed in 25:1–31:18.

35:1–3 *See note on 20:8.* This time, however, an extra admonition forbids the making of a fire on the Sabbath.

35:4–9 *See note on 25:2.*

35:10–19 *See notes on 25:11–28:43.*

35:20–29 *See note on 25:2.*

35:30–36:1 The Lord also gave the two named artisans skill in teaching their trades. This substantiates that they were, most probably, the supervisors or leaders of the construction teams. *See notes on 28:3; 31:1–11.*

36:2–7 The people, stubborn and disobedient at times, nevertheless rose to the occasion and voluntarily brought much more than was needed for the building of the tabernacle. *See note on 25:2.*

36:8–39:43 The report of the work done is repeated in the past tense. This report also highlighted how careful the workers were in carrying out the instructions and blueprints received. The refrain on doing all just as the Lord had commanded Moses is repeated frequently (39:1, 5, 7, 21, 26, 29, 31, 32, 42, 43; 40:19, 21, 23, 25, 27, 29, 32).

36:8–37 *See notes on chapter 26.*

37:1–9 *See notes on 25:16, 17, 18.*

37:10–16 *See note on 25:30.*

37:17–24 *See note on 25:31.*

37:25–28 *See note on 30:1–10.*

37:29 *See notes on 30:22–33, 34–38.*

38:1–7 *See note on 27:1.*

38:8 *See note on 30:18–21.*

38:9–20 *See notes on 27:9, 16.*

38:21–31 The inventory taken calculates out at one-half shekel (cf. 30:13–16) per man twenty years old and up to equal 603,550 men (cf. Num. 1:46 and the first census). Talents were about seventy-five pounds and shekels about half an ounce.

39:1, 2 they made . . . He made. The third-person plural, "they," dominating the manufacturing report (vv. 2–31), is interrupted four times by the singular "he" (vv. 2, 7, 8, 22). The plural undoubtedly refers to Bezalel and/or his associates in operation, whereas the singular marks out what Bezalel worked on by himself.

39:1 *as the* LORD *had commanded Moses.* This repetitive refrain (vv. 1, 5, 7, 21, 26, 29, 31), a quality-control statement, signals to the reader of every era, or to the listener in Israel back then, that God's detailed instructions to Moses on the fabricating of the ephod (vv. 2–7), breastplate (vv. 8–21), and priestly garments (vv. 22–31) were followed to the letter. Obedience in every detail was taken seriously by Israel's artisans.

39:2 *He made the ephod.* See note on 28:5–13.

39:3 *they beat the gold into thin sheets and cut it into threads.* The process adopted to get the delicate strips for braided chains or gold embroidery work conformed well with contemporary Egyptian methods of goldworking.

39:8 *he made the breastplate.* See notes on 28:15–30, 30. The Urim and Thummim were inserted into the breastplate and became an essential part of it, or were seen as a permanent connection with it.

39:22 *He made the robe of the ephod.* See note on 28:31–35.

39:27 *They made tunics . . . for Aaron and his sons.* See notes on 28:39–43.

39:30 *they made the plate of the holy crown.* See note on 28:36–38 on this special plate engraved with its message of God's purity and separation from all the profane and impure.

39:32 *Thus all the work . . . was finished.* Finally, the moment arrived when the different tasks assigned to various artisans were all completed, and the result was ready for formal presentation to Israel's leader. *And the children of Israel.* No individual artisan is singled out for special mention or award; instead, the whole nation was represented as doing everything in accordance with the Lord's instructions to Moses. *so they did.* In what is almost an aside, emphasis is placed on the strict attention paid to the official, divine specifications for all parts of the work for the tabernacle.

39:33 *And they brought the tabernacle to Moses.* Attestations of obedience and accuracy provide, as it were, an envelope (vv. 32, 42, 43) for the concise inventory of all the parts included in that presentation to Moses. None of the individual parts listed, nor the sum of them, reflect just human ingenuity in designing something they wanted to have, but reflect instead just what their Lord required them to have. It was fully His architecture and His design at every level of the undertaking.

39:42, 43 The double repetition of the same quality-control refrain found earlier in the chapter and the three additional phrases emphasizing exact conformity ("indeed," or "behold," and "just so") to all specifications combine to formally mark the completion of these great God-initiated preparations for the place of His presence and the site of their worship. Israel's skillful artisans had done their work with zero tolerance for error.

39:43 *Then Moses looked over all the work.* Fittingly enough, the one who had been with God on the mount and had passed on to the people the blueprints for everything connected with the Lord's tabernacle personally inspected the work and confirmed its successful completion. The term *work* is to be taken as "the end result of professional and skilled craftsmen." *And Moses blessed them.* By this act, Moses set his final and formal seal of approval on the outcome of their earnestness and diligence, and expressed his prayer-wish that good would result to them from their God. This is the only instance recorded in Exodus of Moses' pro-

---

Key Word

Washing: 2:5; 19:10; 29:4, 17; 30:18, 21; 40:12, 30—washing or bathing. The term was used in both religious and cultural settings. The ancient custom of washing a guest's feet was a part of hospitality still practiced in the New Testament period (Gen. 18:4; John 13:5). Ritual washing was an important step in the purification of the priests for service in the tabernacle (40:12). Washing with water symbolized spiritual cleansing, the preparation necessary for entering God's presence (Pss. 26:6; 73:13). The Old Testament prophets used this imagery of repentance (Is. 1:16; Ezek. 16:4). In the New Testament, Paul describes redemption in Christ as "the washing of regeneration" (Titus 3:5).

---

nouncing a blessing on his people. The other appearances of the verb "to bless" occur three times with God as the subject of the verb (20:11, 24; 23:25) and one time with Pharaoh requesting Moses to bless him (12:32).

40:1–33 Finally, the time arrived for the tabernacle to be erected with the Holy of Holies and its accompanying Holy Place to the west, and the courtyard entrance to the east. In terms of pagan religions and their worship of the sun god, some polemic sig-

nificance might be seen in the high priest worshiping God with his back to the rising sun. All who entered the courtyard also turned their backs to the rising sun as they came in to sacrifice and worship.

40:17 The tabernacle was completed almost one year after the Exodus from Egypt. The people were at the foot of Mt. Sinai at that time, where the Book of Leviticus was given in the first month of that second year. The record of Numbers begins with the people still at Mt. Sinai in the second month of that second year after leaving Egypt (cf. Num. 1:1).

40:34 *the cloud covered . . . the glory of the* LORD *filled.* This was the final confirmation for Moses and the people that all the work for setting up God's dwelling place had been properly done and all the tedious instructions obediently followed.

40:36 *taken up.* This first occurred (as recorded in Num. 10:11) fifty days after the tabernacle was finished and erected.

Further Study

Davis, John J. *Moses and the Gods of Egypt.* Grand Rapids: Baker, 1971.

Kaiser, Walter C., Jr. *Exodus*, in Expositor's Bible Commentary. Grand Rapids: Zondervan, 1990.

THE THIRD BOOK OF MOSES CALLED
LEVITICUS

Title

The original Hebrew title of this third book of the law is taken from the first word, translated "and He called." Several OT books derive their Hebrew names in the same manner (e.g., Genesis, "In the beginning"; Exodus, "Now these are the names"). The title *Leviticus* comes from the Latin Vulgate version of the Greek OT (LXX) *Levitikon* meaning "matters of the Levites" (25:32, 33). While the book addresses issues of the Levites' responsibilities, much more significantly, all the priests are instructed in how they are to assist the people in worship, and the people are informed about how to live a holy life. New Testament writers quote the Book of Leviticus more than fifteen times.

Author and Date

Authorship and date issues are resolved by the concluding verse of the book, "These are the commandments which the LORD commanded Moses for the children of Israel on Mount Sinai" (27:34; cf. 7:38; 25:1; 26:46). The fact that God gave these laws to Moses (cf. 1:1) appears fifty-six times in Leviticus' twenty-seven chapters. In addition to recording detailed prescriptions, the book chronicles several historical accounts relating to the laws (see chs. 8–10; 24:10–23). The Exodus occurred in 1445 B.C. (see Introduction to Exodus: Author and Date) and the tabernacle was finished one year later (Ex. 40:17). Leviticus picks up the record at that point, probably revealed in the first month

(Abib/Nisan) of the second year after the Exodus. The Book of Numbers begins after that in the second month (Ziv; cf. Num. 1:1).

Background and Setting

Before the year that Israel camped at Mt. Sinai: (1) the presence of God's glory had never formally resided among the Israelites; (2) a central place of worship, like the tabernacle, had never existed; (3) a structured and regulated set of sacrifices and feasts had not been given; and (4) a high priest, a formal priesthood, and a cadre of tabernacle workers had not been appointed. As Exodus concluded, features one and two had been accomplished, thereby requiring that elements three and four be inaugurated, which is what Leviticus provides. Exodus 19:6 called Israel to be "a kingdom of priests and a holy nation." Leviticus in turn is God's instruction for His newly redeemed people, teaching them how to worship and obey Him.

Israel had, up to that point, only the historical records of the patriarchs from which to gain their knowledge of how to worship and live before their God. Having been slaves for centuries in Egypt, the land of a seemingly infinite number of gods, their concept of worship and the godly life was severely distorted. Their tendency to hold on to polytheism and pagan ritual is witnessed in the wilderness wanderings, e.g., when they worshiped the golden calf (cf. Ex. 32). God would not permit them to worship in the ways of their Egyptian neighbors, nor would He tolerate Egyptian ideas about morality and sin. With the instructions in Leviticus, the priests could lead Israel in worship appropriate to the Lord.

Even though the book contains a great deal of law, it is presented in a historical format. Immediately after Moses supervised the construction of the tabernacle, God came in glory to dwell there; this marked the close of the Book of Exodus (40:34–38). Leviticus begins with God calling Moses from the tabernacle and ends with God's commands to Moses in the form of binding legislation. Israel's King had occupied His palace (the tabernacle), instituted His law, and declared Himself a covenant partner with His subjects.

No geographical movement occurs in this book. The people of Israel stay at the foot of Sinai, the mountain where God came down to give His law (25:1; 26:46; 27:34). They were still there one month later when the record of Numbers began (cf. Num. 1:1).

Historical and Theological Themes
The core ideas around which Leviticus develops are the holy character of God and the will of God for Israel's holiness. God's holiness, mankind's sinfulness, sacrifice, and God's presence in the sanctuary are the book's most common themes. With a clear, authoritative tone, the book sets forth instruction toward personal holiness at the urging of God (11:44, 45; 19:2; 20:7, 26; cf. 1 Pet. 1:14–16). Matters pertaining to Israel's life of faith tend to focus on purity in ritual settings, but not to the exclusion of concerns regarding Israel's personal purity. In fact, there is a continuing emphasis on personal holiness in response to the holiness of God (cf. this emphasis in chs. 17–27). On over 125 occasions, Leviticus indicts mankind for uncleanness and/or instructs on how to be purified. The motive for such holiness is

stated in two repeated phrases: "I am the Lord" and "I am holy." These are used over fifty times. *See note on 11:44, 45.*

The theme of the conditional Mosaic covenant resurfaces throughout the book, but particularly in chapter 26. This contract for the new nation not only details the consequences for obedience or disobedience to the covenant stipulations, but it does so in a manner scripted for determining Israel's history. One cannot help but recognize prophetic implications in the punishments for disobedience; they sound like the events of the much later Babylonian deportment, captivity, and subsequent return to the land (c. 538 b.c.) almost 900 years after Moses wrote Leviticus. The eschatological implications for Israel's disobedience will not conclude until Messiah comes to introduce His kingdom and end the curses of Leviticus 26 and Deuteronomy 28 (cf. Zech. 14:11).

The five sacrifices and offerings were symbolic. Their design was to allow the truly penitent and thankful worshiper to express faith in and love for God by the observance of these rituals. When the heart was not penitent and thankful, God was not pleased with the ritual. (cf. Amos 5:21–27). The offerings were burnt, symbolizing the worshiper's desire to be purged of sin and sending up the fragrant smoke of true worship to God. The myriad of small details in the execution of the rituals was intended to teach exactness and precision that would extend to the way the people obeyed the moral and spiritual laws of God and the way they revered every facet of His Word. *See notes on 11:1–47; 11:44, 45; 13:2.*

Interpretive Challenges
Leviticus is both a manual for the worship of God in Israel and a theology of old covenant ritual. Comprehensive understanding of the ceremonies, laws, and ritual details pre-

scribed in the book is difficult today because Moses assumed a certain context of historical understanding. Once the challenge of understanding the detailed prescriptions has been met, the question arises as to how believers in the church should respond to them, since the NT clearly abrogates OT ceremonial law (cf. Acts 10:1–16; Col. 2:16, 17), the levitical priesthood (cf. 1 Pet. 2:9; Rev. 1:6; 5:10; 20:6), and the sanctuary (cf. Matt. 27:51), as well as instituting the new covenant (cf. Matt. 26:28; 2 Cor. 3:6–18; Heb. 7–10).

Rather than try to practice the old ceremonies or look for some deeper spiritual significance in them, the focus should be on the holy and divine character behind them. This may partly be the reason that explanations which Moses often gave in the prescriptions for cleanness offer greater insight into the mind of God than do the ceremonies themselves. The spiritual principles in which the rituals were rooted are timeless because they are embedded in the nature of God. The NT makes it clear that from Pentecost forward (cf. Acts 2), the church is under the authority of the new covenant, not the old covenant (cf. Heb. 7–10).

The interpreter is challenged to compare features of this book with NT writers who present types or analogies based on the tabernacle and the ceremonial aspects of the law, so as to teach valuable lessons about Christ and new covenant reality. Though the ceremonial law served only as a shadow of the reality of Christ and His redemptive work (Heb. 10:1), excessive typology is to be rejected. Only that which NT writers identify specifically as types of Christ should be so designated (cf. 1 Cor. 5:7, "Christ our Passover").

The most profitable study in Leviticus is that which yields truth in the understanding of sin, guilt, substitutionary death, and atonement by focusing on features which are not explained or illustrated elsewhere in OT Scripture. Later OT authors, and especially NT writers, build on the basic understanding of these matters provided in Leviticus. The sacrificial features of Leviticus point to their ultimate, one-time fulfillment in the substitutionary death of Jesus Christ (Heb. 9:11–22).

Leviticus 1–16 explains how to have personal access to God through appropriate worship, while Leviticus 17–27 details how to be spiritually acceptable to God through an obedient walk.

Outline

I. Laws Pertaining to Sacrifice (1:1–7:38)

1:1–7:38 This section provides laws pertaining to sacrifice. For the first time in Israel's history, a well-defined set of sacrifices was given to them, although people had offered sacrifices since the time of Abel and Cain (cf. Gen. 4:3, 4). This section contains instructions for the people (1:1–6:7) and the priests (6:8–7:38). For a comparison with the millennial kingdom sacrifices, *see notes on Ezekiel 45 and 46.*

A. Legislation for the Laity (1:1–6:7)

1:1–6:7 God had taken the nation at its word, "All that the LORD has spoken we will do" (Ex. 19:8; 24:3–8), and gave detailed instructions as to how they were to sacrifice to Him. Five sacrifices were outlined: the first three were voluntary, the last two compulsory. They were: (1) burnt offering (1:1–17); (2) grain offering (2:1–16); (3) peace offering (3:1–17); (4) sin offering (4:1–5:13); and (5) trespass offering (5:14–6:7). All these offerings were forms of worship to God, to give expression of the penitent and thankful heart. Those who were truly God's by faith gave offerings with an attitude of worship; for the rest, they were external rituals only.

1. Burnt offerings (1:1–17)

1:1 *Now the LORD called to Moses.* Leviticus begins where Exodus left off (see Introduction: Author and Date; Background and Setting). No sooner did the glory cloud come down to rest on the tabernacle in the concluding verses of Exodus than God instructed Moses with the content in Leviticus. The question of how to use the tabernacle in worship is answered here by an audible voice from the divine glory over the ark in the Holy of Holies (cf. Ex. 40:34; Num. 7:89; Ps. 80:1). *tabernacle of meeting.* This is so named since it was the place where Israel would gather to meet the Lord (cf. Ex. 25:8, 22; 26:1–37). See Exodus 25–32 for a detailed description of the tabernacle.

1:2 *Speak to the children of Israel.* This is essential revelation, with reference to their spiritual life, for all the descendants of Jacob, who was also called Israel (cf. Gen. 32:28). *When any one of you brings.* These were completely voluntary and freewill offerings with no specific number or frequency given (1:3). The regulation excluded horses, dogs, pigs, camels, and donkeys, which were used in pagan sacrifices, as well as rabbits, deer, beasts, and birds of prey. The sacrifice had to be from the offerer's herd or he had to purchase it. *an offering.* The Pharisees manipulated this simple concept so that adult children could selfishly withhold the material goods which would help their parents, under the guise of *Corban*, that it was dedicated to the Lord (cf. Mark 7:8–13). *herd . . . flock.* These terms refer to the cattle (1:3), and sheep or goats (1:10), respectively. Only domestic animals could be sacrificed.

1:3–17 See 6:8–13 for the priests' instructions. The burnt offerings were the first sacrifices revealed because these were the ones to be most frequently offered: every morning and evening (Num. 28:1–8), every Sabbath (Num. 28:9, 10), the first day of each month (Num. 28:11–15), and at the special feasts (Num. 28:16–29:40). This offering signified voluntary and complete dedication and consecration to the Lord. It was an offering of repentance for sins committed, with the desire to be purged from the guilt of sinful acts. Designed to demonstrate the sinner's penitence and obedience, it indicated his dedication to the worship of God. The most costly animal was mentioned first, the least costly last. The singing of psalms later became a part of this ritual (cf. Pss. 4; 5; 40; 50; 66).

1:3–9 This section describes the sacrifice of bulls (1:5).

1:3 *burnt sacrifice.* This offering is so called because it required that the animal be completely consumed by the fire, except for the feathers of a bird (1:16) or the skin of the bull, which went to the priest (1:6; 7:8). *a male without blemish.* Since no animal with any deformity or defect was permitted, the priests would inspect each animal, perhaps using a method which the Egyptians employed in their sacrifices, calling for all inspected and approved animals to have a certificate attached to the horns and sealed with wax. A male without blemish was required, as it was the choicest offering of the flock. *at the door . . . before the LORD.* This entrance to the courtyard around the tabernacle where the altar of burnt offering stood (Ex. 40:6) would place the person offering a sacrifice on the north side of the altar (cf. 1:11). God's presence in the cloud rested upon the mercy seat of the ark in the Holy of Holies inside the tabernacle proper (*see note on 1:1*). The offering was brought to and offered before the Lord, not before man.

1:4 *put his hand on the head.* This symbolic gesture pictured the transfer of the sacrificer's sin to the sacrificial animal and was likely done with a prayer of repentance and request for forgiveness (cf. Ps. 51:18, 19). *on his behalf.* This was a substitutionary sacrifice that prefigured the ultimate substitute—Jesus Christ (cf. Is. 53; *see note on 2 Cor. 5:21*). *make atonement.* The word means "cover." The psalmist defines it by saying, "Blessed is he whose transgression is forgiven, whose sin is covered" (Ps. 32:1). Theologically, the "atonement" of the OT covered sin only temporarily, but it did not eliminate sin or later judgment (Heb. 10:4). The one-time sacrifice of Jesus Christ fully atoned for sin, thus satisfying God's wrath forever and insuring eternal salvation (cf.

Burnt Offering
Scripture References
Leviticus 1:3–17; 6:8–13
Purpose
1. To atone for sin in general (1:4)
2. To signify complete dedication and consecration to God; hence it is called the "whole burnt offering."
Consisted of
According to wealth:
1. Bull without blemish (1:3–9)
2. Male sheep or goat without blemish (1:10–13)
3. Turtledoves or young pigeons (1:14–17)
God's Portion
Entirety burned on the altar of burnt offering (1:9), except the skin (7:8)
Priests' Portion
Skin only (7:8)
Offerer's Portion
None

Heb. 9:12; 1 John 2:2), even to those who put saving faith in God for their redemption before Christ's death on the cross (cf. Rom. 3:25, 26; Heb. 9:15).

1:5 *He shall kill.* Making vivid and dramatic the consequences of sin, the person offering the sacrifice killed and butchered the animal (cf. v. 6). *Aaron's sons.* This refers to the immediate descendants of Aaron, i.e., Nadab, Abihu, Eleazar, and Ithamar (cf. Ex. 28:1). In the beginning, there were five priests, including Aaron, who served as the high priest. *shall bring . . . sprinkle the blood.* The priest had to collect the blood in a basin and then offer it to God as a sacrifice to indicate that a life had been taken, i.e., death occurred (cf. 17:11, 14). The price of sin is always death (cf. Gen. 2:17; Rom. 6:23). *the altar.* The altar of burnt offering (cf. Ex. 27:1–8; 38:1–7), which is in the courtyard outside of the tabernacle proper. The prototype experience, before the tabernacle was constructed, is remembered in Exodus 24:1–8.

1:9 wash. This allowed the person sacrificing to cleanse the animal of excrement and, thus, make it clean. *a sweet aroma.* The pleasant smell of burning meat signified the sacrifice of obedience which was pleasing to the Lord. While the costly ritual recognized God's anger for sin committed (cf. 1:13, 17), the penitent heart behind the sacrifice made it acceptable. That was far more significant than the sacrifice itself (cf. Gen. 8:21; 1 Sam. 15:23). This is the first of three freewill offerings to please the Lord; cf. the grain offering (2:2) and the peace offering (3:5).

1:10–13 of the flocks. This section describes the sacrifice of sheep and goats.

1:11 north side. This placed the person sacrificing in front of the tabernacle door (cf. 1:3).

1:14–17 of birds. This section describes the sacrifice of birds. God does not ask the poor to bring the same burnt offering as those financially well off because the relative cost to the one sacrificing was an important factor. This was the kind of sacrifice brought by Joseph and Mary on the eighth day after Christ's birth for Mary's purification (cf. 12:8; Luke 2:22–24).

1:15 The priest . . . wring off. Unlike the livestock being killed by the one offering the sacrifice, the bird was killed by the priest.

1:16 crop . . . feathers. This refers to the neck or gullet of a bird, where food was stored. *east side . . . place for ashes.* This was the closest side to the entrance of the tabernacle compound and provided for the easiest removal of the ashes outside (cf. 6:10, 11).

2. Grain offerings (2:1–16)

2:1–16 See 6:14–23 for the priests' instructions. The grain offering signified homage and thanksgiving to God as a voluntary offering which was offered along with a burnt offering and a drink offering at the appointed sacrifices (cf. Num. 28:1–15). Three variations were prescribed: (1) uncooked flour (2:1–3); (2) baked flour (2:4–13); or (3) roasted firstfruit grain from the harvest (2:14–16). This was the only non-animal sacrifice of the five and shows that there was a place for offering from the fruit of the soil (as in the case of Cain in Genesis 4).

2:1–3 fine flour. The first variation consisted of uncooked flour whose quality of "fine" paralleled the "unblemished" animal in the burnt offering. A portion of this offering was to support the priests (v. 3). Like the drink offering or "libation," the grain offering was added to the burnt offering (cf. Num. 28:1–15).

2:1 oil. *See note on 2:4.* **frankincense.** *See note on 2:15.*

2:2 handful. Unlike the whole burnt offering (1:9), only a representative or memorial portion was given to the Lord. *sweet aroma. See note on 1:9.*

2:3 Aaron's and his sons'. Unlike the burnt offering (cf. 1:9, 13, 17), this offering supplies provision for the priests. *most holy.* This was unique from the others because it was not limited to God alone, like the burnt offering, nor eaten in part by the worshiper, like the peace offering. Only the priest could eat the portion not burned (see 7:9). The sin offering (6:17, 25) and the trespass offering (6:17; 7:1) are also called "most holy."

2:4–13 This variation of the grain offering involved baked flour. The kinds of containers discussed are: (1) oven (2:4); (2) griddle (2:5, 6); and (3) covered pan (2:7–10). The manner of preparation is discussed in 2:11–13.

2:4 unleavened cakes. The notion of leaven as a symbol representing the presence of sin remains valid beyond the context of the Passover and continues to the NT (cf.

Grain Offering

Scripture References

Leviticus 2:1–16; 6:14–23

Purpose

The grain offering accompanied all the burnt offerings; it signified one's homage and thanksgiving to God.

Consisted of

Three types:

1. Fine flour mixed with oil and frankincense (2:1–3)
2. Cakes made of fine flour mixed with oil and baked in an oven (2:4), in a pan (2:5), or in a covered pan (2:7)
3. Green heads of roasted grain mixed with oil and frankincense (2:14, 15)

God's Portion

Memorial portion burned on the altar of burnt offering (2:2, 9, 16)

Priests' Portion

Remainder to be eaten in the court of the tabernacle (2:3, 10; 6:16–18)

Offerer's Portion

None

Matt. 16:6; 1 Cor. 5:6, 7). **anointed with oil.** Anointing is usually reserved for human appointments by God. Here, it was applied to the preparation of a holy sacrifice, set apart as a memorial to the Lord.

2:11 This applies to the offerings of 2:4–10, all of which were to be burned on the altar. **no leaven nor any honey.** Both yeast and honey were edible foods, but were never to be used with a grain offering, since both could induce fermentation, which symbolized sin (*see note on 2:4*).

2:12 This applies to the offering of 2:14–16, which was not to be burned on the altar, but rather roasted by the worshiper (v. 14) before going to the tabernacle.

2:13 the salt of the covenant. This was included in all of the offerings in 2:4–10, 14–16

since salt was emblematic of permanence or loyalty to the covenant.

2:14 firstfruits. These would be offered at the Feast of Firstfruits (23:9–14) and the Feast of Weeks (23:15–22).

2:15 frankincense. A gum resin with a pungent, balsamic odor, used for the incense in the tabernacle sacrifices (cf. Ex. 30:34).

3. Peace offerings (3:1–17)

3:1–17 See 7:11–36 for the priests' instructions. The peace offering symbolizes the peace and fellowship between the true worshiper and God (as a voluntary offering). It was the third freewill offering resulting in a sweet aroma to the Lord (3:5), which served as the appropriate corollary to the burnt offering of atonement and the grain offering of consecration and dedication. It symbolized the fruit of redemptive reconciliation between a sinner and God (cf. 2 Cor. 5:18).

3:1–5 This pertains to cattle, i.e., the herd, used in the peace offering.

3:1, 2 male or female. This is similar to the burnt offering in manner of presentation (cf. 1:3–9), but different in that a female was allowed.

3:4 the fat. All of the fat was dedicated to the Lord (3:3–5, 9–11, 14–16).

3:6–11 This pertains to sheep used in the peace offering.

3:11 as food. The sacrifice was intended to symbolize a meal between God and the one offering it, where peace and friendship were epitomized by sharing that meal together.

3:12–16 This pertains to goats used in the peace offering.

3:17 neither fat nor blood. The details given in the chapter distinctly define which fat was to be burned and not eaten, so that whatever adhered to other parts or was mixed with them might be eaten. As with

---

Peace Offering

Scripture References

Leviticus 3:1–17; 7:11–36

Purpose

The peace offering generally expressed peace and fellowship between the offerer and God; hence it culminated in a communal meal.

There were three types:

1. Thank offering: to express gratitude for an unexpected blessing or deliverance
2. Votive offering: to express gratitude for a blessing or deliverance granted when a vow had accompanied the petition
3. Freewill offering: to express gratitude to God without regard to any specific blessing or deliverance

Consisted of

According to wealth:

1. From the herd, a male or female without blemish (3:1–5)
2. From the flock, a male or female without blemish (3:6–11)
3. From the goats (3:12–17)

Note: Minor imperfections were permitted when the peace offering was a freewill offering of a bull or a lamb (22:23).

God's Portion

Fatty portions burned on the altar of burnt offering (3:3–5)

Priests' Portion

Breast (wave offering) and right thigh (heave offering; 7:30–34)

Offerer's Portion

Remainder to be eaten in the court by the offerer and his family:

1. Thank offering—to be eaten the same day (7:15)
2. Votive and freewill offerings—to be eaten the first and second day (7:16–18)

Note: This is the only offering in which the offerer shared.

---

many facets of the Mosaic legislation, there were underlying health benefits also.

4:1–6:7 The sin (4:1–5:13) and trespass (5:14–6:7) offerings differed from the previous three in that the former were voluntary and these were compulsory. The sin offering differed from the trespass offering in that the former involved iniquity where restitution was not possible, while in the latter it was possible.

4. Sin offerings (4:1–5:13)

4:1–5:13 See 6:24–30 for the priests' instructions. The sin offering atoned for sins committed unknowingly where restitution was impossible. This was a required sacrifice, as was the trespass offering (5:14–6:7). Unintentional sins of commission (4:1–35) and unintentional sins of omission (5:1–13) are discussed. Leviticus 4:1–35 indicates the person committing the sin: (1) the high priest (vv. 3–12); (2) the congregation (vv. 13–21); (3) a leader (vv. 22–26); or (4) an individual (vv. 27–35). Leviticus 5:1–13 unfolds according to the animal sacrificed: (1) lamb/goat (vv. 1–6); (2) bird (vv. 7–10); or (3) flour (vv. 11–13).

4:2 *unintentionally.* The intended meaning is to stray into a sinful situation, but not necessarily to be taken completely by surprise. Numbers 15:30, 31 illustrates the defiant attitude of intentional sin. *ought not . . . does any.* Sins of commission.

4:3–12 Sacrifices for the sin of the high priest are given.

4:3 *the anointed priest.* See Exodus 29:29 and Leviticus 16:32, which defined this person as the high priest. *bringing guilt on the people.* Only the high priest, due to his representative position, was capable of this type of guilt infusion. For example, Achan had brought about the defeat of Israel when he held back the spoils, but the entire nation

Sin Offering

Scripture References
Leviticus 4:1–5:13; 6:24–30

Purpose
To atone for sins committed unknowingly, especially where no restitution was possible

Note: Numbers 15:30, 31: The sin offering was of no avail in cases of defiant rebellion against God.

Consisted of
1. For the high priest, a bull without blemish (4:3–12)
2. For the congregation, a bull without blemish (4:13–21)
3. For a ruler, a male goat without blemish (4:22–26)
4. For a commoner, a female goat or female lamb without blemish (4:27–35)
5. In cases of poverty, two turtledoves or two young pigeons (one for a sin offering, the other for a burnt offering) could be substituted 5:7–10).
6. In cases of extreme poverty, fine flour could be substituted (5:11–13; cf. Heb. 9:22).

God's Portion
1. Fatty portions to be burned on the altar of burnt offering (4:8–10, 19, 26, 31, 35)
2. When the sin offering was for the high priest or congregation, the remainder of the bull was to be burned outside the camp (4:11, 12, 20, 21).

Priests' Portion
When the sin offering was for a ruler or commoner, the remainder of the goat or lamb was to be eaten in the tabernacle court (6:26).

Offerer's Portion
None

was not executed, as was his family (cf. Josh. 7:22–26).

4:5 to the tabernacle. He actually went into the Holy Place.

4:6 seven times. The number of completion or perfection, indicating the nature of God's forgiveness (Ps. 103:12). **the veil of the sanctuary.** The veil marked the entry into the very presence of God in the Holy of Holies.

4:7 altar of sweet incense. See Exodus 30:1–10. This altar was in the tabernacle proper before the veil. It was so close to the ark that Hebrews speaks of it as actually being in the Holy of Holies (Heb. 9:4). This altar was also sprinkled with blood on the Day of Atonement (Ex. 30:10). **altar . . . burnt offering.** The altar in the courtyard on which blood was normally splashed.

4:10 peace offering. See note on 3:1–17.

4:11 offal. This term identifies the major internal organs of an animal, including the intestines' waste content.

4:12 carry outside the camp. This was a symbolic gesture of removing the sin from the people (cf. Heb. 13:11–13 in reference to Christ).

4:13–21 Sacrifices for the sin of the congregation were to follow, essentially, the same procedure as that for the sin of priests (4:3–12).

4:16 The anointed priest. See note on 4:3.

4:22–26 These are sacrifices for the sin of a ruler. The blood of the sacrifice was not sprinkled in the Holy Place, as for the priest or congregation (4:6, 17), but only on the altar of burnt offering.

4:27–35 These are sacrifices for the sin of an individual. Either a goat (4:27–31) or a lamb (4:32–35) could be sacrificed in much the same manner as the offering for a ruler (4:22–26).

5:1–13 Dealing with unintentional sins

continues with an emphasis on sins of omission (vv. 1–4). Lambs/goats (v. 6), birds (vv. 7–10), or flour (vv. 11–13) were acceptable sacrifices.

5:1–5 This call to confession named a few examples of violations for which penitence was the right response: (1) withholding evidence (v. 1); (2) touching something unclean (vv. 2, 3); and (3) rash oath making (v. 4).

5:1 *oath . . . witness.* A witness who did not come forward to testify was sinning when he had actually seen a violation or had firsthand knowledge, such as hearing the violator confess to the sin.

5:4 *swears.* "Speaking thoughtlessly" suggests a reckless oath for good or bad, i.e., an oath the speaker should not or could not keep.

5:5 *he shall confess.* Confession must accompany the sacrifice as the outward expression of a repentant heart which openly acknowledged agreement with God concerning sin. Sacrifice without true faith, repentance, and obedience was hypocrisy (cf. Ps. 26:4; Is. 9:17; Amos 5:21–26).

5:7 *burnt offering.* See notes on 1:3–17.

5:11 *ephah.* About six gallons. *no oil . . . frankincense.* Contrast the grain offering (2:2).

5:13 *grain offering.* See notes on 2:1–16.

5. Trespass offerings (5:14–6:7)

5:14–6:7 See 7:1–10 for the priests' instructions. The trespass offering symbolized an atonement for sin unknowingly committed, where restitution was possible. Like the sin offering (4:1–5:13), this one was compulsory. For sins against the Lord's property, restitution was made to the priest (5:14–19), while restitution was made to the person who suffered loss in other instances (6:1–7).

5:15 *shekel of the sanctuary.* This amounted to twenty gerahs (Ex. 30:13; Lev. 27:25; Num. 3:47) or two bekahs (Ex. 38:26), which is the equivalent of four-tenths of one ounce. God fixed the value of a shekel.

5:16 *one-fifth.* The offender was required to make a 120 percent restitution, which was considerably lower than that prescribed elsewhere in the Mosaic law, e.g., Exodus 22:7, 9. Perhaps this is accounted for by a voluntary confession in contrast to an adjudicated and forced conviction.

6:1–7 While all sins are against God (cf. Ps. 51:4), some are direct (5:14–19) and others are indirect, involving people (6:1–7), as here. These violations are not exhaustive, but

Trespass Offering

Scripture References
Leviticus 5:14–6:7; 7:1–7

Purpose
To atone for sins committed unknowingly, especially where restitution was possible

Consisted of
1. If the offense were against the Lord (tithes, offerings, etc.), a ram without blemish was to be brought; restitution was reckoned according to the priest's estimate of the value of the trespass, plus one-fifth (5:15, 16).
2. If the offense were against a person, a ram without blemish was to be brought; restitution was reckoned according to the value plus one-fifth (6:4–6).

God's Portion
Fatty portions to be burned on the altar of burnt offering (7:3–5)

Priests' Portion
Remainder to be eaten in a holy place (7:6, 7)

Offerer's Portion
None

representative samples used to establish and illustrate the principle.

6:6 your valuation. The priest served as an appraiser to give appropriate value to the goods in question.

B. Legislation for the Priesthood (6:8–7:38)

6:8–7:38 These were laws of sacrifice for the priesthood. Leviticus 1:1–6:7 has dealt with five major offerings from the worshiper's perspective. Here, instructions for the priests are given, with special attention given to the priests' portion of the sacrifice.

1. Burnt offerings (6:8–13)

6:8–13 The burnt offering. *See notes on 1:3–17.*

6:9 on the hearth upon the altar all night. This resulted in the complete incineration of the sacrifice, picturing it as totally given to the Lord, with the smoke arising as a sweet aroma to Him (1:7, 13, 17).

6:10, 11 ashes. This described both the immediate (v. 10) and final (v. 11) disposition of the ash remains, i.e., that which is worthless.

6:12 fat . . . peace offerings. *See note on 3:4.*

6:13 always be burning. The perpetual flame indicated a continuous readiness on the part of God to receive confession and restitution through the sacrifice.

2. Grain offerings (6:14–23)

6:14–23 The grain offering. *See notes on 2:1–16.*

6:15 handful. *See note on 2:2.*

6:16–18 Unlike the burnt offering, the grain offering provided food for the priests and their male children, i.e., future priests.

6:16 in a holy place. This was to be eaten only in the courtyard of the tabernacle.

6:19–23 Aaron, as high priest, was to make a daily grain offering at morning and night on behalf of his priestly family.

6:20 he is anointed. See 8:7–12. **ephah.** *See note on 5:11.*

6:22 The priest . . . in his place. The high priests who succeed Aaron are in view here. **wholly burned.** The priests' offering was to be given completely, with nothing left over.

3. Sin offerings (6:24–30)

6:24–30 The sin offering. *See notes on 4:1–5:13.*

6:25 burnt offering. *See notes on 1:3–17.* **most holy.** *See note on 2:3.*

6:26 priest . . . eat. The priest putting the offering on the brazen altar could use it for food, if the sacrifice was for a ruler (4:22–26) or the people (4:27–35).

6:27, 28 These are instructions on the cleanness of the priest's garments as they relate to blood.

6:30 no sin offering . . . eaten. Those sacrifices made on behalf of a priest (4:3–12) or the congregation (4:13–21) could be eaten.

4. Trespass offerings (7:1–10)

7:1–10 The trespass offering. *See notes on 5:14–6:7.* Verses 7–10 provide a brief excursus on what may be eaten by the priests.

7:1 most holy. *See note on 2:3.*

7:7 *See note on 6:26.*

7:10 mixed with oil or dry. Both were acceptable options.

5. Peace offerings (7:11–36)

7:11–36 The peace offering. *See notes on 3:1–17.* The purposes of the peace offering are given in vv. 11–18. Special instructions which prevented a priest from being "cut off" (vv. 19–27) and the allotment to Aaron and his sons (vv. 28–36) are enumerated.

7:11–15 A peace offering for thanksgiving shall also be combined with a grain offering (see 2:1–16). The meat had to be eaten that

Christ in the Levitical Offerings		
Offering	Christ's Provision	Christ's Character
1. Burnt Offering (Lev. 1:3–17; 6:8–13)	atonement	Christ's sinless nature
2. Grain Offering (Lev. 2:1–16; 6:14–23)	dedication/consecration	Christ was wholly devoted to the Father's purposes
3. Peace Offering (Lev. 3:1–17; 7:11–36)	reconciliation/fellowship	Christ was at peace with God
4. Sin Offering (Lev. 4:1–5:13; 6:24–30)	propitiation	Christ's substitutionary death
5. Trespass Offering (Lev. 5:14–6:7; 7:1–10)	repentance	Christ paid it all for redemption

same day, probably for the reason of health since it would rapidly spoil and for the purpose of preventing people from thinking that such meat had some spiritual presence in it, thus developing some superstitions.

7:13 leavened bread. Contrast the unleavened grain offering (see 2:11).

7:16–18 vow . . . voluntary offering. The priest could eat the meat the same day or next day, but eating on the third day brought punishment.

7:19–21 cut off. Uncleanness was punishable by death. See chapter 22 for more details.

7:22–27 See note on 3:17.

7:27 cut off. See note on 7:19–21.

7:29 offering . . . sacrifice. The worshiper made a peace offering from his sacrifice so that the Lord received the blood (v. 33) and the fat (v. 33). The priests received the breast (vv. 30, 31) and right thigh (v. 33). The worshiper could use the rest for himself.

7:30–32 wave offering . . . heave offering. These were symbolic acts indicating the offering was for the Lord. Bread (Ex. 29:23, 24), meat (Ex. 29:22–24), gold (Ex. 38:24), oil (Lev. 14:12), and grain (Lev. 23:11) all

served as wave offerings. Heave offerings are far less numerous (see Ex. 29:27, 28 and Deut. 12:6, 11, 17). Jewish tradition portrayed the wave offering as being presented with a horizontal motion and the heave offering with a vertical motion, as suggested by Leviticus 10:15. Leviticus 9:21 refers to both as a wave offering.

7:36 He anointed them. See 8:30.

6. Concluding remarks (7:37, 38)

7:37, 38 Moses gives a summary conclusion of 1:3–7:36.

7:37 the consecrations. This refers to the offerings at the ordination of Aaron and his sons (see 8:14–36; Ex. 29:1–46).

II. BEGINNING OF THE PRIESTHOOD (8:1–10:20)

8:1–10:20 Beginnings of the Aaronic priesthood are discussed in this section. Before the time of Aaron, the patriarchs (Gen. 4:3, 4) and the fathers (Job 1:5) had offered sacrifices to God, but with Aaron came the fully prescribed priestly service.

Key Word

Offering: 2:3; 4:35; 6:18; 7:14, 33; 9:4; 10:14—this Hebrew word is derived from the verb *to bring near* and literally means "that which one brings near to God." The fact that the Israelites could approach to present their gifts to God reveals His mercy. Even though the people were sinful and rebellious, God instituted a sacrificial system in which they could reconcile themselves to Him. The sacrifices foreshadowed Jesus' death on the cross, the ultimate offering, the offering that ended the need for any others. Through Christ's sacrificial death, believers have once for all been reconciled to God (Heb. 10:10–18). An appropriate response to Jesus' death is to offer one's life as a living sacrifice to God (Rom. 12:1).

A. Ordination of Aaron and His Sons (8:1–36)

8:1–36 Aaron and his sons were consecrated before they ministered to the Lord. The consecration of Aaron and his sons had been ordered long before (*see notes on Ex. 29:1–28*), but is here described with all the ceremonial details as it was done after the tabernacle was completed and the regulations for the various sacrifices enacted.

8:2 *the garments. See notes on Exodus 28:1–43. the anointing oil.* Oil was used for ceremonial anointing (8:12, 30). *sin offering. See notes on 4:1–5:13, esp. 4:3–12.*

8:6–9 *See notes on Exodus 28:1–43.*

8:8 *the* ***Urim and the Thummim.*** A feature on the breastplate of the high priest by which God's people were given His decision on matters which required a decision. *See note on Exodus 28:30.*

8:11 *seven times. See note on 4:6.*

8:12 *to consecrate him.* This act ceremonially set Aaron apart from the congregation

to be a priest unto God, and from the other priests to be high priest.

8:14–17 *See notes on 4:3–12.*

8:17 *offal. See note on 4:11.*

8:18–21 *See notes on 1:3–17.*

8:23, 24 *right ear . . . right hand . . . right foot.* Using a part to represent the whole, Aaron and his sons were consecrated to listen to God's holy Word, to carry out his holy assignments, and to live holy lives.

8:29 *wave offering. See note on 7:30–32.*

8:35 *keep the charge of the* LORD. The commandment of God ordered Aaron and his sons to do exactly as the Lord had spoken through Moses. Disobedience would meet with death.

B. First Sacrifices (9:1–24)

9:1–24 Since the priests had been consecrated and appropriate sacrifices offered on their behalf, they were prepared to fulfill their priestly duties on behalf of the congregation as they carried out all the prescribed sacrifices in Leviticus 1–7. They rendered them to the Lord.

9:2–4 *sin . . . burnt . . . peace . . . grain offering. See notes on 4:1–5:13; 1:3–17; 3:1–17; and 2:1–16 respectively.*

9:4, 6 *the glory of the* LORD. The Lord's manifestation or presence was going to appear to them to show acceptance of the sacrifices. *See notes on verses 23, 24, where that appearance is recorded.*

9:8–21 Aaron presented sacrifices on his own behalf (vv. 8–14) and on behalf of the people (vv. 15–21).

9:17 *burnt sacrifice . . . morning.* See Exodus 29:41; Numbers 28:4.

9:21 *wave offering. See note on 7:30–32.*

9:22 *lifted his hand toward the people.* The high priest gave a symbolic gesture for blessing, perhaps pronouncing the priestly blessing (Num. 6:24–26; cf. 2 Cor. 13:14).

9:23 *the glory of the LORD appeared.* The Bible speaks often of the glory of God—the visible appearance of His beauty and perfection in blazing light. His glory appeared to Moses in a burning bush in Midian (Ex. 3:1–6), in a cloud on Mt. Sinai (Ex. 24:15–17), and in a rock on Mt. Sinai (Ex. 33:18–23). The glory of God also filled the tabernacle (Ex. 40:34), led the people as a pillar of fire and cloud (Ex. 40:35–38), and also filled the temple in Jerusalem (1 Kin. 8:10, 11). When Aaron made the first sacrifice in the wilderness, as a priest, the "glory of the Lord appeared to all the people." In these manifestations, God was revealing His righteousness, holiness, truth, wisdom, and grace—the sum of all He is. However, nowhere has God's glory been more perfectly expressed than in His Son, the Lord Jesus Christ (John 1:14). It will be seen on earth again when He returns (Matt. 24:29–31; 25:31).

9:24 *fire came out . . . consumed.* This fire miraculously signified that God had accepted their offering (cf. 1 Kin. 18:38, 39), and the people shouted for joy because of that acceptance and worshiped God.

C. Execution of Nadab and Abihu (10:1–20)

10:1 *Nadab and Abihu.* These were the two oldest sons of Aaron. ***censer.*** The vessel in which the incense was burned in the Holy Place (its features are unknown) was to be used only for holy purposes. ***profane fire.*** Though the exact infraction is not detailed, in some way they violated the prescription for offering incense (cf. Ex. 30:9, 34–38), probably because they were drunk (see vv. 8, 9). Instead of taking the incense fire from the brazen altar, they had some other source for the fire and, thus, perpetrated an act, which, considering the descent of the miraculous fire they had just seen and their solemn duty

to do as God told them, betrayed carelessness, irreverence, and lack of consideration for God. Such a tendency had to be punished for all priests to see as a warning.

10:2 *fire went out.* The same divine fire that accepted the sacrifices (9:24) consumed the errant priests. That was not unlike the later deaths of Uzzah (2 Sam. 6:6, 7) or Ananias and Sapphira (Acts 5:5, 10).

10:3 *regarded as holy . . . be glorified.* Nadab and Abihu were guilty of violating both requirements of God's absolute standard. The priests had received repeated and solemn warnings as to the necessity of reverence before God (see Ex. 19:22; 29:44). ***Aaron held his peace.*** In spite of losing his two sons, he did not complain, but submitted to the righteous judgment of God.

10:4 *Mishael . . . Elzaphan.* See Exodus 6:22 for their lineage. This procedure prevented the priests from defiling themselves by handling the dead bodies (Lev. 21:1), and allowed the whole congregation to see the result of such disregard for the holiness of God. ***out of the camp.*** As this was done with the ashes of sacrificed animals (6:11), so it was done with the remains of these two priests who received God's wrath.

10:6 *Eleazar and Ithamar.* These are Aaron's youngest sons who still lived. Later, the line of Eleazar would be designated as the unique line of the high priest (cf. Num. 25:10–13).

10:6, 7 This prohibition against the customary signs of mourning was usually reserved for the high priest only as prescribed in 21:10–12. Here, Moses applies it to Eleazar and Ithamar also.

10:8, 9 *not drink wine or intoxicating drink.* Taken in its context, this prohibition suggests that intoxication led Nadab and Abihu to perform their blasphemous act. Cf. Proverbs 23:20–35; 1 Timothy 3:3; Titus 1:7.

10:11 *that you may teach the children of*

Israel. It was essential that alcohol not hinder the clarity of their minds, since the priests were to teach God's law to all of Israel. They were the expositors of the Scripture, alongside the prophets who generally received the Word directly from the Lord. Ezra would become the supreme example of a commendable priest (Ezra 7:10).

10:12–15 *See notes on 3:1–17; 7:11–36.*

10:16–20 The sin offering had not been eaten as prescribed in 6:26 but, rather, it was wholly burned. It was the duty of the priests to have eaten the meat after the blood was sprinkled on the altar, but instead of eating it in a sacred feast, they had burned it outside the camp. Moses discovered this disobedience, probably from a dread of some further judgment, and challenged not Aaron, whose heart was too torn in the death of his sons, but the two surviving sons in the priesthood to explain their breach of ritual duty. Aaron, who heard the charge, and by whose direction the violation had occurred, gave the explanation. His reason was that they had done all the ritual sacrifice correctly up to the point of eating the meat, but omitted eating because he was too dejected for a feast in the face of the appalling judgments that had fallen. He was wrong, because God had specifically commanded the sin offering to be eaten in the Holy Place. God's law was clear, and it was sin to deviate from it. Moses sympathized with Aaron's grief, however, and having made his point, dropped the issue.

III. Prescriptions for Uncleanness (11:1–16:34)

11:1–16:34 Prescriptions for uncleanness are covered in this section. God used the tangible issues of life which He labeled clean/unclean to repeatedly impress upon Israel the difference between what was holy and unholy. "Clean" means acceptable to God; "unclean" means unacceptable to God. Leviticus 11–15 details the code of cleanness; Leviticus 16 returns to sacrifices on the Day of Atonement.

A. Unclean Animals (11:1–47)

11:1–47 This section contains further legislation on the consumption of animals. Abel's offering hints at a post-fall/pre-flood diet of animals (Gen. 4:4). After the Noahic flood, God specifically had granted man permission to eat meat (Gen. 9:1–4), but here spelled out the specifics as covenant legislation. All of the reasons for the prohibitions are not specified. The major points were: (1) that Israel was to obey God's absolute standard, regardless of the reason for it, or the lack of understanding of it; and (2) such a unique diet was specified that Israel would find it difficult to eat with the idolatrous people around and among them. Their dietary laws served as a barrier to easy socialization with idolatrous peoples. Dietary and hygienic benefits were real, but only secondary to the divine purposes of teaching obedience and separation. *See note on 11:44, 45.*

11:3–23 This section is repeated in Deuteronomy 14:3–20 in almost exact wording. The subject matter includes animals (vv. 3–8), water life (vv. 9–12), birds (vv. 13–19), and insects (vv. 20–23).

11:4 *camel.* The camel has a divided foot of two large parts, but the division is not complete and the two toes rest on an elastic pad.

11:5, 6 *rock hyrax . . . hare.* While not true ruminating animals, the manner in which these animals processed their food gave the distinct appearance of "chewing the cud."

11:9 *fins and scales.* Much like the cud and hoof characteristics, the "no fin and scales" guidelines ruled out a segment of water life commonly consumed by ancient people.

Clean Animals

Mammals
Two qualifications:
  1. cloven hoofs
  2. chewing of the cud
  (Lev. 11:3–7; Deut. 14:6–8)
Birds
Those not specifically listed as forbidden
Reptiles
None
Water Animals
Two qualifications:
  1. fins
  2. scales
  (Lev. 11:9–12; Deut. 14:9–10)
Insects
Those in the grasshopper family
  (Lev. 11:20–23)
Basic Reasons:
  1. Hygiene—Many of the forbidden animals were carriers of disease.
  2. Holiness—Some animals were considered unclean because of their association with pagan cults.

11:13 *among the birds.* Rather than unifying characteristics as in the hoof-cud and no fin-scales descriptions, the forbidden birds were simply named.

11:21 This describes the locust (v. 22), which was allowed for food.

11:24–43 This section deals with separation from other defiling things.

11:26, 27 These prohibited animals would include horses and donkeys, which have a single hoof, and lion and tigers, which have paws.

11:30 *gecko.* A type of lizard.

11:36 *a spring or a cistern.* The movement and quantity of water determined the probability of actual contamination. Water was scarce also, and it would have been a threat to the water supply if all water touched by these prohibited carcasses were forbidden for drinking.

11:44, 45 *consecrate yourselves . . . be holy; for I am holy.* In all of this, God is teaching His people to live antithetically. That is, He is using these clean and unclean distinctions to separate Israel from idolatrous nations who have no such restrictions, and He is illustrating by these prescriptions that His people must learn to live His way. Through dietary laws and rituals, God is teaching them the reality of living His way in everything. They are being taught to obey God in every seemingly mundane area of life, so as to learn how crucial obedience is. Sacrifices, rituals, diet, and even clothing and cooking are all carefully ordered by God to teach them that they are to live differently from everyone else. This is to be an external illustration for the separation from sin in their hearts. Because the Lord is their God, they are to be utterly distinct. In verse 44, for the first time the statement "I am the LORD your God" is made, as a reason for the required separation and holiness. After this verse, that phrase is mentioned about fifty more times in this book, along with the equally instructive claim, "I am holy." Because God is holy and is their God, the people are to be holy in outward ceremonial behavior as an external expression of the greater necessity of heart holiness. The connection between ceremonial holiness carries over into personal holiness. The only motivation given for all these laws is to learn to be holy because God is holy. The holiness theme is central to Leviticus (see 10:3; 19:2; 20:7, 26; 21:6–8).

B. Uncleanness of Childbirth (12:1–8)

12:1–8 Uncleanness is related to the mother's afterbirth, not the child.

Unclean Animals
Mammals
Carnivores and those not meeting both "clean" qualifications
Birds
Birds of prey or scavengers (Lev. 11:13–19; Deut. 14:11–20)
Reptiles
All (Lev. 11:29–30)
Water Animals
Those not meeting both "clean" qualifications
Insects
Winged quadrupeds.
Basic Reasons:
1. Hygiene—Many of the forbidden animals were carriers of disease.
2. Holiness—Some animals were considered unclean because of their association with pagan cults.

12:2 *customary impurity.* This refers to her monthly menstruation cycle (see 15:19–24).

12:3 *eighth day.* Joseph and Mary followed these instructions at the birth of Christ (Luke 2:21). *circumcised.* The sign of the Abrahamic covenant (Gen. 17:9–14) was incorporated into the laws of Mosaic cleanness. Cf. Romans 4:11–13. For a discussion on circumcision, *see note on Jeremiah 4:4.*

12:5 *two weeks . . . sixty-six days.* Apparently, mothers were unclean twice as long (eighty days) after the birth of a daughter as a son (forty days), which reflected the stigma on women for Eve's part in the Fall. This stigma is removed in Christ (*see notes on 1 Tim. 2:13–15*).

12:6 *burnt offering . . . sin offering.* Though the occasion was joyous, the sacrifices required were to impress upon the

mind of the parent the reality of original sin and that the child had inherited a sin nature. The circumcision involved a cutting away of the male foreskin, which could carry infections and diseases in its folds. This cleansing of the physical organ so as not to pass on disease (Jewish women have historically had the lowest incidence of cervical cancer), was a picture of the deep need for cleansing from depravity, which is most clearly revealed by procreation, as men produce sinners and only sinners. Circumcision points to the fact that cleansing is needed at the very core of a human being, a cleansing God offers to the faithful and penitent through the sacrifice of Christ to come.

12:8 *turtledoves . . . pigeons.* Cf. Leviticus 1:14–17; 5:7–10. These were the offerings of Joseph and Mary after Christ's birth (cf. Luke 2:24), when they presented Jesus as their firstborn to the Lord (Ex. 13:2; Luke 2:22). Birds, rather than livestock, indicated a low economic situation, though one who was in total poverty could offer flour (5:11–14).

13:1–14:57 This section covers laws pertaining to skin diseases.

C. Unclean Diseases (13:1–59)

13:2 *bright spot.* This probably refers to inflammation. *a leprous sore.* This is a term referring to various ancient skin disorders that were sometimes superficial, sometimes serious. It may have included modern leprosy (Hansen's disease). The symptoms described in verses 2, 6, 10, 18, 30, and 39 are not sufficient for a diagnosis of the clinical condition. For the protection of the people, observation and isolation were demanded for all suspected cases of what could be a contagious disease. This biblical leprosy involved some whiteness (v. 3; Ex. 4:6), which disfigured its victim, but did not disable him. Naaman was able to exercise his functions as general of Syria's army, although a leper (2 Kin. 5:1, 27). Both OT and NT lepers went almost everywhere, indicating that this disease was not the leprosy of today that cripples. A victim of this scaly disease was unclean as long as the infection was partial. Once the body was covered with it, he was clean and could enter the place of worship (see vv. 12–17). Apparently the complete covering meant the contagious period was over. The allusion to a boil (vv. 18–28) with inflamed or raw areas and whitened hairs may refer to a related infection that was contagious. When lepers were cured by Christ, they were neither lame nor deformed. They were never brought on beds. Similar skin conditions are described in verses 29–37 and verses 38–44 (some inflammation from infection). The aim of these laws was to protect the people from disease; but more importantly, to inculcate into them by vivid object lessons how God desired purity, holiness, and cleanness among His people.

13:45 Unclean! Unclean! Here is the symbol of grief and isolation. This same cry is heard from the survivors of Jerusalem's destruction (cf. Lam. 4:15).

13:47–59 This deals with garments worn by infected persons.

13:59 to pronounce it clean or . . . unclean. The primary purpose of this legislation was to assist the priest in determining the presence of contagious skin disease. The language of the passage indicates disease that affects the clothes as it did the person. This provided more illustrations of the devastating infection of sin and how essential cleansing was spiritually.

D. Cleansing of Diseases (14:1–57)

14:1–32 This section explains the cleansing ritual for healed persons.

14:2 the law of the leper. The sense of this law is a prescription, not for healing from leprosy and other such diseases, but rather for the ceremonial cleansing, which needed to be performed after the person was declared clean.

14:3 out of the camp. The leper was not allowed to return to society immediately. Before the person could enter the camp, some priest skilled in the diagnosis of disease needed to examine him and assist with the ritual of the two birds (vv. 4–7).

14:4–7 The bundle of cedar and hyssop tied with scarlet included the living bird. It was all dipped seven times (cf. 2 Kin. 5:10, 14) into the blood of the killed bird mixed with water to symbolize purification. The bird was then set free to symbolize the leper's release from quarantine.

14:4 hyssop. See note on Exodus 12:22 (cf. Lev. 14:6, 49, 51).

14:8 outside his tent. The movement was progressive until finally he could enter and dwell in his own tent, giving dramatic indication of the importance of thorough cleansing for fellowship with God's people. This was a powerful lesson from God on the holiness He desired for those who lived among His people. This has not changed (see 2 Cor. 7:1).

14:10–20 As part of the leper's ceremonial cleansing ritual, trespass (5:14–6:7), sin (4:1–5:13), burnt (1:3–17), and grain (2:1–16) offerings were to be made.

14:10 one log of oil. Less than one pint.

14:12 wave offering. See note on 7:30–32.

14:17 right ear . . . right hand . . . right foot. See note on 8:23, 24.

14:18 put on the head. This would not have been understood as an anointing for entry into an office, but rather a symbolic gesture of cleansing and healing. There could be a connection with the NT directive to anoint the sick for healing (Mark 6:13; 16:18; James 5:14).

14:33–57 This section covers contami-

Old Testament Sacrifices Compared to Christ's Sacrifice

Leviticus		Hebrews
1. Old Covenant (temporary)	Heb. 7:22; 8:6, 13; 10:20	1. New Covenant (permanent)
2. Obsolete promises	Heb. 8:6–13	2. Better promises
3. A shadow	Heb. 8:5; 9:23, 24; 10:1	3. The reality
4. Aaronic priesthood (many)	Heb. 6:19–7:25	4. Melchizedekian priesthood (one)
5. Sinful priesthood	Heb. 7:26, 27; 9:7	5. Sinless priest
6. Limited-by-death priesthood	Heb. 7:16, 17, 23, 24	6. Forever priesthood
7. Daily sacrifices	Heb. 7:27; 9:12, 25, 26; 10:9, 10, 12	7. Once-for-all sacrifice
8. Animal sacrifices	Heb. 9:11–15, 26; 10:4–10, 19	8. Sacrifice of God's Son
9. Ongoing sacrifices	Heb. 10:11–14, 18	9. Sacrifices no longer needed
10. One year atonement	Heb. 7:25; 9:12, 15; 10:1–4, 12	10. Eternal propitiation

The MacArthur Study Bible, by John MacArthur (Nashville: Word Publishing, 1997) 160. © 1993 by Thomas Nelson, Inc.

nated houses which most likely involved some kinds of infectious bacteria, fungus, or mold.

14:34 *I put the leprous plague.* God's sovereign hand is acknowledged in the diseases that were in Canaan (cf. Ex. 4:11; Deut. 32:39). He had His purposes for these afflictions, as He always does. Uniquely, in Israel's case, they allowed for object lessons on holiness.

14:37 *ingrained streaks, greenish or reddish.* The disease would appear to be some sort of contagious mildew. Leprosy (Hansen's disease), as we know it today, is not the problem here since it is a disease related to the human senses, i.e., the destruction of feeling due to the dysfunction of the nerves (*see note on 13:2*). It is not known to be contagious either, and it couldn't be developed in a house. The matter of cleansing such houses is delineated in verses 38–53.

14:57 *to teach when it is unclean and when it is clean.* The priest needed instruction in identifying and prescribing the course for disease such as that described herein, to teach people the importance of distinguishing holy things.

E. Unclean Discharges (15:1–33)

15:1–33 This section deals with purification for bodily discharges. Several types of discharges by men (vv. 1–18) and women (vv. 19–30) are identified and given prescribed treatment.

15:2–15 These verses describe secretions related to some disease of the male sexual organs. After he became well, he was required to make both a sin and a burnt offerings (v. 15).

15:16–18 These verses refer to natural sexual gland secretions for which no offerings were required.

15:19–24 These verses concern the natural menstrual discharge of a woman for which no offerings were required.

15:25–30 These verses deal with some secretion of blood indicating disease, not menstruation, requiring sin and burnt offerings after she is well.

15:31–33 In all these instructions, God was showing the Israelites that they must have a profound reverence for holy things; and nothing was more suited to that purpose than to bar from the tabernacle all who were polluted by any kind of uncleanness, ceremonial as well as natural, physical as well as spiritual. In order to mark out His people as dwelling before Him in holiness, God required of them complete purity and didn't allow them to come before Him when defiled, even by involuntary or secret impurities. And when one considers that God was training a people to live in His presence, it becomes apparent that these rules for the maintenance of personal purity, pointing to the necessity of purity in the heart, were neither too stringent nor too minute.

F. Purification of the Tabernacle from Uncleanness (16:1–34)

16:1–34 This section covers the Day of Atonement (cf. Ex. 30:10; Lev. 23:26–32; Num. 29:7–11; Heb. 9:1–28), which was commanded to be observed annually (v. 34) to cover the sins of the nation, both corporately and individually (v. 17). Even with the most scrupulous observance of the required sacrifices, many sins and defilements still remained unacknowledged and, therefore, without specific expiation. This special inclusive sacrifice was designed to cover all that (v. 33). The atonement was provided, but only those who were genuine in faith and repentance received its benefit, the forgiveness of God. That forgiveness was not based on any animal sacrifice, but on the One whom all sacrifices pictured—the Lord Jesus Christ and His perfect sacrifice on the cross (cf. Heb. 10:1–10). This holiest of all Israel's festivals occurred in September/October on the tenth day of the seventh month (v. 29). It anticipated the ultimate High Priest and the perfect sacrificial Lamb.

16:1 The death of the two sons of Aaron. Cf. 10:1–3.

16:2 Common priests went every day to burn incense on the golden altar in the part of the tabernacle sanctuary, outside the veil, where the lampstand, table, and showbread were. None except the high priest was al-

lowed to enter inside the veil (cf. v. 12), into the Holy Place, actually called the Holy of Holies, the Most Holy (Ex. 26:33), or the Holiest of All (Heb. 9:3, 8), where the ark of the covenant rested. This arrangement was designed to inspire a reverence for God at a time when His presence was indicated by visible symbols. *appear in the cloud.* This cloud was likely the smoke of the incense which the high priest burned on his annual entrance into the Most Holy Place. It was this cloud that covered the mercy seat on the ark of the covenant (see v. 13). *the mercy seat.* See Exodus 25:17–22. It literally means "place of atonement" and referred to the throne of God between the cherubim (cf. Is. 6). It is so named because it was where God manifested Himself for the purpose of atonement.

16:3 *sin . . . burnt offering.* For these offerings brought by Aaron the high priest, *see notes on 4:1–5:13; 6:24–30 and 1:3–17; 6:8–13,* respectively. The bull was sacrificed first as a sin offering (16:11–14) and later the ram as a burnt offering (16:24).

16:4 For a description of the priests' normal clothing, see Exodus 28:1–43; Leviticus 8:6–19. He wore them later for the burnt offering (cf. v. 24). These humbler clothes were less ornate, required for the Day of Atonement to portray the high priest as God's humble servant, himself in need of atonement (vv. 11–14).

16:5 *two . . . goats.* See 16:7–10, 20–22. One animal would be killed to picture substitutionary death and the other sent to the wilderness to represent removal of sin. *one ram.* Along with the high priest's ram (v. 3), these were to be offered as burnt offerings (v. 24).

16:6–28 The following sequence describes the activities of the high priest and those who assisted him on the Day of Atonement: (1) The high priest washed at the laver in the courtyard and dressed in the tabernacle (v. 4). (2) The high priest offered the bull as a sin offering for himself and his family (vv. 3, 6, 11). (3) The high priest entered the Holy of Holies with the bull's blood, incense, and burning coals from the altar of burnt offering (vv. 12, 13). (4) The high priest sprinkled the bull's blood on the mercy seat seven times (v. 14). (5) The high priest went back to the courtyard and cast lots for the two goats (vv. 7, 8). (6) The high pries sacrificed one goat as a sin offering for the people (vv. 5, 9, 15). (7) The high priest reentered the Holy of Holies to sprinkle blood on the mercy seat and also the Holy Place (cf. Ex. 30:10; vv. 15–17). (8) The high priest returned to the altar of burnt offering and cleansed it with the blood of the bull and goat (vv. 11, 15, 18, 19). (9) The scapegoat was dispatched to the wilderness (vv. 20–22). (10) Afterward, the goatkeeper cleansed himself (v. 26). (11) The high priest removed his special Day-of-Atonement clothing, rewashed, and put on the regular high priest clothing (vv. 23, 24). (12) The high priest offered two rams as burnt offerings for himself and the people (vv. 3, 5, 24). (13) The fat of the sin offering was burned (v. 25). (14) The bull-and-goat sin offerings were carried outside the camp to be burned (v. 27). (15) The one who burned the sin offering cleansed himself (v. 28).

16:8 cast lots. *See note on Proverbs 16:33.* **the scapegoat.** Cf. verses 10, 26. This goat (lit. *Azazel* or "escape goat") pictured the substitutionary bearing and total removal of sin which would later be fully accomplished by Jesus Christ (cf. Matt. 20:28; John 1:29; 2 Cor. 5:21; Gal. 1:4; 3:13; Heb. 9:28; 10:1–10; 1 Pet. 2:24; 1 John 2:2). *See notes on verses 20–22.*

16:9, 10 *See notes on verses 20–22.*

16:12 inside the veil. *See note on verse 2.* The veil separated all from the holy and consuming presence of God. It was this veil in

Herod's temple that was torn open from top to bottom at the death of Christ, signifying a believer's access into God's presence through Jesus Christ (see Matt. 27:51; Mark 15:38; Luke 23:45).

16:13 cloud. *See note on verse 2.* **on the Testimony.** The Testimony included the tablets of stone, upon which were written the Ten Commandments (Ex. 25:16; 31:18), located in the ark under the mercy seat.

16:14 seven times. This number symbolically indicated completion or perfection (cf. v. 19).

16:16 atonement for the Holy Place. The object of this solemn ceremony was to impress the minds of the Israelites with the conviction that the whole tabernacle was stained by the sins of a guilty people. By those sins, they had forfeited the privileges of the presence of God and worship of Him, so that an atonement had to be made for their sins as the condition of God remaining with them.

16:17 himself . . . household . . . assembly. The Day of Atonement was necessary for everyone since all had sinned, including the high priest.

16:20–22 This "sin offering of atonement" (Num. 29:11) portrayed Christ's substitutionary sacrifice (vv. 21, 22) with the result that the sinner's sins were removed (v. 22). *See notes on Isaiah 52:13–53:12* for another discussion of these truths. Christ lived out this representation when He cried from the cross, "My God, My God, why have You forsaken Me?" (Matt. 27:46).

16:21, 22 putting them on the head of the goat. This act was more than a symbolic gesture; it was a picture of the ultimate "substitutionary atonement" fulfilled by the Lord Jesus Christ (cf. Is. 53:5, 6; 10:12; *see note on 2 Cor. 5:21*).

16:27 outside the camp. This represents the historical reality of Christ's death outside of Jerusalem (cf. Heb. 13:10–14).

16:29 *seventh month.* Tishri is September/October. *afflict your souls.* This act of denying oneself was probably with respect to food, making the Day of Atonement the only day of prescribed fasting in Israel's annual calendar.

16:30 *clean from all your sins.* See Psalm 103:12; Isaiah 38:17; Micah 7:19. This day provided ceremonially cleansing for one year, and pictured the forgiveness of God available to all who believed and repented. Actual atonement was based on cleansing through the sacrifice of Christ (cf. Rom. 3:25, 26; Heb. 9:15).

16:34 *once a year.* The better sacrifice of Jesus Christ was offered once-for-all, never to be repeated (cf. Heb. 9:11–10:18). Upon that sacrifice, all forgiveness of sin is based, including that of OT believers.

IV. MANDATES FOR PRACTICAL HOLINESS (17:1–27:34)

17:1–27:34 Stipulations for practical holiness are detailed throughout this section.

17:1–22:33 Holiness issues that pertain to the individual are enumerated.

A. Sacrifice and Food (17:1–16)

17:1–16 Miscellaneous laws relating to sacrifice are discussed.

17:1–9 The Lord warns against sacrificing anywhere other than at the door of the tabernacle of meeting (cf. vv. 5–7).

17:4 *guilt of bloodshed.* An unauthorized sacrifice could result in death.

17:5 *peace offerings.* See notes on 3:1–17; 7:11–34.

17:10–16 Warnings against the misuse of blood are issued (cf. 7:26, 27; Deut. 12:16, 23–25; 15:23; 1 Sam. 14:32–34).

17:11 *life of the flesh is in the blood.* This phrase is amplified by "its blood sustains its life" (17:14). Blood carries life-sustaining el-

ements to all parts of the body; therefore, it represents the essence of life. In contrast, the shedding of blood represents the shedding of life, i.e., death (cf. Gen. 9:4). NT references to the shedding of the blood of Jesus Christ are references to His death. *blood that makes atonement.* Since it contains the life, blood is sacred to God. Shed blood (death) from a substitute atones for or covers the sinner, who is then allowed to live.

17:13, 14 It was customary with heathen hunters, when they killed any game, to pour out the blood as an offering to the god of the hunt. The Israelites, to the contrary, were enjoined by this directive and banned from all such superstitious acts of idolatry.

17:15, 16 This cleansing was necessary because these animals would not have had the blood drained properly. Cf. Exodus 22:31; Deuteronomy 14:21.

B. Proper Sexual Behavior (18:1–30)

18:1–30 Laws are given, relating to sexual practices, which would eliminate the abominations being practiced by the heathen in the land (18:27; cf. Lev. 20:10–21; Deut. 22:13–30). These specific laws assume the general prohibition of adultery (Ex. 20:14) and a father incestuously engaging his daughter. They do not necessarily invalidate the special case of a levirate marriage (cf. Deut. 25:5). The penalties for such outlawed behavior are detailed in 20:10–21.

18:3 *doings.* Repeating the sexual practices or customs of the Egyptians and Canaanites was forbidden by God.

18:4 *I am the LORD your God.* This phrase, used over fifty times, asserts the uniqueness of the one true and living God, who calls His people to holiness as He is holy, and calls them to reject all other gods.

18:5 *if a man does, he shall live by them.* Special blessing was promised to the Israelites on the condition of their obedience to God's Law. This promise was remarkably verified in particular eras of their history, in the national prosperity they enjoyed when pure and undefiled religion prevailed among them. Obedience to God's Law always insures temporal blessings, as this verse indicates. But these words have a higher reference to spiritual life as indicated by the Lord (cf. Luke 10:28) and Paul (cf. Rom. 10:5). Obedience does not save from sin and hell, but it does mark those who are saved (cf. Eph. 2:8, 9; *see notes on Rom. 2:6–10*).

18:6–18 This section deals with consanguinity, i.e., the sins of incest.

18:6 *uncover his nakedness.* This is a euphemism for sexual relations.

18:8 *your father's wife.* Actually, a stepmother is in mind here (cf. v. 7).

18:11 *your sister.* Here, he is forbidden to marry a stepsister.

18:18 *while the other is alive.* The principle on which the prohibitions are made changes slightly. Instead of avoiding sexual involvement because it would violate a relational connection, this situation defaults to the principle of one person at a time, or while the other is still alive, i.e., it forbids polygamy. Commonly in Egyptian, Chaldean, and Canaanite culture, sisters were taken as wives in polygamous unions. God forbids such, as all polygamy is forbidden by the original law of marriage (see Gen. 2:24, 25). Moses, because of hard hearts, tolerated it, as did oth-

ers in Israel in the early stages of that nation. But it always led to tragedy.

18:19 *customary impurity.* This refers to a woman's menstrual period (cf. 15:24).

18:21 *Molech.* This Semitic false deity (god of the Ammonites) was worshiped with child sacrifice (cf. Lev. 20:2–5; 1 Kin. 11:7; 2 Kin. 23:10; Jer. 32:35). Since this chapter deals otherwise with sexual deviation, there is likely an unmentioned sexual perversion connected with this pagan ritual. Jews giving false gods homage gave foreigners occasion to blaspheme the true God.

18:22 *not lie with a male.* This outlaws all homosexuality (cf. 20:13; Rom. 1:27; 1 Cor. 6:9; 1 Tim. 1:10). *See notes on Genesis 19:1–29.*

18:23 *mate with any animal.* This outlaws the sexual perversion of bestiality.

18:29 *cut off.* All the sexual perversions discussed in this chapter were worthy of death, indicating their loathsomeness before God.

18:30 *were committed before you.* Not in their presence, but by the people who inhabited the land before them in time (cf. v. 27), were such sins committed.

C. Neighborliness (19:1–37)

19:1–37 Here are practical applications of holy conduct in society.

19:2 *I the LORD your God am holy.* This basic statement, which gives the reason for holy living among God's people, is the cen-

Christ Fulfills Israel's Feasts

The Feasts (Lev. 23)	Christ's Fulfillment
Passover (March/April)	Death of Christ (1 Cor. 5:7)
Unleavened Bread (March/April)	Sinlessness of Christ (1 Cor. 5:8)
Firstfruits (March/April)	Resurrection of Christ (1 Cor. 15:23)
Pentecost (May/June)	Outpouring of Spirit of Christ (Acts 1:5; 2:4)
Trumpets (Sept./Oct.)	Israel's Regathering by Christ (Matt. 24:31)
Atonement (Sept./Oct.)	Substitutionary Sacrifice by Christ (Rom. 11:26)
Tabernacles (Sept./Oct.)	Rest and Reunion with Christ (Zech. 14:16–19)

The MacArthur Study Bible, by John MacArthur (Nashville: Word Publishing, 1997) 186. © 1993 by Thomas Nelson, Inc.

tral theme in Leviticus (cf. 20:26). *See note on 11:44, 45.* Cf. 1 Peter 1:16. Israel had been called to be a holy nation, and the perfectly holy character of God (cf. Is. 6:3) was the model after which the Israelites were to live (cf. 10:3; 20:26; 21:6–8).

19:3 *revere his mother and his father.* The fifth commandment (cf. Ex. 20:12) to honor one's father and mother is amplified by the use of a different word, *revere.* Because they revered (an attitude), they could then honor (an action).

19:3, 4 In addition to the fifth commandment, the fourth (19:3b), the first (19:4a), and the second (19:4b) were commanded as illustrations of holy behavior (cf. Ex. 20:3–6, 8–11).

19:5–8 *peace offering. See notes on 3:1–17; 7:11–34.*

19:9, 10 This was the law of gleaning (cf. 23:22; Deut. 24:19–22), a practice seen in Ruth 2:8–23.

19:11 Commandments from Exodus 20 are again repeated.

19:12 Cf. Matthew 5:33.

19:13 *wages . . . shall not remain with you all night.* Hired workers were to be paid at the end of a work day. Unsalaried day workers depended on pay each day for their sustenance. *See notes on Matthew 20:1, 2.*

19:14 *the deaf . . . the blind.* Israel's God of compassion always demonstrated a concern for the disabled.

19:16 *take a stand against the life.* This refers to doing anything that would wrongfully jeopardize the life of a neighbor.

19:18 This, called the second great commandment, is the most often quoted OT text in the NT (Matt. 5:43; 19:19; 22:39; Mark 12:31, 33; Luke 10:27; Rom. 13:9; Gal. 5:14; James 2:8).

19:19 These mixtures may have been characteristic of some idolatrous practices.

19:20–22 In the case of immorality with a

betrothed slave, the couple was to be punished (possibly by scourging), but not killed. Afterward, a trespass offering (*see notes on 5:14–6:7*) was to be rendered with appropriate reparation. This is an exception to the norm (cf. Deut. 22:23, 24).

19:23–25 *uncircumcised.* They could not eat from the fruit trees of Canaan for four years after entering the land because the fruit of the first three years was to be considered unclean, and the fourth year the fruit was to be offered to the Lord. Some gardeners say preventing a tree from bearing fruit in the first years, by cutting off the blossoms, makes it more productive.

19:26 *divination . . . soothsaying.* Attempting to tell the future with the help of snakes and clouds was a common ancient way of foretelling good or bad future. These were forbidden forms of witchcraft which involved demonic activity. *See note on Deuteronomy 18:9–12.*

19:27, 28 These pagan practices were most likely associated with Egyptian idolatry and were, therefore, to be avoided. The practice of making deep gashes on the face and arms or legs, in times of grief, was universal among pagans. It was seen as a mark of respect for the dead, as well as a sort of propitiatory offering to the gods who presided over death. The Jews learned this custom in Egypt and, though weaned from it, relapsed into the old superstition (cf. Is. 22:12; Jer. 16:6; 47:5). Tattoos also were connected to names of idols, and were permanent signs of apostasy.

19:29 *prostitute your daughter.* Even the pagans of ancient Assyria at this time forbade such horrendous means of monetary gain.

19:30 *Sabbaths. See note on 19:3, 4.*

19:31 *mediums . . . familiar spirits.* Mediums are humans who act as "go-betweens" to supposedly contact/communicate with the spirits of the dead, who are actually impersonated by demons. Cf. 20:6, 27.

19:32 rise . . . honor. Showing respect for the older man acknowledged God's blessing of long life and the wisdom that comes with it (cf. Is. 3:5).

19:33, 34 stranger. Cf. Exodus 22:21.

19:36 ephah . . . hin. These dry and liquid measures, respectively, were equal approximately to four to six gallons and six to eight pints.

D. Capital/Grave Crimes (20:1–27)

20:1–27 Here, capital and other grave crimes are discussed. Many of the same issues from chapters 18 and 19 are elaborated, with the emphasis on the penalty paid for the violation.

20:2 gives any of his descendants to Molech. Molech (Moloch), the Ammonite god of the people surrounding Israel, required human (especially child) sacrifice. *See note on 18:21.*

20:5, 6 cut him off. This means to kill. It is synonymous with "put to death" in verse 9.

20:5 prostitute themselves. This speaks figuratively of spiritual harlotry.

20:6 medium . . . familiar spirits. *See note on 19:31.* "Familiar spirits" refers to demons (cf. 20:27).

20:9 curses his father or his mother. Doing the very opposite of the command to honor or to revere (cf. 19:3) had fatal consequences. See Mark 7:10, where Jesus referred to this text.

20:10–21 Here are the punishments for violating the prohibitions of sexual sins detailed in 18:1–30; see Deuteronomy 22:13–30.

20:22 may not vomit you out. God repeatedly told Israel that remaining in the land required obedience to the Mosaic covenant (cf. 18:25, 28).

20:27 medium . . . familiar spirits. *See note on 19:31.*

E. Instructions for Priests (21:1–22:33)

21:1–24 Laws for the priests are given, which demanded a higher standard of holy conduct than for the general Israelite.

21:1 defile himself. Coming into contact with a corpse (Num. 19:11) or being in the same room with one (Num. 19:14) made a priest unclean. The exceptions were the dead from the priest's own family (vv. 2–4).

21:5 bald place . . . edges . . . cuttings in their flesh. These were the superstitious marks of grief. *See note on 19:27, 28.* Cf. 1 Kings 18:28.

21:6 the bread of their God. This phrase appears five times in Leviticus 21 (cf. vv. 8, 17, 21, 22). It most likely refers to the bread of the Presence in the Holy Place (cf. 24:5–9; Ex. 25:30; 39:36; 40:23).

21:7, 8 The priest was allowed to marry, but only in the purest of circumstances. A holy marriage union pictured the holy union between God and His people. *See 21:13, 14.* The priests were to be living models of that holy union. Cf. Paul's words regarding pastors in 1 Timothy 3:2, 4; Titus 1:6.

21:9 The priests' children were to live a holy life. The common punishment of stoning (cf. Deut. 22:21) is replaced with burning by fire. Cf. 1 Timothy 3:4; Titus 1:6.

21:10–15 Here is a summary of the standards for the high priest which were the highest and most holy in accord with his utmost sacred responsibility.

21:10 shall not uncover his head nor tear his clothes. These are acts associated with mourning or anguish (cf. the violation in Christ's trial, Matt. 26:65; Mark 14:63).

21:16–23 defect. Just as the sacrifice had to be without blemish, so did the one offer-

Key Word

Blood: 1:5; 3:17; 4:7; 8:15; 9:9; 16:18; 17:10; 20:11—related to the Hebrew word which means "red" (Gen. 25:30) and refers to blood. This may be the blood of animals (Ex. 23:18) or human beings (Gen. 4:10). The word *blood* may also represent a person's guilt, as in the phrase "his blood shall be upon him"; that is, he is responsible for his own guilt (20:9). The Old Testament equates *life* with *blood* (Gen. 9:4; Deut. 12:23), which vividly illustrates the sanctity of human life (Gen. 9:6). According to the New Testament, "without shedding of blood there is no remission" of sin (Heb. 9:22). Thus, the emphasis on blood in the Old Testament sacrifices pointed to the blood that Christ would shed, i.e., the life that He would give on a believer's behalf (Rom. 5:9; 1 Cor. 11:25, 26).

ing the sacrifice. As visible things exert strong impressions on the minds of people, any physical impurity or malformation tended to distract from the weight and authority of the sacred office, failed to externally exemplify the inward wholeness God sought, and failed to be a picture of Jesus Christ, the perfect High Priest to come (cf. Heb. 7:26).

22:1–33 These are additional instructions on ceremonial cleanness for the priests, beginning with a death threat (v. 3, "cut off") to those who might violate these rules.

22:4 leper. Cf. 13:1–14:32; *see note on 13:2*. **discharge.** See notes on 15:1–33.

22:5 creeping thing. See 11:29–38.

22:7 he shall be clean. In the same manner, much water is not made unclean by a small contamination. Time was essential for ceremonial purification.

22:10, 11 buys a person with his money. This portion of the sacrifice assigned to the

support of the priests was restricted to the use of his family. However, an indentured servant was to be treated as one of the priest's family, pertaining to eating the consecrated food. See the laws of release, which show this to be a temporary indenture (25:10; Ex. 21:2–11; Deut. 15:12–18).

22:17–30 This section describes the unacceptable and acceptable sacrifices.

22:31–33 The motive behind obedience to God was His holy nature and grace in delivering the nation.

23:1–27:34 Holiness issues that pertain to the nation collectively are outlined.

23:1–24:9 The special feasts of Israel are explained. Cf. Exodus 23:14–17; Numbers 28:1–29:40; Deuteronomy 16:1–17.

F. Religious Festivals (23:1–44)

23:1–44 This section points to days which are sacred to the Lord. After the Sabbath (v. 3), the feasts are given in the order of the calendar (vv. 4–44).

23:2 proclaim to be holy convocations. These festivals did not involve gatherings of all Israel in every case. Only the feasts of: (1) Unleavened Bread; (2) Weeks; and (3) Tabernacles required that all males gather in Jerusalem (cf. Ex. 23:14–17; Deut. 16:16, 17).

23:3 Sabbath of solemn rest. The Mosaic ordinance of the fourth commandment came first (cf. Gen. 2:1–3; Ex. 20:8–11).

23:4–22 Three events were commemorated in March/April: (1) Passover on the fourteenth (v. 5); (2) Feast of Unleavened Bread on the fifteenth to the twenty-first (vv. 6–8); and Feast of Firstfruits on the day after the Sabbath of Unleavened Bread week (vv. 9–14).

23:5 the LORD's Passover. The festival commemorated God's deliverance of Israel from Egypt (cf. Ex. 12:1–14, 43–49; Num. 28:16; Deut. 16:1, 2).

23:6–8 Feast of Unleavened Bread. This

festival, connected with the Passover, commemorated Israel's hurried departure from Egypt and the associated hardships (cf. Ex. 12:15–20; 13:3–10; Num. 28:17–25; Deut. 16:3–8).

23:9–14 *the firstfruits of your harvest.* This festival dedicated the initial part of the barley harvest in March/April and was celebrated on the day after the Sabbath of Unleavened Bread week. It involved presenting to the Lord a sheaf of barley (cf. 23:10, 11) accompanied by burnt, grain, and drink offerings (cf. Ex. 29:40). Firstfruits symbolized the consecration of the whole harvest to God, and was a pledge of the whole harvest to come (cf. Rom. 8:23; 11:16; 1 Cor. 15:20; James 1:18).

23:15–22 *fifty days.* The Feast of Weeks (May/June) dedicated the firstfruits of the wheat harvest (cf. Ex. 23:16; Num. 28:26–31; Deut. 16:9–12). It occurred on the fiftieth day after the Sabbath preceding the Feast of Firstfruits. It is also known as the Feast of Harvest (Ex. 23:16) and Pentecost, Greek for fifty (Acts. 2:1).

23:23–43 Three events were commemorated in September/October: (1) Feast of Trumpets on the first (vv. 23–25); (2) Day of Atonement on the tenth (vv. 26–32); and (3) Feast of Tabernacles on the fifteenth to the twenty-first (vv. 33–43).

23:23–25 *memorial of blowing of trumpets.* This feast, called the Feast of Trumpets, consecrated the seventh month (September/October) as a sabbatical month (cf. Num. 29:1–6).

23:26–32 *Day of Atonement.* The annual Day of Atonement pointed to the forgiveness and cleansing of sin for the priests, the nation, and the tabernacle (*see notes on 16:1–34*).

23:33–43 *Feast of Tabernacles.* This festival commemorated God's deliverance, protection, and provision during the wilderness wanderings of the Exodus (cf. Ex. 23:16; Num. 29:12–38; Deut. 16:13–15). It is also known as the Feast of Booths (Deut. 16:13) and Feast of Ingathering (Ex. 23:16). The people lived in booths or huts made from limbs (cf. Neh. 8:14–18), remembering their

Jewish Feasts				
	Month on Jewish		Corresponding	
Feast of	Calendar	Day	Month	References
Passover	Nisan	14	Mar.-Apr.	Ex. 12:1–14; Matt. 26:17–20
*Unleavened Bread	Nisan	15–21	Mar.-Apr.	Ex. 12:15–20
Firstfruits	Nisan	16	Mar.-Apr.	Lev. 23:9–14
	or Silvan	6	May-June	Num. 28:26
*Pentecost (Harvest or Weeks)	Silvan	6 (50 days after barley harvest)	May-June	Deut. 16:9–12; Acts 2:1
Trumpets, Rosh hashanah	Tishri	1, 2	Sept.-Oct.	Num. 29:1–6
Day of Atonement, Yom Kippur	Tishri	10	Sept.-Oct.	Lev. 23:26–32; Heb. 9:7
*Tabernacles (Booths or Ingathering)	Tishri	15–21	Sept.-Oct.	Neh. 8:13–18; John 7:2
Dedication (Lights), Hanukkah	Chislev	25 (8 days)	Nov.-Dec.	John 10:22
Purim (Lots)	Adar	14, 15	Feb.-Mar.	Esth. 9:18–32

*The three major feasts for which all males of Israel were required to travel to the temple in Jerusalem (Ex. 23:14–19).

The MacArthur Study Bible, by John MacArthur (Nashville: Word Publishing, 1997) 185. © 1993 by Thomas Nelson, Inc.

wilderness experience. It also celebrated the autumn harvest and will be celebrated in the Millennium (cf. Zech. 14:16).

G. The Tabernacle (24:1–9)

24:1–9 These are additional instructions for the tabernacle relating to the lamps (vv. 1–4) and the bread (vv. 5–9). See Exodus 25:31–40; 27:20, 21; 37:17–24 and Exodus 25:23–30; 39:36; 40:23, respectively.

24:5 Each loaf was made with four quarts of flour.

H. An Account of Blasphemy (24:10–23)

24:10–23 This portion relates to the sin of blasphemy. Cf. Exodus 20:7; 22:28.

24:10–14, 23 *Now the son.* Here is another historical example of blasphemy along similar lines as the Nadab and Abihu account (10:1, 2). The blasphemer was one of the "many other people." The people transferred the guilt of them all to him.

24:12 *put him in custody.* There were no jails in Israel since incarceration was not a penalty for crime. They had merely restrained him, probably in a pit of some sort, until they could establish his punishment. Punishments were corporal, banishment, or, in severe cases, death. Those who lived through the punishment worked to secure restitution for those they had violated.

24:20 Cf. Matthew 5:38. This law of retaliation established the principle that the punishment should fit the crime, but not go beyond it.

I. Sabbatical and Jubilee Years (25:1–55)

25:1–55 Proper care for the Lord's property is prescribed for the sabbatical year (25:1–7) and the Jubilee year (25:8–55).

25:1–7 This involves revitalization of the land. The seventh year of rest would invigorate and replenish the nutrients in the soil.

Whatever grew naturally was free to all for the taking (vv. 6, 7).

25:8–55 The Year of Jubilee involved a year of release from indebtedness (vv. 23–38) and bondage of all sorts (vv. 39–55). All prisoners and captives were set free, slaves released, and debtors absolved. All property reverted to original owners. This plan curbed inflation and moderated acquisitions. It also gave new opportunity to people who had fallen on hard times.

25:8–17 These are general instructions for Jubilee.

25:9 *Jubilee.* This literally means "ram's horn," which was blown on the tenth day of the seventh month to start the fiftieth year of universal redemption.

25:10 *proclaim liberty.* Not only must they let the land lie fallow, but the people were allowed a one-year break from their labor. Those bound by a work contract were released from their commitments and there was the release of indentured servants.

25:14–16 The Jubilee year had an effect on the value of land, which was to be considered in all transactions.

25:17 *you shall not oppress one another.* No one should take advantage of or abuse another person, because cruelty is against the very character of God. Penalties for crime were to be swift and exact.

25:18–22 God's provision in the year of no planting was given, which on a smaller scale had been true for the Sabbath day during the Exodus (cf. Ex. 16:5).

25:20, 21 *enough for three years.* When the important query was asked, God responded by promising to supply enough to last.

25:23–34 Various regulations regarding real estate are outlined.

25:23 *the land is Mine.* God owns the earth and all that is in it (cf. Ps. 24:1). The people of Israel were, in fact, only tenants on the land by the Lord's grace. Therefore, ownership of property was temporary, not permanent.

25:33 *cities of the Levites.* Cf. Numbers 35:1–8; Joshua 21.

25:34 *common-land.* These were fields that the village/city-at-large used to grow crops.

25:35–38 Instructions on dealing with the poor are outlined.

25:35 *like a stranger or a sojourner.* The law required gleanings (leftovers after harvest) for the Israelite as well as the stranger (cf. 19:9, 10; 23:22; Deut. 24:19–21).

25:36 *usury or interest.* Usury or excessive interest was prohibited for all (Ps. 15:5). Even fair interest was otherwise prohibited in dealing with the poor (*see notes on Deut. 23:19, 20; 24:10–13*). The basics of life were to be given, not loaned, to the poor.

25:38 *to give you the land of Canaan.* The Lord cites His generosity in giving them a land that was not theirs as a motive for their generosity toward their countrymen.

25:39–55 The principles for dealing with slavery are laid out.

25:42 *For they are My servants.* The spirit of OT slavery is revealed in these words. God, in effect, ordered that slaves be treated like family, i.e., better than employees, because they are His slaves which He redeemed out of the slave markets of Egypt. God owned not only the land (v. 23), but also the people.

25:44–46 *from the nations.* These slaves included people whom Israel was to either drive out or destroy (i.e., slavery was a humane option) and those who came to Israel in the Exodus from Egypt.

25:47–55 This section deals with an alien who has an Israelite slave.

25:48 *redeemed.* Redemption, a contractual agreement which existed in the slave culture, offered the potential for emancipation to indentured individuals under certain conditions. Slaves could be bought out of slavery or some other sort of indentured status by family members or other interested parties who would pay the ransom price.

25:51–54 *the price of his redemption.* The cost of buying him out of slavery was affected by the Jubilee year, when he could be set free.

25:55 The Israelites, emancipated from Egypt by God, were all God's servants; therefore, they were to treat their own slaves with the same grace and generosity as God had granted them.

J. Exhortations to Obey the Law: Blessings and Curses (26:1–46)

26:1–46 The covenant blessings for obedience (26:3–13) and curses for disobedience (26:14–39) are elaborated (cf. Deut. 28). A provision for repentance is also offered (26:40–45).

26:1, 2 A representative summary of the Ten Commandments (Ex. 20:3–17) was set forth as the standard by which Israel's obedience or disobedience would be measured.

26:1 *image . . . pillar . . . engraved stone.* Israel's neighbors used all of these devices for the worship of their gods.

26:3–13 These blessings will reward obedience.

26:4 *rain in its season.* If the rains did not come at the right times, the people experienced crop failure and famine (cf. 1 Kin. 17; 18).

26:6 *evil beasts.* Dangerous animals such as lions and bears existed in that area. Joseph's brothers claimed that such an animal had killed him (Gen. 37:20).

26:7 *chase your enemies.* God provided victories repeatedly in the conquest of Canaan (cf. Josh. 8–12).

26:9 *make you fruitful, multiply you and confirm My covenant with you.* What God commanded at reation and repeated after the flood was contained in the covenant promise of seed (Gen. 12:1–3), which He will fulfill to the nation of Israel as promised to Abraham (Gen. 15:5, 6).

26:12 *your God . . . My people.* The promise of an intimate covenant relationship with the God of the universe is given (cf. 2 Cor. 6:16).

26:14–39 These punishments will repay disobedience.

26:15 *break My covenant.* By disobeying the commandments and the various laws of the Mosaic covenant, Israel broke this conditional covenant. Unlike the ultimate provisions of the unconditional covenant made with Abraham, all blessings in the covenant of Mosaic law were conditioned upon obedience (cf. Lev. 26:25).

26:16 *wasting disease.* Perhaps tuberculosis or leprosy is in view (the subject of much legislation in Lev. 13; 14), but no certain identification is possible. *your enemies shall eat it.* They will be conquered by their enemies at a time when those enemies will enjoy Israel's harvest.

26:22 *highways shall be desolate.* The activity on a nation's roadway, i.e., messengers, merchants, and people traveling, reflected the well-being of that country. This is a picture of extreme economic siege.

26:25 *the vengeance of the covenant.* God's retribution for Israel's breaking the conditional Mosaic covenant is pledged.

26:29 *eat the flesh.* There will be widespread famine in the land and, thus, the people will even resort to cannibalism, which actually came to pass (cf. 2 Kin. 6:28, 29; Jer. 19:9; Lam. 2:20; 4:10).

26:30 *high places.* These were natural shrines for the worship of idols. Solomon disobeyed God by worshiping Him on the high places (1 Kin. 3:4), and not long afterward, he was serving the gods of his foreign wives (1 Kin. 11:1–9).

26:31–35 All this occurred in the terrible invasion of the northern kingdom of Israel in 722 B.C. by the Assyrians and the destruction of the southern kingdom of Judah in 605–586 B.C. by the Babylonians. In the case of Judah, it was a seventy-year captivity to rest the land for all the Sabbath years that had been violated. See 2 Chronicles 36:17–21.

26:35 *the time it did not rest.* By implication, this is because they had violated the Sabbath repeatedly. This violation became the basis of the later seventy-year Babylonian captivity (cf. 2 Chr. 36:20–21).

26:38 The ten tribes of the northern kingdom of Israel never returned directly from captivity. See 2 Kings 17:7–23; *see note on Acts 26:7.*

26:40–42 *if they confess, . . . I will remember My covenant.* God's covenant was rooted in the relationship He had initiated with His people. True repentance would be honored by Him.

26:42 *Jacob . . . Isaac . . . Abraham.* The reverse chronological order of these names provides a look in retrospect as opposed to the actual historical sequence.

26:46 Much of the content of Leviticus came during Moses' two "forty day and night" visits to Sinai (cf. Ex. 24:16–32:6; 34:2–28; Lev. 7:37, 38; 25:1; 27:34).

K. Redemption of Votive Gifts (27:1–34)

27:1–34 Standard legislation is given for dedicated persons, animals, houses, and lands.

27:2–7 *consecrates by a vow.* This sets the gift apart from the rest of his household and possessions as a gift to the Lord and His service.

27:3 *the shekel of the sanctuary. See note on 5:15.*

27:26 *the firstborn.* The firstborn already belonged to the Lord (Ex. 13:2), so the worshiper could not dedicate it a second time.

27:29 *person under the ban.* Like Achan in Joshua 7.

27:30–32 *tithe.* This general tithe was given to the Levites. Cf. Numbers 18:21–32. This is the only mention of tithe or ten percent in Leviticus. However, along with this offering, there were two other OT tithes which totaled about twenty-three percent annually (cf. the second tithe—Deut. 14:22; and the third tithe every three years—Deut. 14:28, 29; 26:12).

Further Study
Harris, R. Laird. *Leviticus,* in Expositor's Bible Commentary. Grand Rapids, Zondervan, 1990.
Wenham, G. J. *The Book of Leviticus.* Grand Rapids: Eerdmans, 1979.

THE FOURTH BOOK OF MOSES CALLED
NUMBERS

Title

The English title *Numbers* comes from the Greek (LXX) and Latin (Vulgate) versions. This designation is based on the numberings that are a major focus of chapters 1–4; 26. The most common Hebrew title comes from the fifth word in the Hebrew text of 1:1, "in the wilderness [of]." This name is much more descriptive of the total contents of the book, which recount the history of Israel during almost thirty-nine years of wandering in the wilderness. Another Hebrew title, favored by some early church fathers, is based on the first word of the Hebrew text of 1:1, "and He spoke." This designation emphasizes that the book records the Word of God to Israel.

Author and Date

The first five books of the Bible, called the Law, of which Numbers is the fourth, are ascribed to Moses throughout Scripture (Josh. 8:31; 2 Kin. 14:6; Neh. 8:1; Mark 12:26; John 7:19). The Book of Numbers itself refers to the writing of Moses in 33:2; 36:13.

Numbers was written in the final year of Moses' life. The events from 20:1 to the end occur in the fortieth year after the Exodus. The account ends with Israel poised on the eastern side of the Jordan River across from Jericho (36:13), which is where the conquest of the land of Canaan began (Josh. 3–6). The Book of Numbers must be dated c. 1405 B.C., since it is foundational to the Book of Deuteronomy, and Deuteronomy is dated in the eleventh month of the fortieth year after the Exodus (Deut. 1:3).

Background and Setting

Most of the events of the book are set "in the wilderness." The word *wilderness* is used forty-eight times in Numbers. This term refers to land that contains little vegetation or trees and, because of a sparsity of rainfall, it cannot be cultivated. This land is best used for tending flocks of animals. In 1:1–10:10, Israel encamped in "the wilderness in Sinai." It was at Sinai that the Lord had entered into the Mosaic covenant with them (Ex. 19–24). From 10:11–12:16, Israel traveled from Sinai to Kadesh. In 13:1–20:13, the events took place in and around Kadesh, which was located in "the wilderness of Paran" (12:16; 13:3, 26), "the wilderness of Zin" (13:21; 20:1). From 20:14–22:1, Israel traveled from Kadesh to the "plains of Moab." All the events of 22:2–36:13 occurred while Israel was encamped in the plain to the north of Moab. That plain was a flat and fertile piece of land in the middle of the wasteland (21:20; 23:28; 24:1).

The Book of Numbers concentrates on events that take place in the second and fortieth years after the Exodus. All incidents recorded in 1:1–14:45 occur in 1444 B.C., the year after the Exodus. Everything referred to after 20:1 is dated c. 1406/1405 B.C., the fortieth year after the Exodus. The laws and events found in 15:1–19:22 are undated but, probably, all should be dated c. 1443 to 1407

B.C. The lack of material devoted to this thirty-seven-year period, in comparison with the other years of the journey from Egypt to Canaan, communicates how wasted these years were because of Israel's rebellion against the Lord and His consequent judgment.

Historical and Theological Themes
Numbers chronicles the experiences of two generations of the nation of Israel. The first generation participated in the Exodus from Egypt. Their story begins in Exodus 2:23 and continues through Leviticus and into the first fourteen chapters of Numbers. This generation was numbered for the war of conquest in Canaan (1:1–46). However, when the people arrived at the southern edge of Canaan, they refused to enter the land (14:1–10). Because of their rebellion against the Lord, all the adults twenty and over (except Caleb and Joshua) were sentenced to die in the wilderness (14:26–38).

In chapters 15–25, the first and second generations overlap; the first died out as the second grew to adulthood. A second numbering of the people began the history of this second generation (26:1–56). These Israelites did go to war (26:2) and inherited the land (26:52–56). The story of this second generation, beginning in Numbers 26:1, continues through the books of Deuteronomy and Joshua.

Three theological themes permeate Numbers. First, the Lord Himself communicated to Israel through Moses (1:1; 7:89; 12:6–8), so the words of Moses had divine authority. Israel's response to Moses mirrored her obedience or disobedience to the Lord. Numbers contains three distinct divisions based on Israel's response to the word of the Lord: obedience (chs. 1–10), disobedi-

ence (chs. 11–25), and renewed obedience (chs. 26–36). The second theme is that the Lord is the God of judgment. Throughout Numbers, the "anger" of the Lord was aroused in response to Israel's sin (11:1, 10, 33; 12:9; 14:18; 25:3, 4; 32:10, 13, 14). Third, the faithfulness of the Lord to keep His promise to give the seed of Abraham the land of Canaan is emphasized (15:2; 26:52–56; 27:12; 33:50–56; 34:1–29).

Interpretive Challenges
Four major interpretive challenges face the reader of Numbers. First, is the Book of Numbers a separate book, or is it a part of a larger literary whole, the Pentateuch? The biblical books of Genesis, Exodus, Leviticus, Numbers, and Deuteronomy form the Torah. The remainder of the Scripture always views these five books as a unit. The ultimate meaning of Numbers cannot be divorced from its context in the Pentateuch. The first verse of the book speaks of the Lord, Moses, the tabernacle, and the Exodus from Egypt. This assumes that the reader is familiar with the three books that precede Numbers.

Still, every Hebrew manuscript available divides the Pentateuch in exactly the same way as the present text. In them, the Book of Numbers is a well-defined unit, with a structural integrity of its own. The book has its own beginning, middle, and ending, even as it functions within a larger whole. Thus, the Book of Numbers is also to be viewed with singular identity.

The second interpretive question asks, "Is there a sense of coherence in the Book of Numbers?" It is readily evident that Numbers contains a wide variety of literary materials and forms? Census lists, genealogies, laws, historical narratives, poetry, prophecy, and travel lists are found in this book. Nevertheless, they are all blended to tell the story of Israel's journey from Mt. Sinai to the plains of Moab. The coherence of Numbers is reflected in the outline that follows.

A third issue deals with the large numbers given for the tribes of Israel in 1:46 and 26:51. These two lists of Israel's men of war, taken thirty-nine years apart, both put the number over 600,000. These numbers demand a total population for Israel in the wilderness of around two and one-half million at any one time. From a natural perspective, this total seems too high for the wilderness conditions to sustain. However, it must be recognized that the Lord supernaturally took care of Israel for forty years (Deut. 8:1–5). Therefore, the large numbers must be accepted at face value (*see note on 1:46*).

The fourth interpretive challenge concerns the heathen prophet Balaam, whose story is recorded in 22:2–24:25. Even though Balaam claimed to know the Lord (22:18), Scripture consistently refers to him as a false prophet (2 Pet. 2:15, 16, Jude 11). The Lord used Balaam as His mouthpiece to speak the true words He put in his mouth (*see notes on 22:2–24:25*).

I. Israel's First Generation in the Wilderness: The Record (1:1–25:18)

A. The Obedience of Israel Toward the Lord (1:1–10:36)

1:1–10:36 The first ten chapters of Numbers record the final preparations of Israel necessary for their conquest of the land of Canaan. In this section, the Lord spoke to Israel through Moses (1:1; 2:1; 3:1, 5, 11, 14, 44; 4:1, 17, 21; 5:1, 5, 11; 6:1, 22; 7:4; 8:1, 5, 23; 9:1, 9; 10:1), and Moses and Israel responded with obedience (1:19, 54; 2:33, 34; 3:16, 42, 51; 4:49; 7:2, 3; 8:3; 9:5, 18, 23; 10:13, 14–28 [in accordance with 2:34]). These chapters divide into two parts (1:1–6:27 and 7:1–10:36), which both end with an invocation of the Lord's blessing on Israel (6:22–27 and 10:35, 36).

1. The organization of Israel around the tabernacle (1:1–6:27)

1:1–6:27 These six chapters chronologically follow the events recorded in 7:1–10:10. The ordering of Israel around the tabernacle (1:1–4:49) and the purity of the camp of Israel (5:1–6:27) were the final results of the Lord's commands that began in Exodus 25:1. Obeying God's instructions transformed an impure (Ex. 32:7, 8) and disorderly (Ex. 32:25) Israel into a people ready to march into Canaan.

1:1 Now the Lord spoke to Moses. This connects the revelation given here by the Lord with Exodus 25:1ff. and Leviticus 1:1ff. The Word from God directed everything that was done by Israel. **the Wilderness of Sinai.** Israel had been encamped there for eleven months. See Exodus 19:1. **the tabernacle of meeting.** The tabernacle, where the Lord's glory resided in the cloud, had been erected one month earlier (Ex. 40:17). This was God's dwelling place in the midst of his people. In Numbers 1:1–6:27, Israel was organized with the tabernacle as the central feature. **the second year.** Numbers begins in the fourteenth month (377 days) after the Exodus from Egypt.

1:2 a census. In Exodus 30:11–16, the Lord had commanded that a census of the males in Israel over twenty (excluding the Levites) be taken for the purpose of determining the ransom money for the service of the tabernacle. The result of that census is recorded in Exodus 38:25–28. The total number, 603, 550 (Ex. 38:26), equals the number in 1:46.

1:3 go to war. The purpose of this census was to form a roster of fighting men. The Book of Numbers looks ahead to the invasion of the land promised to Abraham (cf. Gen. 12:1–3).

1:4 a man. One leader from each of the twelve tribes was to assist Moses and Aaron in the numbering of the men. These same leaders are mentioned in Numbers 2:1–34 and 10:14–28 as the heads of tribes; in 7:1–88 they bring gifts to the tabernacle.

1:17–46 The tribal order follows the pattern of Jacob's wives: first, the sons of Leah; second, the sons of Rachel; and third, the sons of the maids, except Gad (born of Leah's maid), who replaced Levi in the third-born position (cf. Gen. 29:31–30:24; 35:16–20).

1:46 six hundred and three thousand five hundred and fifty. This number, combined with the twenty-two thousand Levite males a month old and above (3:39), allows for a total population of over two million Israelites. Since this number seems too high for the wilderness conditions and relatively few firstborn sons (3:43), some have reinterpreted the plain meaning of the text by (1) saying *thousand* means "clan" or "chief" here, or (2) stating that the numbers are symbolic. However, if *thousand* is not the meaning in this chapter, 1:46 would read 598 "clans" or "chiefs" with

The First Census of Israel's Tribes

Exodus 38:26; Numbers 1:17–46

Reuben	46,500 (v. 21)
Simeon	59,300 (v. 23)
Gad	45,650 (v. 25)
Judah	74,600 (v. 27)
Issachar	54,400 (v. 29)
Zebulun	57,400 (v. 31)
Ephraim	40,500 (v. 33)
Manasseh	32,200 (v. 35)
Benjamin	35,400 (v. 37)
Dan	62,700 (v. 39)
Asher	41,500 (v. 41)
Naphtali	53,400 (v. 43)
Total	603,550 (v. 46)

only 5,500 individuals. Thus, the meaning *thousand* must be retained. Further, there is no textual indication that these numbers are symbolic. The only conclusion is that God took care of over two million people in the wilderness during the period of forty years (cf. Deut. 8:3, 4). Tampering with the number is tampering with God's purpose for these numbers—to show His power in behalf of Israel.

1:50 *appoint the Levites.* The tribe of Levi, including Moses and Aaron, was not included in this census because it was exempt from military service. The Levites were to serve the Lord by carrying and attending to the tabernacle (cf. 3:5–13; 4:1–33, 46–49).

1:51 *The outsider.* This word often refers to the "alien" or "stranger." The non-Levite Israelite was like a "foreigner" to the transporting of the tabernacle and had to keep his distance lest he die.

1:53 *no wrath.* The purpose of setting the Levites apart and arranging them around the tabernacle was to keep the wrath of the Lord from consuming Israel (cf. Ex. 32:10, 25–29).

2:2 *standard . . . emblems.* The emblems were flags identifying the individual tribes (probably with some sort of insignia). The standards were flags marking each of the four encampments of three tribes each. ***tabernacle of meeting.*** For details, see Exodus 25–30.

2:3 *On the east side . . . Judah.* Judah occupied the place of honor to the east. Genesis 49:8–12 highlights the role and centrality Judah would have in the defeat of Israel's enemies. Judah was the tribe through which the Messiah would be born. ***Nahshon.*** Nahshon appears in the later genealogies of the messianic line (cf. Ruth 4:20; Matt. 1:4).

2:14 *Reuel.* In 1:14; 7:42, this name appears as Deuel. The letters R and D are similar in Hebrew and were easily confused by the scribes who copied the text.

2:17 *move out.* As the tribes marched, the tabernacle was transported in the middle of the tribes of Israel, six in front and six behind.

2:32 *See note on 1:46.*

3:1 *Aaron and Moses.* Because Aaron and his sons are emphasized in this chapter, Aaron is named first. ***Mount Sinai.*** The Lord had first communicated to Moses His choice of Aaron and his sons as priests in Exodus 28:1–29:46 while he was in the midst of the cloud on Mount Sinai (Ex. 24:18).

3:3 *the anointed priests.* Of all the tribe of Levi, only the sons of Aaron were priests. Only priests could offer the sacrifices; the rest of the Levites aided them in the work of the tabernacle (cf. vv. 7–9). ***consecrated.*** The setting apart of Aaron and his sons to the priesthood is recorded in Leviticus 8:1–9:24.

3:4 *Eleazar and Ithamar.* All of the future priests of Israel under the Mosaic covenant were descendants of these two sons of Aaron. Eleazar and his descendants would later be singled out for great blessing (cf. Num. 25:10–13).

The Placement of Israel's Tribes

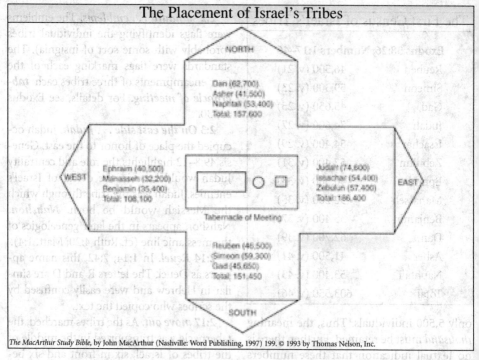

NORTH

Dan (62,700)
Asher (41,500)
Naphtali (53,400)
Total: 157,600

WEST

Ephraim (40,500)
Manasseh (32,200)
Benjamin (35,400)
Total: 108,100

EAST

Judah (74,600)
Issachar (54,400)
Zebulun (57,400)
Total: 186,400

Tabernacle of Meeting

Reuben (46,500)
Simeon (59,300)
Gad (45,650)
Total: 151,450

SOUTH

The MacArthur Study Bible, by John MacArthur (Nashville: Word Publishing, 1997) 199. © 1993 by Thomas Nelson, Inc.

3:6 the tribe of Levi. The specific task of the Levites was to serve Aaron, his sons, and all of Israel by doing the work of the tabernacle, further defined in verses 25, 26, 31, 36, 37; 4:4–33.

3:10 the outsider. Laymen or strangers (cf. 1:51) would die if they participated in priestly activities (cf. v. 38; 16:40).

3:12 firstborn. At the Exodus, the Lord claimed for Himself the firstborn of Israel's males (cf. Ex. 13:1, 2). The firstborn was to act as the family priest. But when the full ministry of the Mosaic economy came in, God transferred the priestly duties to the Levites, perhaps partly because of their holy zeal in the golden calf incident (cf. Ex. 32:29). The Levites substituted for the firstborn.

3:15 Number. Moses took a census of every Levite male who was at least one month old. This included Moses, Aaron, and their sons, because they descended from Amram (v. 19; cf. Ex. 6:20).

3:21–26 Gershon. The Gershonites numbered 7,500 males and were responsible for the coverings of the tabernacle. They were to camp west of the tabernacle.

3:27–32 Kohath. The Kohathites probably numbered 8,300 males. The addition of one Hebrew letter changes the "six" to a "three." This letter was dropped very early in the copying of the text. They were responsible for the holy objects of the tabernacle (including transporting the ark) and were to camp south of the tabernacle.

3:33–37 Merari. The Merarites numbered 6,200 males and were responsible for the wooden framework of the tabernacle. They were to camp north of the tabernacle.

3:38 Moses, Aaron. Moses, Aaron, and his sons were given the place of honor on the east of the tabernacle and gave overall supervision to the Levites. Eleazar oversaw the Kohathites (v. 32), and Ithamar oversaw the Gershonites and Merarites (4:28, 33).

3:43 twenty-two thousand two hundred and seventy-three. This was the total number of Gershonite, Kohathite, and Merarite males born in the twelve and one-half months since the Exodus. The Levites took the place of the first 22,000 firstborns and the rest (273) were redeemed with 1,365 silver shekels (about 170 pounds).

4:1–49 For a discussion of the tabernacle and contents, *see notes on Exodus 25–30.*

4:3 thirty . . . to fifty. This second census of the Levites determined those who would carry the tabernacle on the coming journey to Canaan. Only those between the ages of thirty and fifty were called by the Lord for this task (*see note on 8:24*).

4:4–16 Kohath. The Kohathites carried the furnishings of the tabernacle only after they had been covered by Aaron and his sons. If the Kohathites touched (v. 15) or saw (v. 20) any of the holy things, they would die.

4:21–28 Gershon. *See note on 3:21–26.*

4:29–33 Merari. *See note on 3:33–37.*

4:34–49 numbered. The Kohathites totaled 2,750 (v. 36), the Gershonites 2,630 (v. 40), the Merarites 3,200 (v. 44). All the Levites from thirty to fifty years old in service added up to 8,580 (v. 48).

5:1–4 These verses deal with outward, visible defects.

5:2 leper. One having an infectious skin disease (cf. Lev. 13:1–14:57). **discharge.** A bodily emission indicative of disease, primarily from the sex organs (cf. Lev. 15:1–33).

5:2 corpse. Physical contact with a dead body (cf. Lev. 21:11). All of these prohibitions had sensible health benefits as well as serving to illustrate the need for moral cleanliness when approaching God.

5:3 outside the camp . . . in the midst of which I dwell. God's holy presence in the cloud in the tabernacle demanded cleanness. Therefore, all the unclean were barred from the encampment of Israel.

5:5–10 These verses deal with personal sins, which are not as outwardly visible as the uncleanness of verses 1–4.

5:6 against the LORD. A sin committed against God's people was considered a sin committed against God Himself. There was a need for confession and restitution in addition to the trespass offering (cf. Lev. 5:14–6:7).

5:8 no relative. A supplement to Leviticus 6:1–7. If the injured party had died and there was no family member to receive the restitution called for in verse 7, it was to go to the priest as the Lord's representative.

5:11–31 These verses deal with the most intimate of human relationships and the most secret of sins. Adultery was to be determined and dealt with to maintain the purity of the camp. To accomplish that purity, God called for a very elaborate and public trial. If adultery was proven, it was punished with death, and this ceremony made guilt or innocence very apparent. It was not a trial with normal judicial process, since such sins are secret and lack witnesses, but it was effective. The ceremony was designed to be so terrifying and convicting that the very tendencies of human nature would make it clear if the person was guilty.

5:14 the spirit of jealousy. A mood of suspicion came over the husband that his wife had defiled herself with another man. The accuracy of the suspicion was determined to be right or wrong.

5:15 for bringing iniquity to remembrance. The purpose of the husband's offering was to bring the secret iniquity (if it was present) to light. How this was done is explained in verses 18, 25–26.

5:18 before the LORD. The woman was brought to a priest at the tabernacle. There she was in the presence of the Lord, who knew her guilt or innocence. **uncover the woman's head.** Lit. "unbind the head." In

Leviticus 10:6; 13:45; 21:10, this phrase signifies mourning. This seems to signify the expectation of judgment and consequent mourning if the woman was proven to be guilty. *the bitter water.* This water included dust from the tabernacle floor (v. 17) and the ink used to write the curses (v. 23). The woman was to drink the water (v. 26). If the woman was guilty, the water would make her life bitter by carrying out the curse of making her thigh rot and her belly swell (vv. 21, 27). The public, frightening nature of this test could not fail to make guilt or innocence appear when the conscience was so assaulted.

5:28 *conceive children.* The penalty for the guilty wife was obvious, since the death penalty was called for. In contrast, the innocent wife was assured she would live to bring forth children.

6:1–21 Whereas 5:1–31 dealt with the cleansing of the camp by dealing with the unclean and sinful, 6:1–21 showed how consecration to the Lord was possible for every Israelite. Although only the family of Aaron could be priests, any man or woman could be "priestly" (i.e., dedicated to God's service) for a time (from a month to a lifetime) by means of the vow of a Nazirite. Such a vow was made by people unusually devout toward God and dedicated to His service.

6:2 *the vow of a Nazirite.* The word *vow* here is related to the word *wonder*, which signifies something out of the ordinary. *Nazirite* transliterates a Hebrew term meaning "dedication by separation." The Nazirite separated himself to the Lord by separating himself from (1) grape products (vv. 3, 4), (2) the cutting of one's hair (6:5), and (3) contact with a dead body (vv. 6, 7). The high priest was also forbidden (1) to drink wine while serving in the tabernacle (Lev. 10:9) and (2) to touch dead bodies (Lev. 21:11). Further, both the high priest's crown (Ex. 29:6; 39:30; Lev. 8:9) and the Nazirite's head

(vv. 9, 18) are referred to by the same Hebrew word. The Nazirite's hair was like the high priest's crown. Like the high priest, the Nazirite was holy to the Lord (v. 8; cf. Ex. 28:36) all the days (vv. 4, 5, 6, 8) of his vow.

6:9 *dies . . . suddenly.* If the Nazirite inadvertently came in contact with a dead body, he was to shave his head, on the eighth day bring the prescribed offerings, and begin the days of his vow again. This is a good illustration of the fact that sin can become mingled with the best intentions, and is not always premeditated. When sin is mixed with the holiest actions, it calls for a renewed cleansing.

6:13 *fulfilled.* At the end of the determined time, the Nazirite was released from his vow through offerings and the shaving of his head. His hair was to be brought to the sanctuary at the time of those offerings (cf. Acts 18:18).

6:22–27 Obedient Israel, organized before and consecrated to the Lord, was the recipient of God's blessing (i.e., His favor) pronounced by the priests.

6:24 *bless.* The Lord's blessing was described as His face (i.e., His presence) shining on His people (v. 25) and looking at them (v. 26). God shone forth in benevolence on Israel and looked on them for good. **keep.** The results of the Lord's blessing were His preservation of Israel ("keep"), His kindness toward her ("be gracious," v. 25), and her total well-being ("peace," v. 26).

6:27 *put My name.* The name of the Lord represented His person and character. The priests were to call for God to dwell among His people and meet all their needs.

2. The orientation of Israel toward the tabernacle (7:1–10:36)

7:1–10:36 These four chapters show how the Lord spoke to Moses (7:89) and led Israel (9:22; 10:11, 12) from the tabernacle. As

Israel was properly oriented toward the Lord and obeyed His word, God gave them victory over their enemies (10:35).

7:1–89 As the people of Israel had been generous in giving to the construction of the tabernacle (see Ex. 35:4–29), they showed the same generosity in its dedication.

7:1 finished setting up the tabernacle. According to Exodus 40:17, the tabernacle was raised up on the first day of the first month of the second year. Thus the tabernacle was set up eleven and one-half months after the Exodus from Egypt.

7:2 the leaders of Israel. The leaders of the twelve tribes were those named in 1:5–15 who oversaw the numbering of the people. The order of the presentation by tribe of their offerings to the tabernacle was the same as the order of march given in 2:3–32.

7:6 the carts and the oxen. These were to be used in the transportation of the tabernacle. According to verse 9, the sons of Kohath did not receive a cart because they were to carry the holy things of the tabernacle on their shoulders.

7:12 the first day. I.e., the first day of the first month. The gifts of the leaders to the tabernacle were given over twelve successive days.

7:84–88 Each of the leaders gave the same offerings to the tabernacle. Here, the total of all the gifts was given.

7:89 He spoke to him. With the completion of the tabernacle, the Lord communicated His Word to Moses from the mercy seat in the Holy of Holies (see Lev. 1:1; Num. 1:1).

8:1–4 Exodus 25:32–40 recorded the instructions for the making of the golden lampstand and Exodus 37:17–24 reported its completion.

8:5–26 This ceremony set apart the Levites to the service of the Lord. Their dedication was a feature of the overall description of the dedication of the tabernacle.

8:6 cleanse. In contrast to the priests who were consecrated (Ex. 29:1, 9), the Levites were cleansed. According to verse 7, this cleansing was accomplished by first, the sprinkling of water; second, the shaving of the body; and third, the washing of the clothes. This cleansing of the Levites made them pure so they might come into contact with the holy objects of the tabernacle. Similar requirements were given for the cleansing of the leper in Leviticus 14:8, 9.

8:9 the whole congregation. Since the Levites took the place of the firstborn, who had acted as family priests among the people of Israel (see vv. 16–18), all the congregation of Israel showed their identification with the Levites by the laying on of their hands.

8:19 a gift to Aaron. The Levites were given by God to assist the priests.

8:19 no plague. See note on 1:53.

8:24 twenty-five years old. The Levites were to begin their service in helping the priests at age twenty-five. However, in 4:3 the age of commencement is thirty. A rabbinic suggestion was that the Levites were to serve a five-year apprenticeship. A better solution can be discovered by noting the differing tasks in the two chapters. Numbers 4 dealt with the carrying of the tabernacle, while here they helped in the service in the tabernacle. A Levite began serving in the tabernacle at twenty-five and carrying the tabernacle at thirty. In both cases, his service ended at age fifty. David later lowered the age for beginning service to twenty (see 1 Chr. 23:24, 27; cf. Ezra 3:8).

9:1–14 The call from the Lord to keep the Passover led to an inquiry from those whose uncleanness kept them from obeying. This request led to an amplification of the requirement by the Lord. This was the second Passover.

9:1 the first month. The events recorded in these verses precede the beginning of the census in chapter 1, but follow the dedication of the tabernacle in chapter 7.

9:3 *twilight*. The time between the end of one day and the beginning of the next. See Exodus 12:6.

9:6 *defiled*. They were ceremonially unclean because of contact with a dead body. *See note on 5:2*.

9:10 *posterity*. This word from the Lord was not only for the current situation, but it was a continuing ordinance for Israel. If a person was unable to eat the Passover because of uncleanness or because he was away from the land, he could partake of the Passover on the fourteenth day of the second month.

9:12 This text is alluded to in John 19:36.

9:13 *cut off*. If any Israelite did not keep the Passover at the appointed time and was not unclean or away from the land, he was to be "cut off," which implies that he was to be killed.

9:14 *one ordinance*. A non-Israelite who wished to participate in the Passover would be required to be circumcised.

9:15–23 See Exodus 40:34–38. The cloud, the visible symbol of the Lord's presence, was continually sitting above the tabernacle. The movement of the cloud was the signal to Israel that they were to travel on their journey.

9:15 *tabernacle . . . raised up*. The presence of the Lord arrived when the tabernacle was completed and erected on the first day of the first month of the second year after they had come out of Egypt.

9:16 *cloud . . . fire*. The presence of the Lord which was seen in the cloud by day became a fire that was seen at night (cf. Lev. 16:2).

9:23 *command . . . command*. The text emphasizes that Israel obeyed the Lord at this point in her experience. Throughout the wilderness wanderings, the Israelites could only journey as the cloud led them. When it did not move, they stayed encamped where they were.

10:1–10 Israel was also to be guided by the blowing of the two silver trumpets made by Moses. Both a call to gather and a call to march were communicated with the trumpets.

10:2 *trumpets*. According to a Jewish tradition, these instruments were between twelve and twenty inches long and had a narrow tube that was flared at the end. ***hammered work*.** The same description is given concerning the cherubim above the mercy seat. See Exodus 25:18; 37:7.

10:3, 4 *both . . . one*. The first function of the trumpets was to gather the people to the tabernacle. When both trumpets were blown, all adult males of the congregation were to gather. If only one trumpet was blown, the leaders were to come.

10:5 *advance*. The second purpose of the trumpets was to give a signal indicating that the tribes were to set out on their march. The exact difference between the blowing for the gathering at the tabernacle and for the march is not known. Jewish tradition said the convocation sound was a long steady blast, while the advance signal was a succession of three shorter notes.

10:8 *an ordinance forever*. The blowing of the horns was to be a perpetual ordinance in Israel, calling the people to worship or to war.

10:11–36 Finally, in an orderly and obedient fashion, Israel departed from Sinai as the Lord commanded through Moses.

10:11 *day . . . month . . . year*. Only thirteen months after the Exodus from Egypt and eleven months after the arrival at Sinai, Israel began to march toward Canaan.

10:12 *the Wilderness of Paran*. According to 13:26, Kadesh was in the wilderness of Paran, probably at its northern border. This verse gives a summary of God's leading from Sinai to Kadesh.

10:14–28 The order of march followed by Israel in these verses is in exact conformity to the details given in 2:1–34.

10:14 *standard. See note on 2:2.* **Nahshon.** For the fourth, and final time in the Book of Numbers, the twelve leaders of the first generation of Israel were noted (see chs. 1; 2; 7). In accordance with Genesis 49:8–12, the tribe of Judah was given preeminence as the ruling tribe. It led the march into the Promised Land.

10:29 *Hobab.* As the son of Reuel, Hobab was Moses' brother-in-law. *Reuel.* Reuel was the father-in-law of Moses (see Ex. 2:18). *Come with us.* Moses sought Hobab's help in leading Israel through the wilderness. He promised Hobab a portion of the inheritance of Israel within the land if he would come. The text of Numbers does not explicitly state whether Hobab responded to Moses or not. But Judges 1:16 implies that Hobab agreed to Moses' request. Later, he joined with Judah in the conquest of the land and did receive the blessing of dwelling in the land.

10:33 *journey . . . three days.* The Israelites traveled for three days from Sinai before they encamped for more than one night.

10:35, 36 As Israel traveled and camped, Moses prayed that the Lord would give victory and that His presence would be among her.

B. The Disobedience of Israel Toward the Lord (11:1–25:18)

11:1–25:18 In contrast to Numbers 1–10, a major change takes place at 11:1. Obedient Israel became complaining (11:1; 14:2, 27, 29, 36; 16:1–3, 41; 17:5) and rebellious (14:9; 17:10) Israel. Ultimately, Moses and Aaron rebelled against the Lord as well (20:10, 24). In response to Israel's disobedience, the Lord's anger was aroused (11:1, 10, 33; 12:9;

14:18; 25:3, 4) and He plagued His people (14:37; 16:46, 47, 48, 49, 50; 25:8, 9, 18) as He had Pharaoh and the Egyptians (Ex. 9:14; 12:13; 30:12). Nevertheless, even though God judged that generation of Israel, He will still fulfill His promises to Abraham in the future (23:5–24:24).

1. The complaining of Israel on the journey (11:1–12:16)

11:1–12:16 The complaining of the people and leaders began on the journey from Sinai to Kadesh.

11:1 *the LORD heard it.* Their complaining was outward and loud. *the outskirts of the camp.* God, in His grace, consumed only those who were on the very edges of the encampment of Israel.

11:4 *the mixed multitude.* The word occurs only here in the OT. However, another word, "mixed company," was used in Exodus 12:38. The "mixed multitude" here are non-Israelites who left Egypt with Israel in the Exodus. *meat.* After over a year of eating manna in the wilderness, the mixed multitude wanted the spicy food of Egypt once again.

11:7 *manna.* See Exodus 16:14. *bdellium.* This refers more to appearance than color, i.e., it had the appearance of a pale resin.

11:13, 14 Moses confessed to God that he was not able to provide meat for the people as they demanded. Their complaining was discouraging him so that because of this great burden, Moses desired death from the hand of the Lord.

11:16–30 In response to Moses' despair in leading the people, the Lord gave him seventy men to help.

11:16 *seventy men.* These aides to Moses might be the same seventy referred to in Exodus 18:21–26.

11:17 *the Spirit.* This refers to the Spirit of God. It was by means of the Holy Spirit that Moses was able to lead Israel. In verse 25, the Lord gave the Spirit to the seventy men in fulfillment of the Word He gave to Moses.

11:21 six hundred thousand. Moses rounded off the 603,550 of 1:46; 2:32.

11:23 Has the LORD's arm been shortened? A figure of speech indicating that the Lord was able to do as He had said and provide meat for the 600,000 men of Israel and their families for one month.

11:25 prophesied. Here, the prophesying refers to the giving of praise and similar expressions of worship to the Lord without prior training. The text is clear that this was a one-time event as far as these men were concerned.

11:29 that the LORD would put His Spirit upon them! Moses desired and anticipated the day when all of God's people would have His Spirit within them. By this, he looked forward to the New Covenant. See Ezekiel 36:22–27; Jeremiah 31:31ff.; Joel 2:28.

11:31 a day's journey. The Lord, using a wind, brought a great quantity of quail that surrounded the encampment within one day's journey. **about two cubits above the . . . ground.** The birds flew at a height of about three feet where they were able to be easily captured or clubbed to the ground by the people.

11:32 ten homers. About sixty to seventy bushels.

12:1–16 The brother and sister of Moses opposed his leadership. The immediate occasion was the prophesying of the elders. Moses' position as the spokesman for God to Israel was called into question.

12:1 Ethiopian. Ethiopia, south of Egypt, was inhabited by the descendants of Cush, the firstborn son of Ham (Gen. 10:6, 7). Although the term *Ethiopian* could have been used concerning Zipporah, Moses' first wife, it seems more likely that Moses had

---

Key Word

Elders: 11:16, 24, 25, 30; 16:25; 22:4, 7—a word that means "aged" or "old." In the Old Testament, the word *elder* refers to either an aged, feeble person (Gen. 44:20; Job 42:17) or to a mature person who had authority within the Israelite community (Ex. 3:16; Josh. 8:33). Elders could serve as judges (Ex. 18:12), advisers (Ezek. 7:26), and ruling officials (Deut. 19:12; Ruth 4:2). Their position was one of great honor (Prov. 31:23; Is. 9:15). In addition to age (Hebrew tradition states that an elder had to be a man at least fifty years of age), an elder had to demonstrate his maturity by fearing God, being truthful, and not coveting (Ex. 18:21).

---

remarried after the death of Zipporah. The marriage to the Ethiopian woman had been recent and furnished the pretext for the attack of Miriam and Aaron. Since Miriam is mentioned first, she probably was the instigator of the attack against Moses.

12:2 spoken only through Moses? Miriam and Aaron asserted that God had spoken to them in the same way that He had spoken to Moses.

12:3 very humble. This statement is often cited as evidence that Moses could not have written the Book of Numbers, for he would not have boasted in his own humility. However, the Holy Spirit certainly could inspire Moses to make an accurate statement about himself, probably against his own natural inclination. In this context, Moses was asserting there was nothing that he had done to provoke this attack by Miriam and Aaron. *See note on 16:15.*

12:5 the LORD came down. As in Genesis 11:5, this clause states that the Lord knows and deals with situations on earth. Here, the Lord came down and, in verse 10, departed.

This was God's answer to the attack against Moses.

12:7 *My servant Moses.* This phrase is also repeated in verse 9. A servant of the Lord in the OT is one who responded in faith by obedience to the Word of the Lord. *faithful in all My house.* A reference to Moses' loyal performance of his role as covenant mediator between the Lord and Israel.

12:8 *face to face.* God spoke to Moses without mediation. Also, the Lord did not speak to Moses through visions and dreams, but plainly. It was not that Moses saw the full glory of God (cf. John 1:18), but rather that he had the most explicit, intimate encounters (cf. Deut. 34:10). *the form of the LORD.* This is the likeness or representation of the Lord which Moses was privileged to see. See Exodus 33:23.

12:10 *leprous.* In judgment of Miriam's opposition to Moses, the Lord struck her with leprosy. For the treatment of a leper, see Leviticus 13 and 14. A public sin required a public response from the Lord.

12:16 *Wilderness of Paran. See note on 10:12.*

2. The rebellion of Israel (13:1–19:22)

13:1–14:45 These chapters record the failure of Israel at Kadesh. The people failed to believe the Lord (14:11) and take the Promised Land. Their lack of faith was open rebellion against the Lord (14:9). The NT looks back to these times as an illustration of apostasy (cf. 1 Cor. 10:5; Heb. 3:16–19).

13:1 *the LORD spoke to Moses.* According to Deuteronomy 1:22, 23, the people had first requested the spies be sent out after Moses challenged them to take the land. Here, the Lord affirmed the peoples' desire and commanded Moses to send them.

13:2 *spy out the land of Canaan.* The spies were specifically called to explore the land that God had promised to Israel. This

exploration gave valuable information to Moses for the conquest of the land.

13:3 *heads of the children of Israel.* These leaders were different than those mentioned in Numbers 1; 2; 7; 10. Presumably, the tribal leaders in the four earlier lists were older men. The task for the spies called for some leaders who were younger, probably about forty years of age, based on the ages of Caleb and Joshua.

13:16 *Hoshea ... Joshua.* For reasons not made clear, Moses changed the name of Hoshea, meaning "desire for salvation," to Joshua, meaning "the Lord is salvation."

13:17–20 The spies were to determine the nature of the land itself, as well as the strengths and weaknesses of the people.

13:20 *the season of the first ripe grapes.* Mid-summer (mid to late July).

13:21 *from the Wilderness of Zin as far as Rehob.* These were the southernmost and northernmost borders of the land.

13:22 *Hebron.* This was the first major city the spies came to in Canaan. Abram had earlier built an altar to the Lord here (cf. Gen. 13:18). Abraham and Isaac were buried here (Gen. 49:31). The city had been fortified c. 1730 B.C., seven years before the building of Zoan in Egypt, and later became the inheritance of Caleb (Josh. 14:13–15) and then David's capital when he reigned over Judah (2 Sam. 2:1–4). *the descendants of Anak.* Cf. verse 28. Anak was probably the ancestor of Ahiman, Sheshiai, and Talmai, who were living at Hebron. They were noted for their height (Deut. 2:21; 9:2).

13:23 *the Valley of Eshcol.* Eshcol means "cluster."

13:28 *the people ... are strong.* The spies reported that the land was good; however, the people were too strong to be conquered.

13:30 *Caleb quieted the people.* The verb *quieted* usually occurs in the form of the interjection, *Hush!* This implies that the report of the spies evoked a vocal reaction from the people. Caleb concurred with the report of the other spies, but called the people to go up and take the land, knowing that with God's help they were able to overcome the strong people.

13:32 a bad report. The report of the ten spies was evil because it exaggerated the dangers of the people in the land, it sought to stir up and instill fear in the people of Israel and, most importantly, it expressed their faithless attitude toward God and His promises.

13:33 giants. This term was used in Genesis 6:4 for a group of strong men who lived on the earth before the flood. The descendants of Anak were, in exaggeration, compared to these giants, which led the spies to view themselves as grasshoppers before them.

14:1 all the congregation . . . wept. All of Israel bewailed the circumstances.

14:2 complained. The term means "to murmur." Specifically, they wished they had died in Egypt or the wilderness.

14:4 select a leader and return to Egypt. The faithless people were ready to reject God's leader, Moses.

14:6 tore their clothes. This was an indication of distress (see Gen. 37:29).

14:7–9 Joshua and Caleb reaffirmed their appraisal that the land was good and their confidence that the Lord would deliver it and its people into their hands.

14:10 the glory of the LORD appeared. In response to the people's violent rejection of Joshua and Caleb's challenge, God appeared.

14:11 reject . . . not believe Me. They had refused to trust or rely on God and His power to give them the land of Canaan in spite of the signs that He had done in their midst.

14:12 I will make of you a nation. As in Exodus 32:9, 10, God threatened to wipe out the people and start over again with Moses'

"son." This justifiable threat showed the seriousness with which God took the rebellion on the part of His people.

14:13–19 As in Exodus 32:11–13, Moses interceded for Israel to protect the Lord's reputation with the Egyptians, who would charge the Lord with inability to complete His deliverance of Israel and, thus, deny His power. Second, the Lord's loyal love was the basis on which the Lord could forgive His people.

14:22 ten times. Taken literally this includes: (1) Exodus 14:10–12; (2) Exodus 15:22–24; (3) Exodus 16:1–3; (4) Exodus 16:19, 20; (5) Exodus 16:27–30; (6) Exodus 17:1–4; (7) Exodus 32:1–35; (8) Numbers 11:1–3; (9) Numbers 11:4–34; (10) Numbers 14:3.

14:24 My servant Caleb. Since Caleb was recognized as one who feared and trusted the Lord, God later rewarded his faith (cf. Josh. 14).

14:25 turn and move out into the wilderness. Because of Israel's refusal to enter the land, instead of continuing northward, God commanded them to move southward toward the Gulf of Aqabah.

14:26–35 The Lord granted the Israelites their wish, i.e., their judgment was that they would die in the wilderness (vv. 29, 35: cf. v. 2). Their children, however, whom they thought would become victims (v. 3), God would bring into the land of Canaan (vv. 30–32). The present generation of rebels would die in the wilderness until forty years were completed. The forty years were calculated as one year for each day the spies were in Canaan.

14:37 died by the plague. As an indication of the certainty of the coming judgment, the ten spies who undermined the people's faith were struck by the plague and died.

14:44 they presumed to go up to the

mountaintop. With characteristic obstinacy, the people rejected Moses' counsel and the Lord's command, and went to attack the Amalekites in the hill country. Since the Lord was not with them, they were defeated.

15:1–41 Even though the Israelites had rebelled against the Lord and were under his judgment, the Lord still planned to give the land of Canaan to them. These laws assumed Israel's entrance into the land (15:2, 17).

15:1–16 The law of the grain offering, recorded here, differs from that given in Leviticus 2. The grain offerings in Leviticus were offered separately as a gift to the Lord.

Here, for the first time, grain and drink offerings were allowed to be offered along with either a burnt or a peace offering.

15:4 *ephah . . . hin.* Measurements equal to four to six gallons and six to eight pints.

15:17–21 This regulation pertained to the offering of the firstfruits of the harvest. When the people entered the land of Canaan and began to enjoy its produce, they were to show their devotion to the Lord by presenting to Him a cake baked from the first cuttings of the grain.

15:22 *sin unintentionally.* Sin offerings were prescribed whenever any of the Lord's

Wanderings of the Israelites

Nelson's Complete Book of Bible Maps & Charts (Nashville: Thomas Nelson Publishers, 1996) 55. © 1993 by Thomas Nelson, Inc.

commands were unwittingly disobeyed, i.e., by unintentional neglect or omission. In vv. 24–26, the offerings for the whole community were given. In verses 27–29, the offerings for the individual person who sinned unintentionally were stated.

15:30 *does anything presumptuously.* Lit. "with a high hand." These sins, committed knowingly and deliberately, were described as blasphemous because they were an arrogant act of insubordination against the Lord. Anyone guilty of presumptuous sin was to be excommunicated from Israel and put to death.

15:32–36 This was an illustration of defiant sin. When it was determined that there was a premeditated violation of the Sabbath law, death was required.

15:37, 38 *tassels.* These blue tassels were in the form of a flower or petal and were attached to the clothing of the Israelites to remind them of their need to trust and obey God's commands.

15:41 *the LORD.* This reminder harkens back to Moses' first encounter with the Lord in the desert (Ex. 3:13–22).

16:1–18:32 In 16:1–40, Korah (a Levite), allied with some Reubenites and other leaders of Israel, instigated an organized opposition to the authority of Aaron and the priests. Their argument against Moses and Aaron was that by claiming the unique right and responsibility to represent the people before God, they took "too much upon themselves" based on the promise that "all the congregation is holy, every one of them, and the LORD is among them" (16:3). The Lord dealt with these rebels (16:4–40) and reaffirmed His choice of Aaron (16:41–17:13). Finally, the Lord restated the duties and support of both the priests and Levites (18:1–32). These events took place at some unidentified place and time during Israel's wilderness wanderings.

16:1 *Korah.* Korah was descended from Levi through Kohath. Being a son of Kohath, he already had significant duties at the tabernacle (see 4:1–20). However, he desired further to be a priest (see v. 10).

16:8 *sons of Levi.* Other Levites were involved in this rebellion with Korah.

16:12 *Dathan and Abiram.* These two men of the tribe of Reuben despised Moses, blaming him for taking Israel out of the land of Egypt and failing to bring them into the land of Canaan. Because of Moses' perceived failure, they attacked him, joining with Korah in the rebellion against Moses and Aaron.

16:15 *nor have I hurt one of them.* Moses pled his innocence before the Lord, claiming to have been a true servant-leader. This confirms that Numbers 12:3 could have been written by Moses.

16:16–35 God judged those who rebelled against Moses and Aaron by putting them to death.

16:21 The Lord answered Moses' intercession by calling the people to depart from the tents of the rebels so that only they would be judged.

16:22 *the God of the spirits of all flesh.* This phrase appears only here and in 27:16. Moses called on the omniscient God, who knows the heart of everyone, to judge those who had sinned, and those only.

16:30 *a new thing.* This supernatural opening of the earth to swallow the rebels was a sign of God's wrath and the vindication of Moses and Aaron.

16:32 *their households.* Numbers 26:11 indicates that this did not include their children.

16:36–40 The 250 leaders of Israel had brought censers filled with fire before the Lord (16:17, 18). The censers were holy to the Lord since they had been used in the tabernacle. Therefore, Eleazar was commanded to hammer out the metal censers into a covering for the altar. That covering was to be a perpetual reminder that God had chosen Aaron and his descendants for the priesthood.

16:41–50 Instead of bringing about the repentance of the people, the Lord's wrath only led to more complaining. Though the children of Israel held Moses and Aaron accountable for the people who had been killed by the Lord, it was the intervention of Moses and Aaron for the entire nation that saved them from destruction because of their opposition to God.

16:46 *incense.* Incense was symbolic of prayer. Aaron interceded in prayer and the plague stopped (v. 48).

16:49 *fourteen thousand seven hundred.* See 1 Corinthians 10:10.

17:2 *twelve rods.* These sticks of wood were to bear the names of the twelve tribes, with the tribe of Levi replaced by the name Aaron.

17:4 *before the Testimony.* The Testimony is the Ten Commandments written on two stone tablets kept in the ark of the covenant. The phrase "before the Testimony" is synonymous with "before the ark."

17:8 *the rod of Aaron.* God had stated that the stick of the man He had chosen would blossom (17:5). The stick of Aaron had not only blossomed, but had yielded ripe almonds. Thus, God had exceeded the demands of the test, so there would be no uncertainty of the fact that Aaron had been chosen as high priest.

17:10 *a sign.* Aaron's rod that blossomed and brought forth fruit was to be kept as an indication of God's choice in order to permanently stop the murmuring of the rebellious Israelites.

17:12 *Surely we die.* Finally, the people realized their sin in challenging Aaron's role.

17:13 *comes near.* The people's fear of going near to God led to a reaffirmation of the priesthood of Aaron and his sons in chapter 18.

18:1–7 Only Aaron and his family could minister with the holy articles of the sanctuary of God.

18:1 *the LORD said to Aaron.* Only in verses 1–25 and in Leviticus 10:8 does the Lord speak directly to Aaron alone. *bear the iniquity.* Aaron and his sons, from this point forward, were responsible for any offense against the holiness of the tabernacle or violations of the rules of priesthood.

18:7 *a gift for service.* Even though the priesthood demanded much, the priests were to view it as a gift from the Lord.

18:8–20 In return for their service to the Lord, the priests were to receive a portion of the offerings which the people presented in worship. They could keep all of the parts of the sacrifices not consumed on the altar by fire. Also, the offerings of firstfruits and everything devoted to the Lord were theirs as well.

18:19 *a covenant of salt forever.* Salt, which does not burn, was a metaphor to speak of durability. As salt keeps its flavor, so the Lord's covenant with the priesthood was durable. The Lord would provide through the offerings of His people for His priests forever.

18:21–24 The Levites received the tithes from the people. This was their source of income and compensation for their tabernacle service.

18:25–32 As the Levites themselves received the tithe, they were also required to present a tithe (a tenth) of what they received to the Lord.

19:1–22 Over a period exceeding thirty-eight years, more than 1,200,000 people died in the wilderness because of God's judgment. The Israelites were continually coming into contact with dead bodies, which led to ceremonial uncleanness. Therefore, the

Lord provided a means of purification so that those who came into contact with dead bodies might be cleansed.

19:1–10 The provision given for the preparation of the "water of purification" (cf. Lev. 12–15).

19:2 *a red heifer.* A reddish, brown cow, probably young since no yoke had been put on it. This cow was burned and its ashes were used as the agent of purification (see v. 9).

19:3 *Eleazar.* The son of Aaron was a deputy high priest who was in charge of the slaughter of the red cow. ***outside the camp.*** The red cow was killed outside the camp of Israel and its ashes were stored there as well (see v. 9). Hebrews 13:11–13 picks up the image of "outside the camp" as it relates to Christ's death outside of Jerusalem.

19:6 *cedar wood and hyssop and scarlet.* The cow was totally consumed by the fire along with these three materials, which were also used in the ritual of purification of skin disease (Lev. 14:1–9). The ashes of all these and the cow were mixed to make the agent by which cleansing could take place.

19:11–22 A general statement regarding the use of the "water of purification" (vv. 11–13) is followed by a more detailed explanation of the procedure to be followed.

19:18 *A clean person.* Any clean person, not just priests, could sprinkle the unclean with the water of purification.

20:1–22:1 These chapters record the beginning of the transition from the old generation (represented by Miriam and Aaron) to the new generation (represented by Eleazar). Geographically, Israel moves from Kadesh (20:1) to the plains of Moab (22:1), from where the conquest of the land would be launched. There is an interval of thirty-seven years between 19:22 and 20:1.

3. The rebellion of Moses and Aaron (20:1–29)

20:1–13 Just as the children of Israel failed to trust in the Lord (14:11) and, thus, were not allowed to go into the Promised Land (14:30), Israel's leaders, Moses and Aaron, would also not go into the land because of their failures to trust in the Lord.

20:1 *the first month.* The year is not stated. However, at the end of this chapter, there is a report of the death of Aaron. According to Numbers 33:38, Aaron died on the first day of the fifth month of the fortieth year after the Exodus from Egypt. Thus, the first month, here, must be of the fortieth year. Most of the older generation had died in the wilderness. ***Kadesh.*** As the people had begun their wilderness wanderings at Kadesh (13:26), so they ended them there. Kadesh was located on the northern boundary of the wilderness of Paran (13:26) and on the southeast border of the wilderness of Zin. ***Miriam died.*** Miriam, who led Israel in celebrating the victory over Egypt at the Red Sea (Ex. 15:20, 21), also led the attack against Moses recorded in Numbers 12:1–15. Her death served as a symbol that the old generation would not enter Canaan.

20:2 *no water.* During Israel's forty years in the wilderness, water was their greatest physical need. The Lord had provided it continually, beginning at Horeb (Ex. 17:1–7). The present lack of water stirred the people to contend with Moses.

20:3 *If only we had died when our brethren died.* The situation was so desperate in the people's mind that they wished they had been among those who died in Korah's rebellion (16:41–50).

20:6 *fell on their faces.* As he had done in the past, Moses sought the Lord's counsel (see 14:5; 16:4).

20:8 *Speak to the rock.* Though God told Moses to take his rod with which He had performed many wonders in the past (Ex. 4:1–5; 7:19–21; 14:16; 17:5, 6), he was only to speak to the rock in order for it to yield water.

20:10 *you rebels.* Instead of speaking to the rock, Moses spoke to the people, accusing them of being rebels against God. By his actions, Moses joined the people in rebellion against God (see 27:14).

20:12 *you did not believe Me.* The Lord's evaluation of Moses was that he failed to take God at His Word and, thus, to treat Him as holy to the people. Moses failed in the same way as Israel had at Kadesh thirty-eight years previously (14:11). ***you shall not bring this assembly into the land.*** God's judgment of Moses for his sin of striking the rock was that he would not take Israel into the land of Canaan. The inclusion of Aaron demonstrated his partnership with Moses in the action against the Lord.

20:13 *Meribah.* Lit. "contention, quarreling." The same name was used earlier at the first occasion of bringing water from the rock (Ex. 17:7).

20:14–21 Moses' attempt to pass through the territory of Edom was rejected by the king.

20:14 *your brother Israel.* The people of Edom were descended from Esau, the brother of Jacob (see Gen. 36:1).

20:17 *the King's Highway.* The major north-south trade route from the Gulf of Aqabah north to Damascus, which passed through the Edomite city of Sela.

20:20 *with many men and with a strong hand.* The king of Edom sent out his army to intercept Israel. Since Israel was forbidden by the Lord to engage in warfare with Edom (Deut. 2:4–6), they turned away from Edom's border.

20:22–29 Eleazar succeeded his father,

Aaron, as high priest. Aaron's death further marked the passing of the first generation.

20:22 *Mount Hor.* This is most likely a mountain northeast of Kadesh on the border of Edom.

20:24 *because you rebelled against My word.* Aaron had joined Moses in rebellion against God (v. 12). Aaron's death foreshadowed the death of Moses.

20:29 *mourned . . . thirty days.* This was the same mourning period as for Moses (Deut. 34:8). Since the normal time for mourning was seven days (see Gen. 50:10), the length of this mourning showed the importance of Aaron and the loss to Israel.

4. The resumed complaining of Israel on the journey (21:1–22:1)

21:1–3 Israel's first victory over the Canaanites occurred at Hormah, the place they had previously been defeated (see 14:45).

21:1 *king of Arad.* This raiding king came from a Canaanite city in the south, i.e., the Negev.

21:3 *they utterly destroyed them.* Israel vowed to the Lord that if He would give them victory over Arad, they would

---

Key Word

Vow: 6:2, 21; 15:3; 21:2; 30:2, 3, 9, 13—a vow. A vow to God is a voluntary commitment to do something that pleases Him or to abstain from certain practices to demonstrate devotion to Him. A vivid example of a vow in the Old Testament is the Nazirite vow (6:1–21). Scripture admonishes the believer against making rash vows, since they are made before God, the righteous and holy Judge (Eccl. 5:4). The reason for the warning is that a vow made to Him is binding and must be fulfilled.

completely destroy them, not claiming the spoils of victory for themselves. The Lord responded to this vow and gave victory.

21:4–9 After their victory over Arad, Israel showed again their lack of obedience toward the Lord.

21:4 *by the Way of the Red Sea.* Cf. Deuteronomy 2:1. Since the way through Edom was barred, Moses turned to the south to take Israel around Edom. Thus, Israel journeyed toward Elath on the coast of the Gulf of Aqabah. This long, circuitous route led to impatience and frustration on the part of Israel.

21:5 *this worthless bread.* The people's impatience led them to despise the manna (see 11:6).

21:6 *fiery serpents.* These snake bites inflicted a fiery inflammation.

21:7 *We have sinned.* The people confessed their iniquity and asked that they might be released from the judgment God had sent.

21:9 *a bronze serpent.* One had to fix his gaze upon this snake, a definite act of the will, if he wanted to be healed and live. Note the typological use of this incident in John 3:14, 15.

21:10–20 Israel circled around both Edom and Moab and camped on the north side of the Arnon River in the territory of the Amorites.

21:14 *the Book of the Wars of the Lord.* Apparently, this was a book of victory songs that was current at the time of Moses, possibly written by Moses or a contemporary. The work is cited as evidence that the Arnon River was the northern boundary of Moab.

21:16 *Beer.* Lit. "well." Here, God provided water for Israel. In response, Israel praised the Lord with a song which might have also come from the Book of the Wars of the Lord (vv. 17, 18).

21:21–32 As with Edom (vv. 14–19), Israel requested passage through the land of Sihon, a king of the Amorites. Since there was no requirement from the Lord not to engage the Amorites in warfare, as there had been for Edom, when Sihon brought out his army, he was attacked and defeated by Israel. Israel, thus, took the land bounded by the Arnon River on the south, the Dead Sea and the Jordan River on the west, the Jabbok River on the north, and the land of the Ammonites on the east.

21:27 *those who speak in proverbs say.* These words came from the wise men, probably among the Amorites. The words of verses 27–30 describe the Amorites' defeat of the Moabites north of the Arnon River. Ironically, as the Amorites had taken the land from the Moabites, the Israelites had taken the land from the Amorites. The purpose of these words cited by Moses was to substantiate Israel's right to this land. According to God's commandments, the territory belonging to the Moabites was not to be taken by Israel because the Moabites were descendants of Lot (Deut. 2:9). However, what belonged to the Amorites had been promised to Israel and was theirs for the taking.

21:33–35 The land north of the Jabbok River was under the control of Og, another Amorite king. Og attacked Israel and suffered a devastating defeat. Thus, all of the land in the Transjordan, from the Arnon River in the south to the heights of Bashan in the north, came under Israelite control.

22:1 With their control of Transjordan secured, Israel moved unimpeded to the plains of Moab in preparation for assaulting Canaan.

5. The blessing of Israel by Balaam (22:2–24:25)

22:2–24:25 The narrative changes to

center on Balaam, a pagan prophet. His oracles reassert the faithfulness of the Lord to the Abrahamic covenant and His purpose to bless Israel. In verses 2–40, the events leading to Balaam's words are recorded. This is followed in 22:41–24:24 with the words of his prophecies and the conclusion in 24:25.

22:3 *Moab was exceedingly afraid.* The Moabites were descendants of Lot (see Gen. 19:36, 37). Balak, their king, had seen how the Israelites destroyed the Amorites. Not knowing that Israel was forbidden by God to attack Moab, he was terrified that the same fate awaited him and his people (Deut. 2:9).

22:4 *Midian.* The Midianites were descendants of Abraham through Keturah (see Gen. 25:1–4). They lived south of Moab's border. When Moab communicated to the elders of Midian that they were in danger of being destroyed by Israel as well, they joined with Moab in an alliance to defeat Israel.

22:5 *Balaam.* Balaam was from Pethor, a city on the Euphrates River, perhaps near Mari, where the existence of a cult of prophets whose activities resembled those of Balaam have been found. Balaam practiced magic and divination (24:1) and eventually led Israel into apostasy (31:16). Later, Scripture identifies Balaam as a false prophet (Deut. 23:3–6; Josh. 13:22; 24:9, 10; Neh. 13:1–3; Mic. 6:5; 2 Pet. 2:15, 16; Jude 11; Rev. 2:14).

22:6 *curse this people.* Knowing that Israel was too strong to defeat militarily, Balak called for Balaam to come and curse Israel. A curse was a spoken word that was believed to bring misfortune upon the one against whom the curse was pronounced. Balak acknowledged that Balaam had the reputation of pronouncing curses that actually worked.

22:8 *as the Lord speaks to me.* Throughout these chapters, Balaam himself used the name "Lord," i.e., Israel's God (vv. 13, 18, 19; 23:3, 12; 24:13). In verse 18, he even called the Lord, "the Lord my God." In this verse, it must be assumed that Balaam expected the God of Israel to speak to him. As a pagan prophet, he would anticipate making contact with the gods of any people.

22:9 *God came to Balaam.* Israel's God did communicate to Balaam. However, rather than using the term "Lord," which indicates a covenant relationship, God consistently used the word "God" when He spoke to him (vv. 9, 12, 20). Though Balaam used the word "Lord," the biblical text makes it clear that he did not have a saving relationship with Israel's God.

22:12 *they are blessed.* Balaam could not curse Israel because the Lord had determined to give them blessing only.

22:20 *only the word which I speak to you.* Because of his great desire for the material wealth that would come to him, Balaam desired to go to Balak. He implored the Lord even after God had told him not to go. God acceded to Balaam's request to let him go, but told him that he could speak only the true Word from God.

22:22 *because he went.* Even though God had given Balaam permission to go (v. 20), He knew that his motive was not right. Thus, the anger of the Lord burned against Balaam because God knew that he was not yet submissive to what He required. The result of God's confrontation with Balaam was a reaffirmation of the word given in verse 20, repeated in verse 35, that he was to speak only the words that God wanted him to speak. That Balaam got the message is explicitly stated in verse 38. ***the Angel of the Lord.*** The Angel of the Lord was a manifestation of the presence of the Lord Himself. He was equated with deity (see Gen. 16:7; 18:1, 2; Ex. 3:1–6). *See note on Exodus 3:2.*

22:28 *the Lord opened the mouth of the*

donkey. Balaam's donkey was able to see the Angel of the Lord with His drawn sword (vv. 23, 25, 27). Realizing the danger to herself, she sought to avoid the angel. In doing this, she preserved Balaam as well. Miraculously, the donkey was able to communicate with Balaam.

22:31 the LORD opened Balaam's eyes. The Lord allowed Balaam to see things as they really were, especially those things that are not ordinarily visible to humans and to be submissive to His will as he went to Balak.

22:41–23:12 Balaam's first oracle emphatically stated that Israel could not be cursed (23:8). She was unlike all the other nations of the world (23:9). Balaam even wished to share in her blessing (23:10).

23:5 the LORD put a word in Balaam's mouth. Even though Balak and Balaam offered sacrifices on pagan altars, it was the Lord who gave Balaam his oracle.

23:7 he took up his oracle. This statement introduces each of Balaam's speeches (vv. 6, 18; 24:3, 20, 21, 23).

23:10 Who can count the dust of Jacob? Here is Oriental hyperbole signifying a very populous nation as Jacob's posterity was to be (cf. Gen 13:16; 28:14). **one-fourth of Israel.** The camp was divided into four parts, one on each side of the tabernacle. If one could not count the part, certainly no one could count the whole.

23:13–26 Balaam's second oracle reaffirmed the Lord's determination to bless Israel. The iniquity in Israel was mercifully set aside by the Lord (v. 21) and, therefore, would not stop His plan. The God who supernaturally brought Israel out of Egypt (v. 22) would give victory over all her enemies (v. 24).

23:19 God is not a man. In contrast to the unreliability of man, so well seen in Balaam himself, God is reliable and immutable. He does not change; therefore, His Words always come to pass.

23:27–24:14 Balaam's third oracle focused on the ultimate King (the "Messiah"), who would bring the blessings of the Abrahamic covenant both to Israel and the nations.

23:28 Peor. Also named Beth Peor (Deut. 3:29), it was the location of a temple to Baal (25:3).

24:2 the Spirit of God came upon him. This terminology was regularly used in the OT for those whom God uniquely prepared to do His work (see Judg. 3:10). Unlike the previous two oracles, Balaam does not involve himself in divination before giving this third oracle. He is empowered with the Holy Spirit to utter God's Word accurately.

24:3 whose eyes are opened. His inner eye of understanding had been opened by God's Spirit.

24:7 Agag. In 1 Samuel 15:32, 33, an Amalekite king bore this name. The Amalekites were the first people to attack Israel after they left Egypt (see Ex. 17:8–15). *Agag* may be a proper name or a title of Amalekite rulers, like *Pharaoh* in Egypt.

24:8 God brings him out of Egypt. Because of the verbal similarities between verses 8, 9 with 23:22, 24, the *him* in this verse is usually interpreted to be Israel. However, since the *him* is singular and the closest reference in verse 7 is to the coming king, it is better to see verses 8 and 9 as referring to Israel's king. Numbers 24:9 is a direct quote from Genesis 49:9, which speaks of the ultimate King who will come from Judah, the Messiah.

24:9 Blessed is he who blesses you. These words refer to Genesis 12:3. The ultimate fulfillment of the Abrahamic covenant centers around the coming Messiah. The one who blesses Israel will ultimately reap God's blessing in the future.

24:14 *in the latter days.* Lit. "at the end of days." This term is rightfully used in the OT for the distant future. Balaam's fourth oracle takes the truth communicated in the third and applies it to Moab.

24:15–19 Balaam's fourth oracle predicted the future coming of Israel's king, who would literally "shatter the forehead of Moab" and conquer Edom. He will have total dominion.

24:20–24 Balaam's final three oracles look at the future of the nations. First, Amalek will come to an end (24:20). Second, the Kenites, identical to or a part of the Midianites, will be carried away by Asshur, i.e., Assyria (24:21, 22). Third, Assyria and Eber, probably Israel herself (Gen. 10:21), will be afflicted by Cyprus (this name came to represent the Mediterranean region west of Palestine and in Daniel 11:30 refers to Rome), until Cyprus comes to ruin.

6. The final rebellion of Israel with Baal of Peor (25:1–18)

25:1–18 The final failure of Israel before the conquest of Canaan occurred in the plains of Moab. According to 31:16, the incident was brought about by the counsel of Balaam. Failing to be able to curse Israel, he gave the Moabites and Midianites direction in how to provoke the Lord's anger against His people.

25:1 *Acacia Grove.* This is the region across the Jordan River from Jericho where Israel invaded the land of Canaan (see Josh. 2:1).

25:3 *joined to Baal of Peor.* Israel engaged in acts of sexual immorality with the women of Moab. Since this was part of the pagan cult that was worshiped by the Moabites, the Israelites joined in these idolatrous practices. The Israelites yoked themselves to the false god of the Moabites and the Midianites, referred to as Baal of Peor. This was a violation of the first commandment.

25:6 Cf. verses 14, 15.

25:9 *twenty-four thousand.* This is to be differentiated from the plague involving the golden calf where 23,000 Israelites died (cf. Ex. 32:1–14, 28; 1 Cor. 10:8).

25:10–13 Because of Phinehas's zeal for God's holiness, the Lord made "a covenant of an everlasting priesthood" with him so that through his family line would come all future, legitimate high priests (cf. Ps. 106:30, 31). This promise will extend even into the millennial kingdom (cf. Ezek. 40:46; 44:10, 15; 48:11). This promise comprised the basis for the priestly covenant. *See note on Genesis 9:16.*

25:17 *Harass the Midianites.* Because the Midianites had attacked Israel by their schemes of sexual and idolatrous seduction, the Lord called Israel to attack them in return. This attack is recorded in 31:1–24.

II. ISRAEL'S SECOND GENERATION IN THE PLAINS OF MOAB: A RENEWED OBEDIENCE (26:1–36:13)

26:1–36:13 The final, major section of Numbers records the renewed obedience of Israel. God continued to speak (vv. 1, 2, 52; 27:6, 12, 18; 28:1; 31:1, 25; 33:50; 34:1, 16; 35:1, 9), and the second generation of Israel obeyed. Most of the commandments in this section related to Israel's life after they entered the land.

A. The Preparations for the Conquest of the Land (26:1–32:42)

26:1–32:42 These chapters begin and end speaking of going to war (v. 2; 32:20, 29, 32) and the ensuing inheritance of Canaan (vv. 52–56; 32:32). Israel was being prepared for the conquest of the Promised Land.

26:1–51 This second census, like the first taken over thirty-eight years earlier (1:1–46), counted all the men twenty years of age and older, fit for military service. The great decline in the tribe of Simeon might be due to its participation in the sin of Baal of Peor (see 25:14).

26:9 Dathan and Abiram. These were singled out for special mention because of their part in the rebellion recorded in 16:1–40. Mention of them was a reminder of God's judgment against rebellion. *See note on 16:12.*

26:11 the children of Korah. These sons of Korah were spared judgment because they separated themselves from their father's house (see 16:26).

26:19 Er and Onan. These two sons of Judah did not receive an inheritance in the land because of their great evil (see Gen. 38:1–10).

26:33 Zelophehad. The mentioning of Zelophehad having no sons, but only daughters, laid the basis for the laws of inheritance stated in 27:1–11; 36:1–12.

26:52–56 These census numbers would be used to decide the size of each tribe's inheritance in the land. The exact locations would be determined by lot (see Josh. 13:1–7; 14:1–19:51 for the outworking of these words).

26:57–65 As in the first census (3:14–39), the Levites were counted separately. The total number of Levites was 23,000 (v. 62), an increase of 1,000 over the previous census (see 3:39).

27:1–11 The coming distribution of the land of Canaan presented a dilemma for the family of Zelophehad since he had no sons. His five daughters boldly asked that they inherit their father's name and his inheritance (vv. 1–4). The Lord's decision that the daughters should receive his inheritance became the basis of a perpetual statute in Israel governing inheritances (vv. 5–11).

27:3 he died in his own sin. Zelophehad had not been involved in Korah's rebellion. Instead, he had died under God's judgment in the wilderness, like the rest of the faithless Exodus generation.

27:8–11 The following is the order of in-

The Second Census of Israel's Tribes

Numbers 26:5–51			
Reuben	43,730	(v. 7)	-2,770
Simeon	22,200	(v. 14	-37,100
Gad	40,500	(v. 18)	-5,150
Judah	76,500	(v. 22)	+1,900
Issachar	64,300	(v. 25)	+9,900
Zebulun	60,500	(v. 27)	+3,100
Manasseh	52,700	(v. 34)	+20,500
Ephraim	32,500	(v. 37)	-8,000
Benjamin	45,600	(v. 41)	+10,200
Dan	64,400	(v. 43)	+1,700
Asher	53,400	(v. 47)	+11,900
Naphtali	45,400	(v. 50)	-8,000
Total	601,730	(v. 51)	-1,820

heritance: son, daughter, brother, paternal uncle, and closest relative in the family. This same order (with the exception of the daughter) was followed in Leviticus 25:48, 49, dealing with the various cases of redemption of the land in the Jubilee year.

27:12–14 God reaffirmed that Moses could not enter the land of Canaan, although he was able to see it from Mt. Nebo, across from Jericho (see Deut. 32:49).

27:15–17 Moses' greatest concern was that Israel have a good leader who was like a shepherd. The Lord answered his request in the man Joshua.

27:18 *lay your hand on him.* Joshua already had the inner endowment for leadership—he was empowered by the Holy Spirit. This inner endowment was to be recognized by an external ceremony when Moses publicly laid his hands on Joshua. This act signified the transfer of Moses' leadership to Joshua. The laying on of hands can also accompany a dedication to an office (see Num. 8:10).

27:20 *give some of your authority.* Moses was to pass on some of the "honor" or "majesty" that he had to Joshua. *See Joshua 3:7.*

27:21 *Eleazar . . . shall inquire before the Lord for him.* Moses had been able to communicate directly with God (12:8), but Joshua would receive the Word from the Lord through the high priest. *Urim. See note on Exodus 28:30* for this part of the high priest's breastplate (Ex. 39:8–21) being used as a means of determining God's will (cf. Deut. 33:8; 1 Sam. 28:6).

28:1–29:40 Instructions concerning regular celebrations in Israel's worship calendar had been given previously. Now, poised to enter the land, Moses gave an orderly reiteration and summary of the regular offerings for each time of celebration, adding some additional offerings.

28:3–8 See Exodus 29:38–42.

28:9, 10 These were newly revealed offerings for the Sabbath.

28:11–15 These were newly revealed offerings for the "beginning of the month."

28:16–25 See Leviticus 23:5–8.

28:26–31 See Leviticus 23:18.

29:1–6 See Leviticus 23:23–25.

29:7–11 See Leviticus 23:26–32.

29:12–38 See Leviticus 23:33–43.

30:1–16 This chapter added clarification to the laws regarding vows given in Leviticus 27:1–33. The basic principle for men is restated in verse 2. Then, it was asserted that a man was also responsible for the vows made by women in his household (vv. 3–16). A father or husband could overrule the vow of a daughter or wife, but a man's silence, if he knew of the vow, meant it must be accomplished.

30:2 *a vow . . . some agreement.* A promise to do something or a promise not to do something. Christ could have had this text in mind in Matthew 5:33.

30:9 *a widow or a divorced woman.* These were not viewed as being under a man's authority, so the word of the woman alone sufficed.

31:1–54 This chapter has many links with previous passages in Numbers: vengeance on Midian (vv. 2, 3; 10:2–10); Zur the Midianite (v. 8; 25:15); Balaam (vv. 8, 16; 22:2–24:25); Peor (v. 16; 25:1–9, 14, 15); purification after contact with the dead (vv. 19–24; 19:11–19); care for the priests and Levites (vv. 28–47; 18:8–32). This battle with the Midianites modeled God's requirements for holy war when Israel took vengeance on His enemies (see Deut. 20:1–18).

31:1–11 Israel was commanded by the Lord to take vengeance on Midian because they were responsible for corrupting Israel at Peor (25:1–18).

31:2 *gathered to your people.* A euphemism for death (see Gen. 25:8, 17; 35:29).

Battles in the Wilderness		
1445–1405 B.C.		
Opponent	**Location**	**Scripture**
Amalek	Rephidim	Ex. 17:8–16
Amalek and Canaanites	Hormah	Num. 14:45
Arad	Hormah	Num. 21:1–3
Amorites	Jahaz	Num. 21:21–25
Bashan	Edrei	Num. 21:33–35
Midian	———	Num. 31:1–12

31:12–24 All the Midianites, except the virgin women, were to be put to death. Both the soldiers and the spoil needed to be cleansed.

31:17 The execution of all male children and women of childbearing age insured the extermination of the Midianites and prevented them from ever again seducing Israel to sin. Reference to Midianites later (Judg. 6:1–6) was to a different clan. It was the Midianites living in Moab who were destroyed here.

31:25–54 The plunder was divided equally between those who went and fought and those who stayed.

32:1–42 The tribes of Reuben and Gad desired to live in the land already conquered because they possessed many herds of livestock and the land was good for grazing. Moses gave them, along with the half tribe of Manasseh, portions of the land only on the condition that they would fully participate in the conquest of Canaan.

32:3 *Ataroth . . . Beon.* The places mentioned here cannot be identified, but all lie between the Arnon River to the south and the Jabbok River to the north.

32:8 *Thus your fathers did.* Moses feared that if these two tribes were comfortably settled (1) they would not join with the other ten tribes in conquering Canaan, and (2)

that could be the beginning of a general revolt against entering the land. As the ten spies had dissuaded the people at Kadesh nearly forty years earlier from conquering the land (vv. 9–13; 13:26–14:4), the refusal of these two tribes could cause the people to fail again (v. 15).

32:23 *your sin will find you out.* The two tribes committed themselves to provide their warriors for the conquest of the land. This agreement satisfied Moses, although he added that non-participation would be sin and God would certainly find and judge the tribes for their sin.

32:33 *half the tribe of Manasseh.* Once the agreement was reached with Reuben and Gad concerning settlement on the east side of the Jordan, the half tribe of Manasseh, also rich with flocks, joined in seeking land in that territory. However, verses 39–42 indicate that Manasseh conquered cities not yet taken and settled in the northern area of Gilead.

B. The Summary of the Journey in the Wilderness (33:1–49)

33:1–49 The Lord commanded Moses to write a list of Israel's encampments between Egypt and the plains of Moab. Significantly, forty places were mentioned (not including Rameses and the plains of Moab), reflecting the forty years spent in the wilderness. Some sites recorded earlier are not listed and other sites are only mentioned here. The God who would lead the Israelites in the conquest of Canaan (33:50–56) was the One who had led them through the wilderness.

C. The Anticipation of the Conquest of the Land (33:50–36:13)

33:50–36:13 Entering the Promised Land had been Israel's goal at the beginning of Numbers. This last part of the book anticipated the settlement in Canaan.

From the Wilderness to the Jordan

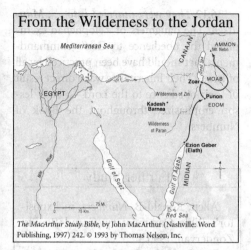

The MacArthur Study Bible, by John MacArthur (Nashville: Word Publishing, 1997) 242. © 1993 by Thomas Nelson, Inc.

33:50–56 God commanded that all of the Canaanites were to be exterminated, along with all their idolatrous symbols.

33:52 *their high places.* These are hills on which Canaanite altars and shrines were placed.

33:56 *I will do to you as I thought to do to them.* If Israel failed to obey God, she would be the object of God's punishment in exactly the same way as the Canaanites were.

34:1–15 God gave precise instruction to Israel concerning the boundaries of the land of Canaan. Sadly, the actual conquest of the land fell far short of these boundaries.

34:13 *give to the nine tribes and to the half-tribe.* The land to be conquered was to be given to the nine and one-half tribes. The other two and one-half tribes already had their inheritance in Transjordan (32:1–42).

34:16–29 The Lord appointed the men who were to assign the portions of the land of Canaan: Eleazar the priest (20:25, 26), Joshua the commander (27:18–23), and the leaders of each of the ten tribes which were to receive an inheritance. None of these men were sons of the leaders listed in 1:5–15.

35:1–8 Forty-eight cities throughout the land were to be given to the Levites. The tribe of Levi did not receive a tribal allotment, but lived among the other tribes. Joshua 21:1–42 gives the list of these forty-eight cities.

35:2 *from the inheritance of their possession.* According to 18:23, the Levites were to have no land as an inheritance in Canaan, so the Levites did not inherit these towns; they only lived in them. ***common-land around the cities.*** The Levites were also given grazing land around the cities, so their animals might feed.

35:9–34 Six of the Levitical cities were to be established as "cities of refuge" (see Deut. 19:1–13). These cities were to be havens providing protection to any person who accidentally killed another person (manslaughter).

35:12 *the avenger.* The meaning of this term is "near of kin." It refers to the person chosen by a family to deal with a loss suffered in that family. Here, the close relative of a homicide victim would seek to avenge his death, but not until proper judgment was made.

35:19 Swift retribution according to the law of Genesis 9:5, 6.

35:24 *the congregation shall judge between the manslayer and the avenger.* The congregation was called to decide the motive of the killer, whether it was with or without hostility. If there was evil intent, the killer was turned over to the avenger to be put to death. If, however, hostility could not be proven to exist between the killer and the victim, then the killer was allowed to remain in the city of refuge.

35:25 *until the death of the high priest.* The manslayer without evil intent was to remain in the city of refuge until the death of the high priest. The death of the high priest marked the end of an old era and the beginning of a new one for the manslayer.

35:30 *witnesses.* No one could be judged guilty of death on the testimony of only one witness. Two or more witnesses were required in all capital cases. *See notes on Deuteronomy 17:6, 7; 19:15.*

35:33 blood defiles the land. Though murder and inadvertent killing polluted the land, murder was atoned for by the death of the murderer. Failure to observe these principles would make the land unclean. If the whole land became unclean, then the Lord would no longer be able to dwell in their midst.

36:1–13 The issue raised here stemmed from a decision regarding female inheritance in 27:1–11. Since a tribe would lose an allotted inheritance in the year of Jubilee if an inheriting woman had married into another tribe, the woman of any tribe who inherited land must marry within her own tribe.

36:12 *They were married into . . . Manasseh.* The daughters of Zelophehad exemplified the obedience to God's commandments that should have been practiced by all of Israel. Their inheritance was a direct result of their obedience to the Lord—a basic lesson emphasized throughout the Book of Numbers.

Further Study

Allen, Ronald B. *Numbers,* in Expositor's Bible Commentary. Grand Rapids: Zondervan, 1990.

Harrison, R. K. *Numbers.* Chicago: Moody, 1990.

THE FIFTH BOOK OF MOSES CALLED
DEUTERONOMY

Title

The English title *Deuteronomy* comes from the Greek Septuagint (LXX) mistranslation of "copy of this law" in 17:18 as "second law," which was rendered *Deuteronomium* in the Latin version (Vulgate). The Hebrew title of the book is translated, "These are the words," from the first two Hebrew words of the book; this is a better description of the book since it is not a "second law," but rather the record of Moses' words of explanation concerning the law. Deuteronomy completes the five-part literary unit known as the Pentateuch.

Author and Date

Moses has traditionally been recognized as the author of Deuteronomy, since the book itself testifies that Moses wrote it (1:1, 5; 31:9, 22, 24). Both the OT (1 Kin. 2:3; 8:53; 2 Kin. 14:6; 18:12) and the NT (Acts 3:22, 23; Rom. 10:19) support the claim of Mosaic authorship. While Deuteronomy 32:48–34:12 was added after Moses' death (probably by Joshua), the rest of the book came from Moses' hand just before his death in 1405 B.C.

The majority of the book is comprised of farewell speeches that the 120-year-old Moses gave to Israel, beginning on the first day of the eleventh month of the fortieth year after the Exodus from Egypt (1:3). These speeches can be dated January–February of 1405 B.C. In the last few weeks of Moses' life, he committed these speeches to writing and gave them to the priests and elders for the coming generations of Israel (31:9, 24–26).

Background and Setting

Like Leviticus, Deuteronomy does not advance historically, but takes place entirely in one location over about one month of time (cf. Deut. 1:3; 34:8 with Josh. 5:6–12). Israel was camped in the central rift valley east of the Jordan River (Deut. 1:1). This location was referred to in Numbers 36:13 as "the plains of Moab," an area north of the Arnon River across the Jordan River from Jericho. It had been almost forty years since the Israelites had left Egypt.

The Book of Deuteronomy concentrates on events that took place in the final weeks of Moses' life. The major event was the verbal communication of divine revelation from Moses to the people of Israel (1:1–30:20; 31:30–32:47; 33:1–29). The only other events recorded were: (1) Moses' recording the law in a book and his commissioning of Joshua as the new leader (31:1–29); (2) Moses' viewing of the land of Canaan from Mt. Nebo (32:48–52; 34:1–4); and (3) his death (34:5–12).

The original recipients of Deuteronomy, both in its verbal and written presentations, were the second generation of the nation of Israel. All of that generation from forty to sixty years of age (except Joshua and Caleb, who were older) had been born in Egypt and had participated as children or teens in the Exodus. Those under forty had been born and reared in the wilderness. Together, they comprised the generation that was on the verge of conquering the land of Canaan under Joshua, forty years after they had left Egypt (1:34–39).

Historical and Theological Themes

Like Leviticus, Deuteronomy contains much legal detail, but with an emphasis on the people rather than the priests. As Moses called the second generation of Israel to trust the Lord and be obedient to His covenant made at Horeb (Sinai), he illustrated his points with references to Israel's past history. He reminded Israel of her rebellion against the Lord at Horeb (9:7–10:11) and at Kadesh (1:26–46), which brought devastating consequences. He also reminded her of the Lord's faithfulness in giving victory over her enemies (2:24–3:11; 29:2, 7, 8).

Most importantly, Moses called the people to take the land that God had promised by oath to their forefathers Abraham, Isaac, and Jacob (1:8; 6:10; 9:5; 29:13; 30:20; 34:4; cf. Gen. 15:18–21; 26:3–5; 35:12). Moses not only looked back, but he also looked ahead and saw that Israel's future failure to obey God would lead to her being scattered among the nations before the fulfillment of His oath to the patriarchs would be completed (4:25–31; 29:22–30:10; 31:26–29).

The Book of Deuteronomy, along with Psalms and Isaiah, reveals much about the attributes of God. Thus, it is directly quoted over forty times in the NT (exceeded only by Psalms and Isaiah) with many more allusions to its content. Deuteronomy reveals that the Lord is the only God (4:39; 6:4), and that He is jealous (4:24), faithful (7:9), loving (7:13), merciful (4:31), yet angered by sin (6:15). This is the God who called Israel to Himself. Over 250 times, Moses repeated the phrase, "the LORD your God" to Israel. Israel was called to obey (28:2), fear (10:12), love (10:12), and serve (10:12) her God by walking in His ways and keeping His commandments (10:12, 13). By obeying Him, the people of Israel would receive His blessings (28:1–14). Obedience and the pursuit of personal holiness is always based on the character of God. Because of who He is, His people are to be holy (cf., 7:6–11; 8:6, 11, 18; 10:12, 16, 17; 11:13; 13:3, 4; 14:1, 2).

Interpretive Challenges

Three interpretive challenges face the reader of Deuteronomy. First, is the book a singular record, or is it only a part of the larger literary whole, the Pentateuch? The remainder of the Scripture always views the Pentateuch as a unit, and the ultimate meaning of Deuteronomy cannot be divorced from its context in the Pentateuch. The book also assumes the reader is already familiar with the four books that precede it; in fact, Deuteronomy brings into focus all that had been revealed in Genesis to Numbers, as well as its implications for the people as they entered the land. However, every available Hebrew manuscript divides the Pentateuch in exactly the same way as the present text. This indicates that the book is a well-defined unit recounting the final speeches of Moses to Israel, and that it may also be viewed as a singular record.

Second, is the structure of Deuteronomy based on the secular treaties of Moses' day? During recent decades, many evangelical scholars have supported the Mosaic authorship of Deuteronomy by appealing to the similarities between the structure of the book and the ancient Near Eastern treaty form of the mid-second millennium B.C. (the approximate time of Moses). These secular suzerainty treaties (i.e., a ruler dictating his will to his vassals) followed a set pattern not used in the mid-first millennium B.C. These treaties usually contained the following elements: (1) preamble—identifying the parties to the covenant; (2) historical prologue—a history of the king's dealing with his vassals; (3) general and specific stipulations; (4) witnesses; (5) blessings and curses; and (6) oaths and covenant ratification. Deuteronomy, it is believed, approximates this basic structure.

While there is agreement that 1:1–5 is a preamble, 1:5–4:43 a historical prologue, and chapters 27, 28 feature blessings and cursings, there is no consensus as to how the rest of Deuteronomy fits this structure. While there might have been a covenant renewal on the plains of Moab, this is neither clearly explicit nor implicit in Deuteronomy.

It is best to take the book for what it claims to be: the explanation of the law given by Moses for the new generation. The structure follows the speeches given by Moses.

Third, what was the covenant made in the land of Moab (29:1)? Many understand this covenant as a renewal of the Sinaitic covenant made nearly forty years before with the first generation. Here, Moses supposedly updated and renewed this same covenant with the second generation of Israel. The second view sees this covenant as a Palestinian covenant which guarantees the nation of Israel's right to the land, both at that time and in the future. A third position is that Moses in chapters 29, 30 anticipated the new covenant, since he knew Israel would fail to keep the Sinaitic covenant. The

Outline

I. Introduction: The Historical Setting of Moses' Speeches (1:1–4)

II. The First Address by Moses: A Historical Prologue (1:5–4:43)
   A. A Historical Review of God's Gracious Acts from Horeb to Beth Peor (1:5–3:29)
   B. An Exhortation to Obey the Law (4:1–40)
   C. The Setting Apart of Three Cities of Refuge (4:41–43)

III. The Second Address by Moses: The Stipulations of the Sinaitic Covenant (4:44–28:68)
   A. Introduction (4:44–49)
   B. The Basic Elements of Israel's Relationship with the Lord (5:1–11:32)
      1. The Ten Commandments (5:1–33)
      2. The total commitment to the Lord (6:1–25)
      3. Separation from the gods of other nations (7:1–26)
      4. A warning against forgetting the Lord (8:1–20)
      5. Illustrations of Israel's rebellion in the past (9:1–10:11)
      6. An admonition to fear and love the Lord and obey His will (10:12–11:32)
   C. The Specific Stipulations for Life in the New Land (12:1–26:19)
      1. Instructions for the life of worship (12:1–16:17)
      2. Instructions for leadership (16:18–18:22)
      3. Instructions for societal order (19:1–23:14)
      4. Instructions from miscellaneous laws (23:15–25:19)
      5. The firstfruits and tithes in the land (26:1–15)
      6. The affirmation of obedience (26:16–19)
   D. The Blessings and Curses of the Covenant (27:1–28:68)

IV. The Third Address by Moses: Another Covenant (29:1–30:20)

V. The Concluding Events (31:1–34:12)
   A. The Change of Leadership (31:1–8)
   B. The Future Reading of the Law (31:9–13)
   C. The Song of Moses (31:14–32:47)
      1. The anticipation of Israel's failure (31:14–29)
      2. The witness of Moses' song (31:30–32:43)
      3. The communicating of Moses' song (32:44–47)
   D. The Final Events of Moses' Life (32:48–34:12)
      1. The directives for Moses' death (32:48–52)
      2. The blessing of Moses (33:1–29)
      3. The death of Moses (34:1–12)

third view seems the best.

I. INTRODUCTION: THE HISTORICAL SETTING OF MOSES' SPEECHES (1:1-4)

1:1-4 This introduction gives the setting of Deuteronomy and its purpose.

1:1 *the words which Moses spoke.* Almost all of Deuteronomy consists of speeches given by Moses at the end of his life. According to verse 3, Moses acted on the authority of God since his inspired words were in accordance with the commandments that God had given. ***to all Israel.*** This expression is used twelve times in this book and emphasizes the unity of Israel, and the universal applications of these words. ***the plain opposite Suph.*** Except for Jordan and the Arabah, the exact location of the places named in 1:1 is not known with certainty, although they may have been along Israel's route north from the Gulf of Aqabah (cf. Num. 33). The plain referred to is the large rift valley that extends from the Sea of Galilee in the north to the Gulf of Aqabah in the south. Israel was camped east of the Jordan River in this valley.

1:2 *eleven days' journey.* The distance from Horeb to Kadesh Barnea was about 150 miles. Kadesh was on the southern border of the Promised Land. This trip took eleven days on foot, but for Israel lasted thirty-eight more years. ***Horeb.*** The usual name in Deuteronomy for Mt. Sinai means "desolation," a fitting name since the area around Sinai is barren and uninviting. ***Mount Seir.*** South of the Dead Sea in Edom.

1:3 *the fortieth year.* The fortieth year after the Exodus from Egypt. The years of divine judgment (Num. 14:33, 34) were ending. ***the eleventh month.*** January-February of 1405 B.C. Numbers 20–36 records the events of the fortieth year.

1:4 *Sihon . . . Og.* The two kings of the Amorites whom the Jews defeated in Transjordan (see 2:24–3:11; Num. 21:21–35).

II. The First Address by Moses: A Historical Prologue (1:5–4:43)

1:5–4:43 These verses mainly contain Moses' first speech. Moses introduced his explanation of the law with a call to enter the land of Canaan (vv. 6–8), which had been promised by the Abrahamic covenant from God (cf. Gen. 15:18–21). Throughout this book, he refers to that covenant promise (1:35; 4:31; 6:10, 18, 23; 7:8, 12; 8:1, 18; 9:5; 10:11; 11:9, 21; 13:17; 19:8; 26:3, 15; 27:3; 28:11; 29:13; 30:20; 31:7, 20–23; 34:4). He then gave a historical review of God's gracious acts (1:9–3:29) and a call to Israel for obedience to the covenant given to them by the Lord at Sinai (4:1–40). This introductory section ends with a brief narrative recounting the appointment of the three cities of refuge east of the Jordan River (4:41–43).

A. A Historical Review of God's Gracious Acts from Horeb to Beth Peor (1:5–3:29)

1:5 *explain.* This means to make clear, distinct, or plain. The purpose of the book was to make the sense and purpose of the law clear to the people as they entered the land. It was to be their guide to the law while living in the land. Moses did not review what happened at Horeb (Sinai), which is recorded by him in Exodus, Leviticus, and Numbers (cf. Ex. 20:1–Num. 10:10), but rather gave Israel instruction in how to walk with God and how to fulfill God's will in the land and be blessed.

1:7, 8 *the land.* The land that the Lord set before Israel to go in and possess was clearly described in verse 7. The mountains of the Amorites referred to the hill country west of the Dead Sea. The plain (Arabah) was the land in the rift valley from the Sea of Galilee in the north to the Dead Sea in the south. The mountains were the hills that run north and south through the center of the land. These hills are to the west of the Sea of Galilee and the Jordan River. The lowland referred to the low, rolling hills that sloped toward the Mediterranean coast (Shephelah). The south (Negev) described the dry wasteland stretching southward from Beersheba to the wilderness. The seacoast referred to the land along the Mediterranean Sea. The boundaries of the land of the Canaanites were given in Numbers 34:1–15. Lebanon to the north marked the northwestern boundary on the coast. The northeast boundary of the land was the Euphrates River. Cf. Numbers 34:1–12.

1:8 *the Lord swore.* God's command to take possession of this land by conquest was based on the promise of the land that had been given in a covenant to Abraham (Gen 15:18–21) and reiterated to Isaac and Jacob (Gen. 26:3–5; 28:13–15; 35:12). These three patriarchs are mentioned seven times in Deuteronomy (1:8; 6:10; 9:5, 27; 29:13; 30:20; 34:4). The Lord sealed His promise to the patriarchs with an oath indicating that He would never change His plan (cf. Ps. 110:4).

1:9–18 See notes on *Exodus 18* for the background.

1:10 *the stars of heaven.* The Lord had promised Abraham that his descendants would be as numerous as the stars in the sky (see Gen. 15:5; 22:17). The nation's growth proved both God's intention and ability to fulfill His original promises to Abraham.

1:11 *a thousand times.* A Semitic way of saying "an infinitely large number."

1:13 *Choose wise . . . men.* The fulfillment of God's promise to give Abraham such a large posterity created a problem for Moses. The nation had become too large for Moses to govern effectively. The solution was the appointment by Moses of men to help him lead the people (see Ex. 18:13–27). These men were to be (1) wise, i.e., men who knew how to apply their knowledge; (2) understanding, i.e., those who had discernment and so were able to judge; and (3) knowledgeable, i.e., experienced and respected. Cf. Exodus 18:21.

1:19–21 See notes on Numbers 10:11–12:16 for the background.

1:22–46 See notes on Numbers 13; 14 for the background.

1:22 *Let us send men before us.* When challenged by Moses to take the land (vv. 20, 21), the people requested that spies be sent first. Moses, it seems, took their request to the Lord, who also approved their plan and commanded Moses to appoint the spies (Num. 13:1, 2). Thus, Moses selected twelve men who went to see what the land was like (Num. 13:17–20).

1:26 *but rebelled.* Israel, at Kadesh Barnea, deliberately and defiantly refused to respond to God's command to take the land (Num. 14:1–9).

1:27 *you complained.* Israel grumbled in their tents that the Lord hated them. They assumed that the Lord brought them from Egypt to have them destroyed by the Amorites.

1:28 *the Anakim.* Lit. "sons of the Anakim" (i.e., the Anakites). The Anakites were early inhabitants of Canaan described as "giants" (2:10, 21; 9:2; Num. 13:32, 33). They were larger than the Israelites and were especially feared because of their military power.

1:32 *you did not believe the LORD your God.* The failure of the people to take the land at the beginning of their time in the wilderness was explained here in the same way as in Numbers 14:11. Israel did not take the Lord at His word and, therefore, did not obey His command. The Israelites' lack of obedience is explained as the outcome of their lack of faith in the Lord.

1:33 *in the fire . . . and in the cloud.* The cloud by day and the fire by night were the means of God's direction for Israel in the wilderness (Ex. 13:21; Num. 9:15–23). The Lord who guided Israel through the wandering journey was the same Lord who had already searched out a place for Israel in the land. As He had directed them in the past, He would direct them also in the future.

1:36–38 *Caleb . . . Joshua.* They were excluded from this judgment because of exemplary faith and obedience (cf. Num. 14:24; Josh. 14:8, 9).

1:37 *The LORD was also angry with me.* Although his disobedience occurred almost thirty-nine years after the failure of Israel at Kadesh (Num. 20:1–13), Moses included it here with Israel's disobedience of the Lord because his disobedience was of the same kind. Moses, like Israel, failed to honor the word of the Lord and thus, in rebellion for self-glory, disobeyed God's clear command and struck the rock rather than speaking to it. Thus, he suffered the same result of God's anger and, like Israel, was not allowed to go into the land (Num. 20:12).

1:41–45 Israel's further defiance of the Lord's command was shown by their presumption in seeking to go into the land after God said they should not. This time they rebelled by attempting to go in and conquer the land, only to be chased back by the Amorites. The Lord showed His displeasure by not helping them or sympathizing with their defeat; for that generation, there was no escape from death in the desert during the next thirty-eight years (cf. Num. 15–19).

1:46 *you remained in Kadesh many days.* These words suggest that Israel spent a large part of the thirty-eight years in the wilderness around Kadesh Barnea.

2:1–3:11 See notes on Numbers 20:14–21:35 for the background.

2:1–23 This section narrates encounters with Israel's relatives, the Edomites (vv. 1–8), Moabites (vv. 9–18), and Ammonites (vv. 19–23).

2:1 *the Way of the Red Sea.* Cf. Numbers 21:4. After spending a long time at Kadesh, the Israelites set out once again at the command of the Lord through Moses. They traveled away from their Promised Land in a southeasterly direction from Kadesh toward the Gulf of Aqabah on the road to the Red Sea. Thus began the wanderings that were about to end. *skirted Mount Seir.* Israel spent many days wandering in the vicinity of Mt. Seir, the mountain range of Edom, south of the Dead Sea and extending down the eastern flank of the Arabah.

2:3 *turn northward.* The departure from Kadesh had been in a southeasterly direction away from the Promised Land, until the Lord commanded Israel to turn again northward in the direction of the Promised Land.

2:4 *your brethren, the descendants of Esau.* Esau was the brother of Jacob (Gen. 25:25, 26). The Edomites, the descendants of Esau, lived in Mt. Seir. According to Numbers 20:14–21, the Edomites refused to allow Israel to pass through their land. Verse 8, reflecting this refusal, states that the Israelites went around the border of the descendants of Esau, i.e., to the east of their territory.

2:5 *I will not give you any of their land.* God had granted to the descendants of Esau an inheritance (Mt. Seir was their possession). In verse 9, the same is said about the Moabites and in verse 19, about the Ammonites.

2:8 *from Elath and Ezion Geber.* Two towns located just north of the Gulf of Aqabah. Israel passed to the east of Edom and to the east of Moab on their journey northward.

2:10 *The Emim.* Apparently a Moabite term (see v. 11) meaning "terrible ones."

These people, numerous and tall, were the pre-Moabite occupants of the land of Moab.

2:12 *their possession which the LORD gave them.* The Horites were Hurrians, a people who lived in various places in Syria and Palestine. Those living in the region of Seir had been displaced by the descendants of Esau. The displacement of the Horites by the Edomites was analogous to the Israelites' possession of their own land.

2:13 *Zered.* A brook that ran into the Dead Sea from the southeast. It seems to have constituted the southern boundary of Moab. In contrast to the disobedience associated with Kadesh, the people obeyed the command to cross over the brook Zered. There was a new spirit of obedience toward the Lord among the people.

2:14 *thirty-eight years.* From 1444–1406 B.C. These were the years from the failure at Kadesh to the obedience at Zered. It was during this time that the rebellious generation, who had been denied access to the Promised Land by the oath of the Lord, had all died.

2:20 *Zamzummim.* Apparently an Ammonite term used to describe their precursors in their land. They were characterized as being as tall as the Anakim. But the Lord had destroyed them and given their land to the Ammonites. This was an encouragement to the Israelites that God could also defeat the Anakim in the land of Canaan and give that land to Israel.

2:23 *the Avim.* The ancient village dwellers of southwestern Palestine along the Mediterranean coast as far as the city of Gaza. *the Caphtorim.* Caphtor probably refers to Crete and may be a reference to an early Philistine group from that island who invaded the coast of Palestine, defeated the Avim, and then dwelt there. These Caphtorim were precursors to the later, greater Philistine invasion of c. 1200 B.C.

2:24–3:29 Moses continues the historical

survey detailing the defeat of two Amorite kings, Sihon and Og, and the takeover of their territory.

2:24 *the River Arnon.* The northern boundary of Moab. Israel was allowed to attack Sihon the Amorite because the Amorites were not relatives of Israel.

2:25 *fear of you.* As the conquest began, God put the fear of Israel into the hearts of their enemies.

2:26 *the Wilderness of Kedemoth.* Kedemoth means "eastern regions." It was probably a few miles north of the Arnon River and near the eastern border of the Amorite state.

2:27 *Let me pass through.* As with the Edomites previously (Num. 20:17), Moses asked to pass peacefully through the territory of Sihon.

2:30 *hardened his spirit.* Sihon, by his own conscious will, refused Israel's request to journey through his land. God confirmed what was already in Sihon's heart, namely arrogance against the Lord and His people Israel, so that He might defeat him in battle

---

Key Word

Rest: 3:20; 12:10; 25:19—means "to be at peace." Rest implies freedom from anxiety and conflict. God promised the Israelites rest in the Promised Land (Ex. 33:14; Deut. 3:1–20; 12:9–10). In the book of Joshua, the idea of rest is related specifically to the conflicts and hostilities Israel had with their neighbors. God promised His people a peaceful place to settle. Obtaining this rest depended on Israel's complete obedience to God's command to drive out the Canaanites (11:23; 14:15). The New Testament writers also speak of the concept of rest. Christians are told that heaven will bring them rest from death, pain, sin, and all other earthly struggles (Heb. 4:1; Rev. 21:4).

---

and give his land to Israel.

2:32 *Jahaz.* The place of battle between Sihon and the Israelites, probably a few miles to the north of Kedemoth (v. 26).

3:1 *Bashan.* A fertile region located east of the Sea of Galilee and the Jordan River, extending from Mt. Hermon in the north to the Yarmuk River in the south. Israel met King Og and his army in battle at Edrei, a city on the Yarmuk River. The Amorite king ruled over sixty cities (vv. 4–10; Josh. 13:30), which were taken by Israel; this kingdom was assigned to the Transjordanic tribes, especially the half tribe of Manasseh (v. 13).

3:8 *this side of the Jordan.* East of the Jordan River, Israel controlled the territory from the Arnon River to Mt. Hermon, a length of about 150 miles Note that the perspective of the speaker was to the east of the Jordan; the west of the Jordan still needed to be conquered. This statement helps date these speeches as pre-conquest.

3:11 *an iron bedstead.* The bedstead may actually have been a coffin, which would have been large enough to also hold tomb objects. The size of the "bedstead," 13? by 6 feet, emphasized the largeness of Og, who was a giant (the last of the Rephaim, a race of giants). As God had given Israel victory over the giant Og, so He would give them victory over the giants in the land.

3:12–20 *See notes on Numbers 32:1–42; 34:13–15* for background.

3:20 *rest.* A peaceful situation with the land free from external threat and oppression. The eastern tribes had the responsibility to battle alongside their western brethren until the conquest was complete (cf. Josh. 22).

3:22 *the Lord your God Himself fights for you.* Moses commanded Joshua not to be afraid because the Lord Himself would provide supernatural power and give them the victory (cf. 1:30; 31:6–8; Josh. 1:9).

Notable Teachers in Scripture

Moses	Renowned as the leader of Israel who first taught God's Law (Deut. 4:5).
Bezalel and Aholiab	Two master craftsmen who were gifted and called to teach others in the construction of the tabernacle (Ex. 35:30–35).
Samuel	The last of Israel's judges before the monarchy, who taught the people "the good and the right way" (1 Sam. 12:23).
David	Prepared his son Solomon to build and staff the temple (1 Chr. 28:9–21).
Solomon	Known for his outstanding wisdom, which he used to teach numerous subjects, including literature, botany, and zoology (1 Kin. 4:29–34).
Ezra	A scribe and priest who was committed not only to keeping the Law himself, but to teaching it to others (Ezra 7:10).
Jesus	Called Rabbi ("teacher," John 1:38; compare Matt. 9:11; 26:18; John 13:13), whose teaching revealed the good news of salvation (Eph. 4:20–21).
Barnabas	One of the teachers among the believers at Antioch (Acts 13:1), who had a lasting impact on Saul after his conversion to the faith (9:26–30).
Gamaliel	A renowned Jewish rabbi who was the teacher of Saul during his youth (Acts 22:3).
Paul	Perhaps the early church's most gifted teacher, known to have taught throughout the Roman world, notably at Antioch (Acts 13:1) and in the school of Tyrannus at Ephesus (19:9).
Priscilla and Aquila	Two believers who taught the way of God to a talented young orator named Apollos (Acts 18:26).
Apollos	A powerful teacher from Alexandria in Egypt, whose teaching paved the way for the gospel at Ephesus (Acts 18:24–26).
Timothy	Pastor-teacher of the church at Ephesus (1 Tim. 1:3; 2 Tim. 4:2).
Titus	Pastor-teacher of a church on the island of Crete (Titus 2:1–15).

Nelson's Complete Book of Bible Maps & Charts (Nashville: Thomas Nelson Publishers, 1996) 189. © 1993 by Thomas Nelson, Inc.

3:23 I pleaded with the LORD. With the victories over Sihon and Og, Moses made one final passionate plea to the Lord to be allowed to enter the Promised Land. However, the Lord would not allow Moses that privilege. He did, however, allow Moses to go to the top of Pisgah and see the land (cf. Deut. 32:48–52; 34:1–4).

3:26 the LORD was angry. See note on 1:37; cf. 4:21–24.

3:29 Beth Peor. Located east of the Jordan River, probably opposite Jericho (*see notes on Num. 22–25* for the background).

B. An Exhortation to Obey the Law (4:1–40)

4:1 O Israel, listen. Moses called the people to hear and obey the rules of conduct that God had given them to observe. Successful conquest and full enjoyment of life in the land was based on submission to God's law. *the statutes and the judgments.* The first are permanent rules for conduct fixed by the reigning authority, while the second deal with judicial decisions which served as precedents for future guidance.

4:2 You shall not add . . . nor take from. The word that God had given to Israel through Moses was complete and sufficient to direct the people. Thus, this law, the gift of God at Horeb, could not be supplemented or reduced. Anything that adulterated or contradicted God's law would not be tolerated (cf. 12:32; Prov. 30:6; Rev. 22:18, 19).

4:3, 4 Moses used the incident at Baal Peor (Num. 25:1–9) to illustrate from the Israelites' own history that their very lives depended on obeying God's law. Only those who had held fast to the Lord by obeying His commands were alive that day to hear Moses.

4:6 the peoples. Israel's obedience of God's law would provide a testimony to the world that God was near to His people and that His laws were righteous. One purpose of the law was to make Israel morally and spiritually unique among all the nations and, therefore, draw those nations to the true and living God. They were from their beginnings to be a witness nation. Though they failed and have been temporarily set aside, the prophets revealed that, in the future kingdom of Messiah, they will be a nation of faithful witnesses (cf. Is. 45:14; Zech. 8:23). *a wise and understanding people.* The nations would see three things in Israel (vv. 6–8). First, the Israelites would know how to apply God's knowledge so as to have discernment and to be able to judge matters accurately.

4:7 God so near to it. Second, faithfulness to the Lord would allow the nations to see that the Lord had established intimacy with Israel.

4:8 statutes and righteous judgments. Third, the nations would see that Israel's law was distinctive, for its source was the Lord, indicating that its character was righteous.

4:9–31 This section carries the most basic lesson for Israel to learn—to fear and reverence God.

4:9 teach them to your children. Deuteronomy emphasizes the responsibility of parents to pass on their experiences with God and the knowledge they have gained from Him to their children (cf. 6:7; 11:19).

4:10 especially concerning the day. One experience of Israel to be passed on from generation to generation was the great theophany (the self-revelation of God in physical form) which took place at Horeb (cf. Ex. 19:9–20:19).

4:12 no form. Israel was to remember that when God revealed Himself at Sinai, His presence came through His voice, i.e., the sound of His words; they did not see Him. God is Spirit (John 4:24), which rules out any idolatrous representation of God in any physical form (vv. 16–18) or any worship of the created order (v. 19).

4:13 the Ten Commandments. Lit. "ten statements," from which comes the term *Decalogue.* These summarize and epitomize all the commandments the Lord gave to Israel through Moses. Though the phrase occurs only here, in 10:4, and in Exodus 34:28, there are twenty-six more references to it in Deuteronomy (*see notes on Matt. 19:16–21; 22:35–40; Mark 10:17–22; Rom. 13:8–10*).

4:15–19 A strong emphasis is made on commandments one and two (cf. Rom. 1:18–23).

4:20 the iron furnace. A fire was used to heat iron sufficiently to be hammered into different shapes or welded to other objects. The iron furnace here suggests that Israel's time in Egypt was a period of ordeal, testing, and purifying for the Hebrews, readying them for usefulness as God's witness nation.

4:24 a jealous God. God is zealous to protect what belongs to Him; therefore, He will not allow another to have the honor that is due Him alone (cf. Is. 42:8; 48:11).

4:25–31 Cf. 8:18, 19. In fact, this section briefly outlines the future judgment of Israel, which culminated in the ten northern tribes being exiled to Assyria (c. 722 B.C.; 2 Kin. 17) and the two southern tribes being deported to Babylon (c. 605–586 B.C.; 2 Kin. 24; 25). Although the Jews returned in the days of Ezra and Nehemiah (c. 538–445 B.C.), they never regained their autonomy or dominance. Thus, the days of promised restoration and return look forward to Messiah's return to set up the millennial kingdom.

4:27 the LORD will scatter you. Moses warned Israel that the judgment for idolatry would be their dispersion among the nations by the Lord (see 28:64–67).

4:30 the latter days. Lit. "the end of days." Moses saw in the distant future a time when repentant Israel would turn again to the Lord and obey Him. Throughout the Pentateuch, "the latter days" refers to the time when Messiah will establish His kingdom (see Gen. 49:1, 8–12; Num. 24:14–24; Deut. 32:39–43).

4:31 the covenant of your fathers. God mercifully will ultimately fulfill the covenant He originally made with Abraham, Isaac, and Jacob with repentant Israel in the future. God will not forget the promise that He has given to Abraham and his seed (cf. Rom. 11:25–27).

4:32–40 A historical apologetic, appealing for the nation's obedience to God's law.

4:32–39 since the day that God created man on the earth. In all of human history, no other nation has had the privilege that Israel had of hearing God speak, as He did in giving the law at Mt. Sinai, and surviving such an awesome experience. Nor had any other people been so blessed, chosen, and delivered from bondage by such mighty miracles as Israel saw. God did this to reveal to them that He alone is God (vv. 35, 39).

4:37 His Presence. Lit. "His face." God Himself had brought Israel out of Egypt. The Exodus resulted from the electing love that God had for the patriarchs and their descendants.

4:40 Such gracious privilege, as remembered in verses 32–39, should elicit obedience, particularly in view of the unconditional promise that the land will be theirs permanently ("for all time") as is detailed in chapters 29 and 30.

C. The Setting Apart of Three Cities of Refuge (4:41–43)

4:41–43 These three verses are a narrative insertion at the end of Moses' speech. The setting aside of three cities on the east side of the Jordan River by Moses showed that Moses willingly obeyed the commandments God gave him. He was an example of the type of obedience that God was calling for in 4:1–40 (cf. Num. 35:14; Josh. 20:18).

III. THE SECOND ADDRESS BY MOSES: THE STIPULATIONS OF THE SINAITIC COVENANT (4:44–28:68)

4:44–28:68 The heart of Deuteronomy is found in this long second speech of Moses. "Now this is the law" (4:44) which Moses explained to Israel (cf. 1:5). After a brief introduction (4:44–49), Moses gave the people a clear understanding of what the law directed concerning their relationship with the Lord in the land (5:1–26:19); then Moses concluded by recounting the blessings or the curses which would come upon the nation as a consequence of their response to the stipulations of this law (27:1–28:68).

A. Introduction (4:44–49)

4:45 *testimonies . . . statutes . . . judgments.* God's instruction to Israel was set forth in: (1) the testimonies, the basic covenant stipulations (5:6–21); (2) statutes, words that were inscribed and, therefore, fixed; and (3) judgments, the decisions made by a judge on the merits of the situation. This law was given to Israel when they came out of Egypt. Moses is not giving further law; he is now explaining what has already been given.

4:48 *Mount Sion.* This reference to Mt. Hermon is not to be confused with Mt. Zion in Jerusalem.

4:49 *Sea of the Arabah.* The Dead Sea.

B. The Basic Elements of Israel's Relationship with the Lord (5:1–11:32)

5:1–11:32 As Moses began his second address to the people of Israel, he reminded them of the events and the basic commands from God that were foundational to the Sinaitic covenant (5:1–33; see Ex. 19:1–20:21). Then, in 6:1–11:32, Moses expounded and applied the first three of the Ten Commandments to the present experience of the people.

1. The Ten Commandments (5:1–33)

5:1 *Hear, O Israel.* The verb *hear* carried the sense of "obey." A hearing that leads to obedience was demanded of all the people (cf. 6:4; 9:1; 20:3; 27:9).

5:2 *a covenant with us in Horeb.* The second generation of Israel, while children, received the covenant that God made with Israel at Sinai.

5:3 *did not make this covenant with our fathers.* The *fathers* were not the people's immediate fathers, who had died in the wilderness, but their more distant ancestors, the patriarchs (see 4:31, 37; 7:8, 12; 8:18). The Sinaitic or Mosaic covenant was in addition to and distinct from the Abrahamic covenant made with the patriarchs.

5:6–21 The first four Commandments involve relationship with God, the last six deal with human relationships; together, they were the foundation of Israel's life before God. Moses here reiterated them as given originally at Sinai. Slight variations from the Exodus text are accounted for by Moses' explanatory purpose in Deuteronomy. *See notes on Exodus 20:1–17* for an additional explanation of these commands.

5:7 *no other gods.* Cf. Exodus 20:3. *Other gods* were non-existent pagan gods, which were made in the form of idols and shaped by the minds of their worshipers. The Israelites were to be totally faithful to the God to whom they were bound by covenant. Cf. Matthew 16:24–27; Mark 8:34–38; Luke 9:23–26; 14:26–33.

5:8 *a carved image.* Cf. Exodus 20:4, 5.

Israel's Other Sacred Times

Besides the Annual Feasts, Israel's time was marked by these other sacred events.

Sabbath Every seventh day was a solemn rest from all work (Ex. 20:8–11; 31:12–17; Lev. 23:3; Deut. 5:12–15).

Sabbath Year Every seventh year was designated a "year of release" to allow the land to lie fallow (Ex. 23:10, 11; Lev. 25:1–7).

Year of Jubilee The 50th year, which followed seven Sabbath years, was to proclaim liberty to those who were servents because of debt, and to return lands to their former owners (Lev. 25:8–55; 27:17–24; Ezek. 46:17).

The New Moon The first day of the Hebrew 29- or 30-day month was a day of rest, special sacrifices, and the blowing of trumpets (Num. 28:11–15; Ps. 81:3).

Dedication (Lights or *Hanukkah*) An eight-day feast in the ninth month (Chislev) commemorating the cleansing of the temple from defilement by Syria, and its rededication (John 10:22).

Purim (Lots) A feast on the 14th and 15th of the 12th month (Adar). The name comes from Babylonian *Pur*, meaning "Lot" (Esth. 9:18–32).

Nelson's Complete Book of Bible Maps & Charts (Nashville: Thomas Nelson Publishers, 1996) 47. © 1993 by Thomas Nelson, Inc.

Reducing the infinite God to any physical likeness was intolerable, as the people found out in their attempt to cast God as a golden calf (cf. Ex. 32).

5:9, 10 third and fourth generations . . . thousands. See note on Exodus 20:5, 6 for an explanation of this often misunderstood text. *those who hate Me . . . love Me.* Disobedience is equal to hatred of God, as love is equal to obedience (cf. Matt. 22:34–40; Rom. 13:8–10).

5:11 take the name . . . in vain. Cf. Exodus 20:7. This means to attach God's name to emptiness. Cf. Psalm 111:9; Matthew 6:9; Luke 1:49; John 17:6, 26.

5:12 as the LORD your God commanded you. Cf. Exodus 20:8–10. These words are missing from Exodus 20:8, but refer back to this commandment given to Israel at Sinai, forty years earlier.

5:15 brought you out from there. Here, an additional reason is given for God's rest after creation (i.e., for the observance of the Sabbath; see Ex. 20:11)—God's deliverance of the people from Egypt. While the Israelites had been slaves in Egypt, they were not allowed rest from their continual labor, so the Sabbath was also to function as a day of rest in which their deliverance from bondage would be remembered with thanksgiving as the sign of their redemption and continual sanctification (cf. Ex. 31:13–17; Ezek 20:12).

5:16–20 Cf. Matthew 19:18, 19; Mark

10:19; Luke 18:20.

5:16 *that your days may be long.* Cf. Exodus 20:12; Matthew 15:4; Mark 7:10; Ephesians 6:2, 3. Paul indicated that this was the first commandment with a promise attached (Eph. 6:2). Jesus also had much to say about honoring parents (see Matt. 10:37; 19:29; Luke 2:49–51; John 19:26, 27).

5:17 *murder.* Cf. Exodus 20:13; Matthew 5:21; James 2:11.

5:18 *adultery.* Cf. Exodus 20:14; Matthew 5:27.

5:19 *steal.* Cf. Exodus 20:15; Ephesians 4:28.

5:20 *bear false witness.* Cf. Exodus 20:16; Colossians 3:9.

5:21 *covet . . . desire.* Cf. Exodus 20:17. Both the lusting after a neighbor's wife and a strong desire for a neighbor's property were prohibited by the tenth commandment (cf. Rom. 7:7).

5:22 *and He added no more.* These Ten Commandments alone were identified as direct quotations by God. The rest of the stipulations of the covenant were given to Moses, who in turn gave them to the Israelites. These basic rules, which reflect God's character, continue to be a means by which God reveals the sinful deeds of the flesh (cf. Rom. 7:7–14; Gal. 3:19–24; 5:13–26). They are also a holy standard for conduct that true believers live by through the Spirit's power, with the exception of keeping the Sabbath (cf. Col. 2:16, 17). *two tablets of stone.* The tablets were written on both sides (see Ex. 32:15).

5:22–27 The frightening circumstances of God's presence at Sinai caused the people to have enough fear to ask Moses to receive the words from God and communicate those words to them, after which they promised to obey all that God said (see v. 27).

5:28, 29 God affirmed that the pledge to be obedient was the right response (v. 28),

and then expressed His loving passion for them to fulfill their promise so they and their children would prosper.

5:30–33 They asked to be given all of God's Word (v. 27), so God dismissed the people and told Moses He was going to give the law to him to teach the people (v. 31). At stake was life and prosperity in the land of promise.

2. The total commitment to the Lord (6:1–25)

6:1–3 *days . . . prolonged.* Moses' concern is that successive generations maintain the obedience to God's laws that insures life and prosperity.

6:3 *a land flowing with milk and honey.* A description that included the richness of the land which the Israelites were soon to possess (see 11:9; 26:9, 15; 27:3; 31:20).

6:4, 5 Cf. Mark 12:29, 30, 32, 33.

6:4 *Hear, O Israel.* See 5:1. Deuteronomy 6:4–9, known as the *Shema* (Heb. for *hear*), has become the Jewish confession of faith, recited twice daily by the devout, along with 11:13–21 and Numbers 15:37–41. *The LORD . . . Lord is one!* The intent of these words was to give a clear statement of the truth of monotheism, that there is only one God. Thus, it has also been translated "the LORD is our God, the LORD alone." The word used for *one* in this passage does not mean "singleness," but "unity." The same word is used in Genesis 2:24, where the husband and wife were said to be "one flesh." Thus, while this verse was intended as a clear and concise statement of monotheism, it does not exclude the concept of the Trinity.

6:5–9 *You shall love the LORD your God.* First in the list of all that was essential for the Jew was unreserved, wholehearted commitment expressed in love to God. Since this relationship of love for God could not be represented in any material way as with idols, it had to be demonstrated in complete obedience to God's law in daily life. Cf. 11:16–21; Matthew 22:37; Luke 10:27.

6:6 these words . . . in your heart. The people were to think about these commandments and meditate on them so that obedience would not be a matter of formal legalism, but a response based on understanding. The law written on the heart would be an essential characteristic of the new covenant to come (see Jer. 31:33).

6:7 teach them diligently to your children. The commandments were to be the subject of conversation, both inside and outside the home, from the beginning of the day to its end.

6:8 hand . . . frontlets between your eyes. The Israelites were to continually meditate on and be directed by the commandments that God had given them. Later in Jewish history, this phrase was mistakenly taken literally and the people tied phylacteries (boxes containing these verses) to their hands and foreheads with thongs of leather.

6:10, 11 the LORD your God brings you into the land. God reiterated that He was going to give Israel the land in fulfillment of the promises He had made to Abraham, Isaac, and Jacob, both with title and prosperity.

6:13 take oaths in His name. An oath was a solemn pledge to affirm something said as absolutely true. The invoking of the Lord's name in the oath meant that a person was bound under obligation before God to fulfill that word (cf. Matt. 4:10; Luke 4:8).

6:15 a jealous God. See note on 4:24.

6:16 Massah. This name actually means "testing" (cf. Ex. 17:1–7; Matt. 4:7; Luke 4:12).

6:20 When your son asks you in time to come. When a young son asked the meaning of the law, his father was to use the following pattern in explaining it to him. First, the Israelites were in bondage in Egypt (v. 21a). Second, God miraculously delivered the

Israelites and judged the Egyptians (v. 21b, 22). Third, this work was in accord with His promise to the patriarchs (v. 23). Fourth, God gave His law to Israel that His people might obey it (vv. 24, 25).

6:25 righteousness for us. A true and personal relationship with God that would be manifest in the lives of the people of God. There was no place for legalism or concern about the external since the compelling motive for this righteousness was to be love for God (v. 5).

3. Separation from the gods of other nations (7:1–26)

7:1–26 This section discusses how the Israelites should relate to the inhabitants of Canaan, including their destruction, the forbidding of intermarriage, and the elimination of all altars and idols. It was God's time for judgment on that land.

7:1 seven nations. These seven groups controlled areas of land usually centered around one or more fortified cities. Together they had greater population and military strength than Israel. Six of these seven are mentioned elsewhere (see Ex. 3:8). The unique nation here is the Girgashites, who are referred to in Genesis 10:16; Joshua 3:10; 24:11; 1 Chronicles 1:14. They may have been tribal people living in northern Palestine.

7:2 utterly destroy them. All the men, women, and children were to be put to death. Even though this action seems extreme, the following considerations need to be kept in mind: (1) the Canaanites deserved to die for their sin (9:4, 5; cf. Gen. 15:16); (2) the Canaanites persisted in their hatred of God (7:10); and (3) the Canaanites constituted a moral cancer that had the potential of introducing idolatry and immorality which would spread rapidly among the Israelites (20:17, 18).

7:3 Nor . . . make marriages. Because of

the intimate nature of marriage, the idolatrous spouse could lead her mate astray (see 1 Kin. 11:1–8 for the tragic example of Solomon).

7:5 destroy their altars. This destructive action would remove any consequent temptation for the Israelites to follow the religious practices of the nations they were to displace from the land.

7:6 a holy people to the LORD your God. The basis for the command to destroy the Canaanites is found in God's election of Israel. God had set apart Israel for His own special use, and they were His treasured possession. As God's people, Israel needed to be separated from the moral pollution of the Canaanites.

7:8 loves you . . . keep the oath. The choosing of Israel as a holy nation set apart for God was grounded in God's love and His faithfulness to the promises He had made to the patriarchs, not in any merit or intrinsic goodness in Israel.

7:9 a thousand generations. *See note on 1:11.*

7:12–15 The Lord promised Israel particular blessings for their obedience, which are further enumerated in 28:1–14.

7:12 the LORD your God will keep with you the covenant. If Israel was obedient to the Lord, they would experience His covenantal mercy. However, the people could

Abominations to God

1. Graven images, idols used for worship	Deut. 7:25, 26
2. Proselytizing to false worship	Deut. 13:14
3. Transvestism	Deut. 22:5
4. Offerings from illicitly earned money	Deut. 23:18
5. Marrying a defiled woman	Deut. 24:4
6. Dishonesty in business	Deut. 25:16
7. An idol maker	Deut. 27:15
8. The evil-minded person	Prov. 3:32; 11:20; 15:26; 26:24, 25
9. A false balance	Prov. 11:1; 20:10, 23
10. The sacrifices of the wicked	Prov. 15:8; 21:27
11. The way of the wicked	Prov. 15:9
12. The justification of the wicked and the condemnation of the just	Prov. 17:15; 29:27
13. A proud look	Prov. 6:17; 16:5
14. A lying tongue	Prov. 6:17; 12:22
15. Hands that shed innocent blood	Prov. 6:17
16. A heart that devises wicked imaginations	Prov. 6:18; 8:7
17. Feet that are swift in running to mischief	Prov. 6:18
18. A false witness	Prov. 6:19
19. One who sows discord among brethren	Prov. 6:19
20. Kings who do evil	Prov. 16:12
21. Scoffing	Prov. 24:8, 9
22. Prayers of the lawless	Prov. 28:9

forfeit the blessings of the covenant through their own disobedience.

7:13 grain . . . new wine . . . oil. These were the three principal food products of Palestine. *Grain* included wheat and barley. *New wine* was the grape juice as it came from the presses. The *oil* was the olive oil used in cooking and in the lamps.

7:15 the terrible diseases of Egypt. Some virulent and malignant diseases such as elephantiasis, ophthalmia, and dysentery were common in Egypt.

7:20 God will send the hornet. The hornet or wasp was a large insect, common in Canaan, that may have had a potentially fatal sting. Here, the reference was probably figurative in the sense of a great army sent into panic when the Lord would inflict His sting on them (see 11:25). *See note on Exodus 23:28.*

7:22 little by little. Even though the Lord promised that the defeat of the people of the land would be quick (4:26; 9:3), the process of settlement would be more gradual to avoid the danger of the land returning to a primitive state of natural anarchy.

7:26 You shall utterly detest it and utterly abhor it. *Detest* and *abhor* were strong words of disapproval and rejection. Israel was to have the same attitude toward the idols of the Canaanites as did God Himself. *it is an accursed thing.* The images or idols were to be set aside for destruction.

4. A warning against forgetting the Lord (8:1–20)

8:2 remember. The people were to recall what God had done for them (cf. 5:15; 7:18; 8:18; 9:7; 15:15; 16:3, 12; 24:9, 18; 25:17), and not forget (cf. 4:9, 23, 31; 6:12; 8:11, 14, 19; 9:7; 25:19; 26:13). *to know what was in your heart.* Israel's forty years in the wilderness was a time of God's affliction and testing so that the basic attitude of the people toward

God and His commandments could be made known. God chose to sustain His hungry people in the wilderness by a means previously unknown to them. Through this miraculous provision, God humbled the people and tested their obedience.

8:3 manna which you did not know. God sustained the people in the wilderness with a food previously unknown to them. See Exodus 16:15 for the start to giving the manna and Joshua 5:12 for its cessation. *man shall not live by bread alone.* Israel's food in the wilderness was decreed by the Word of God. They had manna because it came by God's command; therefore, it ultimately was not bread that kept them alive, but God's Word (cf. Matt. 4:4; Luke 4:4).

8:4 Your garments did not wear out. This miraculous provision is also mentioned in 29:5.

8:5 the LORD your God chastens you. Israel's sojourn in the wilderness was viewed as a time of God's discipline of His children. He was seeking to correct their wayward attitude so they might be prepared to obediently go into the land.

8:6–10 An extensive description of God's abundant blessings for Israel in the land (cf. 7:7–9).

8:7 a good land. In contrast to the desolation of the wilderness, verses 7–9 describe the abundance of Israel's new land.

8:9 iron . . . copper. The mountains of southern Lebanon and the region east of the Sea of Galilee and south of the Dead Sea contained iron. Both copper and iron were found in the rift valley south of the Dead Sea.

8:11 do not forget the LORD your God. Sufficient food would lead to the satisfaction of Israel in the land (vv. 10, 12). This satisfaction and security could lead to Israel forgetting God. Forgetting God means no longer having Him in the daily thoughts of their lives. Israel's forgetfulness would lead to a disobedience of His commandments. Whereas, in the wilderness, Israel had to depend on God for the necessities of life, in the rich land there would be a tempting sense of self-sufficiency.

8:14 *when your heart is lifted up.* Pride was viewed as the root of forgetfulness. In their prosperity, the people might claim that their power and strength had produced their wealth (v. 17).

8:15 *water . . . out of the . . . rock.* Cf. Numbers 20:9–13.

8:16 *to do you good in the end.* God designed the test of the wilderness so that Israel might be disciplined to obey Him. Through her obedience, she received the blessing of the land. Thus, God's design was to do good for Israel at the end of the process.

8:18, 19 *See note on 4:25–31.*

8:19 *if you by any means forget.* Forgetting God would lead to worshiping other gods, which in turn would result in certain destruction. As God destroyed the Canaanites for their idolatry, so also would He judge Israel.

5. Illustrations of Israel's rebellion in the past (9:1–10:11)

9:1–10:11 This part of Moses' speech rehearses the sins of the Israelites at Horeb (cf. Ex. 32).

9:2 *the Anakim.* Moses remembered the people's shock when they heard the original report of the twelve spies concerning the size, strength, and number of the inhabitants of Canaan (Num. 13:26–14:6). Therefore, he emphasized that from a purely military and human point of view—their victory was impossible. The fear of the spies and the people focused on the Anakim, a tall, strong people who lived in the land of Canaan (*see note on 1:28*).

9:3 *a consuming fire.* The Lord was pictured as a fire that burned everything in its path. So the Lord would go over into Canaan and exterminate Canaanites. ***destroy them quickly.*** Israel was to be the human agent of the Lord's destruction of the Canaanites. The military strength of the Canaanites would be destroyed quickly (see Josh. 6:1–11:23), though the complete subjugation of the land would take time (see 7:22; Josh. 13:1).

9:4 *Because of my righteousness.* Three times in verses 4–6, Moses emphasized that the victory was not because of Israel's goodness, but was entirely the work of God. It was the wickedness of the Canaanites that led to their expulsion from the land (cf. Rom. 10:6).

9:6 *a stiff-necked people.* Lit. "hard of neck." A figurative expression for the stubborn, intractable, obdurate, and unbending attitude of Israel. In verses 7–29, Moses illustrated Israel's rebellious attitude and actions toward the Lord.

9:7 *Remember!* Moses challenged Israel to call to mind the long history of their stubbornness and provocation of God which had extended from the time of the Exodus from Egypt for forty years until the present moment on the plains of Moab.

9:10 *the finger of God.* God Himself had written the Ten Commandments on the two tablets of stone at Mt. Sinai (see Ex. 31:18). *Finger* is used in an anthropomorphic sense.

9:14 *blot out their name from under heaven.* God threatened to destroy the people of Israel so completely that He pictured it as an obliteration of all memory of them from the world of men. This threat was taken by Moses as an invitation to intercede for the children of Israel (Num. 14:11–19).

9:19 Cf. Hebrews 12:21.

9:20 *I prayed for Aaron.* Moses interceded on behalf of Aaron, on whom the immediate responsibility for the Israelites' sin of the golden calf rested. Aaron had thus incurred the wrath of God, and his life was in danger (see Ex. 32:1–6). This is the only verse in the Pentateuch which specifically states that Moses prayed for Aaron.

9:22 Taberah . . . Massah . . . Kibroth Hattaavah. These three places were all associated with Israel's rebellion against the Lord. Taberah, "burning," was where the people had complained of their misfortunes (Num. 11:1–3). At Massah, "testing," they had found fault with everything and, in presumption, had put God to the test (Ex. 17:1–7). At Kibroth Hattaavah, "graves of craving," the people had again incurred God's anger by complaining about their food (Num. 11:31–35).

9:23 Kadesh Barnea. There, they sinned by both lack of faith in God and disobedience (cf. Num. 13; 14).

9:24 You have been rebellious against the LORD. Moses concluded that his dealings with Israel as God's mediator had been one of continual rebellion on Israel's part, which led to his intercession (vv. 25–29).

9:28 the land from which You brought us. Moses' prayer of intercession to the Lord on behalf of Israel appealed to the Lord to forgive His people because the Egyptians could have interpreted God's destruction of Israel as His inability to fulfill His promise and His hate for His people.

10:1–3 two tablets of stone like the first. God had listened to Moses' intercession and dealt mercifully with the Israelites who had broken the covenant by rewriting the Ten Commandments on two tablets prepared for that purpose by Moses. The second tablets were made of the same material and were the same size as the first.

10:1 an ark of wood. This refers to the ark of the covenant. Moses telescoped the events in these verses. Later, at the construction of the ark of the covenant, Moses placed the two, new stone tablets within that ark (see Ex. 37:1–9).

10:6–9 These verses show that the priesthood of Aaron and service of the Levites were restored after the incident of the golden calf.

10:6 Moserah, where Aaron died. Aaron was not killed at Sinai, but lived until the fortieth year of the Exodus, which shows the effectiveness of Moses' intercession before the Lord (cf. Num. 20:22–29; 33:38, 39). After Aaron's death, the priestly ministry continued in the appointment of Eleazar. Moserah is the district in which Mt. Hor stands. This is where Aaron died (cf. Num. 20:27, 28; 33:38).

10:8 At that time. This refers to the time that Israel was at Mt. Sinai.

10:9 no portion. The family of Levi received no real estate inheritance in the land of Canaan (see Num. 18:20, 24).

10:10, 11 Because of Moses' intercession, not because of their righteousness, the Israelites were camped on the banks of the Jordan River, ready to enter the Promised Land.

6. An admonition to fear and love the Lord and obey His will (10:12–11:32)

10:12, 13 what does the LORD your God require of you ? This rhetorical question led into Moses' statement of the five basic requirements that God expected of His people (cf. Mic. 6:8): (1) **to fear the LORD your God.** To hold God in awe and submit to Him; (2) **to walk in all His ways.** To conduct one's life in accordance with the will of God; (3) **to love Him.** To choose to set one's affections on the

God Multiplied Abraham's Descendants	
The Promise	**The Reality**
Gen. 15:5	Ex. 32:13
Gen. 22:17	Deut. 1:10
Gen. 26:4	Deut. 10:22
	Deut. 26:5

Lord and on Him alone; (4) *to serve the Lord your God.* To have the worship of the Lord as the central focus of one's life; (5) *to keep the commandments of the Lord.* To obey the requirements the Lord had imposed.

10:14, 15 God, with the same sovereignty by which He controls all things, had chosen the patriarchs and the nation of Israel to be His special people. Cf. Romans 9; 10.

10:16 *Therefore circumcise . . . your heart.* Moses called the Israelites to cut away all the sin in their hearts, as the circumcision surgery cut away the skin. This would leave them with a clean relationship to God (cf. 30:6; Lev. 26:40, 41; Jer. 9:25; Rom. 2:29). *See note on Jeremiah 4:4.*

10:18 *He administers justice.* The sovereign, authoritative God is also impartial (v. 17), as seen in His concern for the orphan, the widow, and the alien (cf. Lev. 19:9–18; James 1:27).

10:20 *to Him you shall hold fast.* The verb means "to stick to," "to cling to," or "to hold on to." As a husband is to be united to his wife (Gen. 2:24), so Israel was to cling intimately to her God.

10:22 *seventy persons.* See Exodus 1:5. One of the great and awesome things God had done for Israel was multiplying the seventy people who went to Egypt into a nation of over two million people.

11:2 *your children.* Moses distinguished between the adults and the children in his audience. The adults were those who had seen the Exodus from Egypt as children and had experienced the Lord's discipline in the wilderness. It was to these adults that Moses could say, "your eyes have seen every great act of the Lord which He did" (v. 7). It was that specially blessed generation of adults that were called to pass on the teaching of what they had learned to their children (v. 19).

11:6 *Dathan and Abiram.* These two

> ### Key Word
>
> **Anger:** 7:4; 11:17; 31:17; 32:21, 22—signifies either "nose," "nostril," or "anger" (Gen. 2:7; Prov. 15:1). This term often occurs with words describing burning. Throughout the Old Testament, figures of speech such as "a burning nose" typically depict anger as the fierce breathing of a person through his nose (Ex. 32:10–12). Most of the Old Testament references using this word describe God's anger (Ps. 103:8; Deut. 4:24–25). The righteous anger of God is reserved for those who break His covenant (Deut. 13:17; 29:25–27; Josh. 23:16; Judg. 2:20; Ps. 78:38).

---

sons of Eliab, of the tribe of Reuben, had rebelled against the authority of Moses, the Lord's chosen leader. The basis of their complaint was that Moses had brought Israel out of Egypt, a fertile and prosperous land, and not brought them into Canaan. Because of their rebellion against Moses, God had judged them by having the earth open and swallow them up (see Num. 16:12–14, 25–27, 31–33). God's judgment of their rebellion was spoken of here by Moses in the context of his contrast between the land of Egypt and the land of Canaan (vv. 10–12).

11:10, 11 *the land which you go to possess.* The land of Canaan was different from Egypt. The land of Egypt depended upon the Nile River for its fertility. By contrast, the land of Canaan depended upon the rains that came from heaven for its fertility.

11:10 *watered it by foot.* Probably a reference to carrying water to each garden or the practice of indenting the ground with foot-deep channels through which irrigating water would flow.

11:13 Cf. 6:5.

11:14 *I will give you the rain for your land.* Since the land of Canaan was dependent on the rainfall for its fertility, God promised, in response to Israel's obedience, to give them the rain necessary for that fertility (vv. 16, 17). **the early rain and the latter rain.** The early rain was the autumn rain from October to January. The latter rain was the spring rain which came through Mar./Apr.

11:18–21 For the children and all subsequent generations, God's great acts had not been seen "with their own eyes," as had been the case with that first generation. God's acts were to be "seen" for them in the Word of Scripture. It was to be in Moses' words that the acts of God would be put before the eyes of their children. The first priority, therefore, was given to Scripture as the means of teaching the law and grace of God (cf. 6:6–9).

11:24 Every place ... your foot treads. In response to the obedience of Israel (vv. 22, 23), the Lord promised to give to Israel all the land they personally traversed to the extent of the boundaries that He had given. This same promise was repeated in Joshua 1:3–5. Had Israel obeyed God faithfully, her boundaries would have been enlarged to fulfill the promise made to Abraham (Gen. 15:18). But because of Israel's disobedience, the complete promise of the whole land still remains, yet to be fulfilled in the future kingdom of Messiah (cf. Ezek. 36:8–38).

11:26–32 As a final motive for driving home the importance of obedience and trust in God, Moses gave instruction for a ceremony which the people were to carry out when they entered the land. They were to read the blessings and the curses of the covenant on Mt. Gerizim and Mt. Ebal (see 27:1–14) as they actually would do later (Josh. 8:30–35).

C. The Specific Stipulations for Life in the New Land (12:1–26:19)

12:1–26:19 Having delineated the general principles of Israel's relationship with the Lord (5:1–11:32), Moses then explained specific laws that would help the people subordinate every area of their lives to the Lord. These instructions were given for Israel "to observe in the land" (12:1).

1. Instructions for the life of worship (12:1–16:17)

12:1–16:17 The first specific instructions that Moses gives deal with the public worship of the Lord by Israel as they come into the land.

12:1–32 Moses begins by repeating his instructions concerning what to do with the false worship centers after Israel had taken possession of the land of the Canaanites (see 7:1–6). They were to destroy them completely.

12:2 the high mountains ... hills ... every green tree. The Canaanite sanctuaries to be destroyed were located in places believed to have particular religious significance. The mountain or hill was thought to be the home of a god; and by ascending the mountain, the worshiper was in some symbolic sense closer to the deity. Certain trees were considered to be sacred and symbolized fertility, a dominant theme in Canaanite religion.

12:3 their altars, ... pillars, ... wooden images ... carved images. These were elements of Canaanite worship, which included human sacrifice (v. 31). If they remained, the people might mix the worship of God with those places (v. 4).

12:5 the place where the Lord your God chooses. Cf. verses 11, 18, 21. Various places of worship were chosen after the people settled in Canaan, such as Mt. Ebal (27:1–8; Josh. 8:30–35), Shechem (Josh. 24:1–28), and Shiloh (Josh. 18:1), which was the center of worship through the period of Judges (Judg. 21:19). The tabernacle, the Lord's dwelling place, was located in Canaan, where the Lord chose to dwell. The central importance of the tabernacle was in direct contrast to the multiple places (see v. 2) where the Canaanites practiced their worship of idols. Eventually, the tabernacle was brought to Jerusalem by David (cf. 2 Sam. 6:12–19).

12:6 *See notes on Leviticus 1–7* for descriptions of these various ceremonies.

12:7 *eat . . . rejoice.* Some of the offerings were shared by the priests, Levites, and the worshipers (cf. Lev. 7:15–18). The worship of God was to be holy and reverent, yet full of joy.

12:8 *every man doing whatever is right in his own eyes.* There seems to have been some laxity in the offering of the sacrifices in the wilderness which was not to be allowed when Israel came into the Promised Land. This self-centered attitude became a major problem in the time of Judges (cf. Judg. 17:6; 21:25).

12:15 *slaughter . . . within all your gates.* While sacrificial offerings were brought to the appointed centers for worship as well as the central sanctuary, the killing and eating of meat for regular eating could be engaged in anywhere. The only restriction on eating nonsacrificial meat was the prohibition of the blood and the fat.

12:17–19 All sacrifices and offerings had to be brought to the place chosen by God.

12:21 *If the place . . . is too far.* Moses envisioned the enlarging of the borders of Israel according to God's promise. This meant that people would live further and further away from the central sanctuary. Except for sacrificial animals, all others could be slaughtered and eaten close to home.

12:23 *the blood is the life.* See Genesis 9:4–6; Leviticus 17:10–14. The blood symbolized life. By refraining from eating blood, the Israelite demonstrated respect for life and, ultimately, for the Creator of life. Blood, representing life, was the ransom price for sins. So blood was sacred and not

to be consumed by the people. This relates to atonement in Leviticus 16; Hebrews 9:12–14; 1 Peter 1:18, 19; 1 John 1:7.

12:29, 30 Cf. 2 Corinthians 6:14–7:1 where Paul gives a similar exhortation.

12:31 *they burn even their sons and daughters.* One of the detestable practices of Canaanite worship was the burning of their sons and daughters in the fire as sacrifices to Molech (cf. Lev. 18:21; 20:2–5; 1 Kin. 11:7; 2 Kin. 23:10; Jer. 32:35).

12:32 *you shall not add . . . nor take away. See note on 4:2.*

13:1–18 After the general prohibition of involvement in Canaanite worship (12:29–31), Moses discussed three ways in which the temptation to idolatry was likely to come to Israel: (1) through a false prophet (vv. 1–5); (2) through a family member (vv. 6–11); or (3) through apostates in some Canaanite city (vv. 12–18).

13:2 *the sign or the wonder comes to pass.* Miraculous signs alone were never meant to be a test of truth (cf. Pharaoh's magicians in Ex. 7–10). A prophet's or a dreamer's prediction may come true, but if his message contradicted God's commands, the people were to trust God and His Word rather than such experience. *Let us go after other gods.* The explicit temptation was to renounce allegiance to the Lord and go after other gods. The result of this apostasy would be the serving of these false gods by worshiping them, which would be in direct violation of the first commandment (5:7).

13:3 *the LORD your God is testing you.* God, in His sovereignty, allowed the false prophets to entice the people toward apostasy to test the true disposition of the Israelites' hearts. And while the temptation was dangerous, the overcoming of that temptation would strengthen the people in their love for God and obedience to His commandments. Cf. 6:5.

The Death Penalty

Crime	Scripture Reference
1. Premeditated Murder	Genesis 9:6; Exodus 21:12-14, 22, 23
2. Kidnapping	Exodus 21:16; Deuteronomy 24:7
3. Striking or Cursing Parents	Exodus 21:15; Leviticus 20:9; Proverbs 20:20; Matthew 15:4; Mark 7:10
4. Magic and Divination	Exodus 22:18
5. Beastiality	Exodus 22:19; Leviticus 20:15, 16
6. Sacrificing to False Gods	Exodus 22:20
7. Profaning the Sabbath	Exodus 35:2; Numbers 15:32-36
8. Offering Human Sacrifice	Leviticus 20:2
9. Adultery	Leviticus 20:10-21; Deuteronomy 22:22
10. Incest	Leviticus 20:11, 12, 14
11. Homosexuality	Leviticus 20:13
12. Blasphemy	Leviticus 24:11-14, 16, 23
13. False Prophecy	Deuteronomy 13:1-10
14. Incorrigible Rebelliousness	Deuteronomy 17:12; 21:18-21
15. Fornication	Deuteronomy 22:20, 21
16. Rape of Betrothed Virgin	Deuteronomy 22:23-27

The MacArthur Study Bible, by John MacArthur (Nashville: Word Publishing, 1997) 270. © 1993 by Thomas Nelson, Inc.

13:5 *put away the evil from your midst.* The object of the severe penalty was not only the punishment of the evildoer, but also the preservation of the community. Paul must have had this text in mind when he gave a similar command to the Corinthian church (cf. 1 Cor. 5:13; also Deut. 17:7; 19:19; 21:21; 22:21; 24:7).

13:6 *your brother . . . friend.* The temptation to idolatry might also come from a member of the immediate family or from an intimate friend. While the temptation from the false prophet would be made openly, based on a sign or wonder, this temptation would be made secretly and would be based upon the intimacy of relationship.

13:10 *until he dies.* The convicting witness would cast the first stone. Love for family and friends was not to take precedence over devotion to God (cf. Luke 14:26).

13:12 *one of your cities.* In mind here is an entire city of Canaan given by God to the Israelites, yet enticed to idolatry.

13:13 *Corrupt men.* Lit. "sons of Belial (worthless)." *Belial* is used of Satan in 2 Corinthians 6:15. It is a way to describe evil, worthless, or wicked men (Judg. 19:22; 1 Sam. 2:12; 1 Kin. 21:10, 13).

14:1 *you shall not cut . . . nor shave.* The two practices, lacerating the body and shaving the head, were associated with mourning customs of foreign religions. Though the actions could in themselves appear to be innocent, they were associated with practices and beliefs reprehensible to the Lord. Cf. Leviticus 19:27, 28; 21:5 1 Kings 18:28; 1 Corinthians 3:17.

14:2 *you are a holy people to the LORD your God.* Again comes the important reminder of their peculiar relation to God. Over 250 times, Moses emphasized to Israel, "the Lord your God."

14:3–21 This summary of clean and unclean animals is drawn from the list in Leviticus 11:2–23. The ground for the allowances and prohibitions of the eating of certain animals was that Israel was to be holy to the Lord (vv. 2, 21). These special dietary laws were to separate them from social mixing with idolatrous people, to prevent them from being lured into idolatry.

14:21 *anything that dies of itself.* Eating the meat of an animal that had died a natural death was prohibited because the animal had not been killed in the proper fashion and the blood drained out (*see note on 12:23*). The animal, however, could be eaten by "the alien who is within your gates." *See notes on Leviticus 17:10–16.* *a young goat in its mother's milk.* This prohibition, no doubt, reflected a common practice in Canaanite religion which was superstitiously observed in the hope that fertility and productivity would be increased (cf. Ex. 23:19; 34:26).

14:22 *tithe.* The tithe (lit. "a tenth") specified in these verses was only that of the agricultural produce which the land would provide. This was a second tithe to be used for the celebration of worship convocations at the sanctuary (vv. 23–26), in addition to the first tithe mentioned, known as the Levitical tithe which went to support the priests and Levites who served the people. Cf. Leviticus 27:30–33 and Numbers 18:21–32. A third welfare tithe was also offered every three years (*see notes on 14:28; 26:12*).

14:23 *eat before the LORD.* The tithe was to be taken to the central sanctuary where the worshipers were to eat a portion in fellowship with the Lord.

14:24 *if the journey is too long.* If certain Israelites lived too far from the sanctuary for it to be practical for them to carry their agricultural tithe there, then they could exchange the tithe locally for silver and subsequently convert the money back into substance at the sanctuary.

14:26 *for wine or similar drink. See notes on Proverbs 20:1; 23:29–35; 31:4–7.*

14:28 *At the end of every third year.* In year three and year six of the seven-year sabbatical cycle, rather than taking this tithe to the central sanctuary, it was instead stored up within the individual cities in the land. This tithe was used to feed the Levites, the orphan, the widow, and the stranger (i.e., foreigner) who lived among the Israelites. Cf. 26:12; Numbers 18:26–32.

15:1 *At the end of every seven years . . . grant a release of debts.* The sabbatical year was established and described in Exodus 23:10, 11; Leviticus 25:1–7. However, while these texts stated that in the seventh year the land was to lie fallow without any crops being planted, only here did Moses prescribe a cancellation of debts. On the basis of verses 9–11, the debt was canceled completely and permanently, not just a cancellation of payment during that year.

15:3 *Of a foreigner you may require it.* The provision for sabbatical release of debts was not intended for a person who stayed only temporarily in the land. That foreigner was still responsible to pay his debts.

15:4 *except when there may be no poor.* Idealistically, there was the possibility that poverty would be eradicated in the land "for the Lord will greatly bless you in the land." The fullness of that blessing, however, would be contingent on the completeness of Israel's obedience. Thus, verses 4–6 were an encouragement to strive for a reduction of poverty while, at the same time, they empasized the abundance of the provision God would make in the Promised Land.

15:8 *willingly lend him sufficient for his need.* The attitude of the Israelites toward the poor in their community was to be one of warmth and generosity. The poor were given whatever was necessary to meet their needs, even with the realization that such "loans" would never have to be paid back. *See note on 23:19, 20.*

15:11 *For the poor will never cease from the land.* Realistically (in contrast to v. 4), the disobedience toward the Lord on Israel's part meant that there would always be poor people in the land of Israel. Jesus repeated this truism in Matthew 26:11.

15:12 *If your brother . . . is sold.* In the context of verses 1–11, the reason for the sale would be default, an alternative repayment of a debt; and a period of servitude would substitute for that repayment. The Hebrew slave would serve his master for six years following the sale, with freedom being declared in the seventh year.

15:13 *you shall not let him go away empty-handed.* When a slave had completed his time of service, his former owner was to make ample provision for him so that he would not begin his state of new freedom in destitution.

15:15 *remember.* The Israelites, formerly enslaved in Egypt, were to treat their own slaves as God had treated them.

15:17 *an awl . . . through his ear.* In certain circumstances, a slave might prefer to remain with the family after the required six years of servitude. He would then be marked with a hole in his ear and become a servant forever (cf. Ex. 21:5, 6).

15:18 *worth a double hired servant.* The slave was worth double to his owner because the owner not only had the service of the slave, but he also did not have to pay out anything for that service as he would for a hired hand.

15:19 *All the firstborn . . . sanctify.* The firstborn was the first to be produced during the bearing life of an animal. It was to be consecrated to the Lord. The firstborn would be sacrificed annually and the offerers would participate in the sacrificial meal (see 14:23). *nor shear.* The firstborn ox or bull was not to be worked, nor was the firstborn sheep or

Israel's Calendar

Month	Of Year			
Pre-/Post-Exilic	Sacred/Civil	Modern Equivalent		Characteristics
Abib/Nisan	1/7	March/April		Latter Rains; Barley Harvest
Ziv/Iyyar	2/8	April/May		Dry Season Begins
Sivan	3/9	May/June		Wheat Harvest; Early Figs
Tammuz	4/10	June/July		Hot Season; Grape Harvest
Ab	5/11	July/August		Olive Harvest
Elul	8/12	August/September		Dates; Summer Figs
Ethanim/Tishri	7/1	September/October		Former Rains; Plowing Time
Bul/Heshvan	8/2	October/November		Rains; Wheat, Barley Sown
Chislev	9/3	November/December		Winter Begins
Tebeth	10/4	December/January		Rains
Shebat	11/5	January/February		Almond Trees Blossom
Adar	12/6	February/March		Latter Rains Begin; Citrus Harvest

The MacArthur Study Bible, by John MacArthur (Nashville: Word Publishing, 1997) 273. © 1993 by Thomas Nelson, Inc.

goat to be shorn in the time before their sacrifice to the Lord.

15:21 *a defect.* An imperfect, firstborn animal was not acceptable as a sacrifice. It was to be treated like any other nonsacrificial animal (see 12:15, 16) and eaten at home (cf. Mal. 1:6–14).

16:1–17 Moses discusses the feasts during which all the men over twenty years of age were to appear before the Lord at the central worship site. If possible, their families were to go as well (see vv. 11, 14). Cf. Exodus 23; Leviticus 23; Numbers 28; 29.

16:1 *the month of Abib.* Abib (which was later called Nisan) occurred in the spring (approximately March/April).

16:1–8 *keep the Passover.* The offering of Passover itself was to be only a lamb (Ex. 12:3–11). However, additional offerings were also to be made during the Passover and the subsequent seven days of the Feast of Unleavened Bread (cf. Ex. 12:15–20; 13:3–10; Lev. 23:6–8; Num. 28:19–25). Therefore, sacrifices from both the flock and the herd were used in keeping the Passover..

16:3 *remember.* This was the key word at Passover time, as it is for the Lord's Supper today (cf. Matt. 26:26–30; Luke 22:14–19; 1 Cor. 11:23–26).

16:5, 6 *at the place . . . God chooses.* The Passover sacrifices could no longer be killed by every family in their house (see Ex. 12:46). From this point on, the Passover sacrifices must be killed at the central place of worship.

16:7 *in the morning . . . go to your tents.* After the sacrifice of the Passover animal, the eating, and the night vigil which followed, the people would return in the morning to their lodgings or tents where they were staying for the duration of the feast.

16:10–12 *the Feast of Weeks.* Seven weeks later this second feast was celebrated. It was also known as the Feast of Harvest (Ex. 23:16), or the day of firstfruits (Lev. 23:9–22;

Num. 28:26–31), and later came to be known as Pentecost (Acts 2:1). With the grain harvest completed, this one-day festival was a time of rejoicing. The outpouring of the Holy Spirit, fifty days after the death of Christ at the Passover, was on Pentecost and gives special meaning to that day for Christians (cf. Joel 2:28–32; Acts 2:14–18).

16:13–15 *the Feast of Tabernacles.* This was also known as the Feast of Ingathering and the Feast of Booths (cf. Ex. 23:16; 34:22; Lev. 23:33–43; Num. 29:12–39).

2. Instructions for leadership (16:18–18:22)

16:18–18:22 This section deals with the responsibilities of the officials who were to maintain pure worship within the land and to administer justice impartially.

16:18 *appoint judges and officers.* Moses had appointed leaders at Sinai to help him in the administration of the people (1:13). Here, he specified that such important leadership should continue in each city. *Judges* were those who adjudicated cases with the application of the law. *Officials* were subordinate leaders of various kinds.

16:19 *a bribe blinds the eyes.* Accepting a bribe was wrong since it perverted the ability of judges to act in fairness to the parties in litigation.

16:21, 22 *wooden image . . . sacred pillar.* A reference to the wooden poles, images, or trees that represented the Canaanite goddess Asherah. A stone pillar symbolic of male fertility was also prevalent in the Canaanite religion. These were forbidden by the first two commandments (5:7–10; Ex. 20:3–6).

17:1 *any . . . defect.* To bring a defective sacrifice to the Lord was to bring something into the sanctuary that was forbidden. Such a sacrifice was an abomination to the Lord. To offer less than the best to God was to despise His name (see Mal. 1:6–8). Offering a less than perfect sacrifice was, in effect, failing to acknowledge God as the ultimate provider of all that was best in life.

17:3–7 *served other gods.* The local judges were to see that false worshipers were executed, so that idolatry was dealt with severely.

17:6, 7 *two or three witnesses.* The execution of the idolater could not take place on the basis of hearsay. There had to be at least two valid witnesses against the accused person in order for a case to be established. One witness was not sufficient in a case of this severity; this standard avoided false testimony. The way in which the execution was carried out emphasized the burden of responsibility for truthful testimony that rested on the witnesses in a case involving capital punishment. The witnesses, by casting the first stone, accepted responsibility for their testimony (cf. 19:15; 1 Cor. 5:13).

17:8–13 *a matter . . . too hard for you to judge.* If a judge thought a case was too difficult for him to decide, he could take it to a central tribunal, consisting of priests and an officiating chief judge, to be established at the future site of the central sanctuary. The decision of that tribunal would be final, and anyone refusing to abide by that court's decision was subject to the death penalty.

17:14 *a king.* The office of king was anticipated by Moses in the Pentateuch (see Gen. 17:16; 35:11; 49:9–12; Num. 24:7, 17). He anticipated the time when the people would ask for a king and, here, gave explicit instruction about the qualifications of that future king.

17:15 *from among your brethren.* How the Lord would make that choice was not explained, but the field was narrowed by the qualification that he must be a fellow Israelite.

17:16, 17 *multiply . . . multiply . . . multiply.* Restrictions were placed on the king: (1) he must not acquire many horses; (2) he must not take multiple wives; and (3) he

Do's and Don'ts for Israel's Future King
1. He must be a Jew (Deut. 17:15)
2. He shall write for himself a copy of the Law (Deut. 17:18)
3. He shall read his copy of the Law all the days of his life (Deut. 17:19)
4. He shall fear the Lord (Deut. 17:19)
5. He shall observe all the words of the Law (Deut. 17:19)
6. Neither he nor the people shall multiply horses (Deut. 17:16)
7. He shall not return to Egypt (Deut. 17:16)
8. He shall not multiply wives for himself (Deut. 17:17)
9. He shall not greatly increase silver and gold for himself (Deut. 17:17)
10. He shall not lift his heart up above his people (Deut. 17:20)
11. He shall not turn aside from God's commandments (Deut. 17:20)

must not accumulate much silver and gold. The king was not to rely on military strength, political alliances, or wealth for his position and authority, but he was to look to the Lord. Solomon violated all of those prohibitions, while his father, David, violated the last two. Solomon's wives brought idolatry into Jerusalem, and this resulted in the kingdom being divided (1 Kin. 11:1–43).

17:18 *write . . . a copy of this law.* The ideal set forth was that of the king who was obedient to the will of God, which he learned from reading the law. The result of his reading of the Pentateuch would be fear of the Lord and humility. The king was pictured as a scribe and scholar of Scripture. Josiah reinstituted this approach at a bleak time in Israel's history (cf. 2 Kin. 22).

17:20 *his heart may not be lifted above his brethren.* The king was not to be above God's law, any more than any other Israelite.

18:1 *all the tribe of Levi.* Unlike the other twelve tribes, none of the tribe of Levi, including the priests, was given an allotment of land to settle and cultivate. The Levites lived in the cities assigned to them throughout the land (Num. 35:1–8; Josh. 21), while the priests lived near the central sanctuary, where they went to officiate in their appropriate course (cf. 1 Chr. 6:57–60). Levites assisted the priests (Num. 3; 4; 8).

18:3–5 *the priest's due.* In place of a land inheritance and in recognition of their priestly duties, the priests had a right to specific portions of the animals offered for sacrifices.

18:6–8 *a Levite.* If a Levite wanted to go to the central sanctuary to minister there in the Lord's name, he was permitted to do so and to receive equal support along with other Levites.

18:9–12 *the abominations of those nations.* Moses gave a strict injunction not to copy, imitate, or do what the polytheistic Canaanites did. Nine detestable practices of the Canaanites were delineated in verses 10, 11, namely: (1) sacrificing children in the fire (see 12:31); (2) witchcraft, seeking to determine the will of the gods by examining and interpreting omens; (3) soothsaying, attempting to control the future through power given by evil spirits; (4) interpreting omens, telling the future based on signs; (5) sorcery, inducing magical effects by drugs or some other potion; (6) conjuring spells, binding other people by magical muttering; (7) being a medium, one who supposedly communicates with the dead, but actually communicates with demons; (8) being a spiritist, one who has an intimate acquaintance with the demonic, spiritual world; and (9) calling up the dead, investigating and seeking information from the dead. These evil practices were the reason the Lord was going to drive the Canaanites out of the land.

18:15–19 *a Prophet like me.* The singular pronoun emphasizes the ultimate Prophet who was to come. Both the OT (34:10) and the NT (Acts 3:22, 23; 7:37) interpret this passage as a reference to the coming Messiah who, like Moses, would receive and preach divine revelation and lead His people (cf. John 1:21, 25, 43–45; 6:14; 7:40). In fact, Jesus was like Moses in several ways: (1) He was spared death as a baby (Ex. 2; Matt. 2:13–23); (2) He renounced a royal court (Phil. 2:5–8; Heb. 11:24–27); (3) He had compassion on His people (Num. 27:17; Matt. 9:36); (4) He made intercession for the people (Deut. 9:18; Heb. 7:25); (5) He spoke with God face to face (Ex. 34:29, 30; 2 Cor. 3:7); and (6) He was the mediator of a covenant (Deut. 29:1; Heb. 8:6, 7).

18:20–22 *who speaks in the name of other gods.* In contrast to the true prophet, Moses predicted there would be false prophets who would come to Israel, speaking not in the name of the Lord, but in the name of false gods. How could the people tell if a prophet was authentically speaking for God? Moses said, "if the thing does not happen," it was not from God. The characteristic of false prophets is the failure of their predictions to come true. Sometimes false prophets speak and it happens as they said, but they are representing false gods and trying to turn people from the true God. They must be rejected and executed (13:1–5). Other times, false prophets are more subtle and identify with the true God, but speak lies. If ever a prophecy of such a prophet fails, he is shown to be false. Cf. Jeremiah 28:15–17; 29:30–32.

3. Instructions for societal order (19:1–23:14)

19:1–23:14 The statutes explained by Moses in this part of Deuteronomy deal broadly with social and community order.

The Law of Witnesses	
OT	NT
Num. 35:30	Matt. 18:16
Deut. 17:6	John 8:17
Deut. 19:15	1 Tim. 5:19
	Heb. 10:28

These laws focus on interpersonal relationships.

19:1–13 See Numbers 35:9–34 for the purpose of the cities of refuge.

19:2 *three cities.* Three cities of refuge were to be set aside in Canaan after the conquest of the land (see Josh. 20:7 for Israel's obedience to this command). These three cities west of the Jordan River were in addition to the three already established east of the Jordan (see 4:41–43 for the eastern cities of refuge).

19:9 *add three more cities.* If the Israelites had been faithful in following the Lord fully, then He would have enlarged their territory to the boundaries promised in the Abrahamic covenant (Gen. 15:18–21). In that case, three more cities of refuge, for a total of nine, would have been needed.

19:14 *your neighbor's landmark.* These *landmarks* referred to stones bearing inscriptions which identified the owner of the property. Moving a neighbor's boundary stone was equivalent to stealing his property (cf. Prov. 22:28; 23:10).

19:15 *by the mouth of two or three witnesses.* More than one witness was necessary to convict a person of a crime. This principle was to act as a safeguard against the false witness who might bring an untruthful charge against a fellow Israelite. By requiring more than one witness, greater accuracy and objectivity was gained (cf. Deut. 17:6; Matt. 18:15–17; 2 Cor. 13:1).

19:16–19 *a false witness.* In some cases, there would only be one witness who would bring a charge against someone. When such a case was taken to the central tribunal of priests and judges for trial and, upon investigation, the testimony of the witness was found to be false, the accuser received the punishment appropriate for the alleged crime.

19:20 *hear and fear.* When the fate of the false witness became known in Israel, it would serve as a deterrent against giving false testimony in Israel's courts.

19:21 *eye for eye.* This principle of legal justice (called *lex talionis,* "law of retaliation") was given to encourage appropriate punishment of a criminal in cases where there might be a tendency to be either too lenient or too strict (*see notes on Ex. 21:23, 24; Lev. 24:20*). Jesus confronted the Jews of His day for taking this law out of the courts and using it for purposes of personal vengeance (cf. Matt. 5:38–42).

20:1–20 The humanitarian principles applicable in war under Mosaic law are in stark contrast to the brutality and cruelty of other nations.

20:1 *do not be afraid.* When Israelites went into battle, they were never to fear an enemy's horses or chariots because the outcome of a battle would never be determined by mere military strength. The command not to be afraid was based on God's power and faithfulness, which had already been proved to Israel in their deliverance from Egypt.

20:2–4 *the priest shall . . . speak to the people.* The role of the priest in battle was to encourage the soldiers by God's promise, presence, and power to be strong in faith. A lack of trust in God's ability to fight for them would affect the strength of their will so that they would become fainthearted. Victory was linked to their faith in God.

20:5–8 *Let him go and return to his*

house. Four exemptions from service in Israel's volunteer army were cited to illustrate the principle that anyone whose heart was not in the fight should not be there. Those who had other matters on their minds or were afraid were allowed to leave the army and return to their homes, since they would be useless in battle and might even influence others to lose courage (v. 8).

20:10–15 offer of peace. Cities outside of Canaan were not under the judgment of total destruction, so Israel was to offer a peace treaty to them. If the city agreed to become a vassal to Israel, then the people would become tributary subjects. However, if the offer of peace was rejected, Israel was to besiege and take the city, killing the men and taking possession of the rest of the people and animals as spoils of war. Note here the principle that the proclamation of peace preceded judgment (cf. Matt. 10:11–15).

20:16–18 utterly destroy. The Canaanite cities were to be totally destroyed, i.e., nothing was to be spared, in order to destroy their influence toward idolatry (cf. 7:22–26).

20:19, 20 you shall not destroy its trees. When besieging a city, armies in the ancient world would cut down the trees to build ramps and weapons, as well as facilities for the long siege. However, Israel was not to use fruit trees in the siege of a city so they could later enjoy the fruit of the land God had given to them (7:12, 13).

21:1–9 it is not known who killed him. This law, which dealt with an unsolved homicide, was not given elsewhere in the Pentateuch. In the event that the guilty party was unknown, justice could not adequately be served. However, the people were still held responsible to deal with the crime. The elders of the city closest to the place where the body of a dead man was found were to accept responsibility for the crime. This precluded inter-city strife, in case relatives sought revenge. They would go to a valley (idol altars were always on high places, so this avoided association with idolatry) and there break the neck of a heifer, indicating that the crime deserved to be punished. But the handwashing of the elders (v. 6) would show that, although they accepted responsibility for what had happened, they were nevertheless free from the guilt attached to the crime.

21:5 This distinctly indicates that final judicial authority in the theocracy of Israel rested with the priests.

21:11–14 a beautiful woman. According to ancient war customs, a female captive became the servant of the victors. Moses was given instruction to deal in a kind way with such issues. In the event her conquerors were captivated by her beauty and contemplated marriage with her, one month was required to elapse, during which her troubled feelings might settle, her mind would be reconciled to the new conditions of conquest, and she could sorrow over the loss of her parents as she left home to marry a stranger. One month was the usual mourning period for Jews, and the features of this period, e.g., shaving the head, trimming the nails, and removing her lovely clothes (ladies on the eve of captivity dressed to be attractive to their captors), were typical signs of Jewish grief. This action was important to show kindness to the woman and to test the strength of the man's affection. After the thirty days, they could marry. If later he decided divorce was appropriate (based on the provisions of 24:1–4), he could not sell her as a slave. She was to be set completely free because "you have humbled her." This phrase clearly refers to sexual activity, in which the wife has fully submitted herself to her husband (cf. 22:23, 24, 28, 29). It should be noted that divorce appears to have been common among the people, perhaps learned from their time in

Egypt, and tolerated by Moses because of their "hard hearts" (*see notes on 24:1–4; Matt. 19:8*).

21:11, 12 *among the captives a beautiful woman.* Such a woman would be from a non-Canaanite city that Israel had captured (see 20:14) since all the Canaanites were to be killed (20:16). These discarded items were symbolic of the casting off of her former life and carried purification symbolism (cf. Lev. 14:18; Num. 8:7).

21:15–17 *has two wives.* In the original, the words literally say "has had two wives," referring to events that have already taken place, evidently intimating that one wife is dead and another has taken her place. Moses, then, is not legislating on a polygamous case where a man has two wives at the same time, but on that of a man who has married twice in succession. The man may prefer the second wife and be exhorted by her to give his inheritance to one of her sons. The issue involves the principle of the inheritance of the firstborn (the right of primogeniture). The firstborn son of the man, whether from the favorite wife or not, was to receive the double portion of the inheritance. The father did not have the authority to transfer this right to another son. This did not apply to sons of a concubine (Gen. 21:9–13) or in cases of misconduct (Gen. 49:3, 4).

21:18–21 *a stubborn and rebellious son.* Cf. 27:16. The long-term pattern of rebellion and sin of a child who was incorrigibly disobedient is in view. No hope remained for such a person who flagrantly violated the fifth commandment (Ex. 20:12), so he was to be stoned to death.

21:22, 23 *hang him on a tree.* After an execution, the body was permitted to hang on a tree for the rest of the day as a public display of the consequences of disobedience. However, the body was not to remain on the tree overnight, but was to be properly buried before sunset. Cf. Galatians 3:13, where Paul quotes this text in regard to the death of the Lord Jesus Christ.

22:1–26:19 While loving God was a person's first duty (cf. 6:5), loving one's neighbor came next (cf. Matt. 22:37–40). In this section, the law of loving one's neighbor is applied to domestic and social relationships.

22:1–4 *hide yourself.* The Israelite must not hide his eyes from such an obvious loss. It was his duty to pursue and bring back the lost property of his neighbor.

22:5 *anything that pertains to a man . . . woman's garment.* Found only here in the Pentateuch, this statute prohibited a man from wearing any item of feminine clothing or ornamentation, or a woman from wearing any item of masculine clothing or ornamentation. The same word translated "abomination" was used to describe God's view of homosexuality (Lev. 18:22; 20:13). This instance specifically outlawed transvestism. The creation-order distinctions between male and female were to be maintained without exception (cf. Gen. 1:27).

22:6 *a bird's nest.* Found only here in the Pentateuch, this law showed that God cared for the long-term provisions for His people. By letting the mother bird go, food could be acquired without killing the source of future food.

22:8 *a parapet.* Found only here in the Pentateuch, this refers to the roof of a home in ancient Israel, which was flat and usually reached by outside stairs. To prevent injury or death from falling, a fence was to be built around the roof. This, too, expressed love for those who might otherwise be injured or killed.

22:9 *different kinds of seed.* The aim of the legislation seems to be to maintain healthy crops by keeping the seeds separate from one another. *See note on Leviticus 19:19.*

22:10 *an ox and a donkey together.* According to the dietary laws prescribed earlier (14:1–8), the ox was a "clean" animal, but the donkey was "unclean." Even more compelling was the fact that these two different animals couldn't together plow a straight furrow. Their temperaments, natural instincts, and physical characteristics made it impossible. As with the seed (v. 9), God is protecting his people's food.

22:11 *garment . . . wool and linen.* See note on Leviticus 19:19.

22:12 *make tassels.* See Numbers 15:38–40 for the purpose of these tassels.

22:13–30 This section is on family life (cf. Lev. 18:1–30; 20:10–21).

22:13–21 An Israelite who doubted the virginity of his bride was to make a formal accusation to the elders of the city. If her parents gave proof of virginity showing the accusation was false, the husband was to pay a penalty and was prohibited from divorcing the woman. However, if she was found not to be a virgin, then she was to be put to death.

22:15 *the evidence of the young woman's virginity.* Probably a blood-stained garment or a bed sheet from the wedding night.

22:19 *shekels.* This word is not in the Hebrew text, but the context suggests it. A shekel weighed four-tenths of an ounce, so the total fine would be about two and one-half pounds of silver.

22:22–29 Adultery was punished by death for the two found in the act. If the adulterous persons were a man with a woman who was pledged to be married to someone else, this consensual act led to the death of both parties (vv. 23, 24). However, if the man forced (i.e., raped) the woman, then only the man's life was required (vv. 25–27). If the woman was a virgin not pledged in marriage, then the man had to pay a fine, marry the girl, and keep her as his wife as long as he lived (vv. 28, 29).

22:30 *A man shall not take his father's wife.* In no case was a man to marry his father's wife or have sexual relations with her. This probably has relations with a stepmother in view, though incest was certainly forbidden (cf. Lev. 18:6–8).

23:1–6 *the assembly of the LORD.* From the sanctification of the home and marriage in the previous chapter, Moses proceeds to the sanctification of their union as a congregation and speaks to the right of citizenship, including being gathered before the presence of the Lord to worship Him. Most likely, this law did not exclude a person from residence in the area where Israel was to live, but from public offices and honors, intermarriage, and participation in the religious rites at the tabernacle, plus later at the temple. The emasculated (v. 1), the illegitimate (v. 2), and the Ammonites and Moabites (vv. 3–6) were not allowed to worship the Lord. The general rule was that strangers and foreigners, for fear of friendship or marriage connections which would lead Israel into idolatry, were not admissible until their conversion to God and the Jewish faith. This purge, however, describes some limitations to the general rule. Eunuchs, illegitimate children, and people from Ammon and Moab were excluded. Eunuchs were forbidden because such willful mutilation (lit. in Hebrew, by crushing, which was the way such an act was generally performed) violated God's creation of man, was associated with idolatrous practices, and was done by pagan parents to their children so they might serve as eunuchs in the homes of the great (cf. 25:11, 12). The illegitimate were excluded so as to place an indelible stigma as a discouragement to shameful sexual misconduct. People from Ammon and Moab were excluded, not because they were born out of incest (cf. Gen 19:30ff.), but on account of their vicious hostility toward God and His people Israel. Many of the Israelites were settled east of the Jordan River in the immediate neighborhood of these people, so God raised this wall to prevent the evils of idolatrous influence. Individuals from all three of these outcast groups are offered grace and acceptance by Isaiah upon personal faith in the true God (cf. Is. 56:1–8). Ruth the Moabitess serves as a most notable example (cf. Ruth 1:4, 16). See Ruth: Interpretive Challenges.

23:2, 3 to the tenth generation. The use of the word *forever* in verses 3 and 6 seems to indicate that this phrase is an idiom denoting permanent exclusion from the worshiping community of Israel. In contrast, an Edomite or Egyptian might worship in Israel in the third generation (see vv. 7, 8). Though these nations had also been enemies, Edom was a near relative, coming from Jacob's family, while individual Egyptians had shown kindness to the Israelites at the Exodus (cf. Ex. 12:36).

23:9–14 Because the camp of Israelite soldiers was a place of God's presence (v. 14), the camp was to be kept clean. Instruction was given concerning nocturnal emission (vv. 10, 11) and defecation (vv. 12, 13). Such instruction for external cleanness illustrated what God wanted in the heart.

4. Instructions from miscellaneous laws (23:15–25:19)

23:15–25:19 Moses selected twenty-one sample laws to further illustrate the nature of the requirements of living under the Sinaitic covenant.

23:15, 16 A fugitive slave was not to be turned over to his master. Evidently, this has in mind a slave from the Canaanites or other neighboring nations who was driven out by oppression or with a desire to know Israel's God.

23:17, 18 Prostitution as a form of worship was forbidden. *Dog* is a reference to male prostitutes (cf. Rev. 22:15).

23:19, 20 This prohibition of lending money at interest to a fellow Israelite is qualified by Exodus 22:25; Leviticus 25:35, 36, which indicates that it restricts its application to the poor and prevents further impoverishment, but it was allowed for foreigners who were engaged in trade and commerce to enlarge their wealth. According to 15:1, 2, it is also clear that money could be legitimately lent in the normal course of business, subject to forgiveness of all unpaid debt in the sabbatical year (cf. 24:10).

23:21–23 Though vows were made voluntarily, they were to be promptly kept once made. Cf. Numbers 30:2.

23:24, 25 Farmers were to share their produce with the people in the land, but the people were not to profit from the farmers' generosity.

24:1–4 This passage does not command, commend, condone, or even suggest divorce. Rather, it recognizes that divorce occurs and permits it, but only on restricted grounds. The case presented here is designed to convey the fact that divorce produced defilement. Notice the following sequence: (1) if a man finds an uncleanness (some impurity or something vile, cf. 23:14) in his wife, other than adultery, which was punished by execution (cf. 22:22); (2) if he legally divorces her (although God hates divorce, as Mal. 2:16 says; He has designed marriage for life, as Genesis 2:24 declares; and He allowed divorce because of hard hearts, as Matt. 19:8 reveals); (3) if she then marries another man; and (4) if the new husband subsequently dies or divorces her; then, that woman could not return to her first husband (v. 4). This is so because she was "defiled" with such a defilement that is an abomination to the Lord and a sinful pollution of the Promised Land. What constitutes that defilement? Only one thing is possible—she was defiled in the remarriage because there was no ground for the divorce. So when she remarried, she became an adulteress (Matt. 5:31, 32) and is thus defiled so that her former husband can't take her back. Illegitimate divorce proliferates adultery. *See notes on Matthew 5:31, 32; 19:4–9.*

24:5 During the first year of marriage, a man was not held responsible for military service or any other duty. He was to devote that year of marriage to the enjoyment and establishment of his marriage.

24:6 Two millstones were needed to grind grain. Neither was to be taken in pledge because it was indispensable to a family's daily subsistence.

24:7 The death penalty would be exacted on kidnappers who kidnaped a brother Israelite for involuntary servitude or as merchandise to sell.

24:8, 9 Moses exhorted the people to follow the commands of the Lord regarding infectious skin diseases (*see notes on Lev. 13:1–14:57*).

24:10–13 *his pledge.* This would often be a cloak, an outer garment, which was given in pledge to guarantee the repayment of a loan. God's people were to act righteously in the lending of money. An example of a righteous lender was one who did not forcefully exact payment and who allowed a poor person to retain his pledge (cloak) overnight if it was necessary to keep him warm. Lending

God's Compassion for Aliens, Widows, and Orphans
Deut. 10:18
Deut. 14:29
Deut. 16:11, 14
Deut. 24:17, 19, 20, 21
Deut. 26:12, 13
Deut. 27:19

to the poor was permitted, but without: (1) interest (23:19, 20); (2) coercion to repay; and (3) extension of the loan beyond the sabbatical year (15:1, 2).

24:14, 15 Day laborers were to be paid on the day they labored because they lived day to day on such wages (cf. Lev. 19:13; Matt. 20:1–16).

24:16 Punishment for a crime was to be borne only by the offender. *See notes on Ezekiel 18.* The death of Saul's seven grandsons (2 Sam. 21:5–9) is a striking exception of national proportion grounded in God's sovereign wisdom, as was the death of David and Bathsheba's first son (2 Sam. 12:14).

24:17, 18 The administration of law should be carried out with equity for all members of society, including those with the least power and influence, e.g., widows, orphans, and immigrants.

24:19–22 The practice of allowing the needy to glean in the field was grounded in the remembrance of Israel's hard service in Egypt (v. 18).

25:1–3 Corporal punishment for crimes committed was to be equitably carried out in the presence of the judges and was limited to forty stripes.

25:4 A worker must be allowed to enjoy the fruit of his own labor (cf. 1 Cor. 9:9; 1 Tim. 5:18; 2 Tim. 2:6).

25:5–10 Levirate marriages (from Latin, *levir,* "husband's brother") provided that the brother of a dead man who died childless was to marry the widow in order to provide an heir. These were not compulsory marriages in Israel, but were applied as strong options to brothers who shared the same estate. Obviously, this required that the brother be unmarried and desired to keep the property in the family by passing it on to a son. Cf. Leviticus 18:16; 20:21, where adultery with a living brother's wife is forbidden. Though not compulsory, this practice reflected fraternal affection; and, if a single brother refused to conform to this practice, he was confronted with contempt and humiliation by the elders. The perpetuation of his name as a member of the covenant people witnessed to the dignity of the individual. Since Numbers 27:4–8 gave daughters the right of inheritance when there were no sons in a family, it is reasonable to read "no child" rather than "no son" in verse 5. Cf. Tamar, Genesis 38:8–10, and the Boaz-Ruth marriage, Ruth 4:1–17.

25:5 Cf. Matthew 22:24; Mark 12:19; Luke 20:28.

25:11, 12 The consequence of the immodest act was the only example of punishment by mutilation in the Pentateuch.

25:13–16 The weights and measures of trade were to be kept equitably so people were not cheated. Obedience meant prosperous years in the land.

25:17–19 The admonition to remember the treachery of the Amalekites was repeated to the new generation (*see notes on Ex.* 17:9–16). For execution of the command, see 1 Sam. 15:1–3.

5. The firstfruits and tithes in the land (26:1–15)

26:1–15 As the stipulation section of Deuteronomy came to an end (chs. 5–25), Moses commanded the people to keep two rituals when they had conquered the land and began to enjoy its produce. These two rituals were the initial firstfruits offering (26:1–11) and the first third-year special tithe (26:12–15). In both cases, there is an emphasis upon the prayer of confession to be given at the time of the rituals (26:5–10, 13–15). These special offerings were given in order to celebrate Israel's transition from a nomadic existence to a settled agrarian community, made possible by the Lord's blessing.

26:2 *the first of all the produce.* Baskets of the firstfruits from the first harvest reaped by Israel, once they were in the land of Canaan, were to be taken to the tabernacle (cf. Ex. 23:19; 34:26; Num. 18:12–17). This is to be distinguished from the annual Feast of Firstfruits (cf. Lev. 23:9–14) celebrated in conjunction with the Passover and the Feast of Unleavened Bread.

26:5 *you shall . . . say before the Lord your God.* The offering of the firstfruits was to be accompanied by an elaborate confession of the Lord's faithfulness in preserving Israel and bringing the people into the land. The essential aspects of the worshipers' coming to the sanctuary were the presentation of the firstfruits, bowing in worship, and rejoicing in the Lord's goodness. In this manner, the visit to the sanctuary was a confession and acknowledgment of God. It was a time of praise and rejoicing because of God's goodness and mercy extended to former generations and evidence of divine sustaining grace at that time. *a Syrian, about to perish.* The word *perish* is better translated as "wandering." "A wandering Syrian" referred to Jacob, who was each Israelite's father or ancestor. When Jacob fled from his home in Beersheba, he passed through Syria (Aram) to Mesopotamia (Aram-naharaim, Gen. 24:10) to live with Laban, his uncle. Re-

---

Key Word
Land: 1:8; 11:8; 19:1; 26:9; 32:52—The common Old Testament word *land* possesses several shades of meaning. In essence, all land belongs to God as its Creator (Ps. 24:1). When God promised the Israelites the land of Canaan, it was His to give. The land of Canaan was so representative of God's covenant with the Israelites (Gen.12:1) that it became one of their identifying characteristics—the "people of the land" (Gen.13:15; 15:7).

turning from there, Jacob was overtaken by Laban after he came through Syria at the Jabbok River, where he not only faced the wrath of Laban, but also that of Esau his brother. Later, the famine in Canaan necessitated his migration to Egypt. When the Israelites became populous and powerful, they were oppressed by the Egyptians, but it was God who responded to their prayers and miraculously delivered them out of Egypt. It was God who enabled them to enter and conquer the land from which the firstfruits were presented before the altar.

26:12 the tithe. I.e., the tithe collected every third year of Israel's existence in the land of Canaan (see 14:28). Apparently, this tithe was not taken to the central sanctuary, but distributed locally to Levites, immigrants, widows, and orphans. For the other regular annual tithes, *see note on 14:22.*

26:13, 14 you shall say before the LORD your God. The confession to be made in connection with the offering of this first tithe consisted of a statement of obedience (vv. 13, 14) and a prayer for God's blessing (v. 15). In this manner, the Israelites confessed their continual dependence on God and lived in obedient expectance of God's continued gracious blessing.

26:15 Look down from . . . heaven. This was the first reference to God's dwelling place being in heaven. From His abode in heaven, God had given the Israelites the land flowing with milk and honey as He had promised to the patriarchs. His continued blessing on both the people and the land was requested.

6. The affirmation of obedience (26:16–19)

26:16–19 The last four verses of the chapter concluded Moses' explanation of the law's stipulations by calling for the total commitment by Israel to the Lord and His commands. These verses can be viewed as the formal ratification of the Sinaitic covenant between the Lord and the second generation of Israel. In accepting the terms of this agreement, acknowledging that the Lord is their God, and promising wholehearted obedience plus a desire to listen to God's voice, the Israelites were assured that they were His people and the chosen over all other nations to receive His blessings and the calling to witness to His glory to all the world. See Exodus 19:5, 6.

26:16 This day. I.e., the first day of the eleventh month of the fortieth year (1:3). Note also, "today" in verses 17, 18.

D. The Blessings and Curses of the Covenant (27:1–28:68)

27:1–28:68 In these two chapters, Moses explained the curses and the blessings associated with the Sinaitic covenant. He first called Israel to perform an elaborate ceremony to ratify the covenant when they entered the land (27:1–26; carried out by Joshua in Josh. 8:30–35). This was to remind the people that it was essential to obey the covenant and its laws. Then, Moses further explained the blessings for obedience and the curses for disobedience (28:1–68).

27:2, 4 whitewash them with lime. Upon arrival in the land of promise, under Joshua, large stone pillars were to be erected. Following the method used in Egypt, they were to be prepared for writing by whitewashing with plaster. When the law was written on the stones, the white background would make it clearly visible and easily read. These inscribed stones were to offer constant testimony to all people and coming generations of their relationship to God and His law (cf. 31:26; Josh. 24:26, 27).

27:3, 8 all the words of this law. This is probably a reference to the entire Book of Deuteronomy.

27:4 Mount Ebal. A mountain in the

center of the Promised Land, just to the north of the city of Shechem. It was at Shechem that the Lord first appeared to Abraham in the land and where Abraham built his first altar to the Lord (Gen. 12:6, 7). This mountain, where the stone pillars with the law and the altar (v. 5) were built, was the place where the curses were to be read (v. 13).

27:5–7 build an altar. In addition to setting up the stones, the Israelites were to build an altar of uncut stones. At this altar, the offerings were to be brought to the Lord, and together the people would rejoice in God's presence. This is what was done when the covenantal relationship was established at Mt. Sinai (Ex. 24:1–8). The burnt offerings, completely consumed, represented complete devotion to God; the peace offerings expressed thanks to Him.

27:12, 13 These . . . these. The Twelve Tribes were divided into two groups of six each. The tribe of Levi was to participate in the first group. The tribes of Manasseh and Ephraim were together as the tribe of Joseph.

27:12 Mount Gerizim. This was the mountain south of Mount Ebal, with the city of Shechem in the valley between, from which the blessings were to be read. Perhaps the actual arrangement provided that the priests stood by the ark of the covenant, in the valley between the two mountains, with six tribes located northward toward Mount Ebal and six southward toward Mount Gerizim. The priests and Levites read the curses and blessings with the people responding with the "men" of affirmation. **to bless.** The blessings that were to be recited from Mount Gerizim were not recorded in this passage, no doubt omitted here to emphasize that Israel did not prove themselves obedient to the covenant and, therefore, did not enjoy the blessings.

27:15–26 Twelve offenses serve as examples of the kind of iniquities that made one

subject to the curse. These offenses might have been chosen because they are representative of sins that might escape detection and, so, remain secret (vv. 15, 24).

27:15 one who makes a carved . . . image. The first curse concerned idolatry, the breaking of the first and second Commandments (5:7–10). **Amen!** To each curse all the people responded, "amen." The Hebrew word means "so be it." The people, thereby, indicated their understanding and agreement with the statement made.

27:16 treats his father or his mother with contempt. The dishonoring of parents was the breaking of the fifth Commandment (5:16).

27:17 landmark. *See note on 19:14.*

27:18 makes the blind to wander. This refers to abusing a blind man.

27:19 perverts the justice. This refers to taking advantage of those members of society who could be easily abused.

27:20 lies with his father's wife. Incest. *See note on 22:30.*

27:21 lies with any kind of animal. This

Key Word

Cursed: 7:26; 13:17; 27:15, 20, 23; 28:16, 19—lit. means "to bind with a curse." A curse is the opposite of a blessing. It wishes or prays illness or injury on a person or an object. God cursed the serpent and the ground after the sin of Adam and Eve (Gen. 3:14, 17). Jeremiah, in despair, cursed the man who brought news of his birth (Jer. 20:14–15). The seriousness of God's covenant with His people is illustrated by the threat of a curse on any who violate it (28:60–61). In the New Testament, Paul taught that Jesus Christ became a "curse" for us, so that we might be freed from the curses of the Law (Gal. 3:13), quoting 21:23.

refers to the sin of bestiality. See 20:15, 16; Exodus 22:19; Leviticus 18:23.

27:22 *lies with his sister.* The committing of incest with either a full sister or a half sister.

27:23 *lies with his mother-in-law.* See Leviticus 18:17; 20:14.

27:24 *attacks his neighbor secretly.* A secret attempt to murder a neighbor.

27:25 *takes a bribe.* This relates to a paid assassin.

27:26 *does not confirm all the words of this law.* The final curse covered all the rest of God's commandments enunciated by Moses on the plains of Moab (cf. Gal. 3:10). Total obedience is demanded by the law and required by God. Only the Lord Jesus Christ accomplished this (2 Cor. 5:21). *Amen!* All the people agreed to be obedient (cf. Ex. 24:1–8), a promise they would soon violate.

28:1–68 In his responsibility as leader and mediator, Moses had previously told the people the promise of God's blessing and the warning that they should not turn to other gods when the covenant was given at Sinai (Ex. 23:20–33). After their rebellion against that covenant, Moses warned them (Lev. 26) of the divine judgment that would come if they disobeyed. Here, Moses gives an exhortation based upon the blessings and the

---

The Blessings of Deuteronomy 28

These are the major themes associated with the blessings of Deuteronomy 28:1–14.

1. Agriculture (vv. 8, 11a, 11c, 12a)
2. Family (v. 11b)
3. Financial (v. 12b)
4. Military (vv. 7, 10, 13)
5. Spiritual (v. 9)

These blessings were obtained by obeying all of God's commandments (vv. 1, 2, 9, 13, 14), walking in His way (v. 9), and not going after other gods to serve them (v. 14).

---

curses of the covenant (see Lev. 26:1–45). The blessings and the curses in this chapter follow the same structure. First, Moses clearly explained that the quality of Israel's future experience would come on the basis of obedience or disobedience to God (28:1, 2, 15). Second, the actual blessings and curses were succinctly stated (28:3–6, 16–19). Third, Moses gave a sermonic elaboration of the basic blessings and curses (28:7–14, 20–68). Just as the curses were given more prominence in the ceremony of 27:11–26, so the curses incurred by disobedience to the covenant were much more fully developed here. The perspective of Moses was that Israel would not prove faithful to the covenant (31:16–18, 27) and, so, would not enjoy the blessings of the covenant; therefore, the curses received much more attention.

28:1–14 See Joshua 21:45; 23:14, 15; 1 Kings 8:56 for blessing fulfillment.

28:1, 2 *diligently obey the voice of the Lord your God.* *Diligently obey* emphasized the need for complete obedience on the part of Israel. The people could not legally or personally merit God's goodness and blessing, but their constant desire to obey, worship, and maintain a right relation with Him was evidence of their true faith in and love for Him (cf. 6:5). It was also evidence of God's gracious work in their hearts.

28:1 *high above all nations.* If Israel obeyed the Lord, ultimate blessing would be given in the form of preeminence above all the nations of the world (see 26:19). The indispensable condition for obtaining this blessing was salvation, resulting in obedience to the Lord, in the form of keeping His commandments. This blessing will ultimately come to pass in the millennial kingdom, particularly designed to exalt Israel's King, the Messiah, and His nation (see Zech. 13:1–14:21; Rom. 11:25–27).

28:3–6 *Blessed.* These beatitudes summarize the various spheres where the blessing of God would extend to Israel's life. God's favor is also intended to permeate all their endeavors as emphasized further in the expanded summary in 28:7–14, on the condition of obedience (vv. 1, 2, 9, 13, 14). They will know victory, prosperity, purity, respect, abundance, and dominance, i.e., comprehensive blessing.

28:6 *come in . . . go out.* An idiomatic way of referring to the normal everyday activities of life (see 31:2). This is a fitting conclusion to the "blessings and curses" (v. 19), since it sums up everything.

28:10 *called by the name of the LORD.* Israel's obedience and blessing would cause all the people of the earth to fear Israel because they were clearly the people of God. This was God's intention for them all along, to be a witness to the nations of the one true and living God and draw the Gentiles out of idol worship. They will be that witness nation in the last days (see Rev. 7:4–10; 14:1) and in the kingdom (see Zech. 8:1–12).

28:13 *the head and not the tail.* Israel was to be the leader over the other nations ("the head") and not to be in subjection to another nation ("the tail").

28:15–68 The curses are outlined as God warned His people of the price of the absence of love for Him and disobedience.

28:15 Cf. Joshua 23:15, 16.

28:16–19 These are parallels to the blessings in verses 3–6.

28:20 *until you are destroyed.* Moses was aware that the Israelites were apt to be unfaithful to God, so he portrays, in extended warnings, the disastrous results of the loss of their land and their place of worship if they disobeyed God. Destruction was the ultimate calamity for Israel's sin (vv. 20, 21, 24, 45, 48, 51, 61, 63).

28:21 Cf. Jeremiah 14:12; 21:6; Ezekiel 5:12; 6:11.

28:22 Cf. Amos 4:9.

28:23 *bronze . . . iron.* The heavens would be as bright as bronze, but no rain would fall from them to water the ground. The earth would be as hard as iron, so any falling rain would run off and not penetrate (cf. Amos 4:7).

28:25 Cf. 2 Chronicles 29:8; Nehemiah 1:8; Jeremiah 15:4.

28:26 Cf. Jeremiah 7:33; 16:4; 19:7; 34:20.

28:27 *the boils of Egypt.* The disease with which God afflicted the Egyptians prior to the Exodus (see Ex. 9:9; Amos 4:10).

28:30 These three curses were in contrast to the exemptions from military service granted in 20:5–7. The exemptions were possible because God would grant His people victory in battle. Disobedience to the Lord, however, would mean that God would no longer fight for His people. Those normally exempted from military service would be forced to fight and be killed. Consequently, the soldier's betrothed wife would be violated and his house and grapes taken by the foreign invader (cf. Jer. 8:10; Amos 5:11; Zeph. 1:13).

28:32 Cf. 2 Chronicles 29:9.

28:35 *sole of your foot . . . head.* Diseases of the skin would afflict the people cursed by God. The disease mentioned here is like that from which Job suffered (see Job 2:7).

28:36 *the king whom you set over you.* Though they had no king at the time of entering the land, Moses anticipated that Israel would have a king over them when this curse came—a future king of Israel who would be taken with them into exile. *to a nation which neither you nor your fathers have known.* The Israelites would be taken captive to a nation other than Egypt, where they had recently been in bondage. This future nation would be particularly steeped in idolatry (cf. 2 Kin. 17:41; Jer. 16:13).

28:37 Cf. 1 Kings 9:8; 2 Chronicles 29:8; Jeremiah 19:8; 25:9, 18; 29:18.

28:38–40 Cf. Isaiah 5:10; Joel 1:4; Micah 6:15.

28:46 Cf. 2 Chronicles 29:8; Jeremiah 18:6; Ezekiel 14:8.

28:49 *a nation . . . from the end of the earth.* God would raise up a nation to act as His own instrument of judgment against His ungrateful people. This foreign nation was described as coming from a far distance, a nation that would arise quickly and one that would completely devastate the land. This was fulfilled first by Assyria (Is. 5:26; 7:18–20; 28:11; 37:18; Hos. 8:1) and then by Babylon (Jer. 5:15; Lam. 4:19; Ezek. 17:3; Hab. 1:6–8).

28:50 Cf. 2 Chronicles 36:17.

28:52–57 Ultimately, an invading nation would besiege all the cities of Judah (*see note on 28:49*). In verses 53–57, Moses gave a revolting description of the Israelites' response to those siege conditions. The unthinkable activity of cannibalism is introduced in verse 53 and, then, illustrated in the verses that follow (see 2 Kin. 6:28, 29; Lam. 2:20; 4:10).

28:52 Cf. 2 Chronicles 32:10; Jeremiah 10:17, 18; Ezekiel 5:2; Hosea 11:6.

28:53 Cf. Jeremiah 19:9.

28:58–63 *this glorious and awesome name, THE LORD YOUR GOD.* Israel's obedience to the law (i.e., the Sinaitic covenant) would lead to fearing the Lord, whose "name" represents His presence and character. The title "LORD (Yahweh)" revealed the glory and greatness of God (see Ex. 3:15). Significantly, the phrase "the LORD your God" is used approximately 280 times in the book of Deuteronomy. The full measure of the divine curse would come on Israel when its disobedience had been hardened into disregard for the glorious and awesome character of God. In verses 15 and 45, Moses described curses for disobedience; hence, the worst of the curses come when disobedience is hardened into failure to fear God. Only

God's grace would save a small remnant (v. 62), thus keeping Israel from being annihilated (cf. Mal. 2:2).

In contrast to the promise made to Abraham in Genesis 15:5, the physical seed of Abraham under God's curse would be reduced as God had multiplied the seed of the patriarchs in Egypt (see Ex. 1:7), He would decimate their numbers to make them as nothing until His restoration of the nation in a future day (see 30:5).

28:59–61 Cf. Amos 4:10.

28:61 *this Book of the Law.* A definite, particular written document was meant (see 31:9), referring not just to Deuteronomy (cf. 31:9), but to the Pentateuch, as far as it had been written. This is evident from verses 60 and 61, which indicate that the diseases of Egypt were written in the book of the law, thus referring to Exodus, which records those plagues.

28:63 Cf. Jeremiah 12:14; 45:4.

28:64 *the LORD will scatter you.* The Jews remaining, after the curses occur, would be dispersed by the Lord ultimately to serve false gods, restlessly and fearfully throughout all the nations of the earth (cf. Neh. 1:8, 9; Jer. 30:11; Ezek. 11:16). This dispersion began with the captivity of the northern kingdom, Israel (722 B.C.), then the southern kingdom, Judah (605–586 B.C.), and is still a reality today. In the future earthly kingdom of Messiah, Israel will experience its regathering in faith, salvation, and righteousness. See. Isaiah 59:19–21; Jeremiah 31:31–34; Ezekiel 36:8–37:14; Zechariah 12:10–14:21. The unbearable nature of Israel's present condition was emphasized since the people longed for another time (v. 67). Cf. Jeremiah 44:7; Hosea 8:13; 9:3; 11:4, 5.

28:68 *but no one will buy you.* Israel would be so abandoned by God that she would not even be able to sell herself into slavery. The curse of God would bring Israel

The Curses of Deuteronomy 28

These are the major themes associated with the curses of Deuteronomy 28:20–68.

1. Agricultural calamity (vv. 17, 18, 30b, 31, 33a, 38–40, 42, 51)
2. Bewilderment and oppression (vv. 28, 29, 33b)
3. Drought (v. 23, 24)
4. Egyptian slavery (v. 68)
5. Exile (vv. 32, 36a, 41, 48b, 63b, 64)
6. Family tragedy
   Husband (v. 56)
   Wife (vv. 30a, 54)
   Children (vv. 32, 41, 53, 55–57)
7. Helplessness (vv. 26b, 27b, 29b, 31d, 32c, 33b)
8. Horror and sign to others (vv. 37, 46)
9. Idolatry in exile (vv. 36b, 64)
10. Military defeat (vv. 25, 26, 29, 32a, 33b, 34, 49, 50)
11. No rest from fear (vv. 65–67)
12. Perish, few in number (vv. 20, 21b, 45, 62, 63a)
13. Pestilence and disease
    Egyptian (vv. 27, 59–61)
    General (vv. 21, 22, 35)
14. Poverty (vv. 43, 44, 48d)
15. Terrible siege (vv. 52–57)

The reasons for God's curses included abandonment of God (v. 20), acts of disobedience (vv. 15, 20, 45, 58), and an attitude of ungratefulness (v. 47).

into a seemingly hopeless condition (cf. Hos. 8:13; 9:3). The specific mention of Egypt could be symbolic for any lands where the Jews have been taken into bondage or sold as slaves. But it is true that after the destruction of Jerusalem in A.D. 70, which was a judgment on the apostasy of Israel and their rejection and execution of the Messiah, this prophecy was actually fulfilled. The Roman general Titus, who conquered Jerusalem and Israel, sent 17,000 adult Jews to Egypt to perform hard labor there and had those who were under seventeen years old publicly sold. Under the Roman emperor Hadrian, countless Jews were sold and suffered such bondage and cruelty.

IV. THE THIRD ADDRESS BY MOSES: ANOTHER COVENANT (29:1–30:20)

29:1–30:20 These chapters contain the third address of Moses, which is a contrast between the covenant at Sinai and the covenant he envisioned for Israel in the future. Though the past had seen Israel's failure to keep the covenant and to trust in God, there was hope for the future. It was this hope that Moses emphasized in the content of these chapters focusing clearly on the themes of the new covenant.

29:1 *These are the words.* The Hebrew text numbers this verse as 28:69 rather than 29:1, seeing it as the conclusion to the second address of Moses. However, as in 1:1, these words introduce what follows, serving as the introduction to Moses' third address. *the covenant . . . in the land of Moab.* The majority of interpreters view the covenant stated here as a reference to the covenant made at Sinai. According to this view, the covenant that God made with Israel at Sinai (Horeb) was renewed in Moab. However, this verse clearly states that the covenant of which Moses now speaks was "besides," or "in addition to," the previous covenant. This was another covenant distinct from the one made at Sinai.

This other covenant is viewed by some interpreters as the Palestinian covenant, which gave Israel the title to the land (see 30:5). However, the emphasis of these two chapters is not on the land, but on the change of Israel's heart (see the contrast between 29:4 and 30:6). It was exactly this change of heart which the later prophets would term "the new covenant" (see Jer. 31:31–34; Ezek. 36:26, 27). In response to Israel's certain failure under the provisions of the Sinaitic covenant (29:23–28), Moses anticipated the new covenant under which Israel would be obedient to the Lord and finally reap His blessings (30:1–10).

29:4 the LORD has not given you . . . eyes to see. In spite of all they had experienced (vv. 2, 3), Israel was spiritually blind to the significance of what the Lord had done for them, lacking spiritual understanding, even as Moses was speaking. This spiritual blindness of Israel continues to the present day (Rom. 11:8), and it will not be reversed until Israel's future day of salvation (see Rom. 11:25–27). The Lord had not given them an understanding heart because the people had not penitently sought it (cf. 2 Chr. 7:14).

29:9 keep the words of this covenant. The spiritual experience of God's faithfulness to Israel should have led to obedience to the stipulations of the Sinaitic covenant in the future, but could not without a transformed

---

Key Word

Swore: 6:13; 7:8; 10:20; 13:17; 19:8; 29:13; 31:7—the verb translated "swore" is related to the word used for the number seven. In effect, the verb means "to bind oneself fully"; that is, "seven times." In ancient times oaths were considered sacred. People were promising to be faithful to their word no matter what the personal cost. The Old Testament describes God as taking an oath (Gen. 24:7; Ex. 13:5). He was not forced to do this; He did not have to swear in order to ensure His own compliance with His word. Instead, He made an oath so that His people would be assured that His promises were completely trustworthy.

---

heart (vv. 4, 18) and the true knowledge of God (v. 6).

29:10, 11 All of you stand today before the Lord your God. All the people were likely stationed in an orderly way before Moses, not as a call to outward order, but inward devotion, to make the covenant a matter of the heart and life.

29:12 enter into covenant . . . and . . . oath. Enter into expresses submission in faith and repentance before God, resulting in heart obedience. The people were to bind themselves in an oath to obey the stipulations of God's covenant (cf. Gen 26:28).

29:14, 15 not with you alone. All of Israel, present and future, were to be bound by the stipulations of the covenant to obey God and be blessed. Thus, they would be able to lead all nations to the blessedness of salvation (cf. John 17:20, 21; Acts 2:39).

29:18 a root bearing bitterness or wormwood. The picture was of a root spreading poison and bitterness into the whole tree. The metaphor indicates permeation of idolatry throughout Israel because of the action of an individual family or tribe, precipitating God's curse and wrath.

29:19 as though the drunkard . . . included with the sober. This could be translated "to destroy the watered land along with the dry land." With either translation, the meaning is that the deceived rebel against the Lord follows only his wicked heart and could not hide within the total community. The idolater would stand out and bear the judgment for his idolatry.

29:20 blot out his name from under heaven. The idolater would have no place among God's people, because God would curse him and then kill him (cf. 25:19: Ex. 17:14). This very strong language reveals how God feels about idolatry, which is forbidden in the Decalogue (Ex. 20:2–7).

29:21 this Book of the Law. See note on 31:9.

29:22 the coming generation . . . and the foreigner. In a future day, both Israel and the nations would see the results of God's judgment on the land of Israel because of Israel's disobedience, as a witness to the holy standard God has established in His law. Cf. Leviticus 26:31, 32.

29:23 Sodom. The punishment the Lord would bring on Israel in the future was likened to that of Sodom and her allies whom the Lord buried in fiery brimstone in the time of Abraham and Lot (see Gen. 19:24–29). It should be noted that Sodom and vicinity resembled paradise, the garden of God, before its destruction (cf. Gen. 13:10).

29:24 This question is answered in verses 25–28.

29:29 The secret things . . . those things which are revealed. That which is revealed included the law with its promises and threats; consequently, that which is hidden can only refer to the specific way in which God will carry out His will in the future, which is revealed in His Word and completed in His great work of salvation, in spite of the apostasy of His people.

30:1–10 The rejection of God by Israel, and of Israel by God and the subsequent dispersion were not the end of the story of God's people. Having anticipated a time when Israel's disobedience would lead to her captivity in a foreign land, Moses looked beyond the destruction of that time of judgment to an even more distant time of restoration and redemption for Israel (cf. Lev. 26:40–45). This future restoration and blessing of Israel would take place under the New Covenant (*see notes on Jer. 31:31–34; 32:36–41; Ezek. 36:25–27*). For a comparison of the New Covenant with the Old Covenant, *see notes on 2 Corinthians 3:6–18*.

30:1–3 you call them to mind. Moses moved to the future when curses would be over and blessings would come. At some future time, after disobedience to the Lord brought on Israel the curses of the covenant, the people will remember that the circumstances in which they found themselves were the consequence of their disobedience and, in repentance, they will return to the Lord. This repentance will lead to a wholehearted commitment of obedience to God's commandments (v. 8) and the consequent end of Israel's distress (v. 3). This is the ultimate salvation of Israel by faith in Christ, spoken of by Isaiah (54:4–8), Jeremiah (31:31–34; 32:37–42), Ezekiel (36:23–38), Hosea (14:1–9), Joel (3:16–21), Amos (9:11–15), Zephaniah (3:14–20), Zechariah (12:10–13:9), Malachi (3:16–4:4), and Paul (Rom. 11:25–27).

30:4, 5 The gathering of Jews out of all the countries of the earth will follow Israel's final redemption. Restoration to the land will be in fulfillment of the promise of the covenant given to Abraham (see Gen. 12:7; 13:15; 15:18–21; 17:8) and so often reiterated by Moses and the prophets.

30:6 the Lord . . . will circumcise your heart. Cf. 10:16. This work of God in the innermost being of the individual is the true salvation that grants a new will to obey Him in place of the former spiritual insensitivity and stubbornness (cf. Jer. 9:25; Rom. 2:28, 29). This new heart will allow the Israelite to love the Lord wholeheartedly, and is the essential feature of the new covenant (see 29:4, 18; 30:10, 17; Jer. 31:31–34; 32:37–42; Ezek. 11:19; 36:26). *See note on Jeremiah 4:4.*

30:7 on your enemies. The curses that had fallen on Israel because of disobedience will, in the future, come upon the nations that have enslaved the Jews. The judgment of God would come upon those who cursed the physical seed of Abraham in fulfillment of Genesis 12:3.

30:8, 9 you will again obey the voice of

the LORD. With a new heart under the New Covenant, Israel would obey all the commandments of the Lord. This would result in the Lord's blessing, which would bring greater prosperity than Israel had ever previously experienced.

30:10 Here is a renewed enforcement of the indispensable fruit of salvation and another echo of the constant theme of this book.

30:11–14 After remembering the failures of the past and the prospects for the future, Moses earnestly admonished the people to make the right choice. The issue facing them was to enjoy salvation and blessing by loving God so wholeheartedly that they would willingly live in obedience to His Word. The choice was simple, yet profound. It was stated in simple terms so they could understand and grasp what God expected of them (v. 11). Although God had spoken from heaven, He had spoken through Moses in words every person could understand (v. 12). They did not have to search at some point beyond the sea (v. 13). The truth was now there, through Moses, in their hearts and minds (v. 14). All the truth necessary for

---

Key Word

Statutes: 4:1, 14; 5:1; 6:1; 7:11; 10:13; 16:12; 28:15; 30:16—conveys a variety of meanings in the Old Testament, including a verb that means "to decree" or "to inscribe" (Prov. 8:15; Is. 10:1; 49:16). It often refers to commands, civil enactments, legal prescriptions, and ritual laws decreed by someone in authority—whether by humans (Mic. 6:16) or by God Himself (6:1). The Law of Moses includes commandments (*miswah*), judgments (*mispat*), and statues (*choq*) (4:1–2). Israel was charged to obey God's statutes and they had pledged to do so (26:16–17).

---

choosing to love and obey God and thus avoid disobedience and cursing, they had heard and known (v. 15). Paul quotes verses 12–14 in Romans 10:6–8.

30:15 Moses pinpoints the choice—to love and obey God is life, to reject God is death. If they chose to love God and obey His Word, they would enjoy all God's blessings (v. 16). If they refused to love and obey Him, they would be severely punished (vv. 17, 18). Paul, in speaking about salvation in the NT, makes use of this appeal made by Moses (Rom. 10:1–13). Like Moses, Paul is saying that the message of salvation is plain and understandable.

30:19 *choose life.* Moses forces the decision, exhorting Israel on the plains of Moab before God (heaven) and man (earth) to choose by believing in and loving God, the life available through the new covenant (see v. 6). Sadly, Israel failed to respond to this call to the right choice (see 31:16–18, 27–29). Choosing life or death was also emphasized by Jesus. The one who believed in Him had the promise of eternal life; while the one who refused to believe faced eternal death (cf. John 3:1–36). Every person faces this same choice.

V. THE CONCLUDING EVENTS (31:1–34:12)

31:1–34:12 Two themes dominate the last four chapters of Deuteronomy: (1) the death of Moses (31:1, 2, 14, 16, 26–29; 32:48–52; 33:1; 34:1–8, 10–12) and (2) the succession of Joshua (31:1–8, 14, 23; 32:44; 34:9). These final chapters are centered around two more speeches by Moses: (1) the Song of Moses (32:1–43) and (2) the Blessings of Moses (33:1–29).

A. The Change of Leadership (31:1–8)

31:1 *Moses went and spoke.* Though some interpreters view this verse as the conclusion to the foregoing address in chapters

29 and 30, it is better to see these words as an introduction to the words of Moses which follow, based upon the general pattern of Deuteronomy. Verses 2–6 are addressed to every Israelite.

31:2 one hundred and twenty years old. This was the age of Moses at his death. According to Acts 7:30, Moses spent forty years in Midian tending sheep. Thus, the life of Moses is broken down into three forty-year periods. His first forty years were spent in Egypt (Ex. 2:1–15). The second forty years were spent in Midian (Ex. 2:15–4:19). His final forty years were spent leading Israel out of Egypt and through the wilderness to the Promised Land. The life and ministry of Moses were completed, but God's work would go on (v. 3a). **go out and come in.** Here is an idiom for engaging in a normal day's work and activity. Though still strong for his age (cf. 34:7), Moses admitted that he no longer could provide the daily leadership necessary for Israel. Furthermore, God would not allow him to enter the land beyond the Jordan River because of his sin at the waters of Meribah (see 32:51).

31:3 God Himself . . . Joshua himself crosses over. Though Joshua was to be the new human leader over Israel (see 31:3–7, 23), it was the Lord Himself who was the real leader and power. He would cross over ahead of them to enable them to destroy the nations.

31:4 Sihon and Og. Israel was assured that the nations of the land would be destroyed by the Lord in the same way that He had recently defeated the Amorite kings, Sihon and Og, on the east side of the Jordan River (see 2:26–3:11). That was a preview of what was to come (v. 5).

31:6–8 Be strong and of good courage. The strength and courage of the warriors of Israel would come from their confidence that their God was with them and would not forsake them. In verses 7 and 8, Moses repeated the substance of his exhortation, this time addressing it specifically to Joshua in the presence of the people to encourage him and to remind the people that Joshua's leadership was being assumed with the full approval of God. This principle for faith and confidence is repeated in 31:23; Joshua 1:5–7; 2 Samuel 10:12; 2 Kings 2:2; 1 Chronicles 22:11–13; 2 Chronicles 32:1–8; Psalm 27:14. The writer of Hebrews quotes verses 6, 8 in 13:5.

B. The Future Reading of the Law (31:9–13)

31:9 Moses wrote this law. At the least, Moses, perhaps with the aid of some scribes or elders who assisted him in leading Israel, wrote down the law that he had explained in the first thirty-two chapters of Deuteronomy (cf. v. 24). However, since the law explained in Deuteronomy had also been given in portions of Exodus through Numbers, it seems best to view this written law as all that is presently found in Scripture from Genesis 1 through Deuteronomy 32:47. After Moses' death, Deuteronomy 32:48–34:12 was added to complete the canonical Torah, perhaps by one of the elders who had served with Moses, even Joshua.

31:11 you shall read this law before all Israel. The law that Moses wrote down was given to the priests who were required to be its custodians and protectors and to read it in the hearing of all Israel at the Feast of Tabernacles during each sabbatical year. This reading of the law every seven years was to remind the people to live in submission to their awe-inspiring God.

C. The Song of Moses (31:14–32:47)

1. The anticipation of Israel's failure (31:14–29)

31:14 *the tabernacle of meeting.* The Lord told Moses to summon Joshua to the tent where He met Israel, and the presence of the Lord appeared in the pillar of cloud standing at the door of the Holy Place (v. 15). This signaled God's confirmation of Joshua, the former military captain (see Ex. 17:9–14) and spy (see Num. 13:16), as Israel's new leader. God's message to Joshua is summed up in verses 16–22.

31:16–21 *they will forsake Me and break My covenant.* After Moses' death, the Lord Himself predicts that in spite of what He has commanded (30:11, 20), the Israelites would forsake Him by turning to worship other gods and, thereby, break the Sinaitic covenant. Having forsaken God, the people would then be forsaken by God with the inevitable result that disaster would fall on them at every turn. This is one of the saddest texts in the OT. After all God had done, He knew they would forsake Him.

31:19, 22 *write down this song.* The song that the Lord gave Moses to teach the Israelites would be a constant reminder of their disobedience to the Lord and the results of that disobedience. The song was written that same day and is recorded in 32:1–43.

31:23 *I will be with you.* Joshua was to assume his lonely role of leadership over Israel with an assurance of the companionship and strength of the Lord. God's presence with him was sufficient to enable him to meet boldly every obstacle that the future could bring (see Josh. 1:5; 3:7).

31:24 *in a book.* The words that Moses had spoken were written down in a book that was placed beside the ark of the covenant (v. 26). Only the Ten Commandments were placed in the ark itself (Ex. 25:16; 31:18). The "Book of the Law" (v. 26) was one of the titles for the Pentateuch in the

rest of Scripture (Josh. 1:8; 8:34).

31:27 *your rebellion and your stiff neck.* See 9:6, 13; 10:16. Moses was well acquainted with Israel's obstinate ways, even in the most gracious of divine provision.

31:29 *you will become utterly corrupt.* Dominated by the practice of idolatry (see 4:16, 25; 9:12), the people would become wicked. ***evil will befall you in the latter days.*** *The latter days* (lit. "at the end of the days") referred to the far distant future. This was the time when the king would come from Judah (Gen. 49:8–12) to defeat Israel's enemies (Num. 24:17–19). Here, it is revealed that it would also be a time when disaster would fall on Israel because of evil done, thus bringing the Lord's wrath. The description of God's judgment on Israel and the nations in this song cannot be limited to the immediate future of the people as they entered the land, but extends to issues which are eschatological in time and global in extent, as the song indicates (32:1–43).

2. The witness of Moses' song (31:30–32:43)

31:30–32:43 This prophetic, poetic song has as its central theme Israel's apostasy, which brings God's certain judgment. The song begins with a short introduction emphasizing the steadfast God and the fickle nation (vv. 1–6). The song describes God's election of Israel (vv. 8, 9) and His care for them from the time of the wilderness wanderings (vv. 10–12) to their possession and initial enjoyment of the blessings in the land (vv. 13, 14). However, Israel's neglect of God's goodness and her apostasy (vv. 15–18) would bring God's future outpouring of wrath on His people (vv. 19–27) and Israel's continuing blindness in the face of God's wrath (vv. 28–33). Ultimately, God's vengeance would strip Israel of all power

Old Testament Songs

Moses	Sung by Moses and the sons of Israel to God as a tribute for rescuing them from the pursing Egyptians at the parting of the Red Sea	Ex. 15:1–18
Israelites	Sung by the people as they dug life-saving wells in the wilderness	Num. 21:14–18
Moses	A song of praise to God by Moses just before his death	Deut. 32:1–44
Deborah and Barak	A victory song after Israel's defeat of the Canaanites	Judg. 5:1–31
Israelite Women	A song to celebrate David's defeat of Goliath	1 Sam. 18:6, 7
Levite Singers	A song of praise at the dedication of the temple in Jerusalem	2 Chr. 5:12–14
Levite Singers	A song of praise, presented as a marching song as the army of Israel prepared for battle	2 Chr. 20:20–23
Levite Singers	A song at the temple restoration ceremony during Hezekiah's reign	2 Chr. 29:25–30

Nelson's Complete Book of Bible Maps & Charts (Nashville: Thomas Nelson Publishers, 1996) 63 © 1993 by Thomas Nelson, Inc.

and turn the nation from idolatry (vv. 34–38). Then God would bring His judgment upon the nations, both His enemies and Israel's (vv. 39–42). The song ends with a call to the nations to rejoice with Israel because God would punish His enemies and spiritually heal both Israel and her land (v. 43). Ezekiel 16 should be studied as a comparison to this chapter. It recites similar matters in graphic and picturesque language.

32:1 *Give ear, O heavens . . . And hear, O earth.* All of creation was called to be an audience to hear the message to Israel, as in 30:19, because the truth Moses was about to proclaim concerned the whole universe. It did so because it involved (1) the honor of God the Creator so disregarded by sinners,

(2) the justification of God so righteous in all His ways, and (3) the manifestation in heaven and earth of God's judgment and salvation (v. 43).

32:2 *my teaching.* Moses imparted instruction that if received would, like rain, dew, raindrops, and showers to the earth, bring benefit to the hearts and the minds of the hearers.

32:3 *Ascribe greatness to our God.* Cf. 3:24; 5:24; 9:26; 11:2; Psalm 150:2. This command refers to the greatness of God revealed in His acts of omnipotence.

32:4 *the Rock.* This word, representing the stability and permanence of God, was placed at the beginning of the verse for emphasis and was followed by a series of phrases which elaborated the attributes of

God as the rock of Israel. It is one of the principal themes in this song (see vv. 15, 18, 30, 31), emphasizing the unchanging nature of God in contrast to the fickle nature of the people.

32:5 *A perverse and crooked generation.* Israel, in contrast to God, was warped and twisted. Jesus used this phrase in Matthew 17:17 of an unbelieving generation and Paul in Philippians 2:15 of the dark world of mankind in rebellion against God.

32:6 *your Father.* The foolishness and stupidity of Israel would be seen in the fact that they would rebel against God who as a Father had brought them forth and formed them into a nation. As Father, He was the progenitor and originator of the nation and the One who had matured and sustained it. This idea of God as Father of the nation is emphasized in the OT (cf. 1 Chr. 29:10; Is. 63:16; 64:8; Mal. 2:10), while the idea of God as Father of individual believers is developed in the NT (cf. Rom. 8:15; Gal. 4:6).

32:7 *Remember the days of old.* A call to reflect on past history and to inquire about the lessons to be learned.

32:8, 9 *the Most High.* This title for God emphasized His sovereignty and authority over all the nations (see Gen. 11:9; 10:32; 14:18; Num. 24:16) with the amazing revelation that, in the plan for the world, God had as His goal the salvation of His chosen people. God ordained a plan where the number of nations (seventy according to Gen. 10) corresponded to the number of the children of Israel (seventy according to Gen. 46:27). Further, as God gave the nations their lands, He established their boundaries, leaving Israel enough land to sustain their expected population.

32:10–14 This description of what God did for Israel is figurative. Israel is like a man in the harsh desert in danger of death, with-out food or water, who is rescued by the Lord.

32:10 *as the apple of His eye.* Lit. "the little man of His eye," i.e., the pupil. Just as the pupil of the eye is essential for vision and, therefore, closely protected, especially in a howling wind, so God closely protected Israel. Cf. Psalm 17:8; Proverbs 7:2.

32:11 *Hovers over its young.* The Lord exercised His loving care for Israel like an eagle caring for its young, especially as they were taught to fly. As the eaglets began to fly and had little strength, they would start to fall. At that point, an eagle would stop their fall by spreading its wings so they could land on them. In the same way, the Lord has carried Israel and not let the nation fall. He had been training Israel to fly on His wings of love and omnipotence.

32:12 *no foreign god.* Moses makes clear that God alone carried Israel through all its struggles and victories, thus depriving the people of any excuse for apostasy from the Lord by interest in false gods.

32:13 *honey from the rock.* This reference to honeycombs, located in the fissures of the faces of a cliff, is used because Canaan had many wild bees. *oil from the flinty rock.* This is likely a reference to olive trees growing in rocky places, otherwise bereft of fruit-growing trees. These metaphoric phrases regarding honey and oil point to the most valuable products coming out of the most unproductive places.

32:14 *rams of . . . Bashan.* See note on 3:1.

32:15 *Jeshurun.* The word means "righteous" (lit. "the upright one"), i.e., a name for Israel which sarcastically expresses the fact that Israel did not live up to God's law after entering the land. God uses this name to remind Israel of His calling and to severely rebuke apostasy. *grew fat and kicked.* Like an ox which had become fat and intractable, Israel became affluent because of the bountiful provisions of God, but instead of being thankful and obedient, she became rebellious against the Lord (cf. 6:10–15).

32:16 foreign gods. Israel turned to worship the gods of the people in the land. These were gods they had not before acknowledged (v. 17).

32:17 demons. Cf. Leviticus 17:7; 2 Chronicles 11:15; Psalm 106:37. The term describes those angels who fell with Satan and constitute the evil force that fights against God and His holy angels. Idol worship is a form of demon worship as demon spirits impersonate the idol and work their wicked strategies through the system of false religion tied to the false god.

32:18–33 For this foolish apostasy, the Lord will severely judge Israel. This visitation of anger is in the form of a divine resolution to punish Israelites whenever they pursue idols, including the next generation of sons and daughters (v. 19). In verses 20–22, Moses quotes the Lord Himself.

32:21 not a nation. As the Lord was provoked to jealousy by Israel's worship of that which was "not God," so He would provoke Israel to jealousy and anger by humiliation before a foolish, vile "no-nation." In Romans 10:19, Paul applied the term "not a nation" to the Gentile nations, generally-speaking. Jews who worship a "no-god" will be judged by a "no-people."

32:22 a fire is kindled . . . to the lowest hell. Cf. 29:20. Once the fire of God's anger was kindled, it knew no limits in its destructive force, reaching even to those in the grave, an indication of God's eternal judgment against those who oppose Him.

32:23 disasters . . . arrows. The disasters (lit. "evil") are described in verse 24. The arrows represent the enemies who would defeat Israel in war and are further described in verses 25–27.

32:27 Our hand is high. This speaks of military arrogance. The only thing that would prevent the Lord from permitting the complete destruction of His people would be His concern that the Gentiles might claim for themselves the honor of victory over Israel.

32:31 rock . . . Rock. A contrast between the gods of the nations ("rock") and Israel's true God ("Rock"). Israel could smite its foes with little difficulty because of the weakness of their gods, who are not like the Rock Jehovah.

32:32 the vine of Sodom. Employing the metaphor of a vineyard, i.e., its grapes and its wine, the wickedness of Israel's enemies was described as having its roots in Sodom and Gomorrah, the evil cities destroyed by God as recorded in Genesis 19:1–29.

32:34 Sealed up among My treasures. The wicked acts of Israel's enemies were known to God and are stored up in His storehouse. At the proper time, God will avenge. Paul uses this image in Romans 2:4, 5.

32:35 Vengeance is Mine, and recompense. The manner and timing of the repayment of man's wickedness is God's prerogative. This principle is reaffirmed in the NT in Romans 12:19; Hebrews 10:30.

32:36 This is the promise that the Lord will judge Israel as a nation, but that the nation is composed of righteous and wicked. God actually helps the righteous by destroying the wicked. "His servants" are the righteous, all who in the time of judgment are faithful to the Lord (cf. Mal. 3:16–4:3). The Lord has judged Israel, not to destroy the nation, but to punish the sinners and show the folly of their false gods (vv. 37, 38). At the same time, the Lord has always shown compassion for those who have loved and obeyed Him.

32:39 I, even I, am He. After showing the

worthlessness of false gods (vv. 37, 38), this declaration of the nature of God was presented in contrast to show that the God of Israel is the living God, the only One who can offer help and protection to Israel. He has the power of life and death with regard to Israel (cf. 1 Sam. 2:6; 2 Kin. 5:7) and the power to wound and heal them (cf. Is. 30:26; 57:17, 18; Jer. 17:14; Hos. 6:1).

32:40–42 I raise My hand. God takes an oath to bring vengeance on His enemies. Here (as in Ex. 6:8; Num. 14:28), the hand is used anthropomorphically of God, who can swear by no greater than His eternal Self (cf. Is. 45:23; Jer. 22:5; Heb. 6:17).

32:43 Rejoice, O Gentiles, with His people. As a result of the execution of God's vengeance, all nations will be called on to praise, with Israel, the Lord who will have provided redemptively for them in Christ and also provided a new beginning in the land. This atonement for the land is the satisfaction of God's wrath by the sacrifice of His enemies in judgment. The atonement for the people is by the sacrifice of Jesus Christ on the Cross (cf. Ps. 79:9). Paul quotes this passage in Romans 15:10, as does the writer of Hebrews (1:6).

3. The communicating of Moses' song (32:44–47)

32:47 it is your life. Moses reiterated to Israel that obedience to the Lord's commands was to be the key to her living long in the land that God had prepared, so he called for this song to be a kind of national anthem which the leaders should see was frequently repeated to animate the people to obey God.

D. The Final Events of Moses' Life (32:48–34:12)

32:48–34:12 The anticipation of and record of Moses' death (32:48–52; 34:1–12) bracket the recording of Moses' blessing given to Israel before his death. This literary unit was composed and added to the text after the death of Moses.

1. The directives for Moses' death (32:48–52)

32:49 Mount Nebo. A peak in the Abarim range of mountains to the east of the north end of the Dead Sea, from where Moses would be able to see across to the Promised Land, which he was not permitted to enter.

32:50 gathered to your people. An idiom for death. See Genesis 25:8, 17; 35:29; 49:33; Numbers 20:24, 26; 31:2.

2. The blessing of Moses (33:1–29)

33:1–29 The final words of Moses to the people were a listing of the blessings of each of the tribes of Israel, Simeon excluded (vv. 6–25). These blessings were introduced and concluded with passages which praise God (vv. 2–5, 26–29). That these blessings of Moses are presented in this chapter as recorded by someone other than Moses is clear because in verse 1, Moses was viewed as already being dead, and as the words of Moses were presented, the clause "he said" (vv. 2, 7, 8, 12, 13, 18, 20, 22, 23, 24) was used.

33:1 the man of God. This is the first use of this phrase in Scripture. Subsequently, some seventy times in the OT, messengers of God (especially prophets) are called "a man of God" (1 Sam. 2:27; 9:6; 1 Kin. 13:1; 17:18; 2 Kin. 4:7). The NT uses this title for Timothy (1 Tim. 6:11; 2 Tim. 3:17). Moses was viewed among such prophets in this conclusion to the book (see 34:10).

33:2 Sinai . . . Seir . . . Paran. These are mountains associated with the giving of the law—Sinai on the south, Seir on the northeast, and Paran on the north. These mountains provide a beautiful metaphor, borrowed from the dawn. God, like the morning sun, is the light that rises to give His beams to all the Promised Land. *saints.* Lit. "holy ones." Probably a reference to the angels who assisted God when the law was mediated to Moses at Mt. Sinai (see Acts 7:53; Gal. 3:19; Heb. 2:2).

33:3 *He loves the people.* Notwithstanding the awe-inspiring symbols of majesty displayed at Sinai, the law was given in kindness and love to provide both temporal and eternal blessing to those with a heart to obey it. Cf. Romans 13:8–10.

33:5 *King in Jeshurun. See note on 32:15.* Since Moses is nowhere else in Scripture referred to as king, most interpret this as a reference to the Lord as King over Israel. However, Moses is the closest antecedent of the pronoun *he* in this clause, and the most natural understanding is that Moses is being referred to as a king. Moses certainly exercised kingly authority over Israel and could be viewed as a prototype of the coming King. Thus, united in the figure of Moses, the coming prophet like unto Moses (18:15) would be the prophet-king.

33:6 *Reuben.* Here is the prayer that this tribe would survive in large numbers (cf. Num. 1:21; 2:11).

33:7 *Judah.* Moses prayed that this tribe would be powerful in leading the nation to be victorious in battle through the help of the Lord.

33:8–11 *Levi.* Moses prayed for the Levites to fulfill their tasks, God granting to them protection from their enemies. Moses omitted Simeon, but that tribe did receive a number of allies in the southern territory of Judah (Josh. 19:2–9) and did not lose their identity (cf. 1 Chr. 4:34–38).

33:12 *Benjamin.* That this tribe would

have security and peace because the Lord would shield them was Moses' request. They were given the land in northern Judah near Jerusalem.

33:13–17 *Joseph.* This included both Ephraim and Manasseh (v. 17), who would enjoy material prosperity (vv. 13–16) and military might (v. 17), which would compensate and reward them for the Egyptian slavery of their ancestor (see Gen. 49:26). Ephraim would have greater military success in the future than Manasseh as the outworking of Jacob's blessing of the younger over the older (see Gen. 48:20).

33:18 *Zebulun . . . Issachar.* Moses prayed that these two tribes from the fifth and sixth sons of Leah would receive God's blessing in their daily lives, particularly through the trade on the seas.

33:20 *Gad.* This tribe had large territory east of the Jordan River and was a leader in gaining the victory in battles in Canaan.

33:22 *Dan.* Dan had the potential for great energy and strength and would later leap from its southern settlement to establish a colony in the north. Cf. Genesis 49:17, 18, where Dan is compared to a serpent.

33:23 *Naphtali.* This tribe would enjoy the favor of God in the fullness of His blessing, having land in the west of Galilee and south of the northern Danites.

33:24 *Asher.* The request is that this tribe would experience abundant fertility and prosperity, depicted by reference to a foot-operated oil press. Shoes of hard metal suited both country people and soldiers.

33:26, 27 *the God of Jeshurun.* Moses concluded his blessings with a reminder of the uniqueness of Israel's God. For *Jeshurun, see note on 32:15.*

33:28, 29 This pledge was only partially fulfilled after the people entered the land,

The Spirit of the Lord Came Upon Them

Person	Scripture
Bezalel	Exodus 31:3; 35:30, 31
Moses	Numbers 11:17
Seventy Elders	Numbers 11:25
Balaam	Numbers 24:2
Joshua	Deuteronomy 34:9
Othniel	Judges 3:10
Gideon	Judges 6:34
Jephthah	Judges 11:29
Samson	Judges 14:6, 19; 15:14
Saul	1 Samuel 10:10; 11:6; 19:23
David	1 Samuel 16:13
Messengers of Saul	1 Samuel 19:20
Amasa	1 Chronicles 12:18
Azariah	2 Chronicles 15:1
Zechariah	2 Chronicles 24:20
Isaiah	Isaiah 61:1
Ezekiel	Ezekiel 3:24; 11:5

but it awaits a complete fulfillment in the kingdom of Messiah.

33:28 *The fountain of Jacob.* This is a euphemism for Jacob's seed, referring to his posterity.

3. The death of Moses (34:1–12)

34:1–12 This concluding chapter was obviously written by someone other than Moses (probably the writer of Joshua) to bridge from Deuteronomy to Joshua.

34:1 *Pisgah.* The range or ridge of which Mt. Nebo was the highest point.

34:1–4 *the LORD showed him.* From the top of the mountain, Moses was allowed to see the panorama of the land the Lord had promised to give (the land of Canaan) to the patriarchs and their seed in Genesis 12:7; 13:15; 15:18–21; 26:4; 28:13, 14.

34:6 *He buried him.* The context indicates that the Lord is the one who buried Moses, and man did not have a part in it. Cf.

Further Study

Deere, Jack S. *Deuteronomy,* in The Bible Knowledge Commentary—Old Testament. Wheaton, Ill.: Victor, 1984.

Merrill, Eugene H. *Deuteronomy,* in New American Commentary. Nashville: Broadman & Holman, 1994.

Jude 9, which recounts Michael's and Satan's dispute over Moses' body.

34:7 *not dim . . . diminished.* Moses' physical vision and physical health were not impaired. It was not death by natural causes that kept Moses from leading Israel into the Promised Land; it was his unfaithfulness to the Lord at Meribah (see Num. 20:12).

34:8 *thirty days.* The mourning period for Moses conformed to that of Aaron (Num. 20:29).

34:9 *spirit of wisdom . . . laid his hands.* Joshua received (1) confirmation of the military and administrative ability necessary to

INTRODUCTION TO THE BOOKS OF
HISTORY

These twelve books of Israel's history extend from Joshua (c. 1405 B.C.) to Nehemiah (c. 424 B.C.)—almost 1,000 years. They begin with Israel's entrance into and possession of the Promised Land after a 430-year period of slavery in Egypt and a 40-year wandering in the wilderness; they conclude with Israel's return to residency in the Promised Land (but not possession of it). Prominent world empires during these centuries included: (1) Assyria (c. 880–612 B.C.); Babylon (c. 612–539 B.C.); and (3) Medo-Persia (c. 539–331 B.C.).

This period of history can be outlined using the following two themes—Kingship and Exile.

Pre-Kingship	Kingship	Post-Kingship
Joshua	1, 2 Samuel	Ezra
Judges	1, 2 Kings	Nehemiah
Ruth	1, 2 Chr.	Esther

Pre-Exile	Exile	Post-Exile
Joshua	Esther	Ezra
Judges		Nehemiah
Ruth		
1, 2 Samuel		
1, 2 Kings		
1, 2 Chronicles		

This was also a prophetic era that included all of the major and minor prophets

of the OT. Apart from those seers who wrote to/about Edom (Obadiah) and Nineveh (Jonah; Nahum) or from Babylon (Ezekiel; Daniel), the historical books relate to the prophets as follows:

1. 1 Kings 12–2 Kings 17—Amos; Hosea (prophets to Israel)
2. 1 Kings 12–2 Kings 25; 2 Chronicles 10–36—Joel; Isaiah; Micah; Zephaniah; Jeremiah; Habbakuk (prophets to Judah)
3. Ezra 1–6—Haggai; Zechariah
4. Ezra 7–10; Nehemiah—Malachi

The books of history begin with the *rise* of Israel in conquering and possessing the Promised Land (Joshua; Judges; Ruth). Transitioning to the *apex* of Israel's history, 1, 2 Samuel; 1 Kings 1–11; 1 Chronicles; and 2 Chronicles 1–9 record the history of the united kingdom. Israel in *decline* with a divided kingdom is reported in 1 Kings 12–22; 2 Kings; and 2 Chronicles 10–36. Esther details a nation in *exile*. With a note of *restoration* hope, Ezra and Nehemiah conclude with a people who once again reside in, but do not possess as once before, God's Promised Land.

Thus, neither the land of promise of the Abraham covenant (Gen. 12; 13; 15; 17) nor the perpetual kingship promise of the Davidic covenant (2 Sam. 7) were fulfilled in history. They must await the future reign of Messiah as foretold by the prophets (Zech. 14).

Chronology of Old Testament Patriarchs and Judges

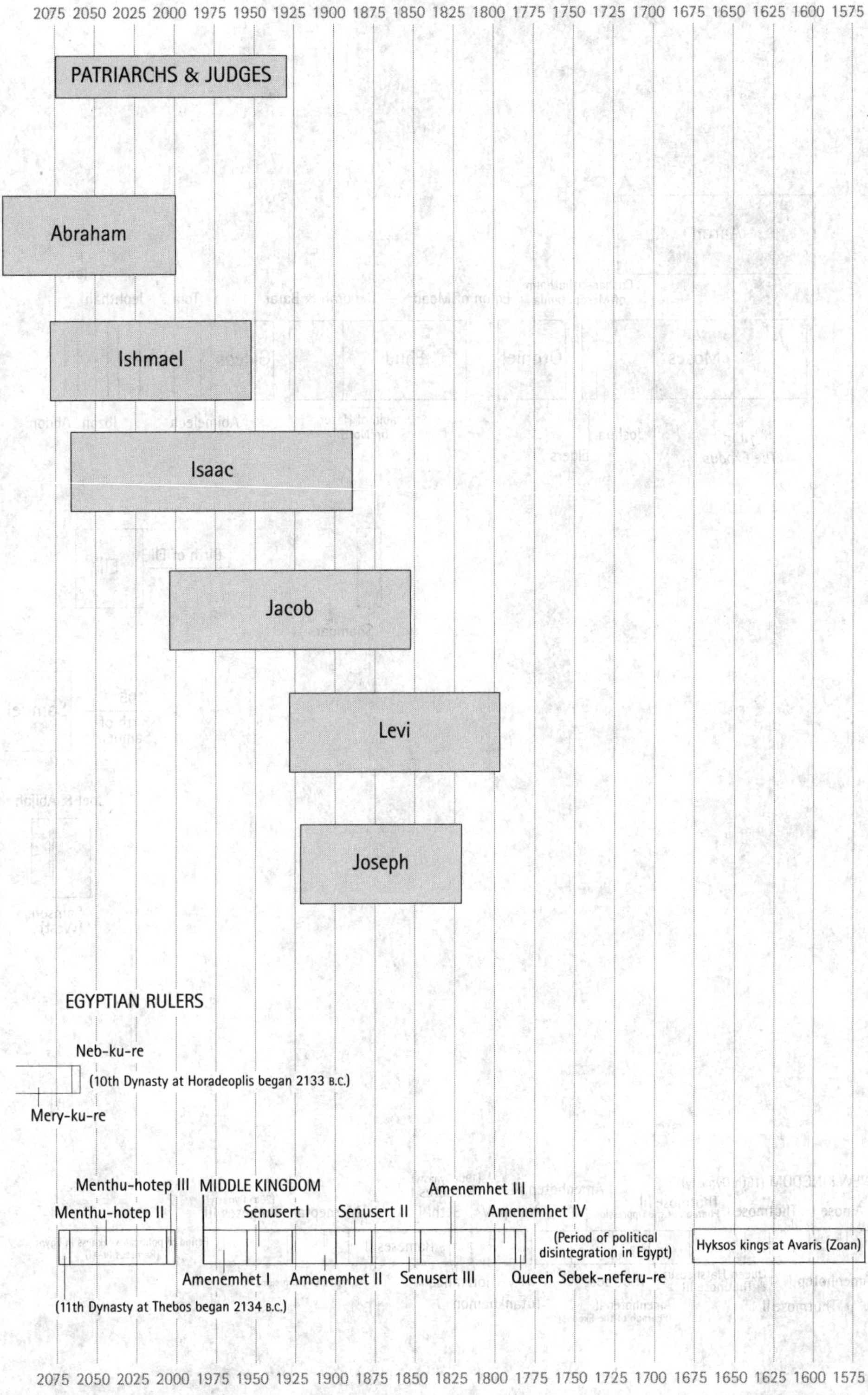

2075 2050 2025 2000 1975 1950 1925 1900 1875 1850 1825 1800 1775 1750 1725 1700 1675 1650 1625 1600 1575

PATRIARCHS & JUDGES

Abraham

Ishmael

Isaac

Jacob

Levi

Joseph

EGYPTIAN RULERS

Neb-ku-re

(10th Dynasty at Horadeoplis began 2133 B.C.)

Mery-ku-re

Menthu-hotep III MIDDLE KINGDOM   Amenemhet III
Menthu-hotep II   Senusert I   Senusert II   Amenemhet IV
                                                              (Period of political
                                                              disintegration in Egypt)   Hyksos kings at Avaris (Zoan)
        Amenemhet I   Amenemhet II   Senusert III   Queen Sebek-neferu-re

(11th Dynasty at Thebos began 2134 B.C.)

2075 2050 2025 2000 1975 1950 1925 1900 1875 1850 1825 1800 1775 1750 1725 1700 1675 1650 1625 1600 1575

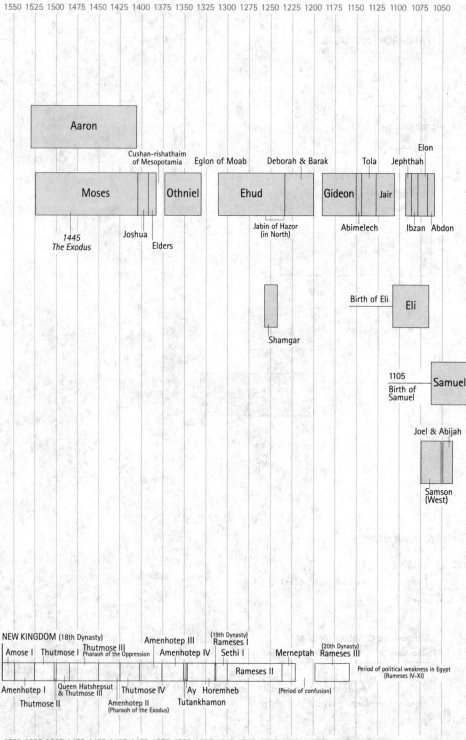

1550 1525 1500 1475 1450 1425 1400 1375 1350 1325 1300 1275 1250 1225 1200 1175 1150 1125 1100 1075 1050

Aaron

Cushan-rishathaim
of Mesopotamia   Eglon of Moab   Deborah & Barak   Tola   Jephthah   Elon

Moses   Othniel   Ehud   Gideon   Jair

1445   Jabin of Hazor   Abimelech   Ibzan   Abdon
The Exodus   Joshua   (in North)
                    Elders

Shamgar

Birth of Eli   Eli

1105
Birth of   Samuel
Samuel

Joel & Abijah

Samson
(West)

NEW KINGDOM (18th Dynasty)   (19th Dynasty)
                    Amenhotep III   Rameses I   (20th Dynasty)
Amose I Thutmose I Thutmose III   Amenhotep IV Sethi I   Merneptah Rameses III
                Pharaoh of the Oppression   Period of political weakness in Egypt
Amenhotep I   Queen Hatshepsut   Thutmose IV   Ay Horemheb   Rameses II   (Rameses IV–XI)
        & Thutmose III   Tutankhamon
Thutmose II   Amenhotep II   (Period of confusion)
                    (Pharaoh of the Exodus)

1550 1525 1500 1475 1450 1425 1400 1375 1350 1325 1300 1275 1250 1225 1200 1175 1150 1125 1100 1075 1050

Chronology of Old Testament Kings and Prophets

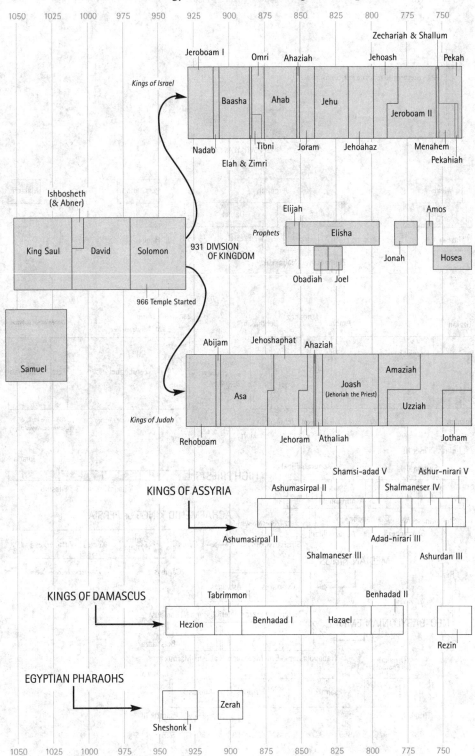

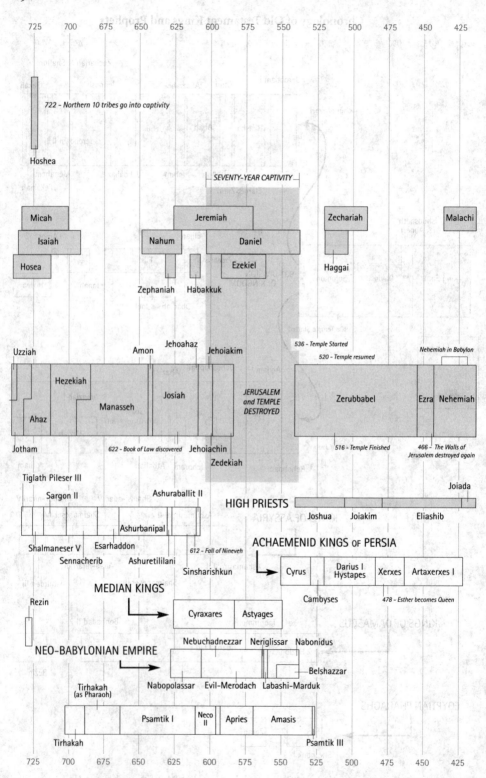

722 – Northern 10 tribes go into captivity

Hoshea

SEVENTY-YEAR CAPTIVITY

Micah

Isaiah

Hosea

Jeremiah

Nahum

Daniel

Zephaniah   Habakkuk

Ezekiel

Zechariah

Haggai

Malachi

536 – Temple Started

520 – Temple resumed

Nehemiah in Babylon

Uzziah

Amon

Jehoahaz

Jehoiakim

Hezekiah

Josiah

Ahaz

Manasseh

Jotham

622 – Book of Law discovered   Jehoiachin

Zedekiah

JERUSALEM
and TEMPLE
DESTROYED

Zerubbabel

Ezra Nehemiah

516 – Temple Finished

466 – The Walls of
Jerusalem destroyed again

Tiglath Pileser III

Sargon II

Ashuraballit II

Ashurbanipal

Shalmaneser V   Esarhaddon

Sennacherib   Ashuretililani

612 – Fall of Nineveh

Sinsharishkun

HIGH PRIESTS

Joiada

Joshua   Joiakim   Eliashib

ACHAEMENID KINGS OF PERSIA

Cyrus   Darius I
Hystapes   Xerxes   Artaxerxes I

Cambyses

478 – Esther becomes Queen

MEDIAN KINGS

Rezin

Cyraxares   Astyages

NEO-BABYLONIAN EMPIRE

Nebuchadnezzar   Neriglissar   Nabonidus

Nabopolassar   Evil-Merodach   Labashi-Marduk

Belshazzar

Tirhakah
(as Pharaoh)

Psamtik I   Neco
II   Apries   Amasis

Tirhakah   Psamtik III

A HARMONY OF THE BOOKS OF
SAMUEL, KINGS, and CHRONICLES

I. The Kingship of God (1 Sam. 1:1–7:17; 1 Chr. 1:1–9:44)
A. Genealogical Tables (1 Chr. 1:1–9:44)
   1. Genealogies of the Patriarchs (1 Chr. 1:1–2:2)
   2. Genealogies of the Tribes of Israel (1 Chr. 2:3–9:44)
B. The Close of the Theocracy (1 Sam. 1:1–7:17)
   1. The Early Life of Samuel (1 Sam. 1:1–4:1a)
      a. Samuel's birth and infancy (1 Sam. 1:1–2:11)
      b. Samuel at Shiloh (1 Sam. 2:12–4:1a)
   2. The Period of National Disaster (1 Sam. 4:1b–7:2)
      a. Israel's defeat and loss of the ark (1 Sam. 4:1b–11a)
      b. Fall of the house of Eli (1 Sam. 4:11b–22)
      c. The ark of God (1 Sam. 5:1–7:2)
   3. Samuel, the Last of the Judges (1 Sam. 7:3–17)
II. The Kingship of Saul (1 Sam. 8:1–31:13; 1 Chr. 10:1–14)
A. Establishment of Saul as First King of Israel (1 Sam. 8:1–10:27)
B. Saul's Reign until His Rejection (1 Sam. 11:1–15:35)
C. The Decline of Saul and the Rise of David (1 Sam. 16:1–31:13)
   1. David's Early History (1 Sam. 16:1–23)
   2. David's Advancement and Saul's Growing Jealousy (1 Sam. 17:1–20:42)
      a. David and Goliath (1 Sam. 17:1–51)
      b. David at the court of Saul (1 Sam. 18:1–20:42)
   3. David's Life of Exile (1 Sam. 21:1–28:2)
      a. David's flight (1 Sam. 21:1–22:5)
      b. Saul's vengeance on the priests of Nob (1 Sam. 22:6–23)
      c. David's rescue of Keilah (1 Sam. 23:1–13)
      d. David's last meeting with Jonathan (1 Sam. 23:14–18)
      e. David's betrayal by the Ziphites (1 Sam. 23:19–24a)
      f. David's escape from Saul in the wilderness of Maon (1 Sam. 23:24b–28)
      g. David's flight from Saul; David's mercy on Saul's life in the cave (1 Sam. 23:29–24:22)
      h. Samuel's death (1 Sam. 25:1)
      i. David's marriage to Abigail (1 Sam. 25:2–44)
      j. David's mercy on Saul's life again (1 Sam. 26:1–25)
      k. David's joining with the Philistines (1 Sam. 27:1–28:2)

       4. Saul's Downfall in War with the Philistines (1 Sam. 28:3–31:13; 1 Chr. 10:1–14)
          a. Saul's fear of the Philistines (1 Sam. 28:3–6)
          b. Saul's visit to the witch of Endor (1 Sam. 28:7–25)
          c. David leaves the Philistines; defeats the Amalakites (1 Sam. 29:1–30:31)
          d. Saul and his sons slain (1 Sam. 31:1–13; 1 Chr. 10:1–14)

III.   The Kingship of David (2 Sam. 1:1–24:25; 1 Kin. 1:1–2:11; 1 Chr. 10:14–29:30)
    A. David's Victories (2 Sam. 1:1–10:19; 1 Chr. 10:14–20:8)
       1. The Political Triumphs of David (2 Sam. 1:1–5:25; 1 Chr. 10:14–12:40)
          a. David is king of Judah (2 Sam. 1:1–4:12; 1 Chr. 10:14–12:40)
          b. David is king over all Israel (2 Sam. 5:1–5:25)
       2. The Spiritual Triumphs of David (2 Sam. 6:1–7:29; 1 Chr. 13:1–17:27)
          a. The ark of the covenant (2 Sam. 6:1–23; 1 Chr. 13:1–16:43)
          b. The temple and the Davidic covenant (2 Sam. 7:1–29; 1 Chr. 17:1–27)
       3. The Military Triumphs of David (2 Sam. 8:1–10:19; 1 Chr. 18:1–20:8)
    B. David's Sins (2 Sam. 11:1–27)
       1. David's Adultery with Bathsheba (2 Sam. 11:1–5)
       2. David's Murder of Uriah the Hittite (2 Sam. 11:6–27)
    C. David's Problems (2 Sam. 12:1–24:25; 1 Chr. 21:1–27:34)
       1. David's House Suffers (2 Sam. 12:1–13:36)
          a. Nathan's prophecy against David (2 Sam. 12:1–14)
          b. David's son dies (2 Sam. 12:15–25)
          c. Joab's loyalty to David (2 Sam. 12:26–31)
          d. Amnon's incest (2 Sam. 13:1–20)
          e. Amnon's murder (2 Sam. 13:21–36)
       2. David's Kingdom Suffers (2 Sam. 13:37–24:25; 1 Chr. 21:1–27:34)
          a. Absalom's rebellion (2 Sam. 13:37–17:29)
          b. Absalom's murder (2 Sam. 18:1–33)
          c. David's restoration as king (2 Sam. 19:1–20:26)
          d. David's kingship evaluated (2 Sam. 21:1–23:39)
          e. David's numbering of the people (2 Sam. 24:1–24:25; 1 Chr. 21:1–30)
    D. David's Preparation and Organization for the Temple (1 Chr. 22:1–27:34)
    E. David's Last Days (1 Kin. 1:1–2:11; 1 Chr. 28:1–29:30)
       1. David's Failing Health: Abishag the Shunammite (1 Kin. 1:1–4)
       2. Adonijah's Attempt to Seize the Kingdom (1 Kin. 1:5–9)
       3. Solomon's Anointing as King (1 Kin. 1:10–40; 1 Chr. 29:20–25)
       4. Adonijah's Submission (1 Kin. 1:41–53)
       5. David's Last Words (1 Kin. 2:1–9; 1 Chr. 28:1–29:25)
          a. David's words for Israel (1 Chr. 28:1–8)
          b. David's words for Solomon (1 Kin. 2:1–9; 1 Chr. 28:9–21)
          c. David's dedication to the temple (1 Chr. 29:1–20)
       6. David's Death (1 Kin. 2:10, 11; 1 Chr. 29:26–30)

IV. The Kingship of Solomon (1 Kin. 2:12–11:43; 1 Chr. 29:21–2 Chr. 9:31)
    A. Solomon's Kingship Begins (1 Kin. 2:12–4:34; 1 Chr. 29:21–2 Chr. 1:17)
       1. Solomon's Kingship Established (1 Kin. 2:12; 1 Chr. 29:21–2 Chr. 1:1)
       2. Solomon's Adversaries Removed (1 Kin. 2:13–46)
       3. Solomon's Marriage to Pharaoh's Daughter (1 Kin. 3:1)
       4. Solomon's Spiritual Condition (1 Kin. 3:2, 3)
       5. Solomon's Sacrifice at Gibeon (1 Kin. 3:4; 2 Chr. 1:2–6)
       6. Solomon's Dream and Prayer for Wisdom (1 Kin. 3:5–15; 2 Chr. 1:7–12)
       7. Solomon's Judging of the Harlots with God's Wisdom (1 Kin. 3:16–28)
       8. Solomon's Officers, His Power, Wealth, and Wisdom (1 Kin. 4:1 –34;
         2 Chr. 1:13–17)
    B. Solomon's Splendor (1 Kin. 5:1–8:66; 2 Chr. 2:1–7:22)
       1. Preparations for the Building of the Temple (1 Kin. 5:1–18; 2 Chr. 2:1–18)
       2. The Building of the Temple (1 Kin. 6:1–38; 2 Chr. 3:1–14)
       3. The Building of the Royal Palace (1 Kin. 7:1–12)
       4. The Making of the Vessels for the Temple (1 Kin. 7:13–51; 2 Chr. 3:15–5:1)
       5. The Dedication and Completion of the Temple (1 Kin. 8:1–66; 2 Chr. 5:2–7:22)
    C. Solomon's Demise (1 Kin. 9:1–11:43; 2 Chr. 8:1–9:31)
       1. Davidic Covenant Repeated (1 Kin. 9:1–9)
       2. Solomon's Disobedience to the Covenant (1 Kin. 9:10–11:8; 2 Chr. 8:1–9:28)
       3. Solomon's Chastening for Breaking the Covenant (1 Kin. 11:9–40)
       4. Solomon's Death (1 Kin. 11:41–43; 2 Chr. 9:29–31)
V. The Kingdom Divided (1 Kin. 12:1–22:53; 2 Kin. 1:1–17:41; 2 Chr. 10:1–28:27)
    A. The Kingdom Divides (1 Kin. 12:1–14:31)
       1. The Division's Cause (1 Kin. 12:1–24)
       2. Jeroboam, King of Israel (1 Kin. 12:25–14:20)
       3. Rehoboam, King of Judah (1 Kin. 14:21–31; 2 Chr. 10:1–12:16)
    B. Judah's Two Kings (1 Kin. 15:1–24; 2 Chr. 13:1–16:14)
       1. Abijam (Joram), King of Judah (1 Kin. 15:1–8; 2 Chr. 13:1–22)
       2. Asa, King of Judah (1 Kin. 15:9–24; 2 Chr. 14:1–16:14)
    C. Israel's Five Kings (1 Kin. 15:25–16:28)
       1. Nadab, King of Israel (1 Kin. 15:25–31)
       2. Baasha, King of Israel (1 Kin. 15:32–16:7)
       3. Elah, King of Israel (1 Kin. 16:8–14)
       4. Zimri, King of Israel (1 Kin. 16:15–20)
       5. Omri, King of Israel (1 Kin. 16:21–28)
    D. Ahab, King of Israel (1 Kin. 16:29–22:40)
       1. Ahab's Sin (1 Kin. 16:29–34)
       2. Elijah the Prophet (1 Kin. 17:1–19:21)
       3. Wars with Syria (1 Kin. 20:1–43)
       4. Naboth Swindled and Killed (1 Kin. 21:1–16)
       5. Ahab's Death (1 Kin. 21:17–22:40)
    E. Jehoshaphat, King of Judah (1 Kin. 22:41–50; 2 Chr. 17:1–21:3)
    F. Ahaziah, King of Israel (1 Kin. 22:51–53; 2 Kin. 1:1–18)

G. Jehoram (Joram), King of Israel (2 Kin. 3:1–8:15)

H. Jehoram, King of Judah (2 Kin. 8:16–24; 2 Chr. 21:4–20)

I. Ahaziah, King of Judah (2 Kin. 8:25–9:29; 2 Chr. 22:1–9)

J. Jehu, King of Israel (2 Kin. 9:30–10:36)

K. Athaliah, Queen of Judah (2 Kin. 11:1–16; 2 Chr. 22:10–23:21)

L. Joash, King of Judah (2 Kin. 11:17–12:21; 2 Chr. 24:1–27)

M. Jehoahaz, King of Israel (2 Kin. 13:1–9)

N. Jehoash (Joash), King of Israel (2 Kin. 13:10–25)

O. Amaziah, King of Judah (2 Kin. 14:1–22; 2 Chr. 25:1–28)

P. Jeroboam II, King of Israel (2 Kin. 14:23–29)

Q. Uzziah (Azariah), King of Judah (2 Kin. 15:1–7; 2 Chr. 26:1–23)

R. Zechariah, King of Israel (2 Kin. 15:8–12)

S. Shallum, King of Israel (2 Kin. 15:13–15)

T. Menahem, King of Israel (2 Kin. 15:16–22)

U. Pekahiah, King of Israel (2 Kin. 15:23–26)

V. Pekah, King of Israel (2 Kin. 15:27–31)

W. Jotham, King of Judah (2 Kin. 15:32–38; 2 Chr. 27:1–9)

X. Ahaz, King of Judah (2 Kin. 16:1–20; 2 Chr. 28:1–27)

Y. Hoshea, King of Israel (2 Kin. 17:1–41)

VI. The Surviving Kingdom of Judah (2 Kin. 18:1–25:30; 2 Chr. 29:1–36:23)

A. Hezekiah, King of Judah (2 Kin. 18:1–20:21; 2 Chr. 29:1–32:33)

B. Manasseh, King of Judah (2 Kin. 21:1–18; 2 Chr. 33:1–20)

C. Amon, King of Judah (2 Kin. 21:19–26; 2 Chr. 33:21–25)

D. Josiah, King of Judah (2 Kin. 22:1–23:30; 2 Chr. 34:1–35:27)

E. Jehoahaz, King of Judah (2 Kin. 23:31–34; 2 Chr. 36:1–3)

F. Jehoiakim, King of Judah (2 Kin. 23:35–24:7; 2 Chr. 36:4–8)

G. Jehoiachin, King of Judah (2 Kin. 24:8–16; 2 Chr. 36:9, 10)

H. Zedekiah, King of Judah (2 Kin. 24:17–25:21; 2 Chr. 36:11–21)

I. Gedaliah, Governor of Judah (2 Kin. 25:22–26)

J. Jehoiachin Released in Babylon (2 Kin. 25:27–30)

K. Cyrus Decrees Rebuilding in Jerusalem (2 Chr. 36:22, 23)

THE BOOK OF
JOSHUA

Title

This is the first of the twelve historical books, and it gained its name from the exploits of Joshua, the understudy whom Moses prayed for and commissioned as a leader in Israel (Num. 27:12–23). *Joshua* means "Jehovah saves," or "the LORD is salvation," and corresponds to the NT name *Jesus*. God delivered Israel in Joshua's day when He was personally present as the saving commander who fought on Israel's behalf (5:14–6:2; 10:42; 23:3, 5; Acts 7:45).

Author and Date

Although the author is not named, the most probable candidate is Joshua, who was the key eyewitness to the events recorded (cf. 18:9; 24:26). An assistant whom Joshua groomed could have finished the book by attaching such comments as those concerning Joshua's death (24:29–33). Some have even suggested that this section was written by the high priest Eleazar or his son, Phinehas. Rahab was still living at the time Joshua 6:25 was penned. The book was completed before David's reign (15:63; cf. 2 Sam. 5:5–9). The most likely writing period is c. 1405–1385 B.C.

Joshua was born in Egyptian slavery, trained under Moses, and by God's choice rose to his key position of leading Israel into Canaan. Distinguishing features of his life include: (1) service (Ex. 17:10; 24:13; 33:11; Num. 11:28); (2) soldiering (Ex. 17:9–13); (3) scouting (Num. 13; 14); (4) supplication by Moses (Num. 27:15–17); (5) the sovereignty of God (Num. 27:18ff.); (6) the Spirit's presence (Num. 27:18; Deut. 34:9); (7) separation by Moses (Num. 27:18–23; Deut. 31:7, 8, 13–15); and (8) selflessness in following the Lord (Num. 32:12).

Background and Setting

When Moses passed the baton of leadership on to Joshua before he died (Deut. 34), Israel was at the end of its forty-year wilderness wandering period c. 1405 B.C. Joshua was approaching ninety years of age when he became Israel's leader. He later died at the age of 110 (24:29), having led Israel to drive out most of the Canaanites and having divided the land among the twelve tribes. Poised on the plains of Moab, east of the Jordan River and the land that God had promised (Gen. 12:7; 15:18–21), the Israelites awaited God's direction to conquer the land.

They faced peoples on the western side of the Jordan River who had become so steeped in iniquity that God would cause the land, so to speak, to spew out these inhabitants (Lev. 18:24, 25). He would give Israel the land by conquest, primarily to fulfill the covenant He had pledged to Abraham and his descendants, but also to pass just judgment on the sinful inhabitants (cf. Gen. 15:16). Long possession of different parts of the land by various peoples had predated even Abraham's day (Gen. 10:15–19; 12:6; 13:7). Its inhabitants had continued on a moral decline in the worship of many gods up to Joshua's time.

Historical and Theological Themes

A keynote feature is God's faithfulness to fulfill His promise of giving the land to Abraham's descendants (Gen. 12:7; 15:18–21; 17:8). By His leading (cf. 5:14–6:2), they inhabited the territories east and west of the Jordan River, and so the word *possess* appears nearly twenty times.

Related to this theme is Israel's failure to press their conquest to every part of the land (13:1). Judges 1 and 2 later describes the tragic results from this sin. Key verses focus on: (1) God's promise of possession of the land (1:3, 6); (2) meditation on God's Law, which was strategic for His people (1:8); and (3) Israel's actual possession of the land in part (11:23; 21:45; 22:4).

Specific allotment of distinct portions in the land was Joshua's task, as recorded in chapters 13—22. Levites were placed strategically in forty-eight towns so God's spiritual services through them would be reasonably within reach of the Israelites, wherever they lived.

God wanted His people to possess the land: (1) to keep His promise (Gen. 12:7); (2) to set the stage for later developments in His kingdom plan (cf. Gen. 17:8; 49:8–12), e.g., positioning Israel for events in the periods of the kings and prophets; (3) to punish peoples that were an affront to Him because of extreme sinfulness (Lev. 18:25); and (4) to be a testimony to other peoples (Josh. 2:9–11), as God's covenant heart reached out to all nations (Gen. 12:1–3).

Interpretive Challenges

Miracles always challenge readers either to believe that the God who created heaven and earth (Gen. 1:1) can do other mighty works, too, or to explain them away. As in Moses' day, miracles in this book were a part of God's purpose, such as: (1) His holding back the Jordan's waters (Josh. 3:7–17); (2) the fall of Jericho's walls (Josh. 6:1–27); (3) the hailstones (Josh. 10:1–11); and (4) the long day (Josh. 10:12–15).

Other challenges include: (1) How did God's blessing on the harlot Rahab, who responded to Him in faith, relate to her telling a lie (Josh. 2)? (2) Why were Achan's family members executed with him (Josh. 7)? (3) Why was Ai, with fewer men than Israel, hard to conquer (Josh. 7; 8)? (4) What does God's "sending the hornet" before Israel mean (Josh. 24:12)? These questions will be addressed in the notes.

Outline

I. Entering the Promised Land (1:1–5:15)

1:2 *the land which I am giving.* This is the land God promised in His covenant with Abraham and often reaffirmed later (Gen. 12:7; 13:14, 15; 15:18–21).

1:4 Borders of the Promised Land are: *west,* the Mediterranean seacoast; *east,* Euphrates River far to the east; *south,* the wilderness over to the Nile of Egypt; *north,* Lebanon.

1:5 The promise of divine power for Joshua's task.

1:6 *I swore to their fathers.* Cf. Genesis 12:7; 15:18–21; 17:8; 26:3; 28:13; 35:12 to Abraham, Isaac, and Jacob.

1:7 *strong and very courageous. See note on Deuteronomy 31:6–8.*

1:8 *This Book of the Law.* A reference to Scripture, specifically Genesis through Deuteronomy, written by Moses (cf. Ex. 17:14; Deut. 31:9–11, 24). *meditate in it.* To read with thoughtfulness, to linger over God's Word. The parts of Scripture they pos-

sessed have always been the main spiritual food of those who served Him, e.g., Job (Job 23:12); the psalmist (Ps. 1:1–3); Jeremiah (Jer. 15:16); and Jesus (John 4:34). *prosperous . . . good success.* The promise of God's blessing on the great responsibility God has given Joshua. The principle here is central to all spiritual effort and enterprise, namely, the deep understanding and application of Scripture at all times.

1:9 *the Lord . . . is with you.* This assurance has always been the staying sufficiency for God's servants such as: Abraham (Gen. 15:1); Moses and his people (Ex. 14:13); Isaiah (Is. 41:10); Jeremiah (Jer. 1:7, 8); and Christians through the centuries (Matt. 28:20; Heb. 13:5).

1:11 *within three days.* In some cases, events that took place before this announcement and these three days (cf. 3:2) are described later on, e.g., Joshua's sending two scouts to check out the land (2:22).

1:12 *half the tribe of Manasseh.* In Genesis 48, Jacob blessed both sons of Joseph,

Joshua's Preparation for Ministry

1. Exodus 17:9, 10, 13–14	Joshua led the victorious battle against the Amalekites.
2. Exodus 24:13	Joshua, the servant of Moses, accompanied the Jewish leader to the mountain of God (cf. 32:17).
3. Numbers 11:28	Joshua was the attendant of Moses from his youth.
4. Numbers 13:16	Moses changed his name from Hosea ("salvation") to Joshua ("the Lord saves").
5. Numbers 14:6–10, 30, 38	Joshua, along with Caleb, spied out the land of Canaan with 10 others. Only Joshua and Caleb urged the nation to possess the land and, thus, only they of the 12 actually entered Canaan.
6. Numbers 27:18	Joshua was indwelt by the Holy Spirit.
7. Numbers 27:18–23	Joshua was commissioned for spiritual service for the first time, to assist Moses.
8. Numbers 32:12	Joshua followed the Lord fully.
9. Deuteronomy 31:23	Joshua was commissioned a second time, to replace Moses.
10. Deuteronomy 34:9	Joshua was filled with the spirit of wisdom.

The MacArthur Study Bible, by John MacArthur (Nashville: Word Publishing, 1997) 305. © 1993 by Thomas Nelson, Inc.

Ephraim and Manasseh, so Joseph actually received a double blessing (Gen. 48:22). This allowed for twelve allotments of the land, with Levi being excluded because of priestly function.

1:13–18 The LORD . . . is giving you this land. God gave these tribes the lands directly across the Jordan River on the east (cf. Num. 32). Yet, it was their duty to assist the other tribes of Israel to invade and conquer their allotted land to the west.

2:1 two men . . . to spy. These scouts would inform Joshua about various features of the topography, food, drinking water, and defenses to be overcome in the invasion. **Acacia Grove . . . Jericho.** The grove (cf. 3:1) was situated in foothills about seven miles east of the Jordan River, and Jericho lay seven miles west of the river. **house of a harlot.** Their purpose was not impure; rather, the spies sought a place where they would not be conspicuous. Resorting to such a house would be a good cover, from where they might learn something of Jericho. Also, a house on the city wall (v. 15) would allow a quick getaway. In spite of this precaution, their presence became known (vv. 2, 3). God, in His sovereign providence, wanted them there for the salvation of the prostitute. She would provide an example of His saving, by faith, a woman at the bottom of social strata, as He saved Abraham at the top (cf. James 2:18–25). Most importantly, by God's grace she was in the Messianic line (Matt. 1:5).

2:2 the king. He was not over a broad domain, but only the city-state. Kings over other city areas appear later during this conquest (cf. 8:23; 12:24).

2:4, 5 Cf. verses 9–11. Lying is sin to God (Ex. 20:16), for He cannot lie (Titus 1:2). God commended Rahab's faith (Heb. 11:31; James 2:25) as expressed in verses 9–16, not her lie. He never condones any sin; yet, none of us are without some sin (cf. Rom. 3:23),

thus the need for forgiveness. But He also honors true faith, small as it is, and imparts saving grace (Ex. 34:7).

2:6 stalks of flax. These fibers, used for making linen, were stems about three feet long, left to sit in water, then piled in the sun or on a level roof to dry.

2:11 God in heaven above and on earth beneath. Rahab confessed the realization that God is the sovereign Creator and sustainer of all that exists (cf. Deut. 4:39; Acts 14:15; 17:23–28), thus the supreme one.

2:15, 16 Her home was on the city wall, with the Jordan River (v. 7) to the east. The rugged mountains to the west provided many hiding places.

2:18 cord. A different word from *rope* (v. 15). Scarlet, unlike drab green, brown, or gray, is more visible to mark the house for protection. The color also is fitting for those whose blood (v. 19) was under God's pledge of safety.

3:3 the ark. This symbolized God's presence going before His people. Kohathites customarily carried the ark (Num. 4:15; 7:9) but, in this unusual case, the Levitical priests transported it, as in Joshua 6:6; 1 Kings 8:3–6.

3:4 two thousand cubits. 1,000 yards.

3:8 stand in the Jordan. The priests were to stand there to permit time for God's words (v. 9) to stimulate reflection on the greatness of God's eminent action in giving the land as He showed His presence (v. 10). Also, it was a preparation to allow the people following to get set for God's miracle which stopped the waters for a crossing (vv. 13–17).

3:10 Canaanite people to be killed or defeated were sinful to the point of extreme (cf. Gen. 15:16; Lev. 18:24, 25). God, as moral judge, has the right to deal with all people, as at the end (Rev. 20:11–15) or any other time when He deems it appropriate for His purposes. The question is not why God chose to

The Peoples Around the Promised Land

1. AMALEKITES	The descendants of Amalek, the fistborn of Esau (Gen. 36:12), who dwelt S of Palestine in the Negev.
2. AMMONITES	The descendants of Ammon, the grandson of Lot by his youngest daughter (Gen. 19:38), who lived E of the Jordan River and N of Moab.
3. AMORITES	A general term for the inhabitants of the Land, but especially for the descendants of Canaan who inhabited the hill country on both sides of the Jordan.
4. CANAANITES	Broadly speaking, these are the descendants of Canaan, son of Ham, son of Noah (cf. Gen. 10:15-18), and included many of the other groups named here.
5. EDOMITES	The descendants of Esau who settled SE of Palestine (cf. Gen. 25:30) in the land of Seir.
6. GEBALITES	People of the ancient seaport later known as Byblos, about 20 mi. N of modern Beirut (Josh. 13:5).
7. GESHURITES	The inhabitants of Geshur, E of the Jordan and to the S or Syria (Josh. 12:5).
8. GIBEONITES	The inhabitants of Gibeon and surrounding area (Josh. 9:17).
9. GIRGASHITES	A tribe descended from Canaan, which was included among the general population of the land without specific geographical identity.
10. GIRZITES	An obscure group which lived in the NW part of the Negev, before they were destroyed by David (1 Sam. 27:8, 9).
11. HITTITES	Immigrants from the Hittite Empire (in the region of Syria) to the central region of the Land (cf. 23:10; 2 Sam. 11:3).
12. HIVITES	Descendants of Canaan who lived in the northern reaches of the Land.
13. HORITES	Ancient residents of Edom from an unknown origin who were destroyed by Esau's descendants (Deut. 2:22).
14. JEBUSITES	Descendants of Canaan who dwelt in the hill country around Jerusalem (cf. Gen. 15:21; Ex. 3:8).
15. KENITES	A Midianite tribe that originally dwelt in the Gulf of Aqabah region (1 Sam. 27:10).
16. MOABITES	The descendants of Moab, the grandson of Lot by his eldest daughter (Gen. 19:37), who lived E of the Dead Sea.
17. PERIZZITES	People included among the general population of the Land who do not trace their lineage to Canaan. Their exact identity is uncertain.

The MacArthur Study Bible, by John MacArthur (Nashville: Word Publishing, 1997) 308. © 1993 by Thomas Nelson, Inc.

destroy these sinners, but why He had let them live so long, and why all sinners are not destroyed far sooner than they are. It is grace that allows any sinner to draw one more breath of life (cf. Gen. 2:17; Ezek. 18:20; Rom. 6:23).

3:16 rose in a heap. The God of all power, who created heaven, earth, and all else according to Genesis 1, worked miracles here. The waters were supernaturally dammed up at Adam, a city fifteen miles north of the crossing, and also in tributary creeks. Once the miracle was completed, God permitted waters to flow again (4:18) after the people had walked to the other side on dry ground (3:17). As the Exodus had begun (cf. Ex. 14), so it ended.

4:1–8 Twelve stones picked up from the riverbed became a memorial to God's faithfulness. They were set up at Gilgal (about one and one-fourth miles from Jericho), which was Israel's first campsite in the invaded land (vv. 19, 20). Placing twelve stones in the riverbed itself commemorated the place that God dried up, where His ark had been held, and where He showed by a miracle His mighty presence and worthiness of respect (vv. 9–11, 21–24).

4:19 tenth day . . . first month. March–April. Abib was the term used by pre-exilic Jews; Nisan later came to be used by post-exilic Israel.

5:1 heard. Reports of God's supernaturally opening a crossing struck fear into the Canaanites. The miracle was all the more incredible and shocking since God performed it when the Jordan River was swollen to flood height (3:15). To the people in the land, this miracle was a powerful demonstration proving that God is mighty (4:24). This came on top of reports about the Red Sea miracle (2:10).

5:2 circumcise. God commanded Joshua to see that this was done to all males under forty. These were sons of the generation who died in the wilderness, survivors (cf. vv. 6, 7) from the new generation God spared in Numbers 13 and 14. This surgical sign of a faith commitment to the Abrahamic covenant (see Gen. 17:9–14) had been ignored during the wilderness trek. Now God wanted it reinstated, so the Israelites would start out right in the land they were possessing. *See note on Jeremiah 4:4.*

5:8 they were healed. This speaks of the time needed to recover from such a painful and potentially infected wound.

5:9 rolled away the reproach. By His miracle of bringing the people into the land, God removed (rolled away) the ridicule that the Egyptians had heaped on them.

5:10 Passover. This commemorated God's deliverance from Egypt, recorded in Exodus 7–12. Such a remembrance was a strengthening preparation for trusting God to work in possessing the new land.

5:12 manna ceased. God had begun to provide this food from the time of Exodus 16 and did so for forty years (Ex. 16:35). Since food was plentiful in the land of Canaan, they could provide for themselves with produce such as dates, barley, and olives.

5:13–15 Commander. The Lord Jesus Christ (6:2; cf. 5:15 with Ex. 3:2, 5) in a preincarnate appearance (Christophany). He came as the Angel (Messenger) of the Lord, as if He were a man (cf. the one of three "angels," Gen. 18). Joshua fittingly was reverent in worship. The commander, sword drawn, showed a posture indicating He was set to give Israel victory over the Canaanites (6:2; cf. 1:3).

II. CONQUERING THE PROMISED LAND (6:1–12:24)

A. The Central Campaign (6:1–8:35)

6:1 Jericho. The city was fortified by a double ring of walls, the outer six feet thick and the inner twelve feet thick; timbers were laid across these, supporting houses on the walls. Since Jericho was built on a hill, it could be taken only by mounting a steep incline, which put the Israelites at a great disadvantage. Attackers of such a fortress often used a siege of several months to force surrender through starvation.

6:3–21 The bizarre military strategy of marching around Jericho gave occasion for the Israelites to take God at His promise (v. 2). They would also heighten the defenders' uneasiness. Seven is sometimes a number used to signify completeness (cf. 2 Kin. 5:10, 14).

6:5 God assured Israel of an astounding miracle, just as He had done at the Jordan.

6:16 The loud shout in unison expressed an expectation of God's action to fulfill His guaranteed promise (vv. 2, 5, 16).

6:17 doomed. The Hebrew term means "utterly destroyed," as in verse 21, i.e., to ban or devote as spoil for a deity. Here, it is required to be retained for God's possession, a tribute belonging to Him for the purpose of destruction.

6:22–25 Joshua honored the promise of safety to the household of Rahab. The part of the wall securing this house must not have fallen, and all possessions in the dwelling were safe.

6:26 God put a curse on whoever would rebuild Jericho. While the area around it was later occupied to some extent (2 Sam. 10:5), in Ahab's reign Hiel rebuilt Jericho and experienced the curse by losing his eldest and youngest sons (1 Kin. 16:34).

6:27 God kept His pledge that He would be with Joshua (1:5–9).

7:1–5 Israel's defeat is similar to an earlier setback against the Amalekites (Num. 14:39–45).

7:2 Ai. A town situated west of the Jordan, in the hills east of Bethel (cf. Gen. 12:8).

7:3 few. The *few* inhabitants of Ai are numbered at 12,000 in 8:25 (cf. 8:3).

7:9 what will You do for Your great name? The main issue is the glory of God (cf. Daniel's prayer in Dan. 9:16–19).

7:15, 24, 25 Achan's family faced execution with him. They were regarded as coconspirators in what he did. They helped cover up his

guilt and withheld information from others. Similarly, family members died in Korah's rebellion (Num. 16:25–34), Haman's fall (Esth. 9:13, 14), and after Daniel's escape (Dan. 6:24).

7:21 I saw. There are four steps in the progress of Achan's sin: "I saw . . . I coveted . . . I took . . . I concealed." David's sin with Bathsheba followed the same path (2 Sam. 11; cf. James 1:14, 15). *a beautiful Babylonian garment.* A costly, ornate robe of Shinar adorned with colored figures of men or animals, woven or done in needlework, and perhaps, trimmed with jewels. This same word is used for a king's robe in Jonah 3:6.

7:24 Achor. Lit. "trouble" (cf. Is. 65:10; Hos. 2:15).

8:3 thirty thousand . . . men. Joshua's elite force was far superior to that of Ai, with a mere 12,000 total population (8:25). This time Joshua took no small force presumptuously (cf. 7:3, 4), but had 30,000 to sack and burn Ai, a decoy group to lure defenders out of the city (vv. 5, 6), and a third detachment of about 5,000 to prevent Bethel from helping Ai (v. 12).

8:7 God will deliver it into your hand. God had sovereignly caused Israel's defeat earlier due to Achan's disobedience (7:1–5). Yet, this time, despite Israel's overwhelming numbers, God was still the sovereign power behind this victory (8:7).

8:18 the spear. Joshua's hoisted javelin represented the go-ahead indicator to occupy Ai. Possibly the raised weapon was even a signal of confidence in God: "For I will give it into your hand." Earlier, Moses' uplifted rod and arms probably signified trust in God for victory over Amalek (Ex. 17:8–13).

8:29 the king of Ai. The execution of Ai's populace included hanging the king. This wise move prevented later efforts to muster a Canaanite army. Further, as a wicked king, he was worthy of punishment according to biblical standards (Deut. 21:22; Josh. 10:26, 27). This carried out the vengeance of God on His enemies.

8:30–35 This ceremony took place in obedience to Deuteronomy 27:1–26 at the conclusion of Joshua's central campaign (cf. 6:1–8:35).

8:30, 31 Thanks is offered to God for giving victory. The altar, in obedience to the instruction of Exodus 20:24–26, was built of uncut stones, thus keeping worship simple and untainted by human showmanship. Joshua gave God's Word a detailed and central place.

B. The Southern Campaign (9:1–10:43)

9:3 inhabitants. Gibeon of the Hivites (v. 7), or Horites (cf. Gen. 36:2, 20), was northwest of Jerusalem and about seven miles from Ai. It was a strong city with capa-

ble fighting men (10:2). Three other towns were in league with it (9:17).

9:4–15 The Gibeonite plot to trick Israel worked. Israel's sinful failure occurred because they were not vigilant in prayer to assure that they acted by God's counsel (v. 14; cf. Prov. 3:5, 6).

9:15 Israel precipitously made peace with the Gibeonites (11:19) who lived nearby, even though God had instructed them to eliminate the people of cities in the land (Deut. 7:1, 2). God permitted peace with cities outside (Deut. 20:11–15).

9:21–23 While honoring the pledge of peace with the Gibeonites (v. 19), Joshua made them woodcutters and water carriers because of the deception. This curse extended the perpetual part (v. 23) of "cursed be Canaan" (Gen. 9:26). Gibeon became a part of Benjamin's land area (Josh. 18:25).

Thirty-Five Cities of Joshua's Conquest			
City	**Scripture**	**City**	**Scripture**
Achshaph	12:20	Hormah	12:14
Adullam	12:15	Jarmuth	12:11
Ai	12:9	Jericho	12:9
Aphek	12:18	Jerusalem	12:10
Arad	12:14	Jokneam	12:22
Beeroth	9:17	Kedesh	12:22
Bethel	12:16	Kiriath-jearim	9:17
Chephirah	9:17	Lachish	12:11
Debir	12:13	Lasharon	12:18
Dor	12:23	Libnah	12:15
Eglon	12:12	Madon	12:19
Geder	12:13	Makkedah	10:16, 17, 28; 12:16
Gezer	10:33; 12:12	Megiddo	12:21
Gibeon	9:17	Shimron	12:20
Gilgal	12:23	Taanach	12:21
Hazor	12:19	Tappuah	12:17
Hebron	12:10	Tirzah	12:24
Hepher	12:17		

Later, Joshua consigned Gibeon as one of the Levite towns (21:17). Nehemiah had help from some Gibeonites in rebuilding the walls of Jerusalem (Neh. 3:7).

10:1–11 Gibeon and three other towns (9:17) were attacked by a coalition of five cities. Israel came to the rescue, with God giving the victory (v. 10).

10:11 large hailstones. The hailstones were miraculous. Note their: (1) source, God; (2) size, large; (3) slaughter, more by stones than by sword; (4) selectivity, only on the enemy; (5) swath, "as far as Azekah"; (6) situation, during a trek down a slope and while God caused the sun to stand still; and (7) similarity, to miraculous stones God will fling down during the future wrath (Rev. 16:21).

10:12–14 sun stood still, and the moon stopped. Some say an eclipse hid the sun, keeping its heat from Joshua's tired soldiers, allowing the temperature to cool for battle. Others suppose that it was caused by a local (not universal) refraction of the sun's rays such as the local darkness in Egypt (Ex. 10:21–23). Another view explains it as only language of observation, i.e., it only seemed to Joshua's men that the sun and moon stopped as God helped them do in one, literal, twenty-four-hour day what would normally take longer. Others view it as lavish poetic description, not literal fact. However, such ideas fail to do justice to 10:12–14, and needlessly question God's power as Creator. This is best accepted as an outright, monumental miracle. Joshua, moved by the Lord's will, commanded the sun to delay (Heb., "be still, silent, leave off"). Possibly, the earth actually stopped revolving or, more likely, the sun moved in the same way to keep perfect pace with the battlefield. The moon also temporarily ceased its orbiting. This permitted Joshua's troops time to finish the battle with complete victory (v. 11).

10:13–15 Book of Jasher? Jasher means "upright." It may be the same as the book called Wars of the Lord (Num. 21:14). The book of Jasher is mentioned again in 2 Samuel 1:18, and a portion is recorded in 1:19–27. The book appears to have been a compilation of Hebrew songs in honor of Israel's leaders and exploits in battle.

10:24 feet on the necks. This gesture (1) symbolized victory and (2) promised assurance of future conquest (v. 25).

10:40–43 A summary of Joshua's southern campaign (cf. 9:1–10:43).

10:42 Tribute belongs to the Lord for all the victories, as "in everything give thanks" (1 Thess. 5:18).

C. The Northern Campaign (11:1–15)

11:1 Hazor. A city five miles southwest of Lake Huleh, ten miles north of the Sea of Galilee. King Jabin led a coalition of kings

The MacArthur Study Bible, by John MacArthur (Nashville: Word Publishing, 1997) 316. © 1993 by Thomas Nelson, Inc.

from several city-states in Galilee and to the west against Joshua, whose victory reports in the south had spread northward.

11:2 south . . . in the lowland. This refers to the deep rift of the Jordan River valley to the south of the Lake of Chinneroth (12:3), later called the Sea of Galilee. Chinneroth was probably a town not far north of the lake. The lowland or foothills are an area somewhat west of the Jordan River, toward the Mediterranean Sea. Here also is the plain of Sharon and the heights of Dor, i.e., foothills extending to Mt. Carmel, nearer the Mediterranean coast and Dor, a seaport city.

11:5 Merom. These copious springs, located a few miles southwest of Lake Huleh and about thirteen miles north from the Lake of Chinneroth, provided the northern armies a rendezvous point.

11:6 hamstring. They cut the large sinew or ligament at the back of the hock on the rear leg, crippling the horses and making them useless.

11:8 Greater Sidon. A city on the Phoenician coast, north of Hazor. *Greater* may refer to surrounding areas along with the city itself. **Misrephoth.** This location lay west of Hazor, also on the Mediterranean.

11:12–15 A summary of Joshua's northern campaign (11:1–15).

D. The Summary of Conquests (11:16–12:24)

11:16, 17 Joshua took all this land. The sweeping conquest covered much of Palestine. **mountain country.** In the south, in Judah. **South.** South of the Dead Sea. **Goshen.** Probably the land between Gaza and Gibeon. **lowland.** Or foothills; this refers to an area between the Mediterranean coastal plain and the hills of Judah. **Jordan plain.** The rift valley running south of the Dead Sea all the way to the Red Sea's Gulf of Aqabah. The hill country of Israel is distinct from

that in 11:16, lying in the northern part of Palestine. The conquest reached from Mt. Halak, about six miles south of the Dead Sea, to Mt. Hermon about forty miles northeast from the Lake of Chinneroth.

11:18 war a long time. The conquest took approximately seven years—c. 1405–1398 B.C. (cf. 14:10). Only Gibeon submitted without a fight (v. 19).

11:20 it was of the LORD to harden their hearts. God turned the Canaanites' hearts to fight in order that Israel might be His instrument of judgment to destroy them. They were willfully guilty of rejecting the true God with consequent wickedness, and were as unfit to remain in the land as vomit spewed out of the mouth (Lev. 18:24, 25).

11:21 Anakim. Enemies who lived in the southern area that Joshua had defeated. They descended from Anak ("long-necked"), and were related to the giants who made Israel's spies feel small as grasshoppers by comparison (Num. 13:28–33). Cf. Deuteronomy 2:10, 11, 21. Their territory was later given to Caleb as a reward for his loyalty (14:6–15).

11:22 Anakim . . . Gath. Some of the Anakim remained in Philistine territory, most notably those who preceded Goliath (cf. 1 Sam. 17:4).

11:23 the whole land. Here is a key summary verse for the whole book, which also sums up 11:16–22. How does this relate to 13:1, where God tells Joshua that he did *not* take the whole land? It may mean that the major battles had been fought and supremacy demonstrated, even if further incidents would occur and not every last pocket of potential resistance had yet been rooted out.

12:1–24 the kings . . . defeated. The actual list of thirty-one kings conquered (v. 24) follows and fills out the summary of "the whole land" in 11:16, 17, 23. The roster shows (1) the kings whom "Moses defeated" east of the

Jordan River earlier (vv. 1–6; cf. Num. 21; Deut. 2:24–3:17); then (2) those whom Joshua conquered west of the Jordan River—a summary (7; 8); central kings (9); southern kings (10–16); and northern kings (17–24).

12:24 The conquest of all these kings, covering areas up and down the "whole land" (11:23), was caused by the Lord's faithful help, which fulfilled His Word. God promised the land in His covenant with Abraham (Gen. 12:7), and reaffirmed that He would give victory in conquest (Josh. 1:3, 6).

III. Distributing Portions in the Promised Land (13:1–22:34)

A. Summary of Instructions (13:1–33)

13:1 *Joshua was old.* By this time he was about 95, in comparison to Caleb's 85 years (14:10). In 23:1, he was 110 and near death (24:29).

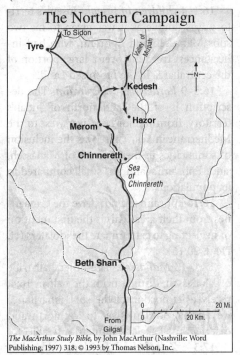

The Northern Campaign

To Sidon
Tyre
Valley of Mizpah
—N—
Kedesh
Merom
Hazor
Chinnereth
Sea of Chinnereth
Beth Shan

0   20 Mi.
0   20 Km.
From Gilgal

The MacArthur Study Bible, by John MacArthur (Nashville: Word Publishing, 1997) 318. © 1993 by Thomas Nelson, Inc.

13:1, 2 *very much land.* Some land had not yet actually been occupied by the Israelites through the previous general victories. Pockets of land in 13:2–6 still lay untouched by specific invasion and occupation (*see note on 11:23*). When Joshua allotted areas to individuals and tribes, they assumed the challenge to drive out lingering resisters; if not, they would disobey God's mandate to be resolute in conquest (Deut. 11:22, 23). Failure to do this thoroughly is a tragic theme in Judges 1.

13:3 *Sihor.* Probably related to the Nile River (Is. 23:3; Jer. 2:18), and possibly a name for that river or an eastern tributary of it. The name could also refer to a seasonal rain trough which runs to the Mediterranean, the Wadi-el-Arish in the desert south of Palestine, northeast of Egypt.

13:7 *divide this land.* God commanded Joshua to devise allotments within boundaries for inheritances as He had prepared for earlier (Num. 32–34). Joshua announced divisions made clear by lot to tribes east of the Jordan (13:8–33), tribes west of the Jordan (Josh. 14–19), Caleb (14:6–15; cf. 15:13–19), his own area (19:49–51), cities of refuge (20:1–9), and Levite towns (ch. 21).

13:22 *Israel also killed . . . Balaam.* This Israelite slaying of the infamous false prophet occurred at an unidentified point during the conquest (cf. 24:9, 10; Num. 21–25; 31:16; 2 Pet. 2:15, 16; Jude 11; Rev. 2:14).

13:33 *to . . . Levi . . . no inheritance.* God did not give this tribe a normal allotment of land. This suited His choice of Levites for the special ministry of the tabernacle service (18:7). God did assign them cities and adjacent lands (14:4; Num. 35:2, 4, 5), scattered at forty-eight places (21:41) throughout all the tribes. This made these religious servants accessible to all the people (cf. ch. 21).

B. West of the Jordan (14:1–19:51)

14:1 *the land of Canaan.* The name for the land west of the Jordan River.

14:5 *so the children of Israel did.* They obeyed in some things, but not in all (*see note on 13:1, 2*).

14:6–9 *Caleb.* This passage reviews what is also recounted in Numbers 13 and 14. This includes a celebration of God's faithfulness (vv. 7–11), and Caleb's specific inheritance (vv. 12–15). Later, he conquered the area (15:13, 14) and conferred blessings on Othniel and his daughter (15:15–19).

14:10 *eighty-five years old.* Given that: (1) Caleb was forty at Kadesh Barnea, (2) the Israelites had wandered in the wilderness thirty-eight years, and (3) the conquering of the land took seven years (c. 1405–1398 B.C.), Caleb was now eighty-five years old.

14:12–14 Based on His promise (v. 9), God granted Caleb's desire for Hebron because of his faithfulness to believe that God would give the land to the Israelites as He promised.

14:15 *Anakim.* See 15:13; *see note on 11:21.*

15:1–12 *the lot of . . . Judah.* The tribe's southern boundary (v. 1) ran from the lower tip of the Salt Sea or Dead Sea in a sweep through the desert over to the wadi, the brook of Egypt (*see note on 13:3*), and along it to the Mediterranean Sea. The eastern limit (v. 5) ran the length of the Salt Sea itself. On the north, it extended from the north end of the Salt Sea by various lines working to the Mediterranean (vv. 5–11). The Mediterranean coastline served as the western border (v. 12).

15:17 *Othniel.* A conqueror like Caleb, who was his father-in-law, he would later be a judge in Israel (Judg. 3:9–11).

15:18, 19 Caleb's daughter sought blessing and exercised faith for it—like father, like daughter.

15:20–62 *the inheritance of . . . Judah.* Judah's cities are grouped in four areas: south (vv. 20–32); lowland or foothills over near the Mediterranean (vv. 33–47); hilly central region (vv. 48–60); Judean wilderness dropping eastward down to the Dead Sea (vv. 61, 62).

15:63 *Jebusites.* The inhabitants of Jerusalem were descendants from the third son of Canaan (Gen. 10:15, 16; 15:21). Joshua killed their king, who had joined a pact against Gibeon (Josh. 10). Israelites called the area "Jebus" until David ordered Joab and his soldiers to capture the city (2 Sam. 5:6, 7) and made it his capital. Judges 1:8, 21 show that the Israelites conquered Jebus and burned it, but the Jebusites later regained control until David's day. Melchizedek had been a very early king (Gen. 14), a believer in the true God, when the site was "Salem" (cf. Ps. 76:2, "Salem" is "Jerusalem").

16:1–4 *children of Joseph.* Joseph's territory was double as it was given to his two sons Manasseh and Ephraim, who had inheritances stretching over a large portion of the central area in the Promised Land.

16:5–9 *border of . . . Ephraim.* The description is of the land north of Judah's territory, from the Jordan River west to the Mediterranean Sea. There was the inclusion of some cities in the territory of Manasseh, since Ephraim's land was small compared to its population.

16:10 Ephraim did not drive the Canaanites from their area. This is the first mention of neglecting to exterminate the idolaters (cf. Deut. 20:16).

17:1–18 *Manasseh.* The other half-tribe of Manasseh, distinct from the half in 16:4, received its portion of the split inheritance west of the Jordan River to the north and east near the Lake of Chinneroth (Galilee).

17:3–6 *Zelophehad.* In Manasseh's tribe, this man had no sons as heirs, but his five daughters received the inheritance. God directed Moses to give this right to women (Num. 27:1–11, cited in v. 4).

17:12–18 *children of Manasseh.* Tribesmen of Manasseh complained that Joshua did not allot them sufficient land for their numbers and that the Canaanites were too tough for them to drive out altogether. He permitted them extra land in forested hills that they could clear. Joshua told them that they could drive out the Canaanites because God had promised to be with them in victory against chariots (Deut. 20:1).

18:1 *Shiloh.* Israel as a whole, having had their first camp at Gilgal (4:20; 5:9), converged on Shiloh for worship at the tabernacle. Shiloh, about nine miles north of Bethel and twenty miles north of Jerusalem, remained the center of spiritual attention, as in Judges 18:31 and 1 Samuel 1:3. Due to Israel's sin, God would later let the Philistines devastate Israel at Shiloh and capture the ark (1 Sam. 4:10, 17). He would also later use Shiloh as an example of judgment (Jer. 7:12).

18:8, 10. Seven tribes were still to receive land (v. 2). Joshua obtained from their twenty-one surveyor scouts (vv. 2–4) descriptions of the seven areas of land, then cast lots to decide the choices. The high priest Eleazar served him, seeking God's will by casting lots (19:51). This was not some act of mere chance, but a means God used to reveal His will (*see note on Prov. 16:33*).

18:11–28 *the lot of . . . Benjamin.* This inheritance lay between Judah's allotment and Ephraim's, and embraced Jerusalem (v. 28).

19:1–9 *Simeon.* This area was a southern portion of Judah's territory, since that allotment was more than Judah needed (v. 9).

19:10–16 *Zebulun.* This allotment lay west of the Lake of Chinneroth (Sea of Galilee) and ran to the Mediterranean Sea.

19:17–23 *Issachar.* Basically, the area ran

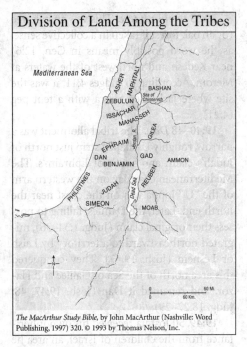

Division of Land Among the Tribes

The MacArthur Study Bible, by John MacArthur (Nashville: Word Publishing, 1997) 320. © 1993 by Thomas Nelson, Inc.

just below the Sea of Galilee from the Jordan River west over to Mt. Tabor, circling southwest almost to Megiddo, north of Manasseh's portion.

19:24–31 *Asher.* This territory was a long, broad strip flanking the Mediterranean Sea on the west, then Naphtali's and Zebulun's claims on the east, running south to Manasseh's. It reached from Mt. Carmel in the south to the area of Tyre in the north.

19:32–39 *Naphtali.* This region took in a long stretch of land with a border at the northern edge of all the Israelite inheritances, a line on the west dividing it from Asher, southward to follow Zebulun's northern border. Then it struck eastward toward the Sea of Galilee with land to the west alongside that sea and down to Issachar's claim, over to the Jordan River. The eastern line ran northward, including the city of Hazor and also Dan, then swung north of Dan. Jesus' Galilean ministry would take place largely in this area (Is. 9:1, 2; Matt. 4:13–17).

19:33 terebinth tree. This was an oak tree (or an oak forest if taken in a collective sense, as the word possibly means in Gen. 12:6) near Kedesh and northwest of the waters at Merom. According to Judges 4:11, it was the site where Jael killed Sisera with a tent peg (4:21).

19:40–48 Dan. The tribal allotment was a narrow, roughly U-shaped strip just north of Judah's claim and south of Ephraim's. The Mediterranean coast lay on the western arm of the "U." Joppa was on the coast near the north end. Later, the Danites, failing to possess their original claim (Judg. 1:34–36), migrated northeastward to a territory by Laish or Leshem (Josh. 19:47). They conquered this area north of the Sea of Galilee and Hazor, and renamed it Dan (Josh. 19:47, 48; Judg. 18:27–29).

19:49, 50 Joshua received his own inheritance from the children of Israel, an area he preferred in the hills of his tribe, Ephraim (Num. 13:8). He built a city, Timnath Serah, about sixteen miles southwest of Shechem. His inheritance was an intrinsic part of God's promise to him, as was also Caleb's inheritance (Num. 14:30).

C. Cities of Refuge (20:1–9)

20:2–9 cities of refuge. Moses had spoken God's Word to name six cities in Israel as refuge centers. A person who inadvertently killed another person could flee to the nearest of these for protection (cf. Num. 35:9–34). Three cities of refuge lay west of the Jordan River, and three lay to the east, each reachable in a day for those in its area. The slayer could flee there to escape pursuit by a family member seeking to exact private justice. Authorities at the refuge protected him and escorted him to a trial. If found innocent, he was guarded at the refuge until the death of the current high priest, a kind of

statute of limitations (Josh. 20:6). He could then return home. If found guilty of murder, he suffered appropriate punishment.

D. Cities of the Levites (21:1–45)

21:1–3 cities to dwell in. God had given Moses His direction to provide forty-eight cities for the Levites, dotted throughout Israel's tribal allotments (Num. 35:1–8). Six were to be the cities of refuge (Num. 35:6).

21:3–42 the children of Israel gave to the Levites. These forty-eight cities (v. 41) were for various branches of the Levite people to live in and have pasture for their livestock (v. 42). People of the other tribes donated the areas, each site giving the Levites a vantage point from which to minister spiritually to the people nearby. In fairness, larger tribes devoted more land, smaller ones less (Num. 35:8). Only the Kohathites were priests, with

The Cities of Refuge

The MacArthur Study Bible, by John MacArthur (Nashville: Word Publishing, 1997) 327. © 1993 by Thomas Nelson, Inc.

other branches of Levites assisting in various roles of ritual worship and manual labors.

21:4 Kohathites. Under God's guiding wisdom, these received thirteen city areas in the vicinity of Jerusalem or at a reasonable distance within allotments of Judah, Benjamin, and Simeon. This would give them access to carry out priestly functions where God would later have the ark moved and the temple situated (2 Sam. 6).

21:43–45 So the LORD gave to Israel all the land. This sums up God's fulfillment of His covenant promise to give Abraham's people the land (Gen. 12:7; Josh. 1:2, 5–9). God also kept His Word in giving the people rest (Deut. 12:9, 10). In a valid sense, the Canaanites were in check, under military conquest as God had pledged (Josh. 1:5), not posing an immediate threat. Not every enemy had been driven out, however, leaving some to stir up trouble later. God's people failed to exercise their responsibility and possess their land to the full degree in various areas.

E. East of the Jordan (22:1–34)

22:1 Reubenites . . . Gadites . . . Manasseh. The tribes from east of the Jordan River had helped their people conquer the land west of the river. Now, they were ready to go back to their families to the east.

22:4 Moses . . . gave you. Clearance from Moses and Joshua for these tribes to possess land east of the Jordan was of God (v. 9; 24:8; Num. 32:30–33).

22:10–34 an altar . . . by the Jordan. The special altar built by the two and one-half tribes near the river, though well-meant, aroused suspicions among the western tribes. They feared rebellion against the Shiloh altar that served all the tribes in unity. When challenged, men of the eastern tribes explained their motives to follow the true God, be in unity with the rest of Israel, and

not be regarded as outsiders. The explanation met with the other Israelites' approval.

IV. RETAINING THE PROMISED LAND (23:1–24:28)

A. The First Speech by Joshua (23:1–16)

23:1 Joshua was old. A long time had passed since he led the conquest c. 1405–1398 B.C.; Joshua had grown old, and was 110 when he died (24:29), c. 1383 B.C. (*see note on 13:1*).

23:5 the LORD . . . will expel them. God was ready to help His people drive the remaining Canaanites out so they could possess their claims fully. Such moves needed to be gradual (Deut. 7:22), but determined, in obedience to God.

23:7, 8 The dangers from being incomplete about possessing all the land included that of intermingling with the godless, as in marriages (v. 12), and adopting their gods, thus drifting from worshiping the true God. The Canaanites would become snares, traps, scourges, and thorns, causing the Israelites to lose the land eventually (vv. 13, 15, 16).

23:15, 16 This actually occurred 800 years later, when Babylon exiled the Israelites c. 605–586 B.C. (cf. 2 Kin. 24; 25).

B. The Second Speech by Joshua (24:1–28)

24:1–25 It was time for worship and thanksgiving because of all God had done leading up to and including the conquest of Canaan.

24:1–5 Joshua reviewed the history recorded in Genesis 11 to Exodus 15.

24:2 the River. The Euphrates, where Abraham's family had previously lived. It is clear here that God's calling of Abraham out to Himself was also a call out of idolatry, as He does with others (cf. 1 Thess. 1:9).

24:6–13 Joshua reviewed the history recorded in Exodus 12 to Joshua 22.

24:8, 15 *Amorites.* Sometimes, this is used as a general term for the entire pagan populace (cf. v. 11) in Canaan, as elsewhere (Gen. 15:16; Judg. 1:34, 35). At other times, the name has a narrower reference to people of the hill country (Num. 13:29), distinct from others.

24:9, 10 *Balaam.* See note on Joshua 13:22 about the unsavory nature of Balaam in Numbers 21–25.

24:12 *I sent the hornet before you.* This description, as in Exodus 23:28, is a picturesque figure (cf. 23:13) portraying God's own fighting to assist Israel (23:3, 5, 10, 18). This awesome force put the enemy to flight, as the feared hornets literally can do (Deut. 7:20, 21).

24:15 *choose . . . this day whom you will serve.* Joshua's fatherly model (reminiscent of Abraham's, Gen. 18:19) was for himself and his family to serve the Lord, not false gods. He called others in Israel to this, and they committed themselves to serve the Lord also (vv. 21, 24).

24:18 The population joined Joshua in claiming total commitment to serve the Lord (cf. Ex. 19:8).

24:26 *Book of the Law.* Joshua expands the five books of Moses, as the canon of revealed Scripture develops. ***by the sanctuary.*** God's tabernacle, including the ark of the covenant, was at Shiloh (21:2). The stone of witness by the holy place (sanctuary) was at Shechem (24:1). This holy place is not a formal tent or building, but a sacred place by a tree (cf. Gen. 12:6; 35:4), just as other places had significance in the past for worship of God (Gen. 21:33).

V. POSTSCRIPT (24:29–33)

24:29–33 *Joshua . . . Eleazar.* Three prominent leaders were buried as the conquering generation was passing on: Joseph, Joshua, and the high priest Eleazar.

24:29 *one hundred and ten years old.* This was c. 1383 B.C. (cf. 14:7–10).

24:31 Faithfulness to God extended only one generation (cf. Judg. 2:6–13).

24:32 *The bones of Joseph.* These remains had been carried by the Israelites in the Exodus (Ex. 13:19) as Joseph had made them promise (Gen. 50:25). He wanted his bones to lie in the land of covenant pledge. So now his people laid them to rest at Shechem, in the land God had promised to Abraham (Gen. 12:7).

Further Study

Campbell, Donald. *Joshua,* in The Bible Knowledge Commentary—OT. Wheaton, Ill.: Victor, 1985.

Davis, John J. and John C. Whitcomb. *A History of Israel from Conquest to Exile.* Grand Rapids: Baker, 1980.

Woudstra, M. H. *The Book of Joshua.* Grand Rapids: Eerdmans, 1981.

THE BOOK OF
JUDGES

Title

The book bears the fitting name *Judges,* which refers to unique leaders God gave to His people for preservation against their enemies (2:16–19). The Hebrew title means "deliverers" or "saviors," as well as judges (cf. Deut. 16:18; 17:9; 19:17). Twelve such judges arose before Samuel; then Eli and Samuel increased the count to fourteen. God Himself is the higher Judge (11:27). Judges spans about 350 years from Joshua's successful conquest (c. 1398 B.C.) until Eli and Samuel judged prior to the establishment of the monarchy (c. 1051 B.C.).

Author and Date

No author is named in the book, but the Jewish Talmud identifies Samuel, a key prophet who lived at the time these events took place and could have personally summed up the era (cf. 1 Sam. 10:25). The time was earlier than David's capture of Jerusalem c. 1004 B.C. (2 Sam. 5:6, 7) since Jebusites still controlled the site (Judg. 1:21). Also, the writer deals with a time before a king ruled (17:6; 18:1; 21:25). Since Saul began his reign c. 1051 B.C., a time shortly after his rule began is probably when Judges was written.

Background and Setting

Judges is a tragic sequel to Joshua. In Joshua, the people were obedient to God in conquering the land. In Judges, they were disobedient, idolatrous, and often defeated. Judges 1:1–3:6 focuses on the closing days of the Book of Joshua. Judges 2:6–9 gives a review of Joshua's death (cf. Josh. 24:28–31). The account describes seven distinct cycles of Israel's drifting away from the Lord, starting even before Joshua's death and with a full departure into apostasy afterward.

Five basic reasons are evident for these cycles of Israel's moral and spiritual decline: (1) disobedience toward God in failing to drive the Canaanites out of the land (Judg. 1:19, 21, 35); (2) idolatry (2:12); (3) intermarriage with wicked Canaanites (3:5, 6); (4) not obeying the judges (2:17); and (5) turning away from God after the death of the judges (2:19).

A four-part sequence repeatedly occurred in this phase of Israel's history: (1) Israel's departure from God; (2) God's chastisement in permitting military defeat and subjugation; (3) Israel's prayer for deliverance; and (4) God raising up "judges," either civil or sometimes local military champions, who led in shaking off the oppressors. Fourteen judges arose, six of them military judges (Othniel, Ehud, Deborah, Gideon, Jephthah, and Samson). Two men were of special significance for contrast in spiritual leadership: (1) Eli, judge and high priest (not a good example) and (2) Samuel, judge, priest, and prophet (a good example).

Historical and Theological Themes

Judges is thematic rather than chronological; foremost among its themes is God's power and covenant mercy in graciously delivering the Israelites from the consequences of their failures, which were suffered for sinful compromise (cf. 2:18, 19; 21:25). In seven historical periods of sin to salvation (cf. Introduction: Outline), God compassionately delivered His people throughout the different geographical areas of tribal inheritances which He had earlier given through Joshua (Josh. 13–22). The apostasy covered the whole land, as indicated by the fact that each area is specifically identified: southern (3:7–31); northern (4:1–5:31); central (6:1–10:5); eastern (10:6–12:15); and western (13:1–16:31).

God's power to rescue shines brightly against the dark backdrop of pitiful human compromise and sometimes bizarre twists of sin, as in the final summary (Judg. 17–21). The last verse (21:25) sums up the account: "In those days there was no king in Israel; everyone did what was right in his own eyes."

Interpretive Challenges
The most stimulating challenges are: (1) how to view men's violent acts against enemies or fellow countrymen, whether with God's approval or without it; (2) God's use of leaders who, at times, do His will and, at times, follow their own sinful impulses (Gideon, Eli, Jephthah, Samson); (3) how to view Jephthah's vow and offering of his daughter (11:30–40); and (4) how to resolve God's sovereign will with His providential working in spite of human sin (cf. 14:4).

The chronology of the various judges in different sectors of the land raises questions about how much time passed and how the time totals can fit into the entire time span from the Exodus (c. 1445 B.C.) to Solomon's fourth year, c. 967/966 B.C., which is said to be 480 years (1 Kin. 6:1; *see note on Judg.*

11:26). A reasonable explanation is that the deliverances and years of rest under the judges in distinct parts of the land included overlaps, so that some of them did not run consecutively, but rather concurrently during the 480 years. Paul's estimate of "about 450" years in Acts 13:20 is an approximation.

Outline

I. INTRODUCTION AND SUMMARY: THE DISOBEDIENCE OF ISRAEL (1:1–3:6)

A. Incomplete Conquest over the Canaanites (1:1–36)

1:1 *after the death of Joshua.* C. 1383 B.C. (cf. Josh. 14:7–10 with Josh. 24:29). Descriptions of the book's setting in Judges 1 and 2 vary between times after Joshua's death and flashbacks summarizing conditions while he was alive (e.g. 2:2–6). Compare Joshua 1:1, "After the death of Moses."

1:2 *Judah shall go up.* This tribe received God's first go-ahead to push for a more thorough conquest of its territory. The reason probably rested in God's choice that Judah be the leader among the tribes (Gen. 49:8–12; 1 Chr. 5:1, 2) and set the example for them in the other territories.

1:6, 7 *cut off his thumbs and big toes.* Removing the king's thumbs hampered effective use of a weapon; taking off his big toes rendered footing unreliable in battle. Thus, the king was rendered unable to fight or rule effectively in the future. The Lord Himself is nowhere said to endorse this tactic, but it was an act of retributive justice for what Adoni-Bezek had done to others. It appears from his confession that he was acknowledging that he deserved it.

1:12–15 *Caleb said.* This repeats the account of Caleb and his family (cf. Josh. 15:13–19)

1:16 *the City of Palms.* Since Jericho was destroyed in the invasion, this refers to the area around Jericho, an oasis of springs and palms (Deut. 34:3).

1:19 *they could not drive out. They* of Judah could not. They had been promised by Joshua that they could conquer the lowland (Josh. 17:16, 18) and should have remembered Joshua 11:4–9. This is a recurring failure among the tribes to rise to full trust and obedience for victory by God's power. Set-

tling for less than what God was able to give (Josh. 1:6–9) began even in Joshua's day (Judg. 2:2–6) and earlier (Num. 13; 14). In another sense, God permitted Israel's enemies to hold out as a test to display whether His people would obey Him (2:20–23; 3:1, 4). Another factor involved keeping the wild animal count from rising too fast (Deut. 7:22).

1:20 *sons of Anak.* Anak was an early inhabitant of central Canaan near Hebron from whom came an entire group of unusually tall people called the Anakim (Deut. 2:10). They frightened the ten spies (Num. 13:33; Deut. 9:2), but were finally driven out of the land by Caleb (Josh. 14:12–15; 15:13, 14; 21:11) with the exception of some who resettled with the Philistines (Josh. 11:22). "The sons of Anak" was used as a term equivalent to "the Anakim."

1:34 *Amorites forced . . . Dan.* Like all other tribes, Dan had a territory given to them, but they failed to claim the power of God to conquer that territory. Later, they capitulated even more by accepting defeat and migrating to another territory in the north, becoming idolatrous (Judg. 18).

B. The Decline and Judgment of Israel (2:1–3:6)

2:1 *the Angel of the* LORD. One of three preincarnate theophanies by the Lord Jesus Christ in Judges (cf. 6:11–18; 13:3–23). This same divine messenger had earlier led Israel out of Egypt (cf. Ex. 14:19). *See note on Exodus 3:2. I will never break My covenant with you.* God would be faithful until the end, but the people would forfeit blessing for trouble, due to their disobedience (cf. v. 3).

2:10 *another generation . . . did not know.* The first people in the land had vivid recollections of all the miracles and judgments and were devoted to faith, duty, and purity. The new generation of Israelites were ignorant of the experiences of their parents and yielded more easily to corruption. To a marked degree, the people of this new generation were not true believers, and were not obedient to the God of miracles and victory. Still, many of the judges did genuinely know the Lord, and some who did not live by faith eventually threw themselves on God's mercy during oppressions.

2:12 they followed other gods. Idol worship, such as the golden calf in the wilderness (Ex. 32), flared up again. Spurious gods of Canaan were plentiful. El was the supreme Canaanite deity, a god of uncontrolled lust and a bloody tyrant, as shown in writings found at Ras Shamra in north Syria. His name means "strong, powerful." Baal, son and successor of El, was "lord of heaven," a farm god of rain and storm; his name means "lord, possessor." His cult at Phoenicia included animal sacrifices, ritual meals, and licentious dances. Chambers catered to sacred prostitution by men and women (cf. 1 Kin. 14:23, 24; 2 Kin. 23:7). Anath, sister-wife of Baal, also called Ashtoreth (Astarte), patroness of sex and war, was called "virgin" and "holy" but was actually a "sacred prostitute." Many other gods besides these also attracted worship.

2:14 the anger of the Lord was hot. Calamities designed as chastisement brought discipline intended to lead the people to repentance.

2:16 the Lord raised up judges. A *judge* or deliverer was distinct from a judge in the English world today. Such a leader guided military expeditions against foes (as here) and arbitrated judicial matters (cf. 4:5). There was no succession or national rule. They were local deliverers, lifted up to leadership by God when the deplorable condition of Israel in the region around them prompted God to rescue the people.

3:1 nations . . . left. The purpose was to

Key Word

Judge: 2:16, 18; 10:2; 11:27; 12:9, 11; 15:20; 16:31—this Hebrew word for *judge* means "to deliver" or "to rule." The judges of Israel had a wide range of responsibilities. Like their modern counterparts, Old Testament judges could decide controversies and hand down verdicts (Ex. 18:16). These judges were also involved in the execution of their judgment in both vindicating the righteous (Ps. 26:1) and destroying the wicked (Ex. 7:3). Many judges were God's appointed military leaders who, empowered by God's Spirit (6:34; 15:14), fought Israel's oppressors and thereby delivered the people. Later, Israel's king functioned as the national judge (1 Sam. 8:5). Ultimately, Israel's perfect Judge is God. He alone is capable of flawlessly judging the wicked and delivering the righteous (Is. 11:4).

use them to test (cf. v. 4) and discipline the sinful Israelites, as well as to aid the young in learning the art of war.

3:5 See notes on 1:1–20.

3:6 See note on 1:19. The Israelites failed God's test, being enticed into (1) marriages with Canaanites and (2) worship of their gods. Disobedience was repeated frequently through the centuries, and led God to use the Assyrians (2 Kin. 17) and Babylonians (2 Kin. 24; 25) to expel them from the land gained here.

II. A Selected History of the Judges: The Deliverance of Israel (3:7–16:31)

A. First Period: Othniel vs. Mesopotamians (3:7–11)

3:10 The Spirit of the Lord came. Certain judges were expressly said to have the Spirit of the Lord come upon them (6:34; 11:29; 13:25;

14:6, 19; 15:14); others, apparently, also had this experience. This is a common OT expression signifying a unique act of God which conferred power and wisdom for victory. But this did not guarantee that the will of God would be done in absolutely all details, as is apparent with Gideon (8:24–27, 30), Jephthah (11:34–40), and Samson (16:1).

B. Second Period: Ehud and Shamgar vs. Moabites (3:12–31)

3:20 *I have a message from God for you.* Ehud claimed he came to do God's will in answer to prayer (v. 15). Calmly and confidently, Ehud acted and, later, credited the defeat of the wicked king to God (v. 28; cf. Ps. 75:6, 7, 10; Dan. 4:25), though it was by the human means of Ehud, just as Jael used a hammer and tent peg (4:21), and Israel's armies used the sword (4:16). By God's power, Ehud's army would kill a greater number (v. 29). Men's evil provokes God's judgment (Lev. 18:25).

3:24 *He is . . . attending to his needs.* The dead king's servants guessed he was indisposed in privacy, literally "covering his feet," a euphemism for bathroom functions.

3:31 *Shamgar.* His extraordinary exploit causes one to think of Samson (15:16). *an ox goad.* This was a stout stick about eight to ten feet long and six inches around, with a sharp metal tip to prod or turn oxen. The other end was a flat, curved blade for cleaning a plow.

C. Third Period: Deborah vs. Canaanites (4:1–5:31)

4:4 *Deborah, a prophetess.* She was an unusual woman of wisdom and influence who did the tasks of a judge, except for military leadership. God can use women mightily for civil, religious, or other tasks, e.g., Huldah the prophetess (2 Kin. 22:14), Philip's daugh-

ters in prophesying (Acts 21:8, 9), and Phoebe a deaconess (Rom. 16:1). Deborah's rise to such a role is the exception in the book because of Barak's failure to show the courage to lead courageously (vv. 8, 14). God rebuked his cowardice by the pledge that a woman would kill Sisera (v. 9).

4:19, 20 *she . . . gave him a drink, and covered him.* Usually, this was the strongest pledge of protection possible.

4:21 *a tent peg and . . . a hammer.* Jael's bold stroke in a tent rather than on a battlefield draws Deborah's and Barak's praise (5:24–27). Her strength and skill had no doubt been toughened by a common Bedouin duty of hammering down pegs to secure tents, or striking them loose to take down tents.

5:1 *sang on that day.* The song (vv. 1–31) was in tribute to God for victory in Judges 4:13–25. Various songs praise God for His help, e.g., Moses' (Ex. 15), David's (2 Sam. 23:1–7), and the Lamb's (Rev. 15:3, 4).

5:10 *white donkeys.* Because of this unusual color, they were a prize of kings and the rich.

5:11 *Far from the noise of the archers, among the watering places.* The wells were at a little distance from towns in the east, away from the battles and often places for pleasant reflection.

5:14 *roots were in Amalek.* Currently, Ephraim as a tribe took the central hill area, which the Amalekites had once held tenaciously.

5:17 *why did Dan remain on ships?* Danites migrated from their territory to Laish north of the Lake of Chinneroth (Sea of Galilee) before the Israelite triumph of Judges 4, though details of it are not given until Judges 18. They became involved with Phoenicians of the northwest in ship commerce (cf. Joppa as a coastal city, Josh.

The Judges of Israel

Judge and Tribe	Scripture References	Period of Oppressors	Oppression/Rest
(1) Othniel (Judah) Son of Kenaz, younger brother of Caleb	Judg. 1:11–15; 3:1–11; Josh. 15:16–19;	Cushan-Rishathaim, king of Mesopotamia	8 years/40 years
(2) Ehud (Benjamin) Son of Gera	Judg. 3:12–4:1	Eglon, king of Moab; Ammonites; Amalekites	18 years/80 years
(3) Shamgar (Perhaps foreign) Son of Anath	Judg. 3:31; 5:6	Philistines	Not given/Not given
(4) Deborah (Ephraim), Barak (Naphtali) Son of Abinoam	Judg. 4:1–5:31 Heb. 11:32	Jabin, king of Canaan; Sisera commander of the army	20 years/40 years
(5) Gideon (Manasseh) Son of Joash the Abiezrite. Also called: Jerubbaal (6:32; 7:1); Jerubbesheth (2 Sam. 11:21)	Judg. 6:1–8:32 Heb. 11:32	Midianites; Amalekites "People of the East"	7 years/40 years
(6) Abimelech (Manasseh) Son of Gideon by a concubine	Judg. 8:33–9:57	Civil war	Abimelech ruled over Israel 3 years
(7) Tola (Issachar) Son of Puah	Judg. 10:1, 2		Judged Israel 23 years
(8) Jair (Gilead-Manasseh)	Judg. 10:3–5		Judged Israel 22 years
(9) Jephthah (Gilead-Manasseh) Son of Gilead by a harlot	Judg. 10:6–12:7 Heb. 11:32	Philistines; Ammonites Civil war with the Ephraimites	18 years/ Judged Israel 6 years
(10) Ibzan (Judah or Zebulun) (Bethlehem-Zebulun; cf. Josh. 19:15)	Judg. 12:8–10		Judged Israel 7 years
(11) Elon (Zebulun)	Judg. 12:11, 12		Judged Israel 10 years
(12) Abdon (Ephraim) Son of Hillel	Judg. 12:13–15		Judges Israel 8 years
(13) Samson (Dan) Son of Manoah	Judg. 13:1–16:31 Heb. 11:32	Philistines	40 years/Judged Israel 20 years

The MacArthur Study Bible, by John MacArthur (Nashville: Word Publishing, 1997) 339. © 1993 by Thomas Nelson, Inc.

19:46). As with some other tribes, they failed to make the trek to assist in the battle of Judges 4.

5:20 *stars . . . fought.* A poetic way to say that God used these heavenly bodies to help Israel. They are bodies representing and synonymous with the heavens, the sky from which He sent a powerful storm and flood (cf. "torrent" of the Kishon River, v. 21) that swept Syrians from their chariots. God also hid the stars by clouds, decreasing Syrian effectiveness due to darkness.

5:24–27 Though this act was murder and a breach of honor, likely motivated by Jael's desire for favor with the conquering Israelites, and though it was without regard for God on her part, God's overruling providence caused great blessing to flow from it. Thus, the words of verses 24–27 are in the victory song.

5:31 The intercessory prayer committed to God's will ends a song that has other aspects: (1) blessing God (v. 2); (2) praise (v. 3); (3) affirming God's work in tribute (vv. 4, 20); and (4) voicing God's curse (v. 23).

D. Fourth Period: Gideon vs. Midianites (6:1–8:32)

6:1 *Midian.* These wandering herdsmen from east of the Red Sea had been dealt a severe blow in Moses' time (Num. 31:1–18) and still resented the Israelites. They became the worst scourge yet to afflict Israel.

6:8 *the LORD sent a prophet.* He used (1) prophets in isolated cases before Samuel, (2) the band of prophets Samuel probably founded (1 Sam. 10:5), and, later, (3) such prophets as Elijah, Elisha, and the writing prophets—major and minor. Here, the prophet is sent to bring the divine curse because of their infidelity (v. 10).

6:11 *the Angel.* This angel (lit. "messenger") of the Lord is identified as "the LORD" Himself (vv. 14, 16, 23, 25, 27). Cf. Genesis 16:7–14; 18:1; 32:24–30 for other appearances. *See note on Exodus 3:2).* ***Gideon threshed wheat in the winepress . . . to hide it.*** This indicated a situation of serious distress; also, it indicated a small amount of grain. This is clear because he is doing it rather than having cattle tread it. It is on bare ground or in the winepress rather than on a threshing floor made of wood, and is done remotely under a tree out of view. The fear of the Midianites caused this.

6:13 Gideon's language indicates a weak theology. The very chastisements of God were proof of His care for and presence with Israel. Cf. Hebrews 12:3–11.

6:17 Like Moses (Ex. 33), Gideon desired a sign; in both incidents, revelation was so rare and wickedness so prevalent that they desired full assurance. God graciously gave it.

6:18–23 In the realization of the presence of God, the sensitive sinner is conscious of great guilt. Fire from God further filled Gideon with awe and even the fear of death. When he saw the Lord, he knew the Lord had also seen him in his fallenness. Thus, he feared the death that sinners should die before Holy God. But God graciously promised life (v. 23). For a similar reaction to the presence of God, see Manoah in 13:22, 23 (cf. Ezek. 1:26–28; Is. 6:1–9; Rev. 1:17).

6:27 *he feared.* Very real human fear and wise precaution interplays with trust in an all-sufficient God.

6:32 Jerubaal (lit. "let Baal contend") became a fitting and honorable second name for Gideon (7:1; 8:29; 9:1, 2). This was a bold rebuke to the non-existent deity, who was utterly unable to respond.

6:36–40 Gideon's two requests for signs in the fleece should be viewed as weak faith; even Gideon recognized this when he said "Do not be angry with me" (v. 39) since God had already specifically promised His presence and victory (vv. 12, 14, 16). But they were also legitimate requests for confirmation of victory against seemingly impossible odds (6:5; 7:2, 12). God nowhere reprimanded Gideon, but was very compassionate in giving what his inadequacy requested. In 7:10–15, God volunteered a sign to boost Gideon's faith. He should have believed God's promise in 7:9, but he needed bolstering, so God graciously gave it without chastisement.

7:2 The people ... are too many. Those of faith, though inadequate by human weakness, gain victory only through God's power (cf. 2 Cor. 3:5; 4:7; 12:7–9). Three hundred men win against an incredible Midianite host (Judg. 7:7, 16–25). God gains the glory by making the outcome conspicuously His act and, thus, no sinful pride is cultivated.

7:5 Everyone who laps. Soldiers who lapped as a dog, scooping water with their hands as a dog uses its tongue, were chosen; in contrast, those who sank to their knees to drink were rejected. No reason for such distinction is given, so that it showed nothing about their ability as soldiers. It was merely a way to divide the crowd. Their abilities as soldiers had no bearing on the victory anyway, since the enemy soldiers killed themselves and fled without engaging Gideon's men at all.

7:10 if you are afraid. God recognized Gideon's normal fear since he was the commander. God encouraged him to take his servant as protection. *See note on 6:36–40.*

7:15 Arise. God said this in 7:9. Newly infused with courage, Gideon is now in step with the Lord.

7:16 Trumpets and torches, at first concealed within clay pitchers, were suddenly displayed at the most startling moment. The shocking impression, caused by blaring noise from the always terrible shouts of Is-

rael (cf. Num. 28:21), and sudden lights surrounding the sleeping hosts, shattered the stillness of the night and conveyed one idea: Each light could mean a legion behind it; thus, they believed an incredible host had moved in to catch the awaking army in a death trap.

7:18 The sword of the LORD and of Gideon! Here was a demonstration of the power of God in harmony with the obedience of man. Such shouts reminded the enemies that the threat of the sword of Gideon and of God was for real. The impression was one of doom and terror, shock and awe.

7:19 beginning . . . middle watch. About 10 P.M.

7:22 every man's sword against his companion. Panic followed shock. Every soldier was on his own, in desperate retreat. In the darkness and crash of sounds, the soldiers were unable to distinguish friend from enemy; and with their swords, they slashed a path of escape through their own men.

8:2 gleaning of the grapes of Ephraim. Ephraim resented being slighted in the call to battle, but was placated by Gideon's compliment. His figures of speech implied that Ephraimite capital punishment of the two fleeing Midianite leaders (7:25) was "the vintage of Ephraim," to use an image drawn from their grape horticulture. It played a more strategic role than taking part in "the vintage of Abiezer," the suicide of the enemy under Gideon's leadership (cf. v. 3).

8:7 thorns. Gideon's threatened discipline of Succoth's leaders for refusing to help their brothers came due. He had them dragged under heavy weights over thorns and briers, which painfully tore their bodies. This was a cruel torture to which ancient captives were often subjected. He did it on his return, not wanting to delay the pursuit (v. 16).

8:9 tower. They probably had defiantly

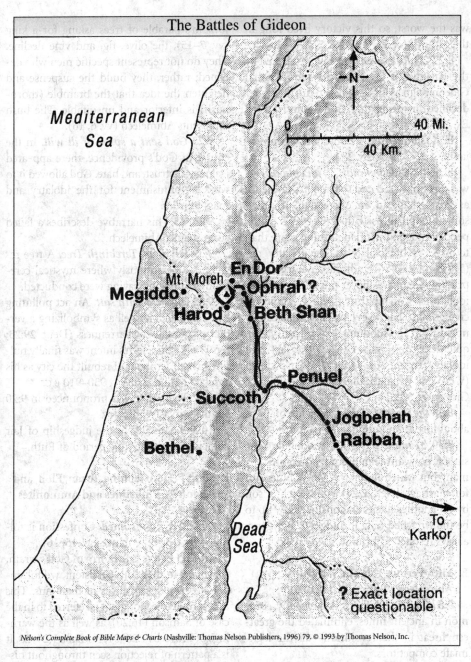

The Battles of Gideon

Mediterranean Sea

Mt. Moreh

En Dor

Megiddo

Ophrah?

Harod

Beth Shan

Penuel

Succoth

Jogbehah

Rabbah

Bethel

Dead Sea

To Karkor

? Exact location questionable

0   40 Mi.

0   40 Km.

-N-

Nelson's Complete Book of Bible Maps & Charts (Nashville: Thomas Nelson Publishers, 1996) 79. © 1993 by Thomas Nelson, Inc.

boasted of their strength and defensibility because of the tower. He kept his promise and more (v. 17).

8:20 Jether . . . kill them! Gideon desired to place a great honor on his son by killing the enemies of Israel and of God.

8:21 killed Zebah and Zalmunna. The earlier Midianite scourge inflicted on Israel was the worst, so this victory lived long in their minds (cf. Ps. 83:11).

8:22, 23 *Rule over us.* Israelites sinned by the misguided motive and request that Gideon reign as king. To his credit, the leader declined, insisting that God alone rule (cf. Ex. 19:5, 6).

8:24 *Ishmaelites.* Synonymous with Midianites (cf. Gen. 37:25, 28).

8:24–27 *Gideon made . . . an ephod.* This was certainly a sad end to Gideon's influence as he, perhaps in an expression of pride, sought to lift himself up in the eyes of the people. Gideon intended nothing more than to make a breastplate as David later did (1 Chr. 15:27) to indicate civil rule, not priestly rule. It was never intended to set up idolatrous worship, but to be a symbol of civil power. That no evil was intended can be noted from the subduing of Midian (v. 28), quietness from wars (v. 28), the fact that idolatry came only after Gideon's death (v. 33), as well as the commendation of Gideon (v. 35).

8:26 *the weight of the gold.* The total was about forty-two pounds.

8:30, 31 *many wives.* Gideon fell into the sin of polygamy, an iniquity tolerated by many but which never was God's blueprint for marriage (Gen. 2:24). Abimelech, a son by yet another illicit relationship, grew up to be the wretched king in Judges 9. Polygamy always resulted in trouble.

E. Fifth Period: Tola and Jair vs. Abimelech's Efforts (8:33–10:5)

9:5 *killed . . . brothers.* This atrocity, common in ancient times, eliminated the greatest threat in the revolution—all the legitimate competitors.

9:6 *Beth Millo.* Lit. "house of the fortress." This was a section of Shechem, probably involving the tower stronghold of verse 46.

9:14 *'You come and reign over us!'* In Jotham's parable of trees asking for a king (vv. 7–15), the olive, fig, and vine decline. They do not represent specific men who declined; rather, they build the suspense and heighten the idea that the bramble (thornbush) is inferior and unsuitable. The bush represents Abimelech (vv. 6, 16).

9:23 *God sent a spirit of ill will.* In the course of God's providence, there appeared jealousy, distrust, and hate. God allowed it to work as punishment for the idolatry and mass murder.

9:26–45 This narrative describes a failed coup against Abimelech.

9:37 *Diviners' Terebinth Tree.* A tree regarded superstitiously where mystical ceremonies and soothsaying were conducted.

9:45 *sowed it with salt.* An act polluting soil and water, as well as symbolizing a verdict of permanent barrenness (Deut. 29:23; Jer. 17:6). Abimelech's intent was finally nullified when Jeroboam I rebuilt the city as his capital (1 Kin. 12:25), c. 930–910 B.C.

9:57 That curse was pronounced in 9:20 for the pervasive idolatry.

10:3–5 Most likely, the judgeship of Jair coincided with the time period of Ruth.

F. Sixth Period: Jephtha, Ibzan, Elon, and Abdon vs. Philistines and Ammonites (10:6–12:15)

10:10 *We have sinned.* Confession is followed by true repentance (vv. 15, 16).

10:13, 14 Here is the form of God's wrath, in which He abandons persistent, willful sinners to the consequences of their sins. This aspect of divine judgment is referred to in the case of Samson (16:20), as well as the warnings of Proverbs 1:20–31; Romans 1:24–28. It is a pattern of rejection seen throughout history (cf. Acts 14:15, 16) even among the Jews (cf. Hos. 4:17; Matt. 15:14).

10:15 *Do to us whatever seems best.* Genuine repentance acknowledges God's right to chasten, so His punishment is seen as just and He is thereby glorified. It also seeks the remediation that chastening brings, because genuine contrition pursues holiness.

11:1 *mighty man of valor.* In a military situation, this means a strong, adept warrior, such as Gideon (6:12). In response to their repentance, God raised up Jephthah to lead the Israelites to freedom from the eighteen years of oppression (v. 8).

11:3 *raiding.* Such attacks would be against the Ammonites and other pagan peoples and brought fame to Jephthah.

11:11 *spoke . . . before the LORD.* This refers to confirming the agreement in a solemn public meeting with prayer invoking God as witness (v. 10).

11:13 *Israel took away my land.* The Ammonite ruler was claiming rights to the lands occupied by the Israelites. Jephthah's answer was direct: (1) those lands were not in the possession of Ammonites when Israel took them, but were Amorite lands; (2) Israel had been there 300 years in undisputed possession; and (3) God had chosen to give them the lands. Thus, they were entitled to them, just as the Ammonites felt they received their lands from their god (cf. v. 24).

11:15 *Israel did not take away the land.* These people initiated the hostility and, being at fault, invited loss of possession (vv. 16–22). This fit perfectly the will of God, who has ultimate rights (cf. Gen. 1:1; Ps. 24:1) to give the land to Israel. God said, "The land is Mine" (Lev. 25:23; cf. Ezek. 36:5).

11:26 *three hundred years.* With an early Exodus from Egypt (c. 1445 B.C.), one can approximate the 480 years covered in Judges to 1 Kings 6:1 (*see note there*), Solomon's fourth year 967/966 B.C.: 38 years from the Exodus to Heshbon; 300 from Heshbon to Jephthah in 11:26; possibly 7 more years for Jephthah; 40 years for Samson, 20 years for

Eli, 20 years for Samuel, 15 or 16 years beyond Samuel for Saul, 40 years for David, and 4 years for Solomon, which totals about 480 years. It is quite possible that 300 has been rounded off.

11:29 *the Spirit . . . came upon Jephthah.* That the Lord graciously empowered Jephthah for war on behalf of his people does not mean that all of the warrior's decisions were of God's wisdom. The rash vow (vv. 30, 31) is an example.

11:30 *made a vow to the LORD.* This was a custom among generals to promise the god of their worship something of great value as a reward for that god's giving them victory.

11:31 *I will offer it.* Some interpreters reason that Jephthah offered his daughter as a living sacrifice in perpetual virginity. With this idea, verse 31 would mean "shall surely be the LORD's" or "I will offer it up as a burnt offering." The view sees only perpetual virginity in verses 37–40, and rejects his offering a human sacrifice as being against God's revealed will (Deut. 12:31). On the other hand, since he was (1) beyond the Jordan River, (2) far from the tabernacle, (3) a hypocrite in religious devotion, (4) familiar with human sacrifice among other nations, (5) influenced by such superstition, and (6) wanting victory badly, he most likely meant a literal, human burnt offering. The translation in verse 31 is "and," not "or." His act came in an era of bizarre things, even inconsistency by leaders whom God otherwise empowered (cf. Gideon in 8:27).

11:34 *his daughter, coming out to meet him.* She was thus to be the sacrificed pledge.

11:35 *Alas.* Jephthah indicated the pain felt by her father in having to take the life of his only daughter to satisfy his pious but unwise pledge.

12:1 *Why did you . . . not call us?* Ephraim's newest threat (cf. 8:1) was their jealousy of Jephthah's success and, possibly, a lust to share in his spoils. The threat was not only to burn the house, but to burn him.

12:4 fugitives. This involved a mockery, referring to the Gileadites as low lifes, the outcasts of Ephraim. They retaliated with battle.

12:6 Shibboleth! The method used for discovering an Ephraimite was the way in which they pronounced this word. If they mispronounced it with an "s" rather than an "sh" sound, it gave them away, being a unique indicator of their dialect.

12:9, 14 thirty sons . . . grandsons. Very large families suggest the fathers' marriage to several wives, a part of life tolerated but never matching God's blueprint of one wife at a time (Gen. 2:24). To have many children had the lure of extending a person's human power and influence.

G. Seventh Period: Samson vs. Philistines (13:1–16:31)

13:3 the Angel of the LORD. In this case, it was a preincarnate appearance of the Lord Himself (vv. 6–22), as elsewhere (see note on 6:11). See note on Exodus 3:2.

13:5 Nazirite. The word is from the Hebrew "to separate." For rigid Nazirite restrictions, such as here in Samson's case, see note on Numbers 6:2. God gave three restrictions: (1) no wine (vv. 3, 4); (2) no razor cutting the hair (v. 5); and (3) no touching a dead body, thus being defiled (v. 6). Such outward actions indicated an inner dedication to God.

13:16 offer it to the LORD. Manoah needed this explanation because he was going to offer this to Him, not as the Lord, or even an angel, but just a human messenger. The instruction is intended to emphasize that this visitor is indeed the Lord.

13:17 What is Your name? This secret name is again indicative that the angel is the Lord.

13:18 Why do you ask My name? That the angel would not divulge His name reminds one of the angel (God) whom Jacob encountered (Gen. 32:24–30), who likewise did not give His name.

13:20 flame went up toward heaven. This miraculous act points to divine acceptance of the offering.

13:22 We shall surely die. This reaction of the fear of death is familiar with those who come into God's presence. Many did die when facing God, as the OT records. It is the terror in the heart of the sinner when in the presence of holy God. Cf. Ezekiel (Ezek. 1:28), Isaiah (Is. 6:5), the Twelve (Mark 4:35–41), Peter (Luke 5:8), and John (Rev. 1:17, 18).

14:1–4 she pleases me well. The Philistines were not among the seven nations of Canaan which Israel was specifically forbidden to marry. Nonetheless, Samson's choice was misdirected (cf. v. 3). Samson sins here, although God is sovereign and was able to turn the situation to please Him (v. 4). He was not at a loss, but used the opportunity to work against the wicked Philistines and provided gracious help to His people. He achieved destruction of these people, not by an army, but by the miraculous power of one man.

14:7 talked. Such conversation was not acceptable in the east, unless a couple was betrothed.

14:8 to get her. It was usually a year until the wedding.

14:9 He took some . . . in his hands. Some scholars suggest that Samson violated his Nazirite standard by coming in contact with a dead body (see note on 13:5). Others reason that Numbers 6 specifies the body of a person, not an animal. Whether or not he

---

Key Word

Riddle: 14:12–19—meaning "an enigmatic saying." In Samson's story, the riddle is used in a contest of wits. Proverbs attributes enigmatic sayings to the wise (Prov. 1:6). When the queen of Sheba tested Solomon's wisdom, her questions are described by this same Hebrew word (1 Kin. 10:1; 2 Chr. 9:1). In the Lord's confrontation with Miriam and Aaron, God describes Himself as speaking in "dark sayings" (the same Hebrew word) to the prophets, but to Moses face-to-face (Num. 12:6–8). Perhaps Paul had this last concept in mind when he admonished the Corinthians that even someone with the ability to understand all mysteries would not amount to anything if that person did not have the love of God (1 Cor. 13:2).

---

sinned here, the context does show instances of him sinning.

14:10 *feast.* The wedding feast usually lasted a week.

14:15 *seventh.* Some ancient authorities read "fourth." The number may be "fourth" (four days starting after the three in v. 14), totaling seven days as in verse 17. Or verse 15 may mean "fourth," and verse 17 that the woman wept for the rest of the seven-day period of verse 12, after the three days of verse 14.

14:16–18 *Samson's wife wept.* She cheated and manipulated, working against Samson's expectations that the men must come up with the answer. The men also cheated and threatened, having murder in their hearts (v. 15) and putting pressure on the woman.

14:19 *his anger.* God blesses the one who had been wronged. Samson's anger may be legitimate—righteous indignation against deceit (cf. Mark 3:5). The battle with the men

at Ashkelon, about twenty-three miles away, was a part of the war between Israel and Philistia.

14:20 *Samson's wife was given.* Another act of treachery was done. The Philistine father had no reason to assume that Samson would not be back, nor had Samson given word about not returning. The father, as a Philistine, did not want his daughter marrying the enemy.

15:1 *wheat harvest.* Samson tactfully made his move when wheat harvest kept men busy. This would have been in May/June. A token of reconciliation was offered as he brought a young goat, showing the father and the daughter that they had nothing to fear.

15:2 *I . . . thought.* This flimsy excuse by the father was an effort to escape the trap that he faced. He feared the Philistines if he turned on the new husband, yet he also feared Samson; so, he offered his second daughter as a way out. This was insulting and unlawful (cf. Lev. 18:18).

15:3 The cycle of retaliation began here, and it ends in 16:30, 31.

15:4 *caught three hundred foxes.* Samson, insulted and provoked to fleshly resentment, took vengeance on the Philistines. It must have taken a while to catch so many foxes or jackals and to keep them penned and fed until the number reached 300. Apparently, he tied them in pairs with a slow-burning torch, sending the pairs down the hills into fields thrashing with fire, igniting all the standing grain so dry at harvest. This was a loss of great proportion to the Philistine farmers.

15:6 *the Philistines . . . burned her and her father.* The general principle of reaping what is sown is apropos here (cf. Gal. 6:7).

15:8 *he attacked them hip and thigh.* This is proverbial for a ruthless slaughter.

15:15 *killed a thousand men.* Cf. 3:31. God gave miraculous power to Samson for destruction, but also to show fearful Israelites (v. 11) that He was with them, in spite of their lack of trust.

15:19 *water came out.* God worked a miracle of supplying a spring in response to Samson's prayerful cry in thirst. He called the place "the spring of him that called" (cf. Jer. 33:3).

16:1–3 God was merciful in allowing Samson to be delivered from this iniquity, but his chastening was only postponed. Sin blinds and later grinds (v. 21).

16:3 *hill that faces Hebron.* This place was about thirty-eight miles from Gaza.

16:4 *loved . . . Delilah.* Samson's weakness for women of low character and Philistine loyalty reappeared (cf. Prov. 6:27, 28). He erred continually by going to her daily (v. 16), allowing himself to be trapped by her deceptions.

16:5 *eleven hundred pieces of silver.* Since there were five rulers of the Philistines, each giving that amount, this was a large sum.

16:7 *And Samson said.* Samson played a lying game and gave away his manhood, here a little, there a little. He also played with giving away his secret—and finally gave it up, i.e., "told her all" (v. 17). He could be bought for a price, and Delilah paid it. Compare Esau selling his birthright (Gen. 25:29–33) and Judas denying Jesus (Matt. 26:14–16).

16:11 *new ropes.* Cf. 15:13.

16:17 *If I am shaven.* His strength came from his unique relation to God, based on his Nazirite pledge. His long hair was only a sign of it. When Delilah became more important to him than God, his strength was removed.

16:20 *he did not know that the Lord had departed from him.* Here was the tragedy of the wrath of abandonment. His sin had caused him to forfeit the power of God's presence. This principle is seen in Genesis 6:3; Proverbs 1:24–31; Matthew 15:14; Romans 1:24–32. *See note on 10:13, 14.*

16:21 *Gaza.* This would be the last town encountered in southwest Palestine as a traveler went from Jerusalem toward Egypt, near the coast. It was nearly forty miles from Samson's birthplace, Zorah. There, he was humiliated.

16:22 *hair . . . began to grow.* His hair grew with his repentance, and his strength with his hair.

16:23 *Dagon.* He was an idol with the head of a man and the body of a fish (*see note on 1 Sam. 5:2*).

16:24 *they praised their god.* It is tragic when a person's sin contributes to the giving of praise to a false god, because God alone is worthy of praise.

16:28 *remember me, I pray!* A prayer of repentance and trust pours forth from Samson.

16:29, 30 Some Philistine temples had roofs overlooking a courtyard, above wooden columns planted on stone foundations. The central pillars were set close together to furnish extra support for the roof. Here the victory celebration and taunts flung at the prisoner below drew a big crowd. The full strength of Samson, renewed by God, enabled him to buckle the columns. As a result, the roof collapsed and the victory was Israel's, not Philistia's. He died for the cause of his country and his God. He was not committing suicide, but rather bringing God's judgment on His enemies and willing to leave his own life or death to God. He was the greatest champion of all Israel, yet a man of passion capable of severe sin. Still, he is in the list of the faithful (cf. Heb. 11:32).

The Geography of the Judges

? Exact location questionable
Elon Name of Judge

Mediterranean Sea

DAN (Northern Settlement)

ASHER
NAPHTALI
Shamgar
ZEBULUN
Elon
Barak
Kedesh
Naphtali?
ISSACHAR
Ophrah?
Gideon
MANASSEH
Kamon
Jair

M A N A S S E H
Tola Shamir
Pirathon Abdon
Zaphon
Jephthah
Shiloh
G A D
E P H R A I M
Deborah
Samson Ehud
BENJAMIN
Ashdod Zorah
Ashkelon Ibzan Bethlehem
J U D A H
Hebron
Gaza Debir?
Othniel
S I M E O N

Jordan River

REUBEN

Dead Sea

0   20 MI.
0   20 Km.

The MacArthur Study Bible, by John MacArthur (Nashville: Word Publishing, 1997) 354. © 1993 by Thomas Nelson, Inc.

III. Epilogue: The Dereliction of Israel (17:1–21:25)

A. The Idolatry of Micah and the Danites (17:1–18:31)

17:1 Chapters 17–21 give miscellaneous appendixes to illustrate the pervasively depraved conditions in the era of the judges.

17:5 Micah had a shrine. A counterfeit shrine and personal idols with a private priest is set up within the tribe of Ephraim (v. 1), whereas God's priests were of the tribe of Levi (cf. v. 13). The defection is one example of personal and family idolatry.

17:6 everyone did . . . own eyes. This is a general characterization of the time, and of sinful behavior in all times. This attitude had

been mentioned much earlier in Israel's history (cf. 21:25; Deut. 12:8).

17:7–13 a Levite. This Levite compromised in departing from one of the forty-eight cities God gave for Levite service to Israel (Josh. 21). Then he sinned grossly by prostituting himself as a priest in a private idolatry.

18:2 On the migration by the tribe of Dan to a new territory, *see note on 1:34.* Dan was an example of tribal idolatry.

18:5 Please inquire of God. The passage does not say if the Levite did in fact seek God's counsel before giving reassurance (v. 6); the Danites should have prayed to seek God's counsel before (1) making this trip and (2) consulting a disobedient priest as one would an oracle.

18:7 Laish. Known also as Leshem (cf. Josh. 19:47), this was a secluded, rich land.

18:14–26 The Danites seized the idols of Micah by force, probably because they believed those false idols were the source of power to give them the land they had found. The apostate Levite who had served Micah as priest sold out again to be a priest for the Danites (vv. 18–20, 30), who were not bothered by his defection, but rather believed in his spiritual power.

18:29 name of the city Dan. This was in the northernmost extremity of the land of Canaan, hence the origin of the phrase, "from Dan to Beersheba," as indicating the land from north to south (cf. 20:1).

18:30 the son of Manasseh. Some manuscripts say "son of Manasseh," others "son of Moses," which may be more probable as Gershom was a son of Moses (Ex. 2:22; 18:3). This idolatrous priestly service continued until the captivity. This is most likely (1) the captivity of Israel by Assyria in 722 B.C. (2 Kin. 15:29; 17:1–6) or, if not, (2) the Philistine captivity of the ark from Shiloh (see Judg. 18:31) in 1 Samuel 4:11.

18:31 *the house of God was in Shiloh.* The ark of God was far away from them, so they justified their idolatry by their distance from the rest of Israel. This caused perpetual idolatry for many generations.

B. The Crime at Gibeah and War Against Benjamin (19:1—21:25)

19:1–10 Here is an example of the kind of personal immorality that went on during this era.

19:1 *concubine.* Priests could marry (Lev. 21:7, 13, 14). Though a concubine wife (usually a slave) was culturally legal, the practice was not acceptable to God (Gen. 2:24).

19:2 *played the harlot.* She should have been killed as the law required and could have been, if there was a devotion to holiness and obedience to Scripture (cf. Lev. 20:10). A priest was not allowed to marry a harlot (Lev. 21:14), so his ministry was greatly tainted. Yet, he made little of her sin and separation and sought her back sympathetically (v. 3).

19:10 *Jebus.* An early title for Jerusalem because of Jebusite control (Judg. 1:21) until David wrested it away to become his capital (2 Sam. 5:6–9). Another early name for the city was Salem (Gen. 14:18; cf. Ps. 76:2).

19:12 *Gibeah.* Jerusalem was still partially out of the control of Israelites. Gibeah was under Israelite control and presumably safer.

19:15 People of the Benjamite town of Gibeah failed to extend the expected courtesy of a lodging. This opened the door to immorality.

19:18 *going to the house of the LORD.* He was headed for Shiloh to return to priestly duty.

19:20 *night in the open square.* The old man knew the danger of such a place at night.

19:22 *perverted men.* Lit. "sons of Belial," i.e., worthless men, who desired to commit sodomy against the Levite. The phrase else-where is used for idolaters (Deut. 13:13), neglecters of the poor (Deut. 15:9), drunks (1 Sam. 1:16), immoral people (1 Sam. 2:12), and rebels against the civil authority (2 Sam. 20:1; Prov. 19:28). *Belial* can be traced to the false god Baal, and is also a term for yoke (they cast off the yoke of decency), and a term for entangling or injuring. It is used in the NT of Satan (2 Cor. 6:15).

19:24 *let me bring them out.* The host showed a disgraceful compromise in his exaggerated desire to extend hospitality to his male guest. He should have protected all in his house, and so should have the Levite, even at the risk of their own lives in guarding the women. His sad view of women was demonstrated by his willingness to hand his daughter or the guest concubine over to indecent men. Lot's plunge from decency was similar (Gen. 19:8). Here, repeated rape and finally murder were the pitiful sequel.

19:25 *the man took his concubine . . . to them.* This is unthinkable weakness and cowardice for any man, especially a priest of God. Apparently, he even slept through the night, or stayed in bed out of fear, since he didn't see her again until he awakened and prepared to leave (cf. v. 28).

19:29 *divided her into twelve pieces.* The Levite's bizarre butchery to divide the woman's body into twelve parts was his shocking summons for aroused Israelite redress. No doubt a message went with each part, and the fact that he "sent" assumes messengers (cf. 1 Sam. 11:7). As he calculated, many Israelites were incensed and desired to avenge the atrocity (cf. 20:30). Nothing could have aroused universal indignation and horror more than this radical summons from the Levite.

20:1 *all the children of Israel came out.* As a result of this tragedy, a national assembly was convened with people coming from the north (Dan) and the south (Beersheba).

as one man before the LORD. This indicated a humble attitude and desire to seek help from God for the nation.

20:13 *the children of Benjamin would not listen.* They hardened their hearts against the justice and decency of turning over the criminals. Even greatly outnumbered in war, they would not yield to what was right (cf. vv. 15–17), so civil war resulted.

20:18 *to inquire of God.* The Lord gave His counsel from the location of the ark at Shiloh, probably through the Urim and Thummim (vv. 27, 28). The tribe of Judah was responsible to lead in battle since God had chosen a leadership role for that tribe (Gen. 49:8–12; 1 Chr. 5:1, 2). *See note on Exodus 28:30.*

20:22–25 The Lord twice allowed great defeat and death to Israel to bring them to their spiritual senses regarding the cost of tolerating apostasy. Also, while they sought counsel, they placed too much reliance on their own prowess and on satisfying their own outrage. Finally, when desperate enough, they fasted and offered sacrifices (v. 26). The Lord then gave victory with a strategy similar to that at Ai (Josh. 8).

20:32 Here was a battle strategy that lured the Benjamite army into a disastrous ambush (cf. vv. 36–46).

20:46 *twenty-five thousand.* The text employs a rounded number for the more exact 25,100 (cf. v. 35).

20:47 The number of Benjamites adds up to the 26,700 (v. 15) in a reasonable way: 18,100 killed (rounded to 18,000 here, v. 44); 5,000 (v. 45); 2,000 (v. 45); 600 survived (v. 47); leaving an estimated 1,000 lost during the final days (v. 48).

21:1 *an oath at Mizpah.* The Israelites made an oath not to "give" their daughters to the 600 surviving Benjamites (20:47). But they realized that the latter would fade as a tribe unless they had wives (cf. 21:6, 7), since the Benjamite women had died in the sack of Gibeah (20:37). Cf. verse 9.

21:8 No one had come from Jabesh Gilead, so the Israelites conquered Jabesh Gilead, which did not help against the Benjamites, and gave 400 virgins from there to the tribe (vv. 12–14).

21:8–16 *Jabesh Gilead.* Israelites placed such a premium on the unity of their tribes that they saw this city's non-cooperation in battle as worthy of widespread death. The passage does not give God's approval to this destruction of men, women, and children (vv. 10, 11). It is another of the bizarre actions of people when they do what is right in their own eyes, which is the point that both begins and ends this dark final section (17:6; 21:25).

21:16 *wives for those who remain.* Having recognized that the 200 others needed wives (vv. 17, 18), they decided to allow them to snatch brides on their own at a dance in Shiloh (vv. 16–22), not believing that this violated their oath of not directly "giving" their daughters.

21:25 Judges 17–21 vividly demonstrates how bizarre and deep sin can become when people throw off the authority of God as mediated through the king (cf. 17:6). This was the expected but tragic conclusion to a bleak period of Israelite history (cf. Deut. 12:8).

Further Study
Davis, John J. and John C. Whitcomb. *A History of Israel from Conquest to Exile.* Grand Rapids: Baker, 1980.
Inrig, Gary. *Hearts of Iron, Feet of Clay.* Chicago: Moody, 1979.
Phillips, W. Gary. *Judges and Ruth.* Nashville: Broadman & Holman, 2004.
Wood, Leon. *Distressing Days of the Judges.* Grand Rapids: Zondervan, 1975.

THE BOOK OF
RUTH

Title

Ancient versions and modern translations consistently entitle this book after Ruth the Moabitess heroine, who is mentioned by name twelve times (1:4 to 4:13). Only two OT books receive their names from women— Ruth and Esther. The OT does not again refer to Ruth, while the NT mentions her just once—in the context of Christ's genealogy (Matt. 1:5; cf. 4:18–22). *Ruth* most likely comes from a Moabite and/or Hebrew word meaning "friendship." Ruth arrived in Bethlehem as a foreigner (2:10), became a maidservant (2:13), married wealthy Boaz (4:13), and discovered herself in the physical lineage of Christ (Matt. 1:5).

Author and Date

Jewish tradition credits Samuel as the author, which is plausible since he did not die (1 Sam. 25:1) until after he had anointed David as God's chosen king (1 Sam. 16:6–13). However, neither internal features nor external testimony conclusively identifies the writer. This exquisite story most likely appeared shortly before or during David's reign of Israel (1011–971 B.C.), since David is mentioned (4:17, 22) but not Solomon. Goethe reportedly labeled this piece of anonymous but unexcelled literature as "the loveliest, complete work on a small scale." What Venus is to statuary and the Mona Lisa is to paintings, Ruth is to literature.

Background and Setting

Aside from Bethlehem (1:1), Moab (the perennial enemy of Israel which was east of the Dead Sea), stands as the only other mentioned geographic/national entity (1:1, 2). This country originated when Lot fathered Moab by an incestuous union with his oldest daughter (Gen. 19:37). Centuries later the Jews encountered opposition from Balak, king of Moab, through the prophet Balaam (Num. 22–25). For eighteen years Moab oppressed Israel during the judges (Judg. 3:12–30). Saul defeated the Moabites (1 Sam. 14:47) while David seemed to enjoy a peaceful relationship with them (1 Sam. 22:3, 4). Later, Moab again troubled Israel (2 Kin. 3:5–27; Ezra 9:1). Because of Moab's idolatrous worship of Chemosh (1 Kin. 11:7, 33; 2 Kin. 23:13) and its opposition to Israel, God cursed Moab (Is. 15; 16; Jer. 48; Ezek. 25:8–11; Amos 2:1–3).

The story of Ruth occurred in the days "when the judges ruled" Israel (1:1), c. 1370 to 1041 B.C. (Judg. 2:16–19) and thus bridges time from the judges to Israel's monarchy. God used "a famine in the land" of Judah (1:1) to set in motion this beautiful drama, although the famine does not receive mention in Judges, which causes difficulty in dating the events of Ruth. However, by working backward in time from the well-known date of David's reign (1011–971 B.C.), the time period of Ruth would most likely be during the judgeship of Jair, c. 1126–1105 B.C. (Judg. 10:3–5).

Ruth covers about eleven to twelve years according to the following scenario: (1) 1:1–18, ten years in Moab (1:4); (2) 1:19–2:23, several months (mid-April to mid-June) in Boaz's field (1:22; 2:23); (3) 3:1–18, one day in Bethlehem and one night at the threshing floor; and (4) 4:1–22, about one year in Bethlehem.

Historical and Theological Themes

All eighty-five verses of Ruth have been accepted as canonical by the Jews. Along with Song of Solomon, Esther, Ecclesiastes, and Lamentations, Ruth stands with the OT books of the Megilloth or "five scrolls." Rabbis read these books in the synagogue on five special occasions during the year—Ruth being read at Pentecost due to the harvest scenes of Ruth 2 and 3.

Genealogically, Ruth looks back almost 900 years to events in the time of Jacob (4:11) and forward about 100 years to the coming reign of David (4:17, 22). While Joshua and Judges emphasize the legacy of the nation and their land of promise, Ruth focuses on the lineage of David back to the patriarchal era.

At least seven major theological themes emerge in Ruth. First, Ruth the Moabitess illustrates that God's redemptive plan extended beyond the Jews to Gentiles (2:12). Second, Ruth demonstrates that women are coheirs with men of God's salvation grace. Third, Ruth portrays the virtuous woman of Proverbs 31:10 (cf. 3:11). Fourth, Ruth describes God's sovereign (1:6; 4:13) and providential care (2:3) of seemingly unimportant people at apparently insignificant times which later prove to be monumentally crucial to accomplishing God's will. Fifth, Ruth along with Tamar (Gen. 38), Rahab (Josh. 2), and Bathsheba (2 Sam. 11, 12)

stand in the genealogy of the messianic line (4:17, 22; cf. Matt. 1:5). Sixth, Boaz, as a type of Christ, becomes Ruth's kinsman-redeemer (4:1–12). Finally, David's right (and thus Christ's right) to the throne of Israel is traced back to Judah (4:18–22; cf. Gen. 49:8–12).

Interpretive Challenges

Ruth should be understood as a true historical account. The reliable facts surrounding Ruth, in addition to its complete compatibility with Judges plus 1 and 2 Samuel, confirm Ruth's authenticity. However, some individual difficulties require careful attention. First, how could Ruth worship at the tabernacle then in Shiloh (1 Sam. 4:4), since Deuteronomy 23:3 expressly forbids Moabites from entering the assembly for ten generations? Since the Jews entered the land c. 1405 B.C. and Ruth was not born until c. 1150 B.C., she then represented at least the eleventh generation (probably later) if the time limitation ended at ten generations. If "ten generations" was an idiom meaning "forever" as Nehemiah 13:1 implies, then Ruth would be like the foreigner of Isaiah 56:1–8 who joined himself to the Lord (1:16), thus gaining entrance to the assembly.

Second, are there not immoral overtones to Boaz and Ruth spending the night together before marriage (3:3–18)? Ruth engaged in a common ancient Near Eastern custom by asking Boaz to take her for his wife as symbolically pictured by throwing a garment of love and care over the intended woman (3:9), just as Jehovah spread His garment over Israel (Ezek. 16:8). The text does not even hint at the slightest moral impropriety, noting that Ruth slept at his feet (3:8, 14). Thus, Boaz became God's answer to his own earlier prayer for Ruth (2:12).

Third, would not the levirate principle of Deuteronomy 25:5, 6 lead to incest and/or polygamy if the nearest relative was already married? God would not design a good plan to involve the grossest of immoralities punishable by death. Implementation of Deuteronomy 25:5, 6 could involve only the nearest relative who was eligible for marriage as qualified by other stipulations of the law.

Fourth, was not marriage to a Moabitess strictly forbidden by the law? The nations or people to whom marriage was prohibited were those possessing the land that Israel would enter (Ex. 34:16; Deut. 7:1–3; Josh. 23:12) which did not include Moab (cf. Deut. 7:1). Further, Boaz married Ruth, a devout proselyte to Jehovah (1:16, 17), not a pagan worshiper of Chemosh—Moab's chief deity (cf. later problems in Ezra 9:1, 2 and Neh. 13:23–25).

Outline

I. Elimelech and Naomi's Ruin in Moab (1:1–5)
II. Naomi and Ruth Return to Bethlehem (1:6–22)
III. Boaz Receives Ruth in His Field (2:1–23)
IV. Ruth's Romance with Boaz (3:1–18)
V. Boaz Redeems Ruth (4:1–12)
VI. God Rewards Boaz and Ruth with a Son (4:13–17)
VII. David's Right to the Throne of Judah (4:18–22)

I. ELIMELECH AND NAOMI'S RUIN IN MOAB (1:1–5)

1:1–5 This introduction to Ruth sets in motion the following events (1:6–4:22), which culminate in Obed's birth and his relationship to the Davidic line of Christ. See Introduction: Background and Setting.

1:1 famine. This disaster sounds similar to the days of Abraham (Gen. 12), Isaac (Gen. 26), and Jacob (Gen. 46). The text does not specify whether or not this famine was God's judgment (cf. 1 Kin. 17, 18, esp. 18:2). **Bethlehem, Judah.** Bethlehem ("house of bread") lies in the territory given to the tribe of Judah (Josh. 15) about six miles south of Jerusalem. Rachel, the wife of Jacob, was buried nearby (Gen. 35:19; cf. 4:11). Bethlehem eventually received the title, "city of David" (Luke 2:4, 11). Later, Mary delivered Christ (Luke 2:4–7; cf. Mic. 5:2) and Herod slaughtered the infants here (Matt. 2:16). This title (Judg. 17:7, 9; 19:1, 2, 18) serves to distinguish it from Bethlehem of Zebulun (Josh. 19:15). **dwell.** Elimelech intended to live temporarily in Moab as a resident alien until the famine passed. **Moab.** See Introduction: Background and Setting.

1:2 Elimelech. His name means "my God is king," signifying a devout commitment to the God of Israel. Most likely, he was a prominent man in the community whose brothers might have included the unnamed close relative and Boaz (cf. 4:3). **Naomi.** Her name means "pleasant." **Mahlon and Chilion.** Their names mean "sick" and "pining," respectively. **Ephrathites.** A title used of people who lived in the area more anciently known as Ephrath (Gen. 35:16, 19; 48:7) or Ephrathah (4:11; Mic. 5:2), but later more prominently called Bethlehem (1:1). Jesse, father of David, is called "an Ephrathite of Bethlehem" (1 Sam. 17:12) and "Jesse the Bethlehemite" (1 Sam. 16:1, 18; 17:58).

1:4 the women of Moab. See Introduction: Interpretive Challenges. **Orpah.** Her name means "stubborn." **Ruth.** Her name means "friendship." **about ten years.** This period would seem to include the entire time of Naomi's residency in Moab.

1:5 the woman survived. Naomi, a widow in Moab whose two sons have died also, believed that the Lord had afflicted her with bitter days until she would die (1:13, 20, 21).

Moab to Bethlehem

Mediterranean Sea

Sea of Chinnereth

Jordan R.

Jericho

Plains of Moab

Bethlehem (Ephrathah)

Heshbon

Medeba

REUBEN

Dibon

Dead Sea

JUDAH

MOAB

Kir Hareseth

The MacArthur Study Bible, by John MacArthur (Nashville: Word Publishing, 1997) 366. © 1993 by Thomas Nelson, Inc.

No reason for the death of these three men in her life is given. Ruth married Mahlon, and Orpah united with Chilion (cf. 4:10).

II. NAOMI AND RUTH RETURN TO BETHLEHEM (1:6–22)

1:6–22 The death of Elimelech and his two sons (1:3, 5) prepared the way for Naomi and Ruth to leave Orpah in Moab (1:6–14), and they returned together to Bethlehem (1:15–22).

1:6 the LORD had visited His people. Obviously the Lord had sent rain to break the famine. The sovereignty of Jehovah on behalf of Israel permeates the pages of Ruth in several ways: (1) God actually worked for good (2:12; 4:12–14), (2) in circumstances perceived by Naomi for bad (1:13, 21), and (3) in the context of prayer/blessing (1:8, 9, 17; 2:4, 12, 20; 3:10, 13; 4:11). The return of

physical prosperity only shadowed the reality of a coming spiritual prosperity through the line of David in the person of Christ.

1:7 she went out. Naomi had friends (1:19), family (2:1), and prosperity (4:3) awaiting her in Bethlehem.

1:8–10 Naomi graciously encouraged her two daughters-in-law to return to their homes (1:8) and to remarry (1:9), but they insisted on going to Jerusalem (1:10).

1:11–13 Naomi selflessly reasoned a second time for their return, because she would be unable to provide them with new husbands (possibly in the spirit of a levirate marriage as described in Deut. 25:5, 6). If Orpah and Ruth waited, they would most likely have become as old as Naomi was then before they could remarry (cf. Gen. 38:11).

1:12 I am too old. Naomi was probably over fifty.

1:13 the hand of the LORD. This is a figure of speech which describes the Lord's work. The Lord is spirit (John 4:24) and therefore does not have a literal hand.

1:14, 15 At the second plea to return, Orpah turned back. Naomi pleaded with Ruth a third time to return.

1:15 her gods. This refers to Chemosh, the chief Moabite deity, who required child sacrifice (2 Kin. 3:27).

1:16–18 Ruth recited her hallmark expression of loyalty to Naomi and commitment to the family into which she married.

1:16 And your God, my God. This testimony evidenced Ruth's conversion from worshiping Chemosh to Jehovah of Israel (cf. 1 Thess. 1:9, 10).

1:17 The LORD do so to me. Ruth's vow bore further testimony to her conversion. She followed the path first blazed by Abraham (Josh. 24:2).

1:19 they came to Bethlehem. A trip from Moab (at least 60–75 miles) would have taken about 7–10 days. Having descended about 4,500 feet from Moab into the Jordan Valley, they then ascended 3,750 feet through the hills of Judea. *all the city.* Naomi had been well known in her prior residency (cf. Ephrathites of Bethlehem, 1:2). The question "Is this Naomi?" most likely reflected the hard life of the last decade and the toll that it had taken on her appearance.

1:20, 21 Naomi . . . Mara; full . . . empty. Naomi's outlook on life, although grounded in God's sovereignty, was not hopeful; thus she asked to be renamed Mara, which means "bitter." Her experiences were not unlike Job (Job 1; 2), but her perspective resembled that of Job's wife (Job 2:10). In reality, Naomi had (1) a full harvest prospect, (2) Ruth plus Boaz, not to mention (3) the hope of God's future blessing.

1:22 Ruth, the Moabitess. This title also appears at 2:2, 21; 4:5, 10. Ruth stands out as a foretaste of future Gentile conversions (cf. Rom. 11). *at the beginning of barley harvest.* Normally the middle to the end of April.

III. BOAZ RECEIVES RUTH IN HIS FIELD (2:1–23)

2:1–23 Two widows, newly at home in Bethlehem after Naomi's ten-year absence, needed the basics of life. Ruth volunteered to go out and glean the fields for food (cf. James 1:27). In so doing, she unintentionally went to the field of Boaz, a close family relative, where she found great favor in his sight.

2:1 relative . . . of the family. This man was possibly as close as a brother of Elimelech (cf. 4:3), but if not, certainly within the tribe or clan. *a man of great wealth.* Lit. "a man of valor" (cf. Judg. 6:12; 11:1) who had unusual capacity to obtain and protect his property. *Boaz.* His name means "in him is strength." He had never married or was a widower (cf. 1 Chr. 2:11, 12; Matt. 1:5; Luke 3:32).

2:2 glean. The Mosaic Law commanded that the harvest should not be reaped to the corners nor the gleanings picked up (Lev. 19:9, 10). Gleanings were stalks of grain left after the first cutting (cf. 2:3, 7, 8, 15, 17). These were dedicated to the needy, especially widows, orphans, and strangers (Lev. 23:22; Deut. 24:19–21).

2:3 she happened to come. Here was a classic example of God's providence at work. *part of the field.* This was possibly a large community field in which Boaz had a plot.

2:4–17 Note throughout how Boaz manifested the spirit of the law in going beyond what the Mosaic legislation required by (1) feeding Ruth (2:14), (2) letting Ruth glean among the sheaves (2:15), and (3) leaving extra grain for her to glean (2:16).

2:4 The LORD be with you. This unusual labor practice speaks to the exceptional godliness of Boaz and his workers.

2:7 sheaves. These were bundles of grain stalks tied together for transport to the threshing floor.

Kinsman-Redeemer

O.T. Qualification	Christ's Fulfillment
1. Blood Relationship	Gal. 4:4, 5; Heb. 2:16, 17
2. Necessary Resources	1 Cor. 6:20; 1 Pet. 1:18, 19
3. Willingness to Buy	John 10:15–18; 1 John 3:16

The MacArthur Bible Handbook, by John MacArthur (Nashville: Thomas Nelson Publishers, 2003) 74. © 2003 by Thomas Nelson Publishers.

2:7, 17 morning . . . evening. Ruth proved to be diligent in her care for Naomi.

2:7 the house. Most likely, this was a temporary shelter built with branches by the side of the field.

2:8 my daughter. Boaz was about forty-five to fifty-five years old as a contemporary of Elimelech and Naomi. He would naturally see Ruth as a daughter (3:10, 11), much like Naomi did also (cf. 2:2, 22; 3:1, 16, 18). Boaz contrasted himself with younger men (3:10). **my young women.** These were the ones who tied up the sheaves.

2:9 young men. The ones who cut the grain with hand sickles (cf. 2:21).

2:10 a foreigner. Ruth remained ever mindful that she was an alien and as such must conduct herself humbly. Possibly she had knowledge of Deuteronomy 23:3, 4. She acknowledged the grace (lit. favor) of Boaz.

2:11 fully reported to me. This indicates Naomi's quickness to speak kindly of Ruth and Boaz's network of influence in Bethlehem. Ruth remained true to her promise (1:16, 17).

2:12 wings . . . refuge. Scripture pictures God as catching Israel up on His wings in the Exodus (Ex. 19:4; Deut. 32:11). God is here portrayed as a mother bird sheltering the young and fragile with her wings (cf. Pss. 17:8; 36:7; 57:1; 61:4; 63:7; 91:1, 4). Boaz blessed Ruth in light of her new found commitment to and dependence on the Lord. Later, he would become God's answer to this prayer (cf. 3:9).

2:14 vinegar. Sour wine mixed with a little oil was used to quench thirst.

2:15 among the sheaves. Boaz granted her request (2:7) to go beyond the law.

2:17 ephah. This amounts to over one-half bushel, weighing about thirty to forty pounds.

2:18 what she had kept back. This was not the gleaned grain, but rather the lunch ration which Ruth did not eat (cf. 2:14).

2:20 His kindness. Naomi began to understand God's sovereign working, covenant loyalty, lovingkindness, and mercy toward her because Ruth, without human direction (2:3), found the near relative Boaz. **one of our close relatives.** The great kinsman-redeemer theme of Ruth begins here (cf. 3:9, 12; 4:1, 3, 6, 8, 14). A close relative could redeem (1) a family member sold into slavery (Lev. 25:47–49), (2) land which needed to be sold under economic hardship (Lev. 25:23–28), and/or (3) the family name by virtue of a levirate marriage (Deut. 25:5–10). This earthly custom pictures the reality of God the Redeemer doing a greater work (Pss. 19:14; 78:35; Is. 41:14; 43:14) by reclaiming those who needed to be spiritually redeemed out of slavery to sin (Ps. 107:2; Is. 62:12). Thus, Boaz pictures Christ who, as a Brother (Heb. 2:17), redeemed those who (1) were slaves to sin (Rom. 6:15–18), (2) had lost all earthly possessions/privilege in the Fall (Gen. 3:17–19), and (3) had been alienated by sin from God (2 Cor. 5:18–21). Boaz stands in the direct line of Christ (Matt. 1:5; Luke 3:32). This turn of events marks the point where Naomi's human emptiness (1:21) begins to be refilled by the Lord. Her night of earthly doubt has been broken by the dawning of new hope (cf. Rom. 8:28–39).

2:22 do not meet you. Ruth the Moabitess would not be treated with such mercy and grace by strangers outside of the family.

2:23 the end of . . . harvest. Barley harvest usually began about mid-April and wheat harvest extended to mid-June—a period of intense labor for about two months. This generally coincided with the seven weeks

Ruth: The Proverbs 31 Wife

The "virtuous" wife of Proverbs 31:10 is personified by "virtuous" Ruth of whom the same Hebrew word is used (3:11). With amazing parallel, they share at least 8 character traits (see below). One wonders (in concert with Jewish tradition) if King Lemuel's mother might not have been Bathsheba, who orally passed the family heritage of Ruth's spotless reputation along to David's son Solomon. Lemuel, which means "devoted to God," could have been a family name for Solomon (cf. Jedediah, 2 Sam. 12:25), who then could have penned Prov. 31:10–31 with Ruth in mind. Each woman was:

1. Devoted to her family (Ruth 1:15–18 // Prov. 31:10–12, 23)
2. Delighting in her work (Ruth 2:2 // Prov. 31:13)
3. Diligent in her labor (Ruth 2:7, 17, 23 // Prov. 31:14–18, 19–21, 24, 27)
4. Dedicated to godly speech (Ruth 2:10, 13 // Prov. 13:26)
5. Dependent on God (Ruth 2:12 // Prov. 31:25b, 30)
6. Dressed with care (Ruth 3:3 // Prov. 31:22, 25a)
7. Discreet with men (Ruth 3:6–13 // Prov. 31:11, 12, 23)
8. Delivering blessings (Ruth 4:14, 15 // Prov. 31:28, 29, 31)

The MacArthur Study Bible, by John MacArthur (Nashville: Word Publishing, 1997) 373. © 1993 by Thomas Nelson, Inc.

between Passover and the Feast of Weeks, i.e., Pentecost (cf. Lev. 23:15, 16; Deut. 16:9–12).

IV. RUTH'S ROMANCE WITH BOAZ (3:1–18)

3:1–18 Encouraged by Ruth's day in Boaz's field, Naomi instructed Ruth in the way she should go to insure a brighter future. Ruth carefully followed Naomi's directions to solicit redemption by Boaz, while the Lord had prepared Boaz to redeem Ruth. Only one potential obstacle remained—a relative nearer than Boaz.

3:1 *security.* Naomi felt responsible, just as she did in 1:9, for Ruth's future husband and home.

3:2 *tonight.* Winnowing (tossing grain into the air to finish separating the grain from the chaff) normally occurred in late afternoon when the Mediterranean winds prevailed. Sifting and bagging the grain would have carried over past dark, and Boaz may have remained all night to guard the grain from theft. *threshing floor.* Usually a large, hard area of earth or stone on the downwind (east) side of the village where threshing took place (loosening the grain from the straw and winnowing).

3:3, 4 Naomi instructed Ruth (1) to put on her best appearance and (2) to propose marriage to Boaz by utilizing an ancient Near Eastern custom. Since Boaz is a generation older than Ruth (2:8), this overture would indicate Ruth's desire to marry Boaz which the older, gracious Boaz would not have initiated with a younger woman.

3:7 *his heart was cheerful.* Using the same language of 3:1 ("security . . . be well"), Boaz is described as having a sense of well-being, which is most readily explained by the full harvest in contrast to previous years of famine (cf. Judg. 18:20; 1 Kin. 21:7).

3:9 *Take your maidservant.* Ruth righteously appealed to Boaz, using the language of Boaz's earlier prayer (2:12), to marry her according to the levirate custom (Deut. 25:5–10). See Introduction: Interpretive Challenges.

3:10 *kindness.* Ruth's loyalty to Naomi, the Lord, and even Boaz is commended by

Boaz. *go after young men.* Ruth demonstrated moral excellence in that (1) she did not engage in immorality, (2) she did not remarry outside the family, and (3) she had appealed for levirate redemption to an older, godly man.

3:11 *virtuous.* In all respects, Ruth personifies excellence (cf. Prov. 31:10). This same language has been used of Boaz ("a man of great wealth" or more likely "a man of valor" in 2:1), thus making them the perfectly matched couple for an exemplary marriage.

3:12 *a relative closer than I.* Boaz righteously deferred to someone else who was nearer in relationship to Elimelech. The nearer relative may have been Boaz's older brother (cf. 4:3) or Boaz may have been his cousin. The fact that the neighbor women said, "There is a son born to Naomi" at Obed's birth would suggest the brother or cousin relationship to Elimelech (4:17).

3:13 *I will perform the duty.* Boaz willingly accepted Ruth's proposal, if the nearer relative was unable or unwilling to exercise his levirate duty. *as the LORD lives.* This is the most solemn, binding oath an Israelite could vow.

3:14 *lay at his feet.* According to the text, no immorality occurred. Boaz even insisted on no appearance of evil.

3:15 *six ephahs.* The Hebrew text gives no standard of measurement; *ephah* has been inserted by the translators only as a possibility. However, six ephahs would weigh about 200 pounds, which was far too much for Ruth to carry home in her shawl. Therefore, deemed most reasonable is six seahs (60–80 pounds), which would have been twice the amount Ruth had previously gleaned (see 2:17).

3:18 *this day.* Naomi knew that Boaz was a man of integrity and would fulfill his promise with a sense of urgency. They needed to wait on the Lord to work through Boaz.

V. BOAZ REDEEMS RUTH (4:1–12)

4:1–22 God's divine plan fully blossomed as Boaz redeemed Naomi's land and Ruth's hand in marriage. Naomi, once empty (1:21), is full; Ruth, once a widow (1:5), is married; but most importantly, the Lord has prepared Christ's line of descent in David, through Boaz and Obed, back to Judah (Gen. 49:10) to fulfill the proper messianic lineage.

4:1 *went up.* Apparently the threshing floor was below the level of the gate. Compare Ruth 3:3, "go down to the threshing floor." *the gate.* This was the normal public place to transact business in ancient times (cf. 2 Sam. 15:2; Job 29:7; Lam. 5:14). *friend.* The Hebrew text is not clear whether Boaz called him directly by name (which is then not mentioned by the author) or indirectly.

4:2 *ten men.* This number apparently comprised a quorum to officially transact business, although only two or three witnesses were needed for judicial proceedings (cf. Deut. 17:6; 19:15).

4:3 *Naomi . . . sold.* This phrase could possibly be translated, "Naomi is about to sell" (cf. Jer. 32:6–15). As a widow, she needed the money for living expenses, knowing that the land would ultimately be returned at Jubilee (Lev. 25:28). *our brother Elimelech.* Boaz and the unnamed relative were most likely either brothers or cousins.

4:4 *Buy it back.* This was authorized by the Mosaic Law (Lev. 25:23–28).

4:5 *you must also buy.* Redeeming both Ruth and the land would not have been required by the letter of the levirate law (Deut. 25:5, 6). Perhaps this exemplified Boaz's desire to obey the spirit of the law (*see note on 2:4–17*), or maybe the redemption of land and marriage had been combined by local tradition. The levirate principle appears first in Scripture at Genesis 38:8 (cf. Matt. 22:23–28).

4:6 *lest I ruin my own inheritance.* He was unwilling to have the family portfolio split between his existing children and the potential offspring of a union with Ruth. ***You redeem.*** The closer relative relinquished his legal right to the land and Ruth. This cleared the way for Boaz to redeem both.

4:7 *took off his sandal.* The Scripture writer explained to his own generation what had been a custom in former generations. This kind of tradition appears in Deuteronomy 25:5–10 and apparently continued at least to the time of Amos (cf. 2:6; 8:6). The closer relative legally transferred his right to the property as symbolized by the sandal, most likely that of the nearer relative.

4:9 *I have bought.* Boaz exercised his legal option to redeem both the land and Ruth before appropriate witnesses.

4:10 *the widow of Mahlon.* Only here is Ruth's former husband identified (cf. 1:5). Therefore, it can also be assumed that Chilion married Orpah. ***I have acquired as my wife.*** Boaz exercised the spirit of the law and became Ruth's kinsman-redeemer (Deut. 25:5, 6). ***the name of the dead.*** Perpetuation of the family name (1 Sam. 24:21) was an important feature that the levirate process provided (cf. Deut. 25:6).

4:11 *We are witnesses.* This affirmation signaled the strong approval of the city. ***like Rachel and Leah.*** Rachel, the most beloved wife of Jacob, was buried nearby (Gen. 35:19); Leah was the mother of Judah (by Jacob), their namesake descendant (Gen. 29:35). This remembrance went back almost 900 years to c. 1915 B.C. ***Ephrathah . . . Bethlehem.*** This was the ancient name of Bethlehem (Gen. 35:19; 48:7). *See note on Ephrathites; 1:2.* Micah later prophetically wrote that this city would be the birthplace of Messiah (5:2).

4:12 *Perez . . . Tamar . . . Judah.* Read Genesis 38:1–30 for the background to these three. Tamar, the widow of Judah's first son Er, when denied a levirate marriage to Judah's remaining son Shelah (38:14), took matters into her own hands and immorally consorted with her father-in-law Judah (38:18). Perez, the first born of twins by Tamar, became the main ancestor of the Ephrathites and Bethlehemites (1 Chr. 2:3–5, 19, 50, 51; 4:4). *See note on 4:18.* ***offspring.*** The firstborn son would be considered the son of Mahlon. Additional sons would legally be the offspring of Boaz (Deut. 25:6).

VI. GOD REWARDS BOAZ AND RUTH WITH A SON (4:13–17)

4:13 *he went in to her.* This is an OT euphemism for sexual intercourse. ***the LORD gave her conception.*** As with Rachel (Gen. 30:22) and Leah (Gen. 29:31), so it was also with Ruth (cf. Ps. 127:3).

4:14 *the LORD . . . has not left you.* This is in contrast to Naomi's worst moments of despair (1:20, 21). ***a close relative . . . his name.*** This refers to Obed, not Boaz (cf. 4:11), who cared for Naomi in her latter years.

4:15 *better . . . than seven sons.* Seven represented the number of perfection and thus seven sons would make the complete family (cf. 1 Sam. 2:5). However, Ruth exceeded this standard all by herself.

4:16 *a nurse to him.* This expresses the natural affection of a godly grandmother for her God-given grandson.

4:17 *the neighbor women gave him a name.* Here is the only place in the OT where a child was named by someone other than the immediate family. ***a son born to Naomi.*** Ruth vicariously bore the son who would restore the family name of Naomi's deceased son Mahlon (cf. 4:1). ***Obed . . . Jesse . . . David.*** This complete genealogy appears identically

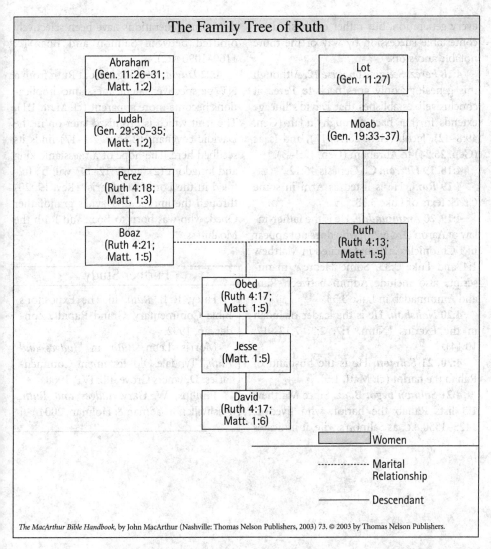

The Family Tree of Ruth

Abraham
(Gen. 11:26–31;
Matt. 1:2)

Lot
(Gen. 11:27)

Judah
(Gen. 29:30–35;
Matt. 1:2)

Moab
(Gen. 19:33–37)

Perez
(Ruth 4:18;
Matt. 1:3)

Boaz
(Ruth 4:21;
Matt. 1:5)

Ruth
(Ruth 4:13;
Matt. 1:5)

Obed
(Ruth 4:17;
Matt. 1:5)

Jesse
(Matt. 1:5)

David
(Ruth 4:17;
Matt. 1:6)

Women

------------ Marital
Relationship

———— Descendant

The MacArthur Bible Handbook, by John MacArthur (Nashville: Thomas Nelson Publishers, 2003) 73. © 2003 by Thomas Nelson Publishers.

in four other biblical texts (4:21, 22; 1 Chr. 2:12–15; Matt. 1:5, 6; Luke 3:31, 32). Boaz and Ruth were the great-grandparents of David.

VII. DAVID'S RIGHT TO THE THRONE OF JUDAH (4:18–22)

4:18–22 Perez . . . David. This representative genealogy, which spans nine centuries from Perez (c. 1885 B.C.) to David (c. 1040 B.C.), specifically names ten generations. The first five (Perez to Nashon) cover the patriarchal times to the Exodus and wilderness wanderings. Salmon to David covers Joshua's lifetime and the judges to the monarchy. This genealogical compression by omission does not signal faulty records, because in Jewish thinking "son" could mean "descendant" (cf. Matt. 1:1). The purpose of a family record did not necessarily include every generation, but rather established incontestable succession by way of the more notable ancestors.

4:18 Perez. *See note on verse 12.* Although this genealogy only goes back to Perez, it conclusively establishes that David's lineage extends further back through Judah (Gen. 49:8–12), Jacob (Gen. 28:10–17), and Isaac (Gen. 26:24) to Abraham (Gen. 12:1–3).

4:18, 19 Hezron. Cf. Genesis 46:12.

4:19 Ram. He is listed as Arni in some Greek texts of Luke 3:33.

4:19, 20 Amminadab. He is the father-in-law of Aaron (Ex. 6:23), who does not appear in 1 Chronicles 2:10, but is cited in Matthew 1:4 and Luke 3:33. Some Hebrew manuscripts also include Admin between Ram and Amminadab in Luke 3:33.

4:20 Nahshon. He is the leader of Judah in the Exodus (Num. 1:7; 2:3; 7:12, 17; 10:14).

4:20, 21 Salmon. He is the husband of Rahab the harlot (cf. Matt. 1:5).

4:21 Salmon begot Boaz. Since Matthew 1:5 lists Rahab the harlot, who lived c. 1425–1350 B.C. as Salmon's wife, it indicates that some generations have been selectively omitted between Salmon and Boaz (c. 1160–1090 B.C.).

4:22 David. Looking back at Ruth from a NT perspective, latent messianic implications become more apparent (cf. Matt. 1:1). The fruit which is promised later on in the Davidic covenant (2 Sam. 7:1–17) finds its seedbed here. The hope of a messianic king and kingdom (2 Sam. 7:12–14) will be fulfilled in the Lord Jesus Christ (Rev. 19; 20) through the lineage of David's grandfather Obed, who was born to Boaz and Ruth the Moabitess.

Further Study

Huey, F. B. *Ruth*, in The Expositor's Bible Commentary. Grand Rapids: Zondervan, 1992.

Morris, Leon, *Ruth*, in *"Judges and Ruth,"* Tyndale Old Testament Commentaries. Downers Grove, Ill.: IVP, 1968.

Phillips, W. Gary. *Judges and Ruth.* Nashville: Broadman & Holman, 2004.

THE FIRST BOOK OF
SAMUEL

Title

First and Second Samuel were considered as one book in the earliest Hebrew manuscripts. They were later divided into the two books by the translators of the Greek version, the Septuagint (LXX), a division also followed by the Latin Vulgate, English translations, and modern Hebrew Bibles. The earliest Hebrew manuscripts entitled the one book *Samuel* after the man God used to establish the kingship in Israel. Later Hebrew texts and the English versions call the divided book 1 and 2 Samuel. The LXX designated them the First and Second Books of Kingdoms and the Vulgate, First and Second Kings, with the English translation of 1 and 2 Kings being titled Third and Fourth Kings in the LXX and Vulgate.

Author and Date

Jewish tradition ascribed the writing of *Samuel* to Samuel himself or to Samuel, Nathan, and Gad (based on 1 Chr. 29:29). But Samuel cannot be the writer because his death is recorded in 1 Samuel 25:1, before the events associated with David's reign even took place. Further, Nathan and Gad were prophets of the Lord during David's lifetime and would not have been alive when the Book of Samuel was written. Though the written records of these three prophets could have been used for information in the writing of 1 and 2 Samuel, the human author of these books is unknown. The work comes to the reader as an anonymous writing, i.e., the

human author speaks for the Lord and gives the divine interpretation of the events narrated.

The Books of Samuel contain no clear indication of the date of composition. That the author wrote after the division of the kingdom between Israel and Judah in 931 B.C. is clear, due to the many references to Israel and Judah as distinct entities (1 Sam. 11:8; 17:52; 18:16; 2 Sam. 5:5; 11:11; 12:8; 19:42–43; 24:1, 9). Also, the statement concerning Ziklag's belonging "to the kings of Judah to this day" in 1 Samuel 27:6 gives clear evidence of a post-Solomonic date of writing. There is no such clarity concerning how late the date of writing could be.

However, 1 and 2 Samuel are included in the Former Prophets in the Hebrew canon, along with Joshua, Judges, and 1 and 2 Kings. If the Former Prophets were composed as a unit, then Samuel would have been written during the Babylonian captivity (c. 560–540 B.C.), since 2 Kings concludes during the Exile (2 Kin. 25:27–30). However, since Samuel has a different literary style than Kings, it was most likely penned before the Exile during the period of the divided kingdom (c. 931–722 B.C.) and later made an integral part of the Former Prophets.

Background and Setting

The majority of the action recorded in 1 and 2 Samuel took place in and around the central highlands in the land of Israel. The nation of Israel was largely concentrated in an area that ran about ninety miles from the hill country of Ephraim in the north (1 Sam. 1:1; 9:4) to the hill country of Judah in the south (Josh. 20:7; 21:11) and between fifteen to thirty-five miles east to west. This central spine ranges in height from 1,500 feet to 3,300 feet above sea level. The major cities of 1 and 2 Samuel are to be found in these central highlands: Shiloh, the residence of Eli and the tabernacle; Ramah, the hometown of Samuel; Gibeah, the headquarters of Saul; Bethlehem, the birthplace of David; Hebron, David's capital when he ruled over Judah; and Jerusalem, the ultimate "city of David."

The events of 1 and 2 Samuel took place between the years c. 1105 B.C., the birth of Samuel (1 Sam. 1:1–28), to c. 971 B.C., the last words of David (2 Sam. 23:1–7). Thus, the books span about 135 years of history. During those years, Israel was transformed from a loosely knit group of tribes under judges to a united nation under the reign of a centralized monarchy. They look primarily at Samuel (c. 1105–1030 B.C.), Saul who reigned c. 1051–1011 B.C., and David who was king of the united monarchy c. 1011–971 B.C.

Historical and Theological Themes

As 1 Samuel begins, Israel was at a low point spiritually. The priesthood was corrupt (1 Sam. 2:12–17, 22–26), the ark of the covenant was not at the tabernacle (1 Sam. 4:3–7:2), idolatry was practiced (1 Sam. 7:3, 4), and the judges were dishonest (1 Sam. 8:2, 3). Through the influence of godly Samuel (1 Sam. 12:23) and David (1 Sam. 13:14), these conditions were reversed. Second Samuel concludes with the anger of the Lord being withdrawn from Israel (2 Sam. 24:25).

During the years narrated in 1 and 2 Samuel, the great empires of the ancient world were in a state of weakness. Neither Egypt nor the Mesopotamian powers, Babylon and Assyria, were threats to Israel at that time. The two nations most hostile to the Israelites were the Philistines (1 Sam. 4; 7; 13; 14; 17; 23; 31; 2 Sam. 5) to the west and the Ammonites (1 Sam. 11; 2 Sam. 10–12) to the east. The major contingent of the Philistines had migrated from the Aegean islands and Asia Minor in the twelfth century B.C. After being denied access to Egypt, they settled among other preexisting Philistines along the Mediterranean coast of Palestine.

The Philistines controlled the use of iron, which gave them a decided military and economic advantage over Israel (1 Sam. 13:19–22). The Ammonites were descendants of Lot (Gen. 19:38) who lived on the Transjordan plateau. David conquered the Philistines (2 Sam. 8:1) and the Ammonites (2 Sam. 12:29–31), along with other nations that surrounded Israel (2 Sam. 8:2–14).

There are four predominant theological themes in 1 and 2 Samuel. The first is the Davidic covenant. The books are literarily framed by two references to the "anointed" king in the prayer of Hannah (1 Sam. 2:10) and the song of David (2 Sam. 22:51). This is a reference to the Messiah, the King who will triumph over the nations who are opposed to God (see Gen. 49:8–12; Num. 24:7–9, 17–19). According to the Lord's promise, this Messiah will come through the line of David and establish David's throne forever (2 Sam. 7:12–16). The events of David's life recorded in Samuel foreshadow the actions of David's greater Son (i.e., Christ) in the future.

A second theme is the sovereignty of God, clearly seen in these books. One example is the birth of Samuel in response to Hannah's prayer (1 Sam. 9:17; 16:12, 13). Also, in relation to David, it is particularly evident that nothing can frustrate God's plan to have him rule over Israel (1 Sam. 24:20).

Third, the work of the Holy Spirit in empowering people for divinely appointed tasks is evident. The Spirit of the Lord came upon both Saul and David after their anointing as king (1 Sam. 10:10; 16:13). The power of the Holy Spirit brought forth prophecy (1 Sam. 10:6) and victory in battle (1 Sam. 11:6).

Fourth, the Books of Samuel demonstrate the personal and national effects of sin. The sins of Eli and his sons resulted in their deaths (1 Sam. 2:12–17, 22–25; 3:10–14; 4:17, 18). The lack of reverence for the ark of the covenant led to the death of a number of Israelites (1 Sam. 6:19; 2 Sam. 6:6, 7). Saul's disobedience resulted in the Lord's judgment, and he was rejected as king over Israel (1 Sam. 13:9, 13, 14; 15:8, 9, 20–23). Although David was forgiven for his sin of adultery and murder after his confession (2 Sam. 12:13), he still suffered the inevitable and devastating consequences of his sin (2 Sam. 12:14).

Interpretive Challenges

The Books of Samuel contain a number of interpretive issues that have been widely discussed:

(1) Which of the ancient manuscripts is closest to the original autograph? The standard Hebrew (Masoretic) text has been relatively poorly preserved, and the LXX often differs from it. Thus, the exact reading of the original autograph of the text is in places hard to determine (see 1 Sam. 13:1). The Masoretic text will be assumed to represent the original text unless there is a grammatical or contextual impossibility. This accounts for many of the numerical discrepancies.

(2) Is Samuel ambivalent to the establishment of the human kingship in Israel? It is claimed that while 1 Samuel 9–11 presents a positive view of the kingship, 1 Samuel 8 and 12 are strongly anti-monarchial. It is preferable, however, to see the book as presenting a balanced perspective of the human kingship. While the desire of Israel for a king was acceptable (Deut. 17:15), their reason for wanting a king showed a lack of faith in the Lord (*see notes on 1 Sam. 8:5, 20*).

(3) How does one explain the bizarre behavior of the prophets? It is commonly held that 1 and 2 Samuel present the prophets as ecstatic speakers with bizarre behavior, just like the pagan prophets of the other nations. But there is nothing in the text which is inconsistent with seeing the prophets as communicators of divine revelation, at times prophesying with musical accompaniment (*see notes on 1 Sam. 10:5; 19:23, 24*).

(4) How did the Holy Spirit minister before Pentecost? The ministry of the Holy Spirit in 1 Samuel 10:6, 10; 11:6; 16:13, 14; 19:20, 23; 2 Samuel 23:2 was not describing salvation in the NT sense, but an empowering by the Lord for His service (see also Judg. 3:10; 6:34; 11:29; 13:25; 14:6, 19; 15:14).

(5) What was the identity of the "distressing spirit from the Lord"? Is it a personal being, i.e., a demon, or a spirit of discontent created by God in the heart (cf. Judg. 9:23)? Traditionally, it has been viewed as a demon (*see note on 1 Sam. 16:14*).

(6) How did Samuel appear in 1 Samuel 28:3–5? It seems best to understand the appearance of Samuel as the Lord allowing the dead Samuel to speak with Saul.

(7) What is the identity of David's seed in 2 Samuel 7:12–15? It is usually taken as Solomon. However, the NT refers the words to Jesus, God's Son in Hebrews 1:5 (*see notes on 2 Sam. 7:12–15*).

Outline

I. SAMUEL: PROPHET AND JUDGE TO ISRAEL (1:1–7:17)

1:1–7:17 This first major division of the book begins and ends in Samuel's hometown of Ramah (v.1; 7:17). The focus of these chapters is on the life and ministry of Samuel. First Samuel 1:1–4:1a concentrates on Samuel as a prophet of the Lord (see the concluding statement of 4:1a, "and the word of Samuel came to all Israel"). The text in 4:1b–7:17 emphasizes Samuel as judge (see 7:17, "there he judged Israel").

A. Samuel the Prophet (1:1–4:1a)

1. The birth of Samuel (1:1–28)

1:1 *a certain man.* This verse resembles the introduction to the birth of Samson in Judges 13:2. The strong comparison also highlights the similarities between the lives of Samson and Samuel. Both men were judges over Israel, fighters of the Philistines, and lifelong Nazirites. *Ramathaim.* Possibly meaning "two heights," the name occurs only here in the OT. Elsewhere, the town is simply called Ramah. It was located about five miles north of Jerusalem. *Elkanah.* Meaning "God has created," he was the father of Samuel. *Zuph.* Zuph is both a place (9:5) and a personal name (1 Chr. 6:35), as here. *Ephraimite.* First Chronicles 6:27 identifies Elkanah as a member of the Kohathite branch of the tribe of Levi. The Levites lived among the other tribes (Josh. 21:20–22). Ephraim was the tribal area where this Levite lived.

1:2 *two wives.* Although polygamy was not God's intention for mankind (Gen. 2:24), it was tolerated, but never endorsed in Israel (see Deut. 21:15–17). Elkanah probably married Peninnah because Hannah was barren. *Hannah.* Meaning "grace," she was probably Elkanah's first wife. *Peninnah.*

Meaning "ruby," she was Elkanah's second wife and the bearer of his first children.

1:3 *This man went up . . . yearly.* All Israelite men were required to attend three annual feasts at the central sanctuary (Deut. 16:1–17). Elkanah regularly attended these festivals with his wives. The festival referred to here was probably the Feast of Tabernacles (September/October) because of the feasting mentioned in 1:9. *the LORD of hosts.* This is the first OT occurrence of *hosts* being added to the divine name. *Hosts* can refer to human armies (Ex. 7:4), celestial bodies (Deut. 4:19), or heavenly creatures (Josh. 5:14). This title emphasizes the Lord as sovereign over all of the powers in heaven and on earth, especially over the armies of Israel. *Shiloh.* Located about twenty miles north of Jerusalem in Ephraim, the tabernacle and ark of the covenant resided here (Josh. 18:1; Judg. 18:31). *Eli.* Meaning "exalted is the LORD," he was the high priest at Shiloh. *Hophni and Phinehas.* Each of Eli's two priestly sons had an Egyptian name: Hophni ("tadpole") and Phinehas ("nubian").

1:4 *an offering.* This was a peace offering since the worshipers ate a portion of the offering (see Lev. 7:11–18).

1:5 *the LORD had closed her womb.* Hannah's barrenness was the result of divine providence like Sarah's (Gen. 16:2) and Rachel's (Gen. 30:2).

1:6 *her rival.* The other wife was an adversary. *provoked her.* Lit. "to thunder against" her; see 2:10 for the same word.

1:7 *did not eat.* Hannah fasted because of the provocation of Peninnah. She did not eat of the peace offerings.

1:8 *your heart grieved?* The idiom used reflects anger, not sadness (see Deut. 15:10 for the same idiom).

1:9 *tabernacle.* The mention of sleeping quarters (3:2, 3) and doors (3:15) implies that at this time the tabernacle was part of a larger, more permanent building complex.

1:11 vow. Hannah pledged to give the Lord her son in return for God's favor in giving her that son. A married woman's vow could be confirmed or nullified by her husband according to Numbers 30:6–15. **Your maidservant.** A humble, submissive way of referring to herself in the presence of her superior, sovereign God. **remember me.** Hannah requested special attention and care from the Lord. **all the days of his life.** A contrast to the normal Nazirite vow, which was only for a specified period of time (see Num. 6:4, 5, 8). **no razor.** Though not specified as such in this chapter, the Nazirite vow is certainly presupposed. The nonshaving of the hair on one's head is one of the three requirements of the vow (Num. 6:5). This expression was used elsewhere only of the Nazirite Samson (Judg. 13:5; 16:17).

1:13 drunk. Public prayer in Israel was usually audible. However, Hannah was praying silently, leaving Eli to surmise that she was drunk.

1:16 wicked. Lit. "daughter of Belial." Cf. 2:12.

1:20 Samuel. The name literally meant "name of God," but sounded like "heard by God." For Hannah, the assonance was most important, because God had heard her prayer.

Old Testament Women

Name	Description	Biblical Reference
Bathsheba	Wife of David; mother of Solomon	2 Sam. 11:3, 27
Deborah	Judge who defeated the Canaanites	Judg. 4:4
Delilah	Philistine who tricked Samson	Judg. 16:4, 5
Dinah	Only daughter of Jacob	Gen. 30:21
Esther	Jewish queen of Persia who saved her people from destruction	Esther 2–9
Eve	First woman	Gen. 3:20
Gomer	Prophet Hosea's unfaithful wife	Hos. 1:2, 3
Hagar	Sarah's maid; mother of Ishmael	Gen. 16:3–16
Hannah	Mother of Samuel	1 Sam. 1
Jezebel	Wicked wife of King Ahab	1 Kin. 16:30, 31
Jochebed	Mother of Moses	Ex. 6:20
Miriam	Sister of Moses; a prophetess	Ex. 15:20
Naomi	Ruth's mother-in-law	Ruth 1:2, 4
Orpah	Ruth's sister-in-law	Ruth 1:4
Rachel	Wife of Jacob	Gen. 29:28
Rahab	Harlot who harbored Israel's spies; ancestor of Jesus	Josh. 2:3–1; Matt. 1:5
Ruth	Wife of Boaz and mother of Obed; ancestor of Jesus	Ruth 4:13, 17; Matt. 1:5
Sarah	Wife of Abraham; mother of Isaac	Gen. 11:29; 21:2, 3
Tamar	A daughter of David	2 Sam. 13:1
Zipporah	Wife of Moses	Ex. 2:21

Nelson's Complete Book of Bible Maps & Charts (Nashville: Thomas Nelson Publishers, 1996) 168. © 1993 by Thomas Nelson, Inc.

1:21 *his vow.* Elkanah supported and joined with his wife in her vow to the Lord. With the birth of Samuel, he brought his votive offering to the Lord (Lev. 7:16).

1:22 *weaned.* As was customary in the ancient world, Samuel was probably breast fed for two to three years. Then he was left to serve the Lord at the tabernacle for the rest of his life.

1:23 *His word.* Probably an earlier word of the Lord not recorded in the text.

1:24 *three bulls ... ephah of flour ... skin of wine.* According to Numbers 15:8–10, a bull, flour, and wine were to be sacrificed in fulfillment of a vow. Hannah brought all three in larger measure than required. An ephah was about three-fourths of a bushel.

1:26 *As your soul lives.* Lit. "by the light of your soul," a common oath formula.

1:27, 28 *asked ... lent.* These terms are from the same Hebrew root used four times in these two verses. Twice in verse 27 it has the usual meaning of "asked." Twice in verse 28 it bears the derived meaning "lent on request." God had given the son Hannah requested, and she gives her gift back to the Giver.

2. The prayer of Hannah (2:1–10)

2:1–10 In contrast to the prayer that came from her bitterness (1:10), Hannah prayed from joy in these verses. The prominent idea in Hannah's prayer is that the Lord is a righteous judge. He had brought down the proud (Peninnah) and exalted the humble (Hannah). The prayer has four sections: (1) Hannah prays to the Lord for His salvation (vv. 1, 2); (2) Hannah warned the proud of the Lord's humbling (vv. 3–8d); (3) Hannah affirmed the Lord's faithful care for His saints (vv. 8e–9b); (4) Hannah petitioned the Lord to judge the world and to prosper His anointed king (vv. 9c–10e). This prayer has a number of striking verbal similarities with David's song of 2 Samuel 22:2–51:

"horn" (2:1; 22:3), "rock" (2:2; 22:2, 3), salvation/deliverance (2:1, 2; 22:2, 3), grave/Sheol (2:6; 22:6), "thunder" (2:10; 22:14), "king" (2:10; 22:51), and "anointed" (2:10; 22:51).

2:1 *horn.* A symbol of strength and power (see Deut. 33:17).

2:2 *rock.* A metaphor for God stressing His strength and the security of those who trust in Him (see Deut. 32:4; Ps. 18:1, 2).

2:3 *proudly ... arrogance.* The majestic and powerful God humbles all those who vaunt themselves against Him. The idea of God's humbling of the proud is shown throughout 1 and 2 Samuel, toward Peninnah, Eli's sons, the Philistines, Goliath, Saul, Nabal, Absalom, Shimei, Sheba, and even David.

2:4–7 Seven contrasts are found in these four verses: (1) mighty and weak; (2) full and hungry; (3) barren and fertile; (4) dead and alive; (5) sick and well; (6) poor and rich; and (7) humbled and exalted.

2:5 *has borne seven.* This is not a personal testimony since Hannah bore only six children (2:21). *Seven* here is a general reference to women whom God blesses.

2:8 *pillars of the earth.* A figure of speech which pictures the earth's stability (cf. Pss. 75:3; 82:5; 104:5).

2:10 *The LORD will judge the ends of the earth.* The Lord will impose His righteous rule on all the nations and peoples (see Is. 2:2–4). *His king.* Moses had already predicted the coming of a king who would exercise God's rule over all the nations of the earth (Gen. 49:8–12; Num. 24:7–9, 17–19). It was this future, victorious king whom Hannah anticipated and Saul and David prefigured. *His anointed.* Previously in the OT, both the tabernacle and its utensils along with the priests (Aaron and his sons) had been anointed with oil. This pictured their consecrated and holy status before the Lord (Ex. 30:26–30). In Samuel, first Saul (10:1), and then David (16:13; 2 Sam. 2:4; 5:3) were anointed as they were inaugurated for the kingship. From this point in the OT, it is usually the king who is referred as "the anointed (of the LORD)" (12:3; 24:6; 26:9, 11, 16; 2 Sam. 1:14, 16; 19:21).

The kings of Israel, particularly David, foreshadowed the Lord's ultimate anointed king. The English word *Messiah* represents the Hebrew word used here meaning "anointed." Thus, this ultimate King who would rule over the nations of the earth came to be referred to as "the Messiah," as here and 2:35; cf. 2 Samuel 22:51.

3. The growth of Samuel (2:11–26)

2:11 ministered to the LORD. As a Levite, the boy Samuel performed services that assisted Eli, the high priest.

2:12 corrupt. Cf. 1:16. "Sons of Belial" was a Hebrew way of saying base, worthless, or wicked men. See 2 Corinthians 6:15, where it is used as a name for Satan. Eli had falsely considered Hannah a wicked woman (1:16). Eli's sons were, in fact, wicked men. **they did not know the LORD.** Eli's sons had no personal experience of, nor fellowship with the Lord. The boy Samuel came to "know the LORD" when the Lord revealed Himself to him (see 3:7).

2:13 the priests' custom. Not content with the specified portions of the sacrifices given to the priests (Deut. 18:3), Eli's sons would take for themselves whatever meat a three-pronged fork would collect from a boiling pot.

2:15 before they burned the fat. The law mandated that the fat of the sacrificial animal was to be burned on the altar to the Lord (Lev. 7:31). In contrast, Eli's sons demanded raw meat, including the fat, from the worshipers.

2:18 But Samuel. The faithful ministry of Samuel before the Lord was in sharp contrast to the disobedience of Eli's sons. **linen ephod.** A close fitting, sleeveless outer vest extending to the hips and worn by priests, especially when officiating before the altar (Ex. 28:6–14).

2:19 little robe. A sleeveless garment reaching to the knees, worn under the ephod (Ex. 28:31).

2:20 the loan. This is the same word used in 1:27, 28 translated there "granted," "asked," "lent." Here, it is a reminder of Hannah's faithfulness to her vow to the Lord. By providing Hannah with additional children, the Lord continued to be gracious to her.

2:22 lay with the women. Eli's sons included in their vile behavior having sexual relationships with the women who served at the tabernacle (see Ex. 38:8). Such religious prostitution was common among Israel's Canaanite neighbors.

2:25 God will judge. Eli's point to his sons was that if God would surely judge when one sinned against another man, how much more would He bring judgment against those who sinned against Him. **the LORD desired to kill them.** Because Eli's sons had persisted in their evil ways, God had already determined to judge them. This divine, judicial hardening, the result of defiant refusal to repent in the past, was the reason Hophni and Phinehas refused to heed Eli's warnings.

2:26 grew in stature, and in favor. In contrast to the apostate sons of Eli, Samuel was maturing both spiritually and socially (cf. Luke 2:52).

4. The oracle against Eli's house (2:27–36)

2:27 man of God. This phrase is usually used as a synonym for "prophet" (see 9:9, 10). **house of your father . . . in Egypt.** Although Eli's genealogy was not recorded in the OT, he was a descendant of Aaron. The Lord had revealed Himself to Aaron in Egypt before the Exodus (see Ex. 4:4–16). Aaron

Locations of Samuel's Ministry

? Exact location questionable

Mediterranean Sea

Aphek • Ebenezer?
• Shiloh
EPHRAIM
Mizpah • Bethel
Ramah • BENJAMIN • Gilgal
• Kiriath Jearim • • Geba
Ashdod • Jerusalem
Ekron • Beth Shemesh
• Gath JUDAH

Dead Sea

0 30 Mi.
0 30 Km.

The MacArthur Study Bible, by John MacArthur (Nashville: Word Publishing, 1997) 380. © 1993 by Thomas Nelson, Inc.

had been divinely chosen to serve the Lord as the first in a long line of priests (Ex. 28:1–4).

2:28 *to be My priest.* The chief duties of the priests were: (1) to place the offerings on the altar; (2) to burn the incense in the holy place; and (3) to wear the linen ephod (see v. 18).

2:29 *My offering.* In recognition of their service to God and His people, the priests were allocated specific parts of the offering which were brought to the sanctuary (see Lev. 2:3, 10; 7:31–36). *honor.* By condoning the sin of Hophni and Phinehas, Eli had shown preference for his sons above the Lord. Therefore, Eli was unworthy of the Lord's blessing.

2:30 *I said indeed.* The Lord had promised that Aaron's descendants would always be priests (Ex. 29:9), and He had confirmed that promise by oath (Num. 25:13). Because

of flagrant disobedience, the house of Eli would forfeit their priesthood. Although the Aaronic priesthood was perpetual, priests could forfeit their position by their sin.

2:31 *will not be an old man in your house.* The judgment of untimely death followed Eli's descendants. Eli's sons died in the flower of their manhood (4:11). Later, Saul massacred the priests at Nob (22:16–19). Ultimately, Solomon removed Abiathar from the priesthood (1 Kin. 2:26, 27), and the priestly line of Eleazar prevailed, as God promised (cf. Num. 25:12, 13).

2:32 *an enemy in My dwelling place.* This probably referred to the desecration of the tabernacle, where the Lord dwelt, at Shiloh by the Philistines (see Jer. 7:12–14).

2:34 *a sign to you.* The death of Eli's two sons on the same day validated the prophecy (cf. 4:11, 17).

2:35 *I will raise up for Myself a faithful priest.* Although some have identified this priest as Samuel and others Christ, it is better to view the prophecy as fulfilled in the accession of Zadok and his family to the priestly office in the time of Solomon (see 1 Kin. 1:7, 8; 2:26, 27, 35). This reestablished the office of high priest in the line of Eleazar and Phinehas (cf. Num. 25:10–13). *I will build him a sure house.* The sons of Zadok will also serve in the millennial temple (see Ezek. 44:15; 48:11). *My anointed.* This refers to the Messiah, who will defeat God's enemies and establish His rule in the Millennium (see v. 10).

2:36 *a morsel of bread.* The judgment corresponded to the sin. Those who had gorged themselves on the sacrifices (vv. 12–17) were reduced to begging for a morsel of food.

5. The Word of the Lord through Samuel (3:1–4:1a)

3:1 *the boy Samuel.* Samuel was no longer a child (2:21, 26). While the Jewish historian Josephus suggested he was twelve years of age, he was probably a teenager at this time. The same Hebrew term translated here "boy" was used of David when he killed Goliath (17:33). *the word of the LORD was rare.* The time of the judges was a period of extremely limited prophetic activity. The few visions that God did give were not widely known. *revelation.* Lit. "vision." A divine revelation mediated through an auditory or visual encounter.

3:3 *before the lamp of God went out.* The golden lampstand, located in the Holy Place of the tabernacle, was filled with olive oil and lit at twilight (Ex. 30:8). The lamp was kept burning from evening until morning (Ex. 27:20, 21). Just before dawn, while the golden lampstand was still burning, Samuel was called to his prophetic ministry. *ark of God.* See Exodus 25:10–22.

3:7 *Samuel did not yet know the LORD.* Samuel had not yet encountered the Lord in a personal way, nor had he received God's Word by divine revelation (see 2:12).

3:8 *Then Eli perceived.* Eli was slow to recognize that God was calling Samuel. This indicates that Eli's spiritual perception was not what it should have been as the priest and judge of Israel (see also 1:12–16).

3:10 *hears.* "To hear with interest," or "to hear so as to obey."

3:11 *ears . . . will tingle.* A message of impending destruction, referring here to Eli's house (see 2 Kin. 21:12; Jer. 19:3).

3:12 *all that I have spoken.* See 2:27–36. The repetition of the oracle against Eli to Samuel confirmed the word spoken by the man of God.

3:13 *made themselves vile.* The LXX reads "his sons blasphemed God." Cursing God was an offense worthy of death (see Lev. 24:11–16, 23). *did not restrain them.* Eli was implicated in the sins of his sons because he did not intervene with judgment. If his sons

were blaspheming God, they should have been stoned (see Lev. 24:15, 16).

3:14 *not be atoned for . . . forever.* Eli's family was apparently guilty of presumptuous sin. For such defiant sin, there was no atonement and the death penalty could be immediately applied (see Num. 15:30, 31).

3:15 *the doors of the house of the LORD.* The doors of the tabernacle compound (see 1:9).

3:17 *God do so to you, and more also.* This is an oath of imprecation. Eli called down God's judgment on Samuel if he refused to tell everything he knew.

3:18 *Let Him do what seems good to Him.* Eli resigned himself to divine sovereignty, without reluctance.

3:19 *the LORD was with him.* The Lord's presence was with Samuel, as it would be later with David (16:18; 18:12). The Lord's presence validated His choice of a man for His service. *let none of his words fall to the ground.* Everything Samuel said with divine authorization came true. This fulfillment of Samuel's word proved that he was a true prophet of God (see Deut. 18:21, 22).

3:20 *Dan to Beersheba.* The traditional limits of the land of Israel from the north to the south. *prophet of the LORD.* Samuel's status as a spokesman of God's message was acknowledged by all throughout Israel.

4:1a *the word of Samuel came to all Israel.* The text of 1:1–3:21 climaxes with the establishment of Samuel as God's spokesman/representative. Observe that "the word of the Lord" (3:21) has become equivalent to "the word of Samuel."

B. Samuel the Judge (4:1b–7:17)

1. The saga of the ark (4:1b–7:1)

4:1b *Philistines.* From the period of the judges through the end of David's reign, the Philistines ("Sea Peoples") were an ever-present enemy of Israel. They were non-Semitic immigrants (see Gen. 10:14; 1 Chr. 1:12; Jer. 47:4, 5; Amos 9:7) who settled along the coastal regions of southern Canaan, organizing their power in five chief cities: Ashdod, Ashkelon, Ekron, Gath, and Gaza (6:17; Judg. 3:13). The introduction of the Philistines into the narrative provides a link between the judgeship of Samuel and the judgeship which Samson was not able to complete (Judg. 13–16). *Ebenezer.* The location of this site has not been specifically identified. Opposite Aphek in Israelite territory, it is possibly modern Izbet Sarteh on the road to Shiloh. When translated, it means "stone of help," and its mention here (and 5:1) and again in 7:12 of another location mark this section as a literary unit. *Aphek.* This site is located near the source of the Yarkon River, at the southern end of the coastal plain of Sharon, approximately five miles east of the Mediterranean Sea. This city marked the northeastern edge of Philistine territory.

4:3 *Why has the LORD defeated us?* The question of the elders reflected their knowledge that the Lord both fought their battles (2:10; 17:47) and allowed their defeat. To be defeated clearly meant that God was not "with" them (Num. 14:42; Deut. 1:42). Instead of inquiring of the Lord for direction, they proceeded to take the matter into their own hands. *Let us bring the ark.* The ark symbolized the presence and power of the Lord. Yet, Israel treated it like a good-luck charm, which would ensure them victory over the Philistines. Knowing that victory or defeat depended on the Lord's presence, they confused the symbol of His presence with His actual presence. In this way, their understanding of God resembled that of the Philistines (4:8).

4:4 *dwells between the cherubim.* A repeated phrase used to describe the Lord (see 2 Sam. 6:2; 2 Kin. 19:15; 1 Chr. 13:6; Pss. 80:1; 99:1; Is. 37:16). It spoke of His sovereign majesty. *Hophni and Phinehas.* These were the two wicked sons of Eli (2:12–17, 27–37), of whom it was said that they "did not know the LORD" (2:12). The fact that they were mentioned together recalls the prophecy that they would die together (2:34).

4:6 *Hebrews.* In Genesis 14:13, the name *Hebrew* was applied to Abram. Consequently, the name came to refer to the physical descendants of Abraham. It was used to distinguish them as a class of people distinct from the foreigners around them. It means that Abram was a descendant of Eber in the line of Shem (cf. 10:25; 11:14–16).

4:7 *God has come into the camp!* The idol, to the Philistine, was thought to be the actual dwelling place of his deity. Hence, when Israel brought the ark into the camp, the Philistines concluded that God was present, an exclamation that reflected a knowledge of God's power.

4:8 *the gods who struck the Egyptians.* Evidently, the news of God's victory over the Egyptians was common knowledge to the Philistines.

4:9 *servants . . . as they have been to you.* Israel's failure to uproot all the inhabitants of Canaan (see Judg. 1:28) caused them to fall under the judgment of God. As a consequence of this judgment, Israel was enslaved to Philistine oppression (see Judg. 10; 13–16). The Philistines feared that they would become servants of the Hebrews.

4:11 *the ark of God was captured.* In spite of their hopes to manipulate God into giving them the victory, Israel was defeated and the ark fell into the hands of the Philistines. The view of having the ark of God being equivalent to having control of God, embraced both by Israel and then the Philistines, is to be contrasted with the power and providence of God in the remaining narrative. **Hophni and Phinehas died.** In fulfillment of 2:34 and 3:12, Eli's sons died together.

4:12 his clothes torn and dirt on his head. The actions of the man of Benjamin were considered to be universal signs of mourning for the dead and of national calamity (cf. 2 Sam. 15:32).

4:13 his heart trembled for the ark of God. Eli's concern for the ark stands in stark contrast to his earlier actions of honoring his two sons over honoring the Lord (2:29, 30; cf. 4:17, 18).

4:18 Eli . . . died. As was the case with Hophni and Phinehas, Eli died. Thus, in fulfillment of the word of the Lord, all of the priestly line through Eli had been wiped out (2:29–34). *See note on 2:31.* **he had judged Israel forty years.** Over that time, Eli fulfilled the office of both priest and judge in Israel.

4:21 Ichabod . . . The glory has departed! Due primarily to the loss of the ark, the symbol of God's presence, Phinehas's wife names her child Ichabod, meaning either "Where is the glory?" or "No glory." To the Hebrew, *glory* was often used to refer to God's presence; hence, the text means "Where is God?" The word *departed* carries the idea of having gone into exile. Thus, to the people of Israel, the capturing of the ark was a symbol that God had gone into exile. Although this was the mind-set of Israel, the text narrative will reveal that God was present, even when He disciplined His people. *See note on Ezekiel 10:18, 19.*

5:1 Ashdod. One of the five chief Philistine cities, inland from the coast (three miles) and approximately thirty-three miles west of Jerusalem.

5:2 Dagon. Ancient literature identifies this deity as a fish god, whose image had the lower body of a fish and the upper body of a man. Dagon seems to have been the leader of

Locations of the Ark's Journey

Mediterranean Sea

Aphek
Shiloh
EPHRAIM
Bethel
BENJAMIN
Ashdod
Kiriath Jearim
Ekron
Jerusalem
Gath
Beth Shemesh
JUDAH
Gaza
Dead Sea
P H I L I S T I A
N

0   30 Mi.
0   30 Km.

The MacArthur Study Bible, by John MacArthur (Nashville: Word Publishing, 1997) 382. © 1993 by Thomas Nelson, Inc.

the Philistine pantheon (Judg. 16:23) and is noted to be the father of Baal. The placing of the ark of God in the temple of Dagon was supposed to be a sign of Dagon's power and Yahweh's inferiority, a visual representation that the god of the Philistines was victorious over the God of the Hebrews. In addition, the textual connection of Dagon reinforces the affinity between the events written her and those in the life of Samson (cf. Judg. 13–16).

5:3 fallen on its face. Ironically, God Himself overturned the supposed supremacy of Dagon by causing Dagon to fall over, as if paying homage to the Lord.

5:4 head . . . hands were broken off. The first display of God's authority over Dagon was not perceived. God's second display of authority, the cutting off of Dagon's head and hands, was a common sign that the enemy was dead (17:54; 31:9; Judg. 7:25; 8:6;

2 Sam. 4:12), and was to be understood as God's divine judgment on the false idol.

5:5 tread on the threshold. Because the head and hands of Dagon fell on the threshold, superstition developed that it was cursed; therefore, the Philistines would not tread on it. **to this day.** This phrase supports the claim that the writer was living at a time removed from the actual event itself (see Introduction: Author and Date). This phrase and phrases equivalent to it are found throughout 1 and 2 Samuel (6:18; 26:6; 30:25; 2 Sam. 4:3; 6:8; 18:18).

5:6 the hand of the LORD was heavy. In contrast to the hands of Dagon being cut off, symbolizing his helplessness against the power of Yahweh, the Lord was pictured to be actively involved in judging the Philistines. The imagery of God's hand is found throughout the ark narrative (4:8; 5:6, 7, 9, 11; 6:3, 5, 9). **tumors.** It has been suggested that this word refers to the sores or boils caused by an epidemic of the bubonic plague carried by rats (6:4, 5). The spread of the disease and its deadly effect (5:6, 9, 12; 6:11, 17) make this a likely view.

5:8 lords of the Philistines. Those men who ruled the chief Philistine cities as kings (*see note on 4:1*). **Gath.** Another main Philistine city, located about twelve miles east of Ashdod (cf. 5:1).

5:10 Ekron. With judgment on Gath, the Philistines sent the ark away to the next main city to see if God was behind their calamity. Located about six miles north of Gath, it was the closest major Philistine city to Israel's border. **the ark . . . to kill us.** The cry of the Ekronites was an admission that the Philistines had gotten the message that God was the source of their troubles. It is curious that the Philistines knew of God's power to strike the Egyptians (4:8), yet they proudly believed themselves stronger than Egypt. The severity of the plagues grew increasingly

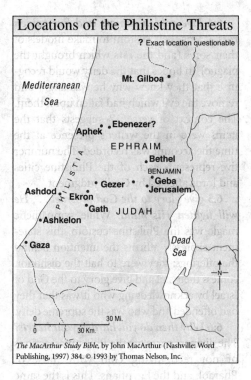

Locations of the Philistine Threats

? Exact location questionable

Mt. Gilboa

Mediterranean Sea

Aphek   Ebenezer?

EPHRAIM

Bethel

BENJAMIN

Gezer   Geba

Ashdod   Jerusalem

Ekron

Gath   JUDAH

Ashkelon

Gaza   Dead Sea

P H I L I S T I A

—N—

0   30 Mi.

0   30 Km.

The MacArthur Study Bible, by John MacArthur (Nashville: Word Publishing, 1997) 384. © 1993 by Thomas Nelson, Inc.

worse in verses 6–12, corresponding with the failure of the Philistines to humble themselves before God. Their actions were similar to those of the Egyptians (Ex. 5–14).

6:2 the priests and the diviners. These men of the Philistines, specifically identified in Scripture as having notable fame (Is. 2:6), were summoned to figure out how to appease God so He would stop the plague. **send it to its place.** The Philistines understood that they had offended God. Their diviners decided to appease His wrath by sending the ark back to Israel.

6:3 trespass offering. The purpose behind this offering was to both acknowledge and compensate for their trespass of dishonoring the God of Israel. These pagans recognized their sin and the need for manifest repentance, which they did according to their religious tradition by means of votive trespass offerings.

6:4 *Five golden tumors and five golden rats.* It was their custom to make models of their sores (and the rats which brought the plague), in hopes that the deity would recognize that they knew why he was angry and remove the evil which had fallen upon them. The context of verse 17 suggests that the items were in the writer's presence at the time the account was recorded. The number five represents each of the Philistine cities and lords affected by God's judgment.

6:5 *give glory to the God of Israel . . . He will lighten His hand.* While sympathetic magic was the Philistine custom, this statement expressly affirms the intention behind the offerings: they were to halt the dishonor, confess their sin, and give glory to the God of Israel by acknowledging who it was that they had offended and who was the supreme deity.

6:6 *Why then do you harden your hearts?* The diviners correlate the Philistines' actions of not recognizing God with those of Pharaoh and the Egyptians. This is the same word *harden* that was used in Exodus 7:14; 8:15, 32. It is an interesting correlation, because the dominant purpose in Exodus 5–14 was that the Egyptians might "know that I am the LORD" (Ex. 7:5).

6:7 *never been yoked.* To know without a doubt that the God of Israel was behind all of their troubles, the diviners devised a plan that would reveal whether God was the One responsible. Using cows which had "never been yoked" meant using animals that were untrained to pull a cart and probably would not go anywhere. *take their calves . . . away from them.* The second element in their plan was to use nursing cows taken away from their calves. For the cows unnaturally to head off in the opposite direction from their calves would be a clear sign that the cause of their judgment was supernatural.

6:9 *Beth Shemesh.* Named "house of the sun" and located in the Sorek Valley, this was a Levitical city about fifteen miles west of Jerusalem. Originally designated for the descendants of Aaron (Josh. 21:16), it was chosen to be the destination of the cows pulling the cart.

6:12 *lowing as they went.* With the moaning from instinctive unwillingness to leave their calves behind, the cows went straight to Beth Shemesh, not turning to the right or left, leaving the inescapable conclusion that God had judged them.

6:13 *reaping their wheat harvest.* Sometime in June. These harvests were accomplished with the whole city participating.

6:14 *Joshua of Beth Shemesh.* The cows stopped in the field of Joshua, where there was a large stone which was verifiable to the writer at the time the account was written. *burnt offering.* Because the cows and cart were used for sacred purposes, they could not be used for normal, everyday purposes. Therefore, the men of Beth Shemesh sacrificed the cows, using the cart for the fire.

6:15 *Levites.* The men of Beth Shemesh, being Levites, were qualified to move the ark. *put them on the large stone.* The stone mentioned was used as a pedestal for both the items of gold and the ark. At the time the account was written, it stood as a witness that God had returned to the land.

6:16 *five lords of the Philistines.* The lords of the Philistines, upon seeing that the ark arrived safely, returned to Ekron.

6:19 *looked into the ark.* This action on the part of the men of Beth Shemesh constituted the sin of presumption. This is first addressed in Numbers 4:20 and is mentioned again in 2 Samuel 6:6, 7. *fifty thousand and seventy men.* Some debate whether this figure is too large. However, retaining the larger number is more consistent with the context of "a great slaughter," and the reference to 30,000 in 4:10 (cf. 11:8). However, a scribal error could have occurred, in which case the number would omit the 50,000 and likely be "seventy," as in Josephus.

6:20 *Who is able to stand?* This question climaxes the narrative of the ark. No one is able to stand against God's judgment. This applied to the people outside the covenant as well as those under the covenant. Presumption before God is unacceptable. ***to whom shall it go?*** The expression was used to denote the desire to take the ark away from them.

6:21 *Kirjath Jearim.* A city located approximately ten miles northeast of Beth Shemesh. It would remain the resting place of the ark until David brought it to Jerusalem (2 Sam. 6:1–19). This location had long been associated with Baal worship (cf. Josh. 15:9, 60; 18:14).

2. Israel's victory over the Philistines and the judgeship of Samuel (7:2–17)

7:2 *twenty years.* Coupled with verse 3, the twenty years designated the period Israel neglected God and chased after foreign gods. After those twenty years, Israel returned to the Lord.

7:3 *prepare your hearts for the Lord . . . and He will deliver you.* This statement recalls the cycle in the Book of Judges: apostasy, oppression, repentance, and deliverance. It previews the contents of this chapter.

7:4 *the Baals and the Ashtoreths.* Most dominant of the Canaanite pantheon, these deities were the fertility gods which plagued Israel. *Baal* and *Ashtoreth* are plurals of majesty, which signify their supreme authority over other Canaanite deities. Ashtoreth represented the female goddess, while Baal represented the male, sky god who fertilized the land.

7:5 *Mizpah.* This city was located eight miles northeast of Kirjath Jearim in Benjamin. It became one of the cities of Samuel's circuit (v. 16). ***I will pray.*** Samuel

was a man of prayer (7:8, 9; 8:6; 12:19, 23; 15:11).

7:6 *drew water, and poured it out before the Lord.* The pouring out of water before the Lord was a sign of repentance. This act is repeated in 2 Samuel 23:16. ***We have sinned against the Lord.*** The symbol of Samuel pouring out the water and the acknowledgment of the people reveal a situation where true repentance had taken place. The condition of the heart superseded the importance or righteousness of the ritual. ***Samuel judged.*** At this point, Samuel is introduced as the judge of Israel. His judgeship encompassed both domestic leadership and the conduct of war. The word links the text back to the last comment about Eli who judged forty years (4:18). Samuel is shown to be the one taking over Eli's judgeship. He served as the last judge before the first king (cf. 1 Sam. 8:5).

7:7 *Israel . . . afraid of the Philistines.* When Israel heard that the Philistines had come up against them for war, they were afraid.

7:10 *the Lord thundered . . . upon the Philistines.* In a literal manner, the Lord did to His enemies what was said by Hannah in her prayer (2:10).

7:11 *Beth Car.* The location is unknown.

7:12 *Ebenezer.* A different location from the one mentioned in 4:1 and 5:1. The name functions as the literary knot for the two ends of this unit (*see note on 4:1*). ***Thus far the Lord has helped us.*** This expression means that the Lord was the One responsible for getting Israel to this point. He was Israel's Sovereign One in times of both faithfulness and rebellion. He fought the battles and provided the blessings.

7:13 *did not come anymore into the territory of Israel.* The Lord gave Israel the victory over the Philistines, discontinuing their threat for the immediate future during Samuel's judgeship. ***all the days of Samuel.***

As the section opened in 4:1 with Samuel pictured as God's agent, so here the section closed with the Lord working powerfully through all the days of Samuel.

7:14 *Ekron to Gath.* These two cities, mentioned earlier as chief Philistine cities (5:8, 10), became the eastern border of the Philistines. The territory to the east of these cities was freed from Philistine control and returned to Israel. *Amorites.* Whereas the Philistines resided in the coastal plains, the Amorites resided in the hills west of Israel between the Jordan Valley and the coastal plain. As with the Philistines, Israel was at peace with the Amorites.

7:16 *a circuit.* The circuit was an annual trip made by Samuel; he would travel to Bethel, Gilgal, Mizpah, and return once again to Ramah, which allowed him to manage the affairs of the people.

7:17 *Ramah.* The first major division of the book (1:1–7:17) ends with Samuel returning to Ramah to judge the people.

II. SAUL: THE FIRST KING OVER ISRAEL (8:1–15:35)

8:1–15:35 This division of the book concentrates on the interaction between Israel, Samuel, and Saul. These chapters begin with the elders of Israel coming to Samuel at Ramah (8:4) and conclude with Samuel's leaving Saul and returning to Ramah (15:34). First Samuel 8:1–12:25 describes the establishment of the kingship over the nation of Israel and the advent of Saul as the first king. These chapters are linked by reference to Samuel's being old (8:1; 12:2) and "heeding the voice" of the people (8:7, 9, 19, 22; 12:1, 14, 15). Chapters 13:1–15:35 recount the failures of Saul as king over Israel. The events of these chapters are bracketed by two interactions between Saul and Samuel that take place in Gilgal (13:4, 7, 8, 12, 15; 15:12, 21, 33).

A. The Rise of Saul to the Kingship (8:1–12:25)

1. The demand of Israel for a king (8:1–22)

8:1 *Samuel was old.* Samuel was about sixty years of age (1043 B.C.). He appointed his two sons to serve as judges in Beersheba, a city about fifty-seven miles south of Ramah.

8:2 *Joel.* The name means "the LORD is God." *Abijah.* The name means "my Father is the LORD."

8:3 *his sons did not walk in his ways.* The perverted desire for riches led Samuel's sons to take bribes and, thereby, pervert justice. These actions were strictly forbidden for judges in Deuteronomy 16:19. The sins of Samuel's sons became the pretext for Israel's demand for a king (vv. 4, 5).

8:5 *Now make us a king . . . like all the nations.* When Israel entered the land, they encountered Canaanite city-states that were led by kings (see Josh. 12:7–24). Additionally, during the period of the judges, Israel was enslaved by nations that were led by kings (Judg. 3:8, 12; 4:2; 8:5; 11:12). However, at the time of the judges, there was no king in Israel (Judg. 17:6; 18:1; 19:1; 21:25). As Israel lived in the land surrounded by nations that had kings, the desire arose for a king in Israel also. According to Deuteronomy 17:14, God knew this would be their desire and He would allow it to occur. However, verse 20 revealed a motive which was definitely counter to the Lord's will. *See note on 8:20.*

8:7 *Heed the voice of the people.* The Lord had predicted that there would be kings over Israel (Gen. 35:11; 36:31; 49:10; Num. 24:7–9, 17; Deut. 17:14; 28:36). Here, the Lord told Samuel to obey the request of

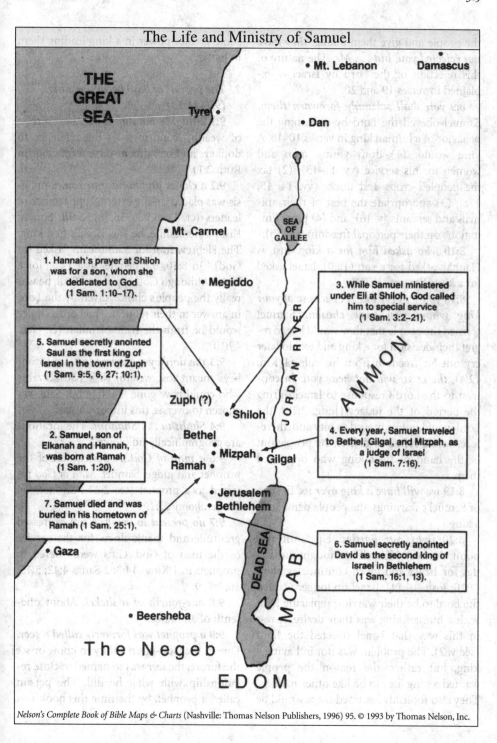

The Life and Ministry of Samuel

THE GREAT SEA

Mt. Lebanon

Damascus

Tyre

Dan

SEA OF GALILEE

Mt. Carmel

1. Hannah's prayer at Shiloh was for a son, whom she dedicated to God (1 Sam. 1:10–17).

Megiddo

3. While Samuel ministered under Eli at Shiloh, God called him to special service (1 Sam. 3:2–21).

JORDAN RIVER

AMMON

5. Samuel secretly anointed Saul as the first king of Israel in the town of Zuph (1 Sam. 9:5, 6, 27; 10:1).

Zuph (?)

Shiloh

Bethel

2. Samuel, son of Elkanah and Hannah, was born at Ramah (1 Sam. 1:20).

Mizpah

Gilgal

Ramah

4. Every year, Samuel traveled to Bethel, Gilgal, and Mizpah, as a judge of Israel (1 Sam. 7:16).

7. Samuel died and was buried in his hometown of Ramah (1 Sam. 25:1).

Jerusalem

Bethlehem

DEAD SEA

MOAB

6. Samuel secretly anointed David as the second king of Israel in Bethlehem (1 Sam. 16:1, 13).

Gaza

Beersheba

The Negeb

EDOM

Nelson's Complete Book of Bible Maps & Charts (Nashville: Thomas Nelson Publishers, 1996) 95. © 1993 by Thomas Nelson, Inc.

the people and give them a king. *they have not rejected you, but . . . Me.* The nature of this rejection of the Lord by Israel is explained in verses 19 and 20.

8:9 *you shall solemnly forewarn them.* Samuel obeyed the Lord by describing the behavior of a human king in verses 10–18. A king would: (1) draft young men and women for his service (vv. 11–13); (2) tax the people's crops and flocks (vv. 14, 15, 17a); (3) appropriate the best of their animals and servants (v. 16); and (4) place limitations on their personal freedom (v. 17b).

8:10 *who asked him for a king.* Just as Hannah asked for a son (1:20), Israel asked for a king. *See note on 9:2.*

8:18 *you will cry out . . . because of your king whom you have chosen.* Samuel warned the people that they would live to regret their decision for a king and would later cry out for freedom from his rule (1 Kin. 12:4). *the LORD will not hear you.* In contrast to the Lord's response to Israel during the period of the judges (Judg. 2:18), the Lord would not be moved to pity and, therefore, would refuse to deliver the people out of the hand of their king who oppressed them.

8:19 *we will have a king over us.* In spite of Samuel's warnings, the people demanded a king.

8:20 *fight our battles.* Up until this point, the Lord Himself had fought the battles for Israel and given continual victory (7:10; Josh. 10:14). Israel no longer wanted the Lord to be their warrior; replacing Him with a human king was their desire. It was in this way that Israel rejected the Lord (see v. 7). The problem was not in having a king, but rather, the reason the people wanted a king, i.e., to be like other nations. They also foolishly assumed there would be

some greater power in a king leading them in battle.

2. The process of Saul becoming king (9:1–11:13)

9:1 *a mighty man of power.* I.e., "a man of wealth," confirmed by the reference to donkeys and servants in verse 3 (cf. Boaz in Ruth 2:1).

9:2 *a choice and handsome son.* Emphasis was placed on the external appearance of leaders (cf. David in 16:18). *Saul.* Son of Kish, a Benjamite, he was Israel's first king. The Hebrew root for *Saul* means "asked (of God)." In 8:10, the people "asked . . . for a king." Although God appointed Saul, he was really the people's choice, given by the Lord in answer to their request. The Lord's choice would be from the tribe of Judah (cf. Gen. 49:10).

9:3 *the donkeys . . . were lost.* Lost donkeys meant lost wealth. Kish had servants who could have gone looking, but Saul was chosen to oversee this important task.

9:4 *Shalisha . . . Shaalim.* The locations are geographically unknown.

9:6 *a man of God.* A description of the prophet and judge, Samuel. *Man of God* referred to a prophet (see 2:27). *See note on Deuteronomy 33:1.*

9:7 *no present to bring.* A gift expressed gratitude and thankfulness for the service of the man of God. Gifts were offered to prophets in 1 Kings 14:3; 2 Kings 4:42; 5:15, 16; 8:8, 9.

9:8 *one-fourth of a shekel.* About one-tenth of an ounce.

9:9 *a prophet was formerly called a seer.* Due to the God-given ability to know or *see* the future, the *seer* was so named in close relationship with what he did. The person called a prophet, by the time this book was written, had been termed a seer in the earlier time of Saul.

9:12 high place. This is essentially Canaanite in background (cf. Deut. 12:2–5). Before the temple was built, the high place was used for worship and sacrifice because it provided the best vantage point for the participation of the people in worship and allowed them to see the sacrifice being made for them.

9:13 he must bless the sacrifice. The sacrifice was offered to the Lord as an act of worship by the man of God.

9:16 anoint him. This represents a setting apart for service to the Lord, which occurs in 10:1. *See note on 2:10.* **commander.** Lit. "one given prominence, one placed in front." The title referred to "one designated to rule" (cf. 1 Kin. 1:35; 2 Chr. 11:22). **their cry has come to Me.** The people had been crying out for deliverance from the Philistines, their long-time rivals, just as they did for liberation from Egypt (cf. Ex. 2:25; 3:9).

9:17 This one shall reign over My people. God identified Saul to Samuel, assuring there was no mistaking whom God was choosing to be king.

9:18 where is the seer's house? A reference to Samuel's house.

9:20 all the desire of Israel? Saul was to become the focus of Israel's hope for military victories over her enemies (cf. 8:19, 20).

9:21 a Benjamite . . . the least of all the families. Saul's humility and timidity was expressed by his proper assessment of his tribe and a humble estimation of his family.

9:22 the hall. The place where those who were invited ate with Samuel after the offering of the sacrifice on the high place (cf. vv. 12, 13).

9:24 the thigh . . . set apart for you. Samuel was following Leviticus 7:28–36. Samuel received the thigh, the portion of the sacrifice reserved for the priest. Samuel's giving of this choice piece of meat to Saul was a distinct honor and reflected Saul's new status as the designated king.

9:25 the top of the house. The roof of Samuel's house provided a place for Saul and his servant to sleep for the night.

9:27 the word of God. Special revelation from God, given to Samuel and intended for Saul. *See note on 3:1.*

10:1 the LORD has anointed you commander. The Lord chose Saul to be the leader of Israel and communicated His choice through the private anointing by Samuel, signifying a setting aside for God's service (see 2:10). **His inheritance?** The inheritance was God's nation, Israel, in the sense that she uniquely belonged to Him (Deut. 4:20; 9:26).

10:2 Zelzah. Only mentioned here, Zelzah was probably near Ramah, located between Bethel and Bethlehem, where Rachel died (Gen. 35:19; 48:7).

10:3 Tabor. This is not the far-distant Mt. Tabor, but a location unknown, probably near Bethel.

10:5 the Philistine garrison. Most likely the garrison in Geba in Benjamin, about five miles north of Jerusalem. **a group of prophets.** Lit. "sons of the prophets." They were young men being trained by Samuel for the prophetic ministry (see 19:18–20). **prophesying.** The prophet, as God's messenger, declared the Word of the Lord (2 Sam. 7:5; 12:1), sometimes accompanied by music (1 Chr. 25:1). Here, *prophesying* connotes praising God and instructing the people with musical accompaniment.

10:6 the Spirit of the LORD will come upon you. The Holy Spirit would enable Saul to declare the Word of the Lord with the prophets. **turned into another man.** With this empowerment by the Holy Spirit, Saul would emerge as another man (cf. 10:9), equipped in the manner of Gideon and Jepthah for deeds of valor (cf. v. 9; Judg. 6:34;

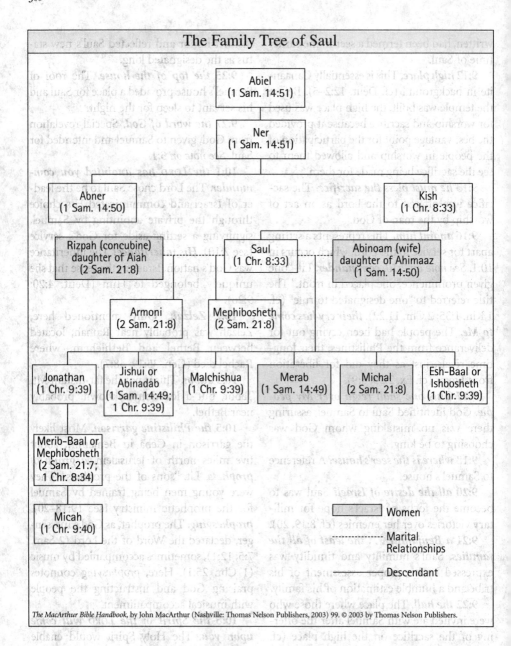

The Family Tree of Saul

Abiel
(1 Sam. 14:51)

Ner
(1 Sam. 14:51)

Abner
(1 Sam. 14:50)

Kish
(1 Chr. 8:33)

Rizpah (concubine)
daughter of Aiah
(2 Sam. 21:8)

Saul
(1 Chr. 8:33)

Abinoam (wife)
daughter of Ahimaaz
(1 Sam. 14:50)

Armoni
(2 Sam. 21:8)

Mephibosheth
(2 Sam. 21:8)

Jonathan
(1 Chr. 9:39)

Jishui or
Abinadab
(1 Sam. 14:49;
1 Chr. 9:39)

Malchishua
(1 Chr. 9:39)

Merab
(1 Sam. 14:49)

Michal
(2 Sam. 21:8)

Esh–Baal or
Ishbosheth
(1 Chr. 9:39)

Merib–Baal or
Mephibosheth
(2 Sam. 21:7;
1 Chr. 8:34)

Micah
(1 Chr. 9:40)

Women

--------------- Marital
Relationships

———— Descendant

The MacArthur Bible Handbook, by John MacArthur (Nashville: Thomas Nelson Publishers, 2003) 99. © 2003 by Thomas Nelson Publishers.

11:29).

10:7 *signs.* The three signs of verses 2–6: (1) the report of the found donkeys; (2) the encounter of the three men going to Bethel; and (3) the encounter with the prophets. *do as the occasion demands.* Saul was to do what his hand found to do (Eccl. 9:10).

10:8 *Gilgal.* The town where Saul eventually would (1) be declared king by Samuel (11:14, 15), and (2) offer sacrifice before the Lord without the prophet Samuel (13:12), also where Samuel killed King Agag (15:33). Gilgal was east of Jericho, but west of the Jordan River. *burnt offerings and . . . peace offerings. See notes on Leviticus 1:3–17; 3:1–17. Seven days.* The appointed time Saul was to wait for Samuel to come and tell him what to do (see 13:8).

10:9 *God gave him another heart.* Lit. "God changed him for another heart," i.e., God prepared Saul for the kingship by having the Holy Spirit come upon him (cf. v. 6).

10:12 *who is their father?* A question asked to find out the identity of the leader of the prophetic band that now included Saul. *a proverb.* A saying of common occurrence.

10:16 *the matter of the kingdom.* He did not tell his uncle the information Samuel gave Saul about becoming king. This might reflect Saul's humility (cf. v. 22).

10:17 *Samuel called the people.* The Lord's choice of Saul was made public at Mizpah, the place of the spiritual revival before Israel's victory over the Philistines (7:5–8).

10:18, 19 *the LORD God of Israel . . . delivered you.* Despite the past faithfulness of God to His people, they still desired a human king to deliver them from the hands of their enemies.

10:20, 21 *chosen.* Probably Saul was selected by the casting of lots (cf. Lev. 16:8–10; Josh. 7:15–18). *See note on Proverbs 16:33.*

10:22 *hidden among the equipment.* Overwhelmed, Saul had hidden himself in the military supplies.

10:23 *taller . . . from his shoulders upward.* Saul's physical stature was impressive; being head and shoulders above the other people gave Saul a kingly presence.

10:25 *the behavior of royalty.* Samuel reminded the people of the regulations governing the conduct of kings according to Deuteronomy 17:14–20.

10:26 *whose hearts God had touched.* Valiant men who were eager to affirm God's choice of Saul and, in response to a divine impulse, joined him.

10:27 *rebels.* Lit. "sons of Belial" (*see note on 2:12*). Those who did not recognize Saul with the respect befitting a king.

11:1 *Nahash the Ammonite.* Nahash, meaning "snake," was king of the Ammonites, the descendants of Lot (cf. Gen. 19:36–38) who lived east of the Jordan River. *Jabesh Gilead.* A town east of the Jordan River, about twenty-two miles south of the Sea of Galilee, in the tribal territory of Manasseh (cf. Judg. 21:8–14).

11:2 *put out all your right eyes.* This barbarous mutilation was a common punishment of usurpers in the ancient Near East which would disable the warriors' depth perception and peripheral vision, rendering them useless in battle.

11:3 *seven days.* The elders at Jabesh were hoping for deliverance from the Israelites west of the Jordan River.

11:4 *Gibeah of Saul.* Saul's home and the first capital city of the monarchy, about three miles north of Jerusalem (cf. 10:26).

11:5 *from the field.* Saul continued to work as a farmer while waiting for the time to answer Israel's expectations of him as the king.

11:6 *the Spirit of God came upon Saul.* This was to fill him with divine indignation and to empower him to deliver the citizens of Jabesh Gilead (cf. 10:6).

11:7 cut them in pieces. Saul divided the oxen in sections to be taken throughout Israel to rouse the people for battle (see a similar action in Judg. 19:29; 20:6).

11:8 Bezek. A city thirteen miles north of Shechem and seventeen miles west of Jabesh Gilead. **children of Israel . . . men of Judah.** This distinction made between Israel and Judah before the kingdom was divided indicates the book was written after 931 B.C. when the kingdom had been divided. See Introduction: Author and Date.

11:11 three companies. A military strategy of dividing up forces, it lessened the possibility of losing everyone to a sneak attack while giving greater military options. **in the morning watch.** The last of the three watches (2:00–6:00 A.M.), this surprise attack was before dawn, before the Ammonites were prepared for battle.

11:13 the LORD has accomplished salvation in Israel. Saul recognized the deliverance of the Lord and refused to kill those who had rebelled against his kingship (10:27).

3. The exhortation of Samuel to Israel concerning the king (11:14–12:25)

11:14 Gilgal. See note on 10:8. **renew the kingdom.** The reaffirmation of Saul's kingship by public acclamation.

11:15 they made Saul king before the LORD. All the people came to crown Saul king that day. The process of entering the kingship was the same for both Saul and David: (1) commissioned by the Lord (9:1–10:16; 16:1–13); (2) confirmed by military victory (10:17–11:11; 16:14–2 Sam. 1:27); and (3) crowned (11:12–15; 2 Sam. 2:4; 5:3). **peace offerings.** Sacrifices of thanksgiving (cf. Lev. 7:13). **rejoiced greatly.** Along with the victory over the Ammonites, there was a great celebration over the nation being united.

12:1 I have heeded your voice. Samuel, obeying the will of the Lord and the people, set the king of God's choice over them, though he had personal reservations about the monarchy.

12:3 Here I am. These familiar words for Samuel throughout his entire life (cf. 3:4, 5, 6, 8, 16) emphasized his availability to God and the people. **Witness.** Samuel requested the people to "testify against" any covenant stipulations that he had violated.

12:7 I may reason with you before the LORD. Despite the nation being unified under the new king, Samuel still wanted to rebuke the nation for ignoring and rejecting what God had done without a king.

12:11 the LORD sent . . . and delivered you. It was the Lord who delivered them through the hands of the judges, not themselves.

12:12 when you saw that Nahash king of the Ammonites came against you. According to the Dead Sea Scrolls and Josephus, Nahash was campaigning over a large area. It was that Ammonite threat that seemingly provoked Israel to demand a human king (8:1–20). **the LORD your God was your king.** The clearest indictment of Israel for choosing a mere man to fight for her instead of the Lord God (cf. 8:20).

12:13 the king whom you have chosen . . . desired. The Lord gave them their request (cf. Ps. 106:15).

12:14 fear the LORD. A reminder of Joshua 24:14. Israel was to stand in awe of the Lord and submit to Him (cf. Deut. 10:12). **you and the king . . . following the LORD your God.** Both the people and the king were given the same command. The standard was the same—obedience to God's commands.

12:15 rebel. "Disobey, not heed, forsake." Echoing the promises of Deuteronomy 28, there would be blessings for obeying and curses for disobeying the commands of the Lord.

12:16 this great thing. Though rain during the wheat harvest (late May to early June) was unusual, the Lord sent the rain and thunder to authenticate Samuel's words to the people.

12:19 Pray for your servants. The people's response to the power of God was their recognition of their sinful motives in asking for a king. They needed Samuel's prayers to intercede for them.

12:20 serve the Lord with all your heart. An often-expressed covenant requirement (Deut. 10:12, 13; 11:13, 14).

12:21 empty things. "Futile things" (i.e., idols).

B. The Decline of Saul in the Kingship (13:1–15:35)

1. The rebuke of Saul (13:1–15)

13:1 one year . . . two years. The original numbers have not been preserved in this text. It literally reads, "Saul was one year old when he became king and ruled two years over Israel." Acts 13:21 states that Saul ruled Israel forty years, but his age at his accession is recorded nowhere in Scripture. Probably the best reconstruction of verses 1 and 2 is, "Saul was one and (perhaps) thirty years old when he began to reign, and when he had reigned two years over Israel, then Saul chose for himself three thousand men of Israel."

13:2 Michmash. This area was located about seven miles northeast of Jerusalem. **Jonathan.** "The Lord has given." Saul's firstborn son and heir apparent to the throne was evidently old enough to serve as a commander in Israel's army at this time, much like David when he killed Goliath (1 Sam. 17:32–37). **Gibeah of Benjamin.** This city was located three miles north of Jerusalem. It was called Gibeah of Saul in 11:4.

Key Word

Name: 12:22; 17:45; 18:30—most likely means "to mark." In biblical history, a person's name often described personal characteristics such as destiny or position (see 1 Sam. 25:25 for the explanation of Nabal's name, which meant "Fool"). Sometimes, God renamed people to reflect a change in their character or status (see Gen. 35:10). The various names of God reveal important aspects of His nature (for example, God Most High, Almighty God, I AM). The name of God should be used with honor and respect (Ex. 20:7). God shared His name with Israel to express His intimate covenantal relationship with them (Ex. 3:13–15).

13:3 Geba. This outpost was located about five miles north-northeast of Jerusalem, one and one-half miles southwest of Michmash. **blew the trumpet.** Saul used the trumpet to summon additional troops for battle.

13:4 an abomination. Israel could expect retaliation from the Philistines for Jonathan's raid. **Gilgal.** This is the town of Saul's confirmation as king by Samuel and the people (11:14, 15). Saul chose Gilgal because of Samuel's word in 10:8.

13:5 thirty thousand chariots. This is probably a scribal error, since the number is too large for the corresponding horsemen. Three thousand is more reasonable and is found in some OT manuscripts. **Michmash.** See note on 13:2. **Beth Aven.** Lit. "house of nothingness." It was less than one miles southwest of Michmash.

13:7 Gad and Gilead. Areas east of the Jordan River. **all the people followed him trembling.** The people were in fear over probable Philistine retaliation.

13:8 seven days . . . the time set by

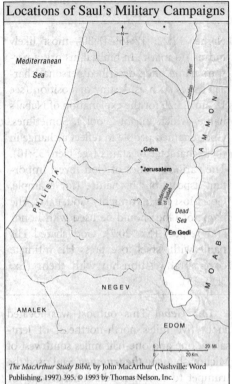

Locations of Saul's Military Campaigns

Mediterranean Sea

Jordan River

AMMON

•Geba

•Jerusalem

PHILISTIA

Wilderness of Judah

Dead Sea

•En Gedi

MOAB

NEGEV

AMALEK

EDOM

0   20 Mi.
0   20 Km.

The MacArthur Study Bible, by John MacArthur (Nashville: Word Publishing, 1997) 395. © 1993 by Thomas Nelson, Inc.

Samuel. This is a direct reference to Samuel's word in 10:8. Saul was commanded to wait seven days to meet Samuel in Gilgal.

the people were scattered. Saul's men were deserting him because of anxiety and fear over the coming battle.

13:9 he offered the burnt offering. Saul's sin was not specifically that he made a sacrifice (cf. 2 Sam. 24:25; 1 Kin. 8:62–64), but that he did not wait for priestly assistance from Samuel. See 10:8. He wished to rule as an autocrat who possessed absolute power in civil and sacred matters. Samuel had wanted the seven days as a test of Saul's character and obedience to God, but Saul failed it by invading the priestly office himself.

13:11 When I saw. Saul reacted disobediently based upon what he saw, not by faith.

He feared losing his men and did not properly consider what God wanted him to do.

13:13 You have not kept the commandment. Saul's disobedience was a direct violation of the command from Samuel in 10:8. **your kingdom . . . forever.** How could this be in light of God's promise that the king would descend from Judah (Gen. 49:10)? This pronouncement would correct the potential contradiction of Saul being from Benjamin, not Judah (cf. v. 14).

13:14 a man after His own heart. Instead of Saul, God was going to choose one whose heart was like His own, i.e., one who had a will to obey God. Paul quotes this passage in Acts 13:22 of David (cf. 16:7). **commander.** Someone else, namely David, had already been chosen to be God's leader over His people.

13:15 from Gilgal to Gibeah. This was about a ten-mile trip westward. Samuel left Saul, realizing that Saul's kingship was doomed. **six hundred men.** This indicates the mass departure of the Israelites (v. 6) and gives a perspective on what Saul saw (v. 5).

2. The wars of Saul (13:16–14:52)

13:17 raiders . . . in three companies. Lit. these were "destroyers" in the Philistine army, divided into three groups.

13:19 no blacksmith. The Philistines had superior iron and metal-working craftsmen until David's time (cf. 1 Chr. 22:3), accounting for their formidable military force.

13:20 mattock. A pickax to work the ground by hand.

13:21 The Philistines charged a high price to sharpen instruments that potentially could be used against them.

13:22 neither sword nor spear. The Philistines had a distinct military advantage over Israel since they had a monopoly on iron weapons.

13:23 *the pass of Michmash.* Some of the Philistines had moved out to a pass leading to Michmash.

14:1 *the other side.* Jonathan and his armorbearer left the Israelite camp to approach the Philistine outpost.

14:2 *pomegranate tree.* These trees are common to Israel's landscape, normally growing as low shrubs with spreading branches. This may have been a particularly large one.

14:3 *Ahijah.* "Brother of the LORD." He was the great-grandson of Eli the high priest, another house which had been rejected of the Lord (2:22–36). ***wearing an ephod.*** The ephod was a white garment worn by the priests that was attached to the body by a belt. A breastplate worn over the ephod had pouches that were used by the priests to carry certain devices used in determining the will of God, i.e., the Urim and Thummim, or sacred lots. *See note on Exodus 28:5–13.* Apparently, Saul chose not to use it for seeking the Lord's will.

14:4 *Bozez . . . Seneh.* Hebrew terms. Bozez may mean "slippery." Seneh means "thorny."

14:6 *uncircumcised.* This was a derogatory term used by the Israelites to describe the Philistines. ***by many or by few.*** Jonathan demonstrated the great faith that should have been demonstrated by the king (cf. 13:11).

14:10 *a sign to us.* This was an unusual manner for determining the will of the Lord, but not without precedent, e.g., Gideon's fleece (Judg. 6:36–40). Jonathan was allowed to determine the will of God by the reaction of his enemies.

14:11 *Hebrews.* The oldest term used by Gentile nations to refer to the people of Israel. ***the holes where they have hidden.*** Many of the Israelites were hiding in fear

over the battle. Apparently, they thought Jonathan and his armorbearer were Israelite deserters coming to the Philistine side.

14:15 *the earth quaked.* The earthquake affirms the fact that divine intervention aided Jonathan and his armorbearer in their raid. The earthquake caused a panic among the Philistines. God would have intervened on Saul's behalf in such a manner had he chosen to be faithfully patient (cf. 13:9).

14:18 *ark of God.* The LXX reads "ephod" instead of "ark," and this seems more likely since the ark was at Kirjath Jearim and the language of verse 19 better fits the ephod (v. 3) than the ark.

14:19 *Withdraw your hand.* Saul, in a hurry, ordered the priest to stop the inquiry into the will of the Lord.

14:21 *Hebrews.* This is a reference to Israelite deserters or mercenaries.

14:22 *the mountains of Ephraim.* A large and partially wooded area north and west of Michmash.

14:23 *So the LORD saved Israel.* The writer uses language similar to that of the Exodus. In spite of their disobedient king, God was faithful to deliver Israel from her enemies. ***Beth Aven.*** *See note on 13:2.*

14:24 *were distressed.* Saul's inept leadership failed to provide for the physical needs of his men, leaving them weak and fatigued. ***Cursed.*** Saul's first foolish oath pronounced a curse upon anyone tasting food until the battle was over. The scene fits chronologically after Jonathan's departure.

14:25 *honey on the ground.* This was a reference to honeycombs found in the forest (v. 27).

14:27 *Jonathan had not heard.* Jonathan apparently had departed before Saul made his oath.

14:29 *My father has troubled the land.* Jonathan saw the foolishness of Saul's oath and how it actually hurt Israel's cause instead of helping it.

14:31 *Aijalon.* This area is located fifteen miles west of Michmash. This would have been a normal path back to the land of the Philistines.

14:32 *ate them with the blood.* The people were so severely hungry because of the oath (v. 24) that they disobeyed the law by eating the meat raw and not draining the blood (cf. Lev. 17:10–14).

14:35 *the first altar.* The first and only altar built by Saul mentioned in Scripture.

14:36 *Let us draw near to God.* Ahijah the priest requested that they first seek the Lord about their course of action.

14:37 *Saul asked counsel of God.* At the request of Ahijah, Saul inquired of the Lord about his battle plan. ***He did not answer him.*** Because of the sin that Saul had caused in his army, God did not answer his inquiry. This would not be the last time that the Lord would refuse to respond to sinful Saul (cf. 28:6).

14:39 *as the Lord lives.* As an encore to his previous oath, Saul followed with another foolish oath, unknowingly jeopardizing his own son's life.

14:41 *taken.* The practice of casting lots was used to distinguish one person or group from another. Jonathan was indicated as the guilty party, though he acted innocently (v. 27).

14:44 *God do so and more also.* Saul, proud and concerned with his own authority and honor, was intent on fulfilling his vow.

14:45 *worked with God this day.* Jonathan, in stark contrast to his father the king, understood the sufficiency of God for the task and relied on Him for the victory.

14:46 *the Philistines went to their own place.* The Philistines were left to continue their retreat unhindered.

14:47, 48 Saul's military accomplishments were significant and expanded Israel's borders in all directions: to the south (Edom), east (Ammon and Moab), north (Zobah), and west (Philistia). The defeat of the Amalekites is recorded in chapter 15.

14:49–51 Saul's children, Jonathan and Michal, would both play significant roles in the life of the next king, David. Nothing further is known of Saul's wife or other children mentioned here.

14:50 *Abner.* A cousin of Saul who commanded his army (cf. 1 Sam. 17:55, 59; 20:25; 26:14, 15).

14:52 *fierce war.* The Philistines' opposition to Israel was persistent and continual to the very last day of Saul's life (1 Sam. 31:1–3). ***strong . . . valiant man.*** Saul looked for the good warriors and attached them to his personal force. David was one such man who would also continue this practice under his rule (2 Sam. 23:8–39).

3. The rejection of Saul (15:1–35)

15:2 *Amalek.* The Amalekites, a nomadic people of the desert and descendants of Esau (Gen. 36:12), became a marked people when they attacked Israel in the wilderness after leaving Egypt (*see notes on Ex. 17:8–16*; cf. Num. 24:20; Deut. 25:17–19; Judg. 6:3–5).

15:3 *utterly destroy.* God gave Saul an opportunity to redeem himself with obedience. The judgment was to be a complete and total annihilation of anything that breathed. God's judgment was severe on those who would destroy His people. It was equally severe to those who disobeyed (cf. Achan in Josh. 7:10–26).

15:4 *Telaim.* The precise location of this area is unknown, but it may be a reference to Telem found in Joshua 15:24.

15:5 *a city of Amalek.* This was possibly modern-day Tel Masos, located about seven miles east-southeast of Beersheba.

15:6 the Kenites. Moses' father-in-law was a Kenite (cf. Judg. 1:16), a people friendly to the Israelites.

15:7 from Havilah . . . to Shur. Saul's victory was extensive, covering much of the Amalekite territory. However, the Amalekites were not completely destroyed (cf. 27:8; 30:1).

15:8 Agag. Another example of Saul's incomplete obedience, in the case of Agag, is recorded because it had such far-reaching implications. Over five centuries later an Agagite named Haman attempted to exterminate the Jewish race from his power base in Persia (cf. Esth. 3:1ff.). **all the people.** The Israelites killed everyone they came across, except for the king.

15:9 Saul and the people spared. Motivated by covetousness, both Saul and the people greedily spared the choice spoil of the land, disobeying God's Word and demonstrating their faithlessness.

15:11 grieved Samuel. Samuel's role as

Key Word

Utterly Destroyed: 15:3, 8, 9, 15, 18, 20—refers to the "setting apart" of inappropriate things, usually because of defilement associated with idol worship. In the ancient world, anything sacred or defiled was considered inappropriate for common use and was therefore subject to complete destruction. According to Deuteronomy 13:12–15, Israel was to destroy everyone and everything that was wicked enough to be considered defiled. Violation of this command cost Achan his life (Josh. 7) and Saul his throne (15:9–11). Paul reminds us that we are all wicked, and as a result are defiled and deserve destruction. Yet God in His mercy has chosen to save those who place their trust in Jesus (Rom. 3:10–26).

---

priest over the people gave him great concern over the poor performance of the king, who was like the kings of other nations (1 Sam. 6:19, 20), i.e., self-centered, self-willed, and disobedient to the things of God.

15:12 Carmel. This is not Mt. Carmel of Elijah's exploits (1 Kin. 18:20ff.), but a Carmel located seven miles south of Hebron. **monument for himself.** Saul, apparently taking credit for the victory, established a monument to himself (cf. Absalom in 2 Sam. 18:18). This foolish act of contemptible pride was Saul's expression of self-worship rather than true worship of God and another evidence of his spiritual weakness. **Gilgal.** The site of Samuel's first confrontation with Saul (13:7b–15) became the site of this pronouncement of judgment.

15:13 I have performed the commandment of the LORD. Saul, either ignorantly or deceitfully, maintained that he did what was commanded (15:20).

15:15 the people spared the best . . . to sacrifice. Saul began to place blame on others, making room for his own excuses just as he had done earlier (cf. 13:11, 12). Then he tried to justify his sin by saying that the animals would be used to sacrifice to the God of Samuel. Saul's disobedience at least pained his conscience so that he could not claim God as his God.

15:17 little in your own eyes. Saul's status before he became king was as a humble and lowly Benjamite (cf. 9:21).

15:19 swoop down on the spoil. Saul and the people greedily took the spoil like a bird of prey diving on its victim.

15:20, 21 I have obeyed the voice of the LORD. Instead of confessing his sin and repenting, Saul continued to justify himself.

15:22 to obey is better than sacrifice. This is an essential OT truth. Samuel stated that God desires heart obedience over the ritual sacrifice of animals (cf. Ps. 51:16, 17;

Is. 1:10–17). The sacrificial system was never intended to function in place of living an obedient life, but was rather to be an expression of it (cf. Hos. 6:6; Amos 5:21–27; Mic. 6:6–8).

15:23 rebellion . . . stubbornness. Saul needed to see that his real worship was indicated by his behavior and not by his sacrifices. He demonstrated himself to be an idolater whose idol was himself. He had failed the conditions (12:13–15) which would have brought blessing on the nation. His disobedience here was on the same level as witchcraft and idolatry, sins worthy of death. **Because you have rejected . . . He also has rejected.** A universal principle is given here that those who continually reject God will one day be rejected by Him. The sins of Saul caused God to immediately depose Saul and his descendants forever from the throne of Israel.

15:24 I have sinned. This overdue confession appears to be generated more by a concern over consequences (regret) than by sorrow over having offended his holy God (repentance). Saul bypasses his personal responsibility by shifting blame to the people.

15:25 return with me. Saul was concerned about having Samuel's visible presence as a show of support in front of the people (cf. 15:30).

15:28 torn the kingdom. Saul's judgment was a settled matter on the day of his disobedience with the Amalekites. Samuel used the illustration as it vividly portrayed how God would take the kingdom from Saul as he had just torn Samuel's robe. **a neighbor of yours.** This was a reference to David (cf. 28:17).

15:29 the Strength of Israel. This was a unique title of God. It could also be translated "the glory of Israel" (cf. Mic. 1:15). **will not lie nor relent.** Samuel emphasized God's

attribute of immutability in regard to the judgment upon Saul.

15:30 honor me. Saul was still thinking of himself and how he could best salvage the situation for self-gain.

15:31 Samuel turned back. Samuel agreed to follow Saul, perhaps seeing this as the wisest course of action for the nation at that time.

15:33 hacked Agag in pieces. This was an act of divine judgment to show the holy wrath of God against wanton sin. Sadly, the Israelites did not exterminate the wicked Amalekites, so they came back later to raid the southern territory and take women and children captive, including David's family (see ch. 30).

15:35 Samuel went no more . . . mourned. Samuel never went to visit the rejected King Saul again in his life (cf. 1 Sam. 28:11–19). On at least one further occasion, Saul sought Samuel (cf. 19:24).

III. DAVID AND SAUL'S TRANSFER OF THE KINGSHIP IN ISRAEL (16:1–31:13)

16:1–31:13 The third major division of Samuel recounts the steady demise of Saul and the selection and preparation of David for the kingship. Chapter 16 begins with Samuel mourning for Saul as one would mourn for the dead. The death of Saul (31:1–13) concludes this last division of the book.

A. The Introduction of David (16:1–17:58)

1. The anointing of David (16:1–13)

16:1 Jesse the Bethlehemite. God's new king of Israel (and ultimately the Messiah; Gen. 3:15; Num. 24:17; 1 Sam. 2:10; Ps. 2) would come from the tribe of Judah (Jesse;

cf. Ruth 4:12, 22; Gen. 49:10) and from Bethlehem of Judah (cf. Mic. 5:2; Matt. 2:2–6). *I have provided Myself.* The king was chosen and provided by God (Deut. 17:15), who orders all things according to the counsel of His own will (Is. 40:14), not according to human desires (8:5, 6; 2 Sam. 2:8, 9).

16:2 Saul . . . will kill me. Saul's unbalanced emotional state was already known in Israel. It is ironic that Samuel's initial reaction to the word of the Lord was fear of Saul instead of rejoicing at God's provision to Israel (and ultimately to all the nations; e.g., 1 Kin. 8:41–43). The route from Ramah to Bethlehem would take Samuel through Gibeah of Saul (cf. 10:26; 11:14). *I have come to sacrifice.* The place of sacrifice could be in any town until the establishment of the house of God in Jerusalem (Deut. 12:11).

16:3 anoint. David's first anointing was performed by Samuel, symbolizing God's recognition/ordination (cf. 2:10). The following two anointings (2 Sam. 2:7; 5:3) were to establish David as king publicly for the benefit of Judah and Israel, respectively.

16:4 the elders of the town trembled. The elders, and no doubt all Israel, had heard of Samuel's execution of Agag (15:33). Israel still closely associated the "seer," or prophet, with the not-so-distant past office of judge.

16:5 Sanctify yourselves. Worship of Yahweh was always preceded by cleansing or washing, both of the outward garments and the inner man (Ex. 19:10, 14; 1 John 1:9).

16:6 Eliab. Lit. "My God is Father." Since Eliab was the first of Jesse's sons to catch Samuel's eye, he must have been an impressive young man by outward appearance.

16:7 his appearance . . . physical stature. Samuel needed to be reminded that God's anointed was not chosen because of physical attributes. This was initially a difficult concept for Samuel as he was accustomed to a king whose only positive attributes were

physical. *the LORD looks at the heart.* The Hebrew concept of *heart* embodies emotions, will, intellect, and desires. The life of the person will reflect his heart (cf. Matt. 12:34, 35).

16:8 Abinadab. Lit. "My Father is noble." Samuel, now more sensitive to the leading of God's Spirit, quickly discerned that Abinadab was not God's anointed.

16:9 Shammah. Lit. "Yahweh hears (or heard)." See 16:8.

16:10 seven . . . sons. With David, Jesse had eight sons. The fact that 1 Chronicles 2:13 indicates seven sons must mean that one of the eight died afterward, and this is not considered in the Chronicles account.

16:11 the youngest . . . keeping the sheep. God's favor/choice often fell on the younger and the least (cf. Jacob, Joseph, Gideon). David, although the youngest, was the firstborn over Israel (Ps. 89:27) whose humble beginnings as a shepherd, and later rule as king, typify Jesus, the ultimate Shepherd and King of Israel.

16:12 ruddy . . . bright eyes . . . goodlooking. God's chosen king was handsome to look at, although that was not the reason for his selection by God. His appearance was, perhaps, enhanced by a genuine faith and joy in Yahweh. See also 17:42.

16:13 anointed him in the midst of his brothers. David's first anointing is before his family/house. His second anointing would be before the assembly of his tribe, Judah; and his third anointing would be before the nation Israel. (*See note on 16:3.*) *the Spirit of the LORD came upon David.* This familiar OT expression relates to empowerment for some God-given task (cf. 10:6, 11; 11:6; 19:20, 23; 2 Sam. 23:2; 2 Chr. 20:14; Is. 11:2; 61:1; Ezek. 11:5; 37:1). David's anointing was an external symbol of an inward work of God. The operation of the Holy Spirit in this case was not for regeneration, but for empowerment to perform his (David's) role in God's program for Israel (cf. Saul, 10:6). After David sinned with Bathsheba (2 Sam. 11, 12), he prayed, "Do not take Your Holy Spirit from me" (Ps. 51:11).

2. David in the court of Saul (16:14–23)

16:14 the Spirit of the LORD departed from Saul. When David's ascent to the throne began, Saul's slow and painful descent began also (cf. 18:12). Without God's empowering Holy Spirit, Saul was effectively no longer king over Israel (15:28), although his physical removal from the throne, and his death, happened many years later. **a distressing spirit.** God, in His sovereignty, allowed an evil spirit to torment Saul (cf. Judg. 9:23; 1 Kin. 22:19–23; Job 1:6–12) for His purpose of establishing the throne of David. This spirit, a messenger from Satan, is to be distinguished from a troubled emotional state brought on by indwelling sin, or the harmful consequences of the sinful acts of others (e.g., spirit of jealousy, Num. 5:14). This demon spirit attacked Saul from without, for there is no evidence that the demon indwelt Saul. **troubled him.** Saul, whose inward constitution was already prone to questionable judgment and the fear of men, began to experience God's judgment in the form of severe bouts of depression, anger, and delusion, initiated and aggravated by the evil spirit assigned to him. There are several NT occasions where God turned people over to demons or Satan for judgment (see Acts 5:1–3; 1 Cor. 5:1–7; 1 Tim. 1:18–20). He also used Satan or demons for the strengthening of the saints. See Job 1:1–2:6; Matthew 4:1ff.; Luke 22:31, 32; 2 Corinthians 12:7–10.

16:16 he will play . . . you shall be well. God used the evil that had befallen Saul to introduce David into the court of the king and to the watching eyes of Israel.

16:18 skillful in playing . . . a handsome person. The writer of Samuel introduces David, the sweet psalmist of Israel (2 Sam. 23:1), before introducing David the warrior. Later proven so skillful in the art of war and killing, David was also a tender musician of exceptional skill and reputation. **the LORD is with him.** The saints of God, OT and NT, are recognized by their fruit (2:26; Luke 2:40). God's approval of David was already recognized by certain people in Israel.

16:19 Send me your son David. This is a verbal link with 16:1, "I have provided myself a king among his (Jesse's) sons." David's lineage was of importance to Saul in the near future when he arranged a marriage between Michal, his daughter, and David. **with the sheep.** David's lowly, humble occupation is emphasized. He gave evidence of that humility and patience as he returned faithfully to his duty following Samuel's anointing.

16:21 he loved him greatly. Saul loved David for his abilities, but later grew to hate him because he knew he was blessed by the Lord (cf. 18:29). **his armorbearer.** David was most likely one of many such young men assigned to Saul's barracks.

3. David, the warrior of the Lord (17:1–58)

17:1 Sochoh . . . Azekah . . . Ephes Dammim. Following the anointing of David and his installation into the court of the king, there is this update on the situation of Israel in regard to Israel's enemies. Sochoh and Azekah were towns of Judah (Josh. 15:20, 35; Jer. 34:7) approximately fifteen miles west and seventeen miles northwest (respectively) of Bethlehem. Ephes Dammim (1 Chr. 11:12, 13; cf., 2 Sam. 23:9), the camp of the Philistines, probably lay one mile south of Azekah.

17:2 Valley of Elah. Where the camp of Israel was, approximately three miles east of

Ephes Dammin.

17:4–7 In human terms alone, Goliath was invincible. However, David counted on the Lord being with him and making the difference (17:34–37).

17:4 *champion.* Lit. "the man between two." An appropriate appellation as Goliath stood between the two armies of the Philistines and Israel, and offered his challenge to a "duel" of hand-to-hand combat, the outcome of which would settle the battle for both sides. *Gath.* One of the five chief, Philistine cities, located five miles west of Azekah. *six cubits and a span.* One cubit measures approximately eighteen inches and one span about nine inches, making Goliath about nine feet nine inches in height (cf. "Egyptian," 1 Chr. 11:23, and "Og of Bashan," Deut. 3:11).

17:5 *five thousand shekels.* 125 pounds.

17:7 *six hundred shekels.* Fifteen pounds.

17:11 *Saul . . . dismayed and greatly afraid.* Saul and Israel had proven themselves to be greatly concerned with outward appearances (10:23, 24; 15:30) and able to be influenced by the fear of men (12:12; 15:24). It is only natural that Goliath would be their worst nightmare come true.

17:12 *Ephrathite.* Ephrath(ah), another name for the Bethlehem in Judah (cf. Ruth 4:11; Mic. 5:2).

17:15 *David occasionally went and returned from Saul.* David's duties were divided between his billet with Saul as one of many armorbearers (16:21), and tending his father's sheep in Bethlehem. Doubtless, David learned important lessons about the weight of responsibility during this time, lessons that were later put to use in ruling over Israel.

17:17 *ephah.* About three-quarters of a bushel.

17:23 *the same words.* Goliath continued to offer the challenge of 17:10, as he had been doing for forty mornings and evenings (17:16).

17:25 *great riches . . . his daughter.* The reward of a daughter in marriage for a great victory over an enemy of Israel was not unusual (cf. Josh. 15:13–17).

17:26 *the reproach from Israel?* David knew that, although Goliath's challenge had been issued to (any) individual of the camp of Israel, Goliath's defiant attitude was a reproach to all Israel.

17:28 *Eliab's anger.* Eliab, perhaps still feeling the sting/rejection of having his "little" brother chosen over him by God/Samuel (16:6, 7), expressed his jealousy in anger (cf. Gen. 37:4, 5, 8, 11).

17:32 *Let no man's heart fail.* Joshua and Caleb exhorted Israel in the same fashion regarding the giant Anakim 400 years before (cf. Num. 13:30; 14:8, 9). The heathens' hearts fail at the name of the Lord God of Israel (cf. Rahab, Josh. 2:11).

17:33 *You are not able.* David's faith, like that of Joshua and Caleb, was met with disbelief on the part of Saul. By all outward appearances, Saul was correct in his assessment, but he failed to consider the Lord's presence in David's life.

17:36 *lion and bear.* Just as David tended his flock of sheep and protected them from the lion and bear, his new responsibility as shepherd over Israel required him to eliminate the threat of Goliath.

17:37 *The LORD . . . He will deliver me.* Just as Jonathan believed earlier (14:6), David had a wholehearted faith in the God of Israel. *the LORD be with you.* One of the first explicit indications in the text that Saul knew that the Lord was with David (cf. 15:28).

17:40 *staff . . . stones . . . sling.* The tools of the shepherd proved to be appropriate weapons also for Israel's shepherd. One of David's honorable and chief men of battle, Benaiah, the son of Jehoiada, killed a formidable Egyptian warrior (2 Sam. 23:20, 21) with a staff like the one David carried toward Goliath.

17:43 *dog*. Goliath uttered a statement of ironic truth about himself of which even he was unaware. As a wild dog can be a threat to the flock and must be chased away or killed, so must Goliath.

17:45 *in the name of the LORD of Hosts*. Goliath came out to battle in his own name; David came to battle in the name of the Lord of all the hosts (armies). Cf. Deuteronomy 20:1–5.

17:46 *all the earth may know*. David fought in the name of the Lord and for the glory of the Lord, whose name and glory will extend to the uttermost parts of the earth, to all nations (cf. Josh. 4:24; 2 Sam. 22:50; Ps. 2).

17:47 *the battle is the LORD's*. Cf. Deuteronomy 31:6; Judges 7:18. David fully understood the chief issue, i.e., the Philistines were in effect challenging the Lord by confronting the Lord's people.

17:50 *no sword*. Iron weapons were scarce in Israel (13:19).

17:51 *cut off his head*. David completed his promise given to Goliath in verse 46a. The Philistines would later do the same with Saul's head (1 Sam. 31:9). ***fled*.** David's exclamation that there is a God in Israel (v. 46) was proven before the Philistines, who were no strangers to the wrath of Yahweh (1 Sam. 5–7). They fled in terror, but did not honor the terms of Goliath if he lost (17:6–9).

17:54 *to Jerusalem*. The Jebusites, who were the inhabitants of Jerusalem, were a stubborn, resistant people (cf. Josh. 15:63; Judg. 1:21; 19:10, 11), particularly to the tribe of Judah. They doubtless began to feel some anxiety about the victory of this Bethlehemite. The head of Goliath was a constant warning to them over the ensuing days

about their future (cf. 2 Sam. 5:6–10).

17:55 *Abner*. *See note on 14:50*. *whose son*. David's lineage was of the utmost importance to Saul at this point, since the victor over Goliath would marry into his family (cf. 17:25; 18:18).

B. David Driven from the Court of Saul (18:1–20:42)

1. The anger and fear of Saul toward David (18:1–30)

18:1 *Jonathan loved him*. Jonathan loved David with a loyalty and devotion indicative of covenantal love (18:3). Hiram of Tyre had much the same covenantal love for David (cf. 2 Sam. 5:11; 1 Kin. 5:1; 9:11). David's later reign from Jerusalem is marked by loyalty to

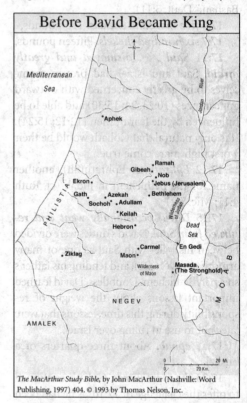

Before David Became King

The MacArthur Study Bible, by John MacArthur (Nashville: Word Publishing, 1997) 404. © 1993 by Thomas Nelson, Inc.

his covenant with Jonathan (2 Sam. 9:1).

18:2 would not let him go home. Saul's interest in keeping David in his household was more self-serving than a token of generous hospitality. Saul was aware of his promise of wife and wealth (17:25) and, no doubt, the stirrings of anxiety/fear were in his heart toward David, who appeared as a threat. Saul preferred to have David in the court to keep a watchful eye on the young upstart.

18:3 covenant. See verse 1. Further mention of this honorable relationship is made in 19:1; 20:8, 13–17, 42; 22:8; 23:18.

18:4 robe . . . belt. Jonathan willingly and subserviently relinquished the outer garments and instruments that signified his position as prince of Israel and heir to the throne. Jonathan, a godly worshiper of Yahweh, quickly discerned that David was God's anointed and, without reservation, offered the robe of succession to the true king of Israel.

18:7 David his ten thousands. This is a song that Saul grew to hate (cf. 21:11; 28:5) because it exalted David over him.

18:8 the kingdom? Saul's jealousy and malice toward David were now explicit. By his own statement, Saul acknowledged that David was the rightful heir to the throne and the one of whom Samuel spoke in Gilgal (15:28).

18:10 the distressing spirit. The painful descent and eventual demise of Saul was marked by the persistent vexing of this spirit. See 16:14. **prophesied.** This means to speak before people, not predict the future. Saul's speeches in the midst of the house were the ravings of a person troubled by an evil spirit like other false prophets (cf. 1 Kin. 22:19–23).

18:11 David escaped . . . twice. As Saul's behavior was becoming increasingly violent, he made more than one attempt on David's life with the javelin. It was evident that God

was with David, as it would be no small feat to dodge a javelin cast by such an experienced warrior as Saul.

18:12 Saul was afraid of David. Saul, faced with the same conclusion reached by Jonathan in verses 1–4, reacted with fear. Saul, a man who viewed life from a human perspective rather than a divine viewpoint, could see David only as a personal threat, rather than a blessing to Israel.

18:13 captain over a thousand. Saul gave David a military commission, intended as kind of honorable exile. But this duty only served to give David opportunity to display his remarkable character and to strengthen his hold on the people's affections.

18:16 loved David. The writer of Samuel, inspired by the Holy Spirit, offers an editorial comment full of truth.

18:17 Merab. Lit. "compensation" or "substitute" (cf. 14:49). Saul's later retraction of the betrothal to Merab (v. 19) was similar to Laban's trickery with Jacob and Rachel (Gen. 29:25). **fight the LORD's battles.** A phrase Saul knew would appeal to David. Saul made the offer out of a treacherous heart, desiring evil and calamity for David. Notice the similarity between Saul's treachery and that of David with Uriah (2 Sam. 11:15).

18:18 son-in-law. The familial lineage was crucial when marrying into the king's family. David asked, "Who am I . . . or my father's family in Israel, that I should be son-in-law to the king?" Saul had asked of David's lineage three times previously (17:55, 56, 58).

18:19 Adriel the Meholathite. Merab married this man and bore children, five of whom were sons later executed by David as punishment for Saul's disregard of Joshua's covenant with the Gibeonites (2 Sam. 21:8; cf. Josh. 9:20).

18:20 Michal. Lit. "Who is like God?" Michal sincerely loved David and perhaps was aware, as Jonathan, of his certain ascent (and right) to the throne. Ironically, Saul offered her to David, not from a benevolent heart, but as a "snare" (v. 21).

18:25 dowry. Lit. "price." Saul resorted to the same treachery in his offer of betrothal to Merab, plotting to eliminate David by placing him in jeopardy with the Philistines. David, already having proved himself wise in many things (16:18), was aware, to some extent, of Saul's intent and acted obediently, valiantly, and wisely.

18:25, 27 foreskins. Such mutilation of the bodies of slain enemies was commonly practiced in ancient warfare. The number indicated the extent of the victory. Saul's intent was to expose David to deadly danger by engaging in such an extensive and hazardous task.

18:27 his men. Cf. 22:2; 25:12, 13; 2 Samuel 23:8–39.

18:29 Saul became David's enemy. All of Saul's plans came to naught. Saul asked for 100 Philistine foreskins; David brought 200. Saul offered Michal as a "snare"; Michal loved David as did Saul's own son, Jonathan. There remained nothing else for Saul to contrive except open hatred toward David.

2. The defense of David by Jonathan and Michal (19:1–20:42)

19:1 kill David. Saul no longer tried to disguise or cover his evil intent toward David, but made known his intent to those who held David in the highest esteem (cf. 16:18; 18:1–4). God, in His mercy, made sure that David had sympathetic ears within Saul's court to inform him of Saul's evil plans (e.g., 19:7; 20:2).

19:4 Jonathan spoke well of David. Jonathan attempted to persuade his father with calm reason. Jonathan's reason was tempered by a godly attitude centered on a remembrance of the Torah (14:6, cf. Num. 11:23; 14:9) and a covenantal loyalty toward and faithfulness for David.

19:4, 5 he has not sinned. Jonathan reminded Saul that David had done nothing to deserve death; in fact, he was worthy of honor for his good works toward the king and Israel. Jonathan knew that the spilling of innocent blood would affect all Israel, not just the house of Saul (Deut. 21:8, 9).

19:6 he shall not be killed. Saul temporarily responded to reason and conviction in his heart. His mental capacity was so unbalanced, however, that this response would not last for long.

19:9 the distressing spirit. Jealousy, rage, and anger once again dominated Saul, who was enraged by David's success against the Philistines. See 6:14; 18:10.

19:10 pin David . . . with the spear. Saul's already diminished capacity for reason was once again clouded by anger, and he responded toward David with murderous intent (cf. 18:10, 11).

19:11 Michal . . . told him. Michal, far from being a "snare" (18:21) to David, was instrumental in saving his life. Michal, at this time in her relationship with David, displayed a covenantal love and faithfulness similar to that of Jonathan. See the title of Psalm 59.

19:13 an image. Hebrew *teraphim.* The writer of Samuel draws a parallel between David/Michal/Saul and Jacob/Rachel/Laban (*see note on 18:17*), in that both Rachel and Michal employed the use of household gods ("teraphim") in trickery and out of loyalty for their husbands rather than their fathers (cf. Gen. 31:30–35).

19:17 He said to me. Michal lied in telling Saul the exact opposite of what she said to

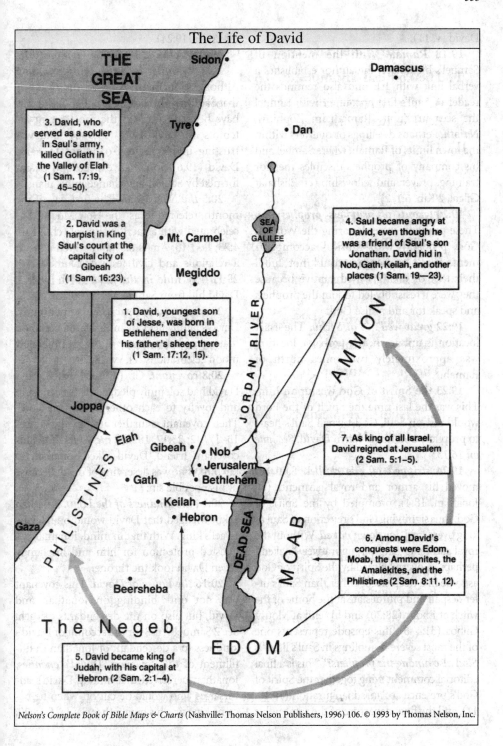

The Life of David

THE GREAT SEA

Sidon •

Damascus •

Tyre •

• Dan

3. David, who served as a soldier in Saul's army, killed Goliath in the Valley of Elah (1 Sam. 17:19, 45–50).

2. David was a harpist in King Saul's court at the capital city of Gibeah (1 Sam. 16:23).

• Mt. Carmel

SEA OF GALILEE

4. Saul became angry at David, even though he was a friend of Saul's son Jonathan. David hid in Nob, Gath, Keilah, and other places (1 Sam. 19—23).

Megiddo

1. David, youngest son of Jesse, was born in Bethlehem and tended his father's sheep there (1 Sam. 17:12, 15).

JORDAN RIVER

AMMON

Joppa

Elah

Gibeah • • Nob

• Jerusalem

7. As king of all Israel, David reigned at Jerusalem (2 Sam. 5:1–5).

• Gath • Bethlehem

PHILISTINES

• Keilah

• Hebron

DEAD SEA

MOAB

Gaza •

6. Among David's conquests were Edom, Moab, the Ammonites, the Amalekites, and the Philistines (2 Sam. 8:11, 12).

Beersheba •

The Negeb

EDOM

5. David became king of Judah, with his capital at Hebron (2 Sam. 2:1–4).

Nelson's Complete Book of Bible Maps & Charts (Nashville: Thomas Nelson Publishers, 1996) 106. © 1993 by Thomas Nelson, Inc.

David (v. 11).

19:18 Ramah. With the mention of Samuel's birthplace, the author establishes a verbal link with 1:1, and also reminds the reader of Saul's first encounter with Samuel the seer in Zuph (Ramathaim Zophim). **Naioth.** Perhaps dwellings or quarters within the town limits of Ramah, where Samuel and his company of prophets-disciples met for training, prayer, and fellowship (cf. Elisha at Gilgal, 2 Kin. 6:1, 2).

19:20 group of prophets prophesying. These prophets were declaring the Word of God, probably with musical accompaniment. Saul's messengers could not fulfill their task of taking David captive because they were irresistibly led to join the prophets and speak for and praise God.

19:22 great well . . . at Sechu. The exact location is unknown; the probable location was approximately two miles north of Ramah.

19:23 the Spirit of God was upon him. This was the last time the Spirit of the Lord would rest on Saul. God turned Saul's heart to prophesy and not to harm David. *See note on 16:13.*

19:24 stripped off his clothes. Saul removed his armor and royal garments (cf. Jonathan, 18:4), prompted by the Spirit of God, thus signifying God's rejection of Saul as king over Israel. **lay down naked.** Without the royal garments, Saul was figuratively "naked," perhaps so overwhelmed by the Spirit of God as to be in a deep sleep. Other than Saul's utter despair and pitiful state at the home of the witch at Endor (28:20) and his end at Mount Gilboa (31:4–6), this episode represents one of the most severe humblings in Saul's life. **"Is Saul also among the prophets?"** This is a final editorial comment tying together the Spirit of God's presence at Saul's inauguration (10:10, 11), and the final departure of the same at his rejection (19:24).

20:1 Naioth in Ramah. *See note on 19:18.*

20:2 my father hide this thing from me? Although Jonathan expressed his certainty that Saul was not seeking David's life, he may have been unaware of the most recent attempts on David's life (19:9–24) and was trusting in his father's oath not to harm David (19:6). Jonathan expected to be informed by Saul of any change in his plans.

20:5 the New Moon. The first day of the month, referred to as "the New Moon," was celebrated with a sacrificial meal (cf. 2 Kin. 4:23; Is. 1:13; Amos 8:5) and served as both a religious and civil festival (Num. 10:10; 28:11–15). **hide in the field.** As in 19:2, 3, David hid from Saul in a secret place.

20:6 a yearly sacrifice. Apparently, David's family held an annual family reunion that coincided with one of the monthly new moon celebrations (cf. vv. 28, 29).

20:8 covenant. Cf. 18:1, 3. Jonathan and David had solemnly pledged their friendship and loyalty to each other before the Lord. Their covenant is further amplified in verses 13–17, 42; 23:17, 18. **kill me yourself.** As his covenant friend, David asked Jonathan to kill him, if he was deserving of death because of his possible sin.

20:14 the kindness of the LORD. Jonathan acknowledged that David would one day be Israel's king. With that in mind, Jonathan requested protection for him and his family when David took the throne.

20:16 the house of David. This covenant was not only binding on Jonathan and David, but also on the descendants of each. See 2 Samuel 9:1–8 for the account of David's kindness to a descendant of Jonathan in fulfillment of this covenant. **David's enemies.** Jonathan perceived that among David's adversaries who would be cut off when he became king was his own father, Saul (cf. 18:29;

19:17).

20:17 *vow.* In response to Jonathan's words, David solemnly pledged to fulfill the covenant between himself and Jonathan. *loved him as . . . his own soul.* A deep concern and affection was the basis of the covenantal relationship between Jonathan and David. This is the affection commanded by God when He said, "Love your neighbor as yourself" (Lev. 19:18; Matt. 22:39).

20:19 *stone Ezel. Ezel* may mean "departure stone." The location of this stone is unknown, but it was a well-known landmark in the field where David was hiding.

20:25 *Abner.* Saul's cousin and commander of his army (*see note on 14:50*).

20:26 *unclean.* At first, Saul did not question David's absence at the feast, assuming that he was ritually unclean and, thus, could not participate in the meal (cf. Lev. 7:20, 21; 15:16).

20:30 *son of a perverse, rebellious woman!* With a vile epithet, Saul was cursing Jonathan, not Jonathan's mother, for having sided with David to his own shame and the shame of the mother who birthed him.

20:41 *bowed down three times.* David's bowing down more than once acknowledged Jonathan as the prince, and expressed humble affection for him.

20:42 *sworn. See note on 20:17.* **the city.** I.e., Gibeah, the home of Saul. From this point until Saul's death, David was an outcast from the royal court.

C. David's Flight from Saul's Pursuit (21:1–28:2)

1. Saul's killing of the priests at Nob (21:1–22:23)

21:1 *Nob.* "The city of the priests" (22:19). The priests dwelt on Mt. Scopus, about one mile northeast of Jerusalem. David went there for necessary supplies and

for comfort and counsel. *Ahimelech.* A great grandson of Eli (1:9), who is possibly the brother of Ahijah (14:3; 22:11), or Abimelech may be another name for Ahijah. Not only is there a rejected king on the throne (15:26–29) but also a disqualified priest (2:30–36). *See note on Mark 2:26.*

21:2 *The king has ordered me.* David, fearing someone might tell Saul where he was, deceived Ahimelech the priest into thinking that he was on official business for the king. He supposed, as many do, that it is excusable to lie for the purpose of saving one's life. But what is essentially sinful can never, because of circumstances, change its immoral character (cf. Ps. 119:29). David's lying led tragically to the deaths of the priests (22:9–18).

21:4 *holy bread.* Consecrated bread was set apart for use in the tabernacle to be eaten only by the priests (Ex. 25:30; Lev. 24:5–9). Ahimelech sought the Lord and received approval (22:10) when he recognized that his spiritual obligation to preserve David's life superseded the ceremonial regulation concerning who could eat the consecrated bread (see Matt. 12:3, 4; Mark 2:25, 26). *kept themselves from women.* Though this was not a spiritual mission or religious journey, David and his men were ceremonially clean (see Ex. 19:15).

21:5 *the vessels.* A euphemism for the bodies of the young men, as in 1 Thessalonians 4:4.

21:5, 6 *bread . . . common.* Since that bread was no longer on the Lord's table, having been replaced by hot bread, it was to be eaten by the priests and in these exigencies, by David under the law of necessity and mercy. *See note on 21:4.* The removal of the old bread and the replacing with new was done on the Sabbath (Lev. 24:8).

21:7 *Doeg, an Edomite.* The head shepherd of Saul's herd, who witnessed the encounter between David and Ahimelech and told Saul (cf. 22:9, 10), had embraced the Hebrew religion and was at the tabernacle, perhaps detained because it was the Sabbath and he could not travel.

21:9 The sword of Goliath. The sword which David had used to behead Goliath in the valley of Elah (17:51) was kept in the place for storing the sacred vestments ("the ephod"), deposited there as a memorial to divine goodness in the deliverance of Israel. *the ephod. See notes on 2:28; 14:3.*

21:10 Achish the king of Gath. One of the kings or lords of the Philistines. *See notes on 4:1; 5:8* for Gath. This seemed to be a dangerous place to go, since David was their greatest enemy and carried Goliath's sword into the giant's hometown.

21:13 changed his behavior. David feared for his life, lacked trust in God to deliver him, and feigned insanity to persuade Achish to send him away. See the titles of Psalms 34; 56. Drooling in one's beard was considered in the East an intolerable indignity, as was spitting in another's beard.

22:1 cave of Adullam. A cave near Adullam was David's refuge. Adullam, which may mean "refuge," was located in the western foothills of Judah (Josh. 15:33), about seventeen miles southwest of Jerusalem and ten

miles southeast of Gath. See titles of Psalms 57; 142, which could possibly refer to 1 Samuel 24:3. *brothers and all his father's house.* David's family members went down from Bethlehem to join David in Adullam, a journey of about twelve miles.

22:2 captain over . . . four hundred men. David became the leader of a formidable force of men united by adverse circumstances. This personal army would soon grow to 600 (23:13).

22:3 Mizpah of Moab. Mizpah means "watch tower," or "place that overlooks." Located on one of the heights of the tableland east of the Dead Sea, this site cannot be exactly identified. *king of Moab.* This ruler was probably a mutual enemy of King Saul. David had Moabite blood from his great-grandmother Ruth, and thus sought refuge for his father and mother in Moab (see Ruth 1:4–18; 4:13–22).

22:4 the stronghold. Transliterated *mesudah*, this may refer to Masada, the mountain fortress above the shores of the Dead Sea, or some unknown location.

22:5 prophet Gad. As the prophet Samuel had helped and advised Saul, so now Gad performed the same functions for David (cf. 2 Sam 24:11, where Gad is called "David's seer"). *forest of Hereth.* Location in Judah

The Psalms in 1 Samuel		
1. 1 Sam. 19:11	When Saul sent men to watch the house in order to kill David.	Ps. 59
2. 1 Sam. 21:10, 11	When the Philistines captured David in Gath	Ps. 56
3. 1 Sam. 21:10–15	When David pretended madness before Abimelech	Ps. 34
4. 1 Sam. 22:1; 24:3	When David fled from Saul into the cave	Ps. 57
5. 1 Sam. 22:1; 24:3	When David was in a cave	Ps. 142
6. 1 Sam. 22:9, 10	When Doeg the Edomite warned Saul about David	Ps. 52
7. 1 Sam. 23:14 (or 2 Sam. 15:23–28)	When David was in the wilderness of Judea	Ps. 63
8. 1 Sam. 23:19	When the Ziphites warned Saul about David	Ps. 54

unknown.

22:6 *tamarisk tree*. Possibly located on a hill outside Gibeah which had been given over to pagan worship (cf. Ezek. 16:24, 25, 31, 39). ***spear*.** A reminder of the threat that Saul was to friend and foe alike (cf. 18:10, 11; 19:9, 10; 20:3).

22:7 *Benjamites!* Saul asked those of his own tribe whether associating themselves with David would provide for them more possessions and privileges than they already had from Saul.

22:8 *my son has made a covenant*. See note on 20:8.

22:8–13 *to lie in wait*. Saul insinuated that David was plotting his death. This was not true, as David would later spare Saul's life (vv. 24, 26).

22:9, 10 *Doeg the Edomite*. See note on 21:7 and the title of Psalm 52.

22:13 *conspired against me*. Saul insisted falsely that Ahimelech was in league with his enemy, David.

22:14 *your bidding*. Ahimelech responded to Saul by defending David's character as loyal to Saul.

22:16–19 This fulfills the curse on Eli's house (*see note on 2:31*), with the exception of Abiathar, who was later dismissed from the priesthood by Solomon (1 Kin. 2:26–29).

22:17 *would not . . . strike the priests*. Although Saul condemned Ahimelech and the priests to death, his servants knew better than to raise their weapons against the priests of the Lord.

22:18 *linen ephod*. See notes on 2:18; 14:3.

22:19 *Nob, the city of the priests*. See note on 21:1. What Saul failed to do righteously to the Amalekites (15:3, 8, 9), he unrighteously did to the citizens of Nob.

22:20 *Abiathar*. Lit. "The father is excellent." A son of Ahimelech (cf. 21:1) who escaped the slaughter and joined David's company, he performed priestly functions for

David for the rest of David's life (cf. 23:6, 9; 30:7; 2 Sam. 8:17). *See note on 22:16–19.*

22:22 *I have caused*. David recognized his responsibility for causing the deaths of the priests' families and animals, acknowledging the devastating consequences of his lie to Ahimelech (cf. 21:1, 2).

2. Saul's life spared twice by David (23:1–26:25)

23:1 *Keilah*. A city located in the western foothills of Judah (see Josh. 15:44), about eighteen miles southwest of Jerusalem and three miles southeast of Abdullam.

23:2 *inquired of the LORD*. Such inquiries were made using the sacred lots, the Urim and Thummim, stored in the priestly ephod which Abiathar had brought to David (v. 6). *See note on Exodus 28:30.*

23:7 *gates and bars*. Lit. "two doors and a bar." Keilah perhaps had only one gateway in its wall. Its two reinforced wooden doors had hinged posts at the sides of the entrance, meeting in the center and secured with a heavy bar spanning the entrance horizontally. Since there was only this one way in and out of the city, Saul believed he had David trapped.

23:11 *deliver me*. David inquired of the Lord again, using the ephod with the Urim and Thummim by which God revealed His will. David wanted to know whether the men of Keilah would be disloyal and surrender him into the hands of Saul. The Lord answered in the affirmative in verse 12.

23:13 *men, about six hundred*. See note on 22:2 when David had only 400 men.

23:14 *strongholds in the wilderness*. The wilderness of Judah is the barren desert area between the hill country and the Dead Sea. Many ravines and caves are found in this rugged region which David used as a place of refuge from Saul. The title of Psalm 63 may refer to this incident or to 2 Samuel 15:23–

28. **Wilderness of Ziph.** The wilderness surrounding Ziph, four miles south of Hebron. **God did not deliver him.** God sovereignly protected David from Saul for the fulfilling of His own divine purposes (cf. Is. 46:9–11).

23:16, 17 strengthened his hand in God. Jonathan encouraged David by reminding him of the Lord's promise to him and concern for him, by emphatically assuring him that the Lord would make him the next king over Israel, as Saul well knew (see 20:30, 31).

23:18 covenant. See notes on 18:3; 20:8.

23:19 hill of Hachilah. Location unknown, somewhere between Ziph and the Dead Sea. See the title of Psalm 54. **Jeshimon?** Another name for the wilderness of Judea.

23:24 Wilderness of Maon. The barren territory in the vicinity of Maon (see Josh. 15:48, 55), about five miles south of Ziph.

23:25 the rock. A landmark in the wilderness of Maon, soon to be given a name (v. 28).

23:26 encircling David. Saul probably divided his forces into two groups and so surrounded David.

23:27 Philistines have invaded the land! Providentially, a messenger came to Saul telling him that the Philistines were invading the land so that he had no choice but to withdraw and postpone his pursuit of David.

23:28 the Rock of Escape. The timely retreat of Saul's men from David's men led to this name.

23:29 En Gedi. An oasis on the western shore of the Dead Sea fourteen miles east of Ziph, where there is a fresh water spring and lush vineyards (Song 1:14), standing in stark contrast to the surrounding wilderness. The limestone that dominates this region is permeated with caves, which provided good hiding places for David.

24:2 three thousand chosen men. See 26:2. These were the most skilled soldiers. **Rocks of the Wild Goats.** The location of this cave is unknown, although "wild goats" emphasizes the inaccessibility of the cave (cf. Job 39:1). See the titles of Psalms 57; 142, which could also possibly refer to 1 Samuel 22:1.

24:3 attend to his needs. Lit. "to cover his feet." This is a euphemism for having a bowel movement, as the person would crouch with his inner garment dropped to his feet.

24:4 the day of which the LORD said to you. David's men, perhaps, believed that God had providentially placed Saul in the same cave where they were hiding so David could kill the king. However, nothing revelatory had previously been said by the Lord that indicated He wanted David to lift a hand against Saul.

24:5 David's heart troubled him. David was able to cut off a piece of Saul's robe undetected. However, touching Saul's clothing was tantamount to touching his person, and David's conscience troubled him on this account.

24:6 LORD's anointed. David recognized that the Lord Himself had placed Saul in the kingship. Thus, the judgment and removal of Saul had to be left to the Lord.

24:11 neither evil nor rebellion. If David were a wicked rebel against the rule of Saul, as Saul had said (22:8, 13), he would have killed Saul when given this opportunity. The corner of the robe was proof to Saul that David was not his enemy.

24:12 Let the LORD judge. David called for the Lord Himself, the only fair and impartial Judge (cf. Judg. 11:27), to decide the fate of David and Saul (also v. 15).

24:13 proverb. A traditional pithy statement that evil deeds are perpetrated only by evil men. A similar point is made by Jesus in

Matthew 7:16, 20.

24:14 *A dead dog? A flea?* David hereby expresses his lowliness and entire committal of his cause to God, who alone is the Judge and to whom alone belongs vengeance.

24:17 *You are more righteous than I.* Upon hearing David's testimony, Saul was moved with emotion and acknowledged that David was more righteous than he was. His testimony to David's righteousness recognized David's right to the kingship.

24:20 *you shall surely be king.* Saul emphatically acknowledged that David would be the ruler over the kingdom of Israel. Saul had already been told by Samuel that God would take the kingdom away from him and give it to a man after his own heart (13:14; 15:28). Jonathan had testified that Saul already knew that David would be king (23:17). However, this recognition did not mean that Saul was ready to give up the kingdom.

24:22 *David swore to Saul.* By solemn oath, David agreed to preserve Saul's family and family name. While most of Saul's family was later killed (2 Sam. 21:8, 9), this pledge was fulfilled in the life of Mephibosheth (*see note on 2 Sam. 21:7*).

25:1 *the Israelites . . . lamented for him.* The death of Samuel, the last of the judges, brought Israel to the end of an era. So widespread was Samuel's influence among the people, that all Israel gathered to lament his death. ***Wilderness of Paran.*** A desert area in the northeast region of the Sinai Peninsula.

25:2 *Carmel.* "Vineyard land," "garden spot." About seven miles south of Hebron and one miles north of Maon. This was the same spot where Saul erected a monument in his own honor (15:12).

25:3 *Nabal.* "Fool." An appropriate name in view of his foolish behavior (v. 25). ***Abigail.*** "My father is joy." The wife of Nabal,

---

Key Word

King: 2:10; 8:6; 10:24; 15:11; 18:22; 21:11, 16; 24:20—may describe a petty ruler of a small city (Josh. 10:3) or a monarch of a vast empire (Esth. 1:1–5). An ancient king's jurisdiction included the military (8:20), the economy (1 Kin. 10:26–29), international diplomacy (1 Kin. 5:1–11), and the legal system (2 Sam. 8:15). He often served as a spiritual leader (2 Kin. 23:1–24), although Israel's kings were prohibited from some priestly functions (13:9–14). The Bible presents David as an example of the righteous king who set his heart on faithfully serving God (Acts 13:22). God's promise to give David an everlasting kingdom (2 Sam. 7:16) has been fulfilled in Jesus Christ, whose human ancestry is through the royal family of David (Luke 2:4).

---

who was intelligent and beautiful in contrast to her evil husband. ***the house of Caleb.*** Nabal was a descendant of Caleb and lived in Caleb's tribal holdings (Josh. 14:13; 15:13), but did not possess the spiritual qualities of his illustrious forefather.

25:4, 5 *shearing his sheep.* While hiding out in the wilderness, David and his men took the job of protecting the flocks of Nabal (vv. 7, 15, 16). Upon hearing that Nabal was shearing his sheep, David sent ten of his men to collect their rightful compensation for the good they had done (v. 8).

25:8 *a feast day.* A special day of rejoicing over the abundance of sheared wool from the sheep (cf. v. 11).

25:10, 11 This pretended ignorance of David was surely a sham. The knowledge of the young king-elect was widespread. Nabal pretended not to know to excuse his unwillingness to do what was right.

25:14 *reviled.* David sent his messengers to "greet" (lit. "bless") Nabal, but David's men were viciously rebuffed by Nabal. This term emphasized the wickedness of Nabal's action.

25:15, 16 The testimony of one of Nabal's men affirmed the value of David's protection. It was like a fortress wall enclosing a city, providing total security.

25:17 *one cannot speak to him.* Nabal was a "son of Belial," a worthless fellow (*see note on 2:12*). Nabal's situation was the product of his own wickedness. His unwillingness to seek the counsel of others ultimately led to his demise.

25:18 *five seahs.* Slightly more than one bushel.

25:19 *did not tell her husband.* Abigail knew that Nabal would disagree with her actions, but knowing the Lord's choice of David (v. 28), she recognized the consequences involved in Nabal's cursing of David. By her actions, she chose to obey God rather than man (see Acts 5:29), as a wife may sometimes need to do.

25:22 *May God do so.* A strong oath of self-imprecation. David swore that he would kill every male in Nabal's household by daybreak.

25:25 *this scoundrel.* I.e., "troublemaker." ***as his name is, so is he.*** A name was not simply a label to distinguish one thing from another, but a profound insight into the character of the one named. "Fool" has the connotation of one who is "morally deficient."

25:28 *an enduring house.* Abigail's perceptive insight fit an essential feature of the Davidic covenant (see 2 Sam. 7:11–16). ***fights the battles of the Lord.*** Unlike the king previously desired by the people (8:20), David was a man who fought the Lord's battles. He was truly God's king.

25:29 *bound in the bundle of the living.* A metaphor that reflects the custom of binding valuables in a bundle to protect them from injury. The point here was that God cared for His own as a man would his valuable treasure. David, she said, enjoyed the protection of divine providence which destined him for great things. On the other hand, God would fling his enemies away like a stone in a sling.

25:30 *ruler over Israel.* Abigail was certain that David would exercise effective rule over Israel after Saul's death. In the meantime, however, she did not want him to do anything to jeopardize his future, endanger his throne, or violate God's will by seeking personal vengeance in anger (vv. 33, 34).

25:37, 38 *heart died . . . became like a stone.* Intoxicated, Nabal apparently suffered a stroke and became paralyzed until he died.

25:43 *Ahinoam of Jezreel.* David's third wife, joining Michal and Abigail. For Jezreel, *see note on 29:1.*

Key Word

Hears: 1:13; 2:23; 4:14; 7:9; 8:18; 17:11; 23:11; 25:24—also means "to listen" or "to obey." This important Old Testament word appears over 1,100 times. It implies that the listener is giving his or her total attention to the one who is speaking. In some cases, the word connotes more than listening and indicates obedience to what has been said. Abraham was blessed not only for hearing, but for obeying God's voice (see Gen. 22:18, where the word is translated "obeyed"). In the third chapter of 1 Samuel, Samuel is listening for God's Word and is determined to obey it. This young man is an example of the kind of person God delights to use—the one who is always ready to receive His Word and follow it.

25:44 Palti . . . from Gallim. Palti means "my deliverance." The location of Gallim is unknown, but was probably a few miles north of Jerusalem. See 2 Samuel 3:13–16 for Michal's return to David.

26:1 hill of Hachilah . . . Jeshimon. See notes on 23:19.

26:2 three thousand chosen men. See 24:2.

26:5 Saul lay. Saul was sleeping in an apparently invulnerable place. He had his commander beside him, inside the camp, surrounded by his entire army. **Abner.** See note on 14:50.

26:6 Ahimelech the Hittite. Mentioned only here, he was one of the many mercenaries who formed a part of David's army. **Abishai the son of Zeruiah, brother of Joab.** See note on 2 Samuel 2:18. He joined with Ahimelech in going down with David into the camp of Saul.

26:9 the LORD's anointed. See note on 24:6.

26:10 As the LORD lives. An oath usually associated with life-or-death matters. The sovereign God would decide when, where, and how Saul would perish, not David.

26:12 spear and the jug. Like the corner of Saul's robe (24:4), these were taken as proof that David had Saul's life in his hand (cf. v. 16). **a deep sleep from the LORD.** As with Adam in Genesis 2:21 and Abraham in Genesis 15:12, the Lord caused Saul to be unaware of what was taking place around him.

26:19 If the LORD . . . the children of men. David set forth two possibilities for why Saul was pursuing him. First, David had sinned against the Lord. If that were the case, he was willing to offer a sacrifice for atonement. Second, evil men had caused Saul's hostility toward David. If that were the case, these men should be judged. **the inheritance of the LORD.** I.e., the land of Israel (cf. 2 Sam. 20:19; 21:3). **Go, serve other gods.** David's

exile from the land was virtually equivalent to forcing him to abandon the worship of the Lord, because there were no sanctuaries devoted to worship of the Lord outside of Israelite territory.

26:20 flea . . . partridge. The flea represents something that was worthless and the partridge something that was impossible to catch. Saul was wasting his time with his pursuit of David.

26:21 I have sinned. As in 24:17, Saul confessed his sin and wrongdoing. Although Saul may have been sincere, he could not be trusted and David wisely did not accept his invitation to return with him. **I have played the fool.** Saul had been foolish in his actions toward David, as had Nabal.

26:25 still prevail. Saul recognized the certain success of David's future as Israel's king (cf. 24:20).

3. David's despair and Philistine refuge (27:1–28:2)

27:1 by the hand of Saul. In direct contrast to Saul's word that David would prevail (26:25), David thought that Saul would ultimately kill him. This anxious thinking and the fear that fell upon him explain David's actions in this chapter. God had told him to stay in Judah (22:5), but he was afraid and sought protection again among the Philistine enemies of Israel (cf. 21:10–15).

27:3 two wives. His third wife, Michal, had been temporarily given to another man by Saul (cf. 25:44).

27:4 sought him no more. Saul was no longer able to pursue David since he was out of the land of Israel.

27:5 the royal city. I.e., Gath. David requested a city of his own in the country so he could be free from the constant surveillance to which he was exposed in Gath, and so he could avoid the pagan influence of that Philistine city.

27:6 Ziklag. This was a city located about thirteen miles northwest of Beersheba that had been an Israelite possession (Josh. 15:31; 19:5), but was then under Philistine control. **to this day.** Ziklag became a part of Judah and was still so at the time of the writing of Samuel, which is clearly in the post-Solomonic, divided kingdom era. See Introduction: Author and Date.

27:7 one full year and four months. For sixteen months David was able to deceive Achish about his actions. He remained there until after Saul's death when he moved to Hebron (2 Sam. 1:1; 2:1, 2).

27:8 Geshurites . . . Girzites . . . Amalekites. These peoples lived in southern Canaan and northern Sinai. **Shur . . . Egypt.** See note on 15:7.

27:9 he left neither man nor woman alive. David left no survivors from his raids in order that Achish might not learn the true nature of his desert exploits (see v. 11).

27:10 Judah . . . Jerahmeelites . . . Kenites. The regions south of the hill country centering around Beersheba. This region was far enough away from Gath so that Achish would be ignorant of David's movements. David implied to Achish that the hostility of Judah toward David was increasing, while in fact he was gaining the appreciation and loyalty of Judah toward himself by raiding their wilderness neighbors. Achish thought David was more securely his servant as his own people turned against him (vv. 2–4), but just the opposite was true.

28:1 You assuredly know. The kindness shown to David and his men by Achish in Gath was not without expectation of reciprocation. This phrase seems to presuppose an understanding of this expectation.

28:2 what your servant can do. Being a man of honor, David would not fail to help those who had shown him kindness. David was drawing attention to the fact that he had

proven himself as a valiant and successful warrior and was assuring Achish of his fidelity and ability. **chief guardians.** In light of David's victory over Goliath (17:49–54) and imagined bad reputation among the Israelites, Achish was expressing considerable trust in David's loyalty and ability, because *chief guardian* literally means "keeper of my head."

D. The Death of Saul (28:3–31:13)

1. Saul's final night (28:3–25)

28:3–13 Having deprived himself of every legitimate means of spiritual input as a result of his own disobedience and rebellion, Saul walked in foolishness again by seeking out the very resource (a medium) he had previously removed from the land. Saul swore to the medium an oath of safety by the very God whom he was disobeying. Yet, the inexorable curiosity of Saul to consult Samuel, in spite of Samuel's death, was satisfied by the medium's willingness to "bring up" Samuel.

28:3 mediums and the spiritists. By divine law, they were banned from Israel (Deut. 18:11), and Israel was not to be defiled by them (Lev. 19:31). Turning to them was tantamount to playing the harlot and would result in God setting His face against the offender and cutting him off from among His people (Lev. 20:6). Mediums and spiritists were to be put to death by stoning (Lev. 20:27). Even Saul understood this and had previously dealt with the issue (see v. 9).

28:4 Shunem. Situated southwest of the hill of Moreh and sixteen miles southwest of the Sea of Galilee; the Philistines designated it as their camp site. **Gilboa.** The mountain range beginning five miles south of Shunem and extending southward along the eastern edge of the plain of Jezreel. See note on 31:1.

28:5 his heart trembled greatly. Saul had hidden himself when he was chosen by lot to be king (10:22). When the Spirit of the Lord came upon him, he was changed (10:6), but after the Spirit had departed (16:14), he was afraid and dismayed by Goliath (17:11, 24). He feared at Gilgal when faced by the overwhelming size of the Philistine army (13:11, 12). Saul was also afraid of David because he knew that the Lord was with David (18:12, 29). But Saul was to fear God (12:24), not people.

28:6 dreams . . . Urim . . . prophets. These were the three basic ways through which God revealed His Word and His will. Dreams and visions were the common manner through which the Lord revealed Himself and His will during the time of Moses (Num. 12:6). The Urim was used by the priest as a means of inquiring of the Lord (Num. 27:21). It was originally put in the breastpiece of judgment with the Thummim and worn over Aaron's heart when he went in before the Lord (*see note on Ex. 28:30*). Somehow, unknown to us, God revealed His will by it. Prophets were formerly called seers (9:9) and were used as a reference for inquiring of the Lord. God also used prophets to declare His Word when people were not interested in it (Amos 7:12, 13). Since Saul had rejected the Lord, God had rejected him (15:23). Saul appears to have had no court prophet in the manner that Gad and Nathan were to David (22:5; 2 Sam. 12); and, by this time, the ephod with the Urim was in David's possession by virtue of Abiathar the priest (23:6).

28:7 Find me . . . a medium. In Saul's desperation, he sought the very source that he had formerly removed from the land (28:3). In spite of the ban, Saul's servant knew exactly where to find a medium. **En Dor.** Located less than four miles northwest of Shunem between Mt. Tabor and the hill of Moreh. Saul risked his life by venturing into the Philistine-held territory to seek out the

counsel of the medium; thus, he went in disguise by night (v. 8).

28:10 swore to her by the LORD. Though blatantly walking in disobedience to God, it is ironic that Saul would swear by the very existence of the Lord as a means of assuring his credibility to the medium. Even more, Saul swore that no punishment would come upon her when the Levitical law required her to be stoned to death (Lev. 20:27).

28:12 the woman saw Samuel. Though questions have arisen as to the nature of Samuel's appearance, the text clearly indicates that Samuel, not an apparition, was evident to the eyes of the medium. God miraculously permitted the actual spirit of Samuel to speak (vv. 16–19). Because she understood her inability to raise the dead in this manner, she immediately knew (1) that it must have been by the power of God and (2) that her disguised inquirer must be Saul.

28:13 a spirit ascending out of the earth. The word translated "spirit" is actually the Hebrew word meaning "God, gods, angel, ruler, or judge." It can also be used to designate a likeness to one of these. From the medium's perspective, Samuel appeared to be "like a spirit" ascending out of the earth. There is no other such miracle as this in all of Scripture.

28:14 old man . . . with a mantle. Obviously, age and clothing do not exist in the realm of the spirits of those who have died, but God miraculously gave such appearances so Saul was able to perceive that the spirit was Samuel. The question arises whether all believers will remain in the form they were in when they died. Samuel may have been as such simply for the benefit of Saul, or he might be in this state until he receives his resurrection body. Since Scripture teaches that the resurrection of OT saints is yet future (see Dan. 12:1, 2), Samuel must have temporarily been in this condition solely for the benefit of

King Saul's Decline and Fall	
Causes	**Results**
A presumptuous sacrifice	Loss of kingdom foretold (13:14)
A foolish curse	Curse falls on Jonathan (14:24, 44)
Spared Agag and flocks	Loss of kingdom (15:28)
Lost fellowship with God	Unanswered prayer (28:6)
Visits a medium	Doom predicted (28:19)
Takes his own life	End of dynasty (31:4, 6)

Nelson's Complete Book of Bible Maps & Charts (Nashville: Thomas Nelson Publishers, 1996) 98. © 1993 by Thomas Nelson, Inc.

Saul.

28:15 *disturbed me.* Samuel's comment expresses agitation caused by Saul's efforts to contact him, since living humanity was not allowed to seek out discussions with the dead (Deut. 18:11; Lev. 20:6). Witchcraft puts the seeker in contact with demons impersonating those who are being sought, since the dead person cannot ordinarily be contacted, except in this unique case.

28:16, 18 *your enemy?* See 15:26–35.

28:19 *will be with me.* This could mean with him in "the abode of the righteous." There is no doubt that Samuel meant this to serve as a premonition of Saul's approaching death.

28:20 *no strength in him.* Already afraid with a heart that "trembled greatly" because of the Philistines (v. 5), Saul's fear was so heightened by the words of Samuel that he was completely deprived of strength and vigor, which was reinforced by a lack of nourishment. The woman met his physical needs, and he returned to his camp to await his doom (vv. 21–25).

2. *David's dismissal by the Philistines (29:1–11)*

29:1 *gathered . . . encamped.* The Philistines were assembling for battle while the Israelites were still camping by the spring. This picks up the story line originally started in 28:1, but which was sidelined to commu-

nicate Saul's encounter with the medium. **Aphek.** Located about twenty-four miles north of Gath (cf. 4:1). **Jezreel.** Only a few miles south of Shunem, and forty miles northeast of Aphek, Jezreel was north of Mt. Gilboa.

29:3 *no fault.* David had proven himself as an honorable and righteous man before Achish, who knew that he could trust David.

29:4 *he become our adversary.* The Philistine lords were not as willing as Achish to give favor and trust to David. Being very shrewd in their estimation of potential hazards, they realized that he might be feigning loyalty to the Philistines in order to seize a strategic moment in the battle when he could betray and fight against them.

29:5 *David, of whom they sang.* The fame of David had spread throughout the land. The Philistine lords were no stranger to the skill and the victories that God had given to mighty David.

29:6 *as the LORD lives.* When seeking the highest standard by which to assure David of his credibility, Achish swore by the existence of David's God. It is evident that the pagan world knows of God, but the irony is that their knowledge does not necessarily lead to repentance.

29:8 *the enemies of my lord the king?* David's fidelity to Achish seemed to be at its climax in this expression of loyalty. David appears to have been fully prepared to do battle on behalf of Achish against his enemies, namely, Israel. In light of David's former refusal to stretch out his hand against the Lord's anointed (24:6, 10; 26:9, 11, 21), David might have been capitulating and compromising. He did not inquire of the Lord before going to live with Achish, nor did he inquire of the Lord as to whether he should go out to battle with Achish. On the other hand, it could be that while David gave the appearance of loyalty, he actually believed the Philistines would not let him go out to battle, just as it actually happened (cf. 27:8–12). The providence of God kept David from fighting against the Lord's anointed and his own countrymen.

29:9 *an angel of God.* The degree to which Achish praised David has led some to believe that his eulogy was merely a formal attempt at flattery.

29:11 *Jezreel.* This was used to designate both a city about fifty-six miles north of Jerusalem as well as the plain of Jezreel, which served as a major battlefield for many nations. The city was situated in the territory of Issachar (Josh. 19:18). It was bounded on the north and south by Megiddo and Beth Shean (1 Kin. 4:12) and on the west and east by Mt. Carmel and Mt. Gilboa.

3. David's destruction of the Amalekites (30:1–31)

30:1 *Ziklag.* Serving as a temporary place of residence for David and his 600 men, Ziklag was located in the Negev and given to David by Achish, king of Gath (27:6). David used it as the base where he would make raids on the neighboring tribes (27:8– 11). ***Amalekites.*** Reaping the consequences of Saul's failure to utterly destroy the Amalekites (1 Sam. 15) and David's raids against them (27:8), David and his men were the victims of a successful raid in

which the Amalekites took all of their wives and livestock captive before burning Ziklag, their city.

30:6 *distressed . . . grieved.* Arriving home to the reality of their great tragedy caused David immense distress and provoked the wickedness of his men to entertain the treasonous idea of stoning him. Having not inquired of the Lord before his departure to support Achish in battle, David desperately needed for God to get his attention. ***strengthened himself in the LORD his God.*** This was the key to David being a man after God's heart (cf. 1 Sam. 13:14; Acts 13:22).

30:7 *Abiathar brought the ephod.* Serving as a source through which one could make direct and specific inquiry into the will of God, the high priest's ephod, which contained the Urim and Thummim, was sought by David. The distress of the moment drew his focus away from the treasonous thoughts of his men and back to God in his desperation to know what God would have him do.

30:9, 10 *Brook Besor.* David, most likely, encountered the brook about thirteen miles south of Ziklag. It consisted of seasonal rivers from the area of Beersheba which ran northwest and emptied into the Mediterranean Sea. Likely, this was during the latter rains (January–April), and the brook was filled with a rampaging runoff that would account for the soldiers who were unable to cross over.

30:14 *southern area of the Cherethites.* Benaiah the son of Jehoiada was over the Cherethites and the Pelethites (2 Sam. 8:18), who are almost always mentioned together. They fled Jerusalem as allies with David (2 Sam. 15:18), and pursued Sheba the son of Bichri with Joab (2 Sam. 20:7). They were hand-picked by David to be present at Solomon's anointing as king. The Cherethites appear to have come from Crete, and to have been a part of the king's bodyguard (2 Sam. 23:20, 23). *southern area of Caleb.* Caleb, the son of Jephunneh, was one of twelve spies chosen to check out the land, and one of only two spies who gave a favorable report (Num. 13:6–30). This was the land assigned to his family (Josh. 14:13, 14).

30:16 *all the great spoil.* The Amalekites had not only what they took from Ziklag, but much more plunder from all their raids. After David conquered the Amalekites (vv. 17, 18), he returned what belonged to Ziklag (vv. 19, 26) and spread the rest all over Judah (vv. 26–31).

30:17 *four hundred young men.* It is obvious from Moses' encounter (Ex. 17:8–16), Saul's failure (1 Sam. 15), and Mordecai's opposition (Esth. 3:1, 10–13) that the Amalekites were wicked people who hated God's people.

30:19 *nothing . . . was lacking.* In spite of David's previous failures, God showed Himself to be more than gracious and abundant in His stewardship of the wives, children, livestock, and possessions of David and his men.

30:22 *worthless men.* From the beginning of David's flight from Saul, he became captain of those who were in distress, discontent, and in debt (22:2), the least likely to exercise kindness and grace to others. This same expression was used of the sons of Eli (2:12), of those who doubted Saul's ability as king (10:27), of Nabal the fool by his servant (25:17), of Nabal the fool by his wife (25:25), of David when he was cursed by Shimei (2 Sam. 16:7), of Sheba the son of Bichri who led a revolt against David (2 Sam. 20:1), and of those who would be thrust away like thorns by David (2 Sam. 23:6).

30:25 *a statute and an ordinance.* In spite of the opposition David received from the worthless men among him, he legislated his practice of kindness and equity into law for the people.

30:26–31 Being no stranger to adversity and a life lived on the run, David realized the important role that so many others had played in his safety and welfare. Being the recipient of such kindness, David missed no opportunity to reciprocate kindness and generosity. It would be presumptuous to think that David was merely paying off debts or buying support; rather, he was giving back as he had received, expressing his debt of gratitude for the kindness and support shown him. *See note on 30:16.*

4. Saul's final day (31:1–13)

31:1–13 See 2 Samuel 1:4–12; 1 Chronicles 10:1–12.

31:1 *Mount Gilboa.* Formerly the site of the Israelite camp, it was turned into the sight of the Israelite massacre. Saul and his sons lost their lives on Mount Gilboa. *See note on 28:4.*

31:2 *Jonathan, Abinadab, and Malchishua.* Three of the four sons of Saul were killed the same day in battle. The fourth son, Eshbaal, would later be referred to as Ishbosheth, meaning "man of shame," an appropriate designation in light of his apparent absence from the battlefield (cf. 2 Sam. 2:8ff.). Jonathan, Ishvi, and Malchishua were named as Saul's sons in 14:49, but Jonathan, Abinadab, and Malchishua are named here; Ishvi and Abinadab are thus one and the same. First Chronicles 8:33 and 9:39 are the only verses naming all four sons.

31:4 *uncircumcised men.* A common term of derision used among Israelites to designate non-Israelites. Circumcision was given as the sign of the Abrahamic covenant in Genesis 17:10–14. *See note on 14:6.* **abuse.** Having engaged in several battles against the Philistines, Saul had succeeded in provoking their hatred and resentment. As the king, Saul had certainly received especially cruel treatment from the hands of his enemies, who would have likely made sport of him and tortured him before his death. *Saul took a sword and fell on it.* Though Saul's suicide is considered by some to be an act of heroism, Saul should have found his strength and courage in God as David did in 23:16 and 30:6 to fight to the end or to surrender. Saul's suicide is the ultimate expression of his faithlessness towards God at this moment in his life.

31:6 all his men. The question is whether *all* was used in a qualified sense or in an absolute sense. In consideration of the context, the meaning was most likely intended to be qualified, not absolute. It is not necessary to conclude that every single one of Saul's 3,000 men died that day and that none escaped. Where such a meaning is intended, the text usually provides more reinforcement, as in Joshua 8:22 where the author specifically states, "And they slew them until no one was left of those who survived or escaped." In fact, Abner the general of Saul's army survived (2 Sam. 2:8). *All* here means those who were personally assigned to Saul's special guard (cf. 31:7).

31:9 cut off his head. There is a parallelism between the death of Saul and the death of Goliath. The giant champion of the Philistines had his head cut off by David and the Philistines fled (17:51). The Philistines had taken revenge and done likewise to the giant champion of Israel, King Saul, who was "taller than any of the people from his shoulders upward" (10:23).

31:10 the Ashtoreths. These were the fertility goddesses of the Canaanites, to whom the Philistines gave homage by placing the weapons of their defeated foe in the temple of the Ashtoreths. As the sword of Goliath was put in the house of the Lord behind the ephod (1 Sam. 21:9), so the weapons of Saul were taken by the Philistines and put in the

---

Suicides in Scripture

Abimelech, the son of Gideon, who had his armor-bearer kill him after being injured by a woman (Judg. 9:54)

Samson, the strong man who destroyed a building, thus killing himself and a multitude of Philistines (Judg. 16:26–30)

Saul, who killed himself after losing a battle to the Philistines (1 Sam. 31:4)

Saul's servant, who killed himself as his master had done (1 Sam. 31:5)

Ahithophel, who hanged himself after his advice was rejected by Absalom (2 Sam. 17:23)

Zimri, who set the palace on fire with himself inside rather than being taken prisoner (1 Kin. 16:18)

Judas Iscariot, who hanged himself after betraying Jesus (Matt. 27:5)

---

temple of the Ashtoreths. Military victory was attributed to the gods, since the belief was that military encounters were battles between the deities of rival nations. *Beth Shan.* Located in the Jordan Valley about sixteen miles south of the Sea of Galilee.

31:11 Jabesh Gilead. Located east of the Jordan River, its people stayed out of the war against Benjamin and suffered severe consequences as a result (Judg. 21). The men of Jabesh Gilead showed kindness and respect to Saul, a Benjamite, by rescuing his body from the wall of Beth Shan because Saul and his sons had saved Jabesh Gilead from the Ammonites (11:9–12) just after he had been chosen as king of Israel. By this act, they honored Saul for his faithfulness to them.

31:12 bodies . . . burned. In light of Saul's head having been cut off and the mutilation that had taken place, it is thought that the citizens of Jabesh Gilead burned his body to hide the damage.

31:13 bones . . . buried. It was considered disrespectful not to bury the dead. Abraham went to great lengths to bury Sarah (Gen. 23:4–15), and Jacob made Joseph swear that he would not bury him in Egypt (Gen. 47:29, 30). **Fasted seven days.** In relation to death, fasting was oftentimes associated with mourning in the Hebrew culture. It was a sign of respect, seriousness, and grief. First Samuel began with the ark of the covenant being captured by the Philistines (1 Sam. 4:11), and in the end Israel's king had been killed by them. Second Samuel will recount how God vindicated His honor by David's defeating the Philistines (2 Sam. 5:17–25), establishing an uncontested kingdom (1 Kin. 2:12), and safely bringing

Further Study

Davis, John J. and John C. Whitcomb. *A History of Israel from Conquest to Exile.* Grand Rapids: Baker, 1980.

Merrill, Eugene. *I and II Samuel,* in The Bible Knowledge Commentary—OT. Wheaton, Ill.: Victor, 1985.

Youngblood, Ronald F. *1, 2 Samuel,* in the Expositor's Bible Commentary. Grand Rapids: Zondervan, 1992.

THE SECOND BOOK OF
SAMUEL

Introduction

See 1 Samuel for the introductory discussion.

I. The Reign of David as King over Israel (1:1–20:26)

A. David's Accession to Kingship over Judah (1:1–3:5)

1:1–3:5 David ascends to the kingship of Judah.

1. The deaths of Saul and Jonathan (1:1–27)

1:1 *the death of Saul.* Second Samuel 1:1–14 begins where 1 Samuel 31:1–13 ends, with the death of Saul (cf. 1 Chr. 10:1–12). *Amalekites.* The mention of these people serves as a reminder of David's obedience to the Lord (1 Sam. 30:1–31) and Saul's disobedience (1 Sam. 15:1–33). *See notes on Exodus 17:8–16. Ziklag. See notes on 1 Samuel 27:6; 30:1.* This town was not so completely sacked and destroyed that David and his 600 men with their families could not stay there.

1:2 *clothes torn and dust on his head.* This was a common sign of anguish and mourning over a death. Cf. 15:32; 1 Samuel 4:12.

1:4–12 See 1 Samuel 31:1–13; 1 Chronicles 10:1–12.

1:6 *chariots and horsemen.* Chariots and horsemen were a symbol of power and strength (cf. 8:4; Ex. 14:9; 1 Sam. 8:11; 13:5; 1 Kin. 4:26; 9:19; 10:26; 1 Chr. 19:6; 2 Chr. 1:14; 9:25; 12:3; 16:8; Dan. 11:40). The Philistines were in pursuit of Saul with an abundant number of warriors, making Saul's escape hopeless.

1:8 *Amalekite.* The man claiming to have killed Saul was from among the people whom David recently slaughtered (v. 1), whom God wanted eliminated (Ex. 17:14; 1 Sam. 15:3), and who would plague Israel for generations (Ex. 17:16) because of Saul's disobedience (1 Sam. 15:9–11).

1:10 *killed him.* The Amalekite claimed responsibility for Saul's death, saying that Saul was still alive when he found him. However, 1 Samuel 31:3–6 makes it clear that Saul died by falling on his own sword, not by the hand of the Amalekite. Thus, this man, who may have witnessed Saul's suicide, claimed to have killed Saul when in reality he had only reached his body before the Philistines, having fabricated the story to ingratiate himself with the new king by killing his enemy and by bringing Saul's crown and bracelet to David. The crown and bracelet in the hands of the Amalekite show that he was the first to pass by the body of Saul.

1:12 *mourned and wept and fasted.* David demonstrates genuine, heartfelt grief for Saul and Jonathan by mourning and weeping, as well as fasting, which were common ways to demonstrate grief (cf. Esth. 4:3; Joel 2:12).

1:14 *the Lord's anointed?* Despite Saul's many attempts on David's life, David would not allow himself to see Saul as just a mere man or human monarch; he remained "the Lord's anointed," who occupied a sacred role before God (cf. 1 Sam. 24:1–15; 26:1–20).

1:15 *execute him!* This most certainly came as a great surprise to the Amalekite, since he intended to win the favor of David by saying he had killed Saul. This event is similar to that of the men who later killed Ishbosheth, thinking they would be able to endear themselves to David (4:5–12).

1:16 *Your blood is on your own head.* David executed the Amalekite on the basis of his own testimony, not on the basis of the truthfulness of his story.

1:17 *lamentation.* David chose to have both Saul and his noble son Jonathan remembered through this lamentation, which would be taught to all Israel as a national war song.

1:18 *the Song of the Bow.* This was the title of the poem in which the word *bow* may have been chosen with reference to

Jonathan, whose bow is mentioned in verse 22. *Book of Jasher.* A poetic collection of Israel's wars in which Israel's events and great men were commemorated (cf. Josh. 10:13).

1:19 *The beauty of Israel.* Lit. the gazelle or antelope of Israel, the chosen symbol of youthful elegance and symmetry, most likely referring to Jonathan. Thus, the song began and ended with Saul's noble son (vv. 25, 26). *high places!* These were open-air worship sites generally established at high elevations. In this case, the high place was Mount Gilboa, where Saul had died. *How the mighty have fallen!* They were not only Israel's slain "beauty," but Saul and Jonathan were mighty men who had fallen in battle. This phrase is repeated as a refrain in verses 25, 27.

1:20 *Gath . . . Ashkelon.* Two chief cities which together could represent all of the Philistine territory. Gath was situated in the eastern part of the Philistine territory, while Ashkelon was in the west by the sea. David did not want the Philistines to rejoice at the calamities of Israel as Israel had rejoiced at the defeat of the Philistines (1 Sam. 18:7).

1:21 *no dew nor rain.* David spoke a curse, seeking the absence of dew or rain on the mountain where Saul and Jonathan had died. *not anointed with oil.* It was necessary in those times to anoint a shield with oil (cf. Is. 21:5) to prevent the leather from being hard and cracked. But, there on Mount Gilboa lay the shield of Saul dried out, a symbol of defeat and death.

1:22 *bow . . . sword.* These two weapons were used by Saul and Jonathan with much power, accuracy, and effectiveness. It was also with the bow that Jonathan helped David escape Saul's wrath (1 Sam. 20:35–42).

1:23 *beloved.* This generous commendation, including Saul who was seeking to kill David, showed David's gracious, forgiving attitude—a model of gracious love (cf. Matt. 5:43–48).

1:26 *Surpassing the love of women.* The bond between David and Jonathan was strong. However, this does not mean that their friendship was necessarily superior to the bond of love between a man and a woman. The commitment shared between the two of them was a noble, loyal, and selfless devotion (cf. 1 Sam. 18:3), which neither of them had ever felt for a woman. Unlike love between a man and a woman in which a sexual element is part of the strong attraction, this love between these two men had no such sexual feature, yet was compellingly strong.

1:27 *weapons of war.* A figurative expression referring to Saul and Jonathan.

2. David anointed by Judah (2:1–7)

2:1 *David inquired of the LORD.* After the death of Saul, David could move about the land freely as the Lord directed him. A contrast can be seen between Saul, who had inquired of the Lord and the Lord would not answer (cf. 1 Sam. 28:6), and David, who also inquired of the Lord and the Lord gave him direction. *cities of Judah?* David sought guidance from the Lord about where to start his reign. David first asked if he should begin in the southern area of Judah. The Lord responded affirmatively and, thus, David sought for a more precise destination. The nucleus of David's future government would come from the cities of Judah. *Hebron.* With the highest elevation of any town in Judah, the city was strategically chosen to be the initial location of David's rule over Israel. Hebron is located twenty miles south-southwest of Jerusalem. Abraham had lived there long before (Gen. 13:18), and later Hebron had been given to Caleb (Josh. 14:13, 14; Judg. 1:20) when Israel occupied the land after the wilderness wanderings.

2:2 *Ahinoam . . . Abigail.* Abigail became David's wife after the death of Nabal (cf. 1 Sam. 25:40–44).

2:4 *anointed David king.* David had already been privately anointed king by Samuel (cf. 1 Sam. 16:3). This anointing recognized his rule in the southern area of Judah. Later, he would be anointed as king over all Israel (cf. 2 Sam. 5:3). ***men of Jabesh Gilead.*** Jabesh, a city of Israel east of the Jordan River, demonstrated its loyalty to Saul by giving him a proper burial (cf. 1 Sam. 31:11–13).

2:7 *your master Saul is dead.* David referred to Saul as "your master" in order not to antagonize the men of Jabesh Gilead. He sought to win Israel over to his side, not force them into submission.

3. David's victories over the house of Saul (2:8–3:1)

2:8 *Abner.* Abner, cousin of Saul and general of his army (1 Sam. 14:50, 51), did not desire to follow the Lord's new anointed king, but placed Ishbosheth on the throne, causing tension between Judah and the rest of the tribes in Israel. ***Ishbosheth.*** His name means "man of shame." Saul's only surviving son was placed as king over the northern tribes of Israel and the eastern ones across the Jordan. ***Mahanaim.*** A town in Gilead east of the Jordan River. Ishbosheth established himself there and reigned for two years in this city. This was the same city where Jacob saw the angels while on his way to Penuel (Gen. 32:2). It was appointed to be a Levitical city from the territory of Gad (Josh. 21:28; 1 Chr. 6:80). It later became a haven for David while fleeing from Absalom (17:24, 27; 19:32; 1 Kin. 2:8), because likely it was well fortified (cf. 18:24).

2:9 *king over Gilead . . . all Israel.* Ishbosheth's power seemed more solidified in the land of Gilead (east of the Jordan River) than in the rest of Israel.

2:10 *the house of Judah.* A natural opposition arose between the tribe of Judah and the rest of Israel since Judah was under the reign of David, while the rest of Israel recognized the reign of Ishbosheth.

2:11 *seven years and six months.* Several years passed before Ishbosheth assumed the throne of Israel, so that Ishbosheth's two-year reign came at the end of David's seven-year-and-six-month reign over Judah. It must have taken Ishbosheth about five years to regain the northern territory from the Philistines.

2:12 *Gibeon.* During the time of Joshua, Gibeon was a very important city (Josh. 10:2). Its people probably had sided with David because Saul had broken a treaty with the Gibeonites and acted treacherously toward them (21:1).

2:13 *Joab the son of Zeruiah.* Joab was the leader of David's army and, thus, led the men against Abner. Although Ishbosheth and David sat on the thrones of their respective territories, Joab and Abner truly had wielded the power and control by leading the military forces. Zeruiah was the sister of David (cf. 1 Chr. 2:16).

2:14 *the young men . . . compete.* Rather than all-out war, Abner proposed a representative contest between champions on behalf of the opposing armies. Because all twenty-four of the contestants lay fallen and dying in combat (vv. 15, 16), the contest settled nothing, but excited passions so that a battle between the two armies ensued (v. 17).

2:18 *Abishai.* Brother of Joab, he was an aide to David throughout his rise to power. Abishai was with David in the camp of Saul when David had opportunity to kill Saul and encouraged the murder of Saul, which David would not allow (cf. 1 Sam. 26:6–9). ***Asahel.*** Another brother of Joab, Asahel was single-minded with dogged determination; though he was extremely fleet-footed, his determination would prove to be fatal (v. 23).

2:21 *take his armor.* To gain the armor of the enemy general, Abner, who was fleeing the defeat, would possess the greatest trophy. Asahel was ambitious to get it, while Abner kept warning him and suggested that he take the armor of some other soldier for his trophy, since he was not able to defeat Abner.

2:22 *How then could I face your brother Joab?* Abner sought to spare Asahel in order to avoid unnecessary vengeance from Joab or David. Abner tried to give Asahel reasons to stop his pursuit, but Asahel was determined. Abner did not wish to strike down Asahel, but Asahel refused to listen, so he was forced to stop his effort with a fatal back stab by the blunt end of his spear.

2:26 *Shall the sword devour forever?* As Abner had earlier proposed that the hostilities begin, he now proposed that they cease.

2:29 *Bithron.* After the death of Asahel, Abner moved through this gorge as he approached Mahanaim (*see note on 2:8*).

3:1 *a long war.* The conflict between Ishbosheth and David did not end in quick victory. There was a gradual transfer of power from the house of Saul to the house of David (v. 10) that lasted at least through the two-year reign of Ishbosheth and maybe longer.

4. David's wives/sons in Hebron (3:2–5)
3:2–5 See 1 Chronicles 3:1–4.

3:2 *Amnon.* He raped and defiled his half-sister Tamar (13:1–22) and later, by the command of Absalom, was killed for his crime (13:23–39).

3:3 *Chileab.* He apparently died before he was able to enter into position to contend for the throne, because nothing more is said about him. This child was born to David by the wife whom David had taken on the death of Nabal (see 1 Sam. 25:3). ***Absalom.*** Lit. "My Divine Father is Peace" or "Divine Father of Peace." Absalom was the son of Maacah, who was a Geshurite princess from

a region in Syria, not Israel. David may have married her as part of a diplomatic agreement made with Talmai, the Geshurite king, to give David an ally north of Ishbosheth. Later Absalom, in fear for his life, fled to Geshur (13:37, 38).

3:4 *Adonijah.* He was a prominent figure in the contention for David's throne at the end of his reign (1 Kin. 1; 2), but was assassinated, allowing the throne to be given to Solomon (1 Kin. 2:25). Haggith was probably married to David after his accession to the throne. ***Shephatiah . . . Abital.*** Shephatiah means "The Lord Judges." Abital means "My Divine Father is Dew" or "My Divine Father of Dew."

3:5 *Eglah.* Eglah is called the "wife of David." This may be because she is the last on the list and serves to draw emphasis to David's polygamy. The inclusion of these sons indicates all who would have been in contention for the throne. ***born to David.*** More children were born to David when he moved to Jerusalem (5:14).

B. David's Accession to Kingship over Israel (3:6–5:16)
3:6–5:16 David assumed the kingdom of all Israel by a similar progression of events as those which led to his assuming the throne of Judah. In both cases, a man comes seeking David's favor (Amalekite, 1:1–13; Abner, 3:6–21). Both of these men are executed for their deeds (Amalekite, 1:14–16; Abner, 3:22–32). In both cases, this is followed by a lament of David (1:17–27; 3:33–39). Close to the middle of both accounts is a brief look at the anointing of David as king (over Judah, 2:1–7; over Israel, 5:1–5). After this, David and his men are successful in defeating their enemies (2:8–3:1; 5:6–12). Each section concludes with a list of the children born to David (Hebron, 3:2–5; Jerusalem, 5:13–16).

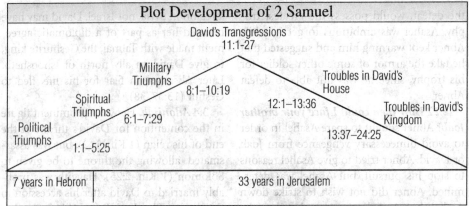

Plot Development of 2 Samuel

David's Transgressions
11:1–27

Military
Triumphs
8:1–10:19

Troubles in David's
House
12:1–13:36

Spiritual
Triumphs
6:1–7:29

Troubles in David's
Kingdom

Political
Triumphs
1:1–5:25

13:37–24:25

7 years in Hebron

33 years in Jerusalem

The MacArthur Bible Handbook, by John MacArthur (Nashville: Thomas Nelson Publishers, 2003) 96. © 2003 by Thomas Nelson, Inc.

1. The deaths of Abner and Ishbosheth (3:6–4:12)

3:6 Abner was strengthening his hold. Abner was the military leader of the country and the one who had put Ishbosheth on the throne and whose power held him there. As time passed, Abner began to make his own move to take the throne.

3:7 Rizpah. By taking Rizpah, the concubine of Saul, Abner made a clear statement to the people that he would take the place of Saul as king over Israel. Going in to the king's concubine was a statement of power and rightful claim to the throne (cf. 16:21, 22 in regard to Absalom). Ishbosheth reacted strongly against Abner, so Abner resented his reaction as an indignity and, compelled by revenge, determined to transfer all the weight of his influence and power to David's side (vv. 9, 10).

3:8 dog's head. This was another way to ask, "Am I a contemptible traitor allied with Judah?" This was a common expression to show disdain (1 Sam. 17:43). Abner used this opportunity to condemn Ishbosheth by reminding him that he would not have been in power had Abner himself not placed him there.

3:9 as the LORD has sworn to him. Abner

seemed to demonstrate the knowledge that David was to be the next king of Israel as God had sworn to David (1 Sam. 13:14; 15:28; 24:20).

3:10 transfer the kingdom. Part of Saul's kingdom had already been transferred to David, namely Judah; however, Abner vowed to complete the process by helping David obtain the rest of the kingdom. **Dan to Beersheba.** This was an expression meaning the whole country (cf. Judg. 20:1), i.e., from Dan in the north to Beersheba in the south.

3:12 Whose is the land? Though Abner's language (vv. 9, 10) implied the conviction that in supporting Ishbosheth he had been going against God's purpose of conferring the sovereignty of the kingdom on David, this acknowledgment was no justification of his motives. He selfishly wanted to be on the winning side and to be honored as the one who brought all the people under David's rule.

3:13 Michal, Saul's daughter. David requested Michal for two reasons. One, it would right the wrong Saul had committed toward David by having given Michal, who was David's wife and who loved him (1 Sam. 18:20, 28), to another man (1 Sam. 25:44). Two, it would serve to strengthen David's claim to the throne of all Israel by inclining some of Saul's house to be favorable to his cause.

3:14 *a hundred foreskins of the Philistines.* David reminded Ishbosheth that he had not only paid the dowry to Saul for his daughter, 100 foreskins of the Philistines, but had delivered double the asking price (1 Sam. 18:25–27). Thus, Michal rightfully belonged to David.

3:16 *Bahurim.* Located just east of Jerusalem, it became the final location where Paltiel (cf. 1 Sam. 25:44) would see Michal. This was also the town of Shimei, the man who cursed David during his flight from Jerusalem before Absalom (16:5). David's soldiers also found refuge in a well at Bahurim while being pursued by Absalom's men (19:16).

3:17 *elders of Israel.* These men were the recognized leaders of the people serving as Ishbosheth's advisers who would have been consulted when important decisions needed to be made (cf. 19:7).

3:18 *My servant David.* David is called "the LORD's servant" more than thirty times in the OT. Abner's words to the elders of Israel clearly recognized David as the servant of the Lord, thus having the right to the throne according to God's sovereign will.

3:19 *Benjamin.* Abner gave special attention to the tribe of Benjamin, because they were Saul's and Ishbosheth's kinsmen (see 1 Sam. 9:1, 2).

3:21 *covenant with you.* This covenant moved beyond the personal agreement made between Abner and David and was operative on the national level, uniting both north and south. *in peace.* The repetition of this phrase in verses 22 and 23 serves to emphasize the fact that David sought to ensure peace with Abner. This also accentuates the fact that David was not involved in Abner's death (vv. 26–30).

3:25 *Abner . . . came to deceive you.* It is ironic that Joab accused Abner of deception in spying on David in verse 25, when in verse 26 he deceived David by not telling him of his request to have Abner returned to Hebron. Joab used this deception to kill Abner, out of personal vengeance for the death of his brother Asahel (v. 27; see 2:19–23).

3:26 *well of Sirah.* The only mention of this location is found here. The town was located less than three miles northwest of Hebron.

3:27 *in the stomach.* Abner died in a similar manner to Joab's brother Asahel, the man he had killed (2:23). However, Abner struck Asahel during battle (cf. 2:18–23) in self-defense, while Joab murdered Abner to avenge the death of Asahel.

3:28 *the blood of Abner.* Since life is in the blood (cf. Gen. 9:4; Lev. 17:11, 14; Deut. 12:23), this expression refers to the life of Abner. David made it clear that he had nothing to do with the murder of Abner, and David sought the Lord's help to punish Joab for his evil deed (v. 39).

3:31 *mourn.* Joab was instructed to mourn for the death of Abner, as was the custom for commemorating the death of an individual. To further demonstrate David's condemnation of the killing of Abner, he instructed "all the people" to mourn the death of Abner, including Joab and his men (vv. 32–34).

3:35–39 David's feelings and conduct in response to Abner's death tended not only to remove all suspicion of guilt from him, but even turned the tide of public opinion in his favor and paved the way for his reigning over all the tribes much more honorably than by the negotiations of Abner (3:17–19).

3:39 *weak . . . harsh.* David had not yet solidified his power enough to exact his own judgment without jeopardizing his command. He was still "weak" and needed time to consolidate his authority. Once that was accomplished, he no longer needed to fear the strength of Joab and Abishai, who were Zeruiah's sons (2:18).

4:1 lost heart . . . troubled. Lit. "his hands became weak or limp" (cf. 17:2; 2 Chr. 15:7). Ishbosheth and all of Israel realized that Abner had been the source of strength and stability for Israel. With Abner dead, Israel was troubled because Ishbosheth no longer had a leader for the army which secured him in power.

4:2 children of Benjamin. It is emphasized that these men were of the tribe of Benjamin (vv. 2, 3), perhaps to show the friction within the house of Saul and his son Ishbosheth, and how the grab for power began once Abner was gone.

4:2, 3 Beeroth . . . Gittaim. Beeroth was a Canaanite town belonging to the tribe of Benjamin. Gittaim was also a village of the tribe of Benjamin.

4:4 Mephibosheth. He may be introduced here to demonstrate that his youth and physical handicap disqualified him from being considered for ruling Israel. He would have been only twelve years old at the time of Ishbosheth's death. For the history of this man, see 9:6–13; 16:1–4; 19:24–30; 21:7.

4:5, 6 It was the custom to secure wheat for the soldiers under their command (v. 2), along with some pay. Under the pretense of that normal routine, they came and killed the king.

4:7 the plain. To avoid easy detection, the men traveled by way of the Arabah (cf. 2:29), i.e., the Jordan Valley. This plain extended about thirty miles from Mahanaim to Hebron.

4:8 the LORD has avenged. The murderers of Ishbosheth came to David and proclaimed, "the LORD has avenged" David. However, as happened earlier to the Amalekite (1:2–15), the men were very surprised

at the response of David. David did not see their deed as the Lord's vengeance, but as murder of an innocent man.

4:9 the LORD . . . has redeemed my life from all adversity. A striking contrast is shown between David and the two murderers who claimed they were performing the Lord's work by killing Ishbosheth. However, David praised the Lord for His providential work through Ishbosheth's life and proclaimed the Lord's deliverance; thus, David condemned the murderers of Ishbosheth and had them executed as he had done to the man who claimed to kill Saul (1:15, 16).

2. David anointed by all Israel (5:1–5)

5:1–3 See 1 Chronicles 11:1–3.

5:1, 2 all the tribes of Israel. The term *all* is used three times (vv. 1, 3, 5) to emphasize that the kingdom established under King David was truly a united monarchy. The "elders" of Israel (v. 3), representing the "tribes" (v. 1), came to David at Hebron with the express purpose of submitting to his rule. Three reasons were given by the Israelites for wanting to make David king: (1) he was an Israelite brother (cf. Deut. 17:15); (2) he was Israel's best warrior and commander; and (3) he had been chosen by the Lord to be the king of Israel.

5:3 King David made a covenant. David bound himself formally to certain obligations toward the Israelites, including their rights and responsibilities to one another and to the Lord (cf. 2 Kin. 11:17). As good as this covenant was, it did not end the underlying sense of separate identity felt by Israel and Judah as the revolt of Sheba (20:1) and the dissolution of the united kingdom under Rehoboam (1 Kin. 12:16) would later demonstrate. **they anointed David.** David's third anointing (2:4; 1 Sam. 16:13) resulted in the unification of the twelve tribes under his kingship.

David's Triumphs

David was a man after God's own heart (1 Sam. 13:14), that is, his will was completely committed to the will of his Lord. As a dedicated servant of God, he was used by God to perform mighty acts for the sake of His chosen people Israel.

King of Judah (2:4)
King of Israel (5:3)
Conquers Jerusalem (5:7)
Returns ark (6:12)
Davidic covenant (7:16)
Defeats Philistines (8:1)
Defeats Moab (8:2)
Defeats Ammon (10:16)
Defeats Syria (10:19)

Nelson's Complete Book of Bible Maps & Charts (Nashville: Thomas Nelson Publishers, 1996) 56. © 1993 by Thomas Nelson, Inc.

5:5 Israel and Judah. The united kingdom was still known by its two component parts.

3. David's conquest of Jerusalem (5:6–12)
5:6–10 See 1 Chronicles 11:4–9.

5:6 Jerusalem. This city is mentioned in the Bible more than any other (from Gen. 14:18 to Rev. 21:10). The city was located in the territory of Benjamin, near the northern border of Judah and was excellently fortified because of its elevation and the surrounding deep valleys, which made it naturally defensible on three sides. In addition, it had a good water supply, the Gihon spring, and was close to travel routes for trade. The city had earlier been conquered by Judah (Judg. 1:8), but neither Judah nor Benjamin had been successful in permanently dislodging the Jebusite inhabitants (Josh. 15:33; Judg. 1:21). By taking Jerusalem, David was able to eliminate the foreign wedge between the northern and southern tribes and to establish his capital. **Jebusites.** A people of Canaanite descent (Gen. 10:16–18). Since the earlier inhabitants of Jerusalem were Amorites (Josh. 10:5), it seems that the Jebusites took control of Jerusalem after the time of the Israelite conquest. **the blind and the lame.** The Jebusites taunted the Israelites and mocked the power of David by boasting that the blind and the lame could defend Jerusalem against him.

5:7 stronghold of Zion. This is the first occurrence of Zion in the Bible and the only one in 1 and 2 Samuel. Referring here to the Jebusite citadel on the southeastern hill, the name was also later used of the temple mount (Is. 10:12) and of the entire city of Jerusalem (Is. 28:16). **City of David.** Both Bethlehem, David's birthplace (Luke 2:4), and Jerusalem, David's place of reign, were called by this title.

5:8 water shaft. A tunnel that channeled the city's water supply from the Gihon spring outside the city walls on the east side into the citadel.

5:9 Millo. Lit. "filling." Stone-filled terraces were built to serve as part of Jerusalem's northern defenses, since the city was most open to attack from that direction.

5:11–16 See 1 Chronicles 14:1–7.

5:11 Hiram king of Tyre. Tyre was a Phoenician port city about thirty-five miles north of Mount Carmel and twenty-five miles south of Sidon. During the latter part of David's reign and much of Solomon's, the friendly Hiram traded building materials for agricultural products. He also provided craftsmen to build David's palace, indicating how the long war had brought the nation to a low place where there were few good artisans. Psalm 30 could possibly refer to the dedication of this house or to the temporary shelter for the ark in Jerusalem (6:17).

5:12 the LORD had established him as

The City of David

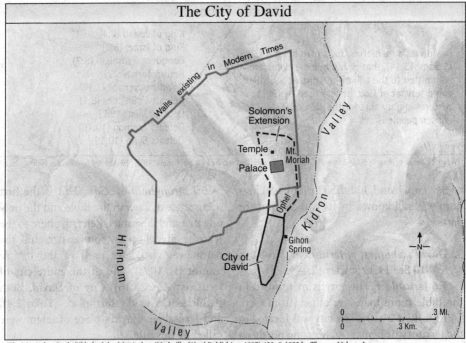

The MacArthur Study Bible, by John MacArthur (Nashville: Word Publishing, 1997) 433. © 1993 by Thomas Nelson, Inc.

king. Witnessing God's evident blessing on his life, David recognized the Lord's role in establishing his kingship.

4. David's wives/sons in Jerusalem (5:13–16)

5:13 more concubines and wives. The multiplication of David's wives and concubines was in direct violation of Deuteronomy 17:17. These marriages probably (cf. 3:3) reflected David's involvement in international treaties and alliances that were sealed by the marriage of a king's daughter to the other participants in the treaty. This cultural institution accounted for some of David's and many of Solomon's wives (see 1 Kin. 11:1–3). In each case of polygamy in Scripture, the law of God was violated and the consequences were negative, if not disastrous.

C. David's Triumphal Reign (5:17–8:18)

5:17–8:18 This section is bracketed by the descriptions of David's military victories (5:17–25; 8:1–14). In between (6:1–7:29), David's concern for the ark of the covenant and a suitable building to house it are recounted.

1. David's victories over the Philistines (5:17–25)

5:17–23 See 1 Chronicles 14:8–17.

5:17 Philistines. The Philistines had remained quiet neighbors during the long civil war between the house of Saul and David, but, jealous of the king who had consolidated the nation, they resolved to attack before his government was fully established. Realizing that David was no longer their vassal, they took decisive military action against his new capital of Jerusalem.

5:18 *Valley of Rephaim.* Lit. "the valley of the giants." It was a plain located southwest of Jerusalem on the border between Judah and Benjamin (Josh. 15:1, 8; 18:11, 16), where fertile land produced grain that provided food for Jerusalem and also attracted raiding armies.

5:20 *Baal Perazim.* The image seen in this name was that of flooding waters breaking through a dam as David's troops had broken through the Philistine assault.

5:21 *images.* The idols that the Philistines had taken into battle to assure them of victory were captured by the Israelites and burned (1 Chr. 14:12).

5:24 *the sound of marching.* The leaves of this tree would rustle at the slightest movement of air, much of which would be generated by a large army marching.

5:25 *Geba . . . Gezer.* Geba was located about five miles north of Jerusalem, and Gezer was about twenty miles west of Geba. David drove the Philistines out of the hill country back to the coastal plain.

2. David's spiritual victories (6:1–7:29)

6:1–11 See 1 Chronicles 13:1–14.

6:2 *Baale Judah.* Lit. "lords of Judah." Also known as Kirjath Jearim (1 Sam. 7:1, 2), this town was located about ten miles west of Jerusalem. *ark of God.* The ark of the covenant represented the glorious reputation and gracious presence of the Lord to Israel. *the Name. See note on Deuteronomy 12:5.* Lord *of Hosts. See note on 1 Samuel 1:3.*

6:3 *new cart.* The Philistines had used a cart to transport the ark (1 Sam. 6:7). But the OT law required that the sacred ark be carried by the sons of Kohath (Num. 3:30, 31; 4:15; 7:9), using the poles prescribed (Ex. 25:12–15). *house of Abinadab.* See 1 Samuel 7:1. *Uzzah and Ahio.* Descendants of Abinadab, possibly his grandsons.

6:6–8 See 1 Chronicles 13:9–12.

6:7 *for his error.* No matter how innocently it was done, touching the ark was in direct violation of God's law and was to result in death (see Num. 4:15). This was a means of preserving the sense of God's holiness and the fear of drawing near to Him without appropriate preparation.

6:8 *David became angry.* Probably anger directed at himself because the calamity resulted from David's own carelessness. He was confused as to whether to carry on the transportation of the ark to Jerusalem (v. 9) and would not move it, fearing more death and calamity might come on him or the people (v. 10). It is likely that he waited for the wrath of God to subside before moving the ark.

6:10 *Obed-Edom the Gittite.* Lit. "servant of Edom." The term *Gittite* can refer to someone from the Philistine city of Gath, but here it is better to see the term related to Gath Rimmon, one of the Levitical cities (cf. Josh. 21:24, 25). Obed-Edom is referred to as a Levite in Chronicles (1 Chr. 15:17–25; 16:5, 38; 26:4, 5, 8, 15; 2 Chr. 25:24).

6:12–19 See 1 Chronicles 15:25–16:3.

6:12 *blessed . . . because of the ark.* During the three months when the ark remained with Obed-Edom, the Lord blessed his family. In the same way, God had blessed Obed-Edom, David was confident that with the presence of the ark, the Lord would bless his house in ways that would last forever (7:29).

6:13 *bearing the ark.* In David's second attempt to bring the ark to Jerusalem, it was transported in the manner prescribed by OT law. *See note on verse 3. six paces.* I.e., after the first six steps, not after every six steps.

6:14 *David danced before the Lord.* Cf. Psalm 150:4. The Hebrews, like other ancient and modern people, had their physical expressions of religious joys as they praised God. *linen ephod.* See 1 Samuel 2:18.

6:16 *Michal . . . despised him.* Michal's

contempt for David is explained by her sarcastic remark in verse 20. She considered David's unbridled, joyful dancing as conduct unbefitting the dignity and gravity of a king because it exposed him in some ways.

6:17 tabernacle. David had made a tent for the ark of the covenant until a permanent building for it could be built. Psalm 30 could possibly refer to this tent or to David's own home (5:11, 12).

6:20 bless his household. David desired the same inevitable success from the Lord as experienced in the household of Obed-Edom (see v. 11). The attitude of Michal aborted the blessing at that time, but the Lord would bless David's house in the future (7:29). **uncovering.** A derogatory reference to the priestly attire that David wore (v. 14) in place of his royal garments.

6:21 before the LORD. David's actions were for the delight of the Lord, not for the maidens.

6:22 humble in my own sight. David viewed himself with humility. It is the humble whom the Lord will exalt (cf. 1 Sam. 7:7, 8).

6:23 Michal . . . had no children. Whether David ceased to have marital relations with Michal or the Lord disciplined Michal for her contempt of David, Michal bore no children. In OT times, it was a reproach to be childless (1 Sam. 1:5, 6). Michal's childlessness prevented her from providing a successor to David's throne from the family of Saul (cf. 1 Sam. 15:22–28).

7:1–17 See 1 Chronicles 17:1–15. These verses record the establishment of the Davidic covenant, God's unconditional promise to David and his posterity. While not called a covenant here, it is later (23:5). This promise is an important key to understanding God's irrevocable pledge of a king from the line of David to rule forever (v. 16). It has been estimated that over forty individual

biblical passages are directly related to these verses (cf. Pss. 89; 110; 132); thus, this text is a major highlight in the OT. The ultimate fulfillment comes at Christ's second advent when He sets up His millennial kingdom on earth (cf. Ezek. 37; Zech. 14; Rev. 19). This is the fourth of five irrevocable, unconditional covenants made by God. The first three include: (1) the Noahic covenant (Gen. 9:8–17); (2) the Abrahamic covenant (Gen. 15:12–21); and (3) the priestly covenant (Num. 3:1–18; 18:1–20; 25:10–13). The new covenant, which actually provided redemption, was revealed later through Jeremiah (Jer. 31:31–34) and accomplished by the death and resurrection of Jesus Christ. *See note on Matthew 26:28.*

7:1 dwelling in his house. See 5:11. David's palace was built with help from Hiram of Tyre. Since Hiram did not become king of Tyre until around 980 B.C., the events narrated in this chapter occurred in the last decade of David's reign. **rest from all his enemies.** David had conquered all the nations around Israel. See 8:1–14 for the details which occur prior to 2 Samuel 7.

7:2 Nathan. Mentioned here for the first time, Nathan played a significant role in chapter 12 (confronting David's sin with Bathsheba) and 1 Kings 1 (upsetting Adonijah's plot to usurp the throne from Solomon). **inside tent curtains.** See note on 6:17.

7:3 Go, do. Nathan the prophet encouraged David to pursue the noble project he had in mind and assured him of the Lord's blessing. However, neither David nor Nathan had consulted the Lord.

7:4–16 The Lord revealed His will to Nathan in this matter, to redirect the best human thoughts of the king.

7:5 Would you build a house? Verses 5–7 are framed by two questions asked by the Lord, both of which pertain to building a temple for Him. The first question, asking if

David was the one who should build the temple, expected a negative answer (see 1 Chr. 17:4). According to 1 Chronicles 22:8; 28:3, David was not chosen by God to build the temple because he was a warrior who had shed much blood.

7:7 'Why have you not built Me a house?' The second question, asking if the Lord had ever commanded any leader to build a temple for His ark, also expected a negative answer. So contrary to Nathan's and David's intentions and assumptions, God did not want a house at that time and did not want David to build one.

7:8–16 a great name. These verses state the promises the Lord gave to David. Verses 8–11a give the promises to be realized during David's lifetime. Verses 11b–16 state the promises that would be fulfilled after David's death. During David's lifetime, the Lord: (1) gave David "a great name" (*see note on Gen. 12:2*); (2) appointed a place for Israel; and (3) gave David "rest" from all his enemies.

After David's death, the Lord gave David: (1) a son to sit on his national throne, whom the Lord would oversee as a father with necessary chastening, discipline, and mercy (Solomon); and (2) a Son who would rule a kingdom that will be established forever (Messiah). This prophecy referred in its immediacy to Solomon and to the temporal kingdom of David's family in the land. But in a larger and more sublime sense, it refers to David's greater Son of another nature, Jesus Christ (cf. Heb. 1:8).

7:11 the LORD . . . will make you a house. Although David wanted to build the Lord a "house," i.e., a temple, instead it would be the Lord who would build David a "house," i.e., a dynasty.

7:12 your seed. According to the rest of Scripture, it was the coming Messiah who would establish David's kingdom forever (see Is. 9:6, 7; Luke 1:32, 33).

7:14 his Father . . . My son. These words are directly related to Jesus the Messiah in Herews 1:5. In Semitic thought, since the son had the full character of the father, the future seed of David would have the same essence of God. That Jesus Christ was God incarnate is the central theme of John's Gospel (see Introduction to John). **If he commits iniquity.** As a human father disciplines his sons, so the Lord would discipline the seed, if he committed iniquity. This has reference to the intermediary seed until Messiah's arrival (any king of David's line from Solomon on). However, the ultimate Seed of David will not be a sinner like David and his descendants were, as recorded in Samuel and Kings (see 2 Cor. 5:21). Significantly, Chronicles, focusing more directly on the Messiah, does not include this statement in its record of Nathan's words (1 Chr. 17:13).

The Davidic Covenant
(Cf. 2 Sam. 23:5; 2 Chr. 21:7; Pss. 89:3, 28; 132:12)
1. God will appoint a place for *His people* (2 Sam. 7:10; 1 Chr. 17:9; Ps. 132:13, 14).
2. God will arrange for the permanence of *His people* (2 Sam. 7:10; 1 Chr. 17:9; Ps. 132:14).
3. God will prevent oppression from *His people*'s enemies (2 Sam. 7:10; 1 Chr. 17:9; Ps. 132:18).
4. God will set up the *Davidic* dynasty—the house of David (2 Sam. 7:12, 16; 1 Chr. 17:10, 11; Ps. 132:11, 12).
5. God will establish the *Davidic* kingdom (2 Sam. 7:12, 13, 16; 1 Chr. 17:11; Ps. 132:17).
6. God will ensure the certainty of the *Davidic* throne (2 Sam. 7:16; 1 Chr. 17:12; Ps. 132:11, 12).

7:15 This is an expression of the unconditional character of the Davidic covenant. The Messiah will come to His glorious, eternal kingdom and that promise will not change.

7:16 *your house ... your kingdom ... Your throne.* Luke 1:32b, 33 indicates that these three terms are fulfilled in Jesus, "and the Lord God will give Him the *throne* of His father David. And He will reign over the *house* of Jacob forever, and of His *kingdom* there will be no end." *forever.* This word conveys the idea of (1) an indeterminately long time or (2) into eternity future. It does not mean that there cannot be interruptions, but rather that the outcome is guaranteed. Christ's Davidic reign will conclude human history.

7:18–29 See 1 Chronicles 17:16–27. David prayed with awe and thanksgiving over God's sovereign claim to bestow the divine blessing on his seed and nation.

7:18 *sat before the LORD.* I.e., before the ark of the covenant in the temporary tent. *Who am I?* David was overwhelmed by the Lord's promise that He would bring His kingdom through David's seed. In verses 18–29, David referred to himself ten times as "your servant" (vv. 19, 20, 21, 25, 26, 27, 28, 29), acknowledging his God-given title, "My servant David" (v. 5).

7:19 *a great while to come.* David recognized that the Lord had spoken about the distant future, not only about his immediate descendant, Solomon. *the manner of man.* Lit. "and this is the law of man." This statement is better taken as a declaration rather than a question, with the idea being that God's covenant promise is for an eternal kingdom, whereby the whole world of man shall be blessed through the coming seed of David. The Davidic covenant is thus a grant, conferring powers, rights, and privileges to David and his seed for the benefit of mankind, a promise that left David speechless (vv. 20–22).

7:23 *Your people ... Your land.* David is remembering aspects of the Abrahamic covenant (cf. Gen. 12; 15; 17). *Israel.* In verses 18–21, David praised the Lord for His favor to him. In verses 22–24, David praised the Lord for the favor shown to the nation of Israel (cf. Deut. 7:6–11).

7:25 *the word ... You have spoken.* In verses 25–29, David prayed for the fulfillment of the divine promise spoken to him.

7:26–29 *Your words are true.* David's prayer indicated that he fully accepted by faith the extraordinary, irrevocable promises God made to David as king and to Israel as a nation.

3. David's victories over the Philistines, Moabites, Arameans, and Edomites (8:1–18)

8:1–14 These verses outline the expansion of David's kingdom under the hand of the Lord (vv. 6, 14). Israel's major enemies were all defeated as David's kingdom extended north, south, east, and west. See 1 Chronicles 18:1–13. This conquering occurred before the event of chapter 7 (see 7:1).

8:1 *Philistines ... subdued.* David's first priority was to deal with the Philistines to the west; these he quickly defeated and subjugated (see 5:25). *Metheg Ammah.* This is probably a reference to the "chief city" of the Philistines, Gath (cf. 1 Chr. 18:1). David defeated his enemies to the west.

8:2 *Moab.* David also defeated the Moabites who lived in Transjordan, east of the Dead Sea. This represented a change from the good relationship David once enjoyed with the Moabite royalty (cf. 1 Sam. 22:3, 4). He defeated his enemies to the east. *he measured off.* This could mean that David spared the young Moabites (whose height was approximately one cord) and executed the adults (whose height was two cords) or that one out of three rows of soldiers was arbitrarily chosen to be spared from execution. Such was a common practice of eastern kings in dealing with deadly enemies.

8:3–8 David defeated his enemies to the north. He had already defeated the Amalekites to the south (1 Sam. 30:16, 17).

8:3 *Hadadezer*. Lit. "Hadad (the personal name of the Canaanite storm god) is my help." Psalm 60 was written to commemorate this battle. ***Zobah*.** An Aramaean kingdom north of Damascus (cf. 1 Sam. 14:47). ***River Euphrates*.** I.e., the most southwesterly point of the Euphrates River around the city of Tiphsah.

8:4 *seven hundred*. The reading of "7,000" in 1 Chronicles 18:4 is preferable. *See note on 1 Chronicles 18:4.* ***hamstrung all the chariot horses*.** Hamstringing the horses disabled them from military action by cutting the back sinews of the hind legs (Josh. 11:6).

8:5 *Syrians*. I.e., Aramaeans, who were peoples located around the city of Damascus as well as in the area of Zobah.

8:7 *shields of gold*. Ceremonial or decorative insignias that were not used in battle, but for decoration.

8:8 *bronze*. First Chronicles 18:8 notes three towns belonging to Hadadezer which yielded bronze that was later used in the construction of the temple.

8:9 *Toi king of Hamath*. Hamath was another Aramaean territory located about 100 miles north of Damascus. The king, Toi, was thankful to see his enemy Zobah crushed and desired to establish good relations with David. So he gave David gifts to indicate that he voluntarily submitted to him as his vassal.

8:12 *Syria*. *Edom* is the preferred variant. These were David's enemies to the south.

8:13 *a name*. The Lord began to fulfill His promise of giving David a great name (see 7:9). ***Syrians*.** There is an alternate manuscript reading that makes this a reference to David's defeat of the Edomites, not the

Syrians. *See note on verse 12.* This reading is supported by Psalm 60 and 1 Chronicles 18:12. ***Valley of Salt*.** An area south of the Dead Sea.

8:15–18 See 1 Chronicles 18:14–17. This is the record of the cabinet under David's rule.

8:15 *judgment and justice*. David ruled his kingdom in a righteous manner, and in the future the Messiah will rule in similar fashion (Is. 9:7; Jer. 23:5; 33:15).

8:16 *Joab*. David's general (2:13; 1 Sam. 26:6). ***Jehoshaphat . . . recorder*.** The keeper of state records, and possibly the royal herald (1 Kin. 4:3).

8:17 *Zadok the son of Ahitub*. Zadok, meaning "righteous," was a Levitical priest descended from Aaron through Eleazar (1 Chr. 6:3–8, 50–53), who, along with his house, was the fulfillment of the oracle by the man of God in 1 Samuel 2:35. Future sons of Zadok will be priests in the millennial kingdom of Messiah (Ezek. 44:15). Later, he became the only high priest in Solomon's reign, fulfilling God's promise to Phinehas (cf. Num. 25:10–13). ***Ahimelech the son of Abiathar*.** See 1 Samuel 22:20, which indicates that Abiathar is the son of Ahimelech. This is best accounted for by a scribal copying error (cf. 1 Chr. 18:16; 24:3, 6, 31). Abiathar was David's priest along with Zadok (15:24, 35; 19:11). Abiathar traced his lineage through Eli (1 Kin. 2:27) to Ithamar (1 Chr. 24:3). With Abiathar's removal (1 Kin. 2:26, 27), God's curse on Eli was completed (1 Sam. 2:33), and God's promise to Phinehas of Eleazar's line was fulfilled (cf. Num. 25:10–13; 1 Sam. 2:35). ***Seraiah was the scribe*.** His name means "The LORD prevails," and he served as the official secretary of David.

8:18 *Benaiah*. His name means "The LORD builds," and he served as the commander of David's personal bodyguard. He later became the commander-in-chief of Solomon's army (1 Kin. 2:34, 35; 4:4), after he killed Joab, David's general (cf. 1 Kin. 2:28–35). *Cherethites and the Pelethites. See note on 1 Samuel 30:14.* *chief ministers.* Though the Hebrew text referred to the sons of David as priests, the LXX referred to them as "princes of the court." The latter reading is supported by 1 Chronicles 18:17, which refers to David's sons as "chief ministers at the king's side."

D. David's Troubled Reign (9:1–20:26)

9:1–20:26 These chapters begin with "the house of Saul" (9:1) and end with "Sheba . . . a Benjamite" (20:1). As with Saul, David is shown to be a failed king, albeit a repentant failure. It was only the grace and mercy of the Lord and His irrevocable covenant that kept David from being removed from the kingship, as Saul had been (cf. 7:15). The emphasis in this section is on the troubles of David, troubles brought on by his own sin.

1. David's kindness to Mephibosheth (9:1–13)

9:1 *show him kindness for Jonathan's sake?* David continued to display loving loyalty toward Jonathan (1 Sam. 20:42) by ministering to the physical needs of his crippled son, Mephibosheth (cf. 4:4).

9:2 *Ziba.* A former servant of Saul, who is first mentioned here.

9:4 *Machir the son of Ammiel.* A man of wealth (see 17:27–29). *Lo Debar.* A city located in Gilead, east of the Jordan River, about ten miles south of the Sea of Galilee.

9:6 *Mephibosheth. See note on 4:4.*

9:7 *restore . . . the land of Saul your grandfather.* The estate belonging to Saul was probably quite substantial. *eat bread at my table.* David desired to honor Mephibosheth by bringing him into the royal palace

and providing for his daily needs (see 2 Kin. 25:29).

9:8 *dead dog.* A *dead dog* was considered contemptible and useless. Mephibosheth saw himself as such in that he knew that he had not merited David's kindness and that there was no way to repay it. David's offer was an extraordinary expression of grace and beauty to his covenant with Jonathan (cf. 1 Sam. 18:3; 20:15, 42).

9:10 *fifteen sons and twenty servants.* This number shows the power and influence of Ziba. It also shows that the land given by David was substantial.

9:12 *Micha.* The descendants of Micha, the son of Mephibosheth, are listed in 1 Chronicles 8:35–38; 9:41–44.

2. David's sins of adultery and murder (10:1–12:31)

10:1–19 See 1 Chronicles 19:1–19.

10:1 *king . . . of Ammon.* I.e., Nahash (*see note on 1 Sam. 11:1*).

10:2 *show kindness to Hanun.* Since Nahash was an enemy of Saul, he was viewed as a friend and supporter of David. It was implied that David and Nahash had entered into a covenant relationship, on the basis of which David desired to communicate his continuing loyalty to Nahash's son, Hanun.

10:3 *the city.* I.e., Rabbah (*see note on 11:1*).

10:4 *shaved off half of their beards.* Forced shaving was considered an insult and a sign of submission (cf. Is. 7:20). *cut off their garments . . . at their buttocks.* To those who wore long garments in that time, exposure of the buttocks was a shameful practice inflicted on prisoners of war (cf. Is. 20:4). Perhaps this was partly the concern of Michal in regard to David's dancing (see 6:14, 20).

10:5 *Jericho.* The first place west of the

The Priestly Lines of Zadok and Abiathar

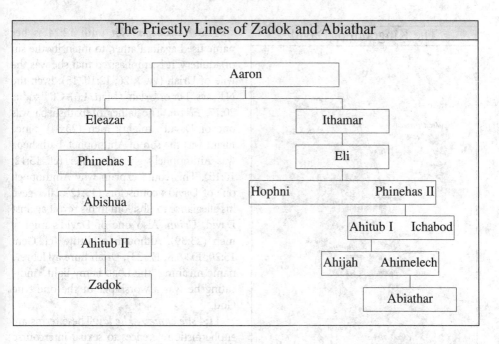

Jordan River that would have been reached by the servants of David as they returned from Rabbah.

10:6 *Beth Rehob.* An Aramaean district located southwest of Zobah (cf. Num. 13:21; Judg. 18:28). *Zoba. See note on 8:3. Maacah.* The region north of Lake Huleh north of Galilee (Deut. 3:14; Josh. 13:11–13). *Ish-Tob.* A city east of the Jordan River, located forty-five miles northeast of Rabbah (Judg. 11:3, 5).

10:6–11 The Ammonite army was in the city ready for defense, while the Syrian mercenaries were at some distance, camped in the fields around the city. Joab divided his forces to deal with both. *See note on 1 Samuel 11:1.*

10:12 *Be of good courage . . . may the Lord do what is good in His sight.* Finding himself fighting on two fronts, Joab urged the army to "be strong" and recognize that the outcome of the battle depended ultimately on the Lord (cf. 15:26). It was a just and necessary war forced on Israel, so they could hope for God's blessing—and they received it (vv. 13, 14).

10:14 *So Joab returned.* He did not attempt to besiege and capture the city of Rabbah at this time because the time was unseasonable (*see note on 11:1*). Cf. 12:26–29.

10:16 *Hadadezer. See note on 8:3. Helam.* The place of battle, about seven miles north of Tob.

10:18 *seven hundred . . . horsemen. See note on 1 Chronicles 19:18.*

10:19 *made peace with Israel.* All the petty kingdoms of Syria became subject to Israel and feared to aid Ammon against Israel.

11:1 *the spring . . . when kings go out to battle.* In the Near East, kings normally went out to battle in the spring of the year because of the good weather and the abundance of food available along the way. *See note on 10:14. David sent Joab.* David dispatched Joab, his army commander, with his mercenary soldiers and the army of Israel to continue the battle against Ammon begun the previous year (10:14). *Rabbah.* The capital of the Ammonites, about twenty-four miles east of the Jordan River opposite Jericho.

The Kingdom of David

HAMATH

(ZOBAH)

Mediterranean
Sea

PHOENICIA

Damascus

Tyre
Dan

Megiddo
Beth Shan

Shechem

Joppa
ISRAEL
Bethel
Rabbah
Ashdod
Bethel
Jericho
(AMMON)
Ashkelon
Gath
Jerusalem
Gaza
Hebron
Dead
Sea
Raphia
Beersheba
(MOAB)

Zoar

Bozrah

Kadesh Barnea
(EDOM)

0   60 Mi.
0   60 Km.

Elath

The MacArthur Study Bible, by John MacArthur (Nashville: Word
Publishing, 1997) 440. © 1993 by Thomas Nelson, Inc.

The previous year, Abishai had defeated the
Ammonite army in the open country, after
which the remaining Ammonites fled behind the walls of the city of Rabbah for protection (10:14). Joab returned the next year
to besiege the city. **But David remained at
Jerusalem.** Stay-ing home in such situations
was not David's usual practice (5:2; 8:1–14;
10:17; but cf. 18:3; 21:17); this explicit remark implies criticism of David for remaining behind, as well as setting the stage for his
devastating iniquity.

11:2 walked on the roof. The higher elevation of the palace roof allowed David to see
down into the courtyard of the nearby house.
That same roof would later become the scene
of other sinful immoralities (see 16:22).

11:3 Bathsheba. Not until 12:24 is her
name used again. Rather, to intensify the sin
of adultery, it is emphasized that she was the
wife of Uriah (vv. 3, 26; 12:10, 15). Even the
NT says "her of Uriah" (Matt. 1:6). Cf. Exodus
20:17. **Eliam.** The father of Bathsheba was
one of David's mighty men (23:34). Since
Eliam was the son of Ahithophel, Bathsheba
was Ahithophel's granddaughter (cf. 15:12;
16:15). This could explain why Ahithophel,
one of David's counselors (15:12), later gave
his allegiance to Absalom in his revolt against
David. **Uriah.** Also one of David's mighty
men (23:39). Although a Hittite (cf. Gen.
15:20; Ex. 3:8, 17, 23), Uriah bore a Hebrew
name meaning "the LORD is my light," indicating he was a worshiper of the one true
God.

11:4 she came . . . he lay. These terms are
euphemistic references to sexual intercourse
(cf. Gen. 19:34), indicating that both
Bathsheba and David were guilty of adultery.
her impurity. Her recent days had involved
menstruation and the required ceremonial
purification (Lev. 15:19–30). They were followed by adulterous intercourse. The fact that
she had just experienced menstruation makes
it plain that Bathsheba was not pregnant by
Uriah when she came to lie with David.

11:5 I am with child. The only words of
Bathsheba recorded about this incident acknowledge the resultant condition of her sin,
which became evident by her pregnancy and
was punishable by death (Lev. 20:10; Deut.
22:22).

11:6, 7 This inane conversation was a ploy
to get Uriah to come home and sleep with
his wife, so it would appear that he had fathered the child, thus sparing David the public shame and Bathsheba possible death.

11:8 wash your feet. Since this washing
was done before going to bed, the idiom
means to go home and go to bed. To a soldier
coming from the battlefield, it said boldly,

"enjoy your wife sexually." Hopefully, David's tryst with Bathsheba would be masked by Uriah's union. *gift of food.* This was designed to help Uriah and Bathsheba enjoy their evening together.

11:9 *Uriah slept.* Wanting to be a loyal example to his soldiers who were still in the field, Uriah did not take advantage of the king's less-than-honorable offer (v. 11).

11:11 *The ark.* The ark of the covenant was residing in either the tent in Jerusalem (6:17) or in a tent with the army of Israel on the battlefield (1 Sam. 4:6; 14:18).

11:13 *made him drunk.* Failing in his first attempt to cover up his sin, David tried unsuccessfully to get Uriah drunk so he would lose his resolve and self-discipline and return to his home and his wife's bed.

11:15 *he may . . . die.* Failing twice to cover up his sin with Bathsheba, the frustrated and panicked David plotted the murder of Uriah by taking advantage of Uriah's unswerving loyalty to him as king, even having Uriah deliver his own death warrant. Thus, David engaged in another crime deserving of capital punishment (Lev. 24:17). This is graphic proof of the extreme to which people go in pursuit of sin and in the absence of restraining grace.

11:18–24 *Joab sent . . . Uriah . . . dead.* He sent a messenger with a veiled message to tell David his wish had been carried out. Joab must have known the reason behind this military deployment.

11:25 *So encourage him.* David hypocritically expressed indifference to those who died, and he consoled Joab, authorizing him to continue the attack against Rabbah.

11:26, 27 *her mourning was over.* The customary period of mourning was probably seven days (Gen. 50:10; 1 Sam. 31:13). Significantly, the text makes no mention of mourning by David.

11:27 *displeased the LORD.* Lit. "was evil in the eyes of the LORD," and would bring forth evil consequences.

12:1–14 Psalm 51 records David's words of repentance after being confronted by Nathan over his sin with Bathsheba (cf. Ps. 32, where David expresses his agony after Nathan's confrontation).

12:1 *the LORD sent Nathan.* The word "LORD" is conspicuously absent from the narrative of chapter 11 until verse 27, but then the Lord became actively involved by confronting David with his sin. As Joab had sent a messenger to David (11:18, 19), so the Lord now sent His messenger to David.

12:1–4 *two men . . . rich . . . poor.* To understand this parable, it is necessary only to recognize that the rich man represented David; the poor man, Uriah; and the ewe lamb, Bathsheba.

12:5 *shall surely die!* According to Exodus 22:1, the penalty for stealing and slaughtering an ox or a sheep was not death, but restitution. However, in the parable, the stealing and slaughtering of the lamb represented the adultery with Bathsheba and the murder of Uriah by David. According to the Mosaic Law, both adultery (Lev. 20:10) and murder (Lev. 24:17) required punishment by death. In pronouncing this judgment on the rich man in the story, David unwittingly condemned himself to death.

12:6 *fourfold.* Exodus 22:1 demanded a fourfold restitution for the stealing of sheep. There is an allusion here to the subsequent death of four of David's sons: Bathsheba's first son (v. 18), Amnon (13:28, 29), Absalom (16:14, 15), and Adonijah (1 Kin. 2:25).

12:7 *anointed.* Earlier, the prophet Samuel's confrontation with the sinful Saul emphasized the same point (1 Sam. 15:17).

12:8 *your master's wives.* This phraseology means nothing more than that God, in His providence, had given David, as king, everything that was Saul's. There is no evidence that he ever married any of Saul's wives, though the harem of eastern kings passed to their successors. Ahinoam, the wife of David (2:2; 3:2; 1 Sam. 25:43; 27:3; 30:5), is always referred to as the Jezreelitess, whereas Ahinoam, the wife of Saul, is distinguished clearly from her by being called "the daughter of Ahimaaz" (1 Sam. 14:50).

12:9 despised. To despise the word of the Lord was to break His commands and thus incur punishment (cf. Num. 15:31). In summarizing David's violations, his guilt is divinely affirmed.

12:10 the sword shall never depart from your house. David's tragic punishment was a lingering one. Since Uriah was killed by violence, the house of David would be continually plagued by violence. These words anticipated the violent deaths of Amnon (13:28, 29), Absalom (18:14, 15), and Adonijah (1 Kin. 2:24, 25).

12:11 adversity . . . from your own house. David had done evil to another man's family (11:27). Therefore, he would receive evil in his own family, such as Amnon's rape of Tamar (13:1–14), Absalom's murder of Amnon (13:28, 29), and Absalom's rebellion against David (15:1–12). **lie with your wives in the sight of this sun.** This prediction was fulfilled by Absalom's public appropriation of David's royal concubines during his rebellion (16:21, 22).

12:13 I have sinned against the Lord. David did not attempt to rationalize or justify his sin. When confronted with the facts, David's confession was immediate. The fuller confessions of David are found in Psalms 32 and 51. **The Lord also has put away your sin.** The Lord graciously forgave David's sin, but the inevitable temporal consequences of sin were experienced by him. Forgiveness does not always remove the consequences of sin in this life, only in the life to come. **you shall not die.** Although the sins of David legally demanded his death (see v. 5), the Lord graciously released David from the required death penalty. There are events in the OT record where God required death and others where He showed grace and spared the sinner. This is consistent with justice and grace. Those who perished are illustrations of what all sinners deserve. Those who were spared are proofs and examples of God's grace.

12:14 the enemies of the Lord. Because of God's reputation among those who opposed Him, David's sin had to be judged. The judgment would begin with the death of Bathsheba's infant son.

12:23 I shall go to him. I.e., David would someday join his son after his own death (cf. 1 Sam. 28:19). Here is the confidence that there is a future reunion after death, which includes infants who have died being reunited with saints who die (*see note on Matt. 19:14;* cf. Mark 10:13–16).

12:24 Solomon. Either "(God is) peace" or "His replacement." Both were true of this child.

12:25 Jedidiah. "Beloved of the Lord" was Nathan's name for Solomon, who was loved in the sense of being chosen by the Lord to be the successor on David's throne, a remarkable instance of God's goodness and grace considering the sinful nature of the marriage.

12:29–31 See 1 Chronicles 20:1–3.

12:29 David . . . took it. David completed what Joab had begun by capturing the city of Rabbah.

12:30 a talent of gold. About 75 pounds.

12:31 put them to work. It is possible here and in 1 Chronicles 20:3 that David imposed hard labor on the Ammonites. But these verses can also be translated with the sense that the Ammonites were cut with saws, indicating that David imposed cruel death on the captives in accordance with Ammonite ways (cf. 1 Sam. 11:2; Amos 1:13).

3. David's family troubles (13:1–14:33)

13:1–22 The rape of Tamar.

13:1, 2 Tamar. "Palm tree." She was David's daughter by Maacah, the daughter of Talmai, King of Geshur (3:3), Absalom's (David's third son) full sister and half-sister of Amnon, David's first son by Ahinoam (3:2). Amnon's love for her was not filial, but lustful, as became clear in the story. Unmarried daughters were kept in seclusion from men, so that none could see them alone. Amnon had seen Tamar because of their family relationship and had conceived a violent passion for her. This was forbidden by God (see Lev. 18:11), yet with the example of Abraham (Gen. 20:12) and the common practice among the surrounding nations of marrying half-sisters, he felt justified and wanted his passion fulfilled with Tamar.

13:3 Jonadab. The son of David's brother, called Shammah in 1 Samuel 16:9; 17:3 and Shimea in 1 Chronicles 2:13. Jonadab was Amnon's cousin and counselor who gave Amnon the plan by which he was able to rape Tamar.

13:12, 13 this disgraceful thing! Lit. "a wicked thing." Tamar appealed to Amnon with four reasons that he should not rape her. First, it was an utterly deplored act in Israel because it violated the Law of God (see Lev. 18:11), and Tamar knew that such action could bring disharmony and bloodshed to the king's family, as it did. **my shame?** Second, as a fornicator, Tamar would be scorned as an object of reproach. Even though resistant to the evil crime perpetuated against her, Tamar would bear the stigma of one defiled. **like one of the fools in Israel.** Third, Amnon would be regarded by

the people as a wicked fool, a God-rejecting man without principles who offended ordinary standards of morality, thereby jeopardizing Amnon's right to the throne. **the king . . . will not withhold me from you.** Fourth, Tamar appealed to Amnon to fulfill his physical desire for her through marriage. She surely knew that such a marriage between half siblings was not allowed by the Mosaic Law (Lev. 18:9, 11; 20:17; Deut. 27:22), but in the desperation of the moment, Tamar was seeking to escape the immediate situation.

13:14 forced. A euphemism for "raped."

13:15 hated her. Amnon's "love" (v. 1) was nothing but sensual desire that, once gratified, turned to hatred. His sudden revulsion was the result of her unwilling resistance, the atrocity of what he had done, feelings of remorse, and dread of exposure and punishment. All of these rendered her undesirable to him.

13:15–17 Amnon's sending Tamar away was a greater wrong than the rape itself because it would inevitably have been supposed that she had been guilty of some shameful conduct, i.e., that the seduction had come from her.

13:18 robe of many colors. See Genesis 37:33. A garment that identified the wearer's special position. For Tamar, the robe identified her as a virgin daughter of the king. The tearing of this robe symbolized her loss of this special position (v. 19).

13:19 put ashes . . . tore her robe . . . laid her hand . . . went away crying bitterly. The ashes were a sign of mourning. The torn robe symbolized the ruin of her life. The hand on the head was emblematic of exile and banishment. The crying showed that she viewed herself as good as dead.

13:20 do not take this thing to heart. Absalom told his sister not to pay undue attention or worry about the consequences of the rape. Absalom minimized the significance of what had taken place only for the moment, while already beginning to plot his revenge in using this crime as reason to do what he wanted to do anyway—remove Amnon from the line of succession to the throne (note also v. 32, where Jonadab knew of Absalom's plans). **desolate.** She remained unmarried and childless. Her full brother was her natural protector, and the children of polygamists lived by themselves in different family units.

13:21 David . . . was very angry. Fury and indignation were David's reactions to the report of the rape (Gen. 34:7). Because he did not punish Amnon for his crime, he abdicated his responsibility both as king and as father. The lack of justice in the land would come back to haunt David in a future day (15:4).

13:22 Absalom hated Amnon. As Amnon hated Tamar (v. 15), Absalom loathed his half-brother, Amnon.

13:23–39 The murder of Amnon.

13:23–27 Baal Hazor. The Benjamite village of Hazor (Neh. 11:33), located about twelve miles northeast of Jerusalem, was the place for a sheep-shearing feast put on by Absalom, to which he invited all his brothers and half-brothers, as well as King David and his royal court (v. 24). David declined, but he encouraged Absalom to hold the feast for "the king's sons" as a means of unity and harmony (vv. 25–27). With David's denial of the invitation, Absalom requested that Amnon go as his representative. Although David had reservations about Absalom's intent, he allowed all his sons to go.

13:28, 29 kill him. Absalom murdered Amnon through his servants (cf. 11:15–17), just as David had killed Uriah through others (11:14–17). Though rape was punishable by death, personal vengeance such as this was unacceptable to God. The due course of law was to be carried out.

13:29 his mule. Mules were ridden by the royal family in David's kingdom (18:9; 1 Kin. 1:33, 38, 44).

13:30 all the king's sons. This exaggeration plunged everyone into grief (v. 31), until it was corrected (v. 32).

13:32 Jonadab . . . answered. Jonadab knew of Absalom's plot to kill Amnon (see v. 20) for the rape of Tamar. Death was prescribed in Leviticus 18:11, 29 ("cut off" means to execute). *See note on verses 28, 29.*

13:34, 37 Absalom fled. The law regarding premeditated murder, as most would view Absalom's act, gave him no hope of returning (see Num 35:21). The cities of refuge would afford him no sanctuary, so he left his father's kingdom to live in Geshur, east of the Sea of Galilee, under the protection of the king who was the grandfather of both Tamar and Absalom (*see note on 13:1, 2*).

13:39 longed to go. David gradually accepted the fact of Amnon's death and desired to see Absalom again, but he took no action to bring him back.

14:1–33 The recall and return of Absalom.

14:1 David was strongly attached to Absalom and, having gotten over the death of Amnon, he desired the fellowship of his exiled son, three years absent. But the fear of public opinion made him hesitant to pardon his son. Joab, perceiving this struggle between parental affection and royal duty, devised a plan involving a wise country woman and a story told to the king.

14:2 Tekoa. A town about ten miles south of Jerusalem (cf. Amos 1:1).

14:2, 3 Joab put the words in her mouth. Joab used a story, as Nathan had (12:1–12), to show David the error of his ways and to encourage him to call Absalom back to Jerusalem.

14:7 leave to my husband neither name nor remnant. The story the woman told involved one brother killing another (v. 6).

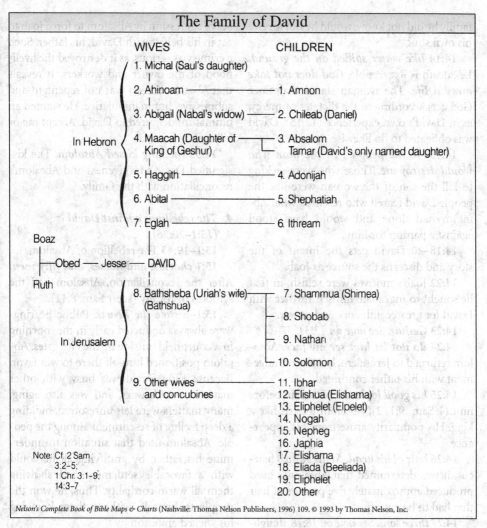

The Family of David

WIVES	CHILDREN
In Hebron	
1. Michal (Saul's daughter)	
2. Ahinoam ——————————	1. Amnon
3. Abigail (Nabal's widow) ——	2. Chileab (Daniel)
4. Maacah (Daughter of ——————	3. Absalom
King of Geshur)	Tamar (David's only named daughter)
5. Haggith ———————————	4. Adonijah
6. Abital ———————————	5. Shephatiah
7. Eglah ———————————	6. Ithream

Boaz
|—Obed — Jesse — DAVID
Ruth

In Jerusalem	
8. Bathsheba (Uriah's wife)———	7. Shammua (Shimea)
(Bathshua)	8. Shobab
	9. Nathan
	10. Solomon
9. Other wives ———————	11. Ibhar
and concubines	12. Elishua (Elishama)
	13. Eliphelet (Elpelet)
	14. Nogah
	15. Nepheg
	16. Japhia
	17. Elishama
	18. Eliada (Beeliada)
	19. Eliphelet
	20. Other

Note: Cf. 2 Sam.
3:2–5;
1 Chr. 3:1–9;
14:3–7

Nelson's Complete Book of Bible Maps & Charts (Nashville: Thomas Nelson Publishers, 1996) 109. © 1993 by Thomas Nelson, Inc.

If the death penalty for murder was invoked (cf. Ex. 21:12; Lev. 24:17), there would be no living heir in the family, leaving that family with no future, a situation the law sought to avoid (Deut. 25:5–10). This would extinguish the last "ember" of hope for a future for her line. Cf. 21:17; Psalm 132:17, where the lamp refers to posterity.

14:9 let the iniquity be on me. The woman was willing to receive whatever blame might arise from the sparing of her guilty son.

14:11 avenger of blood. This is a specific term identifying the nearest relative of the deceased who would seek to put to death the murderer (Num. 35:6–28; Deut. 19:1–13; Matt. 27:25). **not one hair.** This is an expression meaning that no harm will come to the son of the widow in the story.

14:13 against the people of God? The woman asserted that by allowing Absalom to remain in exile, David had jeopardized the future welfare of Israel. If he would be so generous to a son he did not know in a family he did not know, would he not forgive his own son?

14:14 *like water spilled on the ground.* I.e., death is irreversible. *God does not take away a life.* The woman stated that since God acts according to the dictates of mercy, as in David's own experience (12:13), David was obligated to do likewise.

14:15, 16 *the people . . . the man who would destroy me.* Those who were seeking to kill the son of the woman were like the people David feared who resented what Absalom had done and would have stood against a pardon for him.

14:18–20 David gets the intent of the story and discerns the source as Joab.

14:22 Joab's motives were selfish, in that he sought to ingratiate himself further with David for greater influence and power.

14:23 *Geshur. See note on 13:34, 37.*

14:24 *do not let him see my face.* Absalom returned to Jerusalem, but the estrangement with his father continued.

14:25 *his good looks.* As with Saul before him (1 Sam. 9:1, 2), Absalom looked like a king. His popularity arose from his appearance.

14:26 *hair of his head.* At his annual haircut, it was determined that Absalom's head produced approximately five pounds of hair that had to be cut off.

14:27 *three sons. See note on 18:18. daughter . . . Tamar.* Absalom named his daughter after his sister Tamar.

14:28 *two full years.* Whatever were David's errors in recalling Absalom, he displayed great restraint in wanting to stay apart from Absalom to lead his son through a time of repentance and a real restoration. Rather than produce repentance, however, Absalom's non-access to the royal court and all its amenities frustrated him so that he sent for Joab to intercede (v. 29).

14:30–32 *set the field on fire.* This was an act of aggression by Absalom to force Joab to act in his behalf with David, his father. Such a crime was serious, as it destroyed the livelihood of the owner and workers. It reveals that Absalom's heart was not repentant and submissive, but manipulative. He wanted an ultimatum delivered to David: Accept me or kill me!

14:33 *the king kissed Absalom.* The kiss signified David's forgiveness and Absalom's reconciliation with the family.

4. The rebellions against David (15:1–20:26)

15:1–19:43 The rebellion of Absalom.

15:1 *chariots and horses, and fifty men.* After the reconciliation, Absalom had the symbols of royalty (see 1 Sam. 8:11).

15:1–6 *stole the hearts.* Public hearings were always conducted early in the morning in a court held outside by the city gates. Absalom positioned himself there to win favor. Because King David was busy with other matters or with wars, and was also aging, many matters were left unresolved, building a deep feeling of resentment among the people. Absalom used that situation to undermine his father, by gratifying all he could with a favorable settlement and showing them all warm cordiality. Thus, he won the people to himself, without them knowing his wicked ambition.

15:7 *forty years.* The better reading is *four* because the number *forty* could refer neither to the age of Absalom since he was born at Hebron after David had begun to rule (3:2–5), nor the time of David's reign, since he ruled only forty years total (5:4, 5). The four-year period began either with Absalom's return from Geshur (14:23) or with his reconciliation with David (14:33).

15:7–9 *Hebron.* The city of Absalom's birth (3:2, 3), and the place where David was first anointed king over Judah (2:4) and over all Israel (5:3). Absalom said he had made a vow while in Geshur (*see note on 13:34, 37*) that if he was restored to Jerusalem, he would offer a sacrifice of thanksgiving in Hebron, where sacrifices were often made before the temple was built. David, who always encouraged such religious devotion, gave his consent.

15:10–12 Absalom formed a conspiracy, which included taking some of the leading men to create the impression that the king supported this action, and was in his old age sharing the kingdom. All of this was a subtle disguise so Absalom could have freedom to plan his revolution. Absalom was able to do this against his father not merely because of his cleverness, but also because of the laxness of his father (see 1 Kin. 1:6).

15:12 *Ahithophel.* A counselor of David whose advice was so accurate that it was regarded as if it were the very "oracle of God" (16:23). This man was the father of Eliam (23:34) and the grandfather of Bathsheba (11:3; 23:24–39), who may have been looking for revenge on David. *Giloh.* A town in the hill country of Judah (Josh. 15:48, 51), probably located a few miles south of Hebron.

15:13–17 David's escape from Absalom is remembered in Psalm 3. Because he wanted to preserve the city he had beautified, not having a war there, and since he felt that he could find greater support in the country, David left the city with all his household and personal guards.

15:18 *Cherethites . . . Pelethites.* Foreign mercenary soldiers of King David. *See note on 1 Samuel 30:14. Gittites.* Mercenary soldiers from Gath, i.e., Philistines.

15:19–22 *Ittai.* The commander of the Gittites, who had only recently joined David. In spite of David's words, he displayed his loyalty by going into exile with him. Ittai's later appointment as commander of one-

---

Key Word

Ark: 6:2, 4, 10, 12, 17; 7:2; 11:11; 15:24—can be translated "chest" (2 Kin. 12:9) or "sarcophagus" (Gen. 50:26), but most often appears in the phrase which means "ark of the covenant." The ark was a wooden chest overlaid with gold (Ex. 25:10–22), housing the Ten Commandments (Ex. 40:20), Aaron's staff, and a pot of manna (Heb. 9:4). It sat in the Most Holy Place as a reminder of Israel's covenant with God and His presence among them. When the Israelites became careless with the ark (1 Sam. 4:1–11), God allowed it to be captured in order to demonstrate that His covenant relationship with them transcended symbols and superstitions. What He required was continual obedience to His covenant and a contrite heart surrendered to Him (Ps. 51:17; Is. 57:15).

---

third of the army (18:2, 5, 12) was David's way of expressing appreciation for his loyalty.

15:23–28 Psalm 63 has this occasion in view or possibly the one in 1 Samuel 23:14.

15:23 *Brook Kidron.* This familiar valley, running north to south along the eastern side of Jerusalem, separates the city from the Mount of Olives.

15:24–29 *Zadok . . . Abiathar. See notes on 8:17.* They brought the ark to comfort David with assurance of God's blessing, but he saw that as placing more confidence in the symbol than in God and sent it back. David knew the possession of the ark did not guarantee God's blessing (cf. 1 Sam. 4:3).

15:28 *plains of the wilderness.* Probably the region along the western bank of the Jordan River (see 17:16; Josh. 5:10).

15:30 *Mount of Olives.* The hill to the east of the city of Jerusalem was the location for David's contrition and remorse over his sins and their results. This was the location from which Jesus ascended to heaven (Acts 1:9–12).

15:32 *top of the mountain.* This was the place from which David could look toward the city and the temple to the west. ***Hushai the Archite.*** Hushai was of the clan of the Archites who lived in Ephraim on the border with Manasseh (Josh. 16:2) and served as an official counselor to David (v. 37; 1 Chr. 27:33). David persuaded Hushai to return to Jerusalem and attach himself to Absalom as a counselor. His mission was to contradict the advice of Ahithophel (17:5–14) and to communicate Absalom's plans to David (17:21; 18:19).

16:1 *Ziba.* See note on 9:2. ***Mephibosheth.*** Saul's grandson by Jonathan (*see note on 4:4*).

16:3 *where is your master's son?* According to 9:9, 10, Ziba was able to garner such food and drink. His master had been Saul before his death and was then Mephibosheth. ***restore the kingdom of my father.*** Ziba, evidently trying to commend himself in the eyes of David by bringing these gifts, accused his master of disloyalty to the king and participation in Absalom's conspiracy for the purpose of bringing down the whole Davidic house. Thus, the house of Saul would retake

the throne, and he would be king. This was a false accusation (see 19:24, 25), but it was convincing to David, who believed the story and made a severe and rash decision that inflicted injury on a true friend, Mephibosheth.

16:5 *Bahurim.* See note on 3:16.

16:5–8 *Shimei.* Shimei was a distant relative of Saul, from the tribe of Benjamin, who cursed David as "a man of bloodshed" (vv. 7, 8) and "a man of Belial" (*see note on 1 Sam. 2:12*). He could possibly be the Cush of Psalm 7. Shimei declared that the loss of David's throne was God's retribution on his past sins (v. 8), and David accepted his curse as from the Lord (v. 11). It could be that Shimei was accusing David of the murders of Abner (3:27–39), Ishbosheth (4:1–12), and Uriah (11:15–27).

16:9 *Abishai.* See note on 2:18. ***dead dog.*** I.e., worthless and despised (cf. 9:8).

16:10–14 The patience and restraint of David on this occasion was amazingly different than his violent reaction to the slanderous words of Nabal (1 Sam. 25:2ff.). On that occasion, he was eager to kill the man until placated by the wisdom of Abigail. He was a broken man at this later time and knew that while the rancor of Shimei was uncalled for, his accusations were true. He was penitent.

The Psalms in 2 Samuel		
1. 2 Sam. 5:11, 12; 6:17	at the dedication of the house of David	Ps. 30
2. 2 Sam. 8:3, 13	when David fought against Mesopotamia and Syria	Ps. 60
3. 2 Sam. 12:1–14	when Nathan confronted David over sin with Bathsheba	Ps. 51
4. 2 Sam. 15:13–17	when David fled from Absalom his son	Ps. 3
5. 2 Sam. 15:23–28 (or 1 Sam. 23:14)	when David was in the wilderness of Judea	Ps. 63
6. 2 Sam. 16:5; 19:16	concerning the words of Cush a Benjamite	Ps. 7
7. 2 Sam. 22:1–51	the day the Lord delivered David from his enemies/Saul	Ps. 18

16:15 Ahithophel. See note on 15:12.

16:15–23 Absalom set up his royal court in Jerusalem.

16:16 Hushai. See note on 15:32.

16:21, 22 your father's concubines. David had left behind, in Jerusalem, ten concubines to take care of the palace (15:16). In the Near East, possession of the harem came with the throne. Ahithophel advised Absalom to have sexual relations with David's concubines and, thereby, assert his right to his father's throne. On the roof of the palace in the most public place (cf. 11:2), a tent was set up for this scandalous event, thereby fulfilling the judgment announced by Nathan in 12:11, 12.

17:1–4 Ahithophel's second piece of advice to Absalom was that he immediately pursue and kill David to remove any possibility of his reclaiming the throne, which would incline David's followers to return and submit to Absalom.

17:4 all the elders of Israel. The same prominent tribal leaders who had accepted David's kingship in 5:3 had been won over as participants in Absalom's rebellion.

17:7–13 Providentially, the Lord took control of the situation through the counsel of Hushai (see note on 15:32), who advised Absalom in such a way as to give David time to prepare for war with Absalom. Hushai's plan seemed best to the elders. It had two features: (1) the need for an army larger than 12,000 (v. 1), so that Absalom would not lose, and (2) the king leading the army into battle (an appeal to Absalom's arrogance).

17:11 Dan to Beersheba. See note on 3:10.

17:13 ropes. In besieging the town, hooks attached to ropes were cast over the protective wall and, with a large number of men pulling, the walls were pulled down.

17:14 the LORD had purposed. The text notes that Ahithophel's advice was rejected by Absalom because the Lord had determined to defeat the rebellion of Absalom, as

prayed for by David (15:31). God's providence was controlling all the intrigues among the usurper's counselors.

17:16 cross over. Crossing over from the west side to the east side of the Jordan River was the means of protecting David and his people from the immediate onslaught if Ahithophel's plan was followed.

17:17 Jonathan and Ahimaaz. Jonathan was the son of the priest Abiathar, and Ahimaaz was the son of the priest Zadok (15:27). They were designated to take information from Hushai in Jerusalem to David by the Jordan River. **En Rogel.** A spring in the Kidron Valley on the border between Benjamin and Judah (Josh. 15:1, 7; 18:11, 16), less than a miles southeast of Jerusalem.

17:18 Bahurim. See note on 3:16.

17:19 well's mouth. Using an empty cistern as a place for a covering of dry grain was a common practice.

17:23 hanged himself. When Ahithophel saw that his counsel to Absalom had not been followed, he took his own life. He probably foresaw Absalom's defeat and knew that he would then be accountable to David for his disloyalty.

17:24 Mahanaim. See note on 2:8.

17:25 Amasa. Absalom appointed Amasa as commander of the army of Israel, replacing Joab who had accompanied David on his flight from Jerusalem. Amasa was the son of Abigail, either David's sister or his half-sister (1 Chr. 2:17), making him David's nephew. His mother was also the sister of Zeruiah, the mother of Joab. Therefore, Amasa was a cousin of Absalom, Joab, and Abishai. Under his lead, the armies crossed the Jordan River (v. 24) into Gilead, the high-eastern area. Sufficient time had passed for building the large army Hushai suggested, and so David had readied himself for the war (see note on 17:7–13).

17:27 Shobi. A son of Nahash and bro-

David's Troubles	
Causes	Effects
Adultery (11:4) Murder of Uriah (11:17) Amnon's incest (13:14) Absalom usurps throne (16:15, 16) The census (24:2)	Bathsheba bears a son (11:5) Accused, repents, but the child dies (12:10, 13, 19) Amnon murdered (13:28, 29) Absalom murdered (18:14, 15) Plague (24:15)

Consistently illustrated in the life of David's household is the principle that a disobedient life is a troubled life.

Nelson's Complete Book of Bible Maps & Charts (Nashville: Thomas Nelson Publishers, 1996) 56. © 1993 by Thomas Nelson, Inc.

ther of Hanun, kings of the Ammonites (10:1, 2). ***Machir.*** *See note on 9:4.* ***Barzillai.*** An aged, wealthy benefactor of David from Gilead, on the east side of the Jordan River (see 19:31–39; 1 Kin. 2:7).

18:2 A three-pronged attack was a customary military strategy (see Judg. 7:16; 1 Sam. 11:11; 13:17).

18:3 ***You shall not go out!*** David desired to lead his men into the battle; however, the people recognized that the death of David would mean sure defeat and Absalom would then be secure in the kingship. The people's words echo what Ahithophel had earlier pointed out to Absalom (17:2, 3). So David was persuaded to remain at Mahanaim.

18:5 ***Deal gently.*** David ordered his three commanders not to harm Absalom. The four uses of "the young man Absalom" (vv. 5, 12, 29, 32) imply that David sentimentally viewed Absalom as a youthful rebel who could be forgiven.

18:6 ***the woods of Ephraim.*** A dense forest existed east of the Jordan River and north of the Jabbok River in Gilead, where the battle was waged.

18:8 ***the woods devoured more.*** Amazingly, because of the density of the trees and the rugged nature of the terrain, the pursuit through the forest resulted in more deaths than the actual combat (see v. 9).

18:9 ***mule.*** *See note on 13:29.* ***his head***

caught in the terebinth. Either Absalom's neck was caught in a fork formed by two of the branches growing out from a large oak tree or his hair was caught in a tangle of thick branches. The terminology and context (cf. 14:26) favor the latter view.

18:10 ***a certain man.*** One of David's soldiers, who refused to disobey the order of the king recorded in verse 5 to treat Absalom "gently," had done nothing for the suspended prince.

18:11, 12 ***ten . . . thousand.*** Four ounces and twenty-five pounds respectively.

18:14 ***alive.*** The spears of Joab killed Absalom while Joab's armor bearers struck him to make sure that he was dead (v. 15). In this action, Joab disobeyed the explicit order of David (v. 5).

18:16 ***blew the trumpet.*** Joab recalled his soldiers from the battle (cf. 2:28).

18:17 ***a very large heap of stones.*** Absalom was buried in a deep pit that was covered over with stones, perhaps symbolic of stoning, which was the legal penalty for a rebel son (Deut. 21:20, 21). A heap of stones often showed that the person buried was a criminal or enemy (Josh. 7:26; 8:29).

18:18 ***pillar for himself.*** Absalom had memorialized himself by erecting a monument in his own honor (cf. Saul's action in 1 Sam. 15:12). There is today a monument, a tomb in that area, called Absalom's tomb (perhaps on the same site) on which orthodox Jews spit when passing by. **King's Valley.** Traditionally, the Kidron Valley immediately east of the city of Jerusalem. **no son.** According to 14:27, Absalom had three sons, unnamed in the text, all of whom had died before him.

18:19 Ahimaaz. *See note on 17:17.*

18:21 Cushite. Cush was the area south of Egypt.

18:27 good man . . . good news. David believed that the choice of the messenger was indicative of the content of the message.

18:29 I did not know. Ahimaaz concealed his knowledge of Absalom's death as Joab requested (v. 20).

18:32 like that young man! The Cushite's reply was not so much indirect as culturally phrased (cf. 1 Sam. 25:26).

18:33 my son. Repeated five times in this verse, David lamented the death of Absalom, his son (cf. 19:5). In spite of all the harm that Absalom had caused, David was preoccupied with his personal loss in a melancholy way that seems to be consistent with his weakness as a father. It was an unwarranted zeal for such a worthless son, and a warning about the pitiful results of sin.

19:3 the people stole back. Because of David's excessive grief, his soldiers returned from battle not as rejoicing victors, but as if they had been humiliated by defeat.

19:5 disgraced all your servants. Joab sternly rebuked David for being so absorbed in his personal trauma and failing to appreciate the victory that his men had won for him.

19:7 not one will stay with you. Joab, who was the esteemed general of the army, was a dangerous person because of his power. He was also dangerous to David because he had disobeyed his command to spare Absalom, and killed him with no remorse. When he warned David that he would be in deep trouble if he did not immediately express appreciation to his men for their victory, David knew he could be in serious danger.

19:8 sat in the gate. It was at the gate of Mahanaim that David had reviewed his troops as they had marched out to battle (18:4). David's sitting in the gate represented a return to his exercise of kingly authority.

19:9 a dispute. An argument arose in Israel over whether David should be returned to the kingship. David's past military victories over the Philistines and the failure of Absalom argued for David's return. Therefore, David's supporters insisted on knowing why their fellow Israelites remained quiet about returning David to his rightful place on the throne in Jerusalem.

19:11 elders of Judah. Through the priests who had stayed in Jerusalem during the rebellion, David appealed to the leaders of his own tribe to take the initiative in restoring him to the throne in Jerusalem (see 2:4; 1 Sam. 30:26). Though this appeal produced the desired result, it also led to tribal jealousies (vv. 40–43).

19:13 Amasa. *See note on 17:25.* **commander of the army . . . in place of Joab.** David appointed Amasa commander of his army, hoping to secure the allegiance of those who had followed Amasa when he led Absalom's forces, especially those of Judah. This appointment did persuade the tribe of Judah to support David's return to the kingship (v. 14) and secured the animosity of Joab against Amasa for taking his position (cf. 20:8–10).

19:15 Gilgal. *See note on 1 Samuel 10:8.*

19:16 Shimei. *See note on 16:5–8.* Shimei confessed his sin of cursing David and his life was spared, temporarily; but on his deathbed David ordered that Shimei be punished for his crime (1 Kin. 2:8, 9, 36–46).

19:20 house of Joseph. A reference to Ephraim, the descendant of Joseph, a large tribe of Israel which was representative of the ten northern tribes. Here, even Shimei's tribe Benjamin was included.

19:24–30 Mephibosheth. *See note on 4:4.* Mephibosheth also met David, exhibiting the traditional marks of mourning, and explained that he had not followed David into exile because he had been deceived by his servant Ziba (see 16:1–4). He came to David with great humility, generosity of spirit, and gratitude, recognizing all the good the king had done for him before the evil deception (v. 28).

19:29 divide the land. David had previously given the estate of Saul to Mephibosheth to be farmed by Ziba (9:9, 10). Then when David was deceived, he gave it all to Ziba (16:4). Now David decided to divide Saul's estate between Ziba and Mephibosheth since he was either uncertain of the truth of Mephibosheth's story or who was guilty of what, and was too distracted to inquire fully into the matter. It was, in any case, a poor decision to divide the estate between the noble-hearted son of Jonathan and a lying deceiver. Mephibosheth was unselfish and suggested that his disloyal servant take it all; it was enough for him that David was back.

19:31–39 Barzillai. *See note on 17:27.* David offered to let Barzillai live in Jerusalem as his guest, but Barzillai preferred to live out his last years in his own house.

19:37 Chimham. Probably a son of Barzillai (see 1 Kin. 2:7). It is probable that David gave a part of his personal estate in Bethlehem to this man and his seed (see Jer. 41:17).

19:41 stolen you away. Because only the troops of Judah had escorted David as he crossed over the Jordan River, the ten northern tribes complained to David that the men of Judah had "kidnapped" him from them.

19:42 a close relative. The men of Judah answered the men of Israel by stating that David was a member of their tribe. Nor had they taken advantage of their relationship to the king, as some from the northern tribes had done.

19:43 ten shares. The men of Israel replied to the men of Judah that they had a greater right to David, since there were ten northern tribes in contrast to the one tribe of Judah. Contrast the "ten shares" here with the "no share" in 20:1. *you despise us.* The Israel-Judah hostility evidenced here led to the rebellion of Sheba (20:1–22) and, eventually, to the division of the united kingdom (1 Kin. 12:1–24).

20:1–26 The rebellion of Sheba (20:1–26)
20:1 rebel. Lit. "man of Belial." *See note on 1 Samuel 2:12.* **Sheba.** Though nothing is known of this man, he must have been a person of considerable power and influence to raise so sudden and extensive a sedition. He belonged to Saul's tribe, where adherents of Saul's dynasty were still many, and he could see the disgust of the ten tribes for Judah's presumption in the restoration. He sought to overturn David's authority in Israel. *no share . . . inheritance.* Sheba's declaration that the northern tribes had no part in David's realm was similar to words later used in 1 Kings 12:16 when Israel seceded from the united kingdom under Jeroboam.

20:2 Israel deserted David. Once the ten tribes withdrew, Judah was left alone to escort the king to Jerusalem. It seems that the disloyalty of the north continued as long as Sheba lived.

20:3 his concubines. When David returned to Jerusalem, he confined his concubines to a life of abstinence because of their sexual relations with Absalom (16:21, 22).

20:4 Amasa. Amasa was Absalom's general (*see note on 17:25*), whom David promised would be commander of his army after Absalom's death (*see note on 19:13*). Amasa was installed publicly because David thought it would be seen favorably by the ten tribes. He was told to assemble an army in three days to end the insurrection started by Sheba, but could not in such a brief time.

20:6 Abishai. *See note on 2:18.* When Amasa failed to follow David's orders, David did not reinstate Joab, his former general who had Absalom killed against David's orders (see 18:5–15), but appointed Joab's brother Abishai as commander of his forces. *your lord's servants.* Called "Joab's men" in verse 7. Abishai was to take the army of Joab to pursue the rebel leader. Joab went also, determined to take vengeance on his rival Amasa.

20:7 the Cherethites, the Pelethites. *See note on 1 Samuel 30:14.* **mighty men.** Those men are listed in 23:8–39.

20:8 Gibeon. *See note on 2:12.* **Amasa came before them.** Having collected some forces, he marched rapidly and came first to Gibeon, thus assuming the role of commander. It is possible that Joab purposely let the sword fall from its sheath as he approached Amasa, in order that stooping as if to pick up the accidentally fallen weapon, he might salute the new general with his sword already in hand, without generating any suspicion of his intent. He used this ploy to gain the position to stab the new commander, whom he considered as usurping his post.

20:9 my brother? *See note on 17:25.* **by the beard.** Joab, present with his men, seized Amasa by his beard with his right hand, apparently to give the kiss of greeting. Instead, with his left hand, he thrust his sword into Amasa's stomach (cf. 3:27).

20:11 one of Joab's men. Joab was reinstated as commander of David's army by his troops. It is a striking illustration of Joab's influence over the army that he could murder the commander whom David had chosen, a killing right before their eyes, and they

would follow him unanimously as their leader in pursuit of Sheba.

20:14 Abel and Beth Maachah. I.e., Abel Beth-Maacha. About twenty-five miles north of the Sea of Galilee, four miles west of the city of Dan.

20:16–19 This woman (probably a prominent judge in the city) was making an appeal based on the laws of warfare in Deuteronomy 20:10 that required the assaulting army to offer peace before making war. She pleaded for Joab to ask the city if they wanted peace and, thus, avert war (v. 18).

20:19 a mother in Israel. This is a reference to a specially honored city or a recognized capital of the region. *the inheritance of the LORD?* This refers to the land of Israel (see 1 Sam. 10:1).

20:20, 21 The ruthless general was a patriot at heart who, on taking the leader of the insurrection, was ready to end further bloodshed. The woman eagerly responded with the promise of Sheba's head.

20:21 mountains of Ephraim. A large, partially forested plateau that extended into

---

Key Word

Mighty Men: 1:25; 10:7; 16:6; 17:8; 20:7; 23:8, 22—emphasizes excellence or unusual quality. In the Old Testament, it is used for the excellence of a lion (Prov. 30:30), of good or bad men (Gen. 10:9, 1 Chr. 19:8), of giants (Gen. 6:4), of angels (Ps. 103:20), or even God (Deut. 10:17; Neh. 9:32). The Scriptures state that the *mighty man* is not victorious because of his strength (Ps. 33:16) but because of his understanding and knowledge of the Lord (Jer. 9:23–24). The phrase *mighty God* is used three times in the Old Testament, including Isaiah's messianic prophecy of the birth of Jesus (Is. 9:6).

the tribal territory of Benjamin from the north.

20:22 David could not get rid of Joab, though he hated him. He had to ignore the murder of Amasa and recognize Joab as army commander.

20:23–26 Cf. a similar list in 8:15–18.

20:24 *Adoram.* Rendered "Adoniram" in 1 Kings 4:6, 28. He was in charge of the "revenue," a term used to describe the hard labor imposed on subjugated peoples (Ex. 1:11; Josh. 16:10; Judg. 1:28). Adoram oversaw the forced labor on such projects as the building of highways, temples, and houses.

20:25 *Sheva.* He replaced Seraiah (8:17) as David's secretary.

20:26 *Ira.* He was David's royal adviser.

II. EPILOGUE (21:1–24:25)

21:1–24:25 This is the final division of 1 Samuel. Like the Book of Judges (Judg. 17:1–21:25), it concludes with this epilogue that contains material, not necessarily chronological, that further describes David's reign. There is a striking literary arrangement of the sections in this division of the book. The first and last sections (21:1–14; 24:1–25) are narratives that describe two occurrences of the Lord's anger against Israel. The second and fifth sections (21:15–22; 23:8–39) are accounts of David's warriors. The third and fourth sections (22:1–51; 23:1–7) record two of David's songs.

A. The Lord's Judgment against Israel (21:1–14)

21:1–14 This event occurred after the display of David's kindness to Mephibosheth (v. 7; cf. 9:1–13) and before Shimei's cursing of David (cf. 16:7, 8).

21:1 *a famine.* When Israel experienced three years of famine, David recognized it as

divine discipline (cf. Deut. 28:47, 48) and sought God for the reason.

21:1, 2 *Saul and his bloodthirsty house.* By divine revelation, David learned that the famine was a result of sin committed by Saul; namely, that he had slain the Gibeonites. There is no further reference to this event. Saul was probably trying to do as God commanded and rid the land of the remnant of heathen in order that Israel might prosper (v. 2). But in his zeal, he had committed a serious sin; he had broken a covenant that had been made 400 years before between Joshua and the Gibeonites, who were in the land when Israel took possession of it. They deceived Joshua into making the covenant, but it was, nevertheless, a covenant (see Josh. 9:3–27). Covenant-keeping was no small matter to God (see Josh. 9:20).

21:2 *Amorites.* One of the names sometimes used to designate all the pre-Israelite inhabitants of Canaan (Gen. 15:16; Josh. 24:18; Judg. 6:10). More precisely, the Gibeonites were called Hivites (Josh. 9:7; 11:19).

21:3 *the inheritance of the LORD? See note on 20:19.*

21:6 *seven . . . descendants. Seven* symbolized completeness, not necessarily the number of Gibeonites slain by Saul. *Descendants* could be either sons or grandsons. *Gibeah of Saul. See note on 1 Samuel 11:4.*

21:7 *the LORD's oath . . . between David and Jonathan.* Because Mephibosheth was the son of Jonathan, he was spared in accordance with the covenant between David and Jonathan (1 Sam. 20:14, 15) and also between David and Saul (*see note on 1 Sam. 24:22*).

21:8 *Mephibosheth.* A son of Saul, different from the son of Jonathan with the same name. *Rizpah.* Saul's concubine (see 3:7). *Michal.* Since Michal was childless (6:23),

Merab was the actual birth mother of these five sons. She was the wife of Adriel (1 Sam. 18:19). Michal must have adopted them and brought them up under her care. **Barzillai the Meholathite.** A different man than Barzillai the Gileadite (17:27; 19:31).

21:9 before the LORD. These pagans were not bound by the law of Deuteronomy 21:22, 23, which forbade leaving a dead body hanging overnight. Their intention was to let the bodies hang until God signaled He was satisfied and sent rain to end the famine. Such a heathen practice, designed to propitiate their gods, was a superstition of these Gibeonites. God, in His providence, allowed this memorable retaliation as a lesson about keeping covenants and promises. **the beginning of barley harvest.** April (see Ruth 1:22).

21:10 sackcloth . . . spread. Rizpah erected a tent nearby to keep watch over the bodies, to scare away birds and beasts. It was considered a disgrace for a corpse to become food for the birds and beasts (cf. Deut. 28:26; 1 Sam. 17:44, 46; Rev. 19:17, 18). **the late rains.** An unseasonably late spring or early summer shower. Possibly, the rain that ended the drought.

21:11–14 Finally, after the rain had come,

David, encouraged by the example of the woman's devotion to her dead family members, ordered the remains of Saul and Jonathan transferred from their obscure grave in Jabesh Gilead (cf. 1 Sam. 31:11, 12), along with the seven sons' bones, to the honorable family grave in Zelah (cf. Josh. 18:28; 1 Sam. 10:2, "Zelzah"). This location is unknown.

21:14 God heeded the prayer. The famine ended and God restored the land to prosperity.

B. David's Heroes (21: 15–22)

21:15–22 This second section describes the defeat of four Philistine giants at the hands of David and his men. Though these events cannot be located chronologically with any certainty, the narratives of victory provide a fitting preface to David's song of praise, which magnifies God's deliverance (22:1–51). See 1 Chronicles 20:4–8.

21:16 the giant. The Hebrew term used in verses 16, 18, 20, 22 is *rapha*. This was not the name of an individual, but a term used collectively for the *Rephaim* who inhabited the land of Canaan and were noted for their inordinate size (cf. Gen. 15:19–21; Num. 13:33; Deut. 2:11; 3:11, 13). The term *Rephaim* was used of the people called the Anakim (Deut. 2:10, 11, 20, 21), distinguished for their size and strength. According to Joshua 11:21, 22 the Anakim were driven from the hill country of Israel and Judah, but remained in the Philistine cities of Gaza, Gath, and Ashdod. Though the Philistines had succumbed to the power of Israel's army, the appearance of some great champion revived their courage and invited their hope for victory against the Israelite invaders. **three hundred shekels.** Approximately seven and one-half lbs. **a new sword.** Lit. "a new thing." The weapon was not specified.

Key Word

Silver: 8:10, 11; 18:11, 12; 21:4; 24:24—lit. referred to as "the pale metal," was the basic unit of money in the Old Testament (1 Kin. 21:6; Is. 55:1). However, there is no reference to silver coins in the Old Testament because silver was valued by weight in ancient times (Is. 46:6; Jer. 32:9–10). Silver, along with gold, was one of the valuable materials used to construct the tabernacle and the temple (Ex. 25:1–9; 2 Chr. 2:7). In Ecclesiastes, Solomon voices a warning about silver: "He who loves silver will not be satisfied" (Eccl. 5:10).

21:17 Abishai. *See note on 2:18.* **lamp of Israel.** David, who with God's help brought the light of prosperity and well-being to the whole land of Israel, was the symbol of Israel's hope and promise of security. Continued blessing resided in David and his house.

21:18 Gob. Near Gezer (cf. 1 Chr. 20:4), about twenty-two miles west of Jerusalem.

21:19 Elhanan . . . killed the brother of Goliath. The minor scribal omission of "the brother of" (in the Hebrew) belongs in this verse, based on 1 Chronicles 20:5 which includes them, and because the Scripture says clearly that David killed Goliath as recorded in 1 Samuel 17:50. The NKJV gives the most likely solution, that there has been a scribal error in the text which should read, "Elhanan . . . killed the brother of Goliath." A second possible solution is that Elhanan and David may be different names for the same person, just as Solomon had another name (cf. 12:24, 25). A third solution is that there were perhaps two giants named Goliath.

21:20 Gath. About twelve miles south of Geza and twenty-six miles southwest of Jerusalem.

21:21 Jonathan. David's nephew, the son of Shimeah, also called Shammah in 1 Samuel 16:9, different from the son of Saul.

C. David's Song of Praise (22:1–51)

22:1–51 David's song of praise here is almost identical to Psalm 18 and forms the third inset. This song also has many verbal links to Hannah's prayer (*see note on 1 Sam. 2:1–10*) and, together with it, forms the framework for the books of Samuel. This song focuses on the Lord's deliverance of David from all his enemies, in response to which David praised the Lord, his deliverer (vv. 2–4). The major part of the song (vv. 5–46) states the reason for this praise of the Lord.

David first describes how the Lord had delivered him from his enemies (vv. 5–20), then declares why the Lord had delivered him from his enemies (vv. 21–28), and then states the extent of the Lord's deliverance from his enemies (vv. 29–46). The song concludes with David's resolve to praise his delivering Lord, even among the Gentiles (vv. 47–51). *See notes on Psalm 18:1–50* for a detailed explanation.

22:1 all his enemies. Cf. 7:1, 9, 11. David composed this song toward the end of his life when the Lord had given him a settled kingdom and the promise of the messianic seed embodied in the Davidic covenant.

22:2–4 This introduction contains the sum and substance of the whole psalm; David extols God as his defense, refuge, and deliverer in the many experiences of his agitated life.

22:2 rock. *See notes on 1 Samuel 2:2; Deuteronomy 32:4.* **fortress.** This term had previously been used to describe the citadel of Jerusalem (5:9) and the cave of Adullam (1 Sam. 22:1).

22:3 shield. See Genesis 15:1; Deuteronomy 33:29. **horn.** *See note on 1 Samuel 2:1.* **stronghold.** A secure, lofty retreat that the enemy finds inaccessible. As such, the Lord is the refuge of His chosen one, secure from all hostile attacks.

22:5–7 David described how he cried to the Lord in the midst of his distress.

22:5, 6 death. Pictured as (1) violent floods of water like waves ready to break over him and (2) traps set by a hunter to snare him, David faced the reality of imminent death in his personal experience, most frequently when pursued by Saul, but also in Absalom's conspiracy and in certain wars (see 21:16).

22:7 distress. The particular trouble David was referring to was the potential of his imminent death (vv. 5, 6). **His temple.**

God's heavenly dwelling place (cf. Pss. 11:4; 29:9).

22:8–16 In reaffirming the great majesty of God, David described His coming in power from heaven to earth (cf. Ex. 19:16–20; Ezek. 1:4–28; Hab. 3:3–15).

22:14 The LORD thundered. See note on 1 Samuel 7:10.

22:17–20 In personalizing what was just said in verses 8–16, David explained how God reached down from heaven to save him on the earth.

22:20 He delighted in me. This expression that the Lord was "pleased" with David (cf. 15:26) provided a transition to verses 21–28, where David described the basis of God's saving deliverance.

22:21–25 David was not claiming to be righteous or sinless in any absolute sense. Rather, David (1) believed God, (2) was considered righteous by faith, and (3) desired to please the Lord and be obedient to His commands. Thus he was blameless when compared with his enemies.

22:26–28 David stated the basic principles that the Lord follows in delivering or judging people.

22:28 humble . . . haughty. For the idea that the Lord saves the humble but brings the proud low, see also 1 Samuel 2:4–7.

22:29–46 Empowered by God (vv. 29–37), David was able to gain total victory over his enemies (vv. 38–43), both in Israel and throughout the nations (vv. 44–46).

22:29 my lamp. David as the "lamp" of Israel (see note on 21:17) reflected the light of the glory of God, who was the "Lamp" of David himself.

22:50 Paul quotes this in Romans 15:9.

22:51 His king . . . His anointed. These terms are singular and, thus, do not seem to refer to David and his descendants. Rather, they refer to the promised "seed," the Messiah of 7:12. The deliverance and ultimate

triumph of David foreshadow that of the coming Messiah. At the end of his life, David looked back in faith at God's promises and forward in hope to their fulfillment in the coming of a future *king,* the "anointed one" (*see notes on 1 Sam. 2:10*).

D. David's Last Words (23:1–7)

23:1–7 last words. This is David's final literary legacy to Israel, not his final oral speech (see 1 Kin. 2:1–10). This is the fourth inset.

23:1 says. "Declares as an oracle" (cf. Num. 24:3, 15; 1 Sam. 2:30; Prov. 30:1). David realized that the psalms he wrote, as directed by the Holy Spirit, were the very Word of God.

23:2 Spirit. God's Holy Spirit is the divine instrument of revelation and inspiration (cf. Zech. 7:12; 2 Tim. 3:16, 17; 2 Pet. 1:19–21).

23:3, 4 He who rules. These words begin the record of direct speech from God, whose ideal king must exercise His authority with justice, in complete submission to divine sovereignty. Such a king is like the helpful rays of sun at dawn and the life-giving showers that nourish the earth. This ideal king was identified in the OT as the coming Messiah (cf. Is. 9:6, 7).

23:5 my house is not so with God. In response to God's standard for His ideal king, David confessed that his house had not always ruled over God's people in righteousness and in the fear of God and, thus, were not the fulfillment of 7:12–16. Further, none of the kings of David's line (according to 1 and 2 Kings) met God's standard of righteous obedience. **everlasting covenant.** The promise given by the Lord to David recorded in 7:12–16 is here referred to as a "covenant," a binding agreement from the Lord that He will fulfill. In spite of the fact that David and his own household had failed (chs. 9–20), David rightly believed that the Lord would not fail, but would be faithful to His promise of hope for the future in the seed of David, the eternal King, the anointed one (*see note on 7:12*), who would establish a kingdom of righteousness and peace forever.

23:6 sons of rebellion. Lit. "Belial" (*see note on 1 Sam. 2:12*). The wicked enemies of God will be cast aside in judgment when the Messiah, the fulfillment of the Davidic covenant, establishes His rule on the earth (cf. Is. 63:1–6).

E. David's Mighty Men (23:8–39)

23:8–39 This fifth inset recalls David's mighty men. See 1 Chronicles 11:10–41.

23:8 the mighty men. David's bravest warriors and most outstanding soldiers are memorialized. This list appears in 1 Chronicles 11:11–41, with slight variations. According to 1 Chronicles 11:10, these men helped David to become king. The listing of these men is presented in three sets: first, "the three" (vv. 8–12); second, two more honored other than "the thirty," but not attaining to "the three" (vv. 18–23); and third, "the thirty" which is actually thirty-two (vv. 24–39). This list is expanded by sixteen names in 1 Chronicles 11:41–47. **eight hundred.** This is probably a textual error. 1 Chronicles 11:11 has "three hundred," which is the likely number.

23:13–17 three of the thirty. Three of the soldiers mentioned in verses 34–39.

23:13 cave of Adullam. *See note on 1 Samuel 22:1.* **Valley of Rephaim.** *See note on 5:18.*

23:14 stronghold. *See note on 1 Samuel 22:4.*

23:16 poured it out to the LORD. Because David's men brought him water from Bethlehem's well at the risk of their own lives, he considered it as "blood" and refused to drink it. Instead, he poured it out on the ground as a sacrifice to the Lord (cf. Gen. 35:14; Ex. 30:9; Lev. 23:13, 18, 37).

23:18 Abishai. *See note on 2:18.*

23:20 Benaiah. *See note on 8:18.*

23:24 Asahel. *See note on 2:18.*

23:24–39 thirty. A technical term for a small military contingent, named "the thirty" since it usually consisted of around thirty men, whereas thirty-two men are listed here, counting Joab.

23:39 Uriah. Here is inserted a mention of one of David's great soldiers, a reminder of David's great sin (11:1–27), and a preparation for David's further failure recorded in 24:1–10. **thirty-seven.** The three (vv. 8–12) with Abishai (vv. 18, 19) and Benaiah (vv. 20–23), plus the thirty-two men of "the thirty" (vv. 24–39).

F. The Lord's Judgment against David (24:1–25)

24:1–25 This is the sixth and final inset to the Epilogue.

24:1–17 *See notes on 1 Chronicles 21:1–16.*

24:1 Again. A second outbreak of the divine wrath occurred after the three-year famine recorded in 21:1. **against Israel.** The inciting of David to conduct a census was a punishment on Israel from the Lord for some unspecified sins. Perhaps sins of pride and ambition had led him to increase the size of his army unnecessarily and place heavy burdens of support on the people. Whatever the sin, it is clear God was dissatisfied with David's motives, goals, and actions; they brought judgment. **He moved David.** Satan incited David to take this census, and the Lord sovereignly and permissively used Satan to accomplish His will. *See note on 1 Chronicles 21:1.* **number Israel and Judah.** A census was usually for military purposes, which seems to be the case here (see v. 9). Numbering the potential army of Israel had been done in the past (Num. 1:1, 2; 26:1–4). However, this census of Israel's potential army did not have the sanction of the Lord and proceeded from wrong motives. David either wanted to glory in the size of his fighting force or take more territory than the Lord had granted him. He shifted his trust from God to military power (this is a constant theme in the Psalms; cf. 20:7; 25:2; 44:6).

24:2 from Dan to Beersheba. A proverbial statement for all the land of Israel from north to south.

24:3 But why? Although Joab protested the plan, he was overruled by David with no reason for the census being stated by David.

24:5 Aroer. The census began about fourteen miles east of the Dead Sea on the northern bank of the Arnon River, in the southeastern corner of Israel, and continued in a counterclockwise direction through the land. *Jazer.* A town in the territory of Gad about six miles west of Rabbah. Jazer was close to the border of the Ammonite territory.

24:6 Gilead. The Transjordan territory north of Gad. *Dan Jaan.* This was either a village near the town of Dan or a fuller name for Dan itself. Dan is twenty-five miles north of the Sea of Galilee.

24:7 Tyre. The census takers seem to have gone north from Dan and then west towards Sidon before turning south toward Tyre, a city on the coast of the Mediterranean Sea ruled by David's friend Hiram (*see note on 5:11*), but remaining in Israelite territory. *Beersheba.* A major settlement in the south of the land of Israel located about forty-five miles southwest of Jerusalem.

24:9 Israel eight hundred thousand . . . Judah . . . five hundred thousand. First Chronicles 21:5 has "one million one hundred thousand" and "four hundred and seventy thousand," respectively. A solution can be found in seeing the 1 Chronicles figure including all the available men of military age, whether battle-seasoned or not. But the 2 Samuel figure could be 800,000 battle-

seasoned soldiers with the additional 300,000 being of military age who were in reserve but never fought, or it could be the 288,000 in the standing army (1 Chr. 27:1–15) rounded off to 300,000. Either of these two contingents would make up the 1.1 million number of 1 Chronicles 21. As far as Judah was concerned, the number in 2 Samuel is 30,000 more than the 1 Chronicles figure. First Chronicles makes it clear that the numbering was not completed by Joab, because he did not get to the census regarding Benjamin (or Levi) before David came under conviction about completing it all. Joab was glad to stop when he saw the king's changed heart. Because of the procedure selected (*see note on 24:5*), the numbering of Benjamin would have been last, so their number was not included. In the record of 2 Samuel, the figure for Judah included the already-known number of 30,000 troops from Benjamin, hence the total of 500,000. The Benjamites remained loyal to David and Judah.

24:10 David's heart condemned him. Although God's prohibition is not clear in the text, it was clear to David. *sinned greatly . . . done very foolishly.* David recognized the enormity of his willful rebellion against God. David's insight saw the seriousness of his error in relying on numerical strength instead of on the Lord, who can deliver by many or few (see 1 Sam. 14:6).

24:11 Gad. See note on 1 Samuel 22:5.

24:13 famine . . . enemies . . . plague. David was given a choice of three possible punishments for his sin of numbering the people: (1) three years of famine in Israel (*see note on 1 Chr. 21:12*); (2) three months of fleeing from his enemies; or (3) three days of pestilence in the land. Implicit in the threat of pursuit by *enemies* was death by the sword. Famine, sword, and plague were OT punishments of the Lord against His sinful

---

Key Word

Jerusalem: 5:5; 8:7; 11:1; 15:8, 29; 16:15; 17:20; 19:19; 24:16—related to the word for "peace." During the reign of King David, Jerusalem was made the political and religious capital of Israel and became central to the unfolding of God's redemptive plan. Jerusalem is described variously in the Old Testament as the city of God (Ps. 87:1–3), the place where God has put His name (2 Kin. 21:4), a place of salvation (Is. 46:13), the throne of God (Jer. 3:17), and a holy city (Is. 52:1). The prophets foresaw an approaching time when Jerusalem would be judged because of its iniquity (Mic. 4:10–12), but, in pronouncing judgment, they could also see its glorious restoration (Is. 40:2; 44:25–28; Dan. 9:2; Zeph. 3:16–20). This vision of a restored Jerusalem included the hope of a New Jerusalem in which God would gather all His people (Is. 65:17–19; Rev. 21:1–2).

---

people (Lev. 26:23–26; Deut. 28:21–26; Jer. 14:12).

24:14 *fall into the hand of the LORD.* David knew that the Lord would be more merciful than his enemies, so he took the third option.

24:16 relented. Or *repented, grieved,* an expression of God's deep sorrow over man's sin and evil (see 1 Sam. 15:11, 29). ***Araunah the Jebusite.*** Araunah (or Ornan) was a pre-Israelite inhabitant of Jerusalem. He owned a threshing floor north of the citadel of Jerusalem and outside its fortified area.

24:17 *Let Your hand . . . be against me.* Rather than witness the further destruction of his people, David called down God's wrath upon himself and his own family (cf. Ex. 32:32).

24:18–25 See 1 Chronicles 21:18–27.

24:18 *altar.* At this time, the altar associated with the tabernacle of Moses was located at Gibeon (1 Chr. 21:29; 2 Chr. 1:2–6). David was instructed by Gad to build another altar to the Lord at the place where the plague had stopped. This indicated where the Lord's choice was for the building of His temple.

24:24 *costs me nothing.* Sacrifice is an essential part of worship and service to God (see Mal. 1:6–10; 2 Cor. 8:1–5). ***fifty shekels.*** A little more than a pound of silver. First Chronicles 21:25 says David paid 600 shekels of gold. How is this discrepancy resolved? In the initial transaction, David either bought or leased the small threshing floor (usually thirty or forty feet square) and purchased the oxen. Fifty shekels of silver was appropriate. After that, 1 Chronicles 21:25 says he bought "the place," costing 180 times as much, and referring to the entire area of Mt. Moriah.

24:25 *the plague was withdrawn.* This indicates that judgment is not the final action of the Lord toward either Israel or the house of David. God will fulfill the Abrahamic and Davidic covenants (cf. Ezek. 37).

Further Study

Davis, John J. and John C. Whitcomb. *A History of Israel from Conquest to Exile.* Grand Rapids: Baker, 1980.

Merrill, Eugene. *I and II Samuel,* in The Bible Knowledge Commentary—OT. Wheaton, Ill.: Victor, 1985.

Youngblood, Ronald F. *1, 2 Samuel,* in Expositor's Bible Commentary. Grand Rapids: Zondervan, 1992.

THE FIRST BOOK OF THE
KINGS

Title

First and Second Kings were originally one book, called in the Hebrew text, *Kings,* from the first word in 1:1. The Greek translation of the OT, the Septuagint (LXX), divided the book in two, and this was followed by the Latin Vulgate version and English translations. The division was for the convenience of copying this lengthy book on scrolls and codexes; it was not based on features of content. Modern Hebrew Bibles title the books "Kings A" and "Kings B." The LXX and Vulgate connected Kings with the books of Samuel, so that the titles in the LXX are "The Third and Fourth Books of Kingdoms" and in the Vulgate "Third and Fourth Kings."

The Books of 1 and 2 Samuel and 1 and 2 Kings combined represent a chronicle of the entire history of Judah's and Israel's kingship from Saul to Zedekiah. First and Second Chronicles provides only the history of Judah's monarchy.

Author and Date

Jewish tradition proposed that Jeremiah wrote Kings, though this is unlikely because the final event recorded in the book (see 2 Kin. 25:27–30) occurred in Babylon in 561 B.C. Jeremiah never went to Babylon, but to Egypt (Jer. 43:1–7), and would have been at least eighty-six years old by 561 B.C. Actually, the identity of the unnamed author remains unknown. Since the ministry of prophets is emphasized in Kings, it seems that the au-

thor was most likely an unnamed prophet of the Lord who lived in exile with Israel in Babylon.

Kings was written between 561–538 B.C. Since the last narrated event (2 Kin. 25:27–30) sets the earliest possible date of completion and because there is no record of the end of the Babylonian captivity in Kings, the release from exile (538 B.C.) identifies the latest possible writing date. This date is sometimes challenged on the basis of "to this day" statements in 8:8; 9:13, 20, 21; 10:12; 12:19; 2 Kings 2:22; 8:22; 10:27; 14:7; 16:6; 17:23, 34, 41; 21:15. However, it is best to understand these statements as those of the sources used by the author, rather than statements of the author himself.

It is clear that the author used a variety of sources in compiling this book, including "the book of the acts of Solomon" (11:41), "the chronicles of the kings of Israel" (14:19; 15:31; 16:5, 14, 20, 27; 22:39; 2 Kin. 1:18; 10:34; 13:8, 12; 14:15, 28; 15:11, 15, 21, 26, 31), and "the chronicles of the kings of Judah" (14:29; 15:7, 23; 22:45; 2 Kin. 8:23; 12:19; 14:18; 15:6, 36; 16:19; 20:20; 21:17, 25; 23:28; 24:5). Further, Isaiah 36:1–39:8 provided information used in 2 Kings 18:9–20:19, and Jeremiah 52:31–34 seems to be the source for 2 Kings 25:27–29. This explanation proposes a single, inspired author, living in Babylon during the Exile, using these pre-exilic source materials at his disposal.

Background and Setting

A distinction must be made between the setting of the books' sources and that of the books' author. The source material was written by participants in and eyewitnesses of the events. It was reliable information, which was historically accurate concerning the sons of Israel, from the death of David and the accession of Solomon (971 B.C.) to the destruction of the temple and Jerusalem by the Babylonians (586 B.C.). Thus, Kings traces the histories of two sets of kings and two nations of disobedient people, Israel and Judah, both of whom were growing indifferent to God's law and His prophets and were headed for captivity.

The Book of Kings is not only accurate history, but interpreted history. The author, an exile in Babylon, wished to communicate the lessons of Israel's history to the exiles. Specifically, he taught the exilic community why the Lord's judgment of exile had come. The writer established early in his narrative that the Lord required obedience by the kings to the Mosaic Law, if their kingdom was to receive His blessing; disobedience would bring exile (9:3–9). The sad reality that history revealed was that all the kings of Israel and the majority of the kings of Judah "did evil in the sight of the LORD." These evil kings were apostates, who led their people to sin by not confronting idolatry, but sanctioning it.

Because of the kings' failure, the Lord sent His prophets to confront both the monarchs and the people with their sin and their need to return to Him. Because the message of the prophets was rejected, the prophets foretold that the nation(s) would be carried into exile (2 Kin. 17:13–23; 21:10–15). Like every prophecy uttered by the prophets in Kings, this word from the Lord came to pass (2 Kin. 17:5, 6; 25:1–11).

Therefore, Kings interpreted the people's experience of exile and helped them to see why they had suffered God's punishment for idolatry. It also explained that just as God had shown mercy to Ahab (1 Kin. 22:27–29) and Jehoiachin (2 Kin. 25:27–30), so He was willing to show them mercy.

The predominant geographical setting of Kings is the whole land of Israel, from Dan to Beersheba (4:25), including Transjordan. Four invading nations played a dominant role in the affairs of Israel and Judah from 971 to 561 B.C. In the tenth century B.C., Egypt impacted Israel's history during the reigns of Solomon and Rehoboam (3:1; 11:14–22, 40; 12:2; 14:25–27). Syria (Aram) posed a great threat to Israel's security during the ninth century B.C., c. 890–800 B.C. (15:9–22; 20:1–34; 22:1–4, 29–40; 2 Kin. 6:8–7:20; 8:7–15; 10:32, 33; 12:17, 18; 13:22–25). The years from c. 800 to 750 B.C. were a half-century of peace and prosperity for Israel and Judah, because Assyria neutralized Syria and did not threaten to the south. This changed during the kingship of Tiglath-Pileser III (2 Kin. 15:19, 20, 29).

From the mid-eighth century to the late-seventh century B.C., Assyria terrorized Palestine, finally conquering and destroying Israel (the northern kingdom) in 722 B.C. (2 Kin. 17:4–6) and besieging Jerusalem in 701 B.C. (2 Kin. 18:17–19:37). From 612 to 539 B.C., Babylon was the dominant power in the ancient world. Babylon invaded Judah (the southern kingdom) three times, with the destruction of Jerusalem and the temple occurring in 586 B.C. during that third assault (2 Kin. 24:1–25:21).

Historical and Theological Themes

Kings concentrates, then, on the history of the sons of Israel from 971 to 561 B.C. First Kings 1:1–11:43 deals with Solomon's accession and reign (971–931 B.C.). The two divided kingdoms of Israel and Judah (931–722 B.C.) are covered in 1 Kings 12:1; 2 Kings 17:41. The author arranged the material in a distinctive way in that the narration follows the kings in both the north and the south. For each reign described, there is the following literary framework.

Every king is introduced with: (1) his name and relation to his predecessor; (2) his date of accession in relationship to the year of the contemporary ruler in the other kingdom; (3) his age on coming to the throne (for kings of Judah only); (4) his length of reign; (5) his place of reign; (6) his mother's name (for Judah only); and (7) spiritual appraisal of his reign. This introduction is followed by a narration of the events that occurred during the reign of each king. The details of this narration vary widely.

Each reign is concluded with: (1) a citation of sources; (2) additional historical notes; (3) notice of death; (4) notice of burial; (5) the name of the successor; and (6) in a few instances, an added postscript (e.g., 15:32; 2 Kin. 10:36). Second Kings 18:1–25:21 deals with the time when Judah survived alone (722–586 B.C.). Two concluding paragraphs speak of events after the Babylonian exile (2 Kin. 25:22–26, 27–30).

Three theological themes are emphasized in Kings.

First, the Lord judged Israel and Judah because of their disobedience to His law (2 Kin. 17:7–23). This unfaithfulness on the part of the people was furthered by the apostasy of the evil kings who led them into idolatry (2 Kin. 17:21, 22; 21:11), so the Lord exercised His righteous wrath against His rebellious people.

Second, the word of the true prophets came to pass (13:2, 3; 22:15–28; 2 Kin. 23:16; 24:2). This confirmed that the Lord did keep His Word, even His warnings of judgment.

Third, the Lord remembered His promise to David (11:12, 13, 34–36; 15:4; 2 Kin. 8:19). Even though the kings of the Davidic line proved themselves to be disobedient to the Lord, He did not bring David's family to an end as He did the families of Jeroboam I, Omri, and Jehu in Israel. Even as the book closes, the line of David still exists (2 Kin. 25:27–30), so there is hope for the coming "seed" of David (see 2 Sam. 7:12–16). The Lord is thus seen as faithful, and His Word is trustworthy.

Interpretive Challenges

The major interpretive challenge in Kings concerns the chronology of the kings of Israel and Judah. Though abundant chronological data is presented in the book of Kings, this data is difficult to interpret for two reasons.

First, there seems to be internal inconsistency in the information given. For instance, 1 Kings 16:23 states that Omri, king of Israel, began to reign in the thirty-first year of Asa, king of Judah, and that he reigned twelve years. But according to 1 Kings 16:29, Omri was succeeded by his son Ahab in the thirty-eighth year of Asa, giving Omri a reign of only seven years, not twelve (for resolution, *see note on 16:23*).

Second, from extra biblical sources (Greek, Assyrian, and Babylonian), correlated with astronomical data, a reliable series of dates can be calculated from 892 to 566 B.C. Since Ahab and Jehu, kings of Israel, are believed to be mentioned in Assyrian records, 853 B.C. can be fixed as the year of Ahab's death and 841 B.C. as the year Jehu began to reign. With these fixed dates, it is possible to work backward and forward to determine that the date of the division of Israel from Judah was c. 931 B.C., the fall of Samaria 722 B.C., and the fall of Jerusalem 586 B.C. But when the total years of royal reigns in Kings are added, the number for Israel is 241 years (not the 210 years of 931 to 722 B.C.) and Judah 393 years (not the 346 years of 931 to 586 B.C.).

However, it is recognized that in both kingdoms there were some co-regencies, i.e., a period of rulership when two kings, usually father and son, ruled at the same time, so the overlapping years were counted twice in the total for both kings. Further, different methods of reckoning the years of a king's rule and even different calendars were used at differing times in the two kingdoms, resulting in the seeming internal inconsistencies. The accuracy of the chronology in Kings can be demonstrated and confirmed.

A second major interpretive challenge deals with Solomon's relationship to the Abrahamic and Davidic covenants. First Kings 4:20, 21 has been interpreted by some as the fulfillment of the promises given to Abraham (cf. Gen. 15:18–21; 22:17). However, according to Numbers 34:6, the western border of the land promised to Abraham was the Mediterranean Sea. In 1 Kings 5:1ff., Hiram is seen as the independent king of Tyre (along the Mediterranean coast), dealing with Solomon as an equal. Solomon's empire was not the fulfillment of the land promise given to Abraham by the Lord, although a great portion of that land was under Solomon's control.

Further, the statements of Solomon in 1 Kings 5:5 and 8:20 are his claims to be the promised seed of the Davidic covenant (cf. 2 Sam. 7:12–16). The author of Kings holds out the possibility that Solomon's temple was the fulfillment of the Lord's promise to David. However, while the conditions for the fulfillment of the promise to David are reiterated to Solomon (6:12), it is clear that Solomon did not meet these conditions (11:9–13). In fact, none of the historical kings in the house of David met the condition of complete obedience that was to be the sign of the Promised One.

According to Kings, the fulfillment of the Abrahamic and Davidic covenants did not take place in Israel's past, thus laying the foundation for the latter prophets (Isaiah, Jeremiah, Ezekiel, Daniel, and the Twelve) who would point Israel to a future hope under Messiah when the covenants would be fulfilled (see Is. 9:6, 7).

Since the division of 1 and 2 Kings arbitrarily takes place in the middle of the narrative concerning King Ahaziah in Israel, the following outline combines 1 and 2 Kings.

Outline

I. The United Kingdom: The Reign of Solomon (1:1–11:43)

1:1–11:43 The first division of Kings chronicles the reign of Solomon. The literary structure is centered around the building activities of Solomon (6:1–9:9) and climaxes with the failure of Solomon to follow the Lord wholeheartedly (11:1–43).

A. The Rise of Solomon (1:1–2:46)

1:1 *advanced in years.* David was seventy years old (cf. 2 Sam. 5:4, 5).

1:2 *the king may be warm.* In his old age, circulatory problems plagued King David so he had trouble keeping warm. The royal staff proposed a solution—that a young virgin nurse watch over him and, at night, warm him with her body heat. This was in harmony with the medical customs of that day; both the Jewish historian Josephus (first century A.D.) and the Greek physician Galen (second century A.D.) recorded such a practice.

1:3 *Abishag the Shunammite.* Abishag was a beautiful teenager from the town of Shunem, in the territory of Issachar located three miles north of Jezreel (Josh. 19:18; 1 Sam. 28:4; 2 Kin. 4:8). Though from the same town, she is not to be identified with the Shulamite in the Song of Solomon (6:13).

1:4 *the king did not know her.* Although apparently joining David's harem (cf. 2:17, 22–24), Abishag remained a virgin.

1:5 *Adonijah.* Adonijah was the fourth son of David (2 Sam. 3:4) and, probably, the oldest living son; Amnon (2 Sam. 13:28, 29) and Absalom (2 Sam. 18:14, 15) had been killed and Chileab apparently died in his youth, since there is no mention of him beyond his birth. As David's oldest surviving heir, Adonijah attempted to claim the kingship. *chariots and horsemen.* Like Absalom (2 Sam. 15:1), Adonijah sought to confirm and support his claim to kingship by raising a small army.

1:7 *Joab.* David's nephew (1 Chr. 2:16), the commander of the army of Israel (2 Sam. 8:16) and a faithful supporter of David's kingship (2 Sam. 18:2; 20:22). He was guilty of the illegal killings of Abner and Amasa (2:5; cf. 2 Sam. 3:39; 20:10). Adonijah wanted his support in his bid for the throne. *Abiathar.* One of the two high priests serving concurrently during David's reign (2 Sam. 8:17), whose influence Adonijah sought.

1:8 *Zadok.* The other high priest serving during David's reign (2 Sam. 8:17), whose ancestors will serve the millennial temple (see Ezek. 44:15). He had been high priest in the tabernacle at Gibeon under Saul (1 Chr. 16:39). *Benaiah.* The commander of the Cherethites and Pelethites (v. 44), David's official guards distinguished for bravery (see 2 Sam. 23:20). *See note on 1 Samuel 30:14.* He was regarded by Joab as a rival. *Nathan.* The most influential prophet during David's reign (2 Sam. 7:1–17; 12:1–15, 25). *Shimei.* Cf. 4:18. A different individual than the Shimei referred to in 1 Kings 2:8, 36–46; 2 Samuel 16:5–8. *the mighty men.* See 2 Samuel 23:8–39.

1:9 *Zoheleth.* Lit. "Serpent Stone," a standard landmark identified with a previous Jebusite snake worship location. *En Rogel.* Lit. "the spring of the fuller." Typically identified as being located at the north-west confluence of the Kidron and Hinnom valleys to the south of Jerusalem. Here, Adonijah held a political event to court popularity and secure his claim to the throne.

1:11–27 The revolt of Adonijah was defeated by Nathan, who knew the Lord's will (see 2 Sam. 7:12; 1 Chr. 22:9) and acted quickly by having Bathsheba go to David first to report what was happening, after which he would follow (v. 23).

1:11 *Bathsheba the mother of Solomon.*

The mothers of the kings of the Davidic line are continually noted (2:13, 19; 14:21; 15:2; 2 Kin. 8:26; 12:1; 14:2; 15:2, 33; 18:2; 21:1, 19; 22:1; 23:31, 36; 24:8). The queen mother held an influential position in the royal court. For the account of how David sinned with her, see 2 Samuel 11.

1:12 *save . . . the life of your son.* If Adonijah had become king, the lives of Bathsheba and Solomon would have been in jeopardy, because often in the ancient Near East potential claimants to the throne and their families were put to death (cf. 15:29; 16:11; 2 Kin. 10:11).

1:13 *Did you not . . . swear.* This oath was given privately (unrecorded in Scripture) by David, perhaps to both Nathan and Bathsheba. The Lord's choice of Solomon was implicit in his name Jedidiah, meaning "loved by the Lord" (2 Sam. 12:24, 25) and explicit in David's declaration to Solomon (1 Chr. 22:6–13). Cf. verses 17, 20, 35.

1:28–53 See 1 Chronicles 29:21–25.

1:29 *the king took an oath.* David swore another oath to carry out his earlier oath to make Solomon king, and he made good on it that very day.

1:33 *my own mule.* The riding of David's royal mule showed Israel that Solomon was David's chosen successor (see 2 Sam. 13:29). *Gihon.* This spring, which was east of Jerusalem in the Kidron Valley, was Jerusalem's main water supply, located about one-half mile north of En Rogel (v. 9) and hidden from it by an intervening hill. Thus, the sound of Solomon's anointing ceremony could have been heard without being seen by Adonijah's party.

1:34 *anoint him king.* Saul and David had been anointed by Samuel, the Lord's priest and prophet (1 Sam. 10:1; 16:13); Solomon was also to be recognized by priest and prophet. The participation of the prophet Nathan gave Solomon's coronation

evidence of the Lord's blessing. Throughout the book of Kings, God identified His chosen kings through prophets (11:37; 15:28, 29; 16:12; 2 Kin. 9:3). *blow the horn.* The blowing of the trumpet signaled a public assembly where the people corporately recognized Solomon's new status as co-regent with and successor to David (vv. 39, 40).

1:35 *Israel and Judah.* These were two major geographical components of David's and Solomon's kingdoms. Even while still unified, these two separate entities, that would later divide (12:20), were clearly identifiable.

1:39 *tabernacle.* This was the tent David set up in Jerusalem (2 Sam. 6:17; 1 Chr. 15:1) to house the ark of the covenant, not the tabernacle of Moses (see 3:4).

1:41–49 *Adonijah . . . heard it.* The loud shouts hailing Solomon as king reached the ears of those attending Adonijah's feast at En Rogel nearby. A messenger came with the full report of Solomon's coronation, so that the cause of Adonijah was lost and the party ended with the people leaving in fear.

1:42 *Jonathan.* The son of Abiathar, the priest, was an experienced messenger (2 Sam. 15:36; 17:17).

1:50 *horns of the altar.* Cf. 2:28. The *horns* were corner projections on the altar of burnt offering on which the priests smeared the blood of the sacrifices (Ex. 27:2; 29:12). By grasping the horns, Adonijah sought to place himself under the protection of God (see Ex. 21:13, 14).

2:1 *he charged Solomon.* Leaders typically exhorted their successors, e.g., Moses (Deut. 31:7, 8), Joshua (Josh. 23:1–6), and Samuel (1 Sam. 12:1–25). So also David gave Solomon a final exhortation.

2:2 *the way of all the earth.* An expression for death (Josh. 23:14; cf. Gen 3:19). *be strong . . . prove yourself a man.* An expression of encouragement (Deut. 31:7, 23; Josh.

The Kings of the United Kingdom

Saul	1 Samuel 9:1–31:13; 1 Chronicles 10:1–14
David	2 Samuel; 1 Kings 1:1–2:9; 1 Chronicles 11:1–29:30
Solomon	1 Kings 2:10–11:43; 2 Chronicles 1:1–9:31

1:6, 7, 9, 18; 1 Sam. 4:9) with which David sought to prepare Solomon for the difficult tasks and the battles in his future.

2:3 keep the charge of the Lord your God. David admonished Solomon to obey the Mosaic Law so he could have a successful kingship (cf. Deut. 17:18–20).

2:4 His word. The unconditional Davidic covenant was made by the Lord with David in 2 Samuel 7:4–17 and confirmed to Solomon in 1 Kings 9:5, promising the perpetuation of the Davidic dynasty over Israel. *If your sons take heed to their way.* David declared that the king's obedience to the Law of Moses was a necessary condition for the fulfillment of the divine promise. The Book of Kings demonstrates that none of the descendants of David remained faithful to God's Law; none of them met the conditions for the fulfillment of the divine promise. Rather, David's words provided a basis for explaining the Exile. Thus, the ultimate and final King of Israel would appear at a later, undesignated time.

2:5 Abner . . . Amasa. These were victims of Joab's jealousy and vengeance who were killed after warfare had ceased (2 Sam. 3:27; 20:10), thus bringing Joab's punishment as a murderer (Deut. 19:11–13).

2:7 sons of Barzillai. David told Solomon to repay Barzillai's kindness to David (2 Sam. 17:27–29) by showing similar kindness to Barzillai's sons. *eat at your table.* A position of honor that could include a royal stipend (18:19; 2 Sam. 9:7; 2 Kin. 25:29).

2:8 Shimei. He had angrily stoned and vehemently cursed David when David was

escaping from Absalom (2 Sam. 16:5–13). Shimei's actions were worthy of death (Ex. 22:28), and David counseled Solomon through subtle means to arrange for his just punishment (vv. 36–46).

2:10–12 See 2 Samuel 5:5; 1 Chronicles 29:26–28.

2:10 the City of David. I.e., Jerusalem (cf. 8:1).

2:11 forty years. David ruled from c. 1011–971 B.C., probably with Solomon as co-regent during his final year (cf. 11:41).

2:12 firmly established. Solomon's succession enjoyed the Lord's approval, and Solomon experienced unchallenged authority, prosperity, and renown (v. 46).

2:15 all Israel had set their expectations on me. A reference to Adonijah's perceived right to the kingship as the oldest surviving son according to ancient Near Eastern custom.

2:17 give me Abishag. In the ancient Near East, possession of the royal harem was a sign of kingship (cf. 2 Sam. 3:8; 12:8; 16:20–22). Adonijah's request for Abishag was an attempt to support his claim to the kingship and perhaps generate a revolt to usurp the throne. Bathsheba didn't see the treachery (vv. 18–21).

2:22 Ask for . . . the kingdom also. Solomon recognized Adonijah's request as the prelude to his usurping of the throne. Because Adonijah's request violated the terms of loyalty Solomon had previously specified (1:52), he pronounced a formal, legal death sentence on Adonijah (vv. 23, 24).

2:24 as He promised. Solomon viewed

himself as the fulfillment of the Lord's promise to David in 2 Samuel 7:12–16 (see also 5:5; 8:18–21). The ultimate fulfillment will be the Messiah, Jesus, who will return to Israel and set up His kingdom (see Is. 9:6, 7).

2:26 Anathoth. A priestly town, three miles northeast of Jerusalem (cf. Jer. 1:1). There Abiathar, the disloyal high priest (1:7), lived in banishment.

2:27 fulfill the word of the LORD. Solomon's removal of Abiathar from the office of priest fulfilled God's prophecy that Eli's line of priests would be cut off (1 Sam. 2:30–35). This reestablished the line of Eleazar/Phinehas in Zadok (2:35), as promised by God (cf. Num. 25:10–13).

2:28 Joab fled to the tabernacle. Cf. 1:50. He knew he would have been killed already if he had not been so popular with the army. The altar provided no real sanctuary to the rebel and murderer (cf. Ex. 21:14).

2:31 strike him down. Like Adonijah (1:50), Joab sought asylum at the altar (2:28). The protection of the Lord at the altar applied only to accidental crimes, not premeditated murder (Ex. 21:14), so Solomon ordered Benaiah to administer the violent death sought by David (2:6).

2:33 peace forever. This pledge is ultimately to be fulfilled in the Messiah's kingdom (see Is. 2:2–4; 9:6, 7).

2:34 wilderness. The tomb of Joab's father was near Bethlehem (2 Sam. 2:32). Joab's house was probably on the edge of the Judean wilderness, east of Bethlehem.

2:36 do not go out. Shimei had not provoked Solomon directly as Adonijah had. Therefore, Solomon determined to keep Shimei under close watch by confining him to Jerusalem.

2:39 Gath. A major Philistine city about thirty miles southwest of Jerusalem.

2:45 throne of David. In contrast to Shimei's curse (2 Sam. 16:5–8), the Lord's

blessing was to come through the ruler of David's line, not Saul's (cf. 2 Sam. 7:12, 13, 16).

2:46 With the death of Shimei, all the rival factions were eliminated.

B. The Beginning of Solomon's Wisdom and Wealth (3:1–4:34)

3:1 a treaty with Pharaoh. The Pharaoh was probably Siamun, the next-to-last ruler of the weak twenty-first dynasty. Solomon's treaty with Pharaoh signified that he held a high standing in the world of his day. Pharaoh's daughter was the most politically significant of Solomon's 700 wives (cf. 7:8; 9:16; 11:1).

3:2 the high places. The open-air, hilltop worship centers that the Israelites inherited from the Canaanites had been rededicated to the Lord; the use of pagan altars had been forbidden (Num. 33:52; Deut. 7:5; 12:3). After the building of the temple, worship at the high places was condemned (11:7, 8; 12:31; 2 Kin. 16:17–20; 21:3; 23:26). **no house . . . for the name of the LORD.** *Name* represented the character and presence of the Lord (cf. Ex. 3:13, 14). He had promised to choose one place "to put His name for His dwelling place" (Deut. 12:5). The temple at Jerusalem was to be that place (cf. 5:3, 5; 8:16, 17, 18, 19, 20, 29, 43, 44, 48; 9:3, 7). In the ancient Near East, to identify a temple with a god's name meant that the god owned the place and dwelt there.

3:3 except. Solomon's failure in completely following the Lord was exhibited in his continual worship at the high places.

3:4–15 See 2 Chronicles 1:7–13.

3:4 Gibeon. A town about seven miles northwest of Jerusalem, where the tabernacle of Moses and the original bronze altar were located (1 Chr. 21:29; 2 Chr. 1:2–6).

3:5 dream. God often gave revelation in dreams (Gen. 26:24; 28:12; 46:2; Dan. 2:7;

7:1; Matt. 1:20; 2:12, 19, 22). However, this dream was unique—a two-way conversation between the Lord and Solomon.

3:6 great mercy . . . great kindness. These terms imply covenant faithfulness. Solomon viewed his succession to David as evidence of the Lord's faithfulness to His promises to David.

3:7 little child. Since Solomon was probably only about twenty years of age; he readily admitted his lack of qualification and experience to be king (cf. 1 Chr. 22:5; 29:1). *See note on Numbers 27:15–17.*

3:8 a great people. Based on the census, which recorded 800,000 men of fighting age in Israel and 500,000 in Judah (2 Sam. 24:9), the total population was over four million, approximately double what it had been at the time of the conquest of the land (see Num. 26:1–65).

3:9 an understanding heart. Humbly admitting his need, Solomon sought "a listening heart" to govern God's people with wisdom.

3:10 pleased the LORD. The Lord was delighted that Solomon had not asked for personal benefits, e.g., long life, wealth, or the death of his enemies.

3:12 anyone like you. Solomon was one of a kind in judicial insight, as illustrated in verses 16–27.

3:14 lengthen your days. In contrast to riches and honor that were already his, a long life was dependent on Solomon's future obedience to the Lord's commands. Because of his disobedience, Solomon died before reaching seventy years of age (cf. Ps. 90:10).

3:16–27 harlots came to the king. Here is an illustration of how wisely Solomon ruled. In Israel, the king was the ultimate "judge" of the land, and any citizen, even the basest prostitute, could petition him for a verdict (2 Sam. 14:2–21; 15:1–4; 2 Kin. 8:1–6).

3:25 half . . . half. In ordering his servants to cut the child in two, Solomon knew the liar would not object, but out of maternal compassion the real mother would (cf. Ex. 21:35).

3:28 feared the king. Israel was in awe of and willing to submit to the rule of Solomon because of his wisdom from God.

4:1 all Israel. Solomon was in firm control of all the people. Israel's squabbling factions had fallen in line behind the king.

4:2 Azariah . . . the son of. Actually, he was the son of Ahimaaz and the grandson of Zadok, as "son of" can mean "descendant of" (cf. 1 Chr. 6:8, 9). In David's roster of officials, the army commander came first (2 Sam. 8:16; 20:23). Under Solomon, the priest and other officials preceded the military leader.

4:3 scribes. They probably prepared royal edicts and kept official records. **recorder.** Likely, he maintained the records of all important daily affairs in the kingdom.

4:4 priests. Zadok and Abiathar had served together as high priests under David (2 Sam. 8:17; 20:25). Although Abiathar had been removed from priestly service and exiled (2:26, 27, 35), he maintained his priestly title until his death.

4:5 Nathan. Whether this is the prophet Nathan (*see note on 1:8*) or another person by that name is uncertain, but it could be that Solomon was honoring the sons of the prophet.

4:6 over the household. One who managed Solomon's properties, both lands and buildings (cf. 16:9; 18:3; 2 Kin. 18:18, 37; 19:2). **over the labor force.** One who oversaw the conscripted workers of Solomon (cf. 5:13–18).

4:7 twelve governors. Solomon divided the land into twelve geographical districts (different from the tribal boundaries), each supervised by a governor. Each month a different governor collected provisions in his district to supply the king and his staff.

4:20 numerous as the sand by the sea. A clear allusion to the Lord's promise to Abraham in Genesis 22:17. The early years of Solomon's reign, characterized by population growth, peace, and prosperity, were a foreshadowing of the blessings that will prevail in Israel when the Abrahamic covenant is fulfilled.

4:21 all kingdoms. The borders of the kingdoms which Solomon influenced echoed the Lord's promise to Abraham in Genesis 15:18. However, Solomon's reign was not the fulfillment of the Abrahamic covenant for three reasons: (1) Israel still only lived in the land "from Dan as far as Beersheba" (v. 25). Abraham's seed did not inhabit all the land promised to Abraham. (2) The non-Israelite kingdoms did not lose their identity and independence, but rather recognized Solomon's authority and brought him tribute without surrendering title to their lands. (3) According to Numbers 34:6, the Mediterranean Sea is to be the western border of the land of promise, indicating that Tyre was to be a part of the Promised Land. However, Hiram king of Tyre was a sovereign who entered into a bilateral or parity treaty (between equals) with Solomon (5:1–12).

4:22 provision. I.e., the daily provisions for Solomon's palace.

4:24 Tiphsah . . . Gaza. Tiphsah was located on the west bank of the Euphrates River and Gaza on the southwestern Mediterranean coast. These towns represented the northeast and southwest points of Solomon's influence.

4:26 forty thousand stalls. Though the Hebrew text reads 40,000, this was probably a copyist's error in transcribing the text, and it should read 4,000 as in 2 Chronicles 9:25.

4:30 the East . . . Egypt. The people east of

Israel in Mesopotamia and Arabia (cf. Job 1:3) and in Egypt were known for their wisdom. Egypt had been renowned for learning and science, as well as culture. Solomon's wisdom was superior to all at home or abroad (v. 31).

4:31 sons of Mahol. This probably meant "singers," a guild of musicians who created sacred songs.

4:32 proverbs . . . songs. Hundreds of Solomon's proverbs have been preserved in the Book of Proverbs (see Introduction to Proverbs). One of his songs is the Song of Solomon, also called the "Song of Songs" indicating that it was Solomon's finest work.

4:33 trees . . . animals . . . birds. Solomon described and taught about all kinds of plant and animal life, e.g., Proverbs 6:6–8; 28:15; 30:19.

4:34 men of all nations. Solomon acquired an international reputation for his wisdom. Many important visitors came from faraway places to learn from Solomon's wisdom (cf. 10:1–13).

C. The Preparations for the Building of the Temple (5:1–18)

5:1–16 See 2 Chronicles 2:1–18.

5:1 Hiram king of Tyre. Tyre was an important port city on the Mediterranean Sea north of Israel. Two towering mountain ranges ran within Lebanon's borders, and on their slopes grew thick forests of cedars. Hiram I ruled there c. 978–944 B.C. He had earlier provided building materials and workers for David to build his palace (2 Sam. 5:11). Solomon maintained the friendly relations with Hiram established by David. They were beneficial to both as Israel exchanged wheat and oil for timber (see vv. 9–11).

5:4 rest. The guarantee of peace with the peoples surrounding Israel allowed Solomon to build the temple (cf. 4:24).

Solomon's Twelve Districts

King Solomon set up a greatly improved administrative plan for Israel. This was needed because he maintained a large standing army, carried out many large building projects, and had a great number of helpers in his palace. He added some official positions to those established by King David. One of these new positions was the "chief of the prefects," who presided over 12 districts that Solomon had created. The district governors, or prefects, collected taxes and the temple tithe, supplied the royal court with food for one month of the year, and helped with the building projects and with the army (1 Kin. 4:1–19).

Thus, our modern management principles of delegation of authority and responsibility were used by early rulers of Judah and Israel.

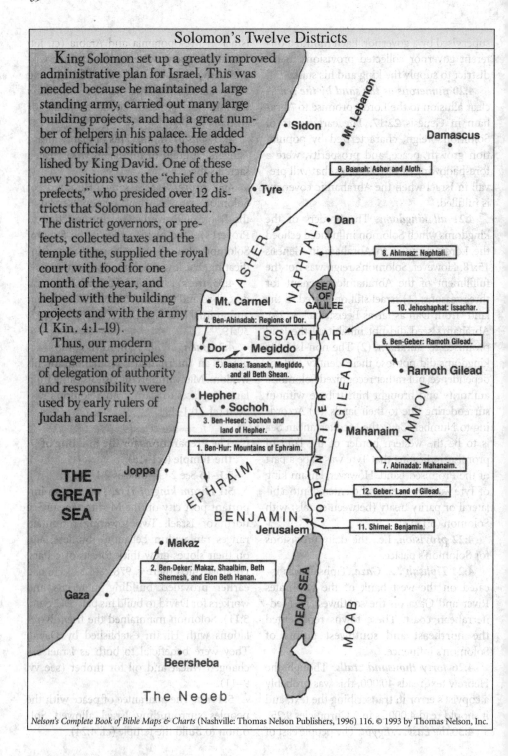

- Sidon
- Mt. Lebanon
- Damascus
- 9. Baanah: Asher and Aloth.
- Tyre
- Dan
- 8. Ahimaaz: Naphtali.
- ASHER
- NAPHTALI
- SEA OF GALILEE
- Mt. Carmel
- 4. Ben-Abinadab: Regions of Dor.
- ISSACHAR
- 10. Jehoshaphat: Issachar.
- Dor
- Megiddo
- 6. Ben-Geber: Ramoth Gilead.
- 5. Baana: Taanach, Megiddo, and all Beth Shean.
- Ramoth Gilead
- GILEAD
- AMMON
- Hepher
- Sochoh
- 3. Ben-Hesed: Sochoh and land of Hepher.
- Mahanaim
- 1. Ben-Hur: Mountains of Ephraim.
- JORDAN RIVER
- 7. Abinadab: Mahanaim.
- Joppa
- EPHRAIM
- 12. Geber: Land of Gilead.
- THE GREAT SEA
- BENJAMIN
- Jerusalem
- 11. Shimei: Benjamin.
- Makaz
- 2. Ben-Deker: Makaz, Shaalbim, Beth Shemesh, and Elon Beth Hanan.
- Gaza
- DEAD SEA
- MOAB
- Beersheba
- The Negeb

Nelson's Complete Book of Bible Maps & Charts (Nashville: Thomas Nelson Publishers, 1996) 116. © 1993 by Thomas Nelson, Inc.

5:5 the name. *Name* represents the character and nature of the person indicated. *See note on 3:2.* **Your son.** Solomon claimed to be the promised offspring of David, the fulfillment of the Lord's promise to David in 2 Samuel 7:12, 13. However, Solomon's later disobedience proved that he was not the ultimate, promised offspring (11:9–13).

5:6 cedars . . . from Lebanon. The cedars of Lebanon symbolized majesty and might (Ps. 92:12; Ezek. 31:3). Because it was durable, resistant to rot and worms, close-grained, and could be polished to a fine shine, its wood was regarded as the best timber for building. The logs were tied together and floated down the Mediterranean Sea to Joppa (see v. 9; 2 Chr. 2:16), from where they could be transported to Jerusalem, thirty-five miles inland. **Sidonians.** These are the inhabitants of the city of Sidon, located on the Mediterranean Sea about twenty-two miles north of Tyre. Here, the term probably referred, in a general sense, to the Phoenicians, who were skilled craftsmen.

5:7 Blessed be the LORD. Perhaps Hiram was a worshiper of the true God, but it is equally possible that he was only acknowledging Jehovah as the God of the Hebrews (cf. 2 Chr. 2:16). **a wise son.** Hiram recognized Solomon's wisdom in seeking to honor his father David's desires.

5:9 food for my household. Tyre's rocky terrain grew great trees, but little good food. Hiram asked Solomon to supply food for his court in exchange for his lumber.

5:13 a labor force out of all Israel. Lit. "conscripted labor." These 30,000 men who labored in Lebanon were Israelites of the land. They were sent to Lebanon, 10,000 a month in rotation. For every month they worked, they were off two months, which meant they worked only four months per year. These Israelite laborers must be distin-

guished from the Canaanite remnant who were made into permanent slaves. *See note on 9:21, 22.* The 30,000 Israelites were free and performed the task of felling trees.

5:16 three thousand three hundred. *See note on 2 Chronicles 2:2.* **people who labored.** According to 2 Chronicles 2:17, 18, these 150,000 laborers (5:15) and their supervisors were non-Israelite inhabitants of the land.

5:18 Gebalites. Inhabitants of Gebal, a town located about sixty miles north of Tyre.

D. The Building of the Temple and Solomon's House (6:1–9:9)

6:1–38 See 2 Chronicles 3:1–17; 7:15–22.

6:1 four hundred and eightieth year. Solomon began to build the temple by laying its foundation (v. 37) 480 years after the Exodus from Egypt. The 480 years are to be taken as the actual years between the Exodus and the building of the temple, because references to numbers of years in the Book of Kings are consistently taken in a literal fashion. Also, the literal interpretation correlates with Jephthah's statement recorded in Judges 11:26. **fourth year.** I.e., 966 B.C. Thus, the Exodus is to be dated 1445 B.C.

6:2 cubits. Normally the cubit was about 18 inches. This would make the temple structure proper 90 feet long, 30 feet wide, and 45 feet high. However, 2 Chronicles 3:3 may indicate that the longer royal cubit of approximately 21 inches was used in the construction of the temple. On this measurement, the temple structure proper would have been 105 feet long, 35 feet wide and 52? feet high. The dimensions of the temple seem to be double those of the tabernacle (see Ex. 26:15–30; 36:20–34).

6:3 vestibule. A porch about fifteen feet long in front of the temple building proper.

6:4 windows. Placed high on the inner side of the temple wall, these openings had

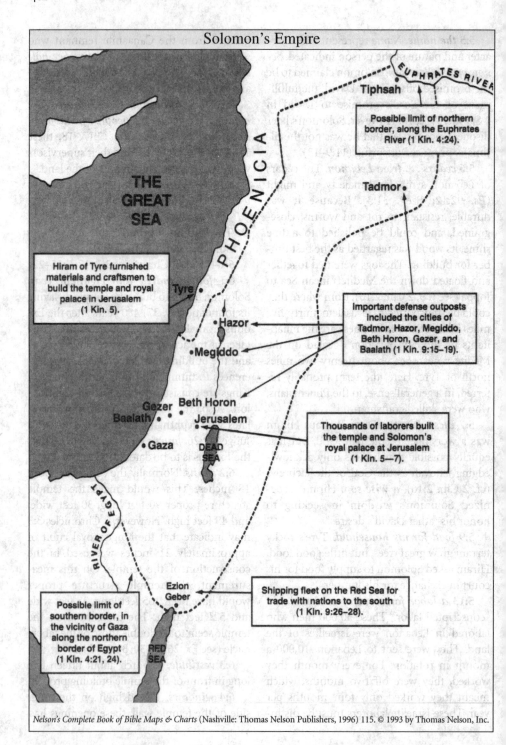

Solomon's Empire

Tiphsah

Possible limit of northern border, along the Euphrates River (1 Kin. 4:24).

EUPHRATES RIVER

Tadmor

THE GREAT SEA

PHOENICIA

Hiram of Tyre furnished materials and craftsmen to build the temple and royal palace in Jerusalem (1 Kin. 5).

Tyre

Hazor

Important defense outposts included the cities of Tadmor, Hazor, Megiddo, Beth Horon, Gezer, and Baalath (1 Kin. 9:15–19).

Megiddo

Gezer **Beth Horon**

Baalath **Jerusalem**

Thousands of laborers built the temple and Solomon's royal palace at Jerusalem (1 Kin. 5—7).

Gaza DEAD SEA

RIVER OF EGYPT

Possible limit of southern border, in the vicinity of Gaza along the northern border of Egypt (1 Kin. 4:21, 24).

Ezion Geber

Shipping fleet on the Red Sea for trade with nations to the south (1 Kin. 9:26–28).

RED SEA

Nelson's Complete Book of Bible Maps & Charts (Nashville: Thomas Nelson Publishers, 1996) 115. © 1993 by Thomas Nelson, Inc.

lattices or shutters capable of being opened, shut, or partially opened. They served to let out the vapors of the lamps and the smoke of incense, as well as to give light.

6:5 *chambers.* Another attached structure surrounded the main building, excluding the vestibule. It provided rooms off the main hall to house temple personnel and to store equipment and treasure (cf. 7:51).

6:6 *lowest . . . middle . . . third.* This attached structure to the temple was three stories high. Each upper story was one cubit wider than the one below it. Instead of being inserted into the temple walls, beams supporting the stories rested on recessed ledges in the temple walls themselves.

6:7 *stone finished at the quarry.* The erection of the temple went much faster by utilizing precut and prefitted materials moved on rollers to the temple site. In addition, the relative quiet would be consistent with the sacredness of the undertaking.

6:8 *doorway . . . stairs.* The entrance to the side rooms of the temple was on the south side, probably in the middle. Access to the second and third stories was by means of a spiral staircase that led through the middle story to the third floor.

6:11–13 During the construction of the temple, the Lord spoke to Solomon, probably through a prophet, and reiterated that the fulfillment of His word to David through his son was contingent on Solomon's obedience to His commands (cf. 2:3, 4; 3:14; 9:4–8). The use of the same words, "I will dwell among the children of Israel," in verse 13 as in Exodus 29:45 implied that Solomon's temple was the legitimate successor to the tabernacle. The Lord forewarned Solomon and Israel that the temple was no guarantee of His presence; only their continued obedience would assure that.

6:16 *the Most Holy Place.* This inner sanctuary, partitioned off from the main hall by cedar planks, was a perfect cube about thirty feet on a side (v. 20) and was the most sacred area of the temple. The Most Holy Place is further described in verses 19–28. The tabernacle also had "a Most Holy Place" (Ex. 26:33, 34).

6:17 *the temple sanctuary.* This was the Holy Place, just outside the Most Holy Place, 60 feet long, 30 feet wide and 45 feet high, that housed the altar of incense, the golden tables of the showbread, and the golden lampstands (7:48, 49).

6:19 *the ark of the covenant of the LORD.* The ark was a rectangular box made of acacia wood. The ark was made at Sinai by Bezalel according to the pattern given to Moses (Ex. 25:10–22; 37:1–9). The ark served as the receptacle for the two tablets of the Ten Commandments (Ex. 25:16, 21; 40:20; Deut. 10:1–5) and the place in the "inner sanctuary" or Most Holy Place where the presence of the Lord met Israel (Ex. 25:22).

6:20 *overlaid it with pure gold.* Cf. verses 21, 22, 28, 30, 32, 35. Gold was beaten into fine sheets, and then hammered to fit over the beautifully embellished wood (vv. 18, 29); it was then attached to every surface in the temple proper, both in the Holy Place and in the Most Holy Place, so that no wood or stone was visible (v. 22).

6:23 *cherubim.* These two sculptured winged creatures, with human faces overlaid with gold (cf. Gen. 3:24; Ezek. 41:18, 19), stood as guards on either side of the ark (see 2 Chr. 3:10–13) and are not to be confused with the cherubim on the mercy seat (see Ex. 25:17–22). The cherubim represented angelic beings who were guardians of God's presence and stood on either side of the ark (8:6, 7) in the Most Holy Place. They were fifteen feet tall and fifteen feet between wing tips (vv. 24–26). *See note on Exodus 25:18.*

6:29 palm trees. An image reminiscent of the Garden of Eden in Genesis 2. The palm tree represented the tree of life from the Garden.

6:31–35 There was distinct and magnificent separation by doors between the inner court of the temple (v. 36) and the Holy Place, as well as between the Holy Place and the Most Holy Place.

6:36 the inner court. This walled-in, open space that surrounded the temple was also called "the court of the priests" (2 Chr. 4:9) or the "upper court" (Jer. 36:10). The wall of that court had a layer of wood between each of the three courses of stone. The alternation of timber beams with masonry was common in Mediterranean construction.

6:37 fourth year . . . Ziv. Cf. 6:1.

6:38 seven years. From foundation to finishing, the temple took seven years and six months to build. *See note on 2 Chronicles 5:1.*

7:1 thirteen years. Having built the house for the Lord, Solomon then built one for himself. Solomon's "house" was a complex of structures that took almost twice as long to build as the temple. The time involved was probably because there was not the same preparation for building or urgency as for the national place of worship. The temple and Solomon's house together took twenty years to complete (cf. 9:10).

7:2–5 the House of the Forest of Lebanon. As a part of the palace complex, Solomon also built this large rectangular building, 150 feet long, 75 feet wide and 45 feet high. It was built of a *forest* of cedar pillars from Lebanon. Three rows of cedar columns supported trimmed cedar beams and a cedar roof.

7:6 the Hall of Pillars. This colonnade

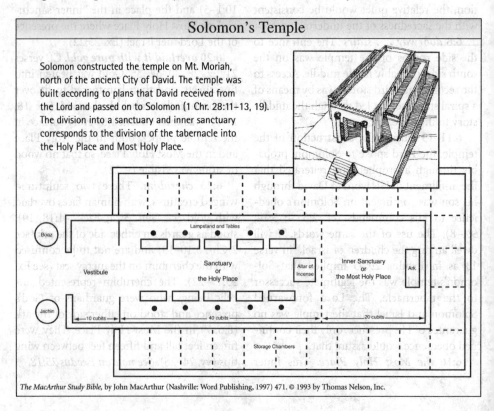

Solomon's Temple

Solomon constructed the temple on Mt. Moriah, north of the ancient City of David. The temple was built according to plans that David received from the Lord and passed on to Solomon (1 Chr. 28:11–13, 19). The division into a sanctuary and inner sanctuary corresponds to the division of the tabernacle into the Holy Place and Most Holy Place.

Boaz

Lampstand and Tables

Vestibule

Sanctuary or the Holy Place

Altar of Incense

Inner Sanctuary or the Most Holy Place

Ark

Jachin

10 cubits — 40 cubits — 20 cubits

Storage Chambers

The MacArthur Study Bible, by John MacArthur (Nashville: Word Publishing, 1997) 471. © 1993 by Thomas Nelson, Inc.

was probably an entry hall or waiting area for the Hall of Judgment, which was most likely used for the transaction of public business.

7:7 the Hall of Judgment. The place where Solomon would publicly hear petitions from Israelites and render judgments was added to the grand palace site.

7:8 house . . . court . . . house. Behind the Hall of Judgment was an open court. Within this court, Solomon built his own personal residence, a palace for his harem, and royal apartments for the Egyptian princess he had married.

7:9–12 A fortune was spent on building, adjacent to the temple, the whole palace with its three parts: (1) the king's home; (2) the courtyard in the middle; and (3) the house of the women on the other side.

7:13 Huram. Although having the same Hebrew name (Hiram), this individual was distinct from the King of Tyre (5:1). Huram had a Tyrian father, but his mother was of the tribe of Naphtali. Second Chronicles 2:14 states that Huram's mother came from the tribe of Dan. Probably one verse refers to her place of birth and the other to her place of residence. Or, if his parents were originally from the two tribes, then he could legitimately claim either. The description of Huram's skills in verse 14 is exactly the same as that of Bezalel who made the tabernacle (Ex. 31:3; 36:1). Huram made the pillars (vv. 14– 22). *See note on 2 Chronicles 2:13, 14.*

7:15 two pillars. One bronze pillar was on each side of the temple's entrance (v. 21). Each pillar was 27 feet high and 18 feet around. *See note on 2 Chronicles 3:15.*

7:16 capitals. These distinctively treated upper ends of the bronze pillars, added 7.5 feet to the height of each pillar.

7:18 pomegranates. One of the fruits of the Promised Land (Num. 13:23; Deut. 8:8),

these were popular, decorative motifs used on the hem of Aaron's priestly garment (Ex. 28:33, 34).

7:21 Jachin . . . Boaz. These names meant "He shall establish" and "In it is strength," respectively. It is likely that each name recalls promises given to the Davidic house, and that they perpetually reminded the worshipers of God's grace in providing the Davidic monarchy, as well as each king's need to depend on God for his success. *See note on 2 Chronicles 3:17.* They were also symbolic of the strength and stability of God's promise of a kingdom forever, even though the temple would come down (see Jer. 52:17).

7:23 the Sea. A huge circular bronze basin corresponding to the laver of the tabernacle. According to verse 26, this great basin's capacity was about 12,000 gallons (*see note on 2 Chr. 4:5*). The sea stood in the courtyard on the temple's southeast side and provided the priests water to wash themselves and their sacrifices (2 Chr. 4:6). It probably also supplied water for the ten movable basins (vv. 38, 39). *See note on 2 Chronicles 4:2.*

7:25 twelve oxen. Huram arranged three oxen facing in each of the four directions of the compass to support the sea. *See note on 2 Chronicles 4:4.*

7:26 two thousand baths. *See note on 2 Chronicles 4:5.*

7:27–37 carts. Huram made ten movable stands of bronze 6 feet square and 4.5 feet high. Each consisted of 4 upright corner poles joined together by square panels. For mobility, the stands rode on four wheels of bronze (v. 30).

7:38 lavers. Huram made ten bronze basins as water containers for the stands. Each measured six feet across and held about 240 gallons of water.

7:40 the shovels and the bowls. Shovels were used to scoop up the ashes that were then emptied into the bowls for disposal. The same tools served the same purpose in the tabernacle (Ex. 27:3).

7:45 burnished bronze. I.e., bronze polished to a high shine.

7:46 between Succoth and Zaretan. Succoth was located on the east side of the Jordan River just north of the Jabbok River (Gen. 33:17; Josh. 13:27; Judg. 8:4, 5). Zaretan was nearby. This location was conducive to good metallurgy, because it abounded in clay suitable for molds and lay close to a source of charcoal for heat, namely, the forests across the Jordan River.

7:48 the altar of gold. The altar of incense stood in front of the Most Holy Place (cf. Ex. 30:1–4). **the table of gold.** The table was made on which the showbread was placed, which the law required to be continually in God's presence (Ex. 25:30).

7:49 lampstands. Ten golden lampstands standing directly in front of the Most Holy Place, five on either side of the doors, provided a corridor of light.

7:51 David had dedicated. Solomon deposited that which David had dedicated to the Lord (2 Sam. 8:7–12) in the side rooms of the temple.

8:1–21 See 2 Chronicles 5:2–6:11.

8:1 elders . . . heads. The *elders* of Israel were respected men who were in charge of local government and justice throughout Israel (Ex. 18:13–26; Num. 11:16–30; 1 Sam. 8:1–9). They advised the king on important matters of state (12:6–11; 1 Sam. 15:30; 2 Sam. 17:5). The *heads* of the tribes or *chief fathers* were the oldest living males within each extended family unit. They were the ones responsible for learning the law and leading their families to obey it.

8:2 seventh month. Solomon finished building the temple in the eighth month of the previous year (6:38; see 2 Chr. 5:1); all its detail signified the magnificence and beauty of God's nature and His transcendent, uncommon glory. The celebration, then, did not take place until eleven months later. Apparently, Solomon intentionally scheduled the dedication of the temple to coincide with the Feast of Tabernacles held in the seventh month, when there would be a general assembly of the people in Jerusalem. That was also a Jubilee year, so it was especially appropriate (Lev. 23:33–36, 39–43; Deut. 16:13–15).

8:4–6 brought up the ark. The ark of the covenant was transported by the priests and the Levites from the tent that David had made for it in Jerusalem (2 Sam. 6:17). They also brought to the temple the tabernacle and all its furnishings which had been located at Gibeon (2 Chr. 1:2–6). The ark was placed in the Most Holy Place (v. 6).

8:7, 8 poles. God had originally commanded that poles be used to carry the ark (Ex. 25:13–15). They were left protruding to serve as a guide so the high priest could be guided by them when he entered the dark inner sanctuary.

8:8 to this day. The phrase is used from the perspective of one who lived and wrote before the destruction of the temple in 586 B.C. The writer of 1 Kings incorporated such sources into his book (cf. 9:13, 21; 10:12; 12:19).

8:9 two tablets of stone. At this time, the ark of the covenant contained only the two tablets inscribed with the Ten Commandments. The pot of manna (Ex. 16:33) and Aaron's rod that budded (Num. 17:10) were no longer in the ark. See Hebrews 9:4.

8:10 the cloud. The cloud was "the glory of the LORD," the visible symbol of God's presence. It signaled the Lord's approval of this new temple. A similar manifestation took place when the tabernacle was dedicated (Ex. 40:34, 35). *See note on Leviticus 9:23.*

8:12–21 See 2 Chronicles 6:1–11.

8:12, 13 Solomon's solemn declaration was addressed to the Lord. Solomon recognized the thick darkness as the manifestation of the Lord's gracious presence among His people (cf. Ex. 19:9; 20:21; Lev. 16:2) and affirmed that he had built the temple so the Lord could dwell there in the glory of thick darkness.

8:14–21 Solomon turned around from addressing the Lord and spoke to the assembly of Israel gathered at the temple. Solomon, in verses 15–19, rehearsed the story of 2 Samuel 7:12–16 and claimed that he, having built the temple, had become the fulfillment of God's promise to his father David (vv. 20, 21). However, Solomon's claim was premature because the Lord later appeared to him and declared the necessity of obedience for the establishment of Solomon's throne (9:4–9), an obedience which would be lacking in Solomon (11:6, 9, 10).

8:22–53 *See note on 2 Chronicles 6:12–40.* Solomon then moved to the altar of burnt offering to offer a lengthy prayer of consecration to the Lord. First, he affirmed that no god could compare to Israel's God, the Lord (vv. 23, 24). Second, he asked the Lord for His continued presence and protection (vv. 25–30). Third, he listed seven typical Israelite prayers that would require the Lord's response (vv. 31–54). These supplications recalled the detailed list of curses that Deuteronomy 28:15–68 ascribed for the breaking of the law. Specifically, Solomon prayed that: (1) the Lord would judge between the wicked and the righteous (vv. 31, 32); (2) the Lord would forgive the sins that had caused defeat in battle (vv. 33, 34); (3) the Lord would forgive the sins that had brought on drought (vv. 35, 36); (4) the Lord would forgive the sins that had resulted in national calamities (vv. 37–40); (5) the Lord would show mercy to God-fearing foreigners (vv. 41–43); (6) the Lord would give victory in battle (vv. 44, 45); and (7) the Lord would bring restoration after captivity (vv. 46–54).

8:22 *spread out his hands.* The spreading of open hands toward heaven was a normal posture of individual prayer (Ex. 9:29; Is. 1:15).

8:27 *heaven . . . cannot contain You.* Solomon confessed that even though the Lord had chosen to dwell among His people in the cloud at the temple, He far transcended containment by anything in all creation.

8:54–61 Solomon arose to pronounce a benediction on the people. His words were substantially a brief recapitulation of the preceding prayer in which he affirmed the faithfulness of the Lord to Israel (v. 56) and exhorted Israel to faithfulness to the Lord (vv. 57–61).

8:62–66 See 2 Chronicles 7:1–10.

8:62 *offered sacrifices.* To complete the temple's dedication, Solomon led the people in presenting peace offerings to the Lord (cf. Lev. 3:1–17; 7:11–21), in which they consumed 22,000 bulls and 120,000 sheep and goats (v. 63). Although the number of sacrifices offered seems high, it was in keeping with the magnitude of this event. Obviously, the single bronze altar could not accommodate such an enormous number of sacrifices. Solomon first had to consecrate the entire middle courtyard, the one directly in front of the temple (v. 64). After consecrating the court, Solomon probably had a series of auxiliary altars set up in the court to accommodate all the peace offerings.

8:65 *the entrance of Hamath to the Brook of Egypt.* The "entrance of Hamath" was located about twenty miles south of Kadesh on the Orontes River and was the northern boundary of the land promised to Israel (Num. 34:7–9; Josh. 13:5). The "Brook of Egypt" is to be equated with Wadi El-Armish in the northeastern Sinai, the

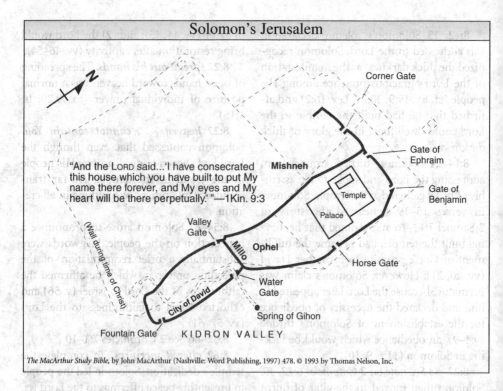

Solomon's Jerusalem

Corner Gate

Mishneh

Gate of Ephraim

Gate of Benjamin

Temple

Palace

"And the LORD said...'I have consecrated this house which you have built to put My name there forever, and My eyes and My heart will be there perpetually.'"—1Kin. 9:3

Valley Gate

(Wall during time of Christ)

Millo

Ophel

Horse Gate

City of David

Water Gate

Spring of Gihon

Fountain Gate

KIDRON VALLEY

The MacArthur Study Bible, by John MacArthur (Nashville: Word Publishing, 1997) 478. © 1993 by Thomas Nelson, Inc.

southern boundary of the land promised to Israel. These locations show that people from all over Israel attended the dedication of the temple.

9:1–9 See 2 Chronicles 7:11–22.

9:1, 2 *finished . . . the king's house.* According to 6:1, Solomon began building the temple in April/May 966 B.C. The temple was completed in October/November 959 B.C. (6:38). The temple dedication and Solomon's prayer to the Lord occurred eleven months after the completion of the temple in September/October 958 B.C. The Lord did not appear to Solomon this second time (cf. 3:5–14) until Solomon had completed the building of his own palace in 946 B.C. (cf. 7:1). Thus, the Lord's response came approximately twelve years after Solomon's prayer and supplication to the Lord recorded in 8:22–53.

9:3 *consecrated.* The Lord made the temple holy by being present in the cloud (cf. 8:10). As proof of the temple's consecration, the Lord told Solomon that He had put His name there (cf. 3:2). *forever.* God was not saying He would dwell in that building forever, since in less than 400 years it was destroyed by the Babylonians (cf. vv. 7–9). He was saying that Jerusalem and the temple mount are to be His earthly throne as long as the earth remains, through the millennial kingdom (see Is. 2:1–4; Zech. 14:16). Even during the eternal state, there will be the heavenly Jerusalem, where God will eternally dwell (see Rev. 21:1, 2). *eyes . . . heart.* These symbolized, respectively, the Lord's constant attention toward and deep affection for Israel. By implication, He promised them access to His presence and answers to their prayers.

9:4–9 See 2 Chronicles 7:17–22.

9:4 *if you walk.* The Lord reiterated to Solomon the importance of obedience to the Mosaic statutes in order to experience the blessings of the Davidic covenant (cf. 2:3, 4).

9:6 *if you . . . turn.* If Israel ("you" is plural) abandoned the Lord to worship other gods, God would expel Israel from the land and destroy the temple (v. 7).

9:9 *this calamity.* The destruction of Jerusalem and exile from the land (v. 8) were predicted by Moses in Deuteronomy 29:24–28. The devastation of the temple, which came in 586 B.C., graphically demonstrated the Lord's anger against Israel's sin, particularly the sin of idolatry.

E. The Further Building Projects of Solomon (9:10–28)

9:10–28 See 2 Chronicles 8:1–18.

9:10 *at the end of twenty years.* The completion of the building of the temple (seven years) and the building of Solomon's palace (thirteen years) would be c. 946 B.C. (*see note on 9:1, 2*).

9:11 *Solomon then gave Hiram twenty cities.* Solomon sold these twenty cities in Galilee to Hiram in exchange for the gold (about 4.5 tons) mentioned in verse 14. Probably these cities lay along the border between Tyre and Israel, just outside the territory of Asher. Later, Hiram gave the towns back to Solomon. *See note on 2 Chronicles 8:2.*

9:13 *to this day.* See note on 8:8.

9:15 *the Millo.* A landfill in the depression between the city of David and the temple and palace complex to the north (see 2 Sam. 5:9). *Hazor.* Ten miles north of the Sea of Galilee, Hazor protected Israel's northeastern entrance from Syria and Mesopotamia. *Megiddo.* Megiddo guarded a crucial pass in the Carmel mountains, which linked the valley of Jezreel and the international coastal highway to Egypt. *Gezer.*

Twenty miles west of Jerusalem, Gezer lay in the coastal plain at the intersection of the coastal highway and the main road to Jerusalem.

9:17 *Lower Beth Horon.* About twelve miles northwest of Jerusalem along a road connecting Gibeon with the western lowlands and providing a western approach to Jerusalem. *See note on 2 Chronicles 8:5.*

9:18 *Baalath.* The designation of several cities in Canaan. *See note on 2 Chronicles 8:6.* *Tadmor.* Probably the same as Tamar, sixteen miles southwest of the Dead Sea on the southeastern boundary of the land (cf. Ezek. 47:19; 48:28). Another Tadmor existed 150 miles northeast of Damascus, which is possibly the reference of 2 Chronicles 8:4.

9:19 *storage cities.* Cities whose primary purpose was to store food (2 Chr. 17:12; 32:28). *cities for his chariots.* Solomon built military outposts for his chariots and horses. To defend his kingdom, these garrisons were probably located along key roads throughout the nation. All the cities listed in verses 15–19 met this requirement.

9:20–23 See note on 2 Chronicles 8:7–10.

9:21, 22 *forced labor.* I.e., "conscripted slave labor." *See note on 5:13.* Only resident aliens permanently became part of this force, since the law did not allow Israelites to make fellow Israelites slaves against their will (Ex. 21:2–11; Lev. 25:44–46; Deut. 15:12–18). Additionally, verse 22 adds that he did not move someone from an established post, even for a specific project.

9:21 *to this day.* See note on 8:8.

9:23 See note on 2 Chronicles 2:2.

9:25 *Solomon offered.* Once the temple had been built, Solomon's practice of sacrificing to God at the various high places ceased (cf. 3:2–4). He kept Israel's three great annual feasts, Unleavened Bread, Pentecost, and Tabernacles (Deut. 16:1–17), at the temple in Jerusalem.

9:26 *Ezion Geber.* Solomon's port located on the modern Gulf of Aqabah.

9:28 *Ophir.* The location of Ophir is unknown. It has been suggested it was located on the southwestern Arabian peninsula. First Kings 10:11, 12 possibly suggests that Ophir was close to or a part of the kingdom of Sheba. *four hundred and twenty talents.* This was about sixteen tons of gold. Second Chronicles 8:18 has 450 talents (*see note on 2 Chr. 8:18*).

F. The Culmination of Solomon's Wisdom and Wealth (10:1–29)

10:1–29 See 2 Chronicles 9:1–28.

10:1 *Sheba.* Sheba was located in southwestern Arabia, about 1,200 miles from Jerusalem. *concerning the name of the* LORD. The primary motive for the queen's visit was to verify Solomon's reputation for wisdom and devotion to the Lord. *hard questions.* Riddles designed to stump the hearer (cf. Judg. 14:12).

10:5 *no more spirit in her.* Lit. the experience "left her breathless."

10:9 *the* LORD *your God.* The queen was willing to credit Solomon's God with giving him wisdom that resulted in just and righteous decisions. Though she recognized the Lord as Israel's national God, there was no confession that Solomon's God had become her God to the exclusion of all others. There is no record that she made any offerings to God at the temple.

10:10 *one hundred and twenty talents.* About four and one-half tons (cf. 9:28).

10:11 *almug wood.* Probably the strong, long-lasting sandalwood, which is black on the outside and ruby red inside.

10:12 *to this day. See note on 8:8.*

10:14 *six hundred and sixty-six talents.* About twenty-five tons of gold.

10:15 Gold also came to Solomon from tolls and tariffs from traders, revenues from loyal administrators, and taxes from Arabian kings who used caravan routes under Solomon's control.

10:16, 17 *shields.* From his gold revenues, Solomon made 200 large shields, containing about 7.5 pounds of gold each, and 300 small shields, having 3.75 pounds of gold each, that were ornamental in design and restricted to ceremonial use.

10:21 *silver.* To show the wealth of Solomon's kingdom, the writer explains that gold was so plentiful that the value of silver dropped to nothing. *House of the Forest of Lebanon.* See note on 7:2–5.

10:22 *merchant ships.* These "ships of Tarshish" were large, all-weather cargo vessels designed to make long ocean voyages.

10:25 *silver and gold . . . horses.* The wisdom God had given to Solomon (v. 24) caused many rulers, like the queen of Sheba (vv. 1–13), to bring presents to Solomon as they sought to buy his wisdom to be applied in their own nations. These gifts led Solomon to multiply for himself horses, as well as silver and gold, precisely what God's king was warned against in Deuteronomy 17:16, 17. Solomon became ensnared by the blessings of his own wisdom and disobeyed God's commands.

10:28 *Keveh.* Keveh was in Cilicia, an area south of the Taurus Mountains in Asia Minor. In antiquity, Cilicia was fabled for breeding and selling the best horses.

10:29 *six hundred shekels.* About fifteen pounds of silver. *one hundred and fifty.* About 3.75 lbs. of silver. *Hittites.* The majority of Hittites lived in Anatolia (Asia Minor). From c. 1720–1200 B.C. a unified kingdom ruled over the Hittites. These kings spread the influence of the Hittites throughout the ancient Near East; the Hittite empire reached the peak of its power c. 1380–1350 B.C. When the Hittite empire collapsed, c. 1200 B.C., many Hittite city-states developed, each with its own king. These rulers were called "the kings of the Hittites" and were scattered in Solomon's day throughout Anatolia and northern Aram (Syria). *Syria.* This familiar geographical area within the bounds set by the Taurus Mountains in the north, the western bend of the Euphrates River and the edge of the desert in the east, the Litani River to the south and the Mediterranean Sea to the west, had Damascus as its major city. *Syria* is actually a later Greek term; the land was known in OT times as Aram.

G. The Decline of Solomon (11:1–43)

11:1–6 *loved many foreign women.* Many of Solomon's marriages were for the purpose of ratifying treaties with other nations, a common practice in the ancient Near East. The practice of multiplying royal wives, prohibited in Deuteronomy 17:17 because the practice would turn the king's heart away from the Lord, proved to be accurate in the experience of Solomon. His love for his wives (vv. 1, 2) led him to abandon his loyalty to the Lord and worship other gods (vv. 3–6). No sadder picture can be imagined than the ugly apostasy of his latter years (over 50), which can be traced back to his sins with foreign wives. Polygamy was tolerated among the ancient Hebrews, though most in the East had only one wife. A number of wives was seen as a sign of wealth and importance. The king desired to have a larger harem than any of his subjects, and Solomon resorted to this form of state magnificence. But it was a sin directly violating God's Law, and the very result which that law was designed to prevent actually happened in Solomon's life.

11:1 *Moabites.* Descendants of Lot (Gen. 19:37) who lived in the land east of the Dead Sea between the Arnon River to the north and the Zered Brook to the south. *Ammonites.* Descendants of Lot (Gen. 19:38)

who were located in the area of the Transjordan beginning about twenty-five miles east of the Jordan River. *Edomites.* Descendants of Esau (Gen. 36:1) who were located in the area south of Moab, southeast of the Dead Sea. *Sidonians. See note on 5:6. Hittites. See note on 10:29.*

11:4 *as . . . David.* Cf. verse 6. David is consistently presented in the Book of Kings as the standard by which other kings were to act and be judged (3:14; 9:4; 14:8; 15:3; 2 Kin. 8:19; 22:2). This was not because David had not sinned (cf. 2 Sam. 11; 12), but because he repented appropriately from his sin (Pss. 32; 51), and because sin did not continue as the pattern of his life.

11:5 *Ashtoreth.* A deliberate distortion of the Canaanite *ashtart,* revocalized based on the Hebrew word for *shame.* She was the goddess of love and fertility, especially worshiped at Tyre and Sidon. *Milcom.* Another name for Molech (v. 7), the national god of the Ammonites. His name seems to mean "the one who rules." The worship of Molech was associated with the sacrifice of children in the fire (Lev. 18:21; 20:2, 3, 4, 5; Jer. 32:35).

11:6 *evil in the sight of the LORD.* The particular evil of Solomon was his tolerance and personal practice of idolatry. These same words were used throughout the book of Kings to describe the rulers who promoted and practiced idolatry (15:26, 34; 16:19, 25, 30; 22:52; 2 Kin. 3:2; 8:18, 27; 13:2, 11; 14:24; 15:9, 18, 24, 28; 17:2; 21:2, 20; 23:32, 37; 24:9, 19). Solomon became an open idolater, worshiping images of wood and stone in the sight of the temple which, in his early years, he had erected to the one true God.

11:7 *Chemosh.* The god of the Moabites, to whom the sacrifice of children as a burnt offering was customary (2 Kin. 3:27). *hill . . . east of Jerusalem.* Probably the Mt. of Olives. This is the area called Tophet in Jeremiah 7:30–34 and the Mt. of Corruption in 2 Kings 23:13.

11:9, 10 *appeared to him twice.* The first time was at Gibeon (3:5), the next at Jerusalem (9:2). On both occasions, God had warned Solomon, so he had no excuses.

11:11 *not kept My covenant.* Solomon failed to obey the commandments to honor God (Ex. 20:3–6), which were part of the Mosaic covenant. Obedience to that covenant was necessary for receiving the blessings of the Davidic covenant (see 2:3, 4). *tear the kingdom away from you.* The Lord's tearing of the kingdom from Solomon was announced in Ahijah's symbolic action of tearing his garment in verses 29–39. The tearing of the robe, picturing the loss of the kingdom, recalls the interaction between Samuel and Saul (1 Sam. 15:27, 28), when the Lord took the kingdom away from Saul because of his disobedience. The great gifts to Solomon followed by his great abuse warranted such a judgment.

11:12 *not do it in your days.* The Lord's great love for David caused Him to temper His judgment with mercy by not disrupting the kingdom in Solomon's lifetime (cf. v. 34). This showed that Solomon's disobedience did not annul the Davidic covenant; the Lord's commitment to fulfill His word to David remained firm (cf. 2 Sam. 7:12–16).

11:13 *one tribe.* The one tribe that remained loyal to the Davidic dynasty was Judah (cf. 12:20). *for the sake of Jerusalem.* The Lord had chosen Jerusalem as the place where His name would dwell forever (9:3). Therefore, Jerusalem and the temple would remain so that the divine promise might stand.

11:14–18 *Hadad the Edomite.* Even though Hadad belonged to the royal family that ruled Edom, he escaped death at the hands of David's army when he was a child, and he fled to Egypt (cf. 2 Sam. 8:13, 14; 1 Chr. 18:12, 13).

11:18 *Midian.* The land directly east of

Edom, to which Hadad first fled on his way to Egypt. *Paran.* A wilderness southeast of Kadesh in the central area of the Sinai Peninsula (cf. Num. 12:16; 13:3).

11:21 *Let me depart.* Like Moses (Ex. 2:10), Hadad's son grew up in Pharaoh's household. As did Moses (Ex. 5:1), Hadad requested that Pharaoh allow him to leave Egypt. Hearing of the deaths of David and Joab, he renounced his easy position and possessions in Egypt to return to Edom in order to regain his throne. His activities gave great trouble to Israel (v. 25).

11:23–25 *Rezon.* After David conquered Zobar (2 Sam. 8:3–8), Rezon and his men took Damascus and established the strong dynasty of Syrian kings that troubled Israel in the ninth century B.C. (cf. 15:18; 20:1).

11:26 *Jeroboam the son of Nebat.* In contrast to Hadad and Rezon, who were external adversaries of Solomon, God raised up Jeroboam from a town in Ephraim as an internal adversary. Jeroboam was from Ephraim, the leading tribe of Israel's ten northern tribes. He was a young man of talent and energy who, having been appointed by Solomon as leader over the building works around Jerusalem, rose to public notice.

11:28 *labor force.* See note on 5:13.

11:29 *Ahijah the Shilonite.* Ahijah was a prophet of the Lord who lived in Shiloh, a town in Ephraim about twenty miles north of Jerusalem. See note on 1 Samuel 1:3.

11:30–32 Here is a monumental prophecy that, because of Solomon's sins, the kingdom would be divided and Jeroboam would rule in the northern area (cf. vv. 35–37).

11:33 See notes on 11:5, 7.

11:36 *a lamp before Me.* A lighted lamp represented the life of an individual (Job 18:6; Ps. 132:17). God promised that David, from the tribe of Judah, would continue to have descendants ruling in Jerusalem (cf. 2 Sam. 21:17; 1 Kin. 15:4; 2 Kin. 8:19).

11:38 *if you heed all that I command you.* The Lord gave the same promise to Jeroboam that He had made to David—an enduring royal dynasty over Israel, the ten northern tribes, if he obeyed God's Law. The Lord imposed the same conditions on Jeroboam for his kingship that He had imposed on David (2:3, 4; 3:14).

11:39 *but not forever.* This statement implied that the kingdom's division was not to be permanent and that David's house would ultimately rule all the tribes of Israel again (cf. Ezek. 37:15–28).

11:40 *kill Jeroboam.* Though the prophecy was private (v. 29), the king heard about it and Jeroboam became a marked man, guilty in Solomon's eyes of rebellion and worthy of the death penalty. ***Shishak.*** Shishak was the founder of the twenty-second dynasty in Egypt. He reigned c. 945–924 B.C. He invaded Judah during the reign of Rehoboam (14:25, 26).

11:42 *forty years.* 971–931 B.C.

II. THE DIVIDED KINGDOM: THE KINGS OF ISRAEL AND JUDAH (12:1–2 KIN. 17:41)

12:1–2 Kin. 17:41 The division of Solomon's kingdom had been predicted by the Lord to Solomon (11:11–13) and through Ahijah to Jeroboam (11:29–37). This section of the Books of Kings shows how the word of the Lord through the prophet was fulfilled and narrates the history of the divided kingdom, Israel (the northern kingdom) and Judah (the southern kingdom), from 931–722 B.C.

A. The Rise of Idolatry: Jeroboam of Israel/Rehoboam of Judah (12:1–14:31)

12:1–14:31 This section describes the disruption of the united kingdom (12:1–24) plus the establishment and royal sanctioning of idolatry in Israel (12:25–14:20) and Judah

(14:21–31). The reigns of Solomon's son, Rehoboam, in the south (c. 931–913 B.C.) and Solomon's servant, Jeroboam, in the north (c. 931–910 B.C.) are discussed. See 2 Chronicles 10:1–12:16.

12:1 *Shechem.* A city located in the hill country of northern Ephraim, thirty miles north of Jerusalem. Shechem had a long and important history as a political and religious center (cf. Gen. 12:6; Josh. 8:30–35; 24:1–28, 32). ***all Israel.*** The representatives of the ten northern tribes assembled to accept Rehoboam as king (cf. 2 Sam. 5:3).

12:2 *heard it.* Jeroboam, in Egypt (11:40), learned about the death of Solomon (11:43).

12:3 *Jeroboam . . . spoke.* The ten northern tribes summoned Jeroboam from Egypt to become their representative and spokesman in their dealings with Rehoboam.

12:4 *yoke.* The hardships that resulted from Solomon's policy of compulsory labor service (cf. 5:13; 9:22; 11:28) and excessive taxes (cf. 4:7) came because the splendor of his courts, the magnitude of his wealth, and the profits of his enterprises were not enough to sustain his demands.

12:6, 7 *the elders.* These were older, experienced counselors and administrators who had served Solomon. They counseled Rehoboam to give concessions to the ten tribes.

12:8–10 *the young men.* The contemporaries of Rehoboam, about forty years of age (cf. 14:21), who were acquainted only with the royal court life of Solomon, recommended that Rehoboam be even harsher on the ten tribes than Solomon had been.

12:10 *My little finger . . . my father's waist!* A proverbial manner of saying he was going to come at them with greater force than Solomon had exhibited (vv. 11–14).

12:15 *from the LORD.* God sovereignly used the foolishness of Rehoboam to fulfill Ahijah's prophecy (11:29–39).

12:16 *David.* These words of Israel (v. 16)

expressed deliberate, willful rebellion against the dynasty of David (cf. v. 19). Defiantly, the Israelites quoted the rallying cry used in Sheba's failed rebellion against David (2 Sam. 20:1). The northern tribes declared that they had no legal tie with David and went their way.

12:17 the children of Israel. People from the northern tribes who had migrated south and settled in Judah.

12:18 Adoram. Sending the chief of taxation and forced labor (Adoniram in 4:6; 5:14) to negotiate with the northern tribes was foolish (cf. v. 4).

12:19 to this day. See note on 8:8.

12:20–24 The kingdom was divided at that point. Israel (the ten northern tribes) had its own king.

12:21 the tribe of Benjamin. The tribe of Benjamin split loyalty and land during the divided kingdom era. According to verse 20, only the tribe of Judah remained completely loyal to the house of David, but in verses 21, 23 it is said that Benjamin was associated with "all the house of Judah," the emphasis being on the tribe of Judah. Certain towns of northern Benjamin, most notably Bethel (v. 29), were included in the northern kingdom. Simeon, the tribe originally given land in the southern section of Judah's territory (Josh. 19:1–9), had apparently migrated north and was counted with the ten northern tribes (cf. 1 Chr. 12:23–25; 2 Chr. 15:9; 34:6). Thus, the ten northern tribes were Reu-ben, Simeon, Zebulun, Issachar, Dan, Gad, Asher, Naphtali, Manasseh, and Ephraim. The southern kingdom was the tribe of Judah only. The twelfth tribe, Benjamin, was split between the two kingdoms. The tribe of Levi, originally scattered throughout both kingdoms (Josh. 21:1–42), resided in Judah during the divided kingdom era (see 2 Chr. 11:13–16).

12:22 the man of God. Cf. 17:24. A com-

mon OT expression designating a man with a message from God who would speak authoritatively on the Lord's behalf (cf. Deut. 33:1; 2 Tim. 3:17). *See note on Deuteronomy 33:1.*

12:24 this thing is from Me. Through the prophet Shemaiah, the Lord commanded Rehoboam and his army not to invade Israel. God, in judgment, had ordained the north-south split (v. 15; 11:29–39), so to attack Israel was to oppose God Himself.

12:25 Shechem. Cf. verse 1. Jeroboam fortified the city of Shechem and made it into his royal residence. Cf. Judges 9:1–47. **Penuel.** Jeroboam also fortified Penuel, a city about ten miles east of the Jordan River on the River Jabbok, asserting his sovereignty over the Israelites east of the Jordan.

12:26 return to the house of David. The

The Land of the Divided Kingdom

The MacArthur Study Bible, by John MacArthur (Nashville: Word Publishing, 1997) 494. © 1993 by Thomas Nelson, Inc.

Lord had ordained a political, not a religious, division of Solomon's kingdom. The Lord had promised Jeroboam political control of the ten northern tribes (11:31, 35, 37). However, Jeroboam was to religiously follow the Mosaic Law, which demanded that he follow the Lord's sacrificial system at the temple in Jerusalem (11:38). Having received the kingdom from God, he should have relied on divine protection, but he did not. Seeking to keep his subjects from being influenced by Rehoboam when they went to Jerusalem to worship, he set up worship in the north (vv. 27, 28).

12:28 two calves of gold. These two calves, probably made of wood overlaid with gold, were presented to Israel as pedestals on which the Lord supposedly sat or stood. He publicly presented them using the very words with which idolatrous Israel had welcomed Aaron's golden calf. He repeated Aaron's destructive sin of trying to make an earthly image of God. *See note on Exodus 32:4.*

12:29 Bethel . . . Dan. Bethel was located about eleven miles north of Jerusalem within the territory of Benjamin (Josh. 18:11–13, 22). It lay at the southern end of Jeroboam's kingdom on the main north-south road to Jerusalem. Israel had long revered Bethel as a sacred place because Jacob had worshiped there (Gen. 28:10–22; 35:1–15). Dan was located in the northernmost part of Jeroboam's kingdom, about twenty-five miles north of the Sea of Galilee. A paganized worship of the Lord was practiced at Dan during the period of the judges (Judg. 18:30, 31).

12:30 this thing became a sin. Jeroboam's policy promoted gross and flagrant violation of the second commandment (Ex. 20:4–6) and led to violation of the first commandment (Ex. 20:3).

12:31 the high places. Jeroboam built minor sanctuaries on high places throughout the land of Israel. Over the centuries these high places became the breeding grounds of Israel's idolatrous apostasy (cf. Hos. 5:1). *See note on 3:2.* **priests.** Jeroboam appointed priests to run his sanctuaries from all his tribes. His action blatantly violated the stipulation that only Aaron's descendants were to hold that office in Israel (Num. 3:10).

12:32 ordained a feast. Jeroboam instituted a religious festival to compete with the Feast of Tabernacles held at the temple in Jerusalem and scheduled it for the fifteenth day of the eighth month (October/November), exactly one month after its divinely ordained Judean counterpart (Ex. 34:22, 23; Lev. 23:33–36, 39, 40).

13:1 man of God. *See note on 12:22.*

13:2 Josiah. He ruled Judah about 300 years later c. 640–609 B.C. (cf. 2 Kin. 22:1–23:30). **sacrifice the priests of the high places.** The prophet predicted that Josiah would slaughter the illegitimate priests of the high places of his day who made offerings on the altar at Bethel. This prophecy was realized in 2 Kings 23:15–20, executing the divine judgment on the non-Levitical priesthood established by Jeroboam (12:31, 32).

13:3 sign. An immediate "wonder" that served to authenticate the reliability of the long-term prediction (cf. Deut. 18:21, 22), this sign came to pass in verse 5. **the ashes on it shall be poured out.** Proper ritual required the disposal of sacrificial ashes in a special "clean" place (Lev. 4:12; 6:10, 11). Contact with the ground would render the ashes "unclean" and nullify the procedure.

13:9 commanded me by the word of the LORD. The prophet's divine commission expressly forbade receiving any hospitality at Bethel. It even required him to return home by a different route from the one by which he came, lest he should be recognized. The prophet's own conduct was to symbolize the Lord's total rejection of Israel's false worship and the recognition that all the people had become apostates.

13:11 *an old prophet.* Here was a spokesman for the Lord who had compromised his ministry by his willingness to live at the very center of the false system of worship, without speaking out against it.

13:18 *He was lying to him.* Why the old prophet deceived the man of God, the text does not state. It may be that his own sons were worshipers at Bethel or perhaps priests, and this man wanted to gain favor with the king by showing up the man of God as an imposter who acted contrary to his own claim to have heard from God. Accustomed to receiving direct revelations, the Judean prophet should have regarded the supposed angelic message with suspicion and sought divine verification of this revised order.

13:20 *the word of the LORD.* The lie arose from his own imagination (cf. Jer. 23:16; Ezek. 13:2, 7), but the true prophecy came from the Lord (cf. Ex. 4:16; Deut. 18:18; Jer. 1:9).

13:22 *your corpse shall not come to the tomb of your fathers.* Israelites buried their dead with the bones of ancestors in a common grave (Judg. 8:32; 2 Sam. 2:32). The lack of such a burial was considered in Israel a severe punishment and disgrace. *See note on Ecclesiastes 6:3–6.*

13:24 *donkey . . . lion.* Both the donkey and the lion acted unnaturally: The donkey did not run and the lion did not attack the donkey or disturb the man's body. Unlike the disobedient prophet, the beasts bent their wills to God's sovereignty.

13:32 *will surely come to pass.* The old prophet instructed his sons to bury him beside the Judean prophet (v. 31). The old prophet was finally willing to identify himself with the message that the man of God from

Judah had given against worship at Bethel.

13:33 *again he made priests.* Unlike the old prophet, Jeroboam did not change his evil ways, but continued appointing priests outside the tribe of Levi to serve the high places (12:30–32).

14:1 *At that time.* Probably indicating a time shortly after the incident recorded in chapter 13. *Abijah.* Meaning "my father is the Lord," Jeroboam's son's name implies that his father desired to be regarded as a worshiper of the Lord at the time of his son's birth. Abijah was referred to as a "child" (vv. 3, 12, 17), a term which can be used from childhood through young adulthood. Of all of Jeroboam's family, Abijah was the most responsive to the Lord (v. 13). Jeroboam's son, Abijah, should not be confused with Rehoboam's son of the same name (*see note on 15:1–8*).

14:2 *disguise yourself.* Probably to avoid recognition by the people. Jeroboam did not want his subjects to know that he was consulting a prophet of the Lord. *Shiloh. See note on 11:29.*

14:3 *take . . . ten loaves.* A simple ordinary food gift added to the disguise (cf. 1 Sam. 9:7, 8; 2 Kin. 8:8). Ten loaves of bread, some cakes, and a jar of honey reflected the means of a common person, not royalty.

14:9 *more evil.* Jeroboam had not only failed to live up to the standard of David, but his wickedness had surpassed even that of Saul and Solomon. He had installed a paganized system of worship for the entire population of the northern kingdom (cf. 16:25, 30; 2 Kin. 21:11).

14:11 *dogs . . . birds.* The covenant curse of Deuteronomy 28:26 was applied to Jeroboam's male descendants.

14:13 *the grave. See note on 13:22.*

14:14 *a king.* I.e., Baasha (15:27–30).

14:15 Ahijah announced God's stern

judgment on Israel for joining Jeroboam's apostasy. Struck by the Lord, Israel would sway like a reed in a rushing river, a biblical metaphor for political instability (cf. Matt. 11:7; Luke 7:24). One day, the Lord would uproot Israel from Palestinian soil and scatter it in exile east of the Euphrates River. The fulfillment of this prophecy is recorded in 2 Kings 17:23.

14:17 Tirzah. Jeroboam had apparently moved his capital from Shechem to Tirzah (cf. 12:25), located in the tribal region of Manasseh, about seven miles northeast of Shechem and thirty-five miles north of Jerusalem. Tirzah was famous for its beauty (Song 6:4).

14:20 twenty-two years. 931–910 B.C.

14:21 seventeen years. 931–913 B.C.

14:22–24 Judah outdid her ancestors in evil, provoking the Lord to jealous anger (v. 22). Signs of idolatrous practice were everywhere (vv. 23, 24). She even practiced sacred prostitution to promote fertility (v. 24). Judah had begun the downward slide toward doom that Israel was in.

14:25 fifth year. 927/926 B.C. **Shishak.** See note on 11:40.

14:27 bronze shields. These bronze shields replaced Solomon's gold shields, which were used as a ransom paid to Shishak. The bronze shields illustrate the sharp decline from the reign of Solomon to Rehoboam.

14:30 war . . . all their days. Many border skirmishes erupted as the armies in the north and south maneuvered for tactical advantage and control of territory (14:19; 15:6). A major battle ultimately erupted during the reign of Abijam (cf. 2 Chr. 13:1–20).

B. Kings of Judah/Israel (15:1–16:22)

15:1–16:22 Having documented the establishment of idolatry in both Israel and Judah (12:1–14:31), the text moves to a quick survey of the kings of Judah and Israel from 913 to 885 B.C. The author notes that the high places remained in Judah (15:14), and the sins of Jeroboam continued in Israel (15:26, 34; 16:13, 19).

15:1–8 Abijam. He was at first called Abijah in 2 Chronicles 13:1, 2. Since Abijam means "father of the sea," and Abijah, "my father is the LORD," he may have had his name changed because of his sin. See notes on 2 Chronicles 13:1–22.

15:2 three years. 913–911 B.C. Parts of years were considered as whole years in this reckoning (cf. v. 9).

15:3 his heart was not loyal. Cf. 11:4, where the same statement was made about Solomon. Cf. verse 14.

15:4 a lamp. See note on 11:36.

15:5 what was right in the eyes of the LORD. This commendation is frequently used in speaking of kings of Judah and means only that they did or did not do what was generally acceptable to God, e.g., verse 11.

15:7 war. See 14:30; 2 Chronicles 13:1–20.

15:9–24 Asa. He was the first of the religiously good kings of Judah (cf. v. 11). See notes on 2 Chronicles 14:1–16:14.

15:10 forty-one years. 911–870 B.C.

15:11–15 Asa did four good things: (1) he removed the "sacred" prostitutes (v. 12); (2) he rid the land of all the idols made by his predecessors (v. 12); (3) he removed the corrupt queen mother and burned the idol she had made; and (4) he placed "holy things," items that he and his father had dedicated to the Lord, back in the temple (v. 15). Though he never engaged in idolatry, Asa's failure was his toleration of "the high places" (v. 14).

15:13 obscene image. This term is derived from the verb "to shudder" (Job 9:6). "Horrible, repulsive thing" suggests a shocking, perhaps even a sexually explicit, idol. Asa

The Kings of the Divided Kingdom

Judah		Israel	
Rehoboam	931–913	Jeroboam I	931–910
Abijah (Abijam)	913–911	Nadab	910–909
Asa	911–870	Baasha	909–886
		Elah	886–885
		Zimri	885
		Tibni	885–880
Jehoshaphat	873–848	Omri	885–874
		Ahab	874–853
		Ahaziah	853–852
Jehoram (Joram)	853–841	Joram (Jehoram)	852–841
Ahaziah	841	Jehu	841–814
Athaliah (queen)	841–835		
Joash (Jehoash)	835–796		
		Jehoahaz	814–798
Amaziah	796–767	Jehoash (Joash)	798–782
Azariah (Uzziah)	790–739	Jeroboam II	793–753
Jotham	750–731	Zechariah	753
		Shallum	752
Ahaz	735–715	Menahem	752–742
		Pekahiah	742–740
Hezekiah	715–686	Pekah	752–732
		Hoshea	732–722
Manasseh	695–642		
Amon	642–640		
Josiah	640–609		
Jehoahaz	609		
Jehoiakim	609–597		
Jehoiachin	597		
Zedekiah	597–586		

The MacArthur Study Bible, by John MacArthur (Nashville: Word Publishing, 1997) 496. © 1993 by Thomas Nelson, Inc.

removed his grandmother, Maacah, the official queen mother, because of her association with this idol. **Brook Kidron.** A seasonal river that ran through the Kidron Valley that marks the eastern boundary of Jerusalem.

15:16 Baasha. Asa, who ruled Judah (c. 911–870 B.C.), enjoyed ten years of peace after Jeroboam's defeat by Abijam (2 Chr. 13:19, 20) until Baasha began attacking. *See notes on 15:27–16:7; 2 Chronicles 16:1–6.*

15:17 Ramah. A strategic town in Benjamin, located about five miles north of Jerusalem along the main north-south highway, built by Baasha, king of Israel, to effectively blockade the city of Jerusalem.

15:18 Ben-Hadad. Ben-Hadad I, the grandson of Hezion (probably Rezon; *see note on 11:23–25,* c. 940–915 B.C.) and the son of Tabrimmon (c. 912–890 B.C.). He was the powerful ruler of the Syrian kingdom (Aramea; *see note on 10:29*), centered in Damascus. The majority of historians think that Ben-Hadad reigned c. 900–860 B.C. and was succeeded by a son or grandson, Ben-Hadad II, who ruled c. 860–841 B.C. (cf. 20:34). Asa sent a sizable gift to influence Ben-Hadad I to break his treaty with Israel, to enter instead a treaty with Judah and invade Israel from the north.

15:20 Ijon . . . Naphtali. The army of

Ben-Hadad I invaded Israel and took cities in the land north of the Sea of Galilee, a conquest giving Syria control of the trade routes to the Mediterranean coast and Israel's fertile Jezreel Valley, and also making Syria a great military threat to Israel. Baasha gave up fortifying Ramah and went to live in Tirzah, the capital of the Northern Kingdom.

15:22 Geba . . . Mizpah. With the threat to Judah from Israel removed, Asa conscripted a Judean labor force to fortify Geba, about six miles northeast of Jerusalem, and Mizpah, about seven miles north of Jeru-salem, using the very building material for those fortifications that Baasha had used at Ramah.

15:25 Nadab . . . two years. 910–909 B.C.

15:27–16:7 Baasha. See note on 15:16.

15:27 Gibbethon. This city, located about thirty-two miles west of Jerusalem, within the territory of Dan, was given to the Levites (Josh. 19:44) but controlled by the Philistines, on whose border it lay.

15:29 he killed all the house of Jeroboam. Baasha, the northern king, in a vicious practice too common in the ancient Near East, annihilated all of Jeroboam's family. This act fulfilled Ahijah's prophecy against Jeroboam (cf. 14:9–11). However, Baasha went beyond the words of the prophecy, since 14:10 specified judgment only on every male, while Baasha killed all men, women, and children.

15:30 This epitaph for wicked Jeroboam of Israel follows through the history of the northern kingdom relentlessly as the standard of sin by which judgment fell on the successive kings (see 15:34; 16:2, 19, 31; 22:52; 2 Kin. 3:3; 10:29, 31; 13:2, 11; 14:24; 15:9, 18, 24, 28).

15:33 twenty-four years. 909–886 B.C.

16:1 Jehu the son of Hanani. Cf. verse 7 This Hanani may have been the prophet who warned Judah's King Asa (2 Chr. 16:7–9). Jehu, like Ahijah before him (14:7–16), delivered the Lord's message of judgment to the king of Israel. The pattern emerges in the Book of Kings that the Lord used His prophets as a legitimate means by which to confront the sin of Israel's kings.

16:2–4 Baasha had angered the Lord by following the sinful paths of Jeroboam. Appropriately, he faced the same humiliating judgment Jeroboam had (14:10, 11). Though he waded through slaughter to his throne, he owed it to the permission of God, by whom all kings reign. His judgment was that no long line of heirs would succeed him; instead, his family would be totally annihilated and their corpses shamefully scavenged by hungry dogs and birds.

16:8–14 Elah . . . two years. C. 886–885 B.C.

16:11 friends. I.e., "relatives able to redeem." Cf. Ruth 2:1. Zimri not only killed Elah and his immediate sons, but all of the extended relatives of Baasha who could help his family.

16:15 seven days. Zimri's reign (885 B.C.) was the shortest of any king of Israel. **Gibbethon.** See note on 15:27.

16:16 Omri. When the soldiers of Israel in the field heard of Elah's death, they immediately acclaimed Omri, the commander of Israel's army, as the new king.

16:21 Tibni. The death of Zimri (vv. 17, 18) automatically placed the kingdom in Omri's hands. Half of the population, including the army, sided with Omri, but the other half backed Tibni. Nothing further is known of Tibni, but he was strong enough to rival Omri for about four years (cf. v. 15 with v. 23).

16:21–28 Omri. He ruled the northern kingdom c. 885–874 B.C.

C. The Dynasty of Omri and Its Influence: The Rise and Fall of Baal Worship in Israel and Judah (16:23–2 Kin. 13:25)

16:23-2 Kin. 13:25 This section is stra-te-gic in the Books of Kings and contains over one-third of the total narrative of the book(s). The coming of the dynasty of Omri to the kingship of Israel brought with it the introduction of Baal worship with official sanction in Israel (16:31, 32). Through intermarriage with the house of Omri, Baal worship penetrated into Judah and corrupted the line of David (2 Kin. 8:18, 27), initiating a gigantic struggle before Baalism was officially eradicated in both Israel and Judah (2 Kin. 9:14–12:21).

1. The introduction of Baal worship (16:23–34)

16:23 twelve years. Omri ruled twelve years (c. 885–874 B.C.), from Asa's twenty-seventh year (16:15) to Asa's thirty-eighth year (v. 29). This notice of his beginning to reign in Asa's thirty-first year must be a reference to his sole rule.

16:24 Samaria. The hill of Samaria, named after its owner, Shemer, was located seven miles northwest of Shechem and stood 300 feet high. Though ringed by other mountains, it stood by itself so that attackers had to charge uphill from every side. This new capital amounted to the northern equivalent of Jerusalem. Its central location gave Israelites easy access to it.

16:29–22:40 Ahab . . . twenty-two years. C. 874–853 B.C.; *see notes on 2 Chronicles 18:1–34.*

16:30 evil . . . more than all who were before him. With Ahab, Israel's spiritual decay reached its lowest point. He was even worse than his father, Omri, who was more wicked than all before him (v. 25). Ahab's evil consisted of perpetuating all the sins of Jeroboam and promoting the worship of Baal in Israel (vv. 31, 32). Of all Israel's kings, Ahab outraged the Lord most (v. 33).

16:31 Jezebel. The wretched wife of Ahab became symbolic of the evil of false religion (cf. Rev. 2:20). **Ethbaal.** His name meant "Baal is alive." The father of Jezebel was the king of Phoenicia (including Tyre and Sidon) who had murdered his predecessor and, according to Josephus, was a priest of the gods Melqart and Astarte.

16:31, 32 Baal. Meaning "lord, husband, owner," Baal was the predominant god in Canaanite religion. He was the storm god who provided the rain necessary for the fertility of the land. The worship of Baal was widespread among the Canaanites with many local manifestations under various other titles, the Tyrians calling him Baal Melqart. The worship of Baal had infiltrated Israel long before the time of Ahab (Judg. 2:11, 13; 3:7; 10:6, 10; 1 Sam. 12:10). However, Ahab gave it official sanction in Samaria through building a temple for Baal (see 2 Kin. 3:2). As David had captured Jerusalem and his son Solomon had built a temple for the Lord there, so Omri established Samaria and his son Ahab built a temple for Baal there.

16:34 Hiel of Bethel built Jericho. The refortification of Jericho was forbidden by God, who had supernaturally destroyed it. But Joshua predicted that a man and his sons would violate God's restriction (*see note on Josh. 6:26*). Two of Hiel's sons died when they sought to help him fortify the city.

2. The opposition of Elijah to Baal worship (17:1–2 Kin. 1:18)

17:1 Elijah. His name means "the LORD is God." The prophet Elijah's ministry corresponded to his name: He was sent by God to confront Baalism and to declare to Israel that the Lord was God and there was no other. **Tishbite.** Elijah lived in a town called Tishbe, east of the Jordan River in the vicinity of the Jabbok River. **not be dew nor rain.** The autumn and spring rains and summer dew were necessities for the crops of Israel. The Lord had threatened to withhold these from the land if His people turned from Him to serve other gods (Lev. 26:18, 19; Deut. 11:16, 17; 28:23, 24). Elijah had prayed for the drought (cf. James 5:17) and God answered. It lasted three years and six months according to James (5:17). The drought proved that Baal, the god of the rains and fertility, was impotent before the Lord.

17:3 Brook Cherith. This was probably a seasonal brook that flowed during the rainy season but dried up when the weather turned hot. It was located east of the Jordan River.

17:6 ravens brought. This was God's supernatural provision, much like the manna and quail during Israel's wilderness wanderings (Ex. 16:13–36).

17:9 Zarephath. A town on the Mediterranean coast about seven miles south of Sidon. Elijah was sent to live there, in a territory controlled by Ahab's father-in-law, Ethbaal. In this way, he showed the power of God in the very area where the impotent Baal was worshiped, as He provided miraculously for the widow in the famine (vv. 10–16).

17:23 your son lives! Canaanite myths claimed that Baal could revive the dead, but here it was the Lord, not Baal, who gave back the boy's life. This conclusively demonstrated that the Lord was the only true God and Elijah was His prophet (v. 24).

17:24 a man of God. *See note on 12:22.* A man of God has a true word from God.

18:1 third year. Cf. James 5:17.

18:2 famine. This was to give Ahab opportunity to repent. He was the cause of national judgment in the famine. If he repented, rain would come.

18:3 Obadiah. His name means "servant of the LORD." He was the manager of Ahab's royal palace and a devout worshiper of the Lord who had demonstrated his devotion to the Lord by protecting 100 of the Lord's prophets from death by Jezebel (vv. 4, 13). This had put him on tenuous ground with Ahab.

18:12 the Spirit of the LORD will carry you. The servant had been asked to tell Ahab that Elijah was present to speak with him (vv. 7, 18), but he was afraid because Ahab was seeking Elijah so intensely. Since Elijah had disappeared from sight earlier (17:5), Obadiah was afraid that the Holy Spirit would carry Elijah away again (cf. 2 Kin. 2:16) and the irrational Ahab would kill him for the false report of Elijah's presence.

18:17 troubler. Such was one who brought misfortune on a community by breaking an oath or by making a foolish oath (Josh. 6:18; 7:25).

18:18 Baals. These were the local idols of Baal (cf. Judg. 2:11). The prophet boldly told Ahab that the calamity of drought and famine was traceable directly to his and his family's patronage and practice of idolatry.

18:19 Mount Carmel. The Carmel range of mountains, rising to 1,800 feet at its highest point, extends about thirty miles to the southeast from the shores of the Mediterranean Sea into the south of the Jezreel Valley. A series of rounded peaks and valleys, it became a symbol of beauty and fruitfulness because of its lush tree cover (Song 7:5; Is. 35:2). It is not known at exactly what point along this ridge the contest between Elijah and the prophets of Baal took place. The queen cared for 850 false prophets who were associated with her.

18:21 falter between two opinions? Lit. "limp along on or between two twigs." Israel had not totally rejected the Lord, but was seeking to combine worship of Him with

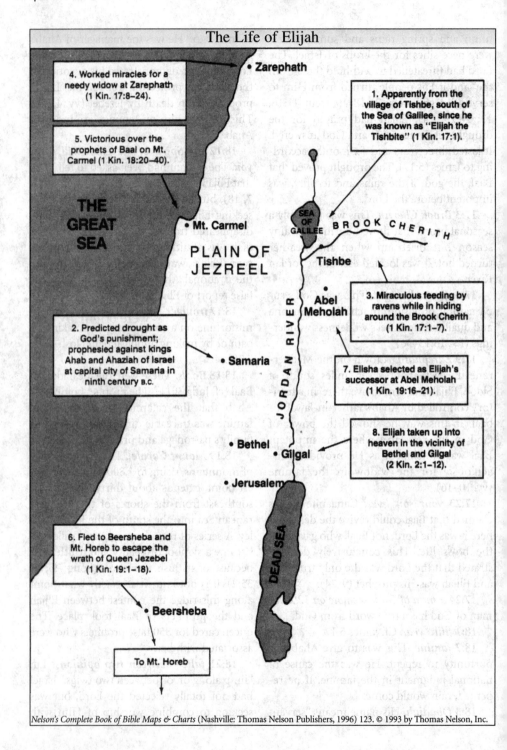

The Life of Elijah

4. Worked miracles for a needy widow at Zarephath (1 Kin. 17:8–24).

1. Apparently from the village of Tishbe, south of the Sea of Galilee, since he was known as "Elijah the Tishbite" (1 Kin. 17:1).

5. Victorious over the prophets of Baal on Mt. Carmel (1 Kin. 18:20–40).

THE GREAT SEA

PLAIN OF JEZREEL

3. Miraculous feeding by ravens while in hiding around the Brook Cherith (1 Kin. 17:1–7).

2. Predicted drought as God's punishment; prophesied against kings Ahab and Ahaziah of Israel at capital city of Samaria in ninth century B.C.

7. Elisha selected as Elijah's successor at Abel Meholah (1 Kin. 19:16–21).

8. Elijah taken up into heaven in the vicinity of Bethel and Gilgal (2 Kin. 2:1–12).

6. Fled to Beersheba and Mt. Horeb to escape the wrath of Queen Jezebel (1 Kin. 19:1–18).

To Mt. Horeb

• Zarephath
SEA OF GALILEE
BROOK CHERITH
• Mt. Carmel
Tishbe
• Abel Meholah
JORDAN RIVER
• Samaria
• Bethel
• Gilgal
• Jerusalem
DEAD SEA
• Beersheba

Nelson's Complete Book of Bible Maps & Charts (Nashville: Thomas Nelson Publishers, 1996) 123. © 1993 by Thomas Nelson, Inc.

the worship of Baal. The issue posed by Elijah was that Israel had to choose who was God, the Lord or Baal, and then serve God wholeheartedly. Rather than decide by his message, Elijah sought a visible sign from heaven.

18:24 *the God who answers by fire.* Since Baal's followers believed that he controlled the thunder, lightning, and storms, and the Lord's followers declared the same (Pss. 18:14; 29:3–9; 104:3), this would prove to be a fair test to show who was God.

18:27 *mocked.* The myths surrounding Baal portrayed him as musing on actions to take, fighting a war, traveling, and even dying and coming back to life. Elijah's sarcastic advice to the prophets of Baal played on these beliefs.

18:28 *the blood gushed out.* Self-laceration was practiced to rouse a god's pity and response in the ancient world, but was prohibited by the OT law (Lev. 19:28; Deut. 14:1).

18:29 *no . . . no . . . no.* This threefold declaration emphasized the lack of response on the part of Baal. The fact that there was no response indicated Baal's impotence and non-existence (Jer. 10:5).

18:31 *twelve stones.* The twelve stones represented the Twelve Tribes, since this contest had significance for both Judah and Israel. Although the tribes had been divided into two nations, they were still one people in the Lord's plans, with the same covenants and a single destiny.

18:32 *two seahs.* This was about four gallons or one-third of a bushel of seed.

18:36 *the evening sacrifice.* This sacrifice was offered around 3:00 P.M. (Ex. 29:38–41; Num. 28:3–8).

18:40 *Seize the prophets.* Taking advantage of the excited feelings of the people over the manifestation of Jehovah as the true God, Elijah called on them to seize the

---

Elijah's Miracles

1. Elijah fed by ravens (1 Kin. 17:1–7)
2. The widow's food was multiplied (1 Kin. 17:8–16)
3. The widow's son resuscitated (1 Kin. 17:17–24)
4. The altar and sacrifice consumed by fire (1 Kin. 18:20–40)
5. Ahaziah's 102 men die by fire (2 Kin. 1:1–17)
6. The Jordan River divided (2 Kin. 2:6–8)
7. Elijah taken to heaven by God's chariot (2 Kin. 2:9–12)

---

priestly imposters and fill the river with their blood, the river that was dried up by their idolatry. ***Brook Kishon.*** This river, which drains the Jezreel Valley from east to the northwest, was in the valley north of Mount Carmel. ***executed them.*** The killing of the 450 prophets of Baal (18:19) fulfilled the law's demands that false prophets be executed (Deut. 13:1–5) and that those embracing idolatry or inciting others to practice it were worthy of death (Deut. 13:13–18; 17:2–7). Further, these deaths were just retribution for Jezebel's killing of the Lord's prophets (vv. 4, 13).

18:41 *eat and drink.* Elijah instructed Ahab to celebrate the end of the drought.

18:42 *bowed down.* Elijah's actions expressed his and Israel's humble submission to God. Elijah prayed for rain this time (cf. 17:1; James 5:17), and God again answered (cf. James 5:18). Since the Lord's curse was lifted, the rains would be coming.

18:45 *Jezreel.* A town located in the tribal allotment of Issachar at the eastern end of the Jezreel Valley, north of Mount Gilboa, about fifty-five miles north of Jerusalem.

Jezreel was Ahab's winter capital (see 21:1), situated between fifteen to twenty-five miles east of the Carmel Range.

18:46 ran ahead. It was customary in the ancient Near East for kings to have runners before their chariots. The prophet showed Ahab his loyalty by rendering to him that service. Empowered by God, Elijah ran on foot ahead of Ahab's chariot the fifteen to twenty-five miles from Mount Carmel to Jezreel.

19:3 he saw. His hope shattered, Elijah fled as a prophet, broken by Jezebel's threats (v. 2), her unrepentant Baalism, and her continuing power over Israel. Elijah expected Jezebel to surrender; when she did not capitulate, he became a discouraged man (vv. 4, 10, 14). **Beersheba.** A city located 100 miles south of Jezreel (18:45, 46) in the Negev, it marked the southern boundary of the population of Judah.

19:4 broom tree. A desert bush that grew to a height of ten feet It had slender branches featuring small leaves and fragrant blossoms. **take my life.** Since Israelites believed that suicide was an affront to the Lord, it was not an option, whatever the distress. So Elijah asked the Lord for death (cf. Jon. 4:3, 8) because he viewed the situation as hopeless. Job (Job 6:8, 9), Moses (Num. 11:10–15), and Jeremiah (Jer. 20:14–18) had also reacted in similar fashion during their ministries.

19:6 cake ... and ... water. As at Cherith and Zarephath (17:6, 19), God provided food and drink for Elijah in the midst of his distress and the surrounding famine.

19:8 forty days. Elijah's trip took over double the time it should have taken. Therefore, the period had symbolic meaning as well as showing literal time. As the people of Israel had a notable spiritual failure and so wandered forty years in the wilderness (Num. 14:26–35), so a discouraged Elijah

was to spend forty days in the desert. As Moses had spent forty days on the mountain without bread and water, sustained only by God as he awaited a new phase of service (Ex. 34:28), so Elijah was to spend forty days depending on God's enablement as he prepared for a new commission from the Lord. As Moses had seen the presence of God (Ex. 33:12–23), so Elijah experienced a manifestation of God. **Horeb.** An alternate name for Mount Sinai, located about 200 miles south of Beersheba.

19:10, 14 Elijah viewed the Israelites as rebels against the Mosaic covenant, a rebellion that his ministry had been unable to arrest (see v. 3). Paul used this incident as an illustration in Romans 11:3.

19:11 the LORD passed by. The three phenomena, wind, earthquake, and fire, announced the imminent arrival of the Lord (cf. Ex. 19:16–19; Ps. 18:7–15; Hab. 3:3–6). The Lord's self-revelation to Elijah came in a faint, whispering voice (v. 12). The lesson for Elijah was that Almighty God was quietly, sometimes imperceptibly, doing His work in Israel (v. 18).

19:15 the Wilderness of Damascus. The Syrian Desert south and east of the city of Damascus, the city located to the northeast of Israel.

19:15–17 The Lord instructed Elijah to anoint Hazael of Syria (see 2 Kin. 8:8), Jehu (see 2 Kin. 9:2), and Elisha (v. 19) for the purpose of commissioning them to destroy Baal worship in Israel. Through these three men, the Lord completed the execution of Baal worshipers that Elijah had begun. Actually, Elijah commissioned only the last of these three men directly; the other two were indirectly commissioned through Elisha. Elisha was involved in Hazael's becoming Syria's king (2 Kin. 8:7–14), and one of Elisha's associates anointed Jehu (2 Kin.

9:1–3). By the time the last of these men died (2 Kin. 13:24), Baalism had been officially barred from Israel.

19:16 Abel Meholah. The hometown of Elisha was located in the Jordan Valley, ten miles south of Beth-Shanon, in the tribal allotment of Manasseh.

19:18 Paul used God's response to Elijah as an illustration in Romans 11:4. **kissed him.** Kissing the image or symbol of Baal was apparently a common act in worship (cf. Hos. 13:2).

19:19 Elisha. This name means "my God is salvation" and belonged to Elisha, the successor to Elijah (see 2 Kin. 2:9–15). **Shaphat.** Elisha's father, whose name meant "he judges." **twelve yoke of oxen.** It was a common practice for several teams of oxen, each with his own plow and driver, to work together in a row. After letting the others pass, Elijah threw his mantle around the last man, Elisha, thus designating him as his successor.

19:20 Go back again. Elijah instructed Elisha to go, but to keep in mind the solemn call of God and not to allow any earthly affection to detain his obedience.

19:21 slaughtered. The slaughter of the oxen was a farewell feast for family and friends, indicating that Elisha was making a decisive break. He followed Elijah and became his servant (lit. "aide," the same term used for Joshua's relationship with Moses in Ex. 24:13; 33:11). Just as Elijah resembled Moses, so Elisha resembled Joshua.

20:1 Ben-Hadad. This was likely Ben-Hadad II of Syria (*see note on 15:18*) who marched on the capital of Israel and demanded surrender by Ahab (vv. 2–6). **thirty-two kings.** These were probably rulers of client city-states in the land of Syria (*see notes on 10:29*).

20:9 I will do . . . I cannot do. Ahab was

The Ministries of Elijah and Elisha

The MacArthur Study Bible, by John MacArthur (Nashville: Word Publishing, 1997) 506. © 1993 by Thomas Nelson, Inc.

willing to give tribute to Ben-Hadad as his vassal (vv. 2–4), but he refused to allow the Syrian king to plunder his palace (vv. 5–8).

20:10, 11 Ben-Hadad boasted that his army would level the hill of Samaria to dust (v. 10). Ahab replied that Ben-Hadad should not boast of the outcome of the battle before it began (v. 11).

20:13 I will deliver it into your hand today. These were the words of assurance given before battles when the Lord was about to fight on Israel's side (Josh. 6:2, 16; 8:1, 18; Judg. 7:2; 18:10; 1 Sam. 23:4; 24:4). Further, the victory would show Ahab that the Lord was in every respect the mighty God He claimed to be. Though the people and king of Israel had dishonored God, He would not utterly cast them off (vv. 14, 15).

20:17–21 The battle strategy was to send out the young leaders who could perhaps draw near to the Syrians without arousing too much alarm and then, at a given signal, initiate a charge, joined by Ahab's main striking force, that would catch the drunken Syrians off guard and throw them into confusion. The glorious victory, won so easily and with such a small force, was granted so that Ahab and the people would know that God was sovereign.

20:22 the spring of the year. Spring was the usual time for battles in the ancient Near East (*see note on 2 Sam. 11:1*), and a prophet warned Ahab that Ben-Hadad would retaliate in the following year.

20:23 gods of the hills. The advisers of Ben-Hadad believed that Israel had won the previous battle because it occurred in mountainous terrain, the area they believed was ruled by Israel's "gods." They counseled Ben-Hadad to strengthen his army and fight Israel again, only on level ground (v. 25). Obviously, this attitude insulted Israel's God, the Lord, who is sovereign over the whole earth (cf. 2 Kin. 19:16–19). That blasphemous depreciation of the Lord's power meant certain defeat for the Syrians (v. 28).

20:26 Aphek. Though several towns in Israel bore the name Aphek, the one mentioned here probably lay about three miles east of the Sea of Galilee, north of the Yarmuk River.

20:27 like two little flocks of goats. Compared to the massive herd of Arameans covering the land, Israel looked like two little goat flocks. Goats were never seen in large flocks or scattered like sheep; hence the description of the two compact divisions.

20:28 man of God. *See note on 12:22.*

20:30 inner chamber. Lit. "a room in a room," a safe, well-hidden place.

20:31 sackcloth . . . and ropes. Sackcloth traditionally symbolized mourning and penitence. Ropes around the heads were symbols of surrender.

20:34 marketplaces. Lit. "streets, outside places." Bazaars were set up in a foreign land (cf. Neh. 13:16), a lucrative market for Israelite goods.

20:35 sons of the prophets. An association of prophets that met and possibly lived together for study, encouragement, and service (*see note on 1 Sam. 10:5*).

20:35, 36 The prophet needed to be wounded as if in battle to carry out the drama. The refusal to do as the prophet said was wrong, as it was a withholding of necessary aid to a prophet of God in the discharge of his duty. It was severely punished as a warning to others (cf. 13:2–24).

20:39–43 The prophet illustrated that, just as a soldier pays dearly for losing a prisoner in war, Ahab will pay for letting Ben-Hadad, the idolatrous enemy of God, live.

20:39 a talent of silver. This was about seventy-five pounds of silver, more than a common soldier could afford and for which debt he would face death.

20:40 your judgment. This "judicial parable" was designed to trap Ahab into announcing the punishment for his own crime (see 2 Sam. 12:1–12). Unknowingly, Ahab declared his own judgment (v. 42).

20:42 utter destruction. By declaring the battles to be holy war (vv. 13, 22, 28), the Lord had put Ben-Hadad and the Syrians under the ban, a reference to something belonging to the Lord and destined to be destroyed (Deut. 7:2; 20:16). By freeing Ben-Hadad, Ahab had disobeyed the law and would suffer the ban in place of Ben-Hadad.

20:43 sullen and displeased. Ahab was resentful and angry because of the Lord's reaction to his actions (cf. 21:4).

21:1 Jezreel. *See note on 18:45.* Ahab had

built a second palace in Jezreel, where he lived when not in the capital at Samaria.

21:2 Give me your vineyard. In Canaanite culture, since land was simply a commodity to be traded and sold for profit, Ahab's offer to Naboth of an exchange of property or offer of purchase was a common transaction in the Near East.

21:3 The LORD forbid. Naboth's words implied that trading or selling his property would be a disregard of the law and, thus, displeasing in God's eyes (cf. 1 Sam. 24:6; 26:11; 2 Sam. 23:17), because the vineyard was his ancestral property. The Lord, the owner of all the land of Israel, had forbidden Israelite families to surrender ownership of family lands permanently (Lev. 25:23–28; Num. 36:7–9). Out of loyalty to God, Naboth declined Ahab's offer.

21:7 You now exercise authority over Israel! This statement can be taken as an exclamation or a question. Either way, Jezebel was rebuking Ahab for not exercising absolute royal power in the matter.

21:8 she wrote letters. Written by the royal scribe, ancient letters were mainly in the form of a scroll sealed in clay or wax with the sender's personal signature. The seal made the contents of the letters a royal mandate and implied that disobedience would certainly lead to some kind of punishment.

21:9 Proclaim a fast. To call an assembly for solemn fasting implied that a disaster threatened the people that could be averted only if they would humble themselves before the Lord and remove any person whose sin had brought God's judgment upon them (cf. Judg. 20:26; 1 Sam. 7:5, 6; 2 Chr. 20:2–4).

21:10 two men. The Mosaic Law required two witnesses in capital cases (Num. 35:30; Deut. 17:6; 19:5). **scoundrels.** Lit. "sons of Belial." These were utterly wicked men. *See note on 1 Samuel 2:12.* **blasphemed God and the**

king. The penalty for cursing God and the king was death (Ex. 22:28).

21:13 outside the city. They hypocritically climaxed their violent murder by killing the innocent Naboth in a place that was in accordance with the Mosaic Law (Lev. 24:14; Num. 15:35, 36). He was stoned to death in the open fields and his sons were killed with him (2 Kin. 9:26), eliminating all possible heirs.

21:19 Elijah's first announcement of judgment applied to Ahab personally. He said that the dogs would lick Ahab's blood in the same place that Naboth died, outside the city of Jezreel. This prophecy was not fulfilled because of his repentance (vv. 27–29), but was partially fulfilled in the licking of Ahab's blood by dogs at the pool in Samaria (22:37, 38).

21:21–24 Elijah's second announcement of judgment applied to Ahab and his house. The judgment was virtually identical with one made to Jeroboam (14:10, 11) and similar to the one made to Baasha (16:3, 4).

21:23 concerning Jezebel. Jezebel was singled out for judgment because of her initiative in driving Ahab in the promotion of Baalism (v. 25). Elijah's prophecy concerning her was literally fulfilled in 2 Kings 9:10, 30–37.

21:27 tore his clothes. The tearing of garments was a common expression of grief, terror, or repentance in the face of great personal or national calamity (Num. 14:6; Josh. 7:6; Judg. 11:35; 2 Sam. 1:2; 3:31).

21:29 days of his son. Since Ahab had truly humbled himself before the Lord, he did not see the disaster forecast for him (v. 19). Instead, God postponed it until the reign of his son, Joram, c. 852–841 B.C. (2 Kin. 9:25, 26). Joram died in the field of Naboth (cf. v. 19).

22:1 three years. Israel had peace for three years following the two years of war

The Kings of Judah (Divided Kingdom)

Rehoboam	1 Kings 12:1–14:31; 2 Chronicles 10:1–12:16
Abijam (Abijah)	1 Kings 15:1–8; 2 Chronicles 13:1–22
Asa	1 Kings 15:9–24; 2 Chronicles 14:1–16:14
Jehoshaphat	1 Kings 22:41–50; 2 Chronicles 17:1–20:37
Joram (Jehoram)	2 Kings 8:16–24; 2 Chronicles 21:1–20
Ahaziah	2 Kings 8:25–29; 2 Chronicles 22:1–9
Athaliah (queen)	2 Kings 11:1–16; 2 Chronicles 22:1–23:21
Joash (Jehoash)	2 Kings 11:17–12:21; 2 Chronicles 23:16–24:27
Amaziah	2 Kings 14:1–22; 2 Chronicles 25:1–28
Uzziah (Azariah)	2 Kings 15:1–7; 2 Chronicles 26:1–23
Jotham	2 Kings 15:32–38; 2 Chronicles 27:1–9
Ahaz	2 Kings 16:1–20; 2 Chronicles 28:1–27
Hezekiah	2 Kings 18:1–20:21; 2 Chronicles 29:1–32:33
Manasseh	2 Kings 21:1–18; 2 Chronicles 33:1–20
Amon	2 Kings 21:19–26; 2 Chronicles 33:21–25
Josiah	2 Kings 22:1–23:30; 2 Chronicles 34:1–35:27
Jehoahaz	2 Kings 23:31–33; 2 Chronicles 36:1–4
Jehoiakim	2 Kings 23:34–24:7; 2 Chronicles 36:5–8
Jehoiachin	2 Kings 24:8–16; 2 Chronicles 36:9, 10
Zedekiah	2 Kings 24:18–25:21; 2 Chronicles 36:11–21

with Syria described in 20:1–34. During this peace, Ben-Hadad, Ahab, and ten other kings formed a coalition to repel an Assyrian invasion. Assyrian records described the major battle fought at Qarqar on the Orontes River in 853 B.C. Though Assyria claimed victory, later events show that they were stopped from further advance southward at that time. With the Assyrian threat neutralized, Ahab turned his attention to the unfinished conflict with Syria.

22:2 Jehoshaphat. The king of Judah, c. 873–848, whose reign is described in verses 41–50. *See notes on 2 Chronicles 17:1–21:3.*

22:3 Ramoth in Gilead. Ramoth was a Levitical city east of the Jordan River in Gilead, on the north border of Gad, the home of Jephthah (Judg. 11:34) and a key administrative center in Solomon's kingdom (4:13). It seems to have been one of the cities that Ben-Hadad should have returned to Israel (20:34).

22:5 inquire for the word of the LORD. Jehoshaphat was willing to help Ahab fight Syria (v. 4), but reminded Ahab of the need to seek the will of the Lord before going into battle (cf. 1 Sam. 23:1–5, 9–13; 2 Sam. 2:1; 5:19–25; 2 Kin. 3:11–20).

22:6 prophets. These 400 prophets of Ahab were not true prophets of the Lord. They worshiped at Bethel in the golden calf center set up by Jeroboam (12:28, 29) and were supported by Ahab, whose religious policy also permitted Baal worship. Their words were designed to please Ahab (v. 8), so they refused to begin with the authoritative

The Kings of Israel (Divided Kingdom)

Jeroboam I	1 Kings 12:25–14:20
Nadab	1 Kings 15:25–31
Baasha	1 Kings 15:32–16:7
Elah	1 Kings 16:8–14
Zimri	1 Kings 16:15–20
Tibni	1 Kings 16:21, 22
Omri	1 Kings 16:21–28
Ahab	1 Kings 16:29–22:40
Ahaziah	1 Kings 22:51–53; 2 Kings 1:1–18
Jehoram (Joram)	2 Kings 2:1–8:15
Jehu	2 Kings 9:1–10:36
Jehoahaz	2 Kings 13:1–9
Jehoash (Joash)	2 Kings 13:10–25
Jeroboam II	2 Kings 14:23–29
Zechariah	2 Kings 15:8–12
Shallum	2 Kings 15:13–15
Menahem	2 Kings 15:16–22
Pekahiah	2 Kings 15:23–26
Pekah	2 Kings 15:27–31
Hoshea	2 Kings 17:1–41

"thus says the LORD" and did not use the covenant name for Israel's God, "LORD."

22:7 *a prophet of the LORD.* Jehoshaphat recognized that the 400 prophets were not true prophets of the Lord, and wished to hear from a true prophet.

22:8 *Micaiah.* His name means "Who is like the LORD?"

22:10 *throne.* A portable, high-backed chair made of wood with arm rests and separate foot stool.

22:11 *Zedekiah.* He was the spokesman for the false prophets. In contrast to verse 6, he used the introductory formula and God's covenant name.

22:15 *Go and prosper.* Micaiah sarcastically repeated the message of the false prophets as he had been encouraged to do

(v. 13). Ahab sensed the sarcasm and demanded that Micaiah tell him the truth (v. 16).

22:17 *sheep that have no shepherd.* The image of the king as a shepherd and his people as the sheep was a familiar one (Num. 27:16, 17; Zech. 13:7). Micaiah's point was that Israel's shepherd, King Ahab, would be killed and his army scattered.

22:22 *a lying spirit.* This must be Satan, whom the Lord allowed to speak through 400 demons who indwelt the 400 false prophets.

22:24 *struck . . . on the cheek.* This was a rebuke by the leader of the false prophets (v. 6) for the perceived insolence of Micaiah and his claim to truly speak for God. It was followed by a sarcastic question asking if the prophet could tell which direction the spirit in Zedekiah had gone.

22:28 *If you ever return.* In accordance with Deuteronomy 18:21, 22, Micaiah declared to Ahab that if he lived to return from the battle, then he had uttered a false prophecy.

22:30 *disguise myself.* Rejecting the prophecy, but fearing it also, Ahab decided not to wear his official robe, but the clothes of an ordinary soldier.

22:31 *only with the king of Israel.* The very Syrian king, Ben-Hadad, whose life Ahab had spared (20:34), singled him out for death.

22:32 *Jehoshaphat cried out.* According to 2 Chronicles 18:31, this was a prayer for the Lord's deliverance. Jehoshaphat's cry showed the Syrians that he was not Ahab.

22:34 *at random.* The Syrian bowman shot at an Israelite soldier, not knowing that it was the disguised Ahab. The arrow found a small groove between the breastplate and the flexible scale armor that covered the lower abdomen and thighs. Instantly, Ahab slumped in his chariot, mortally wounded in the stomach and bleeding to death.

22:38 *while the harlots bathed.* The Hebrew text may read "where" or "while." In either case, the point is the same: Ahab, the spiritual harlot (i.e., idolater), was associated with the physical harlots at his death. *according to the word of the LORD.* Ahab's death fulfilled the prophecies spoken by Elijah (21:19) and Micaiah (v. 17).

22:39 *the ivory house.* Ahab's palace at Samaria had internal walled panels that were made of inlaid ivory, indicative of his kingdom's economic prosperity. *cities that he built.* Archeological excavations show that Ahab strengthened the fortifications of Samaria, Megiddo, and Hazor.

22:41 *fourth year.* A reference to the beginning of Jehoshaphat's reign, after being co-regent with his father Asa, in 870 B.C.

22:42 *twenty-five years.* 873–848 B.C.

22:43 *doing what was right.* Jehoshaphat faithfully followed in his father Asa's footsteps, doing what pleased the Lord. His only major fault, like that of his father, was his failure to close down the high places.

22:44 *made peace.* In 2 Chronicles 19:2, Jehu the prophet rebuked Jehoshaphat for this alliance.

22:45 *made war.* See 2 Kings 3:7–27; 2 Chronicles 17:11; 20:1–30.

22:47–49 Jehoshaphat controlled Edom, which gave him access to Ezion Geber. He sought to emulate Solomon's fleet and wealth (9:26–28), but was unsuccessful. According to 2 Chronicles 20:36, 37, the Lord destroyed his fleet because of Jehoshaphat's alliance to build it with Ahaziah, king of Israel. First Kings 22:49 apparently refers to a subsequent attempt by Ahaziah to continue the joint venture after the disaster.

22:51–2 Kings 1:18 *Ahaziah . . . two years.* 853–852 B.C.

Key Word

Baal: 16:31; 18:19, 21, 26, 40; 19:18; 22:53—lit. means "master," or "husband." Baal refers to pagan gods of fertility and storms throughout the ancient Middle East. Canaanite literature links Baal with the fertility goddess Asherah, who is mentioned numerous times in the Old Testament (2 Kin. 21:7). Worship of these pagan deities included self-mutilation, ritual prostitution, and infant sacrifice. God punished the Israelites for adopting the worship of Baal and Asherah (Judg. 2:11–15; Jer. 19:4–6).

22:53 *he served Baal.* Ahaziah continued the official promotion of Baal worship (cf. 16:31, 32). First Kings ends at this point in the middle of Ahaziah's reign which is picked up in 2 Kings 1:1–18. The explanation for this unusual break is found in Introduction: Title.

Further Study

Davis, John J. and John C. Whitcomb. *A History of Israel from Conquest to Exile.* Grand Rapids: Baker, 1980.

Patterson, R. D. and Hermann J. Austel. *1, 2 Kings,* in Expositor's Bible Commentary. Grand Rapids: Zondervan, 1988.

THE SECOND BOOK OF THE
KINGS

Introduction

See 1 Kings for the introductory discussion and outline.

1:1 *Moab rebelled.* See note on Genesis 19:37, 38; Introduction to Ruth: Background and Setting; cf. 3:4–27.

1:2 *Ahaziah.* This king of the northern kingdom of Israel is not to be confused with Ahaziah of Judah (8:25–9:29). *lattice of his upper room.* Ahaziah's rooftop room was enclosed with crossbars of interwoven reed or wood strips, which shut out direct sunlight while letting in cool breezes. It was not sturdy enough to keep Ahaziah from falling to the ground below (for unexplained reasons). This took place c. 852 B.C. *Baal-Zebub.* This was a local expression of the Baal cult at Ekron (*see note on 1 Kin. 16:31, 32*). Baal-Zebub meant "lord of the flies," suggesting that he was the storm god who controlled diseases brought by flies. On the other hand, the name may have been the sarcastic Israelite parody of Baal-Zebul, meaning "prince Baal" or "exalted lord," a common title for Baal in extrabiblical Canaanite texts. The NT preserved the name in the form Beelzebul, a name for Satan, the prince of the demons (Matt. 10:25; 12:24; Mark 3:22; Luke 11:15). *Ekron.* The northernmost of the major Philistine cities, located about twenty-two miles west of Jerusalem (*see note on 1 Sam. 5:10*).

1:3 *the angel of the LORD.* Although some interpret this as a reference to the preincarnate Christ (e.g., Gen. 16:7–14; Judg. 2:1–4;

see note on Ex. 3:2), probably this reference is to an angelic messenger, like the one sent earlier by the Lord to Elijah (cf. 19:35; 1 Kin. 19:7). The Lord's messenger was in contrast to the messengers of the wicked king (vv. 2, 3, 5). *Elijah.* The record of this unusual prophet to Israel begins in 1 Kings 17:1 and extends to 2 Kings 2:11 (*see note on 1 Kin. 17:1*).

1:4 *you shall surely die.* The Lord's punishment on Ahaziah for consulting a false god instead of the true God was that he would fail to recover from his injuries. This was a merciful application of the Mosaic Law (cf. Ex. 22:20), which demanded death. Cf. verses 16, 17.

1:8 *A hairy man.* Lit. "possessor of hair." This has been interpreted in two ways: (1) Elijah was physically hairy or (2) Elijah wore a garment made of hair. The language supports the second viewpoint that Elijah wore a coarse wool garment girded at the waist with a leather belt. Zechariah 13:4 describes such a garment as belonging to prophets (cf. Matt. 7:15). Further, the NT describes John the Baptist, who came in the spirit and likeness of Elijah, as clothed in camel's hair (Matt. 3:4).

1:9 *Man of God.* A technical title for a man who spoke for God. *See notes on Deuteronomy 33:1; 1 Kings 12:22; 1 Timothy 6:11.*

1:10–12 *fire came down from heaven.* This was the proof that Elijah was a prophet of the Lord and entitled to respect. Additionally, it was an indication that Elijah was like Moses, who also was validated as the Lord's prophet by fire from heaven (Num. 16:35).

1:15 angel of the Lord. See note on 1:3.

1:16 Baal-Zebub. See note on 1:2.

1:17 Jehoram ... Jehoram. The first Jehoram mentioned here was, like Ahaziah (1 Kin. 22:51), a son of Ahab (3:1), who ruled over the northern kingdom of Israel for twelve years, c. 852–841 B.C. (see note on 3:1). The second Jehoram mentioned was the son and successor to Jehoshaphat, who ruled in the southern kingdom of Judah, c. 853–841 B.C. (cf. 8:16–24). **second year.** C. 852 B.C. This was the second year of Jehoram of Judah's co-regency with Jehoshaphat his father (see notes on 3:1; 8:17; 2 Chr. 21:4–20).

3. The influence of Elisha concerning the true God (2:1–9:13)

2:1 by a whirlwind. Lit. "in the whirlwind." This was a reference to the specific storm with lightning and thunder in which Elijah was taken to heaven (v. 11). The Lord's presence was connected with a whirlwind in Job 38:1; 40:6; Jeremiah 23:19; 25:32; 30:23; Zechariah 9:14. **Elisha.** The record of this

prophet, who was the successor to Elijah, begins in 1 Kings 19:16 and extends to his death in 2 Kings 13:20 (see note on 1 Kin. 19:16). **Gilgal.** Although some take this to be the Gilgal located west of the Jordan River near Jericho (cf. Josh. 4:19; 5:9), the close affinity to Bethel (v. 2) and its distance from Jericho (v. 4) seem to indicate that the Gilgal mentioned here was located in the hill country of Ephraim about seven miles north of Bethel.

2:2 Bethel. A town in Benjamin about eight miles north of Jerusalem, where one of Israel's false worship centers was located (see note on 1 Kin. 12:29).

2:3 the sons of the prophets. See note on 1 Kings 20:35. **take away.** The same term was used of Enoch's translation to heaven in Genesis 5:24. The question from the sons of the prophets implied that the Lord had revealed Elijah's imminent departure to them. Elisha's response that he didn't need to hear about it ("keep silent") explicitly stated that Elijah's departure had been revealed by the Lord to him also (cf. v. 5). **from over you.** I.e., from supervising you, an allusion to the habit of students sitting beneath the feet of

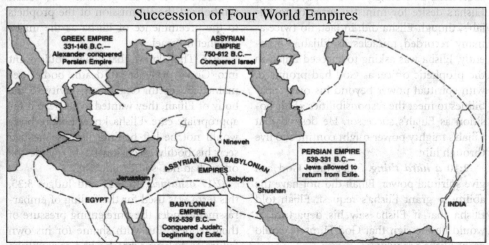

Succession of Four World Empires

GREEK EMPIRE 331–146 B.C.— Alexander conquered Persian Empire

ASSYRIAN EMPIRE 750–612 B.C.— Conquered Israel

PERSIAN EMPIRE 539–331 B.C.— Jews allowed to return from Exile

ASSYRIAN AND BABYLONIAN EMPIRES

Nineveh

Jerusalem

Babylon

Shushan

EGYPT

BABYLONIAN EMPIRE 612–539 B.C.— Conquered Judah; beginning of Exile.

INDIA

Nelson's Complete Book of Bible Maps & Charts (Nashville: Thomas Nelson Publishers, 1996) 287. © 1993 by Thomas Nelson, Inc.

their master, elevated on a platform. Elisha would soon change from being Elijah's assistant to serving as the leader among the prophets.

2:4 *Jericho.* A city about fourteen miles southeast of Bethel in the Jordan River Valley (cf. Josh. 2:1; 6:1), to which Elisha accompanied Elijah (cf. v. 6).

2:8 *water . . . was divided.* Elijah rolled up his cloak into a kind of rod and struck the water of the Jordan River. Immediately, the water parted, leaving a dry path through the river bed for the two prophets to cross. Elijah's act recalled Moses' parting of the Red Sea with his rod (Ex. 14:21, 22) and the parting of the Jordan River when Israel crossed over into the land (Josh. 3:14–17). The crossing put Elijah on the Jordan's east bank, the area where Moses' life came to an end (Deut. 34:1–6).

2:9 *a double portion.* In Israel, the firstborn son inherited a double share of his father's possessions and with it the right of succession (Deut. 21:17). "A double portion of your spirit" was not merely Elisha's request to succeed Elijah in his prophetic ministry, since the Lord had already revealed this succession in 1 Kings 19:16–21. Nor was it Elisha's desire for ministry superior to Elijah's, though Elisha did, in fact, do twice as many recorded miracles as Elijah. Apparently, Elisha was asking to succeed Elijah in the prophetic office, as God had promised, with spiritual power beyond his own capabilities to meet the responsibilities of his position as Elijah's successor. He desired that Elijah's mighty power might continue to live through him.

2:10 *a hard thing.* Since only God can give spiritual power, Elijah did not have the ability to grant Elisha's request. Elijah told Elisha that if Elisha saw his departure, it would be the sign that God Himself would grant Elisha's request.

2:11 *chariot of fire . . . with horses of fire.* The horse-drawn chariot was the fastest means of transport and the mightiest means of warfare in that day. Thus, the chariot and horses symbolized God's powerful protection, which was the true safety of Israel (v. 12). As earthly kingdoms are dependent for their defense on such military force as represented by horses and chariots, one single prophet had done more by God's power to preserve his nation than all their military preparations.

2:12 *My father.* The sons of the prophet recognized the leader of their company as their spiritual father. This title of respect for a person of authority (Gen. 45:8; Judg. 17:10) was later used for Elisha (6:21; 13:14).

2:13 *the mantle of Elijah.* Elijah's cloak (*see note on 1:8*), picked up by Elisha, authenticated him as Elijah's legitimate spiritual successor.

2:14 *water . . . was divided.* Elisha repeated the action of Elijah (v. 8) in using the cloak to part the waters of the Jordan River, allowing Elisha to recross on dry land. This confirmed that Elisha had received from God the same great power as his master, Elijah.

2:15 *bowed to the ground.* This action symbolized the submission of the prophets to the preeminence of Elisha as the major prophet in Israel.

2:16 They knew that when souls went into God's presence at death, bodies remained on earth. Out of sensitivity to the body of Elijah, they wanted to retrieve it for appropriate care. Elisha knew Elijah's body would not be left behind, because he had seen his bodily ascension (v. 11) while the others had not, so he said, "No."

2:17 *ashamed.* In 8:11 and Judges 3:25, this term was used for the feeling of embarrassment under the unrelenting pressure of their request. But with shame for his own failure to believe what he had seen, Elisha was also embarrassed for the prophets, knowing the futile outcome of their search (v. 18). Cf. 1 Kings 18:12.

2:20, 21 bowl . . . salt. Salt purifies water, but the small amount used there could not clean the whole water supply. Rather, the use of salt from a new bowl symbolized the cleansing of the waters that God would miraculously perform. The healing of Jericho's water, through Elisha, freed the city from Joshua's curse, making it habitable for humans once again (cf. Josh. 6:26; 1 Kin. 16:34).

2:23 youths. These were not children, but infidels and idolatrous young men in their late teens or twenties (cf. Gen. 22:12; 37:2; 1 Kin. 20:14, 15). **baldhead.** Baldness was regarded as a disgrace (cf. Is. 3:17, 24). The baldness of Elisha referred to here may be: (1) natural loss of hair; (2) a shaved head denoting his separation to the prophetic office; or more likely, (3) an epithet of scorn and contempt, Elisha not being literally bald. These youths were sarcastically taunting and insulting the Lord's prophet by telling him to repeat Elijah's translation ("go up").

2:24 pronounced a curse. Because these young people of about twenty years of age or older (the same term is used of Solomon in 1 Kin. 3:7) so despised the prophet of the Lord, Elisha called upon the Lord to deal with the rebels as He saw fit. The Lord's punishment was the mauling of forty-two youths by two female bears. The penalty was clearly justified, for to ridicule Elisha was to ridicule the Lord Himself. The gravity of the penalty mirrored the gravity of the crime. The appalling judgment was God's warning to any who attempted to interfere with the prophet's ministry.

2:25 Mount Carmel. For the location, *see note on 1 Kings 18:19.* Elisha associated his prophetic ministry with Elijah's stand against Baalism. **Samaria.** The capital city of the

northern kingdom, located in central Palestine (cf. 1 Kin. 16:24).

3:1 Jehoram. *See note on 1:17.* He was Ahaziah's brother (1 Kin. 22:51). **eighteenth year.** C. 852 B.C. This was Jehoshaphat of Judah's eighteenth year of rule after the death of his father Asa in 870 B.C. Jehoshaphat was co-regent with Asa from 873–870 B.C. Jehoshaphat's son Jehoram was co-regent with his father from 853–848 B.C. (*see notes on 1:17; 8:17*). **twelve years.** 852–841 B.C.

3:2 pillar of Baal. This was probably an image of the god Baal that King Ahab had made and placed in the temple he built to Baal (1 Kin. 16:32, 33). This image was only put in storage, not permanently destroyed, because it reappeared at the end of Jehoram's reign (10:26, 27).

3:3 Jeroboam. C. 931–910 B.C. *See notes on 1 Kings 11:26–14:20; 2 Chronicles 9:29–13:20.*

3:4 Mesha king of Moab. According to the Moabite Stone (discovered at Dihon, Moab, in A.D. 1868 and dated to c. 840–820 B.C.), Moab, which is located east of the Dead Sea between the Arnon River and the Brook Zered, had been Israel's vassal since Omri (c. 880 B.C.). Moab's king, Mesha, was a sheep breeder (cf. Amos 1:1) who supplied the king of Israel with lambs and wool. This was Moab's annual tribute to the Israelite king.

3:5 Moab rebelled. Mesha used Ahab's death as an opportunity to cast off the political domination of Israel with its heavy economic burden. Moab's rebellion took place in 853 B.C. during the reign of Ahaziah (1:1). Jehoram determined to put down Moab's rebellion upon his accession to Israel's throne in 852 B.C. He mobilized Israel for war (v. 6) and asked Jehoshaphat of Judah to join him in the battle (v. 7).

3:8 the Wilderness of Edom. This was the long and circuitous route by the lower bend of the Dead Sea, the arid land in the great depression south of the sea known as the Arabah, or an area of marshes on Edom's western side. According to the Moabite Stone (*see note on 3:4*), Mesha's army controlled the northern approach into Moab. Therefore, an attack from the south had a much better chance of success. It was the most defenseless position, and Mesha could not enlist help from the forces of Edom (v. 9).

3:11 *poured water on the hands.* Probably derived from the custom of washing hands before and after meals. The idiom meant that Elisha had personally served Elijah. Jehoshaphat recognized that Elisha was a true prophet of the Lord (v. 12).

3:13 *What have I to do with you?* A Hebrew idiom that expressed the completely different perspective of two individuals (cf. 2 Sam. 16:10). Elisha sarcastically ordered Jehoram to consult the prophets of his father Ahab, prophets of the northern kingdom's deviant religion (1 Kin. 22:6, 10–12), and the prophets of his mother Jezebel, the prophets of Baal and Asherah (1 Kin. 18:19).

3:14 *regard the presence.* Elisha agreed to seek word from the Lord because of his great respect for Jehoshaphat, the king of Judah, who did what was right in the eyes of the Lord (1 Kin. 22:43).

3:15 *a musician.* The music was used to accompany praise and prayer, which calmed the mind of the prophet that he might clearly hear the word of the Lord. Music often accompanied prophecies in the OT (cf. 1 Chr. 25:1).

3:16 *this valley.* Probably the northeast area of the Arabah, west of the highlands of Moab and southeast of the Dead Sea (see v. 8).

3:20 *the grain offering.* This was offered daily (see Ex. 29:38–41). ***water came by way of Edom.*** Divinely created flash floods from the mountains of Edom caused water to flow

in the direction of the Dead Sea. This water was caught in the canals that had been built in the valley (v. 16).

3:22 *water . . . red as blood.* As the Moabites looked down at the unfamiliar water in the ditches dug in the valley below them, the combination of the sun's rays and the red sandstone terrain gave the water a reddish color, like pools of blood. Unaccustomed to water being in those places and having heard no storm (see v. 17), the Moabites thought that the coalition of kings had slaughtered each other (v. 23) and so went after the spoils. The coalition army led by Israel defeated the Moabites, who had been delivered into their hands by the Lord (see vv. 18, 24).

3:25 *Kir Haraseth.* The coalition army invaded Moab and besieged its capital city, Kir Haraseth, located about eleven miles east of the Dead Sea and about twenty miles northeast of the Arabah.

3:27 *his eldest son . . . offered him.* In desperation, hoping for intervention by his idol god, Mesha sacrificed his oldest son to the Moabite god Chemosh. This was done in plain view of everyone inside and outside the city in an attempt to induce Chemosh to deliver the Moabites from disastrous defeat. ***great indignation against Israel.*** It seems best to understand that the king's sacrifice inspired the Moabites to hate Israel more and fight more intensely. This fierceness perhaps led Israel to believe that Chemosh was fighting for the Moabites. Thus, the indignation or fury came from the Moabites.

4:1 *the sons of the prophets.* See note on *1 Kings 20:35.* ***my two sons to be his slaves.*** According to the Mosaic Law, creditors could enslave debtors and their children to work off a debt when they could not pay (Ex. 21:2–4; Deut. 15:12–18). The period of servitude could last until the next year of Jubilee (Lev. 25:39, 40). Rich people and creditors, however, were not to take advantage of the destitute (see Deut. 15:1–18).

4:2 jar of oil. A flask of oil used to anoint the body.

4:4 shut the door behind you. Since the widow's need was private, the provision was to be private also. Further, the absence of Elisha demonstrated that the miracle happened only by God's power. God's power multiplied little into much, filling all the vessels to meet the widow's need (cf. 1 Kin. 17:7–16).

4:8 Shunem. A town in the territory of Issachar near Jezreel (Josh. 19:18), on the slopes of Mount Moreh, overlooking the eastern end of the Jezreel Valley (*see note on 1 Kin. 1:3*). **a notable woman.** The woman was great in wealth and in social prominence.

4:9 man of God. *See note on 1:9.* The woman recognized Elisha as a prophet uniquely separated to God. Elisha's holiness prompted the woman to ask her husband that a separate, small, walled upper room be provided for the prophet (v. 10). The woman must have feared the "holy" Elisha coming into contact with their "profane" room (cf. Lev. 10:10).

4:12 Gehazi. Elisha's personal servant who was prominent here and in 5:20–27. Gehazi probably is the unnamed servant in verse 43; the term *servant* used there was used in 1 Kings 19:21 of Elisha's relationship to Elijah. Throughout this narrative, Elisha contacted the Shunammite woman through Gehazi (vv. 11–13, 15, 25, 29). Gehazi was involved in this ministry so that he might have opportunity to mature in his service to the Lord.

4:13 I dwell among my own people. This reply expressed her contentment, since she wanted nothing.

4:14 no son, and her husband is old. This remark implied two things: (1) she suffered

the shame of being a barren woman (cf. Gen. 16:1; 18:10–15; 25:21; 30:1, 2; 1 Sam. 1:6); and (2) her husband might die without an heir to carry on his name (Deut. 25:5–10).

4:16 No, my lord. In response to Elisha's announcement that she would have a son, the woman asked Elisha not to build up her hopes if she would be disappointed later. Her reply indicated that she felt having a son was impossible. **Man of God.** *See note on 1:9.*

4:17 conceived . . . bore. This was like Abraham and Sarah (Gen. 21:1, 2).

4:19 My head, my head! The child probably suffered sunstroke. The cries of the boy, the part affected, and the season of the year ("reapers") lead to that conclusion. Sunstroke could be fatal, as in this case (v. 20).

4:23 neither the New Moon nor the Sabbath. The first day of the month and the seventh day of the week were both marked with special religious observances and rest from work (cf. Num. 28:9–15). The husband implied that only on such dates would a person visit a prophet. She apparently concealed the death of the child from him ("It is well") to spare him unnecessary grief, in light of the power of the man of God whom she believed might perform a miracle for the boy.

4:25 Mount Carmel. *See note on 1 Kings 18:19.* The distance from Shunem was about fifteen to twenty-five miles

4:26 "It is well." She withheld the real sorrow of her son's death, waiting to tell the prophet Elisha directly.

4:27 by the feet. The grasping of the feet was a sign of humiliation and veneration.

4:28 See verse 16.

4:29 lay my staff on the face of the child. Elisha sent Gehazi ahead because he was younger and, therefore, faster. He may have expected the Lord to restore the child's life when his staff was placed on him, viewing that staff as representative of his own presence and a symbol of divine power (cf. 2:8).

4:34 *stretched himself out on the child.* Like Elijah (see 1 Kin. 17:17–24), Elisha demonstrated the Lord's power over death by raising their son from the dead. Also, like Elijah, part of the restoration process involved lying on top of the boy's body.

4:38 *Gilgal.* *See note on 2:1.* This was about forty miles south of Shunem. ***sons of the prophets.*** *See note on 1 Kings 20:35.*

4:39 *wild gourds.* Probably a kind of wild cucumber that can be fatally poisonous if eaten in large quantities.

4:41 *flour.* The flour itself did not make the noxious stew edible, but a miraculous cure was accomplished through the flour. Like Elijah (cf. 1 Kin. 17:14–16), Elisha used flour to demonstrate the concern of God for man.

4:42 *Baal Shalisha.* The exact location is uncertain. ***bread of the firstfruits.*** Normally, the firstfruits were reserved for God (Lev. 23:20) and the Levitical priests (Num. 18:13; Deut. 18:4, 5). Though the religion in the northern kingdom was apostate, the man who brought the loaves to Elisha was a representative of godly religion in Israel.

4:43, 44 The multiplication of the loaves in accordance with the word of the Lord through His prophet anticipated the messianic ministry of Jesus Himself (cf. Matt. 14:16–20; 15:36, 37; John 6:11–13).

5:1 *Naaman.* A common name in ancient Syria, meaning "gracious, fair." Four phrases describe the importance of Naaman: (1) he was the supreme commander of the army of Syria as indicated by the term *commander* used of an army's highest ranking officer (Gen. 21:22; 1 Sam. 12:9; 1 Chr. 27:34); (2) he was "a great man," a man of high social standing and prominence; (3) he was "an honorable man in the eyes of his master," a man highly regarded by the king of Syria because of the military victories he had won; and (4) he was "a mighty man of valor," a

term used in the OT for both a man of great wealth (Ruth 2:1) and a courageous warrior (Judg. 6:12; 11:1). Severely mitigating against all of this was the fact that he suffered from leprosy, a serious skin disease (cf. v. 27; *see notes on Lev. 13; 14*). ***king of Syria.*** Either Ben-Hadad I or, more likely, Ben-Hadad II. *See note on 1 Kings 15:18.* ***by him the Lord had given victory to Syria.*** Naaman's military success was attributable to the God of Israel, who is sovereign over all the nations (cf. Is. 10:13; Amos 9:7).

5:2 *raids.* Naaman led the Syrian army in quick penetrations across Israel's border (cf. 1 Sam. 30:8, 15). On one of his raids, he captured a young Israelite girl used as a servant, who ultimately told him of Elisha.

5:3 *the prophet . . . in Samaria!* Elisha maintained a residence in the city of Samaria (6:32).

5:5 *king of Israel.* Jehoram. *See note on 1:17.* ***ten talents of silver, six thousand shekels of gold.*** About 750 pounds of silver and 150 pounds of gold.

5:7 *tore his clothes.* This action was a sign of distress and grief (cf. 1 Kin. 21:27). Jehoram thought that Ben-Hadad expected him to cure Naaman's leprosy. Since Jehoram knew that this was impossible, he thought he was doomed to have a major battle with the Syrians. When Elisha heard of Jehoram's distress, he told the king to send Naaman to him for healing (v. 8).

5:11 *surely come out to me.* Because of his personal greatness (v. 1), his huge gift (v. 5), and diplomatic letter (v. 6), Naaman expected personal attention to his need. However, Elisha did not even go out to meet him. Instead, he sent his instructions for healing through a messenger (v. 10). Naaman was angry because he anticipated a personal, cleansing ceremony from the prophet himself.

5:12 *Abanah . . . Pharpar.* The Abanah

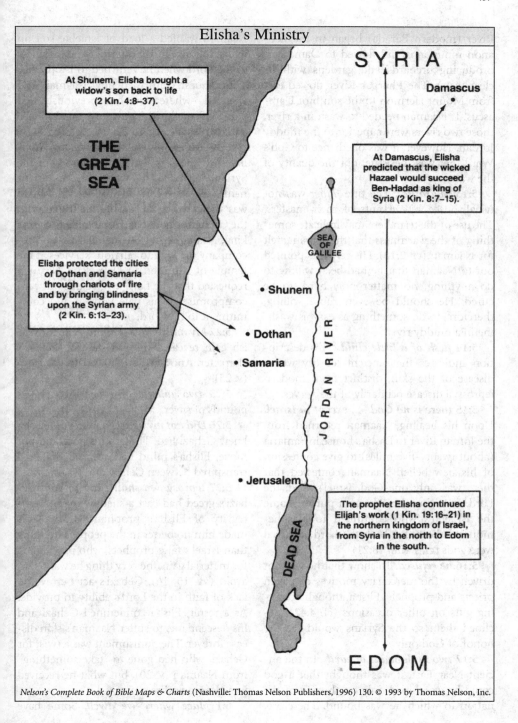

Elisha's Ministry

SYRIA

Damascus

At Shunem, Elisha brought a widow's son back to life (2 Kin. 4:8–37).

At Damascus, Elisha predicted that the wicked Hazael would succeed Ben-Hadad as king of Syria (2 Kin. 8:7–15).

THE GREAT SEA

SEA OF GALILEE

Elisha protected the cities of Dothan and Samaria through chariots of fire and by bringing blindness upon the Syrian army (2 Kin. 6:13–23).

• Shunem

• Dothan

JORDAN RIVER

• Samaria

• Jerusalem

The prophet Elisha continued Elijah's work (1 Kin. 19:16–21) in the northern kingdom of Israel, from Syria in the north to Edom in the south.

DEAD SEA

EDOM

Nelson's Complete Book of Bible Maps & Charts (Nashville: Thomas Nelson Publishers, 1996) 130. © 1993 by Thomas Nelson, Inc.

River (modern Barada) began in the Lebanon mountains and flowed to Damascus, producing orchards and gardens with its clear water. The Pharpar River flowed east from Mount Hermon to the south of Damascus. If Naaman needed to wash in a river, those two rivers were superior to the muddy Jordan. However, it was obedience to God's Word that was the issue, not the quality of the water.

5:13 My father. The title *father* was not usually used by servants of their masters. The use of the term here may indicate something of the warmness that the servants felt for Naaman (cf. 2:12). His servants pointed out to Naaman that he had been willing to do anything, no matter how hard, to be cured. He should be even more willing, therefore, to do something as easy as washing in a muddy river.

5:14 flesh of a little child. This description indicates that ancient leprosy was a disease of the skin, distinct from modern leprosy, a disease primarily of the nerves.

5:15 there is no God . . . except in Israel. Upon his healing, Naaman returned from the Jordan River to Elisha's house in Samaria (about twenty-five miles) to give confession of his new belief. Naaman confessed that there was only one God, Israel's God, the Lord. In saying this, Naaman put to shame the Israelites who continued to blasphemously believe that both the Lord and Baal were gods (cf. 1 Kin. 18:21).

5:16 he refused. To show that he was not driven by the mercenary motives of pagan priests and prophets, Elisha, though accepting gifts on other occasions (cf. 4:42), declined them so the Syrians would see the honor of God only.

5:17 two mule-loads of earth. In the ancient Near East, it was thought that a god could be worshiped only on the soil of the nation to which he was bound. Therefore, Naaman wanted a load of Israelite soil on which to make burnt offerings and sacrifices to the Lord when he returned to Damascus. This request confirmed how Naaman had changed—whereas he had previously disparaged Israel's river, now he wanted to take a pile of Israel's soil to Damascus.

5:18 Rimmon. The Hebrew term *Rimmon* (lit. "pomegranate") is a parody of the Syrian deity, Hadad, whom the Assyrians named *Rananu* (lit. "the thunderer"). Hadad was the storm god, usually identified with the Canaanite god, Baal. As an aide to Syria's king, Naaman's duty demanded that he accompany the king to religious services at the temple of Rimmon in Damascus. Naaman requested that the Lord forgive this outward compromise of his true faith in and commitment to the Lord.

5:22 My master has sent me. A lie for selfish gain revealed the sad state of Gehazi's character. Another lie followed to cover up (v. 25).

5:23 two talents of silver. About 150 pounds of silver.

5:26 Did not my heart go with you. Elisha knew Gehazi lied. Though his body did not move, Elisha's mind had seen all that had transpired between Gehazi and Naaman.

5:27 leprosy . . . shall cling to you. Gehazi's greed had cast a shadow over the integrity of Elisha's prophetic office. This made him no better in the people's thinking than Israel's false prophets, who prophesied for material gain, the very thing he wanted to avoid (vv. 15, 16). Gehazi's act betrayed a lack of faith in the Lord's ability to provide. As a result, Elisha condemned Gehazi and his descendants to suffer Naaman's skin disease forever. The punishment was a twist for Gehazi, who had gone to "take something" from Naaman (v. 20), but what he received was Naaman's disease.

6:1 place where we dwell. Some have

understood the term *dwell* in the sense of *live*. This leads to the conclusion that the sons of the prophets, those specially instructed by Elisha, lived together in a communal setting. However, the term *dwell* can also be understood as "sit before." The term is used this way of David sitting before the Lord in worship (2 Sam. 7:18) and the elders sitting before Ezekiel to hear his advice (Ezek. 8:1; 14:1). Thus, the "place" here refers to a dormitory where Elisha also instructed the sons of the prophets. The growing number of men who wished to be taught led to the need for a larger building.

6:4 Jordan . . . trees. The Jordan Valley had mostly smaller kinds of trees, e.g., willow, tamarisk, and acacia that did not give heavy lumber. The resulting structure would be a humble, simple building.

6:5 iron . . . borrowed. Iron was expensive and relatively rare in Israel at that time and the student-prophet was very poor. The ax head was loaned to the prophet since he could not have afforded it on his own, and would have had no means to reimburse the owner for it.

6:6 made the iron float. Elisha threw a stick in the river at the exact spot where the ax head entered, and the stick caused the heavy iron object to float to the surface. Through this miracle, the Lord again provided for a person who was faithful to Him.

6:8 king of Syria. Either Ben-Hadad I or, more likely, Ben-Hadad II (v. 24). *See note on 1 Kings 15:18.* **making war.** The Syrian king was probably sending raiding parties (v. 23) to pillage and plunder Israelite towns.

6:9 the man of God. I.e., Elisha (v. 12). *See note on Deuteronomy 33:1.* **king of Israel.** I.e., Jehoram. *See note on 1:17.*

6:9, 10 do not pass this place. Elisha, receiving supernatural revelation, continually identified to Jehoram the Israelite towns which the king of Syria planned to attack. Jehoram then took the proper precautions and appropriately fortified those towns in order to frustrate the Syrian plan.

6:11 which of us. The Syrian king was sure someone in his household was revealing his plans to Israel.

6:13 Dothan. A town in the hill country of Manasseh located about ten miles north of Samaria and twelve miles south of Jezreel. Dothan commanded a key mountain pass along a main road that connected Damascus and Egypt (cf. Gen. 37:17). **get him.** The king of Syria's plan was to capture Elisha, who knew all his secrets (v. 12), so that no matter how great Elisha's knowledge might be, he would not be free to inform Israel's king.

Elisha's Miracles

1. The Jordan River divided	2 Kings 2:13, 14
2. Jericho's spring water purified	2 Kings 2:19–22
3. The widow's oil multiplied	2 Kings 4:1–7
4. The widow's son resuscitated	2 Kings 4:8–37
5. Poisonous stew purified	2 Kings 4:38–41
6. The prophets' food multiplied	2 Kings 4:42–44
7. Naaman healed of leprosy	2 Kings 5:1–19
8. Gehazi's leprosy	2 Kings 5:20–27
9. The floating axhead	2 Kings 6:1–7
10. Horses and chariots surrounded the city of Dothan	2 Kings 6:8–17
11. Syrian soldiers blinded	2 Kings 6:18

6:14 *a great army.* In contrast to the smaller raiding parties (vv. 8, 23), the king of Syria sent a sizable force, including horses and chariots, to take Elisha prisoner. Arriving at Dothan, the army encircled the town.

6:16 *those who are with us.* Elisha was referring to God's heavenly army or "host" (cf. Josh. 5:13–15; 2 Chr. 32:7, 8; Dan 10:20; 12:1).

6:17 *open his eyes.* Elisha asked the Lord to enable his servant to see this heavenly host. The Lord gave his servant the ability to see the normally unseen world of God's heavenly armies, here waiting to do battle with the Syrians (cf. Gen. 32:1, 2).

6:18 *blindness.* This word occurs only here and in Genesis 19:11. The term is related to *light* and seems to mean "a dazzling from bright light" (note the "chariots of fire" in v. 17). Both biblical uses of the term involve a miraculous act with angelic presence and both are used in the context of deliverance from danger.

6:19 *Follow me . . . to the man whom you seek.* By going to Samaria himself, Elisha did not lie, but did lead the Syrian army to where he ultimately would be found.

6:20 *inside Samaria!* God delivered a sizable portion of the Syrian army into the hands of the king of Israel without bloodshed. The Syrians discovered they were surrounded and captives of Israel.

6:21 *My father.* See note on 5:13. By using this expression, which conveyed the respect a child had for his father, King Jehoram of Israel acknowledged the authority of Elisha.

6:22 *You shall not kill them.* Elisha, bearing divinely delegated authority, prohibited the execution of the captives. It was uncommon and unusually cruel to put war captives to death in cold blood, even when taken by the point of a sword, but especially by the miraculous power of God. Kindness would testify to the goodness of God and likely stall

future opposition from the Syrian raiders. These kind deeds gained a moral conquest (v. 23).

6:23 *a great feast.* In the ancient Near East, a common meal could signify the making of a covenant between two parties (cf. Lev. 7:15–18).

6:24 *Ben-Hadad. See note on 1 Kings 15:18.* This same Ben-Hadad had laid siege to Samaria earlier (1 Kin. 20:1), which was the result of Ahab's foolish and misplaced kindness (1 Kin. 20:42). *all his army.* In contrast to the smaller raiding parties (vv. 8, 23) and the larger force seeking Elisha's capture (v. 14), Ben-Hadad gathered his entire army, marched to Samaria, and besieged the capital.

6:25 *a donkey's head . . . eighty shekels of silver.* The siege resulted in a terrible famine gripping the city of Samaria. This ignominious body part of an unclean animal (Lev. 11:2–7; Deut. 14:4–8) sold at an overvalued price of about two pounds of silver. *dove droppings . . . five shekels of silver.* Dove droppings was either a nickname for some small pea or root, or literal dung to be used as fuel or food in the desperate situation. Approximately one pint cost about two ounces of silver.

6:26 *Help, my lord, O king!* The woman asked King Jehoram to render a legal decision in her dispute with another woman (*see note on 1 Kin. 3:16–27*).

6:28, 29 *Give your son, that we may eat him.* The curses of the Mosaic covenant, especially for the sin of apostasy, predicted this sort of pagan cannibalism (Lev. 26:29; Deut. 28:52–57). The way in which the woman presented her case without feeling added to the horror of it.

6:30 *tore his clothes.* A sign of distress and grief (*see note on 1 Kin. 21:27*). *sackcloth on his body.* A coarse cloth, made from goat's hair, worn as a sign of mourning (cf. Gen. 37:34). He was not truly humbled for his sins and the nation's or he would not have called for vengeance on Elisha.

6:31 *the head of Elisha.* Jehoram swore an oath to have Elisha killed. The reason Jehoram desired the death of Elisha could have been: (1) the king viewed the siege as the work of the Lord (v. 33), so he assumed that the Lord's representative, the prophet with whom the kings of Israel were in conflict, was involved as well; (2) the king remembered when Elijah had ended a famine (1 Kin. 18:41–46); (3) Jehoram thought that Elisha's clemency to the Syrian army (v. 22) had somehow led to and added intensity to the present siege; or (4) because Elisha had miracle power, he should have ended the famine. But most likely, the reason he wanted Elisha dead was because he expected that his mourning, perhaps counseled by the prophet as an act of true repentance (which it was not; *see note on v. 30*), would result in the end of the siege. When it did not, he sought the prophet's head.

6:32 *the elders were sitting with him.* The elders were the leading citizens of Samaria, whose gathering indicated the high regard in which Elisha was held by the prominent people of Samarian society. *son of a murderer.* This phrase can mean both that: (1) Jehoram was the son of Ahab, who was guilty of murder (1 Kin. 21:1–16); and (2) he had the character of a murderer.

6:33 *why should I wait for the LORD any longer?* Jehoram rightly viewed the Lord as the instigator of the siege and famine in Samaria and declared that he saw no hope that the Lord would reverse this situation.

7:1 *a seah . . . for a shekel.* About seven quarts of flour would sell for about two-fifths of an ounce of silver. *two seahs . . . for a shekel.* About thirteen or fourteen quarts of barley would also sell for about two-fifths of an ounce of silver. These prices, when compared to those in 6:25, indicated that the

next day the famine in Samaria would end. *at the gate.* In ancient Israel, the city gate was the marketplace where business was transacted (cf. Ruth 4:1; 2 Sam. 15:1–5). Normal trade at the city gate of Samaria implied that the siege would be lifted.

7:2 *an officer on whose hand the king leaned. See note on 9:25.* The king depended on this officer as his chief adviser. *you shall see . . . but . . . not eat.* The royal official questioned the Lord's ability to provide food within the day. For that offense against God, Elisha predicted that the officer would witness the promised miracle, but he would not eat any of it. How this prophecy was fulfilled is described in verses 16 and 17.

7:3 *leprous men.* The account of these lepers is used to tell of the siege's end and the provisions for Samaria (vv. 3–11). *at the entrance of the gate.* In the area immediately outside the city gate, four lepers lived, shut out of Samaria because of their disease (Lev. 13:46; Num. 5:3). The lepers knew that living in Samaria, whether just outside or inside the gate, offered them nothing but death.

7:5 *the outskirts of the Syrian camp.* Lit. "the edge of the camp." The normal meaning of this phrase would refer to the back edge of the army camp, the farthest point from the wall of Samaria.

7:6 *the Hittites and . . . Egyptians.* Sometime before the arrival of the lepers, the Lord had made the Syrians hear the terrifying sound of a huge army approaching. They thought the Israelite king had hired two massive foreign armies to attack them. The Hittites were descendants of the once-great Hittite empire who lived in small groups across northern Syria (*see note on 1 Kin. 10:29*). Egypt was in decline at this time, but its army would still have represented a great danger to the Syrians.

7:9 *punishment.* The lepers did not fear that the Syrians would return, but that the

Lord would punish them for their sin of not telling the Israelite king of their discovery.

7:12 *what the Syrians have done to us.* Jehoram greeted the report from the lepers with great suspicion. He thought the Syrians were feigning the pull-back to appear defeated, in order to lure the Israelites out of Samaria for a surprise attack to gain entrance into the city. However, verses 13–15 describe how the leper's report was confirmed.

7:16–20 By repeating words from verses 1 and 2 and by explicit statements ("according to the word of the LORD," v. 16; "just as the man of God had said/spoken," vv. 17, 18), the text emphasizes that Elisha's prophecy in 7:2 literally came to pass.

8:1–6 The chronological question of when the events recounted in these verses took place in Elisha's ministry has been much debated. Interpreters hold to one of three positions: (1) The encounter between the Shunammite woman, the king of Israel, and Gehazi took place toward the end of the reign of Jehoram in Israel. However, this would mean Gehazi was in the presence of the king (vv. 4, 5), although afflicted with leprosy (5:27), and King Jehoram was asking what great things Elisha had done after personally witnessing the events recorded in 6:8–7:19. (2) Because the king of Israel did not know Elisha's exploits, some interpreters place the final encounter during the early reign of Jehu. However, there are still the issues of Gehazi's leprosy and Jehu's being well acquainted with the prophecy of Elijah (9:36, 37; 10:17) that predicted Elisha's ministry (1 Kin. 19:15–18). (3) The best explanation is that the record is out of chronological sequence, being thematically tied to the subject of famine in 6:24–7:20, but having occurred earlier in the reign of King Jehoram of Israel, before the events recorded in 5:1–7:20.

8:1 *a famine . . . for seven years.* Seven-year famines were known in the ancient Near East (cf. Gen. 41:29–32). Since the Shunammite woman would have been only a resident alien in a foreign land, her return within seven years may have aided her legal claim to her property (cf. Ex. 21:2; 23:10, 11; Lev. 25:1–7; Deut. 15:1–6).

8:2 *land of the Philistines.* The area located southwest of Israel along the Mediterranean Sea coastal plain between the Jarkon River in the north and the Besor Brook in the south. The fact that the famine was localized in Israel demonstrated that this was a curse, a punishment for apostasy (cf. Deut. 28:38–40), because of Israel's disobedience of the Mosaic covenant.

8:3 *an appeal to the king.* The Shunammite woman made a legal appeal to the king to support her ownership claim. In Israel, the king was the final arbiter of such disputes (*see note on 1 Kin. 3:16–27*). Providentially, the widow arrived just as Gehazi was describing how Elisha had raised her son from the dead (v. 5).

8:6 *Restore all . . . and all the proceeds.* The king's judgment was to return to the woman everything she owned, including the land's earnings during her absence.

8:7 *Elisha went to Damascus.* It was unusual for a prophet to visit foreign capitals, but not unknown (cf. Jon. 3:3). Elisha went to Damascus, the capital of Syria, to carry out one of the three commands God had given to Elijah at Horeb (1 Kin. 19:15, 16). *Ben-Hadad. See note on 1 Kings 15:18.* Ben-Hadad died c. 841 B.C., the same year as Jehoram of Israel (3:1), Jehoram of Judah (8:17), and Ahaziah of Judah (8:25, 26). *man of God. See note on Deuteronomy 33:1.*

8:8 *Hazael.* His name means "God sees" or "whom God beholds." Hazael was a servant of Ben-Hadad and not a member of the royal family. Assyrian records called Hazael the "son of a nobody," and his lineage was not recorded because he was a commoner.

8:9 *every good thing of Damascus.* The city of Damascus was a trade center between Egypt, Asia Minor, and Mesopotamia. It had within it the finest merchandise of the ancient Near East. Ben-Hadad evidently thought an impressive gift would influence Elisha's prediction. *Your son.* Ben-Hadad approached Elisha with the humble respect of a son for his father (cf. 5:13; 6:21).

8:10 *recover . . . die.* Ben-Hadad wanted to know whether or not he would recover from his present illness. In response, Elisha affirmed two interrelated things: (1) Ben-Hadad would be restored to health; his present sickness would not be the means of his death and (2) Ben-Hadad would surely die by some other means.

8:11 *he was ashamed.* With a fixed gaze, Elisha stared at Hazael because it had been revealed to him what Hazael would do, including the murder of Ben-Hadad (v. 15). Hazael was embarrassed, knowing that Elisha knew of his plan to assassinate the Syrian king.

8:12 *the evil.* Elisha mourned, knowing the atrocities that Hazael would bring on Israel. The harsh actions mentioned here were common in ancient wars (Ps. 137:9; Is. 13:16; Hos. 10:14; 13:16; Amos 1:13; Nah. 3:10). Hazael did prove to be a constant foe of Israel (9:14–16; 10:32; 12:17, 18; 13:3, 22).

8:13 *your servant—a dog.* To call oneself a dog was an expression of humility (*see note on 2 Sam. 9:8*). Hazael sought to deny that he would ever have the power to commit such atrocities. He was trying to convince Elisha that he had no plan to take over the kingship of Syria. *you will become king over Syria.* In response to Hazael's feigned self-deprecation, Elisha affirmed that the Lord willed that Hazael be king over Syria (cf. 1 Kin. 19:15).

8:15 *he died.* Hazael took a bed fur-

nishing, soaked it, and killed Ben-Hadad by suffocation. *Hazael reigned.* Upon Ben-Hadad's death, Hazael took the kingship of Syria and ruled c. 841–801 B.C., during the reigns of Jehoram, Jehu, and Jehoahaz in Israel and Ahaziah, Athaliah, and Joash in Judah.

8:16 *fifth year.* C. 848 B.C., the year Jehoshaphat of Judah died. *Joram.* An alternate name for the king referred to as Jehoram previously (1:17; 3:1, 6). *See notes on 2 Chronicles 21:4–20.*

8:17 *eight years.* 848–841 B.C. *See notes on 2 Chronicles 21:4–20.* Jehoram of Judah served as co-regent with his father Jehoshaphat for the final four years of his reign, 853–848 B.C. Joram (Jehoram) became king of Israel during the second year of this co-regency, 852 B.C. (*see notes on 1:17; 3:1*). Jehoram of Judah ruled alone for eight years after his father's death, until 841 B.C. (cf. 2 Chr. 21:15). Most likely, Obadiah prophesied during his reign.

8:18 *as the house of Ahab.* Jehoram officially sanctioned Baal worship in Judah as Ahab had in Israel (1 Kin. 16:31–33). *the daughter of Ahab.* Jehoram was married to Athaliah, the daughter of Ahab and Jezebel (v. 26). Just as Jezebel incited Ahab to do evil in the sight of the Lord (1 Kin. 21:25), so Athaliah influenced Jehoram. Athaliah's wicked actions are recorded in 11:1–16; 2 Chronicles 22:10–23:15.

8:19 *a lamp . . . forever.* See note on *1 Kings 11:36.*

8:20 *Edom revolted.* Edom had been a vassal of the united kingdom, and of the southern kingdom of Judah since David's reign (2 Sam. 8:13, 14).

8:21 *Zair.* The exact location is unknown.

8:22 *Edom has been in revolt . . . to this day.* During the reign of Jehoram, Edom defeated the Judean army, took some border lands, and became independent of Judah's rule. The continuing sovereignty of Edom proved that none of the future kings of Judah recorded in 2 Kings was the anticipated Messiah because He would possess Edom (cf. Num. 24:18). **Libnah.** A town located in the Shephelah on the border with Philistia, about twenty miles southwest of Jerusalem (Josh. 15:42; 21:13). The revolt of Libnah was probably connected with that of the Philistines and Arabians recounted in 2 Chronicles 21:16, 17.

8:25–29 The reign of Ahaziah (c. 841 B.C.) is not to be confused with that of Israel's King Ahaziah (1 Kin. 22:51–2 Kin. 1:8). *See notes on 2 Kings 9:27; 2 Chronicles 22:1–9.*

8:26 *twenty-two.* This reading is preferred over the *forty-two* of 2 Chronicles 22:2 (*see note there*). **Athaliah.** *See note on verse 18.*

8:27 *like the house of Ahab.* Like his father, Jehoram, Ahaziah continued the official sanctioning of Baal worship in Judah (*see note on v. 18*).

8:28 *Ramoth Gilead.* See note on 1 Kings 22:3.

8:29 *went down to see Joram.* Ahaziah's travel to visit the recuperating Joram (also called Jehoram) king of Israel placed him in Jezreel (west of the Jordan River, southwest of the Sea of Galilee) during Jehu's purge of the house of Omri (see 9:21–29).

9:2 *Jehu.* The Lord had previously told Elijah that Jehu would become king over Israel and kill those involved in the worship of Baal (cf. 1 Kin. 19:17). The fulfillment of the prophecy is recorded from 9:1–10:31. *inner room.* A private room that could be closed off to the public. Elisha commissioned one of the younger prophets to anoint Jehu alone behind closed doors. The rite was to be a secret affair without Elisha present so Jehoram would not suspect that a coup was coming.

9:3 *anointed you king over Israel.* The anointing with olive oil chosen that person to be king (cf. 1 Sam. 10:1; 16:13). This action

of anointing by a commissioned prophet indicated divine investiture with God's sovereign power to Jehu. *flee, and do not delay.* The need for haste by the young prophet underscored the danger of the assignment. A prophet in the midst of Israel's army camp would alert the pro-Jehoram elements to the possibility of the coup.il by a prophet of the Lord confirmed that God Himself had ear

9:7 *avenge the blood.* Jehu was to be the Lord's avenger (cf. Num. 35:12) for the murders of the Lord's prophets (1 Kin. 18:4) and of people like Naboth who served the Lord (1 Kin. 21:1–16).

9:9 *like the house of Jeroboam . . . Baasha.* God would thoroughly annihilate Ahab's line in the same way as Jeroboam's dynasty and Baasha's dynasty had previously ended violently (1 Kin. 15:27–30; 16:8–13).

9:10 *dogs shall eat.* Dogs were considered scavengers in the ancient Near East and they would devour the corpse of Jezebel. *Jezreel.* Formerly the area of Naboth's vineyard (1 Kin. 21:1–16). *none to bury her.* In Israel, the failure to be buried indicated disgrace (*see note on 1 Kin. 13:22*).

9:11 *this madman.* The soldier demonstrated his disdain for Elisha's servant (vv. 1, 4) by referring to him as crazy or demented. In Jeremiah 29:26 and Hosea 9:7 this same term was used as a derogatory term for prophets whose messages were considered crazy. Jehu's response referred to the prophet's "babble," not his behavior.

9:12 *Thus and thus.* This refers to the repeating of the prophecy in verses 4–10.

9:13 *they blew trumpets.* Having laid their cloaks under Jehu's feet with the steps of the house serving as a makeshift throne, the officers blew trumpets acclaiming Jehu as king. A trumpet often heralded such a public proclamation and assembly, including the appointment of a king (cf. 11:14; 2 Sam. 15:10; 1 Kin. 1:34).

Syrian Rulers in Scripture		
Kings	Dates	Scripture References
Hezion (Rezon)	c. 990–930 B.C.	1 Kings 11:23, 25; 15:18
Tabrimmon	c. 930–885 B.C.	1 Kings 15:18
Ben-Hadad I	c. 885–860 B.C.	1 Kings 15:18, 20
Ben-Hadad II	c. 860–841 B.C.	1 Kings 20; 2 Kings 6:24; 8:7, 9, 14
Hazael	c. 841–801 B.C.	1 Kings 19:15, 17
		2 Kings 8; 9:14, 15; 10:32
		12:17, 18; 13:3, 22, 24, 25
Ben-Hadad III	c. 807–780? B.C.	2 Kings 13:3, 24, 25
Rezin	c. 780?–732 B.C.	2 Kings 15:37; 16:5, 6, 9
		(cf. Is. 7:1, 4, 8; 8:6; 9:11)

Nelson's Complete Book of Bible Maps & Charts (Nashville: Thomas Nelson Publishers, 1996) 131. © 1993 by Thomas Nelson, Inc.

4. The overthrow of Baal worship in Israel (9:14–10:36)

9:15 *let no one . . . go and tell it in Jezreel.* For Jehu to succeed in his revolt and to avoid a civil conflict, it was important to take Joram totally by surprise. Therefore, Jehu ordered the city of Ramoth Gilead, where he had been anointed (vv. 2, 3), to be sealed lest someone loyal to Joram escape and notify the king.

9:16 *to Jezreel.* From Ramoth Gilead, Jezreel was straight west across the Jordan River, north of Mount Gilboa.

9:21 *Naboth the Jezreelite.* Providentially, the kings of Israel and Judah met Jehu at the very place where Ahab and Jezebel had Naboth killed (1 Kin. 21:1–16). The alarmed king, aware by then of impending disaster, summoned his forces and, accompanied by Ahaziah, met Jehu as Jehu's men ascended the slope up to the city from the northern side.

9:22 *What peace.* Joram wished to know if Jehu's coming meant peace, apparently unsure of Jehu's rebellious plans. Jehu replied that there could be no true peace in Israel because of Jezebel's influence. *Harlotries,* a common biblical metaphor for idolatry, and *witchcraft,* i.e., seeking information from

demonic forces, described the nature of Jezebel's influence. Idolatry had lured Israel into demonic practices.

9:25 *Bidkar his captain. Captain* originally referred to the third man in a chariot, besides the driver and a warrior; it was his task to hold the shield and arms of the warrior. The term was eventually applied to a high-ranking official (cf. 7:2). Jehu and Bidkar either rode together in one chariot as part of the chariot team or were in different chariots behind Ahab when Elijah gave his prediction to Ahab recorded in 1 Kings 21:17–24. *the LORD laid this burden upon him.* The term *burden* referred to a prophetic oracle, the prophetic utterance of Elijah recorded in 1 Kings 21:19, 20–24. Jehu viewed himself as God's avenging agent fulfilling Elijah's prediction.

9:26 *Naboth . . . sons.* Although their deaths are not expressly mentioned in the record concerning Naboth, they are plainly implied in the confiscation of his property (see 1 Kin. 21:16).

9:27 *Ahaziah king of Judah . . . died.* Ahaziah fled by way of the road to Beth Haggan, a town seven miles southwest of Jezreel. Jehu and his men pursued Ahaziah and wounded him at the ascent of Gur by Ibleam which was just south of Beth Haggan. According to 2 Chronicles 22:9, Ahaziah reached Samaria, about eight miles south of Beth Haggan, where he hid for a while. Ahaziah then fled north to Megiddo, about twelve miles north of Samaria, where he died.

9:29 eleventh year. C. 841 B.C. Cf. 8:25, *twelfth year.* In 8:25, the non-accession-year system of dating was used, so that Joram's accession year was counted as the first year of his reign (*see note on 12:6*). Here, the accession-year dating system was used, where Joram's accension year and his second year were counted as the first year of his reign.

9:30 paint on her eyes. Eyelids were painted with a black powder mixed with oil and applied with a brush. This darkened them to give an enlarged effect. Jezebel's appearance at the window gave the air of a royal audience to awe Jehu.

9:31 Zimri. In referring to Jehu by that name, Jezebel sarcastically alluded to the previous purge of Zimri (1 Kin. 16:9–15). Since Zimri died seven days after beginning to reign, Jezebel was implying that the same fate awaited Jehu.

9:32 eunuchs. Some of Jezebel's own officials threw her out of a second-story window, after which Jehu drove his horses and chariots over her body.

9:34 a king's daughter. Jehu recognized Jezebel's royalty, while denying that she deserved to be the queen of Israel.

9:36 This is the word of the LORD. Where and how Jezebel died fulfilled Elijah's prophetic oracle (1 Kin. 21:23).

10:1 seventy sons. These were the male descendants of Ahab, both sons and grandsons. Ahab had a number of wives (1 Kin. 20:5) and, therefore, many descendants. Since these living relatives could avenge a dead kinsman by killing the person responsible for his death (cf. Num. 35:12), Jehu's life

was in jeopardy while Ahab's male descendants survived. **Samaria.** Ahab's surviving family members were living in the capital city of the northern kingdom, located about twenty-five miles south of Jezreel. **rulers . . . elders . . . those who reared.** Jehu sent the same message (vv. 2, 3) in a number of letters to: (1) the royal officials, who had probably fled from Jezreel to Samaria; (2) the leaders of the tribes of Israel; and (3) those appointed as the custodians and educators of the royal children.

10:3 fight for your master's house. Realizing potential conflict existed between himself and Ahab's family, Jehu was demanding that Ahab's appointed officials either fight to continue the royal line of Ahab or select a new king from Ahab's descendants who would fight Jehu in battle to decide which family would rule Israel (cf. 1 Sam. 17:8, 9; 2 Sam. 2:9).

10:5 he who was in charge of the house . . . city. These two officials were the palace administrator and the city governor, probably the commander of the city's fighting force. **We are your servants.** These officials and leaders transferred their allegiance from the house of Omri to Jehu.

10:6 the heads of the men. As a tangible sign of their surrender, Jehu required the officials to decapitate all of Ahab's male descendants and bring their heads to Jehu at Jezreel by the next day.

10:7 heads in baskets. Out of fear, the officials obeyed Jehu by decapitating Ahab's male descendants. However, they did not personally go to Jehu in Jezreel, probably fearing that a similar fate would await them.

10:8 two heaps. The practice of piling the heads of conquered subjects at the city gate was common in the ancient Near East, especially by the Assyrians. The practice was designed to dissuade rebellion.

10:9 *I conspired . . . killed.* Jehu is referring to his murder of Joram (9:14–24).

10:10 *word of the LORD.* God had prophesied through Elijah the destruction of Ahab's house (1 Kin. 21:17–24).

10:11 *Jehu killed all.* Jehu went beyond God's mandate and executed all of Ahab's officials, a deed for which God later judged Jehu's house (cf. Hos. 1:4).

10:13 *brothers of Ahaziah.* Since the brothers of Ahaziah, the slain king of Judah (9:27–29), had been previously killed by the Philistines (2 Chr. 21:17), these must have been relatives of Ahaziah in a broader sense, like nephews and cousins.

10:14 This slaughter by Jehu was because these people might have stimulated and strengthened those who were still loyal to the family of Ahab.

10:15 *Jehonadab the son of Rechab.* This man was a faithful follower of the Lord and a strict observer of the Mosaic law, leading a life of austerity and abstinence. According to Jeremiah 35:1–16, the Rechabites did not plant fields or drink wine. They shook hands, indicating a pledge of support for Jehu from this influential man.

10:18, 19 *Ahab served Baal a little, Jehu will serve him much.* Though it was in fact a ruse (v. 19), Jehu promised to outdo Ahab's devotion to Baal. The people of Samaria might have thought that Jehu was seeking a military, not a religious, reformation. If so, Jehu was seeking Baal's blessing on his reign as king (v. 20).

10:21 *temple of Baal.* The idolatrous worship center that Ahab had built in Samaria (1 Kin. 16:32). All the worshipers could fit into that one edifice because the number of Baal devotees had been reduced by the influence of Elijah and Elisha and by the neglect and discontinuance of Baal worship under Joram.

10:26 *sacred pillars.* These were wooden idols distinct from the main image *pillar* of Baal (v. 27).

10:27 *a refuse dump.* Lit. "place of dung." This desecration of the site discouraged any rebuilding of the temple of Baal.

10:28 *destroyed Baal from Israel.* Jehu rid the northern kingdom of royally sanctioned Baal worship. It was done, however, not from spiritual and godly motives, but because Jehu believed that Baalism was inextricably bound to the dynasty and influence of Ahab. By its extermination, he thought he would kill all the last vestiges of Ahab loyalists and incur the support of those in the land who worshiped the true God. Jonadab didn't know of that motive, so he concurred with what Jehu did.

10:29 *the sins of Jeroboam.* However, Jehu did continue to officially sanction other idolatry introduced into the northern kingdom by Jeroboam I (cf. 1 Kin. 12:28–33).

10:33 *from the Jordan eastward.* Because Jehu failed to keep the Lord's law wholeheartedly (v. 31), the Lord punished him by giving Israel's land east of the Jordan River to Syria. This lost region was the homeland of the tribes of Gad, Reuben, and half of Manasseh (Num. 32:1–42).

10:36 *twenty-eight years.* 841–814 B.C.

5. The overthrow of Baal worship in Judah (11:1–12:21)

11:1 *Athaliah.* A granddaughter of Omri (8:26) and daughter of Ahab and Jezebel. She was zealous to rule after the death of her son, Ahaziah (9:27) and was dedicated to seeing the worship of Baal officially sanctioned in Judah (*see note on 8:18*). She reigned for six years (v. 3) c. 841–835 B.C. See note on 2 Chronicles 22:10–23:21. ***destroyed all the royal heirs.*** The previous deaths of Jehoram's brothers (2 Chr. 21:4) and Ahaziah's brothers and relatives (10:12–14; 2 Chr. 21:17) left only her grandchildren for Athaliah to put to death to destroy the Davidic line. Though the Lord had promised that the house of David would rule over Israel and Judah forever (2 Sam. 7:16), Athaliah's purge brought the house of David to the brink of extinction.

11:2 *Jehosheba.* She was probably the daughter of Jehoram by a wife other than Athaliah, and so a half-sister of Ahaziah, who was married to the high priest, Jehoida (2 Chr. 22:11). *Joash.* The grandson of Athaliah who escaped her purge. *bedroom.* Lit. "the room of the beds." It was either the palace storeroom where servants kept the bedding or a room in the living quarters of the temple priests.

11:3 *in the house of the LORD.* The temple in Jerusalem. *six years.* 841–835 B.C.

11:4 *seventh year.* The beginning of Athaliah's seventh year of reign, 835 B.C. *Jehoiada.* The high priest during Athaliah's reign (*see note on 2 Chr. 24:15, 16*). He was the husband of Jehosheba (v. 2; 2 Chr. 22:11). *captains of hundreds.* These were the commanders of each 100-soldier unit; 2 Chronicles 23:1, 2 names five of these commanders. The bodyguards were "Carites" associated with the Pelethites (2 Sam. 20:23), who were mercenary soldiers serving as royal bodyguards. The escorts, lit. "runners," were probably another unit of royal bodyguards who provided palace security (see 1 Kin. 14:27). Jehoiada received an agreement of support from the royal guards, sealed with an oath of allegiance, and then presented Joash to them. The military leaders supported the plan to dispose of Athaliah and make Joash king.

11:5–8 Jehoiada outlined his plan to crown Joash as the king. On a selected Sabbath, the royal guards coming on duty, in-cluding priests and Levites (2 Chr. 23:4), would guard the palace as usual. They would especially make sure that no word concerning the coup in the temple courtyard reached Athaliah and those loyal to her. The companies going off duty would not return to their quarters as usual, but would instead report to the temple to form a tight security ring around the young potential king. The successful accomplishment of Jehoiada's plan is recorded in verses 9–12.

11:6 *gate of Sur.* The exact location of this gate is unknown. Verse 19 implies that this gate connected the temple with the palace.

11:10 *spears and shields.* These were probably part of the plunder David captured from King Hadadezer of Zobah (2 Sam. 8:3–12). Dedicated to the Lord by David (2 Sam. 8:7, 11), these articles were stored in the temple. Since the soldiers were already armed, these additional ancient weapons symbolically reassured the soldiers that the temple authorities approved of their actions.

11:12 *the Testimony.* This was a copy of the whole law (Ps. 119:88). According to Deuteronomy 17:18–20, a copy of the law was to be kept with the king always so that it became his guide for life. *anointed.* A priest or prophet customarily anointed kings, as here (9:6; 1 Sam. 10:1; 16:13; 1 Kin. 1:39).

11:14 *pillar.* Either one of the two pillars, Jachin or Boaz, on the temple's front porch (1 Kin. 7:21), or a raised platform in the court of the temple (cf. 2 Chr. 6:13). *people of the land.* Probably Jehoiada chose to stage his coup on the Sabbath during one of the major religious festivals, when those from Judah who were loyal to the Lord would be in Jerusalem.

11:16 *king's house . . . she was killed.* Execution was not appropriate in the temple area since it was a place of worship (cf. 2 Chr.

24:20–22). Thus, the soldiers seized Athaliah and put her to death at one of the entrances to the palace grounds.

11:17 *a covenant.* The renewal of the agreement between the people and the Lord and between the house of David and the people was appropriate because of the disruption under Athaliah. A similar ceremony was held later, during the reign of Josiah (23:1–3). *See notes on Exodus 24:4–8.*

11:18 *the temple of Baal.* A temple in Jerusalem used by Athaliah to promote the worship of Baal in Judah. As Jezebel had promoted Baalism in Israel, her daughter Athaliah had sought its sanction in Judah. During Athaliah's reign as queen, Baalism gained its strongest foothold in Judah. This purge of Baalism in Judah paralleled the earlier purge of Baalism led by Jehu in the northern kingdom (10:18–29).

11:21 *Jehoash.* Jehoash and Joash are variants of the same name, meaning "The LORD gave." *See notes on 2 Chronicles 24:1–27.*

12:1 *seventh year.* 835 B.C. Jehu of Israel began his reign in 841 B.C. (*see notes on 9:29; 10:36*). *forty years.* 835–796 B.C.

12:2 *all the days . . . Jehoiada . . . instructed him.* Joash did what pleased the Lord while Jehoida served as his parental guardian and tutor. After Jehoida died, Joash turned away from the Lord (*see note on 2 Chr. 24:17, 18a*).

12:3 *the high places. See note on 1 Kings 3:2.* As with most kings of Judah, Joash failed to remove these places of worship where, contrary to the Mosaic Law, the people sacrificed and burned incense to the Lord (cf. Deut. 12:2–7, 13, 14).

12:4–16 See 2 Chronicles 24:5–14.

12:4 *the dedicated gifts.* Lit. "holy gifts." These offerings were given to the priests and used to support the temple. These three main offerings were the half-shekel assessed from every male twenty years old and above when-ever a census was taken (Ex. 30:11–16), the payments of personal vows (Lev. 27:1–8), and voluntary offerings (Lev. 22:18–23; Deut. 16:10).

12:5 *his constituency.* This person would be a friend of the priest who either gave offerings or collected the offerings for the priest. Such friends of the priest would make up his "constituency." However, some interpret the Hebrew term to mean "treasurer." This understanding views the individual as a member of the temple personnel who assisted the priests with the valuation of sacrifices and offerings brought to the temple. *repair the damages of the temple.* During the reign of Athaliah, the temple had suffered major damages, and temple articles had been taken for use in the temple of Baal (2 Chr. 24:7). Joash ordered the priests to channel the temple offerings to fund the needed repairs. This was to be in addition to the normal temple expenses.

12:6 *twenty-third year.* C. 813 B.C. Judah seems to have used the non-accession-year system during the reigns of Athaliah and Joash (*see note on 13:1*), which did not count the first year of the reign but began with the second. Joash was twenty-nine years of age.

12:7, 8 The plan of Joash did not work. Either the revenue from these sources was inadequate to support the priests and Levites and also to pay for the temple repairs, or the priests, for some unknown reason, would not fund the temple repairs. Therefore, the priests no longer received the offerings from the people, nor did they fund the temple repairs from the income they had already received.

12:9–16 Joash instituted a new plan. First, a single collection box was to receive all incoming offerings. When the chest was full, only the royal secretary and high priest would be authorized to empty it. Second, from the funds thus generated, men were hired to supervise and pay the carpenters, builders, masons, and stonecutters who worked on the temple repairs. The men involved were so trustworthy that no accounting was taken of them (v. 15).

12:9 priests who kept the door. These were priests who normally screened the people to keep unclean worshipers from entering the temple (25:18; Jer. 52:24). These priests took the offerings from the worshipers, who then personally watched the priests drop them into the chest.

12:16 money from the trespass offerings and . . . sin offerings. The income from these offerings was distinct from the income mentioned in verse 4 and so was not used in the repair of the temple, but remained the property of the priests (see Lev. 4:1–6:7). The temple repairs did not deprive the priests of their income (Lev. 7:7).

12:17 Hazael. See notes on 8:8–15. **Gath.** One of the five major Philistine cities (1 Sam. 5:8), located about twenty-five miles southwest of Jerusalem. Gath had previously belonged to Judah (2 Chr. 11:8).

12:18 all the sacred things. When Joash's army was defeated by Hazael and his leading men killed (2 Chr. 24:23, 24), he averted further attacks against Jerusalem by sending tribute to the king of Syria. This tribute included gifts donated to the temple in Jerusalem by kings of Judah (cf. 1 Kin. 15:15, 18).

12:19 acts of Joash. A more complete account of the reign of Joash is found in 2 Chronicles 22:10–24:27.

12:20 a conspiracy. Some of the officials of Joash conspired against him because he had killed the high priest, Zechariah, the son of the priest, Jehoiada (2 Chr. 24:20–22). **house of the Millo.** Probably a house built on a landfill north of David's city of Jerusalem and south of the temple mount. Cf. 2 Chronicles 24:25. **Silla.** Possibly a ramp

that descended from the landfill to the Kidron Valley.

12:21 Amaziah. See 14:1–22 for the reign of Amaziah.

6. The death of Elisha (13:1–25)

13:1 twenty-third year. 814 B.C. Joash of Judah began his reign in 835 B.C. (see note on 12:1) and Jehu of Israel died in 814 B.C. (see note on 10:36). Thus the twenty-third year of Joash of Judah was calculated according to the non-accession-year system (see notes on 12:6; 13:10). **seventeen years.** 814–798 B.C., i.e., part of seventeen calendar years, with the actual reign counted as sixteen years.

13:2 Jeroboam. For his sins, see notes on 1 Kings 12:25–32. This description of Jeroboam as one who "made Israel sin" occurs in verses 6, 11; 3:3; 10:29, 31; 14:24; 15:9, 18, 24, 28; 17:21, 22; 1 Kings 14:16; 15:30; 16:31.

13:2–7 The record of the reign of Jehoahaz, the king of Israel, has literary and verbal similarities to the Book of Judges: (1) Jehoahaz did evil in the sight of the Lord (v. 2; cf. Judg. 2:11–13; 3:7); (2) the anger of the Lord was aroused against Israel and He delivered them over to their enemies (v. 3; cf. Judg. 2:14, 15; 3:8); (3) Jehoahaz cried out to the Lord who saw their oppression (v. 4; cf. Judg. 2:18; 3:9); (4) the Lord raised up a deliverer for Israel who rescued them out of the hand of their enemies (v. 5; cf. Judg. 2:16, 18; 3:9); and (5) Israel continued in her evil ways with the result of further oppression (vv. 6, 7; cf. Judg. 2:19; 3:12–14).

13:3 Hazael. See notes on 8:8–15. **Ben-Hadad.** Either Ben-Hadad II or, more likely, III (see note on 1 Kin. 15:18). His reign as king of Syria began c. 801 B.C. The length of his rule is unknown.

13:5 a deliverer. The deliverer was not specifically named. This deliverer was: (1) the Assyrian king Adad-Nirari III (c. 810–783 B.C.), whose attack on the Syrians enabled the Israelites to break Syria's control over Israelite territory (see v. 25; 14:25); or (2) Elisha who, as the leader of Israel's military successes (see v. 14; cf. 6:13, 16–23), commissioned Joash to defeat the Syrians (vv. 15–19); or (3) Jeroboam II (c. 793–753 B.C.), who was able to extend Israel's boundaries back into Syrian territory (14:25–27).

13:6 sins . . . of Jeroboam. See note on verse 2. **wooden image.** This idol representing Asherah, a Canaanite goddess and a consort of Baal, had been set up by Ahab (1 Kin. 16:33) and had escaped destruction by Jehu when he purged Baal worship from Samaria (10:27, 28). Along with the other idolatrous religion of Jeroboam II, there were still remnants of Baal worship in the northern kingdom.

13:7 the army. Syria was able to dominate Israel militarily because the Lord had left Jehoahaz only a small army with very few chariots. **dust at threshing.** The army of Israel was so inconsequential, particularly when compared to the armies of Syria and Assyria, that it was likened to the dust left over after grain had been winnowed at a threshing floor.

13:10 thirty-seventh year. C. 798 B.C. Joash of Judah began his reign in 835 B.C. (see note on 12:1). There is a change here to the accession-year system of dating for the reign of Joash of Judah (see note on 13:1). This explains how Jehoahaz of Israel could reign sixteen years with only a fifteen-year advance on Joash of Judah's regnal years (cf. v. 1). **Jehoash.** This king of Israel had the same name as his contemporary, the king of Judah (see note on 11:21). **sixteen years.** 798–782 B.C.

13:12 fought against Amaziah. See notes on 14:8–14.

13:14 Elisha. The last previous reference to Elisha the prophet was in 9:1 when Jehu was anointed king of Israel. Since Jehu and Jehoahaz reigned from 841–798 B.C. (see notes on 10:36; 13:1), nothing was recorded for over forty years of Elisha's life. Elisha began ministering with Elijah during the kingship of Ahab c. 874–853 B.C. (1 Kin. 19:19–21) and so must have been over seventy years of age when these final events of his life took place. **my father.** Jehoash humbly voiced his great respect for Elisha and his dependence on his counsel (see note on 2:12). **the chariots of Israel and their horsemen!** Jehoash acknowledged by this metaphor that the Lord, through Elisha, was the real strength and power of Israel against all her adversaries (see note on 2:11).

13:16 Elisha put his hands on the king's hands. This symbolic act indicated that Jehoash would exert power against the Syrians that came from the Lord through His prophet.

13:17 east window. This window opened toward the east to the Transjordan region controlled by Syria (10:32, 33). **The arrow of the LORD's deliverance.** When Jehoash obeyed Elisha by shooting an arrow out the window, the prophet interpreted the meaning of the action. The shot symbolized the Lord's deliverance for Israel through the defeat of the Syrian army by Jehoash (cf. v. 5). **Aphek.** See note on 1 Kings 20:26.

13:19 three times. Further, Elisha commanded Jehoash to shoot the remaining arrows into the ground (v. 18). Jehoash shot only three arrows into the ground instead of emptying the entire quiver. Because of his lack of faith, Jehoash would win only three victories over the Syrians instead of completely destroying them. The account of these victories is given in verse 25.

13:20 spring. The prophet, who was Israel's defense (v. 14), was dead and it was the season for war campaigns to begin after the rains of winter.

13:21 he revived. A dead man returned to

life after touching Elisha's bones. This miracle was a sign that God's power continued to work in relationship to Elisha even after his death. What God had promised to Jehoash through Elisha when he was alive would surely come to pass after the prophet's death (cf. vv. 19, 25) in the defeat of the enemy, the recovery of the cities that had been taken, and their restoration to the kingdom of Israel (vv. 22–25).

13:22 See note on 8:12.

13:23 His covenant with Abraham, Isaac, and Jacob. During the wicked reign of Jehoahaz (vv. 2–7), the Lord was very patient and did not bring the ultimate military defeat that would lead to exile for Israel. This was because of His agreement with the patriarchs to give their descendants the land (Gen. 15:18–21; 26:2–5; 28:13–15). It was God's promise, not the Israelites' goodness, that motivated God to be merciful and compassionate toward Israel.

D. Kings of Judah/Israel (14:1–15:38)

14:1–15:38 This section quickly surveys the kings and selected events of the northern and southern kingdoms from 796 to 735 B.C. In contrast to the previous nineteen chapters (1 Kin. 17:1–2 Kin. 13:25), which narrated ninety years of history (885–796 B.C.) with a concentration on the ministries of Elijah and Elisha during the final sixty-five years of that period (860–796 B.C.), sixty-two years are covered in these two chapters. The previous section concluded with a shadow of hope: officially sanctioned Baal worship had been eradicated in both Israel (10:18–28) and Judah (11:17, 18); the temple of the Lord in Jerusalem had been repaired (12:9– 15); and the Syrian threat to Israel had been overcome (13:25). However, this section emphasizes that the fundamental problems still remained: the false religion established by Jeroboam I continued in Israel even with the change of royal families (14:24–15:9, 18, 24, 28), and the high places were not removed in Judah, even though there were only good kings there during those years (v. 4; 15:4, 35).

14:1 second year. 796 B.C. **Amaziah.** See notes on 2 Chronicles 25:1–28.

14:2 twenty-nine years. 796–767 B.C.

14:3 not like . . . David. David set a high standard of unswerving devotion to the Lord for the kings of Judah who were his descendants to follow (cf. 1 Kin. 11:4, 6; 15:3). Amaziah did not follow the Lord completely, as David had, because he, like his father Joash, did not remove the high places (v. 4) where, in disregard for Mosaic Law, the people wor-

Resuscitations from the Dead

1. Widow of Zarephath's son, raised by Elijah	1 Kin. 17:22
2. Shunammite woman's son, raised by Elisha	2 Kin. 4:34, 35
3. Man raised when he came into contact with the bones of Elisha	2 Kin. 13:20, 21
4. Widow of Nain's son, raised by Jesus	Luke 7:14, 15
5. Jairus' daughter, raised by Jesus	Luke 8:52–56
6. Lazarus of Bethany, brother of Mary and Martha, raised by Jesus	John 11
7. Dorcas, raised by Peter	Acts 9:40
8. Eutychus, raised by Paul	Acts 20:9–12

The MacArthur Study Bible, by John MacArthur (Nashville: Word Publishing, 1997) 504. © 1993 by Thomas Nelson, Inc.

shiped the Lord (Deut. 12:2–7, 13, 14). Further, according to 2 Chronicles 25:14–16, Amaziah embraced the false gods of the Edomites.

14:5, 6 When firmly in control of the kingdom, Amaziah took revenge on Jozachar and Jehozabad, the officials who assassinated his father Joash (12:20, 21). However, he spared the lives of their sons, in obedience to the Mosaic Law that children were not to die for their fathers' sins (Deut. 24:16; cf. Ezek. 18:1–20).

14:7 For an elaboration of Amaziah's war with Edom, *see the notes on 2 Chronicles 25:5–16.* Edom had revolted in Joram's reign (see 8:20), so the king wanted them subjugated again. *the Valley of Salt.* Probably a marshy plain at the south end of the Dead Sea (*see note on 2 Sam. 8:13*). *Sela . . . Joktheel.* Sela (meaning "rock" in Hebrew) is best identified as Petra (meaning "rock" in Greek), a city carved out of sheer mountain walls located about fifty miles south of the Dead Sea, though some prefer to place it in northern Edom near Bozra on the King's Highway (Judg. 1:36). Renaming a captured city, as Amaziah did with the name Joktheel, implied his control over it.

14:8 *Jehoash . . . of Israel. See notes on 13:10–23. face one another.* Amaziah's challenge to Jehoash constituted a declaration of war. Amaziah, emboldened by his victory over Edom (v. 10), thought he could defeat the stronger army of Israel (cf. 13:25). He was probably also upset by the refusal of Jehoash to establish a marriage alliance with him (v. 9).

14:9 *thistle . . . cedar.* In this parable (cf. Judg. 9:8–15), the thistle (Amaziah), an irritating and worthless plant, sought to become the equal of the majestic cedar (Jehoash), but a wild animal crushed the thistle. Jehoash counseled Amaziah that he was overestimating his power and promi-

nence and should not go to war with Israel lest he be crushed (v. 10).

14:11 *Beth Shemesh.* A town about fifteen miles west of Jerusalem, where the armies of Israel and Judah faced each other in battle.

14:13 *Jehoash . . . captured Amaziah.* Winning the battle, Jehoash also captured Amaziah. Jehoash probably took Amaziah back to Samaria as a hostage (v. 14). The king of Judah was forced to stay in Samaria until the death of Jehoash in 782 B.C. (v. 17). *Gate of Ephraim . . . Corner Gate.* The Corner Gate (cf. Jer. 31:38; Zech. 14:10) was at the northwest corner of the wall around Jerusalem. The Ephraim Gate was in Jerusalem's northern wall facing Ephraim, 600 feet east of the Corner Gate. This northwestern section of the wall of Jerusalem, torn down by Jehoash, was the point where Jerusalem was most vulnerable.

14:14 *he took.* Jehoash plundered both the temple at Jerusalem and the palace of Amaziah. The value of the plundered articles was probably not great, because Jehoash of Judah had previously sent the temple and palace treasures to pay tribute to Hazael of Damascus (12:17, 18). Jehoash probably took hostages from Jerusalem to Samaria to secure additional payments of tribute in view of the small war booty.

14:17 *fifteen years.* 782–767 B.C.

14:18 *the acts of Amaziah.* His apostasy (2 Chr. 25:27), his disastrous war with Israel, the ruinous condition of Jerusalem, the plunder of the temple, and the loss of hostages lost him the respect of his people, who rebelled and killed him.

14:19 *Lachish.* A town about twenty-five miles southwest of Jerusalem to which Amaziah fled seeking to escape death.

14:21 *sixteen years old.* Azariah (Uzziah) (*see note on 15:1*) had actually begun to reign at the age of sixteen in 790 B.C. when his father Amaziah was taken prisoner to Samaria (v. 13). When Amaziah returned to Judah, Azariah ruled with him as co-regent from 782–767 B.C. (v. 17). In 767 B.C. when Amaziah was killed (v. 19), Azariah began his sole rule (15:1). *See notes on 2 Chronicles 26:1–23.*

14:22 Elath. Elath was located on the northern coast of the Gulf of Aqabah and was closely associated with Ezion Geber, a seaport of Solomon (1 Kin. 9:26). Azariah's restoration of Elath to Judah marked the first significant act of his sole rule; his further successes are summarized in 2 Chronicles 26:6–15.

14:23 fifteenth year. C. 782 B.C. This marked the beginning of the sole reign of Jeroboam II. Since his son Zechariah succeeded him in 753 B.C. (see 15:8), Jeroboam II must have had a co-regency with his father Jehoash for eleven years, making a total reign of forty-one years (793–753 B.C.), longer than any other king in the northern kingdom. **Jeroboam.** This was Jeroboam II who, like the other kings of Israel, followed the false religion of Jeroboam I. During the reign of Jeroboam II, the prophets Hosea (Hos. 1:1) and Amos (Amos 1:1) ministered to the northern kingdom. These prophets showed that Jeroboam II's reign was a time of great prosperity and greater spiritual apostasy in Israel.

14:25 restored the territory of Israel. Jeroboam II's greatest accomplishment was the restoration of Israel's boundaries to approximately their extent in Solomon's time, excluding the territory belonging to Judah. The northern boundary was the entrance of Hamath, the same as Solomon's (cf. 1 Kin. 8:65) and the southern boundary was the Sea of the Arabah, the Dead Sea (Josh. 3:16; 12:3). Jeroboam II took Hamath, a major city located on the Orontes River, about 160 miles north of the Sea of Galilee. He also controlled

Damascus, indicating that the Transjordan territory south to Moab was also under his authority. These victories of Jeroboam II were accomplished because the Syrians had been weakened by attacks from the Assyrians, while Assyria herself was weak at this time, suffering from threats on her northern border, internal dissension, and a series of weak kings. **Jonah.** The territorial extension of Jeroboam II was in accordance with the will of the Lord as revealed through the prophet Jonah. This was the same Jonah who traveled to Nineveh with God's message of repentance for the Assyrians (see Introduction to Jonah). **Gath Hepher.** A town located in the tribal area of Zebulun, about fourteen miles west of the Sea of Galilee (Josh. 19:13).

14:25, 26 The explanation for Jonah's prophecy is given here. The Lord had personally witnessed the heavy, bitter affliction borne by everyone in Israel with no human help available (v. 26). Further, the Lord had not decreed Israel's final doom (v. 27). To "blot out the name of Israel from under heaven" meant to annihilate Israel totally, leaving no trace or memory of her (Deut. 9:14; 29:20). Thus, moved with compassion, the Lord used Jeroboam II's reign to rescue His suffering people. However, as the books of Hosea and Amos show, Israel did not respond to God's grace with repentance.

14:28 Without devotion to the Lord, Jeroboam, by might and clever leadership, brought Israel more prosperity than the country had known since Solomon. The people rested in their prosperity rather than God's power. Material blessing was no sign of God's blessing, since they had no commitment to Him.

15:1 twenty-seventh year. 767 B.C. This included the eleven years of Jeroboam II's co-regency with Jehoash (*see note on 14:23*). **Azariah.** The name means "The LORD has helped" (14:21; 15:6, 7, 8, 17, 23, 27; 1 Chr.

3:12). He was also called Uzziah, meaning "The LORD is my strength" (15:13, 30, 32, 34; 2 Chr. 26:1–23; Is. 1:1; 6:1; Hos. 1:1; Amos 1:1; Zech. 14:5). Isaiah the prophet began his public ministry during Azariah's reign (Is. 1:1).

15:2 fifty-two years. 790–739 B.C. Azariah was sixteen when he began his co-regency with his father Amaziah. Azariah's sole rule began in 767 B.C. (*see note on v. 8*).

15:4 Cf. 12:3; 14:4.

15:5 leper. Azariah suffered from leprosy as punishment for usurping the priestly function of burning incense on the altar in the temple (*see notes on 2 Chr. 26:16–18, 19, 20*). The disease eventually killed him (*see note on Is. 6:1*). **isolated house.** Lit. "in a house of freedom." Azariah was relieved of all royal responsibilities. His son Jotham served as co-regent until Azariah's death (750–739 B.C.; *see notes on vv. 2, 32*). As co-regent, Jotham specifically supervised the palace and governed the nation.

15:8 thirty-eighth year. 753 B.C., making Azariah's co-reign with his father Amaziah (*see notes on v. 2; 14:21*) begin in 792–791 B.C. (accession year) or 790 B.C. (non-accession year). **Zechariah.** Zechariah was the fourth and final generation of the dynasty of Jehu

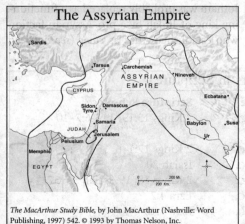

The Assyrian Empire

The MacArthur Study Bible, by John MacArthur (Nashville: Word Publishing, 1997) 542. © 1993 by Thomas Nelson, Inc.

(c. 753/752 B.C.). His death fulfilled the prophecy given by the Lord (cf. 15:12; 10:30).

15:10 Shallum. Shallum killed Zechariah and replaced him as king of Israel. Assyrian records call Shallum "the son of nobody," indicating that he was not from the royal family.

15:13 thirty-ninth year. 752 B.C. Zechariah's reign spanned the last months of Azariah's thirty-eighth year (v. 8) and the first months of the following year.

15:14 Menahem. Menahem had probably been a military commander under Zechariah. **Tirzah.** The former capital of the northern kingdom (1 Kin. 14:17; 15:21, 33), located about nine miles east of Samaria. Menahem was probably stationed with his troops at Tirzah.

15:16 Tiphsah. Since Tiphsah was located on the Euphrates River about 325 miles north of Samaria (1 Kin. 4:24), a majority of interpreters translate this term "Tappuah," a town fourteen miles southwest of Tirzah (Josh. 17:8). **ripped open.** The ripping open of pregnant women was a barbarous practice and elsewhere associated only with foreign armies (8:12; Hos. 13:16; Amos 1:13). Menahem probably did this as a visible reminder of the city's failure to "open up" to his demands.

15:17 thirty-ninth year. 752 B.C. **ten years.** 752–742 B.C. With Menahem, the northern kingdom changed from the non-accession to the accession-year system of computing reigns.

15:19 Pul. Assyrian kings frequently had two names, a throne name for Assyria and another for Babylon. Pul was the Babylonian throne name of the Assyrian king Tiglath-Pileser III (cf. 1 Chr. 5:26) who reigned c. 745–727 B.C.

15:19, 20 Tiglath-Pileser III invaded Israel in 743 B.C. Menahem paid tribute of 1,000 talents of silver (c. 37 tons) raised from the wealthy men of Israel. Each of 60,000 men paid 20 ounces of silver to raise the required 37 tons of silver. For his tribute, Tiglath-Pileser III supported Menahem's claim to the throne of Israel and withdrew his army. By this action, Menahem became a vassal of the Assyrian king.

15:23 fiftieth year. 742 B.C. **two years.** 742–740 B.C.

15:24 sins of Jeroboam. See notes on 13:2; 1 Kings 12:25–32.

15:25 Pekah. See note on verse 27. Pekah was one of Pekahiah's military officers, probably commanding Gilead, since fifty Gileadites accompanied him when he assassinated Pekahiah. Argob and Arieh were either Pekahiah's sons or loyal military officers. Pekah probably represented the anti-Assyrian faction in Israel (cf. 16:5).

15:27 fifty-second year. 740 B.C. **twenty years.** On the basis of Assyrian records, it can be determined that Tiglath-Pileser III deposed Pekah as king of Israel in 732 B.C., evidently using Hoshea as his instrument. Therefore, Pekah reigned c. 752–732 B.C., using the accession-year system of dating (that is, counting the first year as one). For an explanation of this dating system see 1 Kings Introduction: Interpretive Challenges. This included the years 752–740 B.C., when Pekah ruled in Gilead while Menahem (vv. 17–22) and Pekahiah (vv. 23–26) reigned in Samaria

(the Jordan River being the boundary of the split kingdom). Verse 25 seems to indicate that Pekah had an alliance with Menahem and Pekahiah, ruling Gilead for them.

15:29 Ijon . . . Naphtali. The areas of Galilee and Gilead are described here. When Pekah and Rezin, the king of Syria, sought to have Judah join their anti-Assyrian alliance, another invasion by Assyria was provoked (cf. 16:5–9) in 733/732 B.C. Tiglath-Pileser III took Galilee and Gilead and converted them into three Assyrian provinces governed by royal appointees. He also was involved in replacing Pekah with Hoshea as king over the remaining area of Israel (see note on v. 27).

15:30 twentieth year. Jotham of Judah began his reign in 750 B.C. (see note on v. 32). His twentieth year was 732 B.C., according to the non-accession-year system. Assyrian records confirm that Hoshea began to rule Israel in 732 B.C. (see notes on v. 27; 2 Chr. 27:1–9).

15:32 second year. 750 B.C., the year of Pekah's second year of rule in Gilead, according to the accession-year system (see note on v. 27).

15:33 sixteen years. 750–735 B.C. According to verse 30, Jotham reigned until 731 B.C. Jotham was probably replaced as a functioning king of Judah by a pro-Assyrian faction who established Ahaz as ruler (see notes on

Assyrian Rulers in Scripture		
Ruler	**Dates of Rule**	**Scripture Reference**
Tiglath-Pileser III or Tiglath-Pilneser, or Pul(u)	c. 745-727 B.C.	2 Kings 15:19, 29; 16:7–10
Shalmaneser V	c. 727–722 B.C.	2 Kings 17:1–6
Sargon II	c. 722–705 B.C.	Isaiah 20
Sennacherib	c. 705–681 B.C.	2 Kings 18; 19; Isaiah 36; 37
Esarhaddon	c. 681–669 B.C.	Ezra 4:2
Osnapper (a.k.a. Ashurbanipal)	c. 668–627 B.C.	Ezra 4:10

vv. 1, 2) while leaving Jotham as a powerless co-regent. the prophets Isaiah (Is. 1:1) and Micah (Mic. 1:1) ministered to Judah during Jotham's reign.

15:35 *the Upper Gate.* Probably the Upper Benjamin Gate, which stood along the north side of the temple complex facing the territory of Benjamin (cf. Jer. 20:2; Ezek. 9:2; Zech. 14:10). Other accomplishments of Jotham are noted in 2 Chronicles 27:3–6.

15:37 *Rezin . . . Pekah.* See notes on 16:5–9.

E. The Defeat and Exile of Israel by Assyria (16:1–17:41)

16:1–17:41 At this point, the narrative turns to the defeat and exile of Israel by Assyria. In 17:7–23, the prophetic writer states the reasons why Israel was punished by the Lord. A major reason was the sinful religion established by Jeroboam I (17:21–23), which was followed by every king in Israel. Ominously, the section begins with the narrative concerning Ahaz of Judah who "walked in the way of the kings of Israel" (16:3). The kind of punishment that came upon Israel would come later upon Judah for the same reason (17:19, 20).

16:1 *seventeenth year.* 735 B.C., since Pekah's reign began in 752 B.C. (*see note on 15:27*). Although Jotham, the father of Ahaz, was still alive (*see note on 15:30*), Ahaz exercised the sovereign authority in Judah from 735 B.C. to Jotham's death in c. 731 B.C. The prophets Isaiah (Is. 1:1–7:1) and Micah (Mic. 1:1) continued to minister to Judah during the reign of Ahaz. *See notes on 2 Chronicles 28:1–27.*

16:2 *sixteen years.* 731–715 B.C. The principle of "dual dating" was followed here. See 1 Kings Introduction: Interpretive Challenges for an explanation of this principle. In 16:1 and 17:1, Ahaz was recognized as king in the year he came to the throne as a co-

regent, but the year of his official accession was determined as the year when he began to reign alone. Ahaz shared royal power with Azariah (to 739 B.C.) and Jotham from 744 to 735 B.C. (*see note on 17:1*); he exercised total authority as co-regent with Jotham from 735–731 B.C. (*see note on v. 1*); he was sole king from 731 to 729 B.C. and was co-regent with his son Hezekiah from 729 to 715 B.C. (*see note on 18:1*).

16:3 *walked in the way of the kings of Israel.* This does not necessarily mean that Ahaz participated in the calf worship introduced by Jeroboam I at Bethel and Dan, but that he increasingly brought pagan, idolatrous practices into the worship of the Lord in Jerusalem. These are specified in verses 10–16 and parallel those of Jeroboam I in the northern kingdom. This included idols to Baal (2 Chr. 28:2). *made his son pass through the fire.* As a part of the ritual worship of Molech, the god of the Moabites, children were sacrificed by fire (cf. 3:27). This horrific practice was continually condemned in the OT (Lev. 18:21; 20:2–5; Deut. 18:10; Jer. 7:31; 19:5; 32:35). *the abominations of the nations.* Cf. 21:2. *See note on Deuteronomy 18:9–12.*

16:4 *the high places.* Ahaz was the first king in the line of David since Solomon who was said to have personally worshiped at the high places. While all the other kings of Judah had tolerated the high places, Ahaz actively participated in the immoral Canaanite practices that were performed at the high places on hilltops under large trees (cf. Hos. 4:13).

16:5 *Rezin . . . Pekah.* The kings of Syria and Israel wanted to overthrow Ahaz in order to force Judah into their anti-Assyrian coalition. The two kings with their armies besieged Jerusalem, seeking to replace Ahaz with their own king (cf. Is. 7:1–6). The Lord delivered Judah and Ahaz from this threat because of His promise to David (cf. Is. 7:7–16).

16:6 Elath. The Syrians did displace Judah from Elath (*see note on 14:22*). Later this important port town on the Gulf of Aqabah was captured by the Edomites.

16:7 Tiglath-Pileser. *See notes on 15:19, 29.* **your servant and your son.** Ahaz willingly became a vassal of the Assyrian king in exchange for his military intervention. This was a pledge that Judah would serve Assyria from this point on. In support of his pledge, Ahaz sent Tiglath-Pileser III silver and gold from the temple and from the palace trea-

Tiglath-Pileser's Assyrian Campaigns Against Israel and Judah (734–732 B.C.)

From 734 B.C. to 732 B.C. Tiglath-Pileser III mounted one invasion against Judah and two against Israel.

Nelson's Complete Book of Bible Maps & Charts (Nashville: Thomas Nelson Publishers, 1996) 133. © 1993 by Thomas Nelson, Inc.

suries (v. 8). Evidently, the prosperous reigns of Azariah and Jotham had replenished the treasures plundered by Jehoash of Israel fifty years earlier during Amaziah's reign (14:14).

16:9 the king of Assyria heeded him. According to Assyrian records, in 733 B.C. Tiglath-Pileser III's army marched against Damascus, the Syrian capital, laid siege for two years, and captured it. The victorious Assyrian king executed Rezin and deported his subjects to Kir, whose location is unknown.

16:10 the altar. When Ahaz traveled to Damascus to meet Tiglath-Pileser III, he saw a large altar (v. 15) which was most likely Assyrian. Ahaz sent a sketch of this altar to Urijah the high priest in Jerusalem and Urijah built an altar just like it. The serious iniquity in this was meddling with and changing, according to personal taste, the furnishings of the temple, the design for which had been given by God (Ex. 25:40; 26:30; 27:1–8; 1 Chr. 28:19). This was like building an idol in the temple, done to please the pagan Assyrian king, whom Ahaz served instead of God.

16:12, 13 offerings. As did Solomon and Jeroboam before him (1 Kin. 8:63; 12:32), Ahaz dedicated the new altar by offering sacrifices.

16:14–16 bronze altar. Feeling confident about his alterations in the temple, Ahaz moved the old bronze altar dedicated by Solomon (1 Kin. 8:22, 54, 64), which stood in front of the temple between the new altar and the temple itself (v. 14). Ahaz had the bronze altar moved to a spot north of the new altar, thereby relegating it to a place of secondary importance. All offerings from then on were to be given on the altar dedicated by Ahaz, while Ahaz reserved the bronze altar for his personal use in seeking guidance (v. 15). The term *inquire* probably referred here to pagan divination through religious rituals. Deuteronomy 18:9–14 expressly forbade such divination in Israel.

16:17, 18 Ahaz made further changes in the temple at Jerusalem. First, he removed the side panels and basins from the portable stands (cf. 1 Kin. 7:27–29, 38, 39). Second, he removed the large ornate reservoir called "the Sea" from atop the twelve bronze bulls to a new stone base (cf. 1 Kin. 7:23–26). Third, he removed the "Sabbath pavilion," probably some sort of canopy used by the king on the Sabbath. Fourth, he removed "the king's outer entrance," probably a special entrance to the temple used by the king on Sabbaths and feast days (cf. 1 Kin. 10:5).

16:18 *on account of the king of Assyria.* Both items mentioned here were moved into the temple in the hope that if the king of Assyria laid siege to Jerusalem, Ahaz could secure the entrance of the temple from him.

16:20 *Hezekiah.* For his reign, see 18:1–20:21.

17:1 *twelfth year.* 732 B.C. This date for the accession of Hoshea as king of Israel is well established according to biblical and extra-biblical data (*see note on 15:27*). Therefore, Ahaz of Judah must have become co-regent with his father Jotham, who was himself co-regent with his father, Azariah, at that time (*see notes on 15:30, 33*), in 744 B.C. (*see note on 16:2*). *nine years.* 732–722 B.C. according to the accession-year system. Hoshea was imprisoned (v. 4) during the siege of Samaria by Assyria in 724–722 B.C. (v. 5).

17:2 *he did evil.* Though Hoshea was characterized as a wicked king, it is not stated that he promoted the religious practices of Jeroboam I. In this way, he was some improvement over the kings of Israel who had gone before him. However, this did not offset the centuries of sin by Israel's kings or divert her inevitable doom.

17:3 *Shalmaneser.* Shalmaneser V succeeded his father Tiglath-Pileser III as king of Assyria and reigned from 727–722 B.C.

During the siege of Samaria, when the Assyrians began the destruction and captivity of the northern kingdom, Shalmaneser V died and was succeeded by Sargon II (see Is. 20:1), who completed the siege, captured the city, destroyed the nation of Israel, and exiled the inhabitants (v. 6). Sargon II reigned as king from 722–705 B.C. *See note on Hosea 10:14.*

17:4 *So, king of Egypt.* Instead of paying his yearly tribute owed as a vassal of Assyria, Hoshea tried to make a treaty with Osorkon IV (c. 727–716 B.C.), king of Egypt. This was foolish because Assyria was powerful. It was also against God's will, which forbade such alliances with pagan rulers (cf. Deut. 7:2). This rebellion led to Israel's destruction (vv. 5, 6).

17:5 *Samaria . . . besieged.* In 724 B.C., Shalmaneser V invaded Israel and quickly conquered the land and captured Hoshea. However, the capital city of Samaria resisted the Assyrian invaders until 722 B.C. Like all major cities, Samaria had an internal water supply and plenty of stored food that allowed her to endure the siege for three years.

17:6 *king of Assyria.* Sargon II (*see note on 17:3*). *carried Israel away.* The capture of Samaria marked the end of the northern kingdom. According to Assyrian records, the Assyrians deported 27,290 inhabitants of Israel to distant locations. The relocation of populations was characteristic of Assyrian policy during that era. The Israelites were resettled in the upper Tigris-Euphrates Valley and never returned to the Promised Land. Halah was a city northeast of Nineveh. The Habor River was a northern tributary of the Euphrates. The "cities of the Medes" were northeast of Nineveh. Samaria was resettled with foreigners (v. 24). God did what He said He would do in Deuteronomy 28. The Jews were carried as far east as Susa, where the Book of Esther later took place.

17:7–23 In these verses, the writer departs from quoting his written sources and gives his own explanation for the captivity of Israel. Judah is included, though her captivity did not occur until 605/604–586 B.C. at the hands of the Babylonians. Her sins were the same. Here is a very full and impressive vindication of God's action in punishing His privileged but rebellious and apostate people. In verse 7, he begins by stating that the Israelites had sinned against the Lord who had redeemed them from Egypt. Gross perversion of the worship of God and national propensity to idolatry finally exhausted divine patience. The idolatry of Israel is described in verses 7–12. In response to Israel's actions, the Lord sent His prophets to Israel and Judah with a message of repentance (v. 13). However, the people failed to respond to the prophets' messages because, like their fathers, they did not have faith in the Lord (v. 14). Their lack of faith resulted in disobedience to the Lord's commands and the further pursuit of idolatry (vv. 15–17). The idolatry of Israel (and Judah) brought forth the anger of the Lord, which resulted in exile (v. 18). The great sin of both Israel and Judah was their continual following of the wicked pattern of Jeroboam I, departing from the Lord and practicing idolatry, thus bringing down the judgment of captivity predicted by the pro-phets (vv. 19–23).

17:7 feared other gods. The primary cause of Israel's exile was the worship of other gods. The fear of the Lord led to listening to His Word and obeying His ordinances and statutes (Deut. 4:10; 5:29; 6:24), but the fear of the gods of Canaan led Israel to obey the laws of the Canaanite gods (v. 8). The result of this obedience to false gods is recorded in verses 9–12, 16, 17.

17:8 walked in the statutes of the nations. This was expressly forbidden in Leviticus 18:3; 20:23.

17:9 built . . . high places. In addition to their private sins ("secret"), judgment came for public wickedness and idolatry. These were not the high places utilized by Israel for worshiping God before the building of the temple (see note on 1 Kin. 3:2). In direct disobedience to Deuteronomy 12:1–4, the Israelites built new, raised altars in the Canaanite pattern after the temple was constructed. These high places were in all the habitations of Israel, from small fortified structures to large garrison cities, i.e., from the smallest to largest towns. The "high

Shalmaneser's/Sargon's Assyrian Campaigns Against Israel (725/722 B.C.)

In 725 B.C. Shalmaneser V invaded Israel and marched on Samaria. Sargon II took Samaria in 722 B.C.

Nelson's Complete Book of Bible Maps & Charts (Nashville: Thomas Nelson Publishers, 1996) 134. © 1993 by Thomas Nelson, Inc.

place" altars were on wooded hills with images representing the false gods (v. 10; cf. Deut. 16:21, 22).

17:13 Turn from your evil ways. The prophets continually called the people to repentance (cf. Jer. 7:3, 5; 18:11; Ezek. 33:11).

17:14 stiffened their necks. A stubborn refusal to respond (see note on Deut. 9:6; cf. Ex. 32:9; 33:3, 5; 34:9; Acts 7:51).

17:16 a molded image and two calves. The text should be translated "molded images, even two calves." Worship of them was instituted by Jeroboam (see 1 Kin. 12:25–33). **wooden image.** This was built by Rehoboam (see 1 Kin. 14:15, 23). **the host of heaven.** In the ancient Near East, the sun, moon, and stars were deified and worshiped. This astral worship entered Israel and Judah (21:5; 23:4, 5; Ezek. 8:15, 16; Amos 5:26). The worship of the heavenly bodies was prohibited by the Mosaic Law (Deut. 4:19; 17:3).

17:17 pass through the fire. See notes on 3:27; 16:3. **witchcraft and soothsaying.** See note on Deuteronomy 18:9–12. Isaiah prophesied of the devastation these practices would produce (8:19–22).

17:19 Judah followed Israel into sin and judgment.

17:21 He tore Israel. See notes on 1 Kings 11:11–13, 29–39.

17:22 the sins of Jeroboam. See notes on 1 Kings 12:25–32. The sins of that king put in motion an unbroken pattern of idolatrous iniquity. See note on 13:2.

17:23 as it is to this day. The exiles of Israel never returned en masse as did Judah (see note on 1 Chr. 9:1).

17:24 Samaria. After its conquest by the Assyrians, the central hill and coastal plain region of the former northern kingdom of Israel became an Assyrian province, all of which was called "Samaria" after the ancient capital city (cf. vv. 28, 29). The Assyrian king, Sargon II, settled alien people, who came from widely scattered areas also conquered by Assyria, in the abandoned Israelite towns. Babylon and Cuthah were located in southern Mesopotamia. Hamath was a town on the Orontes River in Syria. The exact location of Ava and Sepharvaim are unknown. These people, who intermarried with the Jews who escaped exile, became the Samaritans—a mixed Jew and Gentile people, later hated by NT Jews (cf. Matt. 10:5; John 4:9; see notes on Luke 10:29–36).

17:25 lions among them. Lions were employed occasionally by God as instruments of punishment (cf. 1 Kin. 13:24; 20:36).

17:26 the rituals of . . . God. The newcomers interpreted the lions as a punishment from the God of Israel, whom they viewed as a deity who needed to be placated. Since they did not know how to appease Him, they appealed to Sargon II for help.

17:27, 28 one of the priests. In response, the Assyrian king ordered an Israelite priest back to Samaria from exile to teach the people what the God of the land required in worship.

17:29–32 Though they had been taught the proper way to worship God, these people all placed God alongside their other gods in an eclectic kind of worship that was blasphemy to the one true and living God.

17:30 Succoth Benoth. Lit. "tents of the daughters," probably indicating some deity worshiped by sexual orgies. **Nergal.** Perhaps the Assyrian god of war. **Ashima.** An idol in the form of a bald male goat.

17:31 Nibhaz. A dog-like idol. **Tartak.** Either a donkey or a celestial body, Saturn. **Adrammelech.** Perhaps the same as Molech, worshiped in the form of the sun, a mule, or a peacock. **Anammelech.** A rabbit or a goat idol.

17:33 served their own gods. The religion of the Samaritans was syncretistic; it combined elements of the worship of the Lord with the worship practices of the gods which the Assyrian settlers had brought with them (*see note on v. 24*).

17:34–41 Having shown how the Samaritan people and their religion came into being (vv. 24–33), the writer of Kings shows how the syncretistic worship of the Samaritans continued for generations, even to his own day (cf. v. 41; during the Babylonian exile). The religion of the Samaritans was, at its foundation, no different from Jeroboam I's deviant religion.

III. The Surviving Kingdom: The Kings of Judah (18:1–25:21)

A. Hezekiah's Righteous Reign (18:1–20:21)

18:1–25:21 With the fall of Samaria, the northern kingdom of Israel came to an end (17:5, 6; 18:9–12). This last major division of the Books of Kings narrates the events in the surviving southern kingdom of Judah from 722 B.C. to its captivity and destruction in 586 B.C. These chapters are dominated by the accounts of two good kings, Hezekiah (18:1–20:21) and Josiah (22:1–23:30). However, the reforms of these two godly kings did not reverse the effects of the two worst kings of Judah, Ahaz (16:1–20) and Manasseh (21:1–18). The result of Judah's apostasy was exile, just like it was for Israel (23:31–25:21). The Books of Kings begin with the building of the temple (1 Kin. 5:1–6:38) and end with its destruction (25:8, 9, 13–17), chronicling the sad journey from the establishment of true worship to the destruction of apostasy.

18:1 *third year.* Ca. 729 B.C. Hoshea began to reign in 732 B.C. (*see notes on 15:27; 17:1*). Hezekiah was co-regent with Ahaz to 715 B.C. (*see note on 16:2*). *See notes on 2 Chronicles 29:1–32:32.* With this verse, the writer returned from his digression summarizing the causes of captivity to the historical record of the kings of the southern kingdom, Judah.

18:2 *twenty-nine years.* 715–686 B.C. He reigned by himself for twenty years (715–695 B.C.), and with his son, Manasseh, for nine years (695–686 B.C.). The twenty-nine years given here indicate only those years after his co-regency with Ahaz was over, when he was the actual sovereign. During Hezekiah's reign, the prophets Isaiah (19:2; Is. 1:1; 37:21) and Micah (Mic. 1:1) continued to minister in Judah.

18:4 *removed the high places.* Hezekiah was the first king of Judah to eradicate the high places, i.e., the worship centers built contrary to the Mosaic Law (cf. Deut. 12:2–7, 13, 14). *sacred pillars . . . wooden image.* Hezekiah destroyed the idols used in the worship of Baal and Asherah. *the bronze serpent.* Hezekiah broke the Nehushtan into pieces. This was the bronze snake made by Moses in the wilderness (*see notes on Num. 21:4–9*). Judah had come to worship it as an idol, perhaps influenced by Canaanite religion, which regarded snakes as fertility symbols.

18:5 *He trusted in the Lord God of Israel.* The most noble quality of Hezekiah (in dramatic contrast to his father, Ahaz) was that he relied on the Lord as his exclusive hope in every situation. What distinguished him from all other kings of Judah (after the division of the kingdom) was his firm trust in the Lord during a severe national crisis (18:17–19:34). Despite troublesome events, Hezekiah clung tightly to the Lord, faithfully following Him and obeying His commands (v. 6). As a result, the Lord was with him and gave him success (v. 7).

18:7 *He rebelled against . . . Assyria.* Before he became king, his father had submitted to Assyria. Courageously, Hezekiah broke that control by Assyria and asserted independence (cf. Deut. 7:2).

18:8 *Gaza.* The southernmost city of the

Philistines, located about fifty-five miles southwest of Jerusalem. Since Assyria had controlled Philistia, Hezekiah's invasion defied Assyrian rule and brought the threat of retaliation.

18:9–12 These verses flash back to the time just before Israel's destruction and captivity to give a summary of the fall of Samaria (more fully narrated in 17:5–23) as a graphic reminder of the Assyrian power and the threat this nation still was to Judah. This review sets the scene for the siege of Jerusalem with its reminder of Israel's apostasy against which Hezekiah's faith in the Lord was a bright contrast.

18:13–20:19 This narrative, with a few omissions and additions, is found in Isaiah 36:1–39:8. *See Isaiah notes* for amplification.

18:13 fourteenth year. 701 B.C. Hezekiah began his sole rule in 715 B.C. (*see notes on vv. 1, 2*). This date for the siege of Jerusalem is confirmed in Assyrian sources. **Sennacherib.** He succeeded Sargon II as king of Assyria in 705 B.C. and ruled until 681 B.C.

Hezekiah had rebelled against him (v. 7), probably by withholding tribute when he invaded Philistia. **fortified cities.** *See note on Isaiah 36:1.*

18:14–16 Hezekiah sought to rectify the situation with Sennacherib by admitting his error in rebelling and paying the tribute the Assyrian king demanded. Sennacherib asked for about eleven tons of silver and one ton of gold. To pay, Hezekiah emptied the temple and palace treasuries and stripped the layers of gold off the doors and doorposts of the temple.

18:17–24 The tribute did not satisfy Sennacherib, who sent messengers to demand Hezekiah's surrender.

18:17 Tartan. General of the Assyrian army (cf. Is. 20:1). **Rabsaris.** A high official in the palace. **Rabshakeh.** The word is not a proper noun, but means "commander." He was the spokesman for Sennacherib, who represented the king against Jerusalem on this occasion. **Lachish.** *See note on 14:19.* Sennacherib's conquest of this city was in its

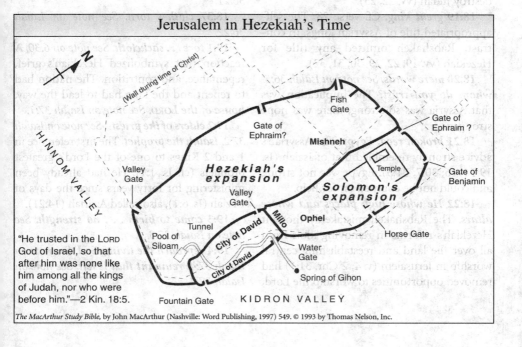

Jerusalem in Hezekiah's Time

(Wall during time of Christ)

N

HINNOM VALLEY

Valley Gate

Hezekiah's expansion

Valley Gate

Tunnel

Pool of Siloam

City of David

City of David

Fountain Gate

Fish Gate

Gate of Ephraim?

Mishneh

Millo

Ophel

Water Gate

Spring of Gihon

KIDRON VALLEY

Gate of Ephraim ?

Temple

Solomon's expansion

Gate of Benjamin

Horse Gate

"He trusted in the LORD God of Israel, so that after him was none like him among all the kings of Judah, nor who were before him."—2 Kin. 18:5.

The MacArthur Study Bible, by John MacArthur (Nashville: Word Publishing, 1997) 549. © 1993 by Thomas Nelson, Inc.

closing phase when he sent the messengers. *great army.* This was a token force of the main army (19:35) with which Sennacherib hoped to bluff Judah into submitting. *aqueduct from the upper pool.* Isaiah had met Ahaz at the same spot to try, unsuccessfully, to dissuade him from trusting in foreign powers (Is 7:3). It was probably located on the higher ground northwest of Jerusalem on the main north-south highway between Judah and Samaria. *Fuller's.* The word means "launderer" and indicates the field where such activity was done, being near the water supply.

18:18 *Eliakim . . . Shebna.* Eliakim was the palace administrator and Shebna, the secretary. *See notes on Isaiah 22:19–22. Joah . . . the recorder.* The position was that of an intermediary between the king and the people (cf. 2 Sam. 8:16).

18:19–25 The Rabshakeh's logic was twofold: (1) Egypt would be unable to deliver Jerusalem (vv. 20, 21, 23, 24); and (2) the Lord had called on the Assyrians to destroy Judah (vv. 22, 25).

18:19 *great king.* Cf. verse 28. The self-appropriated title of Assyrian kings. In contrast, Rabshakeh omitted any title for Hezekiah (vv. 19, 22, 29, 30, 31, 32).

18:20 *mere words. See note on Isaiah 36:5. whom do you trust?* The implication was that Assyria was so strong, there was none stronger.

18:21 *broken reed, Egypt.* The Assyrian's advice strongly resembled that of Isaiah (Is. 19:14–16; 30:7; 31:3). Egypt was not strong and could not be counted on for help.

18:22 *He whose high places and whose altars.* The Rabshakeh mistakenly thought Hezekiah's reforms in removing idols from all over the land and reestablishing central worship in Jerusalem (v. 4; 2 Chr. 31:1) had removed opportunities to worship the Lord,

and thus cut back on honoring Judah's God, thereby displeasing Him and forfeiting His help in war. *this altar.* That all worship should center in Solomon's temple was utterly foreign to the polytheistic Assyrians.

18:23, 24 *See note on Isaiah 36:8, 9.*

18:25 *The Lord said. See note on Isaiah 36:10.*

18:26 *Aramaic . . . Hebrew. See note on Isaiah 36:11.*

18:27 *men . . . on the wall. See note on Isaiah 36:12.*

18:28–32 The Rabshakeh spoke longer and louder in Hebrew, suggesting (1) that Hezekiah could not save the city, but (2) the great king of Assyria would fill the people with abundance if they would promise to surrender to his sovereign control, give tribute to him, and be willing to go into a rich and beneficial exile (vv. 31, 32).

18:32 *take you away. See note on Isaiah 36:17.*

18:32–35 *See note on Isaiah 36:18–20.*

18:36 *held their peace. See note on Isaiah 36:21.*

18:37 *clothes torn. See note on Isaiah 36:22.*

19:1 *tore . . . sackcloth. See note on 6:30.* A reaction that symbolized Hezekiah's grief, repentance, and contrition. The nation had to repent and the king had to lead the way. *house of the Lord. See note on Isaiah 37:1.*

19:2 *elders of the priests. See note on Isaiah 37:2. Isaiah the prophet.* The first reference in 1 and 2 Kings to one of the Lord's greatest prophets (cf. Is. 1:1). He had already been ministering for forty years since the days of Uzziah (Is. 6:1), also called Azariah (14:21).

19:3 *come to birth . . . no strength. See note on Isaiah 37:3.*

19:4 *reproach the living God. See note on Isaiah 37:4. remnant that is left. See note on Isaiah 37:4.*

19:6 Do not be afraid. Sennacherib had blasphemed the Lord by equating Him with other gods. The Lord would personally demonstrate to the Assyrian king His superiority over all other so-called deities.

19:7 spirit. The Lord promised to incline Sennacherib's attitude in such a way that he would leave Jerusalem unharmed and return home. How the Lord did that is recorded in verses 35–37.

19:8 Libnah. See note on Isaiah 37:8.

19:9 Tirhakah king of Ethiopia. See note on Isaiah 37:9.

19:9–13 The king of Assyria sent messengers to summarize the arguments given in the Rabshakeh's ultimatum of 18:19–25.

19:10 deceive. The accusation of deception was first against Hezekiah (18:29), then against the Lord.

19:11–13 The threat repeated the thrust of 18:33–35.

19:12, 13 The conquered cities mentioned here lay between the Tigris and Euphrates rivers in Mesopotamia, and were cities of Syria that had recently fallen to Sennacherib and the Assyrians.

19:14 house of the LORD. Godly Hezekiah returned to the house of the Lord (cf. v. 1) as he should have, in contrast to Ahaz, who in a similar crisis refused even to ask a sign from the Lord (Is. 7:11, 12).

19:15 the One who dwells ... heaven and earth. See note on Isaiah 37:16.

19:16 hear ... see ... hear. See note on Isaiah 37:17.

19:17, 18 See note on Isaiah 37:18, 19.

19:19 You alone. See note on Isaiah 37:20.

19:20 Isaiah the son of Amoz. See note on Isaiah 37:21.

19:21 laughed you to scorn. See note on Isaiah 37:22.

19:22 you reproached and blasphemed? The Lord had heard Sennacherib's reproach against Him (v. 16).

19:23, 24 See note on Isaiah 37:24, 25.

19:25–28 I have brought it to pass. See notes on Isaiah 37:26–29.

19:29 sign. The two years in which they were sustained by the growth of the crops were the two in which Sennacherib ravaged them. He left immediately after the deliverance (v. 36), so in the third year the people remaining could plant again.

19:30, 31 remnant ... remnant. From the remnant of survivors in Jerusalem came descendants who covered the land once again (cf. Is. 1:9, 27; 3:10; 4:3; 6:13; 8:16, 17; 10:20, 22; 11:12, 16; 26:1–4, 8; 27:12; 28:5; 37:4).

Sennacherib's Assyrian Campaign Against Judah (701 B.C.)

Sennacherib moved southward along the coastal plains to Lachish and camped against Jerusalem in 701 B.C.

Nelson's Complete Book of Bible Maps & Charts (Nashville: Thomas Nelson Publishers, 1996) 134. © 1993 by Thomas Nelson, Inc.

False Gods in the Old Testament

1. Rachel's household gods (Gen. 31:19)
2. The golden calf at Sinai (Ex. 32)
3. Nanna, the moon god of Ur, whorshiped by Abraham before his salvation (Josh. 24:2)
4. Asherah, or Ashtaroth, the chief goddess of Tyre, referred to as the lady of the sea (Judg. 6:24–32).
5. Dagon, the chief Philistine agriculture and sea god and father of Baal (Judg. 16:23–30; 1 Sam. 5:1–7)
6. Ashtoreth, a Canaanite goddess, another consort of Baal (1 Sam. 7:3, 4)
7. Molech, the god of the Ammonites and the most horrible idol in the Scriptures (1 Kin. 11:7; 2 Chr. 28:14; 33:6)
8. The two golden images made by King Jeroboam, set up at the shrines of Dan and Bethel (1 Kin. 12:28–31)
9. Baal, the chief deity of Canaan (1 Kin. 18:17–40; 2 Kin. 10:28; 11:18)
10. Rimmon, the Syrian god of Naaman the leper (2 Kin. 5:15–19)
11. Nishroch, the Assyrian god of Sennacherib (2 Kin. 19:37)
12. Nebo, the Babylonian god of wisdom and literature (Is. 46:1)
13. Merodach, also called Marduk, the chief god of the Babylonian pantheon (Jer. 50:2)
14. Tammuz, the husband and brother of Ishtar (Asherah), goddess of fertility (Ezek. 8:14)
15. The golden image in the plain of Dura (Dan. 2)

The MacArthur Study Bible, by John MacArthur (Nashville: Word Publishing, 1997) 61. © 1993 by Thomas Nelson, Inc.

19:31 zeal of the LORD of hosts. The same confirmation of God's promise in 19:7 assured the future establishment of the messianic kingdom. Deliverance from Sennacherib in Hezekiah's day was a down payment on the literal, final restoration of Israel at Christ's Second Coming.

19:32 shall not come . . . build a siege mound. See note on Isaiah 37:33.

19:33 shall he return. See note on Isaiah 37:34.

19:34 For My own sake. Since Sennacherib had directly challenged the Lord's faithfulness to His Word (v. 10), the faithfulness of God was at stake in this contest with the Assyrians (cf. Ezek. 36:22, 23). **for My servant David's sake.** God pledged to perpetuate David's line on his throne (2 Sam. 7:16; cf. Is. 9:6, 7; 11:1; 55:3).

19:35 the angel of the LORD. For identifi-cation, *see note on Exodus 3:2.* For the angel as an agent of destruction, see Genesis 19:15; 2 Samuel 24:16.

19:35–37 killed. See notes on Isaiah 37:36–38.

20:1 In those days . . . sick. The date of Hezekiah's sickness poses three reasonable possibilities: (1) since Hezekiah would be given fifteen years of life and delivered from the Assyrians (v. 6), the sickness occurred c. 701 B.C.; (2) since Berodach-Baladan (v. 12) died in 703 B.C., the sickness occurred shortly before and was followed by the embassy from Babylon that saw the temple treasures (vv. 12–19); or (3) since Berodach-Baladan's greatest power was c. 721–710 B.C., Hezekiah's sickness occurred during those years. The first or second possibility is most likely. **Set your house in order.** An instruction telling Hezekiah to make his final will known to his family (cf. 2 Sam. 17:23). *you shall die, and not live.* The prediction sounded final, but Hezekiah knew God was willing to hear his appeal (cf. Ex. 32:7–14).

20:2, 3 *prayed ... wept bitterly.* Hezekiah reminded the Lord in prayer of his piety and devotion to God. He did not specifically ask to be healed. Based on the interpretation of the date from verse 1, Hezekiah wept because: (1) he thought his death would give Sennacherib cause for boasting; or (2) his son Manasseh was too young to become king.

20:3 *loyal heart.* See note on Isaiah 38:3.

20:6 *fifteen years.* The Lord's immediate (v. 4) response granted the king's request. Having to reverse a prophecy so quickly did not alarm Isaiah as it did Jonah later on (Jon. 4:2, 3). Isaiah resembled Nathan in this respect (2 Sam. 7:3–6). *I will deliver ... this city.* See note on Isaiah 38:6.

20:8–11 *sign ... ten degrees backward.* Here is the first biblical mention of any means of marking time. Hezekiah requested this sign to confirm the Lord's promise of healing.

20:12 *At that time.* Just after Hezekiah's sickness and recovery. *Berodach-Baladan.* Berodach-Baladan, ruler of the city of Babylon, defied Assyria repeatedly between 721 and 710 B.C. He apparently approached Hezekiah (c. 703 B.C.) for help against Sargon, king of Assyria, though interest in the reversal of the sundial (2 Chr. 32:31) and Hezekiah's recovery may have been part of his motivation.

20:13 *Hezekiah was attentive.* The text does not say whether it was because of flattery or out of a desire for help against the Assyrian threat. Cf. *pleased* in Isaiah 39:2.

20:13, 14 *treasures ... treasures.* See notes on Isaiah 39:2, 3.

20:16, 17 *word of the LORD ... carried to Babylon.* Isaiah predicted the Babylonian captivity that would come over a century later (586 B.C.), another prophecy historically fulfilled in all of its expected detail.

20:17 *nothing shall be left.* Hezekiah's sin of parading his wealth before the visitors backfired, though this sin was only symptomatic of the ultimate reason for the captivity. The major cause was the corrupt leadership of Manasseh, Hezekiah's son (21:11–15).

20:18 *sons who will descend from you.* Hezekiah's sons had to go into captivity. See 24:12–16; 2 Chronicles 33:11; Daniel 1:3, 4, 6 for the prophecy's fulfillment.

20:19 *word of the LORD ... good!* A surprising response to the negative prophecy of verses 16–18. It acknowledged Isaiah as God's faithful messenger, and God's goodness in not destroying Jerusalem during Hezekiah's lifetime. *peace and truth ... in my days?* Hezekiah might have reacted selfishly, or perhaps he looked for a bright spot to lighten the gloomy fate of his descendants.

20:20 *tunnel.* See note on 2 Chronicles 32:30.

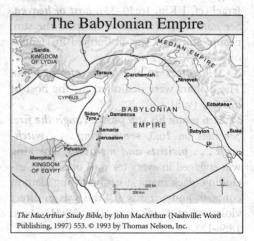

The Babylonian Empire

The MacArthur Study Bible, by John MacArthur (Nashville: Word Publishing, 1997) 553. © 1993 by Thomas Nelson, Inc.

B. Manasseh's and Amon's Wicked Reigns (21:1–26)

21:1 *twelve years old.* Manasseh began to reign as co-regent alongside his father, Hezekiah, in 695 B.C. Since the years of the subsequent royal reigns in Judah total ten years longer than the actual historical period and the dates of the later kings synchronize well with history, it is best to assume a ten year co-regency in Manasseh's long reign. Hezekiah groomed his son as a youth to succeed him as king; however, Manasseh turned out to be the worst king in Judah's history. *fifty-five years.* 695–642 B.C. *See notes on 2 Chronicles 33:1–20.*

21:2 *the abominations of the nations.* Cf. 16:3. The detestable practices of the Canaanites were enumerated in Deuteronomy 18:9–12. Israel's reproduction of these abominable practices of the nations that preceded her in the land was forbidden in Deuteronomy 12:29–31. The idolatry of Manasseh is detailed in verses 3–9 (cf. 17:7–12, 15–17).

21:3 *high places . . . altars . . . wooden image.* Manasseh reversed the reforms of Hezekiah (cf. 18:4), reestablishing the worship of Baal as an official state-sanctioned religion in Judah, just as Ahab had done in Israel (cf. 1 Kin. 16:30–33). *host of heaven.* See note on 17:16. The worship of the sun, moon, and stars was prohibited in Deuteronomy 4:19; 17:2–5.

21:4 *altars in the house of the LORD.* These altars were dedicated to "the host of heaven" (v. 5).

21:6 *made his son pass through the fire.* See note on 16:3. *soothsaying . . . witchcraft . . . piritists and mediums.* The king was engaged in every form of occultism, including black magic, fortune-telling, demon contacts, and wizards. All this was in direct violation of God's law (Lev. 19:31; Deut. 18:9–12).

21:7 *set . . . put.* Manasseh provoked the Lord by "setting" an idol of a Canaanite goddess in the temple where the Lord had "set" His name (see 1 Kin. 8:29; 9:3; 2 Chr. 7:12, 16). Asherah (cf. 23:4; 2 Chr. 15:16) was believed to be the mother of seventy deities, including Baal.

21:8, 9 This alludes to the promise of 2 Samuel 7:10. From the very start of their time in Canaan, the people were called to this obedience, but because the people of Judah did not carefully follow the stipulations of the Mosaic Law, they were again led into idolatry by Manasseh. Their idolatry even exceeded the idolatry of the Canaanites from whom they took the land.

21:10 *the prophets.* Through his spokesman, the Lord announced Judah's judgment. In verses 11–15, the prophetic message to Judah is summarized.

21:11 *Amorites.* A general designation of the original inhabitants of Canaan (cf. Gen. 15:16; Josh. 24:8).

21:13 *the plummet.* These were weighted lines dropped from walls to see whether they were structurally straight (cf. Is. 28:17; Amos 7:7, 8). Walls out of line were torn down. The Lord had measured Jerusalem by the standard of His Word and had determined that the fate of Samaria (Israel) was also to befall Jerusalem. *wipe Jerusalem.* As one would wipe food off a dish, the Lord would wipe Jerusalem clean off the earth, i.e., obliterate her and leave her turned upside down, empty and useless.

21:14 *forsake.* The Lord was going to abandon His people into the hands of enemies who would plunder them (cf. Jer. 12:7). *remnant.* Judah, the only remaining group of the chosen people.

21:15 *provoked Me to anger.* The history of God's people, Israel, was a history of disobedience toward the Lord. With the reign of Manasseh, the sin of God's people climaxed, God's patience was withdrawn, and the judgment of exile became inevitable (cf. 24:1–4).

21:16 very much innocent blood. The reference here is ambiguous and several interpretations have been offered: (1) child sacrifice (cf. v. 6); (2) oppression and persecution of the weak (Jer. 7:6; 22:3, 17; Ezek. 22:6–31); or (3) the martyrdom of God's prophets (cf. v. 10). A combination of all three is most likely. Jewish and Christian tradition alike report that Manasseh had Isaiah sawn in two inside a hollow log (cf. Heb. 11:37).

21:19 two years. 642–640 B.C. Amon continued the idolatrous practices of his father, abandoning the Lord completely (vv. 20–22). *See note on 2 Chronicles 33:21–25.*

21:24 the people of the land. Probably a group of Judah's national leaders who killed the assassins of Amon and installed his son Josiah on the throne. Apparently, they desired to maintain the Davidic dynasty (cf. 2 Kin. 11:14–18).

C. Josiah's Righteous Reign (22:1–23:30)

22:1 thirty-one years. 640–609 B.C. During Josiah's reign, power in the ancient Near East passed from Assyria to Babylon. Nineveh, the capital of Assyria, was destroyed by the Babylonians in 612 B.C., and the Assyrian Empire fell in 609 B.C. Josiah was the last good king of the Davidic line prior to the Babylonian exile. Jeremiah (Jer. 1:2), possibly Habakkuk, and Zephaniah (Zeph. 1:1) were prophets to Judah during the reign of Josiah. *See notes on 2 Chronicles 34:1–35:27.*

22:2 did not turn aside. Josiah had complete devotion to God's approved course of conduct for his life (cf. 23:25). He obeyed the Mosaic stipulations as he came to know them, following the example of David, who

set the pattern for the rulers of God's people (Deut. 17:11, 20; Josh. 1:7).

22:3 eighteenth year. 622 B.C., when Josiah was twenty-six years of age.

22:4 Hilkiah. The high priest was the father of Azariah and the grandfather of Seraiah, the high priest who would be executed at the time of the exile by the Babylonians (cf. 25:8–20).

22:4–7 the doorkeepers. *See note on 12:9.* Josiah used the same procedure as King Joash for collecting funds to repair the temple after its abuse in the days of Manasseh and Amon.

22:8 the Book of the Law. A scroll containing the Torah (the Pentateuch), the revelation of God through Moses to Israel (*see notes on 23:2; Deut. 28:61*). Manasseh may have destroyed all the copies of God's law that were not hidden. This could have been the official copy laid beside the ark of the covenant in the Most Holy Place (Deut. 31:25, 26). It may have been removed from its place under Ahaz, Manasseh, or Amon (cf. 2 Chr. 35:3), but was found during repair work.

22:9, 10 Some believe that Shaphan must have read Deuteronomy 28–30, in which are recorded a renewal of the national covenant and a listing of the terrible threats and curses against all who violate the law of God.

22:11 tore his clothes. Josiah's reaction at the reading of the law was one of immediate contrition, expressed by the common sign of lamentation and grief (see 18:37; 19:1). Josiah's grief sprang from Judah's guilt and God's punishment (v. 13).

22:14 Huldah. This prophetess is otherwise unknown in the OT. She was held in some regard for her prophetic gift, though why she was consulted and not another prophet like Jeremiah or Zephaniah (*see note on 22:1*) is unexplained. Rarely did God speak to the nation through a woman (cf. Miriam, Ex. 15; Deborah, Judg. 5) and never did a woman have an ongoing prophetic ministry identified in Scripture. No woman was inspired to author any of Scripture's sixty-six books. **the wardrobe.** Likely, these were the royal garments or those used by the priests. **the Second Quarter.** This district of Jerusalem was called *second* because it comprised the city's first major expansion. It was probably located on the western hill of Jerusalem, an area enclosed by the city wall and built during the reign of Hezekiah. The expansion of the city during Hezekiah's reign was perhaps to accommodate Jewish refugees who had escaped from the Assyrian invasion of Israel.

22:15–20 Huldah gave God's message to Josiah through his messengers. First, the Lord confirmed to Josiah that He was surely going to bring His judgment upon Jerusalem because of her idolatry (vv. 15–17). Second, the Lord's personal word to Josiah was that he would die "in peace" (v. 20), meaning that he would escape the horrors in store for Jerusalem. This promise was based on Josiah's response of tenderness and humility before the Lord when he heard the scroll de- (vv. 18, 19).

22:20 in peace. His heart was at peace with God and he never lived to see Jerusalem destroyed, but he did die in battle (2 Chr. 35:23).

23:2 Book of the Covenant. Although this designation was used in Exodus 24:7 with reference to the contents of Exodus 20:22–23:33, it seems here to refer to a larger writing. Since the larger part of the Pentateuch focused on the Mosaic covenant, these five books came to be called thusly. Since all the men of Judah and all the inhabitants of Jerusalem were assembled together by Josiah, it seems best to view this as the reading of the whole written law found in Genesis 1

through Deuteronomy 34 (*see notes on Deut. 31:9, 11*).

23:3 pillar. *See note on 11:14.* **a covenant . . . this covenant.** Josiah made a public, binding agreement to completely obey the Lord by doing all that was commanded in the Book of the Covenant that the people had just heard read to them. Following Josiah's example, all the people promised to keep the stipulations of the Mosaic covenant. *See notes on 11:17; Exodus 24:4–8.*

23:4 Asherah. *See note on 21:7.* **the fields of Kidron.** Josiah burned everything in the temple that was devoted to idolatry. This was done in the lower portion of the Kidron Valley, east of the city of Jerusalem (cf. v. 6). **ashes to Bethel.** Located about ten miles north of Jerusalem, Bethel was one of the two original places where Jeroboam I established an apostate worship center (1 Kin. 12:28–33). Bethel was located just north of the border of Judah in the former northern kingdom, which was then the Assyrian province of Samaria. With a decline in Assyrian power, Josiah was able to exert his religious influence in the north. He used the ashes of the burned articles of idolatry to desecrate Jeroboam's religious center (cf. vv. 15–20).

23:5 constellations. Cf. 21:3. The astrologers were also removed. See Isaiah 47:13.

23:6 wooden image. The idol of Asherah (*see note on 21:7*). **graves of the common people.** The Kidron Valley contained a burial ground for the common people (cf. Jer. 26:23). Scattering ashes from the object of idolatry is said in 2 Chronicles 34:4 to have been on the graves of those who sacrificed to that idol. The common people had followed their leaders to apostasy, defilement, and damnation—all symbolized by the act of scattering the ashes.

23:7 booths. Tents (called "Succoth Benoth" in 17:30) used by women who were devoted to Asherah, in which they made hangings and committed sexual sins.

23:8 *Geba to Beersheba.* Geba was located about seven miles northeast of Jerusalem at the far north of Judah, and Beersheba was located c. forty-five miles south of Jerusalem at the southern end of Judah. Thus, this phrase was an idiomatic way of saying "throughout all of Judah."

23:10 *Topheth.* Meaning "a drum," it identified the area in the Valley of Hinnom where child sacrifice occurred (cf. Is. 30:33; Jer. 7:31, 32; 19:5, 6). It, perhaps, was called "drum" because drums were beaten to drown out the cries of the children being sacrificed.

23:11 *horses ... dedicated to the sun.* The horses and the chariots of the sun were probably thought to symbolize the sun blazing a trail across the sky and were a part of worshiping the sun. Recently, a religious shrine with horse figurines has been found in Jerusalem (cf. Ezek. 8:16).

23:12 *on the roof.* Altars were erected on the flat roofs of houses so people could worship the "host of heaven" by burning incense (Jer. 19:13; Zeph. 1:5).

23:13 *Solomon ... had built.* Solomon had built high places east of Jerusalem on the Mt. of Olives, renamed after the desecra-

---

Key Word

High Places: 12:3; 14:4; 15:4; 17:9; 23:8, 15, 20—often refers to a sacred area located on high ground such as a hill or ridge. Before the temple was built, the Israelites worshiped the true God at high places (1 Kin. 3:2–4). However, the Israelites began worshiping pagan gods at these sacred sites. Consequently, the term *high places* in the Old Testament became associated with Israel's religious rebellion and apostasy (1 Kin. 14:23; Ps. 78:58; Jer. 19:5).

---

tion, to be used in worship of foreign gods, e.g., the fertility goddess Ashtoreth from Sidon, the Moabite god Chemosh, and the Ammonite god Molech (1 Kin. 11:7). These altars existed for over 300 years before Josiah finally destroyed them. The placing of human bones defiled them and, thus, rendered these sites unclean and unsuitable as places of worship.

23:15 *the altar ... at Bethel.* Josiah reduced the altar that Jeroboam I had built at Bethel to dust and ashes (see 1 Kin. 12:28–33).

23:16 *tombs.* Seeing tombs nearby, perhaps where idolatrous priests were buried, Josiah had their bones removed and burned on the altar at Bethel to defile it. This action fulfilled a prophecy given about the altar approximately 300 years before (1 Kin. 13:2).

23:17, 18 See 1 Kings 13:1–32, especially verses 31, 32.

23:18 *Samaria.* The former northern kingdom of Israel had become known as Samaria, so named as an Assyrian province (*see note on 17:24*).

23:19 *cities of Samaria.* The desecration of the high place at Bethel was only the beginning of Josiah's desecration of all the high places in the Assyrian province of Samaria.

23:20 *executed all the priests.* These non-Levitical priests, who led apostate worship in the former northern kingdom, were idolaters who seduced God's people into idolatry. They were put to death in accordance with the statutes of Deuteronomy 13:6–18; 17:2–7, and their graves were doubly defiled with burned bones.

23:21, 22 *Such a Passover.* Judah's celebration of this Passover (see Deut. 16:2–8) more closely conformed to the instructions given in the Mosaic Law than any in the previous 400 years of Israel's history. Though the Passover was observed by Hezekiah (2 Chr. 30), no observance had been in exact conformity to God's law since the judges. Further details of this Passover observance are found in 2 Chronicles 35:1–19.

23:23 eighteenth year. C. 622 B.C. All the reforms of Josiah described took place in the same year (cf. 22:3).

23:24 the book . . . found. See 22:8.

23:25 no king like him. Of all the kings in David's line, including David himself, no king more closely approximated the royal ideal of Deuteronomy 17:14–20 than Josiah (cf. Matt. 22:37). Yet, even Josiah fell short of complete obedience because he had multiple wives (cf. vv. 31, 36; *see note on Gen. 2:24*). However, even this righteous king could not turn away the Lord's wrath because of Manasseh's sin (vv. 26, 27). See chapters 17; 18.

23:29 Necho. Pharaoh Necho II (609–594 B.C.) was an ally of Assyria against the growing power of Babylon. For some unstated reason, Josiah was determined to stop Necho and his army from joining the Assyrian army at the Euphrates River to fight Babylon. **Megiddo.** The well-fortified stronghold overlooking the Jezreel Valley about sixty-five miles north of Jerusalem. Megiddo guarded a strategic pass on the route between Egypt and Mesopotamia. Josiah's death is explained with more detail in 2 Chronicles 35:20–27.

D. The Defeat and Exile of Judah by Babylon (23:31–25:21)

23:31 three months. Jehoahaz reigned during 609 B.C., became a prisoner of Pharaoh Necho II, and ultimately died in Egypt. *See note on 2 Chronicles 36:1–4.*

23:33 Riblah in the land of Hamath. Jehoahaz was in prison at Pharaoh Necho II's military headquarters located on the Orontes River in the north Lebanon Valley (*see note on 25:6*). **silver . . . gold.** The tax imposed on Judah, whose king was imprisoned, was 750 pounds of silver and 7.5 pounds of gold.

23:34 Eliakim . . . Jehoiakim. In 609 B.C., Pharaoh Necho II placed Jehoahaz's older brother on the throne of Judah. Necho changed his name from Eliakim, meaning "God has established," to Jehoiakim, "the Lord has established." The naming of a person was regarded in the ancient Near East as sign of authority; so by naming Jehoiakim, Necho demonstrated that he was the lord who controlled Judah. As a vassal of Egypt, Judah risked attack by Egypt's enemy Babylon. *See note on 2 Chronicles 36:5–8.*

23:35 Jehoiakim taxed his people severely to pay tribute to Egypt, though he still had enough to build a magnificent palace for himself (see Jer. 22:13, 14).

23:36 eleven years. 609–597 B.C.

24:1 Nebuchadnezzar. Nebuchadnezzar II was the son of Nabopolassar, king of Babylon from 626–605 B.C. As crown prince, Nebuchadnezzar had led his father's army against Pharaoh Necho and the Egyptians at Carchemish on the Euphrates River in northern Syria (605 B.C.). By defeating the Egyptians, Babylon was established as the strongest nation in the ancient Near East. Egypt and its vassals, including Judah, became vassals of Babylon with this victory. Nebuchadnezzar followed up his victory at Carchemish by invading the land of Judah. Later, in 605 B.C., Nebuchadnezzar took some captives to Babylon, including Daniel and his friends (cf. Dan. 1:1–3). Toward the end of 605 B.C., Nabopolassar died and Nebuchadnezzar succeeded him as king of Babylon, three years after Jehoiakim had taken the throne in Judah (Jer. 25:1). Nebuchadnezzar reigned from 605–562 B.C. **three years.** Nebuchadnezzar returned to the west in 604 B.C. and took tribute from all of the kings of the west, including Jehoiakim of Judah. Jehoiakim submitted to Babylon-ian rule from 604–602 B.C. In 602 B.C., Jehoiakim rebelled against Babylon, disregarding the

Minor Old Testament Rulers

Nationality	Name	Scripture
Amalekite	Agag	1 Sam. 15:8–33
Ammonite	Ammon, King of (unnamed)	Judg. 11:12–28
Ammonite	Baalis	Jer. 40:14
Ammonite	Hanun	2 Sam. 10:1–4
Ammonite	Nahash	1 Sam. 11:12
Canaanite	Adoni-Zedek	Josh. 10:1–27
Canaanite	Bera	Gen. 14:2–24
Canaanite	Jabin	(1) Josh. 11:1–11
Canaanite		(2) Judg. 4:2
Canaanite	Jericho, King of (unnamed)	Josh. 2:2
Edomite	Edom, King of (unnamed)	Num. 20:14–21
Egyptian	Egypt, Pharaoh of (unnamed)	(1) Gen. 12:18–20
Egyptian		(2) Gen. 41:38–55
Egyptian		(3) Ex. 1:8
Egyptian		(4) Ex. 2:15
Egyptian		(5) Ex. 3:10; 5:1
Egyptian		(6) 1 Kin. 3:1
Egyptian	Hophra	Jer. 44:30
Egyptian	Neco	2 Kin. 23:29, 30
Egyptian	Shishak	1 Kin. 14:25, 26; 2 Chr. 12:2–9
Moabite	Balak	Num. 22–24
Moabite	Eglon	Judg. 3:12–30
Moabite	Mesha	2 Kin. 3:4–27
Philistine	Abimelech	(1) Gen. 20
Philistine	Abimelech	(2) Gen. 26
Philistine	Achish	1 Sam. 21:10–14; 27–29
Tyrian	Hiram	1 Kin. 5:1–18
Tyrian	Tyre, Prince of (unnamed)	Ezek. 28:1–10

advice of the prophet Jeremiah (Jer. 27:9–11).

24:2 the LORD sent . . . raiding bands. As punishment for Jehoiakim's disobedience of the Lord's Word through His prophet Jeremiah, the Lord sent Babylonian troops, along with the troops of other loyal nations, to inflict military defeats on Judah.

24:4 innocent blood. See note on 21:16.

24:7 king of Egypt. In 601 B.C., Nebuchadnezzar again marched west against Egypt and was turned back by strong Egyptian resistance. However, though able to defend its own land, Egypt was not able to be aggressive and recover its conquered lands or provide any help for its allies, including Judah.

24:8 eighteen. This reading is preferred over the "eight" of 2 Chronicles 36:9 (see note). **three months.** Having regrouped, Nebuchadnezzar invaded Judah for a second time in the spring of 597 B.C. Before he could enter Jerusalem, Jehoiakim died and was

Nebuchadnezzar's Campaigns Against Judah (605–586 B.C.)

The MacArthur Study Bible, by John MacArthur (Nashville: Word Publishing, 1997) 560. © 1993 by Thomas Nelson, Inc.

took an additional 10,000 Judeans as captives to Babylon, in particular the leaders of the nation. This included the leaders of the military and those whose skills would support the military. Included in this deportation was the prophet Ezekiel (*see notes on Ezek. 1:1–3*). Only the lower classes remained behind in Jerusalem. The Babylonian policy of captivity was different from that of the Assyrians, who took most of the people into exile and resettled the land of Israel with foreigners (17:24). The Babylonians took only the leaders and the strong, while leaving the weak and poor, elevating those left to leadership and, thereby, earning their loyalty. Those taken to Babylon were allowed to work and live in the mainstream of society. This kept the captive Jews together, so it would be possible for them to return, as recorded in Ezra.

24:17 *Mattaniah . . . Zedekiah.* Mattaniah was a son of Josiah and an uncle of Jehoiachin (cf. 1 Chr. 3:15; Jer. 1:3). Mattaniah's name, meaning "gift of the LORD," was changed to Zedekiah, "righteousness of the LORD." Nebuchadnezzar's changing of Zedekiah's name demonstrated his authority as lord over him (*see note on 23:34*). See notes on 2 Chronicles 36:11–21.

24:18 *eleven years.* Zedekiah ruled in Jerusalem, under Babylonian sovereignty, from 597–586 B.C.

24:20 *Zedekiah rebelled.* In 588 B.C., Apries (also called Hophra), the grandson of Necho, became the pharaoh over Egypt. He appears to have influenced Zedekiah to revolt against Babylon (cf. Ezek. 17:15–18).

25:1 *ninth year.* Responding to Zedekiah's rebellion (24:20), Nebuchadnezzar sent his whole army to lay siege against the city of Jerusalem. The siege began in the ninth year of Zedekiah's reign, Jan., 588 B.C. The siege wall was comprised of either wood towers higher than the walls of the city or a dirt rampart encircling the city.

succeeded as king of Judah by his son, Jehoiachin. Jehoiachin ruled for a short time in 597 B.C. *See note on 2 Chronicles 36:9, 10.*

24:10–12 The Babylonian siege of Jerusalem was begun by the troops of Nebuchadnezzar. Later, Nebuchadnezzar himself went to Jerusalem, and it was to the king himself that Jehoiachin surrendered (v. 12).

24:12 *eighth year.* 597 B.C. For the first time, the Books of Kings dated an event in Israelite history by a non-Israelite king. This indicated that Judah's exile was imminent and the land would be in the hands of Gentiles.

24:13 Nebuchadnezzar plundered the treasures of the temple and king's palace, just as the Lord had said he would (cf. 20:16–18).

24:14–16 In 597 B.C., Nebuchadnezzar

Queens of the Old Testament

Name	Scripture	Identification
Michal	1 Sam. 18:20–28; 26:44	Daughter of Saul and first wife of David
Michal	2 Sam. 3:13–16; 6:20–23	Daughter of Saul and first wife of David
Bathsheba	2 Sam. 11; 12	Wife of Uriah, then wife of David and mother of Solomon
Bathsheba	1 Kin. 1; 2	Wife of Uriah, then wife of David and mother of Solomon
Queen of Sheba	1 Kin. 10:1–13	Foreign queen who visited Solomon
Naamah	1 Kin. 14:21, 3	Mother of King Rehoboam of Judah
Maacah	1 Kin. 15:10	Mother of King Abijah and grandmother of King Asa of Judah
Jezebel	1 Kin. 16:31; 18:13, 19; 19:1, 2; 21:1–25	Evil wife of King Ahab of Israel (who promoted Baal worship, persecuted God's prophets, and planned Naboth's murder)
Azubah	1 Kin. 22:42	Mother of King Jehoshaphat of Judah
Jezebel	2 Kin. 9:30–37	Evil wife of King Ahab of Israel (who promoted Baal worship, persecuted God's prophets, and planned Naboth's murder)
Athaliah	2 Kin. 11	Evil daughter of Ahab and Jezebel; mother of King Ahaziah of Judah (only woman to rule Judah in her own right)
Jehoaddin	2 Kin. 14:2	Mother of King Amaziah of Judah
Jecoliah	2 Kin. 15:2	Mother of King Azariah of Judah
Abijah	2 Kin. 18:2	Mother of King Hezekiah of Judah
Hephzibah	2 Kin. 21:1	Mother of King Manasseh of Judah
Meshullemeth	2 Kin. 21:19	Mother of King Amon of Judah
Jedidah	2 Kin. 22:1	Mother of King Josiah of Judah
Hamutal	2 Kin. 23:31; 24:18	Mother of King Jehoahaz and King Zedekiah of Judah
Zebidah	2 Kin. 23:36	Mother of King Jehoiakim of Judah
Nehushta	2 Kin. 24:8	Mother of King Jehoiachin of Judah
Maacah	2 Chr. 15:16	Mother of King Abijah and grandmother of King Asa of Judah
Esther	Esth. 2–9	Jewish wife of King Ahasuerus of Persia

25:2 *eleventh year.* Jerusalem withstood the siege until the eleventh year of Zedekiah, July of 586 B.C. Hezekiah's tunnel guaranteed the city an uninterrupted supply of fresh water (20:20), and an Egyptian foray into Judah gave the city a temporary reprieve from the siege (Jer. 37:5).

25:3 *famine.* After a siege of over two years, the food supply in Jerusalem ran out (Jer. 38:2, 3).

25:4 *the city wall was broken.* The two walls near the king's garden were probably located at the extreme southeast corner of the city, giving direct access to the Kidron

Valley. This gave Zedekiah and his soldiers an opportunity to flee for their lives to the east.

25:5 plains of Jericho. Zedekiah fled toward the Jordan rift valley. Babylonian pursuers caught him in the Jordan Valley south of Jericho, about twenty miles east of Jerusalem.

25:6 Riblah. Located on the Orontes River about 180 miles north of Jerusalem, Riblah was Nebuchadnezzar's military headquarters for his invasion of Judah. This location was ideally situated as a field headquarters for military forces because ample provisions could be found nearby (cf. 23:33). The captured traitor Zedekiah was brought to Nebuchadnezzar at Riblah, where he was blinded after witnessing the death of his sons. The execution of the royal heirs ensured the impossibility of a future claim to the throne or rebellion from his descendants. The blinding made his own future rebellion or retaliation impossible. Jeremiah had warned Zedekiah that he would see Nebuchadnezzar (*see notes on Jer. 32:2–5; 34:3*), while Ezekiel had said he would not see Babylon (*see note on Ezek. 12:10–13*). Both prophecies were accurately fulfilled.

25:8 seventh day. See note on Jeremiah 52:12. This was August of 586 B.C., one month after the Babylonian breakthrough of Jerusalem's walls (vv. 2–4). **Nebuzaradan.** He was the commander of Nebuchadnezzar's own imperial guard, sent by the king to oversee the destruction of Jerusalem. The dismantling and destruction of Jerusalem was accomplished by the Babylonians in an orderly progression.

25:9 First, Jerusalem's most important buildings were burned.

25:10 Second, the Babylonian army tore down Jerusalem's outer walls, the city's main defense.

25:11, 12 Third, Nebuzaradan organized and led a forced march of remaining Judeans into exile in Babylon. The exiles included survivors from Jerusalem and those who had surrendered to the Babylonians before the capture of the city. Only poor, unskilled laborers were left behind to tend the vineyards and farm the fields.

25:13–17 Fourth, the items made with precious metals in the temple were carried away to Babylon. *See notes on 1 Kings 7:15– 49* for a description of these temple items.

25:17 three cubits. See note on Jeremiah 52:22.

25:18–21 Fifth, Nebuzaradan took Jerusalem's remaining leaders to Riblah, where Nebuchadnezzar had them executed. This insured that they would never lead another rebellion against Babylon.

25:18 Seraiah. Seraiah was the grandson of Hilkiah (22:4, 8; 1 Chr. 6:13, 14) and an ancestor of Ezra (Ezra 7:1). Even though Seraiah was executed, his sons were deported (1 Chr. 6:15).

Babylonian Rulers in Scripture

Ruler	Dates of Rule	Scripture Reference
Merodach-Baladan II	721–689 B.C.	2 Kin. 20:12; Is. 39:1
Nebuchadnezzar II	605–562 B.C.	2 Kin. 24; 25; Dan. 1–4
Evil-Merodach	562–560 B.C.	2 Kin. 25:27–30; Jer. 52:31–34
Nergal-Sharezer	560–556 B.C.	Jer. 39:3, 13
Belshazzar	Co-regent with Nabonidus 556–539 B.C.	Dan. 5; 7:1

25:21 *Judah ... carried away captive.* Exile was the ultimate curse brought upon Judah because of her disobedience to the Mosaic covenant (cf. Lev. 26:33; Deut. 28:36, 64). The Book of Lamentations records the sorrow of Jeremiah over this destruction of Jerusalem.

IV. EPILOGUE: THE PEOPLE'S CONTINUED REBELLION AND THE LORD'S CONTINUED MERCY (25:22–30)

25:22–30 The Books of Kings conclude with this brief epilogue. Despite the punishment of the Lord experienced by Israel and Judah, the people were still rebellious (vv. 22–26). However, due to the Lord's mercy, the house of David endured (vv. 27–30). The books of Kings end with a note of hope.

25:22 *Gedaliah.* In an attempt to maintain political stability, Nebuchadnezzar appointed a governor from an important Judean family. A more detailed account of Gedaliah's activities is found in Jeremiah 40:7–41:18. Gedaliah's grandfather, Shaphan, was Josiah's secretary, who had implemented that king's reforms (22:3). His father, Ahikam, was part of Josiah's delegation sent to Huldah (22:14) and a supporter of the prophet Jeremiah (Jer. 26:24).

25:23 *Mizpah.* Located about eight miles north of Jerusalem, Mizpah became the new center of Judah. Mizpah might have been one of the few towns left standing after the Babylonian invasion.

25:24 *oath.* As governor, Gedaliah pledged to the remaining people that loyalty to the Babylonians would ensure their safety.

25:25 *seventh month.* October of 586 B.C., two months after the destruction of Jerusalem (cf. v. 8). *Ishmael.* Elishama, Ishmael's grandfather, was a secretary under Jehoiakim (Jer. 36:12; 41:1). Ishmael probably assassinated Gedaliah because he wished to reestablish the kingship in Judah with himself as king, since he was of royal blood (cf. Jer. 41:1).

25:26 *went to Egypt.* Fearing reprisals from the Babylonians, the people fled to Egypt.

25:27 *thirty-seventh year.* March of 561 B.C. Jehoiachin was about fifty-five years old (cf. 24:8). *Evil-Merodach.* The son and successor of Nebuchadnezzar, he ruled as king of Babylon from 562–560 B.C. To gain favor with the Jews, the king released Jehoiachin from his imprisonment and gave him special privileges.

25:28–30 *spoke kindly to him.* This good word from the king of Babylon to the surviving representative of the house of David served as a concluding reminder of God's good word to David. Through the curse of exile, the dynasty of David had survived. There was still hope that God's good word to David about the seed who would build God's temple and establish God's eternal kingdom would be fulfilled (cf. 2 Sam. 7:12–16). The Book of 2 Kings opened with Elijah being carried away to heaven, the destination of all those faithful to God. The book ends with Israel, and then Judah, being carried away to pagan lands as a result of failing to be faithful to God.

Further Study

Davis, John J. and John C. Whitcomb. *A History of Israel from Conquest to Exile.* Grand Rapids: Baker, 1980.

Patterson, R. D. and Hermann J. Austel. *1, 2 Kings,* in Expositor's Bible Commentary. Grand Rapids: Zondervan, 1988.

THE FIRST BOOK OF THE
CHRONICLES

Title

The original title in the Hebrew Bible read "The annals (i.e., events or happenings) of the days." First and Second Chronicles were comprised of one book until they were divided later into separate books in the Greek OT translation, the Septuagint (LXX), c. 200 B.C. The title also changed at that time to the inaccurate title, "The things omitted," i.e., reflecting material not in 1 and 2 Samuel and 1 and 2 Kings. The English title *Chronicles* originated with Jerome's Latin Vulgate translation (c. 400 A.D.), which used the fuller title "The Chronicles of the Entire Sacred History."

Author and Date

Neither 1 nor 2 Chronicles contains direct statements regarding the human author, though Jewish tradition strongly favors Ezra the priest (cf. Ezra 7:1–6) as "the chronicler." These records were most likely recorded c. 450–430 B.C. The genealogical record in 1 Chronicles 1–9 supports a date after 450 B.C. for the writing. The NT does not directly quote either 1 or 2 Chronicles.

Background and Setting

The immediate historical backdrop encompassed the Jews' three-phase return to the Promised Land from the Babylonian exile: (1) Zerubbabel in Ezra 1–6 (c. 538 B.C.); (2) Ezra in Ezra 7–10 (c. 458 B.C.); and (3) Nehemiah in Nehemiah 1–13 (c. 445 B.C.). Previous history focuses on the Babylonian de-

portation/exile (c. 605–538 B.C.) as predicted/reported by 2 Kings, Jeremiah, Ezekiel, Daniel, and Habakkuk. The prophets of this restoration era were Haggai, Zechariah, and Malachi.

The Jews had returned from their seventy years of captivity (c. 538 B.C.) to a land that was markedly different from the one once ruled by King David (c. 1011–971 B.C.) and King Solomon (971–931 B.C.): (1) there was no Hebrew king, but rather a Persian governor (Ezra 5:3; 6:6); (2) there was no security for Jerusalem, so Nehemiah had to rebuild the wall (Neh. 1–7); (3) there was no temple, so Zerubbabel had to reconstruct a pitiful semblance of the Solomonic temple's former glory (Ezra 3); (4) the Jews no longer dominated the region, but rather were on the defensive (Ezra 4; Neh. 4); (5) they enjoyed few divine blessings beyond the fact of their return; (6) they had little of the kingdom's former wealth; and (7) God's divine presence no longer resided in Jerusalem, having departed c. 597–591 B.C. (Ezek. 8–11).

To put it mildly, their future looked bleak compared to their majestic past, especially the time of David and Solomon. The return could best be described as bittersweet, i.e., bitter because their present poverty brought hurtful memories about what was forfeited by God's judgment on their ancestors' sin, but sweet because at least they were back in the land God had given Abraham seventeen centuries earlier (Gen. 12:1–3).

The chronicler's selective genealogy and

history of Israel, stretching from Adam (1 Chr. 1:1) to the return from Babylon (2 Chr 26:23), was intended to remind the Jews of God's promises and intentions about: (1) the land; (2) the nation; (3) the Davidic king; (4) the Levitical priests; (5) the temple; and (6) true worship, none of which had been abrogated because of the Babylonian captivity. All of this was to remind them of their spiritual heritage during the difficult times they faced, and to encourage them to be faithful to God.

Historical and Theological Themes

First and Second Chronicles, as named by Jerome, recreate an OT history in miniature, with particular emphases on the Davidic covenant and temple worship. In terms of literary parallel, 1 Chronicles is the partner of 2 Samuel, in that both detail the reign of King David. First Chronicles opens with Adam (1:1) and closes with the death of David (29:26–30) in 971 B.C. Second Chronicles begins with Solomon (1:1) and covers the same historical period as 1 and 2 Kings, while focusing exclusively on the kings of the southern kingdom of Judah, thus excluding the history of the ten northern tribes and their rulers, because of their complete wickedness and false worship. It ranges from the reign of Solomon (1:1) in 971 B.C. to the return from Babylon in 538 B.C. (36:23).

Over 55 percent of the material in Chronicles is unique, i.e., not found in 2 Samuel or 1 and 2 Kings. The "chronicler" tended to omit what was negative or in opposition to the Davidic kingship; on the other hand, he tended to make unique contributions in validating temple worship and the line of David. Whereas 2 Kings 25 ends dismally with the deportation of Judah to Babylon, 2 Chronicles 36:22–23 concludes hopefully with the Jews' release from Persia and return to Jerusalem.

These two books were written to the repatriated Jewish exiles as a chronicle of God's intention of future blessing, in spite of the nation's past moral/spiritual failure for which the people paid dearly under God's wrath. First and Second Chronicles may be summarized briefly as follows:

I. A Selected Genealogical History of Israel (1 Chr. 1–9)
II. Israel's United Kingdom Under Saul (1 Chr. 10), David (1 Chr. 11–29), and Solomon (2 Chr. 1–9)
III. Judah's Monarchy in the Divided Kingdom (2 Chr. 10–36:21)
IV. Judah's Release From Their Seventy-Year Captivity (2 Chr. 36:22, 23).

The historical themes are inextricably linked with the theological in that God's divine purposes for Israel have been and will be played out on the stage of human history. These two books are designed to assure the returning Jews that, in spite of their checkered past and present plight, God will be true to His covenant promises. They have been returned by God to the land first given to Abraham as a race of people whose ethnic identity (Jewish) was not obliterated by the deportation and whose national identity (Israel) has been preserved (Gen. 12:1–3; 15:5), although they are still under God's judgment as prescribed by the Mosaic legislation (Deut. 28:15–68).

The priestly line of Eleazar's son Phinehas and the Levitical line were still intact, so that temple worship could continue in the hopes that God's presence would one day return (Num. 25:10–13; Mal. 3:1). The Davidic promise of a king was still valid, although future in its fulfillment (2 Sam. 7:8–17; 1 Chr. 17:7–15). Their individual hope of eternal life and restoration of God's blessings forever rested in the new covenant (Jer. 31:31–34).

Two basic principles enumerated in these two books prevail throughout the OT, namely, obedience brings blessing, disobedience brings judgment. In the Chronicles, when the king obeyed and trusted the Lord, God blessed and protected. But when the king disobeyed and/or put his trust in something or someone other than the Lord, God withdrew His blessing and protection. Three basic failures by the kings of Judah brought God's wrath: (1) personal sin; (2) false worship/idolatry; and/or (3) trust in man rather than God.

Interpretive Challenges

First and Second Chronicles present a combination of selective genealogical and historical records, and no insurmountable challenges within the two books are encountered. A few issues arise, such as: (1) Who wrote 1 and 2 Chronicles? Does the overlap of 2 Chronicles 36:22–23 with Ezra 1:1–3 point to Ezra as author? (2) Does the use of multiple sources taint the inerrancy doctrine of Scripture? (3) How does one explain the variations in the genealogies of 1 Chronicles 1–9 from other OT genealogies? (4) Are the curses of Deuteronomy 28 still in force, even though the seventy-year captivity has cluded? (5) How does one explain the few variations in numbers when comparing Chronicles with parallel passages in Samuel and Kings? These will be dealt with in the notes at the appropriate places.

Outline

I. Selective Genealogy (1:1–9:34)
   A. Adam to Before David (1:1–2:55)
   B. David to the Captivity (3:1–24)
   C. Twelve Tribes (4:1–9:1)
   D. Jerusalem Dwellers (9:2–34)
II. David's Ascent (9:35–12:40)
   A. Saul's Heritage and Death (9:35–10:14)
   B. David's Anointing (11:1–3)
   C. Jerusalem's Conquest (11:4–9)
   D. David's Men (11:10–12:40)
III. David's Reign (13:1–29:30)
   A. The Ark of the Covenant (13:1–16:43)
   B. The Davidic Covenant (17:1–27)
   C. Selected Military History (18:1–21:30)
   D. Temple-Building Preparations (22:1–29:20)
   E. Transition to Solomon (29:21–30)

1:1–9:44 This abbreviated genealogy summarizes the divinely selected course of redemptive history: (1) from Adam to Noah (1:1–4; Gen. 1–6); (2) from Noah's son Shem to Abraham (1:4–27; Gen. 7–11); (3) from Abraham to Jacob (1:28–34; Gen.12–25); (4) from Jacob to the twelve tribes (1:34–2:2; Gen. 25–50); and (5) from the Twelve Tribes to those who had returned to Jerusalem after the seventy-year captivity (2:3–9:44; Ex. 1:1–2 Chr. 36:23). This genealogical listing is unique to the purposes of the chronicler and is not intended necessarily to be an exact duplication of any other lists in Scripture.

I. SELECTIVE GENEALOGY (1:1–9:34)

A. Adam to Before David (1:1–2:55)

1:19 days . . . divided. Peleg, which means "divided," apparently lived when the Lord divided, or scattered, the human race because of Babel (cf. Gen. 11:1–9).

1:28–31 These twelve sons of Ishmael developed Twelve Tribes and settled the great northern desert of Arabia and became Arab peoples.

1:43 kings . . . Edom. Esau's children settled in Edom, east and south of Israel, and are included among the Arab nations.

2:1–7:40 These genealogies reflect the lineage of Jacob/Israel through his twelve sons. The tribe of Judah leads the list, indicating its importance, no doubt because of the Davidic heritage. After Judah, Levi receives the most attention, indicating the importance of their priestly role. Joseph (2:2) is later enumerated in terms of his sons Manasseh and Ephraim. Dan and Zebulun are not mentioned here, although they both are identified in the millennial distribution of land (cf. Ezek. 48:1, 2, 26, 27). The exact reason for these omissions is unknown. Benjamin is given additional attention in 8:1–40. The tribes are mentioned as follows: (1) Judah (2:3–4:23); (2) Simeon (4:24–43); (3) Reuben (5:1–10); (4) Gad (5:11–22); (5) Manasseh-East (5:23–26); (6) Levi (6:1–81); (7) Issachar (7:1–5); (8) Benjamin (7:6–12); (9) Naphtali (7:13); (10) Manasseh-West (7:14–19); (11) Ephraim (7:20–29); and (12) Asher (7:30–40).

2:3–4:23 The family of Judah.

2:7 Achar. This is a variant spelling of Achan, who in Joshua 7:1–26 disobeyed the Lord by taking goods included under God's Jericho ban.

B. David to the Captivity (3:1–24)

3:1–4 2 Samuel 3:2–5.

3:1 David. The chief reason for such

A Short Harmony of Samuel, Kings, and Chronicles

1. Selected Genealogies	-----	1 Chronicles 1–9
2. Samuel's Judgship	1 Samuel 1–8	-----
3. Saul's Reign	1 Samuel 9–31	1 Chronicles 10
4. David's Reign	2 Samuel 1–24	1 Chronicles 11–29
5. Solomon's Reign	1 Kings 1–11	2 Chronicles 1–9
6. Divided Kingdom Pt. 1 (to the Assyrian exile)	1 Kings 12–2 Kin. 17	2 Chronicles 10–27
7. Divided Kingdom Pt. 2 (to the Babylonian exile)	2 Kings 18–25	2 Chronicles 28–36:21
8. Return from Babylon	-----	2 Chronicles 36:22, 23

The MacArthur Study Bible, by John MacArthur (Nashville: Word Publishing, 1997) 566. © 1993 by Thomas Nelson, Inc.

detailed genealogies is that they affirm the line of Christ from Adam (Luke 3:38) through Abraham and David (Matt. 1:1), thus emphasizing the kingdom intentions of God in Christ.

3:5–8 See 14:47; 2 Samuel 5:14–16.

3:10–16 Rehoboam . . . Zedekiah. The reigns of these sons of David are delineated in 2 Chronicles 10:1–36:21.

3:16 Jeconiah. God's curse resulting in no royal descendants from the line of Jeconiah (Jehoiakin), as given by Jeremiah (Jer. 22:30), was enforced by God. Even though Jeconiah was in the line of Christ, the Messiah was not a physical child of that line, thus affirming the curse, yet sustaining the legality of His kingship through Joseph, who was in David's line. His blood birthright came through Mary, who traced her line to David through his son Nathan, not Solomon (cf. Luke 3:31).

3:22 six in all. Only five sons are named, so the number includes their father Shemaiah.

C. Twelve Tribes (4:1–9:1)

4:24–43 The family of Simeon.

4:41 Hezekiah. He ruled Judah c. 715–686 B.C.

4:43 Amalekites. Longstanding enemies of Israel whom God purposed to exterminate. Another branch of the Amalekite family tree had appeared in Persia, represented by Haman, who attempted to exterminate the Jews (Esth. 3:1ff.).

5:1–10 The family of Reuben.

5:2 Judah prevailed. In accordance with Jacob's blessing (Gen. 49:10), the king of Israel is to come from Judah. This prophecy had historical reference to the Davidic covenant (cf. ch. 17; 2 Sam. 7) with full messianic implications.

5:6 Tiglath-Pileser. The king of Assyria (c. 745–727 B.C.) who threatened Judah and made Ahaz pay a tribute (cf. 2 Kin. 16:7–20; 2 Chr. 28:16–21).

Key Word

Sons: 1:43; 3:12; 4:25; 5:14; 7:14; 9:4; 11:22; 22:9; 26:28—lit. "to build." The ancient Hebrews considered their children the "builders" of the future generations. *Ben* can refer to a direct son or to one's future descendants (1 Kin. 2:1; 1 Chr. 7:14). Old Testament names such as Benjamin, meaning "Son of my Right Hand," incorporate this Hebrew noun (Gen. 35:18). In the plural, *ben* can be translated as "children" regardless of gender (see Ex. 12:37; "children of Israel"). God Himself uses this term to describe His unique relationship with Israel: "Israel is My son, My firstborn" (Ex. 4:22).

5:11–22 The family of Gad.

5:22 the captivity. The Assyrian deportation of 722 B.C. is meant (cf. 5:26).

5:23–26 The family of Manasseh (east).

6:1–81 The family of Levi.

6:1–15 This section lists the high-priestly lineage from Levi (6:1) through Aaron (6:3), through Eleazar (6:3, 4), and through Phinehas (6:4), with whom God covenanted for a perpetual priesthood (Num. 25:11–13).

6:8 Zadok. By the time of David's reign, the high priestly line had wrongly been shifted to the sons of Ithamar as represented by Abiathar. When Abiathar sided with Adonijah rather than Solomon, Zadok became the ruling high priest (1 Kin. 2:26, 27) and restored the high-priesthood to the Levitical line through Phinehas (cf. Num. 25:10–13).

6:13 Hilkiah. The high priest who rediscovered the law in Josiah's reign c. 622 B.C. (2 Kin. 22:8–13; 2 Chr. 34:14–21).

6:14 Seraiah. The high priest who was executed by the Babylonians after their occupation of Jerusalem c. 586 B.C. (2 Kin. 25:18–21). **Jehozadak** (Jozadak). The father of

Jeshua, the first high priest in the return (cf. Ezra 3:2; 5:2).

6:16–30 The sons of Levi (6:16–19) and their families (6:20–30) are given here.

6:27, 28 Samuel, a Levite by exceptional, divine direction, offered priestly sacrifices (cf. 1 Sam. 7:9; 10:8; 11:14, 15). The fact that Elkanah was from Ephraim (1 Sam. 1:1) indicates where he lived, not his family history (Num. 35:6–8).

6:31–48 The Levitical musicians are listed as they relate to: (1) Kohath and Heman (6:33–38); (2) Gershon and Asaph (6:39–43); and (3) Merari and Ethan (6:44–47).

6:49–53 This is a repeat of the high-priestly line enumerated in 6:4–8 through Zadok. This repeated genealogy could possibly point to the Zadokian high priesthood for the temple in the Millennium (cf. Ezek. 40:46; 43:19; 44:15; 48:11).

6:54–81 This section rehearses the forty-eight cities given to the Levites instead of a section of land (cf. Num. 35:1–8; Josh. 21:1–42) which signals God's intention for the Jewish nation to have a priesthood and future in the land first given to Abraham (cf. Gen. 12:1–3).

7:1–15 The family of Issachar.

7:6–12 The family of Benjamin.

7:13 The family of Naphtali.

7:14–19 The family of Manasseh (west).

7:20–29 The family of Ephraim.

7:30–40 The family of Asher.

8:1–40 This section enlarges on the genealogy of Benjamin in 7:6–12, most likely because of that tribe's important relationship with Judah in the southern kingdom. Thus, these two tribes taken in captivity together and the Levites make up the returning remnant in 538 B.C.

9:1 all Israel. Even though the northern kingdom of Israel never returned from dispersion in 722 B.C., many from the ten tribes which made up that kingdom migrated

south after the division in 931 B.C. The result was that Judah, the southern kingdom, had people from all tribes, so that when returning from captivity "all Israel" was truly represented.

D. Jerusalem Dwellers (9:2–34)

9:2 first inhabitants. This chapter has genealogies of returning: (1) Israelites (9:3–9); (2) priests (9:10–13); and (3) Levites (9:14–34). **Nethinim.** These were the temple servants (Ezra 8:20), possibly descendants of the Gibeonites (cf. Josh. 9:3, 4, 23).

II. DAVID'S ASCENT (9:35–12:14)

A. Saul's Heritage and Death (9:35–10:14)

9:35–44 This section records Saul's lineage as a transition to the main theme of the rest of the book, which is the kingship of David (c. 1011 B.C.).

10:1–12 See notes on 1 Samuel 31:1–13 (cf. 2 Sam. 1:4–12).

10:13, 14 This summary is unique to 1 Chronicles and provides the proper transition from Saul's kingship to David's reign.

10:14 He killed him. Though Saul killed himself (v. 4), God took responsibility for Saul's death, which was fully deserved for consulting a medium, an activity punishable by death (cf. Deut. 17:1–6). This demonstrates that human behavior is under the ultimate control of God, who achieves His purpose through the actions of people.

11:1–29:30 This section selectively recounts the reign of David with a heavy emphasis on the placement of the ark in Jerusalem and preparation to build the temple.

B. David's Anointing (11:1–3)

11:1–3 See notes on 2 Samuel 5:1–3.

C. Jerusalem's Conquest (11:4–9)

11:4–9 See notes on 2 Samuel 5:6–10.

D. David's Men (11:10–12:40)

11:10–41 *See notes on 2 Samuel 23:8–39.*

11:11 *Jashobeam . . . Hachmonite.* In 27:2, he is called the son of Zabdiel, so Hachmon may be, strictly speaking, his grandfather (27:32). For a variation in name and number (300), *see note on 2 Samuel 23:8.* A copyist's error would best account for 800 being reported in 2 Samuel 23:8.

11:41–47 This adds new material to 2 Samuel 23.

12:1–40 These events predate those of 11:1–47. They are divided between David's time at Ziklag (12:1–22) and Hebron (12:23–40). They summarize the narrative covered in 1 Samuel 27–2 Samuel 5.

12:1 *Ziklag.* Located in the south near the Edomite border, the territory was ruled by the Philistines, who made David a ruler over it during the latter period of Saul's reign when he was pursuing David (1 Sam. 27:6, 7). This was prior to David's taking the rule over all Israel (cf. v. 38).

12:1–14 Men from Benjamin (12:2, 3, 16–18), Gad (12:8–15), Judah (12:16–18), and Manasseh (12:19–22) came to help David conquer enemies on both sides of the Jordan River (v. 15).

12:15 *first month.* March/April when the Jordan River was at flood stage due to melting snow in the north. The Gadites would be crossing from east to west.

12:18 *the Spirit.* A temporary empowerment by the Holy Spirit to assure David that the Benjamites and Judahites were loyal to him and that the cause was blessed by God.

12:19, 20 First Samuel 29 provides the background.

12:21, 22 First Samuel 30 provides the background.

12:23–37 This recounts the period of David's seven-year, six-month reign in Hebron until he was crowned king of the entire nation and was ready to relocate in Jerusalem (2 Sam. 2–5). This narrative comes full circle back to chapter 11:1ff.

12:38–40 This feast was associated with the king's coronation in 2 Samuel 5.

III. DAVID'S REIGN (13:1–29:30)

A. The Ark of the Covenant (13:1–16:43)

13:1–16:43 This section recounts the ark of the covenant being brought from Kirjath Jearim (v. 5) to Jerusalem.

13:1–14 *See notes on 2 Samuel 6:1–11.* First Chronicles 13:1–6 adds new material to the narrative.

13:3 *the ark of our God.* Not only had the ark been stolen and profaned by the Philistines (1 Sam. 5; 6), but when it was returned, Saul neglected to seek God's instruction for it. Scripture records only one occasion when Saul sought God's ark after its return (cf. 1 Sam. 14:18).

13:5 *Shihor.* The "river of Egypt" was a small stream flowing into the Mediterranean Sea which forms the southern boundary of Israel (cf. Josh. 13:3). It is also called the "Brook of Egypt" (Josh. 15:4, 47; Num. 34:5; 2 Chr. 7:8). *Hamath.* On the northern boundary of Israel's territory. *Kirjath Jearim.* A location approximately ten miles west of Jerusalem that the Canaanites called Baalah (cf. 13:6). The ark of God had resided here for the previous twenty years (cf. 1 Sam. 7:1, 2).

13:7–14 *See notes on 2 Samuel 6:1–11.* The violation of divine directives (Num. 4:1–49) for moving the ark proved fatal to Uzza(h) (vv. 7–10).

14:1–7 *See notes on 2 Samuel 5:11–16.* The events of this chapter took place before those of 1 Chronicles 13.

14:3–7 This is a repeat of 1 Chronicles 3:5–9.

14:8–17 The Philistines desired to ruin David before the throne was consolidated. Their plan was to kill David, but God gave

Musical Instruments of the Old Testament

Name	Scripture References
Bagpipe	Dan. 3:5, 7, 10, 15
Bells	(1) Ex. 28:33, 34; 39:25, 26
	(2) Zech. 14:20
Cymbals	(1) 2 Sam. 6:5; Ps. 150:5
	(2) 1 Chr. 13:8; 15:16, 19; 2 Chr. 5:12, 13; Ezra 3:10; Neh. 12:27
Double Pipe	1 Sam. 10:5; 1 Kin. 1:40; Is. 5:12; Jer. 48:36
Harp	(1) 1 Sam. 10:5; Neh. 12:27; Is. 5:12; 14:11; Amos 5:23; 6:5
	(2) Dan. 3:5, 7, 10, 15
Harplike Instrument	Dan. 3:5, 7, 10, 15
Horn, Cornet	Dan. 3:5, 7, 10, 15
Lyre	(1) Gen. 4:21; 1 Sam. 10:5; 2 Sam. 6:5; Neh. 12:27
	(2) Dan. 3:5, 7, 10, 15
Pipe, Reed	Dan. 3:5, 7, 10, 15
Ram's Horn	(1) Josh. 6:4–20; Judg. 7:16–22; 2 Sam. 15:10;
	Pss. 47:5; 150:3; Amos 2:2;
	(2) Ex. 19:13
Sistrum	2 Sam. 6:5
Tambourine	Gen. 31:27; Ex. 15:20; Judg. 11:34; 1 Sam. 10:5; 18:6;
	2 Sam. 6:5; 1 Chr. 13:8; Job 21:12; Pss. 81:2; 149:3; Is. 5:12;
	Jer. 31:4
Trumpet	(1) Num. 10:2–10; 1 Chr. 15:24, 28; 2 Chr. 15:14; 23:13;
	Ps. 98:6; Hos. 5:8
	(2) Ezek. 7:14
Vertical Flute	Gen. 4:21; Job 21:12; 30:3; Ps. 150:4
Zither	Pss. 33:2; 92:3; 144:9

him victory over the Philistines (unlike Saul) and, thus, declared both to the Philistines and Israel His support of Israel's new king. For details, *see notes on 2 Samuel 5:17–23.*

14:12 gods . . . burned. Second Samuel 5:21 reports that the idols were carried away, presenting an apparent contradiction. Most likely the idols were first carried away and then burned later, according to the Mosaic Law (cf. Deut. 7:5, 25).

15:1–29 The chronicler picks up the narrative concerning the ark where it left off at 1 Chronicles 13:14, as David brings the ark from Obed-Edom.

15:1 David built houses for himself. He was able by the alliance and help of Hiram

(18:1) to build a palace for himself and separate houses for his wives and their children. While the ark remained near Jerusalem at the home of Obed-Edom for three months (13:13, 14), David constructed a new tabernacle in Jerusalem to fulfill God's Word in Deuteronomy 12:5–7 of a permanent residency.

15:2 carry the ark. After a lapse of three months (13:14), David followed the Mosaic directives for moving the ark (cf. Num. 4:1–49; Deut. 10:8; 18:5). These directions had been violated when the ark was moved from Kirjath-Jearim to Obed-Edom, and it cost Uzza(h) his life (cf. 13:6–11).

15:4–7 Kohath . . . Merari . . . Gershom.

David conducted the ark's relocation with the same families as had Moses (cf. Num. 4). In the restoration from Babylon, these identical three divisions of Levi participated (cf. 1 Chr. 6:1–48).

15:11 *Zadok . . . Abiathar.* These two high priests, heads of the two priestly houses of Eleazar and Ithamar, were colleagues in the high priesthood (2 Sam. 20:25). They served the Lord simultaneously in David's reign. Zadok attended the tabernacle in Gibeon (1 Chr. 16:39), while Abiathar served the temporary place of the ark in Jerusalem. Ultimately, Zadok prevailed (cf. 1 Kin. 2:26, 27).

15:12 *sanctify yourselves.* This was a special sanctification required on all special occasions, demanding complete cleanliness.

15:13 *broke out.* God's anger "broke out" when the ark had been improperly handled and transported by Uzza(h) (2 Sam. 6:6–8; 1 Chr. 13:9–12).

15:16–24 Eminent Levites were instructed to train the musicians and singers for the solemn procession.

15:25–16:3 *See notes on 2 Samuel 6:12–19.*

16:4–6 *Levites . . . minister.* As soon as the ark was placed in its tent, the Levites began their duties.

16:7–22 *See notes on Psalm 105:1–15.*

16:23–33 *See notes on Psalm 96:1–13.*

16:34–36 *See notes on Psalm 106:1, 47, 48.*

16:37–42 *regularly . . . every day's work.* The ministry was established with continuity.

16:39 *Gibeon.* Located six miles northwest of Jerusalem.

B. The Davidic Covenant (17:1–27)

17:1–27 This section recounts God's bestowing the Davidic covenant. For a full explanation, *see notes on 2 Samuel 7.*

17:1, 10 Second Samuel 7:1, 11 adds that God had and would give David rest from all of his enemies.

17:5 Second Samuel 7:14–17 adds new material.

C. Selected Military History (18:1–21:30)

18:1–21:30 This section selectively recounts David's military exploits.

18:1–11 *See notes on 2 Samuel 8:1–12.*

18:2 Second Samuel 8:2 adds details to the judgment of Moab.

18:4 The numbers here are correct; the number in 2 Samuel 8:4 for the horsemen is 700, which would not seem as consistent with the other numbers, so the 700 probably resulted from a copyist's error.

18:11 Second Samuel 8:12 adds new material.

18:12 Second Samuel 8:13 adds that David was involved.

18:14–17 *See notes on 2 Samuel 8:15–18.*

19:1–19 *See notes on 2 Samuel 10:1–19.*

19:18 *seven thousand.* Second Samuel 10:18 erroneously has 700; this is apparently a discrepancy due to copyist error. ***foot soldiers.*** This is likely more correct than "horsemen" in 2 Samuel 10:18.

20:1–3 *See notes on 2 Samuel 11:1; 12:29–31.* The chronicler was not inspired by God

The Davidic Covenant in Chronicles		
1. 1 Chr. 17:7–27		God to Nathan to David
2. 1 Chr. 22:6-16		David to Solomon
3. 1 Chr. 28:6,7		David to Solomon
4. 2 Chr. 6:8, 9, 16, 17		Solomon to nation
5. 2 Chr. 7:17, 18		God to Solomon
6. 2 Chr. 13:4, 5		Abijah to Jeroboam
7. 2 Chr. 21:7		Chronicle's commentary

The MacArthur Study Bible, by John MacArthur (Nashville: Word Publishing, 1997) 583. © 1993 by Thomas Nelson, Inc.

to mention David's sin with Bathsheba and subsequent sins recorded in 2 Samuel 11:2–12:23. The adultery and murder occurred at this time, while David stayed in Jerusalem instead of going to battle. The story was likely omitted because the book was written to focus on God's permanent interest in His people, Israel, and the perpetuity of David's kingdom.

20:4–8 *See notes on 2 Samuel 21:15–22.* The chronicler chose not to write of some of the darker days in David's reign, especially the revolt of David's son Absalom, for the same reason that the iniquity of the king with Bathsheba was left out.

21:1 There is approximately a twenty-year gap between 20:8 and 21:1, c. 995–975 B.C.

21:1–27 For the explanation of this section, *see notes on 2 Samuel 24:1–25.*

21:1 *Satan . . . moved.* Second Samuel 24:1 reports that it was God who "moved" David. This apparent discrepancy is resolved by understanding that God sovereignly and permissively uses Satan to achieve His purposes. God uses Satan to judge sinners (cf. Mark 4:15; 2 Cor. 4:4), to refine saints (cf. Job 1:8–2:10; Luke 22:31, 32), to discipline those in the church (cf. 1 Cor. 5:1–5; 1 Tim. 1:20), and to further purify obedient believers (cf. 2 Cor. 12:7–10). Neither God nor Satan forced David to sin (cf. James 1:13–15), but God allowed Satan to tempt David and he chose to sin. The sin surfaced his proud heart and God dealt with him for it. *number Israel.* David's census brought tragedy because, unlike the census in Moses' time (Num. 1; 2) which God had commanded, this census by David was to gratify his pride in the great strength of his army and consequent military power. He was also putting more trust in his forces than in his God. He was taking credit for his victories by the building of his great army. This angered God, who allowed Satan to bring the sin to a head.

21:3, 4 *a cause of guilt in Israel?* Joab knew David was operating on a sinful motive, but the king's arrogance led him to ignore the warning.

21:5 *one million one hundred thousand.* Second Samuel 24:9 reports 800,000 and 500,000, respectively. For the resolution of this discrepancy, *see note on 2 Samuel 24:9.*

21:6 *he did not count Levi and Benjamin.* Levites were not soldiers (v. 5) and were not numbered in the Mosaic census (Num. 1:47–55). Benjamin had already been numbered (7:6–11) and the register preserved in the archives of that tribe. From the course followed in the census (2 Sam. 24:4–8), it appears Judah and Benjamin were last to be visited. Before the census could be finished in Judah and begin in Benjamin, David recognized his sin and called for it to stop (cf. 27:24).

21:7 *He struck Israel.* David's sin dramatically affected the entire kingdom in experiencing God's wrath.

21:12 "Three years" here is correct; "seven years" in 2 Samuel 24:13 is most likely a copyist's error, since it seems three years, three months, and three days is the intent.

21:15 *Ornan.* This is a Hebrew name. He is called Araunah in 2 Samuel 24:18, a Jebusite or Canaanite equivalent. He had been converted to worship of the true God.

21:16 This additional detail does not appear in the Hebrew of 2 Samuel 24. The "angel of the LORD" was the executioner poised to destroy Jerusalem, whose menacing destruction was halted (v. 1) because David and the leaders repented as indicated by the "sackcloth" and falling "on their faces."

21:20, 21 This additional detail does not appear in the Hebrew of 2 Samuel 24. "Threshing wheat" was done by spreading the grain out on a high level area and driving back and forth over it with a heavy sled and rollers pulled by oxen. One would drive the oxen while others raked the chaff away from the kernels.

21:25 six hundred shekels. The fifty shekels reported in 2 Samuel 24:24 was for the instruments and oxen alone, while the price here includes the whole property, Mt. Moriah, on which Solomon's temple stood. The threshing floor of Ornan is today believed by some to be the very flat rock under the Moslem mosque, the Dome of the Rock, inside the temple ground in Jerusalem.

21:28–30 This also is new data not included in 2 Samuel 24.

21:29 high place . . . Gibeon. The ark of the covenant resided at Jerusalem in a tent (ch.15) awaiting the building of the temple on Ornan's threshing floor, while the Mosaic tabernacle and altar remained in Gibeon until the temple was completed (cf. 1 Kin. 8:4).

21:30 the sword. Cf. 21:12, 16, 27. David continued to remain at the threshing floor and offer sacrifices because the Lord had appeared to him there (2 Chr. 3:1) and because he feared a menacing angel at Gibeon, the center of worship.

D. Temple—Building Preparations (22:1–29:20)

22:1–29:20 This section recounts David's preparations for Solomon to build the temple. General preparation and various charges are discussed in 22:1–19. The division of labor unfolds in 23:1–27:33. Solomon's final commission comes in 28:1–29:20.

22:1–19 David gives three charges to: (1) the workman (vv. 2–5); (2) Solomon (vv. 6–16); and (3) the leaders (vv. 17–19).

22:1 house. The land David had just purchased (21:22–30), he dedicated for the Jerusalem temple to be built by Solomon (v. 6; 28:9, 10).

22:2 aliens. These were non-Israelite artisans made up of descendants of the Canaan-

ites (2 Chr. 8:7–10) and war captives (2 Chr. 2:7), for whom the Mosaic legislation provided compassion and protection (cf. Ex. 22:21; 23:9; Lev. 19:33; Deut. 24:14, 15) and from whom service was exacted. Only here were the laborers called "aliens" (cf. 1 Kin. 5:13–18).

22:3 iron . . . bronze. David would have acquired the iron technology from the Philistines (1 Sam. 13:19–21), and the bronze would have come from spoils of war (cf. 18:8).

22:4 cedar. This came from Lebanon, the heavily wooded and mountainous country north of Israel, and was provided by the residents of Sidon and Tyre, most likely under the leadership of David's friend, King Hiram (cf. 14:1; 1 Kin. 5:1).

22:5 young. Solomon was born early in David's reign (c. 1000–990 B.C.) and was at this time twenty to thirty years of age. The magnificent and complex challenge of building such a monumental edifice with all its elements required an experienced leader for preparation. **magnificent.** David understood that the temple needed to reflect on earth something of God's heavenly majesty, so he devoted himself to the collection of the plans and materials, tapping the vast amount of spoils from people he had conquered and cities he had sacked (vv. 14–16).

22:6–16 Here is David's careful instruction to Solomon for the building which David could not do because he had killed so many in his battles (v. 8). Cf. 1 Kings 5:3.

22:8–10 David reflects on the covenant God had made with him (cf. 2 Sam. 7; 1 Chr. 17), which included (1) the divine mandate that Solomon build the temple and (2) overtones of the messianic reign.

22:11–13 David's spiritual charge to Solomon resembles the Lord's exhortation to Joshua (cf. Josh. 1:6–9). Solomon asked

God for and received the very "wisdom and understanding" his father, David, desired for him (cf. 1 Kin. 3:3–14; 2 Chr. 1:7–12). He learned the value of such spiritual counsel and passed it on in Ecclesiastes 12:1, 13.

22:14 one hundred thousand . . . gold. Assuming a talent weighed about 75 pounds, this would be approximately 3,750 tons, a staggering amount of gold. **one million . . . silver.** This would be approximately 37,500 tons of silver.

22:17–19 Knowing that Solomon was young and inexperienced (22:5) and that he could not undertake this colossal project alone, David wisely enlisted the loyalty and help of his leaders to transfer their allegiance to Solomon, who would carry out the divine will and the last wishes of his father. The Lord undertook to make Solomon the wisest man on earth (cf. 1 Kin. 3:3–14).

23:1–27:34 This labor-intensive project needed more than building materials. David marshaled his human resources and announced their division of labor as follows: (1) the Levites (23:1–32); (2) the priests (24:1–31); (3) the singers (25:1–31); (4) the gatekeepers (26:1–19); (5) the administrators (26:20–32); (6) the army (27:1–24); and (7) the leaders (27:25–34). Remember, the original readers of Chronicles were the Jews, who returned from exile in Babylon and were rebuilding the destroyed temple. This would remind them of what their fathers' sin forfeited, and how inferior their new temple was.

23:1 he made. For fuller narrative of Solomon's coronation and the attempts to seize his throne, see chapters 28; 29; 1 Kings 1:1–2:9.

23:3 thirty years and above. Numbers 4:3 establishes the age of recognized priests from thirty to fifty years of age. A five-year apprenticeship began at twenty-five (cf. Num. 8:24), and in some cases twenty (1 Chr. 23:24, 27). This number, 38,000, is four times greater than the early census in Moses' time (cf. Num. 4; 26).

23:4 look after. The duties of these Levites are discussed in chapter 24. **officers and judges.** This particular function is covered in 26:20–32.

23:5 gatekeepers. First Chronicles 26:1–19 gives information on them. **praised.** First Chronicles 25 identifies and describes these musicians. **which I made.** David, a gifted musician, was not only the maker, but the inventor of musical instruments (cf. Amos 6:5).

23:6 divisions. The Levites were divided among the three groups with distinct duties, just as they were in Moses' day (Num. 3:14–37) and in Ezra's day (6:16–30). The family of Gershon (23:7–11), Kohath (23:12–20), and Merari (23:21–23) are each discussed.

23:24, 27 twenty years. See note on 23:3.

23:25–32 The duties of the non-priestly Levites are enumerated in their duties to provide the temple service in support of the priests who descended from Levi, through Kohath, through Aaron, through Eleazar and Ithamar (cf. 6:1–3). The original duties of the three families are given specifically in Numbers 3:25, 31, 36, 37.

24:1–31 The divisions and duties of the priests are outlined. Temple worship was carefully structured, without hindering the Holy Spirit or true worship (cf. 1 Cor. 14:40).

24:1 Nadab, Abihu. Consult Leviticus 10:1–3 for their disgrace and demise. **Eleazar.** The line of the high priest would be through Eleazar's offspring in accord with the priestly covenant made by God with Phinehas (Num. 25:11–13).

24:3 Zadok. See notes on 6:8, 49–53. **Ahimelech.** This was the son of Abiathar whom Solomon released from his duties for siding with Adonijah (cf. 1 Kin. 1; 2) and the grandson of another Ahimelech, who was a priest killed by Saul (1 Sam. 22:11–18).

Temple Duties		
Administrative Duties	Supervisors	1 Chronicles 23:4, 5
	Baliffs	1 Chronicles 23:4, 5
	Judges	1 Chronicles 23:4, 5
	Public administrators	1 Chronicles 26:29, 30
Ministerial Duties	Priests	1 Chronicles 24:1, 2
	Prophets	1 Chronicles 25:1
	Assistants for sacrifices	1 Chronicles 23:29–31
	Assistants for purification ceremonies	1 Chronicles 23:27, 28
Service Duties	Bakers of the Bread of the Presence	1 Chronicles 23:29
	Those who checked the weights and measures	1 Chronicles 23:29
	Custodians	1 Chronicles 23:28
Financial Duties	Those who cared for the treasury	1 Chronicles 26:20
	Those who cared for dedicated items	1 Chronicles 26:26–28
Artistic Duties	Musicians	1 Chronicles 25:6
	Singers	1 Chronicles 25:7
Protective Duties	Temple guards	1 Chronicles 23:5
	Guards for the gates and storehouses	1 Chronicles 26:12–18
Individual Assignments	Recording secretary	1 Chronicles 24:6
	Chaplain to the king	1 Chronicles 25:4
	Private prophet to the king	1 Chronicles 25:2
	Captain of the guard	1 Chronicles 26:1
	Chief officer of the treasury	1 Chronicles 26:23, 24

The MacArthur Study Bible, by John MacArthur (Nashville: Word Publishing, 1997) 588. © 1993 by Thomas Nelson, Inc.

Second Samuel 8:17 confirms the Zadok and Ahimelech high priestly combination, one at Jerusalem where the ark was kept and the other at Gibeon serving the tabernacle. *See note on 15:11.*

24:4–19 Priesthood duties were divided up in David's day into twenty-four divisions, sixteen of Eleazar and eight of Ithamar. The reasons Eleazar's family had twice as many divisions were that: (1) he had received the birthright since his older brothers, Nadab and Abihu, had been killed (Lev. 10); (2) he had more descendants; and (3) his descendants had more leadership ability. These divisions each served for either (1) two-week periods annually or, more likely, (2) a one-month period every two years (cf. 27:1–15). These divisions appear again in Nehemiah 10:2–8; 12:1–7; 12:12–21. These divisions extended even into the time of Christ (cf.

Luke 1:5–9). The rest of the time they ministered to people in their own hometowns.

24:5 *divided by lot.* The ancient method of discerning God's will (cf. Prov. 16:33; Acts 1:26) was used to sort out all the duties, so that all cause for pride or jealousy was mitigated (cf. v. 31; 26:13).

24:10 *Abijah.* The division of Zacharias, John the Baptist's father (cf. Luke 1:5).

25:1–31 David, the sweet psalmist of Israel (2 Sam. 23:1), established music as a central feature in the worship of God.

25:1 *the captains of the army.* David relied on his mighty men for help (cf. 11:10). ***Asaph ... Heman ... Jeduthun.*** David's three chief ministers of music (cf. 6:31–48). ***prophesy.*** This is not necessarily to be taken in a revelatory sense, but rather in the sense of proclamation and exhortation through the lyrics of their music (cf. 25:2, 3). Prophesying is not necessarily predicting the future or even speaking direct revelation. It is proclaiming truth (v. 5) to people (cf. 1 Cor. 14:3), and music is a vehicle for such proclamation in praise (v. 3). David and the leaders selected those most capable (v. 7) of leading the people to worship God through their music.

25:5 *seer.* A term used to describe a prophet in that he knew and understood the ways and will of God.

25:9–31 The musicians were divided up into twenty-four divisions (corresponding to that of the priests, 24:4–18) of twelve musicians each, for a total of 288. These would give leadership to the 4,000 instrumentalists (23:5).

26:1–19 Cf. 1 Chronicles 9:17–27 for another discussion of the temple gatekeepers or guards. They had other duties, such as checking out equipment and utensils; storing, ordering, and maintaining food for the priests and sacrifices; caring for the temple furniture; mixing the incense daily burned; and accounting for gifts brought. Their duties (v. 12) are given in 9:17–27.

26:14 *East Gate.* The gate assignments were based on four geographical points. Cf. also north (26:14), south (26:15), and west (26:16).

26:16 *Shallecheth Gate.* A gate assumed to be on the west side, but other details are unknown.

26:18 *Parbar.* Probably a courtyard, extending westward. Verses 17 and 18 indicate a total of twenty-four guards posted at all points of entrance and exit.

26:20–32 This section lists miscellaneous administrative posts handled by the Levites, by those in Jerusalem (26:20–28), and by those outside (26:29–32).

26:20 *treasuries.* The Levites watched over the store of valuables given to the Lord.

This is a general reference to all the precious things committed to their trust, including contributions from David and the people, as well as war spoils given by triumphant soldiers (vv. 26, 27).

26:29–32 *officials and judges.* There were 6,000 magistrates exercising judicial functions throughout the land.

26:31 *fortieth year.* The last year of David's reign (c. 971 B.C.).

27:1–34 First Chronicles 23–26 discusses spiritual leadership, while here the chronicler focuses on the civil aspects of David's kingdom.

27:1–15 This section enumerates the standing army of Israel (288,000 men), which had responsibility to guard the nation and temple. They were divided into twelve divisions, each of which served for one month during the year. When full war occurred, a larger force could be called into action (cf. 21:5).

27:16–22 While twelve officers are named, the tribes of Asher and Gad are not mentioned for unknown reasons.

27:23, 24 Here is further comment on the sinful census detailed in 21:1–30. He didn't try to number all Israelites because they were too many (cf. Gen. 28:14), nor did he finish the census, being interrupted by guilt and judgment.

27:24 *the chronicles of King David.* Daily records were kept of the king's reign. None was kept of this calamity because the record was too painful.

27:25–31 A summary of officials who looked over David's various agricultural assets.

27:32–34 A summary of those whose duties kept them in close contact with the king (cf. 18:14–17), perhaps like a cabinet. When David's son, Absalom, rebelled against him, Ahithophel betrayed David and joined the revolution. Hushan pretended loyalty to Absalom, and his advice caused Absalom's death (cf. 2 Sam. 15:31–17:23).

28:1–29:20 A record is given of David's last assembly in which the king charged Solomon and the people to build the temple for God's glory. These final chapters present the transition from David to Solomon. The chronicler does not mention Adonijah's conspiracy (1 Kin. 1:5–9) or David's weakness (1 Kin. 1:1–4), but looks at the positive contribution of the Davidic kingdom.

28:2–8 For the assembly's sake, David testified to the Davidic covenant originally given by God to him in 2 Samuel 7 (cf. 17:7–27; 22:6–16). David makes it clear that Solomon was God's choice (v. 5) as had been frequently intimated (cf. 2 Sam. 12:24, 25; 1 Kin. 1:13), just as the coming Christ will be God's chosen Son to ultimately fulfill the kingdom promise.

28:8 Cf. Deuteronomy 5:29, 33; 6:1–3.

28:9–21 David turns his words to Solomon with four perspectives: (1) spiritual devotion (28:9, 10); (2) architectural execution (28:11–19); (3) divine intervention (28:20); and (4) human participation (28:21).

28:9, 10 Cf. note on 22:11–13, 18, 19.

28:18 the chariot. Using the imagery of Psalm 18:10, the cherubim are depicted as the vehicle in which God moves.

28:19 in writing. David wrote down the plans under the Holy Spirit's divine inspiration (non-canonical, written revelation). This divine privilege was much like that of Moses for the tabernacle (Ex. 25:9, 40; 27:8; Heb. 8:5).

28:20, 21 Solomon's associates in the building project were God, the owner and general contractor (28:20), plus the human work force (28:21).

29:1–5 David called for consecrated giving to the project (cf. 28:1), based on the example of his generosity (vv. 3, 4). David gave his personal fortune to the temple building, a fortune almost immeasurable.

29:1 young and inexperienced. *See notes on 22:5.*

29:4 three thousand talents. Assuming a talent weighed about 75 pounds, this amounts to almost 112 tons of gold, plus the 7,000 talents of silver which would be 260 tons. The total worth of such precious metals has been estimated in the billions of dollars. **gold of Ophir.** This was held to be the purest and finest in the world (cf. Job 22:24; 28:16; Is. 13:12).

29:6–9 willingly. Here is the key to all freewill giving, i.e., giving what one desires to give. Tithes were required for taxation, to fund the theocracy, similar to taxation today. The law required that to be paid. This, however, is the voluntary giving from the heart to the Lord. The NT speaks of this (cf. Luke 6:38; 2 Cor. 9:1–8) and never demands that a tithe be given to God, but that taxes be paid to one's government (cf. Rom. 13:6, 7). Paying taxes and giving God whatever one is willing to give, based on devotion to Him and His glory, is biblical giving.

29:7 five thousand talents. Assuming a talent weighed about 75 pounds, this amounts to 187 tons of gold. **darics.** A Persian coin, familiar to Jews from the captivity, possibly named after Darius I (cf. Ezra 8:27). The readers of this material in Ezra's day would know it as a contemporary measurement. **ten thousand talents.** This amounts to 375 tons of silver. **eighteen thousand talents.** This amounts to almost 675 tons of bronze. **one hundred thousand talents.** This amounts to 3,750 tons of iron. The sum of all this is staggering, and has been estimated in the billions of dollars.

29:10–15 David responds to the phenomenal offering, involving amazing sacrifices of wealth, with praise in which he acknowledges that all things belong to and come from God. He concludes that God is everything and that man is nothing, much like Psalm 8. This magnificent prayer of thanksgiving gives God all credit, even for the people's generosity (v. 14).

29:16–20 David leads in a prayer of commitment.

29:17 test the heart. Opportunities for giving to God are tests of the character of a believer's devotion to the Lord. The king acknowledges that the attitude of one's heart is significantly more important than the amount of offering in one's hand.

29:20 bowed . . . prostrated. The ultimate physical expression of an inward submission to God in all things.

E. Transition to Solomon (29:21–30)

29:21–30 The chronicler records in selective fashion the final days of David and the enthronement of Solomon. For a more complete treatment, see 1 Kings 1:1–53.

29:22 the second time. This most likely refers to a public ceremony subsequent to the private one of 1 Kings 1:35–39 in response to Adonijah's conspiracy. David's high priest, Zadok, had been loyal to both father and son (1 Kin. 1:32–40; 2:27–29), so

he continued on as high priest during Sol-omon's reign.

29:26–28 Cf. 1 Kings 2:10–12.

29:27 forty years. C. 1011–971 B.C.

29:29 Samuel. This most likely refers to the canonical Book of 1 and 2 Samuel. **seer . . . prophet . . . seer.** All three are different, but synonymous, Hebrew terms referring to the prophetic office from the perspectives of: (1) to understand; (2) to proclaim; and (3) to understand, respectively. **Nathan . . . Gad.** These are non-canonical but reliable historical records that the chronicler utilized. God's Spirit protected the record from error in the original writing (2 Tim. 3:16, 17; 2 Pet. 1:20, 21).

Further Study
Davis, John J. and John C. Whitcomb. *A History of Israel from Conquest to Exile.* Grand Rapids: Baker, 1980.
Merrill, Eugene. *I and II Chronicles,* in The Bible Knowledge Commentary—OT. Wheaton, Ill.: Victor, 1985.
Payne, J. Barton. *1, 2 Chronicles,* in Expositor's Bible Commentary. Grand Rapids: Zondervan, 1988.

THE SECOND BOOK OF THE
CHRONICLES

Introduction

See 1 Chronicles for the introductory discussion.

I. THE REIGN OF SOLOMON (1:1–9:31)

1:1–9:31 This section continues from 1 Chronicles and covers the rule of Solomon (c. 971–931 B.C.; cf. 1 Kin. 3–11). The major theme is Solomon's building God's temple in Jerusalem for the purpose of centralizing and unifying the nation in the worship of God.

A. Coronation and Beginnings (1:1–17)

1:3 Gibeon. *See notes on 1 Chronicles 16:39; 21:29.* The tabernacle remained at Gibeon while the ark resided in Jerusalem, waiting for the temple to be built. **tabernacle.** Built in the days of Moses, this tent was where God met with the people (cf. Ex. 25:22; 29:42, 43; 40:34–38). The center of worship was there until the temple was built (cf. v. 6).

1:4 Kirjath Jearim. *See note on 1 Chronicles 13:5.*

1:5 Bezalel. The Spirit-enabled craftsman who built the bronze altar for the tabernacle (cf. Ex. 31:1–11; 38:1, 2).

1:7–13 The account is paralleled in 1 Kings 3:5–15. Every king of Israel needed to heed God's instructions recorded in Deuteronomy 17:14–20.

1:9 Your promise. A reference to the Davidic covenant in 2 Samuel 7; 1 Chronicles 17.

1:10 Solomon had agreed with his father (cf. 1 Chr. 22:5; 29:1) on his need for wisdom, and that is what he sought from God (cf. 1 Kin. 3:3–15; Prov. 3:15; James 1:5).

1:14–17 1 Kings 10:14–29 and 2 Chronicles 9:13–28 also extol Solomon's wealth.

1:14 chariot cities. Gezer, Hazor, and Megiddo were among the chief cities.

1:16 Keveh. Possibly Cilicia.

1:17 six hundred shekels. Assuming a shekel weighs four-tenths of one ounce, this represents fifteen pounds of silver for one

chariot. **one hundred and fifty.** Assuming the weight is in shekels, this would be about three and three-fourth pounds of silver. Deuteronomy 17:16 warned against the king's amassing horses. **the Hittites.** People, once expelled from Palestine, who lived north of Israel and northwest of Syria.

B. Temple Building (2:1–7:22)

2:1–18 This section reports how Solomon selected men to gather building materials for the temple. This was in addition to the massive supplies stockpiled by David (cf. 1 Chr. 22; 29). This section parallels 1 Kings 5:1–16.

2:1 temple for the name of the LORD. God's covenant name, Yahweh or Jehovah (cf. Ex. 3:14), is in mind. David wanted to build the temple, but was not allowed to do any more than plan and prepare (1 Chr. 23–26; 28:11–13), purchase the land (2 Sam. 24:18–25; 1 Chr. 22), and gather the materials (1 Chr. 22:14–16). **royal house.** See 1 Kings 7:1–12 for details (cf. 7:11; 8:1).

2:2 These numbers are repeated in 2:17, 18. First Kings 5:16 records 3,300 overseers, compared to 3,600 in 2:18. If, however, the additional supervisors (250 in 8:10, but 550 in 1 Kin. 9:23) are added, then both 1 Kings and 2 Chronicles agree that a total of 3,850 men worked. David had done similarly at an earlier date (1 Chr. 22:2).

2:3–10 Compare this text with the contents of 1 Kings 5:3–6. The differences can be accounted for in much the same way as in the Gospels, by combining the narratives of 1 Kings 5:3–6 and 2:3–10 to complete the entire correspondence.

2:7 send me . . . a man skillful . . . skillful men. The Israelites were familiar with agriculture, but not metal working. They needed experts for that.

2:8 algum. A coniferous tree native to Lebanon. Some identify it as sandalwood, a smooth, expensive red wood that could be polished to a high gloss.

2:10 This listing of goods is more complete than that of 1 Kings 5:11. Lebanon traded with Israel regularly for food. *twenty thousand kors.* A kor is the same as a homer and could have measured as much as 7.5 bushels, making this amount about 150,000 bushels *twenty thousand baths.* A bath measured about 6 gallons This would be about 120,000 gallons The 20 kors of "pressed oil" in 1 Kings 5:11 is most likely not a scribal error but a finer grade of oil.

2:11–16 Compare with the context of 1 Kings 5:7–9.

2:12 *God . . . who made heaven and earth.* This was the common identification of the true God when pagans spoke of or were told of Him (cf. 36:23; Ezra 1:2; 5:11, 12; 6:10; 7:12, 21, 23; Jer. 10:11, 12; Acts 4:24; 14:15; 17:24–26; Col. 1:16, 17; Rev. 11:1, 6).

2:13, 14 *Huram.* First Kings 7:14 states that his mother was of the tribe of Naphtali, not Dan, as reported here. This seeming conflict is resolved if she was of Naphtali by birth, but living in the territory of Dan. Or, if his parents were originally from the two tribes, then he could legitimately claim either. He was the parallel to Bezalel, who constructed the tabernacle. *See note on 1:5.*

2:16 *Joppa.* A major coastal port of Israel. Later, Jonah would sail from Joppa (Jon. 1:3); and much later, Peter would be there to receive God's call in a vision (Acts 10:5ff.).

2:17, 18 *See note on 2:2.*

3:1–17 Cf. 1 Kings 6:1–38; 7:15–22 for amplification and additional material on the building of the temple.

3:1 *threshing floor.* See notes on Genesis 22:1–18; 2 Samuel 24:18–25; 1 Chronicles 21:20–30.

3:2 *second month . . . fourth year.* C. April–May of 966 B.C. (cf. 1 Kin. 6:1). The project took seven years and six months to complete, c. October–November 959 B.C. (cf. 1 Kin. 6:37, 38).

3:3 *cubits . . . former measure.* About eighteen inches or possibly the royal cubit of twenty-one inches (cf. Ezek. 40:5).

3:6 *Parvaim.* An unknown location.

3:8 *six hundred talents.* Equal to almost twenty-three tons of gold.

3:9 *fifty shekels.* Equal to one and one-fourth pounds. Most likely, this small amount gilded only the spike heads.

3:10–13 *two cherubim. See note on 1 Kings 6:23.* This free-standing set of cherubim was in addition to the more diminutive set on the ark itself.

3:14 *veil.* Cf. Exodus 26:31–35 on the veil of the tabernacle. The veil separated the Holy Place from the Most Holy Place (the Holy of Holies), which was entered once annually by the high priest on the Day of Atonement (cf. Lev. 16). This highly limited access to the presence of God was eliminated by the death of Christ, when the veil in Herod's temple was torn in two from top to bottom (Matt. 27:51). It signified that believers had immediate, full access to God's presence through their Mediator and High Priest, Jesus Christ, who was the perfect, once-for-all sacrifice (cf. Heb. 3:14–16; 9:19–22).

3:15 *thirty-five cubits.* First Kings 7:15, 2 Kings 25:17, and Jeremiah 52:21 uniformly describe these cast bronze pillars as eighteen cubits high (about twenty-seven feet). Most likely this is accounted for because the chronicler gave the combined height of both as they were lying in their molds (cf. v. 17).

3:17 *Jachin . . . Boaz.* Most likely, these were so named because of the names' meanings rather than in honor of particular people. Jachin means "He shall establish," and Boaz means "In it is strength" (cf. 1 Kin. 7:21).

4:1–5:1 See 1 Kings 7:23–51 for amplification and additional details.

4:1 bronze altar. This is the main altar on which sacrifices were offered (cf. the millennial temple altar, Ezek. 43:13–17). For comparison to the tabernacle's altar, see Exodus 27:1–8; 38:1–7. If the cubit of 18 inches was used rather than the royal cubit of 21 inches, it would make the altar 30 feet by 30 feet by 15 feet high.

4:2 the Sea. This large laver was used for ritual cleansing (cf. Ex. 30:17–21 as it relates to the tabernacle). In Ezekiel's millennial temple, the laver will apparently be replaced by the waters that flow through the temple (Ezek. 47:1–12).

4:3 oxen. First Kings 7:24 reports "buds," which is the more likely translation. These were also around the laver, which was set on top of the twelve oxen.

4:4 twelve oxen. Very likely, the twelve oxen represent the Twelve Tribes who were similarly arrayed around the tabernacle as they set out on their journey in the wilderness (cf. Num. 2:1–34).

4:5 three thousand baths. A bath equaled almost six gallons. First Kings 7:26 reads 2,000 baths. This discrepancy has been reconciled by accounting, here, not only for the water the basin held, but also the water source that was necessary to keep it flowing as a fountain.

4:6 ten lavers. There were no such corresponding lavers in the tabernacle.

4:7, 8 ten lampstands . . . ten tables. The tabernacle had one of each. Everything was large because of the crowds of thousands that came on a daily basis and for special occasions.

4:11–5:1 See notes on 1 Kings 7:40–51. All these details emphasize the great care and concern for worship, and served as a manual for the new temple being built by Zerubbabel after the Jews returned from Babylon.

4:11 Huram. See note on 2:13, 14. He led the actual work which Solomon directed.

5:1 The temple took seven years and six months to build and was completed in Solomon's eleventh year (959 B.C.) in the eighth month (cf. 1 Kin. 6:38). Since it was dedicated in the seventh month (5:3), its dedication occurred eleven months later to coincide with the Feast of Tabernacles. *See note on 1 Kings 8:2.* There is so much emphasis in the OT on the temple because: (1) It was the center of worship that called people to correct belief through the generations; (2) it was the symbol of God's presence with His people; (3) it was the symbol of forgiveness and grace, reminding the people of the seriousness of sin and the availability of mercy; (4) it prepared the people for the true Lamb of God, Jesus Christ, who would take away sin; and (5) it was a place of prayer. (cf. 7:12–17).

5:2–10 *See notes on 1 Kings 8:1–9.*

5:2 The ark was in Jerusalem in a temporary tent (2 Sam. 6:17), not the original tabernacle, which was still at Gibeon (1 Chr. 16:39).

5:11 Most Holy Place. This was to be the last time anyone but the high priest went in, and then only once a year. It took several priests to place the ark in its new home.

5:12 Asaph . . . Heman . . . Jeduthun. *See notes on 1 Chronicles 25.*

5:13, 14 the glory of the LORD. The Lord's presence indwelt the temple, and the first service of worship was held. In the same manner, He descended on the tabernacle (Ex. 40:34–38). He will do likewise on the millennial temple (Ezek. 43:1–5). His glory is representative of His person (cf. Ex. 33), and entering the temple signified His presence.

6:1–11 *See notes on 1 Kings 8:12–21.*

6:11 the covenant of the LORD. The Mosaic Law written on tablets of stone (cf. 5:10).

6:12–40 *See note on 1 Kings 8:22–53.* As Solomon led his people in prayer, he asked

God to help them in many situations: (1) crime (vv. 22, 23); (2) enemy attacks (vv. 24, 25); (3) drought (vv. 26, 27); (4) famine (vv. 28–31); (5) foreigners (vv. 32, 33); (6) war (vv. 34, 35); and (7) sin (vv. 36–39).

6:13 knelt. Solomon, in an unusually humbling act for a king, acknowledged God's sovereignty.

6:18 Solomon marveled that God would condescend to live there. Cf. John 1:14; Colossians 2:9.

6:41, 42 *See notes on Psalm 132:8–10; 1 Kings 8:54–61.*

7:1–3 fire came down. This also occurred when the tabernacle was dedicated (Lev. 9:23, 24). This was the genuine dedication, because only God can truly sanctify.

7:4, 5 *See note on 1 Kings 8:62.*

7:8–10 Solomon's celebration included the special assembly to dedicate the altar on the eighth through the fourteenth days of the seventh month (September–October)

which included the Day of Atonement. It was immediately followed by the Feast of Tabernacles (fifteenth through the twenty-first) and a special assembly on the eighth day, i.e., twenty-second day of the month.

7:8 Hamath . . . Brook of Egypt. Lit. from the northern boundary to the southern boundary.

7:11, 12 *See note on 1 Kings 9:1, 2.* Perhaps years had passed since the dedication of the temple in chapter 6 during which Solomon had also built "the King's house" (cf. 8:1). After all that time, God confirmed that He had heard Solomon's prayer (v. 12).

7:13–16 This section is almost all unique to 2 Chronicles (cf. 1 Kin. 9:3), and features the conditions for national forgiveness of Israel's sins: (1) humility; (2) prayer; (3) longing for God; and (4) repentance.

7:17–22. *See notes on 1 Kings 9:4–9.*

7:17, 18 if . . . then. If there was obedience on the part of the nation, the kingdom

---

2 Chronicles 7:14 and America

"If My people who are called by My name will humble themselves, and pray and seek My face, and turn from their wicked ways, then I will hear from heaven, and will forgive their sin and heal their land."

Unlike ancient Israel, America is not a covenant nation. God has made no promise to our physical ancestors that guarantees our national status. If Israel had to fulfill the conditions for divine blessing, even though God had covenanted with them as His chosen people, America certainly has no inviolable claim on the blessing of God. As long as unbelief and disobedience to the Word of God color the soul of our nation, we cannot expect the blessing of God. Israel didn't get it in her unbelief.

But for those of us who are Christians, the covenant blessings do apply. "If you are Christ's, then you are Abraham's seed, and heirs according to the promise" (Gal. 3:29). All the promises of salvation, mercy, forgiveness of sins, and spiritual prosperity are ours to claim as long as we remain faithful to God.

That is why the spiritual state of the church in our nation is the key to the blessing of the nation as a whole. If God is going to bless America, it will not be for the sake of the nation itself. He blesses the nation, and has always done so, for the sake of His people. If we who are called by His name are not fulfilling the conditions for divine blessing, there is no hope whatsoever for the rest of the nation.

On the other hand, if the church is fit to receive God's blessing, the whole nation will be the beneficiary of that, because the Word of God will be proclaimed with power, God will add to His church, and spiritual blessings of all kinds will result. And those are the truest blessings of all.

would be established and they would have "a man as ruler." Their disobedience was legendary and so was the destruction of their kingdom and their dispersion. When Israel is saved (cf. Zech. 12:14; Rom. 11:25–27), then their King Messiah will set up this glorious kingdom (Rev. 20:1ff.).

C. Wealth/Achievements (8:1–9:28)

8:1 *twenty years.* C. 946 B.C., twenty-four years after Solomon's reign began.

8:2 Cf. 1 Kings 9:10–14. Though these cities were within the boundaries of the Promised Land, they had never been conquered; so Solomon gave Hiram the right to settle them. Hiram, however, returned the Galilean cities which Solomon had given him because they were unacceptably poor. Solomon, apparently, then improved them and settled Israelites there.

8:3–6 Here are additional military campaigns and building projects not mentioned in 1 Kings 9. He was building storage places for his commercial enterprises and fortifying his borders to secure his kingdom from invasion.

8:3 *Hamath Zobah.* A city located in Syria, north of Damascus and in close proximity to but south of Hamath.

8:4 *Tadmor.* A city 150 miles northeast of Damascus. *Hamath.* A city north of Damascus.

8:5 *Beth Horon.* Two cities northwest of Jerusalem. Upper Beth Horon is at 2,022 feet, eleven miles northwest of Jerusalem. Lower Beth Horon is at 1,210 feet, thirteen miles northwest of Jerusalem. They were both on a strategic road that connected Jerusalem with Joppa on the coast.

8:6 *Baalath.* A city originally in Danite territory (Josh. 19:44) c. thirty miles west of Jerusalem.

8:7–10 See notes on Genesis 15:18–21; Deuteronomy 7:1–6; Joshua 15:63. Cf. Exodus 23:23; Numbers 13:28, 29; Judges 3:5; 1 Kings 9:20–23.

8:10 *two hundred and fifty.* See note on 2:2.

8:11 *the daughter of Pharaoh.* Cf. 1 Kings 9:24. First Kings 3:1 mentions the marriage and the fact that Solomon brought her to Jerusalem until he could build a house for her. Until that palace was built, Solomon lived in David's palace, but did not allow her to do so, because she was a heathen and because the ark of God had once been in David's house. He surely knew his marriage to this pagan did not please God (cf. Deut. 7:3, 4). Eventually, Solomon's pagan wives caused tragic consequences (1 Kin. 11:1–11).

8:12–15 This section expands on 1 Kings 9:25, and indicates that Solomon was, in spite of his disobedience in marriage, still faithful to the religious practices required in the temple.

8:13 *three . . . feasts.* These were prescribed in the Mosaic legislation: (1) Unleavened Bread/Passover; (2) Pentecost; and (3) Tabernacles (cf. Ex. 23:14–17; Deut. 16:1–17).

8:17, 18 See notes on 1 Kings 9:26–28. These two ports where Solomon had received ships were located on the eastern gulf of the Red Sea, called Aqabah. Solomon was cultivating peace and commerce, plus using Hiram's sailors to teach his people how to sail.

8:18 *four hundred and fifty talents.* First Kings 9:28 reports 420 talents, probably accounted for by a scribal error in transmission. This was about seventeen tons of gold.

9:1–28 See notes on 1 Kings 10:1–29.

9:8 *His throne.* The thought that Solomon sat on God's throne is not included in the queen of Sheba's words in 1 Kings 10:9. The blessing of God on Israel and on Solomon was to last as long as he followed the Lord as David had (7:17–21).

9:16 *shekels. Bekah,* not *shekel* or *mina,* is

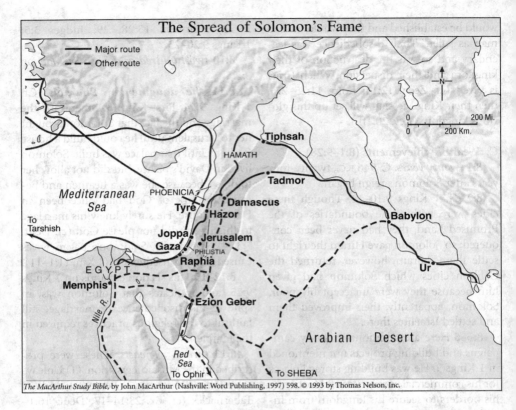

The Spread of Solomon's Fame

— Major route

- - - Other route

0   200 Mi.

0   200 Km.

Tiphsah

HAMATH

Tadmor

Mediterranean Sea

PHOENICIA

Tyre Damascus

Hazor

Babylon

To Tarshish

Joppa Jerusalem

Gaza

PHILISTIA

Raphia

Ur

E G Y P T

Memphis

Nile R.

Ezion Geber

Arabian Desert

Red Sea

To Ophir

To SHEBA

The MacArthur Study Bible, by John MacArthur (Nashville: Word Publishing, 1997) 598. © 1993 by Thomas Nelson, Inc.

the correct unit of weight. Since one mina equals fifty shekels and one shekel equals two bekahs, then the three minas in 1 Kings 10:17 equals the three hundred bekahs here, and both texts agree. This would represent a little less than four pounds.

9:18 *footstool of gold.* The chronicler adds this detail, which is absent in 1 Kings 10:19.

9:25 *four thousand.* This reading is preferable to *forty thousand* in 1 Kings 4:26.

D. Death (9:29–31)

9:29–31 See 1 Kings 11:41–43.

9:29 First Kings 11:41 reports that Solomon's deeds were written in "the book of the acts of Solomon." For the rest of the record of Solomon's life, read 1 Kings 10:26–11:43. In later years, he turned away from

God and, due to the influence of his wives, he led the nation into idolatry. This split the kingdom and sowed the seeds that led to its defeat and dispersion. The Chronicles do not record this sad end to Solomon's life because the focus is on encouraging the returning Jews from Babylon with God's pledge to them for a glorious future in the Davidic covenant.

II. THE REIGN OF THE KINGS OF JUDAH (10:1–36:21)

10:1–36:21 This section records all twenty of the Judean rulers in the divided kingdom from Solomon's son Rehoboam (c. 931 B.C.) to Zedekiah (c. 586 B.C.) when the people were taken captive to Babylon. The righteous kings and the revivals under them are presented, as well as the wicked kings/ queen and their disastrous influence. The northern kingdom is absent since Chronicles focuses on the Davidic line.

A. Rehoboam (10:1–12:16)

10:1–12:16 The reign of Rehoboam (c. 931–913 B.C.). Cf. 1 Kings 12–14.

10:1–11:4 For details on this chapter, *see notes on 1 Kings 12:1–24*. Rehoboam followed foolish and bad advice from novices rather than the good counsel of wise, seasoned people. The result was the division of the nation. Amazingly, with all the strength of Solomon's reign, unity was fragile and one fool in the place of leadership ended it. Rehoboam tried to unite the people by force, but was not allowed to succeed by God (11:1–4).

10:2 *Jeroboam.* He became the first king of the northern kingdom of Israel (c. 931–910 B.C.). The account leading to his return from Egypt is told in 1 Kings 11:26–40.

10:16–19 Here is recorded the beginning of the divided kingdom. Ten tribes followed Jeroboam and were called Israel. The other two tribes, Benjamin and Judah, stayed loyal to David's line, accepted Rehoboam's rule, and were called Judah. However, Benjamin at times demonstrated split loyalties (*see note on 1 Kin. 12:21*).

11:6 *built.* This is to be understood as built further/strengthened/fortified (cf. 11:11, 12).

11:13, 14 The priests and Levites from all the ten northern tribes were rejected by Israel's king, Jeroboam (c. 931–910 B.C.), who saw them as a threat because of their loyalty to Jerusalem and the temple. He appointed his own idolatrous priests, and all true priests moved south and found refuge in Judah with Rehoboam.

11:15 *he appointed.* This is in reference to Jeroboam (cf. 1 Kin. 12:25–33), who es-

tablished idolatry in the north. *Demons* is another term for idols (cf. Lev. 17:7).

11:16, 17 God's blessing rested on Rehoboam for three years because the people's commitment to the ways of God was patterned after David and Solomon.

11:18–23 A summary of Rehoboam's life is given with special emphasis on succession to the throne. This is not a commendation of polygamy or concubinage, which violated God's law for marriage (cf. Gen. 2:24, 25) and resulted in severe trouble and disaffection toward God. Never is polygamy commended in Scripture; its tragic results are usually recorded.

11:21 The chronicler did not include the similar summary of Solomon's wives (cf. 1 Kin. 11:3); but clearly Rehoboam learned this disastrous marital style from his father, Solomon. Even David was a polygamist. Polygamy was often practiced by the kings to secure alliances with nearby nations.

12:1, 2 *fifth year.* C. 926 B.C. Presumably, Rehoboam's three years of blessing preceded a fourth year of spiritual rebellion, which God judged in his fifth year with judgment at the hand of the Egyptians.

12:2–5 *Shishak.* He ruled over Egypt c. 945–924 B.C. An Egyptian record of this invasion written on stone has been found, recording that Shishak's army penetrated all the way north to the Sea of Galilee. He wanted to restore Egypt's once-great power, but was unable to conquer both Israel and Judah. However, he was able to destroy cities in Judah and gain some control of trade routes. Judah came under Egyptian control.

12:6, 7 *humbled themselves.* In the face of the Egyptian conqueror, the leaders responded to the Word of God through the prophet (v. 5) and repented, so that God would end His wrath worked through Shishak.

12:8 *Nevertheless.* A fitting punishment

arose to remind the Jews of their heritage in relationship to Egypt. This was the first major military encounter with Egypt since the Exodus had ended hundreds of years of slavery there. A taste of being enslaved again to a people from whom God had given liberation was bitter. The message was crystal clear—if the Jews would forsake the true worship of God, they would also lose His protective hand of blessing. It was much better to serve God than to have to serve "kingdoms of the nations."

12:9 against Jerusalem. After the parenthetical section (vv. 5–8) describing the state of the beleaguered court, the historian returns to discuss the attack on Jerusalem and the pillage of the temple and palace.

12:9–16 *See notes on 1 Kings 14:25–30.*

12:10, 11 bronze. The pure gold was replaced by bronze, which was carefully guarded.

12:12 Cf. 12:7. God preserved Judah because of her repentance.

12:13 C. 931–913 B.C. By the general revival of true worship, Rehoboam's reign acquired new life and continued many years after the departure of Shishak. Sadly, he faltered (v. 14), probably due largely to his heathen mother (v. 13).

12:16 Abijah. Cf. 11:20, 22. In 1 Kings 15:3, he is called a great sinner. But consistent with his pattern, the writer of the Chronicles highlights the little good he did to indicate that he was still in line with God's covenant promise to David.

B. Abijah (13:1–22)

13:1–22 In the succession of Judah's kings, the reign of Abijah/Abijam is next (c. 913–911 B.C.; cf. 1 Kin. 15:1–8). The disobedient nature of Abijah's reign is mentioned in 1 Kings 15:3, as is his faithless treaty with Syria (16:3).

13:3 *See notes on 1 Kings 15:1–8.* These numbers are large, but not surprising, given the immense number of capable men who could fight, as counted in David's census (cf. 1 Chr. 21:5). Both armies were set for civil war.

13:4 Mount Zemaraim. The exact location is unknown, but it is likely near Bethel (Josh. 18:22) inside Israel's territory.

13:5 covenant of salt. Salt is associated elsewhere with the Mosaic covenant sacrifices (Lev. 2:13), the priestly covenant (Num. 18:19), and the New Covenant symbolic sacrifices in the millennial kingdom (Ezek. 43:24). The preservative quality of salt represents the fidelity or loyalty intended in keeping the covenant. Here, it would refer to God's irrevocable pledge and intended loyalty in fulfilling the Davidic covenant and God's desire for the loyalty of David's lineage to Him if the people are to enjoy the blessings of the covenant.

13:6 For the story of Jeroboam, read 1 Kings 11:26–40 and chapter 10. He was the first king of the northern kingdom, Israel.

13:7 young. He was forty-one (cf. 12:13).

13:8 kingdom of the LORD. Abijah reminds all that the Davidic covenant is God's expressed will concerning who would rule on His behalf in the earthly kingdom. Thus, Judah is God's nation, since the king is in the line of David. **gold calves.** Cf. 11:15; 1 Kings 12:25–33. Israel was full of idols and false priests, having driven out all the Levitical priests and, with them, the true worship of God.

13:10–12 Abijah confessed a national commitment to pure worship and thus confidence in God's favor in battle.

13:15 God struck Jeroboam and all Israel. At the time of certain defeat, with 400,000 troops behind and the same number in front, Judah was saved by divine intervention. What God did is unknown, but the army of Israel began to flee (v. 16), and the soldiers of Judah massacred 500,000 of them in an unimaginable blood bath (v. 17).

13:17 Before the battle, Jeroboam outnumbered Abijah two to one (13:3). After the fray, in which the Lord intervened on behalf of Judah, Abijah outnumbered Jeroboam four to three.

13:19 Bethel. A city located twelve miles north of Jerusalem. Although their exact locations are unknown, Jeshanah and Ephron are believed to be in the vicinity of Bethel.

13:20 he died. Again God acted, in a manner not described, to end the life of this wicked ruler (c. 910 B.C.).

C. Asa (14:1–16:14)

14:1–16:14 The reign of Asa (c. 911–870 B.C.). Cf. 1 Kings 15:9–24.

14:1, 2 First Kings 15:11 says that Asa did as his forefather David had done—honoring God while building the kingdom (vv. 6–8). Times of peace were used for strengthening.

14:3–5 Asa removed elements of false worship that had accumulated over the years of Solomon, Rehoboam, and Abijah (cf. 1 Kin. 15:12, 13). Apparently, he did not remove all the high places or, once removed, they reappeared (cf. 15:17; 1 Kin. 15:14). His son Jehoshaphat later had to remove them (cf. 17:6), although not completely (cf. 20:33). This was done in an effort to comply with Deuteronomy 12:2, 3.

14:8 Asa had an army of 580,000, compared to Abijah's 400,000 (13:3).

14:9–15 A major threat developed from Zerah, the Ethiopian, probably on behalf of the Egyptian Pharaoh, who was attempting to regain control as Shishak had during the days of Rehoboam (cf. 12:7, 8), c. 901–900 B.C.

14:9 Mareshah. Located about eight miles southeast of Gath and twenty-five miles southwest of Jerusalem. Rehoboam had earlier reinforced this city (11:8).

Asa's Legacy of Faith

Second Chronicles 14:1–16:14 records the reign of Asa in Judah (c. 911–870 B.C.). First Kings 15:11 says that Asa did as his forefather David had done—honoring God while building the kingdom (vv. 6–8). Times of peace were used for strengthening. "Asa did what was good and right in the eyes of the LORD his God" (v. 2). He removed elements of false worship that had accumulated over the years of Solomon, Rehoboam, and Abijah (1 Kin. 15:12, 13). Apparently, he did not remove all the high places or, once removed, they reappeared (1 Kin. 15:14; 1 Chr. 15:6). His son Jehoshaphat later had to remove them (2 Chr. 17:6), although not completely (1 Chr. 20:33). This was done in an effort to comply with Deuteronomy 12:2, 3.

Asa had an army of 580,000 men "who carried shields and drew bows; all these were mighty men of valor" (v. 8). Yet a major threat developed from Zerah, the Ethiopian, probably on behalf of the Egyptian pharaoh, who was attempting to regain control as Shishak had done during the days of Rehoboam (2 Chr. 12:7, 8), c. 901–900 B.C. The Ethiopians came against them with "an army of a million men and three hundred chariots" (v. 9).

Asa's appeal to God centered on God's omnipotence and reputation and is well worth memorizing. "LORD, it is nothing for You to help, whether with many or with those who have no power; help us, . . . O LORD, You are our God; do not let man prevail against You!" (v. 11). God's response was to strike the Ethiopian army and overthrow them. "And they carried away very much spoil" (v. 13). It appears that this great horde was a nomadic people who moved with all their possessions and had set up their camp near Gerar. The spoils of Judah's victory were immense.

14:11 Asa's appeal to God centered on God's omnipotence and reputation.

14:13–15 spoil. It appears that this great horde was a nomadic people who moved with all their possessions and had set up their camp near Gerar. The spoils of Judah's victory were immense.

14:13 Gerar. Approximately eight miles south of Gaza on the Mediterranean coast. Egypt does not appear on the scene again for over 150 years (cf. 2 Kin. 17:4).

15:1 Spirit of God. An act of the Holy Spirit, common in the OT, enabling servants of God to speak or act uniquely for Him. **Azariah.** This man was a prophet, mentioned only here, who met Asa as he returned from the victory and spoke to him before all his army.

15:2 The spiritual truth here is basic, namely, that God is present and powerful in defense of His obedient people. Cf. Deuteronomy 20:1; 1 Chronicles 28:9; Isaiah 55:6, 7; Jeremiah 29:12–14; James 4:8. While Asa ruled for forty-one years, eight wicked kings ruled in Israel, including Jeroboam who, along with the others, was a negative illustration of this truth (cf. 12:1ff.).

15:8 the prophecy of Oded. Verse 1 says "Azariah the son of Oded," but "Azariah the son of Oded," which corresponds with verse 1, is the preferred reading. **vestibule.** This refers to the area outside the Holy Place, where the altar of the burnt offering was located.

15:9 Ephraim, Manasseh, and Simeon. This indicates that not all the people in the ten tribes which constituted the apostate northern kingdom of Israel had abandoned God. Many migrated south into Judah, so that all tribes were represented in the mix of Jews in Judah.

15:10 fifteenth year. C. 897 B.C. in May and June. The Feast of Weeks would have been the occasion.

15:11–15 The assembled worshipers en-tered into a renewed promise to obey (cf. Ex. 24:1ff.) and to rigorously enforce the laws which made idolatry punishable by death (cf. Deut. 17:2–5). This was inaugurated with the sacrifices of animals taken in spoil from the Ethiopians (14:15).

15:16–18 See note on 1 Kings 15:11–15.

15:19 thirty-fifth year. C. 875 B.C.

16:1 thirty-sixth year. Since Baasha (c. 909–886 B.C.) died in the twenty-sixth year of Asa's reign (cf. 1 Kin. 15:33), this could not mean that they were at war ten years later. However, if the time reference was to the thirty-fifth year since the kingdom was divided, then the year is c. 896 B.C. in the fourteenth year of Baasha's reign and the sixteenth of Asa's reign. This manner of reckoning was generally followed in the book of the record of the kings of Judah and Israel, the public annuals of that time, from which the inspired writer drew his account (cf. v. 11). This could be a cause for the defections of people from Israel to Judah as described in 15:9. Cf. 1 Kings 15:16, 17. **Ramah.** This frontier town was on the high road about six miles north of Jerusalem. Because of the topography and fortification of that city, this would effectively block all traffic into Jerusalem from the north. Cf. 1 Kings 15:16–22.

16:2–6 Asa resorted to trusting in a pagan king, Ben-Hadad, for protection against the king of Israel in contrast to (1) Abijah (13:2–20) and (2) even earlier in his own battle against Egypt (14:9–15), when they both trusted wholly in the Lord. See note on 1 Kings 15:18.

16:3 my father . . . your father. A previously unmentioned treaty between Abijah (c. 913–911 B.C.) and Tabrimmon (c. 912–890 B.C.).

16:4 Ijon . . . cities. Along with the other cities mentioned, these were located north and east of the Sea of Galilee.

16:6 Geba . . . Mizpah. Located two miles

north-northeast and two miles east of Ramah, respectively.

16:7 Hanani. God used this prophet to rebuke Asa (1) for his wicked appropriation of temple treasures devoted to God to purchase power, and (2) for his faithless dependence on a pagan king instead of the Lord, in contrast to before when opposed by Egypt (14:9–15). **army of the king of Syria has escaped.** Asa forfeited, by this sin, the opportunity of gaining victory not only over Israel, but also Syria. This could have been a greater victory than over the Ethiopians, which would have deprived Syria of any future successful attacks on Judah. Though God had delivered them when they were outnumbered (13:3ff.; 14:9ff.), the king showed his own spiritual decline, both in lack of trust and in his treatment of the prophet of God who spoke truth (v. 10).

16:9 show Himself strong . . . loyal to Him. See note on 15:2. **you shall have wars.** Divine judgment on the king's faithlessness.

16:10–12 During Asa's last six years, he uncharacteristically exhibited the ungodly behavior of: (1) anger at truth (v. 10); (2) oppression of God's prophet and people (v. 10); and (3) seeking man, not God (v. 12).

16:12 thirty-ninth year. C. 872 B.C. He died as a result of what may have been severe gangrene.

16:13 forty-first year. C. 870 B.C.

16:14 great burning. Due to the longevity of his reign and his notable accomplishments, Asa was honored by the people in their memorial of his death. Cremation was rarely used by the Hebrews (cf. 21:19; 1 Sam. 31:13; Amos 6:10). Later, Jehoram was not honored by fire (21:19) because of his shameful reign.

D. Jehoshaphat (17:1–21:3)

17:1–21:3 The reign of Jehoshaphat (c. 873–848 B.C.) Cf. 1 Kings 15:24; 22:1–50.

17:1, 2 Jehoshaphat prepared the nation militarily for any aggression, particularly from the northern kingdom of Israel.

17:3 the Baals. This is a general term used for idols. Cf. Judges 2:11–13.

17:3–9 Jehoshaphat made three strategic moves, spiritually speaking: (1) he obeyed the Lord (vv. 3–6); (2) he removed false worship from the land (v. 6); and (3) he sent out teachers who taught the people the law of the Lord (vv. 7–9).

17:10, 11 Jehoshaphat's spiritual strategy accomplished its intended purpose, i.e., invoking God's blessing and protection, much like it did with Abijah (13:2–20) and Asa (14:9–15). It should be noted that the Jews needed animals for extensive sacrificial uses, as much as for food and clothing.

17:12, 13 These verses indicate the massive wealth that developed under divine blessing (cf. 18:1), as well as formidable military power (vv. 14–19).

18:1–34 See notes on 1 Kings 22:1–39. Ahab was king in Israel. Jehoshaphat arranged for his son (cf. 21:6) to marry Athaliah, daughter of wicked Ahab, then made a military alliance with him. This folly had tragic results: (1) Jehoshaphat drew God's wrath (19:2); (2) after Jehoshaphat died and Athaliah became queen, she seized the throne and almost killed all of David's descendants (22:10ff.); and (3) she brought the wicked idols of Israel into Judah, which eventually led to the nation's destruction and captivity in Babylon. Jehoshaphat had a tendency to rely on other kings as evidenced by this unique report of a marriage alliance with Ahab (v. 1). See also 20:35–37 about an alliance with Ahaziah (c. 853–852 B.C.).

18:5 Evil kings had false prophets who told them what they wanted to hear (cf. Is. 30:10, 11; Jer. 14:13–16; 23:16, 21, 30–36). The true prophet spoke God's Word and was arrested (v. 26).

Prisoners for the Lord

PERSON	SITUATION
Joseph (Gen. 39:7–23; 41:1–45)	Refused to be seduced by his boss' wife, resulting in false accusations of sexual harassment and time in prison; eventually rose to leadership according to God's plan.
Samson (Judg. 16:21–31)	Allowed himself to be tricked by his lover Delilah into revealing the secret of his strength, resulting in arrest by the Philistines, who paraded him as a trophy until God enabled him to take revenge—and his own life in the process.
Micaiah (1 Kin. 22:1–38)	Refused to join other prophets in falsely predicting that Ahab would succeed in battle, resulting in his imprisonment; Ahab did die in battle.
Hanani (2 Chr. 16:7–10)	As a seer of the Lord, condemned King Asa for relying on the Syrians, for which he was put in prison.
Jeremiah (Jer. 37; 38)	Prophesied that Judah would not be able to withstand a siege of the Chaldeans, then was imprisoned on a charge of desertion; later repeated his warnng to King Zedekiah, and was put in a cistern; then warned Zedekiah a third time and was allowed to remain in the court of the prison until the nation fell to Babylon.
John the Baptist (Matt. 14:1–12)	Opposed the marriage of Herod Antipas to Herodias, wife of the tetrarch's half-brother and also his niece, for which John was imprisoned; later executed as a result of Herodias' trickery.
Peter and John (Acts 4:1–21)	Imprisoned as spokesmen of a new movement of Jesus' followers after a man was miraculously healed; released after being sternly warned not to teach about Jesus—a prohibition they immediately ignored.
Paul and Silas (Acts 16:16–40)	Delivered a young woman of Philippi both from demons and the power of her "employers," for which they were slandered, beaten, and jailed; miraculously released and later vindicated because of their Roman citizenship.
Paul (Acts 21:30–28:31)	Mobbed by antagonistic Jews, rescued by Roman soldiers, tried by regional rulers, and ultimately taken in chains to Rome as a prisoner of the empire.

Nelson's Complete Book of Bible Maps & Charts (Nashville: Thomas Nelson Publishers, 1996) 153. © 1993 by Thomas Nelson, Inc.

19:1–3 Having faced possible death that was diverted by God (18:31), Jehoshaphat was rebuked because of his alliances. The prophet condemned the king's alliance with God's enemy, Ahab (1 Kin. 22:2); yet, there was mercy mingled with wrath because of the king's concern personally and nationally for the true worship of God.

19:2 *Hanani.* This same prophet had earlier given Jehoshaphat's father, Asa, a similar warning (16:7–9).

19:4–11 Jehoshaphat put God's kingdom in greater spiritual order than at any time since Solomon. To insure this order, he set "judges" (v. 5) in place and gave them principles to rule by: (1) accountability to God (v. 6); (2) integrity and honesty (v. 7); (3) loyalty to God (v. 9); (4) concern for righteousness (v. 10); and (5) courage (v. 11). All are essentials of spiritual leadership.

20:1, 2 The offspring of Lot, i.e., Moab and Ammon, located east of the Jordan River, and those from Edom to the south (the off-spring of Esau), had intentions of dethroning Jehoshaphat. They had come around the south end of the Dead Sea as far north as En-Gedi, at the middle of the western shore. This was a common route for enemies since they were invisible to the people on the other side of the mountains to the west.

20:3, 4 Jehoshaphat made the appropriate spiritual response, i.e., the king and the nation appealed to God in prayer and fasting. The fast was national, including even the children (v. 13). Cf. Joel 2:12–17; Jonah 3:7.

20:5–12 Jehoshaphat stood in the redecorated center court praying for the nation, appealing to the promises, the glory, and the reputation of God which were at stake since He was identified with Judah. In his prayer, he acknowledged God's sovereignty (v. 6), God's covenant (v. 7), God's presence (vv. 8, 9), God's goodness (v. 10), God's possession (v. 11), and their utter dependence on Him (v. 12).

20:10 Mount Seir. A prominent landmark in Edom.

20:14–17 The Lord responded immediately, sending a message of confidence through the prophet Jahaziel.

20:16 Ascent of Ziz . . . Wilderness of Jeruel. These areas lie between En-Gedi on the Dead Sea and Tekoa, which is ten miles south of Jerusalem and seventeen miles northwest of En-Gedi. This is the pass that leads from the valley of the Dead Sea toward Jerusalem.

20:18–21 Here was the praise of faith. They were confident enough in God's promise of victory to begin the praise before the battle was won. So great was their trust that the choir marched in front of the army, singing psalms.

20:21 the beauty of holiness. The Lord is beautiful in holiness (cf. Ex. 15:11; Ps. 27:4), but the text here would better be translated

"in holy attire," which was referring to the manner in which the Levite singers were clothed in symbolic, sacred clothing (cf. 1 Chr. 16:29) in honor of the Lord's holiness.

20:22–24 Similar to God's intervention in Gideon's day (Judg. 7:15–23), God caused confusion among the enemy, who mistakenly turned upon themselves and slaughtered one another. Some think this may have been done by angels who appeared and set off this uncontrolled and deadly panic. The destruction was complete before Jehoshaphat and his army ever met the enemy (v. 24).

20:25–28 They went back just as they had gone out—with music (cf. vv. 21, 22).

20:29 This is the second time in Jehoshaphat's reign that fear came on the nations (cf. 17:10), which was similar to that when Israel came out of Egypt (Ex. 23:27; Num. 22:3; Josh. 2:9–11; 9:9, 10).

20:31–21:3 *See notes on 1 Kings 22:41–49.*

21:2–5 When the co-regency with his father ended at his father's death, Jehoram killed all who might have threatened his throne.

Key Word
Righteous: 14:2; 20:32; 24:2; 25:2; 26:4; 27:2; 28:1; 34:2—lit. "to be level" or "to be upright." The Hebrew word *righteous* refers to being just or right. The word is used in many settings to describe the righteousness of God (Deut. 32:4; Ps. 111:7, 8), the integrity of one's speech (Job 6:25; Eccl. 12:10), or the lifestyle of a righteous person (Prov. 11:3, 6). Often, this word is used to assess the quality of the kings in 1 and 2 Chronicles. David, as Israel's king, exemplified righteousness in his life (1 Kin. 3:6) and became a standard for judging the kings who succeeded him (see 17:3; 34:2).

E. Jehoram (21:4–20)

21:4–20 The reign of Jehoram (c. 853–841 B.C.). Cf. 2 Kings 8:16–24. Most likely, Obadiah prophesied during his reign.

21:4–10 *See notes on 2 Kings 8:16–22.*

21:11 led Judah astray. Undoubtedly Jehoram was influenced by his marriage to Ahab's daughter (cf. v. 6) and was influenced in the alliance, just like his father (18:1). They had not learned from Solomon's sinful example (cf. 1 Kin. 11:3, 4). His wicked wife, Athaliah, later became ruler over Judah and tried to wipe out David's royal line (22:10).

21:12–15 Elijah, best known for his confrontations with Israel's Ahab and Jezebel (1 Kin. 17:1, 2; Kin. 2:11), prophetically confronted Jehoram's sins of idolatry and murder (21:13). The consequences from God's judgment extended beyond himself to his family and the nation (21:14, 15). This event undoubtedly occurred in the early years of Jehoram's co-regency with his father Jehoshaphat and shortly before Elijah's departure to heaven, c. 848 B.C. (cf. 2 Kin. 2:11, 12).

21:16–20 The consequences of Jehoram's sin were far-reaching. He suffered military losses, his country was ravaged, his capital was taken, his palace was plundered, his wives were taken, all his children but the youngest were killed, he died with a painful disease, and he was buried without honor (21:16–22:1).

21:20 eight years. These were the years of Jehoram's exclusive reign, not including his co-regency with his father.

F. Ahaziah (22:1–9)

22:1–9 The reign of Ahaziah (c. 841 B.C.). Cf. 2 Kings 8:25–29; 9:21–29.

22:1–6 *See notes on 2 Kings 8:25–29.*

22:2 forty-two. This is a copyist's error, easily made due to the small stroke that differentiates two Hebrew letters. The reading

from 2 Kings 8:26 of "twenty-two" should be followed.

22:3 his mother advised . . . wickedly. Athaliah and the rest of Ahab's house who were in the young king's life taught him wickedness and led him to moral corruption, idolatry, and folly in being induced to war with the Syrians (vv. 5, 6).

22:7–9 *See notes on 2 Kings 8:28–9:29.*

G. Athaliah (22:10–23:21)

22:10–23:21 The reign of Athaliah (c. 841–835 B.C.). Cf. 2 Kings 11:1–20.

23:3 as the LORD . . . said. This is one of the most dramatic moments in messianic history. The human offspring of David have been reduced to one—Joash. If he had died, there would have been no human heir to the Davidic throne, and it would have meant the destruction of the line of the Messiah. However, God remedied the situation by providentially protecting Joash (22:10–12) and eliminating Athaliah (23:12–21).

23:11 Testimony. The usual meaning is a copy of the law (cf. Deut. 17:18; Job 31:35, 36).

H. Joash (24:1–27)

24:1–27 The reign of Joash (c. 835–796 B.C.). Cf. 2 Kings 11:17–12:21. Most likely, Joel prophesied during his reign, and his prophecy provides much helpful background to the time.

24:1–14 *See notes on 2 Kings 11:17–12:16.*

24:15, 16 Jehoiada. This man was the high priest of Athaliah's and Joash's reigns (cf. 23:1–24:16) who championed God's cause of righteousness during days of evil by: (1) leading the fight against idols; (2) permitting the coup against Athaliah; and (3) granting the throne to Joash to bring about the subsequent revival.

24:17, 18a After Jehoiada's death, the

leaders of Judah convinced King Joash that they needed to return to idolatry. With the death of the old priest came the turning point in the reign of Joash. He "listened" means Joash gave consent for the idol worship and thus it began.

24:18b, 19 God's righteousness judged the evil of Judah, while at the same time His mercy sent prophets to preach the truth of repentance.

24:20–22 The specific example of Zechariah, son of Jehoiada (not to be confused with Zechariah, son of Berechiah, Zech. 1:1; Matt. 23:35) is alluded to by NT writers in such texts as Acts 7:51, 52; Hebrews 11:37. This priest told the people that faithfulness to the Lord is the condition for blessing (cf. 12:5; 15:2). The conspiracy against this man who spoke the truth was with the king's full authority, and he bore the greatest guilt for the murder (v. 22). *See note on Matthew 23:35.*

24:22 did not remember. Cf. 22:11, where Jehoiada's wife preserved Joash from certain death as an infant, or 23:1–24:1, where Jehoiada devised a plan to dethrone Athaliah and crown Joash king, or 24:2, where Jehoiada is acknowledged as the voice of righteousness for Joash. Yet, Joash willfully ignored all that. Zechariah died pronouncing the just doom that would eventually come to the king.

24:23–25 As Zechariah had prayed (24:22), so God repaid Joash's apostasy with defeat by Syria and death at the hands of his own people.

24:24 small company. As the Lord had previously given victory to Judah's smaller army because of their faithfulness (13:2–20; 14:9–15), He gave Judah defeat at the hands of a lesser force because of their wickedness.

24:25 Unlike righteous Asa (16:13, 14), but like unrighteous Jehoram (21:18–20),

Joash died an ignominious death and received burial without honor.

24:26, 27 *See notes on 2 Kings 12:19–21.*

I. Amaziah (25:1–28)

25:1–28 The reign of Amaziah (c. 796–767 B.C.). Cf. 2 Kings 14:1–20.

25:1–4 *See notes on 2 Kings 14:1–6.*

25:4 Cf. Ezekiel 18.

25:5–16 This section is an elaboration of 2 Kings 14:7.

25:5–13 Amaziah gathered his army, small compared to the army of Jehoshaphat, which was over one million strong (cf. 17:14–19). This shows how the southern kingdom had declined in eighty years.

25:6 one hundred talents. If a talent weighs seventy-five pounds, this represents almost four tons of silver. This wealth was paid to the king of Israel, Jehoahaz, who ordered the mercenaries of Israel to aid Amaziah against Edom.

25:7 man of God. This is a technical term used about seventy times in the OT, always referring to a person who spoke for God. He warned Amaziah not to make idolatrous Israel his ally because the Lord was not with Ephraim, i.e., Israel, the capital of idolatry. *See note on Deuteronomy 33:1.*

25:8 God has power. *See note on 24:24.* The man of God reminded the king sarcastically that he would need to be strong, since God would not help.

25:9, 10 The man of God told Amaziah to cut his losses and trust the Lord. The king obeyed and sent the Israelite mercenaries home in anger.

25:11 Valley of Salt. Most likely, this is located at the southern end of the Dead Sea, where David had been victorious several centuries before (cf. 1 Chr. 18:12, 13). **Seir.** Another name for Edom.

25:12 rock. This mode of execution was

common among pagan nations (cf. Ps. 137:9).

25:13 Samaria. This was the well-known town of Israel from which they launched their attacks. **Beth Horon.** *See note on 8:5.*

25:14–16 Amaziah did the unthinkable from both a biblical and political perspective—he embraced the false gods of the people whom he had just defeated. Perhaps he did this because he was seduced by the wicked pleasures of idolatry and/or because he thought it would help him in assuring no future threat from Edom. However, it only brought destruction to the king, who wanted to silence the voice of God.

25:17–28 *See notes on 2 Kings 14:8–19.*

J. Uzziah (26:1–23)

26:1–23 The reign of Uzziah (Azariah) (c. 790–739 B.C.). Cf. 2 Kings 14:21, 22; 15:1–7. Hosea (Hos. 1:1), Amos (Amos 1:1), Jonah, and Isaiah (Is. 6) ministered during his reign.

26:1–4 *See notes on 2 Kings 14:21, 22; 15:1–4.*

26:5 Zechariah. He was an otherwise unknown prophet during Uzziah's reign, not the priestly spokesman of 24:20, or the prophet Zechariah who wrote the prophetic book to Judah c. 520 B.C. **sought . . . prosper.** This summarizes a major theme in 2 Chronicles.

26:6–15 A summary of Uzziah's prosperity in the realm of: (1) conquering the Philistines (26:6–8); (2) domestic affairs (26:9, 10); and (3) military might (26:11–15).

26:6–8 A description of Judah's military success to the west, east, and south. Israel to the north is not mentioned.

26:6 Gath . . . Jabneh . . . Ashdod. Key Philistine cities southwest of Jerusalem.

26:7 Arabians . . . Gur Baal. This was most likely a nomadic group who lived in an area whose location is unknown. **Meunites.** A nomadic people living in Edom (cf. 20:1).

26:8 Ammonites. Offspring of Lot who lived east of the Jordan.

26:9 Corner Gate. Located in the northwest section of Jerusalem. **Valley Gate.** Located in the southwest section of Jerusalem. **corner buttress.** Located in the east section of Jerusalem.

26:10 Carmel. Though there was a mountain range called Carmel, it was not in the territory under Uzziah; so most likely this should not be taken as a proper name, but rather translated as "fertile field." This fits the rest of the general references in the verse.

26:11–15 With over 300,000 in the army and the development of new weapons, he posed a threat to would-be assailants and, thus, secured the nation in peace.

26:16–18 Uzziah attempted to usurp the role of the priest which is forbidden in the Levitical code (cf. Num. 3:10; 18:7). Proverbs 16:18 indicates that pride precipitates a fall, and it did in his case. Even the king could not live above God's law.

26:19, 20 God judged the king's refusal to heed the law but was merciful, in that He did not kill Uzziah. With leprosy, Uzziah had to submit to the priests in a new way according to the laws of leprosy (cf. Lev. 13; 14) and endure isolation from the temple as well for the rest of his life.

26:21–23 *See notes on 2 Kings 15:5.*

26:22 This is not the canonical Book of Isaiah, but rather a reference to some other volume that the prophet wrote.

26:23 It was in that very year that Isaiah had his vision of God's glory (cf. Is. 6:1ff.).

K. Jotham (27:1–9)

27:1–9 The reign of Jotham (c. 750–731 B.C.). Cf. 2 Kings 15:32–38. Isaiah (Is. 1:11) and Hosea (Hos. 1:1) continued to minister during his reign, plus Micah (Mic. 1:1) prophesied during that time also.

27:1–4, 7–9 *See notes on 2 Kings 15:33–37.*

27:3 wall of Ophel. Located on the south side of Jerusalem.

27:5 Ammonites. See note on 26:8. Jotham repelled the invasion, pursuing the enemy into their own land and imposing a yearly tribute, which they paid for two years until Rezin, king of Syria, and Pekah, king of Israel revolted and attacked. Jotham was too distracted to bother with the Ammonites (cf. 2 Kin. 15:37). **one hundred talents.** If a talent is about 75 pounds, this represents almost four tons of silver. **ten thousand kors.** If a kor is 7.5 bushels, this represents 75,000 bushels.

27:6 Jotham's one failure was in not removing the idolatrous high places and stopping idol worship by the people (cf. v. 2; 2 Kin. 15:35).

L. Ahaz (28:1–27)

28:1–27 The reign of Ahaz (c. 735–715 B.C.). Cf. 2 Kings 16:1–20. Isaiah (Is. 1:1), Hosea (Hos. 1:1), and Micah (Mic. 1:1) all continued to minister during his reign. Second Kings 17:1–9 reports that it was after the twelfth year of Ahaz, when Hosea was king in Israel, that the Assyrians took Israel into captivity (722 B.C.).

28:1–5a See notes on 2 Kings 16:1–6.

28:2 Baals. See note on 17:3.

28:5b–8 Ahaz's gross disobedience earned him God's wrath, by which both Syria and Israel defeated his army, as they had in Jotham's day (cf. 2 Kin. 15:37). This was likely a continuation of the same campaign against Judah begun earlier.

28:5, 6 Damascus. The capital city of Syria, northeast of Judah. **Pekah.** King of Israel (c. 752–732 B.C.).

28:8 Samaria. The capital city of the northern kingdom of Israel.

28:9 Oded. An otherwise unknown prophet, with the same name as an earlier Oded

(cf. 15:1, 8). The prophet said that Israel had won the victory because God was judging Judah. But he protested the viciousness of the killing and the effort to enslave them (v. 10) and warned them of God's wrath for such action (v. 11). Amazingly, the apostate and hostile Israelites complied with the prophet's warning (vv. 12–15).

28:16 kings of Assyria. This is most likely singular, "king," who was Tiglath-Pileser (c. 745–727 B.C.).

28:18 cities . . . lowland. To the southwest of Jerusalem.

28:20, 21 Tiglath-Pileser. See note on 28:16. In spite of temporary relief by the conquest of Damascus and slaughter of Rezin (2 Kin. 16:9), little benefit came from this king to Ahaz because he allied with Assyria.

28:22–27 Ahaz surrendered himself to idolatry with the ignorance of a wicked pagan and a ruthless defiance of God that ruined him and his nation. He was justly dishonored in his burial (v. 27).

M. Hezekiah (29:1–32:33)

29:1–32:33 The reign of Hezekiah (c. 715–686 B.C.). Cf. 2 Kings 18:1–20:21; Isaiah 36–39. Second Kings 18:5 notes that Hezekiah's trust in the Lord had not been equaled by any king who preceded him or by any who followed (cf. 31:21). Isaiah (Is. 1:1), Hosea (Hos. 1:1), and Micah (Mic. 1:1) prophesied during his reign.

29:1, 2 See notes on 2 Kings 18:1, 2.

29:3 first year . . . first month. Hezekiah addressed the spiritual problems first, which reflected his life priorities. Hezekiah correctly diagnosed Judah's ills—she had abandoned the true worship of God. So the king stepped in to reverse the policy of his father (28:22–25) and to repair the temple and return proper temple worship as God had prescribed in His Word (vv. 3–7). He knew such a revival of devotion to God would turn God's wrath away from Judah (v. 10).

29:12–14 Fourteen leaders undertook to collect and prepare for the cleansing of the temple.

29:12 Kohathites . . . Merari . . . Gershonites. The three familial lines of Levi (cf. 1 Chr. 6:1).

29:13, 14 Elizaphan. An important leader among the Kohathites (cf. Num. 3:30; 1 Chr. 15:8). **Asaph . . . Heman . . . Jeduthun.** The three lines of Levitical musicians (cf. 1 Chr. 25:1).

29:15–19 to cleanse. Beginning with the outer courts and working for eight days, they then went inside. But as the Levites were not allowed within the walls of the holy places, the priests had to bring out all the debris to be carted off. This took eight more days.

29:16 Brook Kidron. To the east of Jerusalem, between the temple and the Mount of Olives.

29:20–36 Hezekiah restored true temple worship as practiced in the time of David and Solomon, producing great joy (v. 36).

29:26 instruments of David. The instruments David had made for the temple (cf. 1 Chr. 23:5).

29:34 Levites were more diligent . . . than the priests. Perhaps the priests had become used to participating in all the idol sacrifices they had instituted (cf. 28:25).

30:1–27 Hezekiah reached back to restore the Feast of Unleavened Bread and the Passover (Ex. 12:1–20; Lev. 23:1–8) which apparently had not been properly and regularly observed in some time, perhaps since the division of the kingdom 215 years earlier (v. 5). The Passover would later be revived again by Josiah (35:1–9) and Zerubbabel (Ezra 6:19–22). It celebrated God's for- giveness and redemption of His believing people.

30:1 Israel. These would be the remnant of the ten northern tribes (vv. 6, 25) left in the land or escaped from the enemy after the northern kingdom was taken captive following the invasion by Assyria in 722 B.C. (2 Kin. 17:1–9). Ephraim and Manasseh were the leading tribes.

30:2 second month. This call to Passover was to unite the nation again in worship. Normally, the Passover would be in the first month (March/April). The rule of exception for individuals who were unclean or absent (Num. 9:9–11) was applied to the whole nation.

30:5 Beersheba to Dan. These two cities were at the extreme ends of the country, so this expression was a way of saying, "from south to north."

30:6 return. The nation was required by law to celebrate annually three feasts in Jerusalem: (1) Passover; (2) Pentecost; and (3) Tabernacles (cf. Ex. 23; Lev. 23; Num. 28; 29; Deut. 16). God would have returned to bless the people of the northern apostate and idolatrous kingdom of Israel, if they had returned to Him. Cf. 15:2; 20:20; 26:5; 31:21, where this recurring theme is affirmed.

30:8 stiff-necked. This is the same kind of language used by Stephen in Acts 7:51–53, which in effect says, "Don't be obstinate."

30:9 Not all the people of Israel had been taken captive in the invasion of the Assyrians during Hezekiah's reign (cf. 2 Kin. 17:5–23; 18:9–12).

30:10 Scorn was the response of these tribes, showing their wickedness even after judgment on them had begun. Note verse 18 for the additional, brazen sin of these tribes.

30:13 second month. Normally, Passover and the Feast of Unleavened Bread were held in the first month; however, at this special time, it was better to be one month late, than not at all.

30:14 These altars had been erected to

idols by Ahaz. See 28:25; 29:16. Hezekiah was able to cleanse the city of idols and altars, something his predecessors failed to do.

30:18–20 The attitude of the heart was to prevail over their outward activity (cf. 1 Sam. 15:22; Jer. 7:22, 23; Hos. 6:6). Hezekiah reminded them that God forgives even the most heinous sins, and He did (v. 20).

30:23 This speaks to the authenticity of revival in that the people knew how sinful they had been and how desperately in need of cleansing they actually were. They doubled the time for the feast which pointed to God's salvation and deliverance of the faithful.

30:26 *nothing like this.* This is a telling statement about the spiritual degeneracy of the divided kingdom since the time of Solomon over 215 years earlier.

31:1 *Judah, Benjamin, Ephraim, and Manasseh.* The first two names referred to the southern kingdom; the last two represented the northern kingdom. The Passover had been a real revival, and they carried the conviction of it back to their homes to "utterly destroy" all the idolatry. So the reign of idolatry ended, and the worship of God was restored. The people went home in hope of divine blessing and a future of peace and prosperity.

31:2–19 *divisions of the priests and the Levites.* The priestly service had not been supported by the government during the reign of the wicked kings, so Hezekiah restored that support as God originally ordained it (cf. 8:12–14; 1 Chr. 24:1ff.).

31:6 *tithe.* Since the priests and Levites served the nation, they were to be supported by the people through the taxation of the tithe. According to Leviticus 27:30–33 and Numbers 18:21, 24, the people were to give the tenth (tithe) to supply all the needs of the Levites. They were robbing God when they did not give the tithe (Mal. 3:8). Deuteronomy 12:6, 7 called for a second tithe that was to support the nation's devotion to the temple by being used for the national festivals at the temple in Jerusalem. This was called the festival tithe. Deuteronomy 14:28, 29 called for a third tithe every three years for the poor. The sum of this tax plan totaled about 23 percent annually.

31:7 *third . . . seventh month.* From the time of the Feast of Firstfruits or Pentecost in May/June until the Feast of Tabernacles in September/October.

31:11 *rooms.* These were stone houses, granaries, and cellars to replace the old, decayed ones. In these places, the Levites stored the tithes (v. 12).

31:16 *three years old.* Possibly, this refers to children of the priests who accompanied their fathers and received their portions in the temple. Under three, they were probably still being nursed, needing no food. The families of the priests were cared for (v. 18).

31:17 *twenty years old.* See notes on *1 Chronicles 23:3.* Cf. Numbers 4:3; 28:24.

31:19 *common-lands.* This refers to the forty-eight Levitical cities (cf. Josh. 21:1–42). The tithe taxes collected from everyone were used not only for festivals at the temple, but also for regular daily support of the priests living and leading throughout the Land (*see note on v. 6*).

31:20, 21 See notes on 2 Kings 18:5–7.

32:1–23 Hezekiah's dealings with Sennacherib, king of Assyria (c. 705–681 B.C.). *See notes on 2 Kings 18:13–19:37; Isaiah 36; 37.* The Assyrian king came because Hezekiah, determined to recover the independence of his nation, refused to pay the tribute his father had bound him to pay to Assyria. Sennacherib retaliated, so Hezekiah fortified the city (v. 5) and trusted God (vv. 8, 11), who delivered them (vv. 21, 22) and was glorified (v. 23).

32:24–26 See notes on 2 Kings 20:1–11; Isaiah 38.

32:27–31 See notes on 2 Kings 20:12–20; Isaiah 39.

32:30 A 1,700 foot long tunnel cut through solid rock (below Jerusalem) redirected water from the spring Gihon outside of Jerusalem (to the east) toward the south of Jerusalem into the pool of Siloam within the city to provide water in time of siege. The tunnel was a remarkable feat of engineering and boring skill, often sixty feet below the ground and large enough to walk through. It was discovered in 1838, but not until 1909 was it cleared of the debris left by the destruction of Jerusalem back in 586 B.C. This may not have been the first water shaft, since David may have entered Jerusalem 300 years earlier through a water shaft (cf. 2 Sam. 5:6–8).

32:31 *Babylon.* This empire was gradually gaining power as Assyria declined due to internal strife and weak kings. Assyria was crushed in 612 B.C. and Babylon, under Nebuchadnezzar, became the world ruler (cf. 2 Kin. 20:14).

32:32 *Isaiah.* Cf. Isaiah 1:1.

N. Manasseh (33:1–20)

33:1–20 The reign of Manasseh (c. 695–642 B.C.). Cf. 2 Kings 21:1–18.

33:1–10 See notes on 2 Kings 21:1–10.

33:6 *Hinnom.* This valley to the south and east of the temple was where the worship of Molech involved burning children to death (Ps. 106:37). This was forbidden in Leviticus 18:21; 20:2–5; Deuteronomy 18:10. Such horrible practices appeared in Israel from the time of Ahaz (cf. 28:3).

33:11–17 God's retribution was swift. Manasseh apparently repented, but the spiritual damage was not easily reversed.

33:11 *king of Assyria.* This was most likely Ashurbanipal (c. 669–633 B.C.). Be-

tween 652 and 648 B.C., Babylon rebelled against Assyria. The city of Babylon was defeated temporarily, but Assyria may have felt Manasseh supported Babylon's rebellion, so he was taken to trial in Babylon.

33:12, 13 *Manasseh knew.* This king was very wicked and idolatrous, a murderer of his children, and a desecrater of the temple. God graciously forgave this "chief of sinners" (cf. 1 Tim. 1:15) when he repented. He did what he could to reverse the effect of his life (vv. 15–17). Although the people worshiped God and not idols, they were doing it in the wrong place and wrong way. God had commanded them to offer sacrifices only in certain places (Deut. 12:13, 14) to keep them from corrupting the prescribed forms and to protect them from pagan religious influence. Disobedience to God's requirements in this matter surely contributed to the decline under the next king, Amon (vv. 21–25), whose corruption his successor, Josiah, had to eliminate (34:3–7).

33:14 A wall running from south of the temple and Ophel (west of the Kidron Valley) southeast/northwest reaching to the Fish Gate, northwest of the temple.

33:18–20 See 2 Kings 21:17, 18.

O. Amon (33:21–25)

33:21–25 The reign of Amon (c. 642–640 B.C.). Cf. 2 Kings 21:19–26. See notes on 2 Kings 21:19–24.

P. Josiah (34:1–35:27)

34:1–35:27 The reign of Josiah (c. 640–609 B.C.). Cf. 2 Kings 22:1–23:30. Jeremiah prophesied during this reign (35:24; Jer. 1:2) as did Habakkuk, Zephaniah (Zeph. 1:1), and Nahum.

34:1, 2 See notes on 2 Kings 22:1, 2. At the age of sixteen, Josiah began to cultivate a love for God in his heart, and by age twenty

The Chronicles' Sources

The inspiration of Scripture (2 Tim. 3:16) was sometimes accomplished through direct revelation from God without a human writer, e.g., the Mosaic law. At other times, God used human sources, as mentioned in Luke 1:1–4. Such was the experience of the chronicler as evidenced by the many contributin sources. Whether the material came through direct revelation or by existing resouces, God's inspiration through the Holy Spirit prevented the original human authors of Scripture from any error (2 Pet. 1:19–21). Although relatively few scribal errors have been made in copying Scripture, they can be identified and corrected. Thus, the original, inerrant content of the Bible has been preserved.

1. Book of the Kings of Israel/Judah (1 Chr. 9:1; 2 Chr. 16:11; 20:34; 25:26; 27:7; 28:26; 32:32; 35:27; 36:8)
2. The Chronicles of David (1 Chr. 27:24)
3. Book of Samuel (1 Chr. 29:29)
4. Book of Nathan (1 Chr. 29:29; 2 Chr. 9:29)
5. Book of Gad (1 Chr. 29:29)
6. Prophecy of Ahijah the Shilonite (2 Chr. 9:29)
7. Visions of Iddo (2 Chr. 9:29)
8. Records of Shemaiah (2 Chr. 12:15)
9. Records of Iddo (2 Chr. 12:15)
10. Annals of Iddo (2 Chr. 13:22)
11. Annals of Jehu (2 Chr. 20:34)
12. Commentary on the Book of the Kings (2 Chr. 24:27)
13. Acts of Uzziah by Isaiah (2 Chr. 26:22)
14. Letters/Message of Sennacherib (2 Chr. 32:10–17)
15. Vision of Isaiah (2 Chr. 32:32)
16. Words of the Seers (2 Chr. 33:18)
17. Sayings of Hozai (2 Chr. 33:19)
18. Written instructions of David and Solomon (2 Chr. 35:4)
19. The Laments (2 Chr. 35:25).

The MacArthur Study Bible, by John MacArthur (Nashville: Word Publishing, 1997) 574. © 1993 by Thomas Nelson, Inc.

his character was strong enough in devotion to Him that he went into action to purge his nation.

34:3–7 *See notes on 2 Kings 23:4–20.*

34:8 *repair the house of the LORD.* During the 55-year reign of Manasseh (33:1) and the two-year reign of Amon (33:21), the work of Hezekiah on the temple restoration was undone, which called for another extensive enterprise to "repair and restore" it (vv. 9–13).

34:8–13 *See notes on 2 Kings 22:3–7.*

34:8–33 *See notes on 2 Kings 22:8–23:20.*

34:33 *All his days.* This noble king had a life-long influence by the power of his godly life and firm devotion to God and His Word. The strength of his character held the nation together serving the Lord. It started because, as a young man, he "began to seek God" (cf. v. 3).

35:1–19 The chronicler, probably Ezra,

gave much more attention to this Passover celebration than does 2 Kings 23:21–23.

35:1, 2 Obviously, the temple's contents had been disturbed and the sacrifices/festivals interrupted by lack of attention, idolatrous practices, and foreign intervention. As Hezekiah had restored the Passover in his time (30:1ff.), so did Josiah. This was the central feast in devotion to the Lord (Ex. 12; 13).

35:3 *the holy ark.* The ark of the covenant which was to remain in the Most Holy Place had been removed, probably by Manasseh, who set a carved image in its place (cf. 33:7). The law for the carrying of the ark during the tabernacle days, when it was portable, called for poles to be placed through rings on the sides, and Levites (Kohathites) to carry it by the poles without touching it (cf. Ex. 25:14, 15). Uzza(h) died for touching the ark while he was improperly transporting the ark on a cart (1 Chr. 13:6–10). Now that the temple was built and the ark had a permanent place, it no longer needed to be transported in the old way.

35:6 *Moses.* *See notes on Exodus 12; 13.* The prescribed pattern for the Passover in the temple was followed (vv. 7–17).

35:18 *no Passover.* Hezekiah's Passover (cf. ch. 30) differed. It was not celebrated strictly according to Mosaic Law in that: (1) it was celebrated in the second month (30:2); (2) not all the people were purified (30:18); and (3) not all of the people came (30:10).

35:18, 19 *since . . . Samuel.* C. 1100–1015 B.C. It had been over 400 years since the last Passover like this one, even prior to all the kings of Israel and Judah.

35:20–27 The details of Josiah's tragic death are given. When compared with the account in 2 Kings 23:28–30, the events become clearer. Toward the end of Josiah's reign, the Egyptian Pharaoh Necho (c. 609–594 B.C.) set out on a military expedition to aid the king of Assyria in a war at Carchemish, Assyria's latest capital, 250 miles northeast of Damascus on the bank of the Euphrates River. Fearing such an alliance would present future danger to Israel, Josiah decided to intercept Pharaoh Necho's army and fight to protect his nation. Coming from Egypt, likely by ship to Acco, a northern seaport in Israel, and by land up the coastal plain of Israel, the Egyptian army had landed and proceeded east to the Valley of Megiddo (v. 22), i.e., Jezreel on the plain of Esdraelon. This was the most direct way to Carchemish. There, Josiah met him for battle and was wounded by an arrow. He made it back to Jerusalem (sixty miles south), where he died.

35:21 *God commanded me.* He is referring to the true God; whether he had a true revelation or not is unknown. Josiah had no way to know either, and it is apparent he did not believe that Necho spoke the word of God. There is no reason to assume his death was punishment for refusing to believe. He probably thought Necho was lying and, once victorious with Assyria over Babylon, they would together be back to assault Israel.

35:25 There is no record of Jeremiah's elegy. The people continued to mourn the loss of Josiah up to the writing of the Chronicles in 450–430 B.C., nearly 200 years after the event. In fact, the location of the battle, the town of Hadad-rimmon in the valley of Megiddo, was part of a proverb lamenting Josiah's death even in Zechariah's day (Zech. 12:11), ninety years later.

Q. Jehoahaz (36:1–4)

36:1–4 The reign of Joahaz (c. 609 B.C.). Cf. 2 Kings 23:31–33. Jeremiah continued to prophesy during this reign (Jer. 1:3).

R. Jehoiakin (36:5–8)

36:5–8 The reign of Jehoiakim (Eliakim)

(c. 609–597 B.C.; cf. 2 Kin. 23:34–24:7). *See notes on 2 Kings 23:34–24:7.* Daniel was taken captive to Babylon in 605 B.C. Jeremiah prophesied during this reign (Jer. 1:3), and Habakkuk likely appeared on the scene at this time of kingly abominations.

S. Jehoiachin (36:9, 10)

36:9, 10 The reign of Jehoiachin (c. 597 B.C.). Cf. 2 Kings 24:8–16. *See notes on 2 Kings 24:8–16.* Ezekiel was taken captive to Babylon in 597 B.C. Jeremiah prophesied during this reign.

36:9 *eight years old.* Eighteen years old is preferable, as stated in 2 Kings 24:8, because of the full development of his wickedness (see Ezekiel's description of him in 19:5–9).

T. Zedekiah (36:11–21)

36:11–21 The reign of Zedekiah (Mattaniah) (c. 597–586 B.C.). Cf. 2 Kings 24:17–25:21; Jeremiah 52:4–27. Jeremiah prophesied during this reign (Jer. 1:3) and wrote Lamentations to mourn the destruction of Jerusalem and the temple in 586 B.C. Ezekiel received his commission during this reign (Ezek. 1:1) and prophesied from 592 B.C. to his death in 560 B.C.

36:11–20 *See notes on 2 Kings 24:17–25:21.*

36:20 *See notes on 2 Kings 25:22–30* for the fate of those who remained behind in Jerusalem.

36:21 *Sabbaths.* This suggests that the every-seventh-year Sabbath which God required for the land (Lev. 25:1–7) had not been kept for 490 years dating back to the days of Eli, c. 1107–1067 B.C. (cf. 1 Sam. 1–4). Leviticus 26:27–46 warns of God's judgment in general if this law was violated. Jeremiah 25:1–11 applied this judgment to Judah from 605 B.C. at the time of the first Babylonian deportation until 536 B.C. when the first Jews returned to Jerusalem and started to rebuild the temple (cf. Ezra 3:8).

III. THE RETURN PROCLAMATION OF CYRUS (36:22, 23)

36:22, 23 *See notes on Ezra 1:1–3.* The chronicler ended with a ray of hope because the seventy years were completed (cf. Dan. 9:1, 2) and Abraham's offspring were returning to the land to rebuild the temple.

Further Study

Davis, John J. and John C. Whitcomb. *A History of Israel from Conquest to Exile.* Grand Rapids: Baker, 1980.

Merrill, Eugene. *I and II Chronicles,* in The Bible Knowledge Commentary—OT. Wheaton, Ill.: Victor, 1985.

Payne, J. Barton. *1, 2 Chronicles,* in Expositor's Bible Commentary. Grand Rapids: Zondervan, 1988.

THE BOOK OF
EZRA

Title

Even though Ezra's name does not enter the account of Judah's post-exilic return to Jerusalem until 7:1, the book bears his name ("Jehovah helps") as a title. This is because both Jewish and Christian tradition attribute authorship to this famous scribe-priest. New Testament writers do not quote the Book of Ezra.

Author and Date

Ezra is most likely the author of both Ezra and Nehemiah, which might have originally been one book. Ezra 4:8–6:18 and 7:12–26 are written in Aramaic. Although Ezra never states his authorship, internal arguments favor him strongly. After his arrival in Jerusalem (c. 458 B.C.), he changed from writing in the third person (chs. 1–6) to writing in the first person (chs. 7–10). In the earlier section, it is likely that he had used the third person because he was quoting his memoirs.

Ezra is believed possibly to be the author of both Books of Chronicles. It would have been natural for the same author to continue the OT narrative by showing how God fulfilled His promise by returning His people to the land after seventy years of captivity. There is also a strong priestly tone in Chronicles, and Ezra was a priestly descendant of Aaron (cf. 7:1–5). The concluding verses of 2 Chronicles (36:22, 23) are virtually identical to the beginning verses (1:1–3a), affirming his authorship of both.

Ezra was a scribe who had access to the myriad of administrative documents found in Ezra and Nehemiah, especially those in the Book of Ezra. Very few people would have been allowed access to the royal archives of the Persian Empire, but Ezra proved to be the exception (cf. 1:2–4; 4:9–22; 5:7–17; 6:3–12). His role as a scribe of the law is spelled out in 7:10: "For Ezra had prepared his heart to seek the Law of the LORD, and to do it, and to teach statutes and ordinances in Israel." He was a strong and godly man who lived at the time of Nehemiah (cf. Neh. 8:1–9; 12:36). Tradition says he was founder of the Great Synagogue, where the complete OT canon was first formally recognized.

Ezra led the second return from Persia (c. 458 B.C.), so the completed book was written sometime in the next several decades (c. 457–444 B.C.).

Background and Setting

God had originally brought Israel out of the slave markets of Egypt in the Exodus (c. 1445 B.C.). Hundreds of years later, before the events of Ezra, God told His people that if they chose to break their covenant with Him, He would again allow other nations to take them into slavery (Jer. 2:14–25). In spite of God's repeated warnings from the mouths of His prophets, Israel and Judah chose to reject their Lord and to participate in the worship of foreign gods, in addition to committing the abominable practices that accompanied idolatry (cf. 2 Kin. 17:7–18; Jer. 2:7–13). True to His promises, God brought the Assyrians and Babylonians to issue His chastisement upon wayward Israel and Judah.

In 722 B.C. the Assyrians deported the ten northern tribes and scattered them all over their empire (cf. 2 Kin. 17:24–41; Is. 7:8). Several centuries later, in 605–586 B.C., God used the Babylonians to sack and nearly depopulate Jerusalem. Because Judah persisted in her unfaithfulness to the covenant, God chastened His people with seventy years of captivity (Jer. 25:11), from which they returned to Jerusalem as reported by Ezra and Nehemiah. Cyrus, the Persian, overthrew Babylon in 539 B.C., and the Book of Ezra begins with the decree of Cyrus one year later for the Jews to return to Jerusalem (c. 538 B.C.). It chronicles the reestablishment of Judah's national calendar of feasts and sacrifices, including the rebuilding of the second temple (begun in 536 B.C. and completed in 516 B.C.).

As there had been three waves of deportation from Israel into Babylon (605 B.C., 597 B.C., and 586 B.C.), so there were actually three returns to Jerusalem over a nine-decade span. Zerubbabel first returned in 538 B.C. He was followed by Ezra, who led the second return in 458 B.C. Nehemiah did likewise thirteen years later, in 445 B.C. Complete, uncontested political autonomy, however, never returned. The prophets Haggai and Zechariah preached during Zerubbabel's time, about 520 B.C. and following.

Historical and Theological Themes

The Jews' return from the Babylonian captivity seemed like a second Exodus, sovereignly patterned in some ways after Israel's first redemption from Egyptian bondage. The return trip from Babylon involved activities similar to those of the original Exodus: (1) the rebuilding of the temple and the city walls; (2) the reinstitution of the law, which made Zerubbabel, Ezra, and Nehemiah collectively seem like a second Moses; (3) the challenge of the local enemies; and (4) the temptation to intermarry with non-Jews, resulting in idolatry. Other parallels between the original Exodus and the return from Babylon must have seemed to the returnees like they were given a fresh start by God.

In his account of the return, Ezra drew upon a collection of Persian administrative documents to which he had access as a scribe. The presence of actual royal administrative documents carries a powerful message when accompanied by the resounding line, "the hand of the LORD my God was upon him/me"(7:6, 28). The decrees, proclamations, letters, lists, genealogies, and memoranda, many of them written by the Persian administration, attest to the sovereign hand of God in Israel's restoration.

The primary message of the book is that God orchestrated the past grim situation (captivity) and would continue to work through a pagan king and his successors to give Judah hope for the future (return). God's administration overrides that of any of the kings of this world and, thus, the Book of Ezra is a message of God's continuing covenant grace to Israel.

Another prominent theme that surfaces in Ezra is opposition from the local Samaritan residents whose ancestors had been imported from Assyria (4:2; cf. John 4:4–42). For reasons of spiritual sabotage, Israel's enemies requested to participate in rebuilding the temple (4:1, 2). After being shunned, the enemies hired counselors against the Jews (cf. 4:4, 5). But the Lord, through the preaching of Haggai and Zechariah, rekindled the spirit of the people and their leaders to build, with the words "be strong . . . and work; for I am with you" (Hag. 2:4; cf. 4:24–5:2). The reconstruction resumed

(c. 520 B.C.) and the temple was soon finished, dedicated, and back in service to God (c. 516 B.C.).

Interpretive Challenges

First, how do the post-exilic, historical Books of 1 and 2 Chronicles, Ezra, Nehemiah, and Esther relate to the post-exilic prophets Haggai, Zechariah, and Malachi? For the chronology of Ezra, Nehemiah, and Esther, *see the note on 6:22–7:1* and post-exilic returns to Jerusalem. The two Books of Chronicles were written by Ezra as a reminder of the promised Davidic kingship, the Aaronic priesthood, and appropriate temple worship. Haggai and Zechariah prophesied in the period of Ezra 4–6 when temple construction was resumed. Malachi wrote during Nehemiah's revisit to Persia (cf. Neh. 13:6).

Second, what purpose does the book serve? Ezra historically reports the first two of three post-exilic returns to Jerusalem from the Babylonian captivity. The first return (chs. 1–6) was under Zerubbabel (c. 538 B.C.) and the second (chs. 7–10) was led by Ezra himself (c. 458 B.C.). Spiritually, Ezra reestablished the importance of the Aaronic priesthood by tracing his ancestry to Eleazar, Phinehas, and Zadok (cf. 7:1–5). He reported on the rebuilding of the second temple (chs. 3–6). How he dealt with the gross sin of intermarriage with foreigners is presented in chapters 9; 10. Most importantly, he reports how the sovereign hand of God moved kings and overcame varied opposition to reestablish Israel as Abraham's seed, nationally and individually, in the land promised to Abraham, David, and Jeremiah.

Third, the temple was built during the reign of Cyrus. Mention of Ahasuerus (4:6) and Artaxerxes (4:7–23) might lead one to conclude that the temple could also have been built during their reigns. Such a conclusion, however, violates history. Ezra was not writing about the construction accomplishments of Ahasuerus or Artaxerxes, but rather he continued to chronicle their oppositions after the temple was built, which continued even to Ezra's day. It is apparent, then, that 4:1–5 and 4:24–5:2 deal with rebuilding the temple under Zerubbabel, while 4:6–23 is a parenthesis recounting the history of opposition in the times of Ezra and Nehemiah.

Fourth, the interpreter must decide where Esther fits in the Book of Ezra. A careful examination indicates it took place between the events of chapters 6 and 7. *See notes on Esther.*

Fifth, how does divorce in Ezra 10 correlate with the fact that God hates divorce (Mal. 2:16)? Ezra does not establish the norm, but rather deals with a special case in history. It seems to have been decided (Ezra 10:3) on the principle that the lesser wrong (divorce) would be preferable to the greater wrong of the Jewish race being polluted by intermarriage, so that the nation and the messianic line of David would not be ended by being mingled with Gentiles. To solve the problem this way magnifies the mercy of God in that the only other solution would have been to kill all of those involved (husband, wives, and children) by stoning, as was done during the first Exodus at Shittim (Num. 25:1–9).

Outline

I. THE FIRST RETURN UNDER ZERUBBABEL (1:1–6:22)

A. Cyrus' Decree to Return (1:1–4)

1:1–3a These verses are almost identical to 2 Chronicles 36:22, 23. The pre-exilic history of 1 and 2 Chronicles gave the post-exilic returnees direction regarding the Davidic kingship, the Aaronic priesthood, and temple worship. This book continues the story.

1:1 *first year.* C. 538 B.C. *Cyrus king of Persia.* C. 550–530 B.C. The Lord had prophesied through Isaiah, who said of Cyrus, "He is My shepherd, . . . saying to Jerusalem, 'You shall be built,' and to the temple, 'Your foundation shall be laid' " (Is. 44:28). The historian Josephus records an account of the day when Daniel read Isaiah's prophecy to

Cyrus, and in response he was moved to declare the proclamation of 1:2–4 (538 B.C.). *by the mouth of Jeremiah.* Jeremiah had prophesied the return of the exiles after a seventy-year captivity in Babylon (Jer. 25:11; 29:10–14; cf. Dan. 9:2). This was no isolated event, but rather an outworking of the covenant promises made to Abraham in Genesis 12:1–3. *the LORD stirred up.* A strong expression of the fact that God sovereignly works in the lives of kings to effect His purposes (Prov. 21:1; Dan. 2:21; 4:17). *made a proclamation.* This was the most common form of spoken, public communication, usually from the central administration. The king would dispatch a herald, perhaps with a written document, into the city. In order to address the people, the messenger would either go to the city gate, where people often congregated for social discourse, or gather the people together in a square, occasionally by the blowing of a horn. The herald would then make the proclamation to the people. A document called the Cyrus Cylinder, recovered in reasonably good condition by archeologists, commissioned people from many lands to return to their cities to rebuild the temples to their gods, apparently as some sort of general policy of Cyrus. Whether or not this document was an extension of the proclamation made to the exiles in this passage must remain a matter of speculation (cf. 6:2–5). *put it in writing.* Proclamations were oral statements, usually made by a herald, which were often written down for recordkeeping.

1:2–4 It is possible that Daniel played a part in the Jews' receiving such favorable treatment (cf. Dan. 6:25–28). According to the Jewish historian Josephus, he was Cyrus' prime minister who shared Isaiah's prophecies with Cyrus (Is. 44:28; 46:1–4). The existence of such documents, written over a century before Cyrus was born, led him to

Post-Exilic Returns to Jerusalem				
Sequence	**Date**	**Scripture**	**Jewish Leader**	**Persian Ruler**
First	538 B.C.	Ezra 1–6	Zerubbabel, Joshua	Cyrus
Second	458 B.C.	Ezra 7–10	Ezra	Artaxerxes
Third	445 B.C.	Nehemiah 1–13	Nehemiah	Artaxerxes

The MacArthur Study Bible, by John MacArthur (Nashville: Word Publishing, 1997) 641. © 1993 by Thomas Nelson, Inc.

acknowledge that all his power came from the God of Israel and prompted him to fulfill the prophecy.

1:2 LORD God of heaven. The God of Israel was recognized as the utmost divine authority (cf. 5:12; 6:9, 10; 7:12, 21, 23), who sovereignly dispenses authority to human monarchs. *a house.* This refers to the second temple, which would be built after the return to the land by Zerubbabel.

B. Treasures to Rebuild the Temple (1:5–11)

1:5 whose spirits God had moved. The primary underlying message of Ezra and Nehemiah is that the sovereign hand of God is at work in perfect keeping with His plan at His appointed times. The seventy years of captivity were complete, so God stirred up not only the spirit of Cyrus to make the decree, but His own people to go and build up Jerusalem and the temple (cf. 1:1).

1:6 all those who were around them. A basic similarity to the Exodus is seen throughout Ezra and Nehemiah. One can hear faint echoes of the Egyptians supplying treasures in order to provide splendor for the tabernacle (cf. Ex. 11:2; 12:35, 36). Here, other nations around Israel are called to contribute. They were assisted by some of their captive countrymen, who had been born in Babylon and chose to remain, and perhaps by some Babylonians and Assyrians who were favorably disposed to Cyrus and/or the Jews.

1:7 the articles of the house of the LORD. Cf. 6:5. These were the vessels which Nebuchadnezzar removed when he sacked the temple (c. 605–586 B.C.; 2 Kin. 24:13; 25:14, 15; Dan. 1:2). God had preserved them (2 Chr. 36:7) with the Babylonians (cf. Dan. 5:1–4) for the return as prophesied by Jeremiah (Jer. 27:22).

1:8 Sheshbazzar the prince of Judah. Cf. 1:11; 5:14, 16. Nothing is said about this man biblically, except in Ezra. Most likely, he was a political appointee of Cyrus to oversee Judah. He is not to be confused with Zerubbabel, who was the leader recognized by the Jews (cf. 2:2; 3:2, 8; 4:2, 3; 5:2) and by the Lord (cf. Hag. 1; 2; Zech. 4). While Zerubbabel did not serve as king, he was in the Davidic line of Messiah (cf. Hag. 2:23; Matt. 1:12).

1:9–11 The 2,499 articles counted in verses 9 and 10 are only representative of the total of 5,400 mentioned in verse 11.

1:11 captives. Those whom Nebuchadnezzar had taken into Babylonian captivity from Jerusalem, whose return probably occurred early in the reign of Cyrus (c. 538/537 B.C.). **Babylon to Jerusalem.** A journey taking three to five months (cf. 7:8, 9).

C. Those Who Returned (2:1–70)

2:1–70 This list is given almost identically in Nehemiah 7:6–73 (*see note there*).

2:1 the province. This refers to Judah, reduced from an illustrious, independent, and powerful kingdom to an obscure, servile province of the Persian Empire. The returning Jews were still considered subjects of Cyrus living in a Persian province.

2:2 *Zerubbabel.* This man was the rightful leader of Judah in that he was of the lineage of David through Jehoiachin (cf. 1 Chr. 3:17). He did not serve as king (cf. the curse on Jehoiachin's line, Jer. 22:24–30), but was still in the messianic line because the curse was bypassed (cf. Matt. 1:12; Luke 3:27) in Luke's genealogy by tracing the lineage through David's son, Nathan. His name means "offspring of Babylon," indicating his place of birth. He, rather than Cyrus' political appointee Sheshbazzar (cf. 1:11), led Judah according to God's will. ***Jeshua.*** The high priest of the first return whose name means "Jehovah saves." He is called Joshua in Haggai 1:1 and Zechariah 3:1. His father Jozadak (3:2) had been exiled (cf. 1 Chr. 6:15). He came from the lineage of Levi, Aaron, Eleazar, and Phinehas; thus he was legitimately in the line of the high priest (cf. Num. 25:10–13). ***Nehemiah . . . Mordecai.*** These are not the same men in Nehemiah or Esther.

2:3–20 Various Jewish families are listed.

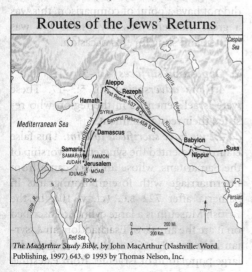

Routes of the Jews' Returns

The MacArthur Study Bible, by John MacArthur (Nashville: Word Publishing, 1997) 643. © 1993 by Thomas Nelson, Inc.

2:21–35 These were people from various Judean cities.

2:36–42 Priests and Levites. See Nehemiah 12:1–9 for additional details.

2:43–54 *Nethinim.* These were temple servants, descendants of the Gibeonites who performed servile duties at the temple.

2:55–58 Here are descendants of Solomon's servants.

2:59–62 Those whose genealogical information could not be verified.

2:63 *Urim and Thummim.* See note on *Exodus 28:30.* These objects, kept in the breastplate of the high priest, were used to determine God's will.

2:64, 65 This gross amount is 12,000 more than the particular numbers given in the catalogue, when added together. Reckoning up the smaller numbers, they amount to 29,818 in this chapter, and to 31,089 in the parallel chapter of Nehemiah. Ezra also mentions 494 persons omitted by Nehemiah, and Nehemiah mentions 1,765 not noticed by Ezra. If, therefore, Ezra's surplus is added to the sum in Nehemiah, and Nehemiah's surplus to the number in Ezra, they will both become 31,583. Subtracting this from 42,360, there is a deficiency of 10,777. These are omitted, because they did not belong to Judah and Benjamin, or to the priests, but to the other tribes. The servants and singers, male and female, are reckoned separately (v. 65) so that, putting all these items together, the number of all who went with Zerubbabel amounted to 50,000 with 8,000 beasts of burden.

2:69 *drachmas . . . minas. Drachma* probably refers to a Persian coin, the daric, named after Darius I. This would have amounted to approximately 1,100 lbs. of gold. A mina weighed about one and two-tenths of a pound, so this would represent three tons of silver (cf. 1 Chr. 29:7).

2:70 *Nethinim.* See note on verses 43–54.

D. Construction of the Second Temple (3:1–6:22)

1. Building begins (3:1–13)

3:1–13 The worship and regular calendar resumed. The altar was probably rebuilt in 537 B.C.

3:1 After their arrival, they were occupied with their own dwellings in and around Jerusalem. After that work was done, they turned to building the altar of burnt offering in time for the feasts, resolved to celebrate as if the temple had been completed. The month (c. September–October 537 B.C.) of the Feasts of Trumpets, Atonement, and Tabernacles (cf. v. 4) was the seventh month. Such an assembly had not convened for seventy years. They obeyed according to Leviticus 23:24–44. Over ninety years later, Nehemiah and Ezra would lead a similar celebration (cf. Neh. 8:13–18).

3:2 *Jeshua . . . and Zerubbabel.* The recognized spiritual and civil leaders, respectively. *See notes on 2:2. as it is written in the Law of Moses.* The burnt offerings were in accord with Leviticus 1:3–17.

3:3 *the people of those countries.* The settlers who had come to occupy the land during the seventy years of Israel's absence were deportees brought in from other countries by the Assyrians and the Babylonians. These inhabitants saw the Jews as a threat and quickly wanted to undermine their allegiance to God (cf. 4:1, 2). *set the altar.* This was all that was needed to reestablish temple worship (cf. v. 6). They reset it on its old foundation ("bases"), so it occupied its sacred site. *burnt offerings.* These were the most common offerings for sin (cf. v. 2).

3:4 *number required by ordinance.* According to Numbers 29:12–38.

3:7 *masons . . . carpenters . . . cedar logs.* The process of rebuilding the temple sounds similar to the original construction under Solomon (1 Kin. 5; 6; 1 Chr. 22; 2 Chr. 2). *Sidon and Tyre . . . Joppa.* The materials were shipped from the Phoenician ports of Sidon and Tyre south to Joppa, the main seaport, about thirty-five miles from Jerusalem. *permission which they had from Cyrus.* Cf. 1:2–4.

3:8 *second month . . . second year.* C. April/May 536 B.C. This officially ended the seventy-year captivity that began in 605 B.C.

3:11 *they sang responsively.* Their song of praise is similar to Psalm 136:1.

3:12 *the first temple.* The temple built by Solomon (cf. 1 Kin. 5–7). *wept with a loud voice.* The first temple had been destroyed fifty years earlier. The old men, who would have been about sixty years or older, knew that this second temple did not begin to match the splendor of Solomon's temple nor did the presence of God reside within it (cf. Hag. 2:1–4; Zech. 4:9, 10). The nation was small and weak, the temple smaller and less beautiful by far. There were no riches as in David's and Solomon's days. The ark was gone. But most disappointing was the absence of God's Shekinah glory. Thus the weeping. *shouted . . . for joy.* For those who did not have a point of comparison, this was a great moment. Possibly Psalm 126 was written and sung for this occasion.

2. Opposition surfaces (4:1–5)

4:1 *the adversaries.* Cf. 5:3–17. These were Israel's enemies in the region who resisted their reestablishment.

4:2 *we have sacrificed to Him.* This false claim represented the syncretistic worship of the Samaritans, whose ancestry came from intermarriage with foreign immigrants in Samaria after 722 B.C. (cf. v. 10). In the British Museum is a large cylinder. Inscribed on it are the annals of Esarhaddon, an Assyrian king (c. 681–669 B.C.), who deported a large population of Israelites from Palestine.

A consequent settlement of Babylonian colonists took their place and intermarried with remaining Jewish women and their descendants. The result was a mongrel race called the Samaritans. They had developed a superstitious form of worshiping God (cf. 2 Kin. 17:26–34).

4:3 we alone. Idolatry had been the chief cause for Judah's deportation to Babylon, and they wanted to avoid it altogether. While they still had their spiritual problems (chs. 9; 10), they rejected any form of mixed religion, particularly this offer of cooperation which had sabotage as its goal (cf. vv. 4, 5). **King Cyrus . . . commanded us.** Cf. 1:2–4 (c. 538 B.C.). This note gave authority to their refusal.

4:5 frustrate. This caused a sixteen-year delay (c. 536–520 B.C.). As a result, the people took more interest in their personal affairs than spiritual matters (cf. Hag. 1:2–6). **Darius.** Darius ruled Persia c. 521–486 B.C.

3. Excurses on future opposition (4:6–23)

4:6–23 This section represents later opposition which Ezra chose to include here as a parenthetical continuation of the theme "opposition to resettling and rebuilding Judah" (see Introduction: Interpretive Challenges). He first referred to the opposition from Israel's enemies under King Ahasuerus (a regal title) or Xerxes (c. 486–464 B.C.), who ruled at the time of Esther (v. 6). Ezra 4:7–23 then recounts opposition in Nehe-miah's day under Artaxerxes I (c. 464–423 B.C.) expressed in a detailed letter of accusation against the Jews (vv. 7–16). It was successful in stopping the work, as the king's reply indicates (vv. 17–23). Most likely, this opposition is that also spoken of in Nehemiah 1:3. This represents the ongoing occurrence of severe animosity between the Israelites and Samaritans, which was later aggravated when the Samaritans built

a rival temple on Mt. Gerizim (cf. John 4:9). The opposition to Zerubbabel picks up again at 4:24–5:2 during the reign of Darius I, who actually reigned before either Ahasuerus or Artaxerxes.

4:6 they wrote an accusation. The word translated *accusation* means "a complaint." Satan, meaning "legal adversary" or "opponent," is a related term.

4:7, 8 letter . . . letter. Two different words are used here. The first is an official document as opposed to a simple letter. The second is the generic term for letter. The context verifies the choices of two different terms, since two different letters are indicated.

4:8–6:18 Since this section contains predominantly correspondence, it is written in Aramaic (also 7:12–26) rather than Hebrew, generally reflecting the diplomatic language of the day (cf. 2 Kin 18:26; Is. 36:11).

4:10 Osnapper. This is most likely another name for the Assyrian king Ashurbanipal, c. 669–633 B.C. **settled . . . cities of Samaria.** The race of Samaritans resulted from the intermarriage of these immigrants with the poor people who were not taken captive to Nineveh (*see note on vv. 2 and 2 Kin. 17:24–41*).

4:11 Artaxerxes. See note on verses 6–23. **beyond the River.** West of the Euphrates River.

4:12 Jews. This name was generally used after the Captivity because the exiles who returned were mainly of Judah. Most of the people of the ten northern tribes were dispersed, and the largest number of returnees came from the two southern tribes.

4:13, 14 This accusation is full of hypocrisy. They did not relish paying taxes either, but they did hate the Jews.

4:15 the book of the records. An administrative document called a "memorandum" kept on file in the royal archives. **city was destroyed.** A reference to Jerusalem's destruction by the Babylonian king Nebuchadnezzar (c. 586 B.C.).

4:19 And I gave the command. The line might better be translated, "I established a decree." In other words, this was no simple routine order given to one person, but a major edict to a large group of people.

4:21 Now give the command. This involved no small order for one or two workers, but the efforts of 50,000 were called to a halt. The king was commissioning a decree of great significance. The original language calls for the difference. This decree would not lose its authority until the king established a new decree.

4:23 letter. Another official document, as opposed to a generic letter, came from Artaxerxes's transfer of authority to the regional leaders to establish the decree. Without the king's official administrative correspondence, the decree could not be established.

4. Construction renewed (4:24–5:2)

4:24 ceased . . . discontinued. For sixteen years, from 536 B.C. to 520 B.C., work on rebuilding was halted.

5:1 Haggai and Zechariah. The Book of Haggai is styled as a "royal administrative correspondence" (cf. Hag. 1:13) sent from the Sovereign King of the universe through the "messenger of the LORD," Haggai (Hag. 1:13). Part of its message is addressed specifically to Zerubbabel, the political leader, and Joshua, the religious leader, telling them to "take courage and work" on the temple because God was with them (Hag. 2:4). These two prophets gave severe reproaches and threats if the people did not return to the building and promised national prosperity if they did. Not long after the exiles heard this message, the temple work began afresh after a sixteen-year hiatus. *See notes on Haggai and Zechariah.*

5:2 prophets of God. These would be in addition to Haggai and Zechariah.

5. Opposition renewed (5:3–6:12)

5:3 Tattenai. Most likely a Persian official. **Who has commanded you.** In other words, "Who issued you a royal decree to build?" Cf. 5:9.

5:5 But the eye of their God was upon the elders. God's hand of protection which led this endeavor allowed the work to continue while official communication was going on with Darius, the Persian king *(see note on 4:5).*

5:8 heavy stones, and timber. This technique of using beams and stone blocks was a well-known form of wall construction. The reason for mentioning it here was it seemed to be a preparation for conflict, or battle. Including this piece of information served as a threat to the Persian official who wanted no such conflict.

5:11 they returned us an answer. They sent back a report (official document for the archives). **a great king of Israel.** Solomon built the first temple (c. 966–960; 1 Kin. 5–7).

5:12 gave them into the hand of Nebuchadnezzar. The expression is used commonly in royal administrative correspondence when a more powerful administrator, such as a king, relinquishes some of his authority to an underling and yet keeps the lower administrative official under his command. The point here is that God, as King of the universe, satisfied His wrath by relinquishing the authority for this administrative action to Nebuchadnezzar. The greatest king the ancient Near East has ever known was just a petty official in the administration of the sovereign Lord.

5:13 Cyrus . . . decree. Cf. 1:2–4.

5:14, 16 Sheshbazzar . . . laid the foundation. This seems to contradict the statement in 3:8–10 that Zerubbabel, Jeshua, and the Jewish workmen laid the foundation, but it actually does not, since Sheshbazzar was the political appointee of the Persian king over the Jews and thus is given official credit for work actually done by them. *See note on 1:8.*

6:1 *King Darius issued a decree.* Rather than a public edict, this was a simple order issued to a small group of officials.

6:1, 2 *Babylon . . . Achmetha.* Achmetha is another name for the Persian capital of Ecbatana, 300 miles northeast of Babylon in the foothills where Cyrus and others had their summer homes.

6:2 *a record was written.* A particular kind of document called a memorandum (4:15; Mal. 3:16). Administrative officials often kept these documents of administrative decisions made, or issues remaining to be settled, to retain the details of administrative action for future reference.

6:3 *first year.* C. 538 B.C. (cf. 1:2–4). *sixty cubits . . . sixty cubits.* These dimensions exceed those of Solomon's temple (cf. 1 Kin. 6:2).

6:5 *Nebuchadnezzar took.* *See note on 1:7.*

6:6, 7 God so favored the Jews (cf. 5:5) that, through Darius, He forbade the officials from interfering with the building project.

6:8–10 Not only could the officials not hinder the building, but they also had to help finance it by giving the Jews some of their portion of taxes collected for the Persian king. The Jews could draw from the provincial treasury.

6:10 *pray for the life of the king and his sons.* This was essentially the same self-serving motive that prompted Cyrus to decree that all captured peoples should return to their countries, rebuild the temples that Nebuchadnezzar and others had destroyed, and placate the offended deities. He wanted all the gods on his side, including Israel's God.

6:11 *pulled . . . erected . . . hanged . . . made a refuse heap.* This was typical punishment for a serious infraction (cf. Rev. 22:18, 19). This was specifically directed at the hostile Samaritans.

6. Temple completed and dedicated (6:13–22)

6:14 *prospered.* Cf. Haggai 1:7–11. *the commandment of the God of Israel . . . the command of Cyrus.* This is not the normal term for commandment, but it is the same word translated "decree" or "administrative order" throughout the book. The message here is powerful. It was the decree from God, the Sovereign of the universe, which gave administrative authority to rebuild the temple. The decrees (same word) of three of the greatest monarchs in the history of the ancient Near East were only a secondary issue. God rules the universe and He raises up kings, then pulls them from their thrones when they have served His administration (cf. Prov. 21:1). *Artaxerxes.* Although he did not contribute to the project under Zerubbabel, he did under Ezra (cf. 7:11–26).

6:15 *Adar . . . sixth year.* The twelfth month (February/March) in 516 B.C.

6:18 *divisions.* Cf. 1 Chronicles 24, where the priestly divisions are delineated. Although David arranged the priests and Levites in order according to families, it was Moses who assigned their rights, privileges, and duties (*see notes on Num. 3; 4*). *the Book of Moses.* I.e., the Pentateuch.

6:19 *Passover.* Cf. Leviticus 23:4–8. Other notable Passovers include Hezekiah's (2 Chr. 30:1–22) and Josiah's (2 Chr. 35:1–19). *first month.* March/April.

6:21 *the filth of the nations.* These were proselytes to Judaism who had confessed their spiritual uncleanness before the Lord, been circumcised, and renounced idolatry to keep the Passover (v. 22).

6:22 *turned the heart of the king of Assyria toward them.* By turning the heart of the king in their favor in allowing them to complete the rebuilding, God encouraged His people. They understood the verse, "The king's heart is in the hand of the Lord" (Prov. 21:1) better through this ordeal. The title "King of Assyria" was held by every king who succeeded the great Neo-Assyrian Empire regardless of what country they may have come from.

6:22–7:1 The Book of Esther fits in this fifty-nine-year gap between the completion of the temple (c. 516 b.c.) under Zerubbabel (chs. 1–6) and the second return (c. 458 b.c.) under Ezra (chs. 7–10). Ezra 4:6 provides a glimpse into this period also.

II. The Second Return under Ezra (7:1–10:44)

7:1–10:44 This section covers the return of the second group to Judah, led by Ezra (c. 458 b.c.).

A. Ezra Arrives (7:1–8:36)

7:1 *Artaxerxes.* King of Persia from 464–423 b.c. ***Ezra.*** See Introduction: Author and Date. ***the son of.*** Ezra traced his lineage back through such notable high priests as Zadok (1 Kin. 2:35), Phinehas (Num. 25:10–13), and Eleazar (Num. 3:4).

7:6 *a skilled scribe.* Ezra's role as a scribe was critical to reinstate the nation since the leaders had to go back to the law and interpret it. This was no small task because many aspects of life had changed in the intervening 1,000 years since the law was first given. Tradition says Ezra had the law memorized and could write it from recall. ***the hand of the Lord his God upon him.*** This refrain occurs throughout the Books of Ezra and Nehemiah. Its resounding presence assures the reader that it was not by the shrewd lead-

Key People in Ezra's Priestly Line	
1. Levi	6. Phinehas
2. Kohath	7. Abishua
3. Amram	8. Zadok
4. Aaron	9. Hilkiah
5. Eleazar	10. Ezra

ership skills of a few men that Judah, with its temple and walls, was rebuilt in the midst of a powerful Medo-Persian Empire. Rather, it was the sovereign hand of the wise and powerful King of the universe that allowed this to happen.

7:7 *Nethinim.* See note on 2:43–54. ***seventh year.*** C. 458 b.c.

7:8, 9 The four-month journey from Babylon to Jerusalem, covering almost 1,000 miles, started in March/April and ended in July/August.

7:10 *seek . . . do . . . teach.* The pattern of Ezra's preparation is exemplary. He studied before he attempted to live a life of obedience, and he studied and practiced the law in his own life before he opened his mouth to teach that law. But the success of Ezra's leadership did not come from his strength alone; rather, most significantly, it came because "the good hand of his God was upon him" (v. 9).

7:11 *copy of the letter.* The original was usually kept for a record. The letter was addressed to Ezra because the decree recorded therein was the critical administrative document. Decrees were commonly embedded in letters. The letter in essence authorized the document into Ezra's hands so he could carry it and read it to its intended audience.

7:12–26 This is a remarkable decree that evidences God's sovereign rule over earthly kings and His intent to keep the Abrahamic, Davidic, and New Covenants with Israel. This section is in Aramaic, as was 4:8–6:18.

7:12 king of kings. Though it was true that Artaxerxes ruled over other kings, Jesus Christ is the ultimate King of kings (cf. Rev. 19:16), who alone can genuinely make that claim since He will rule over all kings in His coming kingdom (cf. Rev. 11:15).

7:14 seven counselors. This number was according to the Persian tradition (cf. Esth. 1:14).

7:17 now therefore. The royal decree protocol recorded in the opening words of verses 13–16 leads up to the section introduced by these words.

7:22 one hundred talents. Approaching four tons in weight. **one hundred kors.** Approximately 750 bushels. **one hundred baths.** Six hundred gallons.

7:25 And you, Ezra. The letter in which the decree was embedded was written to Ezra. The king turned to him in a demonstration of administrative trust and granted him permission to appoint magistrates and judges for the region. The effect of this decision would be to offer a measure of local autonomy to the Jews.

8:1–14 from Babylon. The list that follows no doubt includes those who lived in the surrounding areas. The total number of males in this section is 1,496 plus the men

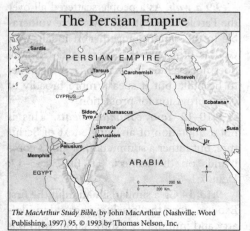

The Persian Empire

The MacArthur Study Bible, by John MacArthur (Nashville: Word Publishing, 1997) 95. © 1993 by Thomas Nelson, Inc.

named; so with the addition of the women and children, the number easily approaches seven to eight thousand. Just as these had not gone with the first group of returnees, so many Jews remained in Babylon after this group had departed. During the seventy years, many of the exiles had settled into a comfortable lifestyle. No small conflict arose between those who returned and those who stayed in Babylon.

8:15 river . . . Ahava. An unknown location where a canal/river flowed into the Euphrates River. This was in Babylon and chosen for the place where the returning Jews would render vows for several days in preparation to leave. **none . . . of Levi.** There were no Levites who chose to return so Ezra pursued such needed men by sending a command to Iddo, who was chief of the Nethinim. Iddo's influence brought 38 Levites and 220 Nethinim (vv. 16–20).

8:17 Nethinim. See note on 2:43–54.

8:21–23 I proclaimed a fast. They would soon begin the long journey. Such travel was dangerous, since the roads were frequented by thieves who robbed for survival. Even messengers traveled with caravans to ensure their safety. Ezra and the people did not want to confuse the king about their trust in God's protection so they entreated Him for safety with a prayerful fast. God honored their prayer of faith with His protection.

8:26 six hundred and fifty talents. Over twenty-five tons. **one hundred talents.** Almost four tons.

8:27 a thousand drachmas. About twenty pounds. See note on 2:69.

8:31 Ahava. See note on verse 15. **first month.** See note on 7:8, 9. The twelve-day delay occurred because of a three-day delay searching for more Levites (v. 15) and the fast which sought God's protection (v. 21).

8:36 they delivered the king's orders. The plural "orders" may account for a change of terminology. This would include the decrees plus other orders in the official correspondence Artaxerxes gave to Ezra to deliver, to support the Jews and their building of the temple.

B. Ezra Leads Revival (9:1–10:44)

9:1 *When these things were done.* This refers to the implementation of the different trusts and duties committed to him. ***priests . . . Levites.*** As was the case before the Assyrian and Babylonian deportations, the spiritual leadership defaulted along with the people (cf. Is. 24:2; Jer. 5:30, 31; 6:13–15; Hos. 3:9; Mal. 2:1–9; 2 Tim. 4:2–4). ***abominations.*** The reason for this exclusiveness was to keep the people pure. In the first settlement, Israel was warned not to make covenants with the nations, which would result in intermarriages and inevitably the worship of foreign gods (Ex. 34:10–17; Deut. 7:1–5). To a great extent, the continual violation of this precipitated the seventy-year exile from which they had just returned. Ezra found out it had happened again and called for immediate repentance. Nehemiah (Neh. 13:23–27) and Malachi (Mal. 2:14–16) later encountered the same sin. It is unthinkable that the Jews would so quickly go down the same disastrous path of idolatry. Neither wrath from God in the exile to Babylon, nor grace from God in the return was enough to keep them from defecting again. ***Canaanites . . . Amorites.*** *See note on Joshua 3:10.*

9:2 *holy seed.* The seed of Abraham that God had set apart (cf. Gen. 13:15, 16; 17:4–14). It was not to be mixed with other nations; and if so, it violated God's covenant (cf. Deut. 7:2, 3). This marriage with Gentile women would bring idolatry into the next generation for certain, so Ezra reacted strongly.

9:3 *tore . . . plucked . . . sat.* An outward expression of a grieving, disturbed spirit

over sin (cf. 2 Chr. 34:27) characterized Ezra as he saw the people returning to their old ways which would bring judgment again.

9:4 *trembled at the words.* In contrast to those who participated in the intermarriage, there were those who saw it as an abomination. They greatly feared the Lord's judgment on them again (cf. Is. 66:2, 5) and sat with Ezra until the gathering of the people for the evening sacrifice, when there was surely public prayer and confession as Ezra fasted, lamented, and prayed (v. 5) in an effort to lead the leaders and people to repent.

9:5–15 Ezra's priestly prayer of intercession and confession is like Daniel's (Dan. 9:1–20) and Nehemiah's (Neh. 1:4–11), in that he used plural pronouns that identified himself with the people's sin, even though he did not participate in it. The use of *we, our,* and *us* demonstrates Ezra's understanding that the sin of the few is sufficient to contaminate the many.

9:8 *a peg in His holy place.* A figure of speech that indicated permanence and prominence.

9:8, 9 *grace . . . mercy.* God had been true to His character and His covenant (cf. Lam. 3:22, 23) in restoring Israel, Jerusalem, and the temple.

9:9 *a wall.* As a people scattered all over the Fertile Crescent, the Jews were vulnerable to the nations. Together in Judah, with God as protector, they were safe. The wall does not exclude the walls of Jerusalem yet to be built, but it speaks more broadly of God's provision for protection.

9:10–12 *Your commandments.* This is not a quotation of any single text of Scripture, but rather a summation of God's commands on the subject (cf. Ex. 34:15–17; Deut. 7:1–6).

9:13, 14 Cf. a similar situation in the first Exodus, when the Israelites engaged in idolatry and immorality led by Aaron, who was then confronted by Moses (Ex. 32:1–35).

9:14 no remnant. Ezra feared that this sin would provoke the ultimate judgment of God and the abrogation of God's unconditional covenants. While God would judge sin, the coming of Messiah and Paul's insights on God's continued faithfulness in His promise to the Jews (Rom. 9–11) assures that God's calling of Israel as a beloved people and nation is irrevocable (Rom. 11:25–29).

9:15 no one can stand before You. All were reckoned guilty and had no right to stand in God's presence, yet they came penitently seeking the grace of forgiveness.

10:1 praying . . . confessing, weeping, and bowing down. Ezra's contrite spirit before the people was evident, and they joined him. These extreme expressions of contrition demonstrated the seriousness of their sin and the genuineness of their repentance.

10:2 Shechaniah. This leader, not involved in the mixed marriages since his name does not appear in the list in verses 18–44 (though his father and five paternal uncles do appear in v. 26), was bold and chose to obey God rather than please his relatives. **hope in Israel in spite of this.** This hope is centered in God's covenant love and forgiveness of truly repentant sinners.

10:3 make a covenant. Shechaniah calls for the people and leaders to accomplish the specific action of divorcing the wives and children and acknowledges that Ezra has counseled a course of action consistent with Scripture (cf. 2 Chr. 29:10). **those who tremble.** Cf. Isaiah 66:2, 5. This refers to those who take the Word of God seriously, especially His judgment on their sin. **according to the law.** They wanted to get in line with God's law as revealed in Deuteronomy 7:2, 3.

10:4 your responsibility. Ezra is acknowledged as the chief spiritual leader with appropriate divine authority and human responsibility to take on the execution of this

formidable task of dealing with divorces for so many (cf. vv. 18–44).

10:5 swear an oath. The oath stands in relation to the covenant specified in verse 3. Cf. Nehemiah 10:28–39 for the content of a later oath under similar conditions.

10:7 they issued a proclamation. A proclamation was delivered orally by a herald. It often had the force of law, as did this one. Not participating in the assembly, as some might have been tempted to do, meant not just losing your property but being ostracized from Israel.

10:8 three days. The message had to go out, and the people were required to respond within seventy-two hours. Since only the territories of Judah and Benjamin were involved, the greatest distance would have been no more than forty to fifty miles.

10:9 all the men. Serious consequences highlighted the gravity of the situation, and thus everyone came. **ninth month.** December/January, the time of the heaviest rains and coldest weather, especially in Jerusalem, which is over 2,500 feet in elevation.

10:11 confession . . . separate. Here are the two essential elements of repentance—agreeing with God and taking righteous action to separate from sin.

10:12–14 all . . . many people. This demonstrates how widespread this sin was among the people. With the heavy rain and the large number of people to be processed, the whole operation could go long; so the people made an administrative suggestion for dealing with the magnitude of the problem. For each unlawful marriage, a questioning or court session could be locally conducted. All of these details had to be treated with great care; thus, delegating the court process was a suggestion much like Jethro's back in the wilderness (cf. Ex. 18).

10:15 opposed this. It is unclear whether these four opposed the delay in dealing with the situation or whether they opposed dealing with the sin at all. It was, however, a good plan and brought about a reasonably fast resolution.

10:16, 17 tenth month . . . first month. It took three months to rectify the situation in all cases, after which the people were prepared to celebrate Passover with a clear conscience.

10:18 *the sons of Jeshua the son of Jozadak, and his brothers.* At the head of the list of those who had intermarried were the descendants and other relatives of the high priest who first returned with Zerubbabel and led in the temple reconstruction. They set the example for all the people in giving the appropriate trespass offering (v. 19).

10:18–44 Given the fact that it took three months to resolve the situation, this list of

113 men could represent only those in leadership (cf. "many people," v. 13). There were apparently more violators among the people. Even though the problem was dealt with directly, it would eventually reappear (cf. Neh. 9–10; 13).

10:44 An appropriate provision was doubtlessly made for the divorced wives and the children.

Further Study

Kidner, Derek. *Ezra and Nehemiah*, in Tyndale Old Testament Commentaries. Downers Grove, Ill.: IVP, 1979.

Martin, John A. *Ezra*, in The Bible Knowledge Commentary—OT. Wheaton, Ill.: Victor, 1985.

THE BOOK OF
NEHEMIAH

Title

Nehemiah ("Jehovah comforts") is a famous cupbearer who never appears in Scripture outside of this book. As with the Books of Ezra and Esther, named after his contemporaries (see Introductions to Ezra and Esther), the book recounts selected events of his leadership and was titled after him. Both the Greek Septuagint (LXX) and the Latin Vulgate named this book *Second Ezra*. Even though the two Books of Ezra and Nehemiah are separate in most English Bibles, they may have once been joined together in a single unit as currently in the Hebrew texts. New Testament writers do not quote Nehemiah.

Author and Date

Though much of this book was clearly drawn from Nehemiah's personal diaries and written from his first-person perspective (1:1–7:5; 12:27–43; 13:4–31), both Jewish and Christian traditions recognize Ezra as the author. This is based on external evidence that Ezra and Nehemiah were originally one book as reflected in the LXX and Vulgate; it is also based on internal evidence, such as the recurrent "hand of the LORD" theme which dominates both Ezra and Nehemiah and the author's role as a priest-scribe.

As a scribe, he had access to the royal archives of Persia, which accounts for the myriad of administrative documents found recorded in the two books, especially in the Book of Ezra. Very few people would have been allowed access to the royal archives of the Persian Empire, but Ezra proved to be the exception (cf. Ezra 1:2–4; 4:9–22; 5:7–17; 6:3–12).

The events in Nehemiah 1 began late in the year 446 B.C., the twentieth year of the Persian king, Artaxerxes (464–423 B.C.). The book follows chronologically from Nehemiah's first term as governor of Jerusalem c. 445–433 B.C. (chs. 1–12) to his second term, possibly beginning c. 424 B.C. (ch. 13). Nehemiah was written by Ezra sometime during or after Nehemiah's second term, but no later than 400 B.C.

Background and Setting

True to God's promise of judgment, He brought the Assyrians and Babylonians to deliver His chastisement upon wayward Judah and Israel. In 722 B.C., the Assyrians deported the ten northern tribes and scattered them all over the then-known world (2 Kin. 17). Several centuries later, c. 605–586 B.C., God used the Babylonians to sack, destroy, and nearly depopulate Jerusalem (2 Kin. 25) because Judah had persisted in her unfaithfulness to the covenant. God chastened His people with seventy years of captivity in Babylon (Jer. 25:11).

During the Jews' captivity, world-empire leadership changed from the Babylonians to the Persians (c. 539 B.C.; Dan. 5), after which Daniel received most of his prophetic revelation (cf. Dan. 6; 9–12). The Book of Ezra begins with the decree of Cyrus, a Persian king, to return God's people to Jerusalem to rebuild God's house (c. 539 B.C.), and chronicles the reestablishment of Judah's national calendar of feasts and sacrifices. Zerubbabel and Joshua led the first return (Ezra 1–6) and rebuilt the temple. Esther gives a glimpse of the Jews left in Persia (c. 483–473 B.C.) when Haman attempted to eliminate the Jewish race. Ezra 7–10 recounts the second return led by Ezra in 458 B.C. Nehemiah chronicles the third return to rebuild the wall around Jerusalem (c. 445 B.C.).

At that time in Judah's history, the Persian Empire dominated the entire Near Eastern world. Its administration of Judah, although done with a loose hand, was mindful of disruptions or any signs of rebellion from its vassals. Rebuilding the walls of conquered cities posed the most glaring threat to the Persian central administration. Only a close confidant of the king himself could be trusted for such an operation. At the most critical juncture in Judah's revitalization, God raised up Nehemiah to exercise one of the most trusted roles in the empire, the King's cupbearer and confidant.

Life under the Persian king Artaxerxes (c. 464–423 B.C.) had its advantages for Nehemiah. Much like Joseph, Esther, and Daniel, he had attained a significant role in the palace which then ruled the ancient world, a position from which God could use him to lead the rebuilding of Jerusalem's walls in spite of its implications for Persian control of that city.

Several other historical notes are of interest. First, Esther was Artaxerxes's stepmother (*see note on Esth. 1:9*) and could have easily influenced him to look favorably upon the Jews, especially Nehemiah. Second, Daniel's prophetic seventy weeks began with the decree to rebuild the city issued by Artaxerxes in 445 B.C. (cf. chs. 1; 2; *see notes on Dan.*

9:24–26). Third, the Elephantine papyri (Egyptian documents), dated to the late fifth century B.C., support the account of Nehemiah by mentioning Sanballat the governor of Samaria (2:19), Jehohanan (6:18; 12:23), and Nehemiah's being replaced as governor of Jerusalem by Bigvai (c. 410 B.C.; 10:16).

Finally, Nehemiah and Malachi represent the last of the OT canonical writings, both in terms of the time the events occurred (ch. 13; Mal. 1–4) and the time when they were recorded by Ezra. Thus, the next messages from God for Israel do not come until over 400 years of silence had passed, after which the births of John the Baptist and Jesus Christ were announced (Matt. 1; Luke 1; 2).

With the full OT revelation of Israel's history prior to Christ's Incarnation being completed, the Jews had not yet experienced the fullness of God's various covenants and promises to them. While there was a Jewish remnant, as promised to Abraham (cf. Gen. 15:5), it does not appear to be even as large as at the time of the Exodus (Num. 1:46). The Jews neither possessed the land (Gen. 15:7) nor did they rule as a sovereign nation (Gen. 12:2). The Davidic throne was unoccupied (cf. 2 Sam. 7:16), although the high priest was of the line of Eleazar and Phinehas (cf. Num. 25:10–13). God's promise to consummate the New Covenant of redemption awaited the birth, Crucifixion, and Resurrection of Messiah (cf. Heb. 7–10).

Historical and Theological Themes

Careful attention to the reading of God's Word in order to perform His will is a constant theme. The spiritual revival came in response to Ezra's reading of "the Book of the Law of Moses" (8:1). After the reading, Ezra and some of the priests carefully explained its meaning to the people in attendance (8:8). The next day, Ezra met with some of the fathers of the households, the priests, and Levites, "in order to understand the words of the Law" (8:13). The sacrificial system was carried on with careful attention to perform it "as it is written in the Law" (10:34, 36).

So deep was their concern to abide by God's revealed will that they took "a curse and an oath to walk in God's Law" (10:29). When the marriage reforms were carried out, they acted in accordance with that which "they read from the Book of Moses" (13:1).

A second major theme, the obedience of Nehemiah, is explicitly referred to throughout the book due to the fact that the book is based on the memoirs or first-person accounts of Nehemiah. God worked through the obedience of Nehemiah; however, He also worked through the wrongly-motivated, wicked hearts of His enemies. Nehemiah's enemies failed, not so much as a result of the success of Nehemiah's strategies, but because "God had brought their plot to nothing" (4:15). God used the opposition of Judah's enemies to drive His people to their knees in the same way that He used the favor of Cyrus to return His people to the land, to fund their building project, and to even protect the reconstruction of Jerusalem's walls. Not surprisingly, Nehemiah acknowledged the true motive of his strategy to repopulate Jerusalem: "My God put it into my heart" (7:5). It was He who accomplished it.

Another theme in Nehemiah, as in Ezra, is opposition. Judah's enemies started rumors that God's people had revolted against Persia. The goal was to intimidate Judah into stopping reconstruction of the walls. In spite of opposition from without and heartbreaking corruption and dissension from within, Judah completed the walls of Jerusalem in only 52 days (6:15), experienced revival after the reading of the law by Ezra (8:1ff.), and celebrated the Feast of Tabernacles (8:14ff.; c. 445 B.C.).

The book's detailed insight into the personal thoughts, motives, and disappointments of Nehemiah makes it easy for the reader to primarily identify with him, rather than "the sovereign hand of God" theme and the primary message of His control and intervention into the affairs of His people and their enemies. But the exemplary behavior of the famous cupbearer is eclipsed by God, who orchestrated the reconstruction of the walls in spite of much opposition and many setbacks; the "good hand of God" theme carries through the Book of Nehemiah (1:10; 2:8, 18).

Interpretive Challenges

First, since much of Nehemiah is explained in relationship to Jerusalem's gates (cf. chs. 2; 3; 8; 12), one needs to see the map "Jerusalem in Nehemiah's Day" for an orientation. Second, the reader must recognize that the time line of chapters 1–12 encompassed about one year (445 B.C.), followed by a long gap of time (over 20 years) after chapter 12 and before chapter 13 (see "Time Line of Nehemiah"). Finally, it must be recognized that Nehemiah actually served two governorships in Jerusalem, the first from 445–433 B.C. (cf. 5:14; 13:6) and the second beginning possibly in 424 B.C. and extending to no longer than 410 B.C.

I. NEHEMIAH'S FIRST TERM AS GOVERNOR (1:1–12:47)

A. Nehemiah's Return and Reconstruction (1:1–7:73a)

1:1–7:73a Nehemiah returns to Jerusalem and successfully leads a fifty-two-day "rebuilding of the wall" project (cf. 6:15).

1. Nehemiah goes to Jerusalem (1:1–2:20)

1:1–2:20 This section details how Nehemiah became the governor of Judah (cf. 5:14; 8:9; 10:1; 12:26).

1:1 *The words of Nehemiah.* The personal records of this famous royal cupbearer, whose name means "Jehovah comforts" (cf. 3:16; 7:7; 8:9; 10:1; 12:26, 47), contribute greatly to this book. Unlike Esther and Mordecai, named after Mesopotamian deities Ishtar and Marduk, Nehemiah was given a Hebrew name. *Hachaliah.* Nehemiah's father is mentioned again in Nehemiah 10:1, but nowhere else in the OT. *Chislev.* This is in November/December 446 B.C., four months before Nisan (March/April), when Nehemiah came before the king to get permission to go to Jerusalem (2:1). *twentieth year.* The twentieth year (c. 446/445 B.C.) in the reign of the Persian king Artaxerxes (c. 464–423 B.C.; cf. 2:1). *Shushan.* Also known as Susa, this city was situated east of Babylon, about 150 miles north of the Persian Gulf. Shushan was one of the Medo-Persian strongholds, a wintering city for many officials and the setting of Esther.

1:2 *Hanani.* Apparently a sibling of Nehemiah (cf. 7:2), he had gone to Jerusalem in the second return under Ezra's leadership (c. 458 B.C.). *Jews . . . Jerusalem.* Nehemiah was deeply concerned about the people and the city, especially during the previous thirteen years, ever since the second return under Ezra (458 B.C.).

1:3 *wall of Jerusalem . . . gates.* The opposition had successfully thwarted the Jews' attempts to reestablish Jerusalem as a distinctively Jewish city capable of withstanding its enemies' assaults, which could possibly lead to another destruction of the newly rebuilt temple (c. 516 B.C.; cf. Ezra 4:7–23).

1:4 *sat down and wept, and mourned for many days.* Although Nehemiah was neither a prophet nor a priest, he had a deep sense of Jerusalem's significance to God and was greatly distressed that affairs there had not advanced the cause and glory of God.

Time Line of Nehemiah

Reference		Date	Event
1:1, 4	Nov./Dec.	446 B.C. (Kislev)	Nehemiah hears of problems and prays.
2:1, 5	Mar./Apr.	445 B.C. (Nisan)	Nehemiah is dispatched to Jerusalem.
3:1; 6:15	July/Aug.	445 B.C. (Ab)	Nehemia starts the wall.
6:15	Aug./Sept.	445 B.C. (Elul)	Nehemiah completes the wall.
7:73b	Sept./Oct.	445 B.C. (Tishri)	Day of Trumpets celebrated (implied).
8:13–15	Sept./Oct.	445 B.C. (Tishri)	Feast of Tabernacles celebrated.
9:1	Sept./Oct.	445 B.C. (Tishri)	Time of confession.
12:27	Sept./Oct.	445 B.C. (Tishri)	Wall dedicated.
13:6		445–433 B.C.	Nehemiah's first term as governor (Neh. 1–12).
13:6		433–424 B.C.	Nehemiah returns to Persia.
No ref.		433–? B.C.	Malachi prophesies in Jerusalem during Nehemiah's absence.
13:1, 4, 7		424–? B.C.	Nehemiah returns and serves a second term as governor (Neh. 13).

The MacArthur Study Bible, by John MacArthur (Nashville: Word Publishing, 1997) 659. © 1993 by Thomas Nelson, Inc.

1:5–11 This prayer represents one of the Scripture's most moving confessions and intercessions before God (cf. Ezra 9:6–15; Dan. 9:4–19).

1:5 *keep Your covenant and mercy with those who love You.* After seventy years of captivity in Babylon, God kept His promise to restore His people to the Promised Land. The promise appeared to be failing, and Nehemiah appealed to God's character and covenant as the basis by which He must intervene and accomplish His pledges to His people.

1:6 *we have sinned against You.* Nehemiah may have believed that the sins of the returnees (cf. Ezra 9; 10) had prompted God to change His mind and withhold His favor from the Jews.

1:7 *commandments . . . statutes . . . ordinances.* Those which are recorded in Exodus, Leviticus, Numbers, and Deuteronomy.

1:8 *Remember.* Not a reminder to God as if He had forgotten, but a plea to activate His Word.

1:8, 9 *the word . . . Moses.* This represents a summary of various Mosaic writings. On *scattering* (v. 8), see Deuteronomy 4:25–28; 28:63–65. On *regathering,* see Deuteronomy 4:29–31; 30:1–5.

1:10 *redeemed by Your great power, and by Your strong hand.* Nehemiah's allusion to the Exodus redemption recalled the faithful and strong hand of God which had brought Israel out of bondage once before; this also grounded his confidence in God's power as the basis of his appeal for a second deliverance that would be as successful as the first.

1:11 *who desire to fear Your name.* Nehemiah alluded to the fact that Israel was the place which God had chosen for His name to dwell (1:9); the people desired to fear His name and, thus, were praying for God's intervention. *in the sight of this man.* The reference to King Artaxerxes anticipated the discussion in 2:1ff. *the king's cupbearer.* As an escort of the monarch at meals, the cupbearer had a unique advantage to petition the king. Not only did the king owe him his life, since the cupbearer tested all the king's beverages for possible poison, thus, putting his own life at risk, but he also became a close confidant. God sovereignly used this relationship between a Gentile and Jew to deliver His people, much as He did with Joseph, Daniel, Esther, and Mordecai.

2:1 *Nisan.* March/April 445 B.C. ***twentieth year.*** See note on 1:1. ***when wine was before him.*** The act of tasting wine to ensure it was not dangerous to the king strengthened the trust between king and cupbearer. So this was the appropriate time for Nehemiah to win Artaxerxes's attention and approval. Not surprisingly, kings often developed so much trust in their cupbearers that the latter became counselors to the kings. ***Now I had never been sad.*** Sadness was a dangerous emotion to express in the king's presence. The king wanted his subjects to be happy, since this reflected the well-being brought about by his administrative prowess.

2:2 *dreadfully afraid.* Nehemiah feared that either his countenance, his explanation, or his request would anger the king, and lead to his death (cf. Esth. 4:11 with 5:1–3).

2:3 *tombs . . . gates.* Nehemiah's deep concern and sadness over the condition of Jerusalem and his people was expressed in his reference to tombs and gates. A tomb was a place to show respect for dead community members who birthed the living generation and passed on their spiritual values to them. Tombs were also the place where the present generation hoped to be honored by burial at death. Gates were emblematic of the life of the city, since the people gathered for judicial procedure or basic social interaction near the gates. The burned gates represented the death of social life, i.e., the end of a community of people.

2:4 *What do you request?* The king rightly interpreted Nehemiah's sad countenance as a desire to take action on behalf of his people and homeland. His immediate response to the king's question illustrates how continual his prayer life was (cf. 1:6). ***God of heaven.*** See note on Ezra 1:2.

2:5 *that I may rebuild it.* The request undeniably referred to the city walls, for there could be no permanence without walls, but it also may have included political and administrative rebuilding as well.

2:6 *the queen.* Since Esther was the queen of the previous king Ahasuerus (Xerxes) c. 486–464 B.C. and the stepmother of Artaxerxes, it could be that she had previously influenced the present king and queen to be favorably disposed to the Jews. ***return?*** This presupposes that (1) Nehemiah was being

Persian Rulers in Scripture

Ruler	Date	Scripture
Cyrus II	c. 539–530 B.C.	2 Chr. 36:22, 23; Ezra 1; Is. 44:28; 45:1; Dan. 1:21; 10:
Darius the Mede		Dan. 5:31; 9:1; 11:1 *(see note on Dan. 5:31)*
Darius I Hystaspes	c. 522–486 B.C.	Ezra 4–6; Hag. 1:1; Zech. 1:1, 7; 7:1
Xerxes I (Ahasuerus)	c. 486–465 B.C. c. 483–473 B.C.	Ezra 4:6; Esth. 1–10
Artaxerxes I Longimanus	c. 464–423 B.C.	Ezra 4:7–23; 7; 8:1; Neh. 2:1–8 (Probably ruler during the time of the prophet Malachi.)
Darius II	c. 423–404 B.C.	Neh. 12:22

dispatched on his desired mission and (2) upon its completion, he would return to Persia (cf. 13:6).

2:7 *let letters be given to me.* Official letters transferred a portion of the king's authority to Nehemiah. In this context, he needed to pass through the lands of Judah's enemies who could harm him or prevent him from rebuilding Jerusalem. The roads upon which messengers, ambassadors, and envoys of all sorts traveled had stations where such letters could be inspected for passage. Three months of travel from Susa to Jerusalem was long, dangerous, and ridden with protocol where letters were required for passage. The danger associated with the passage, but particularly the administrative authority that Nehemiah carried in the letters, led Artaxerxes to send captains of the army and horsemen with Nehemiah for protection (2:9). *See notes on Ezra 1:11; 7:8, 9.*

2:8 *and a letter to Asaph the keeper of the king's forest.* Lumber was a precious commodity. This is illustrated in a document from one ancient city in Mesopotamia in which a forest official is taken to court for cutting down a tree. Forests were carefully guarded, and written permission from the king would assure Nehemiah of the lumber he would need to build the citadel, wall reinforcements, and his own residence from which he would administrate the reconstruction. ***citadel.*** This edifice located next to the temple on the northwest side was a fortified building for the purpose of guarding the temple. It was subsequently rebuilt by Herod and named Antonia. ***the good hand of my God upon me.*** This refrain is common in both Ezra and Nehemiah. It is a frequent reminder in these inspired books that God works through His servants to accomplish His will (cf. Ezra 1:5; 7:6).

2:9–3:1 The journey from Persia to Jerusalem and the preparation period was to be three to four months (cf. 2:1 with 6:15).

2:9 *I went to the governors.* Nehemiah's encroachment upon their provincial control posed a great threat to these officials. If handled improperly, disregard for the other local officials would have put Nehemiah's life and the lives of those in Jerusalem in jeopardy. To prevent such a reaction, God had moved the Persian king to dispatch royal army captains and horsemen to accompany Nehemiah and to guard against such attacks.

2:10 *Sanballat . . . Tobiah.* These men were probably also behind the opposition described in Ezra 4:7–23 which stopped the work in Jerusalem. Sanballat served as governor of Samaria (Horonaim was a town in Moab; he was probably a Moabite) and Tobiah of the region east of the Jordan River. These district magistrates were leaders of Samaritan factions (see ch. 6) to the north and east. They had lost any recourse to prevent Judah from rebuilding, since God's people were authorized to fortify their settlement against attack from enemies such as these two officials. To overtly attack or oppose the Jews would be to oppose the Persian king.

2:11–16 Nehemiah spent three days discerning what course to follow before informing anyone of his plan; then he wisely viewed the terrain in secret and surveyed the southern end of the city, noting the broken and burned conditions of the walls and gates.

2:13, 15 *Valley Gate.* Nehemiah began and ended his trip at the same spot (cf. 3:13) on the west side.

2:13 *Serpent Well.* The exact location is unknown, although it is somewhere in the southern section of Jerusalem. ***Refuse Gate.*** Also known as the Dung Gate. At the southern tip of the city (cf. 3:13; 12:31), a common sewer ran to the Kidron Brook into the Valley of Hinnom.

2:14 *Fountain Gate.* The exact location is

unknown, although it was somewhere in the southern section of Jerusalem, probably on the east side. **King's Pool.** Possibly the pool of Siloam (cf. 3:15).

2:15 the valley. The Kidron Valley, running north and south to the east of the temple mount.

2:17 we may no longer be a reproach. The destruction of the city by Nebuchadnezzar had brought great reproach on Israel, but particularly on their God. Nehemiah assured the Jews (v. 20) that, because God would prosper them in this endeavor for His glory, they should move ahead.

2:18 The sight of Nehemiah's credentials and his motivating message revived their drooping spirits to begin the building despite the bitter taunts of influential men (vv. 19, 20).

2:19 Sanballat . . . Tobiah. See note on 2:10. **Geshem the Arab.** This ruler most likely officiated to the south of Jerusalem.

2:20 God of heaven. Cf. 1:5 and see note on Ezra 1:2. Not only did Nehemiah have the king's permission and was not rebelling, but he had God's protection. Those enemies who tried to intimidate against the work had neither, since they were not commissioned by God or the king.

2. Nehemiah and the people rebuild the walls (3:1–7:3)

3:1–7:3 A detailed account of rebuilding the walls is given.

3:1 Eliashib the high priest. The grandson of Jeshua the high priest in Zerubbabel's era (cf. Neh. 12:10). **built.** On the fourth of Ab, (July/August) 445 B.C. (cf. 6:15). **Sheep Gate.** This is located in the northeast section of Jerusalem (cf. 3:32; 12:39). The narrative moves around the perimeter of Jerusalem in a counterclockwise direction. **Tower of the Hundred . . . Tower of Hananel.** This northern section of Jerusalem opened up to the

central Benjamin plateau where enemy forces could attack most easily from the north. The rest of the perimeter of the city was protected by the natural valley topography.

3:3 Fish Gate. So named because merchants sold fish on the northern side of Jerusalem. Men of Tyre and other coastal towns routinely brought fish to sell (cf. 12:39; 13:16).

3:5 nobles did not put their shoulders to the work of their Lord. One explanation, beyond just the laziness of the rich, is that these nobles had been pledged to Tobiah for personal gain (6:17–19).

3:6 the Old Gate. This is believed to be in the northwest corner of Jerusalem (cf. 12:39).

3:8 the Broad Wall. On the western side of the northern sector (cf. 12:38).

3:11 Tower of the Ovens. On the western side of Jerusalem (cf. 12:38).

3:13 the Valley Gate. See note on 2:13, 15. **the Refuse Gate.** See note on 2:13.

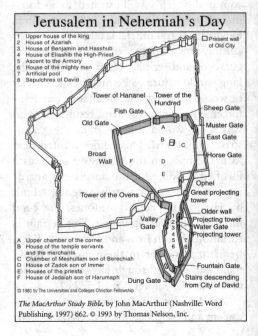

Jerusalem in Nehemiah's Day

1 Upper house of the king
2 House of Azariah
3 House of Benjamin and Hasshub
4 House of Eliashib the High-Priest
5 Ascent to the Armory
6 House of the mighty men
7 Artificial pool
8 Sepulchres of David

☐ Present wall of Old City

Tower of Hananel
Tower of the Hundred
Fish Gate
Sheep Gate
Old Gate
Muster Gate
East Gate
Broad Wall
Horse Gate
Tower of the Ovens
Ophel
Great projecting tower
Older wall
Valley Gate
Projecting tower
Water Gate
Projecting tower
Fountain Gate
Dung Gate
Stairs descending from City of David

A Upper chamber of the corner
B House of the temple servants and the merchants
C Chamber of Meshullam son of Berechiah
D House of Zadok son of Immer
E Houses of the priests
F House of Jedaiah son of Harumaph

© 1980 by The Universities and Colleges Christian Fellowship

The MacArthur Study Bible, by John MacArthur (Nashville: Word Publishing, 1997) 662. © 1993 by Thomas Nelson, Inc.

3:15 *Pool of Shelah.* *See note on 2:14.* **the King's Garden.** In the southeast sector.

3:16 *tombs of David.* Cf. 2:5. Presumably in the southeast sector. **House of the Mighty.** This location is probably associated with David's mighty men (cf. 2 Sam. 23:8–39).

3:19 *the Armory.* Located on the eastern side of Jerusalem.

3:26 *Ophel.* An area south of the temple mount, near the Water Gate, where the Nethinim lived (cf. 11:21; 2 Chr. 27:3; 33:14). **the Water Gate.** Near the Gihon Spring on the east side of Jerusalem (cf. 8:16; 12:37).

3:28 *the Horse Gate.* In the northeast sector.

3:29 *the East Gate.* Possibly located to the east of the temple mount.

3:31 *the Miphkad Gate.* In the northeast sector.

3:32 *the Sheep Gate.* Having traveled around Jerusalem in a counterclockwise direction, the narrative ends where it began (cf. 3:1; 12:39).

4:1–23 This section describes the intimidation and opposition to the project.

4:2 *the army of Samaria.* While it is a possibility that his intentions were to provoke the military force to action, since that would have brought the Persian overlord down on Samaria swiftly, harassment and mockery (v. 3) became the primary strategy to prevent the reconstruction of the walls.

4:4, 5 Nehemiah's dependence on his sovereign God is never more evident than in his prayer (cf. 1:5–11; 2:4).

4:7, 8 *the Ashdodites.* Added to the list of enemies already given are the dwellers of Ashdod, one of the former Philistine cities west of Jerusalem. Apparently, they came to the point where they were at least contemplating a full-scale attack on Jerusalem because of the rapid progress of the wall.

4:9 The Jews exhibited a balance between faith in God and readiness, employing some of the wall builders as guards.

4:10 *so much rubbish.* Lit. "dust," the term refers to the rubble or ruins of the prior destruction (586 B.C.), which they had to clear away before they could make significant progress on the rebuilding of the walls.

4:11, 12 Part of the strategy of the enemy coalition was to frighten and intimidate the Jews by making them think their army would surprise them with a massive force that would engulf them.

4:13–15 *positioned men.* Nehemiah and the others had received word that Sanballat had mustered the army of Samaria (4:2). In fact, God made sure the strategy was known by letting the nearby Jews know, so they would report it to Judah's leaders. Though vigilant, armed, and ready, Nehemiah and those he led consistently gave God the glory for their victories and construction successes.

4:16–18a The threats cut the work force in half, and even those who worked carried weapons in case of attack (cf. v. 21).

4:18b–20 *trumpet.* Among other functions, trumpets were used to sound an alarm in the event of danger or to summon soldiers to battle. Nehemiah kept a trumpeter at his side always, so that the alarm could be sounded immediately. His plan also included continual diligence (vv. 22, 23).

5:1–13 Enemy opposition and difficult times in general had precipitated economic conditions which had a devastating effect on Judah's fragile life. The effect of this extortion on the morale of the returnees was worse than the enemy opposition.

5:1–5 *Jewish brethren.* Perhaps this refers again to the nobles who would not work and had alliances with the enemies (*see note on 3:5*). The people were fatigued with hard labor, drained by the relentless harassment of enemies, poor and lacking the necessities of life, lacking tax money and borrowing for it, and working on the wall in the city rather than getting food from the country. On top of this came complaints against the terrible exploitation and extortion by the rich Jews who would not help, but forced people to sell their homes and children, while having no ability to redeem them back. Under normal conditions, the law offered the hope of releasing these young people through the remission of debts which occurred every seven years or in the fiftieth year of Jubilee (Lev. 25). The custom of redemption made it possible to "buy back" the enslaved individual at almost any time, but the desperate financial situation of those times made that appear impossible.

5:7 *I rebuked the nobles and rulers.* The commitment of the nobles and rulers to the reconstruction project was negligible (cf. 3:5), while their loyalty to Tobiah and others in opposition added to their opportunistic attitudes, placing them close to the status of opposition. They had become the enemy from within. ***exacting usury.*** Usury can refer to normal interest, or it can signify excessive interest. According to Mosaic Law, the Jews were forbidden to take interest from their brothers on the loan of money, food, or anything else. If the person was destitute, they should consider it a gift. If they could pay it back later, it was to be without interest (see Lev. 25:36, 37; Deut. 23:19, 20). Such generosity marked the godly (see Ps. 15:5; Jer. 15:10; cf. Prov. 28:8). Interest could be taken from foreigners (Deut. 23:20). Interest loans were known to exceed 50 percent at times in ancient nations. Such usury took advantage of people's desperation and was virtually impossible to repay, consuming their entire family assets and reducing the debtors to permanent slavery. *See notes on Deuteronomy 23:19, 20; 24:10–13.*

5:8 *we have redeemed.* Nehemiah denounced with just severity the evil conduct of selling a brother by means of usury. He contrasted it with his own action of redeeming with his own money some of the Jewish exiles, who through debt had lost their freedom in Babylon.

5:10 *I also.* Again, Nehemiah set the example by making loans without exacting usury.

5:11 *Restore now to them.* To remedy the evil that they had brought, those guilty of usury were to return the property they had confiscated from those who could not pay the loans back, as well as returning the interest they had charged (*see notes on Luke 19:2–10*).

5:12 *an oath.* The consciences of the guilty were struck by Nehemiah's words, so that their fear, shame, and contrition caused them to pledge the release of their loans and restore property and interest, including setting slaves free. This cancellation of debt had a profoundly unifying effect on both sides of the indebtedness. The proceedings were formally consummated with the people binding themselves by a solemn oath from the priests (acting as administrators) that they would be faithful to the pledge.

5:13 *shook out the fold.* This curse rite from the governor, Nehemiah, called down God's wrath upon anyone who would not follow through with his commitment to release debts. The people agreed and did as they had promised.

5:14 *twentieth year.* See note on 1:1. ***thirty-second year.*** The year Nehemiah returned to Artaxerxes in Persia (c. 433 B.C.; cf. 13:6). ***ate the governor's provisions.*** This refers to the provisions from the Persian administration, but from which he had chosen not to partake because it would have to come from taxing his poverty-stricken people (v. 15). The statement is testimony to the wealth of Nehemiah gained as the king's cupbearer in Persia. Verses 17 and 18 record that he supported 150 men (and their families) with abundant provisions who ruled with him, indicating the personal wealth he had acquired before returning to Jerusalem.

5:15 forty shekels. Approximately one pound of silver. **because of the fear of God.** Nehemiah would not exact usury from his fellow countrymen as his predecessors had, because he viewed it as an act of disobedience toward God.

5:16 we did not buy any land. Even though the time to purchase property from those forced to sell couldn't have been better, Nehemiah maintained a consistent personal policy not to take advantage of another's distress. He worked on the wall rather than spending his time building personal wealth.

5:18 governor's provisions. See note on 5:14. In the ancient Near East, it was customary to calculate the expense of a king's establishment, not by the quantity of money, but by the quantity of his provisions (cf. 1 Kin. 4:22; 18:19; Eccl. 5:11).

5:19 Remember me. The first of four such prayers (cf. 13:14, 22, 31).

6:1 Sanballat, Tobiah, Geshem. See notes on 2:10, 19.

6:2 sent to me. This suggests either a letter or an oral message delivered by messenger to Nehemiah. Satisfied that they could not prevent Nehemiah's project from succeeding by open military engagement (see note on 4:13–15), they decided to overcome him by deception. **plain of Ono.** Located south of Joppa on the western extremity of Judah along the seacoast.

6:3 So I sent messengers. Because Nehemiah knew they were luring him into a trap, he sent representatives, who themselves might have been killed or imprisoned for ransom.

6:5 open letter. Official letters were

Nehemiah's Leadership

Like many biblical leaders, Nehemiah demonstrated an understanding of God's call over his life. Whether as cupbearer to a king or as the rebuilder of Jerusalem, Nehemiah pursued his goals with commitment, careful planning, strategic delegation, creative problem solving, focus on the task at hand, and a continual reliance on God, particularly regarding areas beyond his control. Each of the leadership qualities above can be illustrated from Nehemiah's successful completion of the effort to rebuild the walls of Jerusalem.

First, Nehemiah demonstrated his commitment by his interest and his deep concern over the condition of his fellow Jews in Judah. Next, Nehemiah prayed and planned. He claimed God's promise to bring His people back to the Promised Land, but he didn't assume that he would be part of God's action. He declared himself available (1:11; 2:5).

Even when he arrived in Jerusalem, Nehemiah personally inspected the need before he revealed his plans. Then he enlisted the help of the local leadership. He challenged them to take responsibility for the common good. He placed before them a specific goal—to rebuild the wall. Workers were assigned to work on the wall where it ran closest to their own homes. That way they could see the benefit in having the protective barrier near where they lived.

As the work moved forward, Nehemiah did not allow himself to be distracted by attacks of various kings or tricks from enemies. He took threats seriously enough to arm the people but not so seriously that the work came to a halt. At every turn, we find Nehemiah conferring in prayer with God, placing every decision before Him. Nehemiah succeeded because he never lost sight of the reasons for the work and the source of power with which to accomplish the task.

Seven Attempts to Stop Nehemiah's Work

1. 2:19   Sanballat, Tobiah, and Geshem mocked Nehemiah.
2. 4:1–3   Sanballat and Tobiah mocked Nehemiah.
3. 4:7–23   The enemy threatened a military attack.
4. 6:1–4   Sanballat and Geshem attempted to lure Nehemiah outside of Jerusalem to Ono.
5. 6:5–9   Sanballat threatened Nehemiah with false charges.
6. 6:10–14   Shemaiah, Noadiah, and others were paid to prophesy falsely and discredit Nehemiah.
7. 6:17–19   Tobiah had spies in Jerusalem and wrote Nehemiah letters in order to frighten him.

typically rolled up and sealed with an official signet by the letter's sender or one of his assisting officials. An open or unsealed letter was not only a sign of disrespect and open criticism, but also suggested the information therein was public knowledge. The goal of this document was to intimidate Nehemiah into stopping the work.

6:6 *It is reported among the nations.* The letter suggested that Nehemiah's intent to revolt was common knowledge which would get back to the king of Persia if he did not come to the requested conference. *you and the Jews plan to rebel.* This information would have brought Persian troops against the Jews had it been true. Even though Judah had a reputation for breaking its allegiances with its overlord kings, on this occasion that was not the case. *rebuilding the wall, that you may be their king.* Artaxerxes had commissioned the rebuilding of the wall based on his relationship of trust with Nehemiah. Once the project was accomplished, the king expected Nehemiah to return to Susa. Allegations that Nehemiah was fortifying the city so that he might be made king would seriously violate the Persian king's trust, if not create a war. The plot was an attempt to intimidate Nehemiah with the idea that a wedge was being driven between Nehemiah and Artaxerxes so Nehemiah would come to the meeting with those enemies—a meeting that would have resulted in his death.

6:7 *appointed prophets to proclaim.* If there were such prophets, Sanballat actually hired them to feed incorrect information, thus generating the false rumor (cf. 6:10–14). By dispatching such prophets to make public proclamations that Nehemiah had made himself king, the Persian imperial rule would have appeared to be supplanted.

6:10 *secret informer.* When the open letter failed to intimidate Nehemiah into stopping the work and coming to a meeting, his enemies decided to try intimidation from within. They hired a false prophet (v. 12), Shemaiah, to lure Nehemiah into the Holy Place in the temple for refuge from a murder plot. To enter and shut himself in the Holy Place would have been a desecration of the house of God and would have caused people to question his reverence for God. Shemaiah was the son of a priest who was an intimate friend of Nehemiah. This plan would give them grounds to raise an evil report against Nehemiah, who was not a priest and had no right to go into the Holy Place (cf. v. 13). It could also make the people question his courage (v. 11). Other disloyal Jews included: (1) the nobles (3:5; 6:17); (2) Jews who lived near Sanballat (4:12); (3) Noadiah (6:14); (4) Meshullam (6:17–19); (5) Eliashib (13:4, 7); and (6) the high priest's grandson (13:28). *the house of God.* This is a frequently used name for the temple (cf. 8:16; 10:32–39; 11:11, 16, 22; 12:40; 13:4, 7, 9, 11, 14).

6:15 *Elul.* August/September, 445 B.C. Knowing that the project lasted fifty-two days, it began on the fourth of Ab (July/August) in 445 B.C.

6:16 *this work was done by our God.* While modern readers might be tempted to exalt the leadership qualities which brought the work to completion, Nehemiah's conclusion was seen through the eyes of his enemies, i.e., God works through faithful people, but it is God who works. This is a change from the attitudes indicated in 4:1 and 5:9.

6:17–19 *the nobles of Judah sent many letters to Tobiah.* Nehemiah added a footnote that in the days of building the wall, the nobles of Judah who refused to work (3:5) were in alliance and correspondence with Tobiah because, although his ancestors were Ammonites (2:19), he had married into a respectable Jewish family. Shemaiah was from the family of Arah (Ezra 2:5); his son Jehohanan was the son-in-law of Meshullam who shared in the work of building (3:4, 30). According to 13:4, the high priest, Eliashib, was related to Tobiah (which is a Jewish name). The meddling of these nobles, by trying to play both sides through reports to Tobiah and to Nehemiah (v. 19), only widened the breach as Tobiah escalated efforts to frighten the governor.

7:2 *Hanani.* Cf. 1:2. *the citadel. See note on 2:8.*

7:3 In the ancient Near East, it was customary to open the city gates at sunrise and close them at sunset. Nehemiah recommended that this not be done, because of the hostility of the enemies. Rather, the gates were to be kept shut until well into the heat of the morning when everyone was up and active. When the gates were shut, they were to be guarded by sentinels at watch stations and in front of their own vulnerable homes (v. 4).

3. Nehemiah recalls the first return under Zerubbabel (7:4–73b)

7:5a *my God put it into my heart.* Throughout the book, Nehemiah claimed the hand of God was at work in all circumstances (cf. 2:8, 18; 6:16).

7:5b, 6 *I found a register.* Nehemiah discovered a register of the people made by Ezra in Babylon before the first group returned, a listing of the people who had come with Zerubbabel.

7:6–73a Nehemiah listed those in the first return from Persia to Jerusalem under Zerubbabel in 538 B.C. *See notes on Ezra 2:1–70.* Minor discrepancies are possibly due to Ezra listing those who intended to depart, while Nehemiah listed those who actually arrived; or, it was due to some other unknown reason.

7:65 *consult with the Urim and Thummim.* One of the methods used to discern the will of God on a specific matter. *See note on Exodus 28:30.*

B. Ezra's Revival and Renewal (7:73b–10:39)

7:73b–10:39 God gave revival under Ezra's spiritual leadership.

Key Word

Awesome: 1:5, 11; 4:14; 6:14, 19; 7:2—lit. "to fear." This Hebrew word suggests the virtue that inspires reverence or godly living and respect for God's character (Lev. 19:14; 25:17; Deut. 17:19; 2 Kin. 17:34). Thus while ordinary fear paralyzes a person, godly fear leads to submission and obedience to God. The person who properly fears God follows the will of God (Ps. 128:1) and avoids evil (Job 1:1).

1. Ezra expounds the law (7:73b–8:12)

7:73b–8:12 The revival began with an exposition of God's Word.

7:73b seventh month. The month of Tishri (Sept./Oct.), 445 B.C., less than one week after completing the walls (cf. 6:15). The Feast of Tabernacles usually began on the fifteenth day (cf. 6:14 with Lev. 23:33–44), but here it began on the second (cf. 8:13); and it was a feast to which the whole nation was called. Usually, the Feast of Trumpets occurred on the first day (cf. Lev 23:23–25).

8:1, 2 the Book . . . the Law. In response to the people's request, Ezra brought the Law of the Lord, which he had set his heart to study, practice, and teach to the people (cf. Ezra 7:10). At this time, the law was written on a scroll, as opposed to a text consisting of bound pages. Such a reading was required every seven years at the Feast of Tabernacles (cf. Deut. 31:10–13), even though it had been neglected since the Babylonian captivity until this occasion.

8:1 the Water Gate. See note on 3:26. **Ezra.** This is the first mention of Ezra in the Book of Nehemiah, though he had been ministering in Jerusalem since 458 B.C. (cf. Ezra 7:1–13:44).

8:3 read . . . understand. Here is the general summary of reading and explaining the Scripture from daybreak to noon, a period of at least six hours (more detail is added in vv. 4–8).

8:4 platform . . . beside him. The platform was big enough to hold fourteen people for the long hours of reading and explaining (v. 8). The men, probably priests, stood with Nehemiah to show agreement.

8:5 stood up. In respect for the reading of God's Word, as though they were in the presence of God Himself, the people stood for all the hours of the exposition.

8:6 blessed the LORD. A praise befitting the reading. In a synagogue, the reading is preceded by a benediction. The response of "Amen, Amen" was an affirmation of what Ezra prayed.

8:7, 8 Some of the Levites assisted Ezra with the people's understanding of the Scripture by reading and explaining it.

8:8 gave the sense. This may have involved translation for people who were only Aramaic speakers in exile but, more likely, it means "to break down" the text into its parts so that the people could understand it. This was an exposition or explanation of the meaning and not just translation. **helped them to understand the reading.** In this act of instruction, Ezra's personal commitment to study the law, practice it in his own life, and then teach it (Ezra 7:10) was reflected.

8:9 governor. See note on 5:14. **Ezra the priest.** Cf. Ezra 7:11, 12, 21; 10:10, 16. **wept, when they heard the words of the Law.** When they heard and understood God's Law, they comprehended their violations of it. Not tears of joy, but penitent sorrow (8:10) came forth as they were grieved by conviction (8:11) over the distressing manifestations of sin in transgressing the Lord's commands and the consequent punishments they had suffered in their captivity.

8:10–12 the joy of the LORD is your strength. The event called for a holy day of worship to prepare them for the hard days ahead (cf. 12:43), so they were encouraged to rejoice. The words they had heard did remind them that God punishes sin, but also that God blesses obedience, which was reason to celebrate. They had not been utterly destroyed as a nation, in spite of their sin, and were, by God's grace, on the brink of a new beginning that called for celebration.

2. The people worship and repent (8:13–9:37)

8:13–9:37 The Jews celebrated the Feast of Tabernacles and confessed their history of sins.

8:13 in order to understand the words of the Law. The smaller group that gathered to Ezra consisted of those who had teaching responsibilities: the heads of the father's houses to their families, and the priests and Levites to the general population in the community (Mal. 2:6, 7).

8:14 Cf. Exodus 23:16; Leviticus 23:33–44; Numbers 29:12–38; Deuteronomy 16:13–17 for details on the Feast of Tabernacles.

8:15, 16 they should announce and proclaim. Proclamations such as this carried the authority of the administration represented by leaders such as Nehemiah, who was the governor, and Ezra, the priest and scribe (8:9) who had been used to reestablish the city, its worship, and its social life. The people responded to their directive.

8:16 Water Gate. See notes on 3:26; cf. 12:37. **Gate of Ephraim.** This is believed to have been near the Old Gate (cf. 3:6; 12:39).

8:17 since the days of Joshua . . . very great gladness. Tabernacles had been celebrated since Joshua (2 Chr. 7:8–10; Ezra 3:4), but not with such joy.

8:18 This was more than was required and arose from the exuberant zeal of the people.

9:1 this month. Tishri (September/ October), 445 B.C. (cf. 7:73b; 8:2). **with fasting, in sackcloth, and with dust.** The outward demonstration of deep mourning and heaviness of heart for their iniquity seems to have been done in the spirit of the Day of Atonement which was normally observed on the tenth day of the seventh month (cf. Lev. 16:1–34; 23:26–32).

9:2 separated themselves from all foreigners. This call for divorcing all lawful wives taken from among the heathen was needed, since the last time, prompted thirteen years before by Ezra (see notes on Ezra 10), had only been partially successful. Many had escaped the required action of divorce and kept their pagan wives. Perhaps new defaulters had appeared also, and were confronted for the first time with this necessary action of divorce. Nehemiah's efforts were successful in removing this evil mixture.

9:3 they stood . . . read . . . confessed and worshiped. The succession of events helped to reestablish the essential commitment of Israel to God and His law. They read for three hours about the sins of their fathers and for three more hours confessed that they had done similar evil deeds. In response to all of this, the people worshiped.

9:4–37 This long confession of sin in the context of the recitation of God's mighty redemptive acts on Israel's behalf is an expression of worship (v. 3) that recalls some of the psalms by their theme and worshipful purpose. This season of national humiliation centered on adoring God for His great mercy in the forgiveness of their multiplied iniquities, in delivering them from judgment, protecting them, and blessing them graciously. Apparently, this great prayer of worship offered to God was recited by a group of Levites (vv. 4, 5) indicating it had been prepared and adopted beforehand, probably by Ezra. This prayer initiated the three hours of confession and worship (v. 3), which led to a national promise of obedience to God in the future (v. 38).

9:6 have made heaven. The recitation was sequenced historically, although themes of promise and judgment are traced throughout Israel's history with God. The first feature is the celebration of God's greatness as Creator (cf. Gen. 1; 2). *The host of heaven worships You.* The praise which Israel offered on earth was also echoed in the heavens by angelic hosts.

9:8 *found his heart faithful before You.* The Abrahamic covenant (Gen. 12:1–3; 15:4–7; 17:1–9) was based on God's faithfulness to His Word and given to a man who was faithful to Him. *See notes on Genesis 15:6; Romans 4:3,* where the faithful heart of Abraham is discussed. *a covenant with him to give the land.* The covenant related to salvation, but also involved the Promised Land. The people, having just returned from captivity, emphasized that feature of the covenant, since God had returned them to the land.

9:9–12 This section, comprised of praise and confession, recounts the Exodus (see Ex. 2–15).

9:10 *made a name for Yourself.* God established His righteous reputation over the powers of Egypt by the miracles of immense power.

9:13–19 The months at Sinai are remembered (see Ex. 19–40).

9:17 *They appointed a leader.* The Hebrew of this statement is almost a repeat of Numbers 14:4, which records the dissatisfaction of the people with God's plan and Moses' leadership.

9:19–21 This section remembers the thirty-eight years of wandering in the wilderness (cf. Num. 9–19).

9:21 *They lacked nothing.* The same word is used in Psalm 23:1, "I shall not want." Even during the long season of chastisement, God miraculously cared for their every need.

9:22–25 These verses encompass the period of possessing the Promised Land, as recorded in Numbers 20–Joshua 24.

9:22 *gave them kingdoms and nations.*

Canaan was comprised of a number of politically semi-autonomous groups all loosely connected under the waning authority of Egypt. The Lord divided Canaan into tribal districts, thus apportioning the land for Israel's possession.

9:23 *multiplied their children.* A nation of offspring was another aspect of the promise made to Abraham (Gen. 12:1–3). God told Abraham that his seed would be like the stars of heaven (Gen. 15:5), and Exodus 1:1–3 reminded Israel that their multiplication in Egypt was nothing short of miraculous.

9:24 *subdued before them.* Moses said in Exodus 15:3, "The LORD is a man of war." As Israel's military leader and king, He led them into battle to defeat their enemies and take the land.

9:26–31 This section summarizes the period from the judges to the Assyrian deportation (722 B.C.), even to the Babylonian exile (586 B.C.). See 2 Kings 17–25.

9:26 *who testified against them.* God's prophets brought them to God's court to be judged by His law. This theme is repeated throughout the message (vv. 29, 30, 34).

9:32 *Now therefore.* Having reviewed the faithfulness of God to the Abrahamic covenant (vv. 7, 8) throughout Israel's national history, the prayer turns to the present confessing of their unfaithfulness to (vv. 33–35) and renewed commitment to the Mosaic covenant (vv. 36–38). *kings of Assyria . . . this day.* This statement sweeps across a summary of Assyrian, Babylonian, and Persian domination of the nation for almost four centuries up to that time.

9:36, 37 *in it! . . . over us.* The praise prayer rejoices that the Jews have been returned to the land, but grieves that Gentiles still rule over them.

9:37 *much increase to the kings.* Because

God's people continued in widespread sin, enemy kings enjoyed the bounty that would have been Israel's.

3. Ezra and the priests renew the covenant (9:38–10:39)

9:38–10:39 The nation makes a New Covenant with God to keep the Mosaic Law. Though well intended, as they had been in Exodus 24:1–8, their failure was forthcoming (*see note on 13:10–13*).

9:38 *because of all this.* The history of God's faithfulness, in spite of Israel's unfaithfulness, is the ground of a pledge and promise which the people make to obey God and not repeat the sins of their fathers. *We make a sure covenant and write it.* A covenant was a binding agreement between two parties. In short, it was a formalized relationship with commitments to loyalty. In this case, the nation initiated this covenant with God.

10:1–27 The sealed signatures on the covenant were from the leaders. Surprisingly, Ezra's name is not listed.

10:28 *Nethinim. See note on Ezra 2:43–54. who had separated themselves.* These are those who (1) had followed the demand of Ezra and Nehemiah to divorce pagan spouses or (2) had been left in the land but never joined themselves to any heathen, thus remaining separate. Intermarriage with the nations had previously precipitated an influence in Israel which had culminated in Babylonian slavery, thus playing a major role in Israel's unfaithfulness to the covenant.

10:29 *a curse and an oath.* Covenants characteristically were ratified by an oath ceremony in which the parties swore to the terms of the covenant. A curse rite was often included wherein the slaughtering of an animal indicated similar consequences for the covenant breaker. Israel's pledged adherence to the law was thus solemnly affirmed.

10:30 *not give our daughters . . . nor take their daughters.* Parents controlled marriages, so this part of the covenant came from them. Again, it empasized the serious sin of marrying a heathen from an idolatrous people (see Ezra 10).

10:32–39 The remainder of the conditions the people made in their covenant involved matters of the temple.

10:32, 33 *we made ordinances.* What the people were committing themselves to do by covenant turned into law requiring a one-third shekel temple tax. The Mosaic ordinance required one-half of a shekel (see Ex. 30:11–16), but the severe economic straits of the time led to the reduced amount. By the time of Christ, the people had returned to the Mosaic stipulation of one-half of a shekel. *See note on Matthew 17:24.*

10:34 The carrying of the wood for the constantly burning altar (Lev. 6:12 ff.) had formerly been the duty of the Nethinim, but few of them had returned from Babylon (7:60), so more people were chosen to assist in this task.

10:35–39 Laws for all the offerings and tithes were reinstated so as not to "neglect the house of our God" (v. 39).

10:35–37 *firstfruits . . . firstborn . . . firstborn.* These laws required the firstfruits of the ground (see Ex. 23:19; 34:26; Deut. 26:2), the firstfruits of the trees (see Lev. 19:24; Num. 18:13), the firstborn sons redeemed by the estimated price of the priest (see Num. 18:15), and the firstborn of the herds and flocks (see Ex. 13:12; Num. 18:15, 17). All of this was kept at the storehouses near the temple and distributed for the support of the priests and Levites. The Levites then gave a tenth of what they received to the priests (cf. Num. 18:26).

11:1–13:31 Details of Nehemiah exercising his governorship are given in this section.

C. Nehemiah's Resettlement and Rejoicing (11:1–12:47)

1. Jerusalem is resettled (11:1–12:26)

11:1–12:26 Jerusalem and Judah are resettled.

11:1 cast lots. A method of decision making which God honored (Prov. 16:33). Nehemiah redistributed the population so that one out of every ten Jews lived in Jerusalem. The other nine were free to reestablish their family heritage in the land.

11:3–24 The people who lived in Jerusalem are identified.

11:21 Ophel. *See note on 3:26.*

11:25–36 These are the places where ninety percent of the people lived outside of Jerusalem (cf. Ezra 2:21–23, 27, 34).

12:1–26 Originally there were twenty-four courses of priests, each course serving in the temple for a period of two weeks per year or for one month biannually (see 1 Chr. 24:1–20). Only four of those houses returned from Babylon (see 7:39–42; Ezra 2:36–39), but these were divided into twenty-four courses of which twenty-two are listed here. Perhaps two are omitted because their families had become extinct, because no sons were born since the time Zerubbabel originally named them.

This, then, is a selective rather than exhaustive listing of priests and Levites from the time of Zerubbabel and Jeshua, recording the key priests and Levites through three generations of high priests: (1) Jeshua who came in the initial return with Zerubbabel c. 538 B.C. (vv. 1–11); (2) Joiakim, the son of Jeshua (vv. 12–21); (3) Eliashib (cf. 3:1), the son of Joiakim (vv. 22, 23); and (4) a miscellaneous group who served in the days of Joiakim (vv. 24–26).

12:1 Zerubbabel. *See note on Ezra 2:1.* **Jeshua.** *See note on Ezra 2:2.*

12:10, 11 This record lists six generations of high priests beginning with Jeshua. The Jonathan of verse 11 is the Johanan of verse 22.

12:12–21 Each of the twenty-two families in verses 1–7 is repeated, except one (cf. Hattush; v. 2). Perhaps by the time of Joiakim's high priesthood, this family had become extinct, the fathers having no male offspring.

12:22 Darius the Persian. This refers to Darius II, c. 423–404 B.C.

12:23 book of the chronicles. Lit. "were written on the scroll of the matters of the days." This involved precise genealogical records kept in the administrative archives of Judah.

2. The people dedicate the walls (12:27–43; 13:1–3)

12:27–43 the dedication of the wall. In the same manner marking the dedications of the temple in Solomon's day (2 Chr. 5–7) and the rebuilt temple several decades earlier (Ezra 6:16–18), the rebuilt walls were dedicated with the music of thanksgiving (most likely shortly after the events of ch. 9).

12:30 purified. See Leviticus 16:30 for the sense of moral purity in this symbolic act.

12:31–40 They probably assembled at the Valley Gate on the west. One of the choirs was led by Ezra (v. 36), the other accompanied by Nehemiah (v. 38). Moving in different directions (v. 38), they assembled together in the temple area (v. 40).

12:31 Refuse Gate. *See notes on 2:13.*

12:36 the musical instruments of David. This phrase could refer to the same kind of instruments David's musicians used or the actual instruments constructed in David's time, now being used centuries later. Cf. 1 Chronicles 15:16; 23:5; 2 Chronicles 29:26; Ezra 3:10. **the man of God.** *See note on Deuteronomy 33:1*; cf. Acts 13:22.

12:37 *the Fountain Gate. See note on 2:14.* *the Water Gate. See notes on 3:26;* cf. 8:16.

12:38 *opposite way.* This second choir marched clockwise to the north (cf. 12:31). *Tower of the Ovens. See note on 3:11.*

12:39 *the Gate of Ephraim. See note on 8:16.* *the Old Gate. See note on 3:6.* *the Fish Gate. See note on 3:3.* *the Tower of Hananel. See note on 3:1.* *the Tower of the Hundred. See note on 3:1.* *the Sheep Gate. See notes on 3:1, 32.* *the Gate of the Prison.* Located in the northeast section of Jerusalem.

12:43 *for God had made them rejoice.* The God of all joy (cf. 1 Chr. 12:40; Neh. 8:10; Pss. 16:11; 33:1; 43:4; Gal. 5:22) activated their inner joy which brought corporate celebration. Though these may have been few and far between, moments like this characterized the life of obedience and blessing which God had set before Israel.

3. Various temple responsibilities (12:44–47)

12:44–47 A listing of miscellaneous temple activities is given.

12:44 *specified by the Law.* Cf. Leviticus 7:34–36; Deuteronomy 18:1–5.

12:45 *the command of David . . . Solomon.* Cf. 1 Chronicles 25; 26.

12:47 *the children of Aaron.* The priests.

13:1, 2 *On that day they read from the Book of Moses.* Not surprisingly, as they read on the regular calendar cycle, they were confronted with areas in which their thinking and practice had wavered from the Scriptures, specifically with regard to the requirements of Deuteronomy 23:3–6.

13:2 *Balaam.* See Numbers 22–24.

13:3 This was done in compliance with their recent pledge (cf. 10:26–29) before Nehemiah left for Persia.

II. NEHEMIAH'S SECOND TERM AS GOVERNOR (13:4–31)

13:4–31 Nehemiah left Jerusalem in the thirty-second year of Artaxerxes c. 433 B.C. (cf. 5:14; 13:6) and returned to Persia as he had promised (cf. 2:6). During his absence, the people returned to their former ways, led by the high priest Eliashib (vv. 4, 5). Such a defection called for the needed reforms of verses 10–30. It was during Nehemiah's absence that Malachi also wrote his prophetic book indicting both priests and people for their sinful defection. Possibly having heard of Eliashib's evil, Nehemiah returned to Jerusalem (vv. 4–7). Nehemiah 13 was the last portion of the OT to be written.

13:4 *Tobiah. See note on 2:10.* Eliashib had allied with Israel's enemy for some personal gain and taken it to such an extreme as to desecrate the house of God.

13:6 *I had returned to the king.* Nehemiah returned to Persia as he promised (cf. 2:6) c. 433 B.C., in the thirty-second year of Artaxerxes (cf. 5:14). It is unknown exactly how long Nehemiah remained in Persia, perhaps until c. 424 B.C., but in that interval, the disobedience developed.

13:7–9 Nehemiah's response to the desecration of the temple was similar to Christ's almost five centuries later (cf. Matt. 21:12, 13; John 2:13–17).

13:9 *articles of the house of God.* In order to accommodate Tobiah, they had moved the articles of the house of God from their rightful place and put idols in the temple courts.

13:10–13 In Nehemiah's absence, the Jews violated their previous covenant with God regarding offerings (cf. 10:35–40) as reported by Malachi 1:6–14; 3:8–12. In his presence, it was immediately restored (*see notes on 9:38–10:39*).

13:10 *gone back to his field.* By neglecting the tithe, the people failed to support the Levites. Consequently, they had to abandon their responsibilities in the house of God and perform field labor in order to survive.

13:14 *Remember me.* This refrain is used three times here, once after each rebuke (cf. 13:22, 31).

13:15–17 They went against their previous covenant by violating the Sabbath (cf. 10:31).

13:16 *Tyre.* A Phoenician coastal town twenty miles south of Sidon.

13:18 Jeremiah had rebuked their fathers for the same things (see Jer. 17:21ff.). By such acts, their fathers had brought the misery of exile and oppression, and they were doing the same—increasing God's wrath against them.

13:19–22 Nehemiah had to force compliance with threats.

13:23–29 Both the priests and the people had married pagans of the land in violation of the Mosaic Law (cf. Ex. 34:15, 16; Deut. 7:3), the earlier reforms of Ezra (cf. Ezra 9; 10), and their own covenant (cf. 10:30).

Malachi spoke against this sin (Mal. 2:10–16).

13:23 *Ashdod.* See note on 4:7. *Ammon, and Moab.* Neighboring countries east of the Jordan River whose beginnings can be traced back to Lot's incestuous unions with his two daughters (cf. Gen. 19:30–38).

13:28 Even the grandson of the high priest (cf. 12:10) sinfully married a daughter of Sanballat (*see note on 2:10*).

13:29, 30 Malachi 2:1–8 recognizes the uncleanness within the priesthood.

13:31 *Remember me.* Nehemiah prayed this for the third time (cf. 13:14, 22), desiring God's blessing on his obedient efforts.

Further Study

Kidner, Derek. *Ezra and Nehemiah,* in the Tyndale Old Testament Commentaries. Downers Grove, Ill.: IVP, 1979.

Yamauchi, Edwin. *Nehemiah,* in Expositor's Bible Commentary. Grand Rapids: Zondervan, 1988.

THE BOOK OF
ESTHER

Title

Esther serves as the title of this book without variation through the ages. This book and the Book of Ruth are the only OT books named after women. Like the Song of Solomon, Obadiah, and Nahum, the NT does not quote or allude to Esther.

Hadassah (2:7), meaning "myrtle," was the Hebrew name of Esther, which came either from the Persian word *star* or possibly from the name of the Babylonian love goddess, Ishtar. As the orphaned daughter of her father Abihail, Esther grew up in Persia with her older cousin, Mordecai, who raised her as if she were his own daughter (2:7, 15).

Author and Date

The author remains unknown, although Mordecai, Ezra, and Nehemiah have been suggested. Whoever penned Esther possessed a detailed knowledge of Persian customs, etiquette, and history, plus particular familiarity with the palace at Shushan (1:5–7). He also exhibited intimate knowledge of the Hebrew calendar and customs, while additionally showing a strong sense of Jewish nationalism. Possibly a Persian Jew, who later moved back to Israel, wrote Esther.

Esther appears as the seventeenth book in the literary chronology of the OT and closes the OT historical section. Only Ezra 7–10, Nehemiah, and Malachi report later OT history than Esther. The Esther account ends in 473 B.C. before Ahasuerus died by assassination (c. 465 B.C.). Esther 10:2 speaks as though Ahasuerus's reign has been completed, so the earliest possible writing date would be after his reign around the mid-fifth century B.C. The latest reasonable date would be prior to 331 B.C. when Greece conquered Persia.

Background and Setting

Esther occurred during the Persian period of world history, c. 539 B.C. (Dan. 5:30, 31) to c. 331 B.C. (Dan. 8:1–27). Ahasuerus ruled from c. 486 to 465 B.C.; Esther covers the 483–473 B.C. portion of his reign. The name *Ahasuerus* represents the Hebrew transliteration of the Persian name *Khshayarsha*, while *Xerxes* represents his Greek name.

The events of Esther occurred during the wider time span between the first return of the Jews after the seventy-year captivity in Babylon (Dan. 9:1–19) under Zerubbabel c. 538 B.C. (Ezra 1–6) and the second return led by Ezra c. 458 B.C. (Ezra 7–10). Nehemiah's journey (the third return) from Susa to Jerusalem (Neh. 1; 2) occurred later (c. 445 B.C.).

Esther and Exodus both chronicle how vigorously foreign powers tried to eliminate the Jewish race and how God sovereignly preserved His people in accordance with His covenant promise to Abraham c. 2100–2075 B.C. (Gen. 12:1–3; 17:1–8). As a result of God's prevailing, chapters 9 and 10 record the beginning of Purim—a new annual festival in the twelfth month (February/March) to celebrate the nation's survival. Purim became one of two festivals given outside of the Mosaic legislation still to be celebrated in Israel (Hanukkah, or the Festival of Lights, is the other, cf. John 10:22).

Historical and Theological Themes

All 167 verses of Esther have ultimately been accepted as canonical, although the absence of God's name anywhere has caused some to unnecessarily doubt its authenticity. The Greek Septuagint (LXX) added an extra 107 apocryphal verses which supposedly compensated for this lack. Along with the Song of Solomon, Ruth, Ecclesiastes, and Lamentations, Esther stands with the OT books of the Megilloth, or "five scrolls." Rabbis read these books in the synagogue on five special occasions during the year—Esther being read at Purim (cf. 9:20–32).

The historical genesis for the drama played out between Mordecai (a Benjamite descendant of Saul—2:5) and Haman (an Agagite—3:1, 10; 8:3, 5; 9:24) goes back almost 1,000 years when the Jews exited from Egypt (c. 1445 B.C.) and were attacked by the Amalekites (Ex. 17:8–16), whose lineage began with Amalek, grandson of Esau (Gen. 36:12). God pronounced His curse on the Amalekites, which resulted in their total elimination as a people (Ex. 17:14; Deut. 25:17–19). Although Saul (c. 1030 B.C.) received orders to kill all the Amalekites, including their king Agag (1 Sam. 15:2, 3), he disobeyed (1 Sam. 15:7–9) and incurred God's displeasure (1 Sam. 15:11, 26; 28:18). Samuel finally hacked Agag into pieces (1 Sam. 15:32, 33). Because of his lineage from Agag, Haman carried deep hostility toward the Jews.

The time of Esther arrived 550 years after the death of Agag, but in spite of such a lengthy passage of time, neither Haman the Agagite nor Mordecai the Benjamite had forgotten the tribal feud that still smoldered

in their souls. This explains why Mordecai refused to bow down to Haman (3:2, 3) and why Haman so viciously attempted to exterminate the Jewish race (3:5, 6, 13). As expected, God's prophecy to extinguish the Amalekites (Ex. 17:14; Deut. 25:17–19) and God's promise to preserve the Jews (Gen. 17:1–8) prevailed.

Because of God's faithfulness to save His people, the festival of Purim (named after the Akkadian word for lot—3:7; 9:26), an annual, two-day holiday of feasting, rejoicing, sending food to one another, and giving gifts to the poor (9:21, 22), was decreed to be celebrated in every generation, by every family, in every province and city (9:27, 28). Esther later added a new feature of fasting with lamentation (9:31). Purim is not biblically mentioned again, although it has been celebrated throughout the centuries in Israel.

Esther could be compared to a chess game. God and Satan (as invisible players) moved real kings, queens, and nobles. When Satan put Haman into place, it was as if he announced "Check." God then positioned Esther and Mordecai in order to put Satan into "Checkmate!" Ever since the Fall of man (Gen. 3:1–19), Satan has attempted to sever God's relationship with His human creation and disrupt God's covenant promises with Israel.

For example, Christ's line through the tribe of Judah had been murderously reduced to Joash alone, who was rescued and preserved (2 Chr. 22:10–12). Later, Herod slaughtered the infants of Bethlehem, thinking Christ was among them (Matt. 2:16). Satan tempted Christ to denounce God and worship him (Matt. 4:9). Peter, at Satan's insistence, tried to block Christ's journey to Calvary (Matt. 16:22). Finally, Satan entered into Judas, who then betrayed Christ to the Jews and Romans (Luke 22:3–6). While God was not mentioned in Esther, He was everywhere apparent as the One who opposed and foiled Satan's diabolical schemes by providential intervention.

In Esther, all of God's unconditional covenant promises to Abraham (Gen. 17:1– 8) and to David (2 Sam. 7:8–16) were jeopardized. However, God's love for Israel is nowhere more apparent than in this dramatic rescue of His people from pending elimination. "Behold, He who keeps Israel shall neither slumber nor sleep" (Ps. 121:4).

Interpretive Challenges

The most obvious question raised by Esther comes from the fact that God is nowhere mentioned, as in the Song of Solomon. Nor does the writer or any participant refer to the Law of God, the Levitical sacrifices, worship, or prayer. The skeptic might ask, "Why would God never be mentioned when the Persian king receives over 175 references? Since God's sovereignty prevailed to save the Jews, why does He then not receive appropriate recognition?"

It seems satisfying to respond that if God desired to be mentioned, He could just as sovereignly have moved the author to write of Him as He acted to save Israel. This situation seems to be more of a problem at the human level than the divine, because Esther is the classic illustration of God's providence as He, the unseen power, controls everything for His purpose. There are no miracles in Esther, but the preservation of Israel through providential control of every event and person reveals the omniscience and omnipotence of Jehovah. Whether He is named is not the issue. He is clearly the main character in the drama.

Second, "Why were Mordecai and Esther

so secular in their lifestyles?" Esther (2:6–20) does not seem to have the zeal for holiness like Daniel (Dan. 1:8–20). Mordecai kept his and Esther's Jewish heritage secret, unlike Daniel (Dan. 6:5). The Law of God was seemingly absent in contrast to Ezra (Ezra 7:10). Nehemiah had a heart for Jerusalem that apparently eluded the affections of Esther and Mordecai (Neh. 1:1–2:5).

The following observations help to shed some light on these issues.

First, this short book does not record everything. Perhaps Mordecai and Esther actually possessed a deeper faith than becomes apparent here (cf. 4:16). Second, even godly Nehemiah did not mention his God when talking to King Artaxerxes (Neh. 2:1–8). Third, the Jewish festivals which provided structure for worship had been lost long before Esther, e.g., Passover (2 Kin. 23:22) and Tabernacles (Neh. 8:17).

Fourth, possibly the anti-Jewish letter written by the Samaritans to Ahasuerus several years earlier had frightened them (c. 486 B.C.; Ezra 4:6). Fifth, the evil intentions of Haman did not just first surface when Mordecai refused to bow down (3:1, 2). Most likely they were long before shared by others which would have intimidated the Jewish population. Sixth, Esther did identify with her Jewish heritage at a most appropriate time (7:3, 4). And yet, the nagging question of why Esther and Mordecai did not seem to have the same kind of open devotion to God as did Daniel remains. Further, Nehemiah's prayer (Neh. 1:5–11, esp. v. 7) seems to indicate a spiritual lethargy among the Jewish exiles in Susa. So this issue must ultimately be resolved by God, since He alone knows human hearts.

I. Esther Replaces Vashti (1:1–2:18)

A. Vashti's Insubordination (1:1–22)

1:1 Ahasuerus. See Introduction: Background and Setting. **one hundred and twenty-seven provinces.** The kingdom comprised twenty regions (3:12; 8:9; 9:3) which were further divided into provinces ruled over by governors (3:12). **India to Ethiopia.** Ethiopia, not Asia Minor, is mentioned as representing the western edge of the kingdom to avoid any remembrance of the king's previous defeat by the Greeks c. 481–479 B.C. (cf. 8:9). This description also avoided any confusion with the Ahasuerus of Daniel 9:1.

1:2 Shushan the citadel. Shushan (the Hebrew rendering of the Greek Susa), the winter residence, was one of four capital cities of the Persians; the other three included Babylon, Ecbatana (Ezra 6:2), and Persepolis. The citadel refers to the fortified palace complex built above the city for protection.

1:3 the third year. C. 483 B.C. This probably included the planning phase for Ahasuerus's later campaign against Greece in which the king suffered a humiliating defeat (c. 481–479 B.C.). **Persia and Media.** Cyrus the Persian inherited Media and, thus, the name Media became just as prominent as Persia (c. 550 B.C.).

1:9 Queen Vashti. Greek literature records her name as Amestris. She gave birth (c. 483 B.C.) to Ahasuerus's third son, Artaxerxes, who later succeeded his father Ahasuerus on the throne (Ezra 7:1).

1:12 Vashti refused. Her reason is not recorded, although suggestions have included that (1) her appearance would have involved lewd behavior before drunken men, or (2) that she was still pregnant with Artaxerxes.

1:14 the seven princes. These highest ranking officials (cf. Ezra 7:14) were perhaps equivalent to the magi of Daniel 1:20.

1:19 will not be altered. The irrevocable nature of Persian law (cf. Dan. 6:8, 12, 15) played an important role in how the rest of Esther concluded (cf. 8:8).

1:22 letters. The efficient Persian communication network (a rapid relay by horses) played an important role in speedily publishing kingdom edicts (cf. 3:12–14; 8:9, 10, 14; 9:20, 30).

B. Esther's Coronation (2:1–18)

2:1 After these things. Most likely during the latter portion of the king's ill-fated war with Greece (c. 481–479 B.C.). **he remembered Vashti.** The king was legally unable to restore Vashti (cf. 1:19–22), so the counselors proposed a new plan with promise.

2:5 Mordecai. See Introduction: Historical and Theological Themes. He was among the fourth generation of deported Jews. **Kish.** Mordecai's great grandfather who actually experienced the Babylonian deportation. After Babylon fell to Medo-Persia (c. 539

B.C.), Jews were moved to other parts of the new kingdom. Kish represents a Benjamite family name that could be traced back (c. 1100 B.C.) to Saul's father (1 Sam. 9:1).

2:6 *Jeconiah.* Former king of Judah (also known as Jehoiachin and Coniah) who was deported c. 597 B.C. (cf. 2 Kin. 24:14, 15; 2 Chr. 36:9, 10). Due to his disobedience, the Lord removed his descendants from the line of David to Christ (Jer. 22:24–30). The family of Mordecai and Esther were part of the good figs in Jeremiah 24:1–7.

2:7 *Esther.* See Introduction: Title.

2:8 *Esther also was taken.* It is impossible to tell if Esther went voluntarily or against her will.

2:9 *pleased him.* That she pleased Hegai points to God's providential control.

2:10 *not to reveal it.* Possibly because of the hostile letter mentioned in Ezra 4:6 or the anti-Semitic sentiments of Haman and other like-minded people.

2:14 *the second house.* The place of concubines.

2:15 *obtained favor.* This was according to the Lord's providential plan.

2:16 *Tebeth.* The tenth month corresponding to December/January *the seventh year.* C. 479–478 B.C. Four years had elapsed since Vashti's fall from favor.

2:18 *a holiday.* This probably refers to a remission of taxes and/or release from military service.

II. MORDECAI OVERCOMES HAMAN (2:19–7:10)

A. Mordecai's Loyalty (2:19–23)

2:19 *a second time.* Perhaps the king intended to add the second best to his concubine collection.

2:21 *the king's gate.* This indicates the strong possibility that Mordecai held a posi-

tion of prominence (cf. 3:2; Dan. 2:49). *became furious.* Perhaps in revenge over the loss of Vashti.

2:23 *hanged on a gallows.* The Persian execution consisted of being impaled (cf. Ezra 6:11). It is likely that they were the originators of crucifixion. *book of the chronicles.* The king would five years later (Ahasuerus's twelfth year) read these Persian records as the turning point in Esther (6:1, 2).

B. Haman's Promotion and Decree (3:1–15)

3:1 *After these things.* Sometime between the seventh (2:16) and twelfth year (3:7) of the king's reign. *Haman . . . the Agagite.* See Introduction: Historical and Theological Themes.

3:2 *would not bow.* There is a question as to whether Esther and Mordecai were inclined to obey the Mosaic Law. This refusal may be more likely grounded in the family feud between the Benjamites and the Agagites (see Introduction: Historical and Theological Themes), than Mordecai's allegiance to the second Commandment (Ex. 20:4–6).

3:4 *he was a Jew.* It seems evident, from Haman's fury and attempted genocide, that there were strong anti-Semitic attitudes in Shushan, which seems to explain Mordecai's reluctance to reveal his true ethnic background.

3:6 *the people of Mordecai.* Haman was being satanically used to target the entire Jewish race in an unsuccessful attempt to change the course of redemptive history and God's plans for Israel.

3:7 *Nisan.* The time period March/April. Ironically, the Jews should have been celebrating the Passover to remind them of a former deliverance. *twelfth year.* C. 474 B.C. *they cast.* Haman's court of advisers made decisions superstitiously based on astrology and casting of lots. **Pur . . . lot.** A lot would be like modern dice which were cast to determine future decisions (cf. the Hebrew lot, 1 Chr. 26:14; Neh. 10:34; Jon. 1:7). Proverbs 16:33 states that God providentially controlled the outcome of the lot. **Adar.** February/March. There would have been an eleven-month interval between Haman's decree and its expected fulfillment.

3:8 a certain people. Haman never divulged their identity.

3:9 ten thousand talents. The exact dollar amount is uncertain, but reportedly it would have weighed 375 tons and equaled almost 70 percent of the king's annual revenue. Since this sum would have been derived from the plunder of the Jews, it indicates that they had grown prosperous.

3:10, 11 The king would have easily been eager to eliminate any rebellion against his authority (cf. 3:8), although he did not seem to be interested in the money.

3:10 the enemy of the Jews. Cf. 7:6; 8:1; 9:10, 24.

3:12 sealed . . . king's signet ring. This would be equivalent to the king's signature. The date has been calculated by historians to be April 7, 474 B.C.

3:13 to destroy. An ambitious plot to annihilate the Jews in just one day. Historians have calculated the date to be March 7, 473 B.C. The king had unwittingly approved this provision which would kill his own queen.

3:14 as law. It would be irrevocable (cf. 1:19; 8:5–8).

3:15 perplexed. No specific reason is stated. Most likely, even this pagan population was puzzled at the extreme and deadly racism of the king and Haman.

C. Esther's Intervention (4:1–5:14)

4:1 sackcloth and ashes. An outward sign of inward distress and humiliation (cf. Jer. 6:26; Dan. 9:3; Matt. 11:21). Mordecai real-

ized that he had prompted this genocidal retaliation by Haman.

4:4 she sent garments. Mordecai could then enter the king's gate (cf. 4:2) and talk with Esther directly (cf. Neh. 2:2).

4:5 Hathach. A trusted eunuch who knew of Esther's Jewish background.

4:7, 8 That Mordecai possessed this specific knowledge and a copy of the edict further shows his prominent position in Persia.

4:11 golden scepter. In order to protect the king's life from would-be assassins, this practice prevailed. Seemingly, the king would extend the scepter (a sign of kingly authority) only to those whom he knew and from whom he welcomed a visit (cf. 5:2; 8:4). **these thirty days.** Perhaps Esther feared she had lost favor with the king since he had not summoned her recently.

4:14 relief and deliverance. Mordecai exhibited a healthy faith in God's sovereign power to preserve His people. He may have remembered the Lord's promise to Abraham (cf. Gen. 12:3; 17:1–8). **you . . . will perish.** Mordecai indicated that Esther would not escape the sentence or be overlooked because of her prominence (cf. 4:13). **such a time as this.** Mordecai indirectly appealed to God's providential timing.

4:16 fast. The text does not mention prayer being included such as was Daniel's practice (Dan. 9:3), though it surely was. **perish.** Esther's heroic willingness to die for the sake of her fellow Jews is commendable.

5:2 she found favor. This actually means that Esther first found favor with the God of Israel (cf. Prov. 21:1).

5:3 What is your request? Esther deferred her real wish until 7:2, 3.

5:3, 6 up to half the kingdom. Royal hyperbole that was not intended to be taken at face value (cf. Mark 6:22, 23).

5:4 the banquet. The first of two (cf. 5:4–8; 6:14–7:1) that Esther prepared. God would providentially intervene between the two (6:1, 2).

5:11 *the multitude of his children.* At least ten sons were fathered by Haman (cf. 9:13), who personified sinful pride (cf. Prov. 16:18; 1 Cor. 10:12; Gal. 6:3).

5:13 *avails me nothing.* Haman expressed raging fixation on killing Mordecai.

5:14 *gallows.* A stake on which a human would be impaled to death and/or displayed after death (cf. 2:23). ***fifty cubits.*** Approximately seventy-five feet or almost eight stories high. Perhaps the gallows involved displaying a shorter stake atop a building or wall to attain this height.

D. Mordecai's Recognition (6:1–13)

6:1 *the book.* Five years (cf. 2:16 with 3:7) had intervened since Mordecai's loyal but unrewarded act (cf. 2:23). At exactly the proper moment, God providentially intervened so the king suffered insomnia, called for the book of records, read of Mordecai's unrewarded deeds five years past, and then desired to reward him (cf. Dan. 6:18).

6:4 *Who is in the court?* The drama intensified as Haman arrived at just the wrong time and for just the wrong reason.

6:6, 7 Haman ironically defined the honor

to be given to Mordecai at Haman's expense. To his potential wealth from the Jewish plunder, he thought public acclaim would be added.

6:8 *royal robe . . . royal crest.* An honor which involved being treated as though the recipient were the king himself (cf. 8:15). This is reminiscent of Joseph in Egypt (Gen. 41:39–45). History affirms that horses were adorned with the royal crown.

6:9 *the city square.* Whereas Mordecai had been there the day before in sackcloth and ashes (4:1), he now would arrive with royal honor.

6:10 *Mordecai the Jew.* Cf. 8:7; 9:29, 31; 10:3. Why the king did not remember Haman's edict against the Jews remains unknown.

6:12 *mourning.* Deservedly, Haman has inherited Mordecai's distress (cf. 4:1, 2). What a difference a day makes! His imagined honors had quickly turned to unimaginable humiliation. ***his head covered.*** This is an extreme sign of shame (cf. 2 Sam. 15:30; Jer. 14:3, 4).

6:13 *you have begun to fall.* Neither divine prophecy (Ex. 17:14) nor biblical history (1 Sam. 15:8, 9) stood in Haman's favor. Haman's entourage seemed to have some

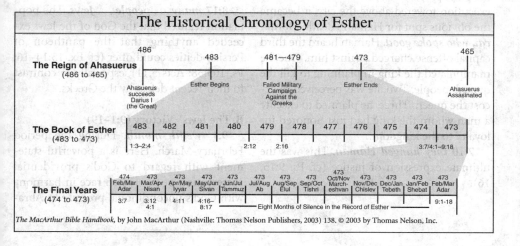

The Historical Chronology of Esther											

The Reign of Ahasuerus (486 to 465): 486 — Ahasuerus succeeds Darius I (the Great); 483 — Esther Begins; 481–479 — Failed Military Campaign Against the Greeks; 473 — Esther Ends; 465 — Ahasuerus Assassinated

The Book of Esther (483 to 473)	483	482	481	480	479	478	477	476	475	474	473
	1:3–2:4				2:12	2:16					3:7/4:1–9:18

The Final Years (474 to 473)	474 Feb/Mar Adar	473 Mar/Apr Nisan	473 Apr/May Iyyar	473 May/Jun Sivan	473 Jun/Jul Tammuz	473 Jul/Aug Ab	473 Aug/Sep Elul	473 Sep/Oct Tishri	473 Oct/Nov Marcheshvan	473 Nov/Dec Chislev	473 Dec/Jan Tebeth	473 Jan/Feb Shebat	473 Feb/Mar Adar
	3:7	3:12 / 4:1	4:11	4:16– / 8:17	Eight Months of Silence in the Record of Esther								9:1-18

The MacArthur Bible Handbook, by John MacArthur (Nashville: Thomas Nelson Publishers, 2003) 138. © 2003 by Thomas Nelson, Inc.

knowledge of this biblical history.

E. Haman's Fall (6:14–7:10)

6:14 *Haman to the banquet.* Like a lamb led to slaughter, Haman was escorted off to his just due.

7:2 *second day.* The first day reference point included the first banquet. This refers to the second banquet on the second day (cf. 5:8). *what is your request?* This was the third time that the king had inquired (cf. 5:3, 6).

7:3 *my people.* This plea paralleled God's message through Moses to Pharaoh, "Let my people go," almost 1,000 years earlier (Ex. 7:16).

7:4 *sold.* This refers back to Haman's bribe (cf. 3:9; 4:7). *destroyed . . . killed . . . annihilated.* Esther recounted the exact language of Haman's decree (cf. 3:13).

7:6 *this wicked Haman.* Similar to Nathan's famous accusation against King David, "You are the man" (2 Sam. 12:7). Haman's honor had quickly turned to humiliation, and then to horror.

7:8 *assault the queen.* Blinded by anger, Ahasuerus interpreted Haman's plea to be an act of violence against Esther, rather than a plea for mercy.

7:9 *Harbonah.* Cf. 1:10. *Look!* Because the place prepared by Haman for Mordecai's execution towered above the city, it became the obvious spot for Haman's death. *Mordecai, who spoke good.* Haman heard the third capital offense charged against him. One, he manipulated the king in planning to kill the queen's people. Two, he was perceived to accost the queen. Three, he planned to execute a man whom the king had just honored for loyalty to the kingdom.

7:10 *they hanged Haman.* This was the ultimate expression of justice (cf. Ps. 9:15, 16).

III. ISRAEL SURVIVES HAMAN'S GENOCIDE ATTEMPT (8:1–10:3)

A. Esther's and Mordecai's Advocacy (8:1–17)

8:1 *the house of Haman.* The property of a traitor, by Persian custom, was returned to the king. In this case, he gave it to his queen, Esther, who put Mordecai over it (8:2). The outcome for Haman's wife Zeresh and his wise men is unknown (5:14; 6:12, 13). Haman's ten sons later died (9:7–10).

8:5 *to revoke.* This proved to be impossible in light of the inflexible nature of the king's edicts (1:19). However, a counterdecree was possible (cf. 8:8, 11, 12).

8:9 *Sivan.* This refers to the period May/June. It had been two months and ten days since Haman's decree (cf. 3:12); eight months and twenty days remained until both decrees became simultaneously effective (cf. 3:13).

8:11 *the king permitted.* Just as the king had permitted Haman, so he permitted the Jews to defend themselves and to plunder their spoil (cf. vv. 10, 15, 16).

8:15 *Mordecai went out.* This second reward exceeded the first (cf. 6:6–9). Blue and white were the royal colors of the Persian Empire.

8:17 *many . . . people . . . Jews.* The population realized that the God of the Jews exceeded anything that the pantheon of Persian deities could offer (cf. Ex. 15:14–16; Ps. 105:38; Acts 5:11), especially in contrast to their recent defeat by the Greeks.

B. The Jews' Victory (9:1–19)

9:1 *twelfth month.* During the period February-March. Here is a powerful statement with regard to God's providential preservation of the Jewish race in harmony with God's unconditional promise to Abraham (Gen. 17:1–8). This providential deliverance stands in contrast to God's miraculous deliverance of the Jews from Egypt; yet, in both cases, the same end had been accomplished by the supernatural power of God.

9:3 the fear of Mordecai. Pragmatically, the nation had a change of heart toward the Jews, knowing that the king, the queen, and Mordecai were the ranking royal officials of the land. To be pro-Jewish would put one in favor with the king and his court and put one on the side of God, the ultimate King (cf. Rev. 19:16).

9:6, 7 Five hundred men died in Shushan.

9:10 did not lay a hand. Unlike Saul, who did take the plunder (cf. 1 Sam. 15:3 with 15:9), the Jews focused only on the mission at hand, i.e., to preserve the Jewish race (cf. vv. 15, 16), even though the king's edict permitted this (8:11).

9:12 further request? Even this pagan king served the cause of utterly blotting out the Amalekites in accord with God's original decree (Ex. 17:14) by allowing for a second day of killing in Shushan to eliminate all Jewish enemies.

9:13 be hanged. I.e., be publicly displayed.

9:15, 16 Over 1,500 years earlier God had promised to curse those who curse Abraham's descendants (Gen. 12:3).

9:15 fourteenth day. Another 300 men died the second day of killing in Shushan, bringing the total dead in Shushan to 810.

9:16 killed. Outside of Shushan, only one day of killing occurred in which 75,000 enemies died.

9:18, 19 This section recounted why Purim would be celebrated for two days rather than one.

C. Purim's Beginning (9:20–32)

9:20–25 A brief summary of God's providential intervention on behalf of the Jews.

9:26 Purim. The first and last biblically revealed, non-Mosaic festival with perpetual significance.

9:29 second letter. An additional letter (cf. v. 20 for the first letter), which added "fasting and lamenting" to the prescribed activity of Purim.

9:32 written in the book. This could be the chronicle referred to in 10:3, or another archival-type document. It certainly does not hint that Esther wrote this canonical book.

D. Mordecai's Fame (10:1–3)

10:1–3 This was apparently a postscript.

10:3 Mordecai . . . was second. Mordecai joined the top echelon of Jewish international statesmen like Joseph, who ranked second in the Egyptian dynasty (Gen. 41:37–45), and Daniel, who succeeded in both the Babylonian (Dan. 2:46–49; 5:29) and Medo-Persian Empires (Dan. 6:28). **speaking peace.** Less than ten years later (c. 465 B.C.), Ahasuerus was assassinated. There are no further details about Esther and Mordecai. What Mordecai did for less than a decade on behalf of Israel, Jesus Christ will do for all eternity as the Prince of Peace (Is. 9:6, 7; Zech. 9:9, 10).

Further Study

Huey, F. B., Jr. *Esther,* in Expositor's Bible Commentary. Grand Rapids: Zondervan, 1988.

Martin, John. *Esther,* in The Bible Knowledge Commentary—OT. Wheaton, Ill.: Victor, 1985.

Whitcomb, John C. *Esther: Triumph of God's Sovereignty.* Chicago: Moody, 1979.

INTRODUCTION TO THE
WISDOM BOOKS

Introduction to the Wisdom Books

The Wisdom section of the OT includes: (1) Job; (2) Psalms; (3) Proverbs; (4) Ecclesiastes; and (5) the Song of Solomon. This general type of literature was common to the ancient Near East, but none other than these five were divinely inspired (2 Tim. 3:16, 17) and, therefore, worthy of one's total confidence in developing a proper worldview.

These OT books portray a wide range of life circumstances from a divine perspective. None are exclusively historical or prophetic in nature, although there can be elements of either one in some contexts. These books are not primarily national in focus, but rather personal. Some are theological in purpose, probing the deeper meaning of life such as Job, Ecclesiastes, and some Psalms; while others expose the more obvious practicalities of life, such as Proverbs, the Song of Solomon, and some Psalms. These contributions concerning wisdom can be summarized as in the following chart.

Each book is distinguished by its own unique literary development. Job is comprised of a series of historical occurrences/dialogues in one man's life. Psalms range from the time of Moses (Ps. 90) to the post-exilic period (Ps. 126) using a poetic/musical form composed by multiple authors. Proverbs develops with a variety of proverbial presentations from long to short. Ecclesiastes explores the themes of "the vanities of life" and "the fear of the LORD" using one man's highly unusual life as the basis. The Song of Solomon employs highly poetic and figurative language with major and minor speakers.

This literature spans time from the patriarchal period (c. 2200 B.C.) or before to post-exilic days (c. 450 B.C.); however, the greatest emphasis is upon the united kingdom reigns of David and Solomon (c. 1011–931 B.C.). These five books of ancient wisdom contain a wealth of timeless truths that are just as applicable today as when they were originally written (Rom. 15:4).

Book	Author	Date	Theme
1. Job	Anonymous	Unknown	How to view suffering
2. Psalms	David and others	c. 1410–450 B.C.	How to view the realities of life
3. Proverbs	Primarily Solomon	c. 971–686 B.C.	How to view wisdom and foolishness in life
4. Ecclesiastes	Solomon	c. 940–931 B.C.	How to view God's purpose in life
5. The Song of Solomon	Solomon	c. 971–965 B.C.	How to view God's intent in marriage

THE BOOK OF
JOB

Title

As with other books of the Bible, Job bears the name of the narrative's primary character. This name might have been derived from the Hebrew word for *persecution,* thus meaning "persecuted one," or from an Arabic word meaning "repent," thus bearing the name "repentant one." The author recounts an era in the life of Job, in which he was tested and the character of God was revealed. New Testament writers directly quote Job two times (Rom. 11:35; 1 Cor. 3:19), plus Ezekiel 14:14, 20 and James 5:11 show that Job was a real person.

Author and Date

The book does not name its author. Job is an unlikely candidate because the book's message rests on Job's ignorance of the events that occurred in heaven as they related to his ordeal. One talmudic tradition suggests Moses as author since the land of Uz (1:1) was adjacent to Midian where Moses lived for forty years, and he could have obtained a record of the story there. Solomon is also a good possibility due to the similarity of content with parts of the Book of Ecclesiastes, as well as the fact that Solomon wrote the other wisdom books (except Psalms, although he did author Pss. 72; 127). Even though he lived long after Job, Solomon could have written about events that occurred long before his own time, in much the same manner as Moses was guided by the Holy Spirit to write about Adam and Eve. Elihu, Isaiah,

Hezekiah, Jeremiah, and Ezra have also been suggested as possible authors, but without support.

The date of the book's writing may be much later than the events recorded in Job. This real possibility is based on: (1) Job's age (42:16); (2) his life span of nearly 200 years (42:16) which fits the patriarchal period (Abraham lived 175 years; Gen. 25:7); (3) the social unit being the patriarchal family; (4) the Chaldeans who murdered Job's servants (1:17) were nomads and had not yet become city dwellers; (5) Job's wealth being measured in livestock rather than gold and silver (1:3; 42:12); (6) Job's priestly functions within his family (1:4, 5); and (7) a basic silence on matters such as the covenant of Abraham, Israel, the Exodus, and the Law of Moses.

The events of Job's odyssey appear to be patriarchal. Job, on the other hand, seemed to know about Adam (31:33) and the Noahic flood (12:15). These cultural/historical features found in the book appear to place the events chronologically at a time probably after Babel (Gen. 11:1–9), but before or contemporaneous with Abraham (Gen. 11:27ff.).

Background and Setting

This book begins with a scene in heaven that explains everything to the reader (1:6–2:10). Job was suffering because God was contesting with Satan. Job never knew that, nor did any of his friends; so they all struggled to explain suffering from the perspective of their ignorance, until finally Job rested in nothing but faith in God's goodness and the hope of His redemption. That God vindicated his trust is the culminating message of the book. When there are no rational or, even, theological explanations for disaster and pain, trust God.

Historical and Theological Themes

The occasion and events that follow Job's sufferings present significant questions for the faith of believers in all ages. Why does Job serve God? Job is heralded for his righteousness, being compared with Noah and Daniel (Ezek. 14:14–20), and for his spiritual endurance (James 5:11). Several other questions are alluded to throughout Job's ordeal, for instance, "Why do the righteous suffer?" Though an answer to that question may seem important, the book does not set forth such a response. Job never knew the reasons for his suffering and neither did his friends.

The righteous sufferer does not appear to learn about any of the heavenly court debates between God and Satan that precipitated his pain. In fact, when finally confronted by the Lord of the universe, Job put his hand over his mouth and said nothing. Job's silent response in no way trivialized the intense pain and loss he had endured. It merely underscored the importance of trusting God's purposes in the midst of suffering, because suffering—like all other human experiences—is directed by perfect divine wisdom. In the end, the lesson learned was that a person may never know the specific reason for his suffering, but he must trust in the sovereign God. That is the real answer to suffering.

The book treats two major themes and many other minor ones, both in the narrative framework of the prologue (chs. 1; 2) and epilogue (42:7–17), and in the poetic account of Job's torment that lies in between (3:1–42:6). A key to understanding the first theme of the book is to notice the debate between God and Satan in heaven and how it connects with the three cycles of earthly debates between Job and his friends. God wanted to prove the character of believers to Satan and to all demons, angels, and people. The accusations are by Satan, who indicted God's claims of Job's righteousness as being untested, if not questionable. Satan accused the righteous of being faithful to God only for what they could get in return. Since Job did not serve God with pure motives, according to Satan, the whole relationship between Job and God was a sham.

Satan's confidence that he could turn Job against God came, no doubt, from the fact that he had led the holy angels to rebel with him (*see note on Rev. 12:4*). Satan thought he could destroy Job's faith in God by inflicting suffering on him, thus showing in principle that saving faith could be shattered. God released Satan to make his point if he could, but he failed, as true faith in God proved unbreakable. Even Job's wife told him to curse God (2:9), but he refused; his faith in God never failed (see 13:15).

Satan tried to do the same to Peter (see Luke 22:31–34) and was unsuccessful in destroying Peter's faith (see John 21:15–19). When Satan has unleashed all that he can do to destroy saving faith, it stands firm (cf. Rom. 8:31–39). In the end, God proved His point with Satan that saving faith can't be destroyed, no matter how much trouble a saint suffers or how incomprehensible and undeserved it seems.

A second and related theme concerns proving the character of God to men. Does this sort of ordeal, in which God and His opponent Satan square off, with righteous Job as the test case, suggest that God is lacking in compassion and mercy toward Job? Not at all. As James says, "You have heard of the perseverance of Job and seen the end intended by the Lord—that the Lord is very compassionate and merciful" (James 5:11). It was to prove the very opposite (42:10–17). Job says, "Shall we indeed accept good from God, and shall we not accept adversity?" (2:10).

God's servant does not deny that he has suffered. He does deny that his suffering is a result of serious, habitual sin. Nor does he understand why he suffers. Job simply commits his ordeal with a devout heart of worship and humility (42:5, 6) to a sovereign and perfectly wise Creator—and that was what God wanted him to learn in this conflict with Satan. In the end, God flooded Job with more blessings than he had ever known.

The major reality of the book is the inscrutable mystery of innocent suffering. God ordains that His children walk in sorrow and pain, sometimes because of sin (cf. Num. 12:10–12), sometimes for chastening (cf. Heb. 12:5–12), sometimes for strengthening (cf. 2 Cor. 12:7–10; 1 Pet. 5:10), and sometimes to give opportunity to reveal His comfort and grace (2 Cor. 1:3–7). But there are times when the compelling issue in the suffering of the saints is unknowable because it is for a heavenly purpose that those on earth can't discern (cf. Ex. 4:11; John 9:1–3).

Job and his friends wanted to analyze the suffering and look for causes and solutions. Using all of their sound theology and insight into the situation, they searched for answers, but found only useless and wrong ideas, for which God eventually rebuked them (42:7). They couldn't know why Job suffered because what happened in heaven between God and Satan was unknown to them. They thought they knew all the answers, but they only intensified the dilemma by their insistent ignorance.

By spreading out some of the elements of this great theme, we can see the following truths in Job's experience:

1. There are matters going on in heaven with God that believers know nothing about; yet, they dramatically affect their lives.

2. Even the best effort at explaining the issues of life can be useless.

3. God's people do suffer. Bad things happen all the time to good people, so one cannot judge a person's spirituality by his painful circumstances or successes.

4. Even though God seems far away, perseverance in faith is a most noble virtue since God is good and one can safely leave his life in His hands.

5. The believer in the midst of suffering should not abandon God, but draw near to Him, so out of the fellowship can come the comfort—even without the explanation.

6. Suffering may be intense, but it will ultimately end for the righteous and God will bless abundantly.

Interpretive Challenges

The most critical interpretive challenge involves the book's primary message. Although often thought to be the pressing issue of the book, the question of why Job suffers is never revealed to Job, though the reader knows that it involves God's proving a point to Satan—a matter that completely transcends Job's ability to understand. James's commentary on Job's case (5:11) draws the conclusion that it was to show God's compassion and mercy, but without apology, offers no explanation for Job's specific ordeal. Readers find themselves putting their proverbial hands over their mouths, with no right to question or accuse the allwise and all-powerful Creator, who will do as He pleases, and in so doing, both proves His points in the spiritual realm to angels and demons and defines His compassion and mercy on earth.

Engaging in "theodicy," i.e., man's attempt to defend God's involvement in calamity and suffering, is shown to be appropriate in these circumstances; though in the end, it is apparent that God does not need or want a human advocate. The Book of Job poignantly illustrates Deuteronomy 29:29, "The secret things belong to the LORD our God."

The nature of Job's guilt and innocence raises perplexing questions. God declared Job perfect and upright, fearing Him and shunning evil (1:1). But Job's comforters raised a critical question based on Job's ordeal: Had not Job sinned? On several occasions, Job readily admitted to having sinned (7:21; 13:26). But Job questioned the extent of his sin as compared to the severity of his suffering. God eventually rebuked Job for his demands to be vindicated of the comforters' accusations (chs. 38–41). But He also declared that what Job said was correct and

what the comforters said was wrong (42:7).

Another challenge comes in keeping separate the preunderstandings that Job and his comforters brought to Job's ordeal. At the outset, all agreed that God punishes evil, rewards obedience, and does so without exception. Job, due to his suffering innocently, was forced to conclude, however, that exceptions are possible in that the righteous also suffer. He also observed that the wicked prosper. These are more than small exceptions to the rule, thus forcing Job to rethink his simple understanding about God's sovereign interaction with His people. The type of wisdom Job comes to embrace was not dependent merely on the promise of reward or punishment.

The long, peevish disputes between Job and his accusers were attempts to reconcile the perceived inequities of God's retribution in Job's experiences. Such an empirical method is dangerous. In the end, God offered no explanation to Job, but He called all parties to a deeper level of trust in the

Outline

B. The Second Cycle (15:1–21:34)

  1. Eliphaz's second speech accuses Job of presumption and disregarding the wisdom of the ancients (15:1–35)

  2. Job's response to Eliphaz appeals to God against his unjust accusers (16:1–17:16)

  3. Bildad's second speech tells Job he is getting just what he deserves (18:1–21)

  4. Job's response to Bildad cries out to God for pity (19:1–29)

  5. Zophar's second speech accuses Job of rejecting God by questioning His justice (20:1–29)

  6. Job's response to Zophar says he is out of touch with reality (21:1–34)

C. The Third Cycle (22:1–26:14)

  1. Eliphaz's third speech denounces Job's criticism of God's justice (22:1–30)

  2. Job's response to Eliphaz is that God knows he is without guilt and, yet, in His providence and refining purpose He permits temporary success for the wicked (23:1–24:25)

  3. Bildad's third speech scoffs at Job's direct appeal to God (25:1–6)

  4. Job's response to Bildad is that God is indeed perfectly wise and absolutely sovereign, but not simplistic as they thought (26:1–14)

D. The Final Defense of Job (27:1–31:40)

  1. Job's first monologue affirms his righteousness and that man can't discover God's wisdom (27:1–28:28)

  2. Job's second monologue remembers his past, describes his present, defends his innocence, and asks for God to defend him (29:1–31:40)

E. The Speeches of Elihu (32:1–37:24)

  1. Elihu enters into the debate to break the impasse (32:1–22)

  2. Elihu charges Job with presumption in criticizing God, not recognizing that God may have a loving purpose, even in allowing Job to suffer (33:1–33)

  3. Elihu declares that Job has impugned God's integrity by claiming that it does not pay to lead a godly life (34:1–37)

  4. Elihu urges Job to wait patiently for the Lord (35:1–16)

  5. Elihu believes that God is disciplining Job (36:1–21)

  6. Elihu argues that human observers can hardly expect to understand adequately God's dealings in administering justice and mercy (36:22–37:24)

III. The Deliverance (38:1–42:17)

A. God Interrogates Job (38:1–41:34)

  1. God's first response to Job (38:1–40:2)

  2. Job's answer to God (40:3–5)

  3. God's second response to Job (40:6–41:34)

B. Job Confesses, Worships, and Is Vindicated (42:1–17)

  1. Job passes judgment upon himself (42:1–6)

  2. God rebukes Eliphaz, Bildad, and Zophar (42:7–9)

  3. God restores Job's family, wealth, and long life (42:10–17)

Creator, who rules over a sin-confused world with power and authority directed by perfect wisdom and mercy. *See notes on Psalm 73.*

Understanding this book requires (1) understanding the nature of wisdom, particularly the difference between man's wisdom and God's, and (2) admitting that Job and his friends lacked the divine wisdom and heavenly circumstances to interpret Job's circumstances accurately, though his friends kept trying while Job learned to be content in God's sovereignty and mercy. The turning point or resolution for this matter is found in Job 28 where the character of divine wisdom is explained: divine wisdom is rare and priceless; man cannot hope to purchase it; and God possesses it all. One may not know what is going on in heaven or what God's purposes are, but one must trust Him. Because of this, the matter of believers suffering takes a back seat to the matter of divine wisdom.

I. The Dilemma (1:1–2:13)

1:1–2:13 This section identifies the main persons and sets the stage for the drama to follow.

A. Introduction of Job (1:1–5)

1:1 *Uz.* Job's home was a walled city with gates (29:7, 8), where he had earned a position of great respect. The city was in the land of Uz in northern Arabia, adjacent to Midian, where Moses lived for forty years (Ex. 2:15). *Job.* The story begins on earth with Job as the central figure. He was a rich man with seven sons and three daughters, in his middle years with a grown family, but still young enough to father ten more children (see 42:13). He was good, a family man, rich, and widely known. *blameless . . . upright . . . feared God . . . shunned evil.* Cf. 1:8. Job was not perfect or without sin (cf. 6:24; 7:21; 9:20); however,

it appears from the language that he had put his trust in God for redemption and faithfully lived a God-honoring, sincere life of integrity and consistency—personally, maritally (2:10), and parentally (1:4, 5).

1:3 *sheep . . . camels . . . oxen . . . female donkeys.* As was typical in the ancient Near East, Job's wealth was not measured in money or land holdings, but in his numerous livestock, like the patriarchs (cf. Gen. 13:1–7). *greatest . . . of the East.* This is a major claim by any standard. Solomon gained a similar reputation, "Solomon's wisdom excelled the wisdom of all the men of the East" (1 Kin. 4:30). The *east* denotes those people living east of Palestine, as the people of the northern Arabian desert did (cf. Judg. 6:3; Ezek. 25:4).

1:4 *on his appointed day.* Each of the seven sons had an appointed day of the week. This reference to the main meal of each day of the week, which moved from house to house, implies the love and harmony of the family members. The sisters are especially noted to show these were cared for with love.

1:5 *send and sanctify.* At the end of every week, Job would offer up as many burnt offerings as he had sons (see Lev. 1:4), officiating weekly ("regularly") as family priest in a time before the Aaronic priesthood was established. These offerings were to cover any sin that his children may have committed that week, indicating the depth of his spiritual devotion. This record is included to demonstrate the righteousness and virtue of Job and his family, which made his suffering all the more amazing. *burnt offerings.* This kind of offering was known as early as Noah (Gen. 8:20).

B. Divine Debates with Satan (1:6–2:10)

1:6 *sons of God.* Job's life is about to be caught up in heavenly strategies as the scene moves from earth to heaven where God is holding council with His heavenly court. It is significant to note that neither Job nor his friends ever knew about this. All of their discussions were conducted without the benefit of knowing about this heavenly dimension. The angelic host (cf. 38:7; Pss. 29:1; 89:7; Dan. 3:25) came to God's throne to render account of their ministry throughout the earth and heaven (cf. 1 Kin. 22:19–22). Like a Judas among the apostles, Satan was with the angels. **Satan.** Emboldened by the success he had with the unfallen Adam in paradise (Gen. 3:6–12, 17–19), he was confident that the fear of God in Job, one of a fallen race, would not stand his tests, for he had fallen himself (see Is. 14:12). In contrast to a personal name, Satan as a title means "adversary," used in either a personal or judicial sense. This arch-demon is the ultimate spiritual adversary of all time and has been accusing the righteous throughout the ages (see Rev. 12:10). In a courtroom setting, the adversary usually stood to the right of the accused. This location is reported when Satan in heaven accused Joshua the high priest (Zech. 3:1). That he is still unsuccessful is the thesis of Romans 8:31–39.

1:7 And the LORD said. Lest there be any question about God's role in this ordeal, it was He who initiated the dialogue. The adversary was not presiding. If anything, Satan raised the penetrating question that might well be asked by anyone, perhaps even Job himself: Does Job serve God with pure motives, or is he in it only as long as the blessings flow? Spiritually speaking, is Job merely a "fair weather" believer in God?

1:7, 8 to and fro on the earth. The picture is of haste. No angel, fallen or holy, is an omnipresent creature, but they move rapidly. In Satan's case, as prince of this world (John 12:31; 14:30; 16:11) and ruler of demons (Matt. 9:34; 12:24), the earth is his domain where he prowls like a "roaring lion, seeking whom he may devour" (1 Pet. 5:8). God gave him Job to test.

1:9–11 Satan asserted that true believers are only faithful as long as they prosper. Take away their prosperity, he claims, and they will reject God. He wanted to prove that salvation is not permanent, that saving faith can be broken and those who were God's could become his. That is the first of the two major themes of this book (see Introduction: Historical and Theological Themes). Satan repeated this affront with Jesus (see Matt. 4), Peter (see Luke 22:31), and Paul (see 2 Cor. 12:7). The OT has many promises from God in which He pledges to sustain the faith of His children. Cf. Psalms 37:23, 28; 97:10; 121:4–7. For NT texts, cf. Luke 22:31, 32; Jude 24.

1:12 power. God allowed Satan to test Job's faith by attacking "all that he has." With God's sovereign permission, Satan was allowed to move on Job, except that he could not attack Job physically.

Job as a Father

1. He was a godly example to his children (1:1).
2. He created a tender, family atmosphere in the home (1:4).
3. He taught his sons to love their sisters (1:4).
4. He pointed their way to God (1:5).
5. He acted as the priest of his home (1:5).
6. He continued to exercise spiritual responsibility for his children, even when they had married and started homes of their own (1:5).
7. He was habitually consistent in exercising his spiritual duties (1:5).
8. He entrusted the lives and welfare of his children to God (1:18–22).

1:13–19 With four rapid-fire disasters, Satan destroyed or removed Job's livestock, servants, and children. Only the four messengers survived.

1:15 *Sabeans.* Lit. "Sheba," part of Arabia. These people were terrorizing robbers, who had descended from Ham (Gen. 10:6, 7) and/or Shem (Gen. 10:21, 28).

1:16 *fire of God ... heaven.* This probably refers to severe lightning.

1:17 *Chaldeans.* A semi-nomadic people of the Arabian desert, experienced in marauding and war (cf. Hab. 1:6–8).

1:19 *great wind.* Most likely, this refers to a tornado-type wind. Cf. Isaiah 21:1; Hosea 13:15.

1:20, 21 *worshiped.* Job heard the other messages calmly, but on hearing about the death of his children, he expressed all the symbols of grief (cf. Gen. 37:34; Jer. 41:5; Mic. 1:16), but also worshiped God in the manner of verse 21. Instead of cursing, he blessed the name of Jehovah. Job's submissive response disproved the adversary's accusations (1:9–11). So far, Job was what God claimed him to be, a true believer with faith that cannot be broken (v. 8).

1:22 *did not sin nor charge God with wrong.* This is better rendered, "sin by charging God with wrong." Hasty words against God in the midst of grief are foolish and wicked. Christians are to submit to trials and still worship God, not because they see the reasons for them, but because God wills them and has His own reasons which believers are to trust (cf. 2 Cor. 4:7–18).

2:1–3a The scene changes again to the heavenly court, where the angels came before the Lord, and Satan was also present, having been again searching the earth for victims to assault. *See notes on 1:6–8.*

2:3 *still he holds fast to his integrity.* God affirmed that Job had won round one. *without cause.* God uses the same expression the adversary used in Job 1 "for nothing (1:9) . . . without cause (2:3)." The message behind God's turn of words is that the adversary is the guilty party in this case, not Job who had suffered all the disaster without any personal cause. He had done nothing to incur the pain and loss, though it was massive. The issue was purely a matter of conflict between God and Satan. This is a crucial statement, because when Job's friends tried to explain why all the disasters had befallen him, they always put the blame on Job. Grasping this assessment from God—that Job had not been punished for something, but suffered for nothing related to him personally—is a crucial key to understanding Job. Sometimes suffering is caused by divine purposes unknowable to us (see Introduction: Historical and Theological Themes).

2:4, 5 *Skin for skin.* Satan contended that what he had done to Job so far was just touching the skin, scratching the surface. Job endured the loss of all that he had, even the lives of his children, but would not endure the loss of his own well-being. If God allowed Satan to make the disaster a personal matter of his own physical body, the Adversary contended, Job's faith would fail.

2:6 *spare his life.* The Lord sovereignly limited the Adversary, although death seemed preferable. Job believed that to be the case (cf. 7:15), as did his wife (2:9).

2:7 *Satan ... struck Job.* This appears to be an exceptional case with no other exact parallel in Scripture. In the Gospels, demons caused physical problems when they dwelled within people (cf. 13:11, 16), but that is not the case here. God's permissive will operated for purposes Job cannot know; God was hidden from him along with the reasons for his suffering. *painful boils.* Although the nature of Job's affliction cannot be diagnosed exactly, it produced extreme physical trauma (cf. 2:13; 3:24; 7:5, 14; 13:28; 16:8; 19:17;

30:17, 30; 33:21). One cannot fully understand Job's conversations throughout the book without considering the extraordinary physical distress he endured in a day without medicine or pain relief. His boils would have been similar to those of the Egyptians (Ex. 9:8–11) and Hezekiah (2 Kin. 20:7).

2:8 potsherd . . . ashes. Suffering terribly, Job took himself to where the lepers go: the ash heap outside the city where he scraped at his sores with a piece of broken pottery, perhaps breaking them open to release the pressure and infection.

2:9 your integrity. Through all this, Job's faith remained strong in the confusion, so that his wife could not accuse him of insincerity as Satan had. Her argument in effect was "let go of your piety and curse God; then He will end your life for blaspheming," (i.e., death under these conditions would be preferable to living). She added temptation to affliction because she advised Job to sin.

2:10 foolish. Not meaning *silly* or *ridiculous,* but acting as one who rejects God or God's revealed will. The word is used of the unwise in the Psalms (14:1; 53:1) and in Proverbs (30:22). Job's wife is not seen or heard of again in this book, except indirectly in 42:13–15. **accept.** Job lived out and explained Deuteronomy 29:29. His words and deeds demonstrated his confidence in God and vindicated God's confidence in him.

C. Arrival of Friends (2:11–13)

2:11–13 Here is one of the most moving scenes in the whole story, as Job's friends came to comfort and commiserate with him in his pain. They expressed all the traditional gestures of grief.

2:11 Temanite. Most likely, Teman was a city of Edom (cf. Gen. 36:4, 11; Jer. 49:7, 20; Ezek. 25:13; Amos 1:12; Obad. 8, 9). **Shuhite.** The Shuhites were descendants of Abraham through Keturah (Gen. 25:2, 6). **Naamath-**

ite. A resident of an unknown location probably in Edom or Arabia, although some have suggested Naamah on the Edomite border (cf. Josh. 15:41).

2:13 his grief was very great. The expression actually meant that Job's disease produced pain that was still increasing. The agony was so great that his friends were speechless for a week.

3:1–42:6 This whole section is poetry—a dramatic poem of speeches attempting to understand Job's suffering.

II. The Debates (3:1–37:24)

3:1–37:24 This section covers the cycles of speeches between Job and his well-meaning friends, including Elihu (chs. 32–37).

A. The First Cycle (3:1–14:22)

3:1–14:22 The first cycle of speeches given by Job and his three friends begins. Job was the first to break the week-long silence with a lament (3:1–26).

1. Job's first speech (3:1–26)

3:1–10 Job began his first speech by cursing the day of his birth, which should have been a day of great rejoicing, and welcomed the day he would finally die. In short, Job says "I wish I'd never been born." See 3; 6; 7; 9; 10; 12–14; 16; 17; 19; 21; 23; 24; 26–31; 40:3–5; 42:1–6 for Job's speeches.

3:1 cursed the day of his birth. Job was in deep pain and despair. What God was allowing hurt desperately; but while Job did not curse God (cf. 2:8), he did curse his birth (vv. 10, 11). He wished he had never been conceived (v. 3) or born because the joys of his life were not worth all the pain. He felt it would have been better to have never lived than to suffer like that; better to have never had wealth than to lose it; better to have never had children than to have them all killed. He never wanted his birthday remembered, and wished it had been obliterated from the calendar (vv. 4–7).

3:8 who curse . . . Leviathan. Job refers to those who pronounce the most powerful curses, even to arousing the destructive sea monster (*see note on 41:1*; cf. Pss. 74:14; 104:26; Is. 27:1).

3:11–26 Job left the matter of never having been born (vv. 1–10) and moved to a desire to have been stillborn (vv. 11–19), then to a desire for the "light" of life to be extinguished in death (vv. 20–23). There is no hint that Job wanted to take his own life, since there was nothing stopping him. Job still trusted God for His sovereign hand in the matter of death, but he did consider the many ways in which death would be a perceived improvement to the present situation because of his pain.

3:23 hedged in. Satan spoke of a hedge of protection and blessing (1:10), whereas Job spoke of this hedge as a prison of living death.

3:24 sighing . . . groanings. These destroyed any appetite Job might have had.

3:25, 26 the thing I greatly feared. Not a particular thing but a generic classification of suffering. The very worst fear that anyone could have was coming to pass in Job's life, and he is experiencing severe anxiety, fearing more.

The Script	
1. Job	Job 3:6–7; 9–10; 12–14; 16–17; 19; 21; 23–24; 26–31; 40:3–5; 42:1–6
2. Eliphaz	Job 4–5; 15; 22
3. Bildad	Job 8; 8; 25
4. Zophar	Job 11; 20
5. Elihu	Job 32–37
6. God	Job 38:1–40:2; 40:6–41:34

Eliphaz's Speeches
1. Eliphaz's first speech kindly protests and urges humility and repentance (4:1–5:27).
2. Eliphaz's second speech accuses Job of presumption and disregarding the wisdom of the ancients (15:1–35).
3. Eliphaz's third speech denounces Job's criticism of God's justice (22:1–30).

2. Eliphaz's first speech (4:1–5:27)

4:1–5:27 Eliphaz. Eliphaz's first speech. See chapters 15; 22 for Eliphaz's other speeches. He spoke profoundly and gently, but knew nothing of the scene in heaven that had produced the suffering of Job.

4:2–6 Job's friend finally spoke after seven days of silence and began kindly by acknowledging that Job was recognized for being a wise man. Unfortunately, with the opening of their mouths for the first speech and those that followed, all the wisdom of their silence departed.

4:7 who ever perished being innocent? Eliphaz, recognizing Job's "reverence" and "integrity" (v. 6), was likely encouraging Job at the outset by saying he wouldn't die because he was innocent of any deadly iniquity, but must be guilty of some serious sin because he was reaping such anger from God. This was a moral universe and moral order was at work, he thought. He had oversimplified God's pattern of retribution. This simple axiom, "the righteous will prosper and the wicked will suffer," does not always hold up in human experience during one's life on earth. It is true that plowing and sowing iniquity reaps judgment, so Eliphaz was partially right (cf. Gal. 6:7–9; 1 Pet. 3:12). But not everything we reap in life is the result of something we have sown (*see notes on 2 Cor. 12:7–10*). Eliphaz was replacing theology with simplistic logic. To say that wherever there is suffering, it is the result of sowing sin is wrong (cf. Ex. 4:11; John 9:1–3).

4:10, 11 Wanting to demonstrate that wicked people experience calamities in spite of their strength and resources, Eliphaz illustrated his point by the destruction that comes on lions in spite of their prowess. Five Hebrew words were used here for *lion,* emphasizing the various characters of wicked people, all of whom can be broken and perish.

4:12–16 *a word was secretly brought to me.* Eliphaz spoke of a mysterious messenger in a vision, eerie fantasy, or a dream. He claimed to have had divine revelation to bolster his viewpoint.

4:17 Here is the conclusion of Eliphaz's revelation—that Job suffered because he was not holy enough, not righteous enough.

4:17–21 This is the content of Eliphaz's message which is, in effect, that God judges sin and sinners among men (described in v. 19 as "houses of clay") as He did among angels (v. 18; cf. Rev. 12:3, 4).

5:1 *holy ones.* Angelic beings (cf. 4:18) are in view. Job was told that not even the angels could help him. He must recognize his mortality and sin, if he would be healed.

5:2–6 Job was told not to be a fool or simpleton, but to recognize that sin is judged, wrath kills, envy slays, foolishness is cursed (vv. 2–5); this wasn't merely a physical matter (v. 6), but it came from man's sin. Sin is inevitable in man; so is trouble (v. 7).

5:7 *sparks.* Lit. "the sons of Resheph," an expression which describes all sorts of fire-like movement (cf. Deut. 32:24; Ps. 78:48; Song 8:6).

5:8 Job's solution was to go to God and repent, his friend thought.

5:9–16 The whole of Eliphaz's argument is based on the moral perfection of God, so he extolled God's greatness and goodness.

However, it lacks the needed perspective of Scripture's special revelation.

5:13 Paul used this line from Eliphaz in 1 Corinthians 3:19 to prove the foolishness of man's wisdom before God.

5:17 *happy is the man whom God corrects.* Eliphaz put a positive spin on his advice by telling Job that enviable or desirable is the situation of the person whom God cares enough about to chasten. "If only Job admitted his sin, he could be happy again" was his advice.

5:18–27 The language of this section, promising blessing for penitence, was strongly reminiscent of Leviticus 26, which elaborated on the blessing of a faithful covenant relationship with God. If Job confessed, he would have prosperity, security, a family, and a rich life.

5:23 *covenant . . . peace.* Even the created order will be in harmony with the person whose relationship with God is corrected through God's disciplinary process.

3. Job's reply to Eliphaz (6:1–7:21)

6:1–7:21 Job's response to Eliphaz was recorded. On top of his physical misery and his tempting wife, he had to respond to ignorance and insensitivity from his friend, by expressing his frustration.

6:2, 3 The heaviness of Job's burden (physical, mentally, emotionally, and spiritually) caused the rashness of his words.

6:4 *the arrows of the Almighty . . . terrors of God.* Here are figures of speech picturing the trials as coming from God, indicating that Job believed these were God's judgments.

6:5–7 These are all illustrations of the fact that Job complained because he believed that he had reason. Even animals expect palatable food.

6:8, 9 *my request.* Job's request was that God would finish whatever process He began. Death was desirable for no other reason than it would bring relief from the inevitable course of events (see ch. 3).

Job's Speeches

1. Job's first speech expresses despair (3:1–26).
2. Job's reply to Eliphaz expresses anguish and questions the trials, asking for sympathy in his pain (6:1–7:21).
3. Job's response to Bildad admits he is not perfect, but may protest what seems unfair (9:1–10:22).
4. Job's response to Zophar tells his friends they are wrong and only God knows and will, hopefully, speak to him (12:1–14:22).
5. Job's response to Eliphaz appeals to God against his unjust accusers (16:1–17:16).
6. Job's response to Bildad cries out to God for pity (19:1–29).
7. Job's response to Zophar says he is out of touch with reality (21:1–34).
8. Job's response to Eliphaz is that God knows he is without guilt and, yet, in His providence and refining purpose He permits temporary success for the wicked (23:1–24:25).
9. Job's response to Bildad is that God is indeed perfectly wise and absolutely sovereign, but not simplistic as they thought (26:1–14).
10. Job's first monologue affirms his righteousness and that man can't discover God's wisdom (27:1–28:28).
11. Job's second monologue remembers his past, describes his present, defends his innocence, and asks for God to defend him (29:1–31:40).
12. Job's answer to God (40:3–5).
13. Job passes judgment upon himself (42:1–6).

6:9 cut me off. This is a metaphor from a weaver, who cuts off the excess thread on the loom (cf. Is. 38:12).

6:10 the words of the Holy One. Job had not been avoiding the revelation of God that he had received. The commands of the Holy One were precious to him and he had lived by them. This was confusing to him, as he could not find any sinful source for his suffering. He would rejoice in his pain if he knew it would soon lead to death, but he could not see any hope for death or deliverance in himself (vv. 11–13).

6:14 kindness . . . even though. Job rebuked his friends with sage words. Even if a man has forsaken God (which he had not), should not his friends still show kindness to him? How can Eliphaz be so unkind as to continually indict him?

6:15–23 Job described his friends as being about as useful with their counsel as a dry river bed in summer. "You are no help," he said in effect (v. 21), "although all I asked for was a little sympathy, not some great gift or deliverance" (vv. 22, 23).

6:19 Tema . . . Sheba. Tema in the north, named for the son of Ishmael (Gen. 25:15; Is. 21:14), and Sheba in the south (Jer. 6:20) were part of the Arabian desert, where water was precious.

6:24–30 Teach me . . . Cause me to understand wherein I have erred. Job was not admitting to having sinned. Rather, he challenged his accusers, "If I've sinned, show me where!" The sufferer indicted his friends for their insensitivity; and while not claiming sinlessness, he was convinced there was no sin in his life that led directly to such suffering.

7:1–21 After having directed his words at his friends in chapter 6, Job then directed them at God. Throughout this section, he used words and arguments that sounded much like Solomon in Ecclesiastes, i.e., "futile labor," "vanity," "trouble," and "breath."

7:1–10 *a time of hard service.* Job felt like a slave under the tyranny of his master, longing for relief and reward (vv. 1, 2); he was sleepless (vv. 3, 4); he was loathsome because of worms and scabs, dried filth, and running sores (v. 5); he was like a weaver's shuttle, tossed back and forth (v. 6); and he was like a breath or cloud that comes and goes on its way to death (vv. 7–10). In this discourse, Job attempted to reconcile in his own mind what God was doing.

7:11 *Therefore.* On the basis of all he had said in verses 1–10, Job felt he had a right to express his complaint.

7:12 *sea, or a sea serpent.* The sea and the whale are two threatening forces that must be watched and curbed because of their destructive force. Job was not like that.

7:13, 14 Even when Job slept, he had terrifying dreams so that he longed for death (vv. 15, 16).

7:17, 18 Why is he so important, Job wonders, that God would spend all this attention on him? Why did God cause all this misery to a person so insignificant as he?

7:19 *till I swallow my saliva?* This strange statement was an Arabic proverb, indicating a brief moment. Job was asking for a moment "to catch his breath," or in the case of the proverb, "to swallow his saliva."

7:21 *not pardon my transgression.* Job conceded the argument of Eliphaz that he must have sinned, not because he was convinced, but because he seemed to find no other explanation (cf. 6:24).

4. Bildad's first speech (8:1–22)

8:1–22 The second, friendly accuser, Bildad, now offered his wisdom to Job. Bildad, also absolutely certain that Job had sinned and should repent, was ruthless in the charges he raised against God's servant. See Job 18; 25 for Bildad's other speeches.

8:2–7 Bildad accused Job of defending his innocence with a lot of hot air and reasoned that Job's circumstances were God's judgment on his sins and those of his family. Again, this is logical, based on the principle that God punishes sin, but it failed to account for the mystery of the heavenly debate between God and Satan (see chs. 1; 2). He was sure something was wrong in Job's relationship with God, thus his call for repentance, with the confidence that when Job repented he would be blessed (vv. 6, 7).

8:3 *does the Almighty pervert justice?* Bildad took Job's claims for innocence and applied them to his simplistic notion of retribution. He concluded that Job was accusing God of injustice when God must be meting out justice. Job tried to avoid outright accusations of this sort, but the evidence led Bildad to this conclusion because he had no knowledge of the heavenly facts.

8:7 In fact, this was Job's outcome (cf. 42:10–17), not because Job repented of some specific sin, but because he humbled himself before the sovereign, inscrutable will of God.

8:8–10 Here, Bildad appealed to past authorities, i.e., godly ancestors who taught the same principle—that where there is suffering, there must be sin. So he actually had history as a witness to his misjudgment.

8:11–19 Bildad further supported his simple logic of cause and effect by illustrations from nature. Again, he accused Job of sin, but surely he had forgotten God as well (v. 13).

Bildad's Speeches
1. Bildad's first speech accuses Job of impugning God (8:1–22).
2. Bildad's second speech tells Job he is suffering just what he deserves (18:1–21).
3. Bildad's third speech scoffs at Job's direct appeal to God (25:1–6).

8:20 *God will not cast away the blameless.* This comment contains a veiled offer of hope. Job could laugh again, but he must take steps to become blameless. But Bildad, like Job, was unaware of the dialogue between the sovereign Judge and Satan the accuser in the opening chapters of the book and unaware that God had already pronounced Job "blameless" twice to heavenly beings (1:8; 2:3), as had the writer (1:1). Cf. Psalms 1:6; 126:2; 132:18.

5. Job's response to Bildad (9:1–10:22)

9:1–10:22 Job, in a mood of deep despair, responded to Bildad's accusations with arguments surrounding God's nature, also raised by Bildad, and started to rationalize something about which he would later admit he knew dangerously little. Job concluded that God is holy, wise, and strong (vv. 4–10); but he wondered if He is fair (v. 22) and why He wouldn't make Himself known to him. Before the mighty God, Job felt only despair. If God is not fair, all is hopeless, he thought.

9:3 *contend with Him.* Job referred to disputing one's innocence or guilt before God as a useless endeavor. Psalm 130:3 illustrates the point, "If You . . . should mark iniquities (keep records of sin), . . . who could stand (innocently in judgment)?"

9:6 *pillars tremble.* In the figurative language of the day, this phrase described the supporting power that secured the position of the earth in the universe.

9:9 *Bear, Orion . . . Pleiades.* Three stellar constellations (cf. Job 38:31, 32). **the chambers of the south.** These were other constellations in the southern hemisphere, unseen by those who could see and name the three in the northern skies.

9:13 *the proud.* Lit. "Rahab." This is symbolic of the ancient mythological sea monster (cf. 3:8; 7:12). God smiting the proud was a poetic way of saying that if the mythi-

cal monster of the sea (a metaphor for powerful, evil, chaotic forces) could not stand before God's anger, how could Job hope to do so? In a battle in God's court, he would lose. God is too strong (vv. 14–19).

9:15, 20 *though I were righteous.* Job means not sinless, but having spiritual integrity, i.e., a pure heart to love, serve, and obey God. He was affirming again that his suffering was not due to sins he was not willing to confess. Even at that, God found something to condemn him for, he felt, making it hopeless to contend with God.

9:24 *covers the faces of its judges.* Job here indicted God for the inequities of His world. He accused God of treating all the same way, unfairly (vv. 21–23), and of even covering the eyes of earthly judges so they would not see injustice. These are the charges that bring about God's rebuke of Job (chs. 38–41) and for which he eventually repented (42:1–6).

9:25, 26 Couriers running with messages, ships cutting swiftly, and eagles swooping rapidly convey the blur of painful, meaningless days of despair.

9:27, 28 If Job promised to change to a happy mood, he would break that promise and God would add that to His list of accusations.

9:29, 30 "God seems to have found me guilty," Job concluded, "so why struggle? Even if I make every effort to clean every aspect of my life, You will still punish me." This reflected his deep despair and hopelessness.

9:32 *that we should go to court together.* Job acknowledged that, as a mere man, he had no right to call on God to declare his innocence or to contend with God over his innocence. Job was not arguing that he was sinless, but he didn't believe he had sinned to the extent that he deserved his severe suffering. Job held on to the same simplistic system of retribution as that of his accusers,

Key Word

Blameless: 1:1, 8; 2:3; 8:20; 9:20–22—means "to be complete." This word signifies a person's integrity: a wholeness and wholesomeness. The word is used as a term of endearment for the Shulamite bride in the Song of Solomon (see "perfect" in 5:2; 6:9). In the Old Testament, blamelessness is frequently associated with the upright (1:1, 8; 2:3; Ps. 37:37; Prov. 29:10) in contrast to the wicked (9:22; Ps. 64:2–4). Job's claim to be blameless agrees with God's assessment of him, but it is not a claim to absolute perfection (1:8; 9:21; 14:16, 17). The psalmist writes that the future of the blameless person is peace, as was the case with Job (42:10–12; Ps. 37:37).

which held that suffering was always caused by sin. Although he knew he was not sinless, Job could not identify any unconfessed or unrepented sins. "Where is mercy?" he wondered.

9:33–35 *any mediator between us.* A court official who sees both sides clearly, as well as the source of disagreement, so as to bring resolution was not found. Where was an advocate, an arbitrator, an umpire, or a referee? Was there no one to remove God's rod and call for justice?

10:2 *condemn me.* Not the condemnation of Job's soul, but Job's physical suffering as a punishment. He held nothing back in his misery (v. 1), but asked God to show him why all this had happened.

10:3 *the work of Your hands.* This is a biblical expression identifying what someone produces, in this case, man as created by God (cf. 14:15; Ps. 102:25; Heb. 1:10).

10:4–7 *see as man sees?* Because he believed he was innocent, Job facetiously, somewhat sarcastically, asked if God was as limited in His ability to discern Job's spiritual condition as were Job's friends. He concluded by affirming that God did know he was innocent and that there was no higher court of appeal (v. 7).

10:8–12 Again, Job returned to the question, "Why was I born?" The answer that God had created him is given in magnificent language, indicating that life begins at conception.

10:13–16 Job wondered if God had planned in His divine purpose not to be merciful to him.

10:17 *renew Your witnesses.* Job said God seemed to be sending people to accuse him. With each witness came another wave of condemnation and increased suffering.

10:18 *brought me out of the womb?* Job returned to the question of why God allowed him to be born. This time he was not just lamenting the day of his birth, but he was asking God for the reason He allowed it to occur.

10:20–22 "Since I was destined to these ills from my birth, at least give me a little breathing room during the brief days left to me, before I die," he said in effect. Death was gloomily described as "darkness."

6. Zophar's first speech (11:1–20)

11:1–20 Zophar the Naamathite now stepped in to interrogate Job. He was quite close to his friends and chose to assault Job with the same law of retaliation. Job must repent, he said, not understanding the heavenly reality. He was indignant at Job's protests of innocence. See Job 20 for Zophar's other speech.

11:2, 3 *a man full of talk be vindicated?* The allegations against Job moved to a new level. Not only was Job guilty and unrepentant; he was also an empty talker. In fact, Job's long-winded defense of his innocence and God's apparent injustice was sin worthy of rebuke, in Zophar's mind.

Zophar's Speeches

1. Zophar's first speech tells Job to get right with God (11:1–20).
2. Zophar's second speech accuses Job of rejecting God by questioning His justice (20:1–29).

11:4 *clean in your eyes.* Job never claimed sinlessness; in fact, he acknowledged that he had sinned (Job 7:21; 13:26). But he still maintained his innocence of any great transgression or attitude of unrepentance, affirming his sincerity and integrity as a man of faith and obedience to God. This claim infuriated Zophar, and he wished God Himself would confirm the accusations of Job's friends (v. 5).

11:6 *secrets of wisdom!* Job would have been much wiser if he had only known the unknowable secrets of God; in this case, the scene in heaven between God and Satan would have clarified everything. But Job couldn't know the secret wisdom of God (vv. 7–9). Zophar should have applied his point to himself. If God's wisdom was so deep, high, long, and broad, how was it that he could understand it and have all the answers? Like his friends, Zophar thought he understood God and reverted to the same law of retaliation, the sowing and reaping principle, to again indict Job. He implied that Job was wicked (vv. 10, 11) and thought he was wise, though actually he was out of control as if he were a "wild donkey man"! (v. 12).

11:13, 14 Zophar set out four steps of Job's repentance: (1) devote your heart to God; (2) stretch your hands to Him in prayer for forgiveness; (3) put your sin far away; and (4) don't allow any sin in your tent. If Job did these things, he would be blessed (vv. 15–19). If Job didn't repent, he would die (v. 20). Zophar was right that the life of faith in God is based on real confession of sins and obedience. He was right that God blesses His people with hope, security, and peace. But, like his friends, he was wrong in not understanding that God allows unpredictable and seemingly unfair suffering for reasons not known on earth. He was wrong in presuming that the answer for Job was repentance.

11:13–20 Zophar started out this section speaking directly to Job, "If you would . . ." and concluded speaking proverbially, "But the eyes of the wicked . . ." In so doing Zophar avoided directly calling Job wicked, but succeeded with even greater force by being indirect. In the end, he told Job that his sin would bring about his death.

7. Job's response to Zophar (12:1–14:22)

12:1–14:22 Job responded in his own defense with strong words, completing the first cycle of speeches.

12:2–4 *you are the people, and wisdom will die with you!* Job began with cutting sarcasm directed at his know-it-all friends (v. 2); and then reminded them that he understood the principles about which they had spoken (v. 3), but concluded they were irrelevant to his situation. On top of that, he despaired at the pain of becoming a derision to his friends, though he was innocent (v. 4).

12:4 *The just and blameless.* If this sounds like presumption, one only needs to recall that this was God's pronouncement on Job (1:8; 2:3).

12:5 *A lamp.* As a torch is to a wanderer, so Job was to his friends. When all was at ease with them, they didn't need him; they even mocked him.

12:6 *God provides.* Job refuted the simplistic idea that the righteous always prosper and the wicked always suffer, by reminding them that God allows thieves and sinners to be prosperous and secure. So why not believe He may also allow the righteous to suffer?

12:7–10 All these elements (animals, birds, plants, and fish) of creation are called as illustrations that the violent prosper and live securely (v. 6). God made it so the more vicious survive.

12:12 *Wisdom is with aged men.* The interrogative nature of the preceding verse may carry over to make this a question also. "Shouldn't aged men be wise?" If this is true, then verse 12 delivers stinging sarcasm against Job's aged friends who gave unwise advice (cf. 15:10), and heard and spoke only what suited them (v. 11).

12:13–13:3 This section gives vivid definition to the wisdom, power, and sovereignty of God (v. 13). Job, despite his questions about his suffering, affirms that God's power is visible in nature, human society, religious matters, and national and international affairs. Job, however, expressed this in terms of fatalistic despair. Job knew all this and it didn't help (13:1, 2), so he did not want to argue with them anymore. He wanted to take his case before God (v. 3).

13:4–19 Job addressed his ineffective counselors.

13:4, 5 Job couldn't hold back from a blistering denunciation of his useless counselors, telling them that their silence would be true wisdom (cf. v. 13).

13:7 *wickedly for God . . . deceitfully for Him?* Job accused his friends of using lies and fallacies to vindicate God, when they asserted that Job was a sinner because he was a sufferer.

13:8 *Will you contend for God?* "Are you wise enough to argue in God's defense?" he asked. To think that is very brash and really mocks God by misrepresenting Him (v. 9) and should lead to fear of chastening (vv. 10, 11).

13:12 *ashes . . . clay.* Ineffective and worthless.

13:14 This is a proverb meaning "Why should I anxiously desire to save my life?" Like an animal who holds its prey in its mouth to preserve it or a man who holds in his hand what he wants to secure, Job could try to preserve his life, but that was not his motive.

13:15 *Though He slay me, yet will I trust Him.* Job assured his accusers that his convictions were not self-serving, because he was ready to die trusting God. But still, he would defend his innocence before God, and was confident that he was truly saved and not a hypocrite (v. 16).

13:17–19 *declaration . . . case . . . vindicated . . . contend.* The language of a courtroom came out strongly. He could not just be silent and die (v. 19). He finished strongly before turning to God in prayer.

13:20–14:22 Job turned to reason with God (v. 3) and pleaded his case.

13:20–22 Job asked God to end his pain and stop frightening him with such terrors (cf. v. 24), then to speak to him. He was concerned with his misery but, even more, with his relation to the God he loved and worshiped.

13:23 *How many are my iniquities and sins?* Job wanted to know this so he could determine if his measure of suffering matched the severity of his sin, and he could then repent for sins about which he was unaware.

13:26 *write bitter things against me.* This a judicial phrase referencing the writing down of a sentence against a criminal, used figuratively for the extreme suffering as if it were a divine sentence as just punishment for extreme sin. Job felt God might be punishing him for sins committed years earlier in his youth.

13:27 *watch closely all my paths.* In another context, these words would speak of protection; but here, Job questioned whether or not God had not held him on too tight a leash. The comment amounts to saying that God is being overly rigorous toward Job's sin, as compared to others.

13:28 This general comment on the plight of man should not be separated from 14:1ff., which it introduces.

14:1–12 Job embraced the fact of God's control over the issues of this life, but challenged their meaning. Life is short (vv. 1, 2), all are sinners (v. 4), and days are limited (v. 5), then comes death (vv. 7–12). In light of this, Job asked God for a little grace instead of such intense judgment (v. 3), and a little rest from all the pain (v. 6), and suggested that a tree has more hope than he did (v. 7).

14:13–17 Job asked to die and remain in the grave until God's anger was over, then be raised to life again when God called him

Job's Living Death

1. Painful boils from head to toe (2:7,13; 30:17)
2. Severe itching/irritation (2:7,8)
3. Great grief (2:13)
4. Lost appetite (3:24; 6:6,7)
5. Agonizing discomfort (3:24)
6. Insomnia (7:4)
7. Worm and dust infested flesh (7:5)
8. Continual oozing of boils (7:5)
9. Hallucinations (7:14)
10. Decaying skin (13:28)
11. Shriveled up (16:8, 17:7; 19:20)
12. Severe halitosis (19:17)
13. Teeth fell out (19:20)
14. Relentless pain (30:17)
15. Skin turned black (30:30)
16. Raging fever (30:30)
17. Dramatic weight loss (33:21)

The MacArthur Study Bible, by John MacArthur (Nashville: Word Publishing, 1997) 704. © 1993 by Thomas Nelson, Inc.

back (vv. 13–15). If he were dead, God wouldn't be watching every step, counting every sin (v. 16); it would all be hidden (v. 17). Here was the hope of resurrection for those who trusted God. Job had hope that if he died, then he would live again (v. 14).

14:18–22 Job returned to his complaint before God, and reverted to a hopeless mood, speaking about death as inevitable (vv. 18–20) and causing separation (v. 21). He was painfully sad to think of it (v. 22).

B. The Second Cycle (15:1–21:34)

15:1–21:34 The second cycle of speeches given by Job and his three friends. Job's resistance to their viewpoint and his appeals energized them to greater intensity in their confrontation.

1. Eliphaz's second speech (15:1–35)

15:1–35 Eliphaz returns for his second session (See Job 4; 5).

15:1–6 He began accusing Job of sinning by attacking God with his complaints. He felt Job was guilty of empty words and had not exhibited godly fear and righteous prayer (v. 4), but rather was sinning in his prayer (vv. 5, 6).

15:7–13 Eliphaz condemned Job for rejecting the conventional wisdom, as if he had more insight than other people (vv. 7–9), and could reject the wisdom of the aged (v. 10) and the kindness of God (v. 11).

15:14–16 A strong statement, with regard to the sinfulness of man (cf. Rom. 3:23), that attacked Job's claim to righteousness. Verse 15 refers to holy angels who fell and brought impurity into the heavens (cf. Rev. 12:1–4). The truth is accurate, that all men are sinners—but irrelevant in Job's case, because his suffering was not due to any sin.

15:17–35 Eliphaz once again returned to the same perspective and indicted Job for sin because Job was suffering. To support his relentless point, he launched into a lengthy monologue about the wicked and their outcomes in life, including many parallels to the sufferings of Job. He had pain, and didn't know when his life would end (v. 20). He suffered from fear, every sound alarmed him, and he thought his destroyer was near (vv. 21, 22). He worried about having food (v. 23). His suffering made him question God (vv. 24–26). Once well-nourished, housed, and rich (vv. 27–29), he would lose it all (vv. 30–33). Eliphaz concluded by calling Job a hypocrite (vv. 34, 35), saying that this was the reason things were going so badly.

2. Job's response to Eliphaz (16:1–17:16)

16:1–17:16 Job responded with his second rebuttal.

16:2–5 *Miserable comforters are you all!* Job's friends had come to comfort him. In spite of seven blissful days of silence at the outset, their mission had failed miserably, and their comfort had turned into more torment for Job. What started out as Eliphaz's sincere efforts to help Job understand his dilemma had turned into rancor and sarcasm. In the end, their haranguing had heightened the frustrations of all parties involved. If the matter were reversed and Job was comforter to his friends, he would never treat them as they treated him. He would strengthen and comfort them.

16:6–9, 12–14 These poignant thoughts from Job lamented his suffering as severe judgment from God, who had worn him out, withered his strength, and chewed him up by severe scrutiny ("sharpens His gaze"). Job refers to God as "my Adversary," who had shattered, shaken, shot at, and sliced him (vv. 12–14).

16:15–20 He had no one to turn to in his sorrow, except God (v. 19), who was silent and had not vindicated him.

16:21 *plead for a man with God.* The pleading would be for a verdict of innocent on behalf of a friend or neighbor in a court setting before the judge/king. God anticipated the need of an advocate, and He has provided One in the person of the Lord Jesus Christ (cf. 1 Tim. 2:5; 1 John 2:1, 2).

17:2 *mockers.* The would-be counselors had become actual enemies and the provocation for Job's tears (cf. 16:20).

17:3 *pledge.* He called on God to promise (by a symbolic handshake) that his case would be heard in the heavenly court.

17:4 *not exalt them.* The blindness of Job's friends toward his innocence came from God, so Job asked that God would not let them succeed in their efforts against him.

17:5 *speaks flattery.* This Hebrew term came to mean "a prey," so that Job was referring to someone who delivers up a friend as prey to some enemy.

17:6 *a byword.* This refers to shame, reproach, and a reputation that is extremely bad (cf. Deut. 28:37; Ps. 69:11). **spit.** The most disdainful act a person could commit to heap scorn and shame on someone as a wicked and unworthy person. Job's friends were aiding him in getting such a reputation (vv. 7, 8).

17:9 *Yet the righteous will hold to his way.* Job, and other righteous people who find themselves in a similar situation, must remain righteous. If they do, Job knew the suffering would produce strength (cf. 2 Cor. 12:7–10).

17:10 Job was not unteachable. He invited his friends to speak again if they had something wise to say, for a change, but not to talk about his restoration because he was done (vv. 11–16).

17:15 *Where then is my hope?* Job's hope was in God alone.

17:16 *gates of Sheol?* A reference to death, also used by Jesus in Matthew 16:18.

3. Bildad's second speech (18:1–21)

18:1–21 Bildad, like his predecessor, ruthlessly attacked Job in his second speech (cf. ch. 8) by telling Job to stop complaining and to become sensible (v. 2). Next, he turned to scorn (vv. 3, 4). Then, he turned to another long tale of the bad outcomes the wicked experience (vv. 5–21).

18:13 The firstborn of death. A poetical expression meaning the most deadly disease death ever produced.

18:14 the king of terrors. This is death, with all its terrors to the ungodly, personified.

18:21 who does not know God. This describes *know* in a redemptive sense and is here applied to an unbeliever.

4. Job's response to Bildad (19:1–29)

19:1–29 Job's response to Bildad's second speech was desperate.

19:1–5 He began with the anguished cry that his friends have become recalcitrant and relentless for mentors (vv. 2, 3), and they have had no effect on his dealing with the sin they imagine is present (v. 4).

19:5–7 Job confessed that if God sent him friends like Bildad, who needs enemies? He feared there was no justice.

19:8–21 Job rehearsed his suffering. God had closed him in, stripped him, broken him, and turned against him (vv. 8–12). His family and friends had failed him (vv. 15–19), so that he was to be pitied because God had caused this to occur (vv. 21, 22).

19:12 build up their road against me. In the ancient world, conquering armies often had their own road crews level out the rough places so their military forces could attack.

19:20 skin of my teeth. This was the origin of a common slang phrase, referring to skin that is thin and fragile. The idea is that he had escaped death by a very slim margin. The loss of all his family, as well as the abuse

of his friends, was added to the terror of God-forsakeness which had gripped him.

19:23–29 At the point of Job's greatest despair, his faith appeared at its highest as he confidently affirmed that God was his Redeemer. He wanted that confidence in the record for all to know (vv. 23, 24). Job wished that the activities of his life were put into words and "inscribed in granite," so all would know that he had not sinned to the magnitude of his suffering. God granted his prayer. God was his Redeemer (cf. Ex. 6:6, Pss. 19:14; 72:14; Is. 43:14; 47:4; 49:26; Jer. 50:34), who would vindicate him in that last day of judgment on the earth when justice was finally done (cf. Jer. 12:1–3; John 5:25, 29; Rev. 20:11–15).

19:26, 27 Job had no hope left for this life, but was confident that "after" he was dead, his Redeemer would vindicate him in the glory of a physical ("in my flesh") resurrection in which he would enjoy perfect fellowship with the Redeemer. That Jesus Christ is the Redeemer of whom Job spoke is the clear message of the gospel. See Luke 2:38; Romans 3:24; Galatians 3:13; Ephesians 1:7; Hebrews 9:12.

19:28, 29 Job warned his friends that their misjudgment of him and verbal violence against him could bring punishment on them.

5. Zophar's second speech (20:1–29)

20:1–29 Zophar spoiled it all, again, for Job with his second and last speech (cf. 11:1–20), in which he admonished Job to reconsider the fate of the wicked.

20:5, 6 wicked . . . hypocrite . . . haughtiness. The application of Zophar's words about this wicked, hypocritical, proud person were aimed at Job. He would, like others so wicked, suffer the consequences of his sins (vv. 7–29).

20:11 The wicked die young.

20:12–22 Evil in a life takes away all the enjoyment, implying that Job had no joy because of sin, such as that in verse 19.

20:23–29 Zophar concluded that more than just losing the enjoyment of life by sin, the wicked fall under the fury of God dispensed for such wickedness.

6. Job's response to Zophar (21:1–34)

21:1–34 Job's reply to Zophar's last speech, ending the second cycle of speeches, refuted the simplistic set of laws by which the mockers lived. He showed that the wicked prosper and, since it is clear that they do (they had argued that *only* the wicked suffer), then by inference, perhaps the righteous suffer. This presented serious problems for their supposed open-and-shut case against Job.

21:1–16 Job called for his friends to be quiet and to listen to some amazing and terrifying truth (vv. 1–6), namely, that the wicked do prosper (vv. 7–13) though they deny God (vv. 14, 15), and they prosper not by their doing, but God's (v. 16).

21:17–22 Playing off Bildad's sentiment (see 18:5, 6, 18, 19), this whole section repeats the assertions of Job's friends about the judgment of sinners. To refute that perspective, Job suggested that his friends were guilty of telling God how He must deal with people (v. 22).

21:23–26 Some of the wicked live and die in prosperity, but others don't, canceling the absolutist nature of his counselors' argument.

21:27, 28 Again, Job referred to the statements of his friends, Zophar in this case (see 20:7), who were trying to prove their "sin-equals-suffering" idea.

21:29–33 Job knew they would not listen to him, so he suggested they ask travelers, any of whom would tell them that wicked people prosper sometimes in this life, but there will be a day of doom for them when they die.

21:34 The boastful words of the counselors were contradicted by facts.

C. The Third Cycle (22:1–26:14)

22:1–26:14 The third cycle of speeches is given by Job and his friends, with Zophar abstaining.

1. Eliphaz's third speech (22:1–30)

22:1–30 In his last speech, Eliphaz got nasty with Job, as his frustration rose.

22:2–4, 12–14 This counselor repeated the emphasis on the almighty nature of God, saying that God was so lofty and transcendent that He had no direct concern at all with Job. God didn't care personally about his complaints and claims to righteousness. God was not involved in the trivia of his life.

22:5–11 This miserable comforter accused Job of wickedness that was great, naming various sins against humanity as the reasons for Job's trouble (vv. 10, 11).

22:15–19 Again, the fate of the wicked was expressed in the simplistic idea that all suffering comes from sin. Contrary to what Job had argued, the wicked characteristically die prematurely, and Job's claim that God prospered them (v. 18a) was counsel that Eliphaz rejected (vv. 18b–20).

22:21–30 Eliphaz painted a picture of the life of blessing in store for Job if only he would return to God and repent of his sin (v. 23), emphasizing again that he did not believe Job was innocent (v. 30). "Stop all the speeches and complaints, repent, and everything will be fine," he thought.

22:24 *Ophir.* A land with high-quality gold, whose location is uncertain (cf. 28:16; Gen. 10:29).

2. Job's response to Eliphaz (23:1–24:25)

23:1–24:25 Job's reply to Eliphaz's third speech was not a rebuttal, but it expressed Job's longing for fellowship with God, so he could experience God's love and goodness and hear from Him the meaning of all his suffering.

23:3 *His seat.* A place of judgment.

23:4 *my case.* Job's claim to innocence.

23:6, 7 *contend.* Job knew God was not going to enter a contest with him to determine, as in a court case, who was right. But he wanted God to at least listen to him, so confident was he that he could make his case and be delivered by his just Judge (cf. 1:8; 2:3).

23:8–12 Even though Job could not sense God's presence, he believed He was present and affirmed his commitment to God's purpose in this test (v. 10) and his continued obedience to God's Word, which were the most important issues in his life (vv. 11, 12).

23:14 *He performs what is appointed for me.* Job's resignation to God's sovereignty faltered at times in practice, but he returned to it repeatedly. This is the great lesson of the book: Trust sovereign God when you cannot understand why things go badly in life.

24:1–25 Job had made the point that the unrighteous prosper in spite of their sin (ch. 21). Extending that theme, he listed the kinds of severe sins which go on in the world and God doesn't seem to do anything to stop them (vv. 2–17), so that the wicked, in general, prosper and live long lives, seemingly unabated. These sins—oppressing the orphans, widows, and poor as well as committing murder, thievery, and adultery—are the very ones forbidden in other parts of the OT.

24:1 *times are not hidden.* Job believed that God knew the appointed times for all activities under the sun (Eccl. 3:1–8), but he bemoaned the fact that God did not inform man about them.

24:2 *remove landmarks.* This ancient practice is addressed in Deuteronomy 19:14; Proverbs 22:28; 23:10: "Do not move the ancient landmark." Corrupt landowners often did this to increase their holdings, particularly where the land was owned by bereaved widows. Taking advantage of widows will be treated by the ultimate court in heaven.

24:7 *spend the night.* It was common practice to take an outer garment as a pledge for money owed. But OT law forbade keeping the garment at night since its owner could get cold and sick (cf. 24:10). *See note on Deuteronomy 24:10–13.*

24:12 *Yet God does not charge them with wrong.* This is a stinging accusation from Job. Human courts prosecuted offenders for most of these social crimes. Job, in essence, was saying, "If human courts punish the wicked, then why doesn't God?"

24:18–21 Again, Job referred to the opinions of his counselors, saying that if their view were correct, all the wicked should be experiencing punishment. But it is obvious they were not.

24:22–25 Job's view was that their punishment would come eventually ("exalted for a little while"). Retribution needed the timing of God's wisdom, when He determined wrongs would be made right. Job was confident that his point could not be refuted.

3. Bildad's third speech (25:1–6)

25:1–6 Bildad made his third speech (the last speech for the three friends), and restated the same theory—that God was majestic and exalted (vv. 2, 3) and man was sinful, especially Job (vv. 4–6).

4. Job's response to Bildad (26:1–14)

26:1–4 Job responded to Bildad's lack of concern for him, showing that all his friend's theological and rational words missed the point of Job's need altogether and had been no help.

26:5–14 As before, in chapters 9 and 12, Job showed that he was not inferior to his friends in describing God's greatness. He understood that as well as they did. He described it as manifested in the realm of the dead called Sheol and Destruction (vv. 5, 6), the earth and sky (v. 7), the waters above (vv. 8–10) and below (v. 12), and the stars (v. 13).

26:7 *hangs the earth on nothing.* A statement that is accurate, given in ancient time, before scientific verification. This indicates the divine authorship of Scripture.

26:10 *a circular horizon.* This describes the earth as a circular globe, another scientifically accurate statement at a time when many people thought the world was flat.

26:11 *pillars of heaven.* A figure of speech for the mountains that seem to hold up the sky (cf. Ps. 104:32).

26:12 *breaks up the storm.* Lit. "Rahab." Cf. 7:12; 9:13; 26:13. This term seems to be widely used to describe various things that wreak havoc.

26:13 *His Spirit.* Cf. 33:4. The Holy Spirit worked mightily in creation (cf. Gen. 1:2). *the fleeing serpent.* This is figurative language for the idea that God brought all constellations into subjection under His authority (cf. 26:12). *Serpent* could be translated "crooked" and refer to any wayward stars or planets being brought under control by God's mighty power.

26:14 *Indeed these are the mere edges of His ways.* Job employed poetic language to remind his counselors that all that could be said and understood by man was only a glimpse of God's powerful hand.

D. The Final Defense of Job (27:1–31:40)

1. Job's first monologue (27:1–28:28)

27:1–12 Job turned from responding to Bildad (26:1–14) to defending his righteousness.

27:2 *who has taken away my justice.* God did not speak to declare Job innocent. Cf. the treatment of Christ in Isaiah 53:8 and Acts 8:33.

27:3–6 Job affirmed his true and steadfast devotion to righteous living, no matter what happened. He refused to live with a guilty conscience (v. 6b). This was no brash claim, because God had recognized Job's virtue (1:8; 2:3).

27:7 Job could have been calling for God to judge his accusers as He judges the wicked.

27:8–10 Job reminded the friends that he would never be hypocritical because he understood the consequences.

27:11 *I will teach you about the hand of God.* Job had pinpointed the issue between him and his friends. They disagreed on the outworking of God's retribution. They agreed that God was powerful, wise, and sovereign. But because Job knew there was no cherished sin in his life that would bring upon him such intense suffering, he was forced to conclude that the simplistic notion that all suffering comes from sin and all righteousness is rewarded was wrong. At the outset, Job himself probably believed as the comforters did, but he had seen that his friends' limitation of God's action was in need of revision; in fact, it was nonsense. Job's immediate comments introduced his exposition on wisdom which follows in Job 28.

27:13–23 Job wanted it made clear he was not denying that the wicked are punished with severe distress, so he agreed that they suffer greatly and affirmed so in this section.

27:18 *house like a moth, like a booth.* These are temporary dwellings which illustrate that the wicked will not live long.

27:23 *clap their hands.* A gesture of mocking.

28:1–28 Though Job had agreed that the

wicked suffer (27:13–23), this explained nothing in his case, since he was righteous. So Job called on his friends to consider that maybe God's wisdom was beyond their comprehension. That is the theme of this chapter. The wisdom of God is not gained by natural or theoretical knowledge. What God does not reveal, we can't know.

28:1–11 References to mining silver, gold, iron, flint, and sapphires, as well as smelting copper. Tremendous effort is made by humans who seek these precious things. Cf. Proverbs 2:1–9.

28:12, 20 These verses sum up the message of the chapter with the point that no amount of effort, even as vigorous and demanding as mining, will yield God's wisdom. It can't be valued or found in the world (vv. 13, 14). It can't be bought for any price (vv. 15–19). The living can't find it (v. 21), and neither can the dead (v. 22; cf. 26:6).

28:16 Ophir. *See note on 22:24.*

28:23 God understands its way, and He knows its place. These are perhaps the most important thoughts in the chapter for the debates. Job and his friends have probed God's wisdom for three times and, basically, have arrived nowhere near the truth. Finally, Job made the point clearly that the divine wisdom necessary to explain his suffering was inaccessible to man. Only God knew all about it, because He knows everything (v. 24). True wisdom belongs to the One who is the almighty Creator (vv. 25, 26). A person can only know it if God declares it to him (cf. Deut. 29:29).

28:28 Behold, the fear of the Lord, that is wisdom. Job had made the connection that the others would not. While the specific features of God's wisdom may not be revealed to us, the alpha and omega of wisdom is to revere God and avoid sin (cf. Ps. 111:10; Prov. 1:7; 9:10; Eccl. 12:13, 14), leaving the unanswered questions to Him in trusting

submission. All a person can do is trust and obey (cf. Eccl. 12:13), and that is enough wisdom (this is the wisdom of Prov. 1:7–2:9). One may never know the reasons for life's sufferings.

2. Job's second monologue (29:1–31:40)

29:1–25 Job did not change his mind about his sin, but he continued to deny that he had earned this pain with his iniquity. The realities of his own words in chapter 28 had not yet fully taken over his mind, so he swung back to despair and rehearsed his life before the events of Job 1 and 2, when he was so fulfilled because God was with him (v. 5). God still was with him, but it seemed as if He were gone.

29:5 When the Almighty was yet with me. Job felt abandoned by God. But God would demonstrate to Job, by addressing his criticisms, that He was with him throughout this ordeal.

29:6 cream . . . oil. He had the richest milk and best olive oil in abundance.

29:7 gate . . . my seat. This was a place in society reserved for city leaders. Job had been one because he was a very wealthy and powerful man.

29:12, 13 poor . . . fatherless . . . perishing man . . . widow's. All over the ancient Near Eastern world, a man's virtue was measured by his treatment of the weakest and most vulnerable members of society. If he protected and provided for this group, he was respected as being a noble man. These things, which Job had done, his accusers said he must not have done or he wouldn't be suffering (see 22:1–11).

29:15, 16 blind . . . lame . . . poor. Contrary to the accusations of his three friends, Job went beyond the standards of the day to care for the widow, the orphan, the poor, the disabled, and the abused.

29:16 searched out the case. Much oppression occurred in unjust courts, but there Job protected the weak.

29:18–20 Job had vigorous health like a widely rooted tree enjoying fresh dew, and he had expected to live a long life with his family ("nest").

29:21–25 Job reminded his friends that there had been a day when no one rejected his insights. He was the one sought for counsel.

29:24 mocked. This is likely a reference to saying something facetiously or jokingly. Job's word was so respected that they didn't believe his humor was humor, but took it seriously.

29:25 as a king. Job was not a king, but some sort of high local official such as a mayor. Mayors, called "hazannu" in Job's day, performed all of the activities Job claimed in the previous section.

30:1–31 Job moved from the recollection of good days in the past (ch. 29) to lament his present losses.

30:2–8 Job described these mockers as dissipated vagabonds who, because of their uselessness and wickedness, were not welcome in society, so were driven out of the land. These base men had made Job the object of their sordid entertainment (vv. 9–15).

30:9 I am their taunting song. Job was

the object of their jeering whereas, in former days, he would not hire their fathers to tend his animals like sheepdogs (30:1).

30:16–19 Job's life ebbed away, suffering gripped him, his bones ached, gnawing pain never relented, his skin ("garment") was changed (v. 30), and he was reduced to mud, dirt, and ashes.

30:20 This caused the most suffering of all—what seemed to be the cruel silence of God (v. 21).

30:23 the house appointed. The grave.

30:24–26 This seems to be saying that God must have some sympathy, if Job has (v. 25), so as not to destroy altogether what is already ruined. Job believed that and reached out for help in his misery but received only evil (v. 26).

30:30 My skin . . . My bones. Job was describing the effect of his disease (see 2:7).

31:1–40 As Job became more forceful in his pursuit of being cleared of false accusations, he intensified the claim that he was innocent, comparatively speaking, and demanded justice. In situations where an individual was innocent, he would attest to it by taking an oath before the king or a deity. This procedure found among Job's neighboring nations was often protocol for court procedures. The repeated "If . . . then" statements amount to the terms of the oath: "If" tells what Job might have done wrong; "then" describes a curse which could result. He accepted the curses (the "then" statements through the chapter) if he deserved them. This represented Job's last attempt to defend himself before both God and man.

In terms of purity (v. 1), sin in general (v. 2, 3), truth (v. 5), covetousness (v. 7), marital faithfulness (v. 9), equity (v. 13), compassion (vv. 16–21), materialism (vv. 24, 25), false religion (vv. 26, 27), love for enemies and strangers (vv. 29–32), secret sin (vv. 33, 34), and business relations (vv. 38–40),

---

Biographical Sketch of Job

1. A spiritually mature man (1:1,8; 2:3)
2. Father of many children (1:2; 42:13)
3. Owner of many herds (1:3; 42:12)
4. A wealthy and influential man (1:3b)
5. A priest to his family (1:5)
6. A loving, wise husband (2:9)
7. A man of prominence in community affairs (29:7–11)
8. A man of benevolence (29:12–17; 31:32)
9. A wise leader (29:21–24)
10. Grower of crops (31:38–40)

The MacArthur Study Bible, by John MacArthur (Nashville: Word Publishing, 1997) 698. © 1993 by Thomas Nelson, Inc.

Job had no pattern of sin. He asked God to answer him (v. 35), and to explain why he suffered.

31:1 made a covenant with my eyes. Job spoke here of purity toward women (cf. Prov. 6:25; Matt. 5:28).

31:33 as Adam. Perhaps this is best taken "as mankind" (cf. Hos. 6:7).

31:35 my Prosecutor had written a book. Job wished that God, the perfect Prosecutor who knows the allegations completely, had written a book that would have revealed God's will and wisdom and the reasons for Job's pain. This would have cleared him of all charges by his friends.

31:40 The words of Job are ended. The speeches which began in Job 3:1 were finished; Job had the first and last word among his friends.

E. The Speeches of Elihu (32:1–37:24)

32:1–37:24 A new participant, who had been there all along with the other three (vv. 3–5), entered the debate over Job's condition. This was the younger Elihu, who took a new approach to the issue of Job's suffering. Angry with the other three, he had some new thoughts, but was very hard on Job. Elihu was full of self-importance and verbose, but his approach was refreshing after listening repetitiously to the others; actually, he was not really helpful to Job. Why was it necessary to record and read these four blustering speeches by this man? Because they happened as part of the story, while Job was still waiting for God to disclose Himself (chs. 38–41).

1. First Speech (32:1–22)

32:2 Buzite. Elihu's ancestry was traced to the Arabian tribe of Buz (cf. Jer. 25:23). The "family of Ram" is unknown.

32:6–8 He may have called it "opinion" (vv. 6, 10, 17), but Elihu claimed it had come by inspiration from God (v. 8; cf. 33:6, 33).

2. Second speech (33:1–33)

33:1–33 The first of Elihu's challenges to Job began with proud claims (vv. 1–7), followed by references to Job's questions/complaints (vv. 8–11). Then came Elihu's answers (vv. 12–33).

33:13 Job had complained that God did not speak to him. Elihu reminded Job that God didn't have to defend His will and actions to anyone.

33:14–18 God does speak, he contended, in many ways such as dreams and visions to protect people from evil and deadly ways (vv. 17, 18).

33:18 the Pit. A reference to the realm of the dead (cf. vv. 21, 24, 30).

33:19–28 Job has lamented that his suffering was not deserved. Elihu answered that complaint by saying he was God's messenger, a mediator to Job to show him that God doesn't act in a whimsical way, but allows suffering as chastening to bring a person to submit to Him as upright (v. 23) and to re-

Elihu's Speeches
1. Elihu enters into the debate to break the impasse (32:1–22).
2. Elihu charges Job with presumption in criticizing God, not recognizing that God may have a loving purpose, even in allowing Job to suffer (33:1–33).
3. Elihu declares that Job has impugned God's integrity by claiming that it does not pay to lead a godly life (34:1–37).
4. Elihu urges Job to wait patiently for the Lord (35:1–16).
5. Elihu believes that God is disciplining Job (36:1–21).
6. Elihu argues that human observers can hardly expect to understand adequately God's dealings in administering justice and mercy (36:22–37:24).

pent (v. 27) that his life may be spared (vv. 24, 28, 30). In other words, God allows suffering for spiritual benefit.

33:32 *I desire to justify you.* Elihu sided with Job and wanted to see him vindicated in his claims to righteousness, so he gave opportunity for Job to dialogue with him as he spoke (v. 33).

3. Third speech (34:1–37)

34:1–37 Elihu addressed Job and his accusers. His approach was to quote Job directly (vv. 5–9), then respond to his complaints; but at times he misinterpreted Job's remarks and at other times he put the words of the accusers in Job's mouth. The most obvious example of the latter wrongdoing was in saying that Job claimed to be sinlessly perfect (v. 6). Job never claimed that; in fact, Job acknowledged his sin (7:21; 13:26). Elihu didn't know it, but God had pronounced Job innocent (1:8; 2:3). In answer to Job's complaints that God seemed unjust, Elihu reminded Job that God was too holy to do anything wrong (v. 10), fair in dealing with people (vv. 11, 12), powerful (vv. 13, 14), just (vv. 17, 18), impartial (vv. 19, 20), omniscient (vv. 21, 22), the Judge of all (v. 23), and the Sovereign who does what He wills to prevent evil (vv. 24–30).

34:9 *For he has said.* Elihu was incorrect. He was putting words into Job's mouth that Job had not uttered.

34:23 *go before God in judgment.* These words do not refer to the judgment of the last days, but to the general accountability toward God that man experiences on a daily basis. The point Elihu made was that God did not need to go through all the trappings of the court to get to the sentence. God "knows their works" (34:25).

34:31–33 God will not be regulated in His dealings by what people may think. He does not consult with men. If He chooses to chasten, He will decide when it is enough.

34:34–37 Apparently, Elihu was convinced that Job needed some more chastening because of how he answered his prosecutors. He continued to defend his innocence and speak to God.

4. Fourth speech (35:1–16)

35:1–16 Elihu again referred to Job's complaints, first of all his thinking that there appeared to be no advantage to being righteous (v. 3), as recorded in 21:15; 34:9. The first part of his answer is that Job gained nothing by sinning or not sinning because God was so high that nothing people do affects Him (vv. 5–7); it only affects other people (v. 8). Job had also complained that God did not answer his prayers when he cried under this oppression (see 24:12; 30:20). Elihu gave three reasons why Job's prayers had not been heard: pride (vv. 10, 12), wrong motives (v. 13), and lack of patient trust (v. 14). Again, all this theoretical talk missed Job's predicament because he was righteous. Elihu was no more help than the other counselors.

35:15, 16 Elihu suggested that, although Job had suffered, his suffering was not the fullness of God's anger or He would have additionally punished Job for the sinfulness of his speeches. He thought God had actually overlooked the folly of Job in his useless words.

36:1–37:24 Elihu had agreed with his three co-counselors that Job had sinned, if nowhere else in the way he questioned God (33:12) by seeing his suffering as indicative that God is unjust (34:34–37) and by feeling that righteousness had no reward (ch. 35). In this final answer to Job, he turned to focus mostly on God rather than the sufferer (v. 2).

5. Fifth speech (36:1–21)

36:4 One who is perfect in knowledge. Elihu made what appeared to be an outrageous claim in order to give credibility to his remarks.

36:5–12 Elihu began by repeating the thought that though God sends trouble, He is just and merciful (v. 6); He watches over the righteous (v. 7); He convicts them of sin (vv. 8, 9); He teaches them to turn from it (v. 10); and He rewards their obedience (v. 11) or punishes their rebellion (vv. 12–14).

36:15 opens their ears in oppression. This was a new insight and perhaps the most helpful thing Elihu said. He went beyond all that had been previously spoken about God's using suffering to chasten and bring repentance. He was saying that God used suffering to open men's ears, to draw them to Himself. But as long as Job kept complaining, he was turning to iniquity rather than drawing near to God in his suffering (vv. 16–21).

6. Sixth speech (36:22–37:24)

36:22–37:24 Instead of complaining and questioning God, as Job had been doing, which was sin (as Job will later confess in 42:6), he needed to see God in his suffering and worship Him (33:24).

36:26 we do not know Him. Though one may have a personal knowledge of God in salvation, the fullness of His glory is beyond human comprehension.

36:27–37:4 Elihu gave a picture of God's power in the rain storm.

36:31 judges . . . gives food. The rain storm can be a disaster of punishment from God or a source of abundant crops.

37:5–13 Elihu described God's power expressed in the cold winter. The storms and the hard winters remind one of the world in which harsh things occur, but for God's

---

Key Word

Affliction: 10:15; 30:16, 27; 36:8, 15, 21— comes from a root meaning "misery" or "poverty." The image evoked by this word is that of a person bowed down under the weight of a heavy burden. Scripture portrays the Lord as seeing the afflictions that bring pain to His people and hearing the anguished cries of those in distress (as in Gen. 16:11; Ex. 2:23–25). The Lord urges us to place our burdens on Him, for he is strong enough to bear them and loves us so much that He will assist us in our time of need (1 Pet. 5:7). Moreover, since He controls all events, we can be assured that He is accomplishing good out of the temporary difficulties we are now facing (Rom. 8:28). The entire story of Job provides vivid example of this fact (42:10–17; 2 Cor. 12:7–10).

---

good purposes of either "correction" or "mercy" (37:13).

37:14–18 These words picture the scene in the sky when the storms have passed, the sunlight breaks through, the warm wind blows, and the sky clears.

37:19, 20 In this passage, Elihu reminded Job that since man can't explain the wonders of God's power and purpose, he ought to be silent and not contend with God. What a man has to say against God's plans is not worthy to utter and could bring judgment.

37:21–23 Elihu illustrated the folly of telling God what to do by describing staring into the golden sun on a brilliant day (vv. 21, 22). One cannot confront God in His great glory; one is not even able to look at the sun He created (v. 21).

37:24 shows no partiality. God is the righteous Judge who will not take a bribe or perform favors in judgment. Thus, in his concluding speech, Elihu had pointed Job and the reader to God, who was ready, at last, to speak (38:1).

III. THE DELIVERANCE (38:1–42:17)

A. God Interrogates Job (38:1–41:34)

1. God's first response to Job (38:1–40:2)

38:1–40:2 God appeared and engaged in His first interrogation of Job, who had raised some accusations against Him. God had His day in court with Job.

38:1 the LORD. Yahweh, the covenant LORD, was the name used for God in the book's prologue, where the reader was introduced to Job and his relationship with God. However, in chapters 3–37, the name Yahweh is not used. God is called El Shaddai, "God the Almighty." In this book, that change becomes a way of illustrating that God has been detached and distant. The relationship is restored in rich terms as God reveals Himself to Job by using His covenant name. **out of the whirlwind.** Job had repeatedly called God to court in order to verify his innocence. God finally came to interrogate Job on some of the comments he had made to his accusers. God was about to be Job's vindicator, but He first brought Job to a right understanding of Himself.

38:2 Job's words had only further confused matters already muddled by useless counselors.

38:3 I will question you. God silenced Job's presumption in constantly wanting to ask questions of God, by becoming Job's questioner. It is important to note that God never told Job about the reason for his pain, i.e., the conflict between Himself and Satan, which was the reason for Job's suffering. He never did give Job any explanation about the circumstances of his trouble. He simply asked Job if he was as eternal, great, power-

---

God's Speeches

1. God's first response to Job (38:1–40:2).
2. God's second response to Job (40:6–41:34).
3. God rebukes Eliphaz, Bildad, and Zophar (42:7–9).
4. God restores Job's family, wealth, and long life (42:10–17).

---

ful, wise, and perfect as God. If not, Job would have been better off to keep quiet and trust Him.

38:4–38 God asked Job if he participated in creation as He did. That was a crushing, humbling query with an obvious "no" answer.

38:4–7 Creation is spoken of using the language of building construction.

38:7 morning stars . . . sons of God. The angelic realm, God's ministering spirits.

38:8–11 God's power over the sea by raising the continents is described, along with the thick clouds that draw up its water to carry rain to the land.

38:12, 13 The dawn rises, and as it spreads light over the earth, it exposes the wicked, like shaking the corners of a cloth exposes dirt.

38:14 clay under a seal. Documents written on clay tablets were signed using personal engraved seals upon which was written the bearer's name. The Hebrew for "takes on form" is *turned.* It conveys the idea that the earth is turned or rotated like a cylindrical seal rolled over the soft clay. Such rolling cylinder seals were found in Babylon. This speaks of the earth, rotating on its axis, an amazing statement that only God could reveal in ancient days. The dawn rolls across the earth as it rotates.

38:15 their light. The light of the wicked is darkness, because that is when they do their works. The dawn takes away their opportunity to do their deeds and stops their uplifted arm ready to harm. Was Job around when God created light? (v. 21).

38:22 treasury. The storehouse of these elements is the clouds.

38:31, 32 Pleiades . . . Orion . . . Mazzaroth . . . Great Bear. Stellar constellations are in view (cf. Job 9:9).

38:33 ordinances of the heavens? The laws and powers that regulate all heavenly bodies.

38:36 wisdom . . . understanding. This is at the heart of the real issue. The wisdom of God which created and sustains the universe is at work in Job's suffering also. See also 39:17.

38:39–39:30 God asked Job humiliating questions about whether he could take care of the animal kingdom. Job must have been feeling less and less significant under the crushing indictment of such comparisons with God.

39:5 onager. A wild donkey.

39:13–18 ostrich. The silly bird that leaves her eggs on the ground lacks sense. God has not given her wisdom. She is almost a picture of Job, who is a mixture of foolishness and strength (v. 18).

39:19–25 Here is a magnificent, vivid picture of a war horse.

40:2 God challenged Job to answer all the questions he had posed. God already knew the answer, but Job needed to admit his weakness, inferiority, and inability to try to figure out God's infinite mind. God's wisdom was so superior, His sovereign control of everything so complete, that this was all Job needed to know.

2. Job's answer to God (40:3–5)

40:3–5 Job's first response to God was "I am guilty as charged. I will say no more." He knows he should not have found fault with the Almighty. He should not have insisted on his own understanding. He should not have thought God unjust. So he was reduced to silence at last.

3. God's second response to Job (40:6–41:34)

40:6–41:34 As if the first was not enough, God's second interrogation of Job began along the same lines, only focusing on two unique animals in God's creation: Behemoth (40:15–24) and Leviathan (41:1–34), two creatures powerful and fearful who embodied all that is overwhelming, uncontrollable, and terrorizing in this world. Man can't control them, but God can.

40:8–14 God unleashed another torrent of crushing rebukes to Job, in which He mocked Job's questionings of Him by telling the sufferer that if he really thought he knew what was best for him rather than God (v. 8), then he should take over being God! (vv. 9–14).

40:15–24 behemoth. While this is a generic term used commonly in the OT for large cattle or land animals, the description in this passage suggests an extraordinary creature. The hippopotamus has been suggested by the details in the passage (vv. 19–24). However, the short tail of a hippo is hardly consistent with verse 17, where tail could be translated "trunk." It might refer to an elephant, who could easily be considered "first" or chief of God's creatures whom only He can control (v. 19). Some believe God is describing His most impressive creation among land animals, the dinosaur species, which fit all the characteristics.

40:23 God was not saying this creature lived in the Jordan River but rather, recognizing that the Jordan was familiar to Job, used it to illustrate how much water this beast could ingest. He could swallow the Jordan! It was a word used to refer to something of enormous size and threatening power.

41:1 Leviathan. This term appears in four other OT texts (Job 3:8; Pss. 74:14; 104:26; Is. 27:1). In each case, leviathan refers to a mighty creature that can overwhelm man but who is no match for God. Since this creature lives in the sea among ships (Ps. 104:26), some form of sea monster, possibly an ancient dinosaur, is in view. Some feel it was a crocodile, which had scaly hide (v. 15), terrible teeth (v. 14) and speed in the water (v. 32). But crocodiles are not sea creatures, and clearly this one was (v. 31). Some have thought it was a killer whale or a great white shark, because he is the ultimate killer beast over all other proud beasts (v. 34). It could also have been some sea-going dinosaur.

41:4 Will he make a covenant with you? "Will this monstrous creature need, for any reason, to come to terms with you, Job? Are you able to control him?" God asked.

41:10 Who then is able to stand against Me? This was the essential question being asked in both the behemoth and leviathan passages. God created these awesome creatures, and His might is far greater than theirs. If Job couldn't stand against them, what was he doing contending with God? He would be better off to fight a dinosaur or a killer shark.

41:11 God did not need to buy anything; He already owned all things. Paul quoted this in Romans 11:35.

B. Job Confesses, Worships, and Is Vindicated (42:1–17)

1. Job passes judgment on himself (42:1–6)

42:1–6 Job's confession and repentance finally took place. He still did not know why he suffered so profoundly, but he quit complaining, questioning, and challenging God's wisdom and justice. He was reduced to such utter humility, crushed beneath the weight of God's greatness, that all he could do was repent for his insolence. Without answers to all of his questions, Job bowed in humble submission before his Creator and admitted that God was sovereign (cf. Is. 14:24; 46:8–11).

Most importantly for the message of the book, Job was still diseased and without his children and possessions, and God had not changed anything, except for the humbling of the heart of His servant. Satan had been proven wrong (1) in the charges he brought against Job and (2) in thinking he could destroy true saving faith. Also, Job's companions were wrong in the charges they brought against him; but most critically, Job himself was wrong in the charges he had raised against God. He expressed his regret that he had not just accepted God's will without complaining and questioning.

42:3, 4 You asked . . . You said. Job twice alluded to statements God had made in His interrogation of him. The first allusion "Who is this who hides counsel without knowledge?" (38:2) indicted Job's pride and presumption about God's counsel. The second, "I will question you, and you shall answer Me" (38:3; 40:7) expressed God's judicial authority to demand answers from His own accuser, Job. The two quotes showed that Job understood the divine rebuke.

42:5 have heard . . . now my eye sees You. At last, Job said he understood God whom he had seen with the eyes of faith. He had never grasped the greatness, majesty, sovereignty, and independence of God so well as he did at that moment.

42:6 repent in dust and ashes. All that was left to do was repent! The ashes upon which the broken man sat had not changed; but the heart of God's suffering servant had. Job did not need to repent of some sins which Satan or his accusers had raised. But Job had exercised presumption and allegations of unfairness against his Lord and hated himself for this in a way that called for brokenness and contrition.

Job as a Husband

1. He modeled godliness for his wife (1:1).
2. Job was the spiritual leader in his home (1:5).
3. Job lovingly corrected his wife's wrong response to the disasters that befell them (2:10).
4. Job was her example in how to suffer righteously by trusting in God (2:10).
5. Job did not hold his wife's wrong response against her—they later started a new family all over again (42:13, 14).

42:7–17 The text goes back to prose, from the poetry begun in 3:1.

2. God rebukes Eliphaz, Bildad, and Zophar (42:7–9)

42:7, 8 you have not spoken of Me what is right. God vindicated Job by saying that Job had spoken right about God in rejecting the error of his friends. They are then rebuked for those misrepresentations and arrogance. This does not mean that everything they said was incorrect, but they had made wrong statements about the character and works of God, and also had raised erroneous allegations against Job.

42:8 seven bulls and seven rams. Since this was the number of sacrifices specified in Numbers 23:1 by Balaam the prophet, perhaps it was a traditional kind of burnt offering for sin.

42:8, 9 As God had been gracious to Job, so He was to Job's friends, by means of sacrifice and prayer. Here, the book points to the need for a sacrifice for sin, fulfilled in the Lord Jesus Christ who gave Himself as an offering for sins and ever lives to intercede (cf. 1 Tim. 2:5). Even before the Levitical priesthood, family heads acted as priests, offering sacrifices and mediating through prayer.

3. God restores Job's family, wealth, and long life (42:10–17)

42:13 seven sons . . . three daughters. While the animals are double the number of Job 1:3, why are not the children? It is obvious that Job still had seven sons and three daughters waiting for him in the presence of God (42:17).

42:14 These names are representative of the joys of restoration. Jemimah means "day light;" Keziah means "sweet smelling;" and Keren-Happuch describes a beautiful color women used to paint their eyelids.

42:15 gave them an inheritance. This was unusual in the East. By Jewish law, daughters received an inheritance only when there were no sons (Num. 27:8). Job had plenty for all.

42:17 So Job died, old and full of days. These concluding words take the reader back to where the account began (1:1). Job died in prosperity, and his days were counted as a blessing. In the words of James (5:11), Job experienced the outcome of the Lord's dealings, that the Lord is "very compassionate and merciful." But the "accuser of the brethren" (Rev. 12:10) is still "going to and fro on the earth" (1 Pet. 5:8) and God's servants are still learning to trust in the all-wise, all-powerful Judge of the universe for what they cannot understand.

Further Study

Smick, Elmer B. *Job*, in Expositor's Bible Commentary. Grand Rapids: Zondervan, 1988.

Zuck, Roy B. *Job*, in The Bible Knowledge Commentary—OT. Wheaton, Ill.: Victor, 1985.

THE BOOK OF
PSALMS

Title

The entire collection of Psalms is entitled *Praises* in the Hebrew text. Later, rabbis often designated it "The Book of Praises." The Septuagint (LXX), the Greek translation of the OT, labeled it "Psalms" (cf. "The Book of Psalms" in the NT: Luke 20:42; Acts 1:20). The Greek verb from which the noun *psalms* comes basically denotes the "plucking or twanging of strings," so that an association with musical accompaniment is implied. The English title derives from the Greek term and its background. The Psalms constituted Israel's ancient, God-breathed (2 Tim. 3:16) "hymnbook," which defined the proper spirit and content of worship.

There are 116 psalms that have superscriptions or titles. The Hebrew text includes these titles with the verses themselves. When the titles are surveyed individually and studied as a general phenomenon, one discovers that there are significant indications that they were appended to their respective psalms shortly after composition and that they contain reliable information (cf. Luke 20:42).

These titles convey various kinds of information such as authorship, dedication, historical occasion, liturgical assignment to a worship director, liturgical instructions (e.g., what kind of song it is, whether it is to have a musical accompaniment, and what tune to use), plus other technical instructions of uncertain meaning due to their great antiquity.

One very tiny, attached Hebrew preposition shows up in the majority of the Psalm titles. It may convey different relationships, e.g., "of," "from," "by," "to," "for," "in reference to," or "about." Sometimes, it occurs more than once, even in short headings, usually supplying "of" or "by" person X . . . "to" or "for" person Y information. However, this little preposition most frequently indicates the authorship of a psalm, whether "of" David, the accomplished psalmist of Israel, or "by" Moses, Solomon, Asaph, or the sons of Korah.

Authorship and Date

From the divine perspective, the Psalter points to God as its author. When approaching authorship from the human side, one can identify a collection of more than seven composers. King David wrote at least seventy-three of the one hundred and fifty psalms; the sons of Korah accounted for ten (Pss. 42; 44–49; 84; 85; 87); and Asaph contributed twelve (Pss. 50; 73–83). Other penmen included Solomon (Pss. 72; 127), Moses (Ps. 90), Heman (Ps. 88), and Ethan (Ps. 89). The remaining fifty psalms remain anonymous in their authorship, although Ezra is thought to be the author of some. The time range of the Psalms extends from Moses, c. 1410 B.C. (Ps. 90), to the late sixth or early fifth century B.C. post-exilic period (Ps. 126), which spans about nine hundred years of Jewish history.

Background and Setting

The backdrop for the Psalms is twofold: (1) the acts of God in creation and history, and (2) the history of Israel. Historically, the psalms range in time from the origin of life to the post-exilic joys of the Jews liberated from Babylon. Thematically, the psalms cover a wide spectrum of topics, ranging from heavenly worship to earthly war. The collected psalms comprise the largest book in the Bible and the most frequently quoted OT book in the NT. Psalm 117 represents the middle chapter (out of 1,189) in the Bible. Psalm 119 is the largest chapter in the entire Bible. Through the ages, the psalms have retained their original, primary purpose, i.e., to engender the proper praise and worship of God.

Historical and Theological Themes

The basic theme of Psalms is living real life in the real world, where two dimensions operate simultaneously: (1) a horizontal or temporal reality, and (2) a vertical or transcendent reality. Without denying the pain of the earthly dimension, the people of God are to live joyfully and dependently on the person and promises standing behind the heavenly/eternal dimension. All cycles of human troubles and triumphs provide occasions for expressing human complaints, confidence, prayers, or praise to Israel's sovereign Lord.

In view of this, Psalms presents a broad array of theology, practically couched in day-to-day reality. The sinfulness of man is documented concretely, not only through the behavioral patterns of the wicked, but also by the periodic stumblings of believers. The sovereignty of God is everywhere recognized, but not at the expense of genuine human responsibility. Life often seems to be out of control and, yet, all events and situations are understood in the light of divine

providence as being right on course according to God's timetable. Assuring glimpses of a future "God's day" bolsters the call for perseverance to the end. This book of praise manifests a very practical theology.

A commonly misunderstood phenomenon in Psalms is the association that often develops between the "one" (the psalmist) and the "many" (the theocratic people). Virtually all of the cases of this occur in the psalms of King David. There was an inseparable relationship between the mediatorial ruler and his people; as life went for the king, so it went for the people. Furthermore, at times this union accounted for the psalmist's apparent connection with Christ in the messianic psalms (or messianic portions of certain psalms).

The so-called imprecatory (curse pronouncing) psalms may be better understood with this perspective. As God's mediatorial representative on earth, David prayed for judgment on his enemies, since these enemies were not only hurting him, but were primarily hurting God's people. Ultimately, they challenged the King of kings, the God of Israel.

Interpretive Challenges

It is helpful to recognize certain recurring genres or literary types in the Psalter. Some of the most obvious are: (1) the wisdom kind with instructions for right living; (2) lamentation patterns which deal with the pangs of life (usually arising from enemies without); (3) penitential psalms (mostly dealing with the "enemy" within, i.e., sin); (4) kingship emphases (universal or mediatorial; theocratic and/or messianic rule); and (5) thanksgiving psalms. A combination of style and subject matter helps to identify such types when they appear.

The comprehensive literary characteristic of the psalms is that all of them are poetry par excellence. Unlike most English poetry, which is based on rhyme and meter, Hebrew poetry is essentially characterized by logical parallelisms. Some of the most important kinds of parallelisms are: (1) synonymous (the thought of the first line is restated with similar concepts in the second line, e.g., Ps. 2:1); (2) antithetic (the thought of the second line is contrasted with the first, e.g., Ps. 1:6); (3) climactic (the second and any subsequent lines pick up a crucial word, phrase, or concept and advance it in a stair-step fashion, e.g., Ps. 29:1, 2); and (4) chiastic or introverted (the logical units are developed in an A . . . B/B . . . A pattern, e.g., Ps. 1:2).

On a larger scale, some psalms in their development from the first to the last verse employ an acrostic or alphabetical arrangement. Psalms 9; 10; 25; 34; 37; 111; 112; 119; and 145 are recognized as either complete or incomplete acrostics. In the Hebrew text, the first letter of the first word of every verse or section begins with a different Hebrew consonant, which advances in alphabetical order until the twenty-two consonants are exhausted. Such a literary vehicle undoubtedly aided in the memorization of the content and served to indicate that its particular subject matter had been covered from "A to Z." Psalm 119 stands out as the most complete example of this device, since the first letter of each of its twenty-two, eight-verse stanzas moves completely through the Hebrew alphabet.

Outline

The one hundred and fifty canonical psalms were organized quite early into five "books." Each of these books ends with a doxology (Pss. 41:13; 72:18–20; 89:52; 106:48; 150:6). Jewish tradition appealed to the number five and alleged that these divisions echoed the Pentateuch, i.e., the five books of Moses. It is true that there are clusters of psalms, such as

(1) those drawn together by an association with an individual or group (e.g., "The sons of Korah," Pss. 42–49; Asaph, Pss. 73–83), (2) those dedicated to a particular function (e.g., "Songs of ascents," Pss. 120–134), or (3) those devoted explicitly to praise worship (Pss. 146–150).

But no one configuration key unlocks the "mystery" as to the organizing theme of this five-book arrangement. Thus, there is no identifiable thematic structure to the entire collection of psalms. A brief introduction and outline for each psalm will be provided with the commentary for individual psalms.

1:1–6 This wisdom psalm basically functions as an introduction to the entire Book of Psalms. Its theme is as big as the whole Bible because it tells of people, paths, and ultimate destinations (for a significant parallel, see Jer. 17:5–8). By two elements of contrast, Psalm 1 separates all people into their respective spiritual categories:

I. By Observation, All People Are Separated Ethically (1:1–4)
   A. A Picture of the Godly (1:1–3)
   B. A Picture of the Ungodly (1:4)
II. By Outcome, All People Are Separated Judicially (1:5, 6)
   A. The Failure of Ungodly People (1:5)
   B. The Fruition of Lifestyles (1:6)
      1. Recognition of the godly (1:6a)
      2. Ruination of the ungodly (1:6b)

1:1 Blessed. From the perspective of the individual, this is a deep-seated joy and contentment in God; from the perspective of the believing community, it refers to redemptive favor (cf. the blessings and cursings of Deut. 27:11–28:6). **walks not . . . nor stands . . . nor sits.** The "beatitude" man (cf. Matt. 5:3–11) is first described as one who avoids such associations as these which exemplify sin's sequential downward drag.

1:2 his delight . . . in the law. Switching to a positive description, the spiritually "happy" man is characterized by the consistent contemplation and internalization of God's Word for ethical direction and obedience.

1:3 *like a tree.* Because of the mostly arid terrain of Israel, a lush tree served as a fitting symbol of blessing in the OT. ***planted.*** Lit. "transplanted." Trees do not plant themselves; neither do sinful people transport themselves into God's kingdom. Salvation is His marvelous work of grace (cf. Is. 61:3; Matt. 15:13). Yet, there is genuine responsibility in appropriating the abundant resources of God (cf. Jer. 17:8), which lead to eventual productivity.

1:4 *The ungodly are not so.* This is an abrupt contrast, lit. "not so the wicked!" ***chaff.*** A frequent OT word picture from harvest time for what is unsubstantial, without value, and worthy only to be discarded.

1:5 *Therefore . . . not stand.* *Therefore* introduces the strong conclusion that the ungodly will not be approved by God's judgment.

1:6 *the LORD knows.* This is far more than recognition; the Lord "knows" everything. In this context, the reference is to personal intimacy and involvement with His righteous ones (contrast Matt. 7:23; cf. 2 Tim. 2:19). ***the way of.*** The repetition of this phrase picks up on the "path" imagery so characteristic of this psalm. It refers to one's total course of life, i.e., lifestyle. Here, these two courses arrive at the ways of life and death, as in Deuteronomy 30:19; Jeremiah 21:8; cf. Matthew 7:13, 14. ***shall perish.*** One day the wicked person's way will end in ruin; a new order is coming, and it will be a righteous order. So Psalm 1 begins with the "blessed" and ends with those who "perish" (cf. Pss. 9:5, 6; 112:10).

2:1–12 Sometimes Psalm 2 is said to share with Psalm 1 in the role of introducing the Psalter (cf. "Blessed" in 1:1 and 2:12). Also, it seems that while the function of Psalm 1 is to disclose the two different "ways" for individuals, Psalm 2 follows up with its application to nations. This psalm is normally termed "royal" and has had a long history of messianic interpretation. Although it has no title, it seems to bear the imprint of David's hand. As such, it fluidly moves from the lesser David through the Davidic dynasty to the greater David—Jesus Christ. Psalm 2 progressively shines its poetic spotlight on four vivid scenes relating to the mutiny of mankind against God:

I. Scene One: Human Rebellion (2:1–3)
II. Scene Two: Divine Reaction (2:4–6)
III. Scene Three: Divine Rule (2:7–9)
IV. Scene Four: Human Responsibility (2:10–12)

2:1 *plot a vain thing.* This is the irony of man's depravity—devising, conspiring, and scheming emptiness (cf. Ps. 38:12; Prov. 24:2; Is. 59:3, 13).

2:2 *against . . . against.* The nations and peoples, led by their kings and rulers (v. 1), direct their hostility toward the Lord and His anointed one. The consecrated and commissioned mediatorial representative referred to David in a near sense and Messiah, i.e., Christ, in the ultimate sense (cf. Acts 4:25, 26).

2:3 *Their bonds . . . Their cords.* Mutinous mankind, instead of understanding that these are God's love-bonds (Hos. 11:4), view them as yoke-bonds (Jer. 5:5).

2:5 *Then.* After mocking them with the laughter of divine contempt, God speaks and acts from His perfectly balanced anger.

2:6 *I have set.* Their puny challenge (v. 3) is answered by this powerful pronouncement. It is as good as done; His king will be enthroned on Jerusalem's most prominent hill.

2:7 *I will declare the decree.* The installed mediator now recites the Lord's previously issued enthronement ordinance. ***You are My***

Son. This recalls 2 Samuel 7:8–16 as the basis for the Davidic king. It is also the only OT reference to the Father/Son relationship in the Trinity, a relationship decreed in eternity past and demonstrated in the incarnation, thus a major part of the NT. **Today I have begotten You.** This expresses the privileges of relationship, with its prophetic application to the Son-Messiah. This verse is quoted in the NT with reference to the birth of Jesus (Heb. 1:5, 6) and also to His resurrection (Acts 13:33, 34) as the earthly affirmations.

2:9 You shall . . . You shall. The supreme sovereignty of "the King of kings" is pictured in its subjugating might. The shepherd's "rod" and the king's "scepter" are the same word in the original. Shepherding and kingly imagery often merged in ancient Near Eastern thought (cf. Mic. 7:14).

2:10–12 The tone of these verses is surprising. Instead of immediate judgment, the Lord and His Anointed mercifully provide an opportunity for repentance. Five commands place responsibility on mutinous mankind.

2:12 Kiss the Son. This symbolic act would indicate allegiance and submission (cf. 1 Sam. 10:1; 1 Kin. 19:18). The word for *Son* here is not the Hebrew word for *son* that was used in verse 7, but rather its Aramaic counterpart (cf. Dan. 7:13), which is a term that would especially be suitable for these commands being addressed to "nations" (v. 1). **perish in the way.** These words pick up the major burden of Psalm 1.

3:1–8 This psalm intermingles both lament and confidence. In its sweeping scope, it becomes a pattern for praise, peace, and prayer amidst pressure. As it unfolds through three interrelated, historical phenomena, David shares his theological "secret" of having assurance in the face of adversity.

I. The Psalmist's Predicament (3:1, 2)
II The Psalmist's Peace (3:3–6)
III. The Psalmist's Prayer (3:7, 8)

3: Title The first of seventy-three psalms attributed to David by superscription. Further information connects its occasion with the Absalom episode (2 Sam. 15–18), although many of its features are more descriptive of persecution in general.

3:1, 2 increased . . . Many . . . Many. The psalmist begins on a low note with his multiplied miseries.

3:2, 3 no help for him . . . But You . . . a shield for me. There is a strong contrast between the allegation and the psalmist's assurance. David's attitude and outlook embraces the theology that Paul summarized in Romans 8:31. Psalm 3 also introduces Divine Warrior language (cf. Ex. 15 as a background).

3:5 I lay down and slept. Since God is known for His sustaining protection, David could relax in the most trying of circumstances.

3:7 Arise, O Lord. This is a battle cry for God to engage the enemy and defend His soldiers (cf. Num. 10:35; Ps. 68:1).

3:8 Salvation belongs to the Lord. This is a broad-sweeping, all-inclusive deliverance, whether in the temporal or eternal realm.

4:1–8 There are certain similarities between Psalms 3 and 4. For example, the former is sometimes labeled a morning psalm (cf. 3:5), while the latter has been called an evening psalm (cf. 4:8). In both, David is besieged with suffering, injustice, and oppression. Additionally, Psalm 4 also exhibits the changing attitudes of the worshiper in his most difficult circumstances. David's movement will be from anxiety to assurance, as he travels down the road of prayer and trust in God. At the end of yet another day of pressure, pain, and persecution, David engages in three conversations which ultimately lead to a point of blessed relaxation:

I. Praying to God for Preservation (4:1)
II. Reasoning with His enemies about Repentance (4:2–5)
III. Praising God for True Perspective (4:6–8)

4: Title Psalm 4 introduces the first of fifty-five assignments to the master, director, or chief overseer of worship services in its title. Further instruction is given in the direction "with stringed instruments." The chief musician, therefore, was to lead the great choir and the string portion of the orchestra in this celebration of worship.

4:1 O God of my righteousness. The ultimate basis for divine intervention resides in God, not in the psalmist. For insight about union with God's righteousness based on His mercy, see Jeremiah 23:6 (cf. 1 Cor. 1:30). **distress.** This is an important word for trying circumstances in the psalms. It pictures the psalmist's plight as being in straits, i.e., painfully restricted. Here, his testimony to God's historical salvation, "you have relieved me," conveys the picture that his Lord had provided space or room for him.

4:2, 3 God's agenda for David (v. 3) is radically contrasted with that of his enemies (v. 2). The term for *godly* or *pious* in the OT is above all else indicating a person blessed by God's grace.

4:4 Be angry, and do not sin. In this context, the admonition means to tremble or shake in the fear of the Lord so as not to sin (cf. Is. 32:10, 11; Hab. 3:16).

4:5 trust. This command reflects the primary word group in the OT for faith-commitment.

4:6–8 The taunting skeptics are cut off by the testimony of the psalmist's rest because of God's personal blessings.

4:8 dwell in safety. The word *safety* introduces a play on words by going back to the term *trust* in verse 5. David evidences a total confidence in God in the midst of his crisis.

5:1–12 Psalm 5 is basically a lament with elements of (1) declarations of innocence and (2) confidence and prayers for protection. David was standing in the presence of

Types of Psalms

Type	Psalms	Act of Worship
Individual and Communal Lament	3–7; 12; 13; 22; 25–28; 35; 38–40; 42–44; 51; 54–57; 59–61; 63; 64; 69–71; 74; 79; 80; 83; 85; 86; 88; 90; 102; 109; 120; 123; 130; 140–143	Express need for God's deliverance
Thanksgiving	8; 18; 19; 29; 30; 32–34; 36; 40; 41; 66; 103–106; 111; 113; 116; 117; 124; 129; 135; 136; 138; 139; 146–148; 150	Make aware of God's blessings Express thanks
Enthronement	47; 93; 96–99	Describe God's sovereign rule
Pilgrimage	43; 46; 48; 76; 84; 87; 120–134	Establish a mood of worship
Royal	2; 18; 20; 21; 45; 72; 89; 101; 110; 132; 144	Portray Christ the sovereign ruler
Wisdom	1; 37; 119	Instruct as to God's will
Imprecatory	7; 35; 40; 55; 58; 59; 69; 79; 109; 137; 139; 144	Invoke God's wrath and judgment against his enemies

The MacArthur Study Bible, by John MacArthur (Nashville: Word Publishing, 1997) 743. © 1993 by Thomas Nelson, Inc.

the Lord when he put his enemies before his God. His prayers have two major concerns: "Help me and harm them!" Therefore, David releases his respective prayers for divine intervention and imprecation with two rounds of contrasting thought which differentiate the enemies of God from the children of God.

I. Round One: Theological Contrast of Retribution with Reconciliation (5:1–8)
   A. David's Prayer for Intervention Expressed (5:1–3)
   B. David's Prayer for Intervention Explained (5:4–8)
II. Round Two: Practical Contrast of the Wayward with the Worshipful (5:9–12)
   A. David's Prayer of Imprecation Expressed (5:10a-c)
   B. David's Prayer of Imprecation Explained (5:9, 10d–12)

5: Title Whereas the instructions to the worship leader in Psalm 4 pertain to a stringed accompaniment, Psalm 5 is to be celebrated in community worship with flute accompaniment (cf. 1 Sam. 10:5; 1 Kin. 1:40; Is. 30:29).

5:1 *Give ear.* This command is built upon the word for *ear.* It takes its place alongside parallel requests that God would pay careful attention to the supplicant and his sufferings (Pss. 17:1; 55:1, 2).

5:2 *My King and my God.* David may have been the anointed theocratic king on earth, but he fully understood that the ultimate King of all Israel and of the whole earth is God (for God's conditional allowance for mediatorial kingship, see 1 Sam. 8:19ff.).

5:3 *in the morning . . . in the morning.* These words have led many people to label this a morning psalm (cf. Ps. 3:5).

5:4–6 *not . . . nor . . . not . . . hate . . . destroy . . . abhors.* These three negatively phrased descriptions follow three directly stated affirmations. This reveals God's perfect standard of justice both in principle and in practice.

5:7 *But as for me.* The psalmist starkly contrasts himself with his enemies. They are haughty; he is humble.

5:8, 9 To man's "hoof" problem, David exposes man's "mouth" problem, with special application to his slick-talking enemies. Proverbs is especially given to exposing the deadliness of mankind's spiritual "hoof" and "mouth" disease, i.e., one's walk and talk. Paul includes these assessments from Psalm 5:9 in his list of fourteen terrible indictments of all mankind in Romans 3:13.

5:8 *Lead me . . . Make Your way straight.* Disciples are to walk in God's way(s), being obedient to His direction for their lives; yet, they are fully dependent upon His grace for responsible progress (cf. Ps. 119:1–5, 26, 27, 30, 32, 33).

5:10–12 The psalmist prays for the just ends of the wicked according to God's revealed standard of justice (Deut. 25:1), and contrastingly urges those who are regarded as righteous by the Lord's grace to joyfully celebrate His blessings.

6:1–10 This lament seems to be quite intensive, for apparently David is sleepless. His circumstances seem hopeless and helpless. The early Christian church regarded this psalm as the first among the "penitential psalms" (cf. Pss. 32; 38; 51; 102; 130; 143). David's cries, coming from the depths of his personal pit of persecution, indicate a radical change in his frame of mind as he addresses two different audiences.

I. Pouring out His Soul Before God: A Defeatist Frame of Mind (6:1–7)
   A. A Tone of Helplessness (6:1–4)
   B. A Tone of Hopelessness (6:5–7)
II. Turning His Attention to His Enemies: A Defiant Frame of Mind (6:8–10)
   A. His Boldness about It (6:8a)
   B. His Basis for It (6:8b–10)

6: Title A new musical direction appears, lit. "upon the eight," indicating either "on an eight-stringed harp" or "upon the octave" (i.e., a lower bass melody to accompany these lyrics of intense lament).

6:1 *in Your anger . . . in Your hot displeasure.* David does not ask for immunity from judgment, but for the tempering of God's discipline with mercy.

6:2, 7 *bones . . . eye.* Many assume that, because the psalmist mentions bodily "parts," his affliction was a grave physical illness. Obviously, his circumstances would have had an affect on his physical dimension. However, in OT anthropology such references are picturesque metaphors for an affliction of his total being (cf. all the parallel, personal references, e.g., "me," "my soul," i.e., my being or person, e.g. "I,").

6:3 *how long?* This is a common exclamation of intense lament (cf. Ps. 90:13; Hab. 2:6; Rev. 6:10).

6:4 *deliver me! . . . for Your mercies' sake!* This introduces a new synonym for salvation, connoting an action of drawing off or out. He desires the Lord to graciously extricate him (cf. Job 36:15; Pss. 18:19; 116:8).

6:5 *no remembrance of You.* There is much about "death" and "the grave," i.e., Sheol, in Psalms. Such language as that of verse 5 does not imply annihilation, but inability to participate temporally in public praise offerings (cf. Hezekiah's reasoning in Is. 38:18).

6:6, 7 Sleep has eluded the psalmist because of his severe sorrow.

6:8–10 Out of his dire straits, boldness surprisingly breaks through as he addresses his enemies. This boldness also has only one basis, that the psalmist's confidence is wholly grounded upon his Lord's attention and ultimate intervention.

7:1–17 This psalm is basically a plea for divine vindication in the light of the oppres-

sor's allegations and actions. David's confidence in the divine Judge is the backbone of Psalm 7 (cf. Abraham in Gen. 18:25). As this truth grips him more and more, he will move from a tense anxiety to a transcendent assurance. This psalm follows David through three progressively calming stages of expression in response to the painfully false accusations that were being hurled against him.

I. Stage One: David's Concern as He Passionately Begs the Attention of the Divine Judge (7:1–5)

II. Stage Two: David's Court Appearance as He Painstakingly Argues His Case Before the Divine Judge (7:6–16)

III. Stage Three: David's Composure as He Patiently Waits for the Verdict of the Divine Judge (7:17)

7: Title This title introduces one of the more enigmatic terms found in superscriptions of the psalms—"a *Shiggaion* (Heb.) of David." It is probably related to the idea of wondering, reeling, veering, or weaving. Although the NKJV translates it "meditation," it more than likely conveys shifting emotions or movements of thought. Consequently, the term may also indicate the song's irregularity in rhythm (cf. Hab. 3:1). "He sang" also indicates that this was a vocal solo. The occasion, "concerning the words of Cush, a Benjamite," cannot be readily identified from the historical books; however, whoever this was or whatever the name represented, some enemy had obviously been falsely charging David (cf. Shimei; 2 Sam. 16:5; 19:16).

7:2 *Lest they tear me like a lion.* Often the psalmist's enemies are symbolized by vicious, attacking animals, with "the king of beasts" occurring frequently (Pss. 10:9; 17:12; 22:13, 16, 21).

7:3–5 Such self-pronounced curses are powerful protestations of innocence (not sinlessness) in the context of being falsely charged (cf. the boldness of Job in 31:5ff.).

7:6 *Arise.* The battle cry relating back to Numbers 10:35 recurs (cf. Pss. 9:19; 10:12; 17:13; 44:26; 102:13).

7:8 *my righteousness . . . my integrity.* These are not declarations of sinlessness, but of innocence in this "court case."

7:9 *the righteous God tests the hearts and minds.* The just Judge has perfect insight (cf. God examining the heart and mind in Jeremiah 17:10; also cf. Acts 1:24; 15:8).

7:11–13 This shows yet another blending of the divine Warrior and divine Judge themes.

7:14–16 Often the principle of exact retribution surfaces in the psalms (cf. the maxim of Prov. 26:27 and the judgment of Hab. 2:15–18).

8:1–9 The beginning and ending of the psalm suggest that it is essentially a hymn of praise. Yet, a major portion qualifies it as a so-called nature psalm, i.e., a psalm of creation. Furthermore, there is a significant focus on the created dignity of man. Through this vehicle, the important subject of Adamic theology comes to the forefront, making this psalm ultimately suitable to the important association of the "One," the Last Adam, i.e., Christ and the "many" (cf. Heb. 2:6–8). Structurally, Psalm 8's beginning and concluding bursts of praise are driven by David contemplating two pairs of radical contrasts.

  I. Introductory Praise (8:1)
  II. Two Pairs of Radical Contrasts (8:2–8)
    A. Between the Nature of "Infants" and Infidels (8:2)
    B. Between Unaided General Revelation and Unveiled Special Revelation (8:3–8)
  III. Concluding Praise (8:9)

8: *Title* Another instrument is referenced in this title, most probably a guitar-like harp associated with Gath in Philistia.

8:1 LORD . . . Lord. Of these twin nouns of direct address to God, the first is His spe-

cially revealed name Yahweh (Ex. 3:14) and the second puts an emphasis on His sovereignty. ***Your name.*** The name of God refers to the revealed person of God, encompassing all of His attributes.

8:2 The introductory irony about infants sets the stage for a contrast between the dependent and the foolishly self-sufficient.

8:3 *Your heavens, the work of Your fingers.* The heavens are created by God (Pss. 33:6, 9; 102:25; 136:5). The anthropomorphism "Your fingers" miniaturizes the magnitude of the universe in the presence of the Creator.

8:4–6 Quoted in the NT at 1 Corinthians 15:27, 28; Ephesians 1:22; Hebrews 2:5–10.

8:4 *What is man.* If the whole universe is diminutive in the sight of the divine Creator, how much less is the significance of mankind! Even the word for *man* used in verse 4 alludes to his weakness (cf. Pss. 9:19, 20; 90:3a; 103:15). ***and the son of man.*** This phrase also looks upon man as insignificant and transitory (e.g., Ps. 90:3b). Yet, the Aramaic counterpart of this phrase is found in Daniel 7:13, which has profound messianic overtones (cf. also Jesus' favorite self-designation in the NT, Son of Man).

8:5–8 These verses consistently emphasize the significance of man, who was created in the image and likeness of God to exercise dominion over the rest of creation (Gen. 1:26–28).

9:1–20 Psalms 9 and 10 go together; so much so, that early Greek and Latin manuscripts treat and number them as one. However, Psalms 9 and 10 evidence two different forms; the first is an individual hymn, while the second is an individual lament.

In the first part (vv. 1–12), praise is prominent and in the second part (vv. 13–20), prayer is prominent. Many subtle patterns weave the thoughts of these verses and lines together. Shifting back and forth between the individual and corporate

perspectives is characteristic, as are introverted (i.e., chiastic) structures. Basically,
David's hymn in Psalm 9 ebbs and flows
through two respective tides of prayer and
praise.

I. First Tide: Divine Justice and Praise
(9:1–12)
  A. Individual Praise and Divine Justice
(9:1–4)
  B. Divine Justice and Corporate Praise
(9:5–12)
II. Second Tide: Divine Justice and Prayer
(9:13–20)
  A. Individual Prayer and Divine Justice
(9:13–16)
  B. Divine Justice and Corporate Prayer
(9:17–20)

9: Title The new element of this title literally reads "upon death of a son." Many conjectures have arisen about this puzzling
phrase, but it is safest to regard these words
as designating a particular tune.

9:1, 2 *I will . . . I will . . . I will . . . I will.*
These four *I wills* launch Psalm 9 with
David's dedication to exuberant worship of
the Lord.

9:1 *Your marvelous works.* This especially references God's extraordinary interventions in history on behalf of His people
(cf. the Exodus events).

**9:4 *You have maintained my right and
my cause.*** This is exactly what God is known
to do (cf. Deut. 10:18; 1 Kin. 8:45, 49).

9:5–10 Verses 5 and 6 reveal the just
Judge's dealings with the godless, verses 7
and 8, His dealings with all men in general,
and verses 9 and 10, His gracious dealings
with dependent disciples.

9:11 *the LORD, who dwells in Zion.* There
is a both/and tension running throughout the
OT, i.e., God is enthroned in and above the
heavens and, also, He symbolically dwells locally in His tabernacle (cf. 1 Kin. 8; Ps. 11:4).

**9:12, 18 *the humble . . . the needy . . . the
poor.*** These designations often stand for the
individual psalmist and/or the corporate
community of disciples he represents. The
terms all point to those who are afflicted,
vulnerable, and, therefore, totally dependent
upon the Lord.

9:15, 16 The "boomerang" principle of
exact retribution returns.

9:17–20 Prominent theological themes
from Psalms 1 and 2 also return as the
psalmist draws this great hymn to a climax.

10:1–18 Whereas Psalm 9 started out
with praise, Psalm 10 begins in despair. In
Psalm 9 the psalmist was confident of the
sure coming of divine justice; in Psalm 10 injustice is rampant and God seems disinter-
ested. However, the psalmist's walking more
by sight than by faith will slowly turn around
as he shifts his focus from empirical observations to theological facts. This is not an
easy turnaround, especially since he is surrounded by so many practical atheists (cf. vv.
4, 11, 13). But hope will begin to dawn for
the helpless (e.g., v. 12). In view of such
kinds of general observations, the psalmist's
expressions in Psalm 10 exemplify how true
believers seem to live in two different worlds
at the same time.

I. From His World of Hostility, Discouragement (10:1–11)
II. From His World of Hope, Encouragement (10:12–18)

10:1 *Why? Why?* Two identical expressions of lament boldly blurt out the
psalmist's question: "God, why do You remain aloof?" (cf. Pss. 13:1; 22:11; 38:21;
44:24; 71:12; 88:14).

10:3 *blesses . . . renounces.* The wicked's
modus operandi is the opposite of what God
demands (Deut. 25:1).

10:5 *His ways are always prospering.*
God seems to be rewarding the ruthless. The

psalmist's questioning insinuation is, "Has God also abandoned His own standards for retribution and reward?" Cf. other "why-do-the-wicked-prosper" inquiries in Job 20:2ff.; Jeremiah 12:1.

10:7–11 Evidences of "hoof" and "mouth" disease (walk/talk) return in application to the wicked. These are enhanced by a return, also, of the ungodly being described as stalking, rapacious beasts.

10:12 *Arise.* The battle cry of Numbers 10:35 also comes back again (cf. Pss. 7:6; 9:19). ***lift up Your hand!*** This is an idiom for God's strength and power, especially as it is used in the context of retaliation.

10:14 *You are the helper of the fatherless.* God is pictured as helper or advocate again but, this time, in association with orphans. He is the defender par excellence of the defenseless (on this imagery, cf. Ex. 22:21ff.; Deut. 10:18ff.; 1 Sam. 1:17; Jer. 7:6).

10:15 *Break the arm of the wicked.* The "hand" of God (vv. 12, 14) is more than sufficiently strong to shatter the arm (another figure for power) of ungodly people.

10:16–18 The confident mood of this great climax outshines the psalm's introductory protestations. The psalmist's great Lord listens (v. 17) and acts (v. 18).

11:1–7 The panic that launched this psalm was not David's but that of his apparently well-meaning counselors. Their mood is one of extreme anxiety, but David's is peace. In view of David's attitude, this psalm can be listed with the psalms of confidence (Pss. 4; 16; 23; 27; 62; 125; 131). Also, the solidarity of the theocratic king and the theocratic people is obvious, as indicated by the shifts back and forth between singular and plural phrasings. The developing verses and lines of this psalm reveal that, although two different "voices" were speaking to David in yet another context of personal and national

crisis, he had made up his mind to trust only in the Lord.

I. Introductory Affirmation (11:1a)
II. The Two Voices
    A. The Voice Urging Flight (11:1b–3)
    B. The Voice Urging Faith (11:4–7)

11:1 *In the LORD I put my trust.* Lit. "I take refuge in the LORD." God is the exclusive refuge for His persecuted children (cf. Pss. 16:1; 36:7).

11:3 These are the words of a committed but confused saint. His philosophical problem is, "In view of the crumbling of the theocratic society, what can one righteous person, out of a shrinking remnant, do?"

11:4a *in His holy temple . . . in heaven.* This emphasizes the transcendent throne room of God; yet, God has sovereign sway over all the affairs of earth (cf. Hab. 2:20).

11:4b–5a *His eyes behold . . . His eyelids test.* God's transcendence previously depicted does not negate His eminence, here presented from the perspective of the divine scrutiny of all people, including the righteous (cf. Jer. 6:27–30; 17:10).

11:5b–6 *His soul hates.* This is undiluted, perfect retribution.

11:7a *For the LORD is righteous.* He loves righteousness. He Himself is the perfect norm or standard for all spiritual integrity.

11:7b *His countenance.* "The upright beholds His countenance" is a better translation (cf. Pss. 17:15; 27:4; 63:2; 1 John 3:2).

12:1–8 People's words do hurt, but the Lord's words heal. These thoughts preoccupy David in Psalm 12. The psalm begins and ends with the reality of the current reign of the wicked. Yet, amidst this very black setting, the gemstone truth of verse 5 shines all the more brightly. These eight verses are characterized by subtle repetitions and bold contrasts. In the development of Psalm 12, David provides a model for passing a spiritual hearing test; genuine disciples listen to and properly respond to radically different sources of speech.

I. Surviving the Propaganda of Depraved Speech (12:1–4)
 A. By Prayer (12:1, 2)
 B. By Petition (12:3, 4)
II. Security in the Protection of Divine Speech (12:5–8)
 A. Its Divine Promises (12:5)
 B. Its Divine Purity (12:6)
 C. Its Divine Perseverance (12:7, 8)

12:1 for the godly man ceases! His words and phraseology are deliberately hyperbolic, yet David's perception, indeed, was that the pious have perished!

12:2–4 These smooth-talking sinners verbally abuse the remnant (vv. 2, 3) and verbally defy their Sovereign (v. 4).

12:3 May the LORD cut off all flattering lips. Here is a call for death in the light of sin. On the obnoxious sin of lying lips, cf. Psalm 5:9; Isaiah 30:10; Daniel 11:32; Romans 3:13.

12:6 pure . . . purified. The Lord's perfect words present a most radical contrast with the profane words of arrogant sinners. The purity of God's person assures the purity of His promises (cf. Ps. 19:7–10).

12:7, 8 The hostile realities of verse 8 call for the heavenly resources of verse 7.

13:1–6 Psalm 13 launches with an explosion of four "How longs?" indicating another lament is about to begin. But David will shift radically from turmoil to tranquility in the space of six short verses through three levels of attitude.

I. Below "Sea Level" Expressions of Despair (13:1, 2)
II. "Sea Level" Expressions of Desires (13:3, 4)
III. "Mountaintop Level" Expressions of Delight (13:5, 6)

13:1, 2 These lines reintroduce the familiar triangle of the psalmist, his God, and his enemies. This three-way relationship produces perplexity and pain. In view of God's apparent absence (v. 1), the psalmist seems left to his own personal resources which are unable to deal with the reality of his enemies (v. 2).

13:4b–5b rejoice . . . rejoice. Using the same verb, the psalmist deliberately contrasts his enemy's celebration with his own confidence in divine deliverance.

14:1–7 Psalm 14 (a wisdom poem), along with its nearly identical twin Psalm 53, contains profound deliberations on human depravity. David's representative desire for deliverance (v. 7) provides the chorus to his two preceding dirges on depravity.

I. The Dirges on Depravity (14:1–6)
 A. The First Dirge: In the Form of a Round, Addresses the Universality of Depravity (14:1–3)
 B. The Second Dirge: In the Form of a Ballad, Addresses the Futility of Depravity (14:4–6)
II. The Chorus on Deliverance (14:7)
 A. The Wish for It (14:7a)
 B. The Worship Attending It (14:7b–c)

14:1 The fool. In the Bible, this designation carries moral rather than intellectual meaning (Is. 32:6).

14:1–3 The *alls* and *nones* of these lines make the indictments universally applicable. No wonder Paul included these indictments in Romans 3:10–12. There is also a common scriptural association of doing with thinking.

14:4–6 The shift from third person affirmations about the wicked (vv. 4, 5) to the second person (v. 6a) intensifies this confrontation with divine judgment.

14:7 Zion! The place on earth where God was pleased to reveal His presence, protection, and power (cf. Pss. 3:4; 20:2; 128:5; 132:13; 134:3).

15:1–5 Whereas Psalm 14 focused on the way of the wicked, Psalm 15 concentrates on the way of the righteous (cf. Ps. 1). The saved sinner is described as exhibiting indications of ethical integrity. These characteristics alternate in triplets of positive and negative descriptions. The whole psalm unfolds through a question-and-answer vehicle and, indeed, it may be regarded as the ultimate question-and-answer session. With its focus on moral responsibility, the psalm offers a sequence of responses to the question of acceptable worship.

I. A Two-Part Question (15:1)
II. A Twelve-Part Response (15:2–5b)
   A. Three Positively Phrased Ethical Characteristics (15:2)
      1. His lifestyle exhibits integrity
      2. His deeds exhibit justice
      3. His speech exhibits reliability
   B. Three Negatively Cast Ethical Characteristics (15:3)
      1. He does not tread over people with his tongue
      2. He does not harm his fellow man
      3. He does not heap reproach upon family or friend
   C. Three Positively Phrased Ethical Characteristics (15:4a–c)
      1. He views the reprobate as rejected
      2. He respects the people of God
      3. He holds himself accountable
   D. Three Negatively Cast Ethical Characteristics (15:4d–5b)
      1. He is not fickle
      2. He is not greedy
      3. He cannot be bought
III. A One-Part Guarantee (15:5c)

15:1 Your tabernacle? Lit. "tent" (cf. Ps. 61:4; for possible background, see 2 Samuel 6:12–17).

15:2–6 Notice the focus on life-and-lip qualities.

15:4 despised . . . honors. Whom God rejects, the psalmist rejects; whom God loves, he loves.

15:5 usury. Interest rates ran as high as fifty percent, but God's law put strict regulations on borrowing and lending (*see notes on Deut. 23:19, 20; 24:10–13*). *He . . . shall never be moved.* This is an important promise in the light of its usage in Psalms and Proverbs (cf. Pss. 10:6; 13:4; 16:8; 46:5; 62:2, 6; Prov. 10:30).

16:1–11 The only prayer of Psalm 16 comes in the first line. The rest of the psalm consists of David's weaving together his personal testimonies of trust in the Lord. In view of this, David's opening prayer is bolstered by two cycles of testimony.

I. David's Introductory Prayer (16:1)
II. David's Testimony (16:2–11)
   A. His Testimony of Communion (16:2–4)
      1. Its divine dimension (16:2)
      2. Its human dimension (16:3, 4)
   B. His Testimony of Confidence (16:5–11)
      1. Its past and present dimensions (16:5–8)
      2. Its present and future dimensions (16:9–11)

16: Title A Michtam of David. Cf. Psalms 56; 57; 58; 59; 60. In spite of many conjectures, this designation remains obscure.

16:1 Preserve me. This is a frequent request begging God to protect the psalmist (cf. Pss. 17:8; 140:4; 141:9).

16:2 O my soul, you have said. The words in italics are supplied because there is a variant in the Hebrew Bible concerning the verb. It may be just as well to regard the verb as a shortened form of "I said" (also occurring at 1 Kin. 8:48; Job 42:2; Ps. 140:13; Ezek. 16:59). *My goodness is nothing apart from You.* I.e., "My well-being is entirely dependent on You."

16:4 The psalmist will have nothing to do with false gods or the people pursuing them.

16:5, 6 These lines use OT metaphors to describe the blessing of God.

16:9 *my glory.* Starting back at verse 7, the psalmist referred to his core of being as literally "my kidneys," then "my heart," now "my glory," and next "my flesh" and "my soul." The anthropological terms stand for the whole person; so, it is best to consider "my glory" as referring to that distinctive way in which man is created in the image of God, i.e., his intelligence and ability to speak.

16:10 These words expressed the confidence of the lesser David, but were applied messianically to the resurrection of the greater David (the Lord Jesus Christ), both by Peter (Acts 2:25–28) and Paul (Acts 13:35).

17:1–15 This "prayer" of David brims with petitions, as many as seventeen of them depending upon the translation of certain Hebrew verb forms. There are many literary parallels with Psalm 16. Although the psalm shows indications of mixed forms, it is essentially a prayer for protection. David is fond of using themes and phrases from the Exodus narrative (cf. Ex. 15; Deut. 32). A logical chiastic development is detected in its verses, with the focus shifting from the psalmist (vv. 1–8) to his enemies (vv. 9–12), remaining on his enemies in vv. 13, 14, then shifting back to David (v. 15). Or viewing its development from another angle, David approaches the divine court with three clusters of appeals in seeking justice.

I. Appeals Dealing with Response and Recognition (17:1–5)
II. Appeals Dealing with Rescue and Relief (17:6–12)
  A. His Need for Rescue Is Presented (17:6–8)
  B. His Need for Relief Is Documented (17:9–12)

III. Appeals Dealing with Retribution and Rest (17:13–15)
  A. His Anticipation of Their Retribution (17:13, 14)
  B. His Assurance of His Own Rest (17:15)

17: *Title* This is the first psalm simply entitled "a prayer" (cf. Pss. 86; 90; 102; 142).

17:1, 2 The introductory language is that of the law court where David stands before the ultimate "chief justice" to present his case.

17:3–5 His basic integrity (vv. 3, 4), especially in view of the present case, was, is, and shall be dependent upon the grace of God (v. 5).

17:8 *the apple of Your eye.* An expression meaning the pupil of the human eye. As a person protects that vital organ of vision, so God protects His people.

17:10 *They have closed up their fat hearts.* Lit. "They have closed their fat." This was a common OT idiom for insensitivity (cf. Deut. 32:15; Job 15:27; Ps. 73:7; Jer. 5:28).

17:13 Divine Warrior language.

17:14, 15 The common grace of God is overlooked by those who are satisfied with temporal prosperities (v. 14), but David brings back the proper perspective on true satisfaction in verse 15. Cf. Jesus' teaching on these vital issues in Matthew 6:19–34.

18:1–50 Psalm 18 is clearly an individual psalm of thanksgiving, also bearing royal characteristics. Its poetry and themes resemble other ancient testimonies to God's great historical deliverances (e.g., Ex. 15; Judg. 5). David's song in 2 Samuel 22:1–51 (*see note there*) closely resembles Psalm 18. Between David's opening (vv. 1–3) and closing (vv. 46–50) praises to God, his life with the Lord is described in three stages.

I. Prelude: His Opening Praises (18:1–3)
II. The Stages of His Life (18:4–45)

A. In the Pit of Peril (18:4–19)
1. His desperation (18:4, 5)
2. His defender (18:6–15)
3. His deliverance (18:16–19)
B. On a Course of Ethical Integrity (18:20–28)
1. The principles of the Lord's direction (18:20–26)
2. The privileges of the Lord's direction (18:27, 28)
C. In the Turbulent Atmosphere of Leadership (18:29–45)
1. Military leadership (18:29–42)
2. Theocratic leadership (18:43–45)
III. Postscript: His Closing Praises (18:46–50)

18: Title This large psalm bears a large title. Although the title seems to refer to only one specific occasion (e.g., "on the day"), it does state that God's deliverance was "from the hand of all his enemies and from the hand of Saul." Therefore, it is preferable that the language of this superscription be understood to summarize the testimony of David's entire life in retrospect.

18:1 love. This is not the normal word for love that often bears covenant meaning (e.g., Deut. 7:8; Ps. 119:97), but it is a rare verb form of a word group that expresses tender intimacy. David's choice of words was intended to express strong devotion, like Peter's in John 21:15–17.

18:2 Military metaphors for the divine Warrior multiply in this verse. Both defensively and offensively, the Lord was all David needed in life's tough battles. On "the horn" (i.e., a symbol of power) of David's salvation, cf. Mary's testimony in Luke 1:47.

18:4 pangs Lit. "cords of death" (cf. Jon. 2:2–9).

18:7–15 This theophany, a vivid, poetic picture of God's presence, rivals other biblical presentations (cf. Ex. 19:16ff.; Deut.

33:2ff.; Judg. 4; 5; Ps. 68:7, 8; Mic. 1:3, 4; Hab. 3; Rev. 19). His presence is largely described by various catastrophic responses by all creation.

18:16–19 His sheer power, exhibited so dramatically in verses 7–15, is now amazingly attested as coming to rescue the psalmist personally.

18:20–24, 37, 38 These verses should not be taken out of context, making David look like an arrogant boaster. As in verses 25–36 and 39–50, both David and the community, although responsible for living with integrity within the covenant relationship, are fully dependent on the resources of God to do so. Therefore, his "boasting" is biblical, since it is ultimately in the Lord (Jer. 9:23, 24).

18:31 a rock. (Cf. vv. 2, 46.) Moses, at the beginning of his great song about the Lord in Deuteronomy 32, called God "the Rock" (v. 4). The Lord is indeed a massive, unshakable foundation and source of protection.

18:50 This concluding verse is another royal messianic affirmation of the Davidic covenant in 2 Samuel 7.

19:1–14 Because of its this psalm's distinct parts and two different names for God, some people have tried to argue that Psalm 19 was really two compositions, one ancient and one more recent. However, the shorter form of the name "God" (cf. the longer form in Gen. 1:1) speaks of His power, especially power exhibited as Creator, while "Lord" fits the relational focus. Consequently, David depicted the Lord God as author of both His world and Hord in a unified hymn. God has revealed Himself to mankind through these two avenues. The human race stands accountable to Him because of His nonverbal and verbal communications. In the light of these intentions, Psalm 19 eloquently summarizes two prominent avenues of God's self-disclosure.

I. God's General Self-Disclosure in the World (19:1–6)
  A. The Publication of the Skies (19:1–4b)
  B. The Prominence of the Sun (19:4c–6)
II. God's Special Self-Disclosure in the Word (19:7–14)
  A. The Attributes of the Word (19:7–9)
  B. An Appreciation for the Word (19:10, 11)
  C. The Application of the Word (19:12–14)

19:1–6 The testimony of the universe comes forth consistently and clearly, but sinful mankind persistently resists it. For this reason, general revelation cannot convert sinners, but it does make them highly accountable (cf. Rom. 1:18ff.). Salvation ultimately comes through special revelation alone, i.e., as the Word of God is effectually applied by the Spirit of God.

19:1 heavens . . . firmament. Both are crucial elements of the creation in Genesis 1 (cf. vv. 1, 8). **declare . . . shows.** Both verbs emphasize the continuity of these respective disclosures. **His handiwork.** An anthropomorphism illustrating God's great power (cf. the "work of His fingers" in Ps. 8:3).

19:2, 3 speech . . . no speech. This is not a contradiction, but shows that the constant communication of the heavens is not with words of a literal nature.

19:4 The message of the created world extends to everywhere.

19:4c–6 Neither the sun nor the heavens are deified as was the case in many pagan religions. In the Bible, God is the creator and ruler over all creation.

19:7–14 The scene shifts from God's world to God's Word.

19:7–9 This section contains six names for God's Word, followed appropriately by six characteristics and six achievements.

19:7, 8 Each of four parallel lines contains a word (a synonym) for God's Word; each describes what His Word is; each pronounces what it effectually accomplishes.

19:7 law. This might better be translated, "His teaching," "a direction," or "instruction" (cf. Ps. 1:2). **testimony.** This word for the Word derives from the root "to bear witness." It, so to speak, bears testimony to its divine author.

19:8 statutes. This synonym looks upon God's Word as orders, charges, and precepts. They are viewed as the governor's governings. **commandment.** This word is related to the verb "to command" or "to order." The Word is, therefore, also perceived as divine orders.

19:9 fear. This is not technically a word for the Word, but it does reflect the reality that Scripture is the manual for worship of God. **judgments.** This term looks upon God's Word as conveying His judicial decisions.

19:12, 13 The psalmist deals respectively with unintentional sins and high-handed infractions (cf. Lev. 4:1ff.; Num. 15:22ff.).

Images of God in the Psalms

Images of God as	Reference in Psalms
Shield	3:3; 28:7; 119: 114
Rock	18:2; 42:9; 95:1
King	5:2; 44:4; 74:12
Shepherd	23:1; 80:1
Judge	7:11
Refuge	46:1; 62:7
Fortress	31:3; 71:3
Avenger	26:1
Creator	8:1,6
Deliverer	37:39, 40
Healer	30:2
Protector	5:11
Provider	78:23–29
Redeemer	107:2

The MacArthur Study Bible, by John MacArthur (Nashville: Word Publishing, 1997) 762. © 1993 by Thomas Nelson, Inc.

David's concerns reflect the attitude of a maturing disciple who, by God's grace and provisions, deals with his sins and does not deny them.

19:14 Be acceptable. Using a term often associated with God's acceptance of properly offered, literal sacrifices, David asks for grace and enablement as he lays his "lip-and-life" sacrifices on the "altar" (cf. Josh. 1:8).

20:1–9 Psalms 20 and 21 are twin warfare events. Psalm 20 is mostly ceremony before a battle, while Psalm 21 is mostly celebration after a battle. In the theocracy, these were to be considered holy wars with the chain of command being as follows: (1) the Lord is commander-in-chief over the anointed king-general and the theocratic people and (2) soldiers. All holy convocations, both before and after battles, involved prayer and praise assemblies dedicated to God, who grants victories through the theocratic king-general. Psalm 20, in anticipation of a military campaign, commemorates a three-phased ceremony regularly conducted by the people in the presence of the commander-in-chief on behalf of the king-general.

I. An Offering of Their Prayers (20:1–5)
II. A Confirmation of Their Confidence (20:6–8)
III. A Reaffirmation of Their Dependence (20:9)

20:1 May the LORD answer you in the day of trouble. This is the prayer of God's people for their king-general (cf. "His anointed," v. 6).

20:2 from the sanctuary . . . out of Zion. These are designations about the place of God's symbolic presence in the ark which David had recaptured and installed in a tabernacle on Mt. Zion. The people's wish was that the Lord Himself would uphold, support, and sustain the king-general with His extending, powerful presence throughout the military campaign.

20:5 your salvation. Here, by contrast, God's salvation is victory in battle.

20:7 Some trust in . . . Trust, boast, and praise must not be directed to the wrong objects but only to God Himself (cf., e.g., Deut. 17:16; 20:1–4; Lev. 26:7, 8; Ps. 33:16, 17; Is. 31:1–3; Jer. 9:23, 24; Zech. 4:6).

20:9 This verse could also be rendered: "LORD, grant victory to the king! Answer us when we call!"

21:1–13 The first part of psalm 21 is a thanksgiving for victory; the last part is an anticipation of future victories in the Lord through the king-general. Two scenarios of victory provide a context for praise and prayer to the commander-in-chief (the Lord) of Israel's king-general.

I. A Present-Past Scenario of Praise: Grounded upon Victories Accomplished in the Lord (21:1–6)
II. A Present-Future Scenario of Prayer and Praise: Grounded upon Victories Anticipated in the Lord (21:7–13)

21:2 Cf. Psalm 20:4, the before; Psalm 21:2, the after.

21:3 You set a crown of pure gold upon his head. This is symbolic of superlative blessing (note the reversal in Ezek. 21:25–27).

21:4 The first part of the verse most likely pertains to preservation of life in battle, and the second part to perpetuation of the dynasty (cf. 2 Sam. 7:13, 16, 29; Pss. 89:4; 132:12).

21:5, 6 The King had given great prominence to the king-general.

21:7 For the king. The human responsibility dimension of the previous divine blessings is identified as the king-general's dependent trust in God. But the sovereign grace of God provides the ultimate basis for one not being "moved" or shaken (cf. Pss. 15:5; 16:8; 17:5; Prov. 10:30).

21:8 Your . . . You. Without denying the

mediatorship of the king-general, these delineations obviously put the spotlight upon the commander-in-chief (God).

22:1–31 This psalm presents the reader with a great contrast in mood. Lament characterizes the first twenty-one verses, while praise and thanksgiving describe the last ten verses. Prayer accounts for this dramatic shift from lament to praise. It is the story of first being God-forsaken and then God-found and filled. It was applied immediately to David and ultimately to the greater David, Messiah. The NT contains fifteen messianic quotations of or allusions to this psalm, leading some in the early church to label it "the fifth gospel."

I. The Psalmist's Hopelessness (22:1–10)
   A. His Hopelessness and National History (22:1–5).
   B. His Hopelessness and Natal History (22:6–10)
II. The Psalmist's Prayer (22:11–21)
   A. A No-Help Outlook (22:11–18)
   B. A Divine-Help Outlook (22:19–21)
III. The Psalmist's Testimonies and Worship (22:22–31)
   A. An Individual Precipitation of Praise (22:22–25)
   B. A Corporate Perpetuation of Praise (22:26–31)

22: Title "The Deer of the Dawn." This unique phrase in the superscription is probably best taken as a tune designation.

22:1 This heavy lament rivals Job 3; Psalm 69; Jeremiah 20:14–18. *My God, My God, why have You forsaken Me?* The repeated noun of direct address to God reflects a personal whisper of hope in a seemingly hopeless situation. *Forsaken* is a strong expression for personal abandonment, intensely felt by David and supremely experienced by Christ on the cross (Matt. 27:46).

22:2–5 The thrust of these verses is "even

though You have not responded to me, You remain the Holy One of Israel who has demonstrated His gracious attention time and time again to Your people."

22:6–8 Reproach and ridicule were overwhelming the psalmist. For messianic applications, cf. Matthew 27:39–44; Luke 23:35.

22:7 *They shoot out the lip.* Lit. "They separate the lip," an idiom for sneering (cf. Job 16:10; Ps. 35:21; Heb. 5:5).

22:8 *He trusted in the Lord.* Lit "he rolled to the Lord." The idea is that he turned his burden over to the Lord (cf. Ps. 37:5; Prov. 16:3).

22:9, 10 The psalmist had a long history of reliance on God.

22:12, 13 This imagery of enemies as rapacious beasts returns (cf. vv. 16, 20, 21).

22:14, 15 These are graphic images showing that the psalmist's vitality and courage had left him.

22:16 *They pierced My hands and My feet.* The Hebrew text reads "like a lion," i.e., "these vicious attacking enemies, like animals, have torn me." Likely, a messianic prediction with reference to crucifixion (cf. Is. 53:5; Zech. 12:10).

22:17 This is a graphic picture of emaciation and exhaustion (cf. Job 33:21; Ps. 102:5).

22:18 *They divide . . . they cast.* All four Gospel writers appeal to this imagery in describing Christ's Crucifixion (Matt. 27:35; Mark 15:24; Luke 23:34; John 19:24).

22:21 *You have answered Me.* A welcomed breaking of God's silence finally arrives. This is fully in keeping with His character (cf. Pss. 20:6; 28:6; 31:22; 118:5).

22:22 The psalmist cannot contain himself; he must testify loudly in the great assembly of God's great mercies. His exuberance is meant to be contagious (cf. Heb. 2:12).

22:27 His testimony expands by soliciting universal praises for universal divine blessings (cf. Pss. 67:7; 98:3).

23:1–6 This psalm is probably the best known passage of the OT. It is a testimony by David to the Lord's faithfulness throughout his life. As a hymn of confidence, it pictures the Lord as a disciple's Shepherd-King-Host. David, by using some common ancient Near Eastern images in Psalm 23, progressively unveils his personal relationship with the Lord in three stages.

I. David's Exclamation: "The Lord Is My Shepherd" (23:1a)
II. David's Expectations (23:1b–5b)
   A. "I Shall Not Want" (23:1b–3)
   B. "I Will Fear No Evil" (23:4, 5b)
III. David's Exultation: "My Cup Runs Over" (23:5c–6)

23:1 *The LORD is my shepherd.* Cf. Genesis 48:15; 49:24; Deuteronomy 32:6–12; Psalms 28:9; 74:1; 77:20; 78:52; 79:13; 80:1; 95:7; 100:3; Isaiah 40:11; Jeremiah 23:3; Ezekiel 34; Hosea 4:16; Micah 5:4; 7:14; Zechariah 9:16 on the image of the Lord as a shepherd. This imagery was used commonly in kingly applications and is frequently applied to Jesus in the NT (e.g., John 10; Heb. 13:20; 1 Pet. 2:25; 5:4).

23:2, 3 Four characterizing activities of the Lord as shepherd (i.e., emphasizing His grace and guidance) are followed by the ultimate basis for His goodness, i.e., "His name's sake" (cf. Pss. 25:11; 31:3; 106:8; Is. 43:25; 48:9; Ezek. 36:22–32).

23:4 *the valley of the shadow of death.* Phraseology used to convey a perilously threatening environment (cf. Job 10:21, 22; 38:17; Pss. 44:19; 107:10; Jer. 2:6; Luke. 1:79). *Your rod and Your staff.* The shepherd's club and crook are viewed as comforting instruments of protection and direction, respectively.

23:5, 6 The able protector (v. 4) is also the abundant provider.

23:5 *You anoint.* The biblical imagery of anointing is frequently associated with blessing (Pss. 45:7; 92:10; 104:15; 133:2; Eccl. 9:8; Amos 6:6; Luke 7:46).

23:6 *And I will dwell.* There is some question concerning the form in the Hebrew text (cf. also Ps. 27:4). Should it be rendered "I shall return" or "I shall dwell"? Whichever way it is taken, by the grace of his Lord, David is expecting ongoing opportunities of intimate fellowship.

24:1–10 The form of Psalm 24 has been disputed. For example, it has been labeled by some as an entrance ceremony (cf. Ps. 15); by others, a hymn of praise; and yet by others, a mixture of both elements. Its occasion has also been contended; however, the view that it might have been used at the time of the bringing of the ark to Jerusalem (2 Sam. 6:12–19; 1 Chr. 13) still has credible appeal. The early church designated it messianically as an ascension psalm (cf. v. 3). The movement of the psalm seems to follow the movement of the people. It traces the community's worship procession, both spatially and spiritually, through three progressive stages.

I. Stage One: Worship of the Creator through Contemplation (24:1, 2)
II. Stage Two: Worship of the Savior through Consecration (24:3–6)
   A. The Probing Questions Inviting Consecration (24:3)
   B. The Proper Qualities Indicating Consecration (24:4–6)
III. Stage Three: Worship of the King through Commemoration (24:7–10)

24:1 *the LORD's.* On His universal ownership, cf. Exodus 19:5; Deuteronomy 10:14; Psalms 50:12; 89:11; in the NT, cf. 1 Corinthians 3:21, 23.

24:2 This is a poetic, not a scientific,

picture of creation (cf. Gen. 1:9, 10; 7:11; 49:25; Ex. 20:4; Deut. 33:13; Job 26:10; Pss. 74:13; 136:6; 2 Pet. 3:5).

24:3 In the liturgy, the questions were most likely asked by the priest. The worshipers would have then responded antiphonally with the "answers." On the form, cf. Psalm 15 and Isaiah 33:14–16.

24:4 These sample qualities do not signify sinless perfection, but rather basic integrity of inward motive and outward manner.

24:7–9 These are bold personifications indicating that the city gates needed to stretch themselves to make way for the awesome entrance of the great King. By so doing, they too participate in worshiping Him.

24:10 *The LORD of hosts.* The divine Warrior possibly comes back into consideration; He, the commander-in-chief, is "the LORD of armies" (cf. 1 Sam. 17:45).

25:1–22 David grapples with the heavy issues of life, avoiding denial and affirming dependence. He must trust God in the face of his troubles and troublemakers. These twenty-two verses follow an acrostic development. On a larger scale, the psalm develops chiastically: Verses 1–7 and 16–22 are parallel sections of prayers for protection and/or deliverance, while the core, verses 8–15, contains affirmations about God and about His dealings with believers.

I. Prayers in Times of Trial (25:1–7)
II. Praise in Periods of Confidence (25:8–15)
III. Petition for Help in Trouble (25:16–22)

25:1 *I lift up my soul.* This is a vivid picture of David's dependence (cf. Pss. 86:4; 143:8).

25:2, 3 *ashamed.* The important phenomenon of shame for the wicked and no shame for the righteous returns (cf. a millennial expression of this great principle in Is. 49:23).

25:4, 5 The noun and verb metaphors

speak of direction for life's pathways (cf. the thrust of Ps. 1).

25:6, 7 *Remember . . . Do not remember . . . remember.* These are not concerns about God forgetting something, but the psalmist's prayer reminds the reader about God's gracious covenant promises and provisions, all of which are grounded in His "goodness' sake" (cf. v. 11, "Your name's sake").

25:8–10 More metaphors for life's paths are used for the purpose of begging divine direction (cf. vv. 4, 5). The last line of verse 10 emphasizes covenant responsibilities on the human side (cf. the divine side in vv. 6, 7).

25:11 *Pardon my iniquity, for it is great.* A maturing disciple develops an increasing sensitivity to sin which drives him more consistently to an appropriation of the promises of God's pardoning grace (cf. v. 18b).

25:12 *Who?* This interrogative device (cf. Pss. 15; 24) serves as an introductory vehicle to the hallmarks of genuine discipleship.

25:14 *The secret.* This could well be rendered the "counsel" or intimate personal communion (cf. Job 29:4; Ps. 55:14; Prov. 3:32).

25:15 *net.* The snare of the hunter or fowler (cf. Ps. 31:4).

25:16–21 Ten rapid-fire prayer requests, asking for relief and encouragement, lie at the heart of these six verses.

25:16 *desolate and afflicted.* These terms speak of isolation and humiliation.

25:22 The shift from the individual to the community is really not surprising, since the welfare of the theocratic people is inextricably connected to the covenant individual (cf. Ps. 51:18, 19).

26:1–12 Psalms 26; 27; and 28 mention the "house" of the Lord because public worship is the central interest. The form of Psalm 26 is mixed, i.e., containing elements of declarations of innocence, prayer, and confidence, (cf. v. 1 as a paradigm). Structurally, four intermingling prayers and proofs reveal the psalmist's passion to worship the Lord in spirit and in truth.

I. His Situation (26:1)
  A. His Prayer for Justice (26:1a)
  B. His Proofs of Commitment (26:1b)
II. His Transparency (26:2–8)
  A. His Prayer for Scrutiny (26:2)
  B. His Proofs of Loyalty (26:3–8)
III. His Eschatological Outlook (26:9–11a)
  A. His Prayers for Final Favor (26:9)
  B. His Proofs of Measurable Difference (26:10–11a)
IV. His Confidence (26:11b–12)
  A. His Prayers Show Confidence in the Person of God (26:11b)
  B. His Proofs Show Confidence in the Provision of God (26:12)

26:1 *Vindicate me.* Lit. "Judge me!" This refers to exoneration of some false accusations and/or charges under the protection of the covenant stipulations of the theocratic law (cf. Pss. 7:8; 35:24; 43:1). ***my integrity.*** Again, this is not a claim to perfection, but of innocence, particularly as viewed within the context of ungrounded "legal" charges (cf. Ps. 7:8; Prov. 10:9; 19:1; 20:7; 28:6). ***I shall not slip.*** Cf. Psalms 18:36; 37:31; contrast Psalm 73:18–20.

26:2 *Examine . . . prove . . . Try.* These three invitations to divine scrutiny are essentially synonymous ways of testing, refining, and purifying (cf. Pss. 11:4, 5; 12:6; 17:3; 66:10; Jer. 17:9, 10).

26:4, 5 This language suggests that David is making a personal application of the characteristics of Psalm 1:1.

26:6 Personal cleansing is a necessary prerequisite for acceptable worship (cf. Ps. 24:3, 4).

26:7 *That I may proclaim.* The Hebrew text literally reads "to hear the sound of praise and to proclaim." This is a reference to the enjoyment of and participation in public worship.

26:8 *Your glory.* God's *glory* most frequently refers to His self-manifestation, e.g., His attributes revealed and exhibited. *See note on Leviticus 9:23.*

26:9–11 This is another sharp contrast between the injurious and the innocent.

26:12 *My foot stands.* Cf. verse 1, "I shall not slip."

27:1–14 This psalm is characterized by strong contrasts such as lament and laud; persecution and praise; plus warfare and worship. In Psalm 27, the psalmist, in the presence of his Lord, engages in three conversations that help him balance the ups and downs of life.

I. He Converses with Himself about Privileges (27:1–6)
II. He Converses with the Lord about Problems (27:7–12)
III. He Converses with Himself about Perseverance (27:13, 14)

27:1 *light.* This important biblical word picture with exclusively positive connotations pictures the light of redemption in contrast to the darkness of condemnation (cf. Pss. 18:28; 36:9; 43:3; Is. 60:1, 19, 20; Mic. 7:8; John 8:12; 12:46; 1 John 1:5).

27:2 *To eat up my flesh.* An allusion to the psalmist's enemies being like vicious beasts (cf. Pss. 7:2; 14:4; 17:12; Job 19:22; Jer. 30:16; 50:7). This wording was also employed to describe slander and defamation (cf. a close Aramaic parallel in Dan. 3:8; 6:24). ***They stumbled and fell.*** This doublet conveys thorough defeat (cf. Is. 3:8; 8:15; 31:3; Jer. 46:6).

27:4 *One thing.* The primary issue in David's life was to live in God's presence and by His purpose (cf. Pss. 15:1; 23:6; cf. Paul's "one thing" in Phil. 3:13).

27:5 *His pavilion.* David portrays the privileges of divine protection as being hidden in God's "booth" or "shelter," a term in parallelism with "tabernacle" or "tent."

27:8, 9 Seek My face, . . . Your face . . . Your face. God's *face* indicates His personal presence or simply His being (Pss. 24:6; 105:4); and seeking His face is a primary characteristic of true believers who desire fellowship with Him (cf. Deut. 4:29; 2 Chr. 11:16; 20:4; Ps. 40:16; Jer. 50:4; Hos. 3:5; Zech. 8:22).

27:10 Even though those nearest and dearest to David might abandon him, his Lord would always be concerned about and care for him (cf. Deut. 31:6, 8; Is. 49:14, 15; Heb. 13:5).

27:14 Wait . . . Wait. This particular word for waiting connotes either a tense or eager and patient anticipation of the Lord (cf. Pss. 37:34; 40:1).

28:1–9 We encounter a radical shift from lamentation and prayer to thanksgiving. The psalmist, without regard for his unchanged circumstances, shows confidence in crisis. David, moving through two cycles of crisis and confidence, magnifies the justice of God.
I. First Cycle: Individual in Outlook—Terminates in Praise (28:1–7)
A. His Personal Crisis (28:1–5b)
B. His Personal Confidence (28:5c–7)
II. Second Cycle: Corporate in Outlook—Terminates in Prayer (28:8, 9)
A. His Reassurance in the Light of Corporate Confidence (28:8)
B. His Request in the Face of Corporate Crisis (28:9)

28:1 silent . . . silent. On the striking picture of God being deaf and dumb regarding his situation, cf. Psalms 35:22; 83:1; 109:1; Isaiah 57:11; 64:12; 65:6; Habukkuk 1:13.

28:2 When I lift up my hands. On this symbolic "posture" representing the heart's attitude in dependent prayer, see Exodus 9:29; 17:11, 12; Psalm 63:4; 1 Tim. 2:8.

28:3–5 The iniquities of the psalmist's

(really God's) enemies bring forth sharp imprecations.

28:6 Because He has heard the voice of my supplications! Contrast verses 1, 2. Through faith, the psalmist will live his life as though God has already intervened.

28:8 His anointed. This is most likely a corporate reference to the people of God being anointed, not to an individual (cf. Hab. 3:13).

28:9 Your inheritance. God amazingly considers His people a most precious possession (cf. Deut. 7:6–16; 9:29; 1 Sam 10:1; Pss. 33:12; 94:5; Eph. 1:18).

29:1–11 This psalm has all the earmarks of the earliest Hebrew poetry (cf. Ex. 15; Judg. 5). As to its general form, it is a hymn. Many of its images appear in parallel literature, especially in referencing pagan gods by various "forces of nature." However, the Lord is the unique Creator and supreme Sovereign over all these phenomena. He alone is "the God of gods" (Dan. 11:36). In view of these realities, three representative realms of the supremacy of God bring forth praise to Yahweh (Jehovah) alone.
I. The Lord's Supremacy over Heavenly Beings (29:1, 2)
II. The Lord's Supremacy over the Forces of Nature (29:3–9)
III. The Lord's Supremacy over Humanity (29:10, 11)

29:1 mighty ones. Lit "sons of God" (cf. Ps. 89:6 in its context of vv. 5–10; cf. the plural form of "gods" in Ex. 15:11). The reference here is most likely to Yahweh's mighty angels.

29:3–9 This is an awesome theophany, depicting dramatic movements in the powerful manifestations of the Lord God; they function to establish His supremacy as the only true God in comparison with any of the so-called gods of Israel's pagan neighbors.

29:3 *The voice of the LORD.* His voice is frequently associated with the thunder (cf., e.g., 1 Sam. 7:10; Job 37:4, 5; Ps. 18:13; Is. 30:30, 31).

29:5 *the cedars . . . the cedars of Lebanon.* These are the grandest of forest trees, in that those of Lebanon were especially impressive.

29:6 *Sirion.* This is the Phoenician name for Mt. Hermon to the north of Dan (cf. Deut. 3:9).

29:8 *the Wilderness of Kadesh.* Kadesh Barnea is in the southern desert country. For its importance in the history of Israel, *see note on Numbers 20:1.*

29:10 *the Flood.* This refers to the universal Flood of Genesis 6–8 (see Gen. 7:17).

30:1–12 A mixture of forms characterize Psalm 30. David speaks out of a cycle of life (i.e., lamentation and laud), especially moving through prayer to praise. In spite of great variety, the psalm is bonded together by praise emphases (cf. vv. 4, 9, 12). The psalmist's beginning and ending pledges to praise provide structure for his prayers and testimonies.

I. His Beginning Pledge of Praise (30:1a)
II. His Look Back on Historic Prayers and Testimonies (30:1b–9)
   A. His Individual Remembrance (30:1b–3)
   B. His Public Reminders (30:4, 5)
   C. His Individual Reflections (30:6–9)
III. His Look Ahead to Continuing Prayers and Testimonies (30:10–12a)
IV. His Concluding Pledge of Praise (30:12b)

30: *Title* The first and last parts of this title, i.e., "A Psalm . . . of David," are common notations in the superscriptions of many psalms. However, the middle words, "a song of dedication," or "consecration of the house," were probably added later, although

they could have referenced David's temporary tent representative of the ark erected on Mt. Zion (2 Sam. 6:17) or his own house (2 Sam. 5:11, 12).

30:2, 3 *You healed me.* God alone is the unique healer (cf. Ex. 15:26; Deut. 32:39; Ps. 107:20). David is extolling God for bringing him back from a near-death experience.

30:5 This stark contrast constitutes one of the most worshipful testimonies from the Scriptures (cf. the principle in Is. 54:7, 8; John 16:20–22; 2 Cor. 4:17).

30:6 David recalls his previous independent attitude and arrogant talk. God had warned the nation and its leaders about such sinfully myopic outlooks (cf. Deut. 8:11–20; note sample failures in Deut. 32:15; 2 Chr. 32:25; Jer. 22:21; Hos. 13:6; Dan. 4:28–37). By the grace of God, David woke up to the fact that he was acting like his arrogant adversaries (cf. Ps. 10:6).

30:8–10 A familiar argument for preservation of life (cf. Pss. 6:5; 28:1; 88:10–12; 115:17; Is. 38:18, 19).

30:12 *my glory.* Now with renewed perspective (contrast v. 6), David recognizes that all he is and has is due to God's unmerited grace (cf. v. 7a).

31:1–24 This psalm contains more of David's problems, prayers, and praises. David will again walk a road that takes him from anguish to assurance. Within the two settings of Psalm 31, the psalmist's testimonies passionately celebrate the sufficiencies of God.

I. The Original, Private Setting (31:1–18)
   A. His Testimony about Security and Salvation (31:1–5)
   B. His Testimony about Discernment and Deliverance (31:6–8)
   C. His Testimony about Reproach and Relief (31:9–18)
II. The Ultimate, Public Setting (31:19–24)

A. His Testimony and Divine Exaltation (31:19–22)

B. His Testimony and Human Exhortation (31:23, 24)

31:2 Bow down Your ear to me. This is a bold "pay-attention-to-my-prayer" demand (cf. Ps. 102:2).

31:3 The language resembles that of Psalm 23:1–3, except it now comes packaged with prayer requests.

31:5 Into Your hand. This is applied to both the lesser David and the greater David (Luke 23:46); here, it involves the common denominator of trust. This is a metaphor depicting God's power and control (cf. v. 15a; contrast vv. 8, 15b).

31:6 I have hated. Cf. Psalm 26:5 on the proper basis for such hatred (cf. Ps. 139:21). **useless idols.** This is a common designation for false gods (cf. Deut. 32:21; 1 Kin. 16:13; Jer. 10:15; 14:22; 16:19; 18:15; Jon. 2:8). On the foolishness of idolatry, see Habukkuk 2:18–20.

31:9, 10 These terms quite frequently are employed metaphysically to convey the non-physical impact of trials and tribulations.

31:11 The psalmist was a reproach to adversaries and personal acquaintances alike, a very painful alienation (cf. Ps. 88:8, 18).

31:13 Fear is on every side. (cf. Jer. 6:25; 20:3, 10; 46:5; 49:29; Lam. 2:22). **They scheme.** On such wicked plotting, cf. Jeremiah 11:19; 18:23.

31:16 This is a request for a personal application of the blessing of Numbers 6:25 (cf. Pss. 4:6; 67:1; 80:3, 7, 19; 119:135).

31:17 On their shame but not his, cf. Psalm 25:2, 3, 20; Jeremiah 17:18.

31:18, 20 His enemies exhibit signs of "mouth" disease.

31:19 Your goodness. As in the case of His other attributes, God being perfectly good is the ground for His doing good things (cf. Ps. 119:68).

31:23 love the LORD. Biblical love includes an attitudinal response and demonstrated

Historical Background to Psalms by David

Psalm	Historical Background	OT Text
Ps. 3	when David fled from Absalom his son	2 Sam. 15:13–17
Ps. 7	concerning the words of Cush a Benjamite	2 Sam. 16:5; 19:16
Ps. 18	the day the Lord delivered David from his enemies/Saul	2 Sam. 22:1–51
Ps. 30	at the dedication of the house of David	2 Sam. 5:11, 12; 6:17
Ps. 34	when David pretended madness before Abimelech	1 Sam. 21:10–15
Ps. 51	when Nathan confronted David over sin with Bathsheba	2 Sam. 12:1–14
Ps. 52	when Doeg the Edomite warned Saul about David	1 Sam. 22:9, 10
Ps. 54	when the Ziphites warned Saul about David	1 Sam. 23:19
Ps. 56	when the Philistines captured David in Gath	1 Sam. 21:10, 11
Ps. 57	when David fled from Saul into the cave	1 Sam. 22:1; 24:3
Ps. 59	when Saul sent men to watch the house in order to kill David	1 Sam. 19:11
Ps. 60	when David fought against Mesopotamia and Syria	2 Sam. 8:3, 13
Ps. 63	when David was in the wilderness of Judea	1 Sam. 23:14; or 2 Sam. 15:23–28
Ps. 142	when David was in a cave	1 Sam. 22:1; 24:3

The MacArthur Study Bible, by John MacArthur (Nashville: Word Publishing, 1997) 745. © 1993 by Thomas Nelson, Inc.

obedience (cf. Deut. 6:4, 5; 10:12; John 14:15, 21; 15:10; 2 John 6). The assurance of both reward and retribution is a biblical maxim (e.g., Deut. 7:9, 10).

31:24 *Be of good courage.* A singular form of this plural imperative was addressed to Joshua in 1:7. It is used nearly twenty times in the OT, particularly in anticipation of battle.

32:1–11 This psalm has been classified by the early church as one of seven penitential psalms (cf. 6; 38; 51; 102; 130; 143). Among these, Psalms 32 and 51 stand out as confessional giants. Historically related to the life of David and especially in connection with the Bathsheba episode (cf. 2 Sam. 11–12), Psalm 51 would have preceded Psalm 32. The overall thrust, intent, and development of Psalm 32 may be summarized as follows: Life's most important lessons about sin, confession, and forgiveness are skillfully shared by David through two avenues of approach.

I. First Avenue: Remembering These Lessons (32:1–5)
  A. Lessons about Results (32:1, 2)
  B. Lessons about Resistance (32:3, 4)
  C. Lessons about Responses (32:5)
II. Second Avenue: Relaying These Lessons (32:6–11)
  A. Lessons about Responses (32:6, 7)
  B. Lessons about Resistance (32:8, 9)
  C. Lessons about Results (32:10, 11)

32: Title "A contemplation" in the heading introduces a new technical term. It could indicate that Psalm 32 was a "*contemplative poem*," or a "psalm of *understanding*," or a "*skillful* psalm."

32:1, 2 *transgression . . . sin . . . iniquity.* Three key OT words for sin occur, appearing respectively as rebellion, failure, and perversion.

32:3, 4 These are vivid descriptions of the physical effects of David's impenitent state.

32:5 David picks up the key terms that he had used to describe sin in verses 1, 2; but now, in a context of personal confession, he identifies those heinous affronts to the person of God as his own. On the priority of confession, cf. Proverbs 28:13; 1 John 1:8–10.

32:6 David slips right back into his teaching mode in this verse, emphasizing that every person who knows the grace of God should not presume upon that grace by putting off confession.

32:8 *instruct . . . teach . . . guide.* This terminology applies to biblical wisdom.

32:9 *horse . . . mule.* I.e., Don't be stubborn. Such animals are used as pointed illustrations of this sin (cf. Prov. 26:3; Is. 1:3; James 3:3).

33:1–22 This psalm is a general hymn of praise. Its two primary themes are: (1) Yahweh is the Lord of nature, and (2) He is Lord of history. In biblical thought, these realms are always related; the Creator sovereignly rules over His total creation, over all creatures throughout time.

I. A Praise Prelude (33:1–3)
II. The Rationale for Praise (33:4, 5)
  A. The Lord's Sovereign Power in Natural History (33:4)
  B. The Lord's Sovereign Providence over Human History (33:5)
III. The Response of Praise (33:6–19)
  A. The Creator's Sovereign Power (33:6–9)
  B. The Creator's Sovereign Providence (33:10–19)
IV. A Prayer Finale (33:20–22)

33:1 *beautiful.* This means that praise to God is proper, suitable, and fitting. On the propriety of praise, cf. Psalm 147:1.

33:3 *a new song.* I.e., a new occasion and impulse for expressing fresh praise to God (cf. Pss. 96:1; 98:1; 149:1).

33:6, 9 God's utterances created a universe out of nothing (cf. "God said" in Gen. 1:3, 6, 9, 11, 14, 20, 24, 26).

33:6 *host.* This designation refers to stars and planets, (cf. Is. 40:26; 45:12) and/or heaven's complement of angels (cf. Ps. 103:20–22). The former emphasis is more prominent in the immediate context.

33:7 *He lays up.* On this picturesque language of God's "heaping up" waters as a "pile" of dirt or sand, cf. Exodus 15:8; Joshua 3:13–16; Psalm 78:13.

33:10, 11 A sharp contrast is drawn between mankind's shaky plans and the Lord's sovereign plans.

33:15 *He fashions their hearts.* This is the potter's word (cf. Gen. 2:7); for the significance of this statement, see Isaiah 29:15, 16.

33:16–19 On the teaching of these verses, cf. the maxim of Zechariah 4:6.

34:1–22 This acrostic psalm is quite similar to Psalm 25, not just in form, but also in major themes (e.g., the emphasis on redemption that concludes Pss. 25; 34). Individual and corporate applications of the Lord's deliverance are found throughout. This psalm unfolds with a praise mode followed by teaching.

I. Personal Testimony (34:1–10)

II. Personal Teaching (34:11–22)

34: *Title* The historical occasion to which this heading alludes is found in 1 Samuel 21:10–15; however, there is nothing obvious in the context of Psalm 34 to make such a specific connection. Abimelech, like Pharaoh, was a dynastic designation, not a proper name.

34:1–3 This is one of the greatest invitations in the Psalms for all the people to join together in praise.

34:2 This is proper boasting because the only proper object is God Himself (cf. Jer. 9:23, 24).

34:7 *The angel of the LORD.* A special manifestation of Yahweh Himself at strategic historical junctures (cf. Gen. 16:7ff.; 18; 19; 31:11ff.; Josh. 5; Judg. 6; 13). A strong case

can be made that these were preincarnate appearances of the Lord Jesus Christ. *See note on Exodus 3:2.*

34:11 This solicitation to wisdom compares with Proverbs 1–9.

34:12–14 This introduces some crucial character qualities of God's people; cf. Psalm 15:1–5.

34:14 This repeats the "pathway" theme of Psalm 1; here, the emphasis is on leaving the evil and doing good (cf. Job 28:28; Prov. 3:7; 16:6, 17; Is. 1:16, 17).

34:18 *broken heart . . . contrite spirit.* These are graphic idioms that describe dependent disciples (cf. Pss. 51:17; 147:3; Is. 57:15; 61:1; 66:2; Matt. 5:3).

34:19–22 The side-by-side realities of human persecution and divine preservation, once again, vividly depict actual life in the real world.

35:1–28 Psalm 35, as to its form, is an individual lament. Its context of literal and legal warfare suggests a scenario of the theocratic king being accused and about to be attacked by a foreign power with whom he had previously entered into a covenant. David presents his "case" before the divine Judge, moving from a complaint about the situation to prayer about the situation; and finally, when the Lord would justly respond to the situation, David praises Him for His righteous intervention. So three cycles of exasperation and expectation in Psalm 35 convey the psalmist's prayers about his opponents to God.

I. First Cycle: The Attacks He Was Experiencing (35:1–10)

II. Second Cycle: The Perjury He Was Experiencing (35:11–18)

  A. He Prays that God Would Examine the Evidence (35:11–16)

  B. He Prays that God Would Act without Delay (35:17)

  C. He Pledges Praise (35:18)

III. Third Cycle: The Mockery He Was
   Anticipating (35:19–28)
   A. He Prays for Judgment Concerning
      Them (35:19–21)
   B. He Prays for Justice Concerning
      Himself (35:22–26)
   C. He Pledges Praise (35:27, 28)

35:1 Plead my cause . . . Fight. The first,
bold prayer solicits the legal advocacy of
God (cf. Prov. 25:8, 9; Is. 3:13), while the second asks the divine Warrior to fight his battles for him (e.g., Ex. 15:3; Deut. 32:41ff.).

**35:3 Say to my soul, "I am your salva-
tion."** David is longing for reassurance (cf.
Ps. 3:8a).

35:4–8 Cf. the imprecations of Psalms 7;
69; 109.

35:7 without cause . . . without cause.
This adds to his defense; all their attacks,
from a covenant or legal standpoint, have
been unjustified.

35:10 LORD, who is like You? This had become a canonized expression of awe at the
uniqueness of Israel's great God (cf. Ex.
15:11; Mic. 7:18).

35:11–14 A strong contrast is drawn between the psalmist's attitude about the covenant
agreement and that of his treaty partner.

35:16 On the painful maimings of mockery, cf. Job 16:9; Psalms 37:12; 112:10;
Lamentations 2:16.

35:17 how long? On laments, cf. Psalm
13:1; Habukkuk 1:2.

35:19 wrongfully. Cf. "without cause"
twice in verse 7.

35:21 "Aha, aha!" This taunting chorus
will return in verse 25.

**35:21, 22 Our eyes have seen it. This you
have seen, O LORD.** What David's enemy al-
legedly saw, the Lord has seen perfectly. David knew that his God would vindicate him
based on the true evidence, all in his favor.

35:23 To my cause. He brings back the
advocacy theme of verse 1.

35:27 Cf. Psalm 40:16. **His servant.** Besides being a polite, third person reference to
the psalmist, the terminology was also used
of an OT disciple regarding himself as
bound to the Lord.

36:1–12 At least three themes may be detected in this psalm: (1) wisdom, verses 1–4;
(2) praise, verses 5–9; and (3) prayer, verses
10–12. Psalm 36 resembles Psalm 14 in its
description of human depravity; it also
brings to mind David's personal confession
found in Psalm 32. Paul used Psalm 36:1 to
summarize his list of fourteen indictments
against the whole race in Romans 3:10–18.
As to its overall structure, David's two different moods in Psalm 36 exemplify his continuing quest for balance about the realities of
human wickedness and divine benevolence.

I. Mood of Deliberation (36:1–9)
   A. His Deliberations on Human Infi-
      delity (36:1–4)
   B. His Deliberations on Divine Fidelity
      (36:5–9)
II. Mood of Dependence (36:10–12)
   A. Implemented through Prayer (36:10,
      11)
   B. Intimated through Perspective
      (36:12)

36: Title The term *servant*, found in
Psalm 35:27, appears in this title. It carries an
association with covenant relationship emphasizing submission to and service for God.
For its application to David within the texts
of Psalms, cf. 78:70; 89:3.

36:1 no fear. This is the opposite of the
attitude that characterizes true disciples. The
word here is actually *dread* or *terror* (cf.
Deut. 2:25; Ps. 119:120; Is. 2:10, 19, 21).

36:2 I.e., the psalmist flatters himself so
much that he is unable to understand
enough to hate his own iniquity.

36:3, 4 Although Paul cites only Psalm
36:1b in Romans 3, the same categories of
characteristic sinfulness also show up in that

context; cf. character: Psalm 36:2 with Romans 3:10–12; communications: Psalm 36:3a with Romans 3:13, 14; and conduct: Psalm 36:3b–4 with Romans 3:15–17.

36:5, 6 These attributes of God are immeasurable.

36:7 *the shadow of Your wings.* Although some take this as referring to wings of the cherubim over the ark, it is probably a general reference to the protective care of a parent bird for its young (Deut. 32:11; Pss. 17:8; 91:4; Ruth 2:12; cf. Jesus' allusion to the word picture in Matt. 23:37).

36:9 *In Your light we see light.* It is likely that this phraseology bears both literal and figurative significance, i.e., God is the source of physical life and also of spiritual life. The Lord is the source and sustainer of all light and life.

36:11 *the foot of pride.* This is most likely military imagery referring to the practice of a victorious king-general symbolically placing his foot on the neck of a prostrated, defeated king-general.

36:12 Cf. Psalms 14:5a; 18:38; Proverbs 24:16.

37:1–40 Psalm 37, an irregular acrostic, is a wisdom poem addressed to man, not God. Verses 12–24 sound very much like the maxims of Proverbs. The covenant promises of the "land" for Israel are prominent in its verses (cf. vv. 3, 9, 11, 22, 29, 34). Its basic theme deals with the age-old question "Why do the ungodly prosper, while the godly painfully struggle through life?" An intricate arrangement puts forth David's answer. In Psalm 37, David mixes and matches six thoughts in order to advance his major message on the eventual arrival of divine justice.

I. An Introductory Overview (37:1, 2)
II. An Initial Expansion (37:3–11)
III. Some Proverbial Perspectives (37:12–24)

IV. An Initial Testimony (37:25, 26)
V. A Final Expansion (cf. vv. 3–11) (37:27–34)
VI. A Final Testimony (cf. vv. 25, 26) (37:35–40)

37:2 Here-today, gone-tomorrow illustrations about the wicked characterize this psalm. On this theme, cf. Job 14:1, 2; Psalms 90:5, 6; 103:15, 16; Isaiah 40:6–8; Matthew 6:30; James 1:10, 11; 1 John 2:17.

37:7, 8 The message of "Relax! Don't react!" returns (cf. v. 1).

37:10 *yet a little while.* Cf. similar terminology in Jeremiah 51:33; Hosea 1:4. The Lord's intervention is imminent.

37:17 *the arms of the wicked shall be broken.* Their members will be shattered for illicitly grabbing their wealth (v. 16b). Cf. Job 38:15; Psalm 10:15; Jeremiah 48:25; Ezekiel 30:21.

37:18 Cf. Psalm 1:6.

37:21 The OT contains both precepts and proverbs about borrowing and lending; cf. Deuteronomy 15:6; 28:12, 44; Psalm 112:1–6; Proverbs 22:7.

37:24 For corroborations of such divine comfort, cf. Psalm 145:14; Proverbs 24:16; Micah 7:8.

37:31 *The law of his God is in his heart.* On God's internalized instruction, cf. Deuteronomy 6:6; Psalms 40:8; 119 (throughout); Jeremiah 31:33; Isaiah 51:7.

37:38 *cut off.* On this truth of judgment, cf. vv. 9, 22, 28, 34, and Psalm 109:13. For a positive presentation in reference to the faithful, cf. Proverbs 23:18; 24:14, 20.

37:39 *salvation . . . from the Lord.* Since salvation belongs to Him (Ps. 3:8), He is the perennial Source of it (cf. Ps. 62:1, 2).

38:1–22 Prayers surround a core of intense lament (vv. 2–20). In many ways, David's laments parallel those of Job. David's perspective is that his painful plight is due, at least in part, to his personal sin. Organizationally, David's opening and closing prayers in Psalm 38 relate to the onslaughts by his enemies.

I. Introductory Prayer (38:1, 2)
II. First Onslaught: The Enemy Within (38:3–10)
III. Second Onslaught: Enemies Without (38:11–20)
IV. Concluding Prayers (38:21, 22)

38: Title To bring to remembrance. Lit. "To cause to remember" (cf. the title to Ps. 70). The psalmist either (1) reminds God of his plight so that He might act, or (2) reminds himself and the community of his historic predicament so that both he and they would fervently pray in similar contexts of acute suffering.

38:1 Cf. Psalms 6:1; 39:11; Jeremiah 31:18.

38:2 Your arrows. The language relates to the divine Warrior motif; on God as archer, cf. Deuteronomy 32:23; Job 6:4; 16:13; Psalm 7:12; Lamentations 3:12, 13.

38:5 my foolishness. On culpable ethical folly, cf. Psalm 69:5. David views this as the reason for the divine chastisements of verses 3ff.

38:11 loved ones . . . friends . . . relatives. Those near and dear to the psalmist had abandoned him to his adversity, adding insult to injury.

38:13, 14 The ultimate example of non-response to tauntings and torturings may be seen in the Suffering Servant of Isaiah 53:7; cf. 1 Peter 2:23.

38:19, 20 Although he had confessed personal sins, the psalmist remained legally innocent in comparison with his persecutors.

39:1–13 Psalm 39 is an exceptionally heavy lament, which compares with Job 7 and much of Ecclesiastes. It also carries on the "here-today, gone-tomorrow" emphasis of Psalm 37 with a new twist, an application

to *all* people, especially the psalmist. In this intense lament, David will break his initial silence with two rounds of requests and reflections about the brevity and burdens of life.

I. Introduction: David's Silence (39:1–3)
II. Round One: The Brevity and Burdens of Life (39:4–6)
  A. His Request for Perspective (39:4)
  B. His Reflection on Perspective (39:5, 6)
III. Round Two: The Brevity and Burdens of Life (39:7–13)
  A. His Reflection on Hope (39:7)
  B. His Request and Reflection on Providence (39:8–11)
  C. His Request for Relief (39:12, 13)

39: Title To Jeduthun. This is most likely a specifically designated worship director (cf. 1 Chr. 9:16; 16:37ff.; 25:1–3; Neh. 11:17).

39:1 I will . . . I will. The form of these expressions intimate strong volitional commitments. **Lest I sin with my tongue.** This sinning could have been in one or both of two ways: (1) directly, by criticizing God for not bringing retribution on the wicked, and/or (2) indirectly, by complaining in the hearing of the wicked.

39:2 His silence did not ease his pain; it seemed to make it all the worse.

39:3 Cf. Jeremiah's predicament in Jeremiah 20:9. **Then I spoke with my tongue.** Contrast the silence of verse 1. Yet, he did not violate the conditions of his original commitment, since he did not vent before people, but unloaded his burdens before God (cf. vv. 4ff.)

39:4 For similar prayers about the brevity and burdens of life, cf. Job 6:11; 7:7; 14:13; 16:21, 22; Psalm 90:12; Ecclesiastes 2:3.

39:5 handbreadths. The psalmist measures the length of his life with the smallest popular measuring unit of ancient times (1 Kin. 7:26); cf. "four fingers" (i.e., about 2.9 in.) in Jeremiah 52:21. **and my age is as**

nothing before You. On "measuring" God's age, cf. Psalm 90:2. *vapor.* For the same Hebrew word, cf. Ecclesiastes 1:2ff., *vanity* (a total of thirty-eight occurrences of this term are in Eccl.); Psalm 144:4. On this concept in the NT, cf. James 4:14.

39:6 *Surely they busy themselves in vain.* On the futility and irony of this phenomenon, cf. Job 27:16 in context; Ecclesiastes 2:18–23; Luke 12:16–20.

39:9 In this verse, the terminology of Psalms 38:13; 39:2 reappears, accompanied by the theology of Job 42.

39:11 *like a moth.* The moth normally represented one of the most destructive creatures; but, here, the delicacy of the moth is intended (cf. Job 13:28; Is. 50:9; 51:8; Matt. 6:19ff.).

39:12 *stranger . . . sojourner.* He considers himself to be a temporary guest and squatter in the presence of God; on the terminology, cf. Leviticus 25:23; Deuteronomy 24:19ff.; 1 Chronicles 29:15; Psalm 119:19; and for the concept in the NT, cf. Hebrews 11:13; 1 Peter 2:11.

39:13 This stark request is parallel in its intention with verse 10.

40:1–17 Psalm 40 begins with a high flight of thanksgiving and ends with a mixture of prayer and lament (cf. the movement of Ps. 27). Furthermore, the last five verses of Psalm 40 are nearly identical to Psalm 70. Crucial associations surface throughout this psalm. The first is between the theocratic king as an individual and the community of the theocratic people. Beyond this, from the vantage point of NT revelation, an association with the greater David is contained in verses 6–8 (cf. Heb. 10:5–7). Historical precedent and prayers for a present plight move the psalm along from beginning to end. Attitudinally, David understood the importance of what would be explicitly commanded through Paul in Romans 12:1, 2.

These elements constitute only a part of the richness of Psalm 40. Two situations constitute the framework for the psalmist's publicized expressions of worship in Psalm 40.

  I. Precedent from a Past Situation
    (40:1–10)
    A. The Merciful Rescue by God (40:1–3)
    B. The Multiple Resources in God
      (40:4, 5)
    C. The Motivational Responses to God
      (40:6–10)
  II. Prayers for a Present Situation
    (40:11–17)

40:2 *a horrible pit . . . the miry clay.* The imagery describes his past hopeless and helpless situation; cf. the language of Psalm 69:2, 14; Jeremiah 38:6ff. God, by His grace, had taken him from no footing to sure footing.

40:3 *a new song.* See note on Psalm 33:3.

40:3, 4 *trust in the LORD . . . the LORD his trust.* The verb and noun forms of this important Hebrew root connote a faith of confident commitment, here in the right object, God alone (cf. the teaching of Jer. 17:7). David's desire was always to make such commitment contagious.

40:5 Cf. the psalmist's pleasant "frustration" in Psalm 139:12–18.

40:6–8 The author of Hebrews dramatically applies these verses to the greater David (10:5–7).

40:6 *Sacrifice and offering You did not desire.* He is not negating the commandment to offer sacrifices, but is emphasizing their being offered with the right attitude of heart (contrast Saul, 1 Samuel 15:22, 23; note the emphases on proper spiritual prerequisites for sacrifices in Pss. 19:14; 50:7–15; 51:15–17; 69:30, 31; Is. 1:10–15; Jer. 7:21–26; Hos. 6:6; Amos 5:21–24; Mic. 6:6–8; Matt. 23:23). *My ears You have opened.* Lit. "ears" or "two ears You have dug for me." This pictures obedience and dedication.

40:7 *In the scroll of the book it is written of me.* Deuteronomy 17:14–20 would apply to the lesser David; cf. possible applications regarding the greater David in passages like Luke 24:27; John 5:39, 46.

40:9 *the good news of righteousness.* This word for *good news* in Hebrew (cf. the root in Is. 40:9; 41:27; 52:7; 60:6; 61:1) is the precursor of the NT terminology for the "gospel" and "preaching the gospel," i.e., "announcing the good news." "Righteousness" is identified as God's righteousness in the next verse (v. 10).

40:10 David's spirit here was encountered previously in Psalm 22:22, 23.

40:12 Cf. both external persecution and internal perversity in Psalm 38.

40:13–17 *See note on Psalm 70.*

41:1–13 The words of this psalm are general and apply to anyone who might be considered "down." The most painful and specific factor addressed here is the insult which is being added to the psalmist's injury (cf. Pss. 6; 38; portions of Job and Jeremiah). While the form and structure of Psalm 41 are quite complex, "blessed" serves as bookends in verses 1 and 13. Within these, other elements include: (1) confidence (vv. 1b–3, 11, 12); (2) prayers (vv. 4, 10); and (3) lament (vv. 5–9), with moments of wisdom and praise. David's message in Psalm 41 speaks of God's tender, loving care in the critical care unit of life.

   I. Recognizes Human Compassion (41:1a)
  II. Revels in God's Care for the Compassionate (41:1b–3)
 III. Requests Grace, Health, and Forgiveness (41:4)
 IV. Rehearses the Meanness that He Has Experienced (41:5–9)
  V. Requests Grace, Health, and Retribution (41:10)
 VI. Revels in God's Care for Him Personally (41:11, 12)
VII. Recognizes Divine Compassion (41:13)

41:1 *Blessed.* On *blessed,* cf. Psalms 1:1; 2:12.

41:2 *And he will be blessed on the earth.* The verb *be blessed* is from the same Hebrew root as the exclamatory description *blessed* of verse 1 (on other occurrences of the verb, cf. Prov. 3:18; 31:28; Song 6:9).

41:3 *You will sustain him on his sickbed.* This pictures God as physician dispensing His tender, loving care

41:4 *for I have sinned against You.* The ancient Near Eastern association of sin and sickness returns (cf. Pss. 31:10; 32:5; 38:3, 4, 18; 40:12). On the explicit combination of "sinning against," cf. Psalm 51:4. This perspective of the psalmist does not negate the reference to his basic "integrity" in verse 12.

41:6 *And if he comes . . . he goes out.* This hypocritical "sick call" really adds insult to injury. The visitor lies to the sick one and gathers "information" for more slander.

41:9 *Even my own familiar friend . . . lifted up his heel against me.* David's close companion betrayed him; he kicked him while he was down. The greater David's experience and the employment of this reference in John 13:18 was to Judas (cf. Matt. 26:21ff.).

41:13 *Blessed be.* The essence of the Hebrew root of *amen* is "it is true," i.e., reliable, confirmed, verified. Note that Book I of the Psalms (Pss. 1–41) closes with a doxology; cf. the endings of the other four books (Pss. 72:18, 19; 89:52; 106:48; 150:6).

42:1–11 As in the case of Psalms 9 and 10, Psalms 42 and 43 were originally probably one. Some ancient manuscripts put them together; Psalm 43 has no title while the rest around it do. In form, Psalm 42 may be considered an individual lament. This psalm also exemplifies a primary characteristic of Book II of the Psalms, i.e., the preference of the ascription "God" (or parallels to it) for the deity. The occasion and situation of Psalm 42 are historically unspecified;

however, the psalmist's situation was obviously intense and greatly aggravated by his surrounding mockers. Consequently, Psalm 42 is a dirge of two stanzas.

I. Stanza One: The Psalmist Sings of His Drought (42:1–5)
 A. The Content of This Stanza (42:1–4)
 B. The Chorus of This Dirge (cf. v. 11) (42:5)
II. Stanza Two: The Psalmist Sings of His Drowning (42:6–11)
 A. The Content of This Stanza (42:6–10)
 B. The Chorus of This Dirge (cf. v. 5) (42:11)

42: Title The references to "the chief musician," i.e., the worship director, and Maskil, a "contemplation" or lesson (cf. Ps. 32:1) are not new; but, the reference to "the sons of Korah" is. On the ancestry of "the sons of Korah," cf. Numbers 26:10ff.; 1 Chronicles 6:16ff.; 2 Chronicles 20:19. A total of eleven psalms are associated with this group, and seven of them are found in Book II (Pss. 42; 44; 45; 46; 47; 48; 49). These people are probably better regarded as the Levitical performers rather than the authors of these psalms (i.e., "For the sons of Korah").

42:1 As the deer pants . . . so pants. On this simile from nature, cf. Joel 1:20. In the psalmist's estimation, he is facing a severe, divine drought.

42:2 My soul thirsts for God. On this desire for the water of God, cf. Psalm 36:8, 9; Isaiah 41:17; 55:1; Jeremiah 2:13; 14:1–9; 17:13; John 4:10; 7:37, 38; Revelation 7:17; 21:6; 22:1, 17.

42:4 When I remember these things, I pour out my soul. Such language also characterizes Jeremiah's Lamentations, indicating a heavy dirge. On "pouring out one's soul" or "heart," cf. 1 Samuel 1:15; Psalm 62:8; Lamentations 2:19. These are attempts

at trying to unburden oneself from intolerable pain, grief, and agony.

42:5 Why are you cast down . . . and . . . disquieted? In this active introspection, the psalmist rebukes himself for his despondency.

42:6 the land of the Jordan . . . the heights of Hermon . . . the Hill Mizar. The Mt. Hermon and the Jordan notations refer to a location in northern Palestine, an area of headwaters which flow southward. These locations signal that a sharp contrast, in the word pictures describing the psalmist's change in condition, is imminent. He is about to move from drought to drowning (cf. vv. 7ff.). The location and significance of Mt. Mizar is not known.

42:7 Deep . . . Your waterfalls . . . Your waves and billows. The psalmist alleges that God is ultimately responsible for the oceans of trial in which he seems to be drowning.

42:8 The LORD will command His lovingkindness. This statement of confidence interrupts his laments (cf. their continuance in vv. 9, 10), providing a few gracious gulps of divine "air" under the cascading inundations of his trials and tormentors.

43:1–5 Psalm 43 might be understood as an epilogue to Psalm 42. The psalmist moves away from introspection toward invocation. However, as verse 5 will indicate, the psalmist's problems had not ended, at least not fully and finally. Nevertheless, spiritual progress is evident. By interrelating the psalmist's two modes of communication in Psalm 43 and then by comparing them with the laments of Psalm 42, one observes indications of that progress as he continued to deal with his despondency.

I. Prayers to God (43:1–4)
 A. Righting Wrongs (43:1, 2)
 B. Restoring "Rights" (43:3, 4)
II. "Pep-talks" to Oneself (43:5)

A. Exhortation (43:5a–b)

B. Encouragement (43:5c–d)

43:1 *Vindicate me . . . plead my cause.* Lit. "Judge me, O God, and argue my case." This combination of legal terms demonstrates respectively that the psalmist was requesting God to be both his divine Judge (cf. Judg. 11:27; 1 Sam. 24:12; Pss. 7:8; 26:1) and defense attorney (cf. Ps. 119:154; Prov. 22:23; 23:11; Jer. 50:34; Lam. 3:58). On both concepts together, as here, cf. 1 Samuel 24:15; Psalm 35:1, 24; Micah 7:9.

43:2 *Why . . . Why?* Since God was his refuge of strength, the psalmist questioned why this apparent divine rejection and why his dejection.

43:3 *Your light and Your truth! Let them lead me; Let them bring me.* These are bold personifications for divine guidance. The psalmist desired that these "messenger-attributes" divinely direct (cf. such "leading" and "guiding" in Gen. 24:48; Pss. 78:14, 53, 72; 107:30; Is. 57:18) so as to bring him successfully to his destination, i.e., Israel's designated place for worship.

43:5 *Why . . . why . . . Hope.* Cf. Psalm 42:5, 11.

44:1–26 Psalm 44 is a national lament following some great, but historically unidentifiable, defeat in battle. Throughout this psalm, there are subtle shifts between speakers of the first person plural (i.e., "we" and "us"; cf. vv. 1–3, 5, 7, 8, 9–14, 17–22) and the first person singular (i.e., "I" or "my"; cf. vv. 4, 6, 15, 16). This may indicate that the psalm was originally sung antiphonally with alterations coming from both the beaten king-general and his defeated nation. The prayers of verses 23–26 may have been offered in unison as a climax. By employing three time frames in Psalm 44, the psalmist tries to understand and deal with a national tragedy.

I. Focus on the Past: The Shock of This National Tragedy (44:1–8)

II. Focus on the Present: The Inscrutability of This National Tragedy (44:9–22)

III. Focus on the Future: A Prayer for an End to This National Tragedy (44:23–26)

44: *Title* The words of this title are the same as those in the title of Psalm 42; however, in the Hebrew text their order is slightly different.

44:1 *We have heard.* There was a rich tradition about God's great acts that the nation's fathers had passed on. Indeed, the rehearsal of holy history was commanded (cf. Ex. 10:1, 2; 12:26ff.; 13:14ff.; Deut. 6:20ff.; Josh. 4:6ff.; Ps. 78:3).

44:2 *You planted.* On the imagery of God's planting His people, cf. 2 Samuel 7:10; Isaiah 5:1ff.; Jeremiah 12:2; also cf. their being planted and taking root in Psalm 80:8–11.

44:3 *For they did not . . . But it was Your right hand.* This is a brief historical summary of the theology of divine grace, intervention, and enablement (cf. Josh. 24:17, 18).

44:4 *Command victories for Jacob.* If the division of the Hebrew consonants is taken at a different point (as it is in some early versions), this line would better fit into the immediate context, reading: "You are my King, my God, who commands (or, orders) victories for Jacob." "Jacob," the original name of the ancient patriarch, is often used to designate the nation of Israel, especially in poetry.

44:5–8 *Through You . . . For I will not trust in my bow . . . But You have saved us.* The defeated king-general picks up the theology of verse 3 and adds his personal commitment to it.

44:9 *But You . . . do not go out with our armies.* The Lord God is viewed here as having apparently resigned His commission as the nation's divine Warrior.

44:11–16 *You have given . . . You sell.* These are graphic descriptions of God superintending the defeat and utter humiliation of the nation.

44:17–21 *But we have not forgotten You . . . If we had forgotten the name of our God.* The nation's recent defeat was painfully perplexing in view of their basic loyalty to God.

44:22 *Yet for Your sake.* They had no specific answers, only this inescapable conclusion—by God's sovereign will, they were allowed to be destroyed by their enemies. Cf. Paul's quote of this verse in Romans 8:36 and its general principle in Matthew 5:10–12; 1 Peter 3:13–17; 4:12–16.

44:23 *Awake! . . . Arise!* Cf. Psalm 35:23. God does not actually sleep. This is only in appearance to man's perception.

44:26 *Arise.* Cf. Numbers 10:35; Psalms 3:7; 7:6. *And redeem us for Your mercies' sake.* The psalm therefore comes full circle from the history of God's gracious redemption (vv. 1–3) to the hope for the same in the near future (v. 26).

45:1–17 Some portions of Psalm 45 convey a secular emphasis, while others suggest a sacred extension. Upon the occasion of a royal wedding, the psalmist offers a three-part song of celebration.

I. Poetic Preface (45:1)
II. Song of Celebration (45:2–16)
  A. The King-Groom (45:2–9)
    1. Endowments of the king-groom (45:2)
    2. Exploits of the king-groom (45:3–5)
    3. Elevation of the king-groom (45:6, 7)
    4. Eminence of the king-groom (45:8, 9)
  B. The Princess-Bride (45:10–15)
    1. A challenge to the princess-bride (45:10–12)
    2. The procession of the princess-bride (45:13–15)
  C. Future Children from this Union (45:16)
III. Poetic Postscript (45:17)

45: *Title* Two new notations are found, "Set to the Lilies" and "A Song of Love." The first most likely had to do with the tune used in accompaniment with its words. The second notation referring to its content probably indicated that this psalm was a wedding song, and even more specifically, a royal wedding composition.

45:1 *My heart is overflowing . . . My tongue.* The psalmist is overwhelmed with emotion on the occasion of the king's marriage; consequently, he puts his stirred-up mind and feelings into words. In verse 2ff., his tongue is the brush that he uses to paint vivid word pictures.

45:2 *You are fairer.* I.e., you are "more beautiful than," or "most handsome among" (cf. an ancient prerequisite for kingship; cf. 1 Sam. 9:2; 10:23; 16:12; 2 Sam. 14:25; 1 Kin. 1:6; Song 5:10; Is. 33:17). *Grace is poured upon Your lips.* The implication is that God has anointed the king's words (cf. Eccl. 10:12; Luke 4:22).

45:3–5 *Gird Your sword.* In these verses, the psalmist wishes the king future victories in battle.

45:6, 7 *Your throne, O God.* Since this king-groom was likely a member of the Davidic dynasty (e.g., 2 Sam. 7), there was a near and immediate application (cf. 1 Chr. 28:5; 29:23). Through progressive revelation (i.e., Heb. 1:8, 9), we learn of the ultimate application to "a greater than Solomon" who is God—the Lord Jesus Christ.

45:9 *Kings' daughters . . . Your honorable women . . . the queen.* This court picture could refer to royal female guests, but also includes the other wives and concubines of the king-groom (cf. the situation with Solomon in 1 Kin. 11:1). Such polygamy, of course, was prohibited by God's Word; unfortunately, it was still common among the kings of Israel. *gold from Ophir.* Although its geographical location is not known, Ophir was well known as the location of the purest gold.

45:10–15 O daughter. The major emphasis of this portion is "Here comes the bride!" However, even in this section, the focus still concentrates, according to ancient Near Eastern precedent, upon the royal groom.

45:16 Instead of Your fathers shall be Your sons. The loyal and joyful poet now speaks of the blessings of anticipated children from this union.

46:1–11 Psalm 46 was the scriptural catalyst for Martin Luther's great hymn, "A Mighty Fortress Is Our God." This psalm also launches a trilogy of psalms (i.e., 46; 47; 48); they are all songs of triumph. Furthermore, it has also been grouped among the so-called "songs of Zion" (cf. Pss. 48; 76; 84; 87; 122). Psalm 46 extols the adequacy of God in facing threats from nature and the nations. God indeed protects (cf. vv. 1, 7, 11) His people upon the earth (cf. vv. 2, 6, 8, 9, 10). The major burden of Psalm 46 is that God provides stability for His people who live in two unstable environments.

I. The Unstable Environment of Nature (46:1–3)
    A. The Affirmation of His Stability (46:1)
    B. The Application of His Stability (46:2, 3)
II. The Unstable Environment of the Nations (46:4–11)
    A. The First Chorus (46:4–7)
    B. The Follow-Up Chorus (46:8–11)

46: Title The new element in this title is "Alamoth." The early Greek translation (LXX) interprets this technical term as "hidden things." However, the Hebrew word normally has to do with "girls" or "young maidens." Consequently, the most likely conjecture about this phrase is that it is a technical musical notation, possibly indicating a song which was to be sung with female voices at a higher range.

46:2 Even though the earth be removed. I.e., "When earth changes and when mountains move (or) shake (or) totter (or) slip" (cf. the language of Is. 24:19, 20; 54:10; Hag. 2:6). These are poetic allusions to earthquakes. Since "the earth" and "mountains" are regarded by men as symbols of stability, when they "dance" great terror normally ensues. But when the most stable becomes unstable, there should be "no fear" because of the transcendent stability of God.

46:3 Though its waters roar. This is an illustration of powerfully surging and potentially destructive floods of waters. These will not erode God's protective fortifications.

46:4 There is a river whose streams. These words about refreshing waters contrast with those about the threatening torrents of verse 3. Cf. the garden of paradise concept often mentioned in ancient Near Eastern literature; but most importantly, cf. the biblical revelation, noting especially the "bookends" of Genesis 2:10 and Revelation 22:1, 2. *the city of God.* These words, in their present setting, refer to Jerusalem, God's chosen earthly residence (cf. Ps. 48:1, 2; Is. 60:14).

46:5, 6 she shall not be moved. These verses pick up some of the key terms about moving, slipping, tottering, sliding, and roaring from verses 1–3; however, because of the presence of God, the forces of nature and the nations are no longer a threat to the people of God who dwell with Him.

46:7 The LORD of hosts is with us. The precious, personal presence (cf. "God with us" in Is. 7:14; 8:8, 10) of the divine Warrior (cf. "LORD of hosts" or "armies," e.g., Pss.

24:10; 48:8; 59:5) secures the safety of His people.

46:8 desolations. This word not only characterizes God's past exploits, but it is also employed in various "Day of the Lord" contexts (e.g., Is. 13:9; Hos. 5:9; Zeph. 2:15).

46:10 Be still, and know that I am God. These twin commands to not panic and to recognize His sovereignty are probably directed to both His nation for comfort and all other nations for warning.

47:1–9 The main concepts of Psalm 47 develop around key words and phrases, e.g., "peoples" and "nations" (vv. 1, 3, 8, 9); "earth" and "all the earth" (vv. 2, 7, 9); and "king" or "reigning (as king)" (vv. 2, 6, 7, 8). The major message of this psalm is that God is the unique Sovereign over all. Structurally, there are two choruses of worship in Psalm 47 which celebrate this universal kingship of the Lord God Most High.

I. First Chorus: God as the Victorious King-Warrior (47:1–5)
  A. Call to Worship (47:1)
  B. Causes for Worship (47:2–5)
II. Second Chorus: God as the Sovereign King-Governor (47:6–9)
  A. Call to Worship (47:6)
  B. Causes for Worship (47:7–9b)
  C. Code of Worship (47:9c)

47:1 all you peoples! The call to worship is universal.

47:3 He will subdue. Or, "He subdues," i.e., an axiomatic truth about the past, present, and future.

47:4 He will choose. Again, "He chooses," serves as a timeless truth. Cf. the election of Israel in Deuteronomy 7:6ff.; Psalm 135:4. On the land of promise as "inheritance," cf. Deuteronomy 32:8, 9; Psalm 105:11. *See notes on Ephesians 1:4; 1 Peter 1:2* for a discussion of the doctrine of divine election. **The excellence of Jacob whom He loves.** The *excellence* or *pride* of Jacob also refers to the

land of Canaan (cf. the term illustratively in Is. 13:19; Is. 60:15; Nah. 2:2). *Whom He loves* is signal terminology for God's special, elective, covenantal love (cf., e.g., Mal. 1:2ff.). This special focus on God's covenant with Israel does not negate the bigger picture involving blessing to all nations sketched out in the original Abrahamic covenant of Genesis 12:1–3.

47:5 God has gone up with a shout. The imagery likely refers to God's presence, after having gone into battle with His people, now ascending victoriously to His immanent "residence" on Mt. Zion and to His transcendent residence in heaven. This procession with the ark of God was accompanied by great shouts and blasts of celebration in verses 5 and 6.

47:9 the shields of the earth. This imagery stands parallel with "the princes of the people." Illustratively, there may be a loose analogy to God's sovereignly appointed, human governors (cf. Rom. 13:1–7) as protectors for the masses.

48:1–14 In Psalm 48, it often appears that Zion is the object of praise. While referring to Zion, this hymn of confidence (cf. Pss. 46; 47) contains several checks and balances showing that it is ultimately God, who dwells in Zion, who is to be praised. Therefore, this perspective must be kept in mind as the lines of Psalm 48 flow back and forth with respective emphases on the city and the great God of that city. Therefore, this psalm, sung with orchestral accompaniment, contrasts two different responses to the God of Zion and the Zion of God.

I. Introduction (48:1–3)
II. The Panic Response of the Provokers of God (48:4–7)
  A. The Chronicling of It (48:4–6)
  B. The Cause of It (48:7)
III. The Praise Response of the People of God (48:8–14)

A. Their Celebration (48:8–13)

B. Their Conclusion (48:14)

48:2 *The joy of the whole earth.* Cf. the judgment context of Lamentations 2:15. *the sides of the north.* *North* is an interpretive translation of a word term that occurs as a Semitic place name, i.e., *Zaphon*. In Canaanite mythology, Zaphon was an ancient Near Eastern equivalent to Mt. Olympus, the dwelling place of pagan gods. If this was the psalmist's intention, the reference becomes a polemical description of the Lord; He is not only King of kings, but also God of all so-called gods. *The city of the great King.* Cf. Psalm 47:2; Matthew 5:34, 35. God Himself has always been the King of kings.

48:3 *God is in her palaces.* Better, "God is in her citadels." The context points to the military connotation of this word.

48:4–7 This dramatic, poetic, rapid-fire, historical rehearsal of events chronicles some serious threat to Jerusalem from a hostile coalition of forces. They had come arrogantly to destroy Jerusalem, the Zion of God, but the God of Zion surprisingly and powerfully devastated them.

48:7 *the ships of Tarshish.* A notable Mediterranean port of uncertain location (cf. Jon. 1:3), possibly Spain.

48:8 *As we have heard, so we have seen.* Cf. the personal, individual testimony of Job (e.g., 42:5). The historical tradition of verses 1–3 had been proven true once again in the events of verses 4–7.

48:11 *the daughters of Judah.* This phrase would refer to the surrounding cities and villages.

48:14 *For this is God.* Other options for translating the Hebrew text of this line are: (1) "For this God is our God," or (2) "For this is God, our God."

49:1–20 Psalm 49 deals with the most real thing about life—the certainty of death. One of its major lessons is that "you really

can't take it with you." Containing these kinds of very practical lessons about life and death, it falls neatly into the category of a didactic or wisdom poem. At places, it sounds very much like portions of Job, Proverbs, and Ecclesiastes. It contains warnings to the rich and famous and words of comfort for the poor. These timeless OT messages undergird many NT passages, such as the accounts about the rich fool in Luke 12:13–21 or the rich man and Lazarus in Luke 16. After a fairly lengthy introduction, the body of the psalm falls into two parts as indicated by the climaxing refrain in verses 12, 20. The wisdom poet of Psalm 49 developed his somber theme in two stages, focusing on death as the universal experience of all people.

I. Introduction (49:1–4)

II. Stage One: The Common Experience of Death (49:5–12)

A. Applying His Teaching through an Important Reflection (49:5, 6)

B. Explaining His Teaching through Important Reminders (49:7–12)

III. Stage Two: The Contrasting Experience in Death (49:13–20)

A. The Assurance of This Contrasting Experience in Death (49:13–15)

B. The Application of This Contrasting Experience in Death (49:16–20)

49:1 *all peoples . . . all inhabitants.* The scope of his message is geographically universal.

49:2 *low and high, rich and poor.* Note the chiastic order (i.e., A-B; B-A) of these descriptives. The scope of his message is also socially universal.

49:3, 4 *wisdom . . . understanding . . . proverb . . . dark saying.* All these are wisdom terms (cf. respectively, Prov. 1:20; 9:1; 14:1; 24:7; then, Prov. 2:3; 3:13; 5:1; 14:29; 18:2; 19:8; next, Prov. 1:6; Ezek. 17:2; and finally, Judg. 14:12ff.).

49:5 the iniquity at my heels. This indicates evil chasing the psalmist.

49:6 Those who trust in their wealth. Mankind's propensity to trust in his own material goods is well attested in Scripture (e.g., Ps. 52:7; Jer. 17:5). Biblically, this is exposed as the epitome of stupidity (cf., e.g., Prov. 23:4, 5; Luke 12:16ff.).

49:7–9 None of them can. No person, regardless of his means, is able to escape death; it is inevitable (Heb. 9:27). This passage anticipates the second death of hell for everyone (cf. Rev. 20:11–15), except for those who by faith have repented of their sin and embraced the only adequate ransom—the one paid by the Lord Jesus Christ with His death on the cross (cf. Matt. 20:28; 1 Pet. 1:18, 19).

49:9b–10a not see . . . For he sees. The irony is obvious; the wealthy person somehow hopes to get around death, yet he witnesses people constantly dying all around him, from the wise to the foolish.

49:12 Nevertheless man . . . does not remain. This refrain (cf. v. 20) is the main point of the psalm. Cf. this concept in Ecclesiastes 3:19. While man and beast both die, man's spirit lives on eternally but beasts have no life after death.

49:14 Like sheep they are laid in the grave; Death shall feed on them. They are considered as sheep once noted for their grazing; now, death shall graze on them. *The upright shall have dominion . . . in the morning.* This harbinger of good news to come (cf. v. 15) interrupts this long series of confirmations of the condemnation of the self-reliant.

49:15 But God will redeem my soul . . . He shall receive me. This is one of the greatest affirmations of confidence in God in the Psalms. Although the faithless person cannot buy his way out of death (v. 7ff.), the faithful one is redeemed by the only Redeemer, God Himself. On the significance of the word *re-*

ceive, cf. Genesis 5:24; 2 Kings 2:10; Psalm 73:24; Hebrews 11:5. So in verse 15, the psalmist expresses his confidence in God, that He would raise him to eternal life.

49:17 he shall carry nothing away. An explicit "you-can't-take-it-with-you" attestation (cf. Job 1:21; Eccl. 5:15; 1 Tim. 6:6, 7).

49:20 A man . . . yet does not understand. The refrain is similar to that of verse 12.

50:1–23 God is quoted throughout the psalm. Consequently, its form resembles the prophetic writings which specialized in delivering divine oracles. Its major burden is to delineate the nature of true worship (i.e., "worshiping in spirit and truth," cf. John 4:24). The psalmist skillfully develops this burden in a polemical fashion to expose the externalism and hypocrisy of false worship. The Lord God, the supreme Judge, levels two felony charges against His professing people.

I. Introduction: The Supreme Judge Enters to Preside (50:1–6)

II. The Supreme Judge Levels Two Charges (50:7–21)

   A. First Charge: Ritualism (50:7–15)

   B. Second Charge: Rebellion (50:16–21)

III. The Supreme Judge Offers a Solution (50:22, 23)

50: Title This is the first psalm entitled "a psalm of Asaph" (cf. Pss. 73–83 in Book III of Psalms). For references to "Asaph," cf. 1 Chronicles 6:39; 15:16ff.; 16:5ff.; 25:1ff.; 2 Chronicles 5:12; 29:30; Ezra 2:40; Nehemiah 12:46. Sometimes, the simple "Asaph" may stand for the longer expression "the sons of Asaph." Each occasion needs to be examined to see what the relationship between a given psalm and "Asaph" might be, i.e., composed by, handed down by, sung by this special Levitical choir. Many older commentators feel that Psalm 50 was authored by the original "Asaph."

50:1 The Mighty One, God the Lord. The

divine Judge is introduced with three significant OT names. The first two are the short and longer forms of the most common word for God in the OT, and the third is the name for Israel's God par excellence, i.e., Yahweh (cf. its historical origin in Ex. 3:14). *From the rising of the sun to its going down.* A common OT idiom conveying from east to west, i.e., all over the planet.

50:2, 3 *God will shine forth.* These verses utilize the language of theophany (cf. Ex. 19:16–19).

50:4, 5 *He shall call to the heavens . . . to the earth . . . His people . . . My saints.* God summons the heavens and the earth as personified witnesses to these charges He is about to level about His professing people (e.g., Deut. 32:1ff.; Is. 1:2ff.).

50:5 *a covenant with Me by sacrifice.* Such a ratification of covenant is serious, sacred business (cf. Ex. 24:3–8). This reference to *sacrifice* will set the stage for His first felony charge in v. 7ff.

50:8 *I will not rebuke you for your sacrifices.* The divine Judge's condemnations are directed not at the act of sacrifice, but at the people's attitude in sacrificing (cf. 1 Sam. 15:22; Pss. 40:6–8; 51:17; 69:30; Is. 1:12; Jer. 7:21–26; Hos. 6:6; Mic. 6:6–8).

50:9–13 *will not take a bull from your house.* God refuses mere ritual; it is an abomination to Him. He, unlike the pagan deities, needs nothing; He created everything and owns everything.

50:14 *Offer to God thanksgiving.* Here is the sacrifice that always pleases Him (cf. Ps. 51:17; Heb 13:15).

50:16–20 *the wicked.* Whereas the first charge dealt with a vertical relationship (cf. the first tablet of the Ten Commandments), this one in verse 16ff. focuses on evidences of horizontal violations of covenant (i.e., rebellion against God in the context of man-

to-fellow-man offenses; cf. the second half of the Ten Commandments).

50:21 *I kept silent . . . But I will rebuke you.* God's longsuffering grace must never be looked upon as laxity (cf. 2 Pet. 3:3–10) or abused. His reckoning for rebellion will indeed be manifested.

50:22 *Now consider this.* Before destruction, mercifully comes an opportunity for deliberation and repentance.

50:23 *Whoever offers praise glorifies Me.* Cf. v. 14. This remains the remedy for mere ritualism. The conclusions of verses 22 and 23 come in chiastic order, heightening the total impact of the psalm's two felony charges (i.e., the recounting of *ritualism*, vv. 7–15; the recounting of *rebellion*, vv. 16–21; the remedy of repentance for *rebellion*, v. 22; the remedy of repentance for *ritualism*, v. 23).

51:1–19 This is the classic passage in the OT on man's repentance and God's forgiveness of sin. Along with Psalm 32, it was written by David after his affair with Bathsheba and his murder of Uriah, her husband (2 Sam. 11; 12). It is one of seven poems called penitential psalms (6; 32; 38; 51; 102; 130; 143). To David's credit, he recognized how horrendous his sin against God was, blamed no one but himself, and begged for divine forgiveness.

  I. Plea for Forgiveness (51:1, 2)
 II. Proffer of Confession (51:3–6)
III. Prayer for Moral Cleanness (51:7–12)
IV. Promise of Renewed Service (51:13–17)
 V. Petition for National Restoration
    (51:18, 19)

51:1 *lovingkindness.* Even though he had sinned horribly, David knew that forgiveness was available, based on God's covenant love.

51:4 *Against You, You only.* David realized what every believer seeking forgiveness must know, that even though he had wronged

Bathsheba and Uriah, his ultimate crime was against God and His holy law (cf. 2 Sam. 11:27). Romans 3:4 quotes Psalm 51:4.

51:5 brought forth in iniquity. David also acknowledged that his sin was not God's fault in any way (vv. 4b, 6), nor was it some aberration. Rather, the source of David's sin was a fallen, sinful disposition, i.e., his since conception.

51:7 hyssop. Old Testament priests used hyssop, a leafy plant, to sprinkle blood or water on a person being ceremonially cleansed from defilements such as leprosy or touching a dead body (cf. Lev. 14:6ff.; Num. 19:16–19). Here, hyssop is a figure for David's longing to be spiritually cleansed from his moral defilement. In forgiveness, God washes away sin (cf. Ps. 103:12; Is. 1:16; Mic. 7:19).

51:8 bones. A figure of speech for the framework of the entire person. David was experiencing personal collapse under guilt (cf. Ps. 32:3, 4).

51:11 Your Holy Spirit from me. This is a reference to the special Holy Spirit anointing on theocratic mediators, not NT indwelling.

51:12 generous Spirit. The Holy Spirit is generous, willing, and eager to uphold the believer.

51:16 You do not desire sacrifice. Ritual without genuine repentance is useless. However, with a right heart attitude, sacrifices were acceptable (see v. 19).

52:1–9 This psalm is a poetic lesson about the futility of evil, the final triumph of righteousness, and the sovereign control of God over the moral events of history. The event in David's life which motivated him to write this psalm is recorded in 1 Samuel 21; 22.

I. The Rashness of the Wicked (52:1–5)
II. The Reaction of the Righteous (52:6, 7)
III. The Rejoicing of the Godly (52:8, 9)

52:1 mighty man. A reference to Doeg, the chief of Saul's shepherds, who reported

to Saul that the priests of Nob had aided David when he was a fugitive (cf. 1 Sam. 22:9, 18, 19).

52:5 God shall likewise destroy. Ultimately, the wicked are in the hands of a holy God (cf. Heb. 9:27).

52:6 see and fear. God's punishment of the wicked serves as a reinforcement to the righteous to obey God. **shall laugh at him.** In the end, the wicked become a laughingstock in a universe controlled by God.

52:8 green olive tree. The psalmist exults (through this simile) that the person who trusts in the mercy of God is productive and secure.

53:1–6 This psalm is nearly identical to Psalm 14 (Ps. 53:1–5a is from Ps. 14:1–5a; Ps. 53:6 is from Ps. 14:7). The major difference is verse 5, in which the psalmist celebrates a military victory over an enemy. Apparently, Psalm 14 is here rephrased to apply to a specified war event, earning it a distinct place in the canon.

I. The Description of Those Who Reject God and His People (53:1–4)
II. The Danger to Those Who Reject God and His People (53:5)
III. The Deliverance of His People (53:6)

53: Title Mahalath. The name of a tune or an instrument.

53:1–4 See notes on Psalm 14. Romans 3:10–12 quotes Psalm 53:1–3.

53:2 God. The reference to "God" rather than "LORD" is another difference between Psalm 14 and 53. "Elohim" is used three times in Psalm 14, but seven times in Psalm 53.

53:5 in great fear. The verse describes a sudden reversal in the fortunes of war. The haughty enemy besieging Israel was suddenly terrified and utterly defeated. Historical examples of such unexpected terrors to Israel's enemy are recorded in 2 Chronicles 20 and Isaiah 37. **scattered the bones.** Perhaps nothing was more disgraceful to a nation at war than to have the bones of its dead army scattered over the land rather than buried.

54:1–7 This psalm apparently comes from the same period of David's life as does Psalm 52. Even though David had recently rescued an Israelite border town from the Philistines, he was still considered a traitor to Saul (1 Sam. 23; 26). In the wake of this emotional devastation, David prayed to God for vindication. The psalm provides encouragement to any believer who has been maligned.

I. The Prayer for Deliverance (54:1–3)
II. The Anticipation of Deliverance (54:4, 5)
III. The Thanksgiving for Deliverance (54:6, 7)

54:1 *by Your name.* In the ancient world,

a person's name was essentially the person himself. Here, God's name includes His covenant protection. *vindicate.* David requests that God will execute justice for him, as in a court trial when a defendant is declared not guilty.

54:2 *Give ear.* An anthropomorphism meaning "listen," "pay attention."

54:3 *strangers.* Either non-Israelites or Israelites who had broken the covenant with God might be called strangers. Since in this case Saul and the Ziphites are the oppressors, the strangers are apostate Israelites (cf. 1 Sam. 23:19; 26:1).

54:5 *in Your truth.* Since God is omniscient, He can execute perfect justice against the wicked.

Anointing of the Holy Spirit in the Old Testament

Old Testament Israel had mediators who stood between God and His people. To empower the OT mediators, the Holy Spirit gave special administrative ability to carry out the management of the nation and military skills which enabled them to defeat the theocracy's enemies. The Lord first anointed Moses with this ministry of the Spirit and then, in a truly dramatic scene, took some of this ministry of the Spirit and shared it with the seventy elders. Thus they were enabled to help Moses administer Israel (Num. 11:17–25).

Also, Joshua (Deut. 34:9), the judges (Judg. 3:10; 6:34), and the kings of united Israel and the southern kingdom were anointed with this special ministry of the Spirit. When the Spirit of the Lord came upon King Saul, for example, he was in effect given "another heart" (1 Sam. 10:6–10). This does not mean that he was regenerated at this point in his life, but that he was given skills to be a king. Later, the theocratic anointing was taken from Saul and given to David (1 Sam. 16:1–14). Saul, from that time on, became a totally incapable leader.

King David, no doubt, had this special ministry of the Spirit in mind with his prayer of repentance in Psalm 51. He was not afraid of losing his salvation when he prayed, "do not take your Holy Spirit from me" (Ps. 51:11), but rather was concerned that God would remove this spiritual wisdom and administrative skill from him. David had earlier seen such a tragedy in the life of Saul when that king of Israel lost the anointing of the Holy Spirit. David was, thus, pleading with God not to remove His hand of guidance.

King Solomon also perceived his youthful inabilities at the beginning of his reign and requested God to give him special wisdom in administering Israel. God was pleased with this request and granted an extra measure of wisdom to the young man (1 Kin. 3:7–12, 28; 4:29–34). Although the OT is silent in this regard about the kings who succeeded Solomon, the theocratic anointing of the Spirit likely came on all of the descendants of David in connection with the Davidic covenant.

When the theocracy went out of existence as Judah was carried away into captivity, and the last Davidic king was disempowered, the theocratic anointing was no longer given (Ezek. 8–11). The kings of the northern tribes, on the other hand, being essentially apostate and not in the Davidic line, never had the benefit of this special ministry of the Spirit.

54:7 *seen its desire.* David anticipates with confidence that which he has seen in the past—the defeat of his enemies.

55:1–23 In this individual lament, David pours out his heart to his Lord because a former close friend has betrayed him (vv. 12–14). There is a strong possibility that this psalm was occasioned by the betrayal of Absalom and/or Ahithophel (cf. 2 Sam. 15–18). Most of the psalm alternates between prayers for his enemy's ruin (vv. 9, 15, 19, 23) and praises for God's blessings (vv. 16, 18, 22). The high point of the psalm for Christians who have been "stabbed in the back" by a confidant is verse 22. Though despairing, David expresses ultimate confidence in God.

I. The Prayer of Distress (55:1–8)
II. The Prayer for Justice (55:9–15)
III. The Prayer of Assurance (55:16–23)

55:3 *bring down trouble.* The verb pictures something being tipped over, crashing down on the victim.

55:6 *wings like a dove.* David expresses his escapist feelings.

55:9 *divide their tongues.* Perhaps this is an allusion to the Tower of Babel, where God destroyed the movement against Him by multiplying languages (cf. Gen. 11:5–9).

55:15 *go down alive into hell.* Since God had done this once with the enemies of Moses (Num. 16:30), David asks Him to perform the same judgment on his enemies.

55:19 *they do not change.* David's enemies were too set in their ways and too secure to pay any attention to God.

55:20 *broken his covenant.* This enemy had broken a treaty in his treachery, even against his allies.

55:21 *war was in his heart.* Though the traitor talked peace, his intention was war.

55:22 *Cast your burden on the Lord.* The word for *burden* implies one's circumstances, one's lot. The psalmist promises that

the Lord will uphold the believer in the struggles of life.

55:23 *the pit of destruction.* Compare the unusual death of Absalom (2 Sam. 18:9–15) and the suicide of Ahithophel (2 Sam. 17:23).

56:1–13 This psalm, apparently written when David had been endangered by the Philistines (1 Sam. 21:10–15), expresses the kind of confidence in the Lord that believers should exude when they find themselves in terrifying circumstances. David's natural reaction was to panic (vv. 3, 4, 11). But he demonstrates in this psalm that the believer can replace potential terror with the composure of trust.

I. Fear and Faith (56:1–4)
II. Destroyer and Deliverer (56:5–9)
III. Trust and Thanksgiving (56:10–13)

56: Title The Silent Dove in Distant Lands. This is possibly a tune name which links Psalm 56 with Psalm 55 (cf. Ps. 55:6ff.). *See note on Psalm 16: Title.*

56:3 *I will trust in You.* Confidence in the Lord is a purposeful decision, replacing an emotional reaction to one's circumstances.

56:5 *All day.* Anguish is intensified by unceasing harassment.

56:7 *In anger.* The anger of God is not an emotional loss of temper, but a judicial outrage resulting from God's holy nature reacting to wickedness and ungodliness.

56:8 *Your bottle . . . Your book.* Figuratively speaking, David asked God to keep a remembrance of all of his sufferings, so that God could eventually vindicate him.

56:11 *What can man do to me?* No human has the power to overcome God's providential control.

56:12 *Vows.* Confident that the Lord would deliver him, David had already vowed to present a thank offering to God (cf. Lev. 7:12; Ps. 50:14).

57:1–11 This is another lament expressing supreme confidence in the Lord in the midst of calamitous circumstances. Though David finds himself hiding from Saul (see Title), he knows that his real refuge is not in the walls of the cave (cf. 1 Sam. 22:1; 24:3), but in the shadow of God's wings.

I. The Plea for Protection (57:1–6)

II. The Proffering of Praise (57:7–11)

57: Title Do Not Destroy. These are possibly the opening words of a known song, implying that this psalm should be sung to the same tune. *See note on Psalm 16:Title.*

57:1 the shadow of Your wings. Metaphorically, God cares for His own as a mother bird protects its young. Symbolically, there may be a reference here to the cherubim wings on the ark of the covenant where God was specifically present (cf. Ex. 37:1–16; Pss. 17:8; 36:7; 61:4; 63:7; 91:1, 4). **I will make my refuge.** When life becomes bizarre, only a person's relationship with his God calms the soul.

57:2 God Most High. God is transcendent, elevated far above His creation and all powerful. **performs all things for me.** God's transcendence (v. 2a) never removes Him from intimate involvement in His peoples' lives.

57:4 lions. The wicked are pictured as menacing animals, ready to destroy their prey with their razor-edged teeth (cf. Pss. 7:2; 10:9; 17:12; 22:13). **set on fire.** The wicked are like a consuming fire.

57:5 Be exalted, O God. A truly godly person wants God's glory to be exhibited more than he wants his own personal problems to be solved.

57:6 a net . . . a pit. This pictures setting a trap, as a hunter might entangle an animal's feet with a net.

57:7–11 These verses were borrowed by David for Psalm 108:1–5.

57:8 my glory! This refers to the mind, that rational, intellectual, emotional part of a person which interacts with and praises

God. *See note on 16:9.* **I will awaken the dawn.** The psalmist cannot wait until morning to praise the Lord for all of His blessings. He must wake up the dawn (personified) so that he can praise the Lord.

57:9 the peoples . . . nations. These are references to Gentiles, nations which would not normally know Jehovah God.

57:10 unto the heavens. David is thinking as broadly (v. 9) and as highly (vv. 10, 11) as he can. God's mercy, truth, and glory are immense and unfathomable (cf. Rom. 11:33; Eph. 3:17, 18).

58:1–11 As a lament against tyranny, the first half of the psalm rehearses a series of charges against wicked leaders and judges; the second half is an imprecatory prayer that they be obliterated. In the end, the psalmist is certain that God will act with ultimate justice.

I. The Indictment of Unjust Leaders (58:1–5)

II. The Imprecation Against Unjust Leaders (58:6–11)

58: Title Do Not Destroy. *See note on Psalm 57: Title. See note on Psalm 16: Title.*

58:1 silent ones. The leaders were silent when they should have spoken up for righteousness.

58:2 weigh out. These wicked rulers meditate on the strategy for wicked schemes.

58:3 as soon as they are born. All people are born totally depraved. Without being made new creatures in Christ by God's power, they are prevented by their wicked nature from pleasing God (cf. Ps. 51:5; Rom. 3:9–18; 2 Cor. 5:17).

58:4 Their poison. The words and actions of these tyrants are like poisonous venom in a serpent's fangs. **deaf cobra.** Like a cobra which cannot hear its charmer are these stubborn rulers, who ignore all encouragements to righteousness.

58:6 Break their teeth . . . fangs. The

psalmist prays that the means of doing evil would be destroyed.

58:7 flow away as waters. An imprecatory prayer that the tyrants would disappear like water seeping into sand in a dry wadi. **arrows . . . cut in pieces.** Apparently, this is a prayer that the intentions of evil would be rendered as ineffective as broken arrows.

58:8 snail which melts away. A simile for that which is transitive, perhaps facetiously based on the idea that a snail depletes itself in its own trail as it moves along.

58:9 Before your pots . . . thorns. An obscure metaphor implying swiftness. The Lord will quickly destroy the wicked rulers.

58:10 wash his feet in the blood. The point of the figure is that the wicked will eventually be defeated and the righteous will share with the Lord in His victory.

58:11 God who judges in the earth. In the end, the righteous will see that Jehovah is not indifferent to injustices.

59:1–17 This is another in a series of laments in which the psalmist pleads for God to defend him against his oppressors. The psalm is a mixture of prayers, unfavorable descriptions of the adversary, imprecations, and praise to God. Though written when David was king of Israel, the psalm recalls an earlier time of anguish when Saul sought to kill David (1 Sam. 19:11). Ultimately, David's strong confidence in God's sovereignty transforms the lament into a song of assurance.

I. A Plea for God's Deliverance (59:1–15)

II. Praise for God's Defense (59:16, 17)

59: Title Do Not Destroy. See note on Psalm 57: Title. **Michtam.** See note on Psalm 16: Title. **Saul sent men . . . to kill him.** The setting for the psalm is 1 Samuel 19:11. David's wife (Saul's daughter) helped David escape through a window in the middle of the night.

59:5 God of hosts. Hosts represent God's angels as His army.

59:6 growl like a dog. Dogs of the ancient world were often wild scavengers. Here, they serve as a simile for Saul's messengers setting an ambush outside of David's house.

59:7 belch with their mouth. This pictures the coarse, uncouth character of Saul's henchmen (cf. v. 12). **swords are in their lips.** Their conversation was dedicated to the assassination of David. **they say, "Who hears?"** A blasphemy implying that God either doesn't exist or doesn't know what happens in the affairs of mankind.

59:8 all the nations. Referring to Gentiles (see note on Ps. 57:9), this phrase and "my people" in verse 11 imply that this psalm was written several years after the event when David was king and involved in international affairs. David wrote his psalms as a prophet under the superintendence of the Holy Spirit (2 Sam. 23:2).

59:11 lest my people forget. The psalmist thinks that if the Lord were to destroy the wicked too quickly, the lesson of God's hatred of evil might not be impressed on the minds of the people.

60:1–12 This psalm is a national lament written after the unexpected military setback alluded to in 2 Samuel 8:13 and 1 Chronicles 18:12. While David and the main part of his army were fighting in the northern part of the country, one of Israel's other neighboring enemies, Edom, successfully attacked the southern part of Judah. David ultimately prevailed in victory. The psalm expresses the feelings of a people shocked and confused by a tragedy which suggested that God had abandoned them. Verses 5–12 are essentially repeated in Psalm 108:6–13.

I. The People's Contemplation of Abandonment (60:1–5)

II. The Lord's Control over the Nations (60:6–8)

III. The People's Confidence in God (60:9–12)

60: Title Joab . . . killed twelve thousand. The Lord soon rewarded their confidence in Him, enabling the armies of Israel to slaughter the Edomites.

60:2 earth tremble. Earthquake imagery is used to illustrate that what appears secure sometimes is not.

60:3 wine of confusion. This metaphor compares the impact of wine on the mind with the confusion which comes from a bewildering event in life.

60:4 banner. God and His truth serve as a rallying point for the perplexed people.

60:5 beloved. This is probably a reference to David. There may be a play on words here in that the Hebrew root for *David* and *beloved* is the same.

60:6 Shechem . . . Succoth. These are two territories on opposite sides of the Jordan River, both occupied by Israel. Jacob had settled in Succoth (east of the Jordan) when he returned from his sojourn with Laban (cf. Gen. 33:17).

60:7 Gilead . . . Judah. All of these key geographical locations in Israel ultimately belonged to God, who was more interested in their welfare than anyone else. **helmet.** Ephraim was the primary source of defense to the north of Israel. **lawgiver.** Judah was the tribe that was to govern Israel—the tribe from which David and his descendants came.

60:8 Moab . . . Edom . . . Philistia. These are the three principal enemies surrounding Israel to the northeast, southeast, and west, respectively. **Moab is My washpot.** The psalmist pictures Moab as a humble, menial servant to God, either being or bringing a washbasin for His use. **Over Edom . . . shoe.** The picture is that of a man entering his house and throwing his shoes to his servant. Edom, like Moab, was a servant under God's sovereign control. **Philistia, shout in triumph.** Here is a victorious battle shout from the pagans, who must realize God's power is behind Israel's victory.

60:12 Through God . . . valiantly. The nation relearned the truth that only God gives victory.

61:1–8 David may have written this wonderful psalm when his own son, Absalom, temporarily drove him away from his throne in Israel (2 Sam. 15–18). The psalm is rich in metaphors and references to God's covenants with Israel. David once again demonstrates a godly response to overwhelming and depressing developments in life.

I. The Cry for Help (61:1, 2)
II. The Confidence in God (61:3–7)
III. The Commitment to Loyalty (61:8)

61:2 From the end of the earth. David's absence from his homeland compounds his feelings of discouragement and exhaustion. The phrase also hints at feelings of estrangement from God. **my heart is overwhelmed.** David's hope and courage were failing. **the rock that is higher.** David expresses his disregard of personal autonomy and his reliance on his God in this metaphor for refuge.

61:3 strong tower. One of four figures of speech in verses 3 and 4 for security; the strong towers stabilized the city walls and served as places of defense and refuge.

61:5 heritage. This refers to the benefits, including life in the Promised Land (cf. Deut. 28–30), of participating in a covenant with God.

61:6 prolong the king's life. In the immediate context, David prays for himself in his struggle with Absalom. Beyond this, here is a prayer for the continuity of the divinely established monarchy. Because he realized that one of his descendants would be the Messiah, David sometimes does not distinguish himself from the messianic dynasty.

61:7 forever. The Davidic covenant guaranteed that, on the basis of God's merciful and faithful dealings with David and the nation, David's descendants would rule on the throne of Israel forever (cf. 2 Sam. 7; Pss. 40:11; 89:4, 33–37).

61:8 *daily perform my vows.* As a regular means of expressing thanksgiving for prayers answered, the psalmist promised daily obedience to his Lord (cf. Ps. 56:12).

62:1–12 Whether Absalom's rebellion is the setting or not (2 Sam. 15–18), David writes this psalm while facing treason from someone. David embraces the problem of his adversaries forthrightly (vv. 3, 4), but his thoughts focus primarily on God (cf. Phil. 4:4–13).

I. Affirming God's Covenant Relationship (62:1, 2, 5, 6)
II. Confronting One's Treasonous Adversaries (62:3, 4)
III. Trusting God's Sovereignty (62:7–10)
IV. Praising God's Power and Mercy (62:11, 12)

62: *Title To Jeduthun.* An official temple musician. *See note on Psalm 39:Title.*

62:1 *silently waits for God.* Silence indicates trust that is both patient and uncomplaining (cf. v. 5).

62:2 *greatly moved.* This means "shaken," or "demoralized."

62:3 *leaning wall and a tottering fence.* A metaphor for imminent collapse. Some apply it to the victim, but as translated here, it refers to the attacker.

62:6 *I shall not be moved.* David demonstrates his increased confidence in the Lord. At first, he would not be "greatly moved" (v. 2). Here, on second thought, he would not be moved at all.

62:9 *low degree . . . high degree.* All men, regardless of social status, are woefully inadequate objects of trust.

63:1–11 In deepest words of devotion, this psalm expresses David's intense love for his Lord. The psalm was written while David was in the Judean wilderness, either during his flight from Saul (1 Sam. 23) or, more likely, from Absalom (2 Sam. 15; cf. 63:11 "the king"). David writes from the perspective of these grammatical tenses:

I. Present—Seeking God's Presence (63:1–5)
II. Past—Remembering God's Power (63:6–8)
III. Future—Anticipating God's Judgment (63:9–11)

63:1 *Early will I seek You.* Eagerness to be with the Lord in every situation is more in view than the time of day. *My soul thirsts.* David longs for God's presence like a wanderer in a desert longs for water. *in a dry and thirsty land.* David writes this psalm while hiding in the wilderness of Judea, but longing to be back worshiping in Jerusalem.

63:3 *better than life.* God's covenant love is more valuable to David than life itself (cf. Phil. 1:21; Acts 20:24).

63:4 *lift up my hands.* As an OT posture of prayer, the upheld hands pictured both the ascent of prayer and the readiness to receive every good gift which comes from God (cf. James 1:17). It was, thus, a posture of trust in God alone.

63:5 *marrow and fatness.* A metaphor comparing the spiritual and emotional satisfaction of the divine presence with the satisfaction of rich banquet food.

63:8 *My soul follows close behind You.* In response to God's repeated invitation to "hold fast" to Him (Deut. 4:4; 10:20; 13:4), the psalmist clings to God. This signifies David's unfailing commitment to his Lord.

63:9 *into the lower parts of the earth.* A reference to the realm of the dead. *See note on Ephesians 4:9.*

63:10 *jackals.* Scavengers, feasting on unburied bodies (*see note on Ps. 53:5*).

63:11 *who swears by Him.* The Mosaic covenant instructed this practice expressing loyalty to the true God alone (cf. Deut. 6:13; 10:20; 1 Kin. 8:31; Jer. 12:16).

64:1–10 This psalm begins with a vivid description of the devious ways of the wicked, especially their speech (vv. 3–5, 8). Still, the psalmist does not fear that God will lose control of the situation. After seeing His justice at work, the righteous will be glad and trust all the more in Him (64:10).

I. The Malevolent Ingenuity of the Wicked (64:1–6)
II. The Memorable Reciprocity by the Lord (64:7–10)

64:1 *Preserve . . . from fear.* This word for *fear* means "dread," and is a different Hebrew word than the fear in verses 4 and 9. The psalmist recognized that the fear of an enemy can be as destructive as an actual assault.

64:3 *sharpen their tongue.* Their intent was to slander with their speech (cf. Ps. 59:7).

64:4 *in secret.* I.e., anonymously.

64:5 *Who will see them?* This was a question of brazen autonomy. They mocked the omniscience of God (cf. Ps. 59:7).

64:6 *inward thought . . . heart . . . deep.* The evil intent of the unrighteous flows from inward depravity.

64:7 *God shall shoot . . . arrow.* The arrows of God, as OT history demonstrates, include natural judgments such as deadly disease, defeat, and calamity.

64:8 *stumble . . . own tongue.* God providentially steers the plots of the wicked to their own demise.

64:9 *shall declare.* Believers should glorify God, not only for His love and mercy, but also for His marvelous acts of judgment on the wicked.

65:1–13 This is a praise psalm, full of hopeful, confident, even enthusiastic feelings in response to God's goodness with no complaints or curses. The setting is a celebration

at the tabernacle, perhaps at the Feast of Unleavened Bread in the spring, or the Feast of Tabernacles in the fall.

I. Praise for Spiritual Blessings (65:1–5)
II. Praise for Natural Blessings (65:6–13)

65:1 *Zion.* Specifically the hill in Jerusalem where Israel worshiped Jehovah, but also synonymous with the Promised Land (cf. Ps. 48:2; also Pss. 3:4; 9:12; 24:3; 68:5; 87:2, 5). *vow . . . performed.* This is likely a reference to vows made by the farmers because of an abundant harvest (cf. Pss. 56:12; 61:8).

65:2 *all flesh will come.* This is referring to the future millennial kingdom when all the world will worship the Lord (cf. Zech. 14:16–19).

65:3 *atonement.* This word, found three times in the Psalms (78:38; 79:9), means to cover sin and its effects. In the OT, atonement was symbolized in sacrificial ritual (cf. Ex. 30:10; Lev. 16:10, 11), though actual forgiveness of sin was ultimately based on the death of Christ applied to the penitent sinner (cf. Heb. 9).

65:5 *confidence . . . earth . . . seas.* Unlike local heathen gods, Jehovah God is not just the God of a single locality. The universal worship of the Lord is required of all people (cf. Rom. 1:18–32) and will be a reality in the messianic era when the kingdom of God will cover the earth (cf. Is. 2:1–4; Zech. 14:9).

65:8 *outgoings . . . morning . . . evening.* This has reference to the nations who live in the east where the sun first makes its morning appearance. Those who live in the west where the sun disappears into darkness rejoice in the Lord.

65:11 *paths drip with abundance.* This pictures a farm wagon dropping its overflow along the path.

66:1–20 This joyful psalm begins with group praise and then focuses on individual worship. The psalmist rehearses some of the major miracles in Israel's history and testifies that God has always been faithful in the midst of serious troubles.

I. Communal Hymn of Praise to God (66:1–12)
  A. For Future Glory (66:1–4)
  B. For Previous Faithfulness (66:5–7)
  C. For Continual Protection (66:8–12)
II. An Individual Hymn of Praise to God (66:13–20)
  A. Through Fulfilled Vows (66:13–15)
  B. For Answered Prayer (66:16–20)

66:1 *joyful shout.* A shout of loyalty and homage, as in 1 Samuel 10:24.

66:4 *All the earth shall worship You.* This praise is not only an acknowledgment of God's universal lordship, but also an intimation of the people's belief in a future, worldwide kingdom where God will be worshiped (cf. Is. 66:23; Zech. 14:16; Phil. 2:10, 11).

66:6 *sea . . . river.* A reference to the crossing of the Red Sea and, possibly, the Jordan River. The OT writers considered the Red Sea crossing the ultimate demonstration of God's power, as well as His care for Israel.

66:9 *feet to be moved.* God had prevented them from prematurely slipping into the realm of the dead.

66:10 *refined us as silver.* God had brought the nation through purifying trials.

66:11 *brought us into the net.* The psalmist speaks of a hunter's net or snare as a metaphor for some extremely difficult situations into which God had brought Israel.

66:12 *ride over our heads.* A picture of a hostile army riding in victory over Israel's defeated troops.

66:13 *pay You my vows.* Paying the vows is spelled out in the following verses as offering sacrifices of dedication which had been previously promised God (cf. Lev. 1; 22:18, 21; Pss. 56:12; 61:8; 65:1).

67:1–7 This brief psalm develops two optimistic themes: the need and result of God's mercy, and the future, universal worship of

God. The psalm reflects the promise to Abraham that God would bless his descendants, and in Abraham, "all the families of the earth" (Gen. 12:1–3).

I. The Prayer for Divine Mercy (67:1, 2)
II. The Plea for Universal Worship (67:3–5)
III. The Prospect of Divine Blessings (67:6, 7)

67:1 *face to shine.* When a king smiled on a supplicant with pleasure, the petitioner was likely to receive his request (cf. Num. 6:24–26; Pss. 31:16; 44:3; 80:3, 7, 19; 119:135; Prov. 16:15).

67:3–7 *peoples . . . nations . . . ends of the earth.* These are references to the inclusion of the Gentile nations in the millennial kingdom (cf. Is. 56:3–8; 60:1–14; Zech. 14:16–19; Matt. 8:11; 25:31–46; Rev. 20:1–10).

68:1–35 This exuberant psalm includes prayer, praise, thanksgiving, historical reminder, and imprecation. It expresses a pride in Jehovah God for His care over His people and His majesty in the universe. The writing of this psalm may have come out of David's jubilant restoration of the ark of the covenant to Jerusalem (cf. 2 Sam. 6:12–15).

I. A Fanfare of Commendation (68:1–6)
II. A Reflection on Faithfulness (68:7–18)
III. An Acclamation of Majesty (68:19–31)
IV. An Invitation to Praise (68:32–35)

68:1 *Let God arise.* The first sentence in this psalm is essentially the same as Numbers 10:35. It was perhaps a fanfare of words announcing the movement of the ark of the covenant (cf. vv. 24–27; also 2 Sam. 6:12–15).

68:4 *His name YAH.* A shortened form of Yahweh, this word is often translated LORD (cf. v. 16; Ex. 3:15). Other names for God in this psalm include God (Elohim, v. 1), Lord (Adonai, v. 11), Almighty (v. 14), LORD God (v. 18), God the Lord (v. 20), and King (v. 24).

68:6 *solitary in families.* God cares for those who have lost families, especially the orphans and widows (v. 5; cf. Ex. 22:22–24; Ps. 10:14; James 1:27). **brings out . . . bound.** This speaks of God's liberating prisoners of war.

68:9 confirmed Your inheritance. God sustains His covenant people.

68:14 snow in Zalmon. *Zalmon* means "black" or "dark mountain." The *snow* pictures the contrast of corpses or bones scattered over the mountain.

68:15 mountain of Bashan. A mountain located across the Jordan River to the east, figuratively described as jealous of Mt. Zion (cf. v. 16), the place which had been chosen for the special presence of God (cf. Jer. 22:20, 21).

68:17 Sinai, in the Holy Place. God's presence had been with the armies in the same way it had been on Mt. Sinai at the giving of the law (cf. Ex. 19).

68:18 ascended on high. Paul quotes this text in Ephesians 4:8 where he applies it to Christ's ascending to the heavens in trumph.

68:22 Bashan . . . sea. Whether the enemy tries to escape by land (Bashan) or by sea, God will bring them back to be destroyed by His people (cf. Amos 9:2–4).

68:24 procession . . . sanctuary. A description of the celebration when the ark of the covenant, a symbol of God's presence, was brought to Mt. Zion (cf. 1 Chr. 15:16–28).

68:27 Benjamin . . . Naphtali. Representative tribes of Israel, two from the south (Benjamin and Judah) and two from the north (Zebulun and Naphtali).

68:29 Kings . . . presents. This section of praise (vv. 28–35) looks forward to the Messiah's reign when the world will universally worship God in the temple in Jerusalem (cf. Is. 2:2–4; 18:7; 45:14; 60:3–7; Ezek. 40–48; Hag. 2:7; Zech. 2:11–13; 6:15; 8:21, 22; 14:16–19).

68:30 pieces of silver. Tribute money, signifying subservience to God.

69:1–36 This psalm is a prayer of desperation. David realizes that because he is hated by others, he may be killed. Though he begs for rescue and calls down curses on his enemies, he concludes the psalm with a high note of praise, with inferences concerning the coming messianic kingdom when all enemies of God's people are dealt with swiftly and severely (cf. Rev. 2:27). Much of this psalm was applied to Christ by the NT writers. This psalm expresses the feelings of any believer who is being horribly ridiculed, but it uniquely refers to Christ.

I. The Prayer of Desperation (69:1–28)
   A. The Description of His Situation (69:1–3)
   B. The Reason for His Situation (69:4–12)
   C. The Hope for His Situation (69:13–18)
   D. The Reproach of His Situation (69:19–21)
   E. The Revenge for His Situation (69:22–28)
II. The Promise of Salvation (69:29–36)

69: Title The Lilies. The name of a tune. *See note on Psalm 45: Title.*

69:4 hate me. Quoted in John 15:25.

69:6 be ashamed. The psalmist fears that his dismal situation may be a stumbling block to other believers.

69:8 alien . . . children. Even the psalmist's family rejected him (cf. Matt. 12:46–50; John 7:3–5).

69:9 has eaten me up. The psalmist has brought hatred and hostility on himself by his unyielding insistence that the behavior of the people measure up to their outward claim of devotion to God. Whenever God was dishonored, he felt the pain because he loved God so greatly. Jesus claimed for Himself this attitude, as indicated in John 2:17; Romans 15:3.

69:11 *sackcloth.* David's wearing of sackcloth, a symbol of grief, brought even more ridicule.

69:12 *sit in the gate.* The highest in society, those who sat in the gate of a city, were usually governmental officials. Even there, city leaders were gossiping about the psalmist. *song of the drunkards.* The dregs of society, the drunkards, ridiculed David in their raucous songs.

69:15 *pit shut its mouth.* The *pit* was another word for Sheol, the realm of the dead. The psalmist felt that death was imminent.

69:21 *gall ... vinegar.* Gall was a poisonous herb. Here, it serves as a metaphor for betrayal. Friends who should provide sustenance to the psalmist had turned against him. Gall in vinegar was actually offered to Christ while He was on the cross (Matt. 27:34).

69:22 *table become a snare.* A snare was a trap for birds. The psalmist prays that the plots of the wicked against him would backfire and destroy them instead.

69:22, 23 Quoted in Romans 11:9, 10.

69:25 Quoted in Acts 1:20 with reference to Judas.

69:26 *the ones You have struck.* Those hostile to the psalmist were ridiculing him as one suffering from God's chastisement. In its messianic application, the suffering of the Messiah was a part of God's plan from eternity past (cf. Is. 53:10).

69:31 *better than an ox or bull.* See Psalm 51:16; also Hebrews 9:11, 12; 10:9–12. *horns and hooves.* Implies a grown animal, one that would be especially valuable.

70:1–5 This prayer for deliverance from one's enemies is nearly identical to Psalm 40:13–17. It substitutes "God" for "Lord" in verses 1, 4, and 5. The historical situation to which David refers is unknown.

Deliverance through God (70:1)
Defeat by God (70:2, 3)
Delight in God (70:4)
Dependence on God (70:5)

71:1–24 One of the features of the psalms is that they engage the circumstances of life. This psalm to God expresses the concerns of old age. At a time in his life when he thinks he should be exempt from certain kinds of troubles, he once again is personally attacked. Though his enemies conclude that God has abandoned him, the psalmist is confident that God will remain faithful.

I. Confidence in God Stated (71:1–8)
II. Confidence in God Practiced in Prayer (71:9–13)
III. Confidence in God Vindicated (71:14–24)

71:3 *continually.* Psalm 71:1–3 is almost the same as Psalm 31:1–3a. One difference, however, is the word *continually,* which the elderly person writing this psalm wants to emphasize. God has *continually* been faithful (cf. vv. 6, 14).

71:7 *a wonder.* A reference to his trials. People are amazed at this person's life, some interpreting his trials as God's care, and others as God's punishment.

71:15 *their limits.* The blessings of God's salvation and righteousness are innumerable.

71:20 *from the depths of the earth.* This does not refer to actual resurrection, but rescue from near-death conditions and renewal of life's strength and meaning.

72:1–20 This is a coronation Psalm, dedicated to the prosperity of Solomon at the beginning of his reign (1 Kin. 2). No NT writer applies any of the psalm to Christ. Still, since the Davidic kings and the Messiah's rule occasionally merge into each other in the OT literature, the messianic inferences here ought not to be missed (vv. 7, 17; cf. Is. 11:1–5; 60–62). This psalm describes a reign when God, the king, nature, all classes of society, and foreign nations will live together in harmony.

I. A Just Reign (72:1–4)
II. A Universal Reign (72:5–11)
III. A Compassionate Reign (72:12–14)
IV. A Prosperous Reign (72:15–17)
V. A Glorious Reign (72:18–20)

72:1 *Your judgments.* A prayer that the king would faithfully mediate God's justice on the nation (cf. Deut. 17:18–20). ***the king's Son.*** A reference primarily to Solomon, emphasizing his bond with the Davidic dynasty; but, it also anticipates Messiah's reign as the culmination of the Davidic covenant (cf. 2 Sam. 7:12, 13; Ps. 2:1–12).

72:3 *mountains . . . peace.* When the king rules with justice and compassion, the earth radiates well-being.

72:7 *Until the moon is no more.* This is primarily referring to the length of the Davidic dynasty and, possibly, also to the mes-

sianic reign (2 Sam. 7:16; Ps. 89:3, 4, 29, 36, 37; Luke 1:30–33). Jeremiah also makes the same kind of observation (cf. Jer. 33:23–26).

72:8 *the River.* Israel's boundaries were to extend to the River Euphrates (cf. Ex. 23:31; 1 Kin. 4:21; Ps. 89:25).

72:10 *Tarshish . . . Seba.* These are countries, near and far, which brought tribute to Solomon (cf. 1 Kin. 4:21; 10:1, 23, 24; Is. 60:4–7; Jer. 6:20). Tarshish is probably in Spain; Sheba, a kingdom in southern Arabia (modern Yemen); and Seba, a North African nation.

72:20 *are ended.* Asaph's psalms immediately follow after this (Pss. 73–83), though David did author some of the psalms included later in the collection (e.g., Pss. 86, 101, 103). This closes Book II (Pss. 42–72) of the Psalms.

73:1–28 This psalm illustrates the results of allowing one's faith in God to be buried under self-pity. The psalmist became

Messianic Prophecies in the Psalms

Prophecy	Psalm	Fulfillment
1. God will announce Christ to be His Son	2:7	Matthew 3:17; Acts 13:33; Hebrews 1:5
2. All things will be put under Christ's feet	8:6	1 Cor. 15:27; Hebrews 2:8
3. Christ will be resurrected from the grave	16:10	Mark 16:6, 7; Acts 13:35
4. God will forsake Christ in His moment of agony	22:1	Matthew 27:46; Mark 15:34
5. Christ will be scorned and ridiculed	22:7,8	Matthew 27:39–43; Luke 23:35
6. Christ's hands and feet will be pierced	22:16	John 20:25, 27;John 20:25, 27; Acts 2:23
7. Others will gamble for Christ's clothes	22:18	Matthew 27:35, 36
8. Not one of Christ's bones will be broken	34:20	John 19:34, 33, 36
9. Christ will be hated unjustly	35:19	John 15:25
10. Christ will come to do God's will	40:7,8	Hebrews 10:7
11. Christ will be betrayed by a friend	41:9	John 13:18
12. Christ's throne will be eternal	45:6	Hebrews 1:8
13. Christ will ascend to heaven	68:18	Ephesians 4:8
14. Zeal for God's temple will consume Christ	69:9	John 2:17
15. Christ will be given vinegar and gall	69:21	Matthew 27:34; John 19:28–30
16. Christ's betrayer will be replaced	109:8	Acts 1:20
17. Christ's enemies will bow down to Him	110:1	Acts 2:34, 35
18. Christ will be a priest like Melchizedek	110:4	Hebrews 5:6; 6:20; 7:17
19. Christ will be the chief cornerstone	118:22	Matthew 21:42; Acts 4:11
20. Christ will come in the name of the Lord	118:26	Matthew 21:9

The MacArthur Study Bible, by John MacArthur (Nashville: Word Publishing, 1997) 754. © 1993 by Thomas Nelson, Inc.

depressed when he contrasted the seeming prosperity of the wicked with the difficulties of living a righteous life. Beginning in verse 15, however, his attitude changes completely. He looks at life from the perspective of being under the control of a sovereign, holy God, and concludes that it is the wicked, not the righteous, who have blundered.

I. Perplexity Over the Prosperity of the Wicked (73:1–14)
  A. Their Prosperity (73:1–5)
  B. Their Pride (73:6–9)
  C. Their Presumption (73:10–14)
II. Proclamation of the Justice of God (73:15–28)
  A. His Perspective (73:15–17)
  B. His Judgments (73:18–20)
  C. His Guidance (73:21–28)

73: Title Asaph. Asaph was a Levite who led one of the temple choirs (1 Chr. 15:19; 25:1, 2). His name is identified with Psalm 73–83, and also Psalm 50 (*see note on Ps. 50: Title*). He either wrote these psalms, or his choir sang them, or later choirs in the tradition of Asaph sang them.

73:4 *no pangs in their death.* The wicked seem to go through life in good health, and then die a painless death.

73:9 *tongue walks through the earth.* The insolent speech of the wicked can be heard anywhere one goes.

73:10 *are drained by them.* Those who associate with the wicked person "drink in" everything he declares (cf. Ps. 1).

73:11 *is there knowledge in the Most High?* The wicked insist on living as if God is not omniscient and does not know what happens on earth.

73:17 *sanctuary of God.* As the psalmist worshiped God at the worship center, he began to understand God's perspective on the fate of the wicked. This is the turning point of the psalm.

73:20 *despise their image.* The wicked are like a bad dream which one forgets as soon as he awakens. Their well-being is fleeting.

73:22 *like a beast before You.* The psalmist confesses his sin of evaluating life secularly and faithlessly.

73:27 *perish . . . You have destroyed.* The psalmist concludes that those who abandon God and attempt to live an autonomous life based on self-chosen idols will eventually endure eternal death.

74:1–23 This community lament expresses the agony of the people in the midst of the most excruciating of circumstances. It was bad enough that Israel's enemies had destroyed the temple (cf. 2 Kin. 25); but even worse, it seemed to the psalmist that God had abandoned them. In this prayer, he reminds God of His bond with Israel plus His past supernatural deeds in the protection of Israel, and begs God to save His covenant nation now (cf. Ps. 137 and Lamentations).

I. The Terror of Abandonment (74:1–11)
II. The Remembrance of Omnipotence (74:12–17)
III. The Plea for Help (74:18–23)

74: Title Asaph. If this psalm reflects the destruction of the temple by Nebuchadnezzar in 586 B.C., Asaph would have been dead by then. Thus, this title may mean that this psalm was written by or sung by a later Asaph choir (*see notes on Pss. 50, 73: Title*).

74:2 *tribe of Your inheritance.* The psalm-ist laments that even though God possessed Israel, He had not protected it.

74:3 *Lift up Your feet.* An anthropomorphism meaning, "Hurry and come to examine the rubble."

74:4 *their banners for signs.* The ravagers had set up their military and pagan religious banners in God's temple.

74:5 *lift up axes.* Like lumberjacks surrounded by trees, the enemy had destroyed everything in sight in the temple of God.

74:8 the meeting places. God allowed only one sanctuary and during Josiah's revival, the high places had been destroyed (cf. 2 Kin. 22; 23). This may be a reference to the several rooms of the temple, or to nonsacrificial religious sites throughout the land.

74:9 our signs. While hostile and pagan signs were everywhere, signs of true Jehovah worship, such as the altars for sacrifice, were missing.

74:13 divided the sea. This is most likely a reference to God's creation activity, rather than to the parting of the Red Sea (cf. Gen. 1:6–8; Ex. 14:26–31). **sea serpents.** This identifies whales, sharks, and other large sea creatures, including dinosaurs.

74:14 Leviathan. *See note on Job 41:1.*

74:15 broke open the fountain . . . flood. This may be a reference to the universal flood (cf. Gen. 7:11), or it may describe creation (Gen. 1:6–8).

74:17 set all the borders. As Creator, God made day and night, also the seasons (v. 16); He divided the land from the sea; and He even established national boundaries.

74:20 the covenant. The people had apostatized (cf. Ex. 16:3–8). God, however, was still in an eternal covenant (the Abrahamic covenant) with the nation (cf. Gen. 17:1–8).

75:1–10 In this psalm, the believing community asserts that, in spite of physical, moral, and societal turmoil, God never loses control of the universe. He gives stability to earthly life, and He will judge the wicked at the appropriate time. Structurally, the psalm revolves around three metaphors: pillars of the earth (v. 3); horns (vv. 5, 6, 11); and God's cup of wrath (v. 8).

I. Divine Stability of the Universe (75:1–3)
II. Divine Justice over the World (75:4–10)

75: Title Do Not Destroy. *See note on Psalm 57: Title.*

75:1 Your name is near. God's name rep-

resents His presence. The history of God's supernatural interventions on behalf of His people demonstrated that God was personally immanent. But OT saints did not have the fullness of God's presence from permanent, personal indwelling of the Holy Spirit (cf. John 14:1, 16, 17; 1 Cor. 3:16; 6:19).

75:3 I set up its pillars firmly. In uncertain times, God stabilizes societies through His common grace.

75:4 Do not lift up the horn. The horn symbolized an animal's or human's strength and majesty (cf. Deut. 33:17; Amos 6:13; Zech. 1:18–21). Lifting up the horn apparently described a stubborn animal who kept itself from entering a yoke by holding its head up as high as possible. The phrase, thus, symbolized insolence or rebellion.

75:8 cup. The cup of wrath describes God's judgment which He forces down the throats of the wicked (cf. Job. 21:20; Is. 51:17; Jer. 25:15–29; Matt. 20:22; 26:39).

75:10 horns . . . cut off. To cut off the horns of the wicked would be to humble them (cf. v. 4).

76:1–12 This psalm teaches that God is willing to use His great power for His people. Some commentators, including the editors of the LXX, have suggested that this psalm was written to celebrate the destruction of Sennacherib's Assyrian army in 701 B.C., as well as the subsequent assassination of Sennacherib himself (vv. 5, 6; cf. 2 Kin. 18; 19; Is. 36; 37). The psalm also includes eschatological overtones (especially vv. 8–12), when Jehovah will defeat His enemies and bring them into judgment.

I. God's Nearness to His People (76:1–3)
II. God's Deliverance of His People (76:4–9)
III. God's Majesty to His People (76:10–12)

76: Title Asaph. *See notes on Psalms 50; 73; 74: Title.*

76:3 broke the arrows . . . shield . . . sword. God destroyed the enemy's weapons.

76:4 mountains of prey. This is probably a poetic description of the attackers.

76:5 the use of their hands. God had crippled the enemy soldiers.

76:10 wrath of man shall praise You. The railings against God and His people are turned into praise to God when God providentially brings the wicked down (cf. Is. 36:4–20; Acts 2:23; Rom. 8:28).

76:12 cut off the spirit of princes. God shatters the attitude of proud governmental leaders who rebel against Him.

77:1–20 This psalm illustrates one cure for depression. The psalmist does not explain the cause of his despair, but he was definitely gloomy. When he thought about God, it only caused him to complain bitterly. But beginning in verse 10, the psalmist's mood starts to change because he commits himself to focusing on God's goodness and past acts of deliverance. His lament then changes into a hymn of praise.

I. The Irritations of a Depressed Soul (77:1–9)

II. The Intention to Refocus the Mind (77:10–15)

III. The Illustrations of God's Past Blessings (77:16–20)

77: Title Jeduthun. *See note on Psalm 39: Title.*

77:2 hand was stretched out. This was the posture for prayer. The psalmist prayed throughout the night.

77:4 hold my eyelids open. The psalmist was so upset that he could neither sleep nor talk rationally.

77:6 my song in the night. The remembrance of happier times only deepened his depression. **spirit makes diligent search.** His spirit continually meditated on possible solutions to his problems.

77:10 years of the right hand of the Most High. The psalmist began to remember the times when God used His right hand (power) to strengthen and protect him.

77:16 waters . . . were afraid. A dramatic picture of God's parting the waters of the Red Sea (cf. v. 19; also Ex. 14:21–31; 15:1–19).

77:17 Your arrows. A metaphor for lightning flashes.

78:1–72 This didactic psalm was written to teach the children how gracious God had been in the past in spite of their ancestors' rebellion and ingratitude. If the children learn well the theological interpretation of their nation's history, hopefully they would "not be like their fathers" (v. 8). The psalmist especially focuses on the history of the Exodus.

I. Exhortation on the Instruction of Children (78:1–11)

II. Lecture on the Graciousness of God (78:12–72)

A. Rehearsal of Israel's History (78:12–39)

B. Reiteration of Historical Lessons (78:40–72)

78:2 parable. The word is used here in the broader sense of a story with moral and spiritual applications. **dark sayings.** This is puzzling, ambiguous information. The lessons of history are not easily discerned correctly. For an infallible interpretation of history, there must be a prophet. The specific puzzle in Israel's history is the nation's rebellious spirit in spite of God's grace.

78:9 children of Ephraim. The act of treachery or apostasy by this largest of the northern tribes is not specifically identified in Israel's history.

78:12 field of Zoan. The regions of Zoan, an Egyptian city.

78:13 waters stand up like a heap. The parting of the Red Sea at the beginning of the Exodus, which allowed Israel to escape from the Egyptian armies, was always considered by the OT saints to be the most spectacular miracle of their history (cf. Ex. 14).

78:15 *split the rocks.* Twice in the wilderness, when Israel desperately needed a great water supply, God brought water out of rocks (cf. Ex. 17:6; Num. 20:11).

78:18 *the food of their fancy.* Instead of being grateful for God's marvelous provisions of manna, the Israelites complained against God and Moses. God sent them meat, but also judged them (Num. 11).

78:19 *prepare a table in the wilderness?* The answer was "yes," but the question implied a sarcastic lack of faith.

78:27 *rained meat.* A poetic description of the quail which dropped into Israel's camp in the wilderness (Num. 11:31–35).

78:41 *limited the Holy One.* The Israelites did this by doubting God's power.

78:42 *did not remember His power.* The generations of Israelites who left Egypt and eventually died in the wilderness were characterized by ignoring God's previous acts of power and faithfulness. The following verses (vv. 42–55) rehearse the plagues and miracles of the Exodus from Egypt, which demonstrated God's omnipotence and covenant love.

78:57 *deceitful bow.* This is a useless bow.

78:60 *tabernacle of Shiloh.* Shiloh was an early location of Jehovah worship in the Promised Land. The capture and removal of the ark from Shiloh by the Philistines symbolized God's judgment (cf. Josh. 18:1; 1 Sam. 1:9; 3:1; 4:1–22).

78:65 *mighty man . . . wine.* The picture is that of a furious, raging warrior entering the battle on Israel's side.

78:68 *the tribe of Judah.* Instead of the prestigious tribes, God chose Judah. In Judah was Mt. Zion where the central worship center of Jehovah was located. Also, David their king, as well as his royal descendants, were from this tribe.

79:1–13 The historical basis for this lamentment psalm was probably Nebuchadnezzar's destruction of the temple in 586 B.C. (cf. Ps. 74; 2 Kin. 25:8–21; Lam. 1–5). The psalm contains (1) prayer for the nation's spiritual needs, (2) curses against the enemies of God's people, and (3) praises in anticipation of God's actions. The psalm helps the believer express his anguish in a disaster when it seems as though God is aloof.

I. The Lamentation Over the National Disaster (79:1–4)
II. The Supplication for Divine Intervention (79:5–13)
   A. The Prayer for Vindication (79:5–7)
   B. The Prayer for Forgiveness (79:8, 9)
   C. The Prayer for Reprisal (79:10–12)
   D. The Praise for Response (79:13)

79:1 *nations.* In this context, the word refers to heathen, pagan people. ***inheritance.*** The inheritance of God was national Israel, and specifically its capital city, Jerusalem, where the temple was located.

79:9 *atonement.* See Psalm 65:3. ***For Your name's sake.*** A defeat of a nation was believed to be a defeat of its god. A mark of spiritual maturity is one's concern for the reputation of God.

79:10 *Where is their God?* The heathen were mocking Israel's God by saying that the destruction of the nation implied that its God was nonexistent.

79:11 *appointed to die.* A prayer for the preservation of the prisoners awaiting execution in the enemy's dungeon.

79:12 *sevenfold into their bosom.* A petition that God would restore His reputation by bringing a much worse destruction of the enemies than what had happened to Israel.

80:1–19 This psalm was probably written from Jerusalem in astonishment at the captivity of the ten northern tribes in 722 B.C. The psalmist recognized that God's people had removed themselves through apostasy from the blessings of the Mosaic covenant.

So he begs God to act and to restore His people to covenant blessings (vv. 3, 7, 14, 19).

I. Prayer for Divine Restoration (80:1–3)
II. Despair over God's Anger (80:4–7)
III. Description of God's Vine (80:8–16a)
IV. Prayer for Divine Restoration (80:16b–19)

80: Title The Lilies. The name of a tune. *See note on Psalm 45: Title.*

80:1 dwell between the cherubim. A reference to the ark of the covenant, a symbol for God's presence. The images of two cherubim sat on top of the ark, facing each other (cf. Ex. 37:1–9).

80:3 face to shine. See note on Psalm 67:1; cf. 80:7, 19.

80:4 God of hosts. See note on Psalm 59:5; cf. 80:7, 14.

80:8 vine out of Egypt. The vine is a metaphor for Israel, whom God delivered out of Egypt and nurtured into a powerful nation (cf. Is. 5:1–7; 27:2–6; Matt. 21:33–40).

80:17 son of man. In this context, this phrase is primarily a reference to Israel. In a secondary sense, the "son of man" may allude to the Davidic dynasty and even extend to the Messiah, since He is so frequently called by that title in the NT.

81:1–16 This psalm was intended to be used in the celebration of one of the feasts of Israel, most likely the Feast of Tabernacles. After the call to worship (vv. 1–5), the psalm presents a message from God in the first person (vv. 6–16). This oracle pleads with Israel to listen to God (v. 13) so He might pour out the blessings of the covenant on the nation.

I. A Call to Joyful Worship (81:1–5)
II. A Call to Godly Obedience (81:6–16)

81: Title instrument of Gath. See note on Psalm 8: Title.

81:2 lute. A musical instrument with a long, narrow neck resembling a guitar.

81:3 New Moon . . . full moon. The seventh month of Israel's year (Tishri; September/October) culminated the festival year with a succession of celebrations. The month began with the blowing of the trumpets, continued with the Day of Atonement on the tenth day, and celebrated the Feast of Tabernacles on the fifteenth day when the moon was full. The Feast of Tabernacles praised God for His care in the wilderness wanderings, and also pointed to the coming kingdom (Matt. 17:1–4).

81:5 language . . . not understand. Possibly the psalmist heard a message, the meaning of which he did not grasp, in which case this message is presented as an oracle in the following verses; or, the psalmist is referring to the Egyptian language, which the Jews did not know.

81:6 hands . . . freed . . . baskets. The Israelites in Egypt were forced to carry bricks and clay in baskets.

81:7 secret place of thunder. This is probably a reference to God's presence on Mt. Sinai at the giving of the law (cf. Ex. 19:16ff.; 20:18ff.). **waters of Meribah.** Meribah, which means "strife" or "dispute," marked places where Israel tempted God (cf. Ex. 17:1–7; Num. 20:1–13; Pss. 95:8; 106:32).

81:14 soon subdue their enemies. One of the blessings of obedience promised to Israel in the Mosaic covenant was victory over their enemies (cf. Num. 33:52–56; Deut. 6:16–19; 7:16–24).

81:16 honey from the rock. This phrase was first used by Moses in his song of praise (Deut. 32:13). Though honey is sometimes found in the clefts of rocks, the intent of the figure here is more likely to valuable food provided from unlikely places.

82:1–8 This psalm, like Psalm 2 and Psalm 58, focuses on the injustices of tyranny. The psalmist pictures God standing in the assembly of earthly leaders, to whom He has delegated authority, and condemning their injustices. The final prayer of the psalmist (v. 8) is that God Himself will take direct control of this world's affairs.

I. The Assembly of World Leaders Before God (82:1)
II. The Evaluation of World Leaders by God (82:2–7)
III. The Replacement of World Leaders with God (82:8)

82:1 *congregation of the mighty.* The scene opens with God having called the world leaders together. *among the gods.* Some have taken this psalm to be about demons or false pagan gods. The best interpretation is that these *gods* are human leaders, such as judges, kings, legislators, and presidents (cf. Ex. 22:8, 9, 28; Judg. 5:8, 9). God, the great Judge, presides over these lesser judges.

82:2–4 *judge unjustly.* God accuses the lesser human judges of social injustices which violate the Mosaic Law (e.g., Deut. 24).

82:5 *darkness.* This signifies both intellectual ignorance and moral iniquity. *foundations of the earth are unstable.* When leaders rule unjustly, the divinely established moral order which undergirds human existence is undermined.

82:6 *I said.* Kings and judges are set up, ultimately, by the decree of God (Ps. 2:6). God, in effect, invests His authority in human leaders for the stability of the universe (cf. Rom. 13:1–7). But God may revoke this authority (v. 7). *"You are gods."* Jesus, in quoting this phrase in John 10:34, supported the interpretation that the *gods* were human beings. In a play on words, He claims that if human leaders can be called *gods,* certainly the Messiah can be called God. *children of the Most High.* These were created by God for noble life.

82:7 *die like men.* In spite of being made in God's image, they were mortal and would die like human beings. *fall like . . . princes.*

The unjust rulers would become vulnerable to the violent deaths which often accompanied tyranny.

82:8 *You shall inherit all nations.* The psalmist prayerfully anticipates the future when God will set up His kingdom and restore order and perfect justice to a sin-cursed world (cf. Pss. 96, 97; Is. 11:1–5).

83:1–18 This psalm, a national lament which includes prayer and imprecations, may be best studied with a map since several individual national enemies of Israel are noted. Second Chronicles 20:1–30 may record the specific historical event prompting this psalm, though some believe that the nations mentioned are only symbolic of all of Israel's enemies. The psalmist begs God to rescue Israel from its enemies as He had done so many times in the past.

I. A Plea for Help (83:1)
II. A Protest Against Israel's Enemies (83:2–8)
III. A Petition for Divine Judgment (83:9–18)

83:2 *Your enemies.* Throughout this psalm, the hostile nations are described as God's enemies.

83:4 *cut them off.* The hostile nations, under Satan's influence, repudiated God's promise to preserve forever the nation of Israel (cf. Gen. 17:7, 8; Ps. 89:34–37).

83:6 *Edom . . . Hagrites.* The list of nations represents Israel's enemies throughout its history. Edom descended from Esau and lived southeast of Israel. The Ishmaelites, descendants from Abraham and Hagar, were Bedouin tribes. The Moabites descended from Lot (cf. v. 8) and were tribal people living east of the Jordan River (cf. Judg. 11:17, 18; Is. 15, 16). The Hagrites were a nomadic tribe living east of the Jordan (1 Chr. 5:10, 19, 20).

83:7 *Gebal . . . Tyre.* Gebal was probably a community south of the Dead Sea, near

Petra in Edom. Ammon, a nation descended from Lot, was located east of the Jordan River. The Amalekites, nomads living southeast of the Jordan River, were descendants of Esau (cf. Gen. 36:12, 16; Ex. 17:8–13; Num. 24:20; Judg. 6:3; 1 Sam. 15:1–8). Philistia was located southwest of Israel (Judg. 14–16). Tyre was northwest of Israel (cf. Ezek. 27).

83:8 Assyria. This dominant nation of the eighth century B.C. took captive the ten northern tribes of Israel in 722 B.C. Assyria used smaller nations, like Moab and Ammon (the children of Lot; cf. Gen. 19:36–38), to accomplish its military goals.

83:9 Midian . . . Jabin. The psalmist reminded God of famous past victories. Gideon had defeated the Midianites (Judg. 7:19–25). Barak and Deborah defeated Jabin and his army commander, Sisera, near the brook Kishon (Judg. 4; 5).

83:11 Oreb . . . Zalmunna. These men were chiefs of the Midianites when they were defeated by Gideon (cf. Judg. 6–8).

83:13–15 The psalmist uses several dramatic similes in his prayer for the destruction of Israel's enemies.

83:18 know . . . Most High. The purpose of the maledictions against the hostile nations is neither personal nor national, but spiritual: that the nations may know and glorify God. *whose name alone is the Lord. Alone* should precede *are* in the next phrase. The Gentile nations need to know that the God of the Bible is the only God.

84:1–12 This psalm, like other psalms of ascent (Pss. 120–134), expresses the joy of a pilgrim traveling up to Jerusalem, then up into the temple to celebrate one of the feasts. The pilgrim focuses his attention, especially, on the thought of being in the very presence of the Lord God. The NT believer-priest, in an even greater way, can come into the presence of the Lord (cf. Heb. 4:16; 10:19–22).

I. The Expectation of Worshiping God (84:1–4)
II. The Expedition to Worship God (84:5–7)
III. The Elation at Worshiping God (84:8–12)

84: *Title instrument of Gath.* See note on *Psalm 8:Title.* **sons of Korah.** These descendants of Levi through Kohath were the gatekeepers and musicians in the temple at Jerusalem (1 Chr. 6:22; 9:17–32; 26:1; see Pss. 42–49; 84; 85; 87; 88).

84:1 lovely is Your tabernacle. The temple worship center was *lovely* because it enabled the OT saint to come into the presence of God (cf. Pss. 27; 42:1, 2; 61:4; 63:1, 2). *Lord of hosts. Hosts* represent God's angelic armies, thus God's omnipotence over all powers in heaven and on earth (cf. vv. 3, 8, 12).

84:2 longs . . . faints . . . cry out. The psalmist is consumed with his happy but intense desire to worship God in the temple.

84:3 sparrow . . . swallow. The psalmist admires these birds who were able to build their nests in the temple courtyards, near the altars of God.

84:4 Blessed. This word is used three times (vv. 4, 5, 12) to describe the happiness of those who, like the sons of Korah, "lodged all around the house of God" (1 Chr. 9:27).

84:6 Valley of Baca. *Baca* can be translated as "weeping" or "balsam tree." The valley was an arid place on the way to Jerusalem. *They make it a spring.* The pilgrims traveling to a festival of worship at Jerusalem turn an arid valley into a place of joy.

84:7 strength to strength. The anticipation of joyously worshiping God in Jerusalem overcame the pilgrims' natural weariness in their difficult journey. *Zion.* See note on *Psalm 87:2.*

84:9 behold our shield. A metaphor for the king, who also would have participated in a festival at the temple (cf. Ps. 47:9; Hos. 4:18). *the face of Your anointed.* The king is regularly described as God's "anointed" (Pss. 2:2; 18:50; 20:6; 28:8; 89:38, 51). The psalmist thus prays that God would look upon the king with favor, blessing his reign with prosperity.

84:10 doorkeeper. One day standing at the door of the temple, or just being near, was better than a thousand days fellowshiping with the wicked.

84:11 sun and shield. This pictures God's overall provision and protection.

85:1–13 The psalmist pledges that God will again demonstrate His covenant love to Israel. God has been merciful in the past; He is angry presently; but He will restore Israel in the future (cf. Deut. 30; Hos. 3:4, 5). Though God judges, He is faithful to His promises. The feelings expressed in this psalm may describe those of the Jews returning from exile in Babylon. Though they were grateful for restoration to their land, they were disappointed that the conditions did not measure up to the glory of the pre-exilic life there (cf. Ezra 3:12, 13).

I. Review of God's Past Mercies (85:1–3)
II. Recognition of God's Present Anger (85:4–7)
III. Revelation of God's Future Salvation (85:8–13)

85: Title sons of Korah. *See note on Psalm 84: Title.*

85:1 favorable to Your land. In the past, God deemed His nation, Israel, to be acceptable.

85:3 fierceness of Your anger. *See note on Psalm 56:7.*

85:7 mercy. The word means "loyal love" or "unfailing love," and specifies God's faithfulness to His people through His covenant relationship.

85:8 peace. Ultimately this comes in the Messiah's kingdom (cf. Matt. 10:34; Luke 2:14).

85:9 salvation . . . who fear Him. Only those who renounce their sinful autonomy and put their trust in the living God will participate in the blessings of salvation and the future kingdom (cf. John 3:3–5). *glory may dwell in our land.* The departure of the glory of God, which signified His presence, is described in Ezekiel 10; 11. God withdrew His glory because of the apostasy of the nation immediately preceding the Babylonian exile (cf. Ezek. 8–11). The return of the glory of the Lord in the future millennial temple is foretold in Ezekiel 43:1–4 (cf. Pss. 26:8; 63:2; Is. 40:3–5; 60:1–3; 62:1–5). *See note on Leviticus 9:23.*

85:10 Mercy . . . truth . . . righteousness . . . peace. These four spiritual qualities, characterizing the atmosphere of the future kingdom of Christ, will relate to each other in perfect harmony and will saturate kingdom life (cf. vv. 10, 13).

85:12 our land . . . increase. Increase in the fertility and productivity of the land will also characterize the future kingdom of Christ (cf. Is. 4:2; 30:23–26; 32:15; Jer. 31:12; Ezek. 36:8–11; Amos 9:13–15; Zech. 8:11, 12).

86:1–17 This psalm is an individual lament (cf. Ps. 56) in which David expresses his distress and overcomes that distress through praise and worship. There is a sense of urgency demonstrated by some fourteen prayer requests. Undergirding the requests is the covenant relationship (vv. 2, 5, 13).

I. The Request for God's Attention (86:1–7)
II. The Testimony to God's Uniqueness (86:8–13)
III. The Plea for God's Deliverance (86:14–17)

86:2 I am holy. David, though recognizing his sinfulness (v. 1), insisted that by the grace of God he had not broken his covenant with the Lord.

86:4 soul . . . soul. The psalmist requests that his inner person would be preserved according to the covenant agreements (cf. Deut. 7; 8; 20).

86:8 Among the gods. David is here contrasting the true God with the imaginary deities of the heathen nations (cf. v. 10; also Ex. 15:11; Ps. 89:6; Is. 46:5–11).

86:9 All nations . . . worship. The psalmists and prophets often look into the future messianic age when all the nations of the world will worship the Lord (cf. Ps. 22:27; Is. 2:3; Zech. 8:21, 22; 14:16–19; Rev. 15:4).

86:11 Unite my heart. The psalmist prays that he would have an undivided heart, singularly loyal to his Lord (cf. Rom. 7:15; James 1:8).

86:14 the proud. The proud (i.e., arrogant, insolent) are those who act independently from God, rebelling against Him and His people (cf. Pss. 119:21, 51, 69, 78, 85, 122).

86:16 the son of Your maidservant. David asks for special favor from God, just as a servant born in the household would receive more than a servant brought in from outside the household (cf. Ps. 116:16).

86:17 a sign. A request for a favorable indication that would demonstrate that God was truly on David's side.

87:1–7 This psalm describes the Lord's love for Jerusalem and exalts this city as the religious center of the world in the coming messianic kingdom (cf. Ps. 48). Though the nations of the world (even including some of Israel's former enemies) will worship the Lord then, Israel will still be the favored nation (cf. Is. 2:2–4; 19:23–25; 45:22–25; 56:6–8; Zech. 8:20–23; 14:16–19).

I. The Lord's Love for Zion (87:1–3)

II. The Lord's Favor of Israel (87:4–6)

III. The Musicians' Exultation over Jerusalem (87:7)

87: Title. sons of Korah. See note on Psalm 84: Title.

87:1 His foundation . . . holy mountains. *His foundation* means "His founded city," namely Jerusalem, located in the hill country of Judea.

87:2 gates of Zion. Zion is a poetic description of Jerusalem, seemingly used by the OT writers when special spiritual and religious significance was being attached to the city. Though God certainly loved other cities in Israel, He did not choose any of them to be His worship center (cf. Pss. 122; 125; 132; 133). The gates represent the access of the potential worshiper into the city where he could come into a special worshiping relationship with God. **More than all the dwellings of Jacob.** The other cities in Israel were not chosen by God to be the place of His special dwelling.

87:3 O city of God! Jerusalem was God's city because there God met His people in praise and offerings.

87:4 Rahab and Babylon. Rahab was a monster of ancient pagan mythology and symbolized Egypt in the OT (cf. Ps. 89:10; Is. 30:7; 51:9). Two of the superpowers of the ancient world, fierce enemies of Israel, will one day worship the Lord in Zion (cf. Is. 19:19–25). **Philistia . . . Tyre . . . Ethiopia.** Three more Gentile nations, ancient enemies of Israel, whose descendants will worship the Lord in Jerusalem (cf. Is. 14:28–32; 18:1–7). This multinational worship is pictured as a great joy to the Lord Himself. **This one was born there.** To be born in Jerusalem will be noted as a special honor in the messianic kingdom (cf. vv. 5, 6; also Zech. 8:20–23).

87:7 All my springs are in you. *Springs* is a metaphor for the source of joyful blessings. Eternal salvation, including the death and resurrection of Christ, is rooted in Jerusalem. The prophets also tell of a literal fountain flowing from the temple in Jerusalem that will water the surrounding land (cf. Joel 3:18; Ezek. 47:1–12).

88:1–18 This lament is unusual in that it does not end on a happy note. The psalmist has been ill or injured since the days of his youth (v. 15) and bemoans God's failure to hear his prayer for good health. He assumes that God is angry with him, but like Job, he knows of no cause for that anger. But, though he does not understand God's ways, the psalmist does turn to God, thus indicating an underlying trust.

  I. Complaints Against God's Action (88:1–9)

  II. Challenges to God's Wisdom (88:10–12)

  III. Charges Against God's Conduct (88:13–18)

88: Title sons of Korah. *See note on Psalm 84: Title.* **Mahalath Leannoth.** *Mahalath* is either the name of a tune or an instrument, possibly a reed pipe which was played on sad occasions. *Leannoth* may mean "to afflict" and describe the despair which permeates this psalm. **Contemplation.** *See note on Psalm 32: Title.* **Heman the Ezrahite.** Heman was a musician from the family of the Kohathites, who founded the Korahite choir (cf. 1 Chr. 6:33; 2 Chr. 5:12; 35:15). He may be the same person who was one of the wise men during Solomon's reign (1 Kin. 4:31). *Ezrahite* may mean "native born," or may be the name of a family clan (cf. 1 Chr. 2:6).

88:4 go down to the pit. *Pit* is one of several references to the grave in this psalm (cf. the dead, vv. 5, 10; the grave, vv. 3, 5, 11; place of destruction, v. 11).

88:5 Adrift among the dead. This expresses the idea that death cuts off all ties to friends and family, as well as to God.

88:7 all Your waves. Like the waves rolling on to the seashore, so God has directed trouble after trouble on the psalmist (cf. v. 17).

88:8 put away my acquaintances. The psalmist claims that the Lord has turned his friends against him. Some see this as a quarantine experience, as from leprosy (cf. v. 18; Job 19:13–20).

88:9 eye wastes away. This could be a description of the psalmist's tears, used as a figure for his collapse under this distress.

88:10 wonders for the dead. The psalmist reminds God, through a series of rhetorical questions, that the dead cannot testify to God's goodness.

88:14 hide Your face? That is, "Why do You not answer my prayers?"

88:15 die from my youth. The psalmist has had some serious illness or injury from the time of his youth.

88:18 Loved one . . . friend . . . acquaintances. *See note on verse 8.*

89:1–52 This psalm describes the author's attempt to reconcile the seeming contradictions between his theology and the reality of his nation's conditions. Through the initial thirty-seven verses, he rehearses what he knows to be theologically accurate: God has sovereignly chosen Israel to be His nation, and David's descendants to rule. The last third of the psalm reflects the psalmist's chagrin that the nation had been ravaged and the Davidic monarchy had apparently come to a disgraceful end.

To his credit, the psalmist refuses to explain away his theology, but instead lives with the tension, hopefully to be resolved at a later time with the promised reestablishment of an earthly kingdom under one of David's descendants (cf. Pss. 110; 132).

  I. God's Manifest Faithfulness to the Davidic Covenant (89:1–37)

    A. God's Covenant Love (89:1–4)

    B. God's Praiseworthiness (89:5–18)

    C. God's Covenant with David (89:19–37)

  II. God's Apparent Neglect of the Davidic Covenant (89:38–52)

A. The Psalmist's Lament (89:38–45)
B. The Psalmist's Consternation
   (89:46–51)
C. The Doxology (89:52)

89: Title *Ethan the Ezrahite*. Possibly the Levitical singer mentioned in 1 Chronicles 6:42; 15:17, 19 *(see note on Ps. 88: Title.).*

89:1 *mercies*. *See note on Psalm 85:7* (cf. vv. 2, 14, 24, 28, 33, 49).

89:2 *You shall establish . . . heavens*. The psalmist exults that the Lord Himself will guarantee the eternality of the Davidic dynasty (cf. 2 Sam. 23:5).

89:3 *covenant with My chosen*. The Davidic covenant, culminating in Messiah's reign, was established in 2 Samuel 7 (cf. 1 Kin. 8:23; 1 Chr. 17; 2 Chr. 21:7; Pss. 110; 132). The covenant was in the form of a royal grant covenant as God, the great King, chose David as His servant king. In this type of covenant, the person with whom the Lord established the covenant could violate the terms of the covenant and the Lord would still be obligated to maintain the covenant.

89:4 *seed . . . forever . . . throne*. The covenant with David was extended to his descendants. The throne promise guaranteed that the rightful heir to the throne would always be a descendant of David (cf. vv. 29, 36; see also 2 Sam. 7:13, 16, 18; Luke 1:31–33). The genealogies of Jesus qualify Him for the throne (cf. Matt. 1:1–17; Luke 3:23–38).

89:5 *faithfulness*. The word suggests constant and habitual actions, meaning here that God was reliable. For God to violate this consistency of actions would be to violate His very nature (cf. vv. 1, 2, 8, 24, 33, 49).

89:6 *sons of the mighty*. Lit. "sons of God," i.e., angels.

89:7 *assembly of the saints*. Lit. "holy ones," which pictures a gathering of the angels around their sovereign Lord.

89:10 *Rahab*. A figurative term for Egypt. *See note on Psalm 87:4.*

89:12 *Tabor and Hermon*. Mountains in Israel pictured joining in praise with the rest of creation.

89:15 *the joyful sound*. This refers to a cheer, a shout of joyful homage to God (cf. Pss. 33:3; 47:5; 95:1; 98:4; 100:1. See note on Ps. 66:1).

89:17 *our horn is exalted*. *See note on Psalm 75:4* (cf. v. 24).

89:18 *shield belongs to the Lord*. The *shield* was a metaphor for the king (*see note on Ps. 84:9*).

89:19 *Your holy one*. The *holy one* was the prophet, Nathan, whom the Lord used to tell David about His covenant with David (2 Sam. 7:4ff.).

89:25 *hand . . . sea . . . rivers*. A reference to the promise of Exodus 23:31 that the Lord would give Israel the land between the Red Sea and the Euphrates River.

89:27 *My firstborn*. The firstborn child was given a place of special honor and a double portion of the inheritance (Gen. 27; 2 Kin. 2:9). However, in a royal grant covenant, a chosen person could be elevated to the level of firstborn sonship and, thus, have title to a perpetual gift involving dynastic succession (cf. Ps. 2:7). Though not actually the first, Israel was considered the firstborn among nations (Ex. 4:22); Ephraim, the younger, was treated as the firstborn (Gen. 48:13–20); and David was the firstborn among kings. In this latter sense of prominent favor, Christ can be called the firstborn over all creation (Col. 1:15), in that He is given the preeminence over all created beings.

89:32 *rod . . . stripes*. The rod was an instrument for inflicting wounds, and the stripes were marks left by such a flogging. God's warning reflects His knowledge of the evident potential for disobedience among the descendants of David (cf. 2 Sam. 7:14). In the lifetime of David's grandsons, for example, the kingdom was split with the ten northern tribes leaving the rulership of the Davidic line (cf. Jer. 31:31; Ezek. 37:16, 17 for the future reunification of the twelve tribes).

89:33 *My lovingkindness.* Though the Lord might have to discipline David's descendants, He would never remove His covenant from this family (cf. 2 Sam. 7:15). Thus, the covenant could be conditional in any one or more generations and, yet, be unconditional in its final outcome (cf. Ezek. 37:24–28).

89:37 *faithful witness in the sky.* God's covenant with David regarding his descendants was as certain as the establishment of the sun (v. 36) and the moon in the heavens (cf. Jer. 33:14–26). The promise involved a kingdom "in the earth" (Jer. 33:15).

89:39 *renounced the covenant.* The Hebrew word behind *renounced* is rare, and it may better be translated "disdained." It seemed to the psalmist that the condition of Israel indicated that God was neglecting His covenant with David (cf. Ezek. 37:1–14). *profaned his crown.* This depicts a serious insult to the dynasty because it is of divine origin.

89:40–45 The ruin is depicted in several images: left with broken hedges, thus defenseless; a stronghold whose ruins invite invaders; a weakling plundered by all his enemies; a soldier with a useless sword; and a youth prematurely old.

89:45 *days of his youth . . . shortened.* This is a figure for the relative brevity of the Davidic dynasty. The dynasty was cut off in its youth.

89:46 *hide Yourself forever?* By God's seeming refusal to answer prayer and restore the Davidic kingship, it seemed as though God was hiding Himself. Of course, the discipline of disobedient kings had been foretold (v. 32). According to the prophets, God would eventually restore Israel and the Davidic throne in an earthly kingdom (cf. Hos. 3:4, 5). Never in the OT is there a sense that this Davidic promise would be fulfilled by Christ with a spiritual and heavenly reign.

89:47. The prosperity of the Davidic kingdom is linked to the welfare of all people (cf. Ps. 72:17; Is. 9:7; 11:1–10). If the kingdom fails, who can survive? (v. 48).

89:49–51. Here is a final plea for God to come to the help of His people, so they can avoid reproach (cf. Is. 37:17–35).

89:52 *Blessed be the LORD.* This blessing, indicating restored confidence, closes not only Psalm 89, but all of Book III (Pss. 73–89) of the Psalms.

90:1–17 The thrust of this magnificent prayer is to ask God to have mercy on frail human beings living in a sin-cursed universe. Moses begins the psalm with a reflection on God's eternality, then expresses his somber thoughts about the sorrows and brevity of life in their relationship to God's anger, and concludes with a plea that God would enable His people to live a significant life. The psalm seems to have been composed as the older generation of Israelites who had left Egypt were dying off in the wilderness (Num. 14).

I. The Praise of God's Eternality (90:1, 2)

II. The Perception of Man's Frailty (90:3–12)

III. The Plea for God's Mercy (90:13–17)

90: Title. *Moses the man of God.* Moses the prophet (Deut. 18:15–22) was unique in that the Lord knew him "face to face" (Deut. 34:10–12). *Man of God* (Deut. 33:1) is a technical term used over seventy times in the OT, always referring to one who spoke for God. It is used of Timothy in the NT (1 Tim. 6:11; 2 Tim. 3:17).

90:1 *our dwelling place.* God was Israel's sanctuary for protection, sustenance, and stability (cf. Deut. 33:27; Ps. 91:9).

90:2 *from everlasting to everlasting.*

God's nature is without beginning or end, free from all succession of time, and contains in itself the cause of time (cf. Ps. 102:27; Is. 41:4; 1 Cor. 2:7; Eph. 1:4; 1 Tim. 6:16; Rev. 1:8).

90:3 You turn man to destruction. The unusual Hebrew word for *destruction* has the idea of crushed matter. Though different from the *dust* of Genesis 3:19, this phrase is no doubt a reference to that passage. Humanity lives under a sovereign decree of death and cannot escape it.

90:4 a watch in the night. A *watch* was a four-hour period of time (cf. Ex. 14:24; Lam. 2:19; 2 Pet. 3:8).

90:5 like a flood. Humankind is snatched from the earth as though it were being swept away by floodwaters. **like a sleep.** Humanity lives its existence as though asleep or in a coma. People are insensitive to the brevity of life and the reality of God's wrath.

90:7 consumed by Your anger. The physical bodies of the human race wear out by the effects of God's judgment on sin in the universe (cf. Deut. 4:25–28; 11:16, 17). Death originates with sin (Rom. 5:12).

90:8 the light of Your countenance. All sin is in clear view to the "face" of God.

90:9 like a sigh. After struggling through his life of afflictions and troubles, a person's life ends with a moan of woe and weariness.

90:10 seventy years . . . eighty years. Though Moses lived to be 120 years old, and "His eyes were not dim nor his natural vigor diminished" (Deut. 34:7), human life was usually more brief and lived under the anger of God. Because of this certain and speedy end, life is sad.

90:11 as the fear of You . . . Your wrath. Instead of explaining away life's curses, a wise person will recognize God's wrath toward sin as the ultimate cause of all afflictions and, consequently, learn to fear God.

90:12 number our days. Evaluate the use of time in light of the brevity of life. **heart of wisdom.** Wisdom repudiates autonomy and focuses on the Lord's sovereignty and revelation.

90:14 Your mercy. *See note on Psalm 85:7.*

90:15 glad . . . afflicted us. A prayer that a person's days of joy would equal his days of distress.

90:17 the beauty of the LORD. The Lord's beauty implies His delight, approval, and favor. **establish the work of our hands.** By God's mercy and grace, one's life can have value, significance, and meaning (cf. 1 Cor. 15:58).

91:1–16 This psalm describes God's ongoing sovereign protection of His people from the ever-present dangers and terrors which surround humanity. The original setting may be that of an army about to go to battle. Most of the terrors mentioned in this psalm are left undefined, no doubt intentionally, so that no kind of danger is omitted from application. Believers in every age can read this psalm to learn that nothing can harm a child of God unless the Lord permits it. However, in light of the many references in the Psalms to the future messianic kingdom (cf. especially Pss. 96–100), this psalm must be read as being literally fulfilled then.

I. The Lord's Protection (91:1–13)
  A. The Confidence (91:1, 2)
  B. The Dangers (91:3–6)
  C. The Examples (91:7–13)
II. The Lord's Pledge (91:14–16)

91:1 secret place of the Most High. An intimate place of divine protection. The use of *Most High* for God emphasizes that no threat can ever overpower Him. **shadow of the Almighty.** In a land where the sun can be oppressive and dangerous, a *shadow* was understood as a metaphor for care and protection.

91:3 snare of the fowler. A fowler trapped birds. Here, the metaphor represents any plots against the believer intended to endanger his life. *perilous pestilence.* The reference here and in verse 6 is specifically to dreaded diseases, plagues, and epidemics (cf. Jer. 14:12; Ezek. 5:12; 14:19).

91:4 *under His wings.* This pictures the protection of a parent bird (*see note on Ps. 57:1*).

91:8 *Only with your eyes.* The righteous are so safe in disaster all around them that they are only spectators.

91:11, 12 This promise of angelic protection was misquoted by Satan in his temptation of the Messiah (see Matt. 4:6).

91:13 *tread . . . lion and the cobra.* In general, a metaphor for God's protection from all deadly attacks (*see notes on Ps. 58:4ff.*).

91:14 *set his love upon Me.* God Himself is the speaker in this section (vv. 14–16), and He describes the blessing He gives to those who know and love Him. The word for *love* means a "deep longing" for God, or a "clinging" to God.

91:16 *long life.* Long life was a specific promise to the OT saint for obedience to the law (e.g., Ex. 20:12; Prov. 3:2). The prophets also promise it to God's people in the future messianic kingdom (cf. Is. 65:17–23).

92:1–15 This psalm expresses the exuberance of the psalmist as he recognizes that God is merciful in salvation, great in His works of creation, just in His dealings with the wicked, and faithful in prospering His children.

I. An Expression of Theistic Optimism (92:1–5)
II. An Observation Concerning Righteous Sovereignty (92:6–9)
III. A Testimony to God's Goodness (92:10–15)

92: *Title for the Sabbath Day.* In the post-exilic community, some psalms were sung throughout the week in connection with the morning and evening sacrifice; others were designated especially for Sabbath worship.

92:2 *lovingkindness . . . faithfulness.* These attributes are constant themes of the psalms (*see notes on Pss. 85:7; 89:5;* see also Luke 10:2).

92:3 *lute.* See note on Psalm 81:2.

92:10 *my horn.* See note on Psalm 75:4. ***anointed with fresh oil.*** This figure is based on a practice of making an animal's horns gleam by rubbing oil on them. Thus God, in effect, had invigorated the psalmist (cf. Pss. 23:5; 133:2).

92:11 *my desire on my enemies.* God granted the psalmist's desire by bringing his enemies to ruin.

92:12 *flourish like a palm tree.* The palm tree and the cedar symbolized permanence and strength (cf. v. 14). They are in contrast to the transience of the wicked, who are pictured as temporary as grass (v. 7). *See notes on Psalm 1.*

92:13 *planted in the house of the LORD.* A tree planted in the courtyard of the temple symbolized the thriving conditions of those who maintain a close relationship with the Lord (*see note on Ps. 52:8*).

93:1–5 Psalms 93 and 95–100 (cf. Ps. 47) are dedicated to celebrating God's sovereign kingship over the world. Psalm 93 glorifies God's eternal, universal kingdom which is providentially administered through His Son (Col. 1:17). Nothing is more powerful than the Lord; nothing is more steadfast than His reign; and nothing is more sure than His revelation.

I. The Lord's Universal Kingdom (93:1–4)
   A. Over the Earth (93:1, 2)
   B. Over the Sea (93:3, 4)
II. The Lord's Authoritative Revelation (93:5)

93:1 *The LORD reigns.* An exclamation of the Lord's universal reign over the earth from the time of creation (v. 2; cf. Pss. 103:19; 145:13) and forever.

93:3, 4 The sea with all its power is nothing in comparison to the power of God. The doubling and tripling of expressions throughout this psalm (vv. 1, 3, 4) are poetic means of generating literary energy and emphasis.

93:5 testimonies are very sure. As God's rule over the earth is stable, so His revelation given through Scripture is trustworthy (cf. Ps. 19:7).

94:1–23 The psalmist's urgent concern in this psalm is that the righteous are being oppressed, the wicked are prospering, and it does not look as though God cares. The psalmist, thus, pleads with God to punish the wicked (cf. Pss. 73; 82).

I. Address to God (94:1, 2)
II. Arrogance of the Wicked (94:3–7)
III. Admonition to the Foolish (94:8–11)
IV. Assurance for the Righteous (94:12–15)
V. Advocacy from God (94:16–23)

94:1 to whom vengeance belongs. Vengeance from God is not in the sense of uncontrolled vindictiveness, but in the sense of just retribution by the eternal Judge for trespasses against His law. **shine forth!** The psalmist asks God to make an appearance; he may even be asking for a theophany (cf. Pss. 50:2; 80:1).

94:7 The LORD does not see. An autonomous and atheistic attitude (*see note on Ps. 59:7*).

94:11 thoughts of man . . . are futile. The wicked designs of the human mind amount to nothing (cf. Ps. 92:5; 1 Cor. 3:20).

94:12 Blessed. To be blessed was to be wise and prosperous in life, as a result of the instruction of God (cf. Ps. 84:5, 12).

94:14 will not cast off His people. God has a permanent commitment to His people, Israel, established through a covenant based on His abiding love (Gen. 15; Jer. 12:15; Mic. 7:18). This important truth serves as a doctrinal basis for Psalms 93–100 and was in-

tended to encourage the nation during difficult times. Paul refers to this in Romans 11:1 as he assures the future salvation of Israel.

94:17 soul . . . settled in silence. Silence here is another term for Sheol, the realm of the dead (cf. Ps. 31:17).

94:18 Your mercy. See note on Psalm 85:7.

94:20 throne of iniquity. A reference to a corrupt judge or ruler. **devises evil by law.** Corrupt judges and rulers counter the very divine moral order of the universe by using law for wickedness rather than for good.

94:23 cut them off in their own wickedness. This portrays destruction while they are sinning.

95:1–11 This psalm, with its references to the wilderness wanderings, may have been composed by David (Heb. 4:7) for the Feast of the Tabernacles (cf. Ps. 81). During this feast, the people of Israel lived in booths, remembering God's provisions for them in the wilderness. After a call to worship (95:1–7a), a prophecy in the voice of the Holy Spirit (cf. Heb. 3:7) breaks in and reminds the people of the dangers of rebellion and tempting God. Verses 7b–11 are quoted verbatim in Hebrews 3:7–11 (cf. Heb. 3:15; 4:3–7) with the warning that those vacillating Jews also were in danger of missing the promised rest (i.e., salvation).

I. Positive Call to Worship (95:1–7a)
II. Negative Warning of Wrath (95:7b–11)

95:1 Rock of our salvation. This metaphor for God was especially appropriate in this psalm, which refers (vv. 8, 9) to the water that came from the rock in the wilderness (cf. Ex. 17:1–7; Num. 20:1–13; 1 Cor. 10:4).

95:3 the great King above all gods. This is a poetic way of denying the existence of other gods (cf. 96:5), which existed only as statues, not persons (cf. Jer. 10:1–10).

95:4 deep places of the earth. This refers to the depths of the seas, valleys, and caverns in contrast with the hills. The point (cf. v. 5) is that God was not a local god like the imaginary gods of the heathens, usually put up in high places, but the universal creator and ruler of the whole earth (*see note on Ps. 65:5*).

95:8 the rebellion. This is a reference to Meribah (translated "rebellion"), the place in the wilderness where the Israelites rebelled against the Lord. Their complaint about lack of water demonstrated their lack of faith in the Lord (Ex. 17:1–7; Num. 20:1–13; Ps. 81:7).

95:9 tested Me. This is a reference to the same event (v. 8), also called *Massah* (translated "testing"), when God brought water out of the rock (Ex. 17:7; cf. Deut. 6:16; 9:22; 33:8). The writer to the Hebrews applies the principle of this event to his readers, suggesting that their inclination to doubt the Lord and return to Judaism was parallel with their fathers' inclination to doubt the Lord and go back to Egypt.

95:10 go astray in their hearts. Their wanderings in the desert were the outworking of straying hearts.

95:11 My rest. The *rest* was originally the Promised Land (i.e., Canaan), where the people came at the end of Israel's forty-year journey in the wilderness. It was analogously applied in the Book of Hebrews to salvation by grace (Heb. 3:7–4:10; cf. Heb. 2:3).

96:1–13 The substance of this psalm, and portions of Psalms 97; 98; 100 are found in 1 Chronicles 16, which was used by David's direction in the dedication of the tabernacle on Mount Zion. The psalm has importance beyond that historical occasion, however, because it anticipates kingdom praise for the Lord from all the nations of the world (vv. 3, 4, 7, 9–13; cf. Is. 2:2–4; Zech. 14:16–19), and even from nature itself. It also expresses the intense joy that will saturate the earth when the Messiah is ruling from Jerusalem (cf. Is. 25:9; 40:9, 10).

I. The Proclamation of Praise (96:1–6)
  A. The Invitation to Praise (96:1–3)
  B. The Recipient of Praise (96:4–6)
II. The Exhortation to Worship (96:7–13)
  A. Worship from the Gentile Nations (96:7–10)
  B. Worship from Personified Nature (96:11–13)

96:1 a new song! This new song was intended for the future inauguration of the millennial rule of the Lord over the earth (cf. Pss. 144:9; 149:1; Rev. 5:9; 14:3).

96:2 Proclaim the good news. Genuine praise includes a testimony to others of God's plan of redemption.

96:3 His glory . . . nations. The glory of the Lord is more than just His majestic splendor. It includes all of the reasons for admiring and praising Him, such as His acts of creation (cf. Ps. 19:2) and redemption (v. 2). **all peoples.** See note on Psalm 67:3.

96:4 feared above all gods. See note on Psalm 95:3.

96:8 an offering. According to the psalmists and prophets, offerings and sacrifices will be presented to the Lord in the millennial kingdom (cf. Ps. 45:12; Ezek. 40–46).

96:9 the beauty of holiness. That is, "worship the LORD because of the splendor of His holiness" (cf. Pss. 29:2; 99; 110:3; 1 Chr. 16:29). *See note on 2 Chronicles 20:21.*

96:10 firmly established. Instead of the continuance of international chaos in human history, the world will be settled and efficiently managed by the Messiah in the millennial kingdom (cf. Ps. 2; Mic. 4:1–5). **judge the peoples righteously.** Not only will the Lord establish international peace and stability in the future messianic kingdom, but He will also rule the world with impeccable justice (cf. v. 13; Is. 11:1–5).

96:11, 12 This is what even inanimate creation awaits (cf. Rom. 8:19–22).

96:13 He is coming. The rule of the Lord

described in this psalm is not the present universal kingdom (Ps. 93), but one which will be established when Christ returns to earth.

97:1–12 The psalmist, though recognizing the Lord's universal rule at the present (v. 9), anticipates a new coming of the Lord to judge the earth. The imagery of the Lord's presence may, in fact, be the basis of some descriptions of the second coming in the NT (cf. Matt. 24; Rev. 19). Special emphasis is also placed on the Lord's righteous judgments on the world in His kingdom, as well as His obliteration of false religions.

I. The Announcement of the Reign of the Lord (97:1, 2)

II. The Effect of the Reign of the Lord (97:3–12)

    A. On His Foes (97:3–9)

    B. On His Friends (97:10–12)

97:1 *multitude of isles.* This refers to all the continents, as well as islands of the world (cf. Is. 42:10; Dan. 2:34, 35, 44; Zech. 14:9).

97:2 *Clouds and darkness.* Such a description emphasizes the terrifying effect of the Lord's presence, both in the past (Ex. 19:16–18) and in the future Day of the Lord (Joel 2:2; Zeph. 1:15; Matt. 24:29, 30).

97:3 *burns up His enemies.* The Lord will utterly destroy His enemies in the future Day of the Lord (cf. Zech. 14:12).

97:4 *His lightnings.* This is perhaps a reference to the Lord's awesome and public coming to rule the world (Matt. 24:26–30).

97:5 *mountains melt.* At the coming of the Lord, the mountains will fade away (cf. Is. 40:3–5; Zech. 14:4, 10).

97:6 *heavens declare His righteousness.* See the parallel description of Christ's coming in glory, e.g., Isaiah 40:5; Matt. 24:29–31 (cf. Rev. 19:11–15).

97:7 *all you gods.* No false gods or false religions will be allowed in the messianic kingdom (cf. Zech. 13:2, 3).

97:8 *Zion.* *See note on Psalm 87:2.* **Be-**

cause of Your judgments. A major reason for joy and well-being in the messianic kingdom will be the perfectly righteous judgments of Christ on the peoples of the world (cf. vv. 1–3; Ps. 48:11; Is. 11:1–5; Zech. 8:3).

97:10 *preserves the souls of His saints.* Here, the doctrine of eternal security is stated. Gratitude for such grace should motivate believers to holiness.

97:11 *Light is sown.* This is a poetic way of describing the ultimate triumph of righteousness and the righteous (cf. Is. 58:8, 10; 60:19, 20; Mal. 4:2).

98:1–9 Like the surrounding psalms, this psalm proclaims the excitement and joy of the whole earth over the rule of the Lord in the kingdom. This psalm is given over entirely to praise, with only a brief mention of the wicked.

I. Celebration of the Lord's Victorious Reign (98:1–6)

    A. Triumphs of the Lord (98:1–3)

    B. Praise to the Lord (98:4–6)

II. Exaltation of the Lord's Righteous Judgments (98:7–9)

98:1 *a new song!* *See note on Psalm 96:1.* ***right hand . . . holy arm.*** These are symbols of power. ***the victory.*** The Lord is often pictured in the OT as a divine Warrior (Ex. 15:2, 3; Pss. 18; 68:1–8; Is. 59:15ff.). According to the prophets, Christ will begin His millennial reign following His victory over the nations of the world which will gather against Israel in the end times (cf. Zech. 14:1–15; Rev. 19:11–21).

98:2 *the nations.* *See notes on Psalms 57:9; 67:3; 82:8.*

98:3 *His mercy and His faithfulness.* *See notes on Psalms 85:7; 89:5.* **salvation.** These words are a metaphor for the Lord's establishment of His righteous kingdom on earth (cf. Is. 46:13; 51:5–8).

98:4 *Shout joyfully.* A great cheer which

greets and welcomes a king (cf. Zech. 9:9; Matt. 21:4–9). **Break forth.** The idea is that of an eruption of praise which could not be contained (cf. Is. 14:7; 44:23; 55:12).

98:5, 6 harp . . . trumpets . . . horn. Instruments normally used in temple worship (cf. 1 Chr. 16:5, 6; 2 Chr. 5:12, 13; 29:25–30; Ezra 3:10–13).

98:8 rivers clap their hands. Different parts of nature are pictured as rejoicing in this global scene of joy (cf. Is. 35:1, 2; Rom. 8:19–21).

98:9 He is coming. See note on Psalm 96:13.

99:1–9 The theme of this psalm is summed up in its last phrase: "the LORD our God is holy"(v. 9). The psalmist encourages praise to the king for His holiness (vv. 3, 5, 9), which is the separateness of God's being from all other creatures and things, as well as His moral separateness from sin. The psalmist also exults in the truth that such a holy God has had an intimate saving relationship with Israel throughout her history (vv. 6–9).

I. Exaltation of the King's Holiness (99:1–5)

II. Examples of the King's Holiness (99:6–9)

99:1 between the cherubim. See note on Psalm 80:1; cf. Psalm 18:6–19; Ezekiel 10:1ff.

99:2 Zion. See note on Psalm 87:2; cf. Hebrews 12:22–24. **peoples.** See notes on Psalms 57:9; 67:3.

99:4 King's strength also loves justice. King's strength may be a kind of epithet for God; or (combining this phrase with v. 3) the psalmist may be saying that a holy name is the strength of a just king. **equity.** I.e., fairness (cf. Is. 11:1–5).

99:5 His footstool. In general, this is a metaphor for the temple in Jerusalem (cf. Is. 60:13; Lam. 2:1); but more specifically, this is a metaphor for the ark of the covenant

(1 Chr. 28:2). Footstools were included with the thrones of the kings of Israel (2 Chr. 9:18).

99:6 Moses . . . Aaron . . . Samuel. Using three of the nation's famous heroes for examples, the psalmist demonstrates that a holy God has had an enduring, intimate, and saving relationship with Israel.

99:7 cloudy pillar. This was a medium of divine direction (cf. Ex. 13:21, 22; 33:9, 10; Num. 12:5; Deut. 31:15ff.). **testimonies . . . ordinance.** Terms used in Psalms for God's Word (see Ps. 119).

99:9 His holy hill. This is the hill in Jerusalem where the temple was built (cf. Pss. 15:1; 24:3), and where it will be located in the future messianic kingdom (cf. Is. 24:23).

100:1–5 This well-known psalm, emphasizing the universal nature of God's kingship, is a benediction to the series of psalms which are occupied with the Lord's kingdom rule (Pss. 93; 95–100). Most of it is a call to praise and thanksgiving, while verses 3 and 5 fix the reasons for that worship.

I. A Call to Praise the Lord (100:1–3)

II. A Call to Thank the Lord (100:4, 5)

100:1 a joyful shout. See note on Psalm 66:1.

100:3 Know. In the sense of experiencing and being completely assured of the truth. **the LORD, He is God.** A confession that Israel's covenant God, Jehovah, is the only true God. **made us.** Though God's actual creation of every human being is understood here, this phrase seems to refer to God's making and blessing Israel as a nation (cf. Deut. 32:6, 15; Ps. 95:6; Is. 29:22, 23; 44:2).

His people . . . His pasture. The shepherd image is often ascribed to the king of Israel, as well as to the Lord (cf. Ps. 78:70–72; Is. 44:28; Jer. 10:21; Zech. 10:3; 11:4–17; also Pss. 23:1; 28:9; 74:1; 77:20; 78:52, 53; 80:1; 95:7). The figure suggests intimate care (cf.

Luke 15:3–6). According to the NT, the Lord is also the Shepherd of saints in the church age (John 10:16).

100:4 His gates . . . courts. The gates and courts were those of the temple.

100:5 the LORD is good. God is the source and perfect example of goodness. *His mercy.* See note on Psalm 85:7. *His truth.* In the sense of keeping His promises, i.e., His faithfulness.

101:1–8 This Davidic psalm expresses the righteous commitments of the mediatorial king (David) to his eternal king (the Lord) in regard to (1) his own personal life and (2) the lives of those who inhabit the kingdom. Possibly, this psalm was used later at the coronations of future kings over Israel. Ultimately, only King Jesus would perfectly fulfill these holy resolutions (cf. Is. 9:6, 7; 11:1–5).

I. Personal Life of the King (101:1–4)
II. Personal Outcome of Kingdom Inhabitants (101:5–8)
  A. The Just (101:6)
  B. The Unjust (101:5, 7, 8)

101:2 perfect way. As the king goes, so go his followers (cf. v. 6). *when will You come to me?* This is not an eschatological expectation, but rather a personal expression of David's need for God's immanent involvement in his earthly kingship. *my house.* The king first starts with his own personal life (cf. v. 7), and then looks beyond to his kingdom (cf. vv. 5, 8).

101:3, 4 This is similar to the "blessed man" in Psalm 1:1.

101:3 my eyes. The king desires to look at nothing but that which is righteous (cf. v. 6).

101:4 wickedness. The king will not engage in wickedness (cf. v. 8).

101:5 slanders . . . haughty look . . . proud heart. Neither character assassination nor pride will be tolerated in the kingdom.

101:6 the faithful of the land. This group

is compared to "the wicked of the land" in verse 8.

101:7 deceit . . . lies. A premium is put on truth as foundational for a kingdom associated with the God of truth (cf. John 14:6).

101:8 the land . . . the city of the LORD. Israel and Jerusalem, respectively.

102:1–28 The non-specific superscription is unique to this psalm which highlights the thoughts of one who is afflicted (cf. Pss. 22; 69; 79; 102; 130; 142), perhaps expressing exilic lament (cf. Pss. 42; 43; 74; 79; 137). Like Job, whose troubles were not the result of God's judgment for personal sin, the psalmist cries out in pain. His only relief comes from refocusing on sovereign God and His eternal purposes. Messianic overtones are present as Hebrews 1:10–12 quotes Psalm 102:25, 26.

I. A Plea for Immediate Divine Help (102:1–11)
II. A Perspective of God's Sovereignty and Eternality (102:12–22)
III. A Prayer for Longer Life (102:23–28)

102:1, 2 Frequently, the Psalms begin with a cry for God's sovereign intervention when human resources have proven insufficient, e.g., Psalms 77:1; 142:1.

102:2 Your face . . . Your ear. Anthropomorphic language (i.e., a figure of speech that attributes human features to God) which points to God's attention and response, respectively.

102:3–5 bones . . . heart . . . bones. These terms describe the emotional and physical toll of the psalmist's ordeal.

102:6 pelican. Possibly a desert owl. The verse describes a desolate situation, extreme loneliness (cf. Is. 34:8–15; Zeph. 2:13–15). *owl.* Owls were unclean animals, cf. Leviticus 11:16–18.

102:7 sparrow. Feeling like a "lonely bird," the psalmist expresses his perceived abandonment by both God and man.

102:10, 11 *a shadow that lengthens.* The time of sunset is used to describe the psalmist's desperate sense that his life will end shortly because God has punished him by withdrawing His presence and strength.

102:12–22 The psalmist radically shifts his focus from earth to heaven—from his dilemma to God—and basks in the eternal nature of God and the eternal outworking of God's redemptive plan.

102:13–16 *Zion.* Earthly Zion or Jerusalem is in view (cf. vv. 16, 21, 22). Perhaps this points to the time of restoration after the Babylonian exile (c. 605–536 B.C.).

102:18 *written.* The psalmist had a sense of the perpetuation of his literary effort.

102:19 *looked down . . . viewed.* The transcendent omniscience of God is in view.

102:22 *the peoples . . . the kingdoms.* This will ultimately be fulfilled in Christ's messianic reign over the world (cf. Ps. 2).

102:23, 24 The psalmist desires to live longer, but acknowledges his mortality compared to God's eternality.

102:24 *the midst of my days.* Lit. at the halfway point of life.

102:25–27 Eternal God created the heavens and earth, which will one day perish (v. 26). Hebrews 1:10–12 applies this passage to the Lord Jesus Christ, who is superior to the angels because: (1) He is eternal, while they had a beginning, and (2) He created, but they were created. This passage clearly affirms the eternality and deity of Christ. The unchangeable God will outlast His creation, even into the new creation (cf. Mal. 3:6; James 1:17; 2 Pet. 3; Rev. 21; 22).

102:28 The realistic hope of one who perceives that though he is about to die, God's purposes on earth will be accomplished in future generations.

103:1–22 Psalms 103 and 104 appear as an intentional pair designed to promote the blessing and exaltation of God. This psalm represents a soliloquy in which David surveys God's goodness and encourages the angels and the works of God's creation to join him in divine praise.

I. A Call for Human Praise (103:1–19)
   A. Personally (103:1–5)
   B. Corporately (103:6–19)
II. A Call for Creation's Praise
   (103:20–22b)
   A. Angels (103:20–21)
   B. Works of Creation (103:22a–b)
III. A Refrain of Personal Praise (103:22c)

103:1 *Bless the LORD.* Cf. 103:2, 22; 104:1, 35.

103:2 *forget not all His benefits.* These earthly gifts from God included: (1) forgiveness of sin (v. 3), (2) recovery from sickness (v. 3), (3) deliverance from death (v. 4), (4) abundant lovingkindness and mercy (v. 4), and (5) food to sustain life (v. 5).

103:3 *diseases.* This is not a promise, but a testimony which should be understood in the light of Deuteronomy 32:39.

103:5 *youth is renewed like the eagle's.* The mysterious way of the long-lived eagle symbolized strength and speed (cf. Ex. 19:4; Jer. 48:40), which also characterizes human youth. As a general rule, a person blessed of God will grow weak and slow down less rapidly than otherwise (cf. Is. 40:29–31, which uses the same language).

103:6–19 The psalmist rehearses the attributes of God with which He blesses the saints.

103:7, 8 *His ways to Moses.* Cf. Moses' request (Ex. 33:13) with God's answer (Ex. 34:6, 7).

103:9 *not always strive.* There will be a final day of accountability, both at death (Luke 16:19–31) and the Great White Throne (Rev. 20:11–15). The Genesis flood served as a stark preview of this truth (cf. Gen. 6:3).

103:10 *not dealt.* God's great mercy

(v. 11) and irreversible, complete justification (v. 12) have redemptively accomplished for believers in Christ, by the death of Christ (cf. 2 Cor. 5:21; Phil. 3:9), what they themselves could not do.

103:13 *As a father.* Unlike the pagan gods, who are apathetic or hostile.

103:14 *dust.* Physically speaking, as Adam was created of dust (Gen. 2:7), so mankind at death decomposes back into dust (Gen. 3:19).

103:15, 16 *days . . . like grass.* Man's life is short and transitory (cf. Is. 40:8).

103:17, 18 *the mercy of the LORD.* Those who appeal to God's mercy by proper fear (v. 17) and obedience (v. 18) will overcome the shortness of physical life with eternal life. Luke 1:50 quotes Psalm 103:17.

103:19 *His throne in heaven.* From everlasting to everlasting, God has always ruled over all things (cf. Pss. 11:4; 47:1–9; 148:8–13). This universal kingdom is to be distinguished from God's mediatorial kingdom on earth.

103:20, 21 *His angels . . . His hosts.* Unfallen, righteous angels who serve God night and day (cf. Ps. 148:2; Rev. 5:11–13).

103:22 *His works.* This refers to God's creation, which is also to His praise (cf. Pss. 148–150, also 1 Chr. 29:10–13).

104:1–35 In vivid poetic detail, the psalmist sings of the Lord's glory in creation (cf. Gen. 1; 2; Job 38–41; Pss. 19:1–6; 148:1–6; Prov. 30:4; Is. 40:1–6; John 1:1–3; Rom. 1:18–25; Col. 1:16, 17). He refers to the original creation (cf. 104:5) without forgetting the fall of man and the cursed earth (104:23, 29, 35). He alternates reciting God's greatness by (1) personal praise to the Creator (104:1, 2, 5–9, 20–30), and (2) declaring God's handiwork to his human audience (104:3, 4, 10–19, 31–35). The flow of the psalm loosely follows the order of creation as first reported in Genesis 1:1–31 but

closes (v. 35) with an allusion to the end-time events recorded in Revelation 20–22.

I. The Heavens and Earth Created (104:1–9)

II. The Needs of Creatures Met (104:10–18)

III. The Sun and Moon (104:19–23)

IV. The Sea and Its Inhabitants (104:24–26)

V. God's Providential Care (104:27–30)

VI. Benediction to the Creator (104:31–35)

104:1–9 This section approximates the first two days of creation (cf. Gen. 1:1–8).

104:1 *very great.* The Creator is greater than His creation. Therefore, the Creator is to be worshiped, not the creation (cf. Ex. 20:3, 4; Rom. 1:29).

104:3 *the waters.* Refers to the original creation with the waters above the heaven (cf. Gen. 1:7, 8).

104:4 *spirits . . . flame of fire.* Hebrews 1:7 attributes these characteristics to angels, describing their swiftness and destructiveness as God's instruments of judgment.

104:5 *foundations.* Cf. Job 38:4.

104:6–9 While this might sound like the worldwide flood of Genesis 6–9, it continues to refer to the creation, especially Genesis 1:9, 10 regarding the third day of creation.

104:10–18 With water (vv. 10–13), vegetation (v. 14), food-producing vines, trees, and grain (v. 15), trees (vv. 16, 17), and cliffs (v. 18), the Creator provides for the basic needs of His creation. This corresponds to the third day of creation (cf. Gen. 1:11–13).

104:13 *upper chambers.* This refers to rain clouds.

104:19–23 This section corresponds to the fourth day of creation in Genesis 1:14–19. The work period of predators (the night) is contrasted with the work time of humans (the day).

104:24–26 This portion corresponds to the fifth day of creation in Genesis 1:20–23.

104:26 *Leviathan.* This term appears in

Christ in the Psalms (Luke 24:44)

Psalms	NT Quote	Significance
2:1–12	Acts 4:25,26; 13:33; Heb. 1:5; 5:5	Incarnation, Crucifixion, Resurrection
8:3–8	1 Cor. 15:27,28; Eph. 1:22; Heb. 2:5–10	Creation
16:8–11	Acts 2:24–31; 13:35–37	Death, Resurrection
22:1–31	Matt. 27:35–46; John 19:23,24; Heb. 2:12; 5:5	Incarnation, Crucifixion, Resurrection
40:6–8	Heb. 10:5–9	Incarnation
41:9	John 13:18,21	Betrayal
45:6,7	Heb. 1:8,9	Deity
68:18	Eph. 4:8	Ascension, Enthronement
69:20,21,25	Matt. 27:34,48; Acts 1:15–20	Betrayal, Crucifixion
72:6–17	-----	Millennial Kingship
78:1,2,15	Matt. 13:35; 1 Cor. 10:4	Theophany, Earthly teaching ministry
89:3–37	Acts 2:30	Millennial Kingship
102:25–27	Heb. 1:10–12	Creation, Eternality
109:6–19	Acts 1:15–20	Betrayal
110:1–7	Matt. 22:43–45; Acts 2:33–35; Heb. 1:13; 5:6–10; 6:20; 7:24	Deity, Ascension, Heavenly Priesthood, Millennial Kingship
118:22,23	Matt. 21:42; Mark 12:10,11; Luke 20:17; Acts 4:8–12; 1 Pet. 2:7	Rejection as Savior
132:12–18	Acts 2:30	Millennial Kingship

The MacArthur Study Bible, by John MacArthur (Nashville: Word Publishing, 1997) 844. © 1993 by Thomas Nelson, Inc.

four other OT passages (Job 3:8; 41:1; Ps. 74:14; Is. 27:1). In each case, Leviathan refers to some mighty creature who can overwhelm man, but who is no match for God. Some form of sea monster, probably a dinosaur, is in view. *See note on Job 41:1.*

104:27–30 All of creation waits on God for His providential care. These verses allude to the sixth day of creation (cf. Gen. 1:24–31).

104:30 *Your Spirit.* This, most likely, should be translated "Your breath," which corresponds to "the breath of life" in Genesis 2:7.

104:31–35 The psalmist closes with a benediction to the Creator in which he prays that the ungodly might no longer spiritually pollute God's universe (104:35). This prayer anticipates the new heaven and new earth (cf. Rev. 21; 22).

104:32 *trembles . . . smoke.* Earthquakes

and fires caused by lightning are in view.

104:35 *sinners . . . wicked.* Although God has been merciful to let His fallen human creation live on (cf. Gen. 3:1–24), those who bless and praise the Lord desire to see the day when (1) sinful people have been abolished from the earth (cf. Rev. 20:11–15), and (2) the curse of the earth is reversed (cf. Rev. 22:3).

105:1–45 Just as Psalms 103 and 104 were matched pairs, so are Psalms 105 and 106 as they look at Israel's history from God's perspective and then Israel's vantage, respectively. This psalm possibly originated by command of David to Asaph on the occasion when the ark of the covenant was first brought to Jerusalem (2 Sam. 6:12–19; 1 Chr. 16:1–7). Psalm 105:1–15 repeats 1 Chronicles 16:8–22.

I. Rejoicing in God's Works for Israel (105:1–3)

II. Remembering God's Works for Israel
(105:4–6)
III. Recounting God's Work for Israel
(105:7–45)
A. Abraham to Joseph (105:7–25)
B. Moses to Joshua (105:26–45)

105:1–5 Ten imperatives call Israel to a time of remembering, celebrating, and spreading the report abroad of the work of God on Israel's behalf as a result of God's covenant with Abraham.

105:6 *seed of Abraham . . . children of Jacob.* Those who were to obey the commands of 105:1–5, i.e., the nation of Israel, are in view.

105:7–12 This section rehearses the Abrahamic covenant.

105:8 *a thousand generations.* A reference to an exceedingly long time (a generation is normally forty years) which would encompass the remainder of human history, i.e., forever (cf. Deut. 7:9; 1 Chr. 16:15).

105:9, 10 The original covenant that God had made with Abraham. He later renewed it with Isaac and then Jacob (cf. Abraham— Gen. 12:1–3; 13:14–18; 15:18–21; 17:1–21; 22:15–19; Isaac—26:23–25; and Jacob— 35:9–12).

105:10 *an everlasting covenant.* From the time of the covenant until the end. Five OT covenants are spoken of as "everlasting": (1) the Noahic covenant, Genesis 9:16; (2) the Abrahamic covenant, Genesis 17:7, 13, 19; (3) the priestly covenant, Leviticus 24:8; (4) the Davidic covenant, 2 Samuel 23:5; and (5) the New Covenant, Jeremiah 32:40.

105:11 *Saying.* This probably has God's promise to Abraham at Genesis 17:8 in view.

105:12 *few in number.* God promised Abraham that He would multiply his small number of descendants to be as numerous as the stars of heaven and the sand of the seashore (cf. Gen. 13:16; 15:5; 17:2, 6; 22:17).

105:13 *one nation to another.* Abraham had migrated from Ur of the Chaldeans to Haran and finally to Canaan (Gen. 11:31). Later, he visited Egypt (Gen. 12:10–13:1).

105:14 *He rebuked.* The Lord struck Pharaoh and his house with great plagues when Sarai was taken to his quarters (Gen. 12:17). Abimelech, king of Gerar, was also rebuked by God (Gen. 20:3–7).

105:15 *Do not touch . . . no harm.* No one passage in the OT records this exact statement. The psalmist most likely is summarizing several occasions, such as Genesis 20:7; 26:11. *My anointed ones . . . My prophets.* With poetic parallelism, God's prophets are termed those whom He chose to represent Him on earth. In Genesis 20:7, Abraham is called a prophet. This title could also apply to Isaac and Jacob.

105:16–25 The history recorded in Genesis 37–50 is in view. Verses 16–22 refer to Joseph's experience in Egypt (cf. Gen. 37–41), while verse 23 looks to Jacob's trek to Egypt that resulted in a 430-year stay (Gen. 42–50; cf. Gen. 15:13, 14; Ex. 12:40). Verses 24 and 25 give an overall summary of Israel's experience in Egypt (cf. Ex. 1:7–14).

105:23 *the land of Ham.* Another name for the area in Egypt where part of the descendants of Ham, the youngest son of Noah, settled (cf. Gen. 9:24; 10:21; Ps. 78:51).

105:23–25 God sovereignly used Egypt to judge Israel (cf. Gen. 15:13).

105:26–36 God's deliverance of Israel from Egypt through the leadership of Moses and Aaron is rehearsed with a special emphasis on the ten plagues, ending with the Passover (cf. Ex. 5–12).

105:28 *darkness.* The ninth plague (cf. Ex. 10:21–29).

105:29 *waters into blood.* The first plague (cf. Ex. 7:14–25).

105:30 *frogs.* The second plague (cf. Ex. 8:1–15).

105:31 *swarms of flies . . . lice.* The fourth

and third plagues, respectively (cf. Ex. 8:16–32). The fifth plague of pestilence (Ex. 9:1–7) and the sixth plague of boils (Ex. 9:8–12) are not mentioned.

105:32, 33 hail . . . flaming fire. The seventh plague (cf. Ex. 9:13–35).

105:34, 35 locusts. The eighth plague (cf. Ex. 10:1–20).

105:36 destroyed . . . the firstborn. The tenth and final plague, which was death to the firstborn of man and beast among the Egyptians (cf. Ex. 11:1–12:51).

105:37–41 The psalmist summarizes Israel's exodus from Egypt. God provided for their financial and physical needs (cf. Ex. 11:2, 3; 12:35; Ex. 15:26); protection by day and night (cf. Ex. 14:19, 20); food needs (Ex. 16:1–36); and water needs (cf. Ex. 17:6; Num. 20:1–11).

105:42–45 The psalmist concludes with a summary that alludes to Joshua's leading the nation back into the high priest, first promised to Abraham, (Josh. 1–12) and then distributed to the twelve tribes of Israel (Josh. 13–24). What God promised (cf. 105:7–12), He delivered.

105:42 He remembered. As promised in verse 8.

105:45 observe . . . keep. This theme of obedience begins (1:6–9) and ends (24:14, 15, 16, 18, 21, 24) the Book of Joshua.

106:1–48 Psalm 106 rehearses God's mercy during Israel's history, in spite of Israel's sinfulness (cf. Neh. 9:1–38; Ps. 78; Is. 63:7–64:12; Ezek. 20:1–44; Dan. 9:1–19; Acts 7:2–53; 1 Cor. 10:1–13). The occasion for this psalm is most likely the repentance (v. 6) of post-exilic Jews who had returned to Jerusalem (vv. 46, 47). Verses 1, 47, 48 seem to be borrowed from 1 Chronicles 16:34–36, which was sung on the occasion of the ark's first being brought to Jerusalem by David (cf. 2 Sam. 6:12–19; 1 Chr. 16:1–7). True revival appears to be the psalmist's intention.

I. The Invocation (106:1–5)
II. The Identification with Israel's Sins (106:6)
III. The Confession of Israel's Sins (106:7–46)
  A. During Moses' Time (106:7–33)
  B. From Joshua to Jeremiah (106:34–46)
IV. The Plea for Salvation (106:47)
V. The Benediction (106:48)

106:1 good . . . mercy. These attributes of God are especially praiseworthy to the psalmist in light of Israel's historical sin pattern (cf. 106:6–46).

106:2, 3 Verse 2 asks the question answered in verse 3.

106:4, 5 The psalmist has the benefits of the Abrahamic covenant in mind (see note on Ps. 105:9, 10). He prays here for personal deliverance (v. 4) and, later, for national deliverance (v. 47).

106:6 We . . . fathers. The psalmist acknowledges the perpetual sinfulness of Israel, including that of his own generation.

106:7–12 This section recalls the crossing of the Red Sea during the Exodus by the nation, when Pharaoh and his army were in pursuit (cf. Ex. 14:1–31).

106:7 rebelled. Cf. Exodus 14:11, 12. **Red Sea.** See note on Exodus 13:18.

106:8 His name's sake. The glory and reputation of God provide the highest motive for His actions. This frequent OT phrase appears six other places in the Psalms (cf. Pss. 23:3; 25:11; 31:3; 79:9; 109:21; 143:11).

106:9 He rebuked the Red Sea. This reliable historical account recalls a true supernatural miracle of God (cf. Ex. 14:21, 22) just as He would later provide a way for the nation to cross the Jordan River into the land (cf. Josh. 3:14–17).

106:10 Quoted in Luke 1:71.

106:11 not one of them left. As recorded in Exodus 14:28 (cf. Ps. 78:53).

106:12 *They sang His praise.* The Song of Moses is in view (cf. Ex. 15:1–21).

106:13–33 This section remembers the nation's wanderings in the wilderness (cf. Num. 14–Deut. 34).

106:13–15 The Jews forgot what God had most recently done on their behalf, but (1) remembered the basics of life that Egypt provided, and (2) doubted that they would have water (cf. Ex. 15:24) or food (cf. Ex. 16:2, 3) in the future.

106:14 *tested God.* According to Numbers 14:22, the nation tested God at least ten times (cf. Ex. 5:21; 6:9; 14:11, 12; 15:24; 16:2, 3; 17:2, 3; 32:1–6; Num. 11:1–6; 12:1, 2; 14:2, 3).

106:16–18 Korah, who is not named here, led the rebellion that is recounted (cf. Num. 16:1–35). God's judgment concluded with fire which consumed 250 men (cf. Num. 16:35).

106:19–23 This section remembers when the nation convinced Aaron to make a golden calf for idol worship while Moses was on the mountain receiving the commandments of God (cf. Ex. 32:1–14; Deut. 9:7–21).

106:19 *Horeb.* This is most likely another name for Mt. Sinai (cf. Ex. 19:11). This special place, called "the mountain of God" (cf. Ex. 3:1; 1 Kin. 19:8), is where Moses received the commandments of God (Deut. 1:6; 5:2; 29:1; Mal. 4:4).

106:21 *God their Savior.* This title, common in the pastoral epistles, is seldom used in the OT outside of Isaiah (19:20; 43:3, 11; 45:15, 21; 49:26; 60:16; 63:8). Here, it refers to physical deliverance. It looks forward to Jesus Christ as spiritual redeemer (Luke 2:11).

106:22 *Ham.* Another name for the part of Egypt that was settled by descendants of Ham, the youngest son of Noah (cf. Gen. 9:24; 10:21).

106:23 *Moses . . . in the breach.* Moses pleaded with God, based on the Abrahamic covenant promises, not to destroy the nation in spite of their idolatry and immoral behavior (cf. Ex. 32:11–14).

106:24–27 This portion recounts (1) the nation's rejection of Joshua's and Caleb's positive report from the high priest, and (2) their desire to return to Egypt (cf. Num. 14:1–4). God responded with judgment (Num. 14:11–38).

106:24 *the pleasant land.* A term used of the high priest which God promised to Abraham for the nation Israel (cf. Jer. 3:19; Zech. 7:14).

106:28–31 This scene recounts Israel's encounter with the prophet Balaam who, on behalf of Balak, king of Moab, tried to curse Israel but was prevented from doing so by God (cf. Num. 22–24; Deut. 23:4; Josh. 24:9, 10; Neh. 13:2). Having failed, Balaam advised Balak to entice Israel with immorality and idolatry (cf. Num. 31:16 with 25:1; 2 Pet. 2:15; Jude 11; Rev. 2:14). Israel sinned and God judged (Num. 25:1–13). Balaam was later killed by Israel (cf. Josh. 13:22).

106:28 *Baal of Peor.* Refers to Baal, a god of the Moabites, whose worship occurred at the location of the mountain called Peor (cf. Num. 23:28). ***sacrifices made to the dead.*** This most likely refers to sacrifices made to lifeless idols (cf. 1 Thess. 1:9). Israel should have been worshiping "the living God" (cf. Deut. 5:26; 1 Sam. 17:26, 36; Pss. 42:2; 84:2; Jer. 10:3–10; Dan. 6:20, 26).

106:30 *Phinehas.* The son of Eleazar, son of Aaron (cf. Num. 25:7).

106:31 *accounted to him for righteousness.* This was a just and rewardable action, evidencing faith in God. As with Abraham (cf. Gen. 15:6; Rom. 4:3; Gal. 3:6; James 2:23), so it was also with Phinehas. This is part of the Mosaic covenant concerning perpetual priesthood through Aaron, from the house of Levi, which was first made by God in Leviticus 24:8, 9 (cf. Jer. 33:17–22; Mal.

2:4–8). This covenant was reaffirmed in Numbers 18:8, 19. In this text, the covenant is further specified to be through the line of faithful Phinehas.

106:32, 33 This scene looks back to Numbers 20:1–13 when Moses, provoked by the continuing rebellion of Israel, wrongly struck the rock in anger (cf. Ex. 11:8; 16:20) and, thus, offended God (cf. Num. 20:12). As a result, both Aaron (cf. Num. 20:22–29) and Moses (Deut. 34:1–8) died prematurely without entering the Promised Land.

106:32 *the waters of strife.* These are the waters of Meribah (cf. Num. 20:13).

106:33 *His Spirit.* This most likely refers to the Holy Spirit of God. The Spirit of God had an extensive ministry in the OT (cf. Gen. 1:2; 6:3; 2 Sam. 23:2; Neh. 9:30; Ps. 139:7; Is. 48:16; Ezek. 2:2; 3:12–14; 8:3; 11:1, 5, 24; Hag. 2:5, Zech. 7:12). Both Isaiah 63:10, 11 and Acts 7:51 point to this particular event.

106:34–39 This section describes the general sins of Israel from the time they entered the Promised Land (Josh. 3; 4) until they were exiled to Assyria (2 Kin. 17) and Babylon (2 Kin. 24; 25). They failed to expel the heathen and sadly conformed to their idolatry.

106:36–38 *idols . . . demons . . . idols.* Demons impersonate idols and encourage idol worship (cf. Deut. 32:17; 2 Chr. 33:5–7; 1 Cor. 10:14–21; Rev. 9:20). The sacrifice of children was not uncommon (cf. Deut. 12:31; 2 Kin. 17:17; Ezek. 16:20, 21).

106:39 *their own works . . . deeds.* God held Israel directly responsible for their sin, without excuse.

106:40–43 From the time of the judges until the Assyrian and Babylonian exiles, God used the hand of His enemies to discipline Israel for their sin.

106:44–46 This emphasizes the unconditional nature of God's covenant with Abraham.

106:45 *for their sake.* A secondary complement to God, who was primarily acting for His name's sake (cf. v. 8). *He remembered His covenant.* This answers the psalmist's prayer of verses 4 and 5 with regard to the Abrahamic covenant that (1) the descendants of Abraham would multiply, and (2) they would possess the high priest (*see note on Ps. 105:9, 10*; cf. Luke 1:72–75).

106:47 The psalmist pleads, on behalf of the nation and in light of the Abrahamic covenant, for the nation to be regathered in Israel. He remembers what the men of Moses' day forgot, i.e., God as their Savior (cf. 106:21). Even though the tribes of Judah and Benjamin returned to Israel in Ezra and Nehemiah, this text looks ahead to the regathering of Israel at the time when the Lord Jesus Christ returns to rule over the promised Davidic (2 Sam. 7) millennial kingdom (Rev. 20) on earth (cf. Ezek. 37:11–28; Hos. 14:4–8; Joel 3:18–21; Amos 9:7–15; Mic. 7:14–20; Zeph. 3:8–20; Zech. 12–14).

106:48 *From everlasting to everlasting.* With the hopeful prayer of 106:47 on his lips, the psalmist closes the fourth book of the Psalms (Pss. 90–106) with a grand benediction focusing on the eternal character of God, Israel's Savior (cf. 1 Chr. 16:36; Pss. 41:13; 90:2).

107:1–43 The common opening line of Psalms 105–107, "Oh, give thanks to the LORD," links together this trilogy of songs which praise God for His goodness and mercy to Israel. Most likely, this psalm has a post-exilic origin (cf. 107:3). The psalm develops two main themes: (1) praising God for His continual deliverance (107:4–32), and (2) remembering God's response to man's obedience/disobedience (107:33–42).

I. The Call to Praise (107:1–3)

II. The Cause of Rejoicing—Deliverance (107:4–32)

III. The Consequences of Obedience/Disobedience (107:33–42)

IV. The Commentary on Wisdom/Understanding (107:43)

107:1–3 All of those who have been delivered (redeemed) from the hand of Israel's enemy focus on God's goodness and everlasting mercy. They had been delivered through the centuries from Egypt to the south (cf. Ex. 12–14), Syria and Assyria to the north (cf. 2 Kin. 19:29–37), the Philistines to the west (cf. 2 Sam. 8:1; 2 Kin. 18:8), and Babylon to the east (cf. Ezra 1). Compare the psalmist's prayer in 106:47 with verse 3.

107:4–32 This portion contains four pictures or actual situations which illustrate the disastrous end of sin in the nation: (1) wandering in the wilderness (vv. 4–9); (2) languishing in prison (vv. 10–16); (3) enduring sickness (vv. 17–22); and (4) tossing on a stormy sea (vv. 23–32). Each picture follows the same sequence of four events: (1) man's predicament (vv. 4, 5, 10–12, 17, 18, 23–27); (2) man's petition (vv. 6a, 13a, 19a, 28a); (3) God's pardon (vv. 6b, 7, 13b, 14, 19b, 20, 28b–30); and (4) man's praise (vv. 8, 9, 15, 16, 21, 22, 31, 32).

107:4–9 Possibly, the psalmist looked back at the desert wanderings of ungrateful, faithless Israel after the miraculous Exodus (Num. 14–Josh. 2).

107:10–16 Possibly, the psalmist thought of the capture and imprisonment of King Zedekiah c. 586 B.C. (cf. 2 Kin. 25:4–7; Jer. 39:4–8; Jer. 52:1–11).

107:17–22 Possibly, the psalmist recalled the mass affliction and subsequent mass healing in Numbers 21:4–9.

107:23–32 Possibly, the psalmist had Jonah and the sailors bound for Tarshish in mind (cf. Jon. 1).

107:33–42 This section contrasts God's blessing in response to man's obedience with God's judgment on man's sin. The psalmist makes his point with four illustrations: (1) descending from prosperity to poverty (vv.

33, 34); (2) being lifted up from barrenness to blessedness (vv. 35–38); (3) falling from the top to the bottom (vv. 39, 40); and (4) being elevated from low to high (vv. 41, 42).

107:33, 34 Perhaps the three years of drought from Ahab's and Jezebel's sins are in view (cf. 1 Kin. 17:1; 18:18).

107:35–38 Perhaps the time of Abraham (Gen. 24:1, 34, 35) or Joshua (Josh. 24:13) is in view.

107:39, 40 Perhaps the Assyrian exile (2 Kin. 17:4–6) or the Babylonian captivity (2 Kin. 24:14, 15) is in view.

107:41, 42 Perhaps the impoverished Jews in Egypt who were made rich with Egyptian gold and other treasures are in view (cf. Ex. 1:13, 14 with 3:21, 22; 11:2; 12:35, 36).

107:43 Perhaps the psalmist has Proverbs 8:1–36, Ecclesiastes 12:13, 14, or Hosea 14:9 in mind as he pens these concluding words.

108:1–13 David combines portions of his own previously written Psalms 57 and 60 to make up this psalm commemorating God's victories (vv. 1–5 are from 57:7–11; vv. 6–13 are from 60:5–12). He deleted the laments that began each psalm (57:1–6 and 60:1–4) while combining his own words of exaltation and confidence in God with only slight word variation. No specific historical occasion behind this psalm is given. *See notes on Psalm 57:7–11 and Psalm 60:5–12.*

I. Personal Exaltation of God (108:1–5)
II. Personal Confidence in God (108:6–13)

109:1–31 This imprecatory psalm of David cannot be conclusively connected by the psalm's general details with any particular incident or person in the king's life such as chronicled in 1 and 2 Samuel; 1 Kings; and 1 Chronicles. David responds here to those who have launched a vicious verbal assault of false accusations against him (cf. 109:2, 3, 20). This psalm is considered messianic in nature, since Acts 1:20 quotes verse 8 in reference to Judas's punishment for betraying Christ (cf. Pss. 41:9; 69:25). David reverses roles with his enemies by moving from being the accused in man's court to being the accuser/prosecutor before the bar of God.

I. The Plaintiff's Plea (109:1–5)
II. The Punishment Desired (109:6–20)
III. The Petition for Justice (109:21–29)
IV. The Praise of the Judge (109:30, 31)

109:1 *O God of my praise!* David begins and ends (cf. v. 30) with praise for the chief justice of the universe. At verse 21, David addresses the Judge as "O God the Lord" and at verse 26 as "O Lord my God."

109:2–5 David's complaint was that the innocent were being accused by the guilty. He asserted that the charges were without cause (109:3). While Doeg the Edomite has been identified by some (cf. 1 Sam. 21; 22; Ps. 52), the most likely candidate would be Saul (cf. 1 Sam. 18–27). Eight of the fourteen historical superscriptions in other psalms refer to the sufferings of David related to Saul's pursuits for the purpose of killing David (cf. Pss. 18; 34; 54; 56; 57; 59; 63; 142).

109:2 In verses 2–5, 20, 25, 27–29, David refers to a group of accusers, in contrast to verses 6–19 where an individual is mentioned. Most likely, the individual is the group leader.

109:6–20 The Mosaic Law had anticipated false accusations and malicious witnesses (cf. Deut. 19:16–21) by decreeing that the false accuser was to be given the punishment intended for the accused. It would appear that David had this law in mind here and verses 26–29. Thus, his imprecations are not malicious maledictions, but rather a call for justice according to the law. These severe words have respect not to the penitent, but to the impenitent and hard-hearted foes of God and His cause, whose inevitable fate is set.

109:8 The apostle Peter cited this verse as justification for replacing Judas the betrayer with another apostle (cf. Acts. 1:20).

109:21–29 David petitioned the court for justice by asking for deliverance for the judge's sake (109:21) and then for his own sake (vv. 22–25). Afterwards, he requested that his enemies be rightfully punished (vv. 26–29).

109:30, 31 David's praise for the divine magistrate (v. 30) was based on his confidence in the compassion and mercy of the judge (v. 31). Second Samuel 22 and Psalm 18 record the general outcome to David's case, which was tried in God's courtroom.

110:1–7 This psalm contains one of the most exalted prophetic portions of Scripture presenting Jesus Christ as both a holy king and a royal high priest—something that no human monarch of Israel ever experienced. It, along with Psalm 118, is by far the most quoted psalm in the NT (Matt. 22:44; 26:64; Mark 12:36; 14:62; Luke 20:42, 43; 22:69; Acts 2:34, 35; Heb. 1:13; 5:6; 7:17, 21; 10:13). While portraying the perfect king, the perfect high priest, and the perfect government, Psalm 110 declares Christ's current role in heaven as the resurrected Savior (110:1) and His future role on earth as the reigning monarch (110:2–7).

This psalm is decidedly messianic and millennial in content. Jesus Christ (Matt. 22:43, 44) verifies the Davidic authorship. The exact occasion of this psalm is unknown, but it could easily have been associated with God's declaration of the Davidic covenant in 2 Samuel 7:4–17.

I. Christ the King (110:1–3)
II. Christ the High-Priest (110:4–7)

110:1 *my Lord.* This title refers to the divine/human King of Israel—the Lord Jesus Christ. Christ's humanity descended from David, which is demanded by the Davidic promise of 2 Samuel 7:12. Using this passage, Christ also declared His deity in the Gospels (Matt. 22:44; Mark 12:36; Luke 20:42–43) by arguing that only God could have been lord to King David. *My right hand.* God the Father invited God the Son in His ascension to sit at the place of honor in the heavenly throne room (cf. Acts. 2:22–36; Heb. 10:10–12). *Your enemies Your footstool.* The footstool was an ancient Near Eastern picture of absolute victory portraying the idea that one's enemy was now underfoot (cf. Pss. 8:6, 7; 47:3; Is. 66:1; 1 Cor. 15:27). This anticipates Christ's Second Advent (cf. Rev. 19:11–21) as a conquering king (cf. Heb. 10:13).

110:2 *the rod.* From the human side, the ancestral staff of Judah is in view (cf. Gen. 49:10). From the divine side, the rod of iron by which King Jesus will subdue the earth is intended (cf. Ps. 2:9). *Zion.* God intends to install His ultimate earthly king in Jerusalem (the southwest side is Zion; cf. Ps. 132:13–18). The earthly Zion (cf. Ps. 2:6; Is. 59:20) is in view, not the heavenly Zion because (1) there are no enemies in heaven, and (2) none of the activities in verses 5–7 will take place in heaven. *Rule.* Christ will rule on the earthly throne of His father David (cf. Luke 1:32), in fulfillment of Isaiah 9:6 and Zechariah 14:9.

110:3 *volunteers.* The redeemed inhabitants of earth will willingly serve the King of kings and Lord of lords. *the day of Your power.* This refers to the power displayed during the millennial reign of Jesus Christ (cf. Zech. 14:1–21; Rev. 19:11–20:6). *beauties . . . womb . . . dew.* This seems to apply to the King and to represent Him as in the constant vigor of youth, a period distinguished by strength and activity, or it may refer to His holiness, eternality, and deity.

110:4 *You are a priest.* The first time in the history of Israel when a king simultaneously served as high priest. Christ (also

known as "Branch," cf. Is. 4:2; Jer. 23:5, 6; Zech. 3:8; 6:12, 13) will build the temple at which the world will worship God (cf. 2 Sam. 7:13; Is. 2:2–4; Ezek. 40–48). *forever.* Christ represents the final and foremost high priest in the history of Israel. *the order of Melchizedek.* This high priest could not be of Aaron's lineage in that he would not be eternal, not be of Judah, not be a king, and not be of the New Covenant (Jer. 31:31–33; Heb. 8; 9). Melchizedek, which means "king of righteousness," served as the human priest/king of Salem in Genesis 14:17–20 and provides a picture of the order of Christ's priesthood (cf. Heb. 5:6; 7:17, 21). The sons of Zadok will serve with Christ in the millennium as His human priestly associates (cf. Ezek. 44:15; 48:11).

110:5 *Your right hand.* The roles have here reversed—the Father now stands at the right hand of the Son. This pictures the Father supplying the needs of the Son (cf. Pss. 16:8; 109:31; Is. 41:13). The Father provides the defeat of His enemies on earth so that His Son can fulfill God's land and nation promises to Abraham (Gen. 12:1, 2) and kingship promise to David (2 Sam. 7:12, 13, 16). *the day of His wrath.* This refers to the Day of the LORD (cf. v. 3 "the day of Your power"), which finds its global expression at the end of Daniel's seventieth week (cf. Dan. 9:24–27). This term exclusively speaks of God's wrath, which will be poured out on an unrepentant world in order to set up Christ's 1,000-year (millennial) reign (cf. Joel 2:1, 11, 31; 3:14; Rev. 6:16, 17; 14:19; 19:15).

110:6 *judge . . . fill . . . execute.* Cf. Psalms 2:8, 9; 50:1–6; Isaiah 2:4; 9:6, 7; Daniel 2:44, 45; 7:26, 27; Joel 3:2, 12; Micah 4:3; Matthew 25:32; Revelation 6:15–17; 14:20; 16:14; 19:19–21.

110:7 *He shall drink.* This pictures a refreshed conqueror who has kingly access to the whole world. This could anticipate the east-west flow of fresh water out of Jerusalem as recorded in Zechariah 14:8. **He shall lift up.** The lifted head pictures Christ's strength in victory (cf. Pss. 3:3; 27:6; 75:10). As Psalm 22:28 reports, "For the kingdom is the LORD's, and He rules over the nations" (cf. Zech. 14:9).

111:1–10 Psalms 111 and 112 are alike in that (1) they both begin with "Praise the LORD!" (as does Ps. 113), and (2) they both are acrostics with twenty-two lines corresponding to the twenty-two letters of the Hebrew alphabet. Psalm 111 exalts the works of God, while Psalm 112 extols the person who fears God. The authors and occasions are unknown.

I. A Word of Praise (111:1)
II. Words about God's Works (111:2–9)
III. A Word of Wisdom (111:10)

111:1 whole heart. Jesus might have had this passage in mind when He stated that the greatest commandment was, "You shall love the Lord your God with all your heart" (Matt. 22:37).

111:2–9 God's works are mentioned five times (vv. 2, 3, 4, 6, 7). Overall, the greater work of redemption seems to be in view (v. 9), without excluding lesser works of a temporal nature (vv. 5, 6).

111:5 food . . . His covenant. It is quite possible that the psalmist has alluded to God's faithfulness in providing food for Jacob through Joseph (Gen. 37–50) in fulfillment of the Abrahamic covenant to make the nation like the stars of the sky (Gen. 15:5).

111:6 the heritage of the nations. Here, it seems even more sure that the psalmist has the Abrahamic covenant in view (cf. Gen. 15:18–21; 17:1–8), specifically the Exodus (Exodus–Deuteronomy) and the conquering/dividing of the high priest (Joshua). *See notes on Deuteronomy 7:1, 2.*

111:9 commanded His covenant forever. In light of verses 5, 6 and Galatians 3:6–9, this appears to look at the redemptive aspects of the Abrahamic covenant, which was declared frequently to be an "everlasting" or "forever" covenant (cf. Gen. 17:7, 13, 19; 1 Chr. 16:15, 17; Ps. 105:8, 10; Is. 24:5).

111:10 The fear of the LORD. *See note on Proverbs 1:7.*

112:1–10 *See note on Psalm 111:1–10.*
I. The Blessing of Obedience (112:1–9)
II. The Emptiness of Sin (112:10)

112:1 who fears the LORD. This psalm begins where 111:10 ended and links the two together.

112:2–9 The desire of every human for prosperity can come only through obedience to the commands of God (cf. Ps. 1:1–3).

112:9 dispersed abroad. Quoted by Paul in 2 Corinthians 9:9.

112:9 His horn. Horns on an animal were an indication of strength and prosperity. This is applied figuratively to the righteous.

112:10 In contrast to the righteous man of verses 2–9, the wicked man lives a worthless existence without strength (cf. Ps. 1:4–6).

113:1–9 Psalms 113–118 comprise a rich six-psalm praise to God commonly known as the Egyptian Hallel (*hallel* meaning "praise" in Hebrew). These were sung at Passover, Pentecost, and Tabernacles, but had the greatest significance at Passover, which celebrated the Jews' deliverance from Egypt (cf. Ex. 12–14). Traditionally, Psalms 113 and 114 were sung before the Passover meal and Psalms 115–118 afterwards. Psalm 118 would most likely be what Christ and the disciples sang before they left the upper room the night Christ was betrayed (cf. Matt. 26:30; Mark 14:26). There are two other notable sets of praise in the Psalter: (1) The Great Hallel (Pss. 120–136) and (2) The Final Hallel (Pss. 145–150).

I. The Call to Praise (113:1–3)
II. The Cause for Praise (113:4–9)
   A. God's Transcendence (113:4, 5)
   B. God's Immanence (113:6–9)

113:1 servants. This refers to the redeemed, all of whom should serve God with obedience. **the name.** The name of God represents all His attributes.

113:2 this time . . . forevermore. Praise is to be rendered always (cf. Eph. 5:20; 1 Thess. 5:18).

113:3 rising . . . going down. From the first moment of consciousness in the morning to the last waking moment before sleep.

113:4, 5 Believers are to praise the only One worthy of praise for His transcendent sovereignty.

113:6–9 humbles. In appearance, God must figuratively lean over from the faraway heavens to examine the earth (cf. Is. 40:12–17). In a far greater way Christ humbled Himself in the incarnation (cf. Phil. 2:5–11).

113:7, 8 the poor. This is borrowed, almost exactly, from Hannah's song in 1 Samuel 2:8. God is responsible for both the rich and the poor (Prov. 22:2). God's compassion reaches out to the poor and needy (cf. Ps. 72:12, 13). Ultimately, Christ came to save those who are poor in spirit (cf. Is. 61:2; Luke 4:18).

113:9 the barren woman. Sarah (Gen. 21:2), Rebekah (Gen. 25:21), and Rachel (Gen. 30:23) would be the most significant since the outcome of the Abrahamic covenant depended on these childless women being blessed by God to be mothers.

114:1–8 *See note on Psalm 113:1–9.* This psalm is the one most explicitly related to the Exodus (Ex. 12–14). It recounts God's response to a captive nation (Israel in Egypt) in order to honor His promises in the Abrahamic covenant (Gen. 28:13–17) given to Jacob (cf. 114:1, "The house of Jacob;" 114:7,

"the God of Jacob").
  I. God Inhabits Israel (114:1, 2)
 II. God Intimidates Nature (114:3–6)
III. God Invites Trembling (114:7, 8)

114:2 Judah . . . Israel. Judah/Benjamin and the northern ten tribes, respectively. **sanctuary . . . dominion.** God dwelt among the peoples as a pillar of cloud by day and a pillar of fire by night (cf. Ex. 13:21, 22; 14:19).

114:3 The sea . . . Jordan. Two miracles of God, i.e., separating the waters began and ended the Exodus. On the way out of Egypt, God parted the Red Sea (Ex. 14:15–31) and forty years later He parted the Jordan River in order for the Jews to enter the Promised Land (Josh. 3:1–17).

114:4 mountains . . . little hills. This refers to the violent appearance of God to Israel at Sinai (cf. Ex. 19:18; Judg. 5:4, 5; Ps. 68:17, 18).

114:5, 6 In poetic imagery, God questioned why the most fixed of geographical features, i.e., water and mountains, could not resist His power and will.

114:7 Tremble. This is the only proper response of helpless nature before the omnipotent God.

114:8 the rock. This refers to the first incident at Massah/Meribah (Ex. 17:5, 6) and/or the second (Num. 20:8–11).

115:1–18 *See note on Psalm 113:1–9.* This praise psalm appears to be antiphonal in nature, following this outline:
   The People (115:1–8)
   The Priests (115:9–11)
   The People (115:12, 13)
   The Priests (115:14, 15)
   The People (115:16–18)

Verses 4–11 are very similar to Psalm 135:15–20. It has been suggested that this psalm is post-exilic (cf. v. 2) and could have first been sung at the dedication of the second temple (cf. Ezra 6:16).

115:1 *to Your name give glory.* God declared He would share His glory with no one (Is. 42:8; 48:11).

115:2 *where is their God?* (cf. Pss. 42:3, 10; 79:10; Joel 2:17; Mic. 7:10). The Jews despised this Gentile taunt.

115:3 Israel's God is alive and rules the earth from His throne room above.

115:4–8 In contrast, Gentiles worship dead gods of their own making, fashioned in the image of the fallen creature (cf. Is. 44:9–20; 46:5–7; Jer. 10:3–16; Rom. 1:21–25). The idol worshiper becomes like the idol—spiritually useless.

115:9–11 This three-verse, priestly admonition (cf. 118:2–4; 135:19, 20) could apply to three different groups: (1) the nation of Israel (115:9); (2) the Levitical priests from the house of Aaron (115:10); and (3) proselytes to Judaism who are God-fearers (115:11). To all three groups, God is their help and shield.

115:16 *the heavens . . . the earth.* These are strong implications that planet earth alone is the dwelling place of life.

116:1–19 *See note on Psalm 113:1–9.* This is an intensely personal "thank you" psalm to the Lord for saving the psalmist from death (116:3, 8). The occasion and author remain unknown, although the language used by Jonah in his prayer from the fish's stomach is remarkably similar. While this appears to deal with physical death, the same song could be sung by those who have been saved from spiritual death.

I. The Lord's Response to the Psalmist's Prayer for Deliverance from Death (116:1–11)

II. The Psalmist's Reaction to God's Deliverance of Him from Death (116:12–19)

116:3 *Sheol.* Another term for grave/death.

116:9 *I will walk.* A vow of obedience.

116:10 *I believed.* Faith in God and His ability to deliver preceded the psalmist's prayer for deliverance. This verse is quoted by the apostle Paul in 2 Corinthians 4:13. It rehearses the principle of walking by faith, not by sight.

116:11 *All men are liars.* Either the psalmist is reacting to his false accusers or to people who say they can deliver him but have not.

116:12 *What shall I render.* God needs nothing and puts no price on His free mercy and grace. The psalmist renders the only acceptable gift—obedience and thanksgiving.

116:13 *the cup of salvation.* This is the only place in the OT where this exact phrase is used. It probably has the meaning of the cup in Psalms 16:5; 23:5; i.e., the redeemed life provided by God, in contrast to Psalm 75:8, which speaks about the cup of God's wrath.

116:14 *I will pay my vows.* Most likely, this refers to vows made during a time of duress (cf. 116:18, 19).

116:15, 16 The psalmist realized what a special blessing his deliverance ("loosed my bonds") was in light of verse 15. Therefore, he reemphasized his role as a servant of God, following the example of his mother.

116:17–19 These verses parallel verses 13 and 14. Jonah made an almost identical statement (Jon. 2:9).

116:17 *the sacrifice of thanksgiving.* This is probably not a Mosaic sacrifice, but rather actual praise and thanksgiving rendered from the heart in the spirit of Psalms 136 and 138 (cf. Pss. 50:23; 100:4; 119:108; Heb. 13:15).

116:19 *the LORD's house.* This refers to (1) the tabernacle in Jerusalem, if written by David or before, or (2) the temple in Jerusalem, if written by Solomon or later.

117:1, 2 *See note on Psalm 113:1–9.* The

seal of redemptive truth is bound up in this diminutive but seminal psalm—its profundity far outdistances its size. This pivotal psalm exhibits three distinguishing features: (1) it is the shortest psalm; (2) it is the shortest chapter in the Bible; and (3) it is the middle chapter of the Bible. That God looked redemptively beyond the borders of Israel in the OT is made clear here. The psalm looks back to God's intent for Adam and Eve in Eden (Gen. 1; 2) and looks ahead to the ultimate fulfillment in the new heavens and earth (Rev. 21; 22).

I. A Global Invitation (117:1)
II. A Grand Explanation (117:2)

117:1 Gentiles! . . . peoples! Paul quoted this verse in Romans 15:11 to make the point that from the very beginning of time God has pursued a worldwide redemptive purpose (cf. Rom. 15:7–13). Other passages quoted by Paul in Romans 15 to make this point include: Deuteronomy 32:43; 2 Samuel 22:50; Isaiah 11:10. While not as obvious in the OT, the NT makes this point unmistakably clear (cf. Acts 10:34, 35; Rom. 1:16; 1 Cor. 12:13; Gal. 3:1–29; Col. 3:11).

117:2 The reasons for such exalted praise as that commanded in verse 1 are: (1) because of God's redemptive kindness, and (2) because of God's eternal truth. Therefore, what God has promised, He will provide (cf. John 6:37–40).

118:1–29 See note on Psalm 113:1–9. This psalm, along with Psalm 110, is intensely messianic and thus the most quoted by the NT (Matt. 21:9, 42; 23:39; Mark 11:9, 10; 12:10, 11; Luke 13:35; 19:38; 20:17; John 12:13; Acts 4:11; Heb. 13:6; 1 Pet. 2:7). Neither the author nor the specific circumstances of the psalm are identified. Two reasonable possibilities could be entertained: (1) it was written during Moses' day in the Exodus, or (2) it was written sometime after

the Jews returned to Jerusalem from exile.

Probably, it was the former, given (1) the nature of the Egyptian Hallel (see Ps. 114); (2) its use by the Jewish community, especially at Passover; (3) the close similarity to Moses' experience in the Exodus; (4) the striking similarity in language (Ps. 118:14 with Ex. 15:2; 118:15, 16 with Ex. 15:6, 12; 118:28 with Ex. 15:2); and (5) the particularly pointed messianic significance as it relates to the redemption provided by Christ our Passover (1 Cor. 5:7). It seems reasonable to propose that Moses possibly wrote this beautiful psalm to look back in worship at the historical Passover and look ahead in wonder to the spiritual Passover in Christ.

I. Call to Worship (118:1–4)
II. Personal Praise (118:5–21)
III. Corporate Praise (118:22–24)
IV. Commitment to Worship (118:25–29)

118:1 Oh, give thanks. Cf. Psalms 105–107; 136. The psalm ends in verse 29 as it began here.

118:2–4 Israel . . . Aaron . . . those who fear the Lord. See note on Psalm 115:9–11. The phrase "His mercy endures forever" is repeated in all twenty-six verses of Psalm 136 (cf. 118:1, 29).

118:5–21 This section contains individual praise by the psalmist, possibly Moses.

118:5–9 The psalmist focuses intensely on the Lord.

118:6 Hebrews 13:6 quotes this verse; cf. Psalm 56:4, 11.

118:10–14 It seems obvious that the leader of the nation is speaking here.

118:12 a fire of thorns. Dried thorns burn easily and quickly.

118:13 You pushed me. This refers to the psalmist's enemy.

118:14 These words are identical to Moses' words in Exodus 15:2.

118:15–18 A declaration of victory.

118:15, 16 The right hand. This is similar to Moses' words in Exodus 15:6, 12.

118:18 This possibly refers to the incident at Meribah where Moses struck the rock (cf. Num. 20:8–13).

118:19–21 The victory against overwhelming odds elicits from the psalmist a great desire to praise God.

118:19 gates of righteousness. Most likely a figurative reference, i.e., spiritual gates through which the righteous pass (cf. Ps. 100:4), rather than to the gates of the temple, e.g., 1 Chronicles 9:23.

118:20 the gate. This points to the entryway which leads to the presence of the Lord. Jesus may have had this psalm in mind when He taught about "the narrow gate" in Matthew 7:13, 14.

118:21 my salvation. The Lord has delivered the psalmist from otherwise certain defeat and death (cf. 118:14, 15).

118:22–26 The NT quotes of verses 22 and 23 and verses 25 and 26 lend strong messianic significance here. If Moses is the author, then the NT writers use a perfect analogy in connecting this passage to Christ. For example, Moses said that God would raise up another prophet like himself (Deut. 18:15). Peter identified this other prophet as the Lord Jesus Christ (cf. Acts 3:11–26). So Moses is a legitimate, biblically recognized type of Christ.

118:22 stone . . . builders rejected . . . chief cornerstone. Peter identified the chief cornerstone in the NT as Christ (Acts 4:11; 1 Pet. 2:7). In the parable of the vineyard (Matt. 21:42; Mark 12:10–11; Luke 20:17), the rejected son of the vineyard owner is likened to the rejected stone which became the chief cornerstone. Christ was that rejected stone. Jewish leaders were pictured as builders of the nation. Now, this passage in verse 22 has a historical basis which is paralleled in its major features by analogy with the rejection of Christ, who came to deliver/save the nation. Moses' experience, as a type of Christ, pictured Christ's rejection. On at least three occasions Moses (stone) was rejected by the Jews (builders) as their God sent the deliverer (chief cornerstone). For examples see Exodus 2:11–15, cf. Exodus 14:10–14; 16:1–3, 11, 12, 20; Acts 7:35.

118:24 the day. This probably refers to (1) the day of deliverance and/or (2) the day the stone was made the chief cornerstone, which they now celebrate.

118:25 Save now, I pray. Transliterated from Hebrew, this becomes "Hosanna." These words were shouted by the crowd to Christ at the time of His triumphal entry into Jerusalem (Matt. 21:9; Mark 11:9, 10; John 12:13). Days later, they rejected Him because He did not provide military/political deliverance.

118:26 Blessed. Christ taught that the nation of Israel would not see Him again after His departure (ascension to heaven) until they could genuinely offer these words to Him at His Second Coming (cf. Matt. 23:39; Luke 13:35). In this historical text, it could have easily been sung by the Jews of Moses' day, especially at the end of the forty years, but prior to Moses' death (cf. Deut. 1–33). **the house of the LORD.** A phrase used in reference to the tabernacle of Moses (cf. Ex. 23:19; 34:26; Deut. 23:18) and later the temple (cf. 1 Kin. 6:1).

118:27 light. Similar to the Mosaic benediction of Numbers 6:25. **the altar.** The altar of burnt offerings, which stood on the east in the court outside the Holy Place (cf. Ex. 27:1–8; 38:1–7).

118:28 This language bears a striking resemblance to Exodus 15:2.

118:29 A repetition of 118:1.

119:1–176 This longest of psalms and

chapters in the Bible stands as the "Mt. Everest" of the Psalter. It joins Psalms 1 and 19 in exalting God's Word. The author is unknown for certain, although David, Daniel, or Ezra have reasonably been suggested. The psalmist apparently wrote while under some sort of serious duress (cf. vv. 23, 42, 51, 61, 67, 71, 78, 86, 87, 95, 110, 121, 134, 139, 143, 146, 153, 154, 157, 161, 169). This is an acrostic psalm (cf. Pss. 9; 10; 25; 34; 37; 111; 112; 145) composed of twenty-two sections, each containing eight lines. All eight lines of the first section start with the first letter of the Hebrew alphabet; thus, the psalm continues until all twenty-two letters have been used in order. The eight different terms referring to Scripture throughout the psalm are: (1) law, (2) testimonies, (3) precepts, (4) statutes, (5) commandments, (6) judgments, (7) word, and (8) ordinances. From before sunrise to beyond sunset, the Word of God dominated the psalmist's life, e.g., (1) before dawn (v. 147), (2) daily (v. 97), (3) seven times daily (v. 164), (4) nightly (vv. 55, 148), and (5) at midnight (v. 62). Other than the acrostic form, Psalm 119 does not have an outline. Rather, there are many frequently recurring themes which will be delineated in the notes.

119:1, 2 Blessed . . . Blessed. This is similar to Psalm 1:1–3. Elsewhere, the psalmist declares that Scripture is more valuable than money (vv. 14, 72, 127, 162) and brings more pleasure than the sweetness of honey (v. 103; cf. Prov. 13:13; 16:20; 19:16).

119:1 walk. This refers to a habitual pattern of living.

119:2 the whole heart. Heart refers to intellect, volition, and emotion (cf. vv. 7, 10, 11, 32, 34, 36, 58, 69, 70, 80, 111, 112, 145, 161). Complete commitment or whole heart appears six times (vv. 2, 10, 34, 58, 69, 145).

119:4 To keep . . . diligently. The psalmist passionately desired to obey God's Word

(cf. vv. 4, 8, 30–32, 44, 45, 51, 55, 57, 59–61, 63, 67, 68, 74, 83, 87, 101, 102, 106, 110, 112, 129, 141, 157, 167, 168).

119:5, 6 Oh. It is hard at times to distinguish where the psalmist's testimony ends and prayer begins (cf. vv. 29, 36, 58, 133).

119:7 I will praise You. The Scriptures provoke singing, thanksgiving, rejoicing, and praise (cf. vv. 13, 14, 54, 62, 108, 151, 152, 160, 164, 171, 172, 175). **righteous.** God's Word reflects the character of God, especially righteousness (cf. vv. 7, 62, 75, 106, 123, 138, 144, 160, 164, 172).

119:9–11 Internalizing the Word is a believer's best weapon to defend against encroaching sin.

119:12 Teach me. The student/psalmist invites the divine author to be his instructor (cf. vv. 26, 33, 64, 66, 68, 108, 124, 135) with the result that the psalmist did not turn aside from the Word (v. 102).

119:14 all riches. Cf. vv. 72, 127.

119:15 meditate . . . contemplate. The psalmist reflected frequently on the Scriptures (cf. vv. 23, 27, 48, 78, 97, 99, 148).

119:16 I will delight. (cf. vv. 24, 35, 47, 70, 77, 92, 143, 174). **I will not forget.** (cf. vv. 93, 176).

119:17 Your servant. The psalmist uses this phrase of himself thirteen times (vv. 17, 23, 38, 49, 65, 76, 84, 122, 124, 125, 135, 140, 176).

119:18 Open my eyes. Perhaps this is the supreme prayer that a student of Scripture could speak since it confesses the student's inadequacy and the divine author's sufficiency (cf. vv. 98, 99, 105, 130).

119:19 a stranger. As a citizen of God's kingdom, the psalmist was a mere sojourner in the kingdom of men.

119:20 breaks with longing. This expresses the psalmist's deep passion for the Word (cf. vv. 40, 131).

119:21 the proud—the cursed. The

psalmist identified with God's rebuke of those who disobey His Word (cf. vv. 53, 104, 113, 115, 118, 126).

119:24 my counselors. The chief means of biblical counseling is the application of God's Word by God's Spirit to the heart of a believer (cf. vv. 98–100).

119:25 Revive me. Revival is greatly desired by the psalmist, who realizes that God and God's Word alone are sufficient (cf. vv. 37, 40, 50, 88, 93, 107, 149, 154, 156, 159).

119:27 Make me understand. Philip asked the Ethiopian eunuch who was reading Isaiah 53, "Do you understand what you are reading?" (Acts 8:30). The psalmist understood God to be the best source of instruction (cf. vv. 34, 73, 100, 125, 144, 169).

119:28 melts from heaviness. This phrase refers to grief or sorrow over sin.

119:29, 30 the way of lying . . . the way of truth. The psalmist desired to emulate the true character of God in contrast to the lying ways of Satan (cf. v. 163).

119:32 run the course. This reflects the energetic response of the psalmist to God's Word.

119:37 looking at worthless things. The psalmist desires to examine the things of greatest value, i.e., God's Word (cf. vv. 14, 72, 127).

119:39 good. The very attributes of God (cf. v. 68) become the characteristics of Scripture: (1) trustworthy (v. 42); (2) true (vv. 43, 142, 151, 160); (3) faithful (v. 86); (4) unchangeable (v. 89); (5) eternal (vv. 90, 152); (6) light (v. 105); and (7) pure (v. 140).

119:41 Your salvation. This reflects a repeated desire (cf. vv. 64, 76, 81, 88, 94, 109, 123, 134, 146, 149, 153, 154, 159, 166).

119:43 hoped. The psalmist waits patiently for the working of God's Word (cf. vv. 49, 74, 81, 114, 147).

119:47, 48 Which I love. The psalmist expresses his great affection for the Word (cf. vv. 97, 113, 127, 140, 159, 163, 163, 167).

119:50 comfort. What the psalmist found in God's Word (cf. vv. 52, 76, 82).

119:68 You are good. The psalmist frequently appeals to the character of God (cf. v. 39): (1) His faithfulness (vv. 75, 90); (2) His compassion (v. 77); (3) His righteousness (vv. 137, 142); and (4) His mercy (v. 156).

119:70 fat as grease. This refers to the proud of verse 69 whose hearts are thick and, thus, the Word is unable to penetrate.

119:73 Your hands. This figuratively refers to God's involvement in human life (Ps. 139:13–16).

119:75 You have afflicted me. The psalmist expresses his confidence in God's sovereignty over human affliction referred to in 119:67, 71 (cf. Deut. 32:39; Is. 45:7; Lam. 3:37, 38).

119:83 a wineskin in smoke. Just as smoke will dry out, stiffen, and crack a wineskin, thus making it useless, so the psalmist's affliction has debilitated him.

119:89 Forever . . . settled in heaven. God's Word will not change and is always spiritually relevant.

119:98–100 The wisdom of God always far surpasses the wisdom of man.

119:105 lamp . . . light. God's Word provides illumination to walk without stumbling.

119:111 rejoicing. The Word brings joy (cf. v. 162).

119:118, 119 . God righteously judges the wicked by His Word.

119:128 See note on v. 21.

119:130 light . . . understanding. This refers to illumination in comprehending the meaning of Scripture.

119:131 panted. As after God Himself (cf. Ps. 42:1, 2).

119:136 *Rivers of water.* The psalmist is brought to sobbing over the sin of others.

119:140 *very pure.* Like silver refined seven times (cf. Ps. 12:6), the Word is without impurity, i.e., it is inerrant in all that it declares.

119:155 *Salvation . . . far.* Salvation is clearly revealed in the Scripture and nowhere else with such unobstructed clarity.

119:160 *The entirety . . . truth.* There is not a speck of untruth in Scripture.

119:161 *in awe.* Just as one stands in awe of God Himself.

119:163 *I hate . . . lying.* Cf. vv. 29, 30.

119:164 *Seven times. Seven* is perhaps used in the sense of perfection/completion, meaning here that a continual attitude of praise characterizes the psalmist's life.

119:173 *Your hand.* An anthropomorphic figure of speech.

119:176 *I have gone astray.* In spite of all that he has affirmed regarding Scripture's power in his life, the psalmist confesses that sin has not yet been eliminated from his life (cf. Rom. 7:15–25). Any decrease of sin in his life should be attributed to the suppression of unrighteousness by the working of God's Word (cf. vv. 9–11).

120:1–7 Psalms 120–136 comprise "the Great Hallel"; cf. "The Egyptian Hallel" (Pss. 113–118) and "The Final Hallel" (Pss. 145–150). Almost all these psalms (fifteen of seventeen) are "Songs of Ascent" (Pss. 120–134), which the Jewish pilgrims sang on their way up to Jerusalem (about 2,700 ft. in elevation) on three prescribed annual occasions. These feasts included: (1) Unleavened Bread; (2) Weeks/Pentecost/Harvest; and (3) Ingathering/Tabernacles/Booths. Cf. Exodus 23:14–17; 34:22, 23; Deuteronomy 16:16. David authored four of these songs (Pss. 122; 124; 131; 133), Solomon one (Ps. 127), while ten remain anonymous. When these psalms were assembled in this way is un-

known. It appears that these songs begin far away from Jerusalem (cf. Meschech and Kedar in Ps. 120:5) and progressively move toward Jerusalem until the pilgrims have actually reached the temple and finished their worship (cf. Ps. 134:1, 2). With regard to Psalm 120, the author and circumstances are unknown, although it seems as if the worshiper lives at a distance among unbelieving people (cf. Ps. 120:5).

I. Petition (120:1, 2)

II. Indictment (120:3, 4)

III. Lament (120:5–7)

120:2 *lying lips . . . deceitful tongue.* Cf. Psalms 52:2–4; 109:2; Romans 3:9–18.

120:4 *Sharp arrows . . . coals.* Lies and false accusations are likened to (1) the pain/injury inflicted in battle by arrows, and (2) the pain of being burned with charcoal made from the wood of a broom tree (a desert bush that grows ten to fifteen feet high).

120:5–7 The psalmist actually lives among pagans who do not embrace his desire for peace.

120:5 *Meshech . . . Kedar.* In Asia Minor (cf. Gen. 10:2) and Arabia (Is. 21:16), respectively.

121:1–8 *See note on Psalm 120:1–7.* The author and circumstances are unknown. This song strikes a strong note of assurance in four stages that God is help and protection to keep both Israel and individual believers safe from harm.

I. God—Helper (121:1, 2)

II. God—Keeper (121:3, 4)

III. God—Protector (121:5, 6)

IV. God—Preserver (121:7, 8)

121:1 *hills.* Most likely those in the distance as the pilgrim looks to Jerusalem, especially the temple.

121:2 *My help.* The psalmist does not look to the creation, but rather the Creator for His help.

121:3 be moved. Cf. Psalm 37:23, 24.

121:3, 4 slumber. Cf. the appearance of sleep, Psalm 44:23. The living God is totally unlike the pagan gods/dead idols (cf. 1 Kin. 18:27).

121:5 your right hand. This represents the place of human need.

121:6 by day . . . by night. Around the clock protection is in view.

121:7, 8 While this seems to have a temporal sense at first glance, there are indications that it looks beyond to eternal life, e.g., all evil (v. 7) and forevermore (v. 8).

122:1–9 See note on Psalm 120:1–7. David expressed his great joy over Jerusalem, which he had settled by defeating the Jebusites (cf. 2 Sam. 5) and bringing the tabernacle and ark for permanent residency (cf. 2 Sam. 6). David's desire/prayer was temporarily fulfilled in Solomon's reign (cf. 1 Kin. 4:24, 25). It is ironic that Jerusalem, which means "city of peace," has been fought over through history more than any other city in the world. Prophetically, David's desire will not be experienced in its fullness until the Prince of Peace (Is. 9:6) comes to rule permanently (Zech. 14:9, 11) as the promised Davidic King (cf. 2 Sam. 7:12, 13, 16; Ezek. 37:24–28).

I. Joy Over Worship (122:1–5)
II. Prayer Over Jerusalem (122:6–9)

122:1 the house of the LORD. A term used of the tabernacle (cf. Ex. 23:19; 34:26; 2 Sam. 12:20), not the temple that would be built later by Solomon.

122:2 standing within your gates. This occurred sometime after the tabernacle and ark of the covenant had arrived in the city of David (2 Sam. 6). David's joy is that the ark has found its proper location.

122:3 compact together. The Jerusalem of David's day (Zion) was smaller than the enlargement by Solomon.

122:4 the Testimony of Israel. This refers to God's command to go up to Jerusalem three times annually (see note on Ps. 120:1–7).

122:6–9 A most appropriate prayer for a city whose name means peace and is the residency of the God of peace (Is. 9:6; Rom. 15:33; Heb. 13:20). Compare prayers for the peace of Israel (Pss. 125:5; 128:6) and other psalms which exalt Jerusalem (Pss. 128; 132; 147). History would prove that bad times had to come (Pss. 79; 137) before the best of times (Rev. 21; 22).

123:1–4 See note on Psalm 120:1–7. The author and situation are unknown.

I. Exalting God (123:1, 2)
II. Enlisting God's Mercy (123:3, 4)

123:1 my eyes. Note the progression from Psalm 121:1. **dwell in . . . heavens.** Cf. Psalms 11:4; 103:19; 113:5.

123:2 servants . . . masters. The psalmist reasons from the lesser to the greater (human to the divine; earthly to the heavenly). One's eyes should be on the Lord to mercifully meet one's needs.

123:3, 4 contempt . . . scorn. This came from unbelieving pagans, perhaps the Samaritans (cf. Neh. 1:3; 2:19).

124:1–8 See note on Psalm 120:1–7. A Davidic psalm which generically recalls past deliverances, possibly the Exodus (v. 5).

I. God's Protection (124:1–5)
II. God's Provision (124:6–8)

124:1, 2 God has preserved Israel from extinction.

124:2 When men rose up. A general statement which could cover the history of Israel from Abraham to David.

124:4, 5 waters . . . stream . . . swollen waters. The Red Sea crossing (Ex. 14) and/or the Jordan River crossing (Josh. 3) are pictured.

124:8 Our help. Cf. Psalm 121:1, 2.

125:1–5 *See note on Psalm 120:1–7.* The author and circumstances are unknown, although the times of Hezekiah (2 Kin. 18:27–35) or Nehemiah (Neh. 6:1–19) have been suggested.

I. The Security of Jerusalem (125:1–3)
II. The Spiritual Purity of Jerusalem (125:4, 5)

125:1 *Mount Zion.* The southwest mount representing Jerusalem and an emblem of permanence, supported by God's covenant promise.

125:1, 2 *forever.* More than a temporal promise is involved here.

125:2 *His people.* Those who trust in the Lord (cf. v. 1).

125:3 *scepter of wickedness.* Assyrian rule if in Hezekiah's time, or Medo-Persian rule if in Nehemiah's day. *the land.* This would be the land promised to Abraham (Gen. 15:18–21).

125:4, 5 The outcome of the upright (v. 4) is contrasted with the crooked (v. 5). The true Israel is distinguished from the false (cf. Rom. 2:28, 29; 9:6, 7).

125:5 *lead them away.* Eternal rather than temporal judgment seems to be in view. *Peace.* God will one day institute a lasting covenant of peace (cf. Ezek. 37:26).

126:1–6 *See note on Psalm 120:1–7.* The author and occasion are not named in the psalm. However, verse 1 points to a time of return from captivity. Most likely, this refers to the Babylonian captivity, from which there were three separate returns: (1) under Zerubbabel in Ezra 1–6 (c. 538 B.C.); (2) under Ezra in Ezra 7–10 (c. 458 B.C.); and (3) under Nehemiah in Nehemiah 1, 2 (c. 445 B.C.). The occasion could be (1) when the foundation for the second temple had been laid (cf. Ezra 3:8–10), or (2) when the Feast of Tabernacles was reinstated (cf. Neh. 8:13–14). This psalm is similar to Psalm 85, which rejoices over Israel's return from Egypt, but contrasts with Psalm 137, which laments the pain of the Babylonian captivity.

I. The Testimony of Restoration (126:1–3)
II. The Prayer for Riches (126:4)
III. The Wisdom of Righteousness (126:5, 6)

126:1 *those who dream.* The actual experience of liberation, so unexpected, seemed more like a dream than reality.

126:2, 3 *The Lord has done.* This was first recognized by the surrounding nations (v. 2) and then the returning remnant (v. 3).

126:4 *Bring back.* A prayer to restore the nation's fortunes at their best. *streams in the South.* The arid region south of Beersheba (called the Negev) which is utterly dry in the summer, but whose streams quickly fill and flood with the rains of spring. In this manner, the psalmist prays that Israel's fortunes will rapidly change from nothing to everything.

126:5, 6 *sow . . . reap.* By sowing tears of repentance over sin, the nation reaped the harvest of a joyful return to the land of Israel.

127:1–5 *See note on Psalm 120:1–7.* The author is Solomon (cf. Eccl. 12:10), but the occasion is unknown. The major message of God being central to and sovereign in life sounds much like portions of Solomon's Ecclesiastes (cf. Eccl. 2:24, 25; 5:18–20; 7:13, 14; 9:1). Psalms 112 and 128 also develop a strong message on the family.

I. God's Sovereignty in Everyday Life (127:1, 2)
II. God's Sovereignty in Family Life (127:3–5)

127:1, 2 God's sovereignty is seen in three realms: (1) building a house, (2) protecting a city; and (3) earning a living. In all three instances, the sovereign intention of God is far more crucial to the outcome than man's efforts. Otherwise, a person's endeavor is in vain (cf. Eccl. 1:2; 12:8).

127:2 *the bread of sorrows.* Food earned with painful labor.

127:3–5 The same principle of God's sovereignty applies to raising a family.

127:3 heritage . . . reward. Children are a blessing from the Lord. There are overtones of God's promise to Abraham to make his offspring like the dust of the earth and stars of heaven (Gen. 13:16; 15:5).

127:4, 5 As arrows are indispensable for a warrior to succeed in battle, so children are invaluable as defenders of their father and mother in time of war or litigation. The more such defenders, the better.

128:1–6 See note on Psalm 120:1–7. The author and occasion are unknown. Psalms 112 and 127 also address issues of the home.

I. The Basics of Fearing the Lord (128:1, 4)
II. The Blessings of Fearing the Lord
  (128:2, 3, 5, 6)
  A. In the Present (128:2, 3)
  B. In the Future (128:5, 6)

128:1 who fears the LORD. See note on Proverbs 1:7. Psalm 112:1–6 also develops this theme. A good working definition is provided by the parallel line, "who walks in His ways." Fathers (Ps. 128:1, 4), mothers (Prov. 31:30), and children (Ps. 34:11) are to fear the Lord. This psalm may have been the basis for Jesus' illustration of the two builders (cf. Matt. 7:24–27).

128:2, 3 Four blessings are recounted: (1) provisions, (2) prosperity, (3) reproducing partner, and (4) flourishing progeny.

128:3 olive plants. Shoots grow off the main root of an olive tree to reproduce.

128:5, 6 Two realms of blessing are mentioned: (1) personal blessing and (2) national blessing.

128:6 children's children. Cf. Psalms 103:17; 112:2; Proverbs 13:22; 17:6 on grandchildren. This prayer is for the prosperity of God's people.

129:1–8 See note on Psalm 120:1–7. The author and occasion are not specified. However, verse 4 indicates a release from captivity, most likely the Babylonian captivity.

I. Israel's Freedom Celebrated (129:1–4)
II. Israel's Foe Imprecated (129:5–8)

129:1 afflicted. From living in Egypt (c. 1875–1445 B.C.), to enduring the Babylonian captivity (c. 605–538 B.C.), Israel had enjoyed little rest from her enemies.

129:2 prevailed. As the Lord had promised Abraham (cf. Gen. 12:1–3).

129:3 plowed on my back. A farming analogy used to describe the deep, but non-fatal, wounds inflicted on Israel by her enemies.

129:4 cut . . . the cords. These cords tied the ox to the plow, and refer to God ending the persecution (cf. Pss. 121; 124).

129:5–8 A three-part imprecatory prayer: (1) be put to shame and defeat (v. 5); (2) be few and short lived (vv. 6, 7); and (3) be without God's blessing (v. 8).

129:6 grass . . . the housetops. Grass with shallow roots, which quickly dies with the first heat, depicts the wicked.

130:1–8 See note on Psalm 120:1–7. The author and occasion are not mentioned. This is the sixth of seven penitential psalms (cf. Pss. 6; 32; 38; 51; 102; 143).

I. Urgent Prayer of the Psalmist (130:1, 2)
II. Unmerited Forgiveness of God (130:3, 4)
III. Unrelenting Patience of the Psalmist
  (130:5, 6)
IV. Unique Hope of Israel (130:7, 8)

130:1 Out of the depths. A figurative expression of severe distress.

130:3, 4 The psalmist basks in the glow of God's undeserved forgiveness (cf. Ps. 143:2).

130:5 in His word I do hope. The psalmist expresses a certain hope since God's Word cannot fail (cf. Matt. 5:18; Luke 16:17; John 10:35).

130:6 watch for the morning. This probably refers to shepherds with a night watch which ends with the sun's rising.

130:7 *hope in the LORD.* The psalmist's hope in God's Word (v. 5) parallels Israel's hope in the Lord.

130:8 *He shall redeem Israel.* This can be taken in both a historical and a soteriological sense (cf. Matt. 1:21; Luke 1:68; Rom. 9–11).

131:1–3 *See note on Psalm 120:1–7.* David is the author, but the circumstances are not apparent.

I. A Personal Testimony (131:1, 2)
II. A National Exhortation (131:3)

131:1 *haughty . . . lofty.* God gives grace to the humble (cf. Prov. 3:34; 16:5; James 4:6). David expresses the greatest of God's ways (cf. Ps. 139:6; Rom. 11:33–36).

131:2 *Like a weaned child.* David has been trained to trust God to supply his needs as a weaned child trusts his mother.

131:3 David exhorts the nation to forever embrace his own personal hope in the Lord.

132:1–18 *See note on Psalm 120:1–7.* The author and occasion are not specifically mentioned. However, the bringing of the tabernacle to Jerusalem in David's time seems likely (cf. 2 Sam. 6:12–19 with 132:6–9). Further, Solomon's quote of verses 8–10 in his dedication of the temple (2 Chr. 6:41, 42) makes that time probable. Psalm 132 has strong historical implications with regard to the Davidic covenant (cf. 2 Sam. 7:10–14; 16; Pss. 89; 132:10, 11) plus pronounced messianic and millennial overtones (Ps. 132:12–18). Essentially, this psalm contains the nation's prayers for David's royal descendants which look ahead, even to Messiah.

I. Israel's First Prayer (132:1)
II. David's Vow to God (132:2–9)
III. Israel's Second Prayer (132:10)
IV. God's Vow to David (132:11–18)

132:1–9 This section focuses on David fulfilling his vow to God to bring the tabernacle to rest in Jerusalem and, thus, his descendants are to be remembered by the Lord.

132:1 *his afflictions.* This seems to be inclusive from the times of being pursued by Saul (cf. 1 Sam. 18–26) through God's judgment because David numbered the people (cf. 2 Sam. 24). Perhaps it focuses on David's greatest affliction, which came from not having the ark in Jerusalem.

132:2–5 Although this specific vow is not recorded elsewhere in Scripture, the historical circumstances can be found in 2 Samuel 6; 1 Chronicles 13–16.

132:2 *the Mighty One of Jacob.* A title last used by Jacob in Genesis 49:24.

132:6–9 The ark was brought from Kirjath Jearim to Jerusalem (cf. 2 Sam. 6; 1 Chr. 13; 15).

132:6 *heard of it in Ephrathah.* This probably refers to David's younger days in Ephrathah, which was an earlier name for Bethlehem (cf. Ruth 1:1, 2; 4:11), when he and his family had heard of the ark, but had not seen it. *found it in the fields of the woods.* After the ark of the covenant was returned by the Philistines in the days of Saul (cf. 1 Sam. 7:1, 2), it rested at the house of Abinadab in Kirjath Jearim until David decided to move to Jerusalem (cf. 2 Sam. 6; 1 Chr. 13–16).

132:7 *His footstool.* God's throne is in heaven (cf. Is. 66:1) and His footstool is on earth (cf. Ps. 99:5), figuratively speaking. Thus to worship at the ark of the covenant on earth would be, so to speak, worshiping at God's footstool.

132:8 *Arise, O LORD.* Since the Holy Place contained the bread of the presence (Ex. 25:30; 1 Sam. 21:6), the psalmist refers to moving the ark to Jerusalem.

132:9 This describes the proper inward attire for the priests who would oversee the move.

132:10–18 This section focuses on God's fulfilling His vow to David to perpetuate the Davidic throne and, thus, his descendants are to be remembered by the Lord.

132:10 A prayer that God's promise and favor would not be withheld from David's descendants on the throne of Judah. *Your Anointed.* As David had been anointed king (1 Sam. 16:13), so a greater King had been anointed, namely Christ, but not yet seated on the throne (cf. Is. 61:1; Luke 4:18, 19).

132:11, 12 God's covenant with David (2 Sam. 23:5) is summarized here from 2 Samuel 7:11–16 and 1 Kings 9:1–9.

132:12 This conditional aspect could interrupt the occupation of the throne, but it would not invalidate God's promise to seat forever the Messiah as king one day in the future (cf. Ezek. 37:24–28).

132:13–18 This section looks forward prophetically to the day when Jesus Christ, the son of David and the son of Abraham (Matt. 1:1), will be installed by God on the throne of David in the city of God to rule and bring peace on earth, especially Israel (cf. Pss. 2; 89; 110; Is. 25; 26; Jer. 23:5, 6; 33:14–18; Ezek. 37; Dan. 2:44, 45; Zech. 14:1–11).

132:13 *Zion.* This refers to earthly Jerusalem.

133:1–3 *See note on Psalm 120:1–7.* The occasion for this Davidic psalm is unknown. Perhaps it was prompted by the nation's coming together in unity at his coronation (cf. 2 Sam. 5:1–3; 1 Chr. 11:1–3). Its teaching on fraternal unity would have been instructive to David's sons, who were antagonistic toward one another, e.g., Absalom murdered Ammon (2 Sam. 13:28–33) and Adonijah tried to preempt Solomon's right to the throne (1 Kin. 1:5–53).

I. Praise of Unity (133:1)
II. Pictures of Unity (133:2, 3)
    A. Oil on Aaron's head (133:2)
    B. Dew on Mt. Zion (133:3)

133:1 *brethren.* Those whose lineage can be traced to Abraham, Isaac, and Jacob. *unity.* While national unity might be on the

---

Seventy-Three Davidic Psalms

Psalms 3; 4; 5; 6; 7; 8; 9; 11; 12; 13; 14; 15; 16; 17; 18; 19; 20; 21; 22; 23; 24; 25; 26; 27; 28; 29; 30; 31; 32; 34; 35; 36; 37; 38; 39; 40; 41; 51; 52; 53; 54; 55; 56; 57; 58; 59; 60; 61; 62; 63; 64; 65; 68; 69; 70; 86; 101; 103; 108; 109; 110; 122; 124; 131; 133; 138; 139; 140; 141; 142; 143; 144; 145.

---

surface, the foundation must always be spiritual unity. This would be the emphasis here, since these songs were sung by Jewish pilgrims traveling to the three great feasts.

133:2 *oil upon.* Most likely, this refers to the anointing of Aaron as high priest of the nation (cf. Ex. 29:7; 30:30), which would picture a rich spiritual blessing as a first priority.

133:3 *the dew of Hermon.* Mt. Hermon, a 9,200-foot peak at the extreme northern portion of Palestine, provided the major water supply for the Jordan River by its melting snow. This reference could be to the Jordan water supply or figuratively to the actual prevalent dew of Hermon being hypothetically transported to Zion. Either way, this pictures a refreshing material blessing as a second, lesser priority. *there.* This seems to refer to Zion. *Life forevermore.* Cf. Psalm 21:4–6.

134:1–3 *See note on Psalm 120:1–7.* This final song in the "songs of ascent" seems to picture the worshipers exhorting the priests to continued faithfulness (134:1, 2) while the priests bestow a final blessing on the faithful as the feast ends and the pilgrims depart Zion for home (134:3).

I. Exhortation to Faithfulness (134:1, 2)
II. Solicitation of Blessing (134:3)

134:1 *servants.* Levites who ministered to God's people. *by night.* The burnt offerings continued day and night (cf. Lev. 6:8–13), as did the Levitical service (cf. 1 Chr. 9:33).

house of the LORD. This refers to the tabernacle up to the time of David (Ex. 23:19; 2 Sam. 12:20) and to the temple from Solomon on (1 Kin. 9:10).

134:2 *Lift up your hands.* A common OT praise practice (cf. Pss. 28:2; 63:4; 119:48; 141:2; Lam. 2:19), which was understood figuratively in the NT (1 Tim. 2:8).

134:3 *The LORD.* The Creator blesses His human creation. *Bless you from Zion!* Since God's presence resided in the tabernacle/temple on Zion, from a human perspective it would be the source of divine blessing.

135:1–21 Psalms 135 and 136 conclude the "Great Hallel." The composer and occasion of Psalm 135 are unknown but likely post-exilic. Psalm 135:15–20 is strikingly similar to Psalm 115:4–11.

I. Call to Praise (135:1, 2)
II. Causes for Praise (135:3–18)
   A. God's Character (135:3)
   B. God's Choice of Jacob (135:4)
   C. God's Sovereignty in Creation (135:5–7)
   D. God's Deliverance of Israel (135:8–12)
   E. God's Unique Nature (135:13–18)
III. Concluding Praise (135:19–21)

135:1, 2 *servants . . . stand . . . in the courts.* Addressed to the priests and Levites (cf. 134:1).

135:3 *the LORD is good.* A consistent theme in the psalms (cf. Pss. 16:2; 25:8; 34:8; 73:1; 86:5; 100:5; 106:1; 107:1; 118:1; 136:1; 145:9).

135:4 *the LORD has chosen.* This refers to God's unique selection of the offering of Abraham, Isaac, and Jacob to enjoy God's covenant blessing (cf. Deut. 7:6–8; 14:2; Ps. 105:6; Is. 41:8, 9; 43:20; 44:1; 49:7). *His special treasure.* Cf. Deuteronomy 26:18, 19. *See note on Psalm 148:14.*

135:5 *the LORD is great.* A common superlative to distinguish the true God of Israel

from the false gods of the other nations (cf. Deut. 7:21; Pss. 48:1; 77:13; 86:10; 95:3; 104:1; 145:3; 147:5).

135:7 *vapors to ascend.* This refers to the water cycle of earthly evaporation and condensation in the clouds.

135:8–12 This is in reference to God's deliverance of Israel from Egypt to the Promised Land.

135:8 *destroyed.* The final plague in Egypt (cf. Ex. 11).

135:9 *signs and wonders.* Cf. Deuteronomy 26:8; 29:3; 34:11.

135:11 *Sihon.* Cf. Numbers 21:21, 32, which recounts Israel's defeat of Sihon, king of the Amorites. *Og.* Cf. Numbers 21:33–35, which recounts Israel's defeat of Og, king of Bashan. *kingdoms of Canaan.* Joshua 6–12 recounts Joshua's conquest of the high priest.

135:12 *gave their land . . . to Israel.* God promised this to Abraham (cf. Gen. 15:18–21).

135:13–18 The living God of Israel (vv. 13, 14) stands decidedly superior to the imaginary gods of the nations (vv. 15–18).

135:18 *make them . . . like them.* Both are worthless and will know nothing of eternal life.

135:19–20 The categories (1) Israel, (2) Aaron, (3) Levi, and (4) you who fear the Lord refer to the nation as a whole (Israel), the priesthood (Aaron and Levi), and the true believers (who fear the Lord).

136:1–26 This psalm, similar to Psalm 135, closes the Great Hallel. Unique to all the psalms, Psalm 136 uses the antiphonal refrain "For His mercy endures forever" after each stanza, perhaps spoken by the people in responsive worship. The author and occasion remain unknown.

I. Call to Praise (136:1–3)
II. Causes for Praise (136:4–22)
   A. God's Creation (136:4–9)
   B. God's Deliverance (136:10–15)

C. God's Care and Gift (136:16–22)
III. Concluding Praise (136:23–26)

136:1 *He is good!* See note on Psalm 135:3.
136:4–9 Cf. Genesis 1.
136:10–15 Cf. Exodus 11–14.
136:16–22 Cf. Numbers 14–36.
136:19 *Sihon.* See note on Psalm 135:11.
136:20 *Og.* See note on Psalm 135:11.
136:23 *lowly state.* Cf. Deuteronomy 7:7; 9:4, 5; Ezekiel 16:1–5.

137:1–9 A psalm which is explicitly about the Babylonian captivity of Judah. Its author and date are unknown.

I. Lamentations (137:1–4)
II. Conditions (137:5, 6)
III. Imprecations (137:7–9)

137:1 *the rivers of Babylon.* The Tigris and Euphrates Rivers. *we wept.* They even wept when the exile was over and the second temple was being built (cf. Ezra 3:12), so deep was their sorrow. *Zion.* The dwelling place of God on earth (Pss. 9:11; 76:2) which was destroyed by the Babylonians (2 Chr. 36:19; Pss. 74:6–8; 79:1; Is. 64:10, 11; Jer. 52:12–16; Lam. 2:4, 6–9; Mic. 3:12).

137:2 *hung our harps.* In captivity, there was no use for an instrument of joy (cf. Is. 24:8).

137:3 *those who carried us away.* The Babylonians taunted the Jews to sing of their once-beautiful but now-destroyed Zion. *the songs of Zion.* Cf. Psalms 46; 48; 76; 84; 87; 122.

137:4 *How shall we sing?* A rhetorical question whose answer is, "We can't!" *the LORD's song.* A unique way to refer to divine inspiration of the psalms.

137:5, 6 Their refusal to sing was not caused by either of two unthinkable situations: (1) they forgot Jerusalem; (2) they did not have Jerusalem as their chief joy. The worst of punishments should be imposed if any one or a combination of these factors were to become true.

137:7 *the sons of Edom.* Edomites had been allied with the Babylonians in the fall and destruction of Jerusalem (cf. Is. 21:11, 12; Jer. 49:7–12; Lam. 4:21; Ezek. 25:12–14; 35:1–15; Obad. 11–14). The psalmist only prayed for that which the Lord had always promised. *The day of Jerusalem.* The day Jerusalem was destroyed. See notes on Psalm 137:1.

137:8 *destroyed.* Cf. Isaiah 13:1–14:23, 46, 47; Jeremiah 50, 51; Habukkuk 1:11; 2:6–17.

137:8, 9 *Happy the one.* These will be God's human instruments used to carry out His prophesied will for the destruction of Babylon.

138:1–8 The next eight psalms were written by David (Pss. 138–145) and are his last in the Psalter. The occasion is unknown, although it is possible that David wrote them in response to the Davidic covenant (cf. 2 Sam. 7:12–14, 16).

I. Individual Praise (138:1–3)
II. International Praise (138:4, 5)
III. Invincible Praise (138:6–8)

138:1 *the gods.* This can refer to either pagan royalty (cf. Ps. 82:1) and/or to the idols they worship.

138:2 *holy temple.* This refers to the Mosaic tabernacle since Solomon's temple had not yet been built. *Your word above ... Your name.* Most likely, this means that God's latest revelation ("Your word") exceeded all previous revelation about God. This would be in concert with David's prayer (2 Sam. 7:18–29) after he received the Davidic promise (2 Sam. 7:12–14, 16).

138:4 *All the kings.* This is in contrast to Psalm 2:1–3, cf. Psalms 68:32; 72:11, 12; 96:1, 3, 7, 8; 97:1; 98:4; 100:1; 102:15; 148:11.

138:6, 7 David sees himself as "the lowly" and his enemies as "the proud."

138:8 *perfect.* This refers to God's completed work in David's life, especially the Davidic covenant (cf. 2 Sam. 7:12–14, 16).

139:1–24 This intensely personal, Davidic psalm expresses the psalmist's awe that God knew him, even to the minutest detail. David might have remembered the Lord's words, "the Lord looks at the heart" (1 Sam. 16:7). The exact occasion is unknown.

I. God's Omniscience (139:1–6)
II. God's Omnipresence (139:7–12)
III. God's Omnipotence (139:13–18)
IV. David's Obeisance (139:19–24)

139:1–6 God knows everything about David.

139:1 *searched me.* As it has been in David's life, he prays later (cf. vv. 23, 24) that it will continue to be so. David understands that nothing inside him can be hidden from God.

139:5 *hedged me.* God used circumstances to limit David's actions.

139:6 *too wonderful.* Cf. Psalm 131:1; Romans 11:33–36.

139:7–12 God was always watching over David, and thus it was impossible to do anything before which God is not a spectator.

139:7 *Your Spirit.* A reference to the Holy Spirit (cf. Pss. 51:11; 143:10).

139:9 *the wings of the morning.* In conjunction with "the uttermost parts of the sea," David uses this literary figure to express distance.

139:13–18 God's power is magnified in the development of human life before birth.

139:13 *formed . . . covered.* By virtue of the divinely designed period of pregnancy, God providentially watches over the development of the child while still in the mother's womb.

139:15 *secret . . . lowest parts.* This language is used figuratively of the womb.

139:16 *Your book.* This figure of speech likens God's mind to a book of remembrance. *none of them.* God sovereignly ordained David's life before he was conceived.

139:17, 18 David expresses his amazement at the infinite mind of God compared to the limited mind of man, especially as it relates to the physiology of human life (cf. vv. 13–16).

139:22 *perfect hatred.* David has no other response to God's enemies than that of hatred, i.e., he is not neutral toward them nor will he ever ally himself with them.

139:23, 24 In light of verses 19–22, David invites God to continue searching his heart to root out any unrighteousness, even when it is expressed against God's enemies.

139:24 *the way everlasting.* David expresses his desire/expectation of eternal life (*see notes on Phil. 1:6*).

140:1–13 Davidic authorship is stated here, but the circumstances are unknown. This is like the earlier psalms in the Psalter that feature the usual complaint, prayer, and confident hope of relief.

I. Concerning David (140:1–5)
  A. "Deliver Me" (140:1–3)
  B. "Protect Me" (140:4, 5)
II. Concerning David's Enemies (140:6–11)
  A. "Thwart Them" (140:6–8)
  B. "Punish Them" (140:9–11)
III. Concerning the Lord (140:12, 13)

140:1–3 The emphasis here is deliverance from evil plans.

140:3 *asps.* A type of snake (cf. Rom. 3:13), signifying cunning and venom.

140:4, 5 The emphasis here is protection from being captured.

140:6–8 The emphasis here is on God's thwarting the plans of David's enemy.

140:7 *covered my head.* God has figuratively been David's helmet in battle.

140:9–11 The emphasis here is on God's turning their evil plans back on them in judgment.

140:12, 13 David expresses unshakeable confidence in the character of God and the outcome for the righteous (cf. Pss. 10:17, 18; 74:21; 82:3, 4).

141:1–10 Another psalm of lament by David whose occasion is unknown. This psalm is comprised of four prayers that have been combined into one.

I. Prayer for God's Haste (141:1, 2)
II. Prayer for Personal Righteousness (141:3–5)
III. Prayer for Justice (141:6, 7)
IV. Prayer for Deliverance (141:8–10)

141:2 *incense . . . evening sacrifice.* David desired that his prayers and stretching forth for God's help (Pss. 68:31; 77:2) be as disciplined and regular as the offering of incense (Ex. 30:7, 8) and burnt offerings (Ex. 29:38, 39) in the tabernacle.

141:3, 4 David prayed that God would protect him from the kind of evil that characterized his own enemy.

141:5 David acknowledged that God would use other righteous people to answer his prayer in verses 3 and 4 (cf. Prov. 9:8; 19:25; 27:6; 27:17).

141:6 *judges . . . overthrown.* That the leaders of the wicked would be punished by being thrown over a cliff (cf. Luke 4:28, 29) is at the heart of David's prayer (cf. v. 5). ***my words . . . sweet.*** This is written in the sense that David's words were true.

141:7 *Our bones.* The basis on which the judges were thrown over the cliff is that they had first done this to the righteous (cf. v. 10).

141:10 *fall into their own nets.* David prays that the wicked will be destroyed by their own devices.

142:1–7 Under the same circumstances as Psalm 57 (according to the superscription), David recounted his desperate days hiding in the cave of Adullam (1 Sam. 22:1) while Saul sought him to take his life (1 Sam. 18–24). It appears that David's situation, for the moment at least, seems hopeless without God's

intervention. Psalm 91 provides the truths that bring the solution.

I. Cry of David (142:1, 2)
II. Circumstances of David (142:3, 4)
III. Confidence of David (142:5–7)

142:4 *no one.* It appears to David that he has been totally abandoned.

142:5 *You are my refuge.* A frequent claim in the psalms (cf. Pss. 7:1; 11:1; 16:1; 18:2; 25:20; 31:1; 46:1; 57:1; 61:3; 62:7; 91:2; 94:22; 141:8; 143:9; 144:2).

142:7 *prison.* The cave in which David was hidden.

143:1–12 No specific background is known for this Davidic psalm, which is the final penitential psalm (cf. Pss. 6; 32; 38; 51; 102; 130).

I. David's Passion (143:1, 2)
II. David's Predicament (143:3–6)
III. David's Plea (143:7–12)

143:1 *faithfulness . . . righteousness.* David fervently appeals to God's character.

143:2 *no one living is righteous.* David admits his own unrighteousness and realizes that if he is to be delivered for the sake of righteousness (cf. 143:11), it will be because of God's righteousness, not his own.

143:6 *a thirsty land.* As a drought-struck land yearns for life-giving water, so persecuted David longs for his life-giving deliverer.

143:7 *Your face.* An anthropomorphism picturing God's attention to the psalmist's plight.

143:10 *Your Spirit.* This refers to the Holy Spirit (cf. Pss. 51:11; 139:7). *See note on Psalm 51:11.*

143:11 *Your name's sake!* David appeals to God's benefit and honor, not his own (cf. Pss. 23:3; 31:3; 79:9).

143:12 *Your servant.* To attack God's servant is to attack God, thus bringing God to the rescue.

144:1–15 This Davidic psalm, in part

(144:1–8), is very similar to Psalm 18:1–15. It could be that this psalm was written under the same kind of circumstances as the former, i.e., on the day that the Lord delivered him from the hand of his enemies, including King Saul (cf. 2 Sam. 22:1–18).

I. God's Greatness (144:1, 2)
II. Man's Insignificance (144:3, 4)
III. God's Power (144:5–8)
IV. Man's Praise (144:9, 10)
V. God's Blessing (144:11–15)

144:1 *my Rock.* David's foundation is God—solid and unshakeable (cf. Pss. 19:14; 31:3; 42:9; 62:2; 71:3; 89:26; 92:15; 95:1). *trains my hands for war.* David lived in the days of Israel's theocracy, not the NT church (cf. John 18:36). God empowered the king to subdue His enemies.

144:2 God provided six benefits: (1) lovingkindness; (2) a fortress; (3) a high tower; (4) a deliverer; (5) a shield; and (6) a refuge.

144:3, 4 Eternal God is contrasted with short-lived man (cf. Ps. 8:4).

144:5–8 Highly figurative language is used to portray God as the heavenly warrior who comes to fight on behalf of David against God's enemies on earth.

144:9 *a new song.* A song of victory that celebrates deliverance/salvation (cf. Pss. 33:3; 40:3; 96:1; 98:1; 144:9; 149:1; Rev. 5:9; 14:3).

144:11 Cf. vv. 7, 8.

144:12 *sons . . . daughters.* God's rescue of David's kingdom from foreigners would bring blessing on families.

144:13, 14 *barns . . . sheep . . . oxen.* Blessing would also come to the agricultural efforts.

144:14 *no breaking in . . . going out . . . outcry.* Peace, not strife, would characterize the land.

145:1–21 David penned this most exquisite conclusion to his seventy-three psalms in the Psalter. Here, the king of Israel extols and celebrates the King of eternity for who

He is, what He has done, and what He has promised. Rich in content, this psalm also duplicates a majestic acrostic design by using the twenty-two letters of the Hebrew alphabet. Psalm 145 begins the great crescendo of praise that completes the psalter and might be called "the Final Hallel" (Pss. 145–150).

I. Commitment to Praise (145:1, 2)
II. God's Awesome Greatness (145:3–7)
III. God's Great Grace (145:8–13)
IV. God's Unfailing Faithfulness (145:14–16)
V. God's Unblemished Righteousness (145:17–20)
VI. Recommitment/Exhortation to Praise (145:21)

145:1 *my God, O King.* David, king of Israel, recognized God as his sovereign (cf. Pss. 5:2; 84:3).

145:11–13 *kingdom.* David refers to the broadest use of kingdom in Scripture—i.e., God the eternal king ruling over all from before creation and eternally thereafter (cf. Ps. 10:16; Dan. 4:3; 7:27).

145:14–16 The emphasis is on God's common grace to all of humanity (cf. Matt. 5:45; Luke 6:35; Acts 14:17; 17:25).

145:20 *the wicked . . . destroy.* The wicked await an eternity of living forever, away from the presence of God in the lake of fire (cf. 2 Thess. 1:9; Rev. 20:11–15).

146:1–10 From this psalm to the conclusion of the Psalter, each psalm begins and ends with "praise the LORD" (Pss. 146–150). Neither the composer nor the occasions are known. Psalm 146 appears similar in content to Psalms 113, 145.

I. Commitment to Praise (146:1, 2)
II. Misplaced Trust (146:3, 4)
III. Blessed Hope (146:5–10)

146:1 *O my soul!* Cf. the beginnings and ends of Psalms 103 and 104.

146:3, 4 *Do not put . . . trust.* This could be (1) a general principle, (2) a reference to the people wanting a human king like the nations (1 Sam. 8:5), or (3) Judah's later dependence on foreign kings for protection (2 Kin. 16:7–9).

146:5 *the God of Jacob.* Including the God of Abraham and Isaac, these are recipients of God's blessing through the Abrahamic covenant (cf. Gen. 12:1–3; Ps. 144:15).

146:6 Man's trust is best placed in the Creator of heaven and earth and the revealer of all truth.

146:7–9b God righteously and mercifully reaches out to those in need.

146:9c *the way of the wicked.* Cf. Psalms 1:4–6; 145:20.

146:10 *shall reign forever.* In contrast to man who perishes (cf. v. 4), the truths of verses 5–9 are not faddish or temporal but rather eternal (cf. Rev. 22:5).

147:1–20 *See note on Psalm 146:1–10.* This seems to be a post-exilic psalm (cf. vv. 2, 3) which might have been used to celebrate the rebuilt walls of Jerusalem (cf. vv. 2, 13; Neh. 12:27, 43). The hard questions that God posed to Job (Job 38–41) and Israel (Is. 40), the psalmist here turns into declarations worthy of praise. Verses 1, 7, 12 each introduce a stanza of praise in this three-part hymn. Verses 2, 3, 19, 20 specifically speak of God's involvement with Israel.

I. Praise the Lord—Part 1 (147:1–6)
II. Praise the Lord—Part 2 (147:7–11)
III. Praise the Lord—Part 3 (147:12–20)

147:2 *builds up Jerusalem.* Ezra and Nehemiah chronicle this portion of Israel's history.

147:3 *heals the brokenhearted.* Cf. Psalm 137 (brokenhearted) with Psalm 126 (healed).

147:6 Each part of the psalm ends with a contrast—here the humble and the wicked (cf. vv. 10, 11, 19, 20).

147:13 *He has strengthened.* This refers

to a means of defense, most likely in reference to the rebuilding of Jerusalem's walls in Nehemiah's time.

147:15–18 This describes the cold weather that Jerusalem can experience in winter. God sovereignly oversees the normal and the extraordinary.

147:19, 20 The psalmist acknowledges God's unique election of Israel from among all the nations (cf. Gen. 12:1–3; Ex. 19:5, 6; Deut. 7:6–8; 14:2; 26:18, 19; 2 Sam. 7:23, 24; Ezek. 16:1–7).

148:1–14 *See note on Psalm 146:1–10.* The author and background for this psalm, which calls for all of God's creation to praise Him, is unknown. There is a connection between the creation praising God and His involvement with Israel.

I. Heaven's Praise (148:1–6)
  A. Who? (148:1–4)
  B. Why? (148:5, 6)
II. Earth's Praise (148:7–14)
  A. Who? (148:7–12)
  B. Why? (148:13, 14)

148:1–4 A representative sample of God's creation in the skies and heavens.

148:2 *all His hosts.* Another term for angels.

148:4 *waters above the heavens.* Cf. Genesis 1:7.

148:5, 6 The psalmist emphatically ascribes creation to God alone.

148:6 Jeremiah 31:35–37; 33:20–22 might be in mind in the sense that the certain, fixed order of creation was a witness to God's unbreakable covenants with Abraham and David.

148:8 *fulfilling His word.* Another way of saying that God sovereignly oversees weather.

148:13, 14 Two reasons are given for earth's praise: (1) His name alone is exalted in heaven (148:13) and (2) He has exalted Israel on earth (148:14).

148:14 *the horn.* This refers in general to

the strength and prosperity of the nation, which became the cause of praise for Israel. This suggests that Israel will enjoy better times than in the past, e.g., during David's and Solomon's reigns or after returning from the Babylonian captivity. **A people near to Him.** Cf. also "My chosen people" (Is. 43:20) and "His special treasure" (Ps. 135:4).

149:1–9 *See note on Psalm 146:1–10.* The composer and occasion for this psalm are unknown.

I. Israel's Praise of God (149:1–5)
II. Israel's Punishment of the Nations (149:6–9)

149:1 *a new song.* A song of testimony concerning salvation (cf. 149:4). *the assembly.* The gathering of the nation for worship.

149:3 *the dance.* Either individual or group, perhaps like David when he brought the ark to Jerusalem (2 Sam. 6:15, 16). *the timbrel.* A tambourine-like instrument which accompanied dancing and singing (cf. Ex. 15:20; 1 Sam. 18:6). See note on 2 Samuel 6:14.

149:6–9 It would appear that this section is eschatological in nature and looks (1) to the millennium when all nations and peoples will acknowledge Christ as king and (2) to Jerusalem as His royal capital (cf. Ezek. 28:25, 26; Joel 3:9–17; Mic. 5:4–15).

149:9 *the written judgment.* This is another way of saying "According to the Scriptures," as God has prophesied the subjection of the nations. *This honor.* The privilege of carrying out God's will.

150:1–6 *See note on Psalm 146:1–10.* This concluding psalm fitly caps the Psalter and

the Final Hallel (Pss. 145–150) by raising and then answering some strategic questions about praise: (1) where? (150:1); (2) what for? (150:2); (3) with what? (150:3–5); and (4) who? (150:6). The author and occasion are unknown.

I. Place of Praise (150:1)
II. Points of Praise (150:2)
III. Proper Means of Praise (150:3–5)
IV. Practitioners of Praise (150:6)

150:1 *sanctuary . . . mighty firmament!* *Sanctuary* most likely refers to the temple in Jerusalem, so the sense would be, "Praise God on earth and in heaven."

150:2 Praise should be for (1) what God has done and (2) who God is.

150:3 *lute.* A harp-like, stringed instrument which was plucked with the finger rather than a plectrum (pick) like the harp.

150:4 *timbrel and dance.* See note on *Psalm 149:3.*

150:6 *everything.* All of God's living creation. This is the fitting conclusion to Book Five of the Psalms (Pss. 107–150) and to the entire Psalter.

Further Study

Lawson, Steven. *Psalms 1–75,* in Holman Old Testament Commentary. Nashville: Broadman & Holman, 2003.

Lawson, Steven. *Psalms 76–150,* in Holman Old Testament Commentary. Nashville: Broadman & Holman, forthcoming.

Ross, Allen P. *Psalms,* in The Bible Knowledge Commentary—OT. Wheaton, Ill.: Victor, 1985.

THE BOOK OF
PROVERBS

Title

The title in the Hebrew Bible is "The Proverbs of Solomon" (1:1), as also in the Greek Septuagint (LXX). Proverbs pulls together the most important 513 of the over 3,000 proverbs pondered by Solomon (1 Kin. 4:32; Eccl. 12:9), along with some proverbs of others whom Solomon might have influenced. The word *proverb* means "to be like;" thus, Proverbs is a book of comparisons between common, concrete images and life's most profound truths. Proverbs are simple, moral statements (or illustrations) that highlight and teach fundamental realities about life. Solomon sought God's wisdom (2 Chr. 1:8–12) and offered "pithy sayings" designed to make people contemplate (1) the fear of God and (2) living by His wisdom (1:7; 9:10). The sum of this wisdom is personified in the Lord Jesus Christ (1 Cor. 1:30).

Author and Date

The phrase "Proverbs of Solomon" is more a title than an absolute statement of authorship (1:1). While King Solomon, who ruled Israel from 971–931 B.C. and was granted great wisdom by God (see 1 Kin. 4:29–34), is the author of the didactic section (chs. 1–9) and the proverbs of 10:1–22:16, he is likely only the compiler of the "sayings of the wise" in 22:17–24:34, which are of an uncertain date before Solomon's reign. The collection in chapters 25–29 was originally composed by Solomon (25:1) but copied and included

later by Judah's king Hezekiah (c. 715–686 B.C.). Chapter 30 reflects the words of Agur and chapter 31 the words of Lemuel, who perhaps was Solomon.

Proverbs was not assembled in its final form until Hezekiah's day or thereafter. Solomon authored his proverbs before his heart was turned away from God (1 Kin. 11:1–11), since the book reveals a godly perspective and is addressed to the "naive" and "young" who need to learn the fear of God. Solomon also wrote Psalms 72 and 127, Ecclesiastes, and Song of Solomon. See Introduction: Author and Date for Ecclesiastes and Song of Solomon.

Background and Setting

The book reflects a threefold setting as: (1) general wisdom literature; (2) insights from the royal court; and (3) instruction offered in the tender relationship of a father and mother with their children, all designed to produce meditation on God. Since Proverbs is wisdom literature, by nature it is sometimes difficult to understand (1:6). Wisdom literature is part of the whole of OT truth; the priest gave the *Law,* the prophet gave a *Word* from the Lord, and the sage (or wise man) gave his wise *Counsel* (Jer. 18:18; Ezek. 7:26). In Proverbs, Solomon the sage gives insight into the "knotty" issues of life (1:6) which are not directly addressed in the Law or the Prophets.

Though it is practical, Proverbs is not superficial or external because it contains moral and ethical elements emphasizing upright living which flows out of a right relationship with God. In 4:1–4, Solomon connected three generations as he entrusted to his son Rehoboam what he learned at the feet of David and Bathsheba. Proverbs is both a pattern for the tender impartation of truth from generation to generation, as well as a vast resource for the content of the truth to be taught. Proverbs contains the principles and applications of Scripture which the godly characters of the Bible illustrate in their lives.

Historical and Theological Themes
Solomon came to the throne with great promise, privilege, and opportunity. God had granted his request for understanding (1 Kin. 3:9–12; 1 Chr. 2:10–11), and his wisdom exceeded all others (1 Kin. 4:29–31). However, the shocking reality is that he failed to live out the truth that he knew and even taught his son Rehoboam (1 Kin. 11:1, 4, 6, 7–11), who subsequently rejected his father's teaching (1 Kin. 12:6–11).

Proverbs contains a gold mine of biblical theology, reflecting themes of Scripture brought to the level of practical righteousness (1:3), by addressing man's ethical choices, calling into question how he thinks, lives, and manages his daily life in light of divine truth. More specifically, Proverbs calls man to live as the Creator intended him to live when He made man (Ps. 90:1, 2, 12).

The recurring promise of Proverbs is that, generally speaking, the wise (the righteous who obey God) live longer (9:11), prosper (2:20–22), experience joy (3:13–18) and the goodness of God temporally (12:21), while fools suffer shame (3:35) and death (10:21). On the other hand, it must be remembered that this general principle is balanced by the reality that the wicked sometimes prosper (Ps. 73:3, 12), though only

temporarily (Ps. 73:17–19). Job illustrates that there are occasions when the godly wise are struck with disaster and suffering.

There are a number of important subjects addressed in Proverbs, which are offered in random order and address different topics, so that it is helpful to study the proverbs thematically as illustrated.

I. Man's Relationship to God
- A. His Trust (22:19)
- B. His Humility (3:34)
- C. His Fear of God (1:7)
- D. His Righteousness (10:25)
- E. His Sin (28:13)
- F. His Obedience (6:23)
- G. Facing Reward (12:28)
- H. Facing Tests (17:3)
- I. Facing Blessing (10:22)
- J. Facing Death (15:11)

II. Man's Relationship to Himself
- A. His Character (20:11)
- B. His Wisdom (1:5)
- C. His Foolishness (26:10, 11)
- D. His Speech (18:21)
- E. His Self-Control (6:9–11)
- F. His Kindness (3:3)
- G. His Wealth (11:4)
- H. His Pride (27:1)
- I. His Anger (29:11)
- J. His Laziness (13:4)

III. Man's Relationship to Others
- A. His Love (8:17)
- B. His Friends (17:17)
- C. His Enemies (16:7)
- D. His Truthfulness (23:23)
- E. His Gossip (20:19)
- F. As a Father (20:7; 31:2–9)
- G. As a Mother (31:10–31)
- H. As Children (3:1–3)
- I. In Educating Children (4:1–4)
- J. In Disciplining Children (22:6)

The two major themes that are interwoven and overlap throughout Proverbs are wisdom and folly. Wisdom, which includes knowledge, understanding, instruction, discretion, and obedience, is built on the fear of the Lord and the Word of God. Folly is everything opposite to wisdom.

Interpretive Challenges

The first challenge is the generally elusive nature of wisdom literature itself. Like the parables, the intended truths are often veiled from understanding if given only a cursory glance, and thus must be pondered in the heart (1:6; 2:1–4; 4:4–9).

Another challenge is the extensive use of parallelism, which is the placing of truths side by side so that the second line expands, completes, defines, emphasizes, or reaches the logical conclusion, the ultimate end, and, in some cases, the contrasting point of view. Often the actual parallel is only implied. For example, 12:13 contains an unstated but clearly implied parallel, in that the righteous person comes through trouble because of his virtuous speech (cf. 28:7).

In interpreting the Proverbs, one must: (1) determine the parallelism and often complete what is assumed and not stated by the author; (2) identify the figures of speech and rephrase the thought without those figures; (3) summarize the lesson or principle of the proverb in a few words; (4) describe the behavior that is taught; and (5) find examples inside Scripture.

Challenges are also found in the various contexts of Proverbs, all of which affect interpretation and understanding. First, there is the setting in which they were spoken; this is largely the context of the young men in the royal court of the king. Second, there is the setting of the book as a whole, understanding that its teachings are to be understood in light of the rest of Scripture. For example,

there is much to be gained by comparing the wisdom Solomon taught with the wisdom Christ personified. Third, there is the historical context in which the principles and truths draw on illustrations from their own day.

A final area of challenge comes in understanding that proverbs are divine guidelines and wise observations, i.e., teaching underlying principles (24:3, 4) which are not always inflexible laws or absolute promises. These expressions of general truth (cf. 10:27; 22:4) usually do have "exceptions," due to the uncertainty of life and unpredictable behavior of fallen men. God does not guarantee uniform outcome or application for each proverb; but in studying them and applying them, one comes to contemplate the mind of God, His character, His attributes, His works, and His blessings. All of the treasures of wisdom and knowledge expressed in Proverbs are hidden in Christ (Col. 2:3).

Outline

I. Prologue

1:1–7 These verses form the Prologue, where the reader is called to serious study for his own benefit. In a few brief words, he is introduced to: (1) the genre of this literature (v. 1); (2) a clear twofold purpose (vv. 2–6); and (3) an all-important motto (v. 7).

A. Title (1:1)

1:1 proverbs. See Introduction: Title. The proverbs are short, pithy sayings which express timeless truth and wisdom. They arrest one's thoughts, causing the reader to reflect on how one might apply divine principles to life situations (e.g., 2:12). Proverbs contain insights both in poetry and prose; yet, at the same time, they can be commands to be obeyed. God's proverbs are not limited to this book alone (see Gen. 10:9; 1 Sam. 10:12; 24:13; Jer. 31:29; Ezek. 12:22; 18:2). **Solomon.** See Introduction: Author and Date. As Solomon became king of Israel, he sought and received wisdom and knowledge from the Lord (2 Chr 1:7–12), which led him to wealth, honor, and fame.

B. Purpose (1:2–6)

1:2–6 The twofold purpose of the book is (1) to produce the skill of godly living by wisdom and instruction (v. 2a; expanded in vv. 3, 4), and (2) to develop discernment (v. 2b, expanded in v. 5).

1:2 wisdom. See Introduction: Historical and Theological Themes. To the Hebrew mind, wisdom was not knowledge alone, but the skill of living a godly life as God intended man to live (cf. Deut. 4:5–8). **instruction.** This refers to the discipline of the moral nature. **understanding.** This word looks at the mental discipline which matures a person for spiritual discernment.

1:3 wisdom, justice, judgment, and equity. Expanding the purpose and terms of verse 2a, Proverbs engages in a process of schooling a son in the disciplines of: (1) wisdom (a different Hebrew word from that in v. 2) discreet counsel, the ability to govern oneself by choice; (2) justice, the ability to conform to the will and standard of God; a practical righteousness that matches one's positional righteousness; (3) judgment, the application of true righteousness in dealing with others; and (4) equity, the living of life in a fair, pleasing way.

1:4 prudence . . . simple. An additional purpose is to impart discernment to the naive and the ignorant. The root of *simple* is a word meaning "an open door," an apt description of the undiscerning, who do not know what to keep in or out of their minds. **young . . . knowledge and discretion.** To make one ponder before possibly sinning, thus to aid in making a responsible choice.

1:5 counsel. The wise believer will have the ability to guide or govern others with truth.

1:6 understand a proverb . . . enigma. Proverbs seeks to sharpen the mind by schooling one in "parabolic speech" and "dark sayings" that need reflection and interpretation. **riddles.** Study of the Scriptures is sufficient to provide the wisdom for the perplexities of life.

C. Theme (1:7)

1:7 The fear of the Lord. The overarching theme of this book and particularly the first nine chapters is introduced—reverence for God (see v. 29; 2:5; 3:7; 8:13; 9:10; 14:26, 27; cf. also Job 28:28; Ps. 34:11; Acts 9:31). See Introduction: Historical and Theological Themes. This reverential awe and admiring, submissive fear is foundational for all spiritual knowledge and wisdom (cf. 2:4–6; 9:10; 15:33; Job 28:28; Ps. 111:10; Eccl. 12:13). While the unbeliever may make statements about life and truth, he does not have true or ultimate knowledge until he is in a redemptive relationship of reverential awe with God.

Note the progression here: (1) teaching about God; (2) learning about God; (3) fearing God; (4) knowing God; and (5) imitating God's wisdom. The fear of the Lord is a state of mind in which one's own attitudes, will, feelings, deeds, and goals are exchanged for God's (cf. Ps. 42:1).

II. PRAISE AND WISDOM TO THE YOUNG (1:8–9:18)

1:8–9:18 This lengthy section features parental praise of wisdom in the form of didactic addresses. These chapters prepare the reader for the actual proverbs that begin in 10:1ff.

1:10–19 Here is a father's warning against enticement by sinners who will succeed if his son fails to embrace wisdom (v. 8).

1:10 *sinners.* This term is reserved in Scripture to describe unbelievers for whom sin is continual and who even endeavor to persuade believers to sin with them (*see note on James 4:8*). The sins of murder and robbery are used as illustrations of such folly.

1:11 *Come with us.* The intimidating force of peer pressure is often the way to entice those who lack wisdom.

1:12 *swallow.* The wicked devise a deceptive plot in which the innocent are captured and victimized, like one who is taken by death itself—as with Joseph (Gen. 37:20ff.), Jeremiah (Jer. 38:6–13), and Daniel (Dan. 6:16, 17). Sheol is the place of death. For the wicked, it is a place of no return (Job 7:9), darkness (Ps. 143:3), and torment (Is. 14:11).

1:13 *We . . . spoil.* This is the enlisting of the innocent without full disclosure of intent. Abundant spoil is promised by this outright robbery, which is made to appear easy and safe for the thieves and murderers.

1:15 *do not walk.* This directly confronts the invitation of verse 11. Sin must be rejected at the first temptation (cf. Ps. 119:114, 115; James 1:15) by refusing even the association that can lead to sin (cf. Ps. 1:1–6). Avoid the beginnings of sin (see 4:14).

1:16 Cf. Romans 3:15.

1:17 *the net is spread.* It would be ineffective to set up a net for catching a bird in full view of the bird. Taken with verse 18, this analogy means that the sinner sets up his trap for the innocent in secret, but ultimately the trap is sprung on the trapper (v. 19), i.e., greed entraps him (cf. 1 Tim. 6:9–11). Stupid sinners rush to their own ruin.

1:20–33 In this section, wisdom is personified and speaks in the first person, emphasizing the serious consequences that come to those who reject it. Similar personifications of wisdom occur in 3:14–18; 8:1–36; 9:1–12.

1:21 *cries out . . . in the city.* While enticement is covert and secret (v. 10), wisdom, with nothing to hide, is available to everyone, being found in the most prominent of public places.

1:22 *How long?* Three questions reveal three classes of those needing wisdom, and the downward progression of sin: (1) the simple or naive, who are ignorant; (2) scorners or mockers, who commit more serious, determined acts; and (3) fools or obstinate unbelievers, who will not listen to the truth. Proverbs aims its wisdom, primarily, at the first group.

1:23 *rebuke.* God's wisdom brings indictments to bear against the sinner for sin that demand repentance. To the person who does repent, God promises the spirit or essence of true wisdom linked to divine revelation.

1:24–26 Sinners who respond with indifference and mockery at God's indictments increase their guilt (cf. Rom. 2:5) and bring upon themselves the wrath of God's mockery and indifference (vv. 26, 27). Some wait to seek God until it is too late. See Deuteronomy 1:45; 1 Samuel 28:6; Psalm 18:41.

1:26, 27 calamity . . . terror . . . destruction . . . distress and anguish. All these terms describe the severe troubles of divine judgment. When sinners who have rejected wisdom call on God in the day of judgment, God will respond to their distress with derision.

1:28–32 God's rejection of sinners is carefully detailed. This is the aspect of God's wrath expressed in His abandonment of sinners. *See notes on Romans 1:24–28.* No prayers or diligent seeking will help them (cf. 8:17).

1:28–30 I will not answer. God will withdraw His invitation to sinners because they have rejected Him. Note the rejection of wisdom (v. 7), knowledge (v. 22), reproof (vv. 23, 24), and counsel (v. 25).

1:31 eat the fruit of their own way. The ultimate punishment is God's giving a people up to the result of their wickedness. Cf. Romans 1:24–28.

1:32 complacency. Willful carelessness or lack of appropriate care is intended.

2:1 my words. Solomon has embraced God's law and made it his own by faith and obedience, as well as teaching. The wisdom of these words is available to those who, first of all, understand the rich value ("treasure") that wisdom possesses. Appropriating wisdom begins when a person values it above all else.

2:2 ear . . . heart. See note on 4:21–23. Once wisdom is properly valued, both the ear and mind are captivated by it.

2:3–6 Cf. James 1:5.

2:3 cry out for discernment. This shows the passionate pleading of a person who is desperate to know and apply the truth of God. The least bit of indifference will leave one bereft of the fullness of wisdom.

2:4 seek . . . search. A desiring search, the most intensive of a lifetime. Cf. Job 28:1–28 for a parallel. Cf. Matthew 13:44.

2:6 His mouth. The words of His mouth are contained in Scripture. It is there that God speaks (cf. Heb. 1:1, 2; 2 Pet. 1:20, 21). True wisdom comes only by revelation.

2:7, 8 the upright. This identifies those who are true believers, who seek to know, love, and obey God and to live righteously. These covenant keepers alone can know wisdom and experience God's protection.

2:9 righteousness . . . justice, equity. Cf. the ethical triad of 1:3.

2:10 wisdom enters your heart. See note on 4:21–23.

2:11 Discretion . . . understanding. Truth is the protector from all evil (see Ps. 119:11, 97–104).

2:12 speaks perverse things. Twisted speech is typical of those who reject wisdom (cf. Prov. 8:13; 10:31, 32).

2:14 Fools love most what is worst and will ultimately result in their greatest hurt.

2:16 immoral woman. She is the harlot repeatedly condemned in Proverbs (cf. 5:1–23; 6:20–29; 7:1–27; 22:14; 23:27), as in the rest of Scripture (Ex. 20:14; Lev. 20:10). Lit. she is "foreign" or "strange" because such women were at first from outside Israel, but came to include any prostitute or adulteress. Her words are the flattering or smooth words of Proverbs 17:14–20.

2:17 forsakes the companion. She leaves the guidance and friendship of her husband (cf. 16:28; 17:9). **forgets the covenant.** In a wider sense, this could be the covenant of Sinai (Ex 20:14); but here, it specifically refers to the marriage covenant of Genesis 2:24, with its commitment to fidelity.

2:18 leads down to death. The destructive nature of this blinding sin leads a person to walk alongside death (see vv. 8, 9, 12, 15). Death in Proverbs is presented as both a

5:3 lips . . . mouth. Seduction begins with deceptive flattery (cf. 2:16). Lips of honey should be part of true love in marriage (Song 4:11).

5:4, 5 in the end. Lit. "the future" of tasting her lips is like "wormwood," a symbol of suffering (cf. Deut. 29:18), and a "sword," the symbol of death. She travels on the road to death and hell (cf. 2:18).

5:5 hell. *See note on 1:12.*

5:6 Her ways are unstable. Her steps willfully and predictably stagger here and there as she has no concern for the abyss ahead.

5:7–14 These verses describe the high price of infidelity. The focus here is on the guilty suffering of the person who yields to lust rather than obeying God's law. Contrast the proper response to such temptation in the case of Joseph (Gen. 39:1–12).

5:9, 10 your honor to others. The consequences of this sin may include slavery, as a commuted punishment, instead of death that should have come for adultery (Deut. 22:22). In that case, "the cruel one" was the judge and the "others" were the masters to whom all the energy of youth was directed in slavery. All personal wealth was lost to outsiders, and one served in a stranger's house, helping him to prosper.

5:11 flesh and . . . body. This could be a reference to venereal disease (cf. 1 Cor. 6:18), or to the natural end of life. At that point, filled with an irreversible regret (v. 12), the ruined sinner vainly laments his neglect of warning and his sad disgrace.

5:14 midst of the assembly. A most painful loss in such a situation is public disgrace in the community. There can be public confession, discipline, and forgiveness, but not restoration to one's former place of honor and service. See 6:33.

5:15–19 Using the imagery of water, the joy of a faithful marriage is contrasted with the disaster of infidelity (vv. 9–14). *Cistern*

and *well* refer to the wife from whom the husband is to draw all his satisfying refreshment, sexually and affectionately (v. 19; cf. 9:17, 18; Song 4:9–11).

5:16, 17 fountains . . . streams. The euphemism refers to the male procreation capacity with the idea of the foolish as a fountain scattering precious water—a picture of the wastefulness of sexual promiscuity. The result of such indiscriminate sin is called "streams of waters in the streets," a graphic description of the illegitimate street children of harlotry. Rather, says Solomon, "let them be only your own" and not the children of such immoral strangers.

5:18 fountain . . . blessed. God offers to bless male procreation when it is confined to one's wife. It should be noted that, in spite of the sinful polygamy of David and Solomon, as well as the disastrous polygamy of Rehoboam (cf. 2 Chr. 11:21), the instruction here identifies God's ideal as one wife (cf. Gen. 2:24).

5:19 graceful doe. The doe has graceful beauty in her face and form and is often used in the poetry of Bible times for the beauty of a woman. *breasts.* This is imagery of affection (cf. Song 1:13; 4:1–7; 7:7, 8).

5:20 Such behavior is presented as having no benefit; thus, to justify such folly is senseless.

5:21, 22 ponders . . . caught. The Lord sees all that man does and in mercy withholds immediate judgment, allowing the sinner time to repent or to be caught in his own sin (cf. Num. 32:23; Pss. 7:15, 16; 57:6; Prov. 1:17; Gal. 6:7, 8). Note the example of Haman (Esth. 5:9–14; 7:1–10). Cf. 15:3; 22:12.

5:23 He shall die. *See note on 2:18.*

6:1 surety . . . pledge. The foolishness here is making one's self responsible for another's debt and pledging to pay if the other defaults (cf. 11:15; 17:18; 20:16; 22:26). While there is precedent for such a practice, it is far better to give to those in need (see Deut. 15:1–15; 19:17) or lend without interest (see Lev. 25:35–38; 28:8).

6:2–4 snared . . . come into the hand. Cf. 22:26, 27. Anyone who becomes responsible for another person's debt is trapped and controlled because he has yielded control of what God has given him as a stewardship. The situation is so serious that it is imperative to take control of one's own God-given resources and get out of such an intolerable arrangement immediately ("deliver yourself," vv. 3, 4) before coming to poverty or slavery. Cf. Gen 43:9; 44:32, 33.

6:6–11 A warning against laziness is appropriate after the discussion on the folly of guaranteeing someone else's debt, since it is often lazy people who want sureties.

6:6 ant . . . sluggard. Cf. 30:25. The ant is an example of industry, diligence, and planning (vv. 7, 8) and serves as a rebuke to a sluggard (a lazy person who lacks self-control). Folly sends a lazy person to learn from an ant (see 10:4, 26; 12:24; 13:4; 15:19; 19:15; 20:4; 26:14–16).

6:11 prowler . . . armed man. The lazy man, with his inordinate devotion to sleep rather than work (vv. 9, 10), learns too late, thus coming to inescapable poverty just as a victim is overpowered by a robber (see 24:33, 34). While laziness leads to poverty (cf. 10:4, 5; 13:4; 20:4, 13), laziness is not always the cause of poverty (cf. 14:31; 17:5; 19:1, 17, 22; 21:12; 28:3, 11).

6:12 A worthless person. A scoundrel (1 Sam. 25:25; Job 34:18), lit. a "man of Belial" (useless; cf. 1 Sam. 2:12; 30:22), a term which came to be used of the devil himself (see 2 Cor. 6:15).

6:13 winks . . . shuffles . . . points. Apparently, this was common in the Near East. Fearing detection, and to hide his intention, the deceiver spoke lies to the victim while giving signals with his eyes, hands, and feet to someone else who was in on the deception to carry out the intrigue.

6:14 discord. The sin of strife, dissent, or creating conflict intentionally recurs in Proverbs (15:18; 16:28; 17:14; 18:19; 21:9, 19; 22:10; 23:29; 25:24; 26:21; 27:15; 28:25; 29:22).

6:15 without remedy. The results of iniquity can be irreversible. A person's punishment will fit his crime when God judges.

6:16–19 six . . . seven. The sequence of these two numbers was used both to represent totality and as a means of arresting one's attention (cf. 30:15, 18; Job 5:19; Amos 1:3). These seven detestable sins provide a profound glimpse into the sinfulness of man. These verses act as a summary of the previous warnings: (1) haughty eyes (v. 13a, "winks"); (2) lying tongue (v. 12b, "perverse mouth"); (3) hands (v. 13c, "fingers"); (4) heart (v. 14a); (5) feet (v. 13b); (6) false witness (v. 12b); and (7) discord (v. 14c).

6:20, 21 See notes on 3:1, 3.

6:22 roam . . . sleep . . . awake. Cf. 3:23, 24. This parallels the three circumstances of life in Deuteronomy 6:6–9; 11:18–20, for which wisdom provides direction, protection, and meditation. The biblical instruction for parents addresses the possible entrance of evil by supplying good and true thoughts, even when sleeping.

6:23 the commandment . . . the law . . . instruction. Each term refers to the Word of God, which provides the wisdom leading to abundant and eternal life (cf. Ps. 19:7–9).

6:24 See notes on 2:16; 5:3. Parental instruction in wisdom is crucial to strengthen a person against the strong attraction of sexual sin. By loving truth and being elevated to wisdom, men are not seduced by lying flattery.

6:25 lust. Sexual sin is rooted in lust (imagination of the sinful act), as implied in

Exodus 20:17 and addressed by Christ in Matthew 5:28. This initial attraction must be consistently rejected (James 1:14, 15).

6:26 crust of bread. Here, the smallest piece of bread demonstrates how the prostitute reduces the life of a man to insignificance, including the loss of his wealth (see 29:3), freedom, family, purity, dignity, and even his soul (v. 32).

6:27–29 Powerful metaphors are given here to describe the obvious danger and destructive consequences of adultery, showing that punishment is a natural and expected consequence.

6:29 touches her. This refers to a touch intended to inflame sexual passion. Paul uses the same expression with the same meaning in 1 Corinthians 7:1.

6:30–35 Adultery is compared to a thief. Unlike the pity extended to a starving thief, who can make restitution (even if it costs all that he has) and put the crime behind him permanently (vv. 30, 31), there is no restitution for the adulterer as he destroys his soul (v. 32; cf. Deut. 22:22). If he lives, he is disgraced for life (v. 33) with a reproach that will never go away. The jealous husband will have no mercy on him either (vv. 34, 35; cf. 27:4; Song 8:6).

6:31 sevenfold. Varying measures of restitution occur in Scripture (cf. Ex. 22:1ff.; Lev. 6:5; Num. 5:7; 2 Sam. 12:6; Luke 19:8), but for the thief, it is severe.

7:1–4 Cf. 2:1–4; 3:1–3; 4:10.

7:2 apple of your eye. This expression refers to the pupil of the eye which, because it is the source of sight, is carefully protected (see Deut. 32:10; Ps. 17:8; Zech. 2:8). The son is to guard and protect his father's teachings because they give him spiritual and moral sight.

7:3 Bind. This is a call to give the truth of divine wisdom a permanent place in the mind and in conduct. Cf. 3:3; 6:21; Deuteronomy 6:8; 2 Corinthians 3:3.

7:6 The drama of seduction by the adulteress, introduced in verse 5 and unfolding to verse 23, is described from the viewpoint of one who is watching from his window.

7:7 simple . . . devoid of understanding. See notes on 1:2–4.

7:8 took the path. Against the advice of 4:14, 15, he put himself right in the harlot's place. "Fleeing immorality" (1 Cor. 6:18) starts by not being in the harlot's neighborhood at night. Cf. v. 25.

7:10 a crafty heart. Lit. "hidden." This is an unfair contest between the simple young man, who lacks wisdom and is void of the truth, and the evil woman, who knows her goal, but hides her true intentions. See notes on 6:26; 23:27, 28.

7:11, 12 These verses break the narrative to describe the woman's modes of operation leading to her successful seduction of the simple man.

7:14 peace offerings. According to the law of peace offerings (Lev. 7:11–18), the meat left over after the sacrifice was to be eaten before the end of the day. She appears very religious in making the invitation that the man join her because she had made her offering and is bringing home the meat that must be eaten.

7:15 It is already night (v. 9) and the meal must be consumed. It cannot be left for morning. Such hypocrisy is concerned about the ceremonial law while aggressively seducing someone to violate God's moral law.

7:16, 17 Egyptian linen. Fine linen was a

Key Proverbs on Marriage	
1. Prov. 5:15–19	6. Prov. 19:14
2. Prov. 6:29	7. Prov. 21:9
3. Prov. 12:4	8. Prov. 24:3,4
4. Prov. 14:1	9. Prov. 27:8
5. Prov. 18:22	10. Prov. 31:10–31

sign of wealth (31:22; Is. 19:9; Ezek. 27:7). Here, the solicitation is direct, as she describes the comfort of her bed with its aromatic spices (cf. Song 1:13; 3:6).

7:18 fill of love. Adultery is not true love, but mere physical gratification.

7:19, 20 She gives the simple man the assurance that there is no fear of discovery of their act, since her husband has taken a large sum of cash, needed because he will be away for a long time (lit. "a full moon"), returning at a set time and not before.

7:21 When the location, time, and setting were allowed, the seduction was easy (cf. v. 26).

7:22 slaughter . . . stocks. Ignorant of the real danger and incapable of resistance, he quickly succumbs like a beast to be butchered or a criminal put in stocks.

7:23 arrow . . . bird. This refers to a mortal wound, as the liver represents the seat of life (Lam. 2:11) and the bird is snared to be eaten (cf. 6:26).

7:24 The appropriate application of this drama is made in the admonition of these verses to avoid her deadly seduction.

7:26 It is not just weak people who fall, but strong people in the wrong place at the wrong time with the wrong thoughts for the wrong reasons.

7:27 Cf. 5:5.

8:1–3 wisdom. See note on 1:21. The openness and public exposure of wisdom contrasts with the secrecy and intrigues of the wicked adulterers in chapter 7.

8:4, 5 simple ones. See note on 1:4.

8:6–8 The virtues of wisdom are summarized in all that is excellent, right, true, and righteous.

8:9 plain. Lit. "clear." The one who applies his mind to the wisdom of God will understand and gain moral knowledge and the insight to recognize truth. Cf. 1 Corinthians 1:18–25.

8:10, 11 The most valuable reality a young person can attain is the insight to order his life by the standard of truth (see notes on 3:14, 15; 8:18–21; also Job 28:12–28; Ps. 19:10).

8:13 The fear of the LORD. See note on 1:7. **arrogance . . . hate.** Wisdom hates what God hates (cf. 6:16–19; Ps. 5:5). The highest virtue is humility (submission to God), and, thus, wisdom hates pride and self-exaltation above all.

8:15, 16 kings . . . rulers . . . princes . . . nobles. In this royal court setting, Solomon addresses his son as a future king. All these leaders should do their work by God's wisdom and justice. Cf. Romans 13:1, 2.

8:17 love. Wisdom's love for the person who receives it is proven by the benefits mentioned in verses 18–21.

8:18–21 Riches and honor. Cf. 3:16; 22:4. Solomon, who was given great wisdom, experienced its wealth of benefits firsthand as a young king (cf. 1 Kin. 3:12–14; 10:14–29).

8:22–31 The LORD possessed me. Cf. 3:19, 20. Personified wisdom existed before everything that God created, so that divine wisdom, like God, was eternally first. Christ used His eternal wisdom in creation (John 1:1–3; 1 Cor 1:24, 30).

8:24–26 Note how these verses parallel the creation account in Genesis. The earth (v. 23) with day one in Genesis 1:1–5; water (v. 24) with day two in Genesis 1:6–8; and land (vv. 25, 26) with day three in Genesis 1:9–13.

8:27 circle on the face of the deep. The

Key Proverbs on Fear of the Lord	
1. Prov. 1:7	6. Prov. 14:26, 27
2. Prov. 3:7, 8	7. Prov. 19:23
3. *Prov. 8:13*	8. Prov. 22:4
4. Prov. 10:27	9. Prov. 28:14
5. Prov. 14:2	10. Prov. 29:25

Hebrew word for circle indicates that the earth is a globe; therefore, the horizon is circular (cf. Is. 40:22). This *deep* that surrounds the earth was the original world ocean that covered the surface of the earth before it was fully formed and given life (cf. Gen. 1:2).

8:29 *sea its limit.* In creation, God limited the waters on the earth (cf. Gen. 1:9; 7:11; 8:2), commanding into existence shorelines beyond which the oceans cannot go. ***foundations.*** This figuratively denotes the solid structure of the earth (cf. Job 38:4; Ps. 24:2).

8:30 *master craftsman.* As translated in Song 7:1 and Jeremiah 52:15, this term describes wisdom as competent and experienced in the craft of creation.

8:31 *my delight.* When God rejoiced over His creation (Gen. 1:31; Job 38:7), wisdom was also rejoicing, especially in the creation of mankind, who in the physical creation alone has the capacity to appreciate wisdom and truth.

8:36 *hate me love death.* Since wisdom is the source of life (see 3:18), anyone who hates wisdom and spurns it is acting as if he loves death.

9:1 *seven pillars.* The significance of seven is to convey the sufficiency of this house as full in size and fit for a banquet.

9:2 *mixed her wine.* Cf. 23:29, 30. Wine was diluted with water as much as one to eight, to reduce its intoxicating power. It was also mixed with spices for flavor (Song 8:2). Unmixed wine is called strong drink (*see note on 20:1*; cf. 20:1; 31:6; Lev. 10:9; Is. 28:7; Luke 1:15).

9:3–5 The call of wisdom is not secret, but public. *See note on 1:21.*

9:5 *Come, eat . . . drink.* Cf. God's banquet call (Is. 55:1–3; Luke 14:16–24; Rev. 22:17).

9:7–9 Wise people receive reproof and rebuke with appreciation; fools do not.

9:10 *The fear of the LORD.* See note on 1:7.

9:11 See Introduction: Historical and Theological Themes.

9:12 Every individual is responsible for his own conduct, so that the choices one makes affect his own life.

9:13–18 The feast of folly is described as offered by the foolish hostess. Note the contrast with lady wisdom in verses 1–6 and similarities to the immoral woman in 7:6–23.

9:13 *clamorous.* Cf. 7:11, 12.

9:17 Forbidden delights sometimes seem sweeter and more pleasant because of their risk and danger.

9:18 *hell.* *See note on 1:12.* Like the adulterer, the flattering words of folly lead to death (see 2:18, 19; 5:5; 7:21–23, 26, 27).

III. PROVERBS FOR EVERYONE (10:1–29:27)

A. From Solomon (10:1–22:16)

10:1–22:16 This large section contains 375 of Solomon's individual proverbs. They are in no apparent order, with only occasional grouping by subject, and are often without a context to qualify their application. They are based on Solomon's inspired knowledge of the Law and the Prophets. The parallel, two-line proverbs of chapters 10–15 are mostly contrasts or opposites (antithetical), while those of chapters 16–22 are mostly similarities or comparisons (synthetical).

10:1 *grief of his mother.* By contrast, *see note on 23:15, 16.* This parental grief is most deeply felt by the mother, who plays a more intimate role in raising a child.

Key Proverbs on Children	
1. Prov. 10:1	6. Prov. 24:21, 22
2. Prov. 13:1	7. Prov. 27:11
3. Prov. 22:6	8. Prov. 28:7
4. Prov. 22:15	9. Prov. 29:3
5. Prov. 23:22–25	10. Prov. 29:15

10:2 death. The greatest of all treasures, life, is gained by righteousness.

10:3 desire of the wicked. For a while, the wicked may seem to realize their desires; in the end, God removes their accomplishments because they are evil (cf. Ps. 37:16–20).

10:4 diligent. This is in contrast to the sluggard (*see notes on 6:6–11*). Poverty by itself is not evil, unless it is the product of laziness.

10:5 gathers . . . sleeps. Cf. 6:6–11; 13:4; 15:19; 24:30–34; 28:19, 20. The timing necessary in agriculture can be applied to the general laying hold of life's opportunities.

10:6 violence. See 10:13; 12:13; 14:3; 18:6, 7. The violence which has gone forth from the wicked later falls back upon his foul mouth (cf. Hab. 2:17; Mal 2:16).

10:7 memory . . . name. This refers to the way a righteous person is remembered by man and God after his death.

10:8 receive commands. To finish the parallelism, the wise listens and is teachable; therefore, he will be lifted up. The fool, always talking, falls because he rejects God's commands.

10:9 Those who have integrity (who live what they believe) exist without fear of some evil being discovered, while those who are perverse and have secret wickedness will not be able to hide it forever. Cf. 11:3; 19:1; 20:7.

10:10 winks with the eye. See 6:13, 14.

10:11 well of life. The Lord is the source of this fountain (Ps. 36:9), which then springs up in the wise man as wise speech (10:11), wise laws (13:14), the fear of the Lord (12:27), and understanding (16:22). *See notes on 3:18; Ezekiel 47:1–12; John 4:10; 7:38, 39.* **violence.** *See note on 10:6.*

10:12 love. True love seeks the highest good for another (cf. 1 Cor. 14:4–7). First Peter 4:8 quotes this verse (cf. James 5:20).

10:13 rod. This first reference to corporal

punishment applied to the backside (cf. 19:29; 26:3) recommends it as the most effective way of dealing with children and fools. See also 13:24; 18:6; 19:29; 22:15; 23:13, 14; 26:3; 29:15.

10:14 mouth of the foolish. The loose tongue of the fool is a recurring subject in Proverbs (cf. vv. 6, 8, 13, 18, 19, 31, 32; 12:23; 13:3; 15:1, 2, 23, 26, 28, 31–33; 17:28; 18:2, 6–8). James parallels this emphasis about the tongue (James 1:26; 3:1–12).

10:15 rich man's . . . poor. While the rich man thinks he has his walled city for protection (cf. 18:11; 28:11), the poor man knows he has nothing. Both should trust in the Lord as their only protection (cf. 3:5, 6; 11:4, 28; 18:10, 11; Ps. 20:7; Eccl. 9:11–18; James 5:1–6).

10:16 wages. The industry of the righteous makes him successful, while the earnings of the wicked provide more opportunities for sinning.

10:18 hatred . . . slander. Both the harboring and venting of hatred are wrong and will be punished. Slander (gossip or lies) is forbidden (cf. 25:10; also 16:28; 18:8; 20:19; 26:20, 22).

10:19 Wisdom restrains the tongue, since much speech risks sin. Cf. Psalm 39:1; James 1:26; 3:2–8.

10:20 tongue . . . heart. These words are used as parallel terms because they are inseparably linked. Cf. Matthew 15:18, 19. **choice silver.** Good words are scarce, precious, and valuable (cf. 15:23; Is. 50:4).

10:21 feed . . . die. Sound teaching benefits many; the fool starves himself to death spiritually by his lack of wise teaching (cf. Hos. 4:6).

10:22 rich. While having more than what one needs is not the object of wisdom, it is generally the result (cf. Deut. 6:11–15; 1 Kin. 3:10–14). See Introduction: Historical and Theological Themes. **no sorrow.** None of the sorrow that is associated with ill-gotten wealth (cf. 13:11; 15:6; 16:19; 21:6; 28:6) is associated with wealth provided by the Lord.

10:24 *fear of the wicked.* The righteous receive what they desire, while the wicked receive what they fear (cf. Heb. 10:26–29).

10:25 *whirlwind.* See 1:27; 6:15; 29:1.

10:27 *fear of the LORD. See note on 1:7.*

10:29 *The way of the LORD.* This is the spiritual path on which God directs man to walk (*see note on Acts 18:25*).

10:30 Cf. Psalm 37:9–11.

11:1 *Dishonest scales.* Cf. 16:11; 20:10, 23. As indicated in Leviticus 19:35, 36; Deuteronomy 25:13–16; Ezekiel 45:10; Amos 8:5; Micah 6:10, God detests dishonesty.

11:2 *pride.* From a root meaning "to boil," or "to run over," indicating an overwhelmingly arrogant attitude or behavior. It is used of ordinary men (Deut. 17:12, 13); kings (Neh. 9:10); Israel (Neh. 9:16, 29); false prophets (Deut. 18:20); and murderers (Ex. 21:14). *the humble.* A rare word, which appears in Micah 6:8: "Walk humbly with your God." This humble and teachable spirit is first of all directed toward God (cf. 15:33; 16:18, 19; 18:12; 22:4).

11:4 *day of wrath.* Money buys no escape from death in the day of final accounting to God, the divine Judge (cf. Is. 10:3; Ezek. 7:19; Zeph. 1:18; Luke 12:16–21).

11:11 Social influence for good or bad is in view.

11:12 *despises.* Lit. one who gossips, slanders, or destroys with words, in contrast to the silence of the wise. *See notes on 10:14, 18.*

11:13 *talebearer.* This depicts someone who is a peddler in scandal, who speaks words deliberately intended to harm rather than merely unguarded speech (cf. Lev. 19:16).

11:14 *multitude of counselors.* As in 15:22; 20:18; 24:6, a good decision is made

with multiple, wise advisers. The more crucial the decision, the more appropriate is corporate wisdom. Note the example of David (2 Sam. 15:30–17:23).

11:15 *See note on 6:1.*

11:16 *gracious woman . . . ruthless men.* While evil people may grasp at wealth, they will never attain the honor due a gracious woman (cf. 31:30).

11:18 *deceptive work.* The efforts of the wicked deceiver do not yield the riches his deception seeks, but the righteous receive a reward from God.

11:20 *abomination.* Defined throughout Scripture as attitudes, this involves words and behaviors which God hates (see 6:16).

11:21 *Though they join forces.* The combined power of the wicked cannot free them from just punishment; while, the unaided children of the righteous find deliverance by reason of their relationship with God.

11:22 *ring of gold.* A nose ring was an ornament intended to beautify a woman in OT times (cf. Gen. 24:47; Is. 3:21; Ezek. 16:12). It was as out of place in a pig's nose as the lack of discretion was in a lovely lady.

11:23 *desire . . . expectation.* These terms refer to outcomes from God's perspective.

11:24–26 *scatters, yet increases.* The principle here is that generosity, by God's blessing, secures increase, while stinginess leads to poverty instead of expected gain. The person who gives receives far more in return (Ps. 112:9; Eccl. 11:1; John 12:24, 25; Acts 20:35; 2 Cor. 9:6–9).

11:28 *trusts in his riches.* Cf. 23:4, 5; *see notes on 1 Timothy 6:17, 19.*

11:29 *inherit the wind.* The person who mismanages his house will see all his possessions blown away, and he will have nothing left in the end. He will serve the one who manages well (15:27).

11:30 *tree of life. See note on 3:18.* *wins souls.* Lit. "to take lives," in the sense of doing them good or influencing them with wisdom's ways (cf. Luke 5:10). The word is also used for capturing people for evil purposes as in 6:25; Psalm 31:13; Ezekiel 13:18.

11:31 recompensed. God's final blessing and reward to the righteous, and His judgment and punishment of the ungodly and sinners come after life on this earth has ended. But there are foretastes of both during life on the earth, as the righteous experience God's personal care and goodness, while the wicked are void of it. Cf. 1 Peter 4:18.

12:1 stupid. From the Hebrew "to graze"; he is as stupid as the brute cattle (cf. Pss. 49:20; 73:22).

12:3 root. The familiar image is of the righteous person being firm like a flourishing tree (Ps. 1; Jer. 17:7, 8).

12:4 excellent wife. *See notes on 31:10; Ruth 3:11.* For the opposite, see 19:13; 21:9, 19; 25:24; 27:15. **rottenness in his bones.** This speaks of suffering that is like a painful and incurable condition.

12:6 Lie in wait. *See notes on 1:11, 12.*

12:7 house. The rewards of wise living are not only to individuals, but extend to one's household or family.

12:9 Better . . . than. This is one of several proverbs which makes a distinct comparison using "better . . . than" (cf. 3:13, 14; 8:11, 19; 12:9; 15:16, 17; 16:8, 16, 19, 32; 17:1; 19:1, 22; 21:9, 19; 22:1; 25:7, 24; 27:5, 10; 28:6). **slighted . . . honors himself.** The obscure person of lowly rank, who can at least afford to hire a servant because of his honest gain, is better than the person who boasts about his prominence but is actually poor.

12:10 regards . . . cruel. Lit. he has concern for the condition of his beast, while the wicked has no concern for people.

12:11 frivolity. Energy expended in worthless pursuits and fantasies is as useless as outright laziness. *See notes on 6:6–11; 20:4; 24:30–34.*

12:12 covet the catch. This refers to the desire for booty gained by the schemes of the wicked, contrasted with a simple life of obedience that produces blessing.

12:14 fruit of his mouth. This deals with the power of words; the reward of wise words is like the reward for physical labor (cf. 10:11; 15:4; 18:4).

12:16 covers shame. A model of self-control, the prudent man ignores an insult (cf. 9:7; 10:12).

12:17 speaks truth. In the court, the truthful witness promotes justice.

12:18 speaks . . . piercings. The contrast here is between cutting words that are "blurted out" (Ps. 106:33) and thoughtful words that bring health. Cf. Ephesians 4:29, 30.

12:20 Deceit. The contrasting parallel is implied, not stated. Those who plan evil by deceit have no joy because of the risks and dangers in their plan, but the righteous who lead by peace fear nothing, and thus have joy.

12:23 conceals. Unlike the fool who makes everyone hear his folly, the wise person is a model of restraint and humility, speaking what he knows at an appropriate time (cf. 29:11). *See notes on 1:4; 10:14.*

12:24 forced labor. Unlike the hardworking people who have charge over their work, the lazy are eventually forced to go to work for the diligent to survive.

12:26 astray. Cf. 1 Corinthians 15:33. This verse could be understood as saying that the righteous person guides his friends carefully, unlike the wicked person who leads his companions astray.

12:27 does not roast. The sluggard lacks commitment to make something of his opportunities (cf. vv. 11, 25).

13:2, 3 The parallels here are implied. A man of good words prospers; but, a man of evil words (thus unfruitful to God) provokes violence against himself.

13:4 *See notes on 6:6, 11.*

13:7 *makes himself rich . . . makes himself poor.* The same pretense is presented in two contrasting weaknesses; one pretends to be rich, while the other pretends to be poor. In contrast, people should be honest and unpretentious (cf. 11:24; 2 Cor 6:10).

13:8 *ransom . . . riches . . . poor . . . rebuke.* Riches deliver some people from punishment, while others suffer because they will not heed the rebuke of laziness, which keeps them poor.

13:9 *light . . . lamp.* This image of life, prosperity, and joy is contrasted with adversity and death (cf. Job 3:20).

13:10 The proud spurn advice from others; the wise accept it.

13:11 Cf. 20:21.

13:12 *tree of life. See note on 3:18.*

13:13 *word . . . commandment.* These terms refer to divine revelation.

13:14 *fountain of life.* The same Hebrew word meaning "well of life." *See note on 10:11.*

13:16 *lays open.* The language vividly shows that a fool displays folly, like a peddler spreads out his wares for others to gaze upon. Cf. 12:23; 15:2.

13:19 The fool's relentless pursuit of evil and hatred of good does not let him taste the sweet blessings of obedience.

13:20 *walks . . . companion.* This speaks of the power of association to shape character. Cf. 1:10, 18; 2:12; 4:14; 16:29; 22:24, 25; 23:20; 28:7, 19; Psalm 1.

13:21 This is a basic theme/general principle throughout Proverbs and is illustrated throughout the OT, which establishes that righteousness brings divine blessing and evil brings divine cursing.

13:22 *leaves an inheritance.* While good people's estates remain with their families, the wealth of the wicked does not. In the

providence of God, it will ultimately belong to the righteous. Cf. 28:8; Job 27:16, 17.

13:23 *lack of justice.* The contrast here is between the poor but industrious man who will be rewarded with provision from his efforts, and the rich man whose efforts are brought to ruin by his deeds of injustice (cf. James 5:1–6).

13:24 *rod . . . disciplines . . . promptly.* Early childhood teaching (*see note on 22:6*) requires both parental discipline, including corporal punishment (cf. 10:13; 19:18; 22:15; 29:15, 17), and balanced kindness and love. There is great hope that the use of the "divine ordinance" of the rod will produce godly virtue (cf. 23:13, 14) and parental joy (cf. 10:1; 15:20; 17:21; 23:15, 16, 24, 25; 28:7; 29:1, 15, 17). Such discipline must have the right motivation (Heb. 12:5–11) and appropriate severity (Eph. 6:4). One who has genuine affection for his child, but withholds corporal punishment, will produce the same kind of child as a parent who hates his offspring.

13:25 This states more directly the teaching of verses 13, 18, 21.

14:1 *builds her house.* Cf. the wise woman building her house (31:10–31) with lady wisdom building her house (9:1–6).

14:3 *rod.* A rare Hebrew word that refers to a small shoot (see Is. 11:1). Here, it is used metaphorically for the proud, inflicting tongue in a fool's mouth, which destroys the fool and others (cf. 11:2; 16:18; 29:23).

14:7 *Go.* Avoid association with all who cannot teach you wisdom. Cf. 1 Tim 4:6, 7; 6:3–5.

14:9 *Fools mock at sin.* While fools ridicule their impending judgment (cf. 1:26), the wise are promised favor with God (cf. Is. 1:11–20) and man (cf. 10:32; 11:27). Cf. 1 Samuel 2:26; Luke 2:40, 52.

14:10 At its depth, suffering and rejoicing are personal and private. No one is able to

Key Word

Wisdom: 1:2; 4:5; 9:10; 14:6; 16:16; 18:4; 23:23; 31:26—can also mean "skill" but is most commonly used to describe daily application of practical wisdom. Proverbs teaches that true wisdom reaches beyond mere knowledge of truth to living a life of moral integrity (8:7–9). Whereas the sinful life leads ultimately to self-destruction, abundant life is found within the wisdom of God (2:6; Job 11:6).

communicate them fully (1 Sam 1:10; 1 Kin. 8:38; Matt 2:18; 26:39–42, 75).

14:12 way of death. See notes on Matthew 7:13, 14.

14:14 backslider in heart. This term, so often used by the prophets (Is. 57:17; Jer. 3:6, 8, 11, 12, 14, 22; 8:5; 31:22; 49:4; Hos. 11:7; 14:4), is used here in such a way as to clarify who is a backslider. He belongs in the category of the fool, the wicked, and the disobedient and he is contrasted with the godly wise. It is a word that the prophets used of apostate unbelievers.

14:17 quick-tempered . . . wicked intentions. The contrast is between the hasty anger that is labeled as folly and the deliberate malice that produces hatred (Ps. 37:7).

14:19 evil will bow. The ancient custom was for the inferior to prostrate himself before the superior or wait humbly before the great one's gate, seeking favor. Good will ultimately humble evil.

14:20 This sad-but-true picture of human nature is not given approvingly, but only as a fact.

14:24 foolishness of fools is folly. This is emphatic language, playing on the word *fool* and showing that the only reward for fools is more folly.

14:25 The truth produces justice, on which the lives of people may depend.

14:26 fear of the LORD. See note on 1:7.

14:27 fountain of life. See note on 10:11.

14:28 multitude of people. This is a truism stating that a king's honor comes from the support of his people as they increase and prosper (cf. 30:29–31).

14:29 Cf. v. 17.

14:30 sound heart . . . body. A healthy mind filled with wisdom is associated with a healthy body (cf. 3:5–8; 17:22). **rottenness to the bones.** See note on 12:4.

14:31 oppresses the poor . . . Maker. It offends the Creator when a person neglects the poor, who are part of His creation (cf. 14:21; 17:5; 19:17; 21:13; 22:2, 7; 28:8; 29:13).

14:32 righteous . . . death. Cf. 23:18. Hope in death for the righteous is a central OT theme (cf. Job 19:25, 26; Pss. 31:5; 49:14, 15; 73:24; Eccl. 11:9; Is. 26:19; Dan. 12:1, 2).

14:33 is made known. Wisdom is quietly preserved in the heart of the wise for the time of proper use, while fools are eager to blurt out their folly (cf. 12:23; 13:16; 15:2, 14).

14:34 exalts. While just principles and actions preserve and even exalt a society, their absence shames a society (cf. 11:11).

14:35 causes shame. Cf. 10:5; 12:4.

15:1 soft answer . . . harsh word. This is the central principle about anger in Proverbs.

15:2 See note on 14:33.

15:3 eyes of the LORD. Cf. 5:21; 22:12. This refers to God's omniscience. Cf. 1 Sam 16:7; 2 Chronicles 16:9; Job 24:23; Psalms 33:13–15; 139:1–16; Jeremiah 17:10.

15:4 tree of life. See note on 3:18. **breaks the spirit.** To crush or wound, thus to destroy one's morale (cf. Is. 65:14).

15:8 External acts of worship, though according to biblical prescription, are repulsive to God when the heart of the worshiper is wicked (cf. Is. 1:12–15; Amos 5:21; Mal. 1:11–14; Heb. 11:4, 6).

15:10 *the way.* The way of truth and righteousness (see 2:13; 10:17).

15:11 *Hell and Destruction.* Cf. 27:20. Hell or Sheol is the place of the dead (*see note on 1:12*). *Destruction* refers to the experience of external punishment. Cf. Job 26:6.

15:13 Cf. v. 4.

15:15 *continual feast.* The joyous, inward condition of the wise man's heart (14:21) is described as a perpetual feast. Real happiness is always determined by the state of the heart (cf. Hab. 3:17, 18; 1 Tim. 4:6–8).

15:16, 17 See note on 12:9 for other "better . . . than" references.

15:16 *fear of the LORD.* See note on 1:7.

15:17 *dinner of herbs.* Vegetables are in view, the typical dinner of the poor.

15:18 "Hotheads" are contrasted with "peacemakers" (cf. 14:17, 29; 15:1; 28:25; 29:11, 22).

15:19 *thorns.* He is too lazy to remove them. *See notes on 6:6, 11.*

15:22 See note on 11:14.

15:24 *hell below.* See note on 1:12.

15:25 When evil people try to take the property of widows, God will intervene (cf. 22:28; 23:10, 11). The most desolate (widows) who have God's help have a more permanent dwelling place than prosperous and self-reliant sinners.

15:27 *bribes.* Cf. 18:5; 24:23; 29:4; Exodus 23:8; Deuteronomy 16:19; Ecclesiastes 7:7; Isaiah 1:23.

15:28 *mouth . . . wicked pours forth.* Wicked people don't guard their words. *See note on 12:23;* cf. Ephesians 4:29.

15:30 *light of the eyes.* This is a comparison, so that the "good report" defines this term. Whatever is good; i.e., sound truth and wisdom, stirs the heart by relieving anxiety and producing a cheerful face (cf. 14:30; 15:13; 17:22).

15:31 *ear that hears . . . wise.* The acquiring of wisdom demands a teachable spirit.

15:33 *fear of the LORD.* See note on 1:7.

16:1 *preparations . . . answer.* Human responsibility is always subject to God's absolute sovereignty (cf. 3:6; 16:2, 9, 33; 19:21; 20:24; 21:1, 30, 31).

16:2 *spirits.* While man can be self-deceived, God determines his true motives (cf. 21:2; 24:12; 1 Sam. 16:7; 1 Cor. 4:4).

16:3 *Commit.* Lit. "roll upon" in the sense of both total trust (3:5–6) and submission to the will of God (Pss. 22:8; 37:5; 119:133). He will fulfill a person's righteous plans.

16:4 The wicked will bring glory to God in the day of their judgment and eternal punishment. *See notes on Romans 9:17–23.*

16:6 By God's mercy and truth, He affects the "atonement" or covering of sin, which for the believing sinner inclines him to depart from evil. *See notes on Leviticus 16:1–34; 17:11* for explanation of atonement. *fear of the LORD.* See note on 1:7.

16:7 This general rule does not preclude persecution from some people. *See note on 2 Timothy 3:12.*

16:8 *righteousness . . . justice.* These words are used as synonyms here.

16:9 *See notes on vv. 1, 2.* Sovereign God overrules the plans of people to fulfill His purposes. See Genesis 50:20; 1 Kings 12:15; Psalm 119:133; Jeremiah 10:23; Daniel 5:23–30; 1 Corinthians 3:19, 20.

16:10 *Divination.* This does not imply any occultic practice forbidden in Leviticus 19:26, but is literally a decision from divine wisdom, via the words of the king who represented God (cf. Rom. 13:1, 2). The king was under mandate (Deut. 17:18–20) to seek out and speak God's wisdom (cf. David in 2 Sam. 14:17–20; Solomon in 1 Kin. 3:9–12; and Christ as King in Is. 11:2).

16:11 See note on 11:1.

16:12 See note on 14:34.

16:14 This points to the king's power of "life or death," which can be abused (cf. 1

Key Proverbs on Mind (Heart)	
1. Prov. 3:5	6. Prov. 18:15
2. Prov. 11:20	7. Prov. 19:21
3. Prov. 14:33	8. Prov. 23:7
4. Prov. 15:13–15	9. Prov. 27:19
5. Prov. 16:9	10. Prov. 28:26

Sam. 22:16–18; Esth. 7–10; Dan. 2:5) or used for good (cf. 2 Sam. 1:1–16; 4:5–12).

16:15 cloud of the latter rain. The late spring rain, which matured the crop, fell before the harvest (cf. 2 Sam. 23:3, 4; Ps. 72:6) and is here compared to the king's power to grace his subjects with encouragement.

16:16 better. Cf. 3:13–16; 8:10, 11, 18, 19. See note on 12:9.

16:17 A plain road represents the habitual course of the righteous in departing from evil. As long as he stays on it, he is safe.

16:19 The proud are those who have plundered the poor.

16:21 sweetness of the lips. "Honeyed words," which reflect intelligence, judiciousness, and discernment in speech. This refers to eloquent discourse from the wise (cf. v. 24).

16:22 wellspring of life. See note on 10:11. The advice of the understanding person brings blessing, while the correction offered by a fool is useless.

16:23 heart. See note on 4:21–23.

16:24 Pleasant words. See note on v. 21; cf. 24:13, 14; Psalm 19:10.

16:25 way of death. Cf. 14:12.

16:26 labors for himself. Labor is hard and often grievous, but necessary, even for the lazy (cf. Eccl. 6:7; Eph. 4:28; 6:7; 2 Thess. 3:10–12).

16:27 ungodly man. See note on 6:12. He literally digs a pit for his neighbor as a hunter would for prey (cf. Pss. 7:15; 62:6), and his speech is incendiary (cf. James 3:6).

16:28 sows. The same root word is used

for the release of flaming foxes in the grain fields of the Philistines (Judg. 15:4, 5; cf. 17:9). **whisperer.** A slanderer or gossip. See note on 6:14; cf. 8:8; 26:20, 22 for the same Hebrew term.

16:30 purses. The idea of winking or squinting the eyes and compressing one's lips was to express the posture showing deep thought and determined purpose.

16:31 This calls for respecting elders. Cf. 20:29.

16:32 slow to anger. See notes on 14:17; 25:28. Cf. Ecclesiastes 9:17, 18; James 1:19, 20.

16:33 lot. See note on 16:1. Casting lots was a method often used to reveal God's purposes in a matter (cf. Josh. 14:1, 2; 1 Sam. 14:38–43; 1 Chr. 25:8–31; Jon. 1:7; Acts 1:26). The high priest may have carried lots in his sacred vest, along with the Urim and Thummim (see note on Ex. 28:30).

17:1 Cf. 15:17.

17:2 wise servant . . . inheritance. A faithful servant will rise above an unworthy son and receive an inheritance (cf. 11:29; 1 Kin. 11:26, 28–38; Matt. 8:11, 12).

17:3 refining pot. This was a heated crucible used to test and refine precious metal. Cf. Psalm 66:10; Isaiah 1:25; 48:10; Jeremiah 6:29; Ezekiel 22:17–22; Daniel 12:10; Malachi 3:3. See 1 Peter 1:7.

17:5 Cf. 14:21, 31.

17:6 Children's children. Godly influence generates mutual love and respect in a family, which extends from generation to generation (cf. Ps. 90 with Ex. 20:12).

17:8 present. This refers to a bribe that brings prosperity to its recipient (v. 23; 15:27).

17:9 Cf. 16:28; 18:8.

17:10 For the theme of a teachable spirit, cf. 9:7, 8; 15:31–33.

17:11 Just retribution comes against people who rebel and, thus, the king's messenger will have no mercy (cf. 16:14; 2 Sam. 20:1–22; 1 Kin. 2:25, 29, 34, 46).

17:12 Fools are less rational in anger than wild bears.

17:13 *evil for good.* Solomon knew this proverb well since his father mistreated Uriah (cf. 2 Sam. 12:10–31). Contrast this with the man who repays evil with good (cf. 20:22; Matt. 5:43–48; 1 Pet. 3:9).

17:14 *releasing water.* The smallest break in the dam sets loose an uncontrollable flood.

17:15 The unjust judge is controlled by his pride, prejudice, bribes, and passions. *See note on 24:23b–25*; cf. Exodus 23:7; Isaiah 5:23.

17:16 Even wealth cannot buy wisdom for those who do not love it. Cf. 4:7.

17:17 The difference between a friend and brother is noted here. A true friend is a constant source of love, while a brother in one's family may not be close, but is drawn near to help in trouble. Friends are closer than brothers because they are available all the time, not just in the crisis. Cf. 18:24.

17:18 *See notes on 6:1, 2–4.*

17:19 *exalts his gate.* The image here is of the proud person who flaunts his wealth with a huge house having a large front door and who, thus, invites death (cf. Jer. 22:13–19).

17:20 *perverse.* Cf. 10:31.

17:21 Cf. 10:1; 15:20; 17:25; 19:26.

17:22 Cf. 14:30; 15:13, 30; 16:14; Job 29:24.

17:23 *See note on v. 8.*

17:24 *ends of the earth.* This refers to the fool's roving fixations in the absence of wisdom.

17:25 Cf. verse 21.

17:26 *punish . . . strike.* Here is a clear statement on political and religious injustice, focusing on the equally bad mistreatment of the innocent and the noble.

17:27 *spares.* Cf. 10:19; 14:29; 15:18; 16:27, 32; 29:20.

17:28 *fool is counted wise.* This is not

saying that fools show wisdom in their silence, but that silence conceals their folly.

18:1 *isolates himself.* This man seeks selfish gratification and accepts advice from no one.

18:2 Cf. Ecclesiastes 10:12–14.

18:3 Sin and punishment are inseparably connected, as evil produces both the feeling of contempt in others and its manifestation, reproach.

18:4 *words . . . deep waters.* Wise speech is like a deep, inexhaustible stream of blessing.

18:5 Cf. 17:26; 28:21.

18:6, 7 The fool self-destructs. Cf. 12:13; 17:14, 19, 28; 19:29; 20:3.

18:8 *tasty trifles.* This comes from a Hebrew word meaning "to swallow greedily." The proverb is repeated in 26:22.

18:9 *slothful . . . destroyer.* To leave a work half done or poorly done is to destroy it. *See notes on 6:1, 11.*

18:10 *The name of the LORD.* This expression, found only here in Proverbs, stands for the manifest perfections of God such as faithfulness, power, mercy, and wisdom, on which the righteous rely for security (cf. Ex. 3:15; 15:1–3; Ps. 27:4, 5)

18:11 This proverb repeats 10:15 and contrasts with verse 10.

18:12 Cf. 16:18.

18:14 *broken spirit.* Cf. 12:25; 15:13. When the spirit is broken, people lose hope.

18:16 *man's gift.* This is not the word for a bribe (cf. 17:23), but rather the word for a present given to someone (cf. Jacob's gift, Gen. 32:20, 21; Joseph's gift, Gen. 43:11; David's gift, 1 Sam. 17:17, 18; and Abigail's gift, 1 Sam. 25:27).

18:17 See verse 13. Cross-examination avoids hasty judgment.

18:18 *lots. See note on 16:33.*

18:19 There are no feuds as difficult to resolve as those with relatives; no barriers are so hard to bring down. Hence, great care should be taken to avoid such conflicts. **bars of a castle.** Cf. Judges 16:3; 1 Kings 4:13; Nehemiah 3:3; Isaiah 45:2.

18:20 the produce of his lips. See notes on 12:14; 13:2, 3. The consequences of one's words should produce satisfaction and fulfillment.

18:21 Death and life. The greatest good and the greatest harm are in the power of the tongue (cf. James 3:6–10).

18:22 Cf. 12:4; 19:14; 31:10–31.

18:23 The rich do not need favors from others, so they do not care how they treat people.

18:24 must himself be friendly. The best text (MT) says "may come to ruin" and warns that the person who makes friends too easily and indiscriminately does so to his own destruction. On the other hand, a friend chosen wisely is more loyal than a brother. **friend.** This is a strong word meaning "one who loves" and was used of Abraham, God's friend (2 Chr. 20:7; Is. 41:8; cf. 1 Sam. 18:1; 2 Sam. 1:26).

19:1 Integrity is better than wealth. Cf. 15:16, 17; 16:8.

19:2 sins. Lit. "to miss the mark." **hastens with his feet.** Rashness, the result of ignorance, brings trouble.

19:3 his heart frets. The fool blames God for his troubles and failures (cf. Gen. 4:5; Is. 8:21; Lam. 3:39–41).

19:4 Wealth makes. Cf. verse 7; 14:20. Lit. wealth adds new friends, while poverty alienates existing friends who grow weary of the demands of the poor.

19:5, 9 For the sin of perjury, cf. 6:19; 12:17; 14:5, 25; 19:9; Deuteronomy 19:18–21.

19:6 Generosity or bribery could be the issue.

19:7 See note on verse 4.

19:10 Neither are suited for possessions

Key Proverbs on Integrity	
1. Prov. 2:7	6. Prov. 19:1
2. Prov. 10:2	7. Prov. 20:6, 7
3. Prov. 10:9, 10	8. Prov. 20:23
4. Prov. 11:3	9. Prov. 28:6
5. Prov. 16:8	10. Prov. 28:18

or responsibilities beyond their capabilities of managing wisely (cf. 30:21–23).

19:11 slow to anger. See note on 14:17.

19:12 This is a call to submit to governmental authority. Cf. Romans 13:1–4; 1 Peter 2:13–17.

19:13 continual dripping. An obstinate, argumentative woman is literally like a leak so unrelenting that one has to run from it or go mad (cf. 21:9, 19). Here are two ways to devastate a man: an ungodly son and an irritating wife.

19:14 One receives inheritance as a family blessing (a result of human birth), but a wise wife (cf. 31:10–31) is a result of divine blessing. Cf. 12:4; 18:22; 31:10–31.

19:15 See notes on 6:6, 11.

19:16 commandment. Wisdom is equated with God's commandments. In a sense, Proverbs contain the applications and implications of all that is in God's moral law.

19:17 See note on 14:31. Cf. Matthew 25:40.

19:18 Chasten. See notes on 3:11, 12; 13:24; 22:6. Cf. Ephesians 6:4.

19:19 Repeated acts of kindness are wasted on ill-natured people.

19:21 See note on 16:1.

19:22 Rich liars are not kind since their lies bring harm; a kind poor man is more desirable.

19:23 fear of the LORD. See note on 1:7.

19:24 The lazy man's lack of action to move his hand from the flat, metal food saucer up to his mouth is because he is too lazy, as explained in 26:15.